Annals Of The Kingdom Of Ireland By The Four Masters, From The Earliest Period To The Year 1616

annala rioghachta eireann.

ANNALS

OF

THE KINGDOM OF IRELAND,

BY THE FOUR MASTERS,

FROM

THE EARLIEST PERIOD TO THE YEAR 1616.

EDITED FROM MSS. IN THE LIBRARY OF THE ROYAL IRISH ACADEMY AND OF TRINITY COLLEGE, DUBLIN. WITH A TRANSLATION, AND COPIOUS NOTES,

BY JOHN O'DONOVAN, LL. D., M. R. I. A.,

PROFESSOR OF THE CELTIC LANGUAGES, QUEEN'S COLLEGE, BELFAST.

"Olim Regibus parebant, nunc per Principes factionibus et studiis trahuntur: nec aliud adversus validissimas gentes pro nobis utilius, quam quod in commune non consulunt. Rarus duabus tribusve civitatibus ad propulsandum commune periculum conventus: ita dum singuli pugnant universi vincuntur."—TACITUS, AGRICOLA, c. 12.

VOL. III.

DUBLIN:
HODGES AND SMITH, GRAFTON-STREET,
BOOKSELLERS TO THE UNIVERSITY.
1851.

DUBLIN:
PRINTED AT THE UNIVERSITY PRESS,
BY M. H. GILL.

ANNALA RIOGHACHTA EIREANN.

ANNALA RIOGHACHTA EIREANN.

AOIS CHRIOSD 1172.

Aois Chriosd mile ced seachtmoġat a dó.

BRIGHDÉIN UA CATHAIN coṁarba Maedóig do écc.

Giollu aeḋa ua muiḋin (do muintir airiḋ loċa con) epscop corcaiġe do écc fear lan do rath dé eisside, tuir óiġe agus ecna a aimsire.

[a] *O'Kane*, O'Caṫain.—This name is anglicised O'Cahan in old law documents, inquisitions, &c., but it is at present made O'Kane, or Kane, in the north of Ireland, and the form O'Kane is adopted throughout this translation. There were several families of the name in Ireland, of whom the most powerful and celebrated were seated in the baronies of Keenaght, Tirkeeran, and Coleraine, in the present county of Londonderry; but it would not appear that the ecclesiastic, whose death is here recorded, was of this sept.

[b] *Successor of Maidoc*, Maodhog, or Aedhan, now anglicised Mogue and Aidan, was the first Bishop of Ferns, and successor of Maodhog is used in these Annals to denote Bishop of Ferns. The word coṁarba signifies successor, either ecclesiastical or lay, but generally the former in these Annals. There were two other ecclesiastical establishments, the abbots of which were called Comharbas of Mogue, or Maidoc, viz. Rossinver, in the county of Leitrim, and Drumlane, in the county of Cavan; but whenever the abbots of these places are referred to, the names of the monasteries are mentioned, as O'Farrelly, Comharba of St. Mogue, at Drumlane; O'Fergus, Comharba of St. Mogue, at Rossinver; but when the Bishop of Ferns is meant, he is simply called Comharba of St. Mogue, without the addition of the name of the place.

[c] *Giolla-Aedha*, i. e. servant of St. Aodh, or Aidus. The word Giolla occurs so frequently, as the first part of the names of men, that I shall explain it here, once for all, on the authority of Colgan. Giolla, especially among the ancients, signified a youth, but now generally a servant; and hence it happened that families who were devoted to certain saints, took care to call their sons after them, prefixing the word *Giolla*, intimating that they were to be the servants or devotees of those saints. Shortly after the introduction of Christianity, we meet many names of men formed by prefixing the word *Giolla* to the names of the celebrated saints of the first age of the Irish Church, as Giolla-Ailbhe, Giolla-Phatraig, Giolla-Chiarain, which mean servant of St. Ailbhe, servant of St. Patrick, servant of

ANNALS OF THE KINGDOM OF IRELAND.

THE AGE OF CHRIST, 1172.

The Age of Christ, one thousand one hundred seventy-two.

BRIGIDIAN O'KANE[a], successor of Maidoc[b], died.

Giolla Aedha[c] O'Muidhin (of the family of Errew of Lough Con[d]), Bishop of Cork, died. He was a man full of the grace[e] of God, the tower of the virginity and wisdom of his time.

St. Kieran. And it will be found that there were very few saints of celebrity, from whose names those of men were not formed by the prefixing of Giolla, as Giolla-Ailbhe, Giolla-Aodha, Giolla-Aodhain, Giolla-Breanainn, Giolla-Bhrighde, Giolla-Chaomain, Giolla-Chainnigh, Giolla-Dachaisse, Giolla-Chaoimhgin, Giolla-Chiarainn, Giolla-Dacholmain, Giolla-Choluim, Giolla-Chomain, Giolla-Chomghaill, Giolla-Domhangairt, Giolla-Finnein, Giolla-Fionnain, Giolla-Mochua, Giolla-Molaisse, Giolla-Moninne, Giolla-Phatruig, &c. &c.

This word was not only prefixed to the names of saints, but also to the name of God, Christ, the Trinity, the Virgin Mary; and some were named from saints in general, as well as from the angels in general, as Giolla-na-naomh, i. e. the servant of the saints; Giolla-na-naingeal, i. e. the servant of the angels; Giolla-De, the servant of God; and Giolla-an-Choimhdhe, i. e. the servant of the Lord; Giolla-na-Trionoide, the servant of the Trinity; Giolla-Chriost, the servant of Christ; Giolla-Iosa, the servant of Jesus; Giolla-Muire, the servant of Mary. These names were latinized by some writers in modern times, Marianus, Christianus, Patricianus, Brigidianus, &c. &c. But when an adjective, signifying a colour, or quality of the mind or body, is postfixed to Giolla, then it has its ancient signification, namely, a youth, a boy, or a man in his bloom, as Giolla-dubh, i. e. the black, or black-haired youth; Giolla-ruadh, i. e. the red-haired youth; Giolla-riabhach, the swarthy youth; Giolla-buidhe, the yellow youth; Giolla-odhar, Giolla-Maol, &c. &c.

The family name O'Muidhin is unknown to the Editor.

[d] *Of Errew of Lough Con*, Αιριό Loċα Con, now Errew on Lough Con, in the parish of Crossmolina, in the barony of Tirawley, and county of Mayo. There was an ancient church here, dedicated to St. Tighernan.—See the year 1413. See also Genealogy, &c., of the Hy-Fiachrach, p. 239, note [i].

[e] *Grace of God*, ꞃαċ ꝺé.—The word ꞃαċ, which is now used to denote prosperity or luck,

Ticcheṙnaċ ua maoileóin coṁorba ciaráin cluana mic nóis do écc.

Ticcheṙnan ua Ruairc ticcheṙna breifne agus Conmaicne agus fer cuṁachta móir fri re fota do ṁarḃaḋ (.i. i tlachtga) la hugó de laci i fiull agus la doṁnall mac Annaḋa uí Ruairc dia ċenél fesin boi imaille friu. Ro dícennaḋ é leó. Ruccsat a cenn agus a ċorp go doċraiḋ co hath cliaṫ. Ro toccbaḋ an cenn uas dorus an dúine ina scaṫ ḋearcc-ṫruaġ do ġaoiḋealaiḃ. Ro crochaḋ ḃeós an corp fria haṫ cliaṫ atuaiṫ agus a ċossa suas.

is employed throughout the *Leabhar Breac* to translate the Latin word *gratia*, from which the modern word grása has been obviously derived.

[f] *Tiernagh O'Malone:* in the original, Ticchernach ua Maoileoin.—The name Ticchernach or Tiġearnach, which is derived from Tiġearna, a lord, and is synonymous with the proper name Dominic, is pronounced Tiernagh, and shall be so written throughout this translation. The name Maoileoin, is written in ancient Irish characters on a tombstone at Clonmacnoise,

MAELIOHAIN EPS.

i. e. Mael-Johannis, Bishop.

The word maol, mael, or moel, like giolla, has two significations, namely, a chief, and a tonsured monk. It was anciently prefixed, like Giolla, to the names of saints, to form proper names of men, as Maol Colaim, Maol Seaċnaill, which mean the servant or devotee of the saints Columb and Secundinus; but when an adjective is post-fixed to MAOL, it has its ancient signification, as Maoldubh, i. e. the black chief.

[g] *Kieran,* Ciarán.—This celebrated Irish saint died in the year 549. *Cluain mac nois,* or, as it is now anglicised, Clonmacnoise, was a famous monastery near the Shannon, in the barony of Garry Castle, and King's County. The name is sometimes written *Cluain muc Nois,* as if it meant the insulated meadow, or pasturage of Nos. The place was more anciently called Druim Tiprad.—See Annals of Inisfallen, at the year 547, and Ussher's *Primordia,* p. 956, and Lanigan's Ecclesiastical History of Ireland, vol. ii. pp. 52–59.

[h] *Tiernan O'Rourke, &c.,* Ticchernan ua Ruairc.—The name Tiġernan, or Tiġearnan, is a diminutive of Tiġearnach, and may be interpreted "Little Dominic." It has been anglicised Tiernan throughout this translation, as this is the form it has assumed in the surname Mac Tiernan, which is still common in the county of Roscommon. Dervorgilla, in Irish Dearḃorgaill, the wife of this Tiernan, who is generally supposed to have been the immediate cause of the invasion of Ireland by the English, died in the monastery of Drogheda, in the year 1193, in the eighty-fifth year of her age. She was, therefore, born in the year 1108, and was in her sixty-fourth year at the death of Tiernan, and in her forty-fourth year when she eloped with Dermot, King of Leinster, in 1152, who was then in the sixty-second year of his age. Dermot was expelled in the seventieth year of his age.—See Dr. O'Conor's Prolegomena ad Annales, p. 146; and also O'Reilly's Essay on the Brehon Laws, where he vainly attempts to clear the character of Dervorgilla from the charge of having wilfully eloped from her husband. The family of O'Ruairc, now usually called in English O'Rourke, were anciently Kings of Connaught, but they were put down by the more

Tiernagh O'Malone[f], successor of Kieran[g] of Clonmacnoise, died.

Tiernan O'Rourke[h], Lord of Breifny and Conmaicne, a man of great power for a long time, was treacherously slain at Tlachtgha[i] by Hugo de Lacy and Donnell[k], the son of Annadh O'Rourke, one of his own tribe, who was along with them. He was beheaded by them, *and* they conveyed his head and body ignominiously to Dublin. The head was placed over the gate[l] of the fortress, as a spectacle of intense pity to the Irish, *and* the body was gibbeted, with the feet upwards, at the northern side of Dublin[m].

powerful family of the O'Conors, and then became chiefs of Breifny. It is stated in the Book of Fenagh, that this Tiernan acquired dominion over the entire region extending from sea to sea, that is, from the sea, at the borders of Ulster and Connaught, to Drogheda. The territories of Breifny and Conmaicne, which comprised Tiernan's principality, would embrace, according to this passage, the counties of Leitrim, Longford, and Cavan, but no part of the county of Meath or Louth.

[i] *Tlachtgha.*—Dr. Lanigan, in his Ecclesiastical History of Ireland (vol. iv. p. 223), says, that Tiernan O'Ruairc was slain on a hill not far from Dublin, by Griffin, a nephew of Maurice Fitz Gerald. Tlachtgha, however, is not near Dublin, but was the name of a hill much celebrated in ancient Irish history for the druidic fires lighted there annually on the 1st of November, in times of paganism, and described as situated in that portion of Meath which originally belonged to Munster. It is the place now called the Hill of Ward, which lies in the immediate vicinity of Athboy in the county of Meath, as is evident from the fact, that in these annals and other authorities Athboy is often called Aṫ buiḋe Tlaċtġa, or Athboy of Tlachtgha, to distinguish it from other places of the name Athboy in Ireland. This Hill of Ward is crowned with a magnificent ancient rath, consisting of three circumvallations, which, connected with the historical references to the locality, and the present local traditions, establishes its identity with the ancient Tlachtgha. The identity of Tlachtgha with the Hill of Ward was first proved by the Editor in a letter now preserved at the Ordnance Survey Office, Phœnix Park. The situation of Tlachtgha has been already given by Mr. Hardiman in a note to the Statute of Kilkenny, p. 84, on the authority of a communication from the Editor.

[k] *Donnell*, in the original Domnall, is still common among the Irish, as the proper name of a man, but always anglicised Daniel. The Editor, however, has used the form Donnell throughout this translation, because it is closer to the original Irish form, and is found in the older law documents, inquisitions, &c., and in the anglicised forms of names of places throughout Ireland, as well as in the family names, O'Donnell and Mac Donnell.

[l] *Over the gate*, uar dorar an dúine.—This was the Danish fortress of Dublin, which occupied the greater part of the hill on which the present castle of Dublin stands.

[m] *The northern side of Dublin.*—The northern side of Dublin, at this time, was near the present Lower Castle-yard. At the arrival of Henry II. the whole extent of Dublin was, in length, from Corn Market to the Lower Castle-yard; and, in breadth, from the Liffey, then covering Essex-street, to Little Sheep-street, now Ship-street, where a part of the town wall is yet standing.

Doṁnall o fearġail toiseaċ Conmaicne do ṁarbaḋ la muinntir riġ Saxan.

Maol maire mac murċaḋa toiseaċ muinntire birn do ṁarbaḋ la haeḋ mac Aenġusa agus la cloinn aeda do uiḃ eaċdaċ ulaḋ.

Diarmaid ua caeḋlaiġi do ecc.

Maiḋm for ċenél neoġain ria fflaiṫbeartac ua maoldoraiḋ agus ria ccenel cconaill. Do bertsad ár aḋḃal forra tria naeṁ miorbal de agus naeṁ Patraicc agus naeṁ ċolaim cille isa cealla ro oirccsed indsin.

Lán ċuairt coiccid Connaċt an ceṫraṁaḋ feaċt do tabairt la giollu macliacc coṁorba Patraicc agus Príoṁaiḋ Erenn, co hardmacha.

Mac Gillepscoip taoiseaċ cloinne aeilabra peċtaire chaṫa Monaiġ do marbaḋ la donnsleḃe uá neochaḋa rí ulaḋ i fiull. Na slána batar etorra .i. maiṫe ulaḋ do ṁarbaḋ Duinnsleḃe ind.

[n] *Chief of Conmaicne.*—That is, of South Conmaicne, or Anghaile, which in latter ages comprised the entire of the county of Longford.

[o] *Mulmurry Mac Murrough, Lord of Muintir Birn.*—The name Maolmaire or Maolmuire, signifies the servant of the Virgin Mary. The name is correctly latinized *Marianus*, by Colgan; but the Editor thinks Mulmurry a more appropriate anglicised form, as it is found in ancient law documents, inquisitions, &c. Mac Murrough has also been adopted throughout, as an anglicised form of Mac Murchaḋa. Muintir Birn, Muinntir birn, was the ancient name of a territory in Tyrone, bordering upon the barony of Trough, in the county of Monaghan.

[p] *The Clann Aodha of Ui Eathach Uladh.*—Clann Aodha, i. e. the clan or race of Hugh, was the tribe name of the Magennises; and it also became the name of their territory; but they aferwards extended their power over all Ui Ethach Cobha, now the baronies of Upper and Lower Iveagh, in the county of Down, and, as O'Dugan informs us, over all Ulidia. Ro gabsat Ulaḋ uile, "They took all Ulidia."—*Topographical Poem.* This territory was called Ui Eathach Uladh, or Ui Eathach Cobha, i. e. descendants of Eochaidh Cobha, to distinguish it from Ui Eathach Mumhan, Ui Eathach Muaidhe, and other tribes and districts called Ui Eathach, in different parts of Ireland.

[q] *Dermot O'Kaelly.*—The Irish name Diarmaid is anglicised *Dermot* in the older law documents, inquisitions, &c., relating to Ireland, and in the family name Mac Dermot. It is now almost invariably rendered Jeremiah, but the Editor prefers the form Dermot, as it comes nearer the original Irish. This family, who now anglicise their name Kelly, were located in the south of ancient Ossory, and were chiefs of the territory of Ui Berchon, now Ibercon, lying along the River Barrow, in the county of Kilkenny. O'Heerin thus speaks of O'Caelluidhe, or O'Kaelly, in his topographical poem:

Ui Ḃearchon an ḃruit ḃuiḋe;
Ri na criche O' Caollaiġe,
Clár na feaḋna ar trom do ṫil,
An fonn os ḃearḃa braoin-ġil.

"Ui Bearchon of the yellow surface;
King of the district is O'Kaelly,
Plain of the tribe, who heavily return,
The land over the bright-watered Barrow."

Donnell O'Farrell, chief of Conmaicne[n], was slain by the people of the King of England.

Mulmurry Mac Murrough[o], Lord of Muintir Birn, was slain by Hugh Magennis and the Clann-Aodha of Ui Eathach Uladh[p].

Dermot O'Kaelly[q] died.

The Kinel Owen[r] were defeated by Flaherty O'Muldorry[s] and the Kinel Connell[t]. They [the Kinel Connell] made prodigious havoc of them, through the holy miracles of God, of St. Patrick, and St. Columbkille, whose churches they [the Kinel Owen] had plundered.

The complete visitation[u] of the province of Connaught was performed the fourth time by Giolla Mac Liag [Gelasius], successor of St. Patrick and Primate of Ireland, to Armagh.

Mac Giolla Epscoip[v], chief of Clann-Aeilabhra, legislator of Cath Monaigh[w], was treacherously slain by Donslevy O'Haughy, king of Ulidia[x]. The chiefs of Ulidia, who were as guarantees between them, put Donslevy to death for it [i. e. *for his crime*].

[r] *Kinel Owen*, Cenel n-eoġain, i. e. the race of Eoghan, the son of Niall of the Nine Hostages. This Eoghan died in the year 465, and was buried at *Uisce Chaoin*, now Eskaheen, an old church in the barony of Inishowen, in the north-east of the county of Donegal. This tribe possessed the present counties of Tyrone and Londonderry, and originally the baronies of Inishowen and Raphoe, but these were, in later ages, ceded to the Kinel Connell.

[s] *O'Muldorry*, O'Maoldoraiḋ.—This name no longer exists in Tirconnell, but there are a few of the name in Dublin and in Westmeath, who anglicise it Muldarry.

[t] *Kinel Connell*, Cenel cconaill, i. e. the race of Conall or Connell, who died in the year 464, and who was the brother of Eoghan, or Owen, ancestor of the Kinel Owen. This tribe possessed, in later ages, the entire of the county of Tirconnell, now Donegal.

[u] *A visitation*, Cuairt.—A journey performed into particular districts by the bishop or abbot, to collect dues, or obtain donations for the erection or repairing of churches or monasteries.

[v] *Mac Giolla Epscoip.*—This name would be anglicised Mac Gillespick, and is the same which in Scotland is now Mac Gillespie.

[w] *Cath Monaigh.*—The territory of Cath Monaigh is somewhere in the present county of Down, but its extent or exact situation has not been discovered.

[x] *Ulidia*, Ulaḋ.—Uladh was the original name of the entire province of Ulster, until the fifth century, when it was dismembered by the Hy-Niall, and the name confined solely to the present counties of Down and Antrim, which, after the establishment of surnames, became the principality of O'h-Eochadha (now anglicised O'Haughy), and his correlatives. The founders of the principality of Oirghialla, or Oriel, in the fourth century, deprived the ancient Ultonians of that part of their kingdom which extended from Lough Neagh to the Boyne; and the sons of Niall of the Nine Hostages, in the

Creaċ fill la mac Anduiḋ uí Ruairc, agus la Saxanachaiḃ ar muinntir na hAnngaile, agus ar muinntir Megiollgan co rugsat bú, agus broid iomda. Sloiġeaḋ leó doriḋisi co hArdachaḋ Epscoip Mél gur ro airgsiot an tír ar meḋón, agus do roċair leo Domhnall ua Fearġail, taoiseaċ muinntire hanġaile don ċur sin.

Seanaḋ cléireaċ nErenn la coigeaḋ connaċt laechaiḃ cleirchiḃ occ tuaim da ġuálann im Ruaiḋri ua Conċoḃair agus im Chaḋla uá nDubṫaiġ Airdepscop Tuáma agus tri teampaill do ċoisearḋaḋ leo.

AOIS CHRIOSD 1173.

Aois ċriosd mile, céd, seachtmoġat, a trí.

Muireḋaċ ua coḃṫaiġ epscop Doire, agus Raṫa boṫ, mac oiġe, leacc loġṁor, gemm gloiniḋe, Reḋla solusta, cisde taisccedha na heccna, craoḃ ċnuasaiġ na canóine, iar ttiodhnacal biḋ agus edaiġ do boċtaiḃ agus do aiḋilgneaċaiḃ, iar noirdneaḋ Saccart agus deochon agus aesa gaċa graidh, iar naṫnuaḋuġad eacclus niomda, iar ccoisreaccaḋ tempall agus relgeaḋ, iar ndenaṁ iolar mainistreaċ agus reiclés, agus gaċa luḃra eccluistacda iar mbuaiḋ ccraḃaiḋ, oiliṫri agus aiṫrigche. Ro faoiḋ a sbiorad do cum niṁi i nDuiḃreicclés Colaim Ċille i nDoire an 10. lá do Febra.

fifth century, seized upon the northern and western parts of Ulster; so that the ancient inhabitants, viz. the Clanna-Rury and Dal-Fiatachs, were shut up within the bounds of the present counties of Down and Antrim; but their country, though circumscribed, still retained its ancient appellation. The writers of Irish history have therefore used the form Ulidia, to denote the circumscribed territory of the Clanna Rury, and Ultonia, to denote all Ulster.—See O'Flaherty's *Ogygia*, Part III. c. 78, p. 372; also Ussher's Primordia, pp. 816, 1048; O'Conor's Dissertations on the History of Ireland, 2nd edit. p. 176; and Lanigan's Ecclesiastical History of Ireland, vol. ii. p. 28.

[y] *Annaly, or Anghaile*, was the tribe name of the O'Farrells, and it also became the name of their country, which comprised the entire of the present county of Longford. According to the genealogical Irish MSS., the O'Farrells derived this tribe name from Anghaile, the great grandfather of Fearghal, from whom they derived their surname in the tenth century.

[z] *Muintir Magilligan*, which is usually called Muintir Giollgain throughout these Annals, was the tribe name of the O'Quins of Annaly, who were seated in the barony of Ardagh, in the present county of Longford, as will be more distinctly shewn in a note under the year 1234.

[a] *Bishop Mel*.—Bishop Mel, who was one of the disciples of St. Patrick, is still the patron saint of the diocese of Ardagh, and the ruins of his original church are still to be seen in the village of Ardagh, in the county of Longford.

The son of Annadh O'Rourke and the English treacherously plundered the inhabitants of Annaly[y] and Muintir Magilligan[z], carrying off many cows and prisoners. They afterwards made another incursion into Ardagh of Bishop Mel[a], and ravaged the country generally, and slew Donnell O'Farrell, chief of Annaly, on that occasion.

A synod of the clergy and laity of Ireland was convened at Tuam, in the province of Connaught, by Roderic O'Conor and Kyley [Catholicus] O'Duffy, Archbishop of Tuam, and three churches were consecrated by them.

THE AGE OF CHRIST, 1173.

The Age of Christ, one thousand one hundred seventy-three.

Murray O'Coffey[b], Bishop of Derry and Raphoe, a son of chastity, a precious stone, a transparent gem, a brilliant star, a treasury of wisdom, and a fruitful branch of the canon,—after having bestowed food and raiment upon the poor and the destitute, after having ordained priests and deacons, and men of every *ecclesiastical* rank, re-built many churches, consecrated many churches and burial-places, founded many monasteries and Regles's [i. e. abbey churches], and fulfilled every ecclesiastical duty; and after having gained the palm for piety, pilgrimage, and repentance, resigned his spirit to heaven in the Duibhregles[c] of Columbkille, in Derry, on the 10th day of February. A great miracle[d]

[b] *Murray O'Coffey*, Muirſḋach ua Coḃṫaiġ. The name Muireaḋach, which is explained ṫiġearna, a lord, by Michael O'Clery, though it would appear to be derived from muir, the sea, is now obsolete as the proper name of a man, but it is preserved in the surname Murray, and has been anglicised Murray throughout this translation. The family name O'Coḃṫaiġ is anglicised Coffey in the northern half of Ireland, but sometimes barbarously, *Cowhig*, in the south. The Editor has adopted O'Coffey throughout this work.

[c] *Duibhregles*.—The Dubh-Regles was the name of the ancient abbey church founded by St. Columbkille at Derry; it was probably called *Dubh*, or black, in contradistinction from the new Templemore, or cathedral church, erected in 1164, by Flaherty O'Brollaghan. Concerning the situation of this old church, see *Trias Thaum.*, p. 398.

[d] *A great miracle, &c.*—This passage is thus rather loosely, but elegantly, translated by Colgan, in his Annals of Derry: "S. Muredachus O Dubhthaich" [*recte* O'Cobhthaigh], "Episcopus Dorensis et Robothensis, vir virginitatis, seu castitatis intactæ, lapis pretiosus, gemma vitrea, sydus præfulgidum, arca et custos Ecclesiæ sedulus, et conservator canonum Ecclesiæ; postquam multos pauperes, et egenos enutrierit; Præsbyteros, Diaconos, aliosque diuersorum ordinum, Deo consecrauerit; postquam diuersa monasteria et Ecclesias extruxerit, et consecrauerit; post palmam pœnitentiæ, peregrinationis, abstinentiæ

Do ronaḋ miorbail mór is in oiḋche atbaṫ .i. an oiḋċe ḋorċa do ḟoillsiuġaḋ o thá iarmeirge co-muichosdoil agus an dar leo an bá forrél do na comfocraiḃe do'n doṁan baoi siḋe for coṁlasaḋ agus ionnaṁail ċaoire moire teneḋ do eirgi ós an mbaile agus a toċt soirḋes. Ro eiriġsed caċ uile, uáir andar leó ro ba lá boí ann agus ro boi aṁlaiḋ sin le muir anoir.

Conaing ua haénġusa cenn canánaċ rosa cré do écc.

Etrú ua miaḋachán, Epscop cluana do écc ina Seandataiḋ iar ndeccḃeathaiḋ.

Cionaeḋ ua Ronáin Epscop glinne da locha do écc.

Maoiliosu mac an bairḋ Epscop ċluana fearta brenainn do écc.

Maolmochta ua maoilseaċnaill abb cluana mic nóis do écc.

Creaċ mór la haeḋ mac aenġusa agus la cloinn aeḋa. Ro airccsed

& reliqua religiosissimæ vitæ exercitia; ad Dominum migrauit in Ecclesia Dorensi, *Dubhrigles* nuncupata, die 10 Febr. Miraculum solemne patratum est ea nocte quâ decessit: nam à mediâ nocte vsque mane tota non solum ciuitas, sed et vicinia ingenti splendore, ad instar iubaris diurni, circumfusa resplenduit: et columna insuper ignea visa est ex ciuitate ascendere, et versus orientalem Austrum tendere. Quo prodigio excitati ciues tanti spectaculi testes vsque ad ortum solis, et venerabundi posteà præcones extitere.—*Quat. Mag.*"—*Trias Thaum.*, p. 504.

The phrase craoḃ cnuasaiġ na canoine, which is translated "conservator canonum ecclesiæ" by Colgan, is more correctly rendered "the fruitful tree of the Canon" in the old translation of the Annals of Ulster.

The account of this miracle is given in the Dublin copy of the Annals of Ulster as follows: A. D. 1173. Do ronaḋ dono mirbuil mor is in aiḋce adbaṫ .i. in aḋaiġ do solustugaḋ oca iarmeirġi co gairm in coiliġ 7 in doman uile for lasaḋ 7 coer mor teineḋ deirġi os in baile 7 a toċt soirḋes 7 eirġi do ċaċ uile in dar leo rob é in laa, 7 ro boi amlaiḋ sein re muir anoir. It is thus rendered in the old English translation: "A. D. 1173. There was a great miracle shewed in the night he died, viz. the night to brighten from the middest to Cockcrow, and all the world burning, and a great flame of fire rising out of the town, and went East and by South; and every body got upp thinking it was day, and was so untill the ayre was cleare."

Here it is to be remarked that neither this translator nor Colgan has rendered the phrase re muir anoir, which literally means *east of the sea*. In the Annals of Kilronan, the reading is 7 ro boi aṁlaiḋ sin co himeal in aieoir, "and it was thus to the borders of the sky." The meaning of re muir anoir is, that the inhabitants of the east coast of Ulster saw the sky illumined over the visible portions of Scotland on the east side of the sea. For the meaning of the preposition le, re, or fri, in such phrases as re muir anoir, see the Editor's Irish Grammar, p. 314, line 1, and p. 439, note [e], and Cormac's Glossary, *voce* Moġ Eime, where fri muir anair is used to express "on the east side of the sea."

[e] *Conaing O'Hennessy*, Conaing ua haénġusa.—The name Conaing, which is explained riġ,

was performed on the night of his death—namely, the dark night was illumined from midnight to day-break; and the people thought that the neighbouring parts of the world which were visible, were in one blaze of light; and the likeness of a large globe of fire arose over the town, and moved in a south-easterly direction; and all persons arose *from their beds*, imagining that it was daylight; and it was also thus on the east side of the sea.

Conaing O'Hennessy[e], head of the canons of Roscrea, died.

Ettru O'Meehan[f], Bishop of Cluain [Clonard], died at an advanced age, after *having spent* a good life.

Kenny O'Ronan[g], Bishop of Glendalough, died.

Maelisa Mac Ward[h], Bishop of Clonfert-Brendan[i], died.

Maelmochta O'Melaghlin[k], Abbot of Clonmacnoise, died.

A great plunder was made by Hugh Magennis and the Clann-Aedha. They plundered the large third[l] of Armagh; but this man was killed in three months after this plundering of Armagh.

a king, in Cormac's Glossary, is now obsolete as the proper name of a man, but is preserved in the family name O'Conaing, under the anglicised form of *Gunning*. The family name Ua h-Aenġura, is now invariably anglicised Hennesy. This family was anciently seated in the territory of Clann Colgan, in the barony of Lower Philipstown, in the King's County, and adjoining the conspicuous hill of Croghan.

[f] *O'Meehan*, Ua Miaḋachan.—This name is still common in most parts of Ireland.

[g] *Kenny O'Ronan*, Cionaeḋ Ua Ronáin.—The name Cionaeḋ is anglicised Kineth by the Scotch; but Kenny by the Irish, in the family name Kenny. It is obsolete among the latter as the proper name of a man. O'Ronan is still common as a family name in many parts of Ireland, but the O' is never prefixed in the anglicised form, which is Ronayne, in the south of Ireland.

[h] *Maelisa Mac Ward*, Maoilisu Mac an Ḃaird.—This family, who were hereditary poets to O'Kelly, were seated at Muine Chasain and Ballymacward, in the cantred of Sodhan, in Hy-Many.—See *O'Flaherty's Ogygia*, p. 327.

[i] *Clonfert*, a bishop's see in the south-east of the county of Galway.

[k] *Maelmochta O'Melaghlin*, Maelmochta ua maoilseaċnaill.—The name Maolmochta signifies the servant or devoted of St. Mochta, or Mocteus, first abbot and patron saint of Louth. This family is generally called O'Maoilseachlainn, or O'Maoileachlainn, which was first correctly anglicised O'Melaghlin, but now incorrectly Mac Loughlin. They are named after their great progenitor, Maelseachlainn or Malachy the Second, Monarch of Ireland, who was dethroned by Brian Borumha, and who died in 1022. The name Mael-Seachnaill signifies servant of St. Seachnall, or Secundinus, the patron of Dunshaughlin in Meath, and the tutelary saint of this family.

[l] *Large third*, trian mór.—Colgan, in the Annals of Armagh (Trias. Thaum. p. 300), thus speaks of the ancient divisions of that city:

"1112. *Arx Ardmachana cum templis, duæ*

trian mór arda maċa. Ro marḃaḋ dan an fear ſin i ccionn trí mís iarr an orccain sin arda macha.

Doṁnall ḃreġach ua maoileċlainn Rí Miḋe do marḃaḋ la mac a aṫar féin la hart ua maoileċlainn agus la muintir Laeġacáin i nDurmaigh ċolaim cille.

Giollu macliacc mac Ruaiḋri coṁarba Patraicc Priomaiḋ Arda maċa agus Erenn uile mac oiġe lán do ġloine croiḋe fri dia agus fri daoinib do ecc go fechtnach iar ffndataiḋ toccaiḋe, 27, marta dia cedaoin iar ccaiscc is in sechtmaḋ bliaḋain ochtmoġat a aoisi. agus baoi siḋe se bliaḋna décc i nabḋaine coluim ċille i nDoire ria ccomarbus Patraicc.

AOIS CRIOSD 1174.

Aois criosd mile, ced, seaċtmoġatt, aceaṫair.

Maoilíosa ua connaċtáin epscop síl Muireaḋaiġ do écc.

Maolpattraicc ua banáin, Epscop Condere 7 ḋal araiḋe fſr airmiḋneaċ lán do naiṁe, do ċſnnsa 7 do ġloine ċroiḋe do écc co feaċtnaċ ind hí ċolaim ċille iar Seandataiḋ ṫoghaiḋe.

Giollu mochaiḋbeo abb mainistreaċ Pſtair 7 Póil i nardmaċa, Moḋ treaḃor tairisi don coimḋeaḋ do écc an 31. do Mhárta Seċtmoġat bliaḋain a aeis.

Flann (.i. Florent) ua Gormáin airdfſr lecchinn arda maċa, 7 Erenn uile, Saoi, eargna eolaċ is in eaccna ḋiaḋa 7 doṁanda, iar mbeiṫ bliaḋain

plateæ in Trian Massain, et tertiani Trian-mor incendio deuastantur."

"Ex hoc loco & aliis dictis suprà ad annum 1092, colligimus ciuitatem Ardmachanam in quatuor olim partes fuisse diuisam. Prima *Rath-Ardmacha*, i. Arx Ardmachana, dicebatur: Secunda *Trian-mor*, id est tertia portio maior: Tertia *Trian Massan*, id est tertia portio Massan. Quarta, *Trian saxon*, id est, tertia portio Saxonum, appellata: quod nomen videtur, adepta ex eo, quod vel mercatores vel (quod verosimiliùs est) studiosi Anglosaxones illi inhabitauerint. Nam Monachi et studiosi Anglisaxones abstractioris vitæ, disciplinæ et bonarum litterarum gratia in magno numero olim Hiberniam frequentare solebant."—See also *Stuart's History of Armagh*.

[m] *Sil-Murray*, Siol Muireaḋaiġ, i. e. the progeny, race, or descendants of Muireadhach Muilleathan, king of Connaught, who died in the year 701. The principal families among them were O'Conor Don, O'Conor Roe, O'Finaghty of Clanconway, O'Flanagan of Clancahill, and Mageraghty. The *Liber Regalis Visitationis* of 1615, places the following fourteen parishes in the deanery of Silmury, which was coexten-

Donnell Breaghach [the Bregian] O'Melaghlin, King of Meath, was slain by the son of his own father [step-brother], Art O'Melaghlin, and by Muintir Laeghachain, at Durrow of Columbkille.

Gilla Mac Liag [Gelasius], the son of Rory, the successor of St. Patrick, and Primate of Armagh, and of all Ireland, a son of chastity, filled with purity of heart towards God and man, died in righteousness, at a venerable old age, on the 27th of March, being the Wednesday after Easter, and in the eighty-seventh year of his age. He had been sixteen years in the abbacy of St. Columbkille, at Derry, before he became successor of St. Patrick.

THE AGE OF CHRIST, 1174.

The Age of Christ, one thousand one hundred seventy-four.

Maelisa O'Connaghtan, Bishop of Sil-Murray[m] [Elphin], died.

Maelpatrick O'Banan[n], Bishop of Connor and Dalaradia[o], a venerable man, full of sanctity, meekness, and purity of heart, died in righteousness, in Hy-Columbkille, at a venerable old age.

Gilla Mochaibeo, Abbot of the monastery of SS. Peter and Paul at Armagh, a diligent and faithful servant of the Lord, died on the 31st day of March, in the seventieth year of his age.

Flann [i. e. Florentius] O'Gorman, chief Lecturer of Armagh, and of all Ireland, a learned sage, and versed in sacred and profane philosophy, after

sive with the territory: Elphin, Kilmacumshy, Shankill, Ballinakill, Kilcorkey, Baslick, Kilkivgan (Kilkeevin), Ballintober, Kilcooley, Killukin (now Killuckin), Ogulla, Roscommon, Fuerty, Drumtemple.

This, however, is not a complete list of all the parishes in Silmurry, for the parishes belonging to monasteries, and those of which the tithes belonged to laymen, are omitted. The list, however, as far as it goes, is very useful to the topographer, as it proves where Moylurg and Silmurry meet. The parishes of Shankill, Killmacumshy, and Kilcorkey, were in Sil-Murry, while Kilcolagh, and all the parishes lying to the north between it and the River Boyle were in Moylurg.—See *Moylurg*.

[n] *O'Banan*, O ḃanain.—There were several distinct families of this name in Ireland. It is now anglicised Bannan and Banon, but incorrectly Banim by the late celebrated novel writer in Kilkenny.

[o] *Bishop of Connor and Dalaradia*, i. e. Bishop of Connor and Down. Dalaradia, according to the Book of Lecan, extended from Newry to Slieve Mis (now Slemmish, in the present county of Antrim), and from the sea to Linn Duachaill, now Magheralin, in the west of the present county of Down.

ar ḟichit i ffrancaiḃ ⁊ i Saxaiḃ acc foghlaim, ⁊ fiche bliaḋan ele ag friochnaṁ ⁊ ag pollaṁnacchaḋ Scol Erenn, atbaṫ co soinṁeaċ is in cét-taóin ria ccaisg iarr an Seachtmoġaḋ bliaḋan a aoisi.

Muirgḟs ua dubṫaiġ abb mainistreċ áṫa dá laarcc for búill do écc.

Ruaiḋri ua cearḃaill tiġearna Ele do ṁarḃaḋ ar lár innsi cloṫrann.

Congalaċ ua Coinfiacla tiġearna tſtḃa do ecc.

Maolruanaiḋ ua ciarḋa tiġearna cairpri do ṁarḃaḋ i meḃail la gallaiḃ áṫa cliaṫ, .i. la mac turnin, ⁊ la mac Aoḋa uí fearġail, ⁊ la ceallaċ ua fionḋalláin tiġearna delbna moire.

Faiṙċe iarṫair miḋe do ċur le caṫair cluana mic nóis do réir cleireaċ Erenn.

Sluaiccéaḋ las in iarla dinoraḋ Muṁan. Sluaiccéaḋ ele la Ruaiḋri dia himdſgail forro. Ot cualattar na goill Ruaiḋri do ṫoċt is in muṁain in airſs caṫa friu, ro ṫoċuirsiot goill áṫa cliaṫ dia saiġiḋ ⁊ ni

[p] *Died happily*, atbaṫ co soinṁeaċ.—Colgan renders this phrase "pie in Domino obdormivit," in his Annals of Armagh. In the Annals of Ulster the phrase is atbaṫ co síṫamail, i. e. "died peaceably." The whole passage is thus rendered in the old translation : "A. D. 1174. Flan O'Gorman, Archlector of Ardmagh and Ireland all, a skillfull notorious man in divine knowledge, and also Mundane, after being 21 yeares in France and England learning, and 20 yeares keeping scoole in Ireland, he died peaceably the 13 Kal. of April, on Wednesday before Easter, in the 70th yeare of his age."

[q] *Maurice O'Duffy*, Muirġeas ua Duḃṫaiġ.—The name Muirġeas, which seems different from Muiris, is anglicised Maurice throughout this translation.

[r] *Ath da laarg* (i. e. aṫ da ġaḃul, *vadum duarum furcarum*, vide *Trias Thaum*., p. 173, n. 23), now the abbey of Boyle. There was an ancient Irish monastery or church here before the erection of the great Cistercian one by Maurice O'Duffy; as we learn from the Irish Calendar of the O'Clerys, that the holy bishop Mac Cainne was venerated here on the 1st day of December :

"Decemb^r 1. The holy bishop Mac Cainne of *Ath-da-larg*."

We learn from the Annals of Boyle and Ware, that in the middle of the 12th century, the abbey of Mellifont, in Louth, sent out a swarm of monks who had settled in several localities before they procured a permanent establishment on the banks of the River Boyle. In August, 1148, they settled at Grellechdinach, where Peter O'Mordha became their first abbot. He was afterwards promoted to the see of Clonfert, and was succeeded in the abbacy by Hugh O'Maccain, who removed the convent to Drumconaind. He was succeeded by Maurice O'Duffy, who remained there nearly three years, when he removed to Bunfinny, now Buninna, near Tonrego, in the county of Sligo, and after having resided there for two years and six months, at length fixed his family at Boyle (opposite the ford of Aṫ dá laarcc), in the year 1161, where this abbey was founded as a daughter of Mellifont, and dedicated to the Virgin Mary.—See Annals of Boyle, at this year.

having spent twenty-one years of study in France and England, and twenty other years in directing and governing the schools of Ireland, died happily[p] on the Wednesday before Easter, in the seventieth year of his age.

Maurice O'Duffy[q], Abbot of the monastery of Ath da laarg[r], on *the River* Boyle, died.

Rory O'Carroll, Lord of Ely[s], was slain in the middle of the island of Inishcloghran[t].

Congalagh O'Coinfiacla[u], Lord of Teffia, died.

Mulrony O'Keary, Lord of Carbury[v], was treacherously slain by the Galls [Ostmen] of Dublin, i. e. by Mac Turnin, assisted by the son of Hugh O'Farrell, and Kellagh O'Finnallan, Lord of Delvin-More[w].

The diocese of Westmeath was annexed to the city of Clonmacnoise, by consent of the clergy of Ireland.

The Earl led an army to plunder Munster; *King* Roderic marched with another army to defend it against them. When the English had heard of Roderic's arrival in Munster, for the purpose of giving them battle, they

This abbey was sometimes called Mainistir Aṫa da laarg, i. e. ford of two forks, but generally Mainistir na Búille, i. e. the monastery of the (River) Boyle. For the meaning of laarcc, see MS. Trin. Coll., Class H. 13. p. 360.

[s] *Ely*, Eile.—O'Carroll's territory, generally called Ely O'Carroll, comprised the baronies of Clonlisk and Ballybritt, in the south of the present King's County.

[t] *Inishcloghran*, Inis cloṫrann.—It is an island in Lough Ree, in the River Shannon. See note under the year 1193.

[u] *O'Coinfiacla.*—This name is now obsolete in Teffia, which is an extensive district in Westmeath. See note under the year 1207.

[v] *Mulrony O'Keary, Lord of Carbury O'Keary*, Maolruanaiḋ ua Ciarḋa tiġearna Cairbre ua Ciarḋa.—This territory, about the situation of which Irish writers have committed most unaccountable blunders, is the barony of Carbury, in the north-west of the county of Kildare. In the translation of the Annals of Clonmacnoise by Connell Macgeoghegan, the translator states, under the year 1076, that "Carbrey O'Kiergie was then called Bremyngham's country." The family name O'Ciardha is now anglicised, correctly enough, Keary, but sometimes incorrectly Carey, and is common in the counties of Meath and Westmeath. Maolruanaiḋ, which signifies *the ruddy chief*, is anglicised Mulrony throughout this translation; for although it is now obsolete as a Christian name, it is preserved in the surname Mulrony.

[w] *Delvin-More*, now the barony of Delvin, in the east of the county of Westmeath.—See *Ogygia*, part iii. c. 82. The family of O'Finnallan were soon after conquered by Hugh de Lacy, who granted this territory to Gilbert Nugent, the ancestor of the present Marquis of Westmeath; and the O'Finnallans have been for many centuries in a state of obscurity and poverty. When the Editor examined the barony of Delvin in 1837, he did not find many of this family in their original locality.

ro hairiseaḋ leo go rangattar go Dúrlas. Tanaic domnall ua briain, ⁊ dál ccais, ⁊ caṫ iarṫair connaċt, ⁊ morċaṫ ṡíl Muireaḋaiġ cenmoṫa dirim dḟſluaiġ ro faccbaḋ las an riġ Ruaiḋri. Ro fiġeaḋ caṫ croḋa eter gallaiḃ, ⁊ gaoiḋelaiḃ an du sin, go ro sraoineaḋ fo deoiḋ tre neart iommbualta for na gallaiḃ, ⁊ ro marḃaḋ secht ccéd décc do gallaiḃ is in caṫ sin, co naċ tearna acht tiorhuairsi becc beo as in caṫ sin do

[x] *Thurles*, in Irish Dúrlas, a name signifying "strong fort," now a small but well-known town in the county of Tipperary. In the Bodleian copy of the Annals of Innisfallen, it is called Durlus Ui Fogarta, i. e. O'Fogarty's Durlus, from its situation in the territory of Elyogarty.

[y] *Dint of fighting*, neart iommbualta.—From this phrase it would appear that both parties fought with stubbornness and bravery. This entry has been abstracted by the Four Masters from the continuation of the Annals of Tighernach. According to Giraldus Cambrensis, the detachment sent from Dublin were slaughtered in Ossory by the Irish, who attacked them early in the morning, while sleeping in their camp. Giraldus also informs us that this party consisted of Ostmen, or Dano-Irish soldiers, and that the number cut off was four hundred, besides four knights by whom they were commanded. Giraldus devotes the third chapter of the second book of his *Hibernia Expugnata* to the description of this event; and as he is so directly opposed to the Irish annalists, and has been followed by Cox, Leland, and others, it is but fair to lay his words before the reader:

"*Interfectio Dublinensium apud Ossyriam.* His ita completis, familiaque tam maris quam terræ successibus egregie refecta: dum Reymundus ob patris, quem audierat, obitum, nobilis videl. viri Guilielmi Giraldidæ, remenso pelago, in Cambriam recessisset: Herueius iterum se constabularium gerens: vt absente Reymundo aliquid agere videretur: Comitem cum familia Cassiliam duxit. Dublinensium autem exercitus in eorum interim auxilium ex edicto veniens, cum apud Ossyriam forte pernoctaret: ecce Limiricensium Princeps Duuenaldus vir sua in gente non improuidus, ipsorum aduentus exploratione certissima præscius, summo diluculo cum manu armata irruens in incautos, 4. milites qui aliis præerant & 400. Ostmannorum viros simul interemit. His autem auditis, Comite Guaterfordiam cum confusione reuerso, casus istius occasione, totus Hiberniæ populus in Anglos vnanimiter insurgunt: ita vt Comes tanquam obsessus, Guaterfordiensi nusquam ab urbe discederet. Rothericus vero Connactiensis Synnenensis fluuii fluenta transcurrens in manu valida Mediam inuasit. Cunctaque eiusdem castra vacua vsque ad ipsos Dubliniæ fines igne combusta, soloque confracta redegit."

Hanmer states, upon what authority the Editor has never been able to discover, that one of the four knights who commanded these Ostmen soldiers was an Irishman, by name O'Grame. As the English and Irish accounts of this event in Irish history differ so much, the Editor thinks it necessary to give here, for the use of the future Irish historian, the various notices of it in the older Irish annals. In the Dublin copy of the Annals of Ulster, it is noticed in the following brief manner:

A. D. 1174. Cath Durluis la Domnall hua mbriain ⁊ la concobur maenmaige for muintir mic naperis .i. rig saxan.

"A. D. 1174. The battle of Thurles by Donnell O'Brien, and by Conor Moinmoy, against

solicited to their assistance the Galls [Ostmen] of Dublin; and these made no delay till they came to Thurles[x]. Thither came Donnell O'Brien and the Dalcassians, the battalion of West Connaught, the great battalion of the Sil-Murray, besides numerous other good troops left there by the King, Roderic. A brave battle was fought between the English and Irish at this place, in which the English were finally defeated by dint of fighting[y]. Seventeen hundred of the

the people of Fitz-Empress, i. e. the king of England."

In the Annals of Boyle, a compilation of the thirteenth century, it is entered thus:

"A. D. 1174. *Bellum Durlas comissum est cum Anglicis et Dubliniensibus a Domnallo Rege Mumunie et Concobaro Maenmaigi cum suis, in quo Anglici defecerunt ad mortem, et Dublinienses perierunt.*"

In the older Annals of Innisfallen, preserved in the Bodleian Library (Rawlinson, 503), the number slain is said to be about seven hundred, not seventeen hundred, as the Continuator of Tighernach, and from him the Four Masters have it. The entry is as follows:

A. D. 1174. Sluaged la Gallaib glasa go tancatar in h-Eli, co ro tinolsatar Domnall ua Briain 7 Tuadmumain go Durlas ui Focarta, co ro cuired cath etarru, co romaid ar Gallaib glasa in cath, in quo dcc. uel paulo plus ceciderunt. Constapla Puirt Lairgi cum ducentis aliis ceciderunt la gallaib i nduni féin.

"A. D. 1174. An army was marched by the green Galls till they came into Ely; and Donnell O'Brien and the men of Thomond flocked to Thurles, and a battle was fought between them, and the green Galls were defeated in the battle, *in quo dcc. vel paulo plus ceciderunt.* The Constable of Waterford, with two hundred others, were slain by the Galls of their own fortress."

In the Dublin copy of the Annals of Innisfallen also, the number slain is stated to be seven hundred. The literal translation of the passage is as follows:

"A. D. 1174. A great army was led by the Earl of Strigule to plunder Munster; and he sent messengers to Dublin, desiring all the Galls left there to join him; and a battalion of knights, officers, and soldiers well armed came to him, and they all marched to Durlus-O'Fogarty. But Donell More O'Brien there defeated the Earl and the knights, and slew four of the knights, and seven hundred of their men. When that news came to the hearing of the people of Waterford, they killed the two hundred who were guarding the town. Then the Earl went on an island near the town [the Little Island], and remained there for a month, and then went back again to Dublin."

The reader is also referred to Ware's Annals, cap. 6, regnant. Hen. II., to *Cambrensis Eversus*, p. 89, Leland's History of Ireland, vol. i. b. 1, p. 99, and the Abbé Mac-Geoghegan's *Histoire d'Irlande*, tom. ii. p. 9, where the Abbé writes: "L'armée étant restée sans chef par la retraite de Reymond, Strongbow en donna le commandement à Hervey. Ce Capitaine voulant tenter fortune, & faire des incursions du côté de Limerick, assembla les troupes de Waterford & de Dublin, & marcha du côté de Cashil; mais ayant été rencontré à Durlas Hy-Ogarta, aujourd'hui Thurles, dans le pays d'Ormond, par Roderick O'Connor le Monarque, son armée fut entiérement défaite, & dix-sept cens Anglois resterent sur le champ de bataille. Wareus donne la gloire de cette action à Donald O'Brien

gallaiḃ imon iarla. Taed side fo méla dia tiġ go Portlairge. Soais ua briain dia tiġ iar ccosccur.

Maelseċlainn ó donnagán tiġearna araḋ do marḃaḋ la hua ccona[ing].

AOIS CRIOSD 1175.

Aois Criosd mile, cét, seachtmoġatt, a cúig.

An tespoc ua briain, espoc ċille dara do écc.

Maoiliosa mac an ċleiriġ ċuirr epscop ulaḋ, do écc.

Giolla domnaill mac carmuic epscop ulaḋ do écc.

Flaiṫbertaċ ua brolċain comorba ċolaim ċille tuir eccna ⁊ eniġ, fear dia ttuccatar cleiriġ Eirenn caṫaoir epscoip ar a ḟeabus ⁊ ar a eaccna ⁊ dia ttarccus comorbus iae, do ecc co feaċtnaċ iar ttreablaid toġaiḋe i nduiḃrecclés ċolaim ċille, ⁊ giollu macliacc ua branáin do oirdneaḋ ina ionaḋ is in abbdaine.

Maiḋm for cenel nEnda ria neaċmarcaċ ua ccaṫain, ⁊ ria niall ua ngairmleaḋaiġ ⁊ ár mór do cor forra.

Maġnus ua maoilseaċluinn tiġherna airṫir miḋi do ċroċhaḋ la gallaiḃ iar ffeallaḋ fair in áṫ truim.

Roi de Limerick, & diminue beaucoup la perte des Anglois. Cet échec causa tant de chagrin au Comte Strongbow, qu'il s'enferma pour quelque tems à Waterford sans voir personne."

Mr. Moore, however, without making any allusion to the Irish accounts of this event, gives full credence to Giraldus's story, and thus manufactures it for the use of posterity: "A reinforcement from the garrison of Dublin, which the Earl had ordered to join him at Cashel, having rested for a night at Ossory on their march, were surprised sleeping in their quarters by a strong party under Donald O'Brian, and the greater number of them put almost unresistingly to the sword."—*History of Ireland*, vol. ii. p. 273. He does not even inform us that the soldiers thus massacred were Ostmen, though Giraldus, and even Sir Richard Cox, distinctly state that they were. Cox says (*Hibernia Anglicana*), p. 27, without, however, quoting any authority, that this massacre was perpetrated by Donald [Fitzpatrick], prince of Ossory, but he observes, that the soldiers cut off were of that sort of the citizens of Dublin called *Easterlings*.

[s] *Waterford*, in Irish, Port Láirge, which is the name of the city of Waterford at the present day in Irish. Both names seem to be of Danish origin, and the latter is most probably derived from a Danish chieftain, Lairge, who is mentioned in these Annals at the year 951.

[a] *Ara*.—The territory of O'Donnagan, and afterwards of a powerful branch of the O'Briens, the chief of whom was styled Mac-I-Brien-Ara, is now called Ara, and sometimes Duharra, and is a half barony in the county of Tipperary bor-

English were slain in this battle, and only a few of them survived with the Earl, who proceeded in sorrow to his house at Waterford[z]. O'Brien returned home in triumph.

Melaghlin O'Donnagan, Lord of Ara[a], was slain by O'Cona[ing[b]].

THE AGE OF CHRIST, 1175.

The Age of Christ, one thousand one hundred seventy-five.

O'Brien, Bishop of Kildare, died.

Maelisa Mac an Chlerigh Cuirr, Bishop of Ulidia (Down), died.

Giolla Donnell Mac Cormac, Bishop of Ulidia, died.

Flaherty O'Brollaghan, successor of St. Columbkille, a tower of wisdom and hospitality, a man to whom, on account of his goodness and wisdom, the clergy of Ireland had presented a bishop's chair, and to whom the presidency of Hy [Iona] had been offered, died in righteousness, after exemplary sickness, in the Duibhregles of Columbkille; and Gilla Mac Liag O'Branan was appointed in his place in the abbacy[c].

The Kinel-Enda[d] were defeated, and a great slaughter made of them by Eachmarcach O'Kane[e], and Niall O'Gormly.

Manus O' Melaghlin, Lord of East Meath, was hanged by the English, after they had acted treacherously towards him at Trim.

dering on the River Shannon.

[b] *O'Conaing.*—The last syllable of this name is effaced in the original, but it is here restored from the Dublin copy of the Annals of Innisfallen. O'Conaing resided at Caislean Ui Chonaing, now corruptly called Castleconnell, in the county of Limerick. See note [j], under the year 1175.

[c] Ƿeaċcnach is used in the *Leabhar Breac* to translate the Latin *pius*, and nemƿechcnaċ, *impius*. O'Clery explains it by the modern word ƿıṗénca, i. e. just, upright.

[d] *Kinel-Enda*, Cınel Enda, otherwise called Tir-Enda, was a territory comprising thirty quarters of land in the present county of Donegal, lying south of Inishowen, between the arms of Lough Foyle and Lough Swilly, that is, between Lifford and Letterkenny. The Kinel-Enda were descended from Enda, the youngest son of Niall of the Nine Hostages, monarch of Ireland.

[e] *Eachmarcach O'Kane*, Eaċmarcaċ Ua Caċáın.—The name Eaċmarcaċ, which signifies horse-rider, *eques*, is anglicised Eghmarkagh in the old translation of the Annals of Ulster. The surname Ua Caċaın, is anglicised O'Cahan throughout the same work, and in most Anglo-Irish records previous to the year 1700; but the form O'Kane is now so well established in the north of Ireland, that the Editor has thought it the best to adopt in this translation. —See p. 2, note [a].

Domnall caemánach mac Diarmada Ri laighen do marbhadh la hua Foirtcern ⁊ la hua nuallain i ffioll.

Mac Domnaill mic donnchadha tigherna Ossraighi do marbhadh i mebhail la domnall ua mbriain.

Taodhg mac Fergail uí Ruairc do marbhadh.

Diarmaid mac taidhg ui briain ⁊ Mathghamain mac toirdhealbhaigh ui briain do dalladh (.i. ina tigh budhéin i ccaislén uí conaing) la domnall ua mbriain ⁊ diarmaid do écc iarttain. Agus mac an leithdercc ui concobhair .i. Mac ui Concobhair corcmodhruadh do marbhadh beos la domnall is in ló cedna.

[f] *Donnell Kavanagh*, Domnall Caomanach.—He was the illegitimate son of Dermot, King of Leinster, and the ancestor of the most distinguished branches of the family of Mac Murrough, now Kavanagh. He was called Caomanach from having been fostered at Cill Chaomain, now Kilcavan, near Gorey, in the county of Wexford. Dermot Mac Murrough's only legitimate son, Conor, was put to death by Roderic O'Conor, monarch of Ireland, to whom he had been given as a hostage by Dermot.—*Hib. Expug.*, lib. i. cc. 10, 17. This Donnell, though illegitimate, became the most powerful of the Mac Murroughs, and attempted to become king of Leinster, but his sister Eva, the wife of the Earl Strongbow, having proved his illegitimacy, he never was able to attain to that dignity.—See *Hibernia Expugnata*, lib. i. c. 3, where Giraldus writes: "Murchardides autem audito eorum aduentu cum viris quasi quingentis (præmisso tamen Duuenaldo naturali eiusdem filio, et quanquam non legitimo, in sua tamen gente præualido) ad eos statim ouanter accessit." See also Pedigree of the Kavanaghs in the Carew Collection of MSS. in the Lambeth Library, No. 635, in which it is stated that Eva, the wife of the Earl Strongbow, to whom Dermot had bequeathed the kingdom of Leinster, proved in England and Ireland that this Donnell, and his brother Eochy, or Enna Kinsellagh, were both illegitimate.

[g] *O'Foirthcern*.—This name is probably that now made O'Fuaraeáin; anglicised Forehan, or Foran.

[h] *O'Nolan*, O'Nuallain.—He was chief of the barony of Fotharta Fea, now the barony of Forth, in the county of Carlow. O'Flaherty informs us (Ogygia, Part iii. c. 65), that the last O'Nuallan who had hereditary possessions here, died not long before his own time. The family are, however, still respectable in the territory.

[i] *The son of Donnell, son of Donough*.—He was Gillapatrick, son of Donnell, son of Donough, who was son of the Gillapatrick, from whom the family of Mac Gillapatrick, now Fitzpatrick, derived their name and origin.

[j] *Ossory*.—The ancient Ossory was a very large territory, extending, in the time of Aengus Oisreithe, in the third century, from the River Barrow to the River Suir, and from the Slieve Bloom mountains to the meeting of the Three Waters; but at the period of the introduction of Christianity it comprised no part of Munster, for it is referred to in all the lives of the primitive Irish saints as forming the south-western portion of Leinster, in fact, what the present diocese of Ossory is. See Life of St. Patrick, quoted

Donnell Kavanagh[f], the son of Dermot, King of Leinster, was treacherously slain by O'Foirtchern[g] and O'Nolan[h].

The son of Donnell, son of Donough[i], Lord of Ossory[j], was treacherously slain by Donnell O'Brien.

Teige[k], the son of Farrell O'Rourke, was killed.

Dermot, the son of Teige O'Brien, and Mahon[l], the son of Turlough[m] O'Brien, were deprived of sight in their own house at Castleconning[n], by Donnell O'Brien; and Dermot died *soon* after; and Mac an Leithdheirg O'Conor, (*i. e.* the son of O'Conor Corcomroe[o]), was also slain by Donnell on the same day.

by Ussher in his Primordia, p. 855, where Ossargy is described as "occidentalis Laginensium plaga." Also the life of St. Cronan, published by Fleming, where we read: "Mater vero ejus Sochla, id est, Larga, vocabatur quæ erat de occidentali Laginiensium plaga, id est Osraigi oriunda." O'Dugan, in his topographical poem, and Keating, in his History of Ireland, reign of Aodh Mac Ainmire, describe Ossory as extending from Slieve Bloom to the sea. In the latter centuries Ossory has been understood as comprising the country of the Fitzpatricks, or the barony of Upper Ossory, in the Queen's county; but its ancient extent is preserved in the diocese.

[k] *Teige*, Taḋg.—This name, which signifies *a poet*, and which was used in the last century as an opprobrious name for a vulgar Irishman, like Paddy in the present century, is now anglicised Timothy and Thady, and sometimes latinised *Thaddæus* and even *Theophilus*.

[l] *Mahon*, Maṫġaṁain, said by Spenser to signify *a bear*, is now anglicised Matthew, as the proper name of a man; but the Editor prefers the form Mahon, as it is used in the Irish Inquisitions and law documents, and also in names of places, and in the family name Mac Mahon.

[m] *Turlough*, Toirḋealḃach, now generally anglicised Terence; but the Editor has used the form Turlough throughout this translation, it being that most commonly found in old law documents, inquisitions, and most Anglo-Irish records.

[n] *Castleconning*, Caislen ui Chonaing, i. e. O'Conaing's, or Gunning's Castle, now corruptly anglicised Castleconnell. O'Conaing was Lord of Aos Greine, the situation of which is thus described in O'Brien's Dictionary:

"Aos-Greine, the small county of Limerick, from the hill called Knockgreine to Limerick, the ancient patrimony of the O'Conuings, whose principal castle, near Limerick, was called *Caislean O'Conaing*, or Castle Connell; Aos-trimaighe from Owny to Limerick." Castleconnell is now a village situated about six miles to the east of Limerick.

[o] *Corcomroe*, Corcmoḋruaḋ.—The barony of Corcumroe, in the west of the county of Clare, preserves the name of this territory, but the territory was unquestionably more extensive than the barony, and comprised not only this barony but also the entire of the barony of Burrin, in the east of which the abbey of Corcumroe is situated. According to the Irish genealogical books, this territory derived its name from Corc Modhruadh, the great grandson of Rury Mor, monarch of Ireland, A. M. 3845, and the ancestor of the families of O'Loughlin Burrin, and O'Conor Corcumroe, the ancient proprietors of these two baronies.

Sluaicchſḋ la Ruaiḋri ua cconcobair la Riġ Ereann i mumain, Ro ionnarb domnall ua mbriain a tuaḋmumain ⁊ ro mill an tír go mor don chur sin.

Concobor mac Concoille abb Reccléra Poil, ⁊ Pſdair, ⁊ comorba Patraicc iarttain do écc hi Roimh iar ndol do accallaim comorba Pſtair.

Giolla colum ua maolmuaiḋ, tiġſrna fſr cceall do marbaḋ la Ruaiḋri mac concobair méġ cochláin tre meabail.

AOIS CRIOSD 1176.

Aois Criosd, mile, céd, seachtmoġad, asé.

Fabar, ⁊ Ceanannus do ḟasuġaḋ do ġallaiḃ ⁊ do uiḃ briuin.

Luġhmaġ do fasuġaḋ do Saxaiḃ.

Niall mac ṁéc lochlainn do ṁarbaḋ la muinntir branáin (.i. dál mbuinne).

[p] *Mac Concoille.*—This name is now obsolete, or translated Cox, or Woods.

[q] *O'Molloy,* Ua Maolmuaiḋ.—This family descends from Maolmuaiḋ, a name signifying noble or venerable chieftain [muaḋ .i. uasal no airmidin, *Cor. Glos.*], who was lord of the territory of Feara Ceall, and was slain in the year 1019. He was descended from Fiacha, the third son of King Niall of the Nine Hostages. The name of this territory is still preserved in that of the small barony of Fircal, in the south-west of the King's County; but we have the most satisfactory evidence to prove that it originally comprised the baronies of Fircal, Ballycowan, and Ballyboy, in the same county. The name Ua Maolmuaiḋ, was originally anglicised O'Mulmoy, but it is now invariably written without the second *m*.

[r] *Mac Coghlan.*—See note on Dealbhna Eathra, at the year 1178.

[s] *Fore,* Fabar, or Fobar.—Ussher (*Primordia*, p. 966) states that Fore is called by the Irish *Baille Leabhair*, the town of books; and he has been followed by Archdall, O'Conor, Lanigan, and all other writers on Irish topography; nor was this etymology questioned till the locality was examined, in 1837, for the Ordnance Survey, by the Editor, who found that this is one of those inadvertent errors into which Ussher has fallen from his want of intimate acquaintance with the Irish language. The Irish name, as now pronounced in Westmeath, is baile ḟobair, which means the town of *Fore*, and not the town of *Books;* and Ussher was led into this error by the similarity of the pronunciation of both combinations, for baile ḟobair and bail' leabair are not very dissimilar to the ear. According to the life of St. Fechin, who founded a monastery here in the seventh century, this place was originally called Gleann Fobhar; and it is probable that the term *Fobhar* was originally applied to the remarkable springs which flow from the hill into the mill-pond at the village of Fore, for the word Fobar, or Fofar, is explained in an old Irish glossary, called

Roderic O'Conor, King of Ireland, marched with an army into Munster; he expelled Donnell O'Brien from Thomond, and much wasted the country on that expedition.

Conor Mac Concoille[p], Abbot of the church of SS. Peter and Paul, and afterwards successor of St. Patrick, died at Rome, having gone thither to confer with the successor of St. Peter.

Gillacolum O'Molloy[q], Lord of Fircall, was treacherously slain by Rory, the son of Conor Mac Coghlan[r].

THE AGE OF CHRIST, 1176.

The Age of Christ, one thousand one hundred seventy-six.

Fore[s] and Kells[t] were laid waste by the English, and by the Hy-Briuin[u].

Louth[v] was laid waste by the Saxons.

Niall, the son of Mac Loughlin, was slain by Muintir Branan, i. e. the Dal-m-Buinne[w].

Deiṁḃriuṡ do'n eagna an éigse, as signifying the same as tobar, a spring. Besides these celebrated rills which turn the mill of St. Fechin, there are in Gleann Fobhar, as it was originally called, two other wells dedicated to St. Fechin, one called tobar na Coġaine, and the other dabach Feichín. For the legend connected with the rills and mill of Fore, see Life of St. Fechin, published by Colgan in *Acta Sanctorum*, 20th January. For some account of the state of Fore in 1682, see Sir Henry Piers's account of Westmeath, published in the first vol. of Vallancey's *Collectanea;* and for a description of the ancient remains there in 1837, see a letter written by the Editor at Rathowen, dated October 13th, 1837, now preserved at the Ordnance Survey Office, Phœnix Park.

[t] *Kells*, Ceanannus.—This name was first anglicised Kenlis.—See Ussher, *De Primordiis*, p. 691. The name signifies the head seat, or residence, and is now translated Headfort, in the name of the seat and title of the present noble proprietor. There is another Ceanannus in the county of Kilkenny, which is also anglicised Kells. The castle of Kells referred to on the next page (or rather reedification of it), stood not many years since opposite Cross-street, in the town of Kells, in the county of Meath, but no part of it now remains. Tradition ascribes its erection to Hugh de Lacy.

[u] *Hy-Briuin*, uiḃ Briuin, i.e. the descendants of Brian, son of Eochaidh Muighmheodhain, monarch of Ireland in the fourth century. There were many septs of this race, but the people here referred to are probably the Hy-Briuin-Breifne, which was the tribe name of the O'Rourkes, O'Reillys, and their correlatives.

[v] *Louth*, Luġṁaġ.—The name is sometimes written Luḃmaġ, and Colgan thinks that it signifies either the plain of Lugh, a man's name, or the plain of herbs: "Lugi campus seu campus herbidus."—*Acta Sanctorum*, p. 731, col. 2, n. 7.

[w] *Dal-Buinne*, Dal mḃuinne, anglicised Dal-

Ingen Ruaidhri ui concobhair (.i. ri Ereann), ben flaithbhertaigh ui maoildoraidh do marbhadh la macaibh ui chairelláin.

Benmidhe ingen donnchadha uí cherbhaill, ben Chonmhaighe ui flainn, baintighherna ua ttuirtre ⁊ fer lí do écc.

Cúmaighe ua flainn tighherna ua ttuirtre, fer lí, ⁊ dal araidhe do marbhadh la coinmidhe la a bhrathair fén ⁊ la feraibh lí.

Saxain do ionnarbhadh do domhnall ua bhriain a luimneach tria forbhairi do dhenamh dó forra.

Caisdiall gall gá dhenamh i cc[er]nannus.

An tiarla Saxanach (.i. Riocard) do écc in áth cliath do bainne aillsi ro gabh ar a choir do miorbhailibh brighde cholaim cille ⁊ na naomh archena isa ceallu ro milleadh lais. At connairc sium féisin brighit andarlais ag a marbhadh.

Boyne.—This tribe was seated near Lough Neagh, in the present county of Antrim; and their territory was nearly coextensive with the district of Killultagh, which was a part of the county of Down in the year 1662, though now in the county of Antrim. According to the Dublin copy of the Annals of Innisfallen, at the year 1176, this tribe of Dal-Buinne was seated in the territory of Moylinny, which extended from Lough Neagh to near Carrickfergus. For the descent of the Dal Buinne, the reader is referred to O'Flaherty's *Ogygia*, part iii. c. 46. For a list of the parish churches and chapels in this territory about the year 1291, see Pope Nicholas's Taxation of the Dioceses of Down and Connor and Dromore, edited by the Rev. William Reeves, M. B.

[x] *Benmee*, benmidhe, denotes *woman or lady of Meath.* It was very common as the proper name of a woman among the ancient Irish, as was also Beanmumhan, meaning "woman, or lady of Munster."

[y] *Of Donough O'Carroll*, Donnchadha uí Cearbhaill.—This was O'Carroll, chief of Oriel, not of Ely O'Carroll. There is a curious entry respecting the death of this Donough O'Carroll of Oriel, in an ancient Antiphonarium, formerly belonging to the cathedral church of Armagh, and now preserved in Ussher's collection of MSS. in the Library of Trinity College, Dublin (Class B. Tab. 1. No. 1). It has been recently published, with a literal English translation, in Petrie's Inquiry into the Origin and Uses of the Round Towers of Ireland, p. 389.

[z] *Cooey O'Flynn*, cumaighe ua flainn.—The name of this family is now anglicised O'Lynn in the north of Ireland, and by some incorrectly made Lindsay. Their territory lay between the Lower Bann, Lough Neagh, and the sea, in the present county of Antrim; but there seems to have been another branch of them in the barony of Loughinsholyn, in the south of the county of Derry, where they gave name to Lough Inish O'Lynn, i. e. the lake of O'Lynn's island, near the village of Desartmartin, and also to Desert Lyn and Monaster Lynn, in the same neighbourhood.

The pedigree of this famous family, who were the senior branch of the Clanna Rury of Uladh, or Ulidia, is thus given in a MS. in Trinity College, Dublin, Class H. 1. 15. p. 266, line 28:

The daughter of Roderic O'Conor, King of Ireland, and wife of Flaherty O'Muldory, was killed by the sons of O'Carellan.

Benmee[x], the daughter of Donough O'Carroll[y], and wife of Cooey O'Flynn, lady of Hy-Tuirtre and Firlee, died.

Cooey O'Flynn[z], Lord of Hy-Tuirtre[a], Firlee, and Dalaradia, was slain by Cumee, his own brother, and the Firlee.

The English were driven from Limerick by Donnell O'Brien, by laying siege to them.

An English castle was in progress of erection at Kells.

The English Earl (i. e. Richard[b]) died in Dublin, of an ulcer which had broken out in his foot through the miracles of SS. Bridget and Columbkille, and of all the other saints whose churches had been destroyed by him. He saw, as he thought, St. Bridget in the act of killing him.

1. Rory, the son of
2. Donnell, who was son of
3. Cumee, or Cu-Midhe.
4. Murtough, or Moriertagh.
5. Alexander.
6. Cumee, or Cu-Midhe.
7. Cooley, or Cu-Uladh.
8. Cumee, or Cu-Midhe.
9. Rory.
10. Foley.
11. Mac Kieran.
12. Hugh, or Aodh.
13. Donnagan.
14. Forgartagh.
15. Flann, the progenitor, *a quo* the O'Lynns [Uı Loınn], &c. &c. up to *Colla Uais*, monarch of Ireland in the fourth century.

The name Cu maighe, meaning *dog*, or *greyhound of the plain*, and Cumidhe, *dog*, or *greyhound of Meath*, were very common among this family. The former is anglicised Cooey, and the latter Cumee, throughout this translation.

[a] *Hy-Tuirtre*, Uı Tuıpτpe, was the ancient name of a territory in the county of Antrim, lying to the east of Lough Neagh. The parishes of Racavan, Ramoan, Donnagorr, and Killead, the church of Dun Chille Bice, now Downkillybegs, in the parish of Drummaul, and the island of Inis Toide, now Church Island, in Lough Beg, were included in this territory, which was the name of a deanery in Colgan's time.—See *Trias Thaum.*, p. 183.

The tribe called the Firlee, and sometimes Fir Li of the Bann, were originally seated on the west side of that river, but at this period they were unquestionably on the east of it. They were probably driven from their original locality by the family of O'Kane, who, at this period, had possession of all the district lying between Lough Foyle and the Bann. For the descent of the Fir Li of the Bann, see *Ogygia*, part iii. c. 76; *Ogygia Vindicated*, Dedication, p. lvi; and Duald Mac Firbis's Genealogical Book, Marquis of Drogheda's copy, pp. 95, 128.

[b] *The English Earl*, i. e. Richard de Clare, Earl of Strigul, commonly called Strongbow. Matthew Paris inserts the death of this earl at the same year; but Pembridge places it about the 1st of

Caislén Sláine i raibe Riocard flemeann co na sluagh, ar ro bás oc milleadh oirgiall ⁊ ua mbriúin ⁊ fer mide do orccain la Maoileachlainn mac meclochlainn la ticchearna cenel neogain ⁊ la cenel neogain budén ⁊ la hairgiallaib. Ro marbsat cúicc céd no ní as uille do na gallaib la taeb ban, leanamh ⁊ each co ná terna duine i mbethaidh as in ccaisdiall. Ro faraighte tri caisteoill im mide ar nabarach ar uamhan cenél neogain .i. caistiall cenannsa, caislén calatroma ⁊ caislen doire Pattraic. Riocard flemenn fein do marbhadh don chur sin.

Baile biataigh do ioḋbairt la Ruaidhri ua concobair Ri Ereann don coimdedh ⁊ do naoimh bearach go brath .i. baile tuama achadh. Isiad Slana na hogh-dilsi go brath. Cadhla ua dubhthaigh airdepscop tuama, aireachtach ua Roduib, flann ua fionnachta, aodh ua floinn, Ruarc ua Maoilbreanainn, Ignaidhe ua mannacháin, Giollu an coimdedh mac an leastair, ua hainligi, ⁊ concobar mac diarmada, a ccoraigheacht an baile sin do bheith ag dia ⁊ ag bearach go brath ó ua cconcobair ⁊ o fior a ionaid.

Domhnall mac toirdealbaigh uí Concobair ticchearna tuaisceirt Connacht, ordan, Smacht ⁊ deghcomhairle na ngaoidheal do écc ⁊ a adhnacal i maigh eo na Saxan.

Domhnall mac toirdhealbaigh uí briain rioghdamhna mumhan do écc.

May, 1177, and Giraldus Cambrensis about the 1st of June. In the Dublin copy of the Annals of Innisfallen, Strongbow is called the greatest destroyer of the clergy and laity that came to Ireland since the time of Turgesius. His character is thus given by Giraldus, who was his cotemporary:

"Comiti vero modus hic erat. Vir subrufus, lentiginosus, oculis glaucis, facie fœminea, voce exili, collo contracto, per cetera fere cuncta, corpore precero, vir liberalis & lenis. Quod re non poterat, verborum suauitate componebat. Togatus & inermis parere paratior, quam imperare. Extra bellum plus militis, quam Ducis: inbello vero plus Ducis quam militis habens: omnia suorum audens consilio: Nihil vnquam ex se vel armis aggrediens, vel animositate præsumens. In prœlio positus fixum suis recuperationis & refugii signum manebat. In vtraque belli fortuna stabilis & constans, nec casibus aduersis desperatione fluctuans; nec secundis vlla leuitate discurrens."—*Hibernia Expugnata*, lib. i. cap. 27, Camden. Francofurti, M.D.CIII. p. 774.

[c] *Slane*, Slaine, now generally called Baile Sláine in Irish. It is a small village near the Boyne, midway between Navan and Drogheda, in the county of Meath. The site of Fleming's Castle is now occupied by the seat of the Marquess of Conyngham.

[d] *Besides women, children, and horses*, le taeb ban leanamh ⁊ each.—This was evidently copied by the Four Masters from the Annals of Ulster, in which the original reads as follows: du in ro marbad cet no ni is moo do ghallaib re taeb ban ⁊ leanum ⁊ ec in caisteoil do marbad

The castle of Slane[c], in which was Richard Fleming with his forces, and from which he used to ravage Oriel, Hy-Briuin, and Meath, was plundered by Melaghlin, the son of Mac Loughlin, Lord of the Kinel-Owen, by the Kinel-Owen themselves and the men of Oriel. They killed five hundred or more of the English, besides women, children, and horses[d]; and not one individual escaped with his life from the castle. Three castles were left desolate in Meath on the following day, through fear of the Kinel-Owen, viz. the castle of Kells, the castle of Galtrim[e], and the castle of Derrypatrick[f]. Richard Fleming himself was slain on this occasion.

A ballybetagh was granted in perpetuity by Roderic O'Conor, King of Ireland, viz. the townland of Toomaghy[g] to God and St. Berach. The following were the sureties of that perpetual gift: Keyly [Catholicus] O'Duffy, Archbishop of Tuam; Aireaghtagh O'Rodiv; Flann O'Finnaghty; Hugh O'Flynn; Rourke O'Mulrenin; Ignatius O'Monahan; Gilla-an-choimhdhe Mac-an-leastair; O'Hanly; and Conor Mac Dermot; who were to guarantee that this townland was to remain for ever the property of God and St. Berach, from O'Conor and his representative.

Donnell, the son of Turlough O'Conor, Lord of the north of Connaught, the glory, the moderator, and the good adviser of the Irish people, died, and was interred at Mayo of the Saxons.

Donnell, the son of Turlough O'Brien, the heir apparent to the kingdom of Munster, died.

co ná térna duine i mbethaid ar in caistel. Thus rendered in the old translation of the Ulster Annals: "where one hundred and more were killed of the Galls, besides women and children, and the horses of the castle, soe as none living escaped out of the castle."

[e] *The castle of Caltruim.*—Caislen Cala Troma, i. e. the castle of Galtrim. Galtrim is now the name of a townland, containing a moat, in a parish of the same name, in the barony of Deece, and county of Meath. The district belonging to this castle was an ancient palatinate, and gave the title of Baron to the family of Hussey, whose ancestor had been a butcher in the town of Athenry, but who was knighted for having killed O'Kelly and his esquire, in the battle of Athenry, in the year 1316. *q. v.*—See *Hibernia Anglicana*, by Sir Richard Cox, p. 96.

[f] Doire Patraic, now Derrypatrick, a townland containing the ruins of an old castle, in a parish of the same name, in the barony of Deece, and county of Meath.—See *Ordnance Map of Meath*, sheet 43.

[g] *Toomaghy*, tuaim achadh.—A ballybetagh was the thirtieth part of a *triocha cead*, or barony. It contained four quarters, or seisreaghs, each seisreagh containing 120 acres of the *large* Irish measure. The name of this ballybetagh is

Doṁnall ua máilli tiġearna uṁaill do écc.

Diarmait mac corbmaic még carṫaiġ ri dſrmuṁan do ġabáil la a ṁac fſin corbmac liathanaċ ⁊ corbmac do ṁarḃaḋ hi ffiull la a ṁuintir buḋein ⁊ diarmait do ġabáil a tiġearnais iaram.

Doṁnall mac giollapatraicc tiġearna osraiġe do écc.

Aoḋ mac giollabroidi ui ruairc do écc.

Doṁnall mac giolla patraic tiġearna cairppre ua cciarḋa, do marḃaḋ i ffiull dua maoileċlainn (.i. Art), ⁊ Art do aiṫriogaḋ la fearaiḃ miḋe, ⁊ riġe (no ticceարnus) do ṫaḃairt do ḋonnchaḋ ua maoileċlainn agus flann a ṁac do ṁarḃaḋ la cairppre ua cciarḋa.

AOIS CRIOSD 1177.

Aois Criosd mile, céṫt seaċtmoġat, a seaċt.

Uiuianus cardinal do ṫeaċt i nErinn. Seanaḋ clſreaċ Erenn do bſiṫ ettir epscopaib ⁊ abbaiḃ iman ccardinal in ath cliaṫ an cſd doṁnaċ don corgus ⁊ ro ċinnsſd deithiḋe iomḋa ná coṁailtear.

Aeḋ O Nell .i. an macaoṁ tóinlescc ticchſrna cenel neoġain re headh ⁊ Rioġḋaṁna Ereann do ṁarḃaḋ la maoileaċlainn ua loċlainn ⁊ la hardġal ua laċlainn ⁊ ardġal feisin do ċoṁṫuitim la hua nell ar an laṫair sin.

Sluaicchſḋ la Iohn do cuirt ⁊ las na ridiriḋiḃ i ndal araiḋe ⁊ co dun

now forgotten. It must have been applied to a large townland, since subdivided into quarters, somewhere near Kilbarry, in the north-east side of the county of Roscommon, where St. Berach's principal church is situated. But the name does not appear in any form on the Down Survey for Connaught, or on the Ordnance Survey.

[h] *Cardinal Vivianus.*—He was sent to Ireland by Pope Alexander III., as apostolic Legate. According to Rogerus Hoveden, and the Chronicle of Man at this year, Vivianus was in the Isle of Man on Christmas-day with King Gothred. After Epiphany he landed at Downpatrick, and on his way to Dublin was taken prisoner by the soldiers of John de Courcy, by whom he was set at liberty. Giraldus Cambrensis states, in his *Hibernia Expugnata*, lib. ii. c. 17, that this Legate held a synod at Dublin, in which he published the King of England's title to Ireland, and pronounced excommunication against all that should oppose it; that he also gave leave to the English, to take out of the churches and monasteries corn and other provisions as often as they should require them, always paying the true value for the same. To which Hanmer most impertinently adds: "He filled his bagges with the sinnes of the people; the English captaines understanding of it, gave him in charge, either to depart the land, or to goe to the warres, and serve for pay with them, and no longer to re-

Donnell O'Malley, Lord of Umallia [the Owles, in the county of Mayo], died.

Dermot, the son of Cormac Mac Carthy, King of Desmond, was taken prisoner by his own son, Cormac Liathanach; but Cormac was treacherously slain by his own people, and Dermot then re-assumed his lordship.

Donnell Mac Gillapatrick [now Fitzpatrick], Lord of Ossory, died.

Hugh, the son of Gilla-Broidi O'Rourke, died.

Donnell, son of Gillapatrick [O'Keary], Lord of Carbury O'Keary, was treacherously slain by O'Melaghlin (i. e. Art), upon which Art was deposed by the men of Meath, and his kingdom (or lordship) was given to Donough O'Melaghlin; and his son Flann was slain by *the inhabitants of* Carbury O'Keary.

THE AGE OF CHRIST, 1177.

The Age of Christ, one thousand one hundred seventy and seven.

Cardinal Vivianus[h] arrived in Ireland. A synod of the clergy of Ireland, both bishops and abbots, *was convened* by this cardinal on the first Sunday in Lent, and they enacted many ordinances not *now* observed.

Hugh O'Neill, *popularly called* an Macaemh Toinleasc, *who had been* for some time Lord of the Kinel-Owen, and heir presumptive to the throne of Ireland, was slain by Melaghlin O'Loughlin[i] and Ardgal O'Loughlin; but Ardgal himself fell on the spot by O'Neill.

An army was led by John De Courcy[j] and the knights into Dalaradia and

ceive money for nought."—*Hanmer's Chronicle*, edition of 1809, pp. 295, 296. See also the same fact given as true history by Sir Richard Cox in his *Hibernia Anglicana*, pp. 33, 34.

[i] *O'Loughlin.*—The name of this family, which was the senior branch of the northern Hy-Niall, is now generally written Mac Loughlin.

[j] *John De Courcy.*—He set out from Dublin, and in four days arrived at Downpatrick. The character and personal appearance of this extraordinary man are thus described by his cotemporary, Giraldus Cambrensis:

"Erat itaque Iohannes vir albus & procerus, membris neruosis & ossosis, staturæ grandis, & corpore perualido, viribus immensis, audaciæ singularis, vir fortis & bellator ab adolescentia. Semper in acie primus, semper grauioris periculi pondus arripiens. Adeo belli cupidus & ardens, vt militi dux præfectus, ducali plerunque deserta constantia Ducem exuens, et militem induens, inter primos impetuosus & præceps: turma vacillante suorum, nimia vincendi cupiditate victoriam amisisse videretur. Et quanquam in armis immoderatus, & plus militis quam Ducis habens, inermis tamen modestus, ac sobrius, & Ecclesiæ Christi debitam reueren-

da Lethghlass. Ro marbhsat Domhnall mac mic Cathasaigh tighearna Dál Araidhe. Ro hoirccceadh ⁊ ro milleadh dun da Lethghlass la Iohn ⁊ las na

tiam præstans, diuino cultui per omnia deditus: Gratiæque supernæ, quoties ei successerat, cum gratiarum actione totum ascribens, Deoq; dans gloriam, quoties aliquod fecerat gloriosum. Sed quoniam, vt ait Tullius, Nihil simplici in genere, omni ex parte perfectum natura expoliuit: nimiæ parcitatis & inconstantiæ nœui, niueum tantæ laudis nitorem denigrauerant. Regis itaque Manniæ Gotredi filia sibi legitime copulata, post varia belli diuturni proelia: & graues vtrinque conflictus, tandem in arce victoriæ plane constitutus, Vltoniam vndique locis idoneis incastellauit. & nusquam (non absque labore plurimo) & inedia, multisque periculis, pace firmissima stabiliuit. Hoc autem mihi notabile videtur: quod grandes hi quatuor Hibernicæ expugnationis postes, Stephanides, Herucius, Reymundus, & Iohannes de Curcy (occulto quidem Dei iudicio, sed nunquam iniusto) legitimam ex sponsis prolem suscipere non meruerunt. Quintum autem his Meylerium adiunxerim, qui legitimam vsque hodie de sponsa prolem non suscepit. Sed hæc de Iohanne Curcy summatim, & quasi sub epilogo commemorantes, grandiaq; eiusdem gesta, suis explicanda scriptoribus reliquentes."—*Hibernia Expugnata*, lib. ii. cap. xvii.

[k] *Donnell, son of Cahasagh*, Domhnall mac Cathasaigh.—In the Dublin copy of the Annals of Ulster, and in the Annals of Kilronan, he is called Domhnall mac mic Cathusaigh, i. e. Donnell, son of the son, i. e. grandson of Cahasagh. In the Dublin copy of the Annals of Innisfallen, the chieftain who contended with De Courcy at Down, on this occasion, is called Rory Mac Donslevy; and it is certain that the family name was Mac Donslevy at this time, though it was originally *O'h-Eochadha* (O'Haughy). The name is latinized *Dunleuus* by Giraldus Cambrensis; but Dr. Hanmer, who knew but little of Irish families or history, supposing that by Dunleuus (which he reads incorrectly *Dunlenus*) Giraldus meant O'Donnell, he speaks throughout of the chief who contended with De Courcy, at Down, as O'Donell! Giraldus, who was cotemporary with Sir John De Courcy, speaks in high terms of the valour of the King of Down, who contended with him on this occasion. It appears that the Pope's Legate, Cardinal Vivianus, happened to be at Downpatrick on De Courcy's arrival, and that he endeavoured to prevail on De Courcy to withdraw his forces from Down, on condition that Dunlevus should pay tribute to the King of England. De Courcy refusing to comply, Dunlevus, encouraged by the suggestions of the Legate, collected his forces, and attacked the English, we are told, with astonishing bravery; but if we believe Giraldus's statement, that he mustered ten thousand warriors, who, fighting manfully (*viriliter*) with spears and battle-axes, were defeated by three hundred English soldiers, commanded by twenty-two knights, we must conclude that his people were either very feeble or very unskilful warriors. Giraldus describes the conquest of Down by De Courcy in the sixteenth chapter of the second book of his *Hibernia Expugnata*, where he writes as follows:

"Videns autem Dunleuus se verbis minime profecturum, corrogatis vndiq; viribus cum 10. bellatorum millibus infra 8. dies hostes in vrbe viriliter inuadit. In hac etenim insula sicut et in omni natione, gens borealis magis bellica semper et truculenta reperitur, &c., &c.

"Prospiciens itaq; Iohannes hostiles acies acriter ad vrbem accedere: quanquam manu modica, tamen perualida, potius obuiam exire, & viribus dimicando, belli fata tentare, quam

to Dun da leathghlas; they slew Donnell, the grandson of Cathasach[k], Lord of Dalaradia. Dun da leathghlas was plundered and destroyed by John and the

exili municipio, quod in vrbis angulo tenuiter erexerat, diutius ab hoste claudi, & fame confici longe præelegit. Igitur atroci bello conserto, in primo eminus sagittarum iaculorumq; grandine perfuso. Deinde cominus lanceæ lanceis, securibus enses confligentes: ad tartara multos vtrinq; transmittunt. Dum igitur acerrimo Martis conflictu, *Iam clypeo clypeus, vmbone repellitur vmbo: Ense minax ensis, pede pes, & cuspide cuspis:* qui gladii Ioannis ictus hic cerneret, qualiter nunc caput ab humeris, nunc armos à corpore, nunc brachia separabat, viri bellatoris vires digne possit commendare. Multis igitur in hoc conflictu se strenue gerentibus: Roger. tamen Poerius adolescens imberbis & flauus, pulcher & procerus (qui postmodum in Lechliniæ & Ossyriæ partibus emicuit) secundam non immerito laudem obtinuit. Post graues itaq; diuq; ambiguos, nimis impari certamine belliq; congressus, tandem Ioannis virtuti cessit victoria: hostium multitudine magna per marinam glisin, quo transfugerant, interempta."

And again, in his short recapitulation of the battles of De Courcy, towards the end of the same chapter:

"In duobus itaque magnis præliis Iohannes apud Dunam victor enituit. In primo post purificationem. In secundo circa Calendas Iulii, in natiuitate Sancti Iohannis, vir de quindecim virorum militibus [al. millibus] victoriam obtinuit cum paucissimis, hostium extincta multitudine. Tertium erat apud Ferly in prædæ captione," &c.

It is stated in the Dublin copy of the Annals of Innisfallen, a work which seems to have been very much interpolated, that John De Courcy on this occasion erected a strong fort of stones and clay at Down, and drew a ditch or wall from sea to sea, but that he was defeated and taken prisoner, and the greater part of his men slain by Rory Mac Donslevy; that he was afterwards set at liberty; and that the English, taking fresh courage, being led on by De Courcy and a valiant knight called Roger Poer, again attacked the Irish and made a great slaughter of them; and took from them the croziers of St. Finghin and St. Ronan, and that then all the English of Dublin went to the assistance of De Courcy. These Annals then add:—"Melaghlin O'Neill [*recte* Mac Loughlin], at the head of the Kinel-Owen, and Rory Mac Donslevy, at the head of the Ulidians, accompanied by the Archbishop of Armagh, Gilla-an-choimdedh O'Carran, the Bishop of Ulidia, and the clergy of the north of Ireland, repaired with their noble relics to Downpatrick, to take it from John De Courcy. A fierce battle was fought between them, in which the Kinel-Owen and Ulidians were defeated, with the loss of five hundred men, among whom were Donnell O'Laverty, chief of Clann Hamill; Conor O'Carellan, chief of Clann-Dermot; Gilla Mac Liag O'Donnelly, chief of Ferdroma; Gilla-an Choimdedh Mac Tomulty, chief of Clann Mongan; and the chiefs of Clann Cartan and Clann Fogarty. The Archbishop of Armagh, the Bishop of Down, and all the clergy, were taken prisoners; and the English got possession of the croziers of St. Comgall and St. Dachiarog, the Canoin Phatruic [i. e. the Book of Armagh], besides a bell called *Ceolan an Tighearna*. They afterwards, however, set the bishops at liberty, and restored the Canoin Phatruic and the bell, but they killed all the inferior clergy, and kept the other noble relics, which" [remarks this compiler] "are still in the hands of the English."

Dr. Hanmer, in describing this battle, states

ridiribh táinic i na ṡochraide. Do ronadh dona caislen leó ann ar a ttugsat maidhm fo dhí ar ulltaibh ⁊ maidhm for cenél eoghain ⁊ for airghiallaibh airm in ro marbhadh conċobhor o caireallain toiseaċ cloinne diarmada ⁊ giollumac-liacc ua donngaile toiseċ ḟer nDroma. Ro gonadh ann beos domhnall ua flaiṫbheartaiġ do ṡoighdibh gur ba marb é iaramh do na gonaibh sin i necclés póil in árdmaċa iar ccaiṫeṁ cuirp crioſt ⁊ a ḟola, iar nongadh ⁊ aith-ricche. Ro marbhadh dona maiṫe iomdha aile leó cenmothaitsidhe. Táinic Iohn do cúirt co na sochraidi an feaċt ceadna i nuibh tuirtre ⁊ i ffearaibh lí. Ro loiscc Cúmidhe ua flainn airṫear ṁaiġe reiṁe. Ro loisccsit dona cul raṫain, ⁊ ceallu iomdha oile.

Niall ua Gairmleadhaiġ tigchearna ḟer maiġe hiṫe ⁊ cenél ennda do mar-

that De Courcy was opposed by Roderic [O Conor] the Monarque and *O'Donnell*, king of *Duune!* See his Chronicle, Dublin edition of 1809, p. 300; and Cox (*Hibernia Anglicana*), p. 32, gravely repeats this blunder as true history. By this expedition and battle were fulfilled, in the opinion of both parties, two prophecies, which would appear to have depressed the spirit of the Ultonians, and animated De Courcy and his superstitious followers for further conquests. The one was a prophecy among the Britons, said to have been delivered by Merlin of Caermarthen, in the latter part of the fifth century, and which had declared that "a white knight, sitting on a white horse, and bearing birds on his shield, would be the first that with force of arms would enter and invade Ulster." ("Miles albus, albo residens equo, aues in clypeo gerens, Vltoniam hostili inuasione primus intrabit.") The other was a prophecy ascribed to Saint Columbkille, who had foreseen this battle not long after the time of Merlin, and who had written in Irish that a certain pauper and beggar, and fugitive from another country ("quendam pauperem & mendicum & quasi de aliis terris fugacem") would come to Down with a small army and obtain possession of the town, and that such would be the slaughter of the citizens that the enemy would wade up to the knees in their blood. Stanihurst, enlarging on a slight hint thrown out by Giraldus in his account of these prophecies, writes that De Courcy, in his anxiety to adapt these prophecies to himself, took every care to adapt himself to the prophecies, and with that view provided for his equipment, on his expedition to Downpatrick, a white horse, a shield with birds painted upon it, and all the other predicted appendages of the predestined conqueror of Ulster; so that he sallied forth like an actor dressed to perform a part! This, however, is overdrawing the picture; for Giraldus says that De Courcy happened by mere chance (*forte*) to ride upon a white horse on this occasion, and had little birds (*aviculas*) painted on his shield, evidently the cognizance of his family; but he distinctly states, however, that De Courcy always carried about with him a book in the Irish language, containing the prophecies of St. Columbkille, as a mirror in which the achievements which he himself was predestined to perform were to be seen; to which Stanihurst, drawing on his imagination, impertinently adds, that he slept with this book under his pillow! "Ad dormiendum proficiscens, eundem sub cubicularis lecti pulvino collocaret." The charge brought by Dr. Hanmer against Cam-

knights who came in his army. A castle was erected by them there, out of which they defeated the Ulidians twice, and the Kinel-Owen and Oriels *once*, slew Conor O'Carellan, chief of Clandermot[l], and Gilla-Macliag O'Donnelly, chief of Feardroma[m]; and Donnell O'Flaherty [now Laverty] was so wounded by arrows on this occasion, that he died of his wounds in the church of St. Paul at Armagh, after having received the body and blood of Christ, and after extreme unction and penance. Many other chieftains were also slain by them besides these. During the same expedition, John [De Courcy] proceeded with his forces to Hy-Tuirtre and Firlee; before his arrival, however, Cumee O'Flynn had set Armoy[n] on fire; but they burned Coleraine and many other churches on this incursion.

Niall O'Gormly, Lord of the men of Magh-Ithe and Kinel-Enda[o], was

brensis, that having malevolent feelings towards De Courcy, he slightly passed over and misrepresented his actions, seems very unfounded, for Cambrensis speaks of the noble achievements of this knight in terms of the highest admiration, saying that he would leave his grand exploits to be blazoned by De Courcy's own writers, evidently alluding to the monk Jocelyn, who was at the time employed by De Courcy to write the Life of St. Patrick. "Sed hæc de Johanne Curcy summatim, & quasi sub epilogo commemorantes, grandiaq; eiusdem gesta suis explacanda scriptoribus reliquentes."—*Hiber. Expugnat.* lib. ii. c. 17.

[l] *Clandermot.*—The name is yet preserved in Clondermot, a parish in the barony of Tirkeeran, in the county of Derry, east of the Foyle. The O'Caireallans are still numerous in this parish, but the name is variously anglicised Carlan, Curland, Carellan, Carelton, &c.

[m] *Feardroma.*—This was an ancient territory in the county of Tyrone, containing Castle-Cauldfield, anciently Ballydonnelly, and the surrounding district.—See note on Ballydonnelly, at the year 1531. It is to be distinguished from the townland of Fordruim, or Fardrome, mentioned in the Donegal Inquisitions, which never at any period belonged to the O'Donnellys.

[n] *Armoy*, Aireṫermuiġe.—The author of the Tripartite Life of St. Patrick, which was translated and published by Colgan, in his *Trias Thaum.*, calls this "*Arthermugia præcipua civitas Dalriedinorum.*" It was anciently a bishop's see, and an ecclesiastical town of consequence; but in Colgan's time it was only a small village in the territory of Reuta. It is still called by its ancient name in Irish, but is anglicised Armoy. It retains at present no monumental evidence of its ancient importance except a part of an ancient round tower, which, however, is no small proof of its ancient ecclesiastical importance. Colgan in his *Acta S. S.*, p. 377, col. 2, note 6, describes it as follows: "Est hodie vicus tantum exiguus in regione Reuta juxta Oceanum octo circiter millibus passuum a Dunliffsia" [Dunluce] "distans."

[o] *Magh-Ithe and Kinel-Enda.*—*Magh Ithe*, i. e. the plain of Ith, is said to have derived its name from Ith, the uncle of Milesius of Spain, who, according to some of the Irish Shanachies, was slain by the Tuatha De Dananns, at Drumline, near Lifford, and buried in this plain.—See Keating's History of Ireland, Haliday's edition,

ḃaḋ la donnchaḋ ua ccairealláin ⁊ la cloinn diarmada ar lár ḋoire ċolaimm ċille ar ro loisccead teaċ fair cetus ⁊ terna niall amaċ ass ⁊ ro marḃaḋ i ndorus an tiċhe iarttain. Da roine doná Donnchaḋ ua cairelláin ogsíṫ fri dia fri colaim cille ⁊ fri muinntir ḋoire annsin tar a cenn fén ⁊ tar ċenn a ṡleaċta .i. a ṁainchine fen, a ṁec, a ua, ⁊ a iarmua tria biṫhe do colaim ċille ⁊ do muinntir ḋoire. Ro iodḃair doná baile biataiġ i fforrad doṁnaiġ ṁóir ḋóiḃ. Do rad dóiḃ ḃeós Mac riaḃaċ .i. corn as ferr boi i nErinn is in aimsir sin i ngioll tri fichit bó. Do ronad imorra teaċ don cleireaċ i monad an tiġe ro loisccead uadha for ua ngairmleadhaiġ. Ro hiocad uile ffris gaċ ar loisccead imbe. Do radsat clann ndiarmada uile lórgnioṁ tar a ccenn fen uatha.

Murċaḋ mac Ruaiḋri ui Concoḃair do ḃreiṫ Mile coca co na ridiriḃ lais go Ros commain do milleaḋ Connaċt ar ulca fri Ruaiḋri. Ro loisccsed doná Connaċtaiġ fo cedoir tuaim do gualann ⁊ ceallu an tire ar ċena ar na hairirsedís goill inntiḃ. Ro chuirset iarttain maiḋm forr na gallaiḃ ⁊ ró diochuirset ar éccin as an tír iatt. Ro ḋall Ruaiḋri a mac murchaḋ i ccionaḋ an turais sin.

p. 266, and note on Druim lighean, in these Annals, at the year 1522. From the situation of the parish church called Domhnach more Muighe Ithe, or the great church of Magh Ithe, now Donaghmore, it is quite evident that Magh Ithe is the tract of level land in the barony of Raphoe, now called the Lagan. The territory of Kinel-Enda lay immediately south of Inishowen, and comprised the parishes of Raymoaghy and Taughboyne.—See Colgan's *Acta Sanctorum*, Life of St. Baithenus. The Editor has a copy of the will of O'Gallagher, who was steward to the celebrated Red Hugh O'Donnell, in which it is stated that Kinel-Enda contained thirty quarters of land.

[p] *Near Donaghmore*, Doṁnaċ mór, i. e. the great church, generally called Doṁnaċ mor Muiġe Iṫe, as in the Tripartite Life of St. Patrick, and in O'Donnell's Life of St. Columbkille, apud Colgan. *Trias Thaum.*, p. 390. It is a parish church, near the village of Castlefin, in the barony of Raphoe and county of Donegal. It was in the territory of Magh-Ithe, of which O'Gormly was lord. From this passage it appears that O'Carellan had seized upon some of O'Gormly's territory, after he had killed him.

[q] *The tan-coloured son.*—This is a fanciful name given to the goblet. The adjective riaḃaċ, pronounced in the south of Ireland as if written riaċ, and anglicised Reagh in names of men and places, signifies tan-coloured, or greyish, and is translated *fuscus*, by Philip O'Sullevan Beare, in his History of the Irish Catholics.—See pp. 123, 145, *et passim.*

[r] *This expedition.*—The Dublin copy of the Annals of Innisfallen contains the following account of this excursion:

"A. D. 1177. A great army was led by the English of Dublin and Tullyard [near Trim] into Connaught. They proceeded first to Ros-

slain by Donough O'Carellan and the Clandermot in the middle of Derry Columbkille. The house in which he was was first set on fire, and afterwards, as he was endeavouring to effect his escape out of it, he was killed in the doorway of the house. Donough O'Carellan then made his perfect peace with God, St. Columbkille, and the family [i. e. clergy] of Derry, for himself and his descendants, and confirmed his own *mainchine* (gifts) and those of his sons, grandsons, and descendants, for ever, to St. Columbkille and the family of Derry. He also granted to them a ballybetagh near Donaghmore[p], and, moreover, delivered up to them the most valuable goblet at that time in Ireland, which goblet was called *Mac Riabhach* [i. e. the tan-coloured son[q]], as a pledge for sixty cows. There was also a house erected for the cleric, in lieu of that burned over the head of O'Gormly, and reparation was made by him for all damage caused by the burning. All the Clandermot gave likewise full satisfaction on their own behalf.

Murrough, the son of Roderic O'Conor, brought Milo de Cogan and his knights with him to Roscommon, to ravage Connaught, to annoy Roderic *his father*. The Connacians immediately burned Tuam and other churches, to prevent the English from quartering in them. They afterwards defeated the English, and forcibly drove them out of the country [of Connaught]; *and* Roderic put out the eyes of his son, in revenge for this expedition[r].

common, where they remained for three nights. Here they were joined by Murrough, the son of Roderic O'Conor, who guided them through the province. King Roderic at the time happened to be on his regal visitation, and was in Iar-Connaught when the news of this irruption into his territories reached his ear. The English proceeded through the Plain of Connaught, burning the country as they passed along, including the churches of Elphin, Fert-Geige, Imleagh Fordeorach, Imleagh an Bhroghadhia, and Dunamon, and making their way to Ath Mogha and Fiodh Monach, and passing over the Togher [causeway] of Moin Coinneadha, and through the great road of Lig Gnathaile, and the ford of Athfinn, near Dunmore, proceeded directly to Tuam; but they made no prey or battle during all this excursion, for the Connacians had fled, with their cattle and other moveable property, into the fastnesses of the country. On this occasion Tuam was evacuated, and the churches of Kilbannan, Kilmaine, Lackagh, Kilcahill, and Roskeen, and the castle of Galway, were burned. The English remained three nights at Tuam, without being able to obtain provisions, or gaining any advantage; here they were informed that the men of Connaught and Munster were on their march to give them battle, which indeed they soon perceived to be true, for they saw that Roderic gave them no time to consider, for he drew up his forces for an engagement. The English took to flight, and escaped to Tochar mona Coinneadha. They were, however, hotly pursued and attacked as

Maiḋm for ua maoildoraiḋ ⁊ for cenel cconaill ria cconcoḃor ua ccairealláin áit in ro marḃaḋ ár cenél ḟnda im mac ui Searraiġ ⁊ im maitib iomḋa archeana.

Doṁnall ua heaġhra ticcḟrna Luiġne do écc.

AOIS CRIOSD, 1178.

Aois Criosd mile, céd, seaċtmoġat a hoċt.

Bachall ċoluim mic luiġḋeaċ do ḃḟiṫ acc iomacallaṁ re na ċleireaċ fḟin co fiadnaċ.

Doṁnall ua foccarta epscop osraiġe do écc.

Giollu criosd ua heothaiḋ epscop Conmaicne do écc.

Concoḃar mac conallaiġ ui luiniġ do ġaḃáil toisiġeaċta cenéil Moen ⁊ doṁnall mac doṁnaill ui ġairmleaḋaiġ do ionnarḃaḋ a maiġ ithe i ninis eoġain do ċum donnchaḋa uí ḋuibdiorma. Cenél moién i ccionn ráiṫe iaraṁ do ċur concoḃair mic conallaiġ a toisiġeaċt, ⁊ a ccḟnnus do ṫaḃairt do ḋoṁnall mac doṁnaill ui ġairmleaḋaiġ. Muinnter doṁnaill .i. mac giollu caeċ uí ederla ⁊ uí flannaġáin do ṁarḃaḋ concoḃair mic conallaiġ i ttoiġ doṁnaill fḟisin i meaḃail ar comairce airċinniġ na hḟsnaiḋe boi ina farraḋ an tan sin. Ro ionnarbsat iaraṁ cenél Moáin doṁnall ua gairm-

they were crossing the Togher, or causeway, where they would have been defeated had not the son of Roderic assisted and guided them. They next proceeded directly to Oran-O'Clabby, and passed the next night there, and on the day following went on their retreat to Athleague, where they were overtaken at the ford by a party of Connacians, who made a vigorous attack upon them, and they did not know their losses until they were clear out of the province. For this, and other previous offences, Murrough O'Conor, the son of Roderic, had his eyes put out by the Sil-Murray, with the consent of his father." Giraldus Cambrensis, in his account of Milo de Cogan's excursion into Connaught (*Hibernia Expugnata*, lib. ii. c. 17), asserts, that the churches were burned by the Connacians themselves, and that the English, who were five hundred and forty in number, lost only three of their men! "Rothericum vero Conactiæ principem cum 3. exercitibus magnis in sylua quadam prope Sinnenum obuium habens, inito graui utrinq; conflictu, demum tribus tantum satellitibus equestribus amissis, & interemptis hostium multis, Dubliniam indemnis euasit."

[s] *Colum Mac Luighdheach.*—This is the Colman, son of Lughaidh (of the race of Niall of the Nine Hostages), whose festival is marked in the Irish Calendar of the O'Clerys, at the 2nd of February. The Editor has not been able to discover this entry in any of the older annals.

[t] *O'Loony.*—The O'Loonys were afterwards

O'Muldory and the Kinel-Connell were defeated by Conor O'Carellan *in a battle*, in which O'Sherry and many other distinguished men of the Kinel-Enda were slain.

Donnell O'Hara, Lord of Leyny [in the now county of Sligo], died.

THE AGE OF CHRIST, 1178.

The Age of Christ, one thousand one hundred seventy-eight.

The crozier of Columb Mac Luighdheach[t] openly conversed with its cleric.

Donnell O'Fogarty, bishop of Ossory, died.

Gilchreest O'Hoey, bishop of Conmaicne [Ardagh], died.

Conor, the son of Conallagh O'Loony[t], assumed the chieftainship of Kinel-Moen[u]; and Donnell, the son of Donnell O'Gormly[v], was banished from Moy Ithe into Inishowen, to Donough O'Duibhdhiorma[w]. In three months afterwards, the Kinel-Moen deposed Conor, the son of Conallagh, and gave back the chieftainship to Donnell, the son of Donnell O'Gormly. The people of Donnell *O'Gormly*, namely, Gilla Caech O'Ederla, and the O'Flanagans, treacherously slew O'Loony in Donnell's own house, *even* while he was under the protection of the Erenagh of Urney[x], who was with him at the time. Upon this the Kinel-Moen drove Donnell O'Gormly from the chieftainship, and set

driven into the wild mountainous district of Muintir-Loony, in the north of the county of Tyrone.

[u] *Kinel-Moen*.—The Kinel-Moen, or race, or descendants of Moen, the principal family of whom were the O'Gormlys, inhabited that tract now called the barony of Raphoe, which was then a part of Tir Eoghain, or Tyrone. In after times this tribe was driven across the river Foyle by the O'Donnells, and their original country was added to Tirconnell.

[v] *O'Gormly*.—An old map of Ulster, preserved in the State Papers' Office, shews the country of O'Gormly, who was originally the chief of Kinel-Moen, as extending from near Derry to Strabane.

[w] *O'Duibhdhiorma*.—The country of O'Duibhdhiorma was called Bredach, and comprised the eastern half of Inishowen. This is to be distinguished from the half cantred of Bredach in Tirawley, in the county of Mayo, the patrimonial inheritance of O'Toghda, who was descended from Muireadhach, son of Fergus, son of Amhalgaidh, *a quo* Tirawley. O'Duibhdhiorma was of the Kinel-Owen, and his family had their tomb in the old church of Moville, near Lough Foyle. The name is still numerous in the barony of Inishowen, but corruptly anglicised to Diarmid, and sometimes, but rarely, to Mac Dermot, though always pronounced O'Ծuıḃḋıaṗma by the natives when speaking Irish.

[x] *Urney*, Eṗnaıḋe, i. e. *Oratorium*.—A parish

leaḋaiġ a toiriġeaċt ⁊ tugsat Ruaiḋri ua flaiṫbertaiġ i ccennus foraiḃ. Meaḃal do ḋernaṁ la triḃ macaiḃ ui flaiṫbertaiġ for cenél Moáin. Domnall mac domnaill ui ġairmleaḋaiġ do ṁarḃaḋ leo, [⁊] Ticchernan mac Raġnaill mic domnaill ⁊ oċtar do ṁaiṫiḃ Cenél moáin immaille friu. Raġnall mac eaċmarcaiġ uí ċaṫáin do ṁarḃaḋ la cenél moáin a ttoraċ an tsraṁraiḋ sin cona ina ḋioġail side do roċair galaċ ua luiniġ ⁊ Muirċeartaċ ua Peatain, ⁊ ar na dioġail ḃeós do ronaḋ in meabail remraite for cenél Moáin.

Gaeṫ mor is in mbliaḋain si. Ro lá fioḋár, Ro trasccair sailġe. Ro trasccair doná sé fichit crann i ndoire colaim cille.

Iohn do cuirt co na allmurchaiḃ do ṫeaċt co maċaire Chonaille, do ronsat oirccne ann. Badar oiḋċe longpuirt i nglionn riġe iaraṁ. Do bert

partly in the county of Tyrone, and partly in the county of Donegal, extending to the south of Lifford.

[y] *O'Flaherty*, in Irish Ua Flaiṫbertaiġ.—This name is still common in the counties of Donegal, Derry, and Tyrone, but, by an aspiration of the initial f, is anglicised Laverty, and sometimes Lafferty.—See note on O'Flainn, where a similar suppression of the initial f takes place in the modern anglicised form O'Lynn.

[z] *Derry-Columbkille.*—This passage is given in the Annals of Kilronan, as follows: "A. D. 1178. Gaoṫ aḋḃal do ṫoiġeċt is in mbliaḋain si, co ro trascair bloiḋ ṁoir do ċoilltiḃ ⁊ d'ḟioḃaiḋiḃ, ⁊ do sailġiḃ ra ṁóra fri lár, ⁊ co trascair sos se fiċit salaċ, uel paulo plus, a ndoire colaim cille.

"A. D. 1178. A great wind occurred in this year, which prostrated a great portion of the woods, forests, and great oaks, and prostrated among the rest six score oaks, *vel paulo plus, in Roboreto Columbæ Cille.*"

The word sail, plur. sailġe, signifies an oak tree. The oak wood of Derry-Columbkille, now Londonderry, is specially mentioned in O'Donnell's Life of Columbkille, as an object for which the saint had a peculiar veneration.

[a] *Machaire Chonaille*, i. e. the plain of Conaille Muirtheimhne, a territory comprising the level part of the present county of Louth, as appears from the ancient Lives of St. Bridget and St. Monenna, and from the Festilogy of Aengus, and other calendars, which place in this territory the churches of Faughard, Iniskeen, Kill Uinche, and Druim Ineascluinn. This district retained the name of Machaire Chonaille in the seventeenth century, as we learn from Archbishop Ussher, who, in his notices of St. Bridget and St. Monenna, has the following notice of this territory: "Intra alterum autem à Dundalkiâ miliarium, in Louthiano Comitatu & territorio olim *Conayl-Murthemni & Campo Murthemene* (in quo Conaleorum gens maximè viget, *de quâ & ipsa sanctissima Monenna procreata est;* ut habet in libri secundi Vitæ illius initio Conchubranus) hodie *Maghery-Conall* dicto, posita est villa *Fochard:* quem *locum nativitatis Brigidæ virginis* habitum fuisse, & in Vitâ Malachiæ notavit olim Bernardus, & hodierna totius viciniæ traditio *Fochardam Brigidæ* eam appellantis etiam nunc confirmat."—*Primordia*, pp. 705, 706. The *Conaleorum gens* here mentioned

up Rory O'Flaherty[y] as their chieftain: *but* the three sons of this O'Flaherty acted a treacherous part towards the Kinel-Moen; they slew Donnell, the son of Donnell O'Gormly, Tiernan, the son of Randal Mac Donnell, and eight other gentlemen of the Kinel-Moen. Randal, the son of Eachmarcach O'Kane, had been slain by the Kinel-Moen in the beginning of this summer, and in revenge of this were slain Galagh O'Loony and Murtough O'Petan; and it was in revenge of this, moreover, the aforesaid act of treachery was committed against the Kinel-Moen.

A violent wind-storm *occurred* in this year; it caused a great destruction of trees. It prostrated oaks. It prostrated one hundred and twenty trees in Derry-Columbkille[z].

John De Courcy with his foreigners repaired to Machaire Conaille[a], *and* committed depredations there. They encamped for a night in Glenree[b], where

were the descendants of Conall Cearnach, the most distinguished of the heroes of the Red Branch in Ulster, who flourished early in the first century.—See O'Flaherty's *Ogygia*, part iii. c. 47.

[b] *In Glenree*, i nglionn riġe, i. e. the vale of the River Righe. Giraldus Cambrensis, in his brief enumeration of the battles of De Courcy, in the sixteenth chapter of the second book of his *Hibernia Expugnata*, calls this his fifth battle, and says that he fought it at the bridge of Newry. In this he is right as to the place; but, it is quite evident from the older Irish Annals that he has transposed the order of the battles, for he was not in Ireland when De Courcy first invaded Ulster. Giraldus came first to Ireland in 1183, and again in 1185, as tutor to the Earl of Moreton, afterwards King John. The bridge of Newry well agrees with the Glenn Righe of the Irish Annals, for the river of Newry was anciently called the Righe, and the valley through which it flows bore the appellation of Glenn Righe. Giraldus states that De Courcy was the victor in this battle: "Quintum apud Pontem Iuori in reditu ab Anglia, unde tamen ad sua victor evasit." But in the Annals of Ulster and Kilronan, and in the Dublin copy of the Annals of Ulster, it is emphatically stated that the English were dreadfully slaughtered here: Ro mebaiḋ for gallaiḃ ⁊ ro cuireḋ ḋerg ár forru. The number of the English slain on this occasion is not stated in the Annals of Ulster or Kilronan, but it is given in the Dublin copy of the Annals of Innisfallen as four hundred; and it is added that the battle was fought at Newry, and that O'Hanvy, chief of Omeath, and one hundred of the Irish, were killed, and that Murrough O'Carroll, King of Oriel, and Rory Mac Donslevy O'Haughy (O'h-Eochaḋa), were victors. The name Rory is, however, incorrect; for, on the death of Donnell, the grandson of Cahasagh, Cu-Uladh, the son of Conor, who was son of Donslevy, son of Eochaidh, became the chief of the Dal-Fiatachs. The pedigree of this Cu-Uladh (i. e. dog of Ulidia) is given by Duald Mac Firbis in his genealogical work, p. 510. He was succeeded by Rory Mac Donslevy, who is introduced in the interpolated Annals of Innisfallen as the chieftain who opposed Sir John De Courcy at Down, in the first battle in 1177. Dr. Hanmer, with that love of dull invention which distin-

Murċaḋ ua cſrbaill ticchſrna Oirgiall ⁊ cu ulaḋ mac duinnſlebe .i. Rí ulaḋ fuabairt bioḋḃaḋ forra gur ro marbaḋ ⁊ gur ro báḋaḋ ceiṫri céd co leiṫ díoḃ. Torċratar céd do na gaoiḋealaiḃ i frioṫguin an ċaṫa im uá nainfeṫ tiġearna uá méiṫ maċa.

Tainic Iohn do cuirt iar ttrioll do orccain dál araiḋe ⁊ uiḃ Tuirtre. Tucc doná cuiniḋe ua flainn ticchſrna ua ttuirtre ⁊ ḟſr lí deaḃaiḋ doſoṁ

guished him, metamorphoses this Rory Mac Donslevy into Roderic O'Conor, Monarch of Ireland.

The exact situation of the valley of Glenree had never been known to any Irish historical or topographical writer in modern times, till it was identified by the Editor of this work when employed on the Ordnance Survey in 1834. Keating, Duald Mac Firbis, O'Flaherty, and all the ancient Bardic writers of the history of Ireland, state that the three Collas, who formed the territory of Oriel, deprived the Ultonians of that portion of their kingdom extending from Gleann Righe, and Loch n-Eathach, westwards. The general opinion was, that the territory of Oirghiall, or Oriel, comprised the present counties of Louth, Armagh, and Monaghan, and that Uladh or Ulidia, the circumscribed territory of the ancient Clanna Rury, was, when formed into shire-ground, styled the county of Down, from Down, its principal town. This having been established, the Editor, during his examination of the ancient topography of Ulster, was led to look for Glenree somewhere on the boundary between the counties of Armagh and Down; and accordingly, on examining the documents, he found that, on an ancient map of the country lying between Lough Erne and Dundalk, preserved in the State Papers' Office, the vale of the Newry River is called "*Glenree*," and the river itself "*Owen Glenree fluvius*." He also found that in the Ulster Inquisitions the remarkable place near Newry called Fathom, is denominated Glenree Magaffee. Oriel, or Oirghialla, anciently extended from this Glenree to Lough Erne, and comprised the counties of Louth, Armagh, Monaghan, and in later ages the whole of the county of Fermanagh, as we learn from O'Dugan, who, in his togographical poem, places Toorsah, the country of O'Flanagan, in the north-west of Fermanagh; Lurg, the country of O'Muldoon, in the north of the same county; and the entire of Maguire's country in it. That the county of Fermanagh was considered a part of Oriel, at least since the Maguires got possession of it, is further corroborated by the fact, that throughout these Annals Maguire is called the pillar and prop of the Oriels. It is stated in a manuscript in Trinity College, Dublin (H. 3. 18. p. 783), that the boundary between Oriel and Ulidia, or the Clann Colla and Clanna Rury, or ancient Ultonians, was made in the west side of Glenree from Newry upwards, and that the Clanna Rury never extended their territory beyond it. This boundary, which consists of a fosse and rampart of great extent, still remains in some places in tolerable preservation, and is called by the strange name of the Danes' Cast, in English, and Gleann na muice duiḃe, i. e. *Valley of the Black Pig*, in Irish. For a minute description of this ancient boundary the reader is referred to Stuart's *Historical Memoirs of the City of Armagh*, Appendix, No. III., pp. 585, 586.

[c] *Hy-Meith Macha.*—Now the barony of Monaghan, in the county of Monaghan. This was otherwise called Hy-Meith Tire, to distinguish it from Hy-Meith Mara, now Omeath, a moun-

Murrough O'Carroll, Lord of Oriel, and Cooley Mac Donslevy, King of Ulidia, made a hostile attack upon them, and drowned and otherwise killed four hundred and fifty of them. One hundred of the Irish, together with O'Hanvy, Lord of Hy-Meith-Macha[c], fell in the heat of the battle.

John De Courcy soon after proceeded to plunder Dalaradia and Hy-Tuirtre; *and* Cumee O'Flynn, Lord of Hy-Tuirtre and Firlee[d], gave battle to him and

tainous district lying between Carlingford and Newry, in the county of Louth. This is evident from the Tripartite Life of St. Patrick, published by Colgan, and from the Irish Calendars, which place in it the churches of Tehallan, Tullycorbet, and Kilmore, all situated in the present barony of Monaghan; and the former authority states that the place called *Omna Renne* was on the boundary between it and Crich Mughdhorn, now the barony of Cremourne, in the county of Monaghan. For the descent of the Hy-Meith, see O'Flaherty's *Ogygia*, part iii. c. 76; and Duald Mac Firbis's Pedigrees. Harris is totally incorrect in his account of the situation of the districts called Hy-Meith.—See his edition of Ware, vol. ii. p. 51.

[d] *Firlee*, Fip li, a tribe and territory situated on the Bann, in the county of Antrim.—*Ogygia*, part iii. c. 76. See note under the year 1176. Giraldus Cambrensis writes this name *Ferly*, and states that De Courcy fought his third battle here, where he lost all his men except eleven. His words are: "Tertium erat apud Ferly in Prædæ captione, vbi ob arctam viæ transitum post graues tandem congressus & anxios: sic pars Iohannis victa succubuit, aliis interemptis, aliis per nemora dispersis, vt vix Iohanni 11. milites superstites adhæsissent. Ipse vero virtutis inuictæ cum tantilla suorum paucitate per 30. milliaria se ab hostili multitudine continue defendendo, equis amissis omnibus vsq; ad Castrum suum duobus diebus & noctibus, ieiunii, armati pedites, miro conatu memoriaq; dignissimo euaserunt."—*Hiber. Expugnata*, l. ii. c. 16.

It may be curious to remark here, as an example of the manner in which Irish history has been manufactured by English writers, how Dr. Hanmer changes the Ferly of Cambrensis into Ferny; and attempts by the sheer force of impudence to break down his evidence in this instance. He says that Cambrensis lightly "overskipped the achievements of De Courcy, partly upon private grudge, for that Sir John De Courcy allowed him not for Vicar-generall in Ireland, and secretary to the state; yet that the certainty of his exploits hath been preserved, and in Latine, committed to paper by a Fryer in the North, the which booke Oneil brought to Armagh, and was translated into English by [George] Dowdall, Primate there Anno 1551." If, however, the account which Hanmer gives of this battle, in direct opposition to Giraldus and the Irish Annals, has been taken from this book, it would appear to be a work compiled at a comparatively modern period, and perhaps first written in Latin on *paper* as he states. Hanmer (or his author) not knowing the situation of *Ferly*, found no difficulty in changing the name to *Ferny*, a well-known territory in Oriel, in which the Mac Mahons were noted rebels in Hanmer's time; and takes occasion to introduce Sir John De Courcy in 1178, as fighting against the rebel Mac Mahon. Now it is worthy of remark here that Hanmer's cotemporary, Spenser, writes that Mac Mahon was of English descent, and that the first of them, an Englishman, named Fitz-Ursula, came to Ireland with his relative Robert de Vere, Earl of Oxford [1385], and de-

co na gallaiḃ isuiḋe. Ro meaḃaiḋ forra. Ro cuir a nár tria ṁiorḃailiḃ patraic, coluim cille ⁊ brenainn. Ocus tearna Iohn fein ar eccin ar co creaċtnaiġṫe co rainic co hAṫ [cliaṫ].

Consṫapla riġ Saxan i nAṫ cliaṫ (.i. hugo), ⁊ i nairṫer miḋe co na ṡochraiḋe do ṫoċt go cluain mic nóis. Ro airgsiot an baile acht na tempaill ⁊ ticche an easpcoip. Do roine dia ⁊ ciarán miorbaile soillsi forra, uair ni ro ċuṁaingsiot taṫaṁ no tionaḃraḋ do ḋénaṁ gur ro élaidsiot a cuirp cluana araḃáraċ.

Abann na gaillme do tracchaḋ fri re laiṫe aicenta. Na huile aiḋme ro báidid innte ó ċen co na hiarcc do ṫionól la luċt an dúin ⁊ an tiri i ccoitcinne.

generating into a wild Irishman, changed his name to Mac Mahon, which is a translation of Fitz-Ursula, or son of the bear. Both stories were evidently invented to turn them to account against the Mac Mahons of Ferny and Oriel who were then very troublesome to the government. But it is well known that the Mac Mahons were not chiefs of Oriel, or Uriel, in De Courcy's time, for it appears, from the concurrent testimony of all the Irish annals, that O'Carroll was then king or chief lord of Oriel, and that the Mac Mahons, who are a collateral branch of the O'Carrolls, were not heard of as chiefs of Oriel for some time after De Courcy's disappearance from Irish history in 1205. Hanmer manufactures the story as follows, and his version of it is gravely quoted as true history by Cox, Leland, Ledwich, and Stuart, who were not able to detect the forgery, but each echoing the tale of his predecessor:

"The third battaile that Sir *John De Courcy* fought was in Ferny, against eleven thousand Irishmen: the occasion was thus, *Courcy* had builded many Castles throughout Vlster, and especially in Ferny [*recte* Ferly], where *Mac Mahon* [*recte* O'Lyn] dwelled; this *Mac Mahon* [*recte* O'Lyn] with solemn protestations vowed to become a true and faithful subject, gave *Courcy* many gifts, and made him his Goship, which is a league of amitie highly esteemed in Ireland. Whereupon *Courcy* gave him two Castles, with their demesnes, to hold of him. Within one month after, this *Mac Mahon* [*recte* O'Lyn], returning to his vomit, brake downe the Castles, and made them even with the ground. Sir *John De Courcy* sent unto him to know the cause that moved him to fall to this villanie: his answer was, that he promised not to hold stones of him, but the land, and that it was contrary to his nature to couche himself within cold stones, the woods being so nigh, where he might better warme himself, with other slender and scornefull answers." He then goes on to give a detailed account of a prey taken, and a battle fought, in which, of the eleven thousand Irishmen, only two hundred escaped with their lives. But the Doctor is obliged to confess that there was a totally different account of this battle (alluding to that already quoted from Cambrensis), which, however, he feels inclined not to believe: "There are," he says, "some out of the schoole of envy, with grace to disgrace Courcy, that report the story otherwise, which deliver not wherein he was to be honoured, but wherein he was foiled, *fortuna de la guerra;* that he was driven, with

his foreigners, and defeated them with great slaughter, through the miracles of Patrick, Columbkille, and Brendan; and John himself escaped with difficulty, being severely wounded, and fled to Dublin[e].

The Constable of the King of England in Dublin and East Meath (namely, Hugo) marched with his forces to Clonmacnoise, and plundered *all* the town, except the churches and the bishop's houses. God and Kieran wrought a manifest miracle against them, for they were unable to rest or sleep, until they had secretly absconded from Cuirr Cluana on the next day.

The River Galliv (Galway) was dried up for a period of a natural day[f]; all the articles that had been lost in it from remotest times, as well as its fish, were collected by the inhabitants of the fortress, and by the people of the country in general.

eleven persons in armes, to travaile a foote some 30. miles, for the space of two dayes, the enemy still pursuing (the which they lay not downe), all fasting without any relief, till he came to an OLD Castle of his owne, which savoureth not altogether of truth, but forwards with the history."—*Hanmer's Chronicle*, Dubl. edit. 1809, p. 309.

[e] *Dublin*, αċ cliαċ.—The latter part of this name is destroyed in the autograph original; but is here restored from Maurice Gorman's copy, which had been made from the autograph before the edge of the paper was worn away. The place to which De Courcy fled on this occasion is not mentioned in the Annals of Ulster or those of Kilronan, or in the Dublin or Bodleian copy of the Annals of Innisfallen; and it is highly probable that he fled to Downpatrick, not to Dublin.

Under this year the Dublin copy of the Annals of Ulster has a brief notice of an attack made upon John De Courcy in the territory of Cuailgne, which is not in any of the other Annals, under this or any other year, except the Dublin copy of the Annals of Innisfallen, in which it is entered under the year 1180, as follows:

"A. D. 1180.—John De Courcy plundered Machaire Chonaille, and Cuailgne, and took a prey of a thousand cows; but Murrough O'Carroll, King of Oriel; Mulrony O'Boylan, Chief of Dartry; and Gillapatrick O'Hanvy, Chief of Mugdorna [Cremourne], pursued and overtook them: a battle ensued, in which the English were routed, and deprived of the prey; and John De Courcy betook himself for shelter to the castle of Skreen-Columbkille, which he himself had built."

Hanmer gives a strange version of this excursion, evidently from the Book of Howth, which is a collection of traditional stories, written by an Anglo-Irish Romancer in the fifteenth or sixteenth century.

[f] *Natural day*, laiṫe aiceanta.—The word aicneḋ is used in ancient Irish writings to denote nature, and aiceanta, natural. O'Flaherty, in his Account of Iar-Connaught (printed for the Archæological Society), notices this occurrence as follows, from which it will be seen that he had other Annals besides those of the Four Masters: "There is an island, where the river issues from the lake, now called Olen na mbrahar, or the Fryars Isle, but anciently Olen na gclereagh, i. e. the Clergy's Isle; for the Irish Annals mention that, anno 1178, from midnight

Maiḋm ria nart ua maoilechlainn, ⁊ ria nuiḃ failġe, ⁊ ria ngallaiḃ for ḋelḃna eaṫra, ⁊ for Mhaoileachlainn mbſcc, ⁊ for dreim do fſraiḃ tſthḃa dú in ro marḃaḋ Muireadhaċ mac an trionnaigh.

Aoḋ ua flaiṫbſrtaiġ ticchſrna iarṫair Connaċt do écc i neanach duin.

Aṁalgaiḋ mág aṁalgaiḋ do marḃaḋ la ríol nanmchadha.

Maelseċlainn bſcc ua maoileċlainn do ġabáil tiġe for Art ua maoileaċlainn, ⁊ Art do téarnuḋ as, ⁊ Flann mac méġ aṁalġaiḋ taoiseaċ calraiġe do marḃaḋ ann la Maelseclainn.

to noon Galway river became dry from Clergy Isle to the sea; and much fish, and goods long afore drowned therein, found by the people of the town."—pp. 28, 29. See note under the year 1191.

[g] *Offaly*, Uí Failġe.—This was originally a very extensive territory in Leinster, and the principality of the O'Conors Faly. Before the English invasion it comprised the present baronies of eastern and western Ophaly, in the County of Kildare, those of upper and lower Philipstown, and those of Geshil, Warrenstown, and Coolestown, in the King's County, as well as those of Portnahinch and Tinnahinch, in the Queen's County. Shortly after the English invasion, however, the Fitzgeralds of Kildare wrested from O'Conor Faly and his correlatives that portion of his original territory of Ui Failghe comprised within the present county of Kildare, and now called the baronies of eastern and western Ophaly. There were then two Ophalys formed out of the ancient Ui Failghe, namely, the English Ophaly, in the county of Kildare, giving the title of baron to a branch of the Fitzgeralds; and the Irish Ui Failghe, extending into the present King's and Queen's Counties, as already specified, and giving the Irish title of King of Ui Failghe to O'Conor Faly, the supposed senior representative of Rosa Failghe, the eldest son of Cathaoir Mor, monarch of Ireland in the second century. See O'Flaherty's *Ogygia*, part iii. c. 59, and an old map of the territories of Leix and Ophaly, made in the reign of Philip and Mary, the original of which on vellum is now preserved in the British Museum, and copies in the MS. Library of Trinity College, Dublin, and at the Ordnance Survey Office, Phœnix Park, Dublin. See note on Clann Maoilughra, or Clanmaliere, under the year 1193.

[h] *Dealbhna Eathra*, called Dealbhna Meg Cochlain in these Annals, at the years 1572 and 1601. This territory comprised the entire of the present barony of Garrycastle in the King's County, except the parish of Lusmagh, which belonged to Sil Anmchadha, or O'Madden's country, and which is still a part of the diocese of Clonfert. — See Colgan's *Acta Sanctorum*, p. 132, col. 2; Keating, in the reign of Niall Cailne; O'Flaherty's *Ogygia*, part iii. c. 82; and De Burgo's *Hibernia Dominicana*, pp. 305, 306.

[i] *Annadown*, Eanach Duin, an ancient cathedral on the margin of Lough Corrib, in the barony of Clare, and county of Galway.—See note [f], *infrà*, A. D. 1179.

[k] *Sil-Anmchadha.*—This was the tribe name of the O'Maddens, and was also applied to their country, which in latter ages comprised the barony of Longford in the county of Galway, and the parish of Lusmagh in the King's County, on the east side of the Shannon.—See *Tribes and Customs of Hy-Many*, published by the Irish Archæological Society in 1843, p. 69, note [x].

A victory was gained by Art O'Melaghlin, the people of Offaly[g], and the English, over the people of Delvin Eathra[h] and Melaghlin Beg, and a party of the men of Teffia; in the battle, Murray, the son of the Sinnagh (the Fox), was slain.

Hugh O'Flaherty, Lord of West Connaught, died at Annadown[i].

Awley Mac Awley was killed by the Sil-Anmchadha[k].

Melaghlin Beg O'Melaghlin took the house of Art O'Melaghlin, who made his escape out of it; but Flann, the son of Mac Awley[l], chief of Calry, was killed by Melaghlin[m].

[l] *Mac Awley.*—He was the chief of Calry an chala, which comprised the parish of Ballyloughloe, in the county of Westmeath.

[m] The Bodleian copy of the Annals of Innisfallen has the following brief notice of the transactions of the English in Munster, which is omitted by the Four Masters: A. D. 1178. Corcach do inriud la mac mic Doṁnaill ua Carthaig 7 la gallaib glasa. Forbais la Miliḋ Cocain 7 la Mac Stemni i Corcaig. Turus la buidin dib go h-Achad da eo, go ro badar da la, 7 da edchi innti, 7 assin go Corcaig aris doib. Iar sin doib ar ammus Puirtlairge go ro thinolsatar na Gaeidil cucu illanairde Lis mor, go ro marbait uile pene.

"A. D. 1178. Cork was plundered by the grandson of Donnell, who was the grandson of Carthach and the green Galls. Cork was besieged by Milo Cogan and Fitz Stephen. A party of their people made an excursion to Aghadoe, where they remained two days and two nights, and then returned again to Cork. After this they went towards Waterford; but the Irish gathered against them at the hill of Lismore, and nearly killed them all."

Under this year also the same Annals record a desolating war between the Irish inhabitants of Thomond and Desmond, during which the whole country extending from Limerick to Cork, and from the plain of Derrymore, near Roscrea, to Brandon Hill, in Kerry, was desolated. In the Dublin copy of the Annals of Innisfallen it is stated, that during this war several of the Eugenian septs fled from their original territories. "A. D. 1178. There was a very great war between the O'Briens and Mac Carthys, so that they desolated the entire country from Limerick to Cork, and from the plain of Derrymore to Brandon Hill, and the greater part of the race of Eoghan fled to the woods of Ivahagh, south of the River Lee, and others to Kerry and Thomond. On this occasion the Hy-Conaill Gabhra and the Hy-Donovane fled southwards over the Mangartan mountain."

Dr. O'Brien, in his History of the House of O'Brien, published by Vallancey, in his own name, in the first volume of the *Collectanea de Rebus Hibernicis*, thus very correctly paraphrases this passage. "A. D. 1178. Donal O'Brien, at the head of the entire Dal Cassian tribe, greatly distressed and reduced all the Eugenians, laid waste their country with fire and sword, and obliged the dispersed Eugenians to seek for shelter in the woods and fastnesses of Ive Eachach, on the south side of the Lee. In this expedition they routed the O'Donovans of Ive-Figeinte, or Cairbre Aodhbha, in the county of Limerick, and the O'Collins of Ive-Conaill Gabhra, or Lower Connallo in said county, beyond the mountain of Mangerton, to the western parts of the county of Cork: here these

AOIS CRIOSD 1179.

Aoir Criorp mile, céd, reacτmoġaτ, a naoi.

Tuaṫal ua Connachtaiġ eppcop τíre briuin colmán ua rcannláin airchinneaċ cluana, giolla domhnaiġ ua forannáin airchinneaċ arda rraτha, ⁊ Maelmaire mac giolla colmain Secnap arda rraṫa do ecc.

two exiled Eugenian families, being powerfully assisted by the O'Mahonys, made new settlements for themselves in the ancient properties of the O'Donoghues, O'Learies, and O'Driscolls, to which three families the O'Mahonys were always declared enemies, to the borders of Lough Leane, where Auliff Mor O'Donoghue, surnamed Cuimsinach, had made some settlements before this epoch." See note under the year 1200.

The territory of Hy-Figeinte, here referred to by Dr. O'Brien, derived its name from the descendants of Fiacha Figeinte, son of Daire Cearb, who was the son of Oilioll Flannbeg, King of Munster, in the latter part of the third century, and comprised the barony of Coshma, and all that portion of the present county of Limerick lying to the west of the River Maigue. Its situation is thus described in the Life of St. Molua, who was descended from Fiacha Fidhgeinte: "Et venit [Molua] ad Mumeniam, et lustravit patriam suam, .i. Nepotes Fidgenti, quæ gens est in medio Mumenie, a media planicie Mumenie usque ad medium Montis Luachra in occidente ad australem plagam fluminis Synna." —*Vitæ S. Molue, Abbatis et Confessoris*, as in the Codex Killkenniensis in Marshe's Library, v. 3. 14. F. 135. In a MS. in Trinity College, Dublin, H. 3. 17. p. 748, it is described thus: hir í crich hua Fidgfinnte o Luachair Bruin co Bruriġ, 7 o Bruriġ co Buair. "The country of the Hy-Fidgeinnte is from Luachair Bruin to Bruree, and from Bruree to Buais." Keating describes this territory as the plain of the county of Limerick: Ui Fidgeinte re raiδτior clár Contae Luimniġ aniu.—*History of Ireland;* Reign of Diarmaid Mac Ceirbheoil and Conall Caol. O'Flaherty has the following notice of it in his *Ogygia*, pp. 380, 381: "*Anno* 366. Crimthannus filius Fidachi Heberio è semine Achaio Mogmedonio sororio suo Temoriæ extremum diem quietè claudenti substituitur Rex Hiberniæ annis tredecim. Transmarinis expeditionibus in Gallia, et Britannia memorabilis erat: uxorem habuit Fidengam è regio Connactiæ stemnate, sed nullam sobolem reliquit.

"Crimthanni regis abavus Fiachus latus vertex rex Momoniæ duos Olillos genuit Flannmor et Flannbeg cognominibus distinctos. Olillus Flannmor rex Momoniæ sobolis expers Olillum Flannbeg fratrem adoptavit. Olillo Flannbeg regi Momoniæ superant Achaius rex Momoniæ, Darius Kearb, ex quo O'Donnowan, Lugaduis et Eugenius.

"Darius Kearb præter Fidachum Crimthanni regis, et Mongfinnæ reginæ Hiberniæ patrem genuit Fiachum Figente, et Achaium Liathanach, ex quo Hy-Liathan in agro Corcagiensi. Fiacho Figente nomen et originem debet Hy-Figenta regio olim variis principibus celebris in media Momoniæ planicie usque ad medium montis Luachra in Kierrigia ad australem Sinanni fluminis ripam; licet hodie hoc nomine vix nota, sed Limericensis comitatus planities appellata."

Nothing has yet been discovered to prove whether the O'Donovans ever returned to their original territory of Cairbre Aobhdha, in the

THE AGE OF CHRIST, 1179.

The Age of Christ, one thousand one hundred seventy-nine.

Tuathal O'Connaghty, Bishop of Tir-Briuin[n]; Colman O'Scanlan, Erenagh of Cloyne; Gilladowny O'Forannan, Erenagh[o] of Ardstraw; and Mulmurry Mac Gillacolum, seachnab[p] (prior) of Ardstraw, died.

present county of Limerick, after this expulsion. It is stated in Lewis's Topographical Dictionary, under the article Croom, that Dermot O'Donovan was possessed of the territory of Coshma in the reign of King John, when he built the Castle of Croom on the River Maigue; but the Editor has not been able to discover any original or trustworthy authority for this statement. It would appear, however, that all the Clann-Donovan were not driven out of Cairbre Aobhdha in 1178, as the name has been very common in many parts of the county of Limerick, particularly the parish of Kilmoylan; and in the year 1551, John Donevan, Rector of Derrygallavan, in the diocese of Limerick, obtained a grant of denization.—(Inrolled 5° Edw. VI. f. r. 19.)

[n] *Bishop of Tir-Briuin.*—There were many territories in Ireland called Tir Briuin and Hy-Briuin, as Tir Briuin na Sinna, Hy-Briuin Breifne, Hy-Briuin Seola, &c. Sir James Ware mentions a Tuathal O'Connachtaigh, Bishop of Hua mbriuin, which he explains by Enaghdune, as attending at the Council of Kells in 1152, who would appear to be the same whose death is here recorded, for Enaghdune was the capital of the Hy-Briuin Seola, or O'Flahertys, and their correlatives.—See Ussher's *Primordia*, p. 955. Roderic O'Flaherty, in his account of the territory of Iar-Connaught, states that the cathedral of the seigniory of the O'Flahertys was "Enaghdun, dedicated to St. Brendan, the 16th of May, Anno Christi 577, there deceased, in the barony of Clare, on the brink of Lough Orbsen." But that "in the time of Malachias Mac Aodha, of West Connaught extraction, archbishope of Tuam [ab an. 1313, ad ann. 1348], after a long debate for many years before and in his time, the cathedrall of Enaghdun was, anno 1321, united to the see of Tuam, by the finall decision of Pope John the Twenty-second." Duald Mac Firbis states, in his Genealogical work, that Aodh, the son of Eochaidh Tirmcharna, was the first that granted Eanach Duin to God and St. Brendan.

[o] *Erenagh,* Airċinneaċ.—This term is explained as follows in Cormac's Glossary: airċindech .i. arcendach, arċos grece, excelsus latine dicitur. Airċindech din .i. erchend oġ, .i. uasal-cend comlan. "Airchindech, i. e. arcendach, *archos* Grece *excelsus* Latine dicitur. Airchindech then, i. e. *erchend ogh*, i. e. a noble perfect head." In the *Leabhar Breac*, fol. 76, *a*, *b*, the term is used to denote a president or superintendent, and is applied to Satan, who is styled "*Airchinnech* of hell and prince of death," airċindech iffirn 7 taisech in ḃais. The first mention made of this office in these Annals occurs at the year 788. Thus Doimṫeach, airċindeach Trefoid móir, decc, i. e. "Doimhtheach, *airchinneach* of the great Trevet, died." From this period forward, however, all the annalists frequently mention this office. Ussher, in his Treatise on Corbes, Herenachs, and Termon Lands, published in the second Number of Vallancey's *Collectanea*, asserts that the office of Herenach and Archdeacon was the same; and Connell Mageoghegan, in his Translation of the

Ard maċa do loscadh ettir templaiḃ ⁊ recclſsaiḃ acht reclſs bricchde ⁊ teampall na ffſrta namá.

Cealla tire heoġain o ṡléḃ bud dſs do ḟolmuġaḋ tre coccaḋ, ⁊ comḟuachaḋ, terce, ⁊ doċmataid.

Ua ruaḋaċán ticchſrna ua neachdaċ do écc do ġalar tri noiḋċi iar na ionnarbaḋ tré ḟáruccaḋ canóine patraicc dó gar roiṁe.

Síḋ do ḋſnaṁ do ḋonnchaḋ ua cairealláin ⁊ do cloinn ndiarmada uile la cenél Móen ⁊ la hua ngairmleaḋaiġ, aṁlaiḃ mac mſnman dſrḃraṫair riḋe mná an donnchaiḋ remraite. Ba hann ro naiḋmsſd a síḋ re aroile i teampall arda sraṫa fo mionnaiḃ na heaccailse ſin, doṁnaiġ móir ⁊ na hſrnaiḋe. Tainic doná ua gairmleaḋaiġ .i. aṁlaoiḃ ar na ṁaraċ do cuingeaḋ tuilleaḋ slána co teaċ donnċaiḋ ui ċairealláin Ro marḃad soṁ fo cſdóir ar lár an aireachta a ndorus an tighe i ffiaḋnaisi a dſrḃſea-ṫor .i. bſn donnċaḋa. Ro marḃaḋ ḃeós triur dia muinntſr i maille friss .i. cionaſḋ mac airt uí ḃracáin, ⁊ mac giollu crioſd mec corbmaic mec reodáin .i. dſrḃ ċoṁalta donncaiḋ ui ċairealláin.

Ardsraṫa Doṁnaċ mor an Earnaiḋe * * * * * * * * * * * * * * do ḟolṁuġaḋ la fſraiḃ maighe hithe.

Annals of Clonmacnoise, always renders airċinnech by archdeacon. In this, however, it is more than probable that both Ussher and Mageoghegan are mistaken. The annalists have another term to express the office of archdeacon, and it is quite certain that the archdeacon was always in holy orders, whereas the *airchinnech* was always a layman, or at least one who had merely received *primam tonsuram*. The origin and duties of the office of Herenach are stated as follows by Sir John Davies, in his letter to the Earl of Salisbury: "For the Erenach: There are few parishes of any compass or extent where there is not an Erenach, which, being an office of the Church, took beginning in this manner: when any lord or gentleman had a direction to build a church, he did first dedicate some good portion of land to some saint or other, whom he chose to be his patron; then he founded the church, and called it by the name of that saint, and then gave the land to some clerke, not being in orders, and to his heires for ever; with this intent, that he should keep the church clean and well repaired, keep hospitality, and give almes to the poore, for the soul's health of the founder. This man and his heires had the name of Erenach. The Erenach was also to make a weekly commemoration of the founder in the church; he had always *primam tonsuram*, but took no other orders. He had a voice in the chapter, when they consulted about their revenues, and paid a certaine yearly rent to the Bishop, besides a fine upon the marriage of every of his daughters, which they call a Loughinipy; he gave a subsidy to the Bishop at his first entrance into the bishoprick, the certainty of all which duties appears in the Bishop's Register; and these duties grew unto the Bishop, first be-

Armagh was burned, as well churches as regleses[q], excepting only Regles Brighde and Teampull na bh-Fearta.

The churches of Tyrone, from the mountain southwards, were left desolate, in consequence of war and intestine commotion, famine, and distress.

O'Rogan, Lord of Iveagh, died of three nights' sickness, shortly after he had been expelled for violating the Canoin-Phatruig[r].

A peace was concluded by Donough O'Carellan and all the Clandermot with the Kinel-Moen and O'Gormly (i. e. Auliffe, the son of Menman, brother-in-law of the aforesaid Donough). This peace was concluded between them in the church of Ardstraw, upon the relics of that church and those of Donaghmore and Urney. On the following day, O'Gormly (Auliffe) repaired to the house of Donough O'Carellan to demand further guarantees, but was killed in the middle of the meeting, in the doorway of the house, in the presence of his own sister, the wife of Donough. Three of his people were also killed along with him; namely, Kenny, son of Art O'Bracan; the son of Gilchreest, son of Cormac Mac Reodan, the foster-brother of Donough O'Carellan[s].

Ardstraw[t], Donaghmore, Urney, * * * * * * * * * * * * * * * were desolated by the men of Magh Ithe.

cause the Erenach could not be created, nor the church dedicated without the consent of the Bishop."

[p] *Seachnab.*—At the year 1089 of these Annals, *Seachnab* is explained by *Prior*: in Cormac's Glossary it is explained *secundus abbas*, i. e. *vice abbot.* The Irish word ꞅeach has the same signification in compound words as the English *vice*, in *vicepresident*, *viceroy*, *vicegerent*, &c.

[q] *Regles* seems to have been abbreviated from the Latin *Regularis ecclesia*, and means a church belonging to the regular, not the secular clergy. O'Flaherty says it is an ecclesiastical word of no great antiquity in the Irish language.—*Ogygia*, p. 16.

[r] *Canoin-Phatruig* is the old name of the ancient manuscript book of the Gospels, commonly called the Book of Armagh.—See a description of this manuscript written by the famous Antiquary Lhuyd, and published by Dr. O'Conor in his *Rerum Hibernicarum Scriptores*, vol. i. *Epist. Nunc.* pp. lvii, lviii, and reprinted, with an English translation, by Sir William Betham, in his Antiquarian Researches, and in the original Latin in Petrie's Essay on the Round Towers of Ireland, pp. 329, 330.

[s] *O'Carellan.*—This passage shews that O'Carellan, Chief of the Clandermot, had seized upon that part of Moy-Ithe, O'Gormly's country, in which Donaghmore-Moy-Itha was situated.

[t] *Ardstraw*, árd ꞅꞃaṫa, an ancient church in Tyrone, formerly the head of a bishop's see, of which Bishop Eoghan, or Eugenius was patron, whose festival was annually celebrated there on the 23rd of August, as was that of Bishop Coibhdhenach on the 26th of November.—See the *Felire Aenguis*, and Irish Calendar of the

Cóicc tiġe ar céd do loisccaḋ hi ccluain mic nois hi ffoġail.

Cluain fſrta brſnainn co na tſmplaiḃ do loisccaḋ.

Loṫra, ardfearta brenainn, Caisiol, tuaim da ġualann, dísſrt ceallaiġ, ceallmſdóin ⁊ balla, iaidsidhe do loisccaḋ uile.

Maelseaċlainn ua maoilmiaḋaiġ taoiseaċ muinntire heolais do ecc.

Iomar ua caṫarasaigh tiġearna na saithne do ecc.

Maoileaċlainn riabaċ o seachnasaiġ ticcearna leiṫe ċenel Aoḋa do marbaḋ la mac donnchaiḋ í ċaṫail.

AOIS CRIOSD 1180.

Aois Criosd mile, céd, ochtmoġatt.

Lorcan ua tuaṫail .i. labras airdeppoc laiġſn, ⁊ legaitt na hſreann do martradh hi Saxain.

O'Clerys' at these days. It was afterwards annexed to the see of Clogher; but about the year 1266 it was separated from the see of Clogher, with other churches in the territory of Hy-Fiachrach Arda Sratha, in the gift of the Kinel-Owen, and incorporated with the see of Londonderry.—See Ussher's *Primordia*, p. 857; O'Flaherty's *Ogygia*, part iii. c. 76; and Ordnance Memoir of the Parish of Templemore.

[u] *Clonfert-Brendan*, Cluain ferta brenainn. The church of Clonfert, the head of an ancient bishop's see, in the barony of Longford, and county of Galway.

[w] *Lorha*, Loṫra.—A small village in the barony of Lower Ormond, about six miles to the north of Burrisokeane. Here are the ruins of two abbeys of considerable extent, but none of an antiquity prior to the Anglo-Norman invasion, though St. Rodanus, the patron of the place, had erected a primitive Irish abbey here in the sixth century. For an account of Rodanus, the reader is referred to his Life, as published by the Bollandists, at 25th April.

[x] *Ardfert-Brendan*, now Ardfert, in the county of Kerry, about four miles to the north of Tralee, where the ruins of several ancient churches are still to be seen.

[y] *Disert-Kelly*, Dísert Ceallaiġ.—The name is now corruptly anglicised Isertkelly, and is applied to an ancient church and parish in the diocese of Kilmacduagh, situated to the south-west of the town of Loughrea, in the county of Galway.—See Ordnance Map of the county of Galway, sheet 114.

[z] *Kilmaine*, Cill meaḋoin, i. e. the middle church, a small village in a barony to which it has given name in the south of the county of Mayo, and not far from the boundary of the county of Galway.

[a] *Balla*, or *Bal*, Balla, a village containing the ruins of an ancient church and round tower in a parish of the same name, in the barony of Carra, and county of Mayo, and about eight miles south-east of Castlebar.—See Life of St. Mochua, published by Colgan, in *Acta Sanctorum*, at 30th of March.

[b] *Muintir-Eolais.*—This territory, which afterwards became the principality of Mac-Rannall,

One hundred and five houses were burned in Clonmacnoise, during a predatory incursion.

Clonfert-Brendan[u], with its churches, were burned.

Lorha[w], Ardfert-Brendan[x], Cashel, Tuam, Disert-Kelly[y], Kilmaine[z], and Balla[a], were all burned.

Melaghlin O'Mulvey, Chief of Muintir-Eolais, died[b].

Ivor O'Casey, Lord of the Saithne[c], died.

Melaghlin Reagh O'Shaughnessy, Lord of half *the territory of* Kinelea, was killed by the son of Donough O'Cahill[d].

THE AGE OF CHRIST, 1180.

The Age of Christ, one thousand one hundred eighty.

Lorcan O'Toole, i. e. Lawrence, Archbishop of Leinster and Legate of Ireland, suffered martyrdom[e] in England.

comprised the southern half of the present county of Leitrim. It extended from Slieve-in-ierin and Lough Allen to Slieve Carbry, and to the west of Ballinamuck, in the county of Longford, and contained the castles of Rinn, Lough-skur, and Leitrim, and the monasteries of Fiodhnacha Muighe Rein, now Fenagh, Maothail, now Mohill, and Cluain Conmaicne, now Cloone. The mountains of Slieve-in-ierin are placed in this territory by the ancient writers.

[c] *Saithne*, an ancient territory in East Meath, the ancient inheritance of the O'Caseys. The Saithne, or O'Caseys, are descended from Glasradh, the second son of Cormac Gaileng, who was of the Munster race, and settled here under King Cormac Mac Art, in the third century.—See O'Flaherty's *Ogygia*, part iii. c. 69; and Mac Firbis's Irish Pedigrees. Giraldus Cambrensis states, in his *Hiber. Expugnata*, lib. ii. c. 24, that Philippus Wigorniensis seized on the lands of O'Cathesie, to the king's use, though Hugh de Lacy had formerly sold them. "Inter ipsa igitur operum suorum initialia, terras, quas Hugo de Lacy alienuerat, terram videlic. Ocathesi & alias quam plures ad Regiam mensam cum omni sollicitudine reuocauit."

[d] *O'Cahill*, ua caṫail.—O'Shaughnessy shortly afterwards became lord of all the territory of Kinelea, and the O'Cahills sunk into comparative insignificance. This territory comprised the southern half of the diocese of Kilmacduagh, in the south-west of the county of Galway, and contained the churches of Kilmacduagh, Beagh, and Kilbecanty, and the castles of Gort, Fedane, and Ardmulduane.

[e] *Suffered martyrdom.*—This is a mistake of the Four Masters, for it is stated under this year in the Bodleian and Dublin copy of the Annals of Innisfallen, as well as in the Annals of Boyle, and in Mageoghegan's translation of the Annals of Clonmacnoise, that he died [a natural death?] in France. The fact is that St. Laurence O'Toole died in the monastery of Augum, now Eu, in Normandy, but an attempt had been made by a maniac to murder him at Canterbury in 1175, and this is the martyrdom alluded to by the Four

Macraiṫ ua daiġre aircinneach doire [do ecc].

Raġnall ua cairealláin do ṁarḃaḋ la cenél Moaín i neneaċ ċolaim ċille for lár doire colaim faḋḟin.

Masters. Ussher has the following curious notice of this distinguished prelate in his *Veterum Epistolarum Hibernicarum Sylloge*, note to the Brief of Pope Alexander III., Epist. xlviii. Anno Christi 1179:

"Est hic Laurentius O'Tolus; cujus Vitam ab Augiensis Collegii monacho descriptam tomo 6. Vit. Sanctor. Novemb. 14. inseruit Laurentius Surius. Patrem habuit, ut author ille indicat, *Muriartach sive* Mauricium O'Tuohail, ad quem *non modica pars Hiberniæ, quæ Lagenia dicitur, iure hæreditario pertinebat:* matrem *Ingen Ybruin* (ita enim legunt duo hujus Vitæ, quæ ego habeo, Manuscripta exemplaria) id est, *filiam Principis*, ex Birnorum, ni fallor, familiâ. Annos natus decem, Dermitio regi (qui alius ab illo Murchardi filio fuit, à quo Angli in Hiberniam sunt introducti) à patre obses datus, durissimè ab eo habitus est: post biennium verò patri restitutus, et Ecclesiæ ministerio ab eo dicatus, sub magisterio Glindelacensis Episcopi vixit. Cùm annorum esset xxv. Ecclesiæ S. Comgeni sive Keivini de Glindelach Abbas, *Clero et populo id postulantibus*, constitutus est: ac demùm Gregorio Dubliniensi Archiepiscopo defuncto, ad Dubliniensem cathedram evectus, anno Domini 1162, *à Gelasio totius Hiberniæ Primate, in ipsâ Dubliniensi Ecclesiâ, multis Episcopis præsentibus, gratias agente populo, solemniter consecratus est.* Anno 1179. unà cum *Catholico* Tuamensi Archiepiscopo et quinque vel sex Hiberniæ Episcopis Romam ad Lateranense concilium profecturus, per Angliam transiit: ubi omnes *pro licentiâ transeundi iuraverunt, quòd neque Regi, neque regno eius damnum quærerent;* quemadmodum in anni illius historiâ refert Rogerus Hovedenus. Laurentium tamen, *ob privilegia in Lateranensi Concilio contra Regiæ dignitatis, zelo suæ gentis, ut ferebatur, impetrata, Anglorum Regi suspectum fuisse*, libro 2. Expugnat. Hibern. cap. 23. narrat Giraldus Cambrensis. Eo tempore, Dubliniensi suæ Metropoli præsens hoc impetratum est ab eo privilegium, ex antiquo Dubliniensis Archiepiscopi Regesto, *quod Crede mihi* appellant, a nobis exscriptum. Obiit apud Augiense Normanniæ castrum (cujus Comes Richardus Strongbous fuerat, qui Dubliniam & Lageniam, Laurentii sedem metropoliticam & provinciam, ipso vivente & vidente subjugavit:) quum patriæ ab Anglis vastatæ calamitatem deplorasset, miserabiliter lingua materna dicens: *Heu popule stulte & insipiens; quid jam facturus es? Quis sanabit aversiones tuas? Quis miserebitur tui?* Atque ita, XVIII. Calendas Decembris, *cùm sextæ feriæ terminus advenisset, in confinio Sabbati subsequentis spiritum sancti viri requies æterna suscepit;* inquit vita eius scriptor. Annum, quem ille tacet, Annales nostri assignant 1180. quo et 14. dies Novembris *in sextam feriam* incidit. Rogerus Hovedenus, & eum secutus Cæsar Baronius in Annalibus suis ad sequentem annum malè referunt. Nam ut ipse Rogerus postea confirmat, anno 1181. *Henricus Rex Angliæ, filius Imperatricis, dedit Ioanni Cumin clerico suo, Archiepiscopatum Divelinice in Hiberniâ*, VIII. *Idus Septembris apud Euesham.* (ideoque Novembris dies 14. qui electionem hanc antecesserat, ad annum 1180, necessariò retrahendus est.) et anno 1182. *Lucius Papa III. ordinavit Ioannem Cumin in sacerdotem III. Idus Martij apud Velletre: deinde consecravit eum in Archiepiscopum Divelinice* XII. *Calend. Aprilis, Dominicâ in ramis Palmarum, apud Velletre*, cui Calendarij quoque ratio suffragatur; quæ anno 1182. Dominicam Paschalem 28. die Martij celebratam fuisse docet. In sanctorum

Macraith O'Deery, Erenagh of Derry [*died*].

Randal O'Carellan was killed by the Kinel-Moen, in defence of St. Columbkille, in the middle of Derry-Columbkille.

verò numerum relatus est Laurentius ab Honorio III. anno 1225. cujus canonizationis Bulla, data Reate, III. Id. Decembr. anno Pontificatus 10. habetur in Laërtij Cherubini Bullario; tomo 1. pag. 49. edit. Rom. anno 1617." For more information about this distinguished prelate, the reader is referred to his Life, as published by Messingham in his *Florilegium*, and to De Burgo's *Hibernia Dominicana*. Dr. Lanigan in his Ecclesiastical History of Ireland, vol. iv. p. 174, and Mr. Moore, in his History of Ireland, vol. ii. p. 308, state that Muirchertach, the father of St. Laurence, was prince of Imaile; but this is as great a mistake as that of the author of St. Laurence's Life, who makes him a son of the King of all Leinster, for O'Toole was at this period Lord of the tribe and territory of Hy-Muireadhaigh, called Omurethi by Giraldus, comprising about the southern half of the present county of Kildare, to wit, the baronies of Kilkea and Moone, Narragh and Rheban, and a part of the barony of Connell. It was bounded on the north by the celebrated hill of Allen, on the north-west by Offaly, which it met at the Curragh of Kildare, and on the west by Laoighis or Leix, from which it was divided by the River Barrow. According to O'Heerin's topographical poem, O'Teige was the ancient chief of Imaile (which was a very small district), but O'Toole was Lord of Hy-Muireadhaigh, which extended along the Barrow northwards as far as the hill of Almhuin, now Allen:

Triall tar Bearbha an buird ealaigh,
O'n tír iothmhair uirmhealaigh,
O Dhinnrigh co Maistin mhir,
Do dhiol m'uirtir o a n-uaisle.
O'Tuathail an mhuir mheadhaigh,
Ar Uibh mearbha Muireadhaigh,
Co h-Almhain an cheoil cochlaigh,
An feoir barrghloin braontorthaigh.

"Pass across the Barrow, of the cattle abounding border,
From the land rich in corn and honey,
From Dinnree to the pleasant Maisdin (Mullamast),
My journey is repaid by their nobility.
O'Toole of the festive fortress,
Is over the vigorous Hy-Muireadhaigh,
As far as Almhuin of melodious music,
Of the fair, grassy, irriguous surface."

The ancient Irish topographical work called *Dinnsenchus*, places in the territory of Ui Muireadhaigh, the old fort of Roeireann, which was situated on the top of the remarkable hill of Mullach Roeireann, now Mullagh-Reelion, about five miles to the south-east of Athy, in the county of Kildare. The name of this territory is preserved even to the present day in that of the deanery of Omurthie, which, according to the Regal Visitation Book of 1615, comprises the following parishes, in the county of Kildare, viz., Athy, Castlereban, Kilberry, Dollardstown, Nicholastown, Tankardstown, Kilkea, Grange-Rosnolvan, Belin, Castledermott, Grange, Moone, Timoling, Narraghmore, Kilcullen, Usk. And this authority adds: "Adjacent to the deanery of Omurthie is the parish church of Damenoge [now Dunamanoge], and the parish church of Fontstown."—See Ledwich's *Antiquities of Ireland*, second Edition, p. 294, where the author ignorantly assumes that Omurethi was O'Moore!

Soon after the death of St. Laurence the O'Tooles, or O'Tuathails, were driven from this beautiful and fertile district of Omurethi by the Baron Walter de Riddlesford, or Gualterus de Ridenesfordia, who, according to Giraldus

Donncaḋ ua caireallain do ṁarbaḋ la cenél cconaill i ndíoġal a ṁeabla ar ua ngairmleaḋaiġ tre mirbailib na naeṁ isa heneaċ ro ṡáraiġ.

Aindilis ua dochartaiġ do écc i ndoire ċolaim ċille.

Caṫ na cconċobor .i. Concobor maenmaiġe mac Ruaiḋri ui Chonċobair ⁊ Concobar ua ceallaiġ (.i. tiġearna ua maine) dú i ttorċair Concobor ua ceallaiġ, taḋg a ṁac, a ḋerbraṫair diarmaid, ⁊ Maoilseachlainn mac diarmada ui ċeallaiġ, ⁊ mac taiḋg ui Concobair (.i. taḋg).

Muirghes ua heidhin tiġerna ua bfiaċrach aiḋne do ṁarbaḋ la feraib Muṁan.

Carrġaṁain ua giolla ultáin taoiseaċ Muinntire Maoil tsionna do ṁarbaḋ la haeḋ Mac carrġaṁna i ninis énḋaiṁ for morloch.

Doṁnall mac taiḋg uí chinnéiḋiġ tiġearna urṁuṁan do éc.

(*Hibernia Expugnata*, lib. ii. c. xxi.), had his castle at Tristerdermot [Disert Diarmada, now Castledermot], in the territory of Omurethi. In the Dublin copy of the Annals of Innisfallen it is stated, under the year 1178, that the English of Wexford set out on a predatory excursion into Hy-Muireadhaigh, and slew Dowling O'Tuathail [O'Toole], king of that territory, and lost their own leader, Robert Poer. But though the O'Tuathails were driven from their original territory about this period, they were still regarded by the Irish as the second highest family in Leinster, and the Annals of Clonmacnoise, as translated by Mageoghegan, record under the year 1214, the death of Lorcan O'Twahall, "young Prince of Leinster, and next in superiority of that province." After their expulsion from the rich plains of Omurethi, the O'Tuohills, or O'Tooles, took shelter in the mountain fastnesses of Wicklow, where in course of time they dispossessed the O'Teiges of Imaile, and other minor families.

It has been the object of the Editor in this note to collect together such evidences as will prove that the father of St. Laurence O'Toole, though not King of all Leinster, was chief of a more important territory than Imaile, a fact which has hitherto escaped our modern historians and topographical writers, who have copied each other without consulting any but printed authorities.

[f] *Violated.*—It is worthy of remark here, that whenever a chief, who had offered insult to a church or sanctuary, happened to be killed, his death is invariably atributed to the miraculous interposition of the patron saint.

[g] *Hy-Many.* — The following parishes, or coarbships, were in Hy-Many, according to a tract in the Book of Lecan, treating of the manners and customs of the O'Kellys, viz.: Clonfert, Kilmeen, Kiltullagh, Kilcommon, Camma (where the Hy-Manians were baptized), Cloontuskert (where the O'Kelly was inaugurated), and Cloonkeen Cairill. The following families were located in Hy-Many, and tributary to O'Kelly, viz., Mac Egan, Chief of the tribe of Clandermot; Mac Gillenan, Chief of Clann Flaitheamhla and Muintir kenny; O'Donnellan, Chief of Clann Breasail; O'Doogan, Chief of Muintir-Doogan; O'Gowran, Chief of Dal-Druithne; O'Docomhlain, Chief of Rinn-na-hEignidi; O'Donoghoe, Chief of Hy-Cormaic, in Moinmoy; and O'Maoilbrighde, Chief of Bredach, which was the best territory in Hy-Many. For further particulars concerning the families and districts of Hy-

Donough O'Carellan was killed by the Kinel-Connell, in revenge of his treacherous conduct towards O'Gormly, and by the miracles of the saints whose guarantee he had violated[f].

Aindileas O'Doherty died at Derry-Columbkille.

A battle, called the battle of the Conors, was fought between Connor Moinmoy, the son of Roderic O'Conor, and Connor O'Kelly, Lord of Hy-Many[g], in which were slain Conor O'Kelly, his son Teige, his brother Dermot, Melaghlin, the son of Dermot O'Kelly, and Teige, the son of Teige O'Conor[h].

Maurice O'Heyne, Lord of Hy-Fiachrach-Aidhne[i], was killed by the men of Munster.

Carroon O'Gilla-Ultain, Chief of Muintir Maoil-t-Sionna, was killed by Hugh Mac Carroon[k], on Inis Endaimh[l], in Mor-loch.

Donnell, the son of Teige O'Kennedy, Lord of Ormond[m], died.

Many, the reader is referred to *Tribes and Customs of Hy-Many*, printed for the Irish Archæological Society in 1843.

[h] *O'Conor.*—It is added in the Annals of Kilronan, that this battle was fought at Magh Sruibhegealain, at the head or extremity of Daire na g-capall.

[i] *Hy-Fiachrach-Aidhne*, Ui Fiachrach Aiḋne. A territory in the south-west of the county of Galway, which, as we learn from the Life of St. Colman Mac Duach, published by Colgan, was originally coextensive with the diocese of Kilmacduagh.

[k] *Mac Carroon*, mac carrġaṁna.—This name is anglicised Caron by O'Flaherty, in his *Ogygia*, part iii. c. 85, and Mac Carrhon by Connell Mageoghegan, who knew the tribe well. The name is now anglicised Mac Carroon. O'Flaherty locates them in the territory of Cuircnia, now the barony of Kilkenny West, in the county of Westmeath. Their ancestor was called Mael Sionna, i. e. Chief of the Shannon, from the situation of his territory on the east side of that river. They are to be distinguished from the O'Caharnys, Sionnachs, or Foxes of Kilcoursey, whose tribe name was Muintir-Tadhgain.

[l] *Inis Endaimh*, is now called Inchenagh, and lies in Lough Ree, not far from Lanesborough. It is curious that Lough Ree is here called mór loċ, or the great lake.

[m] *Ormond*, Urṁuṁain.—Now the baronies of Upper and Lower Ormond, in the county of Tipperary. The territory of Urṁuṁain was anciently very extensive, but it has been for many centuries limited to the baronies now bearing its name. O'Kennedy, who descended from Donnchuan, the brother of Brian Borumha, was originally seated in Glenomra, in the east of the county of Clare, whence they were driven out, at an early period, by the O'Briens and Mac Namaras. O'Heerin thus notices the original situation of O'Kennedy in his topographical poem :

O Cinneidiġ ċorcras ga, ar Ghleann ḟairsing, reiḋ Omra,
Sliocṫ ar nDuinnċuain, tre ċroḋaċṫ, na fuinn fuair gan iarmoraċṫ.

"O'Kennedy, who purples the javelin, *rules* over the extensive, smooth Glenomra,
Of the race of our Donnchuan, who, through valour, obtained the lands without competition."

Maolmuire mac cuinn na mbocht primhṡſnóir Ereann do écc.

Aoḋ ua caiṫniaḋ, tigearna Iorrais do marḃaḋ la hua cceallachain hi ffiull hi ccill ċomáin.

Amhlaiḃ ua toġda taoiseaċ na bréda, do marḃaḋ la hua ngaiḃteċáin taoiseaċ ṁaiġe helſg.

Murchaḋ ua laċtna taoiseaċ an dá ḃac do ḃáḋadh illoch con.

AOIS CRIOSD, 1181.

Aois Criosd mile, ced, ochtmoġatt, a haſn.

Dungal ua caellaiġi espoc Lſithglinne do écc.

Maolmuire ua dunain abb cnuic na Sſngan hi luġmaġ do écc.

Maolciarain ua fiodaḃra comarba ciarain do écc.

Cathrasnſḋ ria fflaithḃſrtaċ ua maeldoraiḋ ticchſrna cenel cconaill for macaiḃ riġ Connaċt Saṫarn cincidisi dú in ro marḃaḋ se meic décc do clannuiḃ ticchſrnaḋ ⁊ toiseaċ Connaċt la cenél cconaill co soċaidib oile do ṡosrclannaiḃ ⁊ dosrclannaiḃ immaille friú cenmotháidsíde. Ro chuirsſtt Connaċtaiġ so daoire dóiḃ fri ré imcén iarsan caṫ sin. Caṫ criċe coirpre ainm in caṫa sin.

[n] *Mac Con-na-mbocht*, i. e. the descendant of Conn of the poor, was the name of the Erenaghs of Clonmacnoise.

[o] *O'Caithniadh.*—This name is now obsolete in Erris, an extensive and remarkably wild barony in the north-west of the county of Mayo, unless it has been changed to O'Cahan, or O'Kane.

[p] *Of Bredagh*, na breḋċa.—This is the name of a district in the barony of Tirawley, comprising the parish of Moygawnagh, and part of that of Kilfian. It is to be distinguished from Bredagh in Inishowen, in the north-east of the county of Donegal, which was the inheritance of O'Duibhdhiorma, of the race of Eoghan, son of Niall of the Nine Hostages.

[q] *Moy-heleag*, maġ helſg.—This is also called maġ heleoġ; it was the ancient name of the level part of the parish of Crossmolina, in the barony of Tirawley, and county of Mayo. The monastery of Errew, on Lough Conn, is in this district, and the family of O'Flynn, a branch of whom were hereditary Erenaghs of this monastery, are still numerous in the parish of Crossmolina. They were till lately in possession of the celebrated reliquary called Mias Tighernain, which is now at Rappa Castle. These O'Flynns are mentioned by Giolla Iosa Mor Mac Firbis, the compiler of the Book of Lecan, as the Brughaidhs, or farmers, or Maghheleag.—See *Genealogies, Tribes and Customs of Hy-Fiachrach*, printed for the Irish Archæological Society in 1844, p. 113, note [k], and p. 239, note [i].

[r] *Da-Bhac*, now generally called the Two Backs; a territory in the south of the barony of Tirawley, in the county of Mayo, lying between Lough Conn and the River Moy.—See

Mulmurry Mac Con-na-mbocht[n], chief senior of Ireland, died.

Hugh O'Caithniadh[c], Lord of Erris, was treacherously slain by O'Callaghan at Kilcommon.

Auliffe O'Toghda, Chief of Bredagh[p], was killed by O'Gaughan, Chief of Moy-heleag[q].

Murrough O'Laghtna, Chief of Da Bhac[r], was drowned in Lough Conn.

THE AGE OF CHRIST, 1181.

The Age of Christ, one thousand one hundred eighty-one.

Dungal O'Kaelly, Bishop of Leighlin, died.

Mulmurry[s] O'Dunan, Abbot of Cnoc-na-Seangan[t] (Louth), died.

Mulkieran O'Fiävra, successor of Kieran, died.

Flaherty O'Muldory, Lord of Tirconnell, defeated the sons of the King of Connaught on the Saturday before Whitsuntide. Sixteen of the sons of the lords and chieftains of Connaught were slain by the Kinel Connell, as well as many others, both of the nobles and the plebeians[u]. They held the Connacians under subjection for a long time after this battle, which was known by the name of Cath Criche Coirpre[v] [i. e. the Battle of the Territory of Carbury].

Tribes of Hy-Fiachrach, pp. 11, 165, 228. The name O'Toghdha, which would be pronounced O'Toffey in this district, is now obsolete. Under this year the Dublin copy of the Annals of Innisfallen, record that John De Courcy fled from Downpatrick, and went to Ath Glaisne [Ardglass?] where he built a castle which he made his residence for some time. According to the Annals of Clonmacnoise he returned to Down in 1181, and repaired his house there.

[s] *Mulmurry*, maelmuire.—Colgan says, *Acta SS.*, p. 737, that this was the celebrated Marianus, the author of the Irish Martyrology, so often quoted by him and other ecclesiastical writers.

[t] *Cnoc-na-Seangan*, i. e. Hill of the ants. This place, which is situated about thirty perches to the east of the town of Louth, is now generally called in English, Pismire Hill. It contains the ruins of a church, but no part of the great abbey is now traceable on it. This abbey was founded and endowed for Augustinian Canons, by Donough O'Carroll, Prince of Oriel, and Edan O'Kaelly, or O'Caollaidhe, Bishop of Clogher.—See *Trias Thaum.*, p. 305; Ware's Antiquities, cap. 26; and also his Bishops of Louth and Clogher, at the name Edan.

[u] *Both of the nobles and the plebeians.*—In the Annals of Kilronan this phrase is given in Latin: "*et alii nobiles et ignobiles cum eis.*"

[v] *Cath Criche Coirpre.*—According to the Annals of Kilronan the persons slain in this battle were the following, viz.: Brian Luighnech and Manus O'Conor; Melaghlin, Murray, and Murtough, three sons of Turlough O'Conor; also Hugh, son of Hugh, son of Rory (O'Flaherty),

Iar naraile liubar itiatt na mſic riog torcratur la flaithbſrtach ir in cath remráite, brian ⁊ Magnur dá mac toirrdealbaig moir, * * * * ⁊ Maolruanaig, dá mac ele Aoda í chonchobair. Do rochair beor Aod mac conchobair ui cellaig, ⁊ giollacrírt mac megoireachtaig uí Rodhuib, Eachmarcach ua muirſdaig, donnchad mac briain luignig ui Concobair, cucuallachta mac Muirchſrtaig uí Concobair, tri huí maoilbrenainn, dá mac giollabuide, ⁊ aod mac mic aoda mic Ruaidri, ⁊ sochaide ele do ſaſrclannaib.

Sloicchſd la domnall mac aſda méc lachlainn, ⁊ la cenel neogain telcha óg i nultoib. Ro meabhratt for ultoib, for uib ttuirtre, ⁊ for ſſraib lí im Ruaidri mac duinnrlebe ⁊ im choinmide ua flainn.

Sluacch la fſraib maige hithe im ua ccathain Eachmarcach, ⁊ im cenel mbinig glinne co rangadar tar tuaim. Ro airccſd fir lí, ⁊ ua ttuirtre uile Ruccrat ilmile do buaib.

Tomaltach ua Conchobair do oirdnead i ccomorbur ratraicc. Cuairt chenél eogain do thabairt lairr, do bſrt a ſſir uaidib ⁊ ro ſaccaib bſnnachtain.

King of West Connaught; and Donough, son of Brian O'Fallon, *et alii multi nobiles et ignobiles cum eis.* The same annals also state that it was Donough, the son of Donnell Midheach O'Conor, that brought Flaherty O'Muldory to assist him in asserting the chieftainship of the territory of Carbury for himself. They also add, that this was called the Battle of Magh Diughbha, and that the bodies of the chieftains were carried to Clonmacnoise, and there interred in the tombs of their ancestors.

[w] *O'Connor.*—According to the Annals of Ulster and of Kilronan, three of the sons of Hugh, son of Turlough O'Conor, were slain in this battle, namely, Melaghlin, Murray, and Murtough.

[x] *O'Murray,* O'Muireadhaig.—In 1585 the head of this family was seated at Ballymurry, in the parish of Kilmaine, barony of Athlone, and county of Roscommon.

[y] *O'Mulrenins,* pronounced in Irish O'Maoil brénainn, *O'Mul-vrénin.*

[z] *Kinel-Binny,* Cenel Binnig.—It would appear from several authorities that this tribe was seated in the valley of Glenconkeine, in the south of the county of Derry.

[a] *Toome,* Tuaim.—This is called Fearrat Tuama, i. e. the *trajectus,* or ferry of Tuaim, in the Tripartite Life of St. Patrick. The place is now called Toome-Bridge, and is situated between Lough Neagh and Lough Beg, and on the boundary between the counties of Antrim and Derry. "Feursait Tuama hodie vulgo vocatur Tuaim est vadum vel trajectus ubi Banna fluvius ex lacu Echach."—*Trias Thaum.,* p. 183.

[b] *Firlee,* Fir lí.—The Tripartite Life of St. Patrick, as translated by Colgan, in *Trias Thaum.,* pp. 127, 146, calls this territory "Leæorum fines," and states that it was on the east side of the River Bann. "Venit (Patricius) in Leæorum fines Bannæ flumini ad orientalem ejus ripam adjacentes." But though the *Firli* were unquestionably seated on the east side of the River Bann, since the twelfth century, it would appear, from the Annotations of Tirechan on the Life of St. Patrick, that they were on the west side of this river in the time of the Irish apos-

According to another book, the sons of kings who were slain by Flaherty in the last mentioned battle were the following, viz. Brian and Manus, two sons of Turlough More; and Mulrony; and * * * two sons of Hugh O'Conor[w]. In that battle also fell Hugh, the son of Conor O'Kelly, and Gilchreest, the son of Mageraghty O'Rodiv; Eachmarcach O'Murray[x]; Donough, the son of Brian Luighneach O'Conor; Cucuallachta, the son of Murtough O'Conor; three of the O'Mulrenins[y]; the two Mac Gillaboys; and Hugh, son of Hugh, who was son of Roderic, together with many others of the nobility.

Donnell, the son of Hugh Mac Loughlin, and the Kinel-Owen of Tullaghoge, made an incursion into Ulidia, and defeated the Ulidians, the Hy-Tuirtre, and the Firlee, together with Rory Mac Donslevy, and Cumee O'Flynn.

The men of Moy-Ithe, together with O'Kane (Eachmarcach), and the Kinel-Binny[z] of the Valley, mustered an army, and crossed Toome[a]. They plundered all *the territories of* Firlee[b] and Hy-Tuirtre, and carried off many thousands of cows.

Tomaltagh O'Conor was consecrated successor of St. Patrick. He performed the visitation of the Kinel-Owen, received his dues from them, and left them his blessing.

tle. The Bann (i. e. the Lower Bann), according to the oldest accounts of that river, flowed between the plains of Li and Eilne, and we learn from Tirechan that the plain of Eilne was on the east side of the river, and consequently the plain of Li, or Lee, was on the west side of it: "Et exiit [Patricius] in Ardd Eolergg et Ailgi, et Lee Bendrigi, et perrexit trans flumen Bandæ, et benedixit locum in quo est cellola *Cuile Raithin* [Coleraine], in *Eilniu*, in quo fuit Episcopus, et fecit alias cellas multas in Eilniu. Et per Buas flumen" [Bush River] "foramen pertulit, et in Dun Sebuirgi" [Dunseverick] "sedit super petram, &c. &c. Et reversus est in campum *Eilni* et fecit multas ecclesias quas Condiri [the clergy of Connor diocese] habent."

Adamnan, in his Life of Columba, says, lib. i. c. 50, that Conallus, Bishop of Cuil Raithin [Coleraine], having collected many presents among the inhabitants of the plain of Eilne, prepared an entertainment for St. Columba; and Colgan, in a note on this passage, conjectures that the plain of Eilne was west of the River Bann, and that which was then called "*an Mhachaire*," i. e. the plain. But that Magh Li was west of the Bann is put beyond dispute by the fact that the church of *Achadh Dubhthaigh*, now Aghadowey, on the west side of the river Bann, is described in ancient authorities, as in *Magh Li*, or Campus Li, on the margin of the Lower Bann.—See Colgan's *Acta Sanctorum*, p. 223; the Irish Calendar of the O'Clerys, at 9th and 22nd of January; and Sampson's Memoir of his Chart and Survey of Londonderry, p. 222. But on the increasing power of the O'Kanes, the Firli were unquestionably driven across the Bann.—See note under the year 1178.

AOIS CRIOSD, 1182.

Aois Criosd míle, céd, ochtmoghatt, a dó.

Aodh ua caellaighi epscop airghiall, ⁊ cenn canánach Ereann do écc.

Domnall ua huallachain airdepscop mumhan do écc.

Sluaicchedh la domhnall mac aedha ui lachlainn go dún bó i ndáil riada. Do radsom cath do ghallaibh is in dú sin Ro meabhaidh for cenél neoghain Ro marbhadh ann dna Raghnall ua breislén, Giolla criosd ó catháin co socaidibh oile i maille friu, Ruccsat Soiscela martain leó don chur sin.

Brian mac toirrdhealbhaigh ui bhriain do mharbhadh la Raghnall mac Commara bicc tre meabhail.

Aodh mac carrghamhna taoiseach muinntire maoiltsionna do marbhadh la giolla ultáin mac carrghamhna.

Murchadh mac taichligh uí dubhda, do marbhadh la Maoilseachlainn ua Maolruanaidh.

Amhlaibh ua ferghail do ghabhail tairisighechta na hangaile ⁊ Aodh do innarbadh.

AOIS CRIOSD, 1183.

Aois Criosd míle, céd, ochtmoghatt, a trí.

Ioseph ua haodha Epscop ua cceinnselaigh [do écc].

Bec ua hegra tigherna luighne Connacht do marbhadh la conchobhar ua diarmata mic Ruaidhri, ar loc mic fearadhaigh ina thigh fein tre meabhail.

[c] *Dunbo, in Dal Riada.*—This is a mistake of the annalists, but not of the Four Masters, as it is found in the older Annals of Ulster and of Kilronan. Dunbo was not in Dalriada at any period, for it is west of the River Bann, in a territory called an Mhachaire, the Plain, in Colgan's time. Dalriada never extended westwards beyond the Bann.

[d] *St. Martin.*—This passage is rendered in the old translation of the Ulster Annals in the British Museum, as follows: "An army by Donell O'Loghlin to Dunbo in Dalriada, and the Galls gave battle to them there, and vanquished Kindred-Owen, and Ranall O'Bryslan was killed there, and Gilli Christ O'Cahan, and many more; and the Galls carried Martin's Gospel with them." From a notice in a manuscript in the Bodleian Library, Laud. 615, p. 81, it would appear that this copy of the Gospels, which was believed to have belonged to St. Martin of Tours, was brought to Ireland by St. Patrick, and that it was preserved at Derry in the time of the writer. There was a cemetery and holy well at Derry dedicated to this St. Martin. In the Dublin copy of the Annals of Ulster, and in the

THE AGE OF CHRIST, 1182.

The Age of Christ, one thousand one hundred eighty two.

Hugh O'Kaelly, Bishop of Oriel, and head of the Canons of Ireland, died.

Donnell O'Huallaghan, Archbishop of Munster, died.

Donnell, the son of Hugh O'Loughlin, marched with an army to Dunbo, in Dal Riada[c], and there gave battle to the English. The Kinel-Owen were defeated, and Randal O'Breslen, Gilchreest O'Kane, and many others, were killed. On this occasion they carried off with them the Gospel of St. Martin[d].

Brian, the son of Turlough O'Brien, was treacherously slain by Randal Macnamara Beg.

Hugh Mac Carroon, Chief of Muintir Maoil-t-Sionna, was killed by Gilla-Ultain Mac Carroon.

Murrough, the son of Taichleach O'Dowda, was killed by Melaghlin O'Mulrony.

Auliffe O'Farrell assumed the lordship of Annaly, and Hugh was expelled[e].

THE AGE OF CHRIST, 1183.

The Age of Christ, one thousand one hundred eighty-three.

Joseph O'Hea, Bishop of Hy-Kinsellagh (died).

Bec O'Hara, Lord of Leyny in Connaught, was treacherously slain by Conor, the grandson of Dermot, who was son of Roderic, in his own house, on Lough Mac Farry.

Annals of Kilronan, the portion of the passage relating to the Gospel reads: 7 soscela martain do ḃreċ do gallaiḃ leo.

[e] Under this year the Annals of Kilronan, of Clonmacnoise, and of Ulster, record the death of Milo de Cogan, the destroyer of all Ireland, both Church and State; also of Reymond de la Gross, Cenn Cuillinn [Kantitunensis?], and the two sons of Fitz-Stephen. The Annals of Kilronan and of Clonmacnoise add, that Milo was killed by Mac Tire, Prince of Ui Mac Caille, now the barony of Imokilly, in the county of Cork. The Irish annalists do not furnish us with any further particulars; but Giraldus Cambrensis, in his *Hibernia Expugnata*, lib. ii. c. 18, calls Mac Tyrus a betrayer: "à proditore Machtyro qui eos *ea nocte hospitari debuerat*, cum aliis quinque militibus improuisis à tergo securium ictibus sunt interempti." Sir Richard Cox, in his *Hibernia Anglicana*, p. 37, magnifies this act of Mac Tyrus into an awful specimen of Irish treachery, and adds, that Milo had been invited by Mac Tyrus to lodge at his house that

Do rala deaḃaiḋ etter ua flaithbertaiġ, an giollu riaḃaċ, ⁊ Mac ui ġairmleaḋaiġ. Ro marḃaḋ ua flaiṫbertaiġ is in iomaireacc sin ⁊ drong mór do cenél Moain.

Ferġal mac Aṁlaiḃ ui ruairc, do marḃaḋ la loċlainn mac doṁnaill ui ruairc.

Giollaultáin mac carrġaṁna taoiseaċ muintire maoiltrionna do marḃaḋ la macaiḃ ui ḃraoin ⁊ la macaibh an trionnaigh ui ċaṫarnaigh go ccuiccear ele a maille friu.

AOIS CRIOSD, 1184.

Aois Criosd mile, ced, ochtmogatt, a cethair.

Giolla iosa ua maoilin Epscop eiriḋe do écc.

Brian breifneċ mac toirrḋelḃaiġ ui conċoḃair do écc.

Maoilíosa ua cerḃaill do oirdneḋ i ccoṁorbus Patraic iar na ḟaccḃáil do ṫomaltaċ ua ċonċoḃair.

Art ua maoileaċlainn tigherna iarṫair ṁiḋe do ṁarḃaḋ i meaḃail la diarmait ua mbriain .i. mac toirrḋelḃaiġ tria forcongra ġall, ⁊ Maoilseaċlainn beacc do ġaḃáil a ionaiḋ, ⁊ maiḋm do sraoineaḋ lais a ccionn trí lá forsan diarmait céna du in ro marbait ile im mac maṫġaṁna í briain.

Caislén do cuṁdaċ la gallaiḃ i ccill áir.

Caislén oile do orccain la Maoilseaċlainn ⁊ la Conċoḃor maenmaiġe ua cconċoḃair. Ro marḃaḋ drong ṁór do gallaiḃ ann.

Deċ ttigche fichet do foirġniḃ cuṁdaiġṫi arda macha do orgain la gallaiḃ miḋe.

Mainistir easa ruaidh do edhbairt la flaithbertach Ua Maoldoraiḋ tiġerna ċinél cconaill do ḋia ⁊ do naoiṁ bernard do raith a anma.

night. The same is repeated by Moore, in his History of Ireland, vol. ii. p. 311, without quoting any authority, which is very unfair, as it turns out that the prejudiced Giraldus is the only authority.

[f] *O'Flaherty.*—This was not O'Flaherty of Iar Connaught, but of Tyrone, where the name is now changed to Laverty, or Lafferty (O'Ḟlaiṫbeartaiġ). In the old translation of the Annals of Ulster preserved in the British Museum, the name of this Tyronian family, Ua Ḟlaiṫbertaiġ, is anglicised O'Lathvertay, which is close enough to the form it has assumed in modern times. The above passage is thus Englished in this translation: "A. D. 1183. A skirmish between Gilla Revagh O'Lathvertay and O'Garm-

A battle was fought between O'Flaherty[f] (Gillarevagh) and the son of O'Gormly, in which O'Flaherty and a great number of the Kinel-Moen were slain.

Farrell, son of Auliffe O'Rourke, was slain by Loughlin, son of Donnell O'Rourke.

Gilla Ultain Mac Carroon, Chief of Muintir Maoil-t-Sionna, and five others, were slain by the sons of the Sinnach (the Fox) O'Caharny[g].

THE AGE OF CHRIST, 1184.

The Age of Christ, one thousand one hundred eighty-four.

Gilla Isa O'Moylin, a bishop, died.

Brian Breifneach, son of Turlough O'Conor, died.

Maelisa O'Carroll was consecrated successor of St. Patrick, after Tomaltach O'Conor had resigned that dignity.

Art O'Melaghlin, Lord of Westmeath, was treacherously slain by Dermot O'Brien (i. e. the son of Turlough), at the instigation of the English, and Melaghlin Beg assumed his place, and in three days afterwards defeated the same Dermot in a conflict, in which many persons were slain, among whom was the son of Mahon O'Brien.

A castle was erected by the English at Killare[h].

Another castle was plundered by Melaghlin and Conor Moinmoy O'Conor, in which many of the English were slain.

Thirty of the best houses in Armagh were plundered by the English of Meath.

The monastery of Assaroe[i] was granted to God and St. Bernard by Flaherty O'Muldory, Lord of Kinel-Connell, for the good of his soul.

leaye's son; and O'Lathvertay and some of Kindred Muan were killed."

[g] Under this year the Dublin copy of the Annals of Innisfallen record the erection of a monastery at Dulcek, by Sir Hugh De Lacy.

[h] *Killare*, Cıllaıṗ.—A parish in the barony of Rathconrath, and county of Meath. Colgan describes it as follows: "Killaria vicus est in regione Mediæ quæ *Magh asuil* appellatur: in quâ sunt tres ecclesiæ; una parochialis viro sancto (Aido) dicata; alia quæ templum Sanctæ Brigidæ, et tertia quæ aula Sanctæ Brigidæ appellatur: et tres etiam fontes quorum aquis in unum confluentibus vicinum non sine miraculo agitur et velociter mouetur molendinum."—*Acta SS.*, p. 423, col. 2, note 31.

Cennfaolaḋ ua gráda comorba cronáin tuama gréne do écc.

Niall mac an triondaiġ ui ċaṫarnaiġ do écc.

Aṁlaiḃ mac ferġail ui ruairc ticcerna breifne do marḃaḋ a ffiull la Mag raġnaill.

Doṁnall ua flannaccáin taoiseaċ cloinne caṫail do écc hi cconga féiċín.

Ferġal ua raġallaiġ do ṁarḃaḋ hi ffiull la Maeileċlainn ua ruairc.

AOIS CRIOSD, 1185.

Aois Criosd mile ced ochtmoġaḋ a cúig.

Maoiliosu ua muireaḋaiġ fer leiġinn doire ċolaim ċille do ecc iar sendataiġ thoġaiḋe.

Pilib Unserra co ngallaiḃ uime do ḃeiṫ in ardmaċa co cenn sé laiṫe cona noiḋċiḃ i meḋon corġais do sonnraḋ.

Giollu criosd mac caṫmaoil ard taoiseaċ cenél fearadaiġ ⁊ na cclann

There are no ruins of the Castle of Killare now visible; but there are considerable remains of the churches mentioned by Colgan.

[i] *Assaroe*, eas ruaḋ.—The remains of this abbey now stand about one mile west of Ballyshannon; one of the side walls and a part of the western gable of the abbey are yet standing. The architecture is very good; but there are at present no windows or architectural features worthy of notice remaining.

[j] *Tomgraney*, Tuaim greine.—An ancient monastery dedicated to St. Cronan, in the barony of Upper Tullagh, in the county of Clare. It is now a small village.

[k] Under this year the Annals of Kilronan record the falling of the great church of Tuam, both its roof and stone work; also the burning by lightning of the fortress of the Clann Mulrony, called the Rock of Lough Key, in which six or seven score of persons of distinction, with fifteen persons of royal descent, were destroyed.

[l] *Philip Unserra*.—He is called Philip Worcester in the old translation of the Annals of Ulster, in the British Museum, and by his cotemporary Giraldus Cambrensis, Philippus Wigorniensis.—See *Topographia Hiberniæ*, dist. 2, c. 50, where there is a strange story told about his conduct at Armagh. Hanmer repeats the same; and Sir Richard Cox, who was always anxious to hide the faults of the English and villify the Irish, has condescended to tell the story in the following strain: *Hibernia Anglicana*, p. 38, ad ann. 1184: "*Philip of Worcester*, Lord Justice or Governour of *Ireland*, came over with a smart party of Horse and Foot; he also brought with him *Hugh Tirrel*, a Man of ill Report: He was not long in the Government, before he seized on the Lands of *O'Cathesie* to the King's Use, though *Lacy* had formerly sold them: He also went a Circuit, to visit the Garrisons, and in *March* came to *Armagh*, where he exacted from the Clergy a great Sum of Mony; thence he went to *Down*, and

Kenfaela O'Grady, successor of Cronan of Tomgraney[j], died.

Niall, son of the Sinnagh (the Fox) O'Caharny, died.

Auliffe, the son of Farrell O'Rourke, Lord of Breifny, was treacherously slain by Mac Rannall.

Donnell O'Flanagan, Lord of Clann-Cahill, died at Conga-Feichin [Cong].

Farrell O'Reilly was treacherously slain by Melaghlin O'Rourke[k].

THE AGE OF CHRIST, 1185.

The Age of Christ, one thousand one hundred eighty-five.

Maelisa O'Murray, Lector of Derry-Columbkille, died at a venerable old age.

Philip Unserra[l] (of Worcester) remained at Armagh with his Englishmen during six days and nights in the middle of Lent.

Gilchreest Mac Cawell, Chief of Kinel-Farry[m] and of the Clans, viz. Clann-

so to *Dublin*, loaden both with Curses and Extorsions. *Tirrel* took a Brewing-Pan from the poor Priests at *Armagh*, and carried it to *Down*, but the House where he lay was burnt, and so were also the Horses in the Stable, so that he was fain to leave the Pan, *for want of Carriage;* and *Philip* had a severe fit of the Gripes, like to cost him his life; both which Punishments (they say) were miraculously inflicted upon them for their sacrilege." Cox, however, should have here stated, on the authority of Giraldus, that Tyrell restored the pan to the poor priests, for Giraldus writes: "Sed eadem nocte, igne, proprio eiusdem hospitio accenso, equi duo qui cacabum extraxerant, cum aliis rebus non paucis, statim combusti sunt. Pars etiam villæ maxima eadem occasione igne est consumpta. Quo viso, Hugo Tyrellus mane cacabum inueniens prorsus illæsum, pecunia ductus, Arthmaciam eum remisit." It looks very strange that the Irish annalists should have passed over this transaction in silence, it being just the sort of subject they generally comment upon.

[m] *Kinel-Farry*, cinel Feaṗaḋaiġ, and the *Clans*. The territory of Kinel-Farry, the patrimonial inheritance of the Mac Cawells (the descendants of Fergal, son of Muireadhach, son of Eoghan, son of Niall of the Nine Hostages) was nearly coextensive with the barony of Clogher, in the county of Tyrone; in which barony all the clans here mentioned were located, except the Hy-Kennoda and the Clann Colla, who were seated in Fermanagh. The Hy-Kennoda gave name to the barony of Tirkennedy, which is situated in the east of Fermanagh, adjoining the barony of Clogher in Tyrone.—See it mentioned at the years 1427, 1468, and 1518. The family of Mac Cathmhaoil, a name generally anglicised Mac Cawell and latinized Cavellus,—who supplied several bishops to the see of Clogher, are still numerous in this their ancient territory, and the name is also found in other counties, variously anglicised Camphill, Cambell, Caulfield, and even Howell; but the natives, when speaking the Irish language, always pronounce the name Mac Caṫṁaoil.

.i. clannt aenġusa, clann duiḃinnreaċt clann ḟoġartaiġ, ui cennfoda, ⁊ clann collu do ḟearaiḃ manaċ cenn coṁairle tuaisceirt Ereann do ṁarḃaḋ la hua néccniġ ⁊ la muinntir ċaoṁáin, ⁊ a ċenn do ḃreiṫ leó go ffríṫ uaṫa i ccionn miosa iarttain.

Maoilseċlainn mac muirċeartaiġ uí laċlainn do ṁarḃaḋ lá gallaiḃ.

Maoiliosa ua dálaiġ ollaṁ ereann, ⁊ alban ard taoiseaċ corcaraiḋe ⁊ corcadain, Saoi oirdeirc ar ḋán, ar eneaċ, ⁊ ar uaisle do écc i ccluain ioraird oca oiliṫre.

Mac ríġ Saxan .i. Seon mac an dara henri do ṫeaċt i nErinn luċt trí ficit long do ġaḃáil a riġe. Ro gaḃ aṫcliaṫ, ⁊ laiġin. Do roine caisdiall oc tiorrait ṗaċtna, ⁊ occ ard ḟionáin. Ro airg muṁa esdiḃ. Ro ḃris tra

[n] *Corcaree*, now a barony in the county of Westmeath. It is bounded on the north and north-east by Loch Dairbhreach, *anglice* Lough Derryvara; on the west by Lough Iron; and on the south and south-east by an irregular line of hills, which divide it from the barony of Moyashel. This territory is mentioned by our genealogists and historians as the inheritance of the descendants of Fiacha Raoidhe, the grandson of the monarch Felimy Reachtmhar, or the Lawgiver.—See O'Flaherty's *Ogygia*, part iii. cap. 69; and Duald Mac Firbis's Pedigrees, p. 106. This was originally the lordship of O'Hionradhain, and not of O'Daly, as we learn from O'Dugan:

> O'Donnchaḋa na ndaġ-ar,
> Ri Tealaiġ min moḋarain;
> O'hionraḋain, saoire sin,
> Rí Chorca Raoiġe roġ loin."

> "O'Donaghoe, of good tillage,
> King of the smooth Tealach Modharain;
> O'Hionradhain, nobler he,
> King of fairest Corca Ree."

[o] *Corca-Adain*, sometimes called Corca-Adaim. This was the original lordship of the O'Dalys; but unfortunately its situation is not to a certainty known. The Editor has been long of opinion that it is identical with the barony of Magheradernon, in the county of Westmeath. At this year, 1185, we find that O'Daly had possession of Corca-Ree, in addition to his own original territory of Corca-Adain; and it is not unreasonable to conclude that the two territories adjoined. Here it is necessary to remark, that, according to O'Dugan's topographical poem, Corca-Adain was in Teffia, or Tir-Mainé, and that Corca-Ree was not; that O'Daly was descended from Mainé, and the original inhabitants of Corca-Ree were not. It may therefore be lawfully assumed, that about this period O'Daly got a grant of Corca-Ree, which adjoined his original territory of Corca-Adain, from the O'Melaghlins, for some great service which that noble poet had rendered them by his sword or pen. That Corca-Ree was not in Teffia may be clearly inferred from Tirechan's annotations on the Life of St. Patrick, in the Book of Armagh. Thus, in describing St. Patrick's travels through Meath, that writer says: "And he (Patrick) built another church (Lecain) in the *country* of *Roide*, at *Caput Art*, in which he erected a stone altar, and another at Cuil-Corre, and he came across the River Ethne (Inny) into the two Teffias." It is, therefore, highly probable that the portion of the country lying between the

Aengus, Clann-Duibhinreacht, Clann-Fogarty, Hy-Kennoda, and Clann-Colla in Fermanagh, and who was the chief adviser of all the north of Ireland, was slain by O'Hegny and Muintir-Keevan, who carried away his head, which, however, was recovered from them in a month afterwards.

Melaghlin, the son of Murtough O'Loughlin, was slain by the English.

Maelisa O'Daly, ollave (chief poet) of Ireland and Scotland, Lord of Corcaree[n] and Corca-Adain[o], a man illustrious for his poetry, hospitality, and nobility, died while on a pilgrimage at Clonard.

The son of the King of England, that is, John, the son of Henry II., came to Ireland with a fleet of sixty ships, to assume the government of the kingdom. He took possession of Dublin and Leinster, and erected castles at Tipraid Fachtna[p] and Ardfinan[q], out of which he plundered Munster; but his people were defeated with great slaughter by Donnell O'Brien. The son of

River Brosnagh (which connects Lough Owel and Lough Ennell) and the baronies of Delvin and Farbil, was anciently called *Feara asail*, or *Magh asail*, and that the tract lying between the same river and the barony of Rathconrath, was called Corca-Adain. Mr. Owen Daly of Moningtown, in the barony of Corcaree, is supposed to be the present head of the O'Dalys of Westmeath.

[p] *Tibraghny*, тıppaıт ғаċтna, i. e. St. Fachna's well, is a townland containing the ruins of an old castle, situated in a parish of the same name, on the north side of the River Suir, in the barony of Iverk, in the south-west of the county of Kilkenny.—See the *Feilire Aenguis*, at the 13th of February and 18th of May, and Irish Calendar of the O'Clerys at the same days, from which it will be seen that this place was in the west of the ancient Ossory. See also the Ordnance Map of the county of Kilkenny, sheets 38 and 39. Sir Richard Cox, in his *Hibernia Anglicana*, p. 40, conjectures that this place is Tipperary; and Dr. Leland, and even Mr. Moore, have taken Cox's guess as true history.—See Leland's *History of Ireland*, vol. i. p. 146; and Moore's, vol. ii. p. 320.

[q] *Ardfinnan*, Ард Ғıonnáın, i. e. St. Finnan's height, or hill. It is situated in the barony of Iffa and Offa, in the county of Tipperary. The ruins of this castle are still to be seen on a rock overlooking the River Suir. Giraldus states (*Hib. Expugnata*, lib. ii. c. 34) that John erected three castles, the first at Tibractia, the second at Archphinan, and the third at Lismore. The Dublin copy of the Annals of Innisfallen also state, that John Earl of Moreton, son of Henry, King of England, came to Ireland this year, accompanied by four hundred knights, and built the castles of Lismore, Ardfinan, and Tiobraid [Tiobraid Fachtna].

For the character of the English servants and counsellors who were in Ireland about the King's son at this period, the reader is referred to Giraldus Cambrensis' *Hibernia Expugnata*, lib. ii. c. 35, where he describes the Normans as "Verbosi, iactatores, enormium iuramentorum authores, Aliorum ex superbia contemptores," &c.; and also to Hanmer's Chronicle, and Campion's *Historie of Irelande*, in which the Normans are described as "great quaffers, lourdens, proud, belly swaines, fed with extortion and bribery."—Dublin Edition of 1809, p. 97.

domhnall ua briain Maidhm ar ġallaibh mic Riġ Saxan Ro ċuir a nár. Do ḋeachaidh dna mac riġ Saxan tairis inunn iarttain do ċosaoid hugo delacii re a aṫair uair asé hugo ba forlamhaiġ a huċt ríġ Saxan ara ċionn in Erinn, ⁊ nír léicc cíos na braiġde ċuigesium ó riġraidh Ereann.

Comhṫoccḃáil coccadh do ḟás i cconnaċtaibh edir na rioġḋamhnaibh .i. ettir Ruaidhri ua conċoḃair ⁊ conċoḃar maenmaiġe, mac Ruaidhri, ⁊ conċoḃar ua diarmada, Caṫal carrać mac conċoḃair maonmaiġe, ⁊ caṫal croibhdearg mac toirrdhealbhaiġ, ro marḃadh soċaidhe ſtorra. Do roine Ruaidhri ⁊ a mac síd ler na huaislib ele iarttain.

Iarṫar connaċt do loscadh taiġib, tſmplaibh la domhnall ua mbriain, ⁊ la gallaibh.

Caṫal carrać mac conċoḃair maonmaiġe mic Ruaidhri do loscadh ċille dálua taiġib, templaibh tar a neisi, tucc a seótta ⁊ a maoine leis. Tuadhmhumha beós do mhilleadh, ⁊ dorccain lá conċoḃar maonmaiġe mac Ruaidhri, ⁊ la gallaibh. Na goill feisne do ṫeaċt leis co ros commain, ⁊ mac Ruaidhri do ṫaḃairt tri míle do ḃuaibh dóibh i ttuarastal.

Amhlaoibh ua muirſdhaiġ epscop ardamaċa, ⁊ ċenél fſradhaigh loċrann solusta nó soillsiccheadh tuaṫ ⁊ ecclas décc, ⁊ foġartać ua cearḃalláin do oirdnſdh ina ionadh.

Diarmaid mag carṫaiġ tiġearna dſsmumhan do mharḃadh la gallaibh corcaiġe.

Domhnall mac giolla pattraicc tiġearna osraiġe do écc.

AOIS CRIOSD, 1186.

Aois Criosd, mile, céd, oċtmogad, asé.

Maolcallann mac adaim mic cleircein epscop cluana fearta brenainn do écc.

Domhnall mac aodha uí laċlainn do ċor a flaiṫſs, ⁊ Ruaidhri ua flaithbeartaiġ doirdnead lá druing do ċenél eoġain ṫealċa óġ.

[r] The death of this bishop is thus noticed in the Annals of Ulster: "A. D. 1185. Amhlaim h-ua Muireḋaiġ, episcopus Ardmaċa ⁊ cenuil Eraḋaiġ, loċrann solusta no soillsiġed tuaiṫ ⁊ eclais, in Christo quieuit i nDun Crutnai, ⁊ a tabairt co h-onorać co Dairi Coluim Cille, ⁊ a adnucal fo cosaibh a aṫar, .i. an espuic h-ui Coḃṫaiġ, .i. i toeb in tem-

the King of England then returned to England, to complain to his father of Hugo de Lacy, who was the King of England's Deputy in Ireland on his (John's) arrival, and who had prevented the Irish kings from sending him (John) either tribute or hostages.

A general war broke out in Connaught among the Roydamnas [princes], viz. Roderic O'Conor, and Conor Moinmoy, the son of Roderic; Conor O'Diarmada; Cathal Carragh, the son of Conor Moinmoy; and Cathal Crovderg, the son of Turlough. In the contests between them many were slain. Roderic and his son afterwards made peace with the other chiefs.

The West of Connaught was burned, as well churches as houses, by Donnell O'Brien and the English.

Cathal Carragh, the son of Conor Moinmoy, who was the son of Roderic, burned Killaloe, as well churches as houses, and carried off all the jewels and riches of the inhabitants. Thomond was also destroyed and pillaged by Conor Moinmoy, the son of Roderic, and by the English. The English came as far as Roscommon with the son of Roderic, who gave them three thousand cows as wages.

Auliffe O'Murray, Bishop of Armagh and Kinel-Farry, a brilliant lamp that had enlightened clergy and laity, died[r]; and Fogartagh O'Carellan was consecrated in his place.

Dermot Mac Carthy, Lord of Desmond, was slain by the English of Cork.

Donnell Mac Gillapatrick, Lord of Ossory, died.

THE AGE OF CHRIST, 1186.

The Age of Christ, one thousand one hundred eighty-six.

Maelcallann, son of Adam Mac Clerken, Bishop of Clonfert-Brendan, died.

Donnell, the son of Hugh O'Loughlin, died; and Rory O'Flaherty [O'Laverty] was elected by some of the Kinel-Owen of Tullaghoge.

paill bic. Thus rendered in the old translation preserved in the British Museum: "A. D. 1185. Auliv O'Mureay, Bishop of Ardmach (Tirone) and Kindred-Feray, a bright taper that lightneth spiritually and temporally, *in Christo quievit* in Dun Cruthny, and [was] brought honourably to Dyry-Columkilly, and was buried at his father's feete, the Bishop O'Coffy, in the side of the church." It looks very odd that a Bishop O'Murray should be the son of a Bishop O'Coffey!

Conn ua breislén (.i. taoiseaċ Fánat) caindeal einiġ, ⁊ ġaiscceḋ ṫuais-cirt Ereann do ṁarbaḋ la mac mic laċlainn, ⁊ lá dréim do ċenél eoġain, ⁊ inis eoġain dorccain fó a biṫin gion go raiḃe cion doiḃ ann.

Giolla Pattraicc mac an ġiolla ċuirr toiseaċ ua mbranáin do ṁarbaḋ lá doṁnall ua laċlainn tré erail muintire branáin fó ḋéin.

Ruaiḋri ua conċobair do ionnarbaḋ i muṁain la conċobar maonmaiġe lá a ṁac ḃúḋéin. Connaċtaiġ do ṁilleaḋ etorra diḃlinib, ⁊ tuccaḋ é dia ṫír do riḋisi tre ċoṁairle ṡil muireḋaiġ, ⁊ do radatt trioċa céd offrann dó.

Hugo delaci Malartaċ ⁊ díscaoilteaċ ceall niomḋa ticcherna gall Miḋe, breifne, ⁊ airġiall. Ar dó dna do ḃeirṫi cíos Connaċt. Ar se ro gaḃ erṁor Eirenn do gallaiḃ. Ró ba lán míḋe uile ó Shionainn go fairrgi do ċaislenaiḃ gall less. Iar ttairccsin iaraṁ caislén derṁaiġe ḋó táinic

[s] *Fanad* was a territory in the north of Tir-Connell, or the county of Donegal, extending from Lough Swilly to Mulroy Lough, and from the sea to Rathmeltan. In the old translation of the Annals of Ulster this passage is rendered as follows: "A. D. 1186. Con O'Brislen, the candle of liberality and courage of the North of Ireland, killed by some of Kindred-Owen, and all Inis Owen spoyled and preyed through that, though innocent of it" [i. e. of the crime, cin co raiḃe cin doiḃ ann].

[t] *Mac Loughlin*.—There were some monarchs of Ireland of this family, but they were at this time only Lords of the Kinel-Owen.

[u] Trioċa céd signifies a cantred, or barony, containing 120 quarters of land. It is thus explained by Giraldus Cambrensis: "Dicitur autem cantaredus tam Hibernica quam Britannica tanta terræ portio quanta 100. villas continere solet."—*Hibernia Expugnata*, lib. ii. c. 18.—See also O'Flaherty's *Ogygia*, pp. 24, 25; and O'Brien's Irish Dictionary, at the word Trioċa. It is translated, "Cantaredus seu Centivillaria regio" by Colgan, in *Trias Thaum.*, p. 19, col. 2, n. 51.

[w] *Hugo de Lacy*.—The character and description of the personal form and appearance of Hugo de Lacy, is thus given by his contemporary, Giraldus Cambrensis:

"Si viri colorem, si vultum quæris, niger, nigris ocellis & defossis: naribus simis, facie à dextris igne casuali, mento tenus turpiter adusta. Collo contracto, corpore piloso, pariter et neruoso. Si staturam quæris, exiguus. Si facturam, deformis. Si mores: firmus ac stabilis, & Gallica sobrietate temperatus. Negotiis familiaribus plurimum intentus. Commisso quoque regimini, rebusque gerendis in commune vigilantissimus. Et quanquam militaribus negotiis plurimum instructus, crebris tamen expeditionum iacturis, Ducis officio non fortunatus: post vxoris mortem vir vxorius, & non vnius tantum, sed plurimarum libidini datus: vir auri cupidus & auarus, propriique honoris & excellentiæ, trans modestiam ambitiosus."—*Hibernia Expugnata*, lib. ii. cap. 20.

[x] *Profaner*, malartaċ.—This word is used in the best Irish manuscripts, in the sense of profaner or defiler, and the verb malartuiġim means, I defile, profane, curse. The following

Con O'Breslen, Chief of Fanad[t], the lamp of the hospitality and valour of the north of Ireland, was slain by the son of Mac Loughlin[t] and a party of the Kinel-Owen; in consequence of which Inishowen was unjustly ravaged.

Gillapatrick Mac Gillacorr, Chief of the Hy-Branain, was slain at the instigation of the Hy-Branain themselves.

Roderic O'Conor was banished into Munster by his own son, Conor Moinmoy. By the contests between both the Connacians were destroyed. Roderic, however, by the advice of the Sil-Murray, was again recalled, and a triochached[u] of land was given to him.

Hugo de Lacy,[w] the profaner[x] and destroyer of many churches; Lord of the English of Meath, Breifny, and Oriel; he to whom the tribute of Connaught was paid; he who had conquered the greater part of Ireland for the English, and of whose English castles[y] all Meath, from the Shannon to the sea, was full; after having finished the castle of Durrow[z], set out, accompanied by

examples of it in the *Leabhar Breac*, fol. 19, *b*, *b*, will prove its true meaning: Uair is menic elnigther 7 malartaigther in pobul uili tria imarbus aenduine; conid aire sin is coir fo cedoir a malairtrium nar ob guasocht do sochaide he 7 na taetsat tria fochaind. "For it is often that all the people are corrupted and defiled through the crime of one man; wherefore it is proper to excommunicate him, that he may not be dangerous to the multitude, and that they may not fall through him." Also at fol. 4, *b*, *b*, Ocus atberim, ol se, a beith malartta, escoitchend tria bithu. "And I say, quoth he, let me be accursed, excommunicated for ever."

[y] *English castles.*—For a curious account of the castles erected by Sir Hugh de Lacy, the reader is referred to *Hibernia Expugnata*, by Giraldus Cambrensis, cap. 19, 21, and 22. Besides his Meath castles he erected one at New Leighlin, in Idrone, called the Black Castle; one at Tachmeho now Timahoe, in the territory of Leix; one at Tristerdermot, now Castledermot, in the territory of Hy-Muiredhaigh, O'Toole's original country; one at Tulachfelmeth, now Tullow, in the county of Carlow; one on the Barrow, near Leighlin; and one at Kilkea, and another at Narragh, in the present county of Kildare.—See also *Hanmer's Chronicle*, Dublin Edition, pp. 321, 322.

[z] Dairmach, now Durrow, situated in the north of the King's County, and close to the boundary of the county of Westmeath, where St. Columbkille erected a famous monastery about the year 550. See Lanigan's Ecclesiastical History of Ireland, vol. ii. p. 118. At the period of the erection of this monastery, Durrow was in the territory of Teffia, and the site was granted to St. Columbkille by Brendan, Chief of Teffia, the ancestor of the Irish chieftain, Fox, or O'Caharny, at whose instigation Sir Hugh de Lacy was murdered. Adamnan, in his Life of Columba, thus speaks of the foundation of a monastery in this place by St. Columbkille: "Vir beatus in mediterraneâ Hiberniæ parte Monasterium, quod Scoticè dicitur Darmaig, divino fundavit nutu." See his Life of Columba, published by Colgan in *Trias Thaum.*, lib. i. cap. 31, lib. ii. c. 2, and lib. iii. c. 19.

amaċ go ttriar gall ina ċoiṁideaċt do ḋéchsain an caislén. Tainic din aon ócclaċ giolla gan ionaċar ó Miaḋaiġ do ḟſraiḃ teathḃa dia ṡoiġiḋ ⁊

Venerable Bede has the following notice of the erection of this monastery (Histor. lib. iii. c. 4):

"Fecerat, (Columba) priusquam Britanniam veniret monasterium nobile in Hiberniâ, quod a copia Roborum *Dearmach* linguâ Scotorum, hoc est, Campus Roborum, cognominatur."

Camden and Mercator thought that by *Dearmach* in this passage, Bede meant *Armagh*, and the former, in pp. 764, 765, of his *Hibernia*, states, that a celebrated monastery was founded at *Armagh* by Columba, about the year 610; but Ussher, who knew Irish topography far better than either of these writers, proves that *Dearmach* was the present *Durrow* in the King's County.

"Columbæ verò *Dearmach* eadem ipsa est quam Giraldus Cambrensis (*Hibern. Expugnat.* lib. ii. c. 34) non *Dernach*, ut habet liber editus, sed ut MSS. *Dervach* vel *Dermach:* (literam enim M aspiratam et V consonam eadem penè sono Hiberni efferunt:) ubi Midiæ illum debellatorem *Hugonem de Lacy, à securibus malè securum, dolo Hibernensium suorum* interemptum fuisse narrat. In regio comitatu ea est, **Durrogh** vulgo appellata: quæ monasterium habuit S. Columbæ nomine insigne; inter cujus Κειμήλια Euangeliorum Codex vetustissimus asservabatur, quem ipsius Columbæ fuisse monachi dictitabant. ex quo, et non minoris antiquitatis altero, eidem Columbæ assignato (quem in urbe **Kelles** sive **Kenlis** dictâ Midenses sacrum habent) diligenti cum editione vulgatâ Latinâ collatione factâ, in nostros usus variantium lectionum binos libellos concinnavimus."—*Primordia*, pp. 690, 691; and *Britannicarum Ecclesiarum Antiquitates*, London, 1687, p. 361.

The Rev. Denis Taaffe, who was well acquainted with the foregoing passage, asserts, nevertheless, that the Darmaig of Adamnan is Durrow, in the county of Kilkenny; but he offers no proof, and is manifestly in error. See his little work entitled the Life and Prophecies of St. Columbkille.

[a] *O'Meyey.*—There are several families of this name in the county of Westmeath, and in the parish of Magheross, in the county of Monaghan.

Mr. Moore, in his History of Ireland, vol. ii. p. 321, states that De Lacy "met his death from a hand so obscure, that not even a name remains associated with the deed." And adds, in a note: "Several names have been assigned to the perpetrator of this act, but all differing so much from each other, as to shew that the real name was unknown. Geoffry Keating, with that love of dull invention which distinguished him, describes the assassin as a young gentlemen in disguise." Keating's account of this murder referred to by Mr. Moore, is thus given in Dr. Lynch's translation of Keating's History of Ireland:

"Hugo de Lacy Midiæ ab Henrico præpositus tanto illicò in indigenas seviendi libidine correptus est, ut nobilem imprimis in eo tractu Colmanorum gentem funditus penè deleverit, aliisque regionis illius proceribus insidias dolosè instruxerit, et laqueis quas tetenderat irretitos vita fortunis spoliaverit. *Quidem autem e nobilitatis flore animosus juvenis* indignissimam hanc suorum cædem, fortunarumque jacturam iniquissimo ferens animo, audax sanè facinus aggressus est. Cum enim Hugo condendo castello Durmagiæ in Midiâ teneretur implicitus, operarios quoscumque idonea mercede conducens, quibus ita familiariter usus est, ut consortio eorum operisque, quandoque se immiscuerit; *juvenis ille nobilis* operarii speciem cultu præ se ferens operam suam ad hoc opus locavit, confus fore, ut facul-

three Englishmen, to view it. One of the men of Teffia, a youth named Gilla-gan-inathar O'Meyey[a], approached him, and drawing out an axe, which he had

tatem aliquando nancisceretur animam illam tanti suorum sanguinis profusione cruentatam hauriendi; nec suâ spe frustratus est; quâdam enim vice Hugonem graviter in opus incumbentem conspicatus, bipennem altè sublatum in tergum ejus adegit, animamque domicilio suo exegit, ac extrusit."

That this story was not invented by the honest Keating, will appear from the following entry in the Dublin copy of the Annals of Ulster, which was transcribed long before he was born.

A. D. 1186. Uga de Laci .i. malartaċ 7 dirscailteċ neimed 7 cell Erenn, a marbad i n-einech coluim cille ic denum caisteoil .i. a nDermaiġ; do marbad d' O Miadaiġ do Tethba.

"A. D. 1186. Hugo de Lacy, i. e. the profaner and destroyer of the sanctuaries and churches of Ireland, was killed in revenge of Columbkille, while making a castle at Durrow; he was killed by O'Meyey of Teffia."

This entry is thus rendered in the old translation of the Annals of Ulster in the British Museum: "A. D. 1186. Hugh de Lacy killed by a workman. Hugh de Lacy, spoyler of churches and privileges" [neimed] "of Ireland, killed by one of Brewny, by the Fox O'Catharny, in revenge of Colum Kill, building a castle in Dorow (his Abby, Anno 640 [540?] ex quo fundata est Daria Ecclesia)." It will be seen that in this passage the translator, who was well acquainted with the English accounts of the murder of De Lacy, renders O' miaḃaiġ, by "*a workman*"! thus: "Hugh de Lacy killed by a workman of Tathva" (do marbad d' O miaḃaiġ do Tethba). But this is so manifest a blunder that it is unnecessary to descend to particulars to refute it; for O' miaḃaiġ is decidedly a family name, not meaning descendant of the labouring man, but descendant of the honourable man, for miaḃ means honour, respect, and miaḃaċ, an honourable or estimable man. In the record of the murder of Hugo De Lacy, preserved in the Annals of Kilronan, it is stated that this O'Meyey was the fosterson of the Fox, Chief of Teffia. The passage is very curious and runs as follows: "A. D. 1186. Uga de Laci do Durmaġ Colaim cille, do denam caislein indti, 7 sluaiġ diairmiḋe do gallaiḃ lais; uair is é ra riġ Miḋe 7 Ḃreḟni, 7 Airgiall, 7 is dó do berta cis Connaċt, 7 ro gaḃ Erinn uile do gallaiḃ. Ro po lan dno Miḋi o Sinainn co fairci do [*recte* d'á] caislenaiḃ, 7 do ġallaiḃ. Iar ttairc-sin do in tsaoṫair sin .i. caislen Durmaiġe do denaim, táinic amach do fechain an caislein, 7 triar do gallaiḃ lais. Tainic dno en occlaċ do feruiḃ miḋe da indsaiġe, 7 a tuagh fa na coim .i. gilla gan inathur o miaḃaiġ, dalta an cSinnaiḃ feissin, 7 tuc én puille do, gur ben a cenn de, 7 gur tuit eitir cend 7 colaind a cloḋh an caislen." "A. D. 1186. Hugo de Lacy *went* to Durrow to make a castle there, having a countless number of the English with him; for he was King of Meath, Breifny, and Oriel, and it was to him the tribute of Connaught was paid, and he it was that won all Ireland for the English. Meath, from the Shannon to the sea, was full of his castles, and English [followers]. After the completion of this work by him, i. e. the erection of the castle of Durrow, he came out to look at the castle, having three Englishmen along with him. There came then one youth of the men of Meath up to him, having his battle-axe concealed, namely, Gilla-gan-inathur O'Meyey, the fosterson of the Fox himself, and he gave him one blow, so that he cut off his head, and he fell, both head and body, into the ditch of the castle."

tuagh fo a ċoimm laiss. Do bḟrt buille do Hugo gur bḟn a cḟnn de gur tuit etir ċḟnn ⁊ ċolainn i cclaḋ an caislén i neneaċ ċolaim ċille. Agus do cuaiḋ giolla gan ionaċar do ṫoraḋ a peaċa ass, ó ġallaiḃ ⁊ o ġaoiḋealaiḃ

Now it is quite clear, from these authorities, that Mr. Moore is wrong in charging Keating with dull invention for having written that the murderer of De Lacy was a young *gentleman* in disguise. He should have remembered that Keating had many documents which he (Mr. Moore) could not understand, and which are probably now lost. As to calling O'Meyey a *gentleman*, we must acknowledge that the term could then be properly enough applied to a youth who had been fostered by an Irish chief of vast territorial possessions, till he had been deprived of them by De Lacy. The scheme of O'Meyey could have been known to the Irish only. The English might have taken it for granted that he was a labourer at the castle. But after all there seems to be no original English authority which calls the murderer of De Lacy a labouring man, nor any authority whatever for it older than Holingshed. Campion, who wrote in 1571, gives the following description of the occurrence, in his *Historie of Ireland*, which savours really of dull invention: "*Lacy* the rather for these whisperings, did erect and edifie a number of Castles, well and substantially, provided in convenient places, one at Derwath, vvhere diverse Irish prayed to be set on worke, for hire. Sundry times came *Lacy* to quicken his labourers, full glad to see them fall in ure with any such exercise, wherein, might they once be grounded & taste the svveetness of a true man's life, he thought it no small token of reformation to be hoped, for which cause he visited them often, and merrily would command his Gentlemen to give the labourers example in taking paines, to take their instruments in hand, and to worke a season. the poore soules looking on and resting. But this game ended Tragically, while each man was busie to try his cunning; some lading, some plaistering, some heaving, some carving; the Generall also himselfe digging with a pykeaxe, a desperate villain of them, he whose toole the Generall used, espying both his hands occupied and his body, with all force inclining to the blow, watched his stoope, and clove his head with an axe, little esteeming the torments that ensued" [no torments ensued, for the murderer, who was as thin as a greyhound, baffled all pursuit.—Ed.] "This Lacy was conquerour of Meth, his body the two Archbishops, *John* of Divelin and *Mathew* of Cashell, buryed in the monastery of Becktye, his head in S. *Thomas* abbey at Divelin."—*Historie of Ireland*, Dublin Edition, pp. 99, 100. See also Hanmer's Chronicle, Dublin Edition, pp. 322, 323, where Hanmer observes of the tragical end of De Lacy: "Whose death (I read in *Holinshed*) the king was not sorry of, for he was always jealous of his greatnesse."

The only cotemporaneous English account of this event are the following brief words of Giraldus Cambrensis, in the 34th chapter of the second book of his *Hibernia Expugnata*, which is headed *Brevis gestorum recapitulatio:* "De Hugonis de Lacy à securibus male securi dolo Hiberniensium suorum apud Dernach [*recte* Deruach] decapitatione." Giraldus would call both the Fox and his fosterson O'Meyey the people of De Lacy, inasmuch as they were inhabitants of Meath, of which he was the chief lord, and of which, it would appear from William of Newburg, he intended to style himself king. The Abbè Mac Geoghegan, in his *Histoire d'Irlande*, tom. ii. p. 36, calls the murderer of De Lacy a young Irish lord disguised as a labouring man, ("un jeune seigneur Irlandois déguisé en ouv-

kept concealed, he, with one blow of it, severed his head from his body; and both head and trunk fell into the ditch of the castle. This was in revenge of Columbkille. Gilla-gan-inathar fled, and, by his fleetness of foot, made his

rier"), in which he is borne out by Keating, and not contradicted by the Irish annals; but he had no authority for stating that Symmachus O'Cahargy (for so he ignorantly calls an Sinnach O'Caharny, or the Fox, Chief of Teffia), who had an armed force concealed in a neighbouring wood, rushed upon, and put to the sword the followers of De Lacy; or that the Irish obtained possession of his body. The fact would appear to be, that his own people buried De Lacy's body in the cemetery of Durrow, where it remained till the year 1195, when, as we learn from Grace's Annals and other authorities, the Archbishops of Cashel and Dublin removed it from the Irish territory ("ex Hybernica plaga"), and buried the body in the Abbey of Bective in Meath, and the head in St. Thomas's church in Dublin. It appears, moreover, that a controversy arose between the canons of St. Thomas's and the monks of Bective, concerning the right to his body, which controversy was decided, in the year 1205, in favour of the former, who obtained the body, and interred it, along with the head, in the tomb of his first wife, Rosa de Munemene.—See Harris's Ware, vol. i. p. 141, and the Abbé Mac Geoghegan (ubi suprà). De Lacy's second wife was Rose, daughter of King Roderic O'Conor, whom he married in the year 1180, contrary (says Holingshed) to the wishes of King Henry II.—See Dublin Copy of the Annals of Innisfallen, A. D. 1180, and Hanmer's Chronicle, Dublin Edition, p. 318. It is stated in Grace's Annals of Ireland, that this Sir Hugh left two sons (but by what mother we are not informed), Walter and Hugh, of whom, according to the Dublin copy of the Annals of Innisfallen, the former became King of Meath, and the latter Earl of Ulster. It also appears from the Irish annals, that De Lacy had, by the daughter of King Roderic O'Conor, a son called William Gorm; from whom, according to Duald Mac Firbis, the celebrated rebel, Pierce Oge Lacy of Bruree and Bruff, in the county of Limerick, who flourished in the reign of Queen Elizabeth, was the eighteenth in descent; and from whom also the Lynches of Galway have descended. (See *Vita Kirovani*, p. 9, and O'Flaherty's Account of Iar-Connaught, printed for the Irish Archæological Society, p. 36.) The race of Walter and Hugh, who were evidently the sons of Hugh I., by his first wife, became extinct in the male line. Walter left two daughters, namely, Margaret, who married the Lord Theobald Verdon, and Matilda, who married Geoffry Genevile. Hugh had one daughter, Maude, who married Walter De Burgo, who, in her right, became Earl of Ulster.—See Hanmer's Chronicle, Dublin Edition, pp. 387, 388, 392. For the different accounts of the death of Hugh de Lacy the reader is referred to Gulielmus Neubrigensis, or William of Newburg, l. 3, c. 9; Holingshed's Chronicle; Camden's *Britannia*, p. 151; Ware's Annals, A. D. 1186; Cox's *Hibernia Anglicana*, p. 40; Leland's History of Ireland, vol. i. pp. 147, 148; Littleton's Life of Henry II., book 5; and Moore's History of Ireland, vol. ii. pp. 321, 322.

It may not, perhaps, be out of place here to remark, that, in our own time, a somewhat similar disaster occurred at Durrow; for its proprietor, the Earl of Norbury, was assassinated by a hand still unknown, after he had completed a castle on the site of that erected by De Lacy, and, as some would think, after having insulted St. Columbkille by preventing the families under

ro ċoill an cláir. Ráinicc iaraṁ i ccſnn an trionnaiġ ⁊ ui braoin, uair assiad ro ḟuráil air an tiarla do marḃaḋ.

Murchaḋ mac taiḋg ui ceallaigh tiġſrna ua máine do marḃaḋ la conċoḃar maonmaiġe.

O brſslein taoiseaċ fánat hi ccenél cconaill do marḃaḋ la mac mic laċlainn.

AOIS CRIOSD, 1187.

Aois Criosd mile, céd, ochtmoghat, a seacht.

Muirċſrtaċ ua maoiluiḋir espoc cluana fearta, ⁊ cluana mic nois decc.

Maoilíosa ua cſrḃaill espucc airġiall décc.

Ruaiḋri ua flaithḃſrtaiġ ticchſrna cenél eoġain do ṁarḃaḋ ar creċ i ttir Conaill la hua maoldoraiġ .i. flaiṫḃſrtach.

Carracc locha cé do loscaḋ do ṫene doait. Ro baiḋſḋ ⁊ ro loisceaḋ inġſn ui eiḋin (.i. duiḃeasa) bſn ċoncobair mic diarmata (tiġſrna maiġe luirg) go seaċt ccéḋaiḃ (no cſṫraċa ar ċéd), nó ní as uille eittir ḟſraiḃ ⁊ mnaiḃ fri ré naon uaire innte.

Giolla iosa mac ailella ui ḃraoin secnap ua maine sſnchaiḋe sccriḃniġe, ⁊ fear dana d'ecc.

his tutelage from burying their dead in the ancient cemetery of Durrow.

[b] *Kilclare*, Coill a' ċláir.—This place, which was originally covered with wood, retains its name to the present day. It is a townland in the parish of Kilbride, in the barony of Kilcoursy and King's County.—See Ordnance Map of the King's County, sheet 8.

[c] *Maelisa O'Carroll.*—He was elected Archbishop of Armagh, and died on his journey towards Rome.—See Harris's Ware, vol. i. p. 180.

[d] *Lough Key.*—The Rock of Lough Key, carraic loċa ce, is the name of a castle on an island in Lough Key, near Boyle, in the county of Roscommon. It is still kept in good repair.

[e] *Magh Luirg*, i. e. *the plain of the track, or road*, generally anglicised Moylurg. The district is now locally called the "Plains of Boyle." This territory was bounded on the north by the River Boyle; on the east partly by the Shannon and partly by the territory of Tir Briuin na Sionna; on the south by Magh Naoi, or Machaire Chonnacht, which it met near Elphin; and on the west by the River Bridoge, which divided it from the district of Airteach. Moylurg extended from Lough O'Gara to Carrick-on-Shannon; from the Curlieu Mountains to near Elphin; and from Lough Key to the northern boundary of the parish of Kilmacumshy. Mac Dermot was Chief of Moylurg, Airteach, and Tir Tuathail; and at the time of dividing the county of Roscommon into baronies, these three territories were joined into one, and called the barony of Boyle. Lat-

escape from the English and Irish to the wood of Kilclare[b]. He afterwards went to the *Sinnagh* (the Fox) and O'Breen, at whose instigation he had killed the Earl.

Murrough, the son of Teige O'Kelly, Lord of Hy-Many, was slain by Conor Moinmoy [O'Conor].

O'Breslen, Chief of Fanat in Tirconnell, was slain by the son of Mac Loughlin.

THE AGE OF CHRIST, 1187.

The Age of Christ, one thousand one hundred eighty-seven.

Murtough O'Maeluire, Bishop of Clonfert and Clonmacnoise, died.

Maelisa O'Carroll[c], Bishop of Oriel (Clogher), died.

Rory O'Flaherty [O'Laverty], Lord of Kinel-Owen, was slain, while on a predatory excursion into Tirconnell, by O'Muldory (Flaherty).

The rock of Lough Key[d] was burned by lightning. Duvesa, daughter of O'Heyne, and wife of Conor Mac Dermot, Lord of Moylurg[e], with seven hundred (or seven score[f]) others, or more, both men and women, were drowned or burned in it in the course of one hour.

Gilla-Isa [Gelasius], the son of Oilioll O'Breen, Sech-Abb [Prior] of Hy-Many, a historian, scribe, and poet, died.

terly, however, by a Grand Jury arrangement, the south-west part of the barony of Boyle has been called the barony of French-Park, from the little town of that name.—See other references to Moylurg at the years 1446 and 1595. The following parishes are placed in the deanery of Moylurg by the *Liber Regalis Visitationis* of 1615; but it must be understood that by Moylurg is there meant all Mac Dermot's lordship, which comprised Moylurg (now the plains of Boyle), Tir Tuathail and Airteach; viz. Kilnamanagh; Ardcarne; Killumod; Assylin, now Boyle parish; Taghboin, now Tibohine; Killcoulagh; Killewekin, now Kulluckin, in Irish Cıll Eıbıcín; Kilrudan, Clonard, and Killicknan, belonging then (as they now also do) to the parish of Taghboyne, or Tibohine."

[f] *Seven score* is interlined in the original: the compilers could not determine which was the true number, and so gave the two readings. In the Dublin copy of the Annals of Ulster, it is stated that the number destroyed on this occasion was "uıı. céτ, no nı ıƿ moo," and in the old translation, the number 700 is written in Arabic figures. Thus: "A. D. 1187. The Carrick of Lough Ce burnt at noone, where the daughter of O'Heiyn was burnt and drowned. Coner Mac Dermot, King of Moyloyrg, and 700 or more, men and women, were burnt and drowned within an hower."

The burning of this fortress is recorded in the Annals of Kilronan, at the years 1185 and 1187;

Caislen cille áir do loscadh ⁊ do múradh for gallaibh la concobar maenmaighe ⁊ lá maelsechlainn mbecc cona terna sgeolanga uatha gan marbadh, ⁊ mudhucchadh. Tuccsat a broidh, a nairm, arceit, allúireacha, ⁊ a neocha leó, ⁊ ro marbaitt dís do ridiribh leó.

Donnchadh ua ruairc do marbadh la muintir eolais hi fFiull.

Druimcliabh do orccain do mac Maelseachlainn uí ruairc do tighearna ua mbriúin ⁊ conmaicne, ⁊ do mhac cathail hui ruairc, ⁊ goill mide amaille friú. Do roine dia, ⁊ colum cille fiort amra innsin, uair ro marbadh mac maelechlainn ui ruairc ria ccionn coicdhisi iar sin hi cconmaicnibh, ⁊ ro dalladh mac cathail huí ruairc la hua maoldoraidh .i. flaithbhertach in enech cholaim chille. Ro marbadh dna sé fichit dasir grádha mhic Maoilsechlainn ar fud conmaicne, ⁊ chairpre droma cliabh tré miorbail dé, ⁊ cholaim chille.

Mac diarmatta, Muirghis mac taidcc, tighearna muighe luircc décc ina thigh fein ar claonloch hi ccloinn cuain.

Raghnall mág cochlain tiecchearna dealbhna do écc.

Aodh mac maoileachlainn ui ruairc tigearna breifne do marbadh la macaibh cuinn még raghnaill.

Aireacttach mac amhalgaidh taoiseach calraighe do écc.

at the former year the number stated to have been destroyed is six or seven score, but at the latter the number destroyed is not stated. In the Annals of Boyle the burning of Carraic Locha Ce is recorded under the year 1186, but the number destroyed is not mentioned.

[g] *Muintir-Eolais*, i. e. the Mac Rannals and their correlatives, who were seated in the southern or level part of the present county of Leitrim. Their country was otherwise called Magh Rein; and they were as often called Conmaicne Maighe Rein, as Muintir-Eolais.

[h] *Drumcliff*, Druim cliabh.—A small village in the barony of Carbury, and county of Sligo, remarkable for the remains of an ancient round tower. O'Donnell, in his Life of St. Columbkille, states that a monastery was founded here by that saint. This is doubted by Dr. Lanigan, in his Ecclesiastical History of Ireland, vol. ii. pp. 132-137; but it must be acknowledged that St. Columbkille was held in peculiar veneration at this place, and was regarded as its patron.—See Irish Calendar of the O'Clerys at 9th of June.

[i] *Son of Melaghlin.*—His name was Aedh, or Hugh, according to the Dublin copy of the Annals of Ulster.

[j] *In revenge of Columbkille*, i neneach cholaim cille.—This phrase, which occurs so frequently throughout the Irish annals, is rendered "in revenge of Columkill" in the old translation of the Annals of Ulster, preserved in the British Museum, in which the above passage is rendered as follows: "A. D. 1187. Drumcliew spoyled by mac Moyleghlin O'Royrck, King of O'Briuin and Conmacne, and by Cathal O'Royrck's son, and the Galls of Meath with them; but God shewed a miracle for Columkill there, for Moylaghlin's son was killed two weeks after, and

The castle of Killare, which was in possession of the English, was burned and demolished by Conor Moinmoy [O'Conor] and Melaghlin Beg: and not one of the English escaped, but were all suffocated, or otherwise killed; They carried away their accoutrements, arms, shields, coats of mail, and horses, and slew two knights.

Donough O'Rourke was treacherously slain by the Muintir-Eolais[g].

Drumcliff[h] was plundered by the son[i] of Melaghlin O'Rourke, Lord of Hy-Briuin and Conmaicne, and by the son of Cathal O'Rourke, accompanied by the English of Meath. But God and St. Columbkille wrought a remarkable miracle in this instance; for the son of Melaghlin[i] O'Rourke was killed in Conmaicne a fortnight afterwards, and the eyes of the son of Cathal O'Rourke were put out by O'Muldory (Flaherty) in revenge of Columbkille[j]. One hundred and twenty of the son of Melaghlin's retainers were also killed throughout Conmaicne and Carbury of Drumcliff, through the miracles of God and St. Columbkille.

Mac Dermot (Maurice, son of Teige), Lord of Moylurg, died in his own mansion on Claenlough, in Clann-Chuain[k].

Randal Mac Coghlan, Lord of Delvin, died.

Hugh, the son of Melaghlin O'Rourke, Lord of Breifny, was slain by the sons of Con Mag Rannal.

Aireaghtagh Mac Awley, Chief of Calry, died[l].

Cathal's son was blinded, with whom the army came, in O'Moyldory's house, in revenge of Columkill, and a hundred and twenty of the chiefest" [followers] "of the sons of Moylaghlin were killed in Conmacne and Carbry of Drumklew, through the miracles of Columkill."

[k] *Clann-Chuain*, Clann Chuain, called also Fir Thire and Fir Siuire; their territory comprised the northern part of the barony of Carra, in the county of Mayo, and was originally a portion of the country of O'Dowda, under whom it was held by O'Quin of Carra; but about the year 1150, O'Quin, in consequence of the barbarous conduct of Rory Mear O'Dowda, who violated his daughter while on a visit at his (O'Quin's) house, renounced his allegiance to him, and placed himself under the protection of Mac Dermot, Chief of Moylurg.—See *Tribes and Customs of Hy-Fiachrach*, printed in 1844, for the Irish Archæological Society, pp. 163, 204, 205. The name Claonloch is now forgotten; it was probably the ancient name of the lake of Castlebar, for we learn from the Book of Lecan that the Clann Chuain were seated on the River Siuir, which flows through the town of Castlebar.

[l] *Chief of Calry*, ταοιρεαċ calραιġe, that is, of Calry-an-chala, which, according to the tradition in the country, and as can be proved from various written authorities, comprised the entire of the parish of Ballyloughloe, in the county of Westmeath.

AOIS CRIOSD, 1188.

Aoiṡ Criosd míle, céd, ochtmoġat, a hocht.

Martain ua brolaigh airdeccnaiḋ gaoiḋeal ⁊ fer léiġinn Arda macha do écc.

Aeḋh ua bechan epscop innsi caṫaiġ do écc.

Amlaoiḃ ua daiġre do toċt co hí dia oiliṫre, ⁊ a ecc ann iar naiṫriġhe toccaiḋe.

Ruaiḋri ua canannain tiġearna ċinél cconaill fri hed, ⁊ rioghdaṁna Ereann beós do marḃaḋ la flaiṫḃeartaċ ua maoldoraiḋ tre meḃail acc droichet Sliccighe iar na bréccaḋ do lar ḋromacliabh amach, ⁊ braṫair ele dó do marḃaḋ amaille fris, ⁊ dream dia ṁuinntir. Maġnas ua gairḃ toiseaċ fer ndroma (ro imbir láṁ ar ua ccanannáin) do ṁarḃaḋ la muinntir eachmarcaiġ uí dochartaiġ i ndioġail uí ċanannáin.

Doṁnall ua canannáin do leoraḋ a ċoirp dia ṫuaiġ fein i ndoire acc bein arcclainge connaidh, ⁊ a écc de tria earccaine raṁṫa ċolaim cille.

Goill ċaisteoil ṁaiġe coba, ⁊ drong do uiḃ eachḋach ulaḋ do ṫoċt ar creich i ttir eoġain go ttorachtatar go leim mic neill, Ro gabsat bú annsin. Do ḋeachaiḋ doṁnall ua laċlainn cona ṫeaġlaċ ina ndeaḋhaiḋ, rucc orra

[m] *O'Broly*, Oḃrolaiġ.—This name still exists in Derry, anglicised Brawly and Broly. This passage is given in the Dublin copy of the Annals of Ulster, as follows: A. D. 1188. Martain hua brolaiġ ardecnaiḋ goeiḋel uile, 7 ard fer leiġinn ard maċa do ec. And thus rendered in the old English translation in the British Museum: "A. D. 1188. Martan O'Brolay, archlearned of the Irish all, and archlector of Armagh, died."

[n] *Inis-Cathy*, Inis Caṫaiġ.—Now called Scattery Island. It is situated in the Shannon, near the town of Kilrush, and is remarkable for the remains of several churches, and a round tower of great antiquity. A church was founded here by St. Senan, a bishop, about the year 540.—See Lanigan's Ecclesiastical History of Ireland, vol. ii. pp. 2–7. It continued to be the seat of a bishop till about this period (1188), when it seems to have been united to the see of Limerick. Ussher, however, who thought that it owed its origin to St. Patrick, informs us that its possessions were divided between the sees of Limerick, Killaloe, and Ardfert: "Atq; hic notandum, Patricium in metropoli Armachanâ successore relicto ad alias Ecclesias constituendas animum adjecisse: in quibus sedes illa Episcopalis fuit in *Sinei* (Shanan) fluminis alveo, *Inis catti* & eodem sensu in Provinciali Romano *Insula Cathay* appellata. Is Episcopatus inter Limiricensem, Laonensem & Ardfertensem hodie divisus."—*Primordia*, p. 873.

[o] *Sincere penitence*, iar naiṫriġhe toccaiḋe, literally, *after choice penance*.—This phrase is

THE AGE OF CHRIST, 1188.

The Age of Christ, one thousand one hundred eighty-eight.

Martin O'Broly[m], chief Sage of the Irish, and Lector at Armagh, died.

Hugh O'Beaghan, Bishop of Inis-Cathy[n], died.

Auliffe O'Deery performed a pilgrimage to Hy [Iona], where he died after sincere penitence[o].

Rory O'Canannan, sometime Lord of Tirconnell, and heir presumptive to the crown of Ireland, was treacherously slain by Flaherty O'Muldory on the bridge of Sligo, the latter having first artfully prevailed on him to come forth from the middle of Drumcliff. The brother and some of the people of O'Canannan were also killed by him. Manus O'Garve, Chief of Fir-Droma (who had laid violent hands on O'Canannan), was afterwards slain by the people of Eachmarcach O'Doherty, in revenge of O'Canannan's *death*.

Donnell O'Canannan wounded his foot with his own axe at Derry, as he was cutting a piece of wood, and died of the wound, in consequence of the curse of the family [clergy] of Columbkille[p].

The English of the castle of Moy-Cova[q], and a party from Iveagh, in Ulidia, set out upon a predatory excursion into Tyrone, and arrived at Leim-mhic-Neill[r], where they seized on some cows; Donnell O'Loughlin pursued them

very frequently given in Latin in the Annals of Ulster thus: "*in bona penitentia quievit*," or "*in bona penitentia mortuus est.*"

p *Columbkille.*—In the Dublin copy of the Annals of Ulster this passage reads as follows: A. D. 1188. Domnall hua canannan do letrad a coiri dia tuaig fein i ndaire i gait arclainne connaid, 7 a ec de tria mirbail colum cille; and thus translated in the old work already referred to: "A. D. 1188. Donell O'Cananan cut his foote by his oune hatchet in Dyry" [when stealing] "a tree for fewell, and died thereof through Columkille's miracles." Here it is to be remarked that i gait is left untranslated; it means "stealing," or "while stealing." In the Annals of Kilronan, the reading is ag buain, i. e. "cutting," or "while cutting," and this is, in the opinion of the Editor, the true reading.

q *Moy-Cova*, mag coba, a plain in the barony of Upper Iveagh, in the county of Down. Its situation appears from the position of the church of Domhnach Mor Muighe Cobha, now Donaghmore, a parish lying nearly midway between Loughbrickland and Newry.—See *Feilire Aenguis*, at 16th November.

r *Leim-mhic-Neill*, i. e. the leap of the son of Niall.—This was the name of a place near Dungannon, in Tyrone, called after Donnagan, the son of Niall, who was son of Maelduin, the son of Aedh Oirdnighe, monarch of Ireland, who died in the year 819.—See Duald Mac Firbis's Pedigrees of the Kinel-Owen, p. 126.

hi ccaḃan na ccrann árd, do rattsat iomairecc dia roile, ro maidh for ġallaiḃ, ro cuirſḋ a nár. Do raḋaḋ eiṁ saḋaḋh do ġallġa for doṁnall a aenar, ⁊ torchair innsin hi frioṫġuin tiġſrna Ailigh, doṁnall mac aoḋa hui laċlainn, rioġḋaṁna Ereann ar cruṫ, ar ċéill, ⁊ ar ṫrebaire. Ruccaḋ an lá sin fſin go hardmaċa. Ro haḋnaicſḋ co nonoir, ⁊ co nairṁiḋin moir iaraṁ.

Edaoin inġſn ui ċuinn baintiġerna muṁan bai aga hoiliṫre i ndoire decc iar mbrſith buaḋa ó ḋoṁan ⁊ o dſṁan.

Sluaicceaḋ la Iohn do cuirt ⁊ la gallaiḃ Ereann hi cconnaċtaiḃ amaille le concoḃar ua ndiarmatta. Tionoiliḋ rí connaċt .i. concoḃar maonmaiġe maiṫe connaċt uile. Tainic doṁnall ua briain co ndruing do ḟſraiḃ Muṁan i rochraitte righ connaċt. Loiscit na goill araill do ċeallaiḃ na tire rſmpa. Ni ro lſiccit sccaoileaḋ doiḃ co rangattar easdara. Ba do ṫeaċt i ttir conaill ón, uair na ro lſiccriott connaċtaiġ niar sia dia ttír iad. Iar bfior sccél do ua maoldoraiḋ do ḟlaiṫbertaċ, teaglomaiḋ síde cenel conaill na ccoinne co druim ċliabh. Od cualadar na goill sin ro loiscсſḋ eásdara co lſir. Soaid tar a naiss. Tiaġaid is in coirrṡliaḃ. Do beartsad connaċtaiġ ⁊ fir muṁan ammus forra. Marḃaid sochaiḋe móir ḋiḃ. Fáccḃaid na goill an tir ar eccin, ⁊ ní ró ṁillsſḋ a beacc don chur sin.

[s] *Cavan na g-crann ard*, Caḃán na ccrann árd, i. e. the hollow of the high trees. This name does not now exist in Tyrone, nor does it occur in the Ulster Inquisitions, or Down Survey. There are two townlands called Cavan-O'Neill in the county of Tyrone, one in the parish of Kildress, near Cookstown, and another in the parish of Aghaloo, near Caledon. Dr. Stuart, in his *Historical Memoirs of the City of Armagh*, p. 163, thinks that this is the place now called Cavanacaw, situated within two miles of Armagh on the Newry road; but this is far from being certain.

[t] *Heat of the conflict*, hi frioṫġuin.—The word frioṫġuin, which occurs so frequently in these Annals, literally means, the retort, or return of the assault, or onset, or the exchange of blows; *Leabhar Breac*, fol. 52, *b*, and 104, *a*; but the Editor has translated it throughout by "the heat of the conflict," or "thick of the battle."

[u] *Spear*.—Gallġai is rendered *a pike* in the old translation of the Annals of Ulster, thus: "A thrust of a Pike was given the King among all, and fell there unhappily, viz. Donell mac Hugh O'Loghlin, King of Ulster [Aileach] and heire of Ireland for personage, witt, liberality and housekeeping, and was caried the same day to Armagh and was honerably buried."

[v] *Of O'Quin*, Ui Chuinn.—This was O'Quin, Chief of Muintir-Iffernan in Thomond, now represented by the Earl of Dunraven. The situation of the territory of O'Quin, from whom Inchiquin derives its name, is thus given in O'Heerin's topographical poem:

with his retainers, and overtook them at Cavan na g-crann ard[s], where an engagement took place between them; and the English were defeated with great slaughter. But Donnell, the son of Hugh O'Loughlin, Lord of Aileach, and presumptive heir to the throne of Ireland, on account of his personal symmetry, intelligence, and wisdom, alone received a thrust from an English spear[t], and fell in the heat of the conflict[u]. His body was carried to Armagh on the same day, and there interred with great honour and solemnity.

Edwina, daughter of O'Quin[v], and Queen of Munster, died on her pilgrimage at Derry, victorious over the world and the devil.

John de Courcy and the English of Ireland made an incursion into Connaught, accompanied by Conor O'Dermot; upon which Conor Moinmoy, King of Connaught, assembled all the chieftains of Connaught, who were joined by Donnell O'Brien, at the head of some of the men of Munster. The English set fire to some of the churches of the country as they passed along, but made no delay until they reached Eas-dara (Ballysadare), with the intention of passing into Tirconnell, because the Connacians would not suffer them to tarry any longer in their country.

As soon as O'Muldory (Flaherty) had received intelligence of this, he assembled the Kinel-Conell, and marched to Drumcliff to oppose them. When the English heard of this *movement*, they burned the entire of Ballysadare, and returned back, passing by the Curlieu mountains, where they were attacked by the Connacians and Momonians. Many of the English were slain, and those who survived retreated with difficulty from the country, without effecting much destruction[w] on this incursion.

D' O'Chuinn an croiḋe neaṁnáir
Muinter fairsing Ifernáin;
Tir toraiḋ an gille ġloin
Fa ċora finne fleaḋoiġ.

"To O'Quin of the good heart belongs
The extensive Muintir-Ifernan;
The fertile district of this splendid man
Is at the festive Corafin."

[w] *Much destruction*, 7 ni ro millsed a beacc. In the Annals of Kilronan the reading is: 7 fagbuid na goill in tir cen a bec do milled don cur sin. "And the English left the country without doing much damage on this occasion." In the Dublin copy of the Annals of Ulster it reads: facbait na goill in tir ar eicin cen a becc do gleuḋ, which is rather incorrectly rendered, "And left the country by force without much fight," in the old translation in the British Museum.

It is added in the Annals of Kilronan, that Murrough, the son of Farrell O'Mulrony, and O'Madden, and many others [*alii multi cum eis*], were slain at the Curlieus on this occasion.

Creach la gallaibh uladh for cenél neoghain co rugurtoir domhnall mac aodha uí lachloinn tighearna cenel neoghain forru, ⁊ ro chuirrst ár for gallaibh, ⁊ atrochair domhnall i frithghuin an chatha sin.

AOIS CRIOSD, 1189.

Aois Criosd, míle, céd, ochtmoghad, anaoi.

Maolcainnigh ua fírcomair fer leiginn doire do bathadh etir áird ⁊ inis eoghain.

Ardmacha do orccain la hiohn do cuirt ⁊ la gallaibh Ereann ina fochair.

Ardmacha do loscadh o crossaibh brighde co reiclés bricin etir rath, ⁊ trian, ⁊ teampall.

Murcha ua cerbaill tigerna oirgiall do écc is in mainistir móir iar naithrighe toghaidhi.

Domhnall mac Muirceartaigh méc lochlainn do marbhadh la gallaibh dal araidhe aca féin.

Echmilidh mac mec cana, sonas ⁊ sobartan tíre heocchain uile do ecc.

Mac na hoidhce ua Maolruanaidh tighearna fer manach do chor as a thighearnas, ⁊ é do dhol do chum ui cherbaill. Tainicc sluagh gall don tír iartain, ⁊ do rad ua cerbaill ⁊ ua maolruanaidh tachar doibh. Maidhidh for ua cerbhaill, ⁊ marbhthar ua maolruanaidh.

Concobhar maonmhaighe (.i. mac Ruaidhri) airdrí connacht eittir gallaibh ⁊ ghaoidhealaibh do marbhadh la druing dia mhuintir féin ⁊ dia oirecht .i. la

[x] *Aird* is now called Ardmagilligan and Tamlaght-ard; it is a parish, situated in the north-west extremity of the county of Londonderry, and is separated from Inishowen by the straits of Loughfoyle. That part of this parish which verges on Lough Foyle is low and level; but the high mountain of Beann Foibhne, now Beneveny, is situated in the southern part of it, from whence it has got the name of Ard, or height.

[y] *The Great Monastery*, i. e. the Abbey of Mellifont, in the county of Louth which was erected by Donough O'Carroll, Chief of Oriel, in the year 1165. This passage is rendered as follows in the old translation of the Annals of Ulster: "A. D. 1189. Murogh O'Carroll, Archking of Argiall, died in the greate Abbey of Melifont after good repentance."

[z] *Eghmily*, Echmilidh.—This name, which is anglicised Eghmily in the old translation of the Annals of Ulster, and Acholy, in the Ulster Inquisitions, is compounded of ech, Lat. *equus*, a horse, and milidh, Lat. *miles*, a soldier. The country of Mac Cann is shewn on an old map preserved in the State Papers' Office, London,

The English of Ulidia took a prey from the Kinel-Owen; but they were overtaken and slaughtered by Donnell, the son of Hugh O'Loughlin, Lord of the Kinel-Owen; but Donnell himself fell fighting in the heat of the battle.

THE AGE OF CHRIST, 1189.

The Age of Christ, one thousand one hundred eighty-nine.

Mulkenny O'Fearcomais, Lector of Derry, was drowned between Aird[x] (Ardmagilligan) and Inishowen.

Armagh was plundered by John De Courcy and the English of Ireland.

Armagh was burned from St. Bridget's Crosses to St. Bridget's Church, including the Rath, the Trian, and the churches.

Murrough O'Carroll, Lord of Oriel, died a sincere penitent in the Great Monastery[y].

Donnell, the son of Murtough Mac Loughlin, was slain by the English of Dalaradia while he was [*staying*] amongst them.

Eghmily[z], the son of Mac Cann, the happiness and prosperity of all Tyrone, died.

Mac-na-h-Oidhche [son of the night] O'Mulrony[a], Lord of Fermanagh, was driven from his lordship, and fled to O'Carroll. Shortly afterwards an English army arrived in that country, to whom O'Carroll and O'Mulrony gave battle; but O'Carroll was defeated, and O'Mulrony killed.

Conor Moinmoy (the son of Roderic), King of all Connaught, both English and Irish, was killed by a party of his own people and tribe[b]; i. e. by Manus,

as the north-eastern angle of the county of Armagh, which borders on Lough Neagh, and through which the River Bann flows on its way into that lake.

[a] *O'Mulrony*, O'Maolruanaiḋ.—There were many distinct families of this name in Ireland. The O'Mulrony here mentioned, was of the same race as Maguire, by whom the former, as well as O'Hegny, who was by far more illustrious, was soon after subdued.

[b] *His own tribe.*—This passage reads as follows in the Annals of Ulster: Concoḃur Maenmaiġi, mac Ruaiḋri, airdri Connaċt, 7 ridamna Erenn uile, do marbaḋ dá luċt graḋa fein tria erail a ḃraṫar; and is thus rendered in the old translation: "Coner Moynmoy mac Roary, archking of Connaught, and to be king of Ireland, was killed by his minions, by his brother's advice."

Maġnus mac floinn ui finaċta (dia ngoirṫi an crosaċ donn), ⁊ la haodh mac briain breifniġ mic toirrdelbaiġ ui conċobair, ⁊ la Muirceartaċ mac caṫail mic diarmata mic taidġ, ⁊ la giolla na naoṁ mac giollacomain, mic muirſdaiġ báin ui maoil Micil dona tuaṫaib. Mairg oireaċt ro coġair adbar aird righ Ereann do ṁarḃaḋ, uair tuccsat urṁor lſiṫe mogha a ccſnnus dó ria síu ro marḃaḋ, Dóiġ tainicc Domnall ua briain dia tiġ go dun leoda, ⁊ boi sſctmain ina ḟarraḋ, ⁊ tuc trí fiċit bo gaċa trioċa céd hi cconnaċtaib dó, ⁊ .x. seóid go nór, ⁊ ni rucc ua briain dſb sin uile, aċt corn diarmata ui briain a ḟſnaṫar fſin, ⁊ do baí Ruaidri mac duinnsleibe ri ulaḋ ina ṫiġ, ⁊ do bai domnall mag cárṫaiġ tiġearna dſsmuṁan ina ṫiġ ⁊ do rad som tuarustal mór dó .i. cuicc eich gaċa trioċait cet hi cconnaċtaib. Bai Maelseaċlainn bſg ri tſmra ina ṫigh, ⁊ rucc tuarustal mor lſis, ⁊ bai ua ruairc ina tiġ, ⁊ rucc tuarustal mor lſis.

Iar marḃaḋ Conċobair maonmaiġi tangus ó ṡiol muireadaiġ ar cſnd Ruaidri ui Choncobair ri Ereann do ṫabairt riġe dó iar nécc a ṁic, ⁊ ó ránaic

[c] *Crossach Donn*, Crosaċ Donn.—The word crosaċ means streaked, seamed, or marked with crosses, and was probably applied to O'Finaghty, from having had the *cicatrices*, or seams of wounds intersecting each other on his face. Shane O'Mullan, a celebrated highwayman, who flourished in the county of Londonderry about one hundred years since, was, according to tradition, called Shane Crosach, from having his face covered with scars of this description.

[d] *The Tuathas.*—Generally called Teora Tuatha, i. e. the three districts. These were Tir Briuin na Sinna, Kinel Dofa, and Corachlann. The tripartite territory called the Teora Tuatha formed a deanery in the diocese of Elphin, comprising the ten parishes following, viz., Aughrim, Kilmore, Clooncraff, Kiltrustan, Kilglass, Bumlin, Termonbarry, Cloonfinlough, Lissonuffy, Kilgefin, and Cloontuskert.—See *Liber Regalis Visitationis* of 1615, and Colgan's *Trias Thaum.*, p. 524, where, speaking of the church of Kilgefin, he points out its situation thus: "Killgeuian ecclesia parochialis Diœcesis Alfinensis in regione et decanatu de Tuatha." From these authorities it is clear that the territory called the Tuatha, or Three Tuathas, comprised that part of the county of Roscommon extending from the northern point of Lough Ree to Jamestown, on the Shannon, from Jamestown to near Elphin, and thence again to Lough Ree. It was bounded on the east by the River Shannon; on the north by the Shannon and the territory of Moylurg; on the west by Sil-Murray, or the Plain of Connaught; and on the south by the modern Hy-Many.—See Map prefixed to the *Tribes and Customs of Hy-Many*, published in 1843, by the Irish Archæological Society. According to these annals, and to O'Dugan's topographical poem, the O'Monahans were originally the chiefs of Tir-Briuin na Sinna (but were subdued by the O'Beirnes); the Mac Branans and O'Mulvihils of Corcachlann or Corca Sheachlann; and the O'Hanlys of Kinel-Dofa.

[e] *To his house.*—This is the phrase used by the Irish annalists to denote "he submitted, or made his submission." On such occasions the

the son of Flann O'Finaghty (usually called an Crossach Donn[c]); Hugh, son of Brian Breifneach, the son of Turlough O'Conor; Murtough, son of Cathal, son of Dermot, the son of Teige; and Gilla-na-naev, the son of Gilla-Coman, who was the son of Murray Bane [the Fair] O'Mulvihil of the Tuathas[d].

Alas for the party who plotted this conspiracy against the life of the heir presumptive to the throne of Ireland! To him the greater part of Leth-Mhogha had submitted as king. Donnell O'Brien had gone to his house[e] at Dunlo[f], where he was entertained for a week; and O'Conor gave him sixty cows out of every cantred in Connaught, and ten articles ornamented with gold; but O'Brien did not accept of any of these, save one goblet, which had once been the property of Dermot O'Brien, his own grandfather. Rory Mac Donslevy, King of Ulidia, had gone to his house. Mac Carthy, King of Desmond, was in his house, and O'Conor gave him a great stipend, namely, five horses out of every cantred in Connaught. Melaghlin Beg, King of Tara, was in his house, and took away a large stipend; and O'Rourke had gone to his house, and also carried with him a great stipend.

After Conor Moinmoy had been slain, the Sil-Murray sent messengers to Roderic O'Conor, *the former* King of Ireland, to tell him of the death of his son[g], and to give [offer] him the kingdom: and as soon as Roderic came to Moy Naei[h], he took the hostages of the Sil-Murray, and of *all* Connaught; for

king to whom obeisance was made, always presented those submitting with gifts. Of this custom we have a remarkable instance on record in the Irish work called Caithreim Toirdhealbhaigh, or Wars of Turlough O'Brien, in which it is stated that at a national assembly held by the Irish at Caol Uisce, near Ballyshannon, O'Neill sent Teige O'Brien one hundred horses as wages of subsidy, and as an earnest of the subordination and obedience due to him from O'Brien; but O'Brien, rejecting the subsidy and denying the superiority of O'Neill, sent him two hundred horses, to be received in acknowledgment of O'Neill's submission to O'Brien.

[f] *Dunlo*, Ꝺun leoꝺa.—It is the name of a townland, which contains that part of the town of Ballinasloe lying to the west of the River Suck, in the county of Galway. Dunlo-street, in Ballinasloe, still preserves the name.

[g] *His son*.—This passage is so confusedly given in the original that the translator has thought it necessary to transpose the order of the language in the translation, but the original is printed exactly as in the autograph.

[h] *Moy Naei*, maᵹ naoı.—This is otherwise called Machaire Chonnacht. The inhabitants of the town of Roscommon and its vicinity, when speaking of the country generally, call the district lying between them and Athlone, the *Barony*, and that between them and Elphin, the *Maghery*; but they say that you are not in the Maghery till you are two miles and a half to the north of the town of Roscommon. The following are the bounds

Ruaiḋri go maġ naoí ro gaḃ gialla ſíl muirſḋaiġ ⁊ Connaċt, ar as ann ro bátar geill Conċoḃair maonmuiġe i ninis cloṫrann for loċ riḃ an tan sin.

Flaiṫbeartaċ ua maoldoraiḋ tiġearna cenél cconaill cona toiċeſtal do bſiṫ illongport is in ccorann, ⁊ connaċtaiġ uile eitir gall ⁊ gaoiḋeal ina naghaiḋ don leiṫ aile.

Concoḃar ua diarmata do marḃaḋ la caṫal carrac mac concoḃair maonṁaiġe a ndioġail a aṫur.

An ceḋ Risdſrd do ríoġaḋ os Saxaiḃ .6. Iulij.

Sluaiġeaḋ la hua Maoildoraiḋ (flaiṫbſrtaċ) do ġabail fri connachtaiḃ gur ro ġab longport is in Corann. Tangatar connaċtaiġ uile eitir ġallaiḃ ⁊ gaoiḋealaiḃ ina aġaiḋ, ar a aoi ni ró ċumaingſet ní ḋó, ⁊ ro ſtar-scarsat fri aroile don chur sin.

AOIS CRIOSD, 1190.

Aois Criosd, mile, céd, nochat.

Diarmait ua raḃartaiġ abb dſrmaiġe do ecc.

Maelseaċlainn ua neaċtain ⁊ Giollabearaiġ ua Sluaġadaiġ do marḃaḋ la toirrḋealbaċ mac Ruaiḋri ui conċoḃair.

Mor inġean toirrḋealbaiġ ui Concoḃair, ⁊ Duibſsa inġſn diarmata mic taiḋg do écc.

Coinne eitir Caṫal croiḃdearcc ⁊ Caṫal carrac hi ccluain fearta brenainn do ḋenaṁ síoḋa ſtorra. Tſccait siol muireaḋaiġ uile is in ccoinne ceḋna im ċomarba Pátraicc, ⁊ im Concoḃar mac diarmata, ⁊ im aireaċtach ua roduiḃ, ⁊ ní ro feadaḋ a síoducchaḋ re roile don chur sin.

of the Maghery, according to the general tradition of the people in the county of Roscommon. It extends northwards as far as Lismacooil, in the parish of Kilmacumshy; eastwards, to Falsk, in the parish of Killuckin; westwards, from the bridge of Cloonfree, near Strokestown, as far as the bridge of Castlereagh; and southwards, to a hill lying two miles and a half north of the town of Roscommon. The natives of the parish of Baslick call a hill in the townland of Drishaghan, in that parish, the navel or centre of the Machaire or plain of Connaught, which conveys a distinct idea of the position of this plain.

[l] *Mac Teige.*—It is added in the Annals of Kilronan, that she was the wife of Cosnamhach O'Dowda.

[k] *Cathal Crovderg*, Caṫal croiḃḋearg, i. e. Cathal, or Cahill, the Red-handed. The name *Cathal*, which means warlike, and appears to be

the hostages that had been delivered up to Conor Moinmoy were on Inishcloghran, an island in Lough Ree, at that time.

Flaherty O'Muldory, Lord of Tirconnell, encamped with his forces in Corran; and all the Connacians, both English and Irish, were against him on the other side.

Conor, grandson of Dermot, was slain by Cathal Carragh, the son of Conor Moinmoy, in revenge of the death of his father.

Richard I. was crowned King of England on the 6th of July.

O'Muldory (Flaherty) marched with his forces against the Connacians, and pitched his camp in Corran. All the Connacians, both English and Irish, came to oppose him; however, they were not able to injure him, and both departed *without coming to an engagement* on that occasion.

THE AGE OF CHRIST, 1190.

The Age of Christ, one thousand one hundred ninety.

Dermot O'Rafferty, Abbot of Durrow, died.

Melaghlin O'Naghtan and Gilla-Barry O'Slowey were slain by Turlough, the son of Roderic O'Conor.

More, daughter of Turlough O'Conor, and Duvesa, daughter of Dermot Mac Teige[i], died.

A meeting was held at Clonfert-Brendan, to conclude a peace between Cathal Crovderg[k] and Cathal Carragh. All the Sil-Murray repaired to this meeting, together with the successor of St. Patrick[l], Conor Mac Dermot, and Aireaghtagh O'Rodiv; but they could not be reconciled to each other on this occasion.

synonymous with the Welsh *Cadell*, is now generally anglicised Charles, as the Christian name of a man, but Cahill as a surname, which is in Irish O'Cathail. Dr. O'Conor, in treating of this king in his suppressed work, *Memoirs of the Life and Writings of Charles O'Conor of Belanagare*, translates his name "Charles the Red-handed."—See p. 32 of that work. O'Flaherty translates it "Cathald Red-fist."—See his account of Hiar Connaught, printed for the Irish Archæological Society in 1845. See also note under the year 1224.

[l] *The successor of St. Patrick*, Comarba Patruic, i. e. the Archbishop of Armagh. He was Thomas, or Tomaltach, O'Conor, who was related to the rival princes, and "a noble and worthy man," who was anxious to restore his native province to tranquillity.—See Harris's Ware, vol. i. p. 62.

Tanaicc ua concoḃair ⁊ siol muireḋaiġ go cluain mic nois in aḋaiġ sin, ⁊ ro eiriġ an coblaċ go moċ ara ḃarach, ⁊ tangatar rompa ar fud na Sionna go rangatar go loċ riḃ. Ro eiriġ anfaḋ anḃail doiḃ ar an loch go ro sccaoilsiot a nartraiġe ó aroile ⁊ ro ṫuairgcc an tanfaḋ an tseṫar i mboí ó concoḃair conar lamaḋ a luaṁaireaċt la méd an anfaiḋ, ⁊ ba is in arṫrach i mboí ua Concoḃair .i. Caṫal croibdercc, bai Aireachtach ua roduiḃ, ⁊ concoḃar mac caṫail. Do cóidh an tseṫar fo uiscce go ro baiḋeḋ i mboi innte cenmotá seisear tearna im Chatal croibdearg. Ro baiḋeaḋ Aireaċtaċ ua roduiḃ, ⁊ Concoḃar mac caṫail, Concoḃar ⁊ Aṁlaiḃ da ṁac Aoḋa még oirechtaiġ, ua Maoilbrenainn, ⁊ mac ui mannaċain co roċaiḋe ele.

AOIS CRIOSD, 1191.

Aois Criosd, mile, céd, nochat a haon.

Ruaiḋri ua Concoḃair do ḟaccḃáil Connaċt ⁊ a ḋol co tir Conaill do saighidh ḟlaiṫḃertaiġ ui maoildoraiḋ, ⁊ i ttír neoġain iar sin diarraiḋ soċraitte ar ṫuairsceart nEreann do ġaḃáil Ríġe Connacht do riḋisi, ⁊ ni ro ḟaomsat ullta fearonn dfaġail dó ó ċonnaċtaiḃ, ⁊ do ċoiḋ roiṁe do ḟaiġiḋ gall na miḋe, ⁊ ní ro sirġettur sidhe leis, ⁊ do ṫaed ar sin is in muṁain, comd eisti sin tuccsat siol muireḋaiġ ferann dó, .i. tir fiachrach, ⁊ cenel aoḋa na hectge.

Aillenn inġen Riaccáin ui maelruanaiḋ, ben aireaċtaiġ ui roduibh do écc.

[m] *It foundered*, do cóidh an tseṫar fo uisce, literally, "the vessel went under water."

[n] *Conor, son of Cathal*, i. e. Conor, Cathal Crovderg's own son. The translator has been obliged to transpose a part of this sentence, which is not properly arranged in the original, but the Irish text is printed exactly as in the autograph.

[o] *Tir Fiachrach*, i. e. *Tir Fiachrach Aidhne*.—The country of the O'Heynes in the south-west of the county of Galway.

[p] *Kinelea of Echtghe*, cenel aoḋa na hEchtge, i. e. the race of Aodh, or Hugh, of Slieve Echtghe, now Slieve Aughtee. This was the tribe name of the O'Shaughnessys and their correlatives, which became also that of their country, for the custom of ancient Ireland was, "not to take names and creations from places and countries, as it is with other nations, but to give the name of the family to the seigniory by them occupied."—See O'Flaherty's *Ogygia Vindicated*, p. 170, and Colgan's *Acta Sanctorum*, p. 354, note 8. O'Shaughnessy's country of Kinelea comprised the south-eastern half of the diocese of Kilmacduagh, in

O'Conor and the Sil-Murray went to Clonmacnoise on that night, and early next morning embarked in their fleet, and sailed up the Shannon until they came to Lough Ree. A violent storm arose on the lake, by which their vessels were separated from each other; and the storm so agitated the vessel in which O'Conor was, that it could not be piloted. Such was the fury of the storm, it foundered[m], and all the crew perished, except O'Conor himself and six others. In this vessel with O'Conor (Cathal Crovderg) were Areaghtagh O'Rodiv and Conor, son of Cathal[n], who were both drowned, as were also Conor and Auliffe, the two sons of Hugh Mageraghty; O'Mulrenin, and the son of O'Monahan, and many others.

THE AGE OF CHRIST, 1191.

The Age of Christ, one thousand one hundred ninety-one.

Roderic O'Conor set out from Connaught, and went to Flaherty O'Muldory in Tirconnell, and afterwards *passed* into Tyrone, to request forces from the north of Ireland, *to enable him* to recover his kingdom of Connaught; but the Ultonians not consenting to aid in procuring lands for him from the Connacians, he repaired to the English of Meath, and these having also refused to go with him, he passed into Munster, whither the Sil-Murray sent for him, and gave him lands, viz. Tir Fiachrach[o] and Kinelea of Echtge[p].

Ailleann, daughter of Regan O'Mulrony, and wife of Aireachtagh O'Rodiv, died.

the county of Galway.—See map prefixed to *Tribes and Customs of Hy-Many*, printed for the Irish Archæological Society in 1843. For a list of townlands in Sir Dermot O'Shaughnessy's country in the year 1543, see *Tribes and Customs of Hy-Fiachrach*, printed for the same Society in 1844, pp. 375, 376. Under this year the Annals of Kilronan record the erection of the castle of Rath Cuanartaighe, but without giving the name of the builder, or the situation of the castle. They also contain the following entry under this year, respecting the drying up of the River Galway: A. D. 1191. In ġaillim do traghadh an ḃliadain si, ⁊ friṫ tuad inntе, ⁊ lam ón ċuirr go ċele di, ⁊ friṫ sleġ innte ⁊ trí duirn ⁊ tri meoir illeiṫed slenna na sleiġe sin, ⁊ lám o'n ngualuinn a fad."

"A. D. 1191. The *River* Galliv dried up this year, and there was a hatchet found in it, *measuring* a hand from one point to the other, and there was a spear found in it measuring three hands and three fingers in breadth, and a hand from the shoulder in length."

See O'Flaherty's Account of Iar-Connaught, published by the Irish Archæological Society, p. 29, and Ware's *Antiq. Hibernicæ*, c. xii., where we read: "In Annalibus Roscomanensibus, ad annum MCXC, fit mentio capitis Hastæ, ad

AOIS CRIOSD, 1192.

Aois Criosd, mile, céd, nochat, adó.

Dorus proinnticce an duibreccléſa colaim cille i nDoire do ḋſnamh la hua cCaṫain na Craibe, ⁊ la hinghin ui Innſirġe.

Taichleac ua Dubda ticchſrna ua nAṁalgaḋa ⁊ ua fFiaċraċ Muaiḋi do ṁarḃaḋ la da ṁac a ṁec féin.

Aeḋ ua Flainn toiseaċ ſil Maoilesuain do écc.

Maiḋm acc Caraid Eacharaḋ ar ġallaiḃ la muinntir Maoiltſionna.

Caiſlén atha an urċair ⁊ caiſlen ċille birgi do ḋſnaṁ iſ in mbliaḋain ſi.

longitudinem unius cubiti, reperti in fluvio Galivæ tum desiccato."—See note under the year 1178.

[q] *Of Creeve*, na craoiḃe.—The district near Coleraine, west of the River Bann. The cataract, now called the Cutt's Fishery, was anciently called Eas Craoibhe.—See O'Flaherty's *Ogygia, Domestica*, cap. 3, where, describing the course of the River Bann, he writes: "Banna inter Leam et Elliam præter Clanbresail regionem scaturiens per Neachum lacum transiens Ændromensem agrum et Fircriviam (Fir na Craoiḃe) Scriniamque in Londinodorensi agro intersecat, et tertio e Culrania, et Cataracta *Eascribe* lapide se in oceanum transfundit, salmonibus totius Europæ longè fæcundissimus."

[r] *O'Inneirghe*, now anglicised Henery.—This family descends from Brian, grandson of Niall of the Nine Hostages, Monarch of Ireland in 406. There are several of this name in the parish of Ballynascreen, in the county of Londonderry, of whom Dr. Henery, of Maghera, in the same county, is at present the most respectable.—See Duald Mac Firbis's Irish Pedigrees, Lord Roden's copy, p. 178, with which the copy in the Royal Irish Academy corresponds.

[s] *Hy-Awley and Hy-Fiachrach*, i. e. the inhabitants of the baronies of Tirawley and Tireragh.

[t] *Sil-Maelruain*.—This was the tribe name of the O'Flynns of Connaught, and it also became the name of their territory, which comprised the entire of the parish of Kiltullagh, and part of the parish of Kilkeevin, in the present county of Roscommon. The present head of this sept of the O'Flynns told the Editor in 1837, that it was the constant tradition in the family, that O'Flynn's country extended southwards as far as the bridge of Glinske, in the county of Galway, but the Editor has not found any authority for extending it beyond the limits of the present county of Roscommon. It comprised the entire of the mountainous district of *Sliabh Ui Fhloinn*, i. e. O'Flynn's mountain, which contains twenty townlands, and lies partly in the parish of Kiltullagh, and partly in that of Kilkeevin. The lake called *Lough Ui Fhloinn*, i. e. O'Flynn's lake (incorrectly anglicised Lough Glynn by Mr. Weld, in his Statistical Account of the county of Roscommon), also lies in this territory, as does the village of Ballinlough, called in Irish baile locha Ui Fhloinn, i. e. the town of O'Flynn's lake. O'Flynn's castle, of which the foundations only are now traceable, stood on the top of the hill between the village and the lake.

The present head of this sept of the O'Flynns is Edmond O'Flynn, Esq., of Newborough (the son of Kelly, son of Edmond, son of Colla), who possesses but a few townlands of the territory.

THE AGE OF CHRIST, 1192.

The Age of Christ, one thousand one hundred ninety-two.

The doorway of the refectory of Duv-regles-Columbkille was made by O'Kane, of Creeve[q], and the daughter of O'Henery[r].

Taichleach O'Dowda, Lord of Hy-Awley and Hy-Fiachrach[s] of the Moy, was slain by his own two grandsons.

Hugh O'Flynn, Chief of Sil-Maelruain, died[t].

The English were defeated at the weir of Aughera[u], by Muintir Maoil-t-Sinna.

The castle of Ath-an-Urchair[w] and the castle of Kilbixy[x] were erected in this year.

Dr. O'Brien, in his Irish Dictionary, printed at Paris in 1768, states that Edmond O'Flin, of Ballinlagh, Esq. (the grandfather of the present Edmond), was then the chief of this ancient family. He also states that "the Right Hon. Lady Ellen O'Flin, Countess de la Hues of Lahnes-Castle, in Normandy, was of the same direct branch of the O'Flins, her ladyship being daughter to Timothy O'Flin, of Clydagh, in the Co. of Roscommon, Esq." The Connaught O'Flynns are of a different race from O'Flynns of Arda, in Munster, and from the O'Flynns, now O'Lynns, of Hy-Tuirtre and Firlee, the warlike opponents of Sir John De Courcy.

[u] *The weir of Aughera*, caraiḋ Eaċaraḋ.—This place is called Acharudh Lobran at the year 1163. The only place near the country of the Muintir Maoil-tsionna, or Mac Carroons, called Aughera, is the parish of Augher, in the barony of Deece, in the county of East Meath. The Mac Carroons were seated in Cuircne in Teffia, which was the western part of the county of Westmeath. According to the Annals of Kilronan the Mac Carroons were defeated this year at Rath Aodha (Rathhugh, near Kilbeggan), by the English, on which occasion the two sons of Mac Carroon, the two sons of Teige Mac Ualgairg [Magoalric], O'Hart, Branan Mac Branan, and many others, both Irish and English, were slain.

[w] *Ath-an-Urchair*, now called in Irish baile áṫa urchuir, and in English Horseleap: it lies in the barony of Moycashel, in the south of the county of Westmeath. Sir Henry Piers of Tristernagh, who wrote in 1682, says, that Sir Hugh De Lacy was murdered here by a mere villain or common labourer, and a native, as he was stooping down to give some directions to the workmen; but this cannot be true, as it appears, from the old Irish annals, that Sir Hugh was murdered in 1186 by O'Meyey, the fosterson of the Fox, prince of Teffia, i. e. six years before this castle was erected.—See note under the year 1186.

Piers says that this place was called *Horseleap*, from Sir Hugh de Lacy having leaped on horseback over the drawbridge of the castle.—See Vallancey's *Collectanea*, vol. i. pp. 84, 85. He describes this castle as a stately structure, and such no doubt it was, but there are no distinct ruins of it at present, except the two piers of the drawbridge; masses of the walls are seen scattered over the hill, but the ground-plan of the building could not now be determined.—See other references to this place at the years 1207 and 1470.

[x] *Kilbixy*, Cill ḃigsi, *recte* Cill ḃigsiġe, i. e.

Creach mór do denam la gallaib laighen ar domnall ua mbriain, go rangattar tré clár cille dalua siar go magh ua ttoirrdhealbaigh, ⁊ ruccsatt dál ccair orra go ro marbsat sochaide diobh. Do ronsat goill caislen cille fiacal, ⁊ caislen cnuic Rafonn don chur sin.

Maidm mor ria ndomnall ua mbriain for ghallaib osraighe go ro cuiredh a nár.

AOIS CRIOSD, 1193.

Aois Criosd mile, ced, nochat, atrí.

Eochaidh ua baoighill do marbadh lá huib fiachrach ardasratha.

Maolpattraicc ua cobthaigh do écc.

Cathal mac gaithéne do écc.

the church of St. Bigseach.—This place is described in the Gloss to the *Feilire* or Festilogy of Aengus at 4th October, as in the territory of Ui Mac Uais (Moygoish), in Meath. It afterwards became an English town of some importance, according to Sir Henry Piers, who wrote in 1682 : "Kilkixy, of old a town of great note, having, as tradition telleth us, twelve Burgesses in their scarlet gowns, a Mayor or Sovereign with other officers suitable to so great a port, &c." The Editor visited this place in 1837, and found but few traces of this ancient town. They were as follows: 1. The Leperhouse, a mere ruin; 2. The site of the castle, but no remains whatever of its walls; 3. A moat surrounded by one circular fosse; 4. Site of the gallows. There is a holy well near the church still bearing the name Tobar Bigsighe, i. e. the well of St. Bigseach, a virgin, whose memory was venerated here, according to the Irish Calendars, on the 28th of June and 4th of October.—See other references to Kilbixy at the years 1430 and 1450.

[y] *Magh-Ua-Toirdhealbhaigh*, a plain near the Shannon, in the parish of Killaloe, in the east of the county of Clare.

[z] Cill Fiacla, now Kilfeakle, an old church, giving name to a parish, in the barony of Clanwilliam, and county of Tipperary, and about four miles and a half to the east of the town of Tipperary. In the Book of Lismore, fol. 47, *b*, *b*, this church is described as in the territory of Muscraighe Breogain, which was the ancient name of the barony of Clanwilliam. See also Annals of Innisfallen, at the years 1192, 1196, and 1205; Colgan's edition of the Tripartite Life of St. Patrick, lib. iii. c. 32; and Lanigan's Ecclesiastical History of Ireland, vol. i. p. 290.

[a] *Knockgraffon*, Cnoc Rafon, i. e. the hill of Raffon, who, according to Keating and the older writers, was the nurse of Fiacha Mulleathan, King of Munster, in the third century. It is a townland in a parish of the same name, in the barony of Middlethird, and county of Tipperary, and about two miles to the north of the town of Cahir. O'Brien has the following notice of this place in his Irish Dictionary, *voce* GRAFANN: "GRAFANN, Knockgraffan, or Raffan, in the county of Tipperary, one of the regal houses of the kings of Munster in ancient times, where Fiacha Muilleathan, and other Momonian kings, had their courts; it was to that seat Fiacha

The English of Leinster committed great depredations against Donnell O'Brien. They passed over the plain of Killaloe, and directed their course westwards, until they had reached Magh-Ua-Toirdhealbhaigh[y], where they were opposed by the Dalcassians, who slew great numbers of them. On this expedition the English erected the castles of Kilfeakle[z] and Knockgraffon[a].

Donnell O'Brien defeated the English of Ossory, and made a great slaughter of them.

THE AGE OF CHRIST, 1193.

The Age of Christ, one thousand one hundred ninety-three.

Eochy O'Boyle was slain by the Hy-Fiachrach of Ardstraw[b].

Mulpatrick O'Coffey died.

Cathal Mac Gaithen died.

brought Cormac Mac Airt, King of Leath-Coinn, prisoner. In after ages it was the estate, together with its annexes, of the O'Sullivans. A very remarkable moat yet remains there to be seen to this day." Again, under the word RAFFAN, he writes; "RAFFAN, Cnoc-Raffan, a beautiful hill near the River Suire, the centre of the primitive estate of the O'Sullivans, descended from Finin, elder brother of Failbhe Flann, ancestor of the Mac Cartys."

The Editor visited Knockgraffon in the year 1840, and found the ancient ruins to consist of a large moat surrounded by a rath of ample dimensions. The moat is about fifty-five feet in perpendicular height, and sixty feet in diameter at top. At the foot of the moat on the west side is a curious platea measuring seventy paces from north to south, and fifty-seven paces from east to west. This place remained in the possession of the descendants of Fiacha Muilleathan, the O'Sullivans, until the year 1192, when the English drove them from their rich plains into the mountains of Cork and Kerry, and erected, within their Rath of Knockgraffon, a strong castle to secure their conquests. Of this castle only one small tower now remains, but the outlines of some of the walls are traceable to a very considerable extent. See Cormac's Glossary, *voce* Ana; and Keating's History of Ireland, reign of Cormac Mac Art.

The Dublin copy of the Annals of Innisfallen records the erection of the castles of Kilkenny and Kilfeakle, by the English, in this year.

[b] *Hy-Fiachrach of Ardstraw*, uí fiaċraċ arda sraċa, i. e. the descendants of Fiachra of Ardstraw. Their territory was situated along the River Derg, in the north-west of the county of Tyrone, and comprised the parish of Ardstraw and some adjoining parishes. Ussher states (*Primordia*, p. 857), that the church of Ardstraw, and many other churches of *Opheathrach*, were taken from the see of Clogher, and incorporated with the see of Derry. This tribe of the Hy-Fiachrach are to be distinguished from those of Connaught, being descended from Fiachra, the son of Erc, who was the eldest son of Colla Uais, monarch of Ireland in the fourth century.—See O'Flaherty's *Ogygia*, P. iii. c. 76.

Derbforgaill (.i. ben tigernain ui Ruairc) ingen murċaḋa ui Maoileachlainn do ecc i mainistir droiċit atha is in cuicceḋ bliaḋan ochtmoġat a haoisi.

Diarmaid mac Conbroġda ui ḋiomusaiġ taoiseaċ cloinne maoilugra, ⁊ ticcherna ua failge fri ré ḟoda do écc.

Cathal oḋar mac méġ carṫaiġ do ṁarḃaoh la doṁnall máġ cartaigh.

Muirchertaċ mac murċaḋa Mec murċaḋa ticcherna ua ccennselaiġ déġ.

Aodh ua maoilbrenainn taoiseaċ cloinne concoḃair do ṁarḃaḋ la gallaibh atha cliath.

[c] *Dervorgilla*, Dearḃforgaill.—She was, therefore, born in the year 1108, was forty-four years of age when she eloped with Dermot Mac Murrough, King of Leinster, who was then in the sixty-second year of his age, a remarkable instance of a *green* old age. Dermot was expelled in eight years afterwards, but, as Dr. O'Conor observes, not for the seduction of this woman.—See O'Conor's *Prolegomena ad Annales*, part ii. p. 146. O'Reilly, in his Essay on the Brehon Laws, attempts to defend the character of this woman; but it cannot be defended, as we have the authority of these Annals, and of the older Annals of Clonmacnoise, to prove that she not only consented to go home with Dermot, but also carried with her, her dowry and cattle.—See Mageoghegan's Translation of the Annals of Clonmacnoise, and note under the year 1172, p. 4.

[d] *Monastery of Drogheda*, Mainistir Droiċit Aṫa.—Colgan observes that, by the Monastery of Drogheda, the Four Masters mean that of Mellifont, which is near that town.—See *Trias Thaum.*, p. 309, and *Acta Sanctorum*, p. 655, 776; see also Lanigan's Ecclesiastical History of Ireland, vol. iv. p. 167, note 22.

[e] *Clanmalier*, clann maoilugra. — This, which was the territory of the O'Dempsys, extended on both sides of the River Barrow, in the King's and Queen's Counties. It appears from an old map of the countries of Leix and Ophaley, made in the reign of Philip and Mary, that the territory of Clanmaliere extended to the margin of the Great Heath of Maryborough, and comprised the barony of Portnahinch in the Queen's County, on the south side of the River Barrow, and the barony of Upper Philipstown, in the King's County, on the north side of that river. This Dermot O'Dempsy was the only man of his name that obtained the chieftainship of all Offaly. He founded, on the site of an ancient church dedicated to St. Evin, about the year 1178, the great Cistercian abbey of Rosglas, now Monasterevin (Mainistir Eiṁín), which he richly endowed.—See his Charter of Foundation published in the *Monasticon Anglicanum*, vol. ii. p. 1031. For the extent of Ui Failghe before the English invasion, see note under the year 1178.

[f] *Murtough, son of Murrough Mac Murrough.*—He was Murtough *na maor* (i. e. of the Stewards), son of Murrough *na nGaedhal* (of the Irish), who was the brother of Dermot *na nGall* (of the English), who first brought the English to Ireland). According to the Book of Leinster, a very important fragment of a MS. preserved in the Library of Trinity College, Dublin (H. 2, 18), Murrough na nGaedhal was the ancestor of the celebrated family of Mac Davy More, or Mac Damore, said by Sir George Carew to be a branch of the Barrys, and also of Mac Vaddock, whose country was situated round Gorey, in the north-east of the county of Wexford, supposed also, but without any proof whatever, except

Dervorgilla[c] (i. e. the wife of Tiernan O'Rourke), daughter of Murrough O'Melaghlin, died in the monastery of Drogheda[d] [Mellifont], in the eighty-fifth year of her age.

Dermot, son of Cubroghda O'Dempsey, Chief of Clanmalier[e], and for a long time Lord of Offaly, died.

Cathal Odhar, the son of Mac Carthy, was slain by Donnell Mac Carthy.

Murtough, the son of Murrough Mac Murrough[f], Lord of Hy-Kinsellagh[g], died.

Hugh O'Mulrenin[h], Chief of Clann-Conor, was slain by the English of Dublin.

mere conjecture, to be of English descent. From Donnell Kavanagh, the illegitimate son of Dermot *na nGall* Mac Murrough, are descended all the Kavanaghs, including the Mac Dermots Láv-derg; and from Enna, another illegitimate son of the same Dermot, are descended the family of the Kinsellaghs, now so numerous in Leinster. The country of Mac Davy More, or Mac Damore, was in the barony of Ballyghkeen, comprising the lands of Glascarrick, &c. In the State Papers' Office, London, is preserved a petition, dated 1611, of Art Mac Dermott Kavanagh, Chief of the Kinsellaghs, and Redmond Mac Davimore, Richard Mac Vaddock, and Donnell Kavanagh Spaniagh, and other gentlemen and freeholders of the countries of Mac Dermott, Mac Davimore, and Mac Vaddock, through their agent, Henry Walsh; and another petition, dated May, 1616, of Redmond Mac Damore, gent., Chief of Mac Damore's country, in the county of Wexford, to the English Privy Council, regarding the new Plantation in Wexfordshire. In this petition Mac Damore states that he holds his lands by descent and not by tanistry. This, however, is not enough to prove his descent from the Barrys, in opposition to the Book of Leinster, a vellum manuscript, at least five centuries old, which traces his pedigree to Murrough *na nGaedhal*, the brother of Dermot *na nGall*. It is highly probable, however, that Murrough *na nGaedhal*, had married a lady of the Barrys, and thus brought the names David and Redmond into this branch of the Mac Murrough family, as the Kavanaghs have that of Gerald, Maurice, Walter, &c., from intermarriages with other English or Anglo-Irish families. The pedigrees of the above septs of the Mac Murroughs are also given in Duald Mac Firbis's Genealogical Book, p. 473, and in Peregrine O'Clery's, p. 82.

[g] *Hy-Kinsellagh.*—The people called Hy-Kinsellagh, were the descendants of Eochy Kinsellagh, King of Leinster, about the year of Christ 358. Their country originally comprised more than the present diocese of Ferns, for we learn from the oldest lives of St. Patrick, that Donaghmore, near Sletty, in the present county of Carlow, was in it. In an ancient Tripartite Life of St. Patrick, quoted by Ussher (*Primordia*, p. 863), it is called the larger and more powerful part of Leinster. "*Ordinavit S. Patricius de gente Laginensium alium episcopum nomine Fyacha virum religiosissimum: qui jussione beatissimi Patricii gentem Ceanselach ad fidem convertit et baptizavit; quæ gens major atque potentior pars Laginensium est.*" The country of Hy-Felmeadha, north, which was the ancient name of the district around Tullow-Ofelimy, in the present county of Carlow, was also in the territory of Hy-Kinsellagh.

[h] *O'Mulrenin*, O'Maoilḃrenainn.—The exact limits of the cantred of Clann-Conor, the terri-

Ua cerbaill tigerna airgiall do gabail la gallaibh, ⁊ a dallad leo o tur, ⁊ a crochadh iarttain.

Inis clothrann do orgain la macaib oirdealb, ⁊ la macaib concobair Maonmaige.

AOIS CRIOSD, 1194.

Aois Criosd, mile, céd, nochat, acethair.

Constantin ua brain [ua briain?] epscop cille dalua do écc.

Domnall mac toirrdealbaig ui briain Ri mumhan, lochrann solusda síodha ⁊ coccadh Redla adanta enig ⁊ engnamha na muimhneach, ⁊ laoch moda archena do écc, ⁊ muirchertach a mhac do gabail a ionaidh.

Goill do thiachtain ar inis ua ffionntain, ⁊ a ccor ar eccin di.

Cúmide ua flainn do marbad la gallaib.

Sloicched la gillebert mac goirdealbaig co heass ruaidh, ⁊ a iompudh arriden gan nach tarba dia Sloiged itir.

tory of O'Mulrenin, cannot now be determined, as this family sunk at an early period under O'Flanagan and O'Conor Roe; but its whereabouts may be ascertained from O'Dugan's topographical poem, which makes the Clann-Conor a subsection of the Clanncahill, whose territory comprised the parishes of Kilmacumshy, Kilcorkey, and Shankill, and parts of the parishes of Creeve and Elphin, in the county of Roscommon. Mael Brenainn, the name of the progenitor of this family, signifies the servant, or devoted of St. Brendan.

[i] *Inishcloghran*, Inis Clothrann, i. e. the island of *Clothra*. This Clothra is said to have been the sister of the famous Meadhbh, or Meave, Queen of Connaught. The island lies in Lough Ree, near St. John's, and is now sometimes called, by the people of the counties of Longford and Roscommon, dwelling in its vicinity, the Seven Church Island, from the ruins of seven old churches still to be seen on it; and sometimes Quaker's Island, from Mr. Fairbrother, the present occupier. These churches, to one of which is attached a very old square belfry, called in Irish Clogás, are said to have been erected by St. Dermot in the sixth century; but some of them were re-edified. The famous Meave of Croghan, Queen of Connaught, was killed on this island by the champion Forby, her own nephew, and the spot on which she perished is still pointed out, and called ionad marbtha Meidhbhe, the place of the killing of Meave. There is also on the highest point of the island the remains of a fort called *Grianan Meidhbhe*.—See Ordnance Map of the Island; and Petrie's Inquiry into the Origin and Uses of the Round Towers of Ireland, p. 358.

[k] *The Sons of Osdealv*, i. e. the Mac Costelloes.—According to the Annals of Kilronan, the island of Inis Clothrann was plundered this year by Gilbert Mac Gosdealv, and his English followers, and the sons of Gilchreest Mac Carroon, viz., Gilla Croichefraich and Auliffe, who had the tribe of Muintir Maeltsinna with them. According to the Dublin copy of the Annals of

O'Carroll, Lord of Oriel, was taken by the English, who first put out his eyes, and afterwards hanged him.

Inishcloghran[l] was plundered by the sons of Osdealv[k], and the sons of Conor Moinmoy.

THE AGE OF CHRIST, 1194.

The Age of Christ, one thousand one hundred ninety-four.

Constantine O'Brain [O'Brien?], Bishop of Killaloe, died.

Donnell, son of Turlough O'Brien, King of Munster, a beaming lamp in peace and war, and the brilliant star of the hospitality and valour of the Momonians, and of *all* Leth-Mogha, died; and Murtough, his son, assumed his place.

The English landed upon [the island of] Inis-Ua-bh-Fionntain[l], but were forcibly driven from it.

Cumee O'Flynn[m] was slain by the English.

Gilbert Mac Costello marched, with an army, to Assaroe[n], but was compelled to return without being able to gain any advantage by his expedition.

Innisfallen, it was plundered by Gilbert de Nangle; and this is correct, for De Nangle was the original name of the Costelloes.

Under this year the Annals of Kilronan record the erection of the Castle of Domhnach maighen, now Donaghmoyne, in the barony of Farney, and county of Monaghan, but do not give the name of the builder. Under this year, also, the Dublin copy of the Annals of Innisfallen record the erection, by the English, of the Castle of Briginis, in Thomond, with the consent of Donnell More O'Brien, who, it was believed, permitted its erection for the purpose of distressing Mac Carthy. The same chronicle also enters under this year the death of the daughter of Godfred, King of the Isle of Mann, and wife of John de Courcy.

[l] *Inis-Ua-bh-Fionntain*, i. e. *insula O'Fintanorum.*—The situation of this island is unknown to the Editor. It is not called from St. Fintan, after whom several places in Ireland are named, but from a family of the name O'Fintan.

[m] *Cumee O'Flynn.*—This is the celebrated chieftain, who, in the year 1178, defeated De Courcy in the territory of Firlee, and cut off all his men except eleven. The name of the person by whom Cumee was slain is not given in the Annals of Ulster, Kilronan, or Innisfallen. Do ṁarḃaḋ do ġallaiḃ is the phrase used by them all, and the old translator of the Annals of Ulster renders the passage: "Cumie Offlin killed by the Galls." The term *Galls* is at this period always applied to the English, though in the previous century it means the Danes, or Scandinavians.

[n] *Assaroe*, eaṡ ruaḋ, i. e. the Red Cataract, but the name is more correctly Eas Aoḋa ruaiḋ, i. e. the cataract of Aodh Ruadh, the son of Badharn, who was drowned here in the year of the world 4518, according to the chronology of these an-

Maolseachlainn mac domhnaill ui ġiollapatraicc tiġerna osraiġe do ecc.

Concobar mac Maġnasa mic duinnsleibe ui eochadha do marbhadh la hUa nannluain i meabhail.

Aedh dall mac toirrdhealbhaiġ ui ċoncobhair do écc.

Sitriucc mac floinn ui ḟindaċta taoiseaċ ċloinne murchadha do éġ.

Donnchadh mac Muirceartaiġ mic toirrdhealbhaiġ do marbhadh la Muirceartach mac domhnaill ui bhriain.

Murchadh mac Amlaoibh uí ċindeidiġ do ṁarbhadh la lochlainn mac micraiṫ uí chinneittiġ i fionġail.

AOIS CRIOSD, 1195.

Aois Criosd, mile, ced, nochatt, a cúicc.

Domhnall ua Conaing easpcop ċille dalua do écc.

Florent mac Ríaccáin ui maoilruanaidh easpcop oile find do écc.

Domhnall ua find comharba cluana fearta brénaind decc.

Eaċmarcach uá caṫáin do écc i recclés póil.

Conċobhar maġ ḟaċtna do écc i recclés doire.

Sitriucc ua gairmleadhaiġ do ṁarbhadh do mac duirn Slebhe.

Slúaiġeadh lá Iohn do cuirti, ⁊ la mac Hugo de laci do gabháil neirt ar ġallaibh laiġean, ⁊ muṁan.

Sluaicchedh la Caṫal ccroibhdercc ua cconcobhair, la mac goisdelbhaiġ go ndreim do ġallaibh, ⁊ do ġaoidhealaibh na midhe imaille fris is in muṁain go rangattar imleach iubhair, ⁊ cairiol go ro loiscceadh ceṫre morċaislein leo ⁊ araile do ṁionċaislenaibh.

Cathal mac diarmada do tocht i cconnachtaibh ar in muṁain, ⁊ ba cosgrach in gach maiġin triasa tudhchaidh go rainig co loch mearg, ⁊ co hinis Rodhba, ⁊ ro gabhait longa cathail croibhdeirg uile lais, ⁊ rug lais iat co

nals, but in the year 3603, according to O'Flaherty's corrected Irish Chronology.—See *Ogygia*, part iii. c. 36. This name is now pronounced *Assaroe*, but the cataract is more generally known by the appellation of the Salmon Leap. It is on the River Samhaoir, now more usually called the Erne, in the town of Ballyshannon.

° *O'Finnaghty.*—There were two families of this name in Connaught, of whom one was Chief of Clann-Murrough, and the other was Chief of Clann-Conway, and had his residence at Dunamon, near the River Suck. These families were

Melaghlin, the son of Donnell, who was the grandson of Gillapatrick, Lord of Ossory, died.

Conor, son of Manus, who was son of Donslevy O'Haughey, was treacherously slain by O'Hanlon.

Hugh Dall (the Blind), the son of Turlough O'Conor, died.

Sitric, the son of Flann O'Finnaghty[o], Chief of Clann-Murrough, died.

Donough, son of Murtough, who was son of Turlough, was slain by Murtough, the son of Donnell O'Brien.

Murrough, the son of Auliffe O'Kennedy, was slain in *fingail*[p] by Loughlin, the son of Magrath O'Kennedy.

THE AGE OF CHRIST, 1195.

The Age of Christ, one thousand one hundred ninety-five.

Donnell O'Conaing [Gunning], Bishop of Killaloe, died.

Florence, the son of Regan O'Mulrony, Bishop of Elphin, died.

Donnell O'Finn, Coarb of Clonfert-Brendan, died.

Eachmarcach O'Kane died in St. Paul's church.

Conor Mag Fachtna died in the abbey church of Derry.

Sitric O'Gormly was slain by Mac Donslevy.

John De Courcy and the son of Hugo De Lacy marched with an army to conquer the English of Leinster and Munster.

Cathal Crovderg O'Conor and Mac Costelloe, with some of the English and Irish of Meath, marched into Munster, and arrived at Imleach Iubhair (Emly) and Cashel. They burned four large castles and some small ones.

Cathal Mac Dermot marched from Munster into Connaught, and passed victoriously through the province. On arriving at Lough Mask and Inishrobe[q], he seized upon all the vessels [i. e. boats] of Cathal Crovderg O'Conor, and

supplanted by that sept of the Burkes called Mac David, who had their chief castle at Glinsk, on the west side of the River Suck, in the county of Galway.—See note under the year 1225.

[p] *Fingail*.—The crime of ꝼıonġaıl was counted worse than simple murder by the Irish. It included patricide, matricide, fratricide, and the murder of any relation.

[q] *Inishrobe*, ınır roḃa, i. e. the island of the River Robe. A small island in Lough Mask, opposite the mouth of the River Robe, not far from the town of Ballinrobe, in the county of Mayo.

caislén na caillighe co ndearna ulca iomḋa ar ar gach leiṫ de co ttainig cathal croibhdearg co ndreim do ġallaiḃ ⁊ do cloinn maoilruana, ⁊ do ronaḋ síḋ fó ḋéoiḋ re mac diarmada ger uo mór na huilc do roine go sin.

AOIS CRIOSD, 1196.

Aois Criosd, míle, céd, nochat, asé.

Recclés Póil ⁊ Petair in Ardmacha cona ttemplaiḃ, ⁊ go mbloiḋ ṁóir don Ráiṫ do loscaḋ.

Muirċertach mac muirċertaiġ uí laċlainn tiġearna ċenél eóġain Rioġḋaṁna Ereann tuir gaiscceḋ, ⁊ eangnaṁa leiṫe cuinn, díorgaoiltiḋ caṫraċ, ⁊ caislén gall, turgbalaiḋ ceall, ⁊ caoiṁneiṁeaḋ, do marbaḋ lá donnchaḋ mac blosgaiḋ uí caṫáin tré comairle ċenel neoġain iar ttabairt na tteora scríne, ⁊ ċánóine Patraig ḋóiḃ im dilsi ḋó. Rugaḋ a ċorp iaroṁ go doire colaim cille, ⁊ ro haḋnacht hiruiḋe go nonóir, ⁊ cátaiḋ.

Slóiġeaḋ lá Ruáiḋri mac duinnsleḃe co ngallaiḃ, ⁊ go macaiḃ toísec connaċt do ḟoiġhiḋ ċenél neoġain, ⁊ na nairṫer, Tangattar dna cenél eóġain telċa ócc, ⁊ fioru airṫir co maċaire árdamaċa ina naġaiḋ, ⁊ do radsat caṫ ḋóiḃ go raoiṁeaḋ for ṁac duinnsleḃe ⁊ ro láḋ dírgár a ṁuin-

[r] *Caislen na-Cailligh**e*.—Now called the Hag's Castle in English: it is situated in Lough Mask, and is a round enclosure of great extent.

[s] *The rath*, or fort, that surrounded the cathedral of Armagh extended, according to tradition, as far south as the present market house.

[t] *Churches and fair nemeds*.—Turgḃálaiḋe ceall ⁊ caoiṁneiṁeaḋ is translated by Colgan "Multarum Basilicarum et Sanctuariorum fundator."—*Vide Trias Thaum*., p. 504, col. 2.

[u] *Blosky O'Kane*.—That this Blosky is the ancestor of the numerous clans of the Mac Closkeys, in the county of Londonderry, can scarcely be doubted. The Erenagh Mac Closkey signed his name Blosganus in the reign of James I., which at once affords a clue to the true original name of this family.

[w] *Honour and respect*.—This passage is translated by Colgan as follows, in his Annals of Derry, *Trias Thaum*., p. 504: "A. D. 1196. Murchertachus Hua Lachlainn, filius Murchertachi, Hiberniæ regis, Princeps de Kinel-eoguin, & expectatione multorum Rex Hiberniæ futurus, turris fortitudinis & defensionis Aquilonaris Hiberniæ, victoriosus Anglicarum Ciuitatum & fortalitiorum expugnator, & multarum Basilicarum & Sanctuariorum fundator, de consilio quorundam procerum de Kinel-eoguin qui per tria Scrinia, & Canones S. Patricij iuramentum fidelitatis ante ipsi præstiterant; manu Dunchadi filij Bloscadii O Cathain dolosè interremptus occubuit: eiusque corpus Doriam delatum ibi cum funebri pompa & honore sepultum est." And thus, very carelessly in the

brought them away to Caislen na-Cailllighe[r] [the Hag's Castle], where he proceeded to commit great ravages in all directions, until Cathal Crovderg, accompanied by a party of the English and of the Sil-Maelruana, arrived and made peace with him (Mac Dermot), although he (Cathal) had thitherto committed great injuries.

THE AGE OF CHRIST, 1196.

The Age of Christ, one thousand one hundred ninety-six.

The Abbey of SS. Peter and Paul at Armagh, with its churches, and a great part of the Rath[s], were burned.

Murtough, the son of Murtough O'Loughlin, Lord of Kinel-Owen, presumptive heir to the throne of Ireland, tower of the valour and achievements of Leth-Chuinn, destroyer of the cities and castles of the English, and founder of churches and fair nemeds[t] (sanctuaries), was killed by Donough, the son of Blosky O'Kane[u], at the instigation of the Kinel-Owen, who had pledged their loyalty to him before the Three Shrines and the Canoin-Phatruig [i.e. the Book of Armagh]. His body was carried to Derry, and there interred with honour and respect[w].

Rory Mac Donslevy, with the English, and the sons of the chieftains of Connaught, marched an army against the Kinel-Owen and Oriors[x]. The Kinel-Owen of Tulloghoge and the men of Orior proceeded to the plain of Armagh to oppose them, and there gave them battle. Mac Donslevy was

old translation of the Annals of Ulster: "A. D. 1195. Murtagh mac Murtagh O'Loghlin, King of Kindred Owen, and that should be King of all Ireland, the supporting Post of Leth-quin for feates of Armes and courage [τυιρ ξαιρ-cιὸ 7 enξnoma leιτι cuιnn], Banisher [*recte* destroyer] of Galls and Castles, Rearer of churches and holiness" [neιmeὸ], "killed by Donogh mac Bloegy O'Cathan, in counsel of all Kindred Owen, after bringing the three schrines and canons of Patrick with him into the south church of Armagh, and he was carryed to Dyry Columkille, and he was buried honorably."

[x] *Oriors*, αιρτερ, i. e. the inhabitants of Orior, i. e. of Upper and Lower Orior, in the east of the county of Armagh. The word αιρτερ signifies Oriental, or Eastern; and the territory and people were so called from their situation in the east of Oriel; and the name of the inhabitants is accordingly latinized *Artheri* and *Orientales*, by Probus, Colgan, O'Flaherty, and other writers. Probus calls this territory *Regio Orientalium*.—See the second Life of St. Patrick, published by Colgan, in *Trias Thaum.*; Ussher's *Primordia*, pp. 857, 1047; O'Flaherty's *Ogygia*, part iii. c. 76; Mac Firbis's Genealogical Book (Marquis of Drogheda's copy), pp. 107, 130; and Dublin P. Journal, vol. i. p. 103.

tire. Torcratar ann dna aoḋ ḋécc do macaiḃ flaṫa, ⁊ toíseaċ Connaċt go sochaidiḃ oile do ḋosscurṡluaġ imaille friú. Ba dia maiṫiḃ Brian buide ua Flaiṫḃertaiġ, mac Maoiliosa ui Concoḃair a Connaċtaiḃ, mac ui Concoḃair Failge, ⁊ mac ui Faolain na nDeise.

Mac Blosccaiḋ uí Cuirin do argain Termainn Dábeócc, ⁊ ro marḃaḋ é fén go ndeargár a ṁuintire ria ccind ṁiosa tria ḟiortaib Dé, ⁊ Dábeóg.

Domṁnall mac Diarmada Mécc Carṫaiġ do ḃriseaḋ caṫa ar Ġallaiḃ Luimniġ ⁊ Muṁan, ⁊ ro ċuir a nDeargár, ⁊ ro diocuir a Luimneaċ, ⁊ ro ḃris dá ṁaiḋm oile forra cén moṫá an maiḋm sin.

Conċuḃar mac Diarmada tiġearna Maiġe Luirg do ḋol hi nurd i mainistir na Búille, ⁊ ro ġaḃ Tomaltach tiġearnus dia éis.

Aoḋ uá Fearġail tiġearna Muintire hAnġaile do marḃaḋ i meaḃail lá macaiḃ Sitrioga uí Cuinn.

Maiṫe muintire hEólais do ṁarḃaḋ la mac Caṫail ui Ruairc hi meaḃail.

Muirċḋaċ Mácc Raġnaill .i. an giolla ruaḋ taoiseaċ muintire hEólais do marḃaḋ la mac Maġnusa uí Conċoḃair tré furáil mic Caṫail ui Ruáirc lás ro marḃaḋ na maiṫe remráite.

Mathgamhain mac Conċobair Maonmaiġe rioġdaṁna Connaċt do mar-

[y] *Desies*, Déise.—At this period the territory of Desies extended from Lismore to Credanhead, in the county of Waterford. The last chief of the Desies, of the family of O'Faelan, was Melaghlin, or Malachy, who was deprived of his principality shortly after the English invasion, when it was granted to Robert Le Poer, whose descendants (now called Powers) for ages after possessed the territory.—See Cambrensis' *Hibernia Expugnata*, lib. i. c. 16; and O'Flaherty's *Ogygia*, P. iii. c. 69.

[z] *Termon-Daveog*, Tearmann Daḃeog, i. e. the sanctuary of St. *Daveog*.—The church of this Termon was situated on an island in Lough Derg, in the county of Donegal, but not a trace of it now remains. For some account of this celebrated island in Lough Derg, commonly called the island of St. Patrick's Purgatory, see Dean Richardson's work entitled Folly of Pilgrimages, and Lanigan's Ecclesiastical History of Ireland, vol. i. p. 368. The stone chair of St. Daveog, or Daibheog, the patron of this Termon, is yet shewn in a townland of Seeavoc, which verges on Lough Derg on the south side. The church lands of Termon Daveog are now called Termon-Magrath.

[a] *Limerick*.—The Dublin copy of the Annals of Innisfallen state, under this year, that Donnell More na Curra Mac Carthy destroyed the castle of Kilfeakle, and slew many of the English there, and took two of their chiefs prisoners; that he also plundered the territory of Imokilly, where he destroyed another castle and slew many of the English; that he and his Eugenian forces joined Cathal Crovderg O'Conor and O'Brien, and marched to Cork, then in the possession of the English, to destroy it; but that he did not suffer the town to be burned, on condition that the

defeated with dreadful slaughter; and twelve of the sons of the lords and chieftains of Connaught, with many of an inferior grade, were slain. Among the chieftains slain were Brian Boy O'Flaherty; the son of Maelisa O'Conor, of Connaught; the son of O'Conor Faly; and the son of O'Faelain (Phelan), of the Desies[y].

The son of Blosky O'Currin plundered Termon-Daveog[z]; but in a month afterwards he himself was slain, and his people were dreadfully slaughtered, through the miracles of God and St. Daveog.

Donnell, the son of Dermot Mac Carthy, defeated the English of Limerick[a] and Munster in a battle, with dreadful slaughter, and drove them from Limerick. He also defeated them in two other battles *in this year*.

Conor Mac Dermot, Lord of Moylurg, embraced Orders[b] in the monastery of Boyle; and Tomaltagh assumed the lordship in his stead[c].

Hugh O'Farrell, Lord of Muintir-Annaly, was treacherously slain by the sons of Sitric O'Quin.

The chiefs of Muintir-Eolais were treacherously slain by the son of Cathal O'Rourke.

Murray Mac Rannall, *surnamed* the Gillaroe[d], Chief of Muintir-Eolais, was slain by the son of Manus O'Conor, at the instigation of the son of Cathal O'Rourke, who had procured the deaths of the above-mentioned chiefs.

Mahon, the son of Conor Moinmoy, Roydamna[e] of Connaught, was slain by O'More (Donnell) and the men of Leix[f], who attempted to prevent him

English should quit it. The same chronicle records an excursion made by the English this year to Fordruim, where they slew O'Kedfy, and the two sons of Buadhach or Victor O'Sullivan, namely, Murtough and Gillycuddy (Ᵹiolla Moċuda). In the margin of this work is the following note, which was probably taken from Dr. O'Brien's copy of the Annals of Innisfallen: "Vide Waræum ad hunc annum, ubi actiones hic descriptas in sensum a reipsâ alienum et Anglis favorabilem, uti in suis passim annalibus, detorquet."

[b] *Embraced Orders*, do dol hi nurd, i. e. took the habit of a monk.—The Annals of Kilronan, under the year 1197, in recording the death of this chief, state, that he died i nouici manaiᵹ, "in the noviceship of a monk."

[c] *In his stead*, dia éis: literally, "after him."

[d] *The Gillaroe*, an Ᵹiolla ruadh, i. e. red or red-haired youth.

[e] *Roydamna*, ríoᵹdamhna, i. e. *materies* of a king, a term applied to the sons of a king, like prince, in the modern acceptation of the word.

[f] *Leix*, laoiᵹis.—This territory, which was the patrimonial inheritance of the family of O'More, comprised a considerable part of the Queen's County. If we take from that county the baronies of Portnahinch and Tinahinch, which belonged to the families of O'Dunn and O'Demp-

bað la hua mórða domnall, ⁊ la laiġiſſ occ coſnam na heðala do bſſt o ġallaibh ffiſſ, ⁊ cathal caſſaċ do maſbað uí móſða ina dioghail.

Conġalach mac fſſġail uí Ruaiſc do maſbað la luiġnib aſ ſliab da én.

Iodnaiðe uá mannachain tiġſſna uá mbſiúin na Sionna do écc.

Cathal mac aſdha uí flaithbſſtaiġ do maſbað la macaib muiſcſſtaiġ miðiġ.

AOIS CRIOSD, 1197.

Aoiſ Cſioſd, míle, céd, noċatt, a ſeaċt.

Sluaiġeað lá Iohn do Cuiſt co nġallaib ulað co hſſſctſaiðe, ⁊ do ſónſatt caiſlén cille Sanctáin, Ró ḟáſaiġeað ⁊ ſo ſolmaiġeð tſioċa céd cianaċta leó. Ro ḟáġaib Roitſel ṗitún co ſoċſaiðe moiſ immaille ffiſ

sey, and were a portion of the territory of Ui Failghe, and the barony of Upper Ossory, which was a part of the ancient Osraighe, and belonged to the Mac Gillapatricks, or Fitzpatricks, the remainder will be Leix.—See Ussher's *Primordia*, pp. 818, 943, and Map of Leix and Ophaley, in the British Museum. The territory of Laoighis, or Leix, was originally divided into seven parts, the boundaries of which met at a stone, called Leac Riada, on the plain of Magh Riada, now Morett, which originally comprised all the Great Heath of Maryborough. These seven districts were under the government of seven petty chiefs, who were all under the jurisdiction of one arch chief, called Righ Riada, who generally resided at Dun Mask, now Dunamase.—See Duald Mac Firbis's Genealogical Book, under the head LAOIGHIS LAIGHEAN. For the bardic account of the original acquisition of this territory by Laoighseach Ceannmhor, the ancestor of the O'Mores, the reader is referred to Mageoghegan's translation of the Annals of Clonmacnoise, reign of Felym Reaghtwar; and to Keating's History of Ireland, reign of Cormac Mac Art.

[g] *In revenge of him*, ina dioġail.—The Annals of Kilronan state that Mahon was slain by an archer of Donnell O'More's people, and that Donnell O'More fell on the same day by the hand of Cathal Carragh, in revenge of his brother. The entry is thus given in the Annals of Kilronan at the year 1196: maṫġamain mac concobaiſ maonmaiġe do maſbað le ſeſſenach .i. Conġoban, do muintiſ Domnaill Ui moſda. Domnall ua moſða ḟéin do tuitim iſ in uaiſ ceðna do laim caṫail caſſaiġ. And thus in the Annals of Boyle, but under the year 1197: "A. D. 1197. Maṫġamain mac Conċubaiſ maenmaiġi *occisus ab aliquo sagittario de familia* Domnaill ui moſða, *et in eadem hora* Domnall ua moſda *cecidit de manu* caṫail caſſaiġ."

[h] *Congalach*, Conġalaċ.—This name is now obsolete, as the Christian name of a man, but is preserved in the surname of Conolly, in Irish O'Conġalaiġ.

[i] *Slieve-dá-én*, ſliab dá én, i. e. the mountain of the two birds.—This mountain, which retains this name to the present day, lies principally in the parish of Kilross, barony of Tirrerill, and county of Sligo, and extends from near Lough

from bearing off the spoil which he had taken from the English; but O'More was killed by Cathal Carrach [O'Conor], in revenge of him[g] [Mahon].

Congalach[h], the son of Farrell O'Rourke, was slain by the men of Leyny, on Slieve-da-én[i].

Iodnaidhe O'Monahan, Lord of Hy-Briuin na-Sinna[k].

Cathal, the son of Hugh O'Flaherty, was slain by the son of Murtough Midheach[l] [Midensis].

THE AGE OF CHRIST, 1197.

The Age of Christ, one thousand one hundred ninety-seven.

John De Courcy and the English of Ulidia marched, with an army, to Eas-Creeva[m], and erected the castle of Kilsanctan[n], and wasted and desolated the territory of Kienaghta[o]. He left Rotsel Pitun, together with a large body of

Gill to Colooney. It is worthy of remark, that there is a lough on the north side of this mountain called *Loch da ghedh*, i. e. the lake of the two geese.—See Map prefixed to the *Tribes and Customs of Hy-Fiachrach*, printed in 1844.

[k] *Hy-Briuin na-Sinna*, now locally called *Tir ua-Riuin*.—It is a beautiful territory lying between Elphin and Jamestown, in the county of Roscommon, and comprising the parishes of Cill mor na Sinna, now Kilmore, Eachdhruim mac n-Aodha, now Aughrim, and Cluain creamha, now Cloncraff. According to the tradition of the district, O'Monahan lived at Lissadorn, near Elphin, now the seat of John Balf, Esq., where there is a well called Monahan's well; and the last of the O'Monahans, who was chief of this territory, was killed here by O'Beirne with a blow of his fist, *unde nomen*, Lissadorn, i. e. *the fort of the fist*.

[l] *Murtough Midheach*, i. e. the Meathian. He was so called from having been fostered in Meath.

Under this year the Dublin copy of the Annals of Innisfallen state, that Gilbert de Nangle was expelled from Meath by the King's Deputy, Hamon de Valentiis [De Valoignes] who took possession of his castles and lands.

[m] *Eas-Creeva*, Eſſcꞃaiḃe, now called the Salmon Leap, or the Cutt's Fishery, is a cataract on the River Bann, to the south of Coleraine, in the county of Londonderry.

[n] *Kilsanctan*, Cill Sanctáin.—In the Annals of Kilronan it is called caiſlen cille Santail, and in the old translation of the Annals of Ulster, "the Castle of Killsandle." It was situated on the east side of the River Bann, not far from Coleraine. There is still a remarkable mound near the Salmon Leap on the Bann, called Mountsandall.—See Ordnance Map of Londonderry, sheet 7.

[o] *Kienaghta*, Cianaċta, now the barony of Keenaght, in the north-west of the county of Londonderry.—The tribe called Cianaċta, i. e. the race or progeny of Cian, were descended from Cian, the son of Oilioll Olum, King of Munster in the third century. After the establishment of surnames the principal family of the Cianachta of this territory took the surname of O'Conor, and is distinguished in the Irish Annals by the appellation of O'Conor of Glenn Geimhin.

isin ccaistiall hísin, ⁊ ro ġabsat ag indradh, ⁊ occ argain tuaṫ ⁊ ceall ar. Tainig iaroṁ Roitsel Phitun ar creiċ co port doire, ⁊ ro airg cluain í, eanaċ, ⁊ dírgbruach, Rug dna flaiṫbeartaċ ua maoildoraiḋ tigearna conaill ⁊ eóġain co nuaṫaḋ do ċlandaiḃ néill an tuaiscirt forra, Ro fiġeḋ iomairg eatarra for traiġ na huaċonġḃála, ⁊ ro cuireaḋ a nár im mac ardgail ṁéc loċlainn tria ṁíorḃail colaim ċille, cainniġ, ⁊ breacain isa cealla ro airccseatt.

p *The territories and the churches*, tuaṫ ⁊ ceall.—By this phrase the annalists often mean lay and ecclesiastical property. Idir tuaṫ ⁊ cill generally means "both laity and clergy."

q *Cluain-I, Enagh, and Dergbruagh*, cluain i, eanaċ ⁊ dírgbruach.—The Editor has been able after much study and attention, to identify these three churches, though Colgan, a native of this part of Ireland, had done much to confound them. Cluain í is the present townland of Clooney, containing the ruins of an old church, in the parish of Clondermot, not far from the city of Londonderry; Eanaċ is the old church of Enagh, situated between the two loughs of the same name, in the north of the parish of Clondermot; and Dírgbruach, i. e. the *red brink*, is the townland of Gransha, in the same parish. Colgan, in *Trias Thaum.*, p. 505, gives an incorrect translation of the following part of the this passage, viz.: Táinig iaraṁ Roitsel Pitun ar creiċ go port doire ⁊ ro airg cluain í, eanach ⁊ dírgbruach. "Rotsellus Pitun venit ad portum Dorensem, Ciuitatem ipsam, Ecclesiis de *Cluain* an *Eanach*, & Dearg-bhruach spoliatis, invasurus."

Here he reads Cluain í, Eanach, "*Cluain an Eanach*," as if i were an abbreviation of the article in or an; but in this he is undoubtedly mistaken, for we learn from the older Irish Annals of Ulster and of Kilronan, that three churches are distinctly mentioned in the passage, viz., Cluain i, and Eanach, and Deargḃruaċ. The passage runs as follows in the Annals of Ulster: A. D. 1197. Tainic dno Roitsel Pitun co port Daire, co ro airc cluaini ⁊ enach ⁊ derc-bruaċ. And thus rendered in the old translation of the Ulster Annals, preserved in the British Museum, MSS. add. 4795. "This Rochel Pitun came to Port Dyry, and spoyled Cluain hie and Anagh and Dergbruagh."

Colgan, who thought that he understood the passage correctly, concluded that only two churches are mentioned, and took for granted that *Cluain i Eanagh* was the name of one church, and this he evidently took to be the one now in ruins between the two lakes Enagh already mentioned. Thus in the note on his wrongly made name of *Cluain an Eanach*, he writes: "Est Capella Diœcesis Dorensis, juxta Eanach arcem nobilissimæ familiæ O'Cathanorum; a qua et Cluain Enaich appellatur."—*Trias Thaum.*, p. 450, n. 51. And again, in his notice of the church of *Eanach*, he writes: "Ecclesia vulgo Eanach dicta (juxta quem est arx nobilissimæ familiæ O'Cathanorum) tertio tantum milliari versus aquilonem distat ab ipsa civitate Dorensi."—*Trias Thaum.*, p. 377, col. 2.

The Editor, who took for granted that Colgan's knowledge of the topography of this part of Ireland was next to perfect, as he was a native of Inishowen, was very much puzzled by these notes; but on examining the parish of Clondermot in 1834, he found that *Cluain i* and *Eanach* were two distinct townlands, containing each the ruins of an old church. O'Donnell, in his Life of Columbkille, distinctly points out

forces, in the castle, out of which they proceeded to plunder and ravage the territories and the churches[p]. Rotsel Piton afterwards came on a predatory excursion to the harbour of Derry, and plundered the churches of Cluain-I, Enagh, and Dergbruagh[q]. But Flaherty O'Muldory, Lord of Kinel-Owen and Kinel-Conell, with a small party[r] of the northern Hy-Niall, overtook him; and a battle was fought between them on the strand of Faughanvale[s], in which the English and the son of Ardgal Mac Loughlin were slaughtered, through the miracles of SS. Columbkille, Canice[t], and Brecan, whose churches they had plundered.

the situation of *Cluain i*, which he calls simply *Cluain*, in the following words:

"In loco quodam quem *Cluain* vocant, a Dorensi oppido ad adversam Feabhalii lacus marginem non procul distanti templum excitavit." (Columba). O'Donnell then goes on to state, that Nicholas Boston [Weston], an English Bishop, had, not long before his own time (1520), pulled down this church and commenced erecting a palace with the materials obtained from its ruins, at a place called *Bunseantuinne*, not far from Derry. "Paucis retro ab hinc annis, Episcopus Anglicus, Nicholaus Boston dictus, præfatum templum demolitus, ex ejus ruderibus palatium molitus est, sed consummare non potuit vindicante Deo." &c.—*Trias Thaum.*, p. 399, col. 1.

The place called Deargbruagh by the annalists is called the "Grange of Dirgebroe," in an inquisition taken at Derry, in the year 1609, and is now, beyond dispute, the townland of Gransha, or Grange, in the parish of Clondermot, but its church has been totally destroyed.—See Ordnance Map of Londonderry, sheets 13 and 14.

[r] *A small party*, uaċaḋ.—This word is used throughout these annals to denote "a few, or a small party."—See O'Brien's Dictionary, *in voce*. In the old translation of the Annals of Ulster the passage is rendered thus, under the year 1196 [*recte* 1197]: "An°. 1196. An army by John de Coursy with the Galls of Vlster to Eas-Krivy, and made the castle of Killsandle, and wasted the Trichaced of Kyanaght" [out] "of that castle. In that castle was Rochel Pitun left with a number to him. This Rochel Pitun came to Port Dyry, and spoyled Cluain hie and Anagh and Dergbruagh. Flaithvertagh O'Moildory, King of Kindred Owen overtooke him with a few of Conels and Owens, and broke of them uppon the shore of Vochongvail, that most of them were killed through the miracles of Columkill, Cainegh, and Brekan, whom they spoyled [i. e. whose churches they had plundered]." There is no reference to Ardgal Mac Loughlin in this translation, but his name is inserted in a more modern hand in the Dublin copy of the Annals of Ulster. The son of Ardgal Mac Loughlin seems to have joined the English on this occasion, as he is stated to have been slain through the miracles of the patron saints of the district.

[s] *Faughanvale.*—Colgan writes it *Nuachongbail.* There are several other places of this name in Ireland: one near the foot of Croaghpatrick, in the county of Mayo; a second in the county of Westmeath, on the borders of the county of Longford; a third on the River Boyne, to the west of Drogheda; and a fourth in the county of Clare. The name is translated *Nova habitatio* by Colgan.—See *Acta Sanctorum*, p. 141, note 8.

[t] *Canice*, caınnech.—He is the patron saint of the territory of Kienaghta, in which he was born in the year 516.—See Colgan, *Trias*

Mac etiġ do ċianaċtaiḃ do ḟlat altóra teampaill ṁóir doire colaim ċille, ⁊ cſiṫre cuirn bad fearr ro ḃaoi in Erinn do breiṫ eiste, .i. mac Riaḃaċ, mac solas, corn uí maoilḋoraiḋ, ⁊ cammcorainn corn uí ḋoċartaiġ, Ro brisitt imorra ⁊ do all a nionnṁassa, ⁊ a lossa ḋíḃ. Foriṫ [friṫ] imorra na seóid is in trſs ló iar ná ngoid, ⁊ an tí ro goid, ⁊ ro crochaḋ lá flaiṫḃeartaċ ag croiss na riaġ i neneaċ ċoluim cille isa haltóir ro ṡáraiġ.

Flaiṫḃſrtaċ ua maoilḋoraiḋ tiġearna cenél cconaill, eoġain, ⁊ airġiall cosnaṁaċ tſṁra, ⁊ rioġḋaṁna Ereann uile; Conall ar láoċḋact eriḋe, Cúċulainn ar ġaisceaḋ, Guaire ar eneaċ, Mac luġaċ ar ócclaċus décc (an dara la februari) iar ttreablaid toġaiḋe, i nimis Saimer isin trioċatmaḋ bliaḋain a ḟlaiṫiusa, ⁊ isin noṁaḋ bliaḋain ar ċaogatt a aoise. Agus ro haḋnact i nDruim ṫuama co nónoir aṁail ro baḋ díor.

Gabais eaċmarcaċ ua doċartaiġ (.i. an giolla sronṁaol) cſnnus ċenél cconaill fó ċédóir, ⁊ i ccionn coicṫiḋisi iaroṁ tainig Iohn do cuirt co soċraite ṁóir imaille fris tar tuaim hi ttír eógain, airsiḋe co hardsraṫa iarsin timċeall go doire colaim ċille. Airisit cóicc haiḋċe ann. Tiaġaid iaraṁ co cnoc nascain dia niomarcar tairis. Teccait dna cenél conaill im eċmarcaċ ua nDoċartaiġ dia saiġiḋ, ferṫar caṫ ſtorra, ⁊ torcratar soċaiḋe mor aḋiú ⁊ anall. Gid iad cenél conaill ann ro díthiġit iſttriḋe uair tor-

Thaum., p. 182; and *Acta Sanctorum*, p. 190; also Lanigan's *Ecclesiastical History of Ireland*, vol. ii. pp. 200, 202.

[u] *Mac Etigh.*—In the Annals of Ulster and Kilronan he is called Mac Gilla Edich.

[w] *Their jewels.*—A nionmasa ⁊ a lossa.—In the Annals of Ulster the reading is: ⁊ tall a ninnmasa ⁊ a lasa díḃ; which in the old translation is rendered, "broke their gilt and silver off them."

[x] *Defender of Tara*, cosnaṁaċ tſmra.—This might also be translated *contender for* Tara, i. e. for the sovereignty of Ireland.

[y] *Connell ... Cuchullin.*—These were two of the most distinguished of the Red Branch heroes, who flourished in Ulster under Concovar Mac Nessa in the first century.

[z] *Guaire in hospitality.*—He is here compared to Guaire Aidhne, King of Connaught, who was so distinguished for hospitality and bounty that he became the personification of generosity among the Irish bards. Guaire was King of Connaught for thirteen years, and died in the year 662.—See *Tribes and Customs of Hy-Fiachrach*, printed for the Irish Archæological Society in 1844, p. 391.

[a] *Mac Lughach in feats of arms.*—He was the best spearsman among the Fiana Eireann, or Irish Militia, in the third century. He was the son of Daire Derg, and grandson of Finn Mac Cumhaill, the Fingal of Mac Pherson's Ossian, and was called Mac Lughach, from his mother Lugha.—See Book of Lismore, fol. 204, *b*, where St. Patrick is introduced as asking the senior

Mac Etigh[u], one of the Kienaghts, robbed the altar of the great church of Derry, and carried off the four best goblets in Ireland, viz. Mac Riabhach, Mac Solas, the goblet of O'Muldory, and the goblet of O'Doherty, called Cam-Corainn. These he broke, and took off their jewels[w] and brilliant gems. On the third day after this robbery, these jewels and the thief were discovered. He was hanged by Flaherty [O'Muldory] at Cros-na-riagh (i. e. the Cross of Executions), in revenge of Columbkille, whose altar he had profaned.

Flaherty O'Muldory, Lord of Kinel-Connell, Kinel-Owen, and Oriel, defender of Tara[x], heir presumptive to the sovereignty of all Ireland, a Connell in heroism, a Cuchullin[y] in valour, a Guaire[z] in hospitality, and a Mac Lughach in feats of arms[a], died on Inis Saimer[b], on the second day of February, after long and patient suffering, in the thirtieth year of his reign, and fifty-ninth of his age, and was interred at Drumhome[c] with due honour.

Eachmarcach O'Doherty (i. e. Gilla Sron-mael) immediately after assumed the chieftainship of Kinel-Connell. A fortnight afterwards John De Courcy, with a numerous army, crossed Toome into Tyrone, thence proceeded to Ardstraw, and afterwards marched round to Derry-Columbkille, where he and his troops remained five nights. They then set out for the hill of Cnoc-Nascain[d], to be conveyed across it; but the Kinel-Connell, under the conduct of Eachmarcach O'Doherty, came to oppose them, and a battle was fought between them, in which many fell on both sides. The Kinel-Conell were much

Caoilti Mac Ronain, who this Mac Lughach was, thus: Cia dar mac Mac Lugach, ro fiarfaiger díc a réir, a Cailti, ar Patraic. Mac do Daire Derg mac Finn, ar Cailti. "Whose son was Mac Lughach, I asked of thee last night, O Cailti, said Patrick. He was the son of Daire Derg, the son of Finn, replied Cailti."

[b] *Inis Saimer*, an island in the River Erne, immediately under the Cataract of Eas Aodha Ruaidh, at Ballyshannon. For the origin of the name Inis Saimer, see Keating's History of Ireland, Haliday's Edition, p. 164; and O'Flaherty's *Ogygia*, part iii. c. 2. O'Muldory had a house on this island. The monastery of Eas Aodha Ruadh is not on this island, but on the north side of the river, about one mile to the west of the town of Ballyshannon.

[c] *Drumhome*, druim thuama, a church and parish in the barony of Tirhugh, and county of Donegal. This church is referred to under the Latinized name of *Dorsum Tommæ* by Adamnan in his *Vita Columbæ*, lib. iii. c. 23. It is also mentioned in O'Donnell's Life of Columba, lib. iii. c. 61; in Ussher's *Primordia*, p. 969; and also in the Irish Calendar of the O'Clerys, at 23rd September, where it is stated that it is one of St. Adamnan's churches.

[d] *Cnoc Nascain*, was the ancient name of a hill near Lough Swilly, in the barony of Inishowen, but the name is now obsolete.

cratar dá céd díoḃ im eaċmarcaċ fessin, im ḋonnchaḋ ua tairceirt toiseaċ cloinne Sneḋgile cong einiġ, ⁊ eangnaṁa, ceille, ⁊ comairle cenél cconaill uile im ġiolla mbriġde ua ndoċartaiġ, im ṁag nduḃain, im Mhág ḟfrġail, ⁊ im ṁacaiḃ ua mbaoiġill, ⁊ im ṡaorċlandaiḃ oile, ⁊ ro airccsfd inis eoġain, ⁊ do ḃeartsatt bóraiṁe ṁór leó este, ⁊ iompoiḋitt iar sin.

Conċoḃar ua caṫáin do écc.

Concoḃar mac taiḋg tiġearna maiġe luirg ⁊ ṁaiġe aoí, tuir ordain, aireċais, einiġ, ⁊ comairce connacht uile décc iar naiṫriġe ṫoġaiḋe i mainis-tir aṫa dalaarg.

Macraiṫ ua laiṫḃertaiġ tanaisi tíre heoġain ⁊ Maolruanaiḋ ua cai-relláin toísec cloinne diarmada do ṁarḃaḋ.

Doṁnall mac Raġnaill méc Raġnaill do ṁarḃaḋ do ṁacaiḃ méc duiḃ-dara i fiull.

Ruaiḋri ua flaiṫḃfrtaiġ tiġearna iarṫair connacht do ġaḃail lá caṫal croiḃdearg lá riġ connacht.

AOIS CRIOSD, 1198.

Aois Criosd, mile, céd, noċatt, a hocht.

Giolla macliacc ua branáin do aṫċur a ċoṁarbais uaḋa, ⁊ giollacrist ua cfrnaiġ do oirdneaḋ ina ionaḋ in abbḋaine colaim cille do réir toġa laoċ ⁊ cléireaċ tuaiscirt Ereann i ccoitċinne.

Ruaiḋri ua conċoḃair Rí Connacht ⁊ Ereann uile eittir ġallaiḃ ⁊ gaoiḋe-

[e] *Tower*, tuir.—The word tuir properly means a prop, pillar, support, or fulcrum, and tor means a tower. But as Colgan has translated tuir throughout his works by the Latin *turris*, the translator has adopted the word *tower*, but it should be understood in the sense of support, or prop, throughout.

[f] *Roderic O'Conor*, Ruaiḋri ua Conċoḃair.—The name Ruaiḋri, which is to be distinguished from Ruḋraiġe, seems to be of Danish origin in Ireland. It first occurs in the Irish Annals at the year 780.—See O'Conor's edition of the first part of the Annals of the Four Masters, p. 295; but Ruḋraiġe is found among the Irish as the proper name of a man at the earliest period of their history.—*Id.*, pp. 26, 59, 293. Throughout this translation the name Ruaiḋri is anglicised Rory, except in the name of this last monarch of Ireland, which is made Roderic for the sake of distinction. During ten years of his life this unfortunate prince reigned over Connaught only, for the eighteen following he was acknowledged by the greater part of the Irish chieftains as monarch of all Ireland; but finally, upon the unnatural revolt of his sons, he retired, according to the Annals of Kilronan,

slaughtered, for two hundred of them were slain, besides Eachmarcach himself and Donough O'Tairchirt, Chief of Clann-Snedhgile [Clann-Snelly], the prop of the hospitality, valour, wisdom, and counsel of all the Kinel-Conell; and also Gilla-Brighde O'Doherty, Mag-Duane, Mag-Fergail, the sons of O'Boyle, and many other nobles. The English then plundered Inishowen, and carried off a great number of cows from thence, and then returned.

Conor O'Kane died.

Conor, the son of Teige, Lord of Moylurg and Moynai, tower[e] of the grandeur, splendour, hospitality, and protection of all Connaught, died after exemplary penance in the monastery of Ath-da-laarg (Boyle).

Magrath O Laverty, Tanist of Tyrone, and Mulrony O'Carellan, Chief of Clann-Dermot, were slain.

Donnell, son of Randal Mac Ranall, was treacherously slain by the sons of Mac Duvdara.

Rory O'Flaherty, Lord of West Connaught, was taken prisoner by Cathal Crovderg, King of Connaught.

THE AGE OF CHRIST, 1198.

The Age of Christ, one thousand one hundred ninety-eight.

Gillamacliag O'Branan resigned his abbacy; and Gilchreest O'Kearney was elected coarb of St. Columbkille by the universal suffrages of the clergy and laity of the north of Ireland.

Roderic O'Conor[f], King of Connaught and of all Ireland, both the Irish and

in 1183, into the abbey of Cong, which had been founded and endowed by himself, where he spent the last thirteen years of his life. The late Dr. O'Conor, in his suppressed work, *Memoirs of the Life and Writings of Charles O'Conor of Belanagare*, has endeavoured to invest the life and character of this weak monarch with heroic dignity and interest, asserting that "in his adversity his fortitude was not of that ignoble species, which flows from resentment;" but that "his constancy shone forth in all its lustre, without any alloy from temerity, revenge, and despair," p. 28. But Mr. Moore, who has weighed his character without any bias from family pride, has come to the conclusion, that "the only feeling his name awakens is that of pity for the doomed country which at such a crisis of its fortunes, when honour, safety, independence, national existence, were all at stake, was cursed, for the crowning of its evil destiny, with a ruler and leader so utterly unworthy of his high calling."—*History of Ireland*, vol. ii.

laiḃ décc hi ccanánċaiḃ i ccunga iar naiṫriġe toġaiḋe, ⁊ iar mbreiṫ buaḋa ó ḋoman, ⁊ o ḋeaṁan, ⁊ ruccaḋ a ċorp co cluain mic nóir, ⁊ ro haḋnaiceaḋ don taoḃ tuaiḋ daltoir ṫeampaill móir cluana mic nóir.

Mac briain bréifniġ mic toirrḋealḃaiġ uí concoḃair do ṁarḃaḋ la caṫal carrac mac concoḃair maonṁaiġe.

Caṫalan ua maolḟaḃaill tiġearna cairrge braċaiġe do ṁarḃaḋ dua dérain, ⁊ uá dérain feisin do ṁarḃaḋ ina ḋioġail fó ċédóir.

Sluáicceaḋ la Iohn de cuirt hi ttír eóġain ar fud na cceall, ⁊ ro haircceaḋ, ⁊ ro milleaḋ Ardsraṫa, ⁊ raṫboṫ lair, Rainic iaroṁ doire colaim ċille, ⁊ baoi ainnriḋe di oiḋċe for ḟeaċtmain ag milleaḋ insi heoġain ⁊ an tíre arċeana, ⁊ ní raġaḋ ass itir ineallṁa muna toirreaḋ aoḋ ó néll luċt cóicc long co cill * * * i laṫarnaiḃ, ⁊ ro loisc ní don ḃaile, ⁊ ró ṁarḃ oċt ffir ḋécc do ġallaiḃ, Ro ṫionóilset goill maiġi line, ⁊ dail araiḋe tri ċéd do roċtain aoḋa, ⁊ ní ro raṫaiġ aoḋ naċ ní co ro doirtset ina ċeann ag

p. 340. The only remark which the Editor deems necessary to add here on the history of this unfortunate monarch is, that it is stated in the *Historia Familiæ De Burgo*, preserved in the Library of Trinity College, Dublin, that Rickard More, the son of William Fitz Adelm De Burgo, in the battle of Leithridh, near Dublin, deprived him of his arm and kingdom with one stroke of his sword! a fact which, if true, has been concealed by all other writers on Irish history. The descendants of Roderic have been long extinct in Ireland, in the male line; but, if we believe the author of *Vita Kirovani*, and O'Flaherty, the Lynches of Galway descend from him in the female line.—See Account of West Connaught, printed for the Irish Archæological Society, p. 36. According to Duald Mac Firbis, the Lacys of the county of Limerick have sprung from William, the son of Sir Hugh De Lacy, by the daughter of Roderic O'Conor.

[g] *Carrick-Braghy*, carraic braċaiḋe, a territory comprising the north-western part of Inishowen, where the family of O'Maelfabhaill is still in existence; but the name is anglicised Mulfaal, and sometimes, incorrectly, Mac Paul.

[h] *John De Courcy.*—This passage is also given in the Annals of Ulster and of Kilronan, nearly word for word as in the text of the Four Masters, except that they add that some of the English of Moylinny and Dalaradia were dressed in iron mail. It is rendered as follows in the old translation of the Annals of Ulster. The Irish phrases in brackets are from the Dublin copy of the Ulster Annals. "A. D. 1198 [*recte* 1199]. An army, by John de Courcy, into Tirowen among the churches [ar fut na ceall], viz., Ardsraha and Rathboth spoyled by him, untill he came to Dyry, and was there nine nights, spoyling of Inis Owen and the country about, and [*would not have*] went [gone] from thence for a long tyme [⁊ ní raġaḋ ar ffri re fota], untill [unless] with five ships Hugh O'Neale went [had gone] to Killaharna and burnt part of the town, and killed forty wanting two. There were the Galls of Moyline and Dalnaray, three hundred before them in iron plate and without iron, and wist nothing untill they rushed upon

the English, died among the canons at Cong, after exemplary penance, victorious over the world and the devil. His body was conveyed to Clonmacnoise, and interred at the north side of the altar of the great church.

The son of Brian Breifneagh, who was the son of Turlough O'Conor, was slain by Cathal Carragh, the son of Conor Moinmoy.

Cathalan O'Mulfavil, Lord of Carrick-Braghy[g], was slain by O'Dearan, who was himself slain immediately afterwards in revenge of him.

An army was led by John De Courcy[h] into Tyrone, among the churches; and Ardstraw and Raphoe were plundered and destroyed by him. He afterwards went to Derry, where he remained a week and two days, destroying Inishowen and the country generally. And he would not have withdrawn all his forces from thence had not Hugh O'Neill sailed with five ships to Kill[i] * * * in Latharna, burned a part of the town, and killed eighteen of the English. The English of Moylinny[k] and Dalaradia mustered three hundred men, and marched against Hugh, who had no intimation of their approach until they

them, burning the town. Then they fought in the midest of the towne [ar lar in baile] untill the Galls were put to flight, and gave them five overthrows after untill they went to their ships, and killed but five of O'Neal's men. Then went John away [from Dyry] hearing of this."

[i] *Kill * * in Larne*, cill * * * i Laṫarna.—In the Annals of Ulster this name is written cill, with a blank left for the latter part of the name, exactly as in the text of the Four Masters; but in the Annals of Kilronan it is written cill a Laṫarna, i. e. a church in the territory of Latharna; and in the old translation of the Annals of Ulster it is made Killaharna. Latharna is now called Larne, and is the name of a village in the east of the county of Antrim; but it was originally a tuath, cinament, or regiuncula, near Lough Laoigh in Ulster.—See Colgan's *Trias Thaum.*, p. 188, and 5th Index. There can be little doubt that the cill, or church, whose name is here left imperfect by the annalists, is the celebrated church of Cill Ruaḋ, now anglicised Kilroot—but anciently Kilroegh and Kilreugh—which was certainly in this district.—See the Calendar of the O'Clerys, at 16th October. This church, whose patron saint was a Bishop Colman, son of Cathbhadh, is described as situated on the brink of Loch Laoigh in Dalaradia, in Ulster. See also the *Feilire*, or Festilogy of Aengus, at the same day, where this church is described, as for bru locha laiġ i n-Ulltaiḃ, "on the brink of Loch Laigh in Uladh." For the descent of the tribe originally seated in the regiuncula of Latharna, the reader is referred to Duald Mac Firbis's Genealogical work, Marquis of Drogheda's copy, p. 248.

[k] *Moylinny*, Maġ line.—This name is still preserved as that of a townland in the parish of Antrim, in the county of Antrim. But Moylinny, before the present arrangement of the baronies in the county of Antrim, was a territory which extended from Lough Neagh to Carrickfergus.—See note ', p. 23, on *Dal Buinne*. For its boundaries in 1609, see note under the year 1503.

losccaḋ an baile. Ro ḟſraḋ iomaireacc eatorra iaroṁ, ⁊ ro ṁuiḋ for ġallaiḃ, ⁊ tuccaḋ cóicc maḋmanna forra ó ṫá sin co ndeaċsat ina longaiḃ, ⁊ ní ro marḃaḋ do muintir aoḋa aċt coigear namá. Iar cclos na sccél sin do Iohn ro ḟagaiḃ an baile i raiḃe .i. doire colaim cille.

Coccaḋ eitir cenél conaill ⁊ eoġain, ⁊ cenél conaill do coimċſngal la hua neccniġ in acchaiḋ cenél eoġain, ⁊ ro boi coinne ſtorra do naiḋm a ccaradraḋ hi ttermann dábeócc. Tainic trá aoḋ ua néill go ccenél eoġain imme do ṫoirmeascc na coinne, ⁊ ro ionnsaiġ ua héiccniġ, ⁊ ro ṁeaḃaiḋ fair co bfarccaiḃ braiccde lá hua neill.

Do deachaiḋ aoḋ go ccenél eoġain is in ló ċſdna, co ndernsat creiċ for cenél conaill hi maċaire Maiġe híoṫa, ⁊ tucsat bóraiṁe díriṁe iar marḃaḋ leó uí ḋuiḃdiorma for sceiṁleaḋ marcsluaiġ.

Sluaiġeaḋ lá haoḋ ua néll ⁊ lá cenél neoġain doriḋisi go maċaire Maiġe híoṫa do tabairt ċaṫa do cenél cconaill, ⁊ ro ḟágaibsſt cenél cconaill a longport leó, ⁊ do rónaḋ bloḋaḋ siṫe ⁊ cadaċ ſtorra don ċur sin.

Caṫal croibdearg ua concoḃair do denaṁ sióḋa fri caṫal carraċ mac concoḃair maonmaiġe, ⁊ a ṫaḃairt don tír, ⁊ fearann do ṫaḃairt dó.

AOIS CRIOSD, 1199.

Aois Criosd, mile, ced, nochatt, anaoi.

Maolíosa mac giolla eráin, airċindeaċ ċille moire ua nialláin, ⁊ aḋḃar coṁarba Patraic décc.

Sanctus Mauritius ua baottáin décc in hí colaimm ċille.

Do rónsat goill ulaḋ trí slóiġ ṁóra hi tír neoġain, ⁊ an tres slóiġ do rónsat, ro ġaḃsat longport ag doṁnaċ mór maiġe ioṁċláir, ⁊ do ċuirsſt

[l] *O'Hegny*.—He was at this period the Chief of all Fermanagh, the Maguires not having as yet acquired any power over that territory.—See O'Flaherty's *Ogygia*, part iii. c. 76.

[m] *A skirmish*, sceiṁleaḋ marcsluaiġ, a skirmish of cavalry. In the old translation of the Annals of Ulster, it is rendered "Nell O'Duivdirma was killed uppon a skirmish."

[n] *The plain of Moy Itha*.—This, as already observed, was the level part of the barony of Raphoe, now called the Lagan.

[o] *Kilmore-Oneilland*, cill mór ua nialláin.—Now the parish of Kilmore, in the barony of Oneilland, and county of Armagh, about three miles east of the city of Armagh.

[p] *Donaghmore-Moy-Imclare*, Domnaċ mor muiġe imċláir.—Now Donaghmore, a church and parish in the barony of Dungannon, and

poured round him, while he was burning the town. A battle was then fought between them, in which the English were defeated. The English were routed five successive times before they retreated to their ships; and there were only five of Hugh's people slain. As soon as John [De Courcy] had heard of this, he left the place where he was [*determined upon making conquests*], that is, Derry-Columbkille.

A war broke out between the Kinel-Connell and the Kinel-Owen. The Kinel-Connell joined O'Hegny[l] against the Kinel-Owen; and they had a meeting at Termon Daveog, for the purpose of forming a league of amity with him. Hugh O'Neill, however, repaired thither to prevent the meeting, and attacked and defeated O'Hegny, who delivered him hostages.

On the same day Hugh and the Kinel-Owen went to the plain of Magh Ithe, and plundered the Kinel-Connell. From this place they drove off a vast number of cows, after killing O'Duvdirma in a skirmish[m] between the cavalry.

Hugh O'Neill and the Kinel-Owen made a second incursion into the plain of Moy Itha[n], to give battle to the Kinel-Connell; but the Kinel-Connell left their camp to them, upon which terms of peace and friendship were agreed on between the parties.

Cathal Crovderg O'Conor made peace with Cathal Carragh, the son of Conor Moinmoy, brought him into his territory, and gave him lands.

THE AGE OF CHRIST, 1199.

The Age of Christ, one thousand one hundred ninety-nine.

Maelisa, son of Gilla-Ernain, Erenagh of Kilmore-Oneilland[o], and intended successor of St. Patrick, died.

Sanctus Mauritius O'Baedain died in Hy-Columbkille.

The English of Ulidia made three great incursions into Tyrone, and on the third incursion they pitched their camp at Donaghmore-Moy-Imclare[p], and sent

three miles west of the town of Dungannon. This church was founded by St. Patrick, who placed there a St. Columba, called in Irish Colum Ruis Glanda. The place where this church stands was called Ros Glanda, from a well named Glan, before St. Patrick's time, as we learn from the Festilogy of Aengus, at the 6th September: Roſſ ᵹlanda ainm in baile ppiuſ .i. ᵹlan ainm na tibpad pil ann, 7 domnach mop ainm indiu; "Ross Glanda *was* the name of the place

drong mór dia muintir do ṁilleaḋ ⁊ do ċreachaḋ an tíre. Tainic dna aoḋ ó néill ind oirsr an tslóiġ comá comṗainic dó, ⁊ do na gallaiḃ, ⁊ ro la a nár, ⁊ an do srna uaḋa ro élaiḋset san aiḋċe gan naċ tairsreaṁ co ndeaċatar tar tuaim.

Sluaicceaḋ la Ruaiḋri ua nduinnsleḃe co ní do ġallaiḃ miḋe, ⁊ ro airccset mainistir Phóil, ⁊ Peattair co nár ḟáccaiḃset innte aċt aon ḃó.

Doṁnall ua doċartaiġ tiġearna cenél nénda ⁊ árda mioḋair décc.

Donnchaḋ uaiṫneaċ mac Ruaiḋri ui Conċoḃair do ṁarḃaḋ la Saxaiḃ luimniġ.

Roḋuḃ mac roéḋig toiseċ cenél aongusa do ṁarḃaḋ lá gallaiḃ ar creċ in ua nearca ċéin.

Caṫal croiḃdearg ua conċoḃair do ionnarbaḋ a riġe Connaċt, ⁊ caṫal carraċ do ġabáil a ionaiḋ.

Sluaiċċeaḋ lá haoḋ ua néill i fóiriṫin caṫail croiḃdeirg go bfsraiḃ maiġe híoṫa, ⁊ co nairġiallaiḃ gu rangattar tsġ baoiṫin airtiġ. Soirset iaroṁ go

(*baile*) first, i. e. from Glan, the name of the well which is there; and Domnach mor is its name at this day." See also the Irish Calendar of the O'Clerys at the same day, where it is added that Domhnach mor Moighe Iomchlair is in Tir Eoghain, now Tyrone. Magh Imchlair was the ancient name of the plain in which the church of Donaghmore stands. It is explained by Colgan as follows: "*Imchlair*, quæ et aliquando *Maghclair*, .i. campus planus, sive planities legitur vocata; est ager regionis Tironiæ, non procul a *Dungenainn*, et in ecclesia eiusdem regionis *Domnach mor* dicta colitur S. Columba Præbyter 6. Septemb."—*Trias Thaum.*, p. 184, c. 1.

[q] *Toome.*—This passage is given as follows in the Dublin copy of the Annals of Ulster: A. D. 1200. Do ronsat gaill ulaḋ tri crecha i tir neogain, 7 in tris crech do ronsat do gabsat longport ic domnach mor muiġi imclair, do cuirset crech mor imach. Tainig aeḋ ua neill in aircis na creiċe co ro comrac do 7 na gaill 7 co ro maiḋ ar ġallaiḃ, 7 co tarait ar diarmiḋe forro, 7 ro eladur san aiḋċe co ndeċadar tar Tuaim. It is rendered as follows in the old translation: "A. D. 1199" [*recte* 1200]. "The Galls of Vlster this yeare prayed" [preyed] "thrice in Tyrowen, and the third tyme they camped at Donnaghmore, and sent forth a great army. Hugh O Neale came to prevent them, and fought with the Galls and broke of them, and slaughtered a great number of them, and they stole away by night, untill they went beyond Toame."

[r] *O'Donslevy*, ua duinnsleiḃe; more correctly mac Duinnsleḃe, in the Dublin copy of the Annals of Ulster. It is thus rendered in the old translation: "A. D. 1199. An army by Rory Mac Dunleve to" [with] "some of the Galls of Meath, and spoyled the Abbey of Paul and Peter, so as they left but one cowe."

[s] *Kinel-Enda and Ard-Mire.* — Kinel-Enda was the ancient name of the district situated between the Rivers Foyle and Swilly, in the county of Donegal.—See p. 19, note [d]. Ardmire, or Ard Miodhair, was the name of a ter-

forth a large body of their troops to destroy and plunder the country. Hugh O'Neill set out to oppose this host; and they came to an engagement, in which the English were slaughtered, and such as escaped from him fled secretly by night, tarrying nowhere until they had passed Toome[q].

Rory O'Donslevy[r], and some of the English of Meath, mustered a body of troops, and plundered the Monastery of SS. Peter and Paul (at Armagh), and left only one cow there.

Donnell O'Doherty, Lord of Kinel-Enda and Ard-Mire[s], died.

Donough Uaithneach, the son of Roderick O'Conor, was slain by the English of Limerick.

Roduv Mac Roedig, Chief of Kinel-Aengusa, was slain by the English, on a predatory incursion, in Hy-Earca-Cein[t].

Cathal Crovderg O'Conor was banished from the kingdom of Connaught; and Cathal Carrach assumed his place.

Hugh O'Neill, with the men of Moy-Itha and the men of Oriel, marched to Tibohine-Artagh[u], to relieve Cathal Crovderg O'Conor. They returned again,

ritory lying westwards of Kinel-Enda, in the direction of Lough Finn. It is to be distinguished from Ceann Maghair, near Fanaid. The O'Dohertys were afterwards settled in the territory, now the barony of Inishowen, which had been previously possessed by families of the Kinel-Owen race, who were all tributary either to Mac Loughlin, or O'Neill; but after the settlement of the O'Dohertys, who were of the Kinel-Connell race, the inhabitants of Inishowen generally paid tribute to O'Donnell.

[t] *Hy-Earca-Cein.*—This was the ancient name of a tribe situated in a valley in the present barony and county of Antrim.—See Colgan's *Trias Thaum.*, p. 183, col. 2, note 221.

The Kinel-Aengusa were a tribe of the Clanna Rury, in the same neighbourhood. They descend, according to Duald Mac Firbis, from Aengus, the second son of Maelcobha, and the Chiefs of Leath Cathail, now the barony of Lecale, in the county of Down, were of them.—See his Genealogical Book (Lord Roden's copy), p. 568: Da mac Maoilcoḃa .i. blaṫmac, a quo ríoġraiḋ ulaḋ, ⁊ aongus, a quo cinel n-aongusa: as diḃ ríoġraiḋ leiṫe caṫail.

[u] *Tibohine-Artagh*, Teaċ ḃaoiṫin airtiġ, i. e. the house, or church of St. Baoithin, of the territory of Airteach. It is now the name of a parish church in the diocese of Elphin.—See the *Feilire Aenguis* at 19th of February, where this church is described as lying to the west of Croghan, in Connaught: "fri cruachain Connacht aniar;" and the Irish Calendar of the O'Clerys at the same day, where the saint is called "Bishop Baoithin, the son of Cuanach, of Airteach."—See also Colgan's *Trias Thaum.*, p. 370, col. 1, notes 17, 18, 19; and *Acta Sanctorum*, pp. 369, 370; also Erck's Ecclesiastical Register; Beaufort's Ecclesiastical Map of Ireland; and Archdall's Monasticon (at Tibohin). The parish called after this church is still sometimes locally called Airteach; but the territory

ranngadar earrdara, ⁊ rucc orra cathal carrach co maithibh connacht, ⁊ uilliam burc go ngallaibh luimnigh maille friu. Feachar iomaireacc eatorra, ⁊ ro raoineadh for thuaisceirt Ereann, ⁊ ro fágbhadh ann ua heccnigh tighearna oirghiall, ⁊ sochaidhe cenmothá soin.

Sluaigheadh lá Iohn do Cuirt co ngallaibh uladh, ⁊ lá mac hugo de laci co ngallaibh midhe hi poiritin chathail croibhdeirg go rangadar cill mic duach. Tainicc iarom cathal carrach co cconnachtaibh imaille friu, ⁊ ro chathaighsit fri aroile. Sraointear for gallaibh uladh ⁊ midhe airm hi rabattar cúicc catha, ni théarna acht dá chath díbh, ⁊ ro leanadh iad alláthair an chatha go rinn dúin for loch ribh, ⁊ ro gabhadh iomchumang for Iohn ainnridhe, ⁊ ro marbhadh drong mór do ghallaibh, ⁊ ro báidhidh araill díobh ar ní fuarattar conair theichidh acht a ndeachaidh i neathraibh tar loch soir uatha.

Ruarc ua Maoilbrénainn toisech cloinne conchobhair do écc.

Ri Saxan Iohn do righadh os Saxain .6. April.

Murchadh mac cochláin tighearna dealbhna sethra do écc.

of Airteach was more extensive than the present parish of Tibohine.—See note under the year 1197. There is another parish church called Teagh Baoithin, in the barony of Raphoe, but the name is now anglicised *Taughboyne*, though always pronounced Tiboyne by the Scotch settlers, and Tibweeheen by those who speak the Irish language. This is called after St. Baoithin, or Baithenus, son of Brendan, son of Fergus, the relative and companion of St. Columbkille, and his immediate successor in the abbacy of Iona.

[w] *Kilmacduagh*, Cill mic Duach, i. e. the church of Mac Duach, an ancient cathedral church in the barony of Kiltartan, and county of Galway. This church was erected by Guaire Aidhne, King of Connaught, about the year 610, for his kinsman, Colman Mac Duach, who is the patron saint of the Hy-Fiachrach Aidhne, a tribe who possessed the entire of the present diocese of Kilmacduagh before the English invasion.—See Colgan, *Acta Sanctorum*, p. 245; and *Tribes and Customs of Hy-Many*, printed for the Irish Archæological Society in 1842, p. 71, note [b], and map to the same work.

[x] *Rindown*, Rinn dúin, i. e. the point or peninsula of the *dun*, or earthen fort. This peninsula extends into Lough Ree, in the parish of St. John's, barony of Athlone, and county of Roscommon, and is about eight miles to the north of the town of Athlone.—See Ordnance Map of the county of Roscommon, sheet 46. This peninsula contains the ruins of a castle of great size and strength, and of a military wall, with gates and towers, of considerable extent and magnificence, measuring five hundred and sixty-four yards in length, and dividing the *Rinn*, or point, from the main land by extending from water to water. It is stated in the Irish Annals that the Danish tyrant, Turgesius, built a fortress on Lough Ree, and it has been conjectured that by him was erected the *dun*, or fort, from which this point of land was denominated Rinn dúin.—See a very curious description of this place, by Mr. Petrie, in the Irish

however, and on coming to Easdara (Ballysadare), were overtaken by Cathal Carragh, with the chiefs of Connaught, and William Burke, with the English of Limerick: a battle was fought between them, in which the *forces of* the north of Ireland were defeated; and O'Hegny, Lord of Oriel, and many others beside him, were slain.

John de Courcy, with the English of Ulidia, and the son of Hugo De Lacy, with the English of Meath, marched to Kilmacduagh[w] to assist Cathal Crovderg O'Conor. Cathal Carragh, accompanied by the Connacians, came, and gave them battle: and the English of Ulidia and Meath were defeated *with such slaughter that*, of their five battalions, only two survived; and these were pursued from the field of battle to Rindown[x] on Lough Ree, in which place John was completely hemmed in. Many of his English were killed, and others were drowned; for they found no passage by which to escape, except by crossing the lake in boats.

Rourke O'Mulrenin, Chief of Clann-Conor[y], died.

John was crowned King of England on the sixth of April.

Murrough Mac Coghlan, Lord of Delvin Eathra, died[z].

Penny Journal, No. 10, pp. 73, 74, 75.

[y] *Clann-Conor.*—See note under year the 1193.

[z] The Annals of Kilronan and of Clonmacnoise enter these transactions under the year 1200; and the former contain a much fuller and more detailed account of the battles between the two rivals of the house of O'Conor in this and the two succeeding years. The Annals of Clonmacnoise add, that soon after this slaughter of the English at Lough Ree, Cathal Carragh was treacherously taken prisoner by Hugh De Lacy, who confined him in the Castle of Nobber (an Obaıṗ), there to be kept until he should give them their pay. The whole passage is thus translated by Connell Mageoghegan: "A. D. 1200. Cahall Crovedearg O'Connor, accompanied with the forces of John De Coursey and Hugh Delacie, passed through Connought, untill they came to Tyrefiaghragh Aynie, where they were mett by Cahall Carragh O'Connor, with all his Irish and English forces, and were overthrown and pursued to Royndown (now called Teagh Eoyn, or John's house, neer Loghrie). John Coursey was driven to take boate when he came to that place, and his people knew not where to betake themselves for their safety, but only by sailing into the islands of Loghrie, where an infinite number of them were slain and drowned. Soone after Cahall Carragh was taken deceiptfully by the English of Meath, and by Hugh Delacy the younger, and was conveighed to the Castle of the Obber, there to be safely kept, untill he had given them their pay, which he was content to give in part, and for the rest to give security, by which means he was sett at Liberty, and immediately went to Munster to Macarthie and William Burke. And for John Coursey, after slaying of his people, [he] returned to Ulster again."

AOIS CRIOSD, 1200.

Aois Criosd, míle, dá ċéd.

Caḋhla ua duḃṫaiġ airdepscop tuama decc iar sſndataiḋ.

Uairéirġe mac maoilmórḋa mic uairéirġe uí neaċtain uasal sruiṫ do sruiṫiḃ cluana mic nóis, fſr lán do ḋeserc, ⁊ dá gaċ sóalċiḋ arċſna, ⁊ ceann cele ndé cluana décc an deaċmaḋ lá do ṁarta.

Maoleóin ua carmacáin coṁarba commáin décc.

Aoḋ ua néill do aiṫriġaḋ lá cenél neóġain, ⁊ conċoḃar ua loċlainn do riġaḋ ina ionaḋ, ⁊ do rónaḋ creaċ lais hi ttir nenda, Ro ṁarḃ daoine, ⁊ rucc buar iomdha.

Do ḋeachaiḋ tra Eccneaċán ua doṁnaill tiġſrna cenél conaill co loingſs cenél conaill ar muir lais, ⁊ cona slóġ ar tír, ⁊ ro ġaḃsat longport ag gaoṫ an ċairrgín, tangattar clann diarmada don leiṫ oile go Port Rois do

Under this year the Annals of Kilronan state that Gormgal O'Quin, *Dux*, or Captain of Muintir Gillagan, was taken prisoner by the English, who plundered his people, and reduced them to great distress for want of food and raiment. They also record the erection of the Castle of Granard under this year, but without giving the name of the builder. The Dublin copy of the Annals of Innisfallen state that it was built by Richard Tuite, as a stronghold against O'Reilly in south Breifny; and this appears to be correct: for Granard is very close to the ancient *dunchladh*, boundary wall, or ditch, between Breifny and Annally, extending from Lough Gawna to Lough Kinclare.

Under this year also the Annals of Ulster and of Kilronan record the death of Rowland Mac Uchtry, King of the Gall-Gaels in Scotland.

[a] *Kyley O'Duffy*, caḋhla ua duḃṫaiġ.—This is the prelate called *Catholicus Tuomenensis* by Giraldus Cambrensis, in his *Hibernia Expugnata*, lib. i. c. 34. He succeeded Edan O'Hoisin in the year 1161. In the year 1175 he was sent to England, together with Laurence O'Toole, Archbishop of Dublin, and Concors, Abbot of St. Brendan's, by King Roderic O'Conor, to negotiate with King Henry II.; and they waited on the King at Windsor, where a grand council was held, and a convention ratified, by which Henry granted to his liegeman Roderic, that as long as he continued to serve him faithfully he should be a king under him ready to do him service as his vassal, and that he should hold his hereditary territories as firmly and peaceably as he had held them before the coming of Henry into Ireland. Roderic was likewise to have under his dominion and jurisdiction all the rest of the island, and the inhabitants, kings and princes included, and was bound to oblige them to pay tribute through his hands to the King of England, &c.—See this treaty in Rymer's *Fœdera*, vol. i.; and also as given in the original Latin in Cox's *Hibernia Anglicana*, p. 29; and an abstract of it in Leland's History of Ireland, vol. i. p. 104; and in Moore's History of Ireland, vol. ii. p. 287.

THE AGE OF CHRIST, 1200.

The Age of Christ, one thousand two hundred.

Kyley [Catholicus] O'Duffy[a], Archbishop of Tuam, died at an advanced age.

Uaireirghe, son of Mulmora, the son of Uaireirghe O'Naghtan, one of the noble sages of Clonmacnoise, a man full of the love of God, and of every virtue, and head of the Culdees of Clonmacnoise, died on the tenth of March.

Malone O'Carmacan, Successor of St. Coman[b], died.

Hugh O'Neill was deposed by the Kinel-Owen, and Conor O'Loughlin was elected in his stead. The latter plundered Tir-Enda, killed many persons, and drove off many cows.

Egneghan O'Donnell, Lord of Tirconnell, sailed with the fleet of Tirconnell [thirteen vessels] by sea, and despatched his army by land, and pitched his camp at Gaeth-an-Chairrgin[c]. The Clandermot repaired to Port-Rois[d] on the

[a] In the year 1179, Cadhla, or Catholicus O'Duffy, attended the second Council of Lateran, together with Laurence O'Toole, Archbishop of Dublin; Constantine, Bishop of Killaloe; Brictius, Bishop of Limerick; Augustin, Bishop of Waterford; and Felix, Bishop of Lismore: but on their passage through England, they were obliged to take an oath that they would not say or do anything at the council prejudicial to King Henry or his kingdom.—See note under the year 1180, p. 51. According to the Dublin copy of the Annals of Innisfallen, he died in the Abbey of Cong, in the year 1201.

[b] *Successor of St. Coman*, i. e. abbot of Roscommon.

[c] *Gaeth-an-Chairrgin*, i. e. the inlet of Carrigin.—Carrigin is a village three miles to the south of the city of Londonderry, on the west side of the River Foyle. The word ȝaeṫ, or ȝaoṫ, enters into the names of three other places in the county of Donegal, as Ȝaoṫ Ɗóꞃ (Gweedore), Ȝaoṫ ḃeaꞃa (Gweebarra), Ȝaoṫ Ꞁuaċꞃoıꞅ (Loughros Bay), all on the western coast.

[d] *Port-Rois*, i. e. the port or harbour of Ross.—This is not the Portrush in the parish of Ballywillin, in the county of Antrim, but Rosses Bay, a short distance to the north of Derry. This story is very confused in the original. It should be told thus: "Egneghan O'Donnell, Lord of Tirconnell, despatched the ships of Tirconnell, thirteen in number, by sea, ordering their commanders to meet him at Gaeth-an-Chairrgin. He then marched the remainder of his forces by land, and pitched his camp at Gaeth-an-Chairrgin. As soon as the Clann-Dermot, his opponents, had heard of this division of his forces, they marched to Port-Rois (Rosses Bay), to intercept the passage of the ships, and prevent them from joining the land forces; but the crews of the thirteen ships attacked and defeated them. This shews how unequal they were to compete with the combined forces of O'Donnell.

gabail fris an loingsir. Od ċonncadar foirne na ttrí long ndécc baoi an coblaċ indsin, Ro léccsit foċaib iatt gor raoiṁeaḋ for cloinn nDiarmada. Ticc macc Laċloinn (.i. Concoḃar becc mac Muirċertaiġ), ina ḃfóiriṫin, ⁊ ro gonaḋ a eaċ foo, ⁊ ro trasccraḋ somh di, torcair iaroṁ lá Cenél cConaill in eneaċ Colaim Ċille, a ċoṁarba, ⁊ a scrini ro diṁiġneaḋ fecṫ riaṁ. As triaran dímiaḋ céona ro marḃadh Murċaḋ ua Cricáin tiġearna ua Fiaċ-rach. Leanait muinter Écneaċáin an maiḋm iarttain gur ro ċuirseat ár ar Eoġanchaiḃ ⁊ ar cloinn nDiarmada.

Sluaicceaḋ lá Meilir ⁊ lá Gallaiḃ Laiġen go Cluain mic Nóis i cCoinne Caṫail Ċarraiġ. Ro ḃatar dí oiḋċe i cCluain, ⁊ airccṫir leó an baile eitir croḋ ⁊ biaḋ, ⁊ do ċóiḋreaḋ ro a ṫeimplaiḃ.

Caṫal Croiḃḋearg do dol is in Muṁain do ṡaiġiḋ mic Mec Carṫaiġ ⁊ Uilliam Burc.

Germaide ua Baoigellán do ṁarḃaḋ la hua nDoṁnaill .i. la hÉcc-neaċán.

Iomaireacc eidir ua nDoṁnaill ⁊ ua Ruairc, Ualgarcc, ⁊ Conċoḃar na glaisḟéne ua Ruairc. Ro ṁaiḋ for uiḃ Briúin, ⁊ ro cuireaḋ dersgár a muintire eidir ḃáḋaḋ, ⁊ ṁarḃaḋ, ⁊ ro báiṫeaḋ Concoḃar fein don ċur sin, occ Leic Uí Ṁaoildoraiḋ do ṡonnradh ro fighsedh an iomargoil sin.

[e] *Murrough O'Creaghan*, Murċaḋ na Crioċán.—This name would be now anglicised Morgan Creighan, or Cregan.

[f] *Hy-Fiachrach*, i. e. Hy-Fiachrach of Ardstraw.—See note under the year 1193.

[g] *The Clann-Dermot*, Clann Diarmada.—These were a tribe of the Kinel-Owen, who inhabited and gave name to the present parish of Clondermot (anciently Clandermot), on the east side of the River Foyle, in the barony of Tirkeerin, and county of Londonderry.

[h] *Meyler*, i. e. Meyler Fitz-Henry, natural son of King Henry I., by Nesta, the mother of Maurice Fitzgerald. He was made Lord Justice of Ireland in the year 1199.—See Harris's Ware, vol. ii. p. 102; and Cox's *Hibernia Anglicana*, p. 46. His personal form and character are described as follows by his cotemporary, Giraldus Cambrensis: "Meylerivs vero vir fuscus, oculis nigris, & toruis, vultuque acerrimo. Staturæ paulo mediocri plus pusillæ. Corpore tamen pro quantitatis captu perualido. Pectore quadrato, ventreq; substricto, brachiis ceterisq; membris ossosis, plus neruositatis habentibus, quam carnositatis. Miles animosus & æmulus. Nihil vnquam abhorrens, quod aggredi quis vel solus debeat vel comitatus. Primus in prælium ire: vltimus conserto prœlio redire consuetus: in omni conflictu omnis strenuitatis opera seu perire paratus, seu præire: adeo impatiens & præceps: vt vel vota statim, vel fata complere dignum ducat. Inter mortis & Martis triumphos, nil medium ponens: adeo laudis cupidus & gloriæ, quod si viuendo forte non valeat: vincere velit vel moriendo. Vir itaq; fuisset cumulata laude dignus vterque, si ambitione posthabita,

other side, to attack the fleet: when the crews of the thirteen vessels perceived their intentions, they attacked and defeated the Clann-Dermot. Mac Loughlin (Conor Beg, son of Murtough) came to their assistance; but his horse was wounded under him, and he himself was dismounted. He was afterwards slain by the Kinel-Connell, in revenge of Columbkille, his coarb and shrine, that he had violated some time before. And it was for the same violation that Murrough O'Creaghan[e], Lord of Hy-Fiachrach[f], was killed. Egneghan's troops followed up the route, and slaughtered the Kinel-Owen and the Clann-Dermot[g].

Meyler[h], and the English of Leinster, marched to Clonmacnoise against Cathal Carragh (O'Conor), where they remained two nights: they plundered the town of its cattle and provisions, and attacked its churches.

Cathal Crovderg O'Conor went into Munster, to the son of Mac Carthy and William Burke [to solicit their aid].

Gerrmaide O'Boylan[i] was slain by O'Donnell (Egneghan).

A battle was fought between O'Donnell [on the one side], and O'Rourke (Ualgarg) and Conor na-Glaisfene O'Rourke [on the other]. The Hy-Briuin (O'Rourkes) were defeated, and their men dreadfully cut off, both by drowning and killing. Conor himself was drowned on this occasion. This battle was fought at Leckymuldory[k].

Christi Ecclesiam debita deuotione venerantes, antiqua & autentica eiusdem iura non tantum illibata conseruassent: Quinimo tam nouæ, tamque cruentæ conquisitionis (plurima quippe sanguinis effusione, Christianæq; gentis interemptione fœdatæ) partem placabilem Deoq; placentem, laudabili largitione contulissent. Verumtamen quod mage stupendum est, amplioriq; dolore dolendum: postremum hoc vitium toti fere militiæ nostræ à primo adventu, vsque in hodiernum constat commune fuisse."—*Hibernia Expugnata*, lib. ii. c. x. This Meyler was the founder of the abbey of Great Connell, in the county of Kildare, in which he was buried in the year 1220.—See Archdall's *Monasticon*, at Great Connell, county of Kildare, where there are some curious notices of this "Tameless tamer of the Irish all."

[i] *O'Boylan*, ua baoıġeallάın.—The O'Boylans were chiefs of the territory of Dartry-Coininsi, now the barony of Dartry, in the county of Monaghan. O'Dugan calls them the blue-eyed, white-handed, red-lipped host, the griffins of splendid horses, and the bold kings of Dartry.

[k] *Leckymuldory*, leac uı ṁaoılḋopaıḋ, i. e. O'Muldory's flag-stone, or flat surfaced rock. The Editor, after a minute examination of the topographical names in O'Muldory's country, has come to the conclusion that this is the remarkable flat surfaced rock called the leac, under the cataract at Bellice, now Belleek, on the River Erne, about two miles to the east of Ballyshannon.—See it described in the notes under the years 1409, 1522. Hy-Briuin, or Hy-Briuin Breifne, was the tribe name of the O'Rourkes and their correlatives.

Donnchaḋ uaitneach mac Ruaiḋri uí Concoḃair do ṁarḃaḋ la gallaiḃ luimniġ.

Mathġaṁain mac giollapatraicc uí chiarrda do ṁarḃaḋ la gallaiḃ cluana ioraird.

Cluain ioraird do loscaḋ dua ciarḋa do ḟoġail for na gallaiḃ batar innte.

Creach la caṫal croibdearg i Muṁain gur ro loisg caislén uí ċonaing, ⁊ margaḋ luimniġ, ⁊ caislen uilcín, ⁊ tuc uilcín cona ṁnaoi illaiṁ lais iar marḃaḋ di ridere ḋécc, ⁊ iolar daoine cenmóthát.

Fiaċra ua flainn taoiseaċ ṡil Mhaoilruain do écc.

Cathal carraċ do ġabáil Riġe connaċt, ⁊ caṫal croibdearg do ionnarbaḋ do i nultaiḃ go rainig co teaġ ui Eigniġ tiġearna fearmanaċ, ⁊ airide do ḟaiġiḋ Iohn do cuirt gur ro naiḋm a cura friss.

AOIS CRIOSD, 1201.

Aois Criosd, mile, da chéd, a haon.

Tomaltach ua concoḃair coṁorba Pattraicc, ⁊ Príoṁaiḋ na hEreann décc.

Conn ua meallaiġ espcop eanaiġ dúin, gém gloiniḋe ecclastacḋa décc.

Iohannes de monte celion cardinál coṁorba peadair do ṫoċt ó Roiṁ co hérinn. Senaḋ mór do ṫeaglamaḋ ina ḋáil co háṫ cliaṫ eidir espcopaiḃ,

[l] *To injure the English*, dfoġail for na gallaiḃ, i. e., not for the sake of destroying the monastery, but to take revenge of the English; or rather, he ran the risk of committing sacrilege to wreak his vengeance on the English.

[m] *Besides them*, cenmótát.—This phrase is very generally used throughout these Annals, though it has little or no meaning, and might be left untranslated throughout.

[n] *Banished into Ulster.*—This is a repetition, for it is mentioned under the last year.

[o] Under this year the Dublin copy of the Annals of Innisfallen contain the following notice of the affairs of Munster, of which the Four Masters have collected no account: "A. D. 1200. A great army was mustered by William De Burgo, and all the English of Munster, joined by Murtough Finn, Conor Roe, and Donough Cairbreach, the three sons of Donnell More O'Brien; and they marched through Munster to Cork. They encamped for a week at Kinneigh, where Auliffe More O'Donovan, King of Cairbre Aodha, and Mac Costello were slain. Then came Mahon O'Heney, the Pope's Legate, and the bishops of Munster, and made peace between the O'Briens [on the one side] and the

Donough Uaithneach, the son of Roderic O'Conor, was slain by the English of Limerick.

Mahon, the son of Gilla Patrick-O'Keary, was slain by the English of Clonard.

Clonard was burned by O'Keary, to injure the English[l] who were in it.

Cathal Crovderg O'Conor made a predatory incursion into Munster, and plundered Castleconning [Castleconnel], the market of Limerick, and Castle-Wilkin; and led Wilkin and his wife away captives, after having killed thirteen knights, and many other persons besides them[m].

Fiachra O'Flynn, Chief of Sil-Mailruana, died.

Cathal Carragh assumed the government of Connaught, and Cathal Crovderg was banished by him into Ulster[n]. He arrived at the house of O'Hegny, Lord of Fermanagh, and went from thence to John de Courcy, with whom he formed a league of amity[o].

THE AGE OF CHRIST, 1201.

The Age of Christ, one thousand two hundred one.

Tomaltagh O'Conor, successor of St. Patrick, and Primate of Ireland, died.

Conn O'Melly, Bishop of Annaghdown, a transparently bright gem of the Church, died.

Johannes de Monte Celion, the Pope's Legate, came to Ireland, and convoked a great synod of the bishops, abbots, and every other order in the Church,

Mac Carthys, O'Donohoes, and the rest of the Eugenians" [on the other].

In a marginal note is the following observation in Latin: "O'Donovan, Rex Carbriæ Aodha; nam ab anno 1178 relagatus erat O'Donovan ex ditione sua de Cairbre Aodhbha in regione Limiricensi in occidentalem partem regionis Corcagiensis. Vid. supra ad istum annum." The substance of this passage is thus given by Dr. O'Brien, in his History of the House of O'Brien, published by Vallancey, in the first volume of his *Collectanea de Rebus Hibernicis*, under the title of Law of Tanistry. "A. D. 1200. He [Mortogh Fionn O'Brien] marched at the head of the Dal-Cassians, his brothers, Connor Ruadh and Donough Cairbreach, serving as officers under him, against the Eugenians, whom he greatly harassed, and slew Auliff O'Donovan, chief of that family, with many others of the Eugenian nobility. After which a peace was concluded between him and Donall Mor Mac Carthy, surnamed na Curadh, King of Desmond, by the mediation of Mahon O'Heney, Archbishop of Cashel, who was the Pope's Legate in Ireland at that time."—See note under the year 1254.

⁊ abbadaiḃ, ⁊ gaċ grad eccailsi, ⁊ sochaide do saorclandaiḃ Ereann imaille friú. Ro ordaigsiot iaroṁ a ccaingne uile iar na ccóir eittir ecclais ⁊ tuaiṫ.

Senad connaċt (immon cairdinal céona) laochaiḃ, cléirchiḃ occ aṫ luain hi cind coicṫidhisi iaroṁ, ⁊ ro cindsiot a ccaingne feḃ roba teċta.

Niall ua floinn do ṁarḃad lá gallaiḃ ulad i meaḃail.

Maghnus mac diarmada uí laċlainn do ṁarḃad lá muirċeartaċ ua néll, ⁊ muirċeartaċ do ṁarḃad ina ċionaid.

Conċoḃar mac muirghesa uí eidin décc.

Tadhg ua braoin tigearna luighne mide décc.

Muireadaċ mac neill mic an trionnaigh ui caṫarnaigh décc.

Murchad ua Madadáin leṫ toiseċ sil nanmċada do ghuin ina ċenn do ṡoighit ⁊ a écc treṁit.

Sluaighead lá caṫal croiḃdearg, ⁊ la huilliam búrc cona soċraide gall ⁊ gaoideal hi cconnaċtaiḃ o ṫa luimneaċ go tuaim dá ualann, aissiде go

[p] *Lune*, luighne.—This was a territory of considerable extent in ancient Meath; and its name is still preserved as that of a barony, anglicised Lune, and now corruptly pronounced in Irish luiḃne; but the ancient territory of Luighne was much more extensive than the modern barony, for we learn, from the Tripartite Life of St. Patrick, that Domhnach mor Muighe Echnach, now Donaghmore, near Navan, was situated in it.

[q] *Forces.*—The account of the death of Cathal Carragh, and of the actions of William Fitz-Adelm De Burgo, is given as follows in the Annals of Clonmacnoise, as translated by Macgeoghegan: "A. D. 1201. Cahall Crovedearg and William Burk, with all their forces of English and Irishmen, came to Connaught, pass'd from Limbrick to Twayme, from thence to Owran, from thence to Alfyn, from thence to the Carrick of Loghke, from thence to the Abbey of Athdalaragh, where the chambers and roomes of that abbey were the lodgings of the armie. Cahall mac Connor O'Dermott went to prey the lands of Mac Dermott" [*recte* Hy-Diarmada], "and was slain by Teige mac Connor Moenmoye there; also Cahall Carragh O'Connor, King of Connaught, came in view of the said forces to a place called Gurthin Cowle Lwachra, and from thence he went to the skirmish between his forces and them, who finding his people discomfited, and put to flight, was killed himself, by the miracles of St. Quæran, together with Kollye mac Dermott O'Moylerwayne, and many others.

"Cathal Crovdearge and William Burk, after committing these great slaughters, went with their forces to Moynoye and Moylorge, over Donleoy into Moynemoye, from thence to West Connought, until they came to Cowynge of St. Ffehine, where they kept their Easter. At that time William Burke, and the sonne of O'Flathvertye, privily consulted and conspired together to kill Cahall Crovederge O'Connor, which God prevented, for they were by great oaths sworn to each other before, which whosoever wou'd breake was to be excommunicated with booke, bell, and candle.

"William Burk sent his forces to distrain for

at Dublin, at which also many of the nobles of Ireland were present. By this synod many proper ordinances, for the regulation of the Church and the State, were enacted.

A fortnight afterwards the same Legate called a meeting of the clergy and laity of Connaught at Athlone, at which meeting many excellent ordinances were established.

Niall O'Flynn [O'Lynn] was treacherously slain by the English of Ulidia.

Manus, the son of Dermot O'Loughlin, was slain by Murtough O'Neill; and Murtough was killed in revenge of him.

Conor, the son of Maurice O'Heyne, died.

Teige O'Breen, Lord of Lune[p], in Meath, died.

Murray, son of Niall, who was son of the Sinnagh (the Fox) O'Caharny, died.

Murrough O'Madden, Chief of half Sil-Anmchadh, was wounded in the head by an arrow, and died of the wound.

Cathal Crovderg and William Burke, at the head of their English and Irish forces[q], marched from Limerick, through Connaught, to Tuam, and proceeded

his pays and wages throughout Connought, who were soone cut off, for six or seven hundred of them were soone after slain. William Burk afterwards repaired to Limbrick, and Cahall Crovederge tooke upon him the name of King of Connought again."

The Annals of Kilronan, which may be considered the chronicle of the district, contain a much fuller account of the battles between these two rivals of the house of O'Conor. The account of the profanation of the abbey of Boyle, and of the death of Cathal Carragh, is given as follows, under the year 1202: "A great army was led into Connaught by Cathal Crovderg, joined by William Burke, the sons of Donnell O'Brien, viz., Murtough and Conor Roe, and by Fineen Mac Carthy. They marched to the monastery of Ath-dalarac, on the *River* Boyle, and took up their quarters in it; and they remained there for three days, during which time they profaned and defiled the whole monastery; and such was the extent of the profanation that the archers of the army had women in the hospital of the monks, in the houses of the cloister, and in every apartment throughout the whole monastery; and they left nothing in the monastery without breaking or burning, except the roofs of the houses only, and even of these they broke and burned many. They left no part of the monastery to the monks excepting only the dormitory and the house of the novices. On this occasion William Burke commenced the erection of a cashel [or circular wall] around the great house of the guests, on which he bestowed two days' work. On the third day after the commencement of this wall, Cathal Carragh, King of Connaught, was killed by the English, as were also Dermot, son of Gilchreest, son of Dermot, who was son of Teige O'Mulrony, and Tomaltagh, son of Taichleach O'Dowda, and many others. They then departed from the monastery, after which William Burk dismissed

huarán go hoilfinn go carraic loċa cé, go mainistir aṫa da loarg, ⁊ arιad tiġe na mainistre robtar boṫa longpuirt dóiḃ. Do ċóiḋ din caṫal mac diarmada for creċ in uiḃ diarmada.

Rucc tadg mac concoḃair maonmaiġe fair. Ro fiġeaḋ eargal eatorra, ⁊ torċair caṫal.

Dala caṫail carraiġ riġ connacht tionolaiḋ side a soċraide, ⁊ tainic do ṡoiġiḋ an tslóiġ go riacht guirtin cúil luaċra hi ccomḟoċraiḃ don ṁainistir. Batar samlaiḋ ucht ré hucht co cenn seċtṁaine, ⁊ deabaiḋ gaċ laoi etorra. Hi foirċenn na ree hisin do deachaiḋ caṫal carraċ do déccsin na deaḃṫa. Sraintear sruṫṁaiḋm dia ṁuintir ina ċenn, ⁊ tairṫear eisein ina ttrecommarcc, ⁊ ro marḃaḋ é, ba tria fiorṫaiḃ dé ⁊ ciaráin inosin. Ro marḃaḋ ḃeós an collaiḋ mac diarmada uí ṁaoilruanaiḋ don deaḃaiḋ sin i maille re soċhaiḋiḃ ele. Luiḋ caṫal croibdearg ⁊ uilliam búrc cona sloġaiḃ ar a haiṫle i muiġ luircc, i muiġ naoi, airriḋe co hiarṫar connaċt. Rangattar conga ḟeiċin, ⁊ ar innte do rónsat an caiscc. Ciḋ tra, act ro cogradh lá huilliam burc, ⁊ lá cloinn Ruaiḋri uí flaiṫbertaiġ feall do ḋénaṁ for caṫal croiḃdearg, ⁊ ro ṡaor dia é don ċur sin tria ṡlánaḋ na

the sons of O'Brien and Mac Carthy and their forces. The resolution to which Cathal Crovderg and William Burke then came, was to despatch their archers throughout Connaught to distrain for their wages, and William Burke and his attendants, and Cathal Crovderg, repaired to Cong. Then a miraculous report was bruited abroad, and it is not known whether it proceeded from a man, or from the spirit of God in the shape of a man, namely, that William Burke was killed! There was not a way or road in Connaught through which this report had not passed. On hearing this news a resolution was adopted by the tribes of Connaught, as unanimously as if they had all met in council for the purpose, and this was, that each person should kill his guest [i. e. the soldier billeted on him]. This was done: each tribe killed the number billeted among them, and their loss, according to the report of their own people, was nine hundred, *vel amplius*. When William Burke had heard of the killing of his people he sent for O'Conor. A forewarning of his intention reaching O'Conor, he shunned the place where William was. William then set out for Munster, having lost the greater part of his people."

[r] *Oran*, uarán, now Oran.—A well-known place, containing the ruins of a church and round tower, in the barony of Ballymoe, and county of Roscommon.—See *Trias Thaum.*, p. 136, where the name is thus explained: "*Huaran* enim sive *fuaran* idem Hibernis sonat quod fons vivus, sive viva vel frigida aqua è terra scaturiens." See also the year 1556, at which mention is made of Gillacolumb O'Clabby, Coarb of St. Patrick, at this place. The place is still called Uaran Ui Chlabaiġ, and "Patrons" are yet held there annually on St. Patrick's day (17th March), and on the last Sunday in July, called Garland Sunday. Not many years ago the senior of the

from thence *successively* to Oran[r], to Elphin, to the Rock of Lough Key, and to the monastery of Ath-da-Loarg (Boyle); and the houses of the monastery served them as military quarters.

At this time Cathal Mac Dermot went on a predatory excursion into Hy-Diarmada[s]: Teige, the son of Conor Moinmoy, overtook him, and a battle was fought between them, in which Cathal [Mac Dermot] was slain.

As to Cathal Carragh, King of Connaught, he assembled his forces, and marched against this army, and arrived at Guirtin Cuil luachra[t], in the vicinity of the monastery. They remained confronting each other for a week, during which daily skirmishes took place between them. At the end of this time Cathal Carragh went forth to view a contest; but a body of his people being violently driven towards him, he became involved in the crowd, and was killed. This happened through the miracles of God and St. Kieran. Ancolly, the son of Dermot O'Mulrony, and many others, were also killed in this battle. After this Cathal Crovderg and William Burke passed with their forces through Moylurg and Moy-Nai, and thence through West Connaught, and arrived at Cong, where they spent the Easter. William Burke and the sons of Rory O'Flaherty, however, conspired to deal treacherously by Cathal Crovderg, but God protected him on this occasion from their designs, through the guarantee of the ecclesiastical witnesses to their league of mutual fidelity.

O'Clabbys used to appear at the *Patrons*, and point out to the people the extent of the Termon lands possessed by his ancestors, on which occasion the people were accustomed to make a collection for his support. The O'Clabbys, now Clabbys, are numerous in the county, but have retained no property in this Termon.

Colgan calls this church *nobilissima ecclesia de Huaran*, but little of its magnificence, however, remains at present, there being at the place but a mere fragment of the ruins of the church, and the base of its *clogás*, or round tower, measuring about fifteen feet in height. The *uaran*, or spring, from which the place derives its name, is still accounted a holy well, and frequented by pilgrims. It has a small stone cross over it before which the pilgrims kneel. Traces of the foundations of other buildings are also observable in the field adjoining the church, which shew the ancient importance of the place.

[s] *Hy-Diarmada.*—This was the tribe name of the family of O'Concannon, in the county of Galway. The chief of the name had his seat, in 1585, at Kiltullagh, in the county of Galway.—See *Tribes and Customs of Hy-Many*, printed for the Irish Archæological Society in 1843, p. 19. The Hy-Diarmada are to be distinguished from the Clann-Diarmada, who were at Dun Doighre, now Duniry, in the barony of Leitrim, in the county of Galway.

[t] *Guirtin Cuil luachra*, i. e. the little field of the rushy corner or angle. This name is now ob-

heaccailse baoi eatorra im ðílsi fri aroile. Tangadar muintir uilliam búrc iarttain do ṫobaċ a ttuarasdail for connaċtaiḃ, lingit connaċtaiġ forrasoṁ, ⁊ marḃait 700. diḃ. Soair uilliam co luimneaċ iar sin ⁊ gaḃaiṫ caṫal croiḃdearg riġe ċóigiḋ connaċt.

Slóigheaḋ la hualgarcc ua Ruairc do ḋul i ccenél cconaill, ⁊ ar roch-tain dóiḃ isin ccrích Rugsat bú ⁊ gaḃála. Rug ua domnaill éccneachán forra occ leic uí maoildoraiḋ. Feachar scaindear stoirra go raeiṁeḋ for uiḃ briúin cona soċraide, ⁊ ro laaḋ a ndeargár eitir ṁarḃaḋ ⁊ ḃaḋaḋ. Ḃa don ċur sin ro baiḋeaḋ conċoḃar na glaissene.

Cenél neoġain do ṫocht for creich naile i ccenél conuill isin ló ċéṫna. Do rala sttarra ⁊ ua domnaill gur ró sraoineaḋ for cenél neóghain ⁊ ro marḃaḋ gearrṁaidi ua baoiġealláin co sochaiḋiḃ aile do chenél neóghain i maille fris.

Tigernán mac domnaill mic caṫail ui Ruairc do ṁarḃaḋ la mag fiaċraċ ⁊ lá cloinn chathail, ⁊ an teoġanaċ mag fiaċraċ do ṁarḃaḋ ar an láṫair sin.

AOIS CRIOSD, 1202.

Aois Criosd, mile, da céd, adó.

Muirċertaċ ua carmacain epscop cluana ferta brenainn do écc.

Maolcolaimm ua bronain airċindeaċ toraiġe décc.

Domnall ua brolċáin sriórir ⁊ uasal ṡeanóir, Saoí dearrscaiġṫe ar ċéill, ar ċruṫ, ar ḋelḃ, ar ṁíne, ar ṁorḋaċt, ar ċraḃaḋ, ⁊ ar eagna déġ iar ndeiġḃeṫhaiḋ an seaċtmaḋ lá ficet April.

solete, for the oldest men in the parish of Boyle never heard of it.

[u] *O'Carmacan*, O Carmacáin, now anglicised Gormican. The family of this name were seated in the parish of Abbey-Gormican, in the north-west of the barony of Longford, in the county of Galway, which parish derived its name from a monastery founded by a chief of this tribe. The name is written O'Gormagan in the Galway Inquisitions.

[w] *Maelcolum*, Maolcolaimm, i. e. the servant of, or devoted to, St. Columba. This name is made Malcolm in Scotland.

[x] *Of Tory*, Toraiġe, and sometimes called Toir-inis, i. e. the island of the tower.—It is an island off the north coast of the county of Donegal, where St. Columbkille is said to have erected a monastery and *cloigtheach*, or round tower belfry, in the sixth century.—See O'Donnell's Life of Columba, lib. i. c. 73, lib. ii. c. 20, and Calendar of the O'Clerys, at 9th June. For the early history of this island the reader is referred

The people of William Burke afterwards went to demand their wages from the Connacians; but the Connacians rushed upon them, and killed seven hundred of them. William then returned to Limerick, and Cathal Crovderg assumed the regal sway of Connaught.

Ualgarg O'Rourke mustered an army, and marched into Tirconnell. On their arrival in the country, they seized upon a number of cows and other property. O'Donnell (Egneghan) overtook them at Leck-I-Muldory, where a battle was fought between them, in which the Hy-Briuin (O'Rourkes) and their army were defeated and cut off with terrible havoc, both by killing and drowning. It was on this occasion that Conor na-Glais-fene (O'Rourke) was drowned.

On the same day the Kinel-Owen made another predatory incursion into Tirconnell; and a conflict took place between them and O'Donnell, in which the Kinel-Owen were defeated, and Gearrmaidi O'Boylan and many others of the Kinel-Owen were slain along with him.

Tiernan, the son of Donnell, who was the son of Cathal O'Rourke, was slain by Mag-Fiachrach and the Clann-Cahill; but Mag-Fiachrach, *surnamed* Eoganach [i. e. the Tyronian] was killed on the same spot.

THE AGE OF CHRIST, 1202.

The Age of Christ, one thousand two hundred two.

Murtough O'Carmacan[u], Bishop of Clonfert-Brendan, died.

Maelcolum[w] O'Bronan, Erenagh of Tory[x] (island), died.

Donnell O'Brollaghan, a prior, a noble senior, a sage illustrious for his intelligence, personal form, and comeliness, and for his mildness, magnanimity, piety, and wisdom, after having spent a good life[y], died on the twenty-seventh of April.

to Keating's History of Ireland, Haliday's Edition, pp. 122, 180, 182; and O'Flaherty's *Ogygia*, part iii. c. 7. See also *Battle of Magh Rath*, printed for the Irish Archæological Society in 1842, p. 106, note [x]. A St. Ernan, son of Colman, son of Maen, son of Muireadhach, who was son of Eoghan, ancestor of the Kinel-Owen, was the most distinguished saint of this island next after St. Columbkille.

[y] *A good life.*—Thus expressed in Latin, in the Annals of Ulster: "*Domnall h Ua Brolchain, Prior, &c. &c., post magnam tribulationem et optimam penitenciam in quinta Kalendas Maij uitam finiuit.*"

Maolfinnein mac colmáin seanóir togaide ⁊ conn craiḃdeċ ua flannagáin déġ.

Doṁnall carrac ua doċartaiġ (.i. rioġ ṫaoiseaċ árda mioḋair) do ṁarbaḋ lá muintir baoiġill iar narġain ceall ⁊ tuaṫ iomḋa.

Conċoḃar ruaḋ mac doṁnaill uí ḃriain do ṁarḃaḋ lá a dearḃraṫair fẋin ⁊ lá muirċsrtaċ mac doṁnaill mic toirrḋealḃaiġ uí briain.

Toirrḋealḃaċ mac Ruaiḋri uí ċonċoḃair do éluḋ a geiṁeal, ⁊ caṫal croiḃdearg ḋo ḋenaṁ sioḋa fris, ⁊ ferann do tabairt dó. Toirrḋealḃaċ iarom do ionnarbaḋ lá caṫal ⁊ síḋ do denoṁ ris fo ċédóir tria impiḋe na ngall.

Doṁnall mac muircsrtaiġ uí maoileachlainn do écc.

Diarmaitt mac airt uí maoileachloinn do ṁarbaḋ la mac lochlainn uí concoḃair.

AOIS CRIOSD, 1203.

Aois Criosd, mile, da ċed, atrí.

An teascop mac giolla ċeallaiġ í ruaiḋin epscop cille mic duach do ecc.

Doire colaim ċille do loscaḋ o ṫa relecc Martain co tiopprait aḋaṁnain.

Mainistir do ḋenaṁ lá ceallaċ ar lár croi la gan nach dliġeḋ tar sárucċaḋ muintiri la foḋéin, ⁊ ro ṁill an baile co mór. Cleiriġ an tuaisceirt do ṫionol co haoín ionaḋ do ḋul go hí .i. Florent ua cśrballán epscop ṫire heogain, Maolíosa ua doriġ epscop ṫíre conaill, ⁊ abb recclésa póil ⁊ peadair in ardmaċa, aṁalgaiḋ ua ferġail abb reccl̃esa doire, ⁊ ainmire ua coḃṫaiġ, ⁊ drong ṁór do ṁuintir doire, ⁊ sochaiḋe do cléircib an tuaisceirt genmoṫaitsíḋe. Tiagaid iaroṁ co hí, ⁊ scaoiltear leó an ṁainis-

[z] *O'Boyles*, muintir ḃaoiġill.—According to O'Dugan's topographical poem, the O'Boyles were chiefs of Cloch Chinnfhaolaidh, now Cloghineely, in the north-west of the barony of Kilmacrennan, and of Tir Ainmire, now the barony of Boylagh, and Tir Boghaine, now Bannagh barony, in the west of Tirconnell, now the county of Donegal.—See notes under the years 1284 and 1343.

[a] *At once*, fo ċédóir .i. fo ċéd uair.—This adverbial expression, which occurs so frequently throughout these Annals, signifies *at once, without delay, sine mora.*

[b] *Awley*, Aṁalgaiḋ.—This name, which has been anglicised Awley throughout this translation, existed among the Irish from a remote pe-

Maelfinen Mac Colman, a venerable senior, and Conn Craibhdheach (the Pious) O'Flanagan, died.

Donnell Carragh O'Doherty, Royal Chieftain of Ardmire, was slain by the O'Boyles[a], after he had plundered many churches and territories.

Conor Roe, the son of Donnell O'Brien, was slain by his own brother, i. e. Murtough, son of Donnell, who was son of Turlough O'Brien.

Turlough, the son of Roderic O'Conor, escaped from confinement; and Cathal Crovderg made peace with him, and gave him land. He afterwards expelled him, but, at the intercession of the English, made peace with him at once[a].

Donnell, the son of Murtough O'Melaghlin, died.

Dermot, the son of Art O'Melaghlin, was slain by the son of Loughlin O'Conor.

THE AGE OF CHRIST, 1203.

The Age of Christ, one thousand two hundred three.

The son of Gillakelly O'Ruaidhin, Bishop of Kilmacduagh, died.

Derry-Columbkille was burned, from the cemetery of St. Martin to the well of St. Adamnan.

A monastery was erected by Kellagh without any legal right, and in despite of the family of Iona, in the middle of Iona, and did considerable damage to the town. The clergy of the north of Ireland assembled together to pass over into Iona, namely, Florence O'Carolan, Bishop of Tyrone [i. e. of Derry]; Maelisa O'Deery, Bishop of Tirconnell [Raphoe], and Abbot of the church of SS. Peter and Paul at Armagh; Awley[b] O'Fergahail, Abbot of the regles of Derry; Ainmire O'Coffey; with many of the family [clergy] of Derry, besides numbers of the clergy of the north of Ireland. They passed over into Iona; and, in accordance with the law of the Church, they pulled down the aforesaid monas-

riod of their history. It is to be distinguished from Amhlaoibh, which they derived from their connexion with the Danes, and which has been anglicised Auliffe in this translation. This latter is identical with the Danish Amlaff, Anlaff, Olaf, and Olé. The surname O'Ferghail was, and is still, very common in Tirconnell, but usually written O Firghil. It was the name of the hereditary Erenaghs of Kilmacrenan, by whom the O'Donnells were inaugurated. It is now pronounced as if written O'Frighil, by a metathesis or transposition of letters, not unusual in many words in the modern Irish, and always anglicised Freel, without the prefix O'.

tir remepertmar do réir ḋliġeḋ na heccailsi, ⁊ ro hóirdneḋ an taṁalgaiḋ reṁráite in abḋaine ia tria ṫoġa gall ⁊ gaoideal.

Diarmaitt mac muirceartaiġ uí Loċlainn co ndruing do ġallaiḃ do ḋul ar creċ hi ttír neoġain, ⁊ ro airgsit Scrin colaim cille, ⁊ rugsat dream do cenél eoġain orra, ⁊ sraointer leó for ḋiarmaitt co na ġallaiḃ, ⁊ ro marḃaḋ diarmaid fsirin tria ṁiorḃailiḃ na Scrine.

Slóiġeaḋ la mac hugo de laci co ndruing do ġallaiḃ miḋe i nultaiḃ co ro díoċuirseḋ Iohn do cuirt a hultoiḃ iar ccor ċaṫa sturra i ndun da leṫglas, in ro marbhadh sochaiḋe.

Muirceartaċ teṫbaċ mac conċoḃair ṁaonṁaiġe mic Ruaiḋri uí conċoḃair do marḃaḋ la diarmaid mac Ruaiḋri ⁊ la haoḋ mac Ruaiḋri .i. dá dearbráṫair a aṫar féin ar faithche ċille mic duach.

Maiḋm ria ndoṁnall mac meg carṫaiġ ⁊ ria ndesṁuṁain for ġallaiḃ dú hi ttorċratar searccatt ar céd nó ní as uille.

Faolan mac faolain tiġerna ua ffaolain do ecc i mainistir Congalaiġ.

[c] *Galls*, i. e. the northmen or inhabitants of Scotland who were not of the Gaelic or Scotic race.

[d] This passage is translated by Colgan as follows: "A. D. 1203. Kellachus extruxit Monasterium in Insulâ Hiensi, contra ius & æquitatem renitentibus loci senioribus. Quo facto audito Clerus Aquilonaris Hiberniæ indicit publicum conuentum; ad quem Florentius O'Kervallan-Episcopus Tironiæ, Moelia O'Dorigh Episcopus Tirconalliæ, & Abbas Monasterij SS. Petri & Pauli Ardmachæ; Amalgadius Hua Fergail, Abbas Dorensis, Anmirius O Cobhthaich, & multi alij de Clero convenerunt. Et posteà omnes profecti sunt ad Insulam Hiensem, & Monasterium jam memoratum à Kellacho ibi extructum, destruxerunt: & prædictum Amalgadium, communibus suffragiis electum, Hiensi Monasterio præficiunt."—*Trias Thaum.*, p. 501.

[e] *Screen-Columbkille*, Scrín Colaim cille.—This is not the shrine of Columbkille in Ardmagilligan, as assumed by Archdall and Sampson, but the present old church of Ballynascreen, in the barony of Loughinsholin. This Colgan clearly shews in *Trias Thaum.*, p. 494, col. 2: "Hic locus est Diœcesis Dorensis jacens in valle de *Gleann Conncadhain*, unde diversus ab alio cognomine loco ejusdem Diocesis." The valley of Gleann Concadhain here mentioned by Colgan still retains its name, which is correctly anglicised Glenconkeyne in the Ulster Inquisitions, and other Anglo-Irish official documents. It is a wide and beautiful valley in the west of the barony of Loughinsholin, and county of Londonderry, bounded on the south by the remarkable mountain of Sliabh Callain, Anglicè Slieve Gallion, and on the north by the Dungiven and Banagher mountains. According to the tradition of the country, which is corroborated by written documents, this district, which was the patrimonial inheritance of O'Henery, comprised the parishes of Ballynascreen, Kilcronaghan, and Desertmartin.

There is a remarkable esker, or long hill, to the south of the old church of Ballynascreen, in the west of this district, called Eisgir Mhic Lochlainn, which tradition points out as the site of a

tery; and the aforesaid Awley was elected Abbot of Iona by the suffrages of the Galls[c] and Gaels[d].

Dermot, the son of Murtough O'Loughlin, went on a predatory excursion into Tyrone, and plundered the Screen-Columbkille[e]. He was encountered, however, by a party of the Kinel-Owen, who defeated Dermot and his English; and Dermot himself was killed through the miracles of the Shrine.

An army was led by the son of Hugo de Lacy and a party of the English of Meath into Ulidia; and they banished John de Courcy from thence, after they had defeated him in a battle fought at Dundaleathglas (Downpatrick), in which many had been slain.

Murtough the Teffian, son of Conor Moinmoy, who was the son of Roderic O'Conor, was slain by Dermot, the son of Roderic, and Hugh, the son of Roderic, namely, by his own two paternal uncles, on the green of Kilmacduagh.

A victory was gained by Donnell, the son of Mac Carthy, and the people of Desmond, over the English; in the conflict one hundred and sixty persons, or more, were slain.

Faelan Mac Faelan[f], Lord of Hy-Faelain[g], died in the monastery of Connell[h].

great battle fought between the two rival chiefs. O'Neill and Mac Loughlin, in which the latter was defeated and slain, and there can be little, if any, doubt that this tradition alludes to this Dermot O'Loughlin.—See note at 1526.

[f] *Mac Faelan.*—He is called Mackelan in the work attributed to Maurice Regan.—See Harris's Ware, vol. ii. pp. 192, 193.

[g] *Hy-Faelain.*—This was the name of the tribe and territory of the O'Byrnes. Before the English invasion, their country comprised the present baronies of Clane and Salt, and the greater portion, if not the entire, of those of Ikeathy and Oughteranny, in the present county of Kildare, as appears from the Irish calendars, and other documents, which place in this territory the town of Naas, and the churches of Claenadh, now Clane; Laithreach Briuin, now Laraghbrine, near Maynooth; Domhnach Mor Moighe Luadhat, now Donaghmore parish; Cluain Conaire, now Cloncurry; and Fiodhchuillinn, now Feighcullen. Shortly after the English invasion, however, the Hy-Faelain, or O'Byrnes, were driven from their original level territory, and forced to take refuge in the mountain fastnesses of Wicklow, where they dispossessed other minor families, and became very powerful.—See the Feilire or Festilogy of Aengus, and Calendar of the O'Clerys, at 18th May, 8th June, 8th August, 2nd and 16th September, and 27th October. See also note on Hy-Muireadhaigh, under the year 1180. It is quite clear, from the authorities here referred to, that, previous to the English invasion, the families of O'Toole and O'Byrne, with their correlatives and followers, were in possession of the entire of the present county of Kildare, with the exception, perhaps, of a very small portion adjoining the present county of Carlow.

[h] *Connell,* Congalaiġ.—Now the abbey of

Cenandus Ath truim ⁊ an droichett nua do losccaḋ.
Sitricc teabthaċ ua ceallaiġ Maine do écc.

AOIS CRIOSD, 1204.

Aois Criosd, mile, dá chéd, a ceaṫair.

Sitriucc ua Sruithén airchinneaċ na congḃala, .i. cenn ua Murtele ⁊ toiseaċ cloinne Snéḋgile ar ṫotacht décc iar ndéiġ pendainn, ⁊ a aḋnacal is in tempall do rónaḋ leis féin.

John de Cuirt indredhac ceall, ⁊ tuaṫ do ionnarbaḋ lá mac hugo de laci

Great Connell, in the county of Kildare. According to Ware this abbey was founded, under the invocation of the B. V. Mary and St. David, by Myler Fitz-Henry, Lord Justice of Ireland, in the year 1202.—See Harris, Ware, vol. ii. p. 262. It looks strange that the chief of Hy-Faelain should die in this monastery the year after its erection. It is probable that, after being subdued, he consented to become a monk in the great abbey erected in his territory by the English conqueror.—See Archdall's *Monasticon*. The ruins of this abbey, which was one of great extent and magnificence, are now almost totally destroyed, and nothing remains to attract the notice of the antiquary, but the figure of a bishop and an old Latin inscription in the Gothic character, which has been often published.

[i] Under this year the Annals of Kilronan contain the following curious passage, which is altogether omitted by the Four Masters:

"A. D. 1203. William Burke marched with the English of Munster and Meath into Connaught, and erected a castle at Meelick in Sil-Anmchadha, and where he erected it was around the great church of the town, which was filled all round with stones and clay to the tops of the gables; and they destroyed West Connaught, both churches and territories." The erection of this castle is also given in the Annals of Clonmacnoise, but entered under the year 1202, and it is added, that it was broken down the same year by the King of Connaught.

[k] *Sitric O'Sruithen.*—His death is entered in the Annals of Ulster as follows, under the year 1205.

"A. D. 1205. Sitriuc hua Sruiṫen oirċinnec na congḃala .i. cenn hua murtele, ⁊ toiseċ clainne Sneidgile ar toċuct, *post optimam penitentiam feliciter finiuit vitam, et sepultus est in templo quod factum est apud ipsum.*"

[l] *Conwal*, Congḃail.—This is generally called Congḃail Glinne Suiliġe, i. e. Conwall of the vale of the River Swilly; it is an ancient parish church, now in ruins, near the River Suileach (Swilly), in the barony of Kilmacrenan, and county of Donegal.—See the *Feilire Aengus*, and the Irish Calendar of the O'Clerys, at 8th of February, and Colgan's *Acta Sanct.*, p. 406; also Erck's Ecclesiastical Register, p. 44. The ruins of this church are to be seen on the right of the road as you go from Letterkenny to Dunglow, about two miles from the former.

[m] *Clann-Snedhgile*, Clann Sneḋgile, were a tribe of the Kinel-Connell, seated in Glenswilly, to the west of Letterkenny. They descend from Snedhgil, son of Airnealach, son of Maelduin, son of Kinfaela, son of Garbh, son of Ronan, son of Lughaidh, son of Sedna, son of Fergus Kin-

Kells, Trim, and Droichead Nua (Newbridge) were burned.

Sitric (the Teffian) O'Kelly, of Hy-Maine, died[i].

THE AGE OF CHRIST, 1204.

The Age of Christ, one thousand two hundred four.

Sitric O'Sruithen[k], Erenagh of Conwal[l], i. e. head of the Hy-Murtele, and chief man of all the Clann-Snedhgile[m] for his worth, died, after exemplary penance, and was interred in the church which he had himself founded.

John de Courcy[n], the plunderer of churches and territories, was driven by

fada, who was son of Conall Gulban, ancestor of the Kinel-Connell.

[n] *John de Courcy.* — This is the last notice of De Courcy in these Annals. It is entered in the Annals of Ulster under the year 1205. At the year 1204 the Annals of Kilronan state that a battle was fought between Hugo de Lacy, with the English of Meath, and John de Courcy, with the English of Ulidia, in which John de Courcy was taken prisoner, but afterwards set at liberty, ιαρ nα ċροſſαḋ ḋó ḋul co Ιαρuſαlem, having been prohibited from going to Jerusalem. Under the year 1205 the same Annals record, that John de Courcy brought a fleet from the Innsi Gall, or the Hebrides, to contest Ulidia with the sons of Hugh de Lacy and the English of Meath, but that he effected nothing by this expedition except the plundering of the country; that he was compelled to go away without making any conquest, and that after this he entered into a league of amity with O'Neill and the Kinel-Owen. In the interpolated Dublin copy of the Annals of Innisfallen it is stated, that John de Courcy gained a great victory at Carrickfergus in 1207; but this must be a mistake. In the Annals of Clonmacnoise, as translated by Connell Mageoghegan, it is stated, under the year 1203, that Sir John de Courcy and his forces were, in a long encounter, overthrown at Downdalethglass [Down] by Hugh de Lacy, and himself banished into England; but under the next year the same Annals would seem to contradict this entry, or, if not, to give us to understand that De Courcy returned from England. The passage is as follows:

"A. D. 1204. John de Courcy and the Englishmen of Meath fell to great contentions, strife, and debate among themselves, to the utter ruin and destruction of Ulster. John was gone to the country of Tyreowne, and Hugh Delacie went to England."

The Dublin copy of the Annals of Innisfallen, in noticing the doings of King John in Ireland, state that he summoned the sons of Hugh de Lacy to appear before him to answer for the death of the valiant knight John de Courcy, who was treacherously killed by them. Mr. Moore thinks (History of Ireland, vol. iii. p. 3) that this was the great Sir John de Courcy, conqueror of Ulster; but this is not the fact, for the Sir John de Courcy killed by the De Lacys was Lord of Rathenny and Kilbarrock, in the county of Dublin.—See Grace's Annals of Ireland at the year 1210, and Campion's Historie of Ireland, Edition of 1809, p. 109. Ware supposes that this Lord of Kilbarrock and Rathenny was the natural son of the great Sir John de Courcy, but this does not appear probable, for

hi tír eoġain ar comairce cenél neoġain go rainicc go carraicc ḟerġusa, ⁊ ro marbsat goill ulaḋ sochaiḋe dia ṁuinntir.

we find that the Earl Richard (Strongbow) had granted Rathenny to Vivian de Cursun and his heirs, as fully as Gilcolm before held them: and it is most likely that the Sir John de Courcy, Lord of Rathenny, was the son of this Vivian. The great Sir John de Courcy had a brother, Jordanus de Courcy, who was killed by his own people in the year 1197, as appears from the Dublin copy of the Annals of Innisfallen, and who was possibly the ancestor of the Mac Patricks of Kingsale and Ringrone.

The truth seems to be that the conqueror of Ulster went to England in 1205. The archives of the Tower of London furnish us with the mandate of King John to the Ulster knights, who had become sureties for their chief, directing them to cause him to appear and perform his service by a term to be assigned by his Lord Justice of Ireland; together with the King's safe conduct to De Courcy, and the names of the hostages delivered on his part.—See *Rotuli Literarum Patentium in Turri Londinensi asservati*, an. 1201 ad. 1216, vol. i., part i., London, 1835.

Here we lose sight of Sir John de Courcy, conqueror of Ulster, as he is called, for we have no trustworthy records to prove what was his ultimate fate. The Book of Howth, now preserved among the manuscripts in the Lambeth Library, P. 628, contains a detailed account, professing to be authentic, of his subsequent history, of which the Editor is tempted to give here a brief outline.

Immediately after his defeat at Down, De Courcy offered the combat to Hugh de Lacy, which this cowardly lord refused, alleging that as he was the representative of the king in Ireland, it would be beneath his dignity to enter the lists with a rebellious subject. De Lacy next proclaimed De Courcy as a rebel, and offered a large reward to any who should seize him and deliver him into his hands. This having proved ineffectual, he next bribed the servants and followers of De Courcy, and held out great rewards to them for betraying him. To this they agreed, and gave De Lacy the following information: that De Courcy was a man of such gigantic strength, and always so well armed in public and private, that no one man durst lay hands upon him. However, that upon Good Friday yearly he wears no arms, but remains alone, doing penance, in the church-yard of Down; that if De Lacy would have a troop of horse in readiness near Down, he could, by their (the betrayers') directions, apprehend their master. These directions were followed. De Courcy was attacked unarmed: seeing no other weapon at hand he ran to a wooden cross that stood in the churchyard, and, tearing its shaft from the socket, he dealt such powerful blows of it upon his enemies, that he killed thirteen of them upon the spot. He was, however, finally overpowered, fettered, and delivered a prisoner into the hands of De Lacy, who conveyed him to London, where he was confined in the tower and condemned to perpetual imprisonment. For this service King John conferred the Earldom of Ulster upon De Lacy, who, instead of rewarding the betrayers of De Courcy, caused them to be hanged.

In this condition would De Courcy have passed the remainder of his life, had it not been for some difference that arose between John, King of England, and Philip, King of France, about the right to some fort in Normandy, who, to avoid the shedding of Christian blood, agreed to put it to single combat. King Philip had in readiness a French knight of so great prowess and renown, that King John found no subject

the son of Hugo de Lacy into Tyrone, to seek the protection of the Kinel-Owen. He arrived at Carrickfergus, and the English of Ulidia slew great numbers of his people.

of his realm willing to encounter him. At length he was informed by one of his officers, that there was a mighty champion confined in the Tower of London, who would prove more than a match for the French knight. King John, right glad to hear this, sent to De Courcy, calling upon him to support the honour of England; and who, after repeated denials, is at last prevailed upon to accept the challenge. He sends for his own sword to Ireland, which was a ponderous weapon, of exceeding good temper, and which he had often imbrued in the blood of the men of Ulster. The rigours of his imprisonment were softened, and his strength restored by proper nourishment and exercise. The day came, the place is appointed, the list provided, the scaffolds set up, the princes with their nobility on each side, with thousands in expectation. Forth comes the French champion, gave a turn and rests him in his tent. De Courcy is sent for, who all this while was trussing of himself with strong points, and answered the messengers, that if any of them were invited to such a banquet they would make no great haste. Forth, at length, he comes, gave a turn, and went into his tent. When the trumpets sounded to battle the combatants came forth and viewed each other. De Courcy looked his antagonist in the face with a wonderful stern countenance, and passed by. The Frenchman, not liking his grim look, gigantic size, and symmetric proportions, stalked still along, and when the trumpets sounded the last charge, De Courcy drew out his ponderous sword, and the French knight, being seized with a sudden panic, ran away, and fled into Spain; whereupon the English sounded victory, clapped their hands, and cast up their caps.

The two kings, disappointed in their anticipated pleasure of seeing a combat between mighty champions, intreated De Courcy to give them some proof of his bodily strength. Complying with their request, he ordered a strong stake to be driven firmly into the ground, on which were placed a coat of mail and a helmet. He then drew his sword, and looking with a frowning and threatening aspect upon the kings, he cleft the helmet and coat of mail, and sent the weapon so deeply into the wood, that no one but himself could draw it out. Then the kings asked him what he meant by looking so sternly at them, and he answered in a sullen tone, that had he missed his blow, he would have cut off both their heads. His words were taken in good part, on account of the services he had performed. King John gave him his liberty, as well as great gifts, and restored him to his possessions in Ulster. He then sailed to England, and coming to Westchester, committed himself to the mercy of the sea, but was put back again by contrary winds, which rose upon a sudden at his embarkation. This he did for fifteen days successively, and upon every repulse he was admonished at night in a vision, that all his attempts to cross the sea to Ireland were vain, for that it was preordained that he should never set foot upon Irish ground, because he had grievously offended there by pulling down the master and setting up the servant. De Courcy recollected that he had formerly translated the cathedral church of Down, which had been dedicated to the Holy Trinity, into an abbey of black monks brought thither from Chester, and that he had consecrated the same in honour of St. Patrick. On being driven back the fifteenth time his visions had so powerfully wrought upon

Uilliam búrc do indradh connacht eitir chill ⁊ tuaith ⁊ ro dioghail dia ⁊ na naoimh indsin fair uair ro ég do ghalur iongnáth do badh adhnár dairnéis.

Muirchertach ua flaithbhertaigh tighearna iarthair connacht do écc.

his imagination, that he submitted to the decrees of heaven, passed sentence upon himself, returned to France, and there died about the year 1210.

Dr. Leland observes (History of Ireland, v. i. b. i. c. 6, p. 180), that those who reject the superstitious addition, have yet adopted the romantic part of the narrative without scruple, though both evidently stand upon the same original authority. It is quite certain, however, that it stands upon no *original* authority, but is a mere story invented in the fifteenth or sixteenth century to flatter the vanity of the Howth family, whose ancestor, Sir Armoric Tristeram, or St. Laurence, married De Courcy's sister, and followed his fortunes into Ireland. Leland adds, that this romantic part of the history of Sir John De Courcy was invented by Irish bards and romancers, and writes as follows: "But it would not be worth while to detain the reader by this romantic tale, merely for the sake of refuting it, if we did not conceive it to be a specimen not unworthy of regard of the narrative of Irish bards and romancers, and the liberties they assumed of enlarging and embellishing the real incidents of their times. They who lived in earlier times are not so easily detected. But we see with what caution we are to receive their narratives, when, in times less obscure, and when confronted by other evidence, this order of men have hazarded such bold fictions, and with such ease and such success have obtruded the marvellous and the affecting upon their unrefined hearers for real history. But as we find in these instances that the tales of the Irish bards were founded upon facts, we may reasonably conclude that their predecessors took the same course: that they sophisticated the truth by their additions, but were not entirely inventors."

There can be little doubt, however, that this story about Sir John de Courcy was not invented by any Irish bard, for it has not been found in any Irish manuscript in prose or verse. It is evidently a story got up in the fifteenth or sixteenth century, on the slender basis of an Anglo-Irish tradition, and was first committed to writing, with other stories of a similar character, in that repertory of Anglo-Irish traditions and legends, the Book of Howth.

A similar story is told in the mountainous districts of Kerry and Beare, and Bantry, about Donnell O'Sullivan Beare, who fought with as much valour and desperation in the reign of Elizabeth, as Sir John de Courcy did in the reign of Henry II., and who was, perhaps, as great a hero as Ireland ever produced. But stories of this description are poetical inventions of later ages, when tradition, through the want of written records, had fallen into that degree of obscurity which left romantic writers at full liberty to raise as bright a fabric of fable as they pleased, on the slender basis of true history. They often, no doubt, owe their origin to vivid traditional reminiscences of the valour of noble warriors, whose real characters, if described by writers who could keep within the bounds of nature and of truth, would afford abundance of shining virtues to be held up for the admiration of posterity.

We have already seen that Giraldus Cambrensis states that Sir John de Courcy had no legitimate son. According to the Dublin copy of the Annals of Innisfallen, he was married in the year 1180 to [Affrica] the daughter of Godfred, King of the Isle of Man; and she died in the year

William Burke[c] plundered Connaught, as well churches as territories; but God and the saints took vengeance on him for that; for he died of a singular disease, too shameful to be described.

Murtough O'Flaherty, Lord of West Connaught, died.

1193, having borne no children up to the middle of the year 1186, when Giraldus's historical notices of the Irish invaders end. Campion, who compiled his *Historie of Ireland* in 1571, asserts, that "Courcye dying without heires of his body, the Earldome of Vlster was entirely bestowed upon Hugh de Lacye, for his good service."—See Dublin edition of 1809, p. 100. But Dr. Smith, in his *Natural and Civil History of Cork*, states that, "notwithstanding what Giraldus Cambrensis asserts, in the second book of his History, that John de Courcey, Earl of Ulster, had no issue, there is a record extant in the Tower of London (Rot. Pat. 6 Johan. M. Dors.), that Milo de Courcey, son of John de Courcey, was an hostage for his father upon his enlargement from the Tower to fight the French champion." —Vol. ii. pp. 228, 229, of the third edition. It is also stated in a Pedigree of the Mac Carthys, of Loch Luigheach, now Corraun Lough, in Kerry, now preserved in the Library of the Royal Irish Academy, that this branch of the Mac Carthys descend from a daughter of Sir John de Courcy.

Lodge enters fully into the question of the legitimacy of the issue of De Courcy in vol. iv. pp. 30–32, edition of 1754, and thinks that wearing the hat in the royal presence is conclusive as to lawful issue; but the antiquity of the privilege has not been proved by documentary evidence sufficient to establish it to the satisfaction of the historian. Mr. Moore seems satisfied that De Courcy had one legitimate son, Milo, but agrees with Leland in doubting the story of Hanmer, and his legendary authority, the Book of Howth. He writes, "that he" [Sir John De Courcy] "did not succeed, as some have alleged, in regaining his place in the royal favour, may be taken for granted from the fact that, though he left a son to inherit his possessions, both the title and property of the earldom of Ulster were, on his decease" [*qr.* before his decease?] "transferred to his rival, Hugh de Lacy."—*History of Ireland*, vol. iii. p. 4.

The Patent Roll referred to by Dr. Smith mentions a Milo de Curcy, *juvenis*, son of John de Curcy, Junior, but contains not a word to shew who this John de Curcy, Jun., was, or about the combat with the French champion. On the strength of the traditional story, however, the heads of the Mac Patricks, or De Courcys of Cork, have claimed and exercised the privilege of appearing covered in the royal presence. It may not be impertinent to remark, however, that no mention is made of this privilege in the works of Hanmer or Campion. The former merely states that King John gave De Coury, Earl of Ulster, "great gifts, and restored him to his former possessions in Ireland."—Dublin edition of 1809, p. 368. And the latter writes in 1571, "Lord Courcye, a poore man, not very Irish, the ancient descent of the *Courcyes* planted in Ireland with the Conquest."—*Historie of Ireland*, Dublin edition, 1809, p. 10.

Mr. Burke states, in his Peerage, but upon what authority the Editor knows not, that Almericus, the twenty-third Lord Kingsale, in observance of the ancient privilege of his house, appeared in the presence of King William III. covered, and explained to that monarch, when his Majesty expressed surprise at the circumstance, the reason thus:—"Sire, my name is Courcy; I am Lord of Kingsale, in your Majesty's kingdom of Ireland; and the reason of my appearing covered

AOIS CRIOSD, 1205.

Aoir Criorð, míle, dá céð, a cúicc.

An tairðeascoc ua Leienni [Heinni] do ðol i mainċini, ⁊ a écc ro ċedóir.
Donait ua bſcða erpcop ua namalgaða do écc.

in your Majesty's presence is, to assert the ancient privilege of my family, granted to Sir John de Courcy, Earl of Ulster, and his heirs, by JOHN, King of England." Burke adds: "The King acknowledged the privilege, and giving the Baron his hand to kiss, his Lordship paid his obeisance, and continued covered." The oldest authority the Editor has been able to find for this privilege is Smith's Natural and Civil History of Cork, first published in 1750, in which it is added, by Smith himself, but without citing any authority whatever, to Hanmer's account of Sir John de Courcy's enlargement from prison to fight the French champion. He also adds: "The privilege of being covered in the royal presence is enjoyed to this day by his lordship, being granted to his great ancestor, the Earl of Ulster, by King John. On the 13th of June, 1720, the late Lord Gerald de Courcy was by his Grace the Duke of Grafton, presented to His Majesty King George I., when he had the honour to kiss his hand, and to assert his ancient privilege. And that on the 22nd of June, 1727, he was presented by the Lord Carteret to His Majesty George II., by whom he was graciously received, had the honour of kissing his hand, and of being also covered in his presence." He then adds: "In May, 1627, Sir Dominick Sarsfield was created Lord Viscount Kinsale, to the great prejudice of this ancient and noble family, and set up his arms in the town. But, upon a fair hearing before the Earl Marshal of England, he was obliged to renounce the title of Kinsale, and take that of Kilmallock. The lords of Kinsale were formerly the first barons of Ireland, but are said to have lost their precedency *anno* 1489. James lord Kinsale, having missed being at a solemn procession at Greenwich, King Henry VII. gave the title of Premier Baron of Ireland to the lords of Athenry, who have ever since enjoyed the same; but this fact is disputed." It may be here remarked, that as the Barony of Athenry is now extinct, the title of Premier Baron of Ireland reverts to the De Courcys, and that the late John de Courcy, twenty-sixth Baron of Kinsale, exercised the ancient privilege of his ancestors on George the Fourth's visit to Ireland in 1821.

[o] *William Burke.*—The Annals of Clonmacnoise, as translated by Connell, the son of Niall Mageoghegan, in the year 1627, record the death of William Burke at an. 1204, in the following words: "William Burke took the spoyles of all the churches of Connaught, viz.: of Clonvicknose, Clonfert, Milick, Killbyan, the churches of O'Fiaghragh, Twayme, Kill-Beneoine, Killmeoyne, Mayo of the English, Cownga of St. Fechin, the abbey of Athedalaragh, Ailfynn, Uaran, Roscommon, with many other churches. God and the Patrons of these churches shewed their miracles upon him, that his entrails and fundament fell from his privie place, and it trailed after him even to the very earth, whereof he died impenitently without Shrive or Extream Unction, or good buryall in any church in the kingdom, but in a waste town." Mageoghegan then adds the following remarks by way of annotation, though he incorporates them with the text:

"These and many other reproachable words

THE AGE OF CHRIST, 1205.

The Age of Christ, one thousand two hundred five.

The Archbishop O'Heney[p] retired into a monastery, where he died soon after.

Donat O'Beacdha, Bishop of Tyrawley, died.

my author layeth down in the old book, which I was loath to translate, because they were utter'd by him for the disgrace of so worthy and noble a man as William Burke was, and left out other his reproachfull words, which he (as I conceive) rather declear'd of an Evill will he did bear towards the said William then" [i. e. than] "any other just cause."

This is the famous William Fitz Adelm de Burgo, who is generally called the *Conqueror* of Connaught. Mageoghegan's defence of him, in opposition to all the Irish authorities, is to no effect; and should any one be inclined to reject the testimony of the Irish writers altogether, the following character given of him by his own countryman and contemporary, Giraldus Cambrensis, must have some weight in corroborating their veracity: "Erat autem Aldelmi filius vir corpulentus, tam staturæ quam facturæ, inter parum mediocribus maiores satis idoneæ: vir dapsilis & curialis. Sed quicquid honoris cuiquam impendit, semper in insidiis, semper in dolo, semper propinans sub melle venenum, semper latens anguis in herba. Vir in facie liberalis & lenis, intus vero plus aloes quam mellis habens. Semper

"*Pelliculam veterem retinens, vir fronte politus,*
Astutam vapido portans sub pectore vulpem.
Semper
Impia sub dulci melle venena ferens.

"Molliti sermones eius super oleum: sed ipsi sunt iacula. Cuius hodie venerator, cras eiusdem spoliator existens, vel delator. Imbellium debellator, rebellium blanditor: Indomitis domitus, domitis indomitus, hosti suauissimus, subdito grauissimus: nec illi formidabilis, nec isti fidelis. Vir dolosus, blandus, meticulosus, vir vino Veneriq; datus. Et quanquam auri cupidus, & curialiter ambitiosus: non minus tamen curiam diligens quam curam."—*Hibernia Expugnata*, lib. ii. cap. xvi.

Duald Mac Firbis, in his account of the English families of Ireland, attempts, in the pedigree of the Earl of Clanrickard, to defend the character of Fitz Adelm, by stating that Giraldus was prejudiced against him; and it must be admitted, on comparing the character which Giraldus gives of William Fitz Adelm with that of Fitz Stephen, the uncle of Cambrensis, that there was more or less of prejudice in the way: but still, when it is considered that De Burgo's character, as drawn by Cambrensis, does not much differ from that given of him in the Annals of Clonmacnoise, it is clearly unfair to conclude that both are false, though it may be allowed that both are overdrawn, as Giraldus was undoubtedly prejudiced, and as the Irish ecclesiastic, who compiled the Annals of Clonmacnoise, could not be expected to give an impartial account of an invader and conqueror, who had plundered the church of Clonmacnoise and all the most sacred churches of Connaught.

[p] *The Archbishop O'Heney.*—In the Annals of Innisfallen, at the year 1192, he is called the Pope's Legate. According to the Annals of Mary's Abbey, Dublin, he died in the Abbey of Holycross, in the county of Tipperary—See

Saoirḃreṫaċ ua doiréḋ oirċinneaċ doṁnaiġ móir, ⁊ patraicc ua moġróin, décc.

Maġnus ua caṫáin mac tiġerna cianaċta, ⁊ ḟer na craoiḃe, tuir gaisccedh, ⁊ beoḋaċta an tuaisceirt do ġuin do ṡoiġit, ⁊ a ecc iaroṁ.

Mac Guillḃealaiġ uí ċerḃaill tiġerna éle do ṁarḃaḋ lá gallaiḃ.

Conċoḃar ua braoin breaġmaine do écc ina ailiṫre i ccluain mic nois.

Raġnall mac diarmata ticcerna cloinne diarmata do écc.

Doṁnall mac concoiccriċe taoiseċ muintire Sercaċáin do écc.

Doṁnall ua faoláin tiġearna na nDéisi muṁan do écc.

Tadcc mac caṫail croiḃderce do écc do ġalar en oiḋċe i ccluain mic nois.

Maelir mac Maelir do dul ar éccin ar luimneach, ⁊ coġaḋ mór dírgi

Harris's edition of Ware's Bishops, pp. 469, 470.

q *Donaghmore*, Doṁnaċ mor, is a church near Castlefin, in the county of Donegal, of which the O'Deerys were Erenaghs, according to the Ulster Inquisitions.

r *Kianaghta*, Cianaċta, is the present barony of Keenaght, in the north-west of the county of Londonderry. It derives its name from the tribe name of the family of the O'Conors of Glengevin, who descend from Cian (son of Olioll Olum, King of Munster), and who were chiefs of it, previous to the O'Kanes.

s *Firnacreeva*, Fir na craoiḃe, i. e. the men of the bush or branch; latinized *Fircrivia* by O'Flaherty. This was the name of a tribe of the O'Kanes seated on the west side of the Bann. "Bann, fluvius inter Leam et Elliam" [*recte* Elniam] "præter Clanbreasail regionem scaturiens per Neachum lacum Oendromensem agrum et FIRCRIVIAM Scriniamque in comitatu Derriensi, intersecat, et tertio a Culraniâ et cataracta Eascrive [eas craoiḃe] lapide in oceanum transfundit."—*Ogygia*, part iii. c. 3. This tribe of the O'Kanes had some time previously driven the Firlee eastwards across the Bann; and the latter settled in Magh Elne, where they certainly were seated in the time of Sir John de Courcy; for it appears from these Annals, at the year 1177, that Cumee O'Flynn was then in possession of the ecclesiastical town of Armoy, called Airther Maighe, i. e. the eastern part of the plain, because it was in the east of Magh Eilne, into which the Firlee had been driven by the O'Kanes.

t *Tower*, tuir.—The word tuir properly means prop or support. This passage is rendered as follows in the old translation of the Annals of Ulster: "A. D. 1205. Manus O'Cahan, son to the King of Kienaght and men of Krive, the upholder of martiall feats, and stoutnes of the North of Ireland, was slayne with the shot of an arrow."

u *The son of Guill-bhealach*.—In the pedigree of O'Carroll, given by Duald Mac Firbis, he is called Finn mac Goill an bhealaigh, and is made the twenty-fourth in descent from Eile Rigdhearg, from whom O'Carroll's country, in the now King's County, was called Eile, or Ely.—See note under the year 1174, p. 15.

w *Brawney*, breaġṁaine, an ancient territory, now a barony in the county of Westmeath, ad-

Saerbrehagh [Justin] O'Deery, Erenagh of Donaghmore[q], and Patrick O'Muron, died.

Manus O'Kane, son of the Lord of Kianaghta[r] and Firnacreeva[s], tower[t] of the valour and vigour of the North, was wounded by an arrow, and died of the wound.

The son of Guill-bhealach[u] O'Carroll, Lord of Ely, was slain by the English.

Conor O'Breen, of Brawney[w], died on his pilgrimage to Clonmacnoise.

Randal Mac Dermot, Lord of Clandermot, died.

Donnell Mac Concogry, Chief of Muintir Searcachan, died.

Donnell O'Faelain (Phelan), Lord of the Desies of Munster[x], died.

Teige, the son of Cathal Crovderg, died of one night's sickness at Clonmacnoise.

Meyler, the son of Meyler[y], took possession of Limerick by force; on ac-

joining Athlone and the Shannon.

[x] *Desies of Munster*, Deiṡi Muṁan.—This name is still preserved in the two baronies of Desies, in the present county of Waterford, but the ancient territory was much more extensive than the present baronies. Keating informs us (Reign of Cormac Mac Art) that the country of the southern Deisi extended from Lismore to Ceann Criadain —now Credan head, at the eastern extremity of the county of Waterford,—and from the River Suir southwards to the sea; and that of the northern Deisi from the Suir to the southern boundary of Corca Eathrach, or the Plain of Cashel, comprising the present baronies of Middlethird and Iffa and Offa East, in the south of the county of Tipperary. The country of the northern Deisi was otherwise called Magh Feimhin, which comprised, according to Keating, the baronies of Clonmel-third and Middle-third. The two districts formed the see of St. Declan of Ardmore, which became united to that of Lismore, and is now comprised under its name. These united dioceses extend northwards to about midway between Cashel and Clonmel, and there also ended the country of the northern Deisi.—See Ussher's *Primordia*, pp. 782, 866, 867; O'Flaherty's *Ogygia*, part iii. c. 69; and Lanigan's *Ecclesiastical History of Ireland*, vol. i. p. 282. The Deisi were originally seated near Tara, in Meath, and their country there is still called Deiṡe Teaṁraċ, *Anglice* Deece barony. In O'Heerin's topographical poem it is stated that O'Bric and O'Faelain were the ancient kings or head chiefs of the Desies, and that their sub-chiefs were as follows: O'Meara of Hy-Fatha (now Offa barony); O'Neill of Hy-Owen Finn, O'Flanagan of Uachter Tire, Anglice Upperthird; O'Breslen of Hy-Athele, as far as the sea to the south-east; O'Keane of Hy-Foley, along the River Moghan; O'Bric of Hy-Feathach, from Leac Logha (cloċ labraiṡ?) to Liathdruim, now Leitrim, on the boundary of the counties of Cork and Waterford.

[y] *Meyler*.—This passage is given as follows in Mageoghegan's translation of the Annals of Clonmacnoise: "A. D. 1205. Meyler the younger, son of Meyler Bremyngham, besieged Limbrick, and at the last tooke the same per force, for which there arose great dissention between the English of Meath. In which dissention Cowley

etir ġallaiḃ na Miḋe ⁊ ġoill Maoilir triḋ sin, ⁊ cuulaḋ mac conmédha uí laeghachain taoiseach síl Ronain do ṁarḃaḋ ar an ccoccaḋ sin la cenél fiachach mic néill.

AOIS CRIOSD, 1206.

Aois Criosd, míle, dá chétt, a sé.

Domhnall ua muirédhaigh airdfherleiginn doire do écc.

Maolpéttair ua calmáin comharba cainnigh tuir crábhaiḋ ⁊ eccna tuaisceirt Ereann do écc.

Flaiṫbértaċ ua flaiṫbértaiġ prióir ḋuine géimin, ⁊ giollapatraicc ua falaċtaiġ airchinneaċ ḋúin cruiṫne do écc.

Eiccnéchán ua domhnaill do ḋénaṁ creaċ ⁊ marbṫa i ttír eoġain.

Comharba patraicc do ḋol i ccénd Righ Saxan do ċuinġiḋ sochair ċeall, ⁊ do ċosaoid ar gallaibh Ereann.

Mac Convey O'Leygaghan was killed by those of Kynaleaghe; he was Chief of Sileronan, with many other hurts done among the Englishmen themselves."

[f] *O'Laeghaghan.* — This family was otherwise called Mac Conmeadha, now Mac Namee. O'Dugan makes O'Ronain Chief of Cairbre Gabhra, which was in North Teffia; but whether O'Ronain and O'Laeghachain of Sil Ronain were the same, or of the same tribe, the Editor has not been able to determine, for the tribe name of one family may agree with the surname of another, and yet be very different. Nothing will determine those points but positive evidence of their localities, and of their exact pedigrees.

[g] *Race of Fiacha*, cinel fiaċa mic néill, i. e. the race of Fiagha, son of Niall. This Fiagha was the third son of Niall of the Nine Hostages, monarch of Ireland in the beginning of the fifth century. His descendants were the Mageoghegans and O'Molloys, whose country extended from Birr to Killare, as we learn from an entry in Mageoghegan's translation of the Annals of Clonmacnoise, at the year 1207. But in later ages the name Kinel Fhiacha, or Kineleaghe, was applied to Mageoghegan's country only, which comprised the present barony of Moycashel. It should be here remarked that the country of Kinel-Fhiacha was never accounted a portion of Teffia, as asserted by some of our modern writers. The men of Teffia were the descendants of Maine, the fourth son of King Niall of the Nine Hostages, and their country was sometimes called Tir Mainé. The families of Teffia were the Foxes, or O'Caharny, who were originally lords of all Teffia, but were in latter ages seated in the barony of Kilcoursy (in the north-west of the present King's County), which bore their tribe name of Muintir-Tagan; the Magawleys of Calry an chala, comprising the parish of Ballyloughloe in Westmeath; the O'Breens of Brawney; the Mac Carghamhnas (anglicised Caron by O'Flaherty, and Mac Carrhon by Connell Mageoghegan, but now always Mac Carroon) of Muintir Maoiltsinna, placed by O'Flaherty near the Shannon, in the territory of Cuircnia, now the barony of Kilkenny West;

count of which a great war broke out between the English of Meath and the English of Meyler, during which Cooley, the son of Cumee O'Laeghaghan[z], was slain by the race of Fiacha[a], the son of Niall [i. e. the Mageoghegans, &c.]

THE AGE OF CHRIST, 1206.

The Age of Christ, one thousand two hundred six.

Donnell O'Murray, Chief Lector at Derry, died[b].

Mulpeter O'Calman, Coarb of St. Canice[c], and tower of the piety and wisdom of the north of Ireland[d], died.

Flaherty O'Flaherty, Prior of Dungiven[e], and Gillapatrick O'Falaghty, Erenagh of Dun-crun[f], died.

Egneghan O'Donnell took a prey, and killed some persons in Tyrone.

The successor of St. Patrick went to the King of England on behalf of the churches of Ireland[g], and to complain of the English of Ireland.

the O'Dalys of Corca Adain; the O'Quins of Muintir Gilligan, in the present county of Longford; and a few others, who all sunk into insignificance and obscurity shortly after the English invasion.—See note under the year 1207.

[b] This passage is thus translated by Colgan: "Domnaldus O'Muireduich Archiscolasticus seu supremus professor S. Theologiæ Dorensis Ecclesiæ obiit."—*Trias Thaum.*, p. 504.

[c] *St. Canice* is the patron saint of the barony of Keenaght, in the county of Londonderry, in which the chief church seems to be that of Drumachose.

[d] *North of Ireland.*—The coarb of St. Canice, in the north of Ireland, was the abbot of Termonkenny, in the territory of Kienaghta, now the barony of Keenaght, in the county of Londonderry, of which territory St. Canice was a native and the principal patron. The Annals of Ulster give a quotation from an ancient poem on the high character of this ecclesiastic, and the old translator anglicises his name Mael-Peter O'Calman.

[e] *Dungiven*, Ꝺun ᵹeimhin, a village in the barony of Keenaght, in the county of Londonderry. Ꝺun ᵹeimhin signifies the fortress of Geimhin, a man's name, but no historical account of his tribe or period has been discovered by the Editor.

[f] *Dun-crun*, Ꝺun cruiṫne, translated *arx Cruthænorum* by Colgan in *Trias Thaum.*, p. 181, col. 2. The name is now sometimes anglicised Duncroon, and is a townland in the parish of Ardmagilligan, in the county of Londonderry. There was a church erected here by St. Patrick, and a shrine finished for St. Columbkille by the celebrated brazier, Conla.—See Tripartite Life of St. Patrick, lib. ii. c. 125; and O'Donnell's Life of St. Columbkille, lib. i. c. 99. See also Sampson's Memoir of a Map of Londonderry, p. 487, and the note given above under the year 1203.

[g] *On behalf of the churches of Ireland*, roċur ceall n-Ereann.—The Primate went to England to request that the King would compel the English chiefs in Ireland to restore their lands and other liberties to the Irish churches. It appears

Tomaltaċ, mac Concoḃair, mic Diarmata mic Taiḋg tiġearna Maiġe Luirg ⁊ Airtigh, ⁊ na haiciḋeċta en branan Cloinne Maolruanaiḋ do écc.

Creaċ la hEccneċán ua nDoṁnaill in Uiḃ Farannain, ⁊ hi cCloinn Diarmata. Ro ġabhsat bú iomda, ⁊ ro marbhsatt daoine. Ruccsat Uí Diarmatta, Uí Forannáin ⁊ Uí Gairmlſḋhaiġ orra. Ro marḃaḋ, ⁊ ro báiḋſḋ soċaiḋe ſcorra, ⁊ ruccsat Cenél cConaill an ccreich so ḋſóiḋ iar morsaoṫar.

Ruaiḋri ua Gaḋra ticcerna Sleḃe Luġa do ecc.

Aodh mac Murchaḋa Uí Ċeallaiġ ticcſrna Ua Maine, ⁊ Caiṫniaḋ ua Caiṫniaḋ tiġearna Iorrair do écc.

Aoḋ ua Goirmġiallaiġ ticcſrna Partraiġe cſra do marḃaḋ lá fearaiḃ cſra.

Ruaiḋri ua Toġda taoiseaċ na Breḋcha la hUa nAmalgaiḋ do ecc.

Gillibert ua Flannaccáin, ⁊ Ioṁar mac Murchaiḋ cáċ díoḃ ḋo marḃaḋ aroile is Ros Comáin.

from charters in the Book of Kells, now in the Library of Trinity College, Dublin, that the word soċar means *advantage*, *benefit*, or *freedom*. It is in this sense the opposite of doċar.

In Harris's edition of Ware's Bishops (under *Eugene Mac Gillivider*, p. 64), he gives the following translation of this passage from what he calls anonymous Annals: "The comarb of Patrick (Eghdon Mac Gilluys), went to the King of England's house, for the good of the churches of Ireland, and to complain of the GALLS (i. e. the English) of Ireland." Harris took this extract from the old English translation of the Annals of Ulster, preserved in the British Museum, which contains the above quotation, word for word.—See note under the year 1216.

[h] *Tomaltagh*, tomaltaċ.—In the Annals of Kilronan he is styled na carrge, i. e. *of the rock*. Charles O'Conor of Belanagare states in one of his manuscripts, that he built the castle and chief seat of the family on one of the islands of Lough Key, and that this seat obtained the name of Mac Dermot's Rock, which it retains to this day.—See *Memoirs of the Life and Writings of Charles O'Conor of Belanagare*, p. 305.

[i] *Moylurg, Airtech, &c.*—Mac Dermot, or, as the family were more anciently called, O'Mulrony, was Chief of Moylurg, Airteach, and Tirtuathail, all included in the old barony of Boyle.

[k] *Clann-Dermot*, clann Diarmada, i. e. the O'Carellans. These, as well as the O'Forannans and O'Gormlys, were of the Kinel-Owen race, and were at this period seated on both sides of the River Mourne, and of the arm, or narrow part, of Lough Foyle. The O'Donnells afterwards drove them out of the plain of Magh Ithe, and established families of the Kinel-Connell in their place.

[l] *Sliabh Lugha*.—The name of this territory is still well known in the county of Mayo, and its limits pointed out. It comprises the parishes of Kilkelly, Kilmovee, Killeagh, Kilcolman, and Castlemore-Costello, in the south-east of the county of Mayo, that is, that part of the barony of Costello included in the diocese of Achonry.

Tomaltagh[h], the son of Conor, son of Dermot, who was the son of Teige, Lord of Moylurg, Airtech, and Aicidheacht[i], and chief hero of the Clann-Mulrony, died.

Egneghan O'Donnell plundered Hy-Farannan and Clann-Dermot[k]; he took many cows, and killed persons. He was overtaken by the Hy-Dermot, the O'Farannans, and the O'Gormleys; *and a struggle ensued, in which* many were killed and drowned on both sides; but the Kinel-Connell ultimately bore off the prey, after much labour.

Rory O'Gara, Lord of Sliabh Lugha[l], died.

Hugh, the son of Murrough O'Kelly, Lord of Hy-Many, and Caithniadh O'Caithniadh, Lord of Erris[m], died.

Hugh O'Goirmghialla, Lord of Partry[n] in Carra, was slain by the men of Carra.

Rory O'Toghda, Chief of Bredagh[o] in Hy-Awley [Tirawley], died

Gilbert O'Flanagan and Ivor Mac Murrough slew each other at Roscommon[p].

According to Downing, in his brief, but curious and valuable account of the county of Mayo, the country of the Galengi, i. e. the O'Haras and O'Garas, comprised the entire of the diocese of Achonry. The O'Garas were afterwards driven out of Sliabh Lugha by the family of Costello, and in later ages were possessed of the territory of Coolavin only, in which they had their chief castle at Moy-O'Gara, near the margin of Lough Gara. In an inquisition taken at Castlemore, on the 14th of July, 1607, this name is anglicised Slewlowe.

[m] *Erris*, ιορρυρ, an extensive and remarkably wild barony in the north-west of the county of Mayo. The family of O'Caithniadh are now extinct, or the name changed, in this barony.

[n] *Partry*, ραρτραιγε.—This name is still well known in the county of Mayo, as a territory forming the western portion of the barony of Ceara, and now believed to be coextensive with the parish of Ballyovey, or Odhbha Ceara, which is locally called the parish of Partry, and in which there is a range of mountains still called Slieve Partry; but it would appear, from the writings of the Mac Firbises of Lecan, that the territory of Partraighe extended originally into the present parish of Ballintober.—See *Tribes, Genealogies, and Customs of the Hy-Fiachrach*, printed for the Irish Archæological Society in 1844, p. 152, note [k], and p. 189, note [q]. The family name, O'Goirmghialla, is now called in Irish O'Ȝορmγύιl, which is anglicised Gormilly, Gormly, and even Gorman, which latter is an unpardonable corruption.—See *Tribes, &c. of Hy-Fiachrach*, pp. 47, 187, 202, note [b].

[o] *Of Bredagh*, να bρεοchα.—This territory which contained fifteen ballys, or sixty quarters of land, of the large old Irish measure, comprised the parish of Moygawnagh, in the west of the barony of Tirawley, in the county of Mayo, and a part of the adjoining parish of Kilfian.—See *Genealogies, Tribes, and Customs of Hy-Fiachrach*, pp. 10, 11, 165, 228.

[p] Roγ chomαιn, i. e. *Boscus Sancti Comani*,

Muirceartach mac carrgamhna taoisech muintire maoiltrionna do écc.

Sloiccheadh la mac hugo de laci co ngallaibh midhe ⁊ laighean i ttelach nócc. Ro loisccedh cealla, ⁊ arbanna lais, ⁊ ni rucc geill náid sidirsdha aodhae uí neill don chur sin.

Sloiccheadh las an lucht ccedna i cciannachtaibh. Ro loiscset cealla ciannachta uile, ⁊ ruccsat buar dirímhe.

AOIS CRIOSD, 1207.

Aois Criosd, mile, da céd, a seacht.

Creach la heiccnechan ua ndomnaill a bfearaibh manach go ro gabhsat bú. Ruccsat fir manach foirlion forra, ⁊ ro marbsat Ua domhnaill tigearna tíre Conaill, tuir engnamha, ⁊ einigh an chuiccidh ina fhimsir, ⁊ torchrattar drong do shaorclannaibh ele i maille fris. Ittiat na huaisle do rochrattar ann, an giolla riabhach mac ceallaigh uí baoighill, donnchadh conallach mac concobhair maonmaighi, ⁊ Mathgamhain mac domhnaill midhigh uí concobhair ⁊ laochraid iomda cenmothát.

Domhnall mac fearghail uí ruairc ticcerna urmóir breifne do écc.

Muirfedhach mac Ruaidhri uí Concobhair, ⁊ Amhlaibh ua ferghail taoisech muintire hAnghaile do écc.

Diarmait ua madagáin tighearna síl nanmchadha do écc.

Taissi Ruaidhri ui concobhair Rí Connacht do thabhairt a talmain, ⁊ a ccur hi sccrín chloiche.

now the town of Roscommon, which gives name to the county. St. Coman's well, called Dabhach Chomáin, is still in existence, and lies in a field to the east of the town, in the townland of Ballypheasant.

[q] These two passages are rendered, in the old translation of the Annals of Ulster, as follows: "A. D. 1206. An army by Hugh de Lacy to Tule Og, and burned Churches and Corne, but caried neither pledg nor hostage with them for that tyme. An army by de Lacy in Kyanaght, burnt many churches, and tooke many cowes."

[r] Under this year the Annals of Clonmacnoise record the death of the abbot Cahal O'Malone, a man of great riches and learning. They also contain the following passage relative to the town of Ballyloughloe, near Athlone, in the county of Westmeath, of which town the Four Masters have collected no early notice. "A. D. 1206. The sons of Art O'Melaghlyn preyed the town of Balleloghloe, and burnt part thereof? were overtaken by Melaghlyn Begg O'Melaghlyn, Sile Crowherfrey Mac Carrhon, and certain English forces, where in pursuite that rowte of Meathmen were discomfitted and putt to flight, killed Mortagh, or Morrogh, son of

Murtough Mac Carroon, Chief of Muintir Maoil-t-Sionna, died.

An army was led by the son of Hugo de Lacy, and the English of Meath and Leinster, into Tullaghoge (in Tyrone), and burned churches and corn, but obtained neither hostages nor pledges of submission from Hugh O'Neill on this occasion.

The same people led another army[q] into Kienaghta, and burned all the churches of that territory, besides driving off a countless number of cows[r].

THE AGE OF CHRIST, 1207.

The Age of Christ, one thousand two hundred seven.

Egneghan O'Donnell set out upon a predatory excursion into Fermanagh, and seized upon cows; but a considerable muster of the men of Fermanagh pursued him, and slew O'Donnell, Lord of Tirconnell, tower of the warlike prowess and hospitality of the province in his time; and some others of his nobility were slain along with him. The following were the nobles who fell on this occasion: Gillareagh, the son of Kellagh O'Boyle; Donough Conallagh, the son of Conor Moinmoy; and Mahon, the son of Donnell Midheach (i. e. the Meathian) O'Conor. Many other heroes fell besides these[s].

Donnell, the son of Farrell O'Rourke, Lord of the greater part of Breifny, died.

Murray, the son of Roderic O'Conor, and Auliffe O'Farrell, Chief of Annaly, died.

Dermot O'Madden, Lord of Sil-Anmchadha, died.

The remains of Roderic O'Conor, King of Connaught, were disinterred, and deposited in a stone shrine.

Melaghlyn Begg, Mortagh mac Donnagh Koyle, and also Morrogh mac Morrogh O'Kelly was taken."

They also record the death of Robert, son of Hugh Delacie, under the same year.

[s] *Besides these.*—This passage is better given in the Annals of Kilronan. The literal translation is as follows:

"A. D. 1207. A prey was taken by Egneghan O'Donnell in Fermanagh; but the men of Fermanagh overtook him with a more numerous host than he had, and slew O'Donnell, King of Tirconnell, till then the tower of valour, hospitality, and bravery of the north of Ireland. Some of his chieftains also fell, viz., Gillareagh, son of Kellagh O'Boyle; Mahon, son of Donnell, the Meathian O'Conor; Donough Conallagh, the son of Conor Moinmoy O'Conor, *et alii multi*

Caṫal croiḃḋſrcc ó Concoḃair Rí Connaċt do ionnarbaḋ Aoḋa uí Ḟlaiṫḃeartaiġ ⁊ a crioch do ṫaḃairt dia mac fſin dAoḋ mac caṫail.

Coccaḋ mor eittir ġallaiḃ laiġean fſin .i. eittir Maoilir ⁊ Seffraiġ marer, ⁊ Uilliam marurccal gur milleaḋ laiġin, ⁊ fir muṁan ſtorra.

Coccaḋ mór fór eittir hugo de laci ⁊ maoilir, go ro milleaḋ uile muintir Mhaoilir.

Crſch mor la caṫal carraċ mac diarmata mic taiḋg, ar ċorbmac mac tomaltaiġ mic diarmata, ⁊ ar ua fFloinn Earra, co ruccsat drem do Connaċtaibh fair .i. diarmait mac Maġnusa mic Muircſrtaiġ uí ċoncoḃair, ⁊ corbmac mac tomaltaiġ, Concoḃar god o hſġra tiġſrna luighne, ⁊ donnchaḋ ua duḃda tiġearna ua naṁalgaḋa, ⁊ ua fFiachraċ go ro chuirriot cliachaiḋ go ro muidh for caṫal ċarraċ, ⁊ go ro gaḃaḋ é fſin, ⁊ go ro dallaḋ, ⁊ ro marḃaḋ muirġſr a ṁac, ⁊ Mac Chonġránna uí Ḟlannaccáin co soċaiḋiḃ ele.

Creach ṁór la Maoilir ócc, ⁊ la Muircſrtaċ ua mbriain, ⁊ lá toirr-

nobiles, et ignobiles, cum eis occisi sunt. The son of Mac Mahon, the men of Fermanagh, and the Oriels *victores fuerunt.*"

[t] *Geoffrey, Mares, and William Mareschal.*—The former is generally called Geffry de Marisco, or De Mariscis, by English writers.—See Hanmer's Chronicle, Dublin Edit. of 1809, pp. 382–385. He was made Custos or Governor of Ireland in 1216, and Lord Justice in 1226.—See Harris's Ware, vol. ii. p. 103. William Mareschal, or Marshal, was Earl of Pembroke, and Prince of Leinster in Ireland, in right of his wife, the granddaughter of Dermot Mac Murrough.—See Hanmer's Chronicle, Dublin Edit. of 1809, p. 343, *et sequen.*

[u] These passages are thus given in the Annals of Clonmacnoise, as translated by Mageoghegan: "A. D. 1207. There arose great warrs in Lynster between the Englishmen there, vizt. between Meyler and Geffry March, and also William Mareschall, which soone brought all Lynster and Munster to utter destruction.

"There arose also the like contention and strife between Meyler and Hugh Delacie, that between the said partys the land of Fohartíes was wasted, preyed, and destroyed."

[v] *Cathal.*—This passage is given more fully in the Annals of Kilronan, but under the year 1208, as follows: "A. D. 1208. Cathal, son of Dermot, son of Teige O'Mulrony, King of Moylurg, was taken prisoner by Cathal Crovderg in violation of the guarantee of the bishops who were securities between them, namely, Ardgal O'Connor, Murray O'Duffy, Clement O'Sneyey. He was, however, set at liberty, through the guarantee of those bishops, without giving a hostage or pledge. After this he went out of the country and took a great prey, which he drove on as far as Lough Macnean. A week afterwards he set out on a predatory excursion into Tir-Oiliolla [Tirerrill], and drove off a prey into the Curlieus, and over the Curlieus into Moylurg. A great force overtook him here, namely, Dermot, son of Manus, son of Turlough O'Conor; Manus, son of Murtough, son of Turlough O'Conor; Cormac, son of Tomaltagh of the Rock; Murray,

Cathal Crovderg O'Conor, King of Connaught, expelled Hugh O'Flaherty, and gave his territory to his own son, Hugh *O'Conor*.

A great war broke out among the English of Leinster; i. e. between Meyler, Geoffrey, Mares, and William Mareschal[t]. Leinster and Munster suffered severely from them.

Another great war broke out between Hugo de Lacy and Meyler; and the result was, that nearly all Meyler's people were ruined[u].

Cathal[v] Carragh, son of Dermot, who was son of Teige [O'Mulrony], took a great prey from Cormac, son of Tomaltagh Mac Dermot, and O'Flynn of the Cataract[w], but was overtaken by some of the Connacians, namely, Dermot, son of Manus, who was son of Murtough[x] O'Conor; Cormac, son of Tomaltagh; Conor God O'Hara, Lord of Leyny; and Donough O'Dowda, Lord of Tirawley and Tireragh; and a battle ensued, in which Cathal Carragh was defeated. He was taken prisoner, and blinded; and his son, Maurice, with the son of Cugranna O'Flanagan, and many others, were killed (in the battle).

Meyler Oge, Murtough O'Brien, and Turlough, the son of Roderic O'Conor,

son of Tomaltagh of the Rock; Donslevy, son of Rory O'Gara, Lord of Sliabh Lugha; Flaherty O'Flanagan, Chief of Clann Cahill; and Gilla-na-nech O'Monahan, King of Hy-Briuin na Sinna. When his Breifnian archers perceived that they were overtaken by this great force, they fled as soon as they had crossed Lec Damhaighe, and Mac Dermot, being left accompanied by his own followers only, he was rushed upon, and his son Maurice, and many others of his people, were slain, and he was himself at length taken prisoner, and his people routed. When this great force had dispersed, the counsel which the sons of Tomaltagh of the Rock adopted was, to put out Mac Dermot's eyes, and this was accordingly done."

Under this year the Annals of Ulster and of Kilronan record a battle between the son of Randal Mac Sorley and the men of Skye [Sciadh], in which a countless multitude were slaughtered.

[w] *Of the Cataract*, i. e. of Eαr uι ḟlαιnn, or Assylyn.—This was the name of a small cataract, now nearly removed by the wearing down of the rock, on the River Boyle, about one mile to the west of the town of Boyle. There was an ancient church on the north side of the river, opposite this cataract, originally called Eαr Ꝺαchonnα, i. e. St. Dachonna's cataract, and Eαr mic n-eιnc, i. e. the cataract of the son of Erc, that being the saint's patronymic name, from his father Erc; but in later ages, Eαr Uι Ḟhloιnn, O'Flynn's cataract, from the family of O'Flynn, who were the hereditary Erenaghs, or wardens, of the church, and the comharbas of St. Dachonna.—See note under the year 1209.

[x] *Dermot, son of Manus, who was son of Murtough.*—This Murtough O'Conor was the celebrated Muircheartach Muimhneach, or the Momonian, the eleventh son of Turlough More O'Conor, monarch of Ireland, and the ancestor of that warlike clan of the O'Conors, called Clann-Muircheartaigh.

ḋealḃaċ mac Ruaiḋri uí Concoḃair i ttír ḟiaċraċ aiḋne co ro airccsiot cúicc baile ḋécc.

Caṫal mac Ruaiḋri mac an tsionnaiġ uí Ċaṫarnaiġ tiġearna tſṫba do écc.

Sluaiccheaḋ la macaiḃ Hugo de laci, ⁊ la gallaiḃ miḋe go caislén aṫa an urċair go rabattur seċtmain for mís acc forḃaisi fair go ro ḟáccbaḋ an caislén leó, ⁊ trioċa ċéd ḟſrcceall, ⁊ go hionnarbaḋ Maoilir as in tír.

AOIS CRIOSD, 1208.

Aois Criosd, mile, da céd a hocht.

Dauid bſrtnac epscop Puirt Lairge do ṁarḃadh la hUá bfaoláin dona deisibh.

[y] *Fifteen ballys*, cúicc baile ḋécc.—A bally was at this period, the thirtieth part of a triocha ced, or barony.

[z] *Teffia*, teaṫḃa.—This was anciently a large territory, comprising, according to several ancient Irish and Anglo-Irish authorities, about the western half of the present county of Westmeath. It appears from various ancient authorities that it comprised the following baronies: 1. The barony of Rathconrath; 2. That part of the barony of Magheradernon, lying to the west of the River Brosnagh, and of the lakes of Lough Oul and Lough Ennell; 3. The barony of Cuircne, now Kilkenny West; 4. The barony of Brawney; 5. Clonlonan (into which the O'Melaghlins were afterwards driven), with that part of it which was added to the King's County, by the procurement of the celebrated Terence Coghlan; and 6. The barony of Kilcoursey in the King's County.—See O'Flaherty's *Ogygia*, part iii. c. 85, where it is stated that the lands assigned to the Tuites, Petits, and Daltons were in Teffia.

In the fourth century the southern half of this territory of Teffia was granted by the Monarch Niall of the Nine Hostages, to his son Maine, from whom it is sometimes, but not frequently, called Tir-Maine of Meath, and among whose descendants it was afterwards subdivided into petty territories, the lords of which were tributary to the archchief, who was looked upon as the representative of Maine, though not always of the senior branch of his descendants. North Teffia was divided from South Teffia by the River Eithne, now the Inny, and was granted in the fourth century to Carbry, the brother of Maine. This territory is frequently called Cairbre Gabhra in the old Irish authorities, but for many centuries before the English invasion, North Teffia was the principality of the O'Farrells, who gave it their tribe name of Anghaile, or South Conmaicne.

South Teffia was subdivided into the following lordships or chieftainries, viz.: 1. Breaghmhaine, now Brawney, the lordship of O'Breen; 2. Machaire Chuircne, which was originally the lordship of O'Tolairg, but was in the possession of the Dillons from the period of the Anglo-Norman invasion till the seventeenth century; 3. Calry-an-chala, and sometimes Calry-Teaffa, the lordship of Magawly, now the parish of Ballyloughloe; Muintir Tadhgain, the lordship of the Fox, or O'Caharny, now the barony of Kil-

made a predatory incursion into Tir-Fachrach Aidhne, and plundered fifteen ballys[y] (townlands).

Cathal, son of Rory, who was son of the Sinnagh (the Fox) O'Caharny, Lord of Teffia[z], died.

The sons of Hugo de Lacy and the English of Meath marched to the castle of Athnurcher [now Ardnurcher], and continued to besiege it for five weeks, when it was surrendered to them, as was also the territory of Fircal[a]; and Meyler was banished from the country[b].

THE AGE OF CHRIST, 1208.

The Age of Christ, one thousand two hundred eight.

David Breathnach (Walsh), Bishop of Waterford[c], was slain by O'Faelan of the Desies.

coursey, in the King's County; 5. Corca Adaim, or Corca Adain, now in all probability the barony of Magheradernon.

[a] *Fircal*, Feara Ceall, was, as already shewn, a territory in the south of ancient Meath, comprising the present baronies of Ballycowen, Ballyboy, and Fircall, or Eglish, in the King's County.

[b] Under this year the Annals of Clonmacnoise have the following entries, altogether omitted by the Four Masters:

"A. D. 1207. The English of Meath and Lynster, with their forces, went to Killaloe to build a castle, near the Borowe [béal borúṁa], and were frustrated of their purpose, did neither castle nor other thing worthy of memory, but lost some men and horses in their journey, and so returned to their houses back again.

"Moriertagh mac Bryen an Tleyve besieged the castle of Byrre, and at last burnt the whole town.

"The castle of Athroynny, in Lease [Ballyroane, in the Queen's County], was spoyled altogether by the said Mortagh and the sons of O'Connor of Connought" [who] "slewe many of the inhabitants, and after taking away all the cowes, sheep, harnesses, and other things therein, they burnt the town.

"The Castle of Kinnetty, the Castle of Byrre, and the Castle of Lothra, were broken downe and quite destroyed by the said Mortagh O'Bryen."

Under this year, also, the Dublin copy of the Annals of Innisfallen state, that the churches of Tigh Damhnad [Tedavnet], Kilmurrigan, and Clones" [in Ulster], "were burned by Hugo de Lacy.

[c] *Waterford*, Port Lairge.—Port Lairgé is the present Irish name of the city of Waterford. See note [z] under the year 1174, p. 18. Neither Ware nor Harris has any notice of this David as a bishop.—See Harris's edition of Ware's Bishops, under O'Heda, and Robert of Bedford, pp. 551, 552. His name does not occur in any of the Irish annals known to the Editor, except Mageoghegan's translation of the Annals of Clonmacnoise, in which his death is noticed as follows: "A. D. 1207. David Breathnagh, Bushopp

Creachsloiccheaḋ la hAodh Ua neill i ninis Eoġain. Rucc ua doṁnaill .i. doṁnall mór cona soċraitte fair, Ro cuirsiot caiṫiorgail etorra in ro marbaḋ ár dírimhe ar gach leiṫ. Torċair is in maiḋm sin doṁnall mac murchaḋa, ⁊ ár aḋbal do ċenél Eoġain imaille friss. Torcrattar i ffrioṫġuin an ṁaḋma Caṫbarr o doṁnaill, Ferġal ua baoiġill, Corbmac Ua doṁnaill, dauid ua doċartaiġ, ⁊ dream do ṁaiṫib ċenel cconaill cenmoṫátt. Ro sraoinead fo deoiḋ tre neart iommbualta for cenél neoghain.

Sluaiccheaḋ la hUa ndoṁnaill (Doṁnall mór) for ċenél neoġain, ⁊ for Aoḋ ua neill go rucc for creaċaiḃ ⁊ braiġdiḃ an tire gur snaḋmaḋ sídh eittir Ua ndoṁnaill ⁊ Ua neill, ⁊ ro naidmsiot a ccarattradh friaroile i nacchaiḋ gall ⁊ gaoiḋeal no ċuirfeaḋ ina naghaiḋ.

Duiḃinnsi mág aenġusa ticcerna cloinne hAoḋa ua neachdaċ do ṁarḃaḋ la mac duinnsleiḃe uí Eochaḋa.

Fínġin mac diarmata mic corbmaic ṁég cárṫaiġ do ṁarḃaḋ la a braiṫriḃ feisin.

Ualġarcc ua ruairc do ċor a tigearnas ḟer mbreifne, ⁊ Art mac doṁnaill mic ferġail do ġabail a ionaiḋ a huċt gall.

Iohannes episcopus norbus do ċor do Riġ Saxan i nErinn dia ḃeiṫ ina lustis innte, ⁊ Saxoin descoitċionnucchaḋ la coṁarba Peattair fodaiġ an esscoip do ċor cum coccaḋ i nerinn, go mbáttar Saxain gan aifrionn gan baistteaḋ gan ongaḋ, gan aḋnacal inaṫéċta fri ré trí mbliadhan.

of Waterford, was killed by O'Foylan of the Desies." *Breathnach*, as a family name, is now always anglicised Walsh. Waterford was made an episcopal see in 1096, and united to the see of Lismore in 1363.—See Harris's Ware, vol. i. p. 533; and Lanigan's Ecclesiastical History of Ireland, vol. iv. pp. 15, 16, 45.

[d] *David O'Doherty*.—He is the ancestor of the family of Mac Devitt, now so numerous in the barony of Inishowen.

[e] *Duvinnsi*, duiḃinnsi.—This name signifies the black, or black-haired man, of the island.

[f] *Iveagh*, Uí Eaċdach.—The name of two baronies in the county of Down. At this time O'Haughey was Chief of all Iveagh, and Magennis of only a portion of it called Clann Aedha.

[g] *Fineen*, Fínġin.—This name, which is very common in the family of Mac Carthy, signifies the fair offspring. It is Latinized *Florentius* by O'Sullevan Beare, throughout his History of the Irish Catholics, and now always anglicised *Florence*. The name Finnen is translated *Albinus* by Colgan.—See his *Acta Sanctorum*, p. 353, note 3.

[h] *Ualgarg*, ualġarcc.—This name, which was very common among the family of O'Rourke, is now obsolete, as the Christian or baptismal name of a man; but is preserved in the family of Magoalric, a collateral branch of the

A prey was taken by Hugh O'Neill in Inishowen. O'Donnell (Donnell More) overtook him with his forces; and a battle was fought between them, in which countless numbers were slaughtered on both sides. In this battle fell Donnell Mac Murrough, and a great number of the Kinel-Owen with him. In the heat of this conflict fell also Caffar O'Donnell, Farrell O'Boyle, Cormac O'Donnell, David O'Doherty[d], and other chiefs of the Kinel-Connell. The Kinel-Connell were at length routed by dint of fighting.

An army was led by O'Donnell (Donnell More) against Hugh O'Neill and the Kinel-Owen; and he seized upon the spoils and hostages of the country. A peace, however, was afterwards concluded between O'Neill and O'Donnell, who entered into an alliance to assist each other against such of the English or Irish as should oppose them.

Duvinnsi[e] Magennis, Lord of Clann-Aodha, in Iveagh[f], was slain by the son of Donslevy O'Haughy.

Fineen[g], son of Dermot, son of Cormac Mac Carthy, was slain by his own brothers.

Ualgarg[h] O'Rourke was deprived of the lordship of Breifny; and Art, son of Donnell, who was son of Farrell, assumed his place through the influence of the English.

John, Bishop of Norwich[i], was sent by the King of England into Ireland as Lord Justice; and the English were excommunicated by the successor of St. Peter for sending the Bishop to carry on war in Ireland; so that the English were without mass, baptism, extreme unction, or lawful interment, for a period of three years.

O'Rourkes, now very numerous in the county of Leitrim. It is derived from uaill, pride, and garg, fierce.

[i] *John, Bishop of Norwich, Johannes Episcopus Norbus.*—His name was John de Gray. He was chosen by King John's recommendation to the archbishopric of Canterbury in 1205; but Pope Innocent III. refused to confirm his election, and procured the election of Cardinal Stephen Langton, an Englishman then at Rome, in his place, and consecrated him with his own hands. The King, enraged at this conduct of the Pope, wrote him a sharp letter, upbraiding him with his unjust proceedings, which caused His Holiness to lay the whole kingdom under an interdict. This event is stated as follows in Mageoghegan's translation of the Annals of Clonmacnoise, under the year 1207: "An English Bushop was sent over into this land, by the King of England, to govern the land as Deputie thereof: he was Bushop of Norway [Norwich], and was Excommunicated by the Pope, together with all Englishmen in England, which Excommunication hung over them for the space of two

Muirceartaċ mac domnaill ui ḃriain tiġearna tuaḋṁuṁan do ġabáil lá gallaiḃ luimnigh tar sarúccaḋ trí nepscop tre ḟoráil ḋonnchaiḋ ċairḃriġ a ḋearbraṫar féin.

Diarmaitt ua caoṁáin taoiseċ o tuaim da ḃoḋar go gleóir do écc.

Amlaiḃ ua Roṫláin taoiseċ calraiġe cúile cearnatan do marḃaḋ la hua Móráin.

AOIS CRIOSD, 1209.

Aois Criosd, míle, da céd, a naoi.

Cele ua duḃṫaigh epscop Maiġe eo na Saxan, giollacrist ua cearnaiġ comorba condere, ⁊ flaiṫbeartach ua flainn comarba daconna easa mic neirc do écc.

or three years, in so much that their churches did not use the Sacraments durcing the said space." Hanmer says that this excommunication extended to Ireland also; but he should have said, to the English in Ireland.—See his Chronicle, Dublin Edition of 1809, pp. 373, 377.

[k] This passage is rendered as follows in Mageoghegan's translation of the Annals of Clonmacnoise: "A. D. 1207. Mortagh mac Donnell O'Bryen, prince of Thomond, was taken by the Englishmen of Lymbrick against the wills of three Bushopps, by the procurement of his own brother Donnagh Carbreagh mac Donnell O'Bryen."

[l] *O'Keevan*, ua caoṁain, now sometimes anglicised Kavanagh, but totally different from the Kavanaghs of Leinster. The Connaught Kavanaghs are yet numerous in the district here mentioned, but they have all dwindled into peasants, or small farmers.—See *Tribes, &c. of Hy-Fiachrach*, pp. 109, 167, 248, 35[illegible].

[m] *From Toomore to Gleoir.*—Tuaim-da-bhodhar is now anglicised *Toomore*. It is the name of an old church and parish near the River Moy, in the barony of Gallen and county of Mayo.—See *Tribes, &c. of Hy-Fiachrach*, printed for the Archæological Society in 1844, p. 242, note [o], and map prefixed to the same work. According to a tradition in the county of Sligo, Gleoir was the ancient name of the river now called the Culleen or Leafony river, which takes its rise to the south of Tawnalaghta townland, in the parish of Kilglass, and barony of Tireragh, and running northwards, empties itself into the sea at Pollacheeny, in Cabrakeel townland. From the position of this river, and the old church of Toomore, or Toomour, it is quite clear that the O'Caomhains possessed, or at least were the head chiefs of all the territory of Coolcarney, and the western portion of the barony of Tireragh, verging on the River Moy, near its mouth, and that their territory comprised the parishes of Toomore, Attymass, and Kilgarvan, in the county of Mayo, and the parish of Kilglass, in the county of Sligo.—See Map prefixed to *Tribes, Genealogies, and Customs of Hy-Fiachrach*, printed for the Irish Archæological Society in 1844.

[n] *O'Rothlain*, now pronounced by the Irish in the county of Sligo as if written O'Roithleain, and incorrectly anglicised *Rowley*. It might be more analogically anglicised Rollin, which would sound better. For the extent of the territory of this tribe of the Calry, see note under Cool-

Murtough, the son of Donnell O'Brien, Lord of Thomond, was taken prisoner by the English of Limerick, in violation of the guarantee of three bishops, and by order of his own brother, Donough Cairbreach[k].

Dermot O'Keevan[l], Lord of *that tract of country* extending from Toomore to Gleoir[m], died.

Auliffe O'Rothlain[n], Chief of Calry of Coolcarney, was slain by O'Moran[o].

THE AGE OF CHRIST, 1209.

The Age of Christ, one thousand two hundred nine.

Kele O'Duffy[p], Bishop of Mayo[q] of the Saxons; Gilchreest O'Kearney, Coarb (Bishop) of Connor[r]; and Flaherty O'Flynn, Coarb of Dachonna[s] of Eas-mic n-Eirc [Assylyn], died.

carney, at the year 1225.—See also *Tribes, &c., of Hy-Fiachrach*, printed for the Irish Archæological Society in 1844, pp. 167, 423.

[o] *O'Moran.*—He had his seat at Ardnarea, on the east side of the River Moy, at Ballina-Tirawley, and his territory extended thence to Toomore.—See *Tribes, Genealogies, and Customs of Hy-Fiachrach*, pp. 167, 245.

[p] *Kele O'Duffy.*—He is called Celestin, or Cele O'Dubhai, in Harris's edition of Ware's Bishops, p. 602.

[q] *Mayo*, maᵹ eo, translated by Colgan, *campus quercuum*, the plain of the oaks, though it more probably means plain of the *yews*. This place, which contained a monastery and a cathedral, was founded by St. Colman, an Irishman, who had been bishop of Lindisfarne, in the north of England, and who, returning to his native country in the year 664, purchased from a chieftain part of an estate on which he erected the monastery of Maigeo, in which he placed about thirty English monks, whom he had taken with him from Lindisfarne, and whom he had first established on Inis Bo Finne. Ussher states (*Primordia*, p. 964) that the see of Mayo was annexed to Tuam in 1559, and that Eugenius Mac Brehoan was the last Bishop of Mayo.—See also O'Flaherty's *Ogygia*, part i. c. 1; Harris's edition of Ware's Bishops, p. 602; and Lanigan's *Ecclesiastical History of Ireland*, vol. iii. p. 79.

[r] *Connor*, conneıṗe, now a small town in the barony and county of Antrim. Until the year 1442 it was the head of a bishop's see, founded by Mac Nise, who died in the year 507.—See Colgan's *Acta Sanctorum*, p. 190; and Harris's *Ware*, vol. i. p. 218. It was united to the see of Down in the year 1442. In the old Irish Annals, and other documents, the Bishop of Down is often called the Bishop of Uladh, or Dal Araidhe, while the Bishop of Connor, is always called after his cathedral church. Immediately before the English invasion, the territory of Dal Araidhe, comprising the diocese of Down, was possessed by Mac Donslevy, and Hy-Tuirtre and Firlee, comprising the diocese of Connor, by O'Lynn.—See note [o], under the year 1174, p. 13.

[s] *Dachonna.*—In the Irish Calendar of the O'Clerys, at the 8th of March, he is styled

Art mac domhnaill mic fferghail ui Ruairc tighearna breifne do marbhadh la corbmac mac airt uí maoilsechlainn, ⁊ la corbmac mac airt uí ruairc, ⁊ ualgarcc ua Ruairc do ghabáil ticcernais ina dhiaidh.

Donnchadh ua fferghail ticcerna na hanghaile do ecc.

Ri Saxan do techt i nerinn seacht ccéd long. Is ann ro ghabhsat in ath-cliath. Baoi athaidh ainnsein acc leghadh sccisi na mara de iar ttorrachtain

Mochonna Mac Eirc, Abbot of Eas-mic nEirc, in the county of Rescommon; and in the Feilire Aenguis, at the same day, the place is distinctly called eas mic nEirc, i. e. the cataract of the son of Eirc, i. e. of Dachonna. Eas mic nEirc, now Eas ui Fhloinn, an old church about one mile to the west of the town of Boyle. Colgan, and after him Lanigan, confounds this with the great Abbey of Boyle. The Editor has adduced various evidences to shew that Eas mic n-Eirc is not the great Abbey of Boyle, in a letter, describing the localities in the neighbourhood of Lough Key, written at Boyle, July 23, 1837, and now preserved at the Ordnance Survey Office, Phœnix Park. In this he has proved that Eas mic nEirc was the ancient name of the present Assylyn, and Ath da laarg that of the great Abbey of Boyle, and that Eas mic nEirc was also often called Eas Dachonna, from St. Dachonna, otherwise Mochonna mac nEirc, the patron saint of the place. See note under the year 1463.

[t] *Seven hundred ships*, seacht ccéd long.—The Dublin copy of the Annals of Ulster has the same number: "A. D. 1210. Ri Saxan do thaidhecht i n-Erinn co longais diarmhidhe .i. dcc. long. The King of England came to Ireland with a great fleet, i. e. seven hundred ships.' The exact number of ships brought by King John to Ireland is not stated in any other of the Irish Annals. In the Annals of Kilronan his fleet is styled loingess adhbhal, "a prodigious fleet," at the year 1209; and cobhlach mór, "a great fleet," at 1210. In the old translation of the Annals of Ulster, the entry is given briefly as follows, without mentioning the number of ships: "A. D. 1209. The King of England came to Ireland with a great navy." In the Annals of Clonmacnoise, as translated by Mageoghegan, the account of the acts of King John in Ireland is entered as follows under the year 1209.

"A. D. 1209. The King of England, with a great Company of men and ships, came into Ireland, and landed at Dublin, came from thence to Tibreydultan, called Ardbreackan, in Meath, where Cahall Crovederg O'Connor came to the King's house, banished Walter Delacie out of Meath into England, whereupon the King and O'Connor, with his Fleett, departed, and went to Carrickfergus, and banished Hugh Delacie from out of Ulster into England.

"O'Neal came then to the King of England's house and departed from him again, without hostages or securitie: O'Connor return'd to his own house from thence [and] the King of England lay siege to Carrickffergus, and compelled the Warde to leave the same, and did put a strong ward of his own in the same, and from thence the King came to Rathwry, or Rathgwayrie, [where] O'Connor came again to the King's house and yealded him four hostages, viz[t]. Connor God O'Hara, prince of Lawyne in Connought, Dermott mac Connor O'Moyleronie, Ffyn O'Carmackan, chieftaine of Klyn Kelly, and Torvean mac Gollgoyle. The King of England went soon after for England, and conveighed his [these] hostages with him."

It is given in the Annals of Kilronan as fol-

Art, son of Donnell, who was son of Farrell O'Rourke, Lord of Breifny, was slain by Cormac, the son of Art O'Melaghlin, and Cormac, the son of Art O'Rourke; and Ualgarg O'Rourke assumed the lordship as his successor.

Donough O'Farrell, Lord of Annaly, died.

The King of England came to Ireland with seven hundred ships[t], and landed at Dublin, where he remained until he had recruited himself after the fatigues

lows, under the year 1210, which seems the true Connaught account of the event.

"A. D. 1210. Johannes, the son of Fitz-Empress, King of England, came to Ireland with a great fleet this year. On his arrival he levied a great army of the men of Ireland, to march them to Ulster, to take Hugh De Lacy, or banish him from Ireland, and to take Carrickfergus. Hugh departed from Ireland, and those who were guarding Carrickfergus left it and came to the King, and the King left a garrison of his own there. He afterwards dispatched a fleet of his people to the Isle of Mann, who plundered the island, and killed many of its inhabitants. Cathal Crovderg O'Conor, King of Connaught, and his Connacian forces, were on this expedition. On their arrival in the north, the King of England had told the King of Connaught to return to him at the expiration of a fortnight, and the latter promised that he would do so, and bring his son Hugh O'Conor with him to be delivered up as a hostage. This, however, the King did not require; but he said, 'Bring him, that he may receive a charter for the third part of Connaught.' But when O'Conor returned home, the advice which he and his wife and people adopted was,—the worst that could be,—not to bring his son to the King. However, O'Conor repaired to the King of England, and as he did not bring his own son, the king obtained the following persons in his stead, viz., Dermot, son of Conor Mac Dermot, King of Moylurg; Conor O'Hara, King of Leyny in Connaught; Finn O'Carmacan, a servant of trust to O'Conor; and Torbert, son of the King of the Gall-Gaels, one of O'Conor's lawgivers (peaċtaiṗiḃ). The King of England then returned, and brought these chieftains with him into England. He left the chief government of Ireland to the English bishop, and told him to build three castles in Connaught. The English bishop soon after raised an army in Meath and Leinster, and marched to Athlone, and there erected a bridge across the ford, and a castle on the site of O'Conor's castle."

In the Dublin copy of the Annals of Innisfallen, a somewhat different account of King John's actions in Ireland is entered under the year 1211, which the Editor is tempted to insert here; for, although he has some suspicions of its authenticity, he thinks that the compiler had original documents which are now lost, or, at least, not preserved in Ireland.

"A. D. 1211" [*recte* 1210]. "John, King of England, with a large fleet and a numerous army, set sail for Ireland, and landed at Waterford. Thither Donough Cairbreach, the son of Donnell More O'Brien, repaired, to make his submission to him, and received a charter for Carrigogonnell, and the lordship thereunto belonging, for which he was to pay a yearly rent of sixty marks.

"Cathal Crovderg, the son of Turlough More O'Conor, King of Connaught, repaired with a great body of troops to make his obeisance unto him.

"King John proceeded from Waterford to Dublin, with the intention of banishing from

do, ⁊ tanaic o Athcliaṫ go Tiopraitt Ulltain i Midhe. Do coidh Caṫal Croibhdherg ó Concobhair ina tech. Ro hionnarbaḋ Ualtera de Laci as in Miḋe hi Saxain. Do ċoid iaraṁ an Rí ⁊ na maiṫe bai ina ḟarraḋ go Carraic Fergura co ro ḋioċuir Hugo de Laci a hUlltaiḃ hi Saxain. Aodh ó Néill do ḋol fo ṫogairm an Riġ ⁊ a ṫeaċt for ccúlaiḋ gan giallaḋh. An Riġ do ḃeiṫ i ḃforbairi for an ccarraicc co ro faccbaḋh dó í, ⁊ tucc a ṁuintir fein innte. Tanaicc ó Concobhair iaroṁ dia ṫiġ iar ndein.

Do coidh iaroṁ Rí Saxan go Raith nGuaire, ⁊ tanaicc Ua Concobhair dorididhisi dia foighidh, ⁊ ro bai an Rí acc iarraiḋ a ṁeic ar Ua cConcobhair do ġiall fri coṁall dó. Ni ṫárd Ua Concobhair a ṁac uaḋa, aċt do rad cethrar dia ṁuintir dia ċionn, .i. Concobhar Godd ó hEġra tiġearna Luiġne, ⁊ Diarmait mac Concobhair uí Maoilruanaiḋ tiġearna Ṁuiġi Luircc, Fionn Ua Carmacáin, ⁊ Toirḃeard mac Riġ Gallgaoidhel do aes grada uí Concobhair, ⁊ do ċóid an Rí go Saxain, ⁊ rucc na braiġde sin lais.

Ireland Walter de Lacy (who afterwards passed into France). The King marched from Dublin into Meath, and dispatched a large fleet northwards to a fortress of the English called Carlingford, to command the sons of Hugh de Lacy, viz., Walter, Lord of Meath, and Hugh, Earl of Ulster, and then Lord Deputy of Ireland, to appear before him to answer for the death of the valiant knight, John de Courcy" [Lord of Rathenny and Kilbarrock.—*Grace*], "who was treacherously slain by them, and to answer to such questions as should be asked of them, for their apparent ill conduct. When Hugh de Lacy had discovered that the King was going to the north, he burned his own castles in Machaire Conaille, and in Cuailgne, before the King's eyes, and also the castles which had been erected by the Earl of Ulster and the men of Oriel, and he himself fled to Carrickfergus, leaving the chiefs of his people burning, levelling, and destroying the castles of the country, and, dreading the fury of the King, he himself went over the sea.

"When the King saw this disrespect offered him, he marched from Drogheda to Carlingford, where he made a bridge of his ships, across the harbour, by which he landed some of his troops on the other side, and proceeded thence to Carrickfergus, partly by sea and partly by land, and laid siege to the castle, which he took."

According to the Itinerary of King John, by the accurate and trustworthy T. D. Hardy, Esq., the King was at Crook, near Waterford. on the 20th of June, 1210, and was on his return, at Fishguard, on the 26th of August, the same year. For an account of his movements in Ireland at this period, the reader is referred to the Rev. Mr. Butler's curious work on the History of the Castle of Trim.

Hanmer, Cox, and Leland, assert that O'Neill submitted to King John on this occasion; but, if we believe the Irish accounts, he refused to give him hostages.

[u] *Tiopraid Ulltain*, i. e. St. Ulltan's well.—There was a place so called in Westmeath in Colgan's time.—See his *Acta Sanctorum*, p. 242, note 25; and Lanigan's *Ecclesiastical History of Ireland*, vol. iii. p. 52. There is a holy well

of his voyage, and then set out for Tioprait Ulltain[u] in Meath, where Cathal Crovderg O'Conor came into his house [i. e. *made his submission to him*]. He banished Walter de Lacy to England, and then proceeded, with his nobles, to Carrickfergus, whence he also banished Hugo de Lacy to England. Hugh O'Neill repaired *hither* at the King's summons, but returned home without giving him hostages. The King besieged Carrick until it surrendered, and he placed his own people in it. O'Conor then returned home.

The King of England then went to Rathguaire[w], whither O'Conor repaired again to meet him; and the King requested O'Conor to deliver him up his son, to be kept as a hostage. O'Conor did not give him his son, but delivered up four of his people instead, namely, Conor God O'Hara, Lord of Leyny; Dermot, son of Conor O'Mulrony, Lord of Moylurg; Finn O'Carmacan; and Torvenn, son of the King of the Gall-Gaels[x], one of O'Conor's servants of trust. The King then returned to England, bringing these hostages with him.

called Tobar Ulltain in the townland of Ballynaskea, near the old church of Rathcore in Meath.—See Ordnance Map of Meath, sheet 48; and there is also a townland called TobarUlltain in the parish of Killinkere, in the barony of Castlerahen, and county of Cavan, and not far from the boundary of the county of Meath. This townland contains a holy well dedicated to St. Ulltan, which was formerly visited by pilgrims; but it is more than probable that Mageoghegan is right in making the Tobar Ulltain, visited by King John on this occasion, another name for Ardbraccan.—See p. 162, *supra*.

[w] *Rathguaire* is so called by those who speak Irish at the present day, but anglicised *Rathwire*. It lies in the parish of Killucan, in the east of the county of Westmeath, and about three miles north north-west of Kinnegad.—See *Circuit of Ireland by Muircheartach Mac Neill*, published by the Irish Archæological Society in 1841, p. 49, note 151. The castle of Rathwire is thus described by Sir Henry Piers in 1682, in his Chorographical Description of the County of Westmeath: "Rathwire is the first place of note that presents itself to our view, and that at a distance, if you come from the east, situate in the barony of Farbill, on a high rising ground, built as of design not to overlook, but to awe the whole country; founded (as tradition goes) by Sir Hugh de Lacy, who was one of the first English conquerors, and fixed in this country in or very near the reign of Henry the Second. It seems, by what to this day remains of the ruins, to have been a strong, well-built fort, for the manner of building at that time capacious and of good receipt; now only remain some portions of the outwalls and heaps of rubbish."—*Collectanea de Rebus Hibernicis*, p. 61. See also a notice of this place at the year 1450, where it is mentioned that this town was plundered and burned by Mageoghegan. There is scarcely a vestige of it now remaining.

[x] *Gall-Gaels*. — Of this people O'Flaherty writes as follows: "Gallgaidelios vero existimo Gaideliós insulas Britanniæ adjacentes tum incolentes, Nam Donaldum filium Thadæi O Brian, quem Anno Christi 1075 Manniæ, ac Insularum

AOIS CRIOSD, 1210.

Aois Criosd, míle, dá céd, a deich.

Goill do ṫeacht co caoluiscce. Aoḋ ó néill, ⁊ doṁnall ua doṁnaill do ṫionol ċuca go ro marḃait leo na goill im Henri mbecc. Ro roinnsiot a nionnṁusa, ⁊ a nédála for na sloġaibh.

Toirrdelḃach mac Ruaiḋri uí concoḃair do ḋenaṁ creiċe i muiġ luirg, ⁊ rucc lsir is in Seġais í do ṡaighiḋ diarmata a ḃraṫar. Luiḋ Aoḋ mac caṫail ina deadhaiḋ co ndeachaiḋ toirrdelḃaċ is in tuaisceart ar teicheḋ roimhe.

Braighde Connacht do ṫoiḋecht i nerinn, concoḃar god o hEġra tiġearna luighne, ⁊ diarmait mac concoḃair uí maoilruanaiḋ, fionn ua carmacáin, ⁊ aireaċtach mac donnchaiḋ.

Muirchertach muimhnech mac toirrdealḃaiġ moir do ecc.

Coccaḋ mór do eirġe eitir Riġ Saxan ⁊ Ri bretan, teacta do ṫocht o Righ Saxan ar cend an gailleasbuicc, ⁊ maiṫe ġall nereann imon ngaill-esscop do ḋol fo ṫoġairm Righ Saxan, ⁊ Riocard diúid do ḟaccbail ina iustis i nerinn, ⁊ an iustis do ṫocht co háṫ luain ar dáigh go ccuirfeaḋ a

proceres regni sui protectorem acceperunt, Inse Gall, & Gallgædelu regem Hibernicè dictum reperio. Hebrides vero sunt, quas nostri Inse-gall dixerunt."—*Ogygia*, c. 75, p. 360.

y *Cael-uisge*, i. e. *narrow water*,—now called Caol-na-h-Eirne,—is that part of Lough Erne near Castle Caldwell, where the lake becomes narrow. No remains of the castle are now visible; nor does it appear that it was left standing for any considerable period.

z *Henry Beg*.—This passage is given as follows in Mageoghegan's translation of the Annals of Clonmacnoise:

"A. D. 1210. The Castle of Keyleuskie was made by Gilbert Mac Cosdealvie" [now Costello]. "O'Neale came with his forces to the place, caused them to desist from building thereof, killed the builders with the constable of the place, called Henry the younger."

In the Dublin copy of the Annals of Innisfallen this castle is said to have been built by Henry, the King of England's son, upon an island [*recte* caol?] of Lough Erne, and that he was slain by O'Neill and Mac Mahon.

a *Mac Donough*.—This passage is copied incorrectly by the Four Masters, from mere carelessness: indeed they have left many entries imperfect throughout their compilation. It stands more correctly in the Annals of Kilronan, as follows:

"A. D. 1211. Braiġde Connaċt do toiġeaċt i n Erinn .i. Diarmaid mac Conċubair mic Diarmada riġ muiġe luirc, 7 Concubar O heaġra ri luiġni 7 find O Carmacan, 7 toirbeard mac Gallgoedil. Aireaċtaċ mac Duinnċaṫaiġ occisus est.

THE AGE OF CHRIST, 1210.

The Age of Christ, one thousand two hundred ten.

The English came to Cael-uisge[y]. Hugh O'Neill and Donnell O'Donnell, assembling their forces, marched thither, and slew the English, together with Henry Beg[z], and distributed their goods and property among their troops.

Turlough, the son of Roderic O'Conor, took a prey in Moylurg, and carried it with him to Seghais [the Curlieus], to his brother Dermot. Hugh, the son of Cathal, pursued him; but Turlough fled before him to the North.

The hostages of Connaught arrived in Ireland, viz. Conor God O'Hara, Lord of Leyny; Dermot, son of Conor O'Mulrony; Finn O'Cormacan; and Aireachtach Mac Donough[a].

Murtough Muimhneach[b], son of Turlough More [O'Conor], died.

A great war broke out between the King of England and the King of Wales: and ambassadors came from the King of England into Ireland for the English bishop; and the chiefs of the English of Ireland repaired, with the English bishop, to attend the summons of the King of England: and Richard Tuite[c] was left in Ireland as Lord Chief Justice.

"A. D. 1211. The hostages of Connaught arrived in Ireland, viz., Dermot, son of Conor Mac Dermot, King of Moylurg; Conor O'Hara, King of Leyny; Finn O'Carmacan, and Torbert, son of the Gall-Gael. Aireaghtagh Mac Doncahy *occisus est.*" Here it is to be observed that the death of Aireaghtagh is a distinct entry, and has nothing to do with the account of the returning of the hostages. The list of these hostages is given correctly by the Four Masters under the last year.

[b] *Murtough Muimhneach*, i. e. the Momonian, so called because he was fostered in Munster. He was the son of Turlough More O'Conor, Monarch of Ireland and the ancestor of the warlike and restless clan of the O'Conors called Clann Muircheartaigh. In the Annals of Clonmacnoise, as translated by Mageoghegan, his death is entered as follows: "A. D. 1210. Mortagh Moyneagh mac Terlagh, Tanist, or next successor of the kingdom of Connought, died." This Murtough Muimhneach had four sons, namely, Manus, Conor Roe, Donough Reagh, and Conor Gearr, who raised great disturbances in Connaught in their time.—See the Book of Lecan, fol. 72, *et sequen.*, and Duald Mac Firbis's Genealogical Book, Lord Roden's copy, p. 219.

[c] *Richard Tuite.*—This is a mistake of the Four Masters, for Richard Tuite was not Lord Justice of Ireland. His name does not appear in the list published in Harris's edition of Ware's works, vol. ii., or in any of the older Irish annals. This entry is given as follows in Mageoghegan's translation of the Annals of Clonmacnoise, which is more correct than the ac-

bhraithre co Luimnech, go port Láirge, 7 co Loch garman 7 co mbiadh féin in Athcliath, 7 in Ath luain. Do rala dó gur ro thuitset cloca caislén atha luain ina chenn gur bo marbh gan anmain Riocard diuid cona shacart, 7 co ndreim dia mhuintir immaille friss tria mhiorbailibh Dé, naoimh Pedair, 7 naoimh Chiarain.

Clann Ruaidhri uí Concobhair, 7 Tadhg mac Concobhair Maonmhuighe do thocht tar Sionainn anair isna tuathaibh, 7 dream do muintir Anghaile imaille friu 7 ruccsat creich leo i nDitreibh Cheneoil Dobhta. Do thaeth Aodh mac Cathail,

count of the transaction manufactured by the Four Masters: "A. D. 1210. The English Bushopp that was Deputie and Richard Tuite founded a stone castle in Athlone, wherein there was a Tower of stone built, which soon after fell and killed the said Richard Tuite, with eight Englishmen more. My author sayeth that this befell by the miracles of St. Quæran, of St. Peter, and St. Paule, upon whose Land the said Castle was built." After this it is stated that the English bishop went to England. The Annals of Kilronan also state that the bridge of Athlone was erected by the English bishop this year, and also its castle, on the site of O'Conor's castle, namely, on the site of one erected in 1129 by Turlough More O'Conor, then King of Connaught.

The fact is, that the Four Masters have disarranged this passage, as appears by the original Irish of it given in the margin of Mageoghegan's translation of the Annals of Clonmacnoise. It is as follows: Caislén cloiche do dhénamh ag ath luain la gallaibh .i. las an ngaillesbog, 7 la Riocard De Uide. Tor cloiche do deanamh is an chaislén, 7 a thuitim co ro marbh Riocard 7 ochtar gall maille fris .i. tria fearta aibh Ciarain, Poil 7 Peadair sa fearann ar a ndearnadh an caislen sin. In the Annals of Kilronan, and in Grace's Annals, it is stated that Richard Tuite was killed by the fall of a stone at Athlone, in the year 1211. The Four Masters should have arranged the passage as follows, as is evident from the older annals: "Previous to his being called to England, this Lord Justice (John de Gray) went to Athlone to erect a castle there, that he might send his brothers [or relations] to Limerick, Waterford, and Wexford, and that he himself might make Dublin and Athlone his principal quarters. For this purpose he raised forces in Leinster and Meath (where Richard Tuite had been the most powerful Englishman since the flight of the De Lacys to France), and marched to Athlone, where he erected a bridge across the Shannon, and a castle on the site of the one which had been built by Turlough More O'Conor, in the year 1129. But it happened, through the effects of the anathema pronounced against this warlike bishop by the Coarb of St. Peter, and the miraculous interposition of St. Peter and St. Kieran, into whose sanctuaries he was extending the outworks of the castle, that he lost, on this occasion, Richard Tuite, the most distinguished of his barons, as also Tuite's chaplain, and seven other Englishmen, for one of the towers of the castle fell, and overwhelmed them in the ruins."

This Richard Tuite received large grants of land in Teffia in Westmeath, and was made baron of Moyashell. His pedigree is traced by Mac Firbis to Charlemagne, but upon what authority the Editor has not been able to discover. Thus, the pedigree of Andrew Boy Tuite, of the castle of Moneylea, near Mullingar, runs as follows: "Andrew Boy, son of Walter, son of An-

The Justice went to Athlone, with the intention of sending his brothers to Limerick, Waterford, and Wexford, that he himself might reside in Dublin and Athlone (alternately); but it happened, through the miracles of God, St. Peter, and St. Kieran, that some of the stones of the castle of Athlone fell upon his head, and killed on the spot Richard Tuite, with his priest and some of his people, along with him.

The sons of Roderic O'Conor and Teige, the son of Conor Moinmoy, accompanied by some of the people of Annaly, came across the Shannon, from the east side, into the Tuathas[d], and carried a prey with them into the wilderness of Kinel-Dofa[e]. Hugh, the son of Cathal Crovderg, pursued them; and a battle

drew, son of Edmond, son of Andrew, son of Geoffry, commonly called *an Gilla Gorm*, son of Thomas, son of James, son of Thomas, son of John, son of Richard, son of Rickard, surnamed *of the Castles*, son of Thomas, son of Maurice, son of Rickard More, son of John Tuite, son of the King of Denmark, son of Drobard, son of Richard, son of Luibincus, or Lamard, son of Arcobal, son of Rolandus, son of Oliver, son of Carolus Magnus, King of France.

In the Annals of Kilronan is the following curious account of the affairs of Connaught at this period: "A. D. 1210. Donough Cairbreach O'Brien with his forces, and Geoffry Mares with his forces, composed of the English of Munster, and Hugh, son of Roderic O'Conor, joined by the son of O'Flaherty, marched into Connaught as far as Tuam, and proceeding thence to Loch na n-Airneadh in Ciarraighe, they seized upon great preys, and remained a fortnight, or nearly twenty nights, in Ciarraighe, the Connacians opposing them. After this O'Conor and his people came on terms of peace with Donough Cairbreach and Geoffry Mares, and the conditions were these, that they should be permitted to pass to Athlone to the English bishop, and that O'Brien and Geoffry Mares should make peace between O'Conor and the English bishop. This was accordingly done, and Turlough, the son of Cathal Crovderg, and the sons of other distinguished men of Connaught, were given into the hands of the English bishop."

[d] *Into the Tuathas*, iſ na tuaṫaiḃ.—There were three territories of this name on the west side of the Shannon. The sentence would be more correct thus, "do ṫoċt tar Sionainn aniar iſ na tuaṫaiḃ," i. e. came across the Shannon westwards into the Tuathas. For the situation and exact extent of the territory called the Tuathas, in the county of Roscommon, the reader is referred to *Tribes and Customs of Hy-Many*, printed for the Irish Archæological Society in 1843, p. 90, note [b], and the map prefixed to the same. The celebrated mountain anciently called Sliaḃ ḃáġna na d-Tuaṫ, now Slieve Baune, extends through the Tuathas from north to south, nearly parallel with the Shannon. The word tuata is the plural of tuat, a territory or district, and the districts or Tuathas here referred to were three in number, namely, Tir Briuin na Sinna, Corca Eachlann, and Kinel-Dofa. See the next note.

[e] *Kinel-Dofa*, cenel doḃṫa.—This was in latter ages called Doohy-Hanly, from its chief, O'Hanly, the senior of the Kinel-Dofa. It was the ancient name of a territory in the present county of Roscommon, extending along the Shannon from Caradh na-dtuath (now

croiḃdſircc ina ndiaiḋ, ⁊ do beartsat deaḃaiḋ dia roile ⁊ ro ṁeaḃaiḋ ar ṁacaibh Ruaiḋri gur ro cuireaḋ dar Sionainn sair doridiri iatt iar ffacc-ḃail daoine ⁊ each.

AOIS CRIOSD, 1211.

Aois Criosd, míle, dá ched, a haon ndécc.

Sitriocc ua laiġenáin coṁarba coṁgaill do ecc.

Caislen cluana heoais do ḋénaṁ lá gallaiḃ ⁊ lás an ngaillespoc, ⁊ crſchṡluaiccheaḋ do ḋenaṁ leó i ttír eoġain. Aoḋ ó néill do ḃreiṫ orra, ⁊ ro sraoineaḋ reṁe for gallaiḃ, ⁊ ro ċuir a nár im Maoilir mac Robſrd.

Tomas mac uċtraigh go macaiḃ Raġnaill mic Soṁairlich do teċt co doire ċoluim ċille foirſnn sé long seaċtmoġat, ⁊ an baile do orgain ⁊ do milleaḋ leo. Lodar assiḋe co hinis eoġain, ⁊ ro ṁillſet in insi uile.

called Caranadoe Bridge) to Drumdaff, in the southern extremity of the parish of Kilgefin. It was divided from Carcachlann, or Corca Sheachlann, the country of Mac Brannan, by the ridge of the mountain called Slieve Baune, the western face of which belonged to Mac Brannan, and the eastern to O'Hanly; and tradition says that there were standing stones and crosses on the ridge of the mountain which marked the boundary between them. According to the most intelligent of the natives, the following are the townlands of this mountain, which were in Corcachlann, viz.: Aghadangan, Corrowhawnagh (in Bumlin parish); Cloonycarron, Carryward, Ballymore, Ballybeg (in Lissonuffy parish); Leckan, Aghalahard, Reagh, Killultagh, Aghaclogher (in Cloonfinlough parish). All the other townlands of the mountain lying east of these belonged to Kinel-Dofa. Treanacreeva at Scramoge Bridge was also on the boundary between both territories.

Kinel-Dofa, or O'Hanly's country, comprised the following parishes, viz., the entire of the parishes of Kilglass and Termonbarry, Cloontuskert and Kilgefin; one townland of the parish of Bumlin, now called North Yard; the east half of the parish of Lissonuffy (as divided by the ridge of Slieve Baune, as aforesaid). The desert or wilderness of Kinel-Dofa (in which St. Berach, or Barry, founded his church of Cluain Coirpthe), is thus described by the Rev. John Keogh, of Strokestown, author of the Irish Herbal, who wrote in 1682:

"The woods, the chiefest in the county of Roscommon, are lodged about the saide mountaine (Slieve Bawn), situate most upon the north-east side of it, and beyond the north part thereof, Montaugh (móinteaċ), is an aggregate of many and great bogs several miles long, and in some parts thereof two miles in breadth, intercepted betwixt the said mountain and the River Shannon, interspersed here and there with some little islands of profitable land, interrupted one from another by interpositions of the said bogs."

O'Dugan speaks of O'Hanly's country as follows:

Duṫaiḋ do'n ḟeaḋain airmġér,
Cenel doḃṫa nolúṫ aiṁreḋ;
Ḃí cóiṁḟearc um ċríḋe
Ar oireaċt ó n-ainliġe.

was fought between them, in which the sons of Roderic were defeated, and again driven eastwards across the Shannon, leaving some of their men and horses behind.

THE AGE OF CHRIST, 1211.

The Age of Christ, one thousand two hundred eleven.

Sitric O'Laighenain[f], Coarb of St. Comgall [of Bangor], died.

The castle of Clones was erected by the English and the English bishop, and they made a predatory incursion into Tyrone; but Hugh O'Neill overtook them, and routed and slaughtered them, *and slew, among others*, Meyler, the son of Robert.

Thomas Mac Uchtry and the sons of Randal Mac Sorley[g] came to Derry with a fleet of seventy-six ships, and plundered and destroyed the town. They passed thence into Inishowen, and ravaged the entire island [*recte* peninsula].

"The country of the tribe of sharp weapons
Is Kinel-Dofa fast and uneven;
There dwells affection in my heart
For the people of O'Hanly."

The following pedigree, as given by Duald Mac Firbis, will shew how O'Hanly descends from Dofa:

Loughlin, son of
Hugh, or Aedh, who was the son of
Conor, or Conchobhar.
Donnell, or Domhnall.
Ivor, or Imhar.
Donnell.
Amlaff, or Amhlaoibh.
Ivor mor.
Murtough, or Muircheartach, who found the white steed which Teige O'Conor had, and from which he was styled an eiċ ġil, or of the White Steed.
Raghnall, who fought at the battle of Clontarf in 1014.
Morough, or Murchadh.
Teige, or Tadhg.
Donnell.
Teige.
Murtough, or Muircheartach.
Anly, or Ainlighe, *a quo* O'Hanly.
Hurly, or Urthuile.
Muldoon, or Maelduin.
Cluthechar.
Funis.
Dofa, or Dobhtha, the progenitor of the Kinel-Dofa, and from whom St. Berach, or Barry, the patron saint of the district, was the fifth in descent.
Aengus.
Erc the Red.
Brian.
Eochy Muighmheodhain, Monarch of Ireland in the fourth century.

[f] *O'Laighenain*, now anglicised Lynam.

[g] *Mac Sorley*, mac Somairle, anglicised Mac

Sloicċeaḋ la connactaiḃ tria ṫoġairm an ġailleaspuic ⁊ ġillibeirt mic goisdelḃaiġ co hEssruaiḋ, ⁊ do ronsat caislen occ caol uisce.

Ruaiḋri, mac ruaiḋri, mic toirrdealḃaiġ ui concoḃair, do marḃaḋ la luiġniḃ Connaċt.

Corbmac mac Airt uí maoileaċloinn do buain delḃna do na gallaiḃ, ⁊ Maoileachlainn mac airt do ṫaḃairt maḋma ar na gallaiḃ do ḃai ag coiṁett dealḃna, ⁊ a cconstabla Robeard ḋúncomair do marḃaḋ.

Cugaela ua heidhin do ecc.

Raġnailt ⁊ Cailleċ dé dí ingin Ruaiḋri ui Concoḃair do écc.

AOIS CRIOSD, 1212.

Aois Criosd, mile, da céd, a dodecc.

Druimċaoin cona tempall do loscaḋ la cenél neoġain gan ced dua néill.

Fergal ua caṫáin tiġearna ciannaċta ⁊ ḟer na craoiḃe do ṁarḃaḋ la gallaiḃ.

Gillibert mac goisdelḃaiġ do ṁarḃaḋ i ccaislen ċaoiluisce, ⁊ an caislen fesin do loscaḋ la hua neicnigh.

Caislen cluana heoais do loscaḋ la hAoḋ ua neill, ⁊ la tuaisceart erenn.

Donnchaḋ ua heiḋin do ḋallaḋ la hAoḋ mac caṫail croiḃdeirg gan ced dua concoḃair.

Maiḋm caille na ccrann do ṫaḃairt la corbmac mac Airt ui maoilseċ-

Sawairle in the old translation of the Annals of Ulster. Samhairle, anglicised Sorley, was a name very common among the Mac Donnells of Scotland. Thomas Mac Uchtry was Earl of Athol in Scotland, and the son of Alan de Gallaway.

[h] *Cael-uisge*, caol uisge, i. e. *narrow water*, is now called Caol na h-Eirne, and is that narrow part of Lough Erne near Castle Caldwell. No remains of the castle are now visible.

[i] *Duncomar.*—This passage is given as follows in Mageoghegan's translation of the Annals of Clonmacnoise:

"A. D. 1211. Cormack mac Art O'Melaghlin expelled the Englishmen out of Delvyn, and gave a great overthrow to a company of Englishmen that were left to defend that contrey, in which discomfiture Robertt Dongomer, their constable and chief head, was slain, together with Gillernew Mac Coghlan, the Prince of Delvyn's son."

[k] *Raghnailt.*—A woman's name, corresponding with the man's name Raghnall, or Randall.

[l] *Caillech De*, i. e. *the Nun of God.*—It would

An army was led by the Connacians, at the summons of the English bishop and Gilbert Mac Costello, to Assaroe; and they erected a castle at Cael-uisge[h].

Roderic, the son of Roderic, who was son of Turlough O'Conor, was slain by the inhabitants of Leyny, in Connaught.

Cormac, the son of Art O'Melaghlin, wrested Delvin from the English; and Melaghlin, the son of Art, defeated the English, who were maintaining possession of that territory, and killed their constable, Robert of Duncomar[i].

Cugaela O'Heyne died.

Raghnailt[k] and Caillech De[l], two daughters of Roderic O'Conor, died.

THE AGE OF CHRIST, 1212.

The Age of Christ, one thousand two hundred twelve.

Drumquin[m], with its churches, was burned by the Kinel-Owen, without the consent[n] of O'Neill.

Farrell O'Kane, Lord of Kienaghta and Firnacreeva, was slain by the English.

Gilbert Mac Costello was slain in the castle of Cael-uisge; and the castle itself was burned by O'Hegny.

The castle of Clones[o] was burned by Hugh O'Neill and the [men of the] north of Ireland.

Donough O'Heyne was deprived of sight by the son of Cathal Crovderg, without the consent of the O'Conor.

The victory of Caill-na-gcrann[p] was gained by Cormac, the son of Art

appear to be the feminine form of Cele De, which is Latinized Deicola by Giraldus Cambrensis, and Anglicised Culdee.

[m] *Drumquin*, ᴅꞃuım ċaoın.—This is the name of a townland and village in the barony of Omagh, in the county of Tyrone, and about six miles to the west of the town of Omagh.—See Ordnance Map of Tyrone, sheet 33.

[n] *Without the consent*, ᵹan ċeaᴅ ᴅua neıll, "*O'Nello invito.*" Ᵹan ċeaᴅ ᴅo is an idiomatic expression, generally denoting "*in despite of,*" or "*in defiance of.*" This passage is thus rendered in the old translation of the Annals of Ulster: "A. D. 1212. Drumkyn with its churche burnt by Kindred Owen, without O'Neil's licence."

[o] *Clones.*—A well-known town in the county of Monaghan. A round tower and large stone cross, with antique ornaments, and now or lately used as the market cross, point out the antiquity of this town.

[p] *Caill-na-gcran*, caıll na ccꞃann, written coıll na ccꞃann, in the Annals of Kilronan, i. e. *the wood of the* [*great*] *trees.*—This place is now called

lainn ⁊ la hAoḋ mac Concoḃair maonmaiġe ar ġallaiḃ dú in ro láḋ a nár im piarus Masan ⁊ im macaiḃ Sleiṁne.

Donnchaḋ mac cana toiseċ ċenél Aonġusa do ecc.

Doṁnall ó daiṁín do ṁarḃaḋ la macaiḃ méġ laċlainn i ndorus recles a doire.

Creach las in ngiolla riaclach ua mbaoiġill co ndruing do cenél cconaill a maille friss for araill do ċenel eoġain baoi for comairce uí ṫairċeirt, .i. an giolla riaḃach toiseaċ cloinne Sneiḋgile ⁊ cloinne fíngin. Rucc imorro ó taircheirt forra, ⁊ fearaiḋ deaḃaiḋ friú ⁊ marḃtar é buḋ deirin ag cosnamh a einigh.

Teach do ġaḃáil la diarmait mac Ruaiḋri uí Concobair for Aoḋ mac Maġnusa uí Concoḃair hi ccill colmain ḟinn hi ccorann gur ro loisccit cuicc fir ḋécc ar ḟiċit ann.

Maidm do ṫabairt do ḋoṁnall mac doṁnaill bregaiġ í maoilsechlainn for ċorbmac Ua maoileachlainn dú in ro marḃaḋ giolla crioṡd mac colgan co soċaiḋe ele amaille friṡ.

Doṁnall mac doṁnaill uí maoileaċlainn do ṁarḃaḋ ar creiċ la muinter Maoilir.

Sluaicceaḋ la gallaiḃ Muṁan go Roscré go ndearnsat caislén ann.

Kilmore, or Great Wood, and is situated in the parish of Killoughy, barony of Ballyboy, and King's County.—See Ordnance Map of that county, sheet 24. The name Coill na g-crann has been long obsolete, but we have the clearest evidence to prove its situation and modern name. Thus, the writer of the old Irish story called the Battle of Moylena (*Cath Maighe Lena*), in describing the rout of the Munster forces coming to the battle field of Moylena, which is about two miles to the north of Tullamore, states that they marched by Coill na g-crann, which was then, he says, called *Coill Mhor* (or Great Wood). But, if we had no other evidence, the following passage in the Annals of Clonmacnoise would be sufficient to shew the situation and modern name of this place. In these annals the above passages are given more fully than by the Four Masters, and were thus translated, in the year 1627, by Connell Mageoghegan of Lismoyny, who knew this place well:

"A. D. 1211. The English Bushop came over into this land again, and was Deputie thereof, and went, with all the English forces, of Ireland to Cloneis, in the north, where he built a castle. The English Bushop sent certain of the army to Magmahon's Land to take the preys of the Land; they were overtaken and mett by Magmahon, [who] slew divers of them about Myler mac Robert, and Myler himself, and divers of the Englishmen of Lynster, took and caused them to leave the prey and horses, and gave them many fierce onsetts as well by night as by day from thence forward.

"The said Deputie came from thence to Lynster, and sent for the forces of Munster, who

O'Melaghlin, and Hugh, the son of Conor Moinmoy, over the English, in which the latter, together with Pierce Mason and the sons of Sleviny, were slaughtered.

Donough Mac Cann, Chief of Kinel-Aengusa[q], died.

Donnell O'Devine was slain by the sons of Mac Loughlin in the doorway of the abbey-church of Derry.

A prey was taken by Gillafiaclagh O'Boyle, accompanied by a party of the Kinel-Connell, from some of the Kinel-Owen, who were under the protection of O'Taircheirt (Gillareagh), Chief of Clann-Sneidhghile and Clann-Fineen. O'Taircheirt overtook them (the plunderers), and gave them battle, but was killed while defending his guarantee[r].

Dermot, the son of Roderic O'Conor, *forcibly* took the house of Hugh, the son of Manus O'Conor, at Kilcolman-Finn[s], in Corran. Thirty-five men were burned in the house on this occasion.

Donnell, the son of Donnell Breaghagh [the Bregian] O'Melaghlin, defeated Cormac O'Melaghlin in a battle, in which Gilchreest Mac Colgan and many others were slain.

Donnell, the son of Donnell O'Melaghlin, was slain, while on a predatory excursion, by the people of Meyler.

An army was led by the English of Munster to Roscrea, where they erected

came accordingly, with Donnogh Carbreagh O'Bryen, and marched with all their forces to Killnegrann in Ffercall, now called Kilmore, where they were met by Cormac mac Art O'Melaghlyn, who discomfitted them, where they left all their cowes, horses, gold, silver, and other things to the said Cormack."

[q] *Kinel-Aengusa.*—This is anglicised Kindred Eneas in the old translation of the Annals of Ulster. It was the tribe name of the Mac Canns and their correlatives, who were seated in the present county of Armagh, where the Upper Bann enters Lough Neagh. There were several other tribes of this name in the province of Ulster, as well as in other parts of Ireland.

[r] *While defending his guarantee*, ag copnaṁ a einiġ, while defending those whom he had guaranteed to protect.—This, which is a Brehonic legal phrase, occurs very frequently throughout the Irish annals. This passage is rendered as follows in the old translation of the Annals of Ulster: "A. D. 1212. An army by Gillafiaglagh O'Boyle, and some of Kindred Connell, vppon Tirowen, being in protection with the Conells and especially of O'Tirchirt" [7 ꞅiat ap eineċ ceneoil conaill uile 7 hui taipcepc co ꞅonnaḋaċ]. "O'Tirchert came uppon them, fought with them, where Gillariavagh O'Tirchert was slayne, King of Snedgaile and Clanfynin, *in saving his credit*."

[s] *Kilcolman-Finn*, cill Colmáin Finn.—This is certainly the present Kilcolman, an old church near Ballaghaderreen, in the barony of Costello, and county of Mayo; but it is at least nine miles from the nearest boundary of the present barony of Corran, in the county of Sligo. The festival

Assaiḋe go cill achaiḋ go rucc Muirceartaċ mac briain orra cona ṡloiġ go ttard deabaid doiḃ. Ro loiteadh Maoileachlainn mac caṫail ċarraiġ gur bó marḃ dia ġonaiḃ.

AOIS CRIOSD, 1213.

Aois Criosd, mile, dá ċéTT, a trí decc.

Gilla na naoṁ ua Ruaḋan epscop luiġne, ⁊ Muiriccen ua muireccein epscop cluana mic nois do écc.

Ainmire ua cobtaigh abb Reclesa doire coluim cille uasal cléreċ toġaiḋe ar ċraḃaḋ, ar ċeannsa, ar ḋeirc, ar eccna, ⁊ ar gaċ maiṫ arċeana [do ecc].

Tomás mac uchtraigh ⁊ Ruaiḋri mac Raġnaill do orccain ḋoire ċoluim cilli ⁊ do ḃreith seóid ṁuintire doire, ⁊ tuaisceirt Ereann arċeana a lár teampaill an Recclesa, ⁊ a mbreiṫ leo go cúil raiṫin.

of St. Colman Finn, or Colman the Fair, is marked in the Irish Calendar of the O'Clerys at the 4th of April.

[t] *Killeigh*, cill aċaiḋ, anciently called cill aċaiḋ droma foda, and referred to in the *Feilire Aenguis*, at 25th of June, as in Ui Failghe.—It is a fair-town in the barony of Geshil, in the King's County, about four miles to the south of Tullamore. Here are still some remains of a great abbey, and also a holy well dedicated to the two St. Sinchells. This place is to be distinguished from Killoughy in the barony of Ballyboy, in the same neighbourhood. The Murtough, son of Brian, who opposed the English here, was son of Brian Breifneach O'Connor, who died in 1184.

It is to be suspected that this entry refers to the same event as that already given under the year 1211, namely, the victory of Coill na gcrann, for we find the different compilers of the annals of Ireland, whose works have been amalgamated (frequently without much skill) by the Four Masters, often repeat the same events, as having found them entered in different forms and under different years in the compilations of more ancient writers. The present entry is given somewhat differently in Mageoghegan's translation of the Annals of Clonmacnoise, as follows:

"A. D. 1212. The Englishmen of Ireland made a voyadge" [an expedition] "to Roscre, where they built a castle.

"The Englishmen of Meath with their greatest forces took their journey to Killnegrann in Ffercall, where they were mett by Cormack mac Art O'Melaghlyn, and were quite overthrown by Cormack, with a slaughter of the chiefest and principallest Englishmen in Meath, as Ferrus Mersey, the two sons of Leyvnie Wanie, and William Howard, and many others of them; that they left all their cattle, both horses and cowes, gold and silver, and shirts of mail; and pursued them to the abbey of Kilbeggan, and the place called Bealagh-monie-ne-Sirrhyde. Melaghlyn mac Cahall Carragh O'Connor was killed by Geffray March of that journey."

According to the Annals of Kilronan the per-

a castle. From thence they proceeded to Killeigh[t], where they were overtaken by Murtough, the son of Brian [O'Conor], and his army, who gave them battle; in which Melaghlin, the son of Cathal Carragh [O'Conor] received wounds of which he died[u].

THE AGE OF CHRIST, 1213.

The Age of Christ, one thousand two hundred thirteen.

Gilla-na-naev O'Rowan, Bishop of Leyny, and Muirigen O'Muirigen, Bishop of Clonmacnoise, died.

Ainmire O'Coffey, Abbot of the Church of Derry-Columbkille, a noble ecclesiastic, distinguished for his piety, meekness, charity, wisdom, and every other good quality [died][w].

Thomas Mac Uchtry and Rory Mac Randal plundered Derry-Columbkille, and carried off, from the middle of the church of Derry, all the precious articles of the people of Derry, and of the north of Ireland, which they brought to Coleraine[x].

sons slain were Perris Messat and Walter Dunel.

[u] Under this year the Annals of Clonmacnoise record the death of William Petitt, and contain the two entries following, which the Four Masters have very much shortened:

"A. D. 1212. Mortagh O'Bryen, Donnell mac Donnell O'Melaghlyn, Cowlen O'Dempsie, and Donnell Clannagh Mac Gillepatrick, gave an overthrow to Cormack mac Art O'Melaughlyn, where were killed Gillechrist mac Murrough Macoghlan, and Donslevey mac Connor O'Melaghlyn, with many others.

"Donnell mac Donnell Bregagh O'Melaghlyn, next in succession of Meath and Irish of Ireland, made a journey to take a prey from Meyler, was overtaken by Meyler himself, and great forces of both English and Irishmen, who killed the said Donnell with many others with him, at the River of Rahan in Ffercall."

[w] *Died.*—This passage is thus translated by Colgan: "Anmirus O'Cobhthaich, Abbas Dorensis, vir sapientia, religione, mansuetudine, et eleemosynis selectissimus, obiit."—*Trias Thaum.*, p. 505. In the Dublin copy of the Annals of Ulster, the character of this Ainmire O'Coffey is thus given: "A noble ecclesiastic, distinguished for his piety, descent, meekness, majesty, mildness, charity, and every other goodness, *post optimam penitentiam ingressus est viam universe carnis in Dubrecles Coluim Cille.*"

[x] *Coleraine*, cúil raiṫin, now locally but corruptly called in Irish cúr-raṫain, but more correctly anglicised *Coleraine*. This name is translated "*Secessus filicis*," in the Tripartite Life of St. Patrick, lib. ii. c. 136, published by Colgan in his *Trias Thaum.*, where its situation is distinctly pointed out as "*in aquilonari Bannæi fluminis margine*," i. e. on the north (eastern) side of the River Bann. Colgan, who was well acquainted with the situation of places in the north of Ireland, shews that Cuilraithin is the place now called Coleraine: "civitas *Dalriedæ* seu Reuta,

Ua caṫain, ⁊ fir na craoiḃe do ṫeaċt go doire do gaḃail tighe ar ṁacaibh még lachlainn. Ro marḃaḋ cellóir mór Reicclesa doire etorra occa nettargoire. Do roine dia ⁊ coluim cille miorḃail innsin uair ro marḃaḋ an fer tionoil ⁊ toichestail baí leo, .i. Maṫġaṁain ṁág aiṫne i neneach ċoluim ċille i ndorus in duiḃreiclésa.

Caislen cuile Raṫain do ḋenaṁ la tomas mac uċtraiġ ⁊ la gallaiḃ ulaḋ, ⁊ ro sccaoileaḋ relcce, ⁊ cuṁdaiġṫe an baile uile do ċum an ċaislein sin cenmoṫá an tempall.

Aoḋ ua neill do ṫaḃairt maḋma ar ġallaiḃ ⁊ ro la a nḋescár, ⁊ ro loiscceaḋ beós lais an carrlongport isin ló cetna eittir ḋaoinibh, ⁊ innilibh.

Donn ó breisléin taoiseaċ fánatt do ṁarbaḋ da ṁuintir féin i meabail.

Fionn ua brolċáin maor í ḋoṁnaill (.i. doṁnall mor) do ḋol i cconnaċtaiḃ do ċuingiḋ ċíosa í ḋoṁnaill. Arreaḋ do ċoiḋ cettus co cairpre droma cliaḃ. Ro taḋaill side cona ċaoiṁtecctaibh do tigh an ḟiliḋ Muireḋhaiġ lesa an doill ua [uí] ḋálaiġ, ⁊ ro ġaḃ for miocorttaḋ mór frisin bfiliḋ ar ba haiteach roṁ a huċt tféin (gion gur bo hé a ticcearna ro coṁairleicc do). Ro lonnaiġeaḋ an fear dána friss, ⁊ ron gaḃ biail mbiṫġéir ina laiṁ co ttaratt beim ndó go ffarccaiḃ marḃ gan anmain. Teitt féin iarsin ar iomġaḃail uí ḋoṁnaill hi cCloinn Riocaird. Iar na ḟios sin dUa doṁnaill do ronaḋ léirtionol slóiġ lais ina deadhaiḋ, ⁊ ní ro airis co rainicc

Culraine vulgo dicta."—*Trias Thaum.*, p. 183, col. 2, note 127.

[y] *O'Kane.*—In the old translation of the Annals of Ulster this passage is rendered thus:

"O'Kathan and the men of Kriv came to Dyry to take house vppon the Maglaghlans, and killed between them the great *Caller* of the Church of Dyry. God and Columkille shewed a great miracle, viz., the gatherer and bringer, Mahon Magaithne, [was] killed at Columkill his prayer justly in the church doore."

[z] *Prior*, cellóir in the original. It is thus explained in O'Brien's Dictionary. "Cealloir, the superior of a cell or monastery; ex., ni ceallóir na sub-ceallóir ṫu; you are neither superior nor vicar."

[a] *Castle.*—This passage is thus rendered in the old translation of the Ulster Annals:

"A. D. 1213. The castle of Cailrathan, built by Thomas Mac Ughtry and Galls of Vlster, and" [they] "broke down all the stones, pavements, and fences, of all the town for that work, the church only excepted."

The Irish text is thus given in the Dublin copy of the same annals:

Caistel cula raṫain do denum le Tomas mac uċtraiġ 7 le gallaiḃ Ulaḋ 7 ro scaileḋ reilce 7 claċana 7 cumdaiċi in baile uile cenmoṫa in tempall amain cuice fein.

[b] *Carlongphort*, now Carlingford, a decayed

O'Kane[y] and the [sept of] Firnacreeva, came to Derry to take the house of the son of Mac Loughlin. The great prior[z] of the abbey church of Derry, who interposed to make peace between them, was killed. God and St. Columbkille wrought a miracle on this occasion; for Mahon Magaithne, the person who had gathered and mustered the army, was killed in the doorway of the church of Duvregles, in revenge of Columbkille.

The castle[a] of Coleraine was erected by Thomas Mac Uchtry, and the English of Ulidia; and all the cemeteries and buildings of the town were thrown down excepting only the church to supply materials for erecting this castle.

Hugh O'Neill defeated and dreadfully slaughtered the English, and, on the same day, burned Carlongphort[b] (Carlingford) both people and cattle.

Donn O'Breslen, Chief of Fanad, was treacherously killed by his own people.

Finn O'Brollaghan, steward of O'Donnell (Donnell More) went to Connaught to collect O'Donnell's tribute. He first went to Carbury of Drumcliff, where, with his attendants, he visited the house of the poet Murray O'Daly of Lissadill[c]; and, being a plebeian representative of a hero, he began to wrangle with the poet very much (although his lord had given him no instructions to do so). The poet, being enraged at his conduct, seized a very sharp axe, and dealt him a blow which killed him on the spot, and then, to avoid O'Donnell, he fled into Clanrickard. When O'Donnell received intelligence of this, he collected a large body of his forces, and pursued him to Derrydonnell[d] in

town in the barony of Lower Dundalk, and county of Louth. This passage is rendered as follows in the old translation of the Annals of Ulster:

"A. D. 1213. Hugh O'Neile broke of the Galls, and had a great slaughter of them, and burnt the Cairlongfort the same day, both men and cattle."

The same work gives the following entry immediately after the foregoing:

"John, King of England, gave England and Ireland into the Pope's hands, and the Pope surrendered them to himself againe, and 1000 marks to him, and after every yeare 700 out of England, and 300 out of Ireland."

But this passage is not in the Dublin copy of the Annals of Ulster, or in the Annals of Kilronan.

[c] *Lissadill*, lıor a ꝺoıll, i. e. the *Lis*, or fort of the blindman; it is situated in the southwest of the barony of Carbury, near the Bay of Sligo. On an old map of the coast of the counties of Mayo, Sligo, and Donegal, made in the reign of Elizabeth or James I., preserved in the State Papers' Office, London, Lissadill is marked as a castle.

[d] *Derrydonnell*, ꝺoıre uí ḋomnaıll, i. e. *Roboretum Odonnelli*.—A townland containing the ruins of a castle in the parish of Athenry, and about three miles to the east of Oranmore, in the county of Galway. The territory of Clan-

doire í doṁnaill i ccloinn Riocaird, conaḋ uaḋ ro ġaḃ ainmniuccaḋ, ar a ḃeiṫ adhaiḋ longpoirt ann. Ro ġaḃ for creaċloisccaḋ an tíre gur ḃo riaraċ Mac uilliam dó fó ḋeoiḋ, ⁊ co ro ḋioċuir Muiredhaċ dia ċomairge i ttuaḋṁumain. Do ṫaed ua doṁnaill ina ḋiaiḋ, ⁊ geiḃiḋ for inoraḋ, ⁊ orccain na criche féin coros aṫcuir donnchaḋ cairbreċ ua briain Muiredhaċ uaḋa i nuċt muintire luimniġ. Ro lean ua doṁnaill é co dorus luimniġ, ⁊ baí i fforbaisi ⁊ hi ḃforlongport ag móin uí ḋoṁnaill conaḋ uaḋ ainmnighṫear. Ro ḋiocuirsiot luċt luimniġ Muiredhaċ uaḋaiḃ for forċongra ui ḋoṁnaill co nach ffuair a imḋiden acht a ṫairḃirt ó láiṁ do láiṁ go riaċt ath cliath duiḃlinne.

Soais ó doṁnaill don chur sin iar sireadh, ⁊ iar ccor cuarta connacht uile go hiomlan. Do ronaḋ Sloiccead ele lais doriḋise gan iompuireaċ gan fosuccaḋ is in mbliadain céttna ḃeos co hAthcliaṫ gur ba héiccen do luċt Atha cliaṫ Muiredhaċ do ċor uaḋaiḃ go halbain, ⁊ bai annsaiḋe co ndearna teóra dreċta aḋmolta do ċuingiodh siodha, ⁊ maithme nanacail ar Ua ndoṁnaill, ⁊ ba hé an trear dán dibh sidhe, A ḋomhnaill deaḋlaṁ fo sith, ⁊c. Do radadh sith dósomh ar a aḋmoltaibh, ⁊ gaḃaiḋ O doṁnaill ina ṁuintear é iaroṁ, ⁊ do raḋ forba, ⁊ fearann do reir ro ba data lais.

Creach la Corbmac ua maoileachlainn for ċaislen chinn claip go ro

rickard comprised six baronies in the county of Galway, namely, Leitrim, Loughreagh, Dunkellin, Killartan, Clare, and Athenry.—See *Tribes and Customs of Hy-Many*, printed for the Irish Archæological Society in 1843, pp. 17, 18; and Map to the same, on which doire ui ḋoṁnaill is shewn due east of the town of Galway, and on the boundary between the territories of Clann Fergaile and Hy-Many; see also Ordnance Survey of the county of Galway, sheet 95.

[e] *Mac William.*—This was Richard de Burgo, the son of William Fitz-Adelm, and the great Lord to whom King Henry III. granted the province of Connaught in the year 1225. On this occasion O'Daly addressed a poem to De Burgo, stating the cause of his flight, and imploring his protection. It begins, cread agaiḃ aoiḋiġ a gcéin? i. e. "What brings a guest to you from afar?" In this poem (of which there is a good copy on paper in the Library of the Royal Irish Academy), the poet calls himself O'Daly of Meath (see note [n], under the year 1185, pp. 66, 67), and states that he was wont to frequent the courts of the English, and to drink wine from the hands of kings and knights, of bishops and abbots; that, not wishing to remain to be trampled under the feet of the Race of Conn, he fled to one who, with his mail-clad warriors, was able to protect him against the fury of the King of Derry and Assaroe, who had threatened him with his vengeance, though indeed the cause of his enmity was but trifling,

Clanrickard,—a place which was named from him, because he encamped there for a night;—and he proceeded to plunder and burn the country, until at last Mac William[e] submitted to him, having previously sent Murray to seek for refuge in Thomond. O'Donnell pursued him, and proceeded to plunder and ravage that country also, until Donough Cairbreach O'Brien sent Murray away to the people of Limerick. O'Donnell followed him to the gate of Limerick, and, pitching his camp at Monydonnell (which is named from him), laid siege to that town; upon which the people of Limerick, at O'Donnell's command, expelled Murray, who found no asylum anywhere, but was sent from hand to hand, until he arrived in Dublin.

O'Donnell returned home on this occasion, having first traversed and completed the visitation of all Connaught. He mustered another army without much delay in the same year, and, marching to Dublin, compelled the people of Dublin to banish Murray into Scotland; and here he remained until he composed three poems in praise of O'Donnell, imploring peace and forgiveness from him. The third of these poems is the one beginning, "Oh! Donnell, kind hand for [granting] peace," &c. He obtained peace for his panegyrics, and O'Donnell afterwards received him into his friendship, and gave him lands and possessions, as was pleasing to him.

Cormac O'Melaghlin plundered the castle of Kinclare[f], burned the bawn,

for that the fugitive had only killed a plebeian of his people who had the audacity to affront him!

> beag ar bfala rir an bfear,
> baċlaċ do beiṫ dom ċáineaḋ,
> mé do ṁarbaḋ an ṁogaḋ;
> a Dé! an ádbar anfolaḋ?

> "Small is our difference with the man,
> A shepherd was abusing me,
> And I killed that clown;
> O God! is this a cause for enmity?"

He calls upon the puissant knight Rickard, the son of William, to respect the order of the poets, who are never treated with harshness by chieftains, and to protect the weak against the strong. He next bestows some verses of panegyric upon him,—describes the splendour of his house and its inmates,—calls him the chief of the English, the lord of Leinster, the King of Connaught, the proprietor of the forts of Croghan, of Tara, of Mac Coisi's wall of stone, and of Mur mic an Duinn, then called Caislen Ui Chonaing,—and hints that he might yet invite the poets of the five provinces to his house. He then tells Rickard that whatever deeds of valour any one may have achieved, he cannot be truly renowned without protecting the venerable or the feeble; and that he now has an opportunity of making himself illustrious by protecting O'Daly of Meath, a poet, whose verses demand attention, and who throws himself on his generosity. He concludes by reminding him of his duties as King of the famous province of Connaught.

[f] *Of Kinclare*, chinn cláir.—This name is now

loiscc an baḋbḋun, ⁊ go raoiṁiḋ for na gallaiḃ co ttuccaḋ eiċ ⁊ eitte iomḋa uatha.

Morsluaiġeaḋ la gallaiḃ Ereann dionnsaicchiḋ Corbmaic mic Airt gur comraicsiot acc droichſt tine. Feachar iomairſcc ſcorra, ⁊ ro ṁeaḃaiḋ for ṁac airt, ⁊ do roċair Ruaiḋri ua ciarḋa is in deaḃaiḋ sin, ⁊ ro díoċuireaḋ mac Airt a dealḃna, ⁊ ro hairccſoh a ṁuintir. Do ċóiḋsiot na goill go hAṫ luain, ⁊ do ronaḋ caislen leó ann. Do ronsat bſós caislen ċinneitiġ, caislen biorrae, ⁊ caislen durmaiġe.

Creach la corbmac mac Airt i ndealbna co ro aircc Maoilseachlainn bſcc ⁊ go ro ionnarb ar an tír. Ro marḃ dná uilliam Muilinn, ⁊ ro ġaḃ fſin tiġſnas dealbhna.

obsolete, but the situation of the place is distinctly pointed out in Mageoghegan's translation of the Annals of Clonmacnoise, in which it is stated that it was originally called Claire Athmoynie, and situated to the west of Lismoyny (which was the name of Mageoghegan's own house), and is still that of a townland in the parish of Ardnurcher, or Horseleap, in the barony of Moycashel, county of Westmeath.—See Ordnance Map of that county, sheet 37. The transactions of the O'Melaghlins in this year are given in the Annals of Clonmacnoise as follows:

"A. D. 1213. Cormack mac Art O'Melaghlyn took a great prey from the town of Ardinurcher, and the next morrow after took the spoyles of the Castle of Ardinurcher, and markett of the same; he tooke many other small preys and booties.

"The said Cormack mac Art tooke a prey from the Castle of Kynnclare, together with the spoiles of the Bawne and Markett of the said town, and also killed many of the Englishmen, that they left him twenty-eight horses, with eight other harnished horses, and shirts of Mail, and burnt many men in the said town, [and] returned to his own house without loss. All the forces of the English of Ulster, Munster, Lynster, and Meath, together with all the Irish forces that owed service to the King of England throughout all the provinces and parts of Ireland, assembled, and mett together at the bridge of Tynnie to assault the said Cormack mac Art O'Melaghlyn, whom they did also meet at a place then called Clare Athmoynie, now called Killclare [*sic*], adjoining to Lissmoyne and weast, fought couragiously withall, where four principall men of the said Cormack's army were slain, as Rowrie O'Kiergy, and others. The English army came from thence to Delvyn Mac Coghlan, and so to Clonvicknose, where they built a Castle; also they finished and aided the Castles of Dorrowe, Byrre, and Kynnety of that voyage [expedition]."

"Cormack mac Art O'Melaghlyn went to Athboye" [Ballyboy] "and there devised a stratagem to make the Ward come out of the Castle, and killed ten of them immediately, and took all theirs and spoyles of the towne with him. Soone after he departed the contrey, and came after a long space into the contrey again, tooke all the spoyles of Melaughlyn Begg O'Melaghlyn, and killed some of his people, and among the rest, killed the knight called William Moylyn, and took the possession of the country again against them.

"Cormack mac Art tooke the spoyles of the

and defeated the English, and carried away from them many horses and accoutrements.

The English of Ireland led a great army against Cormac, the son of Art [O'Melaghlin]. They met him at the bridge of Tine[g], where a battle was fought between them, in which the son of Art was defeated, and Rory O'Keary was killed. The son of Art was then banished from Delvin, and his people were plundered. The English then went to Athlone, where they erected a castle. They also erected the castle of Kinnity[h], the castle of Birr[i], and the castle of Durrow[k].

Cormac, the son of Art, went on a predatory excursion into Delvin, and plundered Melaghlin Beg, whom he banished from that country: he also slew William of the Mill, and assumed the lordship of Delvin himself[l].

Castle of Smerhie, together with all the cowes, horses, and other cattle in the towne, was overtaken and fought withall by the English of the towne, where the English forces were overthrown, three of their knights slain, with their Constable and Cheif man, and Cormack broght himself, men, and prey home salfe and sound."

[g] *Bridge of Tine*, droichet Tine.—This name would be anglicised Drehidtinny. It must have been the name of some old wooden bridge on the Brosna or on the Silver River; but there is no bridge or place at present bearing the name in the King's County, or in the county of Westmeath. The name Tinnycross, a townland in the parish of Kilbride, barony of Ballycowan, and King's County, would seem to retain a portion of this name, viz., *Tinny;* but as Tinnycross is but an anglicised form of tiġ na croise, i. e. *house of the cross*, it cannot be considered as bearing any analogy to droichet Tine.

[h] *Kinnity*, cenn eitiġ, i. e. the head of Etech, so called, according to a note in the *Feilire Aenguis*, at the 7th of April, from Etech, an ancient Irish heroine, whose head was interred here.—It is the name of a townland and parish in the barony of Ballybrit, in the King's County.

[i] *Birr*, biorra.—Now generally called Parsonstown, from the family name of the present noble and distinguished proprietor, Lord Ross. This name is explained by O'Clery as "a watery plain," thus: Ḃiorrae .i. maġ uisge: oir as ionann bir 7 uisge: Ionann for rae 7 maġ. "Biorra, i. e. a plain of water: for *bir* means water; and *rae* means a plain." A monastery was founded here, according to the Irish Calendar of the O'Clerys, by St. Brendan, the son of Neman, who died on the 29th of November, A. D. 572.

[k] *Durrow*, durṁaiġ.—A castle had been finished at this place by Sir Hugh de Lacy, the elder, so early as the year 1186. In the Annals of Clonmacnoise, as translated by Connell Mageoghegan, it is stated, more correctly, that the English on this occasion "finished and aided the Castles of Dorrowe, Byrre, and Kynnety."

[l] Under this year the Annals of Clonmacnoise state, that Finn O'Dempsey, and his brother Donough, were most deceitfully taken by Geffrey March [De Marisco], who conveyed Finn to Dublin, where he was bound to a horse's tail, and so dragged through all the streets, and afterwards hanged.

AOIS CRIOSD, 1214.

Aois Criosd, mile, dá céd, a ceathair decc.

An tespcop ó ceallaiġ .i. easpcop ó ffiaċrach do ecc.

Ardġar ua concoḃair epscop ṡl Muireḋaiġ do ecc.

Bennmiḋe ingen eccniġh bean aoḋa uí neill baintiġearna oiliġ décc iar ndeiġbeathaiḋ.

Creach do ḋenamh la hAoḋ mac Maoilreachlainn ui laċlainn for comorba ċoluim ċille, ⁊ Aoḋ buiḋerin do ṁarbaḋ la gallaiḃ ria ccind bliadhna tria ḟiortaibh dé ⁊ ċoluim cille.

Caṫal mac diarmatta mic taidg tiġearna Muiġe luircc, tuir ordain Connacht do écc.

Brian mac Ruaiḋri í ḟlaiṫbertaiġ mac tiġearna iarṫair Connacht do ecc.

Creach criche cairpre do ḋenaṁ la hualgarcc ua ruairc ar ṗilip mac goisdelḃaiġ co rucc bú iomḋa lais.

AOIS CRIOSD, 1215.

Aois Criosd, mile, dá céd, a cuicc decc.

Dionisius ua longargáin airdepscop caisil decc hi Roiṁ.

Conċobar ua henne epscop ċille dálua do écc ar sliġidh occ tionntuḋ do iarsan cceṫramaḋ coṁairle generailte bai in ecclais lateranensis.

[m] *Bishop of Hy-Fiachrach*, easpog ua ffiaċrach.—He was Bishop of the Hy-Fiachrach Aidhne, whose country was co-extensive with the diocese of Kilmacduagh. He could not have been bishop of the northern Hy-Fiachrach, or Killala, as Cormac O'Tarpaidh was bishop of that see from 1207 to 1226.—See Harris's Edition of Ware's Bishops, pp. 649, 650.

[n] *Of* [*O*] *Hegny*, egniġ.—The Four Masters have omitted the uí by mere oversight. In the Annals of Ulster the reading is, Bennmiḋe ingen hui Eigniġ, &c., and in those of Kilronan: "Bennmide ingen hí Eicniċ .i. bean Oeda hí néill, .i. ri Oiliġ, *in bona penitentia quieuit.*"

[o] *Elagh*, oileach.—This was one of the four royal palaces of Ireland, and its ruins are situated on a hill about six miles north of Derry. Colgan thus speaks of it in *Trias Thaum.*, p. 181, col. 1, note 169: "A priscis scriptoribus *Ailech Neid*, hodie vulgo Ailech appellatur. Fuit perantiqua Regum Hiberniæ sedes, et post tempora fidei per easdem derelicta, Temoria denuo repetita et restaurata. Jacet in Peninsula Borealis Ultoniæ *Inis Eoghuin* dicta

THE AGE OF CHRIST, 1214.

The Age of Christ, one thousand two hundred fourteen.

O'Kelly, Bishop of Hy-Fiachrach[m], died.

Ardgar O'Conor, Bishop of Sil-Murray [Elphin], died.

Benmee, daughter of [O'] Hegny[n], and wife of Hugh O'Neill, Queen of Aileach[o], died, after having spent a virtuous life.

A depredation was committed by Hugh, the son of Melaghlin O'Loughlin, on the coarb of Columbkille; but Hugh himself was killed before the expiration of a year afterwards, through the miracles of God and Columbkille.

Cathal Mac Dermot, the son of Teige, Lord of Moylurg, and tower of the glory[p] of Connaught, died.

Brian, the son of Rory O'Flaherty, the son of the Lord of West Connaught, died.

The territory of Carbury [Co. Sligo], the possession of Philip Mac Costello, was preyed by Ualgarg O'Rourke, who carried off a number of cows[q].

THE AGE OF CHRIST, 1215.

The Age of Christ, one thousand two hundred fifteen.

Dionysius O'Lonargan, Archbishop of Cashel, died at Rome.

Conar (Cornelius) O'Heney, Bishop of Killaloe, died on his return from the fourth General Council of Lateran.

tertio lapide a civitate Dorensi."

[p] *Glory*, ordan.—The word ordan, which occurs so frequently in these Annals, is explained glóir, no airechas, glory, nobility, in the Gloss to Fiach's Hymn, in the *Liber Hymnorum;* uasal ġradh, i. e. noble grade or dignity, in a MS. in Trin. Col. Dublin, H. 3, 18, p. 550; it is glossed ard ainm, i. e. high name or fame, in the *Amhra Shenain*, preserved in the *Leabhar Breac*, fol. 121, *a*; grádh no uaisle, dignity or nobility, by Michael O'Clery, in his Glossary of ancient Irish words; and ard uaisle, no aireachas, high nobleness, or dignity, in a paper MS. in Trinity College, Dublin, H. 1, 15, p. 946. Colgan translates tuir ordain 7 oireachais iarthair domhain, supremum caput *ordinum* & procerum occidentis."—*Trias Thaum.*, p. 298.

[q] Under this year (1214) the Annals of Kilronan record the erection, by the English, of the castles of Clonmacnoise and Durrow; and they add that, shortly after the completion of the castle of Clonmacnoise, Cormac, the son of Art O'Melaghlin, who had been expelled from Delvin, returned into that territory, and plundered

Annuḋ ua muireḋhaiġ, espcop Conmaicne, ⁊ Maolpóil ua muireḋhaiġ prioir dúine ġeimin do ecc.

Trad ua maoilfábaill toiseċ ċenél ḟerġusa cona ḃraiṫriḃ, ⁊ co ndruing móir ele immaille friú do ṁarḃaḋ la Muireaḋaċ mac mormair Leaṁna.

Donnchaḋ ua duibdíorma toiseaċ na mbréḋċa do écc, i nduibreccles doire.

Aongus ua cairelláin toiseaċ cloinne diarmata do ṁarḃaḋ la a braiṫriḃ fen.

Murchaḋ mac caṫmaoil toiseċ ceneoil ḟearadhaiġ do écc.

Maġ cana toiseċ ċenél aenġusa do ṁarḃaḋ la a braiṫribh.

Ruaiḋri ua floinn ticcerna derlais do ecc.

Gilla cuitrigh maċ carrgaṁna taoiseċ muintire maoiltrionna decc.

Giolla caoiṁgin ua ceallaiġ berġ do ġabáil la gallaiḃ i mainistir peatair acc athluain, ⁊ a crochaḋ leo in athtruim.

Taḋg mac eitigein taoiseaċ cloinne diarmata do ecc.

the castle of Clonmacnoise of its cattle, and defeated the English who were defending it.

Under this year, also, the Annals of Ulster and of Kilronan mention the appearance of a certain character, called *Aedh Breige*, or the false, or pretended, Hugh, who was styled the Cobhartach, the Aider, Liberator, or Deliverer. He was evidently some person who wished to make it appear that he came to fulfil some Irish prophecy, but failed to make the intended impression.

[r] *Bishop of Conmaicne.*—That is, bishop of the see of Ardagh, which comprises the country of the eastern Conmaicne; that is, Annaly, the territory of O'Farrell, in the county of Longford; and Muintir Eolais, that of Mac Rannall, in the county of Leitrim. These two families descend from Cormac, the illegitimate son of Fergus, the dethroned King of Ulster, by Meave, Queen of Connaught, in the first century.—See O'Flaherty's *Ogygia*, part iii. c. 46, where, by a mere oversight in the construction of a Latin sentence, the situation of these territories is reversed. The diocese of Ardagh, however, was extended beyond the country of these tribes at the synod of Rath Breasail, about the year 1118, when it was defined thus: "the diocese of Ardagh, from Ardcana to Slieve-an-ierin, and from Ceis Coran to Urchoilten."

[s] *O'Mulfavill*, Ua maolfabaill.—This name, which is Anglicised Moylfavill in the old translation of the Annals of Ulster, is still common in Inishowen, but Anglicised Mulfaal, and sometimes Mac Paul. The same name is Anglicised Lavelle in Connaught, though pronounced in Irish O'Mullaville. The territory of the Kinel-Fergus, of whom O'Mulfaal was chief, was called Carraic Bhrachaidhe, and comprised the northwest part of Inishowen.

[t] *The Great Steward of Lennox*, mormaor leaṁna.—See O'Flaherty's *Ogygia*, part iii. c. 81. Leaṁain, now the Leven, is a river flowing out of Loch Lomond, and uniting with the Clyde at the town of Dumbarton. It gave name to a district coextensive with the present Dumbartonshire in Scotland. O'Flaherty thinks that the great

Annudh O'Murray, Bishop of Conmaicne[r] [Ardagh], and Maelpoil O'Murray, Prior of Dungiven, died.

Trad O'Mulfavill[s], Chief of Kinel-Fergusa, with his brothers, and a great number of people who were with them, were slain by Murray, the son of the Great Steward of Lennox[t].

Donough O'Duvdirma[u], Chief of Bredagh, died in the Duvregles of Derry.

Aengus O'Carellan, Chief of the Clann-Dermot[w], was slain by his own kinsmen.

Murrough Mac Cawell, Chief of Kinel-Farry, died.

Mac Cann, Chief of Kinel-Aengusa, was slain by his kinsmen.

Rory O'Flynn [O'Lynn], Lord of Derlas[x], died. Gillacutry Mac Carroon, Chief of Muintir Maoil-t-sionna, died.

Gillakevin O'Kelly of Bregia, was taken prisoner in the monastery of St. Peter at Athlone, by the English, and afterwards hanged by them at Trim.

Teige Mac Etigen, Chief of Clann-Dermot, died[y].

Stewarts of Leamhain, or Lennox, were descended from Maine Leamhna, the son of Corc, King of Munster, by Mongfinna, the daughter of Feradhach, King of the Picts. In the year 1014 Muireadhach (a name which the Scotch write Murdoch), the *mormaer* of Leamhain, assisted Brian Borumha in the battle of Clontarf against the Danes, which the Irish writers urge as an evidence of his Munster descent; and some have thought that they discovered a strong resemblance between the pronunciation of the dialect of the Gaelic which is spoken in this territory, and that spoken in Munster.

[u] *O'Duvdirma.*—This name is yet common in Inishowen, but sometimes corrupted to Mac Dermot. Bredach was the north-east part of Inishowen.

[w] *Clann-Dermot*, clann διαρмαδα, was the tribe name of the Mac Egans, situated in the district lying round Duniry, in the south of the present county of Galway.

[x] *Derlas*, δεɼlaɼ, called δúɼlaɼ in the Annals of Ulster and of Kilronan. It was the name of the seat of O'Lyn, Chief of Hy-Tuirtre. This name, which signifies *a strong fort*, was applied to many other places in Ireland, and is sometimes Anglicised Thurles. The Editor has met several forts of this name in Ireland, but none in Hy-Tuirtre in the county of Antrim. The most remarkable fort of the name remaining in Ireland is situated in the parish of Kilruane, in the barony of Lower Ormond, in the county of Tipperary: it consists of three great circular embankments and two deep trenches.

[y] Under this year the Dublin copy of the Annals of Innisfallen record, that a great war broke out between Dermot of Dundronan, the son of Donnell More na Curra Mac Carthy, and his brother Cormac Finn; that the English were assisting on both sides; and that during this war the English acquired great possessions, and made great conquests of lands, on which they built castles and strong forts for themselves, to defend them against the Irish. The following were the castles erected on this occasion:

The castle of Muintir Bhaire, in Kilcrohane

AOIS CRIOSD, 1216.

Aois Criosd, mile, da cett, a sé decc.

Maṫġamain ua laiṫbſrtaiġ tiġearna cloinne doṁnaill do écc.

Giolla arnáin ua martain ollaṁ Erenn i mbreitſmnus do écc.

Tomaltaċ mac aoḋa mic aireaċtaiġ uí roḋuiḃ do ṁarḃaḋ la domhnall mac aſdha mic diarmatta.

Eachḋonn mac gilliuidhir comarba patraicc, ⁊ prioṁaiḋ na hErenn do écc hi Roimh iar ndſiġhbſchaiḋ.

Maoilreaċlainn mac diarmata do ṁarḃaḋ dfearaiḃ ceall, ⁊ do ṁuintir Mhaoilir.

Murchaḋ mac Ruaiḋri uí Concoḃair do écc.

parish, erected by Mac Cuddihy.—See Ordnance Map of the County of Cork, sheet 129.

The castles of Dun na mbarc [Dunnamarc] and Ard Tuilighthe, by Carew.—See Ordnance Map of the county of Cork, sheet 118.

The castles of Dun Ciarain [Dunkerron] and Ceapa na Coise [Cappanacusha], near the Kenmare River, in Kerry, by Carew.—See Ordnance Map of Kerry, sheet 92.

The castle of Dunloe, in Kerry, by Maurice, son of Thomas Fitzgerald.—See Ordnance Map of Kerry, sheet 65.

The castle of Killforgla [Killorglin], and the castle of the Mang [Castlemaine], in Kerry, by the same Maurice.—See Ordnance Map of Kerry, sheets 47, 56.

The castles of Moylahiff, of Cala na feirse [Callanafersy], of Cluain Maolain [Cloonmealane], and of Curreens [now Currans], by the son of Maurice Fitzgerald.—See Ordnance Map of Kerry, sheets 46, 47, 48, 56.

The castle of Arlioch, by Roche.

The castles of Dunnagall and Dun na scad [Baltimore], by Sleviny. The ruins of the former are marked on the Ordnance Map of the County of Cork, sheet 150, on Ringarogy Island, in the parish of Creagh, in the east division of the barony of West Carbery; and the ruins of the castle of Baltimore, which was anciently called dún na séad, are shewn on the same sheet, at Baltimore village.

The castle of Traigh-bhaile, near the harbour of Cuan Dor [Glandore], was erected by Barrett. This castle was afterwards called Cloghatradbally, and belonged to Donell na Carton O'Donovan, Chief of Clann-Loughlin, who died on the 10th of May, 1580, and to his son and grandson. It was situated in the townland of Aghatubridmore, in the parish of Kilfaughnabeg, and is now generally called Glandore Castle. See Ordnance Map of Cork, sheet 142.

The castles of Timoleague and Dundeady were erected by Nicholas Boy de Barry.—For their situation see Ordnance Map of the County of Cork, sheets 123, 144.

[a] *Clann-Donnell*, clann doṁnaill.—These were a distinguished sept of the Kinel-Moen, originally seated in the present barony of Raphoe, but afterwards driven across the Foyle by the O'Donnells.—See the year 1178, where it is stated that Rory O'Laverty was elected chief of all Kinel-Moen, in place of Donnell

THE AGE OF CHRIST, 1216.

The Age of Christ, one thousand two hundred sixteen.

Mahon O'Laverty, Chief of the Clann-Donnell[z], died.

Giolla Arnain O'Martan, Chief Ollave (professor) of law in Ireland, died.

Tomaltagh, the son of Hugh, who was the son of Oireaghtagh O'Rodiv, was slain by Donnell, the son of Hugh Mac Dermot.

Eachdonn Mac Gilluire[a], Coarb of St. Patrick and Primate of Ireland, died at Rome, after a well-spent life.

Melaghlin, the son of Dermot[b], was slain by the men of Fircall[c] and the people of Meyler.

Murrough, the son of Roderic O'Conor, died.

O'Gormly, who was deposed. This is sufficient evidence to shew that O'Laverty was of the race of the Kinel-Moen.

[a] *Eghdonn Mac Gilla-Uidhir.*—He is called Eugene Mac Gillivider in Harris's edition of Ware's Bishops, p. 62. His death is entered in the Annals of Ulster, as follows: "A. D. 1216. Echdonn mac Gille uidir, comarba patraic, 7 primaiṫ Erenn port generale consilium Lateranense Rome feliciter obdormiuit." Thus rendered in the old translation: "A. D. 1216. Eghdon Mac Gilluir, Coarb of Patrick and Primate of Ireland, *post generale Consilium Lateranense Romæ feliciter obdormiuit.*"—See note under the year 1206.

[b] *Melaghlinn, the son of Dermot.*—His surname was O'Dempsey, according to Mageoghegan's translation of the Annals of Clonmacnoise.

[c] *Fircall.*—The territory of Feara-Ceall, as already observed, comprised the baronies of Ballycowan, Ballyboy, and Fircal, *alias* Eglish, in the King's County. It was the most southern territory of ancient Meath, and the hereditary principality of the O'Molloys, descended from Fiacha, the son of Niall of the Nine Hostages. It was bounded on the north by Muintir-Thadhgain, or Fox's country, and Kinel-Fiacha, or Mageoghegan's country, both which it joined near Kilbeggan; on the west by Delvin Eathra, or Mac Coghlan's country; on the east by Offaly, O'Conor Faly's country; on the south-east by Hy-Regan, or Duthaidh Riagain, O'Dunne's country; and on the south by Ely O'Carroll, from which it was separated by the Abhainn Chara, which falls into the Little Brosna, near the town of Birr.—See *Feilire Aenguis*, preserved in the *Leabhar Breac* of the Mac Egans, fol. 9, in which Kinnity (church) is placed on the frontiers of Ely and Feara Ceall: "Finán cam Cind etiġ i ccoicrich heli 7 fer cell." "Finan Cam of Kinnity, on the frontiers of Ely and Feara Ceall." The following places are mentioned by the old Irish writers as in this territory, viz.: Rathain (now Rahen); Durrow; Magh-leana, now the parish of Moylena, *alias* Kilbride, containing the town of Tullamore; Lann Elo (now Lynally); Coill-na-gerann (now called Kilmore and Greatwood, and situated in the parish of Killoughy); Pallis; Ath-buidhe (now Ballyboy); Eglish; Baile-an-duna; Drumcullen. O'Dugan honours the Feara ceall with the following quatrain:

Caiślén ċille dalua do dénam la Seaffraiġ mares, ⁊ an gailleasboc fós do dénamh tighe innte ar eiccin.

An tres Henry do ríoghadh os Saxain 19. October.

AOIS CRIOSD, 1217.

Aois Criosd, míle, dá céd, a secht décc.

Giolla tiġearnaigh mac giolla Ronain epscop Airġiall, ⁊ cenn canánać Ereann do écc iar bpennainn, ⁊ iar naithrighe.

Diarmait mac concobair mic diarmata tiġearna muiġi luircc do écc.

Mór inġen uí briain, .i. domnaill ben caṫail croibdeircc do écc.

Domnall ua gadra do ecc.

Niall mac mic lochlainn uí Concobair do écc.

Donnchadh ua maoilbrenainn taoiseać cloinne concobair do écc.

Tadg ua feargail do marbad la Murchadh carrać ua ffergail.

Giolla Patraicc mac acadain taoiseać cloinne fermaiġe do écc.

Rí fear ceall na g-cloidheam sean
O'Maoilmhuaidh,—saor an sloinneadh,—
Ro faomadh gać lann leisean;
Rann na aonar aigesean.

"King of Feara Ceall of ancient swords
Is O'Molloy,—noble the surname,—
Every sword was vanquished by him;
He has a division to himself alone."

[d] *The castle of Killaloe.*—This passage is given in the Annals of Clonmacnoise, as translated by Connell Mageoghegan, as follows: "A. D. 1216. Geffrey Marche" [De Marisco] "founded a Castle at Killaloe, and forced the inhabitants to receive an English Bushop." The name of this bishop was Robert Travers. He was afterwards deprived (in 1221), and the see continued to be filled almost exclusively by Irishmen till the Reformation, there having been but one Englishman, namely, Robert de Mulfield, who succeeded in 1409.—See Harris's edition of Ware's Works, vol. i. pp. 521–593.

[e] Under the year 1216 the Annals of Kilronan contain the following entries, which the Four Masters have omitted:

"A. D. 1216. A synod of the clergy of the world at Rome at Lateran, with the Pope Innocentius, and soon after this synod (council), Pope Innocentius *quieuit in Christo.*

"John, King of England, was deposed by the English this year, and died of a fit. (In the Annals of Clonmacnoise, as translated by Mageoghegan, it is stated that he died in the Abbey of Swynshead, being "poyson'd by drinking of a cup of ale wherein there was a toad pricked with a broach.") "The son of the King of France assumed the government of England, and obtained her hostages."

"Gilla Croichefraich Mac Carroon and the priest O'Celli died, both having been crossed and ordered to go to the River [Jordan].

"The abbot O'Lotan, a learned and pious

The castle of Killaloe[d] was erected by Geoffrey Mares. The English Bishop also built a house there by force.

Henry III. was crowned in England on the 19th of October[e].

THE AGE OF CHRIST, 1217.

The Age of Christ, one thousand two hundred seventeen.

Gillatierny Mac Gillaronan, Bishop of Oriel (Clogher), and head of the canons of Ireland, died, after penance and repentance[f].

Dermot, the son of Conor Mac Dermot, Lord of Moylurg, died.

More, daughter of O'Brien (Donnell), and wife of Cathal Crovderg [O'Conor], died.

Donnell O'Gara died.

Niall, the grandson of Loughlin O'Conor, died.

Donough O'Mulrenin, Chief of the Clann-Conor, died.

Teige O'Farrell was slain by Murrough Carragh O'Farrell.

Gillapatrick Mac Acadhain, Chief of Clann-Fearmaighe[g], died.

man, *in pace quieuit.* Gregory, son of Gilla-na-naingel, abbot of the monks of Ireland, *in pace quieuit*, in the East, being expelled by the monks of Drogheda, through envy and jealousy.

"The Archbishop O'Rooney was cruelly and violently taken prisoner by Maclisa O'Conor, and the Connacians, who cast him in chains, a thing of which we never heard a parallel, i. e. the fettering of an archbishop.

"Patricius, Bishop of Knockmoy, *quieuit.*"

[f] *Repentance*, ıar bpſnaınь 7 naıchpıcche.—In the Annals of Ulster at 1218, and of Kilronan in 1217, this phrase is given in Latin thus: "Ȝılla tıġſpnaıġ mac Ȝılla Ronáın eppuc áıpġıall 7 cſnn canánaċ Epenn *in bona penitentia quieuit.*"

[g] *Clann-Fearmaighe.*—The natives still remember the name of this territory, and that of the adjoining one of Muintir Kenny, both which are contained in the present barony of Dromahaire, in the county of Leitrim; Muintir-Kenny lying principally between Lough Allen and the boundary of the county of Roscommon, and Clann-Fermaigh, comprising all the valley of Glanfarne. The following chiefs are placed in the district of West Breifny, and tributary to O'Rourke, in O'Dugan's topographical poem, viz.: Mac Tiernan of Tealach Dunchadha, now the barony of Tullyhunco, in the county of Cavan; Magauran, Chief of Tealach Eachdhach, now the barony of Tullyhaw, in the same county; Mac Consnamha, now Mac Kinnaw (and sometimes ridiculously anglicised Forde), Chief of Muintir-Kenny, and Mac Cagadhain, Chief of Clann-Fermaighe, both in the present barony of Dromahaire, in the county of Leitrim; Mac Darcey, Chief of Kinel-Luachain, a territory which comprised the present parish of Oughteragh, at the foot of Slieve-an-ierin; and Mac Clancy, and his correlatives in Dartry and Calry, territories nearly all in-

Domhnall mac Murchaḋ ṁéġ coċláin tiġearna urṁóir dealḃna do ṁarḃaḋ do ṁacaiḃ Maoileaċlainn méaġ coċlin i meaḃail i liaṫdruim.

Caṫal fionn ó lacṫna taoiseaċ an dá ḃac do marḃaḋ la hua fflóinn ṁaighe heleocc i ffiull ina tigh féin.

Corbmac mac Tomaltaiġ doirdnedh.

AOIS CRIOSD, 1218.

Aois Criosd, mile, da chéd, a hocht décc.

Clemens espcop luighne do écc.

Giolla na naoṁ ua gormġaile Saccart ráṫa lúraiġ do écc ina oilithre.

cluded in the present barony of Rossclogher, in the north of the county of Leitrim.

[h] *Liathdruim.*—There is no place in the territory of Delvin Mac Coghlan, now called Liathdruim, unless we may suppose Leitra, in the parish of Clonmacnoise, to be a corruption of it. See Ordnance Map of the King's County, sheet 13. There is a place called Liathdruim, Anglice Leitrim, in the parish of Monasteroris, in the same county.—See Ordnance Map, sheet 11.

[i] *Moy-h Eleog*, maġ heleoġ.—A level district in the parish of Crossmolina, in the barony of Tirawley, in the county of Mayo.—See note under the year 1180. The territory of the Two Backs lies principally between Lough Conn and the River Moy.

[k] This entry should be made a part of the second paragraph under this year, relating to Dermot mac Dermot, Lord of Moylurg, for so it is given in the more ancient and more correct Annals of Ulster and of Kilronan. It stands thus in the Annals of Ulster:

A. D. 1218. Diarmaid mac Conchuḃair mic Diarmada riġ Muiġe luirg mortuus est. Cormac do gabail riġi da éis.

In the Annals of Kilronan, which is the Chronicle of the district, this Cormac is called the son of Tomaltagh of the Rock, the son of Conor.

Under this year the Annals of Kilronan contain the following entries, which have been altogether omitted by the Four Masters;

"A. D. 1217. Oisin, Abbot of Abbeyderg [in the county of Longford], died.

"The fishermen of all Ireland, from Waterford and Wexford in the south, to Derry-Columbkille in the north, went to the Isle of Mann to fish, where they committed aggressions, but were all killed in Mann in retaliation for their violence.

"The Abbots of all Ireland went to England, to the general chapter held there this year; but their attendants were dispersed, and the most of them were slain in England; and the Abbot of Drogheda was deprived of his abbacy at this chapter."

"Every fruit tree produced abundance of fruit this year."

"The English of Ulidia mustered a plundering army, with which they proceeded to Armagh, and totally plundered it. O'Fotuelan was the person who guided them, for he had promised the people of Armagh that the English would not plunder them so long as he should be with them (the English). In a week after, O'Neill

Donnell, the son of Murrough Mac Coghlan, Lord of the greater part of Delvin, was treacherously slain by the sons of Melaghlin Mac Coghlan, at Liathdruim[h].

Cathal Finn O'Laghtna, Chief of the Two Bacs, was treacherously slain in his own house by O'Flynn of Moy-h-Eleog[i].

Cormac, the son of Tomaltagh [Mac Dermot], was inaugurated[k].

THE AGE OF CHRIST, 1218.

The Age of Christ, one thousand two hundred eighteen.

Clemens, Bishop of Leyny [Achonry], died.

Gilla-na-naev O'Gormally, priest of Rathloury[l], died on his pilgrimage.

Roe and Mac Mahon came and took a great prey from the English, namely, one thousand two hundred cows. The English and O'Fotuelan pursued them, but the Kinel-Owen turned upon them, and killed fourteen men who were clad in coats of mail, besides the Constable of Dundalk; and O'Fotuelan was killed in revenge of St. Patrick."

[l] *Rathloury*, Raṫ Luraiġ, i. e. St. Lurach's fort.—This church, about the situation of which our topographical writers have committed so many strange blunders, is still well known; it is the head of a deanery in the county of Londonderry, and is situated in the town of Maghera, anciently called Machaire Ratha Luraigh, where the church, grave, and holy well of St. Lurach are still to be seen, and where his festival was celebrated on the 17th of February.—See Calendar of the O'Clerys at this day. The situation of this church, which some have supposed to be the same as Ardstraw, was well known to Ussher.—See his *Primordia*, pp. 856, 857, where he says that the bishopric of Ardstraw, together with that of Rathlurig, then a deanery called *Rathloury*, was annexed to the see of Derry. Its situation was also well known to Ware and even to Harris.—See Harris's edition of Ware's Bishops, p. 286, under *Flathberty O'Brolcain*, where it is stated that "the episcopal see was translated from *Ardsrath* to *Maghere*, which was dedicated to St. *Luroch*, whose festival is celebrated on the 17th of February." In a Latin epitaph on a tombstone in the cemetery of the Roman Catholic chapel of Maghera, the late Dr. Makeever, P. P. of Maghera, is called *Parochus Rathlurensis*. The patron saint is now locally called St. Loury. The cathedral church of the Kinel-Owen was originally at Ardstraw, in the north-west of Tyrone, whence it was afterwards translated to Rath Luraigh, in the present town of Maghera, in the county of Londonderry. In course of time the ancient bishopric of Ardstraw became a part of the see of Clogher; but on the elevation of Derry into a bishop's see in the year 1158, the bishopric of Rath Luraigh was made a part of its diocese; and finally, by the power of German O'Cervallan, and his tribe of the Kinel Owen, the bishopric of Ardstraw was separated from the diocese of Clogher, and annexed to that of Derry, about the year 1266.—See note under the year 1179.

Maoiliosa ua daiġre airchinneach doire ċoluim ċille do écc an toċtmaḋ la do ḋecember iar mbſiṫ cſṫraċat bliaḋain ina airchindeaċ, ⁊ iar ndenaṁ gaċa maiṫſsa for caoṁnaccair do gnioṁ hi ccill ⁊ i ttuaiṫ.

Tſmpall mainistre na buille do ċoisreaccaḋ.

Muircſrtaċ ua floinn ticcſrna ua ttuirtre do marḃaḋ la gallaiḃ, ⁊ Conġalach ua cuinn taoiseaċ Maiġe lugad, ⁊ ṡil ccaṫaraicch uile, tuir ġaiscceḋ, einigh, ⁊ oirdearcais tuaiscirt Ereann do ṁarḃaḋ la gallaiḃ beós is in ló céḋna.

Ruaiḋri, ⁊ Maoilseaċlainn da ṁac ṁég coċláin do écc i mainistir ċille bſccain.

Lochlainn ua Concoḃair do écc ⁊ mainistir cnuic muaiḋe.

[m] *Maelisa O'Deery.*—This passage is thus translated by Colgan: "Moelisa Hua Doighre Archidnechus Dorensis in hospitalitatiis, aliisque bonis operibus prædicabilis, postquam munus Archidnechi quadraginta annis exercuerat; obiit Doria 8 Decembris." The airċinneach was not the archdeacon, as many respectable antiquaries have supposed.

[n] *Moy-Lughad,* maġ lugad.—This is called Magh Lughach in the Annals of Kilronan. There were several districts in Ireland of this name, but the one here mentioned is a level district in Hy-Tuirtre, in the present county of Antrim, which is mentioned in these Annals at A. M. 2859, and in Keating's History of Ireland (Haliday's edition, p. 178), as cleared of wood in the time of Neimhidh, the leader of the second colony into Ireland. This passage is rendered in the old translation of the Annals of Ulster as follows: "A. D. 1218. Murtagh O'Flyn, King of Turtry, was killed by the Galls, Congalach O'Cuin, the Candle of feats and courage of the North of Ireland, Prince [ríg toirech] of Moye Luga and Kindred Cathasay, all" [both] "killed the same day."

[o] *Kilbeggan,* cill beccain.—Now a town in the south of the county of Westmeath. There is not a vestige of the monastery now remaining, but its site is pointed out about one hundred perches to the south of the town. Its burial ground still remains, but the site of the monastery is now a green field.

[p] *Loughlin O'Conor.*—He was the tenth son of Turlough More O'Conor, Monarch of Ireland.—See Book of Lecan, fol. 72, *b*, col. 4.

[q] *Knockmoy,* Cnoc muaiḋe, i. e. *Collis Muadiæ.*—Now the Abbey of Knockmoy, in the barony of Tiaquin, in the county of Galway, and about six miles to the south-east of Tuam. This is the first mention made of this monastery by the Four Masters. According to Grace's Annals of Ireland, the Abbey of Knockmoy, which was otherwise called *de Colle Victoriæ,* was founded by Cathal Crovderg, King of Connaught, in the year 1189; but the Dublin copy of the Annals of Innisfallen, and Ware's Antiquities at Galway, and also his annals, place its foundation in the year 1190. It is the general opinion of Irish historians that Cathal Crovderg founded this abbey for Cistercian monks, in commemoration of a victory, which he had gained at the hill of Knockmoy, and hence called it *de Colle Victoriæ.* In a compilation of the sixteenth century, now at the Convent of Esker, near Athenry, it is stated that the Abbey of cnoc buaḋ, i. e. monasterium *de Colle Victoriæ,* was

Maelisa O'Deery[m], Erenagh of Derry, died on the 18th of December; having been Erenagh of Derry for forty years, and having done all the good in his power, both in Church and State.

The church of the monastery of Boyle was consecrated.

Murtough O'Flynn, Lord of Hy-Tuirtre, was slain by the English; and Congalagh O'Quin, Chief of Magh Lugad[n], and of all Sil-Cathasaigh, and tower of the valour, hospitality, and renown of the north of Ireland, was also slain by the English on the same day.

Rory and Melaghlin, two sons of Mac Coghlan, died in the monastery of Kilbeggan[o].

Loughlin O'Conor[p] died in the monastery of Knockmoy[q].

founded by Carolus O'Conor about the year 1220; but this is totally wrong in the name and date of the foundation, for the original Irish name is not cnoc buaiḋ, *the hill of the victory*, but cnoc muaiḋe, the hill of Muaidh, a woman's name, denoting *good*, or noble (maiṫ no uaſal); and this name is unquestionably older than the time of Cathal Crovderg, for the plain adjoining the hill of Knockmoy was called Magh Muaidhe at a very early period. The Editor has discovered no contemporaneous or trustworthy account of the battle said to have been fought and won by Cathal Crovderg at this place, and is inclined to think that *Collis Victoriæ* is but a fanciful translation of the ancient Irish name of the hill, as if it were cnoc mbuaiḋ. Of such fanciful translations we have several instances in other parts of Ireland, as *de Rosea Valle*, for Roſ ġlaſ; *de Viridi ligno*, for Newry, or Iubaṗ Cinn ꞇṗaġa; *de Valle salutis*, for mainiſꞇiṗ an ḃealaiġ, &c. The Book of Howth, and from it Hanmer, in his Chronicle (Dublin edition of 1809, pp. 338–341), give an account, but without mentioning the place, of a "bloody battaile" between O'Conor and Sir Armoric St. Lawrence, in which Sir Armoric and all his small band of steel-clad warriors were annihilated; but it is a mere romance, and should not be received as history without being corroborated by some cotemporaneous English or Irish authority. Dr. Ledwich says, that the battle in commemoration of which the Abbey of Knockmoy was built, was fought in Ulster! "In the height of the battle," writes the doctor, "O'Conor vowed to build an abbey *in his own country*, if he was crowned with success, and he erected Knockmoy, in Irish, *Cnocmugha*, the *hill of slaughter*, and in monkish writers styled 'Monasterium de Colle Victoriæ,' to perpetuate the remembrance of O'Conor's victory."—*Antiquities of Ireland*, second edition, p. 520.

Dr. Leland, however, with that display of philosophic inference from legendary events, which renders his work worthless as an authority, treats as true history the account of this supposed battle contained in the Book of Howth, which he quotes (but without knowing that it was the Book of Howth), as a MS. in the Lambeth Library, P. No. 628, and draws the following conclusion, which shews that a man may be a sound logician, though a bad judge of the authenticity of historical monuments. After describing the fictitious battle, he writes: "An advantage gained with such difficulty and so little honour, was yet sufficient for the levity and vanity of Cathal. He founded an abbey

Creac do dénamh la gallaibh mide, ⁊ la muirchertach carrach ua ffergail ar uibh briúin na Sionna, ⁊ diarmait mac toirrdealbaigh mic maoileachlainn, ⁊ dream do chonnachtaibh do breith forra go raimhid forr na gallaibh go ttorchratar tuilleadh ar chéd eittir mharbhadh, ⁊ bádhadh díobh. Do rochair mac uí Concobair i ffritheghuin na sgainnre go noruing dia mhuintir a maille fris.

AOIS CRIOSD, 1219.

Aois Criosd, mile, dá chéd, a naoi décc.

Aodh ua maoileóin epscop cluana mic nois do bathadh.

Fonachtán ua bronáin comorba coluim cille do ecc, ⁊ flann ua brolcháin do oirdneadh ina ionadh is in comhorbus.

Maelsechlainn mac Concobair maonmaighe do marbhadh la Maghnus mac toirrdealbaigh í Concobair iar ngabháil tighe fair i ccluain tuaiscirt.

Sluaicchеadh la hUa ndomhnaill .i. domhnall mor i ngairbhtrian connacht da

upon the field of action called *de Colle Victoriæ;* and by this weak and inconsiderate mark of triumph, raised a trophy to the romantic valour of his enemies."

Mr. Moore says, in opposition to all writers, that this battle was fought on the site of the abbey, between two rivals of the house of O'Conor, but he quotes no authority, and we must therefore conclude that he drew his account of the event by inference from other collateral facts. The truth would seem to be that there is no evidence to prove that such a battle was ever fought, and it is, therefore, but fair to assume that the name *de Colle Victoriæ* is but a fanciful Latinized translation of cnoc Muaide, or Knockmoy.

' *Hy-Briuin of the Shannon,* otherwise called *Tir Briuin na Sionna,* now *Tir ui Bhriuin.*—A beautiful district in the county of Roscommon, lying between Elphin and Jamestown, of which O'Manachain, now Monahan, was chief up to the year 1249, but after that period it became the lordship of O'Beirne. To this circumstance O'Dugan refers in the following lines:

Muintir Beirn, croda an cathal,
Ar macaibh O'Mannachán;
Tre gleó, tre brig, tre bagar,
As leó tír a d-tangadar.

"The O'Beirnes, a brave battalion,
Are over the race of O'Monahan ;
By fighting, by vigour, by threatning,
The district into which they came is their's."

ˢ Under this year the Annals of Ulster and of Kilronan record the death of Gilla-Ernan O'Martan, chief Brehon of Ireland, who had retired into a monastery; and the latter annals record the death of the poet O'Maelrioc, the most distinguished of the poets of Ireland, next after the O'Dalys; also the death of O'Nioc, Abbot of Kilbeggan; and they also record the burning of that part of the town of Athlone belonging to Meath.

ᵗ *In his place.*—This passage is thus rendered,

A depredation was committed by the English of Meath, and by Murtough Carragh O'Farrell on the Hy-Briuin of the Shannon[r]. Dermot, the son of Turlough, who was the son of Melaghlin, and some of the Connacians, overtook them, and defeated the English, of whom upwards of one hundred persons were either slain or drowned. The son of O'Conor and some of his people fell fighting, in the heat of the conflict[s].

THE AGE OF CHRIST, 1219.

The Age of Christ, one thousand two hundred nineteen.

Hugh O'Malone, Bishop of Clonmacnoise, was drowned.

Fonaghtan O'Bronan, Coarb of St. Columbkille, died; and Flann O'Brollaghan was appointed in his place[t].

Melaghlin, the son of Conor Moinmoy, was slain by Manus[u], the son of Turlough O'Conor, who had taken his house (by force) at Cloontuskert[w].

An army was led by O'Donnell (Donnell More) into the Rough Third of

word for word, in the old translation of the Annals of Ulster: "A. D. 1219. Fonaghtan O'Bronan, Coarb of Colum-kill, died. Flan O'Brolcan was put in his place in the coarbship;" and thus by Colgan, in *Trias Thaum.*, p. 506: "Fanactanus O'Broin, Abbas Dorensis, obiit; et in ejus locum Flannius O'Brolchain suffactus est."

In the Dublin copy of the Annals of Ulster it is stated, that on the death of O'Bronan, a dispute arose between the people of Derry and the Kinel-Owen, about the election of a successor; that the people of Derry elected Mac Cawell, and that Hugh O'Neill and the Kinel-Owen elected Flann O'Brollaghan, and established him in the coarbship; that soon after a dispute arose between the people of Derry and O'Brollaghan, when the latter was expelled; that after this the people of Derry and the Kinel-Owen elected Murtough O'Milligan, the Lector of Derry, who enjoyed his professorship and the abbacy for a year, *vel paulo plus*, when a dispute arose between him and Godfrey O'Deery, the Erenagh, about the professorship, when the matter was referred to the Coarb of St. Patrick, who settled their differences, and decided, by consent of all the parties, that John Mac Infhir leighinn should be appointed to the professorship.

[u] *Manus*, maġnuṗ.—He was the tenth son of Turlough More O'Conor, Monarch of Ireland.—See Book of Lecan, fol. 72, *b*, col. 4.

[w] *Cloontuskert*, cluain tuaiṗcipt.—There are two places of this name in Connaught, but the one here referred to is unquestionably that situated near the River Suck, about five miles south of Ballinasloe, in the county of Galway, where are the ruins of an extensive monastery erected by O'Kelly. Conor Moinmoy O'Conor, the father of Melaghlin O'Conor, who had his house here, made great efforts to wrest the territory of Moinmoy from the O'Kellys of Hy-Many, and erected a castle at Ballinasloe, in the very heart of their country.

bFuair braiġde, ⁊ úṁla uí ruairc, ⁊ ui Raiġilliġ, ⁊ caṫa aoḋa finn uile ⁊ ġabail dó iar sin tre ḟearaiḃ manach go ro milleaḋ lais gaċ conair tres a ttuaṫcaiḃ etir ċill, ⁊ tuaiṫ doneoċ bai i ffrithsabhra fris.

Ualtra de lacy, ⁊ mac uilliam burc do ṫeaċt a Saxoibh.

Duḃdara mac Muireaḋaiġ ui maille do ṁarbaḋ i nġleiṁeal la caṫal croibhdhearcc ina longphort féin tré na ṁíġníoṁaibh.

Enda mac danair uí ṁaoilċiaráin do écc.

AOIS CRIOSD, 1220.

Aois Criosd, míle, da ċéd, a fiċe.

Iacobus do toċt i nErinn ina léġaideċ on bPapa do ḟioḋiuccad, ⁊ dorduccḣaḋ dal ecclastacda na hEreann, ⁊ a dol for cculaibh doridisi.

Diarmait mac Ruaidri (.i. mac toirrdhealbaiġ ṁoir) Concoḃair do marbaḋ la tomás mac uċtraiġ ag teċt a hinnsibh gall, ar ttionól coblaiġ do ḋiarmait ag teċt do ġabáil riġe connacht. Maolruanaiḋ ua duḃda do ḃaṫaḋ ar an ccoḃlaċ cceDna.

Maolseachlainn, mac maoilseċlainn ḃicc do bathaḋ ar loċ riḃ.

Diarmait mac briain daill do marbaḋ do ṁac maṫġaṁna ui ḃriain tre ṁeabail.

Sluaiġeaḋ la ualtra de lacy, ⁊ la gallaiḃ miḋe go hath liacc go ndéarn-

[x] *Rough Third of Connaught*, garbṫrian Connaċt.—Connell Mageoghegan, in his translation of the Annals of Clonmacnoise, states that the rough third of Connaught comprised the counties of Leitrim, Longford, and Cavan. "A. D. 765. The Rules of St. Quæran and St. Aidan were preached in the three thirds of Counaught, whereof the two Brenyes and Annally, counties of Leytrym, Longford, and Cavan were one third part called the Rough Third Part of Connaught."

[y] *Race of Aedh Finn*, cáṫ aeḋa finn, i. e. the O'Rourkes, O'Reillys, and their correlatives, descended from Aedh Finn, son of Feargna, the son of Fergus, son of Muireadhach, son of Eoghan Sriabh, son of Duach Galach, who was son of Brian, the brother of the Monarch Niall, of the Nine Hostages, and ancestor of the most distinguished families of Connaught.

[z] *O'Malley*, ua maille.—The O'Malleys were chiefs of Umhall, a territory comprising the baronies of Murrisk and Burrishoole, in the west of the county of Mayo. It was divided into two parts, called Upper and Lower Umhall, the former comprising the barony of Murrisk, and the latter that of Burrishoole. These divisions are called the Owles by English writers.—See map prefixed to ***Genealogies, Tribes, and Customs of Hy-Fiachrach***, printed for the Irish Archæological Society in 1844.

[a] Under this year the Annals of Kilronan

Connaught[x], and obtained hostages and submission from O'Rourke and O'Reilly, and from all the race of Aedh Finn[y]. He afterwards passed through Fermanagh, and destroyed every place through which he passed, both lay and ecclesiastical property, wherein there was any opposition to him.

Walter de Lacy and the son of William Burke returned from England.

Duvdara, the son of Murray[z] O'Malley, was put to death for his crimes by Cathal Crovderg O'Conor, while in fetters in O'Conor's fortress.

Enda, the son of Danar O'Mulkieran, died[a].

THE AGE OF CHRIST, 1220.

The Age of Christ, one thousand two hundred twenty.

Jacobus came to Ireland as the Pope's Legate, to regulate and constitute the ecclesiastical discipline of Ireland, and then returned home[b].

Dermot, the son of Roderic (who was son of Turlough More O'Conor), was slain by Thomas Mac Uchtry, as he was coming from the Insi Gall (Hebrides), after having there collected a fleet, for the purpose of acquiring the kingdom of Connaught. Mulrony O'Dowda was drowned on the same expedition.

Melaghlin, the son of Melaghlin Beg [O'Melaghlin], was drowned in Lough Ree.

Dermot, the son of Brian Dall, was treacherously slain by the son of Mahon O'Brien.

An army was led by Walter de Lacy and the English of Meath to

contain the following entries, of which the Four Masters have collected no account: "A. D. 1219. The Coarb of Feichin of Fore *mortuus est.*" "Cluain Coirbthe [Kilbarry] was burned, both its houses and church, in this year, and Drogheda was carried away by the flood.

[b] *Returned home.*—In the Annals of Clonmacnoise, as translated by Mageoghegan, this passage is given as follows:

"A. D. 1220, Jacob, the Pope's Legate, came to Ireland this year, went about all the Kingdome for the Reformation of the Inhabitants, and constituted many wholesome rules for their Salvation."

But in the Annals of Kilronan, under the year 1221, this entry is given differently, thus: A. D. 1221. Iacop Penciail do ṫíċt mar legáid ó Róim do reḋuġaḋ ḋál eglasdaċda, 7 eireaġa na n-eċ d'ór, 7 d'airgeḋ do ṫimsuġaḋ dó o ċleirciḃ Erenn tre Simóntaċt, 7 imṫeaċt do a h-Erinn is in mbliaḋain céḋna. "A. D. 1221. Jacob Penciail came to Ireland as a Legate from Rome, to settle the ecclesiastical affairs, and he collected horse-loads of gold and silver from the clergy of Ireland by simony, and he departed from Ireland the same year."

sat urṁór caisléin ann. Sluaiġeaḋ ele la caṫal croiḃḋ̄rcc tar Sionainn soir ir in ccalaḋ, gur gaḃ eccla na goill go ndearnsat síṫ le hua cconcobhair, ⁊ co ro sccaoilsiot connaċtaigh an caislén.

An cairneach riaḃach ṁag flannchaḋa, ⁊ fḟrġal mag saṁradain do marḃad la hAodh ua ruairc .i. mac doṁnaill mic fearġail, ⁊ la cloinn fḟrmaighe.

AOIS CRIOSD, 1221.

Aois Criosd, míle, da céd, fiċe a h-áoin.

Sanct dominic [do ecc].

Corbmac ab comair do ṁarḃaḋ.

Mac hugo de laci do ṫecht ⁊ nErinn do nsṁṫoil Ríġ Saxan, ⁊ táinig i mbáiḋ aoḋa uí nell. Do ċóiḋriod ar aon i naġaiḋ gall Ereann, ⁊ do

[c] Aṫ liag, now called baile aṫa liag and Anglicised Ballyleague. The name aṫ liag was originally applied to the ford on the Shannon at Lanesborough. Ballyleague is now the name of that part of the village of Lanesborough, on the west side of the Shannon, in the province of Connaught.—See *Tribes and Customs of Hy-Many*, printed for the Irish Archæological Society, in 1843, and the map prefixed to the same work. The Athliag on the Shannon is called *Athliag Finn* in the work called Dinnsenchus, where it is explained *the ford of Finn's* [Mac Cumhaill's] *stones*. There is another place on the River Suck, called anciently Athliag Maenacain, i. e. St. Maenacan's Stony-ford, now Anglicised Athleague.

[d] *Caladh*.—This territory is still well known in the country, and contains the parish of Rathcline, in the west of the county of Longford. This passage is given as follows, in Mageoghegan's translation of the Annals of Clonmacnoise.

"A. D. 1220. Walter Delacie and the English of Meath, with their forces, went to Athliag, where they founded a castle, which they finished almost; whereupon, Cahall Crovederg, King of Connought, with his forces, went to the west" [*recte* east] "of the river of Synen, and the Englishmen, seeing them encamped at Calace, were strocken with fear, and came to an attonement of Truce; the Englishmen returned to their own houses, and Cahall Crovederg broke down the said Castle." The passage is better given in the Annals of Kilronan, but under the year 1221, as follows:

A. D. 1221. Caislen Aṫa liag do ḟuabairt do ḋenuṁ do Ualtra Delaci, ⁊ do ṡluaġ na miḋe uile. Od ċualadar imorru Connaċta sin tancodar tairis iniar co rancodar tri lar Muintire h Angoile, ⁊ a mag mbreaġmuiḋe gur loiscedor Daingsn hí Chuinn, ⁊ co ndeaċadar tremit siar is in Calaḋ, cur facbad dóib in caislen ar éicin, ⁊ tre cóir síṫa.

"A. D. 1221. The Castle of Ath liag was attempted to be made by Walter De Lacy and the forces of all Meath. But when the Connacians heard of this, they came across [the Shannon] from the West, and proceeded through the middle of Muintir-Annaly, and Magh Breagh-

Athliag[c], where they erected the greater part of a castle. Another army was led by Cathal Crovderg, eastwards across the Shannon, into the territory of Caladh[d], and the English, being stricken with fear, made peace with him; and the Connacians destroyed the castle.

The Cairneach Riabhach[e] Mac Clancy[f], and Farrell Magauran[g], were killed by Hugh, the son of Donnell, who was son of Farrell O'Rourke, and by the Clann-Fermaighe[h].

THE AGE OF CHRIST, 1221.

The Age of Christ, one thousand two hundred twenty-one.

St. Dominic [died].

Cormac, Abbot of Comar[i], was killed.

The son of Hugo de Lacy came to Ireland, without the consent of[k] the King of England, and joined Hugh O'Neill. Both set out to oppose the English of

mhuidhe, and burned O'Quin's fortress, and passing through it westwards into the territory of Caladh [i. e. Caladh na h-Anghaile], they compelled the castle to be left to them, on conditions of peace."

[e] *The Cairneach Riabhach*, i. e. *sacerdos fuscus*, the swarthy or tan-coloured priest. O'Clery explains the word cáirneach by sagart, a priest. It was the name of a celebrated saint, who flourished in the sixth century, and had his principal church at Dulane, near Kells in Meath.—See Battle of Magh Rath. pp. 20, 146.

[f] *Mac Clancy*, mag ḟlannchaḋa, was chief of Dartry, now the barony of Rossclogher, in the north of the county of Leitrim.

[g] *Magauran*, mac Saṁraḋáin. This name is sometimes Anglicised Magovern and Magowran. The head of the family was chief of the territory of Tealach Eachdhach, now the barony of Tullyhaw, in the north-west of the county of Cavan.

[h] *Clann-Fermaighe.*—See note under the year 1217. Under this year the Annals of Kilronan record the death of Gilchreest Magorman, the great priest of Taghshinny" [in the county of Longford],—"a senior distinguished by his piety, charity, wisdom, learning, and writings,—on his pilgrimage in the sanctuary of Inisclogbran" [in Lough Ree].

They also record the coming of Lucas de Letreuille [Netterville] into Ireland, as Primate of all Ireland, and remark that he was the first Englishman that became Primate of Ireland. For more of this Primate's history, see Harris's Ware, vol. i. pp. 64, 65.

[i] *Comar.*—This place is called *Domhnach Combuir*, in the sixth life of St. Patrick, upon which Colgan writes the following note in *Trias Thaum.*, p. 114, col. 2, note 142: "*Domnach commuir* hodie sine addito vocatur *Comar*, estque nobile cœnobium Diocesis Dunensis et Connerensis." It is now a village on the north-west branch of Lough Cuan, or the Lake of Strangford, in the barony of Castlereagh, and county Down.

[k] *Without the consent of*, do nḟiṁċeoil.—In the Dublin copy of the Annals of Ulster the phrase is da inndeoin, which would mean "*in despite*

ḋeaċattar céttur go cúlraṫain, ⁊ ro rcaoilriot a cairlén. Loittur iaraṁ i míḋe, ⁊ i laiġniḃ gur ro millriot ile don cur roin. Tionólaid trá goill Ereann ceṫre caṫa fiċet go dealccain. Tánicc aoḋ ó neill ⁊ mac hugo ceṫre caṫa coṁmóra ina naġaiḋ co ttuccrat goill annrinn a ḃreṫ féin dua nell.

AOIS CRIOSD, 1222.

Aoir Criorð, míle, dá céd, fiċe adó.

An terrcop mag Gelain errcop ċille dara decc.

Ailbin ua maolṁuaiḋ errcop ferna décc.

Maoilira ua floinn rrioir eara mic nerc décc.

Taḋg ua baoiġill ronur ⁊ taccaḋ tuairċirt Ereann, tiodnaicṫeaċ réd, ⁊ maoine daor gaċa dána décc.

Niall ó néll do ráruccaḋ doire im ingin uí caṫáin. Ro ḋíoġail dia ⁊ colum cille innrin uair nír bó cian a raoġal rom dia ér.

of." The whole passage is thus rendered in the old translation of the Ulster Annals:

"A. D. 1221. Hugo de Lacy his son, came into Ireland against the King of England's will, and came to Hugh O'Neale, and they on both sides went against the Galls of Ireland, and spoyled much in Meath, Leinster, and Vlster, and broke down the castle of Culrathan. And the Galls of Ireland gathered 24 Battles" [battalions] "to Delgain, and Hugh O'Neale and Hugh de Lacye's son came against them 4 Battles" [battalions] "where the Galls gave O'Neale his own will" [co tucrat gaill breṫ a beoil fein d' O Neill].

[l] Under this year the Annals of Kilronan record the death of Dermot O'Culeachain, "a learned historian and scribe; a man who had more books and knowledge than any one of his time,—he who had transcribed the Mass Book of Knock, and a befitting Office Book for Dermot Mageraghty, his tutor, and for Gillapatrick, his own foster-brother, who were successively coarbs of Achadh Fabhair" [Aghagower, in the county of Mayo].

[m] *Albin O'Mulloy.*—He was raised to this dignity in the year 1186. He was the great rival of Giraldus Cambrensis, to whom the bishopric of Ferns had been offered by John Earl of Moreton, afterwards King John; but Giraldus refusing to accept of it, Albin O'Molloy, then Abbot of Baltinglass, was elected bishop. It is stated in the Dublin copy of the Annals of Innisfallen, that this "righteous philosopher preached an excellent sermon at a synod in Dublin, in the year 1185, on the chastity of the clergy, and proved satisfactorily before the archbishop, John Cumin, and the whole convocation, that the Welsh and English clergy, by their vicious lives and bad examples, had corrupted the chaste and unspotted clergy of Ireland, a thing which gave great offence to Giraldus, who was called Cambrensis."

For more particulars of the history of this remarkable prelate, the reader is referred to Harris's Ware, vol. i. pp. 439, 440; and Lanigan's

Ireland, and first went to Coleraine, where they demolished the castle. They afterwards went into Meath and Leinster, and destroyed a great number of persons on that occasion. The English of Ireland mustered twenty-four battalions at Dundalk, whither Hugh O'Neill, and the son of Hugo de Lacy, came to oppose them with four great battalions. The English upon this occasion gave his own demands to O'Neill[l].

THE AGE OF CHRIST, 1222.

The Age of Christ, one thousand two hundred twenty-two.

Mag-Gelain, Bishop of Kildare, died.

Albin O'Mulloy[m], Bishop of Ferns, died.

Maelisa O'Flynn, Prior of Eas-mac-neirc[n], died.

Teige O'Boyle, the Prosperity and Support of the North of Ireland, and bestower of jewels and riches upon men of every profession, died.

Niall O'Neill violated[o] Derry with the daughter of O'Kane, but God and St. Columbkille were avenged for that deed, for he did not live long after it.

Ecclesiastical History of Ireland, vol. iv. p. 277.

[n] *Eas-mac-neirc*, now called Eaꞅ uı Ḟhloınn, from the family of O'Flynn, who were the hereditary Erenaghs of the place. Ware thought (Antiq. c. 26, at Roscommon), that this place might have been the same as Inchmacnerin, an island in Lough Key; but this notion cannot be reconciled with the statements of the older writers, who never speak of it as an island, and agree in placing it near the River Ḃúıll (Boyle). Colgan thought that it was the very monastery which, many centuries later, fell into the possession of the Cistercian order, and became so famous under the name of the Abbey of Boyle; "*Eas mac neirc* Monasterium ad ripam Buellii fluvii in Conaciâ. Hodié vocatur Monasterium Buellense etque ordinis Cisterciensis."—*Act. SS.* p. 494. But Colgan, who knew but little of the localities about Lough Key, is unquestionably wrong, for the great Cistercian Abbey of Boyle was that called Ath-da-Laarc. O'Donnell, in his Life of Columbkille, lib. i. c. 104, distinctly points out the situation of Eas mic Eirc, as follows:

"Inde ultra Senannum versus occidentem progressus pervenit [Columba] ad eum locum cui praeterlabentis Buellii fluminis vicina catharacta nomen fecit *Eas-mic-Eirc*, eumque Deo sacravit." The place is now called Assylyn, which is but an anglicised form of Eaꞅ uı Ḟhloınn, and is situated on the north bank of the River Boyle, about a mile west of the town. The ruins of the church still remain, and, in the memory of the old inhabitants, a part of a round tower was to be seen adjoining it.

[o] *Violated.*—In the old translation of the Annals of Ulster this passage is rendered as follows: "A. D. 1222. Neal O'Neal forcibly took away O'Cathan his daughter, and God and Columbkill miraculously shortened his days." The word ꞅáꞃuġaḋ in this sense means to profane or violate. We cannot understand from this

Giolla mochoinni ua caṫail tiġearna ċeneoil aoḋa ṫoir ⁊ ṫiar do marḃaḋ la Sſcnasaċ mac giolla na naomh uí Sſchnasaigh iar na ḃraṫ da ṁuintir féin.

Mor ingean ui ḃaoiġill bſn Amhlaiḃ uí beolláin décc.

AOIS CRIOSD, 1223.

Aois Criosd, míle, da céd, fiċe, a trí.

Mailiosa mac toirrdhealbaiġ uí Chonċoḃair prioir innsi mſdoin decc.

Dubṫach ua dubṫaigh abb conga decc.

Sloiccheaḋ la hua ndomhnaill (domhnall mór) co cruachain ċonnacht,

sentence what Niall O'Neill did to the daughter of O'Kane; it merely states that he profaned Derry by some misconduct towards the daughter of O'Kane. The sarugaḋ would be committed by taking her a prisoner from the sanctuary, in order to detain her as a hostage; by violating her person, without carrying her away; or by forcing her away in abduction, with a view of marrying her.—See note under 1223, on bacall mor ċolmain cille mic Duaċ.

p *Maelisa, the son of Turlough O'Conor.*—According to the Book of Lecan, fol. 72, *b*, col. 4, this Maelisa was the eldest of the three sons of Turlough More O'Conor, monarch of Ireland, by his married wife. It appears that he embraced a religious life in his youth, and left his younger brothers to contend with each other for the sovereignty of Connaught, and crown of Ireland.

q *Inishmaine*, Inis mſdoin, i. e. the middle island.—It is situated in the east side of Lough Mask, in the county of Mayo, between the islands called Inis Cumhang and Inis Eoghain. It contains the ruins of a small but beautiful abbey.

r *Croghan*, Cruaċain, now generally called Rathcroghan.—It is situated in the parish of Kilcorkey, nearly midway between Belanagare and Elphin, in the county of Roscommon. This was the ancient palace of the Kings of Connaught, so celebrated in the Bardic histories of Ireland as having been erected in the first century by Eochaidh Feidhleach, monarch of Ireland, the father of the celebrated Meave, Queen of Connaught. As the remains at Rathcroghan have never been minutely described by any of our topographical writers, the Editor is tempted here to give a list of the forts and other ancient remains still visible at the place. It may be described as the ruins of a town of raths, having the large rath called Rathcroghan, placed in the centre. This great rath is at present much effaced by cultivation; all its circumvallations (for such it originally had) are destroyed, and nothing remains of it but a flat, green moat, said to be hollow in the centre, and to contain a large, round chamber with a conical roof. The natives of the district believe that there were apertures all round the moat which admitted light and air to this internal chamber, which is now inhabited only by Queen Mab and her attendant fairies. The following are the present names of the raths and other artificial features which stand around it. Many of them are clearly modern, though the features to which they are applied are ancient.

Gilla Mochoinni O'Cahill, Lord of Kinelea East and West, was slain by Shaughnessy, the son of Gilla-na-naev O'Shaughnessy, after having been betrayed by his own people.

More, daughter of O'Boyle, and wife of Auliffe O'Beollain [Boland], died.

THE AGE OF CHRIST, 1223.

The Age of Christ, one thousand two hundred twenty-three.

Maelisa, the son of Turlough O'Conor[p], Prior of Inishmaine[q], died.

Duffagh O'Duffy, Abbot of Cong, died.

An army was led by O'Donnell (Donnell More) to Croghan[r], in Connaught,

1. Rath Screig, to the north, in the townland of Toberrory; 2. Cuirt mhaol, near Rath Screig, in the same townland; 3. Rath Carrain, a fort containing a cave, in the same townland; 4. Rath-beg, in the townland of Rathcroghan, lying to the north-west of the great central rath; 5. Rathmore, lying about five hundred paces to the north-west of Rathbeg; 6. Knockaun-Stanly, i. e. Stanly's Hillock, a fort lying a quarter of a mile to the north-west of Rathcroghan; 7. Rath-na-dtarbh, i. e. Fort of the Bulls, due west of Rathcroghan; 8. Rath-na-ndealg, i. e. Fort of the Thorns, which gives name to a townland, lies a short distance to the west of Rath-na-dtarbh; 9. Rath fuadach, lies to the south-west of Rathcroghan, in the parish of Baslick, and gives name to the townland in which it is situated; 10. Caisiol Mhanannain, i. e. Manannan's stone fort, lies to the south-west, about a quarter of a mile from Rathcroghan, in the townland of Glenballythomas. This caisiol or circular cyclopean fort of stone, is now level with the ground, but its outline can yet be traced; 11. Roilig na Riogh, i. e. the Cemetery of the Kings, lies a quarter of a mile to the south of Rathcroghan. This was the royal cemetery of Connaught in pagan times, and has been much celebrated by the bards. It is of a circular form, is surrounded with a stone wall now greatly defaced, and it measures one hundred and sixteen paces in diameter. It exhibits several small tumuli, now much effaced by time. One of these was opened by the uncle of the late Mr. O'Conor, of Mount Druid, who found that it contained a small square chamber of stone-work, without cement, in which were some decayed bones.

Close to the north of Roilig-na-Riogh is a small hillock, called Cnocan na gcorp, i. e. the Hillock of the Corpses, whereon, it is said, the bodies of the kings were wont to be laid while the graves were being dug or opened. About two hundred paces to the north of the circular enclosure called Roilig-na-Riogh is to be seen a small circular enclosure, with a tumulus in the centre, on the top of which is a very remarkable red pillar-stone which marks the grave of Dathi, the last pagan monarch of Ireland, and the ancestor of the O'Dowdas of Tir Fiachrach. This stone stood perpendicularly when seen by the Editor in the year 1837, and measured seven feet in height, and four feet six inches in width at its base, and three feet near the top. It gradually tapered, and was nearly round at the top. It is called the coirthe dearg, or red pillar-stone, by

arraiḋe hi ttuaṫaiḃ connacht, ⁊ tar Suca siar gur ṁill ⁊ gur ċreachloiscc gach tir gur a rainicc co ffuair a mbraiġde ⁊ a nuṁla.

Seachnusach mac giolla na naoṁ uí ṡeachnusaiġ do ṁarbaḋ do ċloinn ċuiléin, ⁊ sárucchaḋ na bachla ṁoire Cholmáin cille mic duach uime.

Murchaḋ carraċ ua fearġail do marbaḋ daon urcor saiġde, ag dénaṁ greissi ar Aoḋ mac Amlaoibh uí fearġuil.

AOIS CRIOSD, 1224.

Aois Criosd, míle, da céd, a ceathair.

Mainistir. S. Froinsiais i nAṫluain do ṫionnsgnaḋ lá caṫal croiḃdearg ua cconcoḃair la riġ connacht in easpuccóideacht cluana mic nóis ar brú na sionna allanoir.

Duald Mac Firbis, in his account of the monarch Dathi, in the pedigree of the O'Dowdas. See *Tribes and Customs of Hy-Fiachrach*, printed for the Irish Archæological Society in 1844, pp. 24, 25, note [m].

12. Cathair na Babhaloide, the caher or stone Fort of the feasting Party, lies about three quarters of a mile to the east of Rathcroghan; 13. Carn Ceit, lies one mile to the south-west of Rathcroghan; it is a tumulus raised over the celebrated Ceat Mac Magach, a Connacian champion who flourished in the first century, and was contemporary with the heroes of the Red Branch in Ulster.

There are two large stones lying flat on the ground, about one hundred paces to the northwest of Rathcroghan, the one a large square rock called Milleen Meva, the other, measuring nine feet in length, two feet in breadth, and about two feet in thickness, is called Misgan Meva.

There are also some curious natural caves near this fort of Rathcroghan, in connexion with which there are some wild legends told in the neighbourhood, and there are also some written ones in ancient Irish manuscripts. The reader will find all the above forts accurately shewn on the Ordnance Map of the county of Roscommon, sheets 21 and 22.

[s] *Clann-Cuilen.*—Until the year 1318 the territory of the Clann Cuileain, which belonged to the Mac Namaras of Thomond, was a small district lying eastwards of the River Fergus in the county of Clare, and containing the following parishes, viz., Quin, Tulla, Cloney, Dowry, Kilraghtis, Kiltalagh, now included in the parish of Inchacronan, Templemaley, Inchacronan, and Kilmurry-na-Gall. But after the year 1318, in which the Hy-Bloid were defeated by the descendants of Turlough O'Brien, aided by the Mac Namaras, the latter got possession of nearly the entire country lying between the River Fergus and the Shannon.

[t] *Bachal mor*, i. e. the great crozier.—This relic is yet extant, but in very bad preservation. It is in the cabinet of George Petrie, Esq., Author of the Essay on the Round Towers, and ancient Ecclesiastical Architecture of Ireland.

[u] *Colman Mac Duach*, i. e. Colman the son of *Duach*, who founded the church called Kilmacduagh, situated in the barony of Kiltartan, in the county of Galway, about the year 620. He was of the illustrious tribe of Hy-Fiachrach

thence into the Tuathas of Connaught, and westwards across the Suck, and plundered and burned every territory which he entered, until he had received their hostages and submissions.

Shaughnessy, the son of Gilla-na-naev O'Shaughnessy, was slain by the Clann-Cuilen[s], a deed by which the Bachal mor[t] of St. Colman[u], son of Duach, was profaned[v].

Murrough Carragh O'Farrell was slain [at Granard, An. Ult.] by an arrow, in a battle against Hugh, the son of Auliffe O'Farrell[w].

THE AGE OF CHRIST, 1224.

The Age of Christ, one thousand two hundred twenty-four.

The Monastery of St. Francis at Athlone, was commenced by Cathal Crovderg O'Conor, King of Connaught, in the diocese of Clonmacnoise, on the eastern bank of the Shannon.

Aidhne, in the south of the province of Connaught, and nearly related to Guaire Aidhne, King of that province, so famed in Irish history for unbounded hospitality. See Colgan's *Acta SS.*, p. 248.

[v] *Was profaned*, do ṡáruġaḋ.—When parties had sworn on a crozier or any relic to observe certain conditions, such as to offer protection to a man in case he made his appearance, and that such an oath was afterwards violated, the crozier or relic, in the language of these Annals, was said to be profaned. The true application of the word ṡáruġaḋ will appear from the following passage in these Annals at the year 907 :

A.D. 907. Sáruccaḋ Ardmacha la Cernachan mac Duilgen .i. cimbiḋ do ḃreiṫ as in cill, 7 a ḃáḋaḋ hi loch Cuirr fri h-ardmacha aniar. Cernachan do ḃaḋaḋ la Niall mac Aoḋa, riġ in tuaisceirt is in loċ cedna hi ccionn ṡáraiġṫe Padraicc.

It is translated by Colgan as follows in his Annals of Armagh :

"907. *Basilica Ardmachana sacrilegam vim passa per Kernachanum filium Dulgeni ; qui quendam Captiuum eo refugij causa effugientem*, ex Ecclesia sacrilego ausu *extraxit*, et in lacu de *Loch Kirr vrbi versus occidentem adiacenti, suffocauit, sed Kernachanus iustam tanti sacrilegij pœnam, mox luit, per Niellum filium Aidi Regem Aquilonaris* partis : et posteà totius Hiberniæ in eodem lacu suffocatus."—*Trias Thaum.* p. 296; see also note on Termon Caelainne under the year 1225.

[w] Under this year the Annals of Kilronan have the following entries, which have been omitted by the Four Masters :

"A. D. 1223. Clonmacnoise was burned, including two churches, and many valuable articles.

"A great storm occurred the day after the festival of St. Matthew, which destroyed all the oats throughout Ireland that remained unreaped in the fields.

"Finn O'Carmacan, a steward to the King of Connaught, and who held much land, died.

"Twenty-six feet were added to the church of Tigh Sinche [Taghshinny, in the county of

Maolmuire ó connmaic espoc ua bfiaċraċ ⁊ cenél aoḋa do écc.

Espoc Conmaicne, .i. an gaillespoc decc.

Muirgius canánaċ mac Ruaiḋri uí ċonċoḃair aon bá dearrscnaiġṫi do ġaoiḋelaiḃ illegionn, i ccanntaireaċt, ⁊ a ndénaṁ uérsa décc, ⁊ a aḋnacal i ccunga.

Maolcaoiṁġin ua Scingin airċinneaċ arda carna décc.

Maoilisu mac an espuic uí ṁaoilḟaġṁair pearsún ua bfiaċraċ ⁊ ua naṁalgaḋa, ⁊ aḋḃar espuic ar eccna, do marḃaḋ do mac donnchaḋa uí ḋuḃda mar nar ḋú dó uair noċar ṁarḃ neaċ duiḃ duḃda riaṁ cleireaċ gó sin.

Cioṫ aḋḃal aḋuaṫṁar dfearṫain i ccuid do connaċtaiḃ, .i. i ttir maine i Sodain, ⁊ in uiḃ diarmata ⁊c. diar ḟás teḋm, ⁊ galar aiḋḃreċ do ceṫraiḃ

Longford], by the priest of the town, namely, Mael-Magorman.

"William de Lacy came to Ireland and made the Crannog [wooden house] of Inis Laeghachain; but the Connacians came upon the island by force, and let out the people who were on it, on parole." This latter entry is given in Mageoghegan's translation of the Annals of Clonmacnoise under the year 1222, as follows: "A. D. 1222. William Delacie and the English of Meath, with their forces, founded a castle at Loghloygeaghan; the Connoghtmen of the other side came with their forces to Loghloygeachan" [and] "the ward of the said castle came forth to the principalls of Connoght, and as soone as they were out of the Castle the Connoughtmen broke the same, and so departed."

[x] *The Bishop of Hy-Fiachrach and Kinelea*, easpoc ua ffiaċraċ ⁊ ċinel aoḋa.—By this the Annalists mean the Bishop of Kilmacduagh; but they have expressed it incorrectly, for the Kinel-Aodha were Hy-Fiachrach, as much as the inhabitants of the rest of the diocese of Kilmacduagh. They should have called O'Conmaic Bishop of Hy-Fiachrach Aidhne, which would express the diocese of Kilmacduach without adding another word; or have called him Bishop of Coill Ua bh-Fiachrach and Kinel Aodha na h-Echtghe, which would express and distinguish the two districts of which the diocese consisted, namely, the countries of O'Heyne and O'Shaughnessy: but the fact is, that the Four Masters who compiled this work from various sources, have left many entries imperfectly arranged.

[y] *Conmaicne*, i. e. of the people and district so called, on the east side of the Shannon. The principal families among the eastern Conmaicne were the O'Farrells and Mac Rannalls, whose territories are comprised in the diocese of Ardagh. The name of this bishop was Robert, but his surname no where appears. He was an Englishman, and had been the eleventh abbot of St. Mary's Abbey, Dublin, before he was elevated to the see of Ardagh.—See Ware's Bishops by Harris, p. 250.

[z] *Maurice*.—The natives of Cong still point out his tomb in the Abbey, but some suppose it is the tomb of his father Roderic.

[a] *Poetical compositions*, a ndenaṁ uersa, literally "in making of verses." In the Annals of Kilronan, the term employed is uersoḟnṁuiḋeaċt, i. e. in verse-making. In the Lowland Scotch a *maker* signifies, "a poet."

[b] *Ardcarne*, Ard cárna.—A vicarage in the

Mulmurry O'Conmaic, Bishop of Hy-Fiachrach and Kinelea[x] [Kilmacduagh] died.

The Bishop of Conmaicne[y] [Ardagh], i. e. the English bishop, died.

Maurice[z], the Canon, son of Roderic O'Conor, the most illustrious of the Irish for learning, psalm-singing, and poetical compositions[a], died, and was interred at Cong.

Mulkevin O'Scingin, Erenagh of Ardcarne[b], died.

Maelisa, son of the Bishop O'Mulfover, parson of Hy-Fiachrach and Hy-Awley, and *materies* of a bishop for his wisdom, was killed by the son of Donough O'Dowda, a deed strange in him, for none of the O'Dowda's had ever before killed an ecclesiastic.

A heavy and awful shower[c] fell on a part of Connaught, namely, on Hy-Many[d], Sodan[e], in Hy-Diarmada[f], and other districts, from which arose a mur-

diocese of Elphin, situated in the barony of Boyle and county of Roscommon, and about four miles to the east of the town of Boyle. This church was founded by St. Beo-Aedh, a bishop who died on the 8th of March, 524; and it continued for some time to be the head of a bishop's see. For some account of the patron saint of this church, the reader is referred to Colgan's *Acta Sanctorum*, at 8th of March; the *Feilire Aenguis*, and Irish Calendar of the O'Clerys, at the same day; and also to Lanigan's Ecclesiastical History of Ireland, vol. i. p. 462. Archdall places Ardcharn in the county of Westmeath, which is a very strange blunder, as Colgan, his authority, had described it as in Maghluirg, in Connaught.

Considerable ruins of the church of Ardcarne are still to be seen; and in the field lying between the church and the high road are shewn slight remains of the walls of an abbey, and the foundations of some of the houses which constituted the ancient village of Ardcarne.

[c] *A heavy and awful shower*, cioċ anḃal aḃuaḋmap.—This shower is also mentioned in the Annals of Kilronan, but not in any way connected with the death of Cathal Crovderg, of which the Four Masters represent it as an ominous presage. The literal translation is as follows: "A. D. 1224. A shower fell in parts of Connaught, namely, in Tirmany, in Soghan, in Hy-Diarmada, and in Clann-Teige, of which there grew a great murrain among the cows, after having eaten of the grass and herbage; and the people, after having taken of their milk and flesh, contracted many diseases."

[d] *Hy-Many*, ui maine.—O'Kelly's country, originally extending from Athenry to the Shannon, and from the borders of Thomond to Lanesborough, on the Shannon.

[e] *Sodan*.—This was the country of the O'Mannins, and, as appears from various authorities, was included in the present barony of Tiaquin, in the county of Galway. For a list of the townlands in the occupation of different persons of the name of O'Mannin in this territory, in the year 1617, the reader is referred to *Tribes and Customs of Hy-Many*, printed for the Irish Archæological Society in 1843, p. 164.

[f] *Hy-Diarmada*, uí Diapmada.—This was the tribe name of the O'Concannons, which also be-

na ccríoċ remraiti iar ccaitsiṁ an ḟeóir do ḟliuch an cioṫ ra ḋóiḃ. Do gnioḋ ḃeos laċt na ninnileḋ sin galraiġṫi inṁeoḋonċa go héxaṁail do na daoiniḃ do ṫoimleḋ é. Ba deṫḃir na dearḃairḋi si do ṫeċt i cConnaċtaiḃ is in mbliaḋain si uair ba mór an tolc, ⁊ an timneḋ do rala ḋóiḃ innte, .i. caṫal croibdearg mac toirrḋealḃaiġ ṁóir uí ċonċoḃair, Rí Connaċt, aon ar

came that of their country. The head of the O'Concannons was seated at a place called Kiltullagh, in the county of Galway, in 1585, and his country was then considered a part of Hy-Many.—See *Tribes and Customs of Hy-Many*, p. 19, note [l].

[8] *Cathal Crovderg*, Caṫal croiḃḋearg, i.e. Cathal, or Charles of the Red Hand.—The obituary of Cathal Crovderg is thus given in the Dublin copy of the Annals of Ulster, with which those of Kilronan agree.

"A.D. 1224. Caṫal croiḃderg hua concobuir, rí connaċt, ⁊ rí gaiḋel Erenn ar toṫuċt aḋbaṫ i mainistir cnuic muaide u°. Kal. Iunii, in taen gaiḋel is ferr tainig o brian boroma anuas ar uaisli, ⁊ ar onoir; togbalach tresaġmur toṫuċtuċ na tuaṫ; soḃartanaċ saiḋbir suaiṫniġ soineṁail na síṫċana, dóiġ is ré reiṁes do gabad deċmaiḋ co dliġtech ar túr i n-iaṫ Erenn; columain connail craiḋbeċ certbriaṫraċ creiḋṁi ⁊ cristaiḋeċta; certaiġṫeoir na cintaċ, ⁊ na coiḃḋenach; múġaiġṫeoir na méirleċ ⁊ na malartaċ; coimetaiġcoitċenn caṫbuaḋaċ in recta roo ḋlestaiġ, d'á tuc Dia deġonóir i talṁain, ⁊ in flaiṫius nemḋa ċall ar neg in aibit ṁanaiċ do, iar mbreiṫ buaḋa ó doman ⁊ o deman."

Thus rendered in the old translation of the Annals of Ulster, in which it is incorrectly placed under the year 1223.

"A. D. 1223. Cathal Crovderg O'Coner, King of Connaught, and King of the Irish of Ireland, died at the Abbey of Knock-moy, 5 *Kal. Junij*. The best Irishman that was from the time of Brien Boroma, for gentility and honor; the upholder, mighty and puissant, of the country; keeper of peace, rich and excellent. For in his time was tieth payd and established in Ireland first legally. Threshold, meek and honest, of belief and Christianity; corrector of transgressors and thieves; the banisher of" [the] "wicked and robbers" [múġaiġṫeoir na méirleċ ⁊ na malartaċ]; "the defender of the right Law, conning and couragious; to whom God gave great honour in this life, and everlasting" [life] "in heaven, dying in a Munck's habit, overcoming the world and the Devill."

Cathal Crovderg was the son of Turlough More O'Conor, Monarch of Ireland, and the brother of Roderic O'Conor, the last of the Irish monarchs. According to the traditional story told about him in the neighbourhood of Ballintober, in the county of Mayo, he was the illegitimate son of King Turlough by Gearrog Ny-Moran of the territory of Umhall. The traditional story, which is very vivid, and believed to be true, runs as follows:

"Shortly before the English invasion of Ireland, the King of Connaught, who was of the family of O'Conor, having no issue by his lawful queen, took to his bed a beautiful girl, out of the territory of Umhall, by name Gearrog Ny-Moran, who soon exhibited symptoms of fertility. When the Queen of Connaught heard of this demonstration of her own barrenness, she became, like Sarah of old, jealous in the highest degree, and used every means in her power to persecute the King's concubine. She even had recourse to witches, who were then numerous in the province, but without success, until at last, shortly

rain and dreadful distemper among the cattle of the aforesaid territories, after they had eaten of the grass moistened by this shower, and the milk of these cattle produced a variety of inward maladies in the people who used it. · It was no wonder that these ominous signs should appear this year in Connaught, for great was the evil and affliction which they suffered in this year, viz., the death of Cathal Crovderg[g], son of Turlough More O'Conor, King of Connaught, a man

before Gearrog was about to be delivered, a celebrated witch, more skilful than the rest, who lived in the neighbourhood of Ballytoberpatrick, in the county of Mayo, presented the Queen with a magical string, with three intricate knots, telling her, that as long as she kept it in her possession Gearrog Ny-Moran, against whom its magical properties were directed, could never be delivered of a child. Before, however, the string had been fully indued with the intended charm, the King's child thrust his right hand into the external world, but farther he could not move; for, as soon as the last word of the incantation had been pronounced, he was fixed, spell-bound, in his awkward position. He continued thus for several days and nights, and though his mother wished for death she could not die. At length a certain good man, who had heard of the magical string, and of the pitiable condition of O'Moran's daughter, called one day at the palace, with a view to destroy the properties of the string, and the Queen, who held him in high esteem, having no suspicion of his design, bade him welcome and asked him the news. He answered, with some expression of annoyance on his countenance, that the principal news in the west of Connaught, was, that Gearrog Ny-Moran had brought forth a son for the King of Connaught. When the Queen heard this from the lips of one on whom she placed the utmost reliance, she took the magical string, which she was persuaded to believe would for ever prevent O'Moran's daughter from giving birth to a roydamna, and cast it into the fire in his presence, calling down all sorts of execrations on the head of the old sorceress, who had so much deceived her. No sooner had the last knot of the string been destroyed by the action of the fire, than the King's son, who had been so long kept spell-bound by its influence, was ushered upon the theatre of his future greatness; but his *crov*, or that part of the hand, from the wrist out, which he had thrust into the world before the magical string was perfected, was as red as blood, from which he received the cognomen of Cροιб-δεαρɼ, or '*the Red-handed*' *Crov-derg*.

"The Queen of Connaught, who was of a most powerful family, continued to persecute the red-handed child and his mother, with all the perseverance of a jealous barren woman; but the child, who had all the appearance of royalty in his countenance, was sheltered by the clergy of the province; and when the Queen discovered that he was lurking in one monastery, he was secretly sent away to another. In this manner was he sheltered for three years in the monasteries of Connaught. At last the Queen's fury rose to such a height against the clergy, that they gave up all hopes of being able to protect the child any longer. His mother then fled with him into Leinster, where, for many years, disguised, she supported him by labouring work. When the boy grew up, although he was constantly told of the royalty of his birth, and of the respectability of the O'Morans, still, having no hopes of being able to return to his native province as long as the Queen lived, he was obliged to apply himself to common

mó do ṁudaiġ do merlechaib, ⁊ dearccairdib Erenn ré haimsir imċéin, aon ar mó ro ḟár do ċleirċib, boċtaib, ⁊ aidelgneachaib, aon ar uille inar ḋoirtheardair dia gac mait, ⁊ gac mór suailċe dá ttáinic duaislib Ereann a ccomfoccus dia reiṁsir, óir as é ro congaib é fén ar aon mnaoi ṗósda gan truailledh a ġenmnaidheachta tar a héis có a báṡ. As ré a linn beos ar mó ro gabadh deachmadh go dliġteach céttus i nErinn. An Rí fírén foirccliḋi si, ⁊ an caitmiledh condail craibteċ ceirtbreṫaċ d'écc an tochtmadh lá fichet do ṡamradh (dia luain do ṡainnriudh) i naibíd manaiġ léṫ i mainistir cnuic

labouring work for subsistence; and it was observed by the clowns of Leinster, that he exhibited no appearance of industry, or taste for agricultural pursuits, but was constantly telling stories about Kings, wars, and predatory excursions.

"Time rolled on, and the poor boy with the red hand was necessitated to pass his time in misery, in the society of Leinster clowns and buddaghs, whom he held in the highest contempt. At length a Connaught Bollscaire, or bearer of public news, passing through Leinster, happened to come into the very field in which Crovderg was employed, with several others, reaping rye. They immediately recognized by his dress that he was a Bollscaire, and, therefore, inquired what proclamation he was publishing. He replied in the set words of his commission, that the King of Connaught was dead, and that the people, assembled in council, had declared that they would have no king but Cathal Crovderg his son; and, he added, I, and many others, have been for several weeks in search of him in different parts of Ireland, but without success; some, who wish to support the claim of rivals to the throne of Connaught, have reported that the Queen, his step-mother, had him secretly assassinated, but others are of opinion, that he lurks in some obscure place, disguised in humble garb, and that he will return home as soon as he will hear of this proclamation. He will be at once known by his right hand, which is as red as blood from the wrist out.

"The heart of Cathal bounded with joy at the news, and he stood on the ridge for some minutes in a reverie. His comrades told him to get on with his work, that he was always last, and that there never was a good workman from his province. Hereupon, Cathal pulled off the mitten, with which he constantly kept the *red hand* concealed, and exhibited it to the Bollscaire; and his eye beamed, and his countenance glowed with all the majesty of his father's, when he first mounted the throne of Connaught. The Bollscaire recognizing him at once by his resemblance to his father, fell prostrate at his feet. Cathal cast the sickle on the ridge, saying: 'Slán leat, a ċorrán, anois do'n ċloiḋeaṁ,' i. e. 'Farewell, sickle, now for the sword.' And to this day, Slán chaṫail faoi an treagal, i. e. Cathal's farewell to the rye, meaning a farewell never to return, has been a common proverb among the Sil-Murray and their followers.

"He returned home without delay, and was solemnly inaugurated King of Connaught on Carnfree, near Tulsk, in the presence of the twelve chieftains and twelve coarbs of Sil-Murray; and though he found many rivals in the province before him, he put them all down by his superior wisdom and valour. When he had restored his native province to tranquillity he did not forget his old friends the friars, who had made

who, of all others, had destroyed most of the rebels and enemies of Ireland, he who had most relieved the wants of the clergy, the poor, and the destitute, he who, of all the Irish nobility that existed in or near his time, had received from God most goodness, and greatest virtues, for he kept himself content with one married wife, and did not defile his chastity after her death until his own death, in whose time most tithes were lawfully received in Ireland; this just and upright king, this discreet, pious, and justly-judging hero, died on the 28th day of the summer (on Monday), in the habit of a Grey Friar, in the monastery of Knockmoy[h], (which monastery, together with its site and lands, he himself had

such efforts to save him from the fury of the Queen. He erected several monasteries for them on an extensive scale, and in magnificent style, namely, the monastery of Ballintober in Mayo, which was three years in building, and which was roofed and shingled with oak timber; the monastery of Athlone, on the Shannon; and also that of Knockmoy, in the county of Galway."

Notwithstanding the evidence of this vivid tradition, we must conclude from the Book of Lecan, fol. 72, b, col. 4, that Turlough More O'Conor, King of Ireland, had three sons by his married wife, namely, Maelisa, Coarb of St. Coman, who was his eldest son and heir, Aedh Dall, and Tadhg Aluinn.

Dr. O'Conor, in his suppressed work, *Memoirs of the Life and Writings of Charles O'Conor of Belanagare*, who was his own grandfather, alludes to the traditions preserved in the country about the valour of "Charles the Red-handed," but makes no allusion whatever to the story above given, which, though in great part fabulous, is generally believed to be true by the story-tellers and farmers in the counties of Mayo and Galway. But to enter upon the proofs of the legitimacy or illegitimacy of Cathal Crovderg would swell this note to a length which would interfere with the elucidation of other entries in those Annals, and the Editor must, therefore, reserve the discussion of the question for another work.

Ledwich, in his Antiquities of Ireland, second edition, p. 520, says, that there is a monument to Cathal Crovderg in the Abbey of Knockmoy; but the monument in that abbey to which he alludes, but which he evidently never saw, is that of Malachy O'Kelly, who died in 1401, and of his wife Finola, the daughter of O'Conor, who died in 1402. Ledwich was of opinion that the fresco paintings on the north wall of the choir of this abbey, were executed in the seventeenth century, "when," he says, "the confederate Catholics possessed themselves of the abbeys of Ireland, which they everywhere repaired, and, in many instances, adorned with elegant sculptures;" but it is quite clear, from the style of these paintings, and from the legible portion of the inscriptions, among which may be clearly read, in the black letter, orate pro anima Malachie, that they belong to the period of the aforesaid Malachy O'Kelly, by whom the abbey of Knockmoy seems to have been repaired if not in great part re-edified; for it is quite obvious, from the style of the abbey of Ballintuber, which unquestionably exhibits the architecture of the latter part of the twelfth century, that there is no part of that of Knockmoy as old as the period of Cathal Crovderg.

[h] *Knockmoy.*—According to the Annals of Clonmacnoise, as translated by Mageoghegan,

muaiḋe iar na heḋbairt dó buḋén do dia, ⁊ do na manchaiḃ roiṁe sin guna ronn ⁊ fearonn, ⁊ a aḋnacal innte co huasal onórach. A bpurt loċa mesca do geneaḋ caṫal croiḃdearcc, ⁊ a oilsṁain in uiḃ diarmata ag taḋcc ua ċoinċeanainn. Aoḋ ó concoḃair a mac do gaḃáil riġi Connaċt tar a éis gan cáirde uair bádar braigde Connaċt ar a láiṁ ré nécc a aṫar. As ré huċt gaḃala riġe don aoḋ sa tucc ró deara mac ui mannaċáin do ḋallaḋ tré éccsin mná do taḃairt, ⁊ a láṁa ⁊ a ċosa do ḃén do neoċ oile iar ndénaṁ méirle dó. Do ċoiṁéd smaċta flaṫa innsin.

Aoḋ mac Conċoḃair maonṁoiġi décc ag toiḋeċt ó Ierusalém, ⁊ ó sruṫ Iordanén dó.

Donnċaṫaiġ mac airsċtaiġ uí Raḋuiḃ toísec cloinne tomaltaiġ décc ina oiliṫri acc torus Pattraicc.

Maoilseaċlainn mac taiḋg uí ċeallaiġ tiġearna ó maine do écc.

Giolla na naomh crom ó Seaċnusaiġ tiġearna leṫe iarṫaraiġe cenél aoḋa na heċtgi décc.

Doṁnall ó ceallaiġ tiġearna ó maine décc.

Cúċsnann ua coinċsnainn décc.

Maṫġaṁain mac ceṫsrnaiġ uí céirin tiġearna ciarraiġe loċa na nairneaḋ décc.

Cathal Crovderg died at Broyeoll in Connaught. Bruigheol, or Briola, is in Clann-Uadagh, near the River Suck, in the county of Roscommon. The entry is as follows:

"A. D. 1223. Cahall Crovederge O'Connor, King of Connoght, and King of the Irish of Ireland, one that used reverence and bounty towards the Church, and both ritch, fortunate, and happy, died in Broyeoll in Connought, and Hugh mac Cahall, his son, was constituted King of Connoght in his place."

[i] *Harbour of Lough Mask*, port locha measca.—This place is now called Caladh Locha Measca, and Ballincalla, and is a parish in the barony of Kilmaine, and county of Mayo, verging on Lough Mask. Culaḋ, in this part of Ireland, signifies a landing place for boats, and is synonymous with port; though in the county of Roscommon it means a wet meadow, or a strath or holm on the margin of a lake or river.

[k] *A robbery*, iar ndenaṁ méirle.—This passage is given more satisfactorily in the Annals of Kilronan, as follows: "Hugh O'Conor, his own son, assumed the government of Connaught after him, and right worthy of the dignity he was, for he had been a king for his efficiency, might, and puissance, in his father's life-time, and he had the hostages of Connaught in his hands. And God permitted his succession, for such was the strictness of his law, that no evils were committed in Connaught at his accession, but one act of plunder on the road to Croagh-patrick, for which the perpetrator had his hands and feet cut off; and one woman was violated by the son of O'Monahan, for which he was deprived of sight."

granted to God and the monks), and was interred therein nobly and honourably. Cathal Crovderg was born at the Harbour of Lough Mask[i], and fostered in Hy-Diarmada by Teige O'Concannon. The government of Connaught was assumed without delay by Hugh O'Conor, his son, for the hostages of Connaught were in his (Hugh's) hands at the time of his father's death. Hugh, upon his accession to the government, commanded the son of O'Monahan should be deprived of sight as a punishment for his having violated a female, and ordered the hands and feet of another person to be cut off for having committed a robbery[k]. This *was done* to maintain the authority of a prince.

Hugh, the son of Conor Moinmoy [O'Conor], died on his return from Jerusalem and the River Jordan.

Donncahy, the son of Aireaghtagh O'Rodiv, Chief of Clann-Tomalty[l], died on his pilgrimage, at Toberpatrick[m].

Melaghlin, the son of Teige O'Kelly, Lord of Hy-Many, died.

Gilla na-naev Crom [the Stooped] O'Shaughnessy, Lord of the Western half of Kinelea of Echtge, died.

Donnell O'Kelly, Lord of Hy-Many, died.

Cucannon O'Concannon died.

Mahon, the son of Kehernagh O'Kerrin, Lord of Kerry of Lough-na-narney[n], died.

[l] *Clann-Tomalty*, clann τomalτaiġ.—This tribe was situated in the plains of Roscommon, not far from Rathcroghan, but they sunk into obscurity, and were deprived of property at so early a period, that the extent, or even exact position, of their cantred, cannot now be determined.

[m] *Toberpatrick*, τopaρ paτρaic, i. e. St. Patrick's well.—This is certainly the Abbey of Ballintober, in the county of Mayo. There are countless other places in Connaught so called.

[n] *Kerry of Lough-na-narney*, ciaρρaiġe loċa na náiρneaḋ.—This territory is now simply called ciuρρaiġe by the natives of it, who speak the Irish language remarkably well. It comprises the parishes of Annagh, Bekan, and Aghamore, which form about the southern half of the barony of Costello, in the south-east of the county of Mayo. Colgan, and after him O'Flaherty, have supposed, that the territory of Kierrigia de Loch nairne was co-extensive with the barony of Belathamhnais, otherwise called Costello, in the county of Mayo.—See *Trias Thaum.*, p. 137; and *Ogygia*, part iii. c. 46, p. 276. But this, which is put as a mere conjecture by Colgan, is certainly incorrect; for the mountainous district of Sliabh Lugha, which belonged to the Galengæ, and of which the Kierrigii never possessed any portion, formed the greater part of that barony. The boundary of the diocese of Achonry runs across the barony of Costello, in such a manner as to divide it into two almost equal parts. That part of the barony to the north of this boundary is, even at this very day, called Sliabh Lugha,

An tarḃar gan ḃuain go feil briġde, ⁊ an treaḃaḋ aga denaṁ do briġ an ċoccaiḋ, ⁊ na doininde.

Mainistir do ṫógḃáil la Muiris mac gSpailt (ó ttátt gSpaltaiġ cille dara, ⁊ gearaltaiġ dSmuṁan) in eóchaill in easscoboitteacht cluana is in Muṁain do ḃraiṫriḃ S. ffroinsiais.

and was O'Gara's original country; and the part of the barony lying to the south of the said boundary is Kerry of Lough-na-narney. The lake of Loċ na n-áirneaḋ, i. e. *Lake of the Sloes*, from which this territory took its name, is situated on the boundary between the parishes of Bekan and Aghamore, in the barony of Costello, and is now more generally called Mannin Lough. Downing, who wrote about the year 1682, when the name of this lake was well remembered, puts the situation of this lake beyond dispute by stating that the castle of Mannin is in Lough Arny. "There is likewise," he says, "a small lough in the barony, called Lough Arny in former times. In the west end thereof stands an antient ruin of a castle called Mannin." See Map to the *Genealogies, Tribes, and Customs of Hy-Fiachrach*, printed for the Irish Archæological Society in 1844, on which this lake and its castle are shewn, as well as the true boundary line between Kerry of Lough-na-narney and Sliabh Lugha, or O'Gara's country.

[o] *Maurice Fitzgerald.*—He was the grandson of the Maurice Fitzgerald who came to Ireland with the Earl Strongbow, and who died on the 1st of September, 1177. For the origin of the family of Fitzgerald the reader is referred to the History of the Earls of Desmond, by the celebrated Daniel O'Daly, published at Lisbon in 1655, under the title of "*Initium Incrementum et Exitus Familiæ Giraldinorum, Desmoniæ Comitum Palatinorum Kyerria in Hiberniâ, ac persecutionis Hæreticorum Descriptio, ex nonnullis fragmentis collecta, ac Latinitate donata.*" In this work O'Daly deduces the pedigree of the Fitzgeralds from Troy, and places their ancestors among the followers of Æneas into Italy, where they settled in Tuscany, or Etruria, from whence some of the family passed into Normandy, thence into England, and, in process of time, into Ireland. But the Editor is of opinion that there is no authentic monument of the history of this family earlier than the time of William the Conqueror, with whom they seem to have come into England, though Mr. Burke, in his pedigree of the Duke of Leinster, asserts that his ancestor Otho was a Baron of England in the 16th year of Edward the Confessor.

The character of Maurice Fitzgerald, the first of this family that came to Ireland, and who was one of the principal heroes of the English Conquest, is given as follows by his contemporary, Giraldus Cambrensis :

"Erat autem Mauritius vir venerabilis & verecundus : vultu colorato, decentique : mediocri quodam modicitate, tam mediocribus minor quam modicis maior. Vir tam animo quam corpore modificato : nec illo elato, nec hoc dilatato: Innata vir bonitate bonus & tamen longe cura propensiore bonus fieri, quam videri malens. Mauricio modus, in omnibus seruare modum : vt credi possit suarum partium, suique temporis tam censura morum, quam facetiarum exemplum. Vir breuiloquus et sermone perpauco sed ornato: puta, plus pectoris habens quam oris, plus rationis quam orationis : plus sapientia [sapientiæ ?] quam eloquentia. Et tamen cum sermonem res exigebat : ad sententiam dicendam, sicut serus, sic scientissimus. Rebus quoque in Martiis, vir animosus : et nulli fere strenuitate secundus. Ad capessenda tamen pericula, nec impetuosus nec præceps : sed sicut prouidus in aggrediendis :

The corn remained unreaped until the Festival of St. Bridget [1st February], when the ploughing was going on, in consequence of the war and inclement weather.

A monastery was erected by Maurice Fitzgerald[o], from whom the Fitzgeralds of Kildare and Desmond are descended, at Youghal[p], in the diocese of Cloyne, in Munster[q], for Franciscan friars[r].

sic pertinax erat in aggressis. Vir sobrius, modestus, et castus: stabilis, firmus, atque fidelis. Vir quidem non expers criminis: crimine tamen omni notabili carens et enormi."—*Hibernia Expugnata*, lib. i. c. 42.

It is stated by some popular Irish writers that this first Maurice Fitzgerald was appointed Chief Governor of Ireland by Henry II. in 1173; but this seems to be an error, as no original authority has yet been found for it, and his name does not appear in the list of Chief Governors of Ireland given in Harris's Ware, vol. ii. c. 15, p. 102, nor in any other trustworthy authority that the Editor has ever seen; but his grandson, the Maurice mentioned in the text, was Lord Justice of Ireland in the year 1229, and again in 1232. This Maurice is said to have been the first who brought the orders of Friars Minors and Preachers into Ireland. By a mandatory letter of Henry III., dated 26th November, 1216, he was put into possession of Maynooth, and all the other lands of which his father died seised in Ireland; and was put also into possession of the castle of Crome in the county of Limerick. According to the tradition among the O'Donovans, as stated in the Pedigree of the late General O'Donovan, by John Collins, he was the first that drove the head of that family from the castle of Crome, or Croom, in the county of Limerick; but the Editor has not been able to find any cotemporaneous authority for this statement, nor any authority whatever older than a manuscript, entitled *Carbriæ Notitia*, written in 1686, which formed No. 591 of the Sale Catalogue of the books and MSS. of the late Lord Kingsborough, in which it is stated as follows: "But let us pass from the rough seas to the smooth plains, whereof we shall find few till we pass Clancahill, a territory belonging to the Donovans, a family of Royall Extraction amongst the Irish. They came hither from Coshma, in the county of Limerick, and" "built there the famous Castle of Crome, which afterwards falling to the Earle of Kildare, gave him his motto of Crome-a-boo, still used in his scutcheon." Dr. Smith, who has used the information in this MS. throughout his Natural and Civil History of Cork, repeats the same passage, vol. i. p. 25, but quotes no authority whatever.

This Maurice died on the 20th of May, 1257, in the habit of St. Francis, and was succeeded by his son Maurice Fitz-Maurice Fitzgerald, who was appointed Lord Justice of Ireland on the 23rd of June, 1272.—See Lodge's Peerage, and a curious pedigree of the Fitzgeralds, in the handwriting of Peregrine O'Clery, in the Library of the Royal Irish Academy, and another in the copy from the Autograph of Duald Mac Firbis, in the same Library.

[p] *Youghal*, Eochaill, a well-known town in the county of Cork, situated on the River Blackwater, about twenty miles east of Cork.

[q] *In Munster*, ir in mumain, i. e. ir *in*, in *the*, and mumain *Munster*; the article an or in being sometimes prefixed to names of territories and countries in the Irish language.

[r] Under this year the Annals of Kilronan contain the following entry relative to the son of

AOIS CRIOSD, 1225.

Aois Criosd, míle, dá céd, fiche a cúig.

Aṁlaoiḃ ua beólláin airchinneaċ droma cliaḃ, Saoi eccna, ⁊ biattaċ coitċinn décc.

Ua Maoilḃrénainn ab mainistre na buille décc do biṫin cuislinne do leicceaḋ dó.

Maolbríġde ua maiccin ab topair padraicc, mac oiġe ⁊ eccnaiḋe décc. As les ro tionnscnaḋ teampal tobair patraic, ⁊ ro forbaiḋ gona Shancctair, ⁊ crosaiḃ iar mor ṡaoṫar a nónóir patraic, ⁊ Muire, eóin, ⁊ na napstal.

Giolla an ċoiṁḋeḋ mac giolla ċarraiġ uasal ṡaccart ⁊ pearsún tiġe baoiṫin deg.

Dionis ó maoilċiarain airċinneaċ arda carna décc.

Giollacoirpṫe ua muġroin decc, ⁊ a aḋnacal i cconga ḟéin.

Coiṁéirġe mór ṡluaiġ do ḋénaṁ lá hua néll i cconnaċtaiḃ do conġnaṁ le cloinn Ruaiḋri uí concoḃair, .i. toirrḋealḃaċ ⁊ aoḋ tré forconġra duinn óig ṁécc oireaċtaiġ ríoġtaoíseaċ Síl Muireḋaiġ a ndioġail a ḟearainn do ḃén de duu concoḃair (.i. aoḋ). Acċ ċéna ó ro iompaiḋ macc oireċtaiġ

Hugh de Lacy: "A. D. 1224. The son of Hugo came to Ireland, despite of the King of England, and a great war and contention arose between him and the English of Ireland, all of whom rose up against him and banished him to O'Neill, King of Aileach. Thither the English and Irish of Ireland pursued them, with their forces, namely, Hugh, the son of Cathal Crovderg, King of Connaught; Donough Cairbreach O'Brien, King of Munster; Dermot Cluasach Mac Carthy, King of Desmond; and all the other chiefs of Ireland, except the Kinel-Connell and Kinel-Owen. They marched to Muirtheimhne and Dundalk, where they demanded hostages of the sons of Hugo and of O'Neill. Then came O'Neill with his English and Irish forces, and distributed them on the passes of Sliabh Fuaid and the Gates of Emania, and the woods of Conaille; and the English were challenged to approach them in those places. However, when the English of Ireland perceived that they occupied such strong positions, they came to the resolution of making peace with the sons of Hugo, and to leave the conditions to the award of the King of England. The English of Ireland then dispersed without obtaining tribute or reward from Hugh O'Neill."

[s] *Biatagh*, biatach, a public victualler.—Sir Richard Cox thought that this term was the same as Buddagh, a clown or villain; but the two words are essentially different in their application and derivation, biatach being derived from biaḋ, food, and bodaċ, which is a name of contempt, from a different radix. The Biatagh was endowed with a quantity of land called a baile biataiġ, or ballybetagh, which was the thirtieth part of a *triocha ced*, or barony, and contained

THE AGE OF CHRIST, 1225.

The Age of Christ, one thousand two hundred twenty-five.

Auliffe O'Beollan (Boland) Erenagh of Drumcliff, a wise and learned man, and a general Biatagh[s], died.

O'Mulrenin, abbot of the monastery of Boyle, died in consequence of having been blooded.

Maelbrighde O'Maigin, Abbot of Toberpatrick[t], a son of chastity and wisdom, died. By him the church of Toberpatrick, together with its sanctuary and crosses, had been, with great exertions, begun and finished, in honour of St. Patrick, the Blessed Virgin Mary, St. John, and the Apostles.

Gilla-an-Choimhdhe Mac Gillacarry, a noble priest, and parson of Teach Baoithin, died.

Dionysius O'Mulkieran[u], Erenagh of Ardcarne, died.

Gilla-Coirpthe O'Muron, died, and was buried at Conga-Fechin (Cong).

O'Neill mustered a great force at the request of Donn Oge Mageraghty, royal Chieftain of Sil-Murray, who wanted to be revenged of O'Conor (i. e. Hugh[w]), for having deprived him (Mageraghty) of his lands, and marched into Connaught to assist the sons of Roderic, viz., Turlough and Hugh. But

four quarters or seisreaghs, each containing one hundred and twenty acres of land. The ancient Irish had two kinds of farmers, the one called Biataghs and the other Brughaidhs (Brooees), who seem to have held their lands of the chief under different tenures; the former, who were comparatively few in number, would appear to have held their lands free of rent, but were obliged to entertain travellers, and the chief's soldiers, when on their march in his direction; and the latter would appear to have been subject to a stipulated rent and service. According to the *Leabhar Buidhe*, or the Yellow Book of the Mac Firbises of Lecan, preserved in the Manuscript Library of Trinity College, Dublin, H. 3, 18, p. 921, it appears that the Brughaidh, or farmer, called bruġaıḋ ceḋaċ, was bound by law to keep one hundred labourers, and one hundred of each kind of domestic animals. For a curious dissertation on the tenure of the Irish Biataghs, the reader is referred to Harris's Ware, vol. ii. c. 10, pp. 157, 158; and *Statute of Kilkenny*, edited by Mr. Hardiman for the Irish Archæological Society, pp. 4, 5.

[t] *Toberpatrick.*—Now Ballintober, in the county of Mayo, where the ruins of a great abbey and of a small church, dedicated to St. Patrick, may be seen.

[u] *O'Mulkieran*, O maoılċıapáın.—This name is still common in the vicinity of Boyle and Ardcarne.

[w] *Hugh*, Aoḋ, i. e. Hugh, the son of Cathal Crovderg, who succeeded his father as King of Connaught.

in aġaidh aoḋa do rónsat Síol muirsdhaiġ ⁊ iarṫar ċonnacht im aoḋ ua flaiṫḃsrtaiġ tiġearna iartair Connaċt, ⁊ gaoidil an ċuiccid dormór coiṁérġi ina aġaidh aċt mac diarmata, .i. corbmac mac tomaltaiġ. Dála uí néll nír hairirsead les go rainig lár síl muireadhaiġ. Airisde go feadha aṫa luain, go mbaoí dá oídċe ag Muilleann guanaċ gur lomairccsetur loċ nén go rucc seóid uí concoḃair as. Teccaid airsíde go carn fraich. Ríoġtar toirrdealḃaċ mac Ruaidri annsin, ⁊ téd aoḋ ua nell cona muintir dia

[x] *Faes of Athlone*, feaḋa aṫa luain, i. e. *the woods of Athlone.*—This was the name of O'Naghtan's country, containing thirty quarters of land in the barony of Athlone, and county of Roscommon.—See Inquisition taken at Athlone, on the 26th of October, 1587, and another taken at Roscommon, on the 23rd of October, 1604; also *Tribes and Customs of Hy-Many*, printed for the Irish Archæological Society in 1843, pp. 175, 176, and the map prefixed to the same.

[y] *Muilleann Guanach.*—In the Annals of Ulster and of Kilronan this name is written muillib uanaċ, and muillib uainiḋe, in the Annals of Connaught. The Editor has not been able to find this name in any form in the Faes, or in any part of the county of Roscommon. The whole passage is given somewhat more intelligibly in the Annals of Ulster, and thus Englished in the old translation:

"A. D. 1224. A great army by Hugh O'Neale into Connought with the sons of Rory O'Coner, and consent of all Sylmurea, only Mac Dermot, viz., Cormac mac Tumultach, that he went along Conought southerly into the woods of Athlone, that they were two nights at the Mills of Vonagh, and prayed Loghnen, and brought O'Conner's Juells and goods out of it. He came after to Carnefrich and prayed" [*recte* inaugurated] "Tirlagh mac Roary there, and went in haste home, hearing" [that] "a great army of Galls and Mounstermen about Donogh Kerbregh O'Brian and Geffry Mares, with Hugh O'Coner and Mac Dermot coming uppon him; and" [these] "having not overtaken O'Neile, they followed Roary's son until they dog'd him to O'Neile againe. Mounster in that journey killed Eghmarkagh O'Branan, Chief of Corkaghlyn at Kill-Kelly, after banishing Roary's son out of Connaght, Hugh mac Cathall Crovderg reigned in Connaght after him." The account of the coming of O'Neill into Connaught on this occasion is also given in Mageoghegan's translation of the Annals of Clonmacnoise, but incorrectly entered under the year 1224, as follows: "A. D. 1224. Hugh O'Neale and Tyreowen" [*recte* the Kinel-Owen], "with their forces, accompanied with Terlagh O'Conor and his brothers, the sonns of Rowrie O'Connor, with their forces also, wasted and destroyed all Moyntyrr Arteagh, and the most part of the countrey of Moynoye. Donn Mac Oyreaghty made a retraite upon Hugh O'Connor, and afterwards went to O'Neale. O'Connor returned to the Deputie, Geffrey March his house in Athlone; whereupon the said Geffrey March sent his letters to all parts of Ireland, and assembled together his forces of the five Provinces, which being so assembled and gathered together, the Deputie and O'Connor, with their great forces, sought to banish O'Neal and the sons of Rowrie O'Connor, from out of Connought," [and] "pursued them. O'Neale returned to his own house, and left the sons of Rowrie O'Connor in Connought, between whom and the forces of the Deputie and O'Connor all Connought was wasted. Upon the Deputies and O'Connor's going to

when Mageraghty turned against Hugh, the Sil-Murray also, and the inhabitants of West Connaught, with Hugh O'Flaherty, Lord of West Connaught, as well as all the Irish of the province, with the exception of Mac Dermot (Cormac, the son of Tomaltagh), conjointly rose out against him. As to O'Neill he made no delay until he arrived in the very centre of Sil-Murray, whence he marched to the Faes of Athlone[x]; and he remained two nights at Muilleann Guanach[y], and totally plundered Lough Nen[z], from whence he carried off O'Conor's jewels. Thence he proceeded to Carnfree[a], where Turlough, the son of Roderic, was inaugurated; and then O'Neill, with his people, returned home; for all their own people were faithful to the sons of Roderic,

Twayme, from Esroe to Clonvicknose, in so much that there was not in all those Contreys, the door of a church unburnt, with great slaughters of both partys. Eachmarkagh Mac Brannan, Chieftaine of Corckaghlan, was killed. Mories Mac Murrogh, with his brothers, Mahon Mac Connor Menmoye, Neal O'Teig, Teig mac Gilleroe O'Connor, Flann O'Ffallawyn, and others, were all killed. The sons of Rowrie O'Connor left Connought. Hugh O'Connor took hostages of all the Provence, and Geffrey March the Deputie, with the most part of the English, returned to their houses."

[z] *Lough Nen*, loċ nén.—This is the place now called *Loch-na-n-éan*, or lake of the birds. It lies to the west of the castle of Roscommon, and is said to have been originally a deep lake; but at present it is generally dried up in summer, in consequence of drains which were sunk to carry off the water; but in winter the drains are not sufficient for this purpose, and the land becomes inundated.

[a] *Carnfree.*—This carn, which was called after Fraech, the son of Fiodhach of the Red Hair, was the one on which the O'Conor was inaugurated. It is situated in the townland of Carns, in the parish of Ogulla, in the barony and county of Roscommon. The situation of this carn, so often mentioned in Irish history, was never before pointed out by any of our topographical writers. One of the legends given in the *Dinnseanchus* points out its situation very distinctly in the following words: "They conveyed the body of *Fraech* to *Cnoc na Dala* (Hill of the Meeting) to the SOUTH-EAST of *Cruachain*, and interred him there; so that it is from him the *carn* is named: unde dicitur *Carn Fraeich*, i. e. the *carn* of Fraech."—*Book of Lecan*, fol. 243, p. *a*, col. *a*.

It is a small carn of stones and earth, situated to the south of the village of Tulsk, and about three miles to the south-east of Rathcroghan, in the townland of Carns, to which this carn and a small green mound, or tumulus, situated to the east of the carn, give name. This carn, though small, is a very conspicuous object in the plain of Croghan; and a good view of it, as well as of Rathcroghan, may be had from the street of Elphin. Not far from this carn, in the same field, is a long standing stone, called cloċ ḟada na ᵹcarn, which was probably erected here as a boundary. The Editor visited this place on the 10th of August, 1837, and made every search for the inauguration stone of the O'Conors, but could find no such stone, nor tradition respecting it. It is probable that it was either destroyed or carried away several centuries since. The green moat to the east of Carnfree is the *Dumha Sealga*, so

ttighiḃ. (o roba tairisi lá cloinn Ruaiḋri a nairecta buḋén) aċt maḋ aos graḋa aoḋa namá, .i. mac diarmada, ⁊ dáuiṫ ua floinn, ⁊c.

Así coṁairle ar ar cinneaḋ annsin le ṁac caṫail croiḃdeirg, dul i cceann gall co cúirt aṫa luain, óir do rala go roḋánaċ dóraṁ maiṫe gall Ereann do ḃeiṫ coṁċruinn ainnsiḋe an ionbaiḋ sin, ⁊ báttar caraid a nurmór dóraṁ alos a aṫar, ⁊ ar aſon fesin uair bá tuarustlaċ tioḋlaicṫeċ iad araon dóiḃ. Fiadhaidid goill roiṁe siṁ go lúṫgáireċ ⁊ congḃaid ſtorra é go lán graḋaċ athaiḋ iar sin. Tuccsaṁ an iursír ⁊ inar lór lais do ṁaiṫiḃ gall ar ċſna ina coimbaiḋ annsin, donnchaḋ cairbreċ ua briain, ⁊ ua maoilseclainn gona soċraidiḃ.

Iar cclos an comcruinniġṫi sin do luċt moigi haí, ⁊ do ṫuaṫaiḃ Connaċt, ro teċsiod rompa i ccriċ luiġne, ⁊ i ttír naṁalgaiḋ gona mbuar ⁊ innileaḋa, ⁊ ro faccaiḃsiod meic Ruaiḋri in uaṫaḋ socraidi. Teccaid clann Ruaiḋri uí concoḃair rompa iarom an líon báttur co cill ċeallaiġ ar cúl a mbó ⁊ a mbuair. Imtusa aoḋa go ngallaiḃ uime cuirid siorṫa siuḃlaċa uaṫa darccain aosa gráiḋ cloinne Ruaiḋri, ⁊ congbaid trom a slóiġ ina ttimċel re hionnsaiġiḋ do tabairt orra buḋén. Téd aoḋ mac Ruaiḋri mic Muirceartaiġ, doṁnall ua flaiṫbſertaiġ, tiġearnán mac caṫail miccárain, ⁊ mac toirrdealḃaiġ mic Ruaiḋri danacul coda dá naos graiḋ. Teccaid goill im aoḋ mac caṫail croiḃdeirg iarsin i ttimċeal toirr-

celebrated in the Dinnseanchus and Lives of St. Patrick.

[b] *Had paid them wages, &c.*, uair ba tuarustlaċ, tioḋlaicṫeaċ iad araon dóiḃ.—The tuarastal was the stipend or wages paid by the superior to his assistant. It never means tribute, or even rent, but a stipend or salary for work or service done. The Annalists here look upon the English as hireling soldiers, who were employed in the service of the King of Connaught. They do not appear to have been aware of the mandate, dated 12th June, 1225, issued by King Henry III., directing William Earl Marshall, the Lord Justice, to seize on the whole country of Connaught, stated to have been forfeited by O'Conor, and to deliver it to Richard de Burgo; or, if they were aware of it, they may not have been willing to acknowledge the King's right to make such a grant.

[c] *Troops.*—All this is much better told in the Annals of Kilronan, in which it is stated that the sons of Roderic were left with a few Roydamnas, chieftains, horse-boys, and servants: ⁊ ro faġbuit meic Ruaiḋri gan tinol airecta, ⁊ ni raiḃe na ḃfarrad aċt uaṫaḋ riḋamnaḋ ⁊ taoiseċ, ⁊ gille ech, ⁊ gille friṫeolma.

[d] *Kilkelly*, cill ceallaiġ, i. e. the church of St. Ceallach.—An old church in a village and parish of the same name, in the barony of Costello, and county of Mayo. See it marked on the map prefixed to ***Genealogies, Tribes, and Customs of Hy-Fiachrach***, printed for the Irish Archæological Society in 1844, and noted in the explanatory Index to the same Map, p. 484.

excepting only the supporters of Hugh, namely, Mac Dermot, David O'Flynn, &c.

The resolution then adopted by the son of Cathal Crovderg, was to repair to the English to the Court of Athlone; for it happened, fortunately for him, that the chiefs of the English of Ireland were at that very time assembled there, and the greater part of them were friendly to him, on his father's account as well as on his own, for both had paid them wages[b] [for military services], and had been bountiful towards them. The English received him with joy, and kept him among them with much affection for some time afterwards. He then engaged in his cause the Lord Justice, and as many of the chiefs of the English of Ireland as he considered necessary, together with Donough Cairbreach O'Brien, and O'Melaghlin, with their forces.

When the inhabitants of Moynai and of the Tuathas of Connaught had heard of this muster, they fled into the territory of Leyny and Tirawley, with their cows and other cattle, and left the sons of Roderic attended by only a few troops[c]. The sons of Roderic O'Conor afterwards proceeded to Kilkelly[d] with all the troops they had, and placed themselves in defence of their cows and flocks. As for Hugh [O'Conor], and the English who accompanied him, they despatched light marauding parties to plunder the retainers of the sons of Roderic, but detained the main body of their army about them for the purpose of making an attack upon [the sons of Roderic] themselves. Hugh, the son of Roderic, Donnell O'Flaherty, Tiernan, the son of Cathal Miccarain[e], and the son of Turlough, son of Roderic, went to protect some of their Aes graidh[f].

[e] *Cathal Miccarain.*—He is called Cathal Miogharan by Duald Mac Firbis, in his Pedigree of the O'Conors, in Lord Roden's copy of his Genealogical Book, p. 219. He was the fifteenth son of Turlough More O'Conor, Monarch of Ireland.—See also the Book of Lecan, fol. 72, *b*, col. 4. This Cathal, who was one of the illegitimate sons of King Turlough, left one son, Conor, of whose descendants no account is preserved.

[f] *To protect some of their Aes gradha*, ᴅanacul coᴅa ᴅa naoꞅ ᵹꞃaiᴅ, i. e. to protect their stewards and chief servants of trust. Aoꞅ ᵹꞃáiᴅ is used throughout these Annals in the sense of "servants of trust." It is stated in the Annals of Kilronan that they went on this occasion to protect the cows and people of Farrell O'Teige, who had taken an oath to be faithful to them, but that he was the first of the Connacians that violated his oath to the sons of Roderic; and that he brought in their stead Hugh, the son of Cathal Crovderg, and the English, to protect his cows and people; that it was on this occasion the English came in collision with Turlough, the son of Roderic, who, perceiving the treachery of O'Teige, made a judicious and clever retreat by the help of Donn Oge Mageraghty, Flaherty

ḋealḃaiġ. Iar na airiuċċaḋ sin ḋósoṁ cuirir a ġlasláiṫ i réṁṫús roiṁe, Donn ócc máġ oireaċtaiġ gona anraḋaiḃ, Flaiṫḃeartaċ ua Flannagáin, ⁊ uaṫaḋ daṁsaiḃ eoganaċ baoi ina ḟoċair, ordaiġis iad dia nimdíḋen ina ndeóiḋ go ttéarnadar samlaiḋ ona mbioḋḃaḋaiḃ gan aon do ṫuitim díoḃ. Do rala an lá sin drong do siorṫaiḃ aoḋa ui ċonċoḃair i ccenn eaċmarcaiġ mic branáin go ndeachaiḋ do ċosnaṁ a ḃóiċreċe orra go ttorċair eaċmarcaċ don anḃforlann galccaḋ baoí na aġaiḋ. Leanais aoḋ ó conċoḃair go ngallaiḃ uime mac ruaiḋri an oiḋċe sin go mílecc go mbaoí teóra hoiḋċe iarsin ag argain luiġne do gaċ leṫ. Bá hiondoċonaiġ do rala dó eaġra annsin. Siṫ do ḋenaṁ iar ná argain tar cenn an tioruairri do ḟáccḃaḋ da hinnilíḃ illuiġniu.

Ar ann báttar meic Ruaiḋri mun amsa a ccoṁġar do loċ mic Fearadaiġ i nglenn na moċart. Comairliġis aoḋ ré na ġallaiḃ annsin na tuaṫa dionnsaiġiḋ dia nargain, Síol Muireadhaiġ, ⁊ clann tomaltaiġ dinnraḋ mar an cedna ó do ḃáttar ar tteċeḋ roiṁe. Iar ccinneaḋ na coṁairle si lottar rompa i sliġiḋ naċ smuainfeaḋ gall co bráṫ dul treimpe .i. hi bfioḋ ngatlaiġ go riacttsat áṫ tíġe in messaiġ gur airccsiod cúil cernaḋa iar ndilgenn a ḋaoine dóiḃ. Gaċ ar gaḃ go duḃċonga do luċt

O'Flanagan, and some of the Tyronian route of soldiers, who covered their retreat.

[g] *Tyronian soldiers.*—These were some of the soldiers left by O'Neill to assist Turlough, the son of Roderic, whom he had set up as King of Connaught. In the Annals of Kilronan these are called beaġán don Rúṫ Eoġanaċ, i. e. some of the Eugenian, or Kinel-Owenian, *route, turma*, or company of soldiers.

[h] *Him.*—In the Annals of Kilronan it is stated that Mac Brannan displayed great valour in defending himself, but that he was overwhelmed by too many men of might.

[i] *Meelick*, Miliuc.—A church, near which are the ruins of one of the ancient Round Towers, in a parish of the same name, in the barony of Gallen, and county of Mayo.

[k] *Then left*, do ḟaccḃaḋ.—That is, the number not seized upon by the plunderers previously to the ratification of the peace.

[l] *Lough Macfarry*, loċ mic Feraḋaiġ, called loċ mic Eruḋaiġ, in the Annals of Connaught, and loċ mic Aireaḋaiġ, in those of Kilronan. This name is now forgotten; but the Editor thinks that it was the old name of the Lake of Templehouse, in the county of Sligo.

[m] *Inhabitants of the Tuathas.*—This is better told in the Annals of Kilronan, thus: "The resolution which the son of Cathal Crovderg then adopted, was to go with the English in pursuit of the cows of the Tuathas, of the Sil-Murray, and of the Clann-Tomalty, by a way which no Englishman had ever passed before, that is, by Fidh Gadlaigh, until they arrived at Attymas, and they received neither javelin nor arrow on that rout. They plundered Coolcarney, where they seized upon the cows and destroyed the people. Some attempted to escape from them into the Backs;

The English, with Hugh, the son of Cathal Crovderg, then set out to surround Turlough; but the latter, on perceiving this, ordered his recruits in the van, and Donn Oge Mageraghty, with his Calones, Flaherty O'Flanagan, and a few Tyronian soldiers[g], who were with him in the rear, to cover the retreat, by which means they escaped from the enemy without the loss of a man. On the same day some of Hugh O'Conor's marauding parties encountered Eachmarcach Mac Branan, who had gone to protect his cows against them; and Eachmarcach fell by the overwhelming force of the warriors who fought against him[h]. Hugh O'Conor, and the English, pursued the sons of Roderic that night to Meelick[i], and for three nights afterwards continued plundering Leyny in all directions. This was unfortunate to O'Hara, who had to make peace with them, in consideration of the inconsiderable number of its cattle then left[k] in Leyny.

The sons of Roderic were at this time stationed near Lough Macfarry[l], in Gleann-na-Mochart. Hugh then proposed to the English that they should pursue and plunder the inhabitants of the Tuathas[m], the Sil-Murray, and Clann-Tomalty, as they had fled before him [with their cattle]; and this being agreed upon, they set out, taking a road which the English *alone* would never have thought of taking[n], viz. they passed through Fiodh Gatlaigh, and marched until they reached Attymas[o]; and they plundered Coolcarney[p], after

but such of these as were not drowned in the attempt were killed or plundered. It was pitiful! Such of them as proceeded to Dubhchonga were drowned, and the fishing weirs with their baskets, were found full of drowned children. Such of the flitting Clann-Tomalty as escaped the English and the drowning, fled to Tirawley, where they were attacked by O'Dowda, and left without a single cow."

[n] *Would never have thought of taking*, nač ṡmuainfeaḋ gall co bṗaċ ḋul ṫreimpe, that is, Hugh, who was intimately acquainted with the passes and population of the country, conducted the English by a rout which they themselves would never have thought of. The Annals of Connaught and of Kilronan describe these transactions more fully than those of the Four Masters.

[o] *Attymas*, aṫ ṫiġe an meṡṡaiġ.—A parish forming about the southern half of the territory of Coolcarney, in the barony of Gallen, and county of Mayo.—See Map to *Genealogies, Tribes, and Customs of Hy-Fiachrach*, printed in the year 1844, and Explanatory Index to the same, p. 477.

[p] *Coolcarney*, Cúil Ceaṗnaḋa.—This territory retains its name to the present day. It is situated in the barony of Gallen, and county of Mayo, and comprises the parishes of Kilgarvan and Attymas, which are divided from the county of Sligo by a stream called Sruthan geal. According to the Book of Hy-Fiachrach, Cuil Cearnadha extended from Beul atha na nidheadh, six miles from Ballina, to the road or pass of Breachmhuighe (Breaghwy), which is the name

an tecṁe ro báidit a normór. As amlaiḋ do gebṫi na cesganna uas a ccairrib lomlán do leanbaib iar na mbáthaḋ. Gach a tteasna don toirc sin díob ó ġallaib, ⁊ on iombáṫaḋ remráite lodar i ttír namalgaiḋ go ndeaċaiḋ ó dúbda fúṫa gonár ḟáccaib aon bó aca.

Maḋ iad clann Ruaidri tra arí comairle do rónsat ag loċ mic fearadaiġ sgaoileaḋ ó aroile dóib go sgerdís soċraide gall ré haoḋ. Donn mag oireċtaiġ, ⁊ aroile dia maiṫib do ċor do saiġiḋ uí flaitbaertaiġ a ffir comluiġi ⁊ comċodaiġ. Meic muirceartaiġ uí concobair, ⁊ tiġearnan mac caṫail do dul ar cúl a mbó ⁊ a muintear, ⁊ Síṫ do ḋénaṁ dóib tar a ccenn go bfágbaidís goill mac caṫail croibdeirg. As ann baoi aoḋ mun am soin i moiġ neó, ⁊ tiaġaid meic muirceartaiġ muininiġ ina ċenn ar Shlanaib ⁊ ċomaircib.

Maḋ an ṫaob ṫear do connaċtaib dana nír bó ciúin dóib don dul soin, uair tangadar goill laiġen ⁊ muṁan im muirceartaċ ua briain, goill dersmuṁan beós, ⁊ Sirriam corcaiġe ina ttreċomurc gur marbsat a ndaoine doneoċ ar a rucsat diob, ⁊ gur ionnradar a mbruiġ ⁊ a mbailte. Bá holc tra lá haoḋ mac caṫail croibdeirg a ttoċtroṁ don turus sin uair ní hé ro ṫóċuir iad, acht tnuṫ, ⁊ format dá ngabáil fén ré gaċ maiṫer dá ccualadar dfáġail don iursís gona ġallaib i cconnaċtaib an tan soin. As don ruaṫar so do marbaid cetre meic méc murchaiḋ ar én láṫair.

Bá truacch tra an neṁsén do ḋeonaiġ día don ċuicceḋ do bfer baoi i nErinn an ionbaiḋ si, uair ní ċoitcleaḋ an mac occlaoiċ aroile aċt gá creachaḋ ⁊ arccain fona cuṁang. Do cuirid beós mná, ⁊ leniṁ, fainn, ⁊ foḋaoine dfuaċt ⁊ ġorta don ċoccaḋ sin.

of a townland in the parish of Castleconor, lying to the east of Ardnarea.

[q] *After having destroyed its people*, iar ndilgenn a daoine doib.—The word dilgenn or dilgeann signifies destruction, or depopulation. O'Clery writes it dilġionn, according to the modern Irish orthography, and explains it sgrios, no dioláiṫriuġadh. The compound uile-dilgenn means total destruction, extirpation, or annihilation. —See Annals of Tighernach at the year 995.

[r] *Duvconga.*—This place is now called béal áṫa conga in Irish, and Anglicised Bellacong and Ballycong. It is situated near Ballymore Lough, in the parish of Attymas, in the barony of Gallen, and county of Mayo.—See Ordnance Map of the county of Mayo, sheet 40; and also *Genealogies, Tribes, and Customs of Hy-Fiachrach*, pp. 242, 243, and map to the same.

[s] *The baskets of the fishing weirs*, na cesganna uas a ccairrib.—In the Annals of Kilronan the reading is, na carranna co na ceascandaib; and in the Annals of Connaught, na cairr co na cessachaib, i. e. the weirs and baskets. The children that had been carried away by the floods were found entangled in the baskets, which were placed for nets in the *carrys* or fishing weirs.

having *nearly* destroyed its people[q]. Some of them fled to Duvconga[r], but the greater part of these were drowned; and the baskets of the fishing weirs[s] were found full of drowned children. Such of them as on this occasion escaped from the English, and the drowning aforesaid, passed into Tirawley, where they were attacked by O'Dowda, who left them not a single cow.

As to the sons of Roderic, the resolution they adopted, at Lough Macfarry, was to separate from each other, until the English should leave Hugh; to send Donn Mageraghty, and others of their chieftains, to O'Flaherty, their sworn friend and partisan; and the sons of Murtough O'Conor, and Tiernan, the son of Cathal[t], to take charge of their people and cows, and to obtain peace on their behalf, until the English should leave (Hugh) the son of Cathal Crovderg. Hugh was at this time at Mayo, and the sons of Murtough Muimhneach [O'Conor] went to him under protection and guarantee[u].

As to the inhabitants of the southern side of Connaught, they were not in a state of tranquillity at this period, for the English of Leinster and Munster, with Murtough O'Brien, the English of Desmond, and the sheriff of Cork, had made an irruption upon them, and slew all the people that they caught, and burned their dwellings and villages. Hugh, the son of Cathal Crovderg, was displeased at their coming on this expedition; for it was not he that sent for them, but were themselves excited by envy and rapacity, as soon as they had heard what good things the Lord Justice and his English followers had obtained in Connaught at that time. During this incursion the four sons of Mac Murrough were slain on the same spot.

Woeful was the misfortune, which God permitted to fall upon the best province in Ireland at that time! for the young warriors did not spare each other, but preyed and plundered each other to the utmost of their power. Women and children, the feeble, and the lowly poor[w], perished by cold and famine in this war!

[t] *Tiernan, the son of Cathal.*—He was the son of Cathal O'Conor, who was one of the sons of Turlough More O'Conor, Monarch of Ireland.

[u] *Under protection and guarantee*, ap rlánaib 7 comaipcib, that is, they had persons to guarantee their safety on their arrival in his presence, to make their mock peace. In the Annals of Kilronan it is stated that the sons of Murtough "went into his house [to make their submission] under sureties and guarantees."

[w] *The poor.*—The Annals of Kilronan state, that during this war women, children, young lords, and mighty men, as well as feeble men, perished of cold and famine. Do cuipic mna

Iar ndul tra do macaib muirceartaiġ muiṁniġ do láṫair aoḋa ui con-ċoḃair do réir mar do ráiḋsinar, do ċuaiḋ ar náḃárac go cill mfḋóin. Comraicit trí slóiġ na ngall ann sin re roile, ⁊ ar bfg nár bó lán an tríoċa céd ina mbattar lfṫ ar lfṫ eidir gallaiḃ ⁊ gaoiḋealaiḃ. Tainicc aoḋ ó flaiṫbeartaicc ar ċoraiḃ ⁊ ar slánaiḃ maiṫe gall, ⁊ ḋonnchaḋa cairbriġ uí briain a cairdfsa criosd hi ccfnn aoḋa uí concobair, ⁊ an iurdís co ndearna síṫ tar cfnn a ḃuair, ⁊ a ḋaoine ris, ar macaiḃ Ruaiḋri daṫċor uaiḋ. Imtiġir aoḋ iar sin, ⁊ a ġoill imaille ris co tuaim dá ġualann, ⁊ leiccis goill laiġean, ⁊ dfsmuṁan uaiḋ annsin. Iompaíḋis féin ar ccúla do ċom uí flaiṫbfrtaiġ óir níor ḃó tairise lais eisiḋe, uair battar meic Ruaiḋri roiṁe sin allaniar do loċ aicce, ⁊ donn ócc mág oireaċtaiġ araon riú.

Annsin ro scar mac maġnusa ré cloinn Ruaiḋri gur innsaiġ hi ttír naṁalgaiḋ ar cfnn a ḃó, ⁊ a ṁuintire go bfuair iatt go roḃánac gan ċreachaḋ gan arccain. Rucc leis iad iaraṁ fó ḋídean uí Ruairc, ⁊ é iar ccreachaḋ Pilip meic goisdelbaiġ.

Donnchaḋ cairbreac ua briain daná do ċuir siḋe drong dia ṁuintir roiṁe go néḋalaiḃ aiḋbliḃ. Iar ná fios sin daoḋ mac Ruaiḋri ⁊ deoġan ó eiḋin lodur rompa uaṫaḋ dfġdaoine gur muiḋeaḋ for muiṁneċaiḃ, gor beanaḋ a neḋala ḋíoḃ, ⁊ gur congbaḋ braiġde dá maiṫiḃ uaṫa. Iar na clos sin do donnchaḋ cairbreac ticc do láṫair aoḋa mic Ruaiḋri go ndearna síṫ báitte coimdel ris, ⁊ gur ġaḃ do laiṁ gan toiḋeacht na aġhaiḋ doriḋisi dia lécceaḋ

⁊ leinḃ ⁊ óigtiġeirn ⁊ treoin ⁊ etreoin re fuaċt ⁊ re gorta don ċogaḋ sin.

[x] *Of his gossip*, a ċairdeasa Criosd.—This term is used in the modern language to denote a gossip, or one who is a sponsor for a child at baptism.—See O'Brien's Dictionary *in voce*.—See also Harris's Ware, vol. ii. p. 72, for *Gossipred*. Hanmer says, that it was a league of amity highly esteemed in Ireland.—See note [d] under the year 1178, p. 42, *supra*.

[y] *Donn Oge*.—It is stated in the Annals of Kilronan that Donn Oge Mageraghty was O'Flaherty's son-in-law: Do roine sim comairli aili ann sin .i. impoḋ do ċum I Flaiṫbertaiġ ar cula, uair nír tairisi leis mar do fáguib e, uair do badar meic Ruaiḋri alla aniar do loċ aige, ⁊ a ċliamain fein .i. Donn Og maille friu. "He then came to another resolution, namely, to return back to O'Flaherty, for he did not like how he left him; for he had on the west side of the lake the sons of Roderic, and his own son-in-law, that is, Donn Oge along with them."

[z] *Manus*.—According to the Book of Lecan, fol. 72, *b*, col. 4, he was the ninth son of Turlough More O'Conor, monarch of Ireland. His descendants took the surname of Mac Manus, and were seated in Tir Tuathail, in the north-east of the barony of Boyle, in the county of Roscommon.

[a] *After having first plundered*, iar ccreachaḋ. That is, on his passage through the present

The sons of Murtough Muimhneach [O'Conor] having come before Hugh O'Conor, as we have stated, he went on the next day to Kilmaine, where the three English armies met; and nearly the whole of the triocha ched (cantred) was filled with people, both English and Irish. Hugh O'Flaherty, under the protection and guarantee of the chiefs of the English, and of his gossip[x], Donough Cairbreach O'Brien, came to Hugh O'Conor and the Lord Justice, and made peace with O'Conor, on behalf of his people and cows, on condition that he should expel the sons of Roderic. After this, Hugh and his English went to Tuam, where he dismissed the English of Leinster and Desmond; after which he returned back to (watch) O'Flaherty, for he did not confide in him, as O'Flaherty had, some time before, the sons of Roderic at the west side of the lake, together with Donn Oge[y] Mageraghty.

The son of Manus[a] then parted from the sons of Roderic, and set out for Tirawley, in quest of his cows and people, and fortunately found them there, without having been plundered or molested. He then took them with him, under the protection of O'Rourke, after having first plundered[a] Philip Mac Costello.

Donough Cairbreach O'Brien sent a detachment of his people before him, with immense spoils; but Hugh, the son of Roderic, and Owen O'Heyne, having heard of this movement, went before them with a few select men, defeated the Momonians, deprived them of their spoils, and detained some of their nobles as hostages. When Donough Cairbreach heard of this, he came to Hugh, the son of Roderic, and made a solemn peace[b] with him, and bound himself never

barony of Costello, which lay on his way to O'Rourke, he plundered Mac Costello. In the Annals of Kilronan, the language of this passage is much better than that written by the Four Masters. It runs thus: Is ann sin ro ḋeiliġ meic Maġnusa re macaiḃ Ruaiḋri, 7 do ċuatar a ttir naṁalgaiḋ ar cenn a mbo 7 a muintear, 7 fuaradar iad go soḋánaċ can indrad can argain, 7 rugsat leo iat a nuċt I Ruairc, 7 do ronsat creiċ moir ar Philip mac Goisdealbh. "Then the sons of Manus separated from the sons of Roderic, and they went to Tirawley in quest of their cows and people, and found them in good condition, without having been plundered or molested, and they took them with them to O'Rourke, and *on their way* they took a great prey from Philip Mac Costello."

[b] *A solemn peace*, síṫ báiṫṫe coinnel, i. e. a peace of the extinguishing of candles, i. e. a peace so solemn, that he who should violate it would incur excommunication, of which ceremony the extinguishing of the candles formed the last and most terror-striking part. Mageoghegan expresses it, "a peace so solemn that whoever would break it was to be excommuni-

a aos graiḋ cuige. Giḋeadh ní ro ċomaill siom a coingioll do mac Ruaiḋri (iar bfaġail a ṁuintire ḋó uaiḋ) uair tainicc ar an céd sluaiġeaḋ ina aġaiḋ la haoḋ mac caṫail croiḃḋerg.

Téd aoḋ ⁊ an iusdís gona ġallaiḃ iarsin go calaḋ innsi crſṁa gur béccin dó flaiṫbeartaicch inis crſṁa, ⁊ oilén na circe go nairṫraiġiḃ an loċa do taḃairt ar laiṁ aoḋa. Triallais an iusdís iar sin dia ṫiġ. Ted aoḋ ó concoḃair dia ioḋlacaḋ uiḋe ċian dá slíġiḋ gur ḟáġaiḃ an iúsdís uaṫaḋ do ṁaiṫiḃ a muintire aicce imaille re hiomad fénneḋ, ⁊ fearóġlaoċ óir níor ḃó tairisi lais connaċtaiġ acṫmaḋ bſcc. Tuccsom annsin maiṫe a oireaċta illaiṁ gall a ngioll ré a ttuarastlaiḃ, .i. flaiṫbeartaċ ó flannaccain, fſr-ġal ua taiḋg, ⁊ aroile do maitiḃ connaċt, ⁊ as dóiḃ fén do béccin a bfuas-laccaḋ.

As a haiṫle sin iompaíḋis ua flaiṫbeartaiġ, meicc muirceartaiġ, ⁊ na huaisle arċéna ar aoḋ mac caṫail croiḃḋeirg iar nimṫeċt troimṫionóil na ngall uaiḋ, ⁊ ro gabsat le macaiḃ Ruaiḋri. Cuiris aoḋ o concoḃair annsin teċta ⁊ sgriḃne do ṡaiġiḋ an iustís dia foillsiuġaḋ sin ḋó, ⁊ diar-raiḋ fuilleaḋ soċraiḋi. Nir ḃó haiṫesc fó lár dóraṁ sin, uair do sreccra-

cated with book, bell, and candle."—See note under the year 1200.

[c] *Lord Justice.*—He was Geoffry de Marisco, or De Mariscis, or Geffry March, as he is called by Mageoghegan, in his translation of the Annals of Clonmacnoise, at the years 1225, 1226. He was succeeded by Richard de Burgo, the great Lord of Connaught, on the 10th of March, 1227. See list of the Chief Governors of Ireland given in Harris's Ware, vol. ii. p. 103, where it is incorrectly stated that Hubert de Burgh, afterwards Earl of Kent, was appointed Lord Justice of Ireland, on the 10th of March, 1227, and Richard de Burgo appointed Lord Deputy of Ireland, on the same day and year.

[d] *Inis Creamha.*—This is a small island in Lough Corrib, near the Castle of Cargins, and belonging to the barony of Clare, in the county of Galway. The name is translated Wildgarlick Isle by Roderic O'Flaherty, in his Account of West Connaught, where he speaks of it as follows: "Iniscreawa, or Wildgarlick Isle, is near Cargin, in the barony of Clare; a small island, where the walls and high ditch of a well fortified place are still extant, and encompass almost the whole island. Of this isle, Macamh Insicreawa, a memorable ancient magician, as they say, had his denomination."—See *Territory of Hiar Connaught*, by Roderic O'Flaherty, printed for the Irish Archæological Society in 1845, p. 25. The walls here referred to by O'Flaherty still remain, and are of a cyclopean character. The natives assert that this was the castle of Orbsen, from whom Loch Orbsen, now Lough Corrib, took its name.—See Map to *Tribes and Customs of Hy-Many*, printed in 1843, on which the position of this island is shewn.

The transaction narrated in the text is thus stated by O'Flaherty, in his Account of West Connaught: "Anno 1225. The Lord Justice of Ireland coming to the port of Iniscreawa, caused

again to oppose him, on condition that Hugh would restore him his Aes graidh. But he did not adhere to this his covenant with the son of Roderic; for, after obtaining his people from him, he came in the first army that Hugh, the son of Cathal Crovderg, marched against him.

After this, Hugh [the son of Cathal Crovderg O'Conor], and the Lord Justice[c], with his English, set out for the port of Inis Creamha[d]; and O'Flaherty was compelled to surrender the island of Inis Creamha, and Oilen na Circe[e], and all the vessels [boats] on the lake, into the hands of Hugh. The Lord Justice then returned home, and was escorted a great part of the way by Hugh O'Conor, with whom he left a few of the chiefs of his people, together with many soldiers[f] and warriors; for the Connacians were not faithful to him, except very few. After this Hugh gave up to the English the chiefs of his people, as hostages for the payment of their wages[g], as Flaherty, O'Flanagan, Farrell O'Teige[h], and others of the chiefs of Connaught, who were *subsequently* obliged to ransom themselves.

After the departure of the main army of the English from Hugh, the sons of Cathal Crovderg, O'Flaherty, the son of Murtough[i], and all the other nobles, revolted against him, and joined the sons of Roderic. Hugh O'Conor then despatched messengers and letters to the Lord Justice, to inform him of the circumstance, and request additional[k] forces. His request was by no means

Odo O'Flaherty, Lord of West Connaught, to deliver that island, Kirke Island, and the boats of Lough Orbsen, into the hands of Odo O'Connor, King of Connaught (Cathald Redfist's son), for assurance of his fidelity."—p. 25.

[e] *Oilen na Circe*, now Castlekirk island, in the north-west part of Lough Corrib, containing the ruins of a very ancient castle.—See *Hiar Connaught*, by Roderic O'Flaherty, pp. 22, 24.

[f] *Soldiers*, ꝼenneḋ.—According to the Annals of Kilronan, the Lord Justice left with Hugh, the son of Cathal Crovderg, on this occasion, a few [uaṫaḋ] of the chiefs of the English and many archers [ꝼeiꞃꝼeanuiġ imḋa]."

[g] *Wages*, ꞇuaꞃaꞅꞇluiḃ.—In the Annals of Kilronan, the reading is, a ngill ꞃe ꞇꞇuaꞃuꞅdal, i. e. in pledge for their pay or stipend, i. e. the reward or wages to be paid them by the King of Connaught for their services in war. This had nothing to do with the tribute to be paid to the King of England in accordance with the Treaty of Windsor.

[h] *O'Teige* is now anglicised Teige, and sometimes Tighe. The name is common in the neighbourhood of Castlereagh, in the county of Roscommon.

[i] *The son of Murtough*, mac Muiꞃcheꞃꞇaiġ, i. e. the sons of the celebrated Muirchertach Muimhneach, or Murtough the Momonian O'Conor, who, according to the Book of Lecan, was the eleventh son of Turlough More, monarch of Ireland.

[k] *Additional.*—Fuilleḋ is the old form of the modern word ꞇuilleaḋ, *more*. In the Annals of

dar goill go soinniṁ sairésccaiḋ é. Aċt cſna ba tuillṁeaċ dóibsioṁ an turus sin óir fá mór a nédala, ⁊ bá bſcc a nimreasgna. Cuirṫear goill laiġean cuigsioṁ annsin im uilliam ccras, ⁊ im macaiḃ griffín. Iar mbreṫ na soċraidi sin aissioṁ ionnsaiġiḋ meic Ruaiḋri tar tóċar siar, ⁊ gaḃais roiṁe in uiḃ diarmata mar a ccuala meic Ruaiḋri do ḃeiṫ gan líon soċraide, uair ní rangattar a luċt combáda iad mun am soin, ⁊ cuirir feḋlimiḋ a ḃraṫair, ⁊ araile do ṁaiṫiḃ a ṁuintire, ⁊ soċraide mór do glasláṫaiḃ gall dionnsaḋ eoġain uí eḋin in uiḃ bfiaċraċ aiḋne co mbádar aḋaiġ longpuirt in ard raṫain fa comair na tíre darccain a muċa na maiḋne ar ccionn.

Foillsiġtear dua flaiṫbeartaiġ, ⁊ do macaiḃ muirceartaiġ (badar ag ionnsaiġiḋ mac Ruaiḋri) goill do ḋul do creachaḋ a bfir comluiccė, Eoġan ó heiḋin, ⁊ a mbeṫ an ard raṫain, nír faillicceaḋ sin siusoṁ oir do lſnsat iatt déntoil ⁊ dénaontaiḋ go rangadar i ccoṁfoccus dóiḃ. Do ġníad comairle ré roile annsin, .i. tuaṫal mac muirceartaiġ, ⁊ taicleċ ua

Kilronan, the reading is, diarraiḋ tuilleaḋ socruide.

[l] *Struggle trifling*, ba becc a nimsſrgna.—In the Annals of Kilronan the reading is: do geiḃtſs étála ⁊ ni faġdais gáḋ na himeasarcain, i. e. "They used to obtain the spoils, but did not expose themselves to the danger of the conflict." The word imsergna, which is used by the Four Masters, is thus explained in O'Clery's Glossary of ancient Irish Words: imseargna, .i. imeasorgain, .i. bruiġean. "*Imseargna*, i. e. striking on every side, i. e. conflict." Both forms of the word are correctly explained in the Irish Dictionaries of O'Brien and O'Reilly, both having taken them from O'Clery.

[m] *William Grace*, Uilliam Ccrás.—In the Annals of Kilronan he is called Uilliam Crás, i. e. *Gulielmus Crassus*. Cras, or Gras, was the soubriquet of Raymond le Gras, and afterwards became a family name, which is now always incorrectly written Grace. It is derived from the French *Gras*, or *Gros*.

[n] *The togher*, i. e. the causeway. This causeway, which was called tóċar mona coineaḋa, is still well known, and its situation pointed out by the natives, though the country is very much improved. It is situated in the parish of Templetogher, in the barony of Ballimoe, and county of Galway. Hugh O'Conor, who had his residence in the plain of Croghan, marched on this occasion across the ford at Ballimoe, and directing his course south-westwards crossed this causeway, and proceeded into Hy-Diarmada, or O'Concannon's country, where he had heard his rival was staying.—See note [r], under the year 1177, pp. 34, 35, 36. Also note under the year 1255.

[o] *Recruits*, glaslaáṫaiḃ, i. e. raw recruits, or soldiers lately enlisted. The Annals of Kilronan call them gaillḟeirséanċaiḃ, i. e. English archers.

[p] *Ardrahin*, ard raṫain, a fair-town in the barony of Dunkellin, and county of Galway, and a vicarage in the diocese of Kilmacduagh. Here is still to be seen a small portion of the

an ineffectual one, for the English responded to his call cheerfully and expeditiously; and well was their promptness rewarded, for their spoil was great, and their struggle trifling[l]. The English of Leinster, under the conduct of William Grace[m] and the sons of Griffin, were sent to aid him. On the arrival of these forces, Hugh proceeded westwards, across the Togher[n] [the Causeway], against the sons of Roderic, and advanced to Hy-Diarmada, where he had heard they were stationed, without any considerable forces, for their allies had not as yet joined them; and he sent his brother Felim, and others of the chiefs of his people, and a great number of the English recruits[o] into Hy-Fiachrach Aidhne, to plunder Owen O'Heyne. These encamped for one night at Ardrahen[p], with a view to plunder the country early in the morning following.

O'Flaherty and the sons of Murtough [O'Conor], who were then on their way to join the sons of Roderic, having received intelligence that the English had gone to plunder their sworn partisan, Owen O'Heyne, and were stationed at Ardrahen, did not abandon their friend, but, with one mind and accord, followed the English until they came very close to them. They then held a council[q], and came to the resolution of sending Tuathal, the son of Murtough[r]

ruins of an ancient cloigtheach, or Round Tower.

[q] *They then held a council*, do ġniat coṁairle re roile ann sin.—This attack on the English at Ardrahen is much better described in the Annals of Kilronan, particularly in giving the names of persons, which are so confusedly given by the Four Masters. It runs as follows: "O'Flaherty and the sons of Murtough [O'Conor], as they were coming to join the sons of Roderic, heard of the English having set out to plunder their sworn ally O'Heine, and of their being at Ardrahen; and they adopted the resolution of going to Ardrahen, attacking the English early in the morning, and burning the town over their heads. They travelled all night, and early in the morning arrived on the green of the town. The resolution they then came to was, to sent first into the town Tuathal, the son of Murtough, and whomsoever of the Irish chieftains he would wish to accompany him, while O'Flaherty, and the other son of Murtough, was to remain outside the town. The Irishman selected to accompany Tuathal O'Conor, was Taichleach, the son of Hugh O'Dowda; and they entered the town with great courage and boldness, and the English fled out of the town, one party of them passing eastwards and another westwards. They were pursued eastwards. The party who fled to the west came in collision with the Irish who were at the back of the town, and routed them, though there were not living among the Irish any people more vigorous than they; but fortune did not favour them. The party who fled eastwards were pursued by Tuathal [O'Conor] and Taichleach O'Dowda. Tuathal first wounded the constable of the English, who fell by the hand of Taichleach. It was indeed fortunate for the sons of Roderic that they were not in this conflict," &c.

[r] *Tuathal, the son of Murtough.*—From the

dubda go noirim amaille riú do ċur do ḟoiġid an baile cetus ua flaiṫbear-taiġ ⁊ mac muirceartaiġ iman mbaile sechtair guna soċraidiḃ. Luid tuaṫal, ⁊ taiċleaċ gona bfianláċ go mſnmnaċ meardána i ttrecommusc gall is in mbaile go ttucsat tiuġ ḟuabairt bioḋbaiḋ orro. Maiḋtear for ġallaiḃ soir ⁊ siar as a haiṫle. Lſnaitriom aos na maḋma soir. Loitir tuaṫal consttapla na ngall dá ced ḟurgaṁ. Aṫġonais taiċleaċ é gur fag-baḋ an consdapla gan anmain de síḋe. Dála na ngall ar ar muiḋeaḋ as an mbaile don taoiḃ araill ro eiriġ ua flaiṫbeartaiġ, ⁊ mac muirceartaiġ doiḃ. Giḋeaḋ tarla dainṡén daiḃriḋe gur ḃriseattar goill orra fó ceḋóir. As don toirc sin do marḃaḋ matġaṁain mac aoḋa mic conċoḃair maonmaiġe, giolla criosd mac diarmada, niall mac feargail ua taiḋg, ⁊c. Act ċſna ro marḃaḋ an fear ro ṁarḃ niall ó taiḋg, .i. braṫair ċolén uí ḋíomusaiġ.

Dala mac Ruaiḋri coindrecaid ar aḃarac re hua fflaiṫbeartaiġ, ⁊ sir an ccuid oile dá naos coṁta go ttangatar rompa a ndeas go druim cſnan-náin. Luid aoḋ mac caṫail croiḃdeirg gona ġallaiḃ ina ndiaiḋ. Comair-liġtear ag aireaċtaiḃ cloinne Ruaiḋri annsin gaċ aon dioḃ do saiġid a mſnnata fesin, ⁊ do gníat samlaid act donn ócc mag oireċtaiġ namá. Cid tra act iar ffágḃáil na suireaċ, .i. cloinne Ruaiḋri uí concoḃair annsin in uaṫaḋ soċraide lodar do ḟaiġid aoḋa uí nell, ⁊ donn mág oireaċ-taiġ imaille riú.

Ionnsaiġis aoḋ mac caṫail croiḃdeirg ua flaiṫbeartaiġ annsin go ttuc gell, ⁊ edireaḋa uaiḋ. Tainic roiṁe iaraṁ go cill meaḋóin, ⁊ go moiġ neó i ndiaiḋ mic muirceartaiġ, ⁊ tiġſrnáin mic caṫail miccarain go ndearnsat síṫ tar cſnn a mbuair ⁊ a muintire, ⁊ go ndeaċsat do laṫair

manner in which this name is given by the Four Masters, one would suppose that this Tuathal was one of the O'Dowda family; but the more ancient annals shew that he was Tuathal, the son of the celebrated Muircheartach Muimhneach O'Conor, and the brother of Manus O'Conor.

[s] *They joined*, coindrecaid.—In the Annals of Kilronan the reading is, ro comruiceadar, i. e. they met. The word coindrecaid is often used to translate the Latin word *conveniunt*.—See Book of Lecan, fol. 75, *b*, *a*; Book of Ballymote, fol. 23, p. *b*, col. *a*, line 29; and Duald Mac Firbis's Genealogical Book, p. 575.

[t] *Druim Ceanannain*.—The Editor could not find any place of this name in the county of Galway. There is a Liscananaun in the parish of Lackagh, in the barony of Clare, and county of Galway.

[u] *Residence*.—Mſnnad, is explained by O'Clery, in his Vocabulary, at the word muireaḋaċ, thus: "Muireadhaċ .i. tiġearna. muireaḋaċ gaċ

[O'Conor], and Taichleach O'Dowda, with numerous forces, into the town, while O'Flaherty and the [other] son of Murtough were to remain with their forces outside. Tuathal and Taichleach, with a strong body of their soldiers, marched spiritedly and boldly into the town, and made a powerful attack upon the English there, who were routed east and west. They pursued those who fled eastwards. Tuathal wounded the constable of the English with his first shot; and Taichleach, by another shot, gave him so deep a wound, that he was left lifeless. As to the English who were routed westwards from the town, they were met by O'Flaherty and the [other] son of Murtough; but it happened, through their evil destiny, that the English routed them immediately. On this occasion Mahon, the son of Hugh, who was son of Conor Moinmoy; Gilchreest Mac Dermot; Niall, the son of Farrell O'Teige, and others, were slain; but the man who slew Niall O'Teige, i. e. the brother of Colen O'Dempsey, was slain himself also.

As to the sons of Roderic, they joined[s] O'Flaherty and their other allies the next morning, and proceeded southwards to Druim-Ceanannain[t]; but Hugh, the son of Cathal Crovderg, with his English, set out after them. The tribes who supported the sons of Roderic now held a consultation, and came to the resolution that each of them should return to his own residence[u], which all accordingly did, excepting Donn Oge Mageraghty; and the princes, i. e. the sons of Roderic, being thus left with only a small force, went to Hugh O'Neill[v], accompanied by Donn Mageraghty.

Hugh, the son of Cathal Crovderg, then attacked O'Flaherty, and took hostages and pledges from him. He then proceeded to Kilmaine and Mayo, in pursuit of the sons of Murtough[w] and Tiernan, the son of Cathal Migaran [O'Conor] who came before him under the guarantee of Donough Cairbreach,

meannatta, .i. tiġearna ar ġaċ ionadh: mínnad .i. ionad."

[v] *Went to Hugh O'Neill*, lodar do ṡaiġiḋ Aoḋa uí neill.—The compound preposition, or prepositional phrase, do ṡaiġiḋ, is now obsolete, and d'ionnṡaiġiḋ, or do ċum, used in its place. This passage is given somewhat differently in the Annals of Kilronan, thus: "The resolution they adopted was that each of them should return to his people and cattle, and leave the sons of Roderic. The sons of Roderic then left the country, for they had no English or Irish forces at hand, and Donn Oge went again to O'Neill. And nothing resulted from this expedition, but that the best province in Ireland was injured and destroyed between them.

[w] *Murtough*, i. e. the celebrated Muircheartach Muimhneach O'Conor.

aoḋa uí Conċaḃair ar slánaiḋeaċt donnchaḋa cairbriġ, ⁊ maiṫe na ngall. Ba cuṁsanaḋ na ionam sin uair ní raiḃe cill na tuaiṫ i cconnaċtaiḃ an tan soin gan lot ⁊ láinṁilleḋ.

Teóm diofulaing do teccḃáil i ccríċ ċonnaċt an ionḃaiḋ si, .i. treaḃlaid trom ṫſraiġṫi gur folmaiġeaḋ mór mbailte ḋi gan elaiḋṫeċ bſṫa dfáġḃáil ionnta.

Flann mac aṁlaoiḃ uí ḟallamain toiseċ cloinne huadaċ do ṁarḃadh dfeḋlimiḋ mac caṫail croiḃdeirg don coccaḋ sin. Taḋg ua fínnaċta fear gráiḋ daoḋ mac Ruaiḋri do ṁarḃaḋ lá muintir méc aoḋagáin is in coccaḋ ceḋna.

Amlaoiḃ mac fearcair uí ḟallaṁain toiseċ a dúṫċusa fén do ḃfearr don cenel da mboi do ecc.

Muireaḋaċ ua fínnaċta toíseċ cloinni murchaḋa décc in arṫraċ ar loċ oirbsion, ⁊ é slán ag dol inn.

Teaċ do ġaḃáil for concoḃar mac taiḋg uí ċeallaiġ (tiġſrna ua maine) ⁊ for ardġal a ḃraṫair lá macaiḃ taiḋg uí ċeallaiġ, ⁊ a loscaḋ ann ar aon.

Duarcán ó hſġra, taḋg ó hſġra, ⁊ éḋaoín ingean diarmata mic doṁnaill uí eġra décc.

[x] *A necessary tranquillity*, cuṁsanaḋ na ionam.—In the Annals of Kilronan the reading is: is cumsanaḋ sangus a leas sin, uair ni raibe ceall na tuaṫ gan ṁilleaḋ ín lá sin a Connuċtuiḃ. Iar nairgniḃ ⁊ iar marḃaḋ bo in tire ⁊ a daoine, ⁊ ar cur caiċ re fuaċt ⁊ re gorta, do ḟás teiḋm mórġalair is in tir uile .i. cenel tesċa trés a ḃfolṁuiġṫe na baileaḋa gan duine beo dfacḃáil inntiḃ.—"This rest was wanting, for there was not a church or territory in Connaught, which had not been destroyed by that day. After the plundering and killing of the cattle, people had been broken down by cold and hunger, and a violent distemper raged throughout the whole country, i. e. a kind of burning disease, by which the towns were desolated, and left without a single living being."

[y] *Clann-Uadach*, a territory in the barony of Athlone, and county of Roscommon, comprising the entire of the parish of Camma, and the greater part, if not the entire, of that of Dysart. Briola, in the parish of Dysart, is referred to in old manuscripts as in this territory.—See *Tribes and Customs of Hy-Many*, printed for the Irish Archæological Society, in 1843, p. 19; and map to the same. O'Fallon resided at Milltown, in the parish of Dysert, in the year 1585, as appears from a curious document among the *Inrolments tempore Elizabethæ*, in the Auditor General's Office, Dublin, dated 6th August, 1585, and entitled "Agreement between the Irish chieftains and inhabitants of Imany, called O'Kelly's country, on both sides of the River Suck in Connaught, and the Queen's Majesty."

[z] *Clann-Murrough*, Clann Murchaḋa.—Ac-

and the chiefs of the English, and on condition that he should spare their people and cattle. This was a necessary tranquillity[x], for there was not a church or territory in Connaught at that time that had not been plundered and desolated.

An oppressive malady raged in the province of Connaught at this time: it was a heavy burning sickness, which left the large towns desolate, without a single survivor.

Flann, the son of Auliffe O'Fallon, Chief of Clann-Uadagh[y], was slain by Felim, the son of Cathal Crovderg, in this war; and Teige O'Finaghty, one of the officers [Aes graidh] of Hugh, the son of Roderic, was slain by the people of Mac Egan during the same war.

Auliffe, the son of Fearcair O'Fallon, chieftain of his own tribe, and the best of them, died.

Murray O'Finaghty, Chief of Clann-Murrough[z], died in a vessel on Lough Oirbsen (Lough Corrib), which he had gone into in good health.

A house was attacked upon the son of Teige O'Kelly (Lord of Hy-Many), and upon Ardgal his brother, by the sons of Teige O'Kelly, and both were burned within it.

Duarcan O'Hara, Teige O'Hara, and Edwina, daughter of Dermot, the son of Donnell O'Hara, died.

cording to O'Dugan's topographical Poem, there were two chiefs of the O'Finaghtys in Connought (gió enmuicne ní hionann), one called Chief of Clann Murchadha, and the other Chief of Clann Conmhaigh. The latter name is still remembered and now pronounced Clanconow, but the former is totally forgotten. According to Duald Mac Firbis, and the tradition in the country, the O'Finaghtys were seated on both sides of the River Suck, and their territory comprised, before the English invasion, forty-eight ballys, or large Irish townlands. Some think that the sept of them called Clann-Murrough were on the east side of the River Suck, in the present county of Roscommon, and that called Clannconow, or Clanconway, on the west of the same river, in the now county of Galway, and that each sept had twenty-four ballys, or ninety-six quarters of land. Both septs were dispossessed soon after the English invasion by that family of the Burkes called Mac Davids, who descended from a furious heroine, named Nuala na meadoige, the daughter of O'Finaghty, who was the mother of David Burke, the ancestor of Mac David, Lord of Clanconow, and by whose treachery the O'Finaghtys, her own tribe, were dispossessed. In the year 1628, Sir Ulick Burke, only son of Edmond Burke, of Glinske, Lord of Clanconow, was created a baronet of Ireland, and from him the present Sir John Burke, of Glinsk Castle, the present head of this family, is descended.—See *Genealogies, Tribes, &c., of Hy-Fiachrach*, p. 108, note [b].

Muiṁniġ ⁊ goill do ḋul fo tearmann caolainne, ár na ngall do cor don toisc sin tre feartaiḃ dé ⁊ caolainne.

An tarḃar gá ḃuain a haiṫle na féli bríġde.

[a] *The Momonians, &c.*—This entry relating to the plundering of Tearmann Caelainne, is entered in the Annals of Kilronan under the year 1224. These annals state that when O'Neill (after having inaugurated Turlough, the son of Roderic, as King of Connaught) had heard that Donough Cairbreach O'Brien and Geoffry Mares were coming into Connaught, he retreated with all possible expedition; and that the Momonians and English not finding O'Neill in Connaught before them, pursued the sons of Roderic, and banished them to O'Neill a second time, &c. &c. They then add: "The English and the Momonians then attacked Tearmann Caoilfinn, but the English were slaughtered through the miracles of Caoilfinn."

[b] *Tearmann Caelainne*, i. e. the Termon, or sanctuary of the virgin, St. Caelainn. The situation of this place has not been pointed out by any of our historical or topographical writers. Duald Mac Firbis, indeed, in his Genealogies of the Irish Saints, p. 733, states that it is in Connaught. Thus: "Caolḟionn ó Tſrmonn Caolainne i cconachtaiḃ," i. e. "Caolfionn of Termon Caolainne in Connaught." It appears from an Inquisition taken on the 27th of May, 1617, that Termon-Kealand belonged to the monastery of Roscommon. The Editor, when examining the localities of the county of Roscommon for the Ordnance Survey, found that this place is still well known, and that its ancient name is not yet forgotten, though Termonmore is that more generally used. It is situated in the parish of Kilkeevin, and about one mile to the east of the town of Castlereagh, in the county of Roscommon, where the virgin, St. Caellain, is still vividly remembered, and curious legends told about her miracles. Her holy well, called Tobar Caelainne, is situated in the townland of Moor, in the same parish, and from it an old road led across the bog to the Termon, where her nunnery church stands in ruins.—See Ordnance Map of the county of Roscommon, sheets 20 and 26, whereon the ruins of her church and nunnery, and also her holy well, called Tobercaelainne, are shewn.

This virgin was the patron saint of the tribes called Ciarraighe or Kierrigii, of the original settlement, of whom in this neigbourhood, as well as in the present barony of Costello, in the county of Mayo, the following account is preserved in a vellum MS. in Trinity College, Dublin, H. 3, 17, p. 875.

Cuin tancatar Ciarraigi a Conaċtaib? Nīn. In-aimsir Aeḋa mic Eaċach Tirmcarna. Cia diḃ táinic ar túr? Nīn. .i. Coirbri mac Conaire tainic a Muṁain a ndeas iar na indarba eirti. Tainic tra co n-a muinter uile co hAeḋ mac Eachach Tirmcarna. Bai ingſn dſrscaiṫech la coirḃri; ro chuindiġ Aeḋ ar a hathair hí. Tainic sí feaċt aon do ṫiġ a haṫar. Ro ġaḃ a haṫair fein toirsi móir i n-a fiaḋnaisi. Ro fiarḟaiḋ in ingſn de cid dia mbui. Mo ḃeiṫ gan fſrann for deoraiġſċt ar sé. Tangar on riġ ar cſnn na hinġine iar sin. Ro ċind imorru an inġin na raġaḋ tria biṫhu co tardta fſrann maiṫ dia haṫair. Do ḃéarsa do ar Aeḋ, doneoċ a ticfa timcheall i n-aen lo do na foithriḃ sea siar, ⁊ do béarṫar Caelaind craiḃṫeach fris na dilsi. Timċeallaiḋ sin iaraṁ co mor an tir sin aṁail a duḃraḋ ris ⁊ do soith fa deoiġ dia ṫiġ. Beiriḋ a muinter is na fſrandaiḃ sin. Cairiġiḋ Connacta co mor an ti Aeḋ ar a met leo do raḋ d'fſrand do choirbri, ⁊ arbeartatar coirbri do marḃuṫ. Ní fſtaiḋṫſr

The Momonians[a] and English attacked Tearmann Caelainne[b], but the English were slaughtered on this occasion, through the miracles of God and St. Caelainn.

The corn remained unreaped until after the festival of St. Bridget [the 1st of February[c]].

sin, ar Aedh, ór ata Caelainn a n-dilsi fris féin, 7 sria ferann. Acht cena dénter lind agaibh do, 7 tabar deoch neimhe do acon lind sin, gur ob marbh de. Do gnitér iaram amhlaidh sin an fled, gur bo urlamh. Foillsighter iaram ón choimhdi do Chaelainn in ní sin. Tig sidhe do saighidh na fleighi. Cidh dia rum saraidhis, a Aedh? ar sí. Saraidhfetsa tusa fod righi ind. Toirghiar duit ind, ar an righ. Gebad, ar Caelainn. Beir do bhreith dono, ar an righ. Berad, ar sí. Ar is tria lind ro foibris a marbhadh, ar sí, a mheath no éag firéinaigh, ar si, .i. ri Connacht dia neaba lind Ciarraighe co brath; conad de sin na dénaid ciarraighe lind do righ Connacht do ghnáth. Ferann dam féin, ol in chailleach. Raghaidh ar an righ. Do bhertar in Termann mór di iaram; conad and fil i ceall aniu.

"When first did the Kierrigii come into Connaught? Not difficult. In the time of Aedh, son of Eochy Tirmcharna. Which of them came first? Not difficult. Coirbri, son of Conairi, who came from the south of Munster, when he had been expelled. He came with all his people to Aedh, the son of Eochy Tirmcharna. Coirbri had a famous daughter. Aedh asked her of her father. She came one time to her father's house; her father conceived great grief in her presence; his daughter asked him from what it arose. 'My being without land in exile,' said he. Messengers came afterwards from the King to see the daughter, but she determined that she would not go to the King until he should give a good portion of land to her father. 'I will give him,' said Aedh, 'as much of the wooded lands to the west, as he can pass round in one day; and Caelainn, the Pious, shall be given as guarantee of it.' Coirbri afterwards went round a great extent of that country, according to the mode directed, and finally returned to his house. He brought his people into these lands. The Connacians greatly criminated Aedh for the too great extent of land, as they deemed, which he had given, and said that Coirbri should be killed. 'This cannot be done,' said Aedh, 'for Caelainn is guarantee for himself and for his land. But, however, let some beer be made by you for him, and give him a poisonous draught in that beer, that he may die of it.' A feast was, therefore, afterwards prepared. This thing was afterwards revealed by the Lord to Caelainn. She came to the feast. 'Why hast thou violated my guarantee,' said she to Aedh. 'I will violate thee as regards thy kingdom.' Accept thy own award, in compensation for it,' said the King. 'I will,' said Caelainn. 'Pass thy sentence, then,' said the King. 'I will,' said she. 'Because it is through the medium of beer thou hast attempted to destroy him [Coirbri], may the King of Connaught meet decline or certain death, if ever he drink of the beer of the Kierrigii.' Hence it happens that the Kierrigii never brew any beer for the Kings of Connaught. 'Grant land to myself,' said the Nun. 'Choose it,' said the King. The Termonmore was afterwards given, where her church is at this day."

[c] Under this year the Annals of Clonmacnoise, as translated by Mageoghegan, record that Moylemorrey O'Connor of Affalie [Offaly], was killed at Rosseglassie" [now Monasterevin], "by Cowlen O'Dempsie."

Under this year also the Dublin copy of the

AOIS CRIOSD, 1226.

Aois Criosd míle da ċéd fiċe a sé.

Donum dei epscop na Miḋe do écc.

Connmach ua tarppa espoc Luiġne do écc.

Aoḋ mac duinn uí soċlaċáin airċinneaċ conga, Saoi ċanntaire, Sccribniġ, ⁊ ċeard nesaṁail esiḋe do écc.

Maṫa ua maoilmoiċerġe do ecc.

Tiġearnán mac caṫail miccarain mic Toirrḋealḃaiġ ṁóir Ríoġdaṁna bá mó eneach, ⁊ eangnaṁ, ⁊ as mó do rinne do nḟéiṫiḃ fuaiṫḟnta fodáanacha tainic dá cinid ré haimsir esiḋe, do ṁarḃaḋ do ḋonnchaḋ ó ḋuḃda ⁊ dá ċloinn.

Nuala ingḟn Ruaiḋri uí conċoḃair baintiġearna ulaḋ décc i cconga feċin, ⁊ a haḋnacal go honórach i tteampall canánaċ conga.

Doṁnall mac Ruaiḋri uí flaiṫbeartaiġ do ṁarḃaḋ do ṁacaiḃ muircḟrtaiġ uí ḟlaiṫbeartaiġ iar ngaḃáil tiġe fair dóiḃ fḟn, ⁊ dfeḋlim mac caṫail croibhḋeirg.

Fearġal ua taiḋg an teaġlaiġ, toiseċ teaġlaiġ caṫail croiḃḋeirg, ⁊ aoḋ mac caṫail do ṁarḃaḋ lá donnsleḃe ó ngaḋra.

Aoḋ mac doṁnaill uí ruairc do marḃaḋ do caṫal ó raġaillig ⁊ do ċonċoḃar mac corbmaic uí maoilruanaiḋ ar loċ aillinne.

Muirġḟs mac diarmata do ṁarḃaḋ.

Annals of Innisfallen record the erection of the castles of Dublin and Trim by the English.

[d] *Donum Dei.*—He is called "Donum Dei, Bushopp of Meath," in Mageoghegan's translation of the Annals of Clonmacnoise; but in the Annals of Multifernan he is called "Deodatus *electus* Midie."—See Harris's edition of Ware's Bishops, p. 142, where it is conjectured that he was never consecrated.

[e] *A learned singer.*—In the Annals of Kilronan, it is stated that he made a kind of musical instrument for himself which had never been made before, and that he was skilled in the arts of poetry, embroidery, and penmanship, and every other known science.

[f] *O'Mulmoghery,* O Maolmoċeirġe.—This name is still common in the county of Donegal, but anglicised *Early,* because moċeirġe signifies *early rising.* Maolmoċeirġe signifies *chief of the early rising.* The word maol, when not prefixed to the name of a saint, signifies a king or chief, as in the present instance, but when prefixed to the name of a saint, it means one tonsured in honour of some saint, as we learn from Colgan: "*Mail,* seu ut variè scribitur Hibernis *maol, mael, moel,* idem nunc quod *do-*

THE AGE OF CHRIST, 1226.

The Age of Christ, one thousand two hundred twenty-six.

Donum Dei[d], Bishop of Meath, died.

Connmagh O'Tarpy (Torpy), Bishop of Leyny, died.

Hugh, the son of Donn O'Sochlaghan, Erenagh of Cong, a learned singer[e], a scribe, and a man expert in many trades, died.

Matthew O'Mulmoghery[f] died.

Tiernan, the son of Cathal Miccaruinn, who was son of Turlough More, a Roydamna [prince], the most hospitable man and most expert at arms, and whose exploits had been more various and successful than those of any of his tribe for a long time, was slain by Donough O'Dowda and his sons.

Nuala, daughter of Roderic O'Conor, and Queen of Ulidia[g], died at Conga Fechin [Cong], and was honourably interred in the church of the Canons at Cong.

Donnell, the son of Rory O'Flaherty, was slain by the sons of Murtough O'Flaherty, after they and Felim, the son of Cathal Crovderg, had attacked and taken the house in which he was.

Farrell O'Teige, surnamed an Teaghlaigh, Chief of the household[h] of Cathal Crovderg, and Hugh, the son of Cathal, were slain by Donslevy O'Gara.

Hugh, the son of Donnell O'Rourke, was slain on Lough Allen[i] by Cathal O'Reilly and Conor, the son of Cormac O'Mulrony.

Maurice Mac Dermot was slain.

minus vel rex, idem nunc quod *calvus, tonsus, vel coronatus*."—*Acta Sanctorum*, p. 188, n. 4. See also p. 386, n. 1, of the same work.

[g] *Queen of Ulidia.*—She was the wife of Mac Donslevy, who was at this period styled King of Uladh; but by this is not to be understood the entire province of Ulster, but only that part of it lying eastwards of Glenree, Lough Neagh, and the Lower Bann.

[h] *Of the household*, teaġlaiġ.—In the Annals of Kilronan: *Dux* loċta tiġe Caṫail Croiḃdeirg ⁊ a ṁic na ḋiaiḋ, i. e. "Leader or chief of the household of Cathal Crovderg, and of that of his son after him." The word loċt tiġe is anglicised *Loghty*, and *Loghtee* in some Anglo-Irish documents, in which the term is used to denote mensal lands, or lands set apart for the maintenance of the chief's table.—See Harris's Ware, vol. ii. p. 70. There was a celebrated territory in Oriel, called luċt tiġe Meg Maṫġamna, anglicised "the Loughty," as appears from several ancient maps of Ulster.

[i] *Lough Allen*, loċ aillinne.—A well known lake in the county of Leitrim, near the source of the Shannon.

Caislén cille móire do leaccaḋ lá caṫal ó Raiġilliġ.

Aodh mac caṫail croiḃḋeirg do ġaḃáil Aodha uí ḟlaiṫḃertaiġ, ⁊ a tabairt i láiṁ ġall.

AOIS CRIOSD, 1227.

Aois Criost, mile, dá céd, fiche, aseacht.

Concobar mac Neill uí chatharnaiġ do ṁarḃaḋ la haṁsaiḃ laiġneaċ ro baoi i fochair Riġ Connacht.

Enrí ua maoileaċloinn ⁊ muircertaċ ua maoileaċloinn do ṁarḃaḋ la galloiḃ.

Maolseachlainn ua conċoḃair failġe do ṁarḃaḋ lá cuilén ua ndíomusaiġ.

Giollacoluim ua Maoilmuaiḋ do ṁarḃaḋ la hua Mórdha.

Goill Ereann do coṁcruinniuccaḋ go háṫcliaṫ. Aoḋ mac caṫail croiḃḋeirg Ri connaċt do ṫoċuireaḋ dóiḃ. Iar ndul dó dá saiġiḋ ro ṫionnscainsiod feallaḋ fair. Uilliam marusccál a ḟear caradraiḋ do ṫocht ċuicce gona soċraide, ⁊ é da breiṫ daiṁḋeoin gall ar lár na cúirte amaċ, ⁊ a iodlacaḋ dó go ndeachaiḋ i cconnaċtaiḃ.

Aoḋ mac caṫail croiḃḋeirg do ḋénaṁ coinne iar sin ag laṫaiġ caíċtuṫbil ré huilliam mares mac Seafraiḋ .i. iustis erenn, ⁊ ní deachaiḋ siom tar

[k] *Demolished*, do leaccaḋ, literally, was thrown down. In the Annals of Kilronan, the verb used is do ḃriseaḋ, and in the Annals of Ulster do scailed, and in the old translation the passage is rendered: "The Castle of Kilmore broken down by Cahall O'Rely."

[l] The passage is given as follows in the Annals of Ulster: A. D. 1226. Feiḋlim hua Concoḃair do ġaḃail taiġi ar Domnall hua ḟlaiṫbertaiġ gur marḃ 7 gur loisc é féin 7 a braṫair. Aeḋ hua flaṫbertaiġ do ġaḃail la hAeḋ mac caṫail croiḃdeirg 7 a tobairt illaim ngall. And thus rendered in the old translation: "Felim O'Conor, taking a house uppon Donell O'Flaithvertay, killed and burned himselfe and his brother. Hugh O'Flaithvertay committed by Hugh mac Cathal Crovderg & did deliver him into the hands of the Galls."

[m] *Henry O'Melaghlin.*—This entry is given as follows in Mageoghegan's translation of the Annals of Clonmacnoise, but under the year 1226, "Henry O'Melaghlyn, son of the knight O'Melaughlyn, was killed by the Englishmen of Ardinurcher. Murtagh mac Melaghlyn Begg was also killed by the English."

[n] *Assembled at Dublin.*—In the Annals of Kilronan this passage is entered under the year year 1226. It begins thus: Cuirt do denaṁ do ġallaiḃ aṫa cliaṫ 7 Erenn a nAṫ cliaṫ, 7 aoḋ mac Caṫail Croiḃdeirg do gairm fuirre,

The Castle of Kimlore was demolished[k] by Cathal O'Reilly.

Hugh, the son of Cathal Crovderg, took Hugh O'Flaherty prisoner, and delivered him up into the hands of the English[l].

THE AGE OF CHRIST, 1227.

The Age of Christ, one thousand two hundred twenty-seven.

Conor, the son of Niall O'Caharny [Fox], was slain by the Leinster soldiers, who were along with the King of Connaught.

Henry O'Melaghlin[m] and Murtough O'Melaghlin were slain by the English.

Melaghlin O'Conor Faly was slain by Cuilen O'Dempsy.

Gilla-Colum O'Molloy was slain by O'More.

The English of Ireland assembled at Dublin[n] and invited thither Hugh, the son of Cathal Crovderg, King of Connaught. As soon as he arrived they began to deal treacherously by him; but William Mareschal, his friend, coming in with his forces, rescued him, in despite of the English, from the middle of the Court, and escorted him to Connaught.

Hugh, the son of Cathal Crovderg, appointed a conference at Lathach Caichtubil[o] with William Mares (de Marisco), the son of Geoffry Lord Justice

i. e. A Court [Council] was formed by the English of Dublin and of Ireland, at Dublin, and they summoned Hugh, the son of Cathal Crovderg to it."

The account of this transaction is more fully given in Mageoghegan's translation of the Annals of Clonmacnoise, as follows: "A. D. 1226. Hugh O'Connor, King of Connaught, went to the English Court of Dublin; by the compulsarie means of the English they tooke his sonn and daughter as hostages, with the hostages of all the principall men in Connought; upon examining of some criminall causes there objected to the said Hugh, he was found guilty in their censure, and being to be apprehended for the same, a speciall friend of his then within, and of great favour and power with the King of England, did assist Hugh, and by the help of his sword and strength of his hand he conveighed Hugh away from them, and so departed to Connaught in safety. Within a week after the Englishmen kept court in Athlone, whereunto the Connoughtmen came, and tooke captive William March, the Deputie's son, and tooke other principal men belonging to him, and also killed a good knight at his taking."

[o] *Lathach Caichtubil.*—This *Lathach*, or slough, is now dried up, but the old men living near Athlone still point out its situation and exact extent. The name is still preserved in that of a village and townland lying immediately to the west of Athlone, in the parish of St. Peter, viz. *Beal-Lathaich*, i. e. the *os*, mouth, or entrance, into the *Lathach*. The name of this village is

laṫaiġ anonn aċtṁaḋ uathaḋ deaġḋaoine, .i. corbmac mac tomaltaiġ, Diarmaid mac maġnusa, maġnus mac muirċeartaiġ uí ċonċobair, taḋġ mac maṫġaṁna uí ċerin, ⁊ Ruaiḋri ua maoilḃrénainn. Uilliam mares do ṫeaċt oċtar marcaċ ina coṁḋail. O do ċuiṁniġ ó conċobair an ḟeall rémraite erġis i ccoinne na ngall, gresis a muintir fóṫa ionnsaiġiḋ fén uilliam mares gur ġabarsair é fó ċéḋóir. Cioḋ iad a ṁuintir ann ro ḟreaccair-siod greasaċt uí Concobair ro lśiccsiod fona gallaiḃ iad gur moiḋsiod orra, marḃaitt Constapla aṫa luain, gaḃaid maiġistir Sleṁne ⁊ hugo airddin. Cuirit aoḋ na goill sin i mbraiġdśnus tar laṫaiġ suas. Luiḋ roiṁe gon a ḟocraide ar a haiṫle gur airgśdair margaḋ aṫa luain, ⁊ gur loisccearsair an baile go hiomlán. Ḃá gníoṁ socair do ċonnaċtaiḃ an gníoṁ so, óir fuairsioṁ a mac, a inġean, ⁊ braiġde connaċt ar ċeana bat-tar ar laṁaibh gall do coṁḟuasglaḋ ar na braiġdiḃ rémraite genmótá Síṫ dfagail dfearaiḃ connaċt.

Donnsléḃe ó gaḋra tiġearna sléḃe luġa do ṁarḃaḋ don ġiolla ruaḋ mac a dearbraṫar fén iar ngabáil tiġe in oiḋċe fair, ⁊ an giolla ruaḋ do ṁar-ḃaḋ inn iar sin tré imdeall aoḋa uí conċobair.

Aoḋ mac Ruaiḋri uí concobair, ⁊ mac uilliam búrc do ṫoiḋeċt slóġ lan-mór i ttuaisceart Connaċt gur loiscsiot inis mśḋóin gur airccsiod an críoċ i ttangadar, ⁊ gur ġaḃsat a braiġde.

Sluaiġeaḋ lá seaffraiḋ mares ⁊ la toirrḋealḃaċ mac Ruaiḋri uí conco-

now correctly enough Anglicised Bellaugh, and sometimes, but incorrectly, Bellough, and even Bullock. The Irish, however, call it distinctly béal laṫaiġ, and understand it as referring to the laṫaċ which lay between it and Athlone.—See map prefixed to the *Tribes and Customs of Hy-Many*, printed for the Irish Archæological Society in 1843, on which this name is given.

[p] *Sliabh Lugha*, i. e. Looee's mountain.—This territory still retains its name, and comprises the northern half of the barony of Costello, in the county of Mayo, viz., the parishes of Kilbeagh, Kilmovee, Kilcolman, and Castlemore-Costello, being the portion of the barony of Costello included in the diocese of Achonry. The remaining parishes in this barony are in the diocese of Tuam, and constitute the territory of Kerry of Lough-na-narney.—See note under the year 1224.

[q] *By the devise*, Tre imdeall.—In the Annals of Ulster the phrase is written tre imdell. The whole entry is thus rendered in the old translation: "A. D. 1226. Dunleve O'Grada was killed by [the son of] his own brother, and he was killed therefor himselfe soone by the devise of Hugh O'Conner."

[r] *The son of William Burke*, i. e. Rickard More, the son of William Fitz-Adelm.

[s] *Geoffrey Mares*.—In Mageoghegan's trans-

of Ireland. A few only of his chiefs went with him across the *Lathach* [slough], namely, Cormac, the son of Tomaltagh [Mac Dermot], Dermot, the son of Manus, the son of Murtough O'Conor, Teige, the son of Mahon O'Kerrin, and Rory O'Mulrenin. William Mares set out to meet them, accompanied by eight horsemen. But when O'Conor recollected the treachery already mentioned, he rose up against the English and excited his people to attack them; and he himself attacked William Mares, and at once took him prisoner. His people responded to O'Conor's incitement, rushed upon the English, and defeated them; they killed the constable of Athlone, and took Master Slevin and Hugo Arddin prisoners. Hugh sent these Englishmen across the *Lathach* to be imprisoned; and then, advancing with his troops, he plundered the market of Athlone and burned the whole town. This achievement was of great service to the Connacians, for he [O'Conor] obtained his son and daughter, and all the other hostages of Connaught, who had been in the hands of the English, in exchange for the aforesaid prisoners; and obtained moreover a peace for the men of Connaught.

Donslevy O'Gara, Lord of Sliabh Lugha[p], was slain by Gillaroe, his own brother's son, after the latter had, on the same night, forcibly taken a house from him; and Gillaroe himself was afterwards put to death for this crime by the devise[q] of Hugh O'Conor.

Hugh, son of Roderic O'Conor, and the son of William Burke[r], marched with a great army into the North of Connaught, and they burned Inishmaine, plundered the country into which they came, and took hostages.

An army was led by Geoffrey Mares[s] [de Marisco] and Turlough, the son

lation of the Annals of Clonmacnoise these transactions are given somewhat more copiously, as follows:

"A. D. 1226. Geffrey March, Deputie of Ireland, with a great army, went to Connought to expell Hugh O'Connor from out of that provence, which he did accordingly, and established the two sons of Rowrie O'Connor, named Terlagh and Hugh, in the possession and superiority thereof.

"Hugh O'Connor, that was before King of Connought, returned from Tyrconnell, into which he was banished by Geffrey March, brought with him his wife, son, and his brother Felym O'Connor, and came to a place in Connought called Gortyn Cowle Lwachra, out of which place Mac Meran, his porter, fled from him, and betraid him to the sons of Terlagh O'Connor, who came privilie to the said Gortyn, without knowledge of the said Hugh. O'Connor, knowing them to be then about the house, tooke one of his sons, his brother Ffelym tooke the

ḃair i maġ aoí go ndearnsat caislén isRinn dúin, ⁊ gur gaḃsat braiġdi sil muirſdhaiġ.

Aoḋ mac caṫail croiḃdeirg do ḋul i ttir conaill doċum uí ḋoṁnaill, ⁊ a iompóḋ bu ḋeas dorídisi, ⁊ a bſn do ṫabairt les. Meic toirrḋealḃaiġ do teccḃáil cuicce a ccomfoccus na sſgsa, a bſn ⁊ a eaċraiḋ do ḃén de, ⁊ an bſn do ċor illaiṁ gall.

Sluaicċeaḋ oile lá toirrḋealḃaċ ḃeós, ⁊ lá gallaiḃ miḋe in iarṫar connaċt co ndearnsat creaċ mór ar aoḋ mac Ruaiḋri ui flaiṫḃſrtaiġ. A ndul airíde i ccrich ceara, ⁊ braiġde mac muirceartaiġ do gabáil doiḃ, ⁊ nuiṁir do buaiḃ feolmaiġ ar ceċ trioċa céd do toirrḋealḃaċ uaṫa.

Cúmara o doṁnalláin do marḃaḋ i ngemil la Ruaiḋri mac duinnsleḃe a ndiogail a aṫar.

Brian mac concoḃair uí diarmata do marḃaḋ.

Caislén aṫa liacc do ḋénaṁ la Seffraiḋ marés.

AOIS CRIOSD, 1228.

Aois Criost, mile, da ċéd, fiċe a hoċt.

Aoḋ mac caṫail croiḃdeirg uí ċoncoḃair rí connaċt do ṁarḃaḋ hi ccuirt Seffraiḋ máres tre meaḃail ar aslaċ gall iar ná ḋíoċur do ċonnaċtaiḃ.

other son, and so departed safely, save only that the Lady Ranelt, Hugh his wife, and daughter of O'Fferall, was taken. Melaughlyn mac Hugh mac Bryen O'Connor was killed, and the said Ranelt delivered to the Englishmen.

"The Englishmen immediately founded a castle in Rindowne, now called Teagh Eoyn, or John his house, neer Loghree."

[t] *Moynai*, maġ naoi.—Now Maghery-Connaught, lying between Strokestown and Castlereagh, and Roscommon and Elphin.

[u] *Rindown*, Rinn dúin.—A peninsula on Lough Ree, in the county of Roscommon.—See note under the year 1199. In Mageoghegan's translation of the Annals of Clonmacnoise, at this year, he calls this castle "Rindowne," and adds, "now called Teagh Eoyn, or John his House, neer Loghree."—See a curious account of this castle, written by Mr. Petrie, in the 10th Number of the Irish Penny Magazine, September 5th, 1840, pp. 73–75.

[w] *The sons of Murtough.*—In the Annals of Kilronan they are called clann muirċeartaiġ muiṁniġ, i. e. the sons of Murtough Muimhneach O'Conor, who was one of the sons of Turlough More O'Conor, Monarch of Ireland.

[x] *Athleague*, now Ballyleague, the western, or Connaught part of the village of Lanesborough, on the Shannon. It is in the parish of Cloontuskert, and the barony of south Ballintober.—

of Roderic O'Conor, into Moynai[t], erected a castle at Rindown[u], and took the hostages of the Sil-Murray.

Hugh, the son of Cathal Crovderg, went to Tirconnell to O'Donnell, and returned again southwards, taking his wife with him; but he was met by the sons of Turlough very near Seaghais [Curlew Mountains], who took his wife and his horses from him, and his wife was given up into the hands of the English.

Another army was led by Turlough, and the English of Meath, into the West of Connaught, and they committed a great depredation on Hugh, the son of Rory O'Flaherty. They proceeded thence into the country of Carra; they took hostages from the sons of Murtough[w], and Turlough obtained from them a number of fat beeves out of every cantred in their possession.

Cumara O'Donnellan was slain, while in fetters, by Rory Mac Donslevy, in revenge of his father.

Brian, the son of Conor O'Diarmada, was slain.

The castle of Athleague[x] was erected by Geoffrey Mares [De Marisco].

THE AGE OF CHRIST, 1228.

The Age of Christ, one thousand two hundred twenty-eight.

Hugh, the son of Cathal Crovderg O'Conor, King of Connaught, was treacherously killed by the English in the court [mansion] of Geoffrey Mares, at the instigation of the English, after he had been expelled by the Connacians[y].

See Ordnance Map of the county of Roscommon, sheet 37. According to the Annals of Clonmacnoise, as translated by Connell Mageogeghan, this castle was erected by William Delacie and the English of Meath. Under this year the same annals record the erection of the castle of Rahen O'Swaine (now Rahen, near Tullamore, in the King's County), by Symon Clifford, who gave an annuity of four hundred [?] to the Prior and Convent of Dorrowe.

[y] *Connacians.*—The account of the murder of Hugh O'Conor is more satisfactorily given in Mageoghegan's translation of the Annals of Clonmacnoise as follows:

"A. D. 1227. Hugh O'Connor came to an atonement with Geffrey March, and was again restored to his kingdome of Connoght by the said Deputie, and being afterwards in the Deputie's house was treacherously killed by an Englishman, for which cause the Deputie the next day hanged the Englishman that killed him for that fowle fact. The cause of killing the King of Connaught was, that after the Wife of that Englishman that was so hanged by the

Coccaḋ mor do eirġe hi cconnaċtaiḃ etir da ṁac Ruaiḋri ui conċoḃair, .i. etir aoḋ ⁊ toirrḋealḃaċ, iar marḃaḋ an aoḋa remraite, ar ní ṫucc an mac bá só uṁla don mac ba sine gur millseat Connaċta eatorra ⁊ ro fásaiġeaḋ leó ó Eassdara co haḃainn ua ffiaċraċ ro ḋſs aċt maḋ beacc hi Sleiḃ luccha, ⁊ luċt airtiġ nama.

Niall mac congalaiġ uí Ruairc tiġearna dartraicċe, ⁊ cloinne fſrmaiġe do ṁarḃaḋ lá dá ṁac airt mic domnaill uí Ruairc, .i. art ⁊ aṁlaoiḃ. Aṁlaiḃ gſrr mac néill mic conġalaiġ do ṁarḃaḋ hi foċraccaḋ lá haṁlaiḃ mac airt céona.

Fſrġal mac sitriucca uí ruairc do ṁarḃaḋ la macaiḃ néll mic conġalaiġ uí Ruairc.

Muirċſrtaċ mac flaiṫbeartaicch uí ḟlannaccáin do ṁarḃaḋ la macaiḃ taiḋg uí gaḋra.

Aoḋ mac donnchaiḋ uí fearġail do ṁarḃaḋ lá haoḋ mac aṁlaoiḃ uí fearġail.

Dauid ua floinn taoiseaċ síl ṁaoilruain, ⁊ Ruaiḋri ua maoilḃrenainn décc.

Riocard mac uilliam burc do ṫeċt ó Riġ Saccsan ina iustís in erinn.

Aoḋ mac Ruaiḋri uí concoḃair do gaḃail riġe Connaċt do rſir ṫoccha an iustís go maiṫiḃ connaċt ar bélaiḃ toirrḋealḃaiġ a ḃráṫar fá sine inás.

Deputie, had so washed his head and body with sweet balls and other things, he, to gratifie her for her service, kissed her, which the Englishman seeing, for meer jealousie, and for none other cause, killed O'Connor presently at unawares." Dr. Leland had this passage furnished him by Charles O'Conor, of Belanagare, and has given its substance in a note in his History of Ireland, vol. i. p. 208, b. 2, c. 1.

[z] *Airteach* is a territory in the present county of Roscommon, comprising the parish of Tibohine, lately in the west of the barony of Boyle, but at present in the barony of Frenchpark. It adjoins Sliabh Lugha, which is the northern part of the barony of Costello, in the county of Mayo.—See map to *Tribes and Customs of Hy-Fiachrach*, on which the relative position of these territories is shewn.

[a] *Dartry* is generally called Dartry-Mac Clancy, as being the territory of Mac Clancy. It looks wild and romantic at the present day, and was anciently formidable in its mountains and fastnesses. It comprises the entire of the present barony of Rossclogher, in the north of the county of Leitrim, for which it is at present the most usual popular appellation. In this territory were situated the castles of Rossclogher (from which the barony took its name), Dun-Carbry, and the *Crannog* of Inishkeen, an island in Lough Melvin, as well as all the islands of that beautiful lake, with the monasteries of Doire Melle, Carcair Sinchill, Bealach Mith-

A great war broke out in Connaught between the two sons of Roderic O'Conor, Hugh and Turlough, after the death of the Hugh above-mentioned, for the younger son did not yield submission to the elder; and they destroyed Connaught between them, and desolated the *region extending* from Easdara [Ballysadare], southwards, to the river of Hy-Fiachrach, excepting only a small portion of Sliabh Lugha, and the territory of the people of Airtech[a].

Niall, the son of Congalagh O'Rourke, Lord of Dartry[a] and Clann Fearmaighe, was slain by the two sons of Art, the son of Donnell O'Rourke, namely, Art and Auliffe; and Auliffe Gearr, the son of Niall, who was son of Congalagh, was slain, while bathing, by Auliffe, the son of the same Art.

Farrell, the son of Sitric O'Rourke, was slain by the sons of Niall, the son of Congalagh O'Rourke.

Murtough, the son of Flaherty O'Flanagan, was slain by the sons of Teige O'Gara.

Hugh, the son of Donough O'Farrell, was slain by Hugh, the son of Auliffe O'Farrell.

David O'Flynn, Chief of Sil Maelruain, and Rory O'Mulrenin, died.

Richard, the son of William Burke, came to Ireland, from the King of England, as Justiciary[b].

Hugh, the son of Roderic O'Conor, assumed the kingdom of Connaught, by the election of the Justiciary and the chiefs of Connaught, in preference to Turlough, his elder brother[c].

idhein (now Ballaghmeehin), and Rossinver. The ancestors of the family of Mac Clancy, with their neighbours the Calry Laithim, or Calry of Lough Gile, in the barony of Carbury, in the county of Sligo, who settled in this part of Connaught at a very remote period, have sprung from a stock totally different from the Hy-Bruin-Breifne and Conmaicne, who occupied the remaining part of the county of Leitrim; but we have no accurate record of how they were enabled to settle here. The Mac Clancys, and their correlatives, in this neighbourhood, are not of the race of Milesius of Spain, being, if we can depend on the Bardic pedigrees, descended from Daire, the Plunderer, who deduced his lineage from Ith, the uncle of that Milesius.—See O'Flaherty's *Ogygia*, part iii. c. 67. There was another family of this name in the county of Clare, but of a totally different lineage, being descended from the same stock as the Mac Namaras. Both now Anglicise their name Clancy.

[b] *Justiciary.*—This passage is given in the Annals of Kilronan under the year 1227. According to the list of the Chief Governors of Ireland, given in Harris's Ware, vol. ii. p. 103, Richard de Burgo was appointed Lord Deputy of Ireland on the 10th of March, 1227.

[c] *Elder brother.*—The sons of Roderic O'Co-

Maolseaċlainn mac toirrdealbaiġ mic Ruaiḋri uí ċoncobair do ṁarbaḋ lá haodh ri Connaċt.

Gorta dioḟulaincc i cconnaċtaiḃ tri coccaḋ cloinne Ruaiḋri. Ro hairccitt cealla ⁊ tuaṫa. Ro ḋioċuirit a clerig ⁊ a hollamain hi ccríochaiḃ cianaiḃ coṁaiġtiḃ, ⁊ atbaṫ cid araill diḃ dfuaċt ⁊ do ġorta.

Dauid ua floind taoiseach síl Mhaeilruain do éġ.

Aéḋ mac donnchaiḋ uí ferġail do marbaḋ la haeḋ mac aṁlaoiḃ uí ḟer-ghail.

AOIS CRIOSD, 1229.

Aois Criost, míle, da ċed, fiċe anaoí.

Maineistir S. Frainseis hi ccorcaiġ do ṫoġḃáil la mag carṫaiġ mór, diarmaitt.

Muirḟdaċ ua garmġaile prióir innsi mic nérin saoi ċonnacht hi ccraḃaḋ ⁊ in eccna [decc].

Diarmait ua fiaiċ abb reiclesa gillamolairi uí Giollarain ṫuaim décc, ⁊ a adnacal in ardċarna.

nor, King of Ireland, are set down in the following order, in the Book of Lecan: Aedh, Tadhg, Concobhar Maenmaighe, Muireadhach, Toirdhelbhach, Murchadh, Diarmaid."—Fol. 73. But it is highly probable that they are set down in the order of their celebrity, rather than in that of their births.

[d] *Melaghlin*, Maolseaċlainn.—He was the son of Toirdhealbach, who was the fifth son of Roderic O'Conor, Monarch of Ireland.

[e] *Famine.*—Thus rendered in the old translation of the Annals of Ulster:

"A. D. 1228. Hugh mac Roary tooke the kingdome of Connaght and prayed [preyed] Church and Laity of Connaght, and their Clerks & Learned men were banished into strange countrys."

[f] Under this year, 1228, the Annals of Ulster state that the justiciaryship of Ireland was assumed by Rickard, the son of William Burke.

Giustísecht na h-Erenn do ġabail do mac uilliam burc .i. ricard. Thus rendered in the old translation: "The Justiceship of Ireland taken by Mac William Bourk."

A. D. 1228. Under this year the Annals of Kilronan contain the following passages, which have been altogether omitted by the Four Masters:

"A. D. 1228. Rinn duin was plundered by Felim O'Conor and Conor Boy, the son of Turlough, and Teige, the son of Cormac, were killed, and the justiciary came to Tearmann Caoluinne, and the town was burned, as was also the church of Imleach Urchadha.

"Felim gained the victory of Cluanacha over the sons of Roderic, and over Conor, the son of Cormac."

[g] *O'Gormally*, O Gormġaile.—In the Annals

Melaghlin[d], the son of Turlough, who was the son of Roderic O'Conor, was slain by Hugh, King of Connaught.

An intolerable dearth prevailed in Connaught, in consequence of the war of the sons of Roderic. They plundered churches and territories; they banished its clergy and *ollaves* into foreign and remote countries, and others of them perished of cold and famine[e].

David O'Flynn, Chief of Sil-Maelruain, died.

Hugh, son of Donough O'Farrell, was slain by Hugh, son of Auliffe O'Farrell[f].

THE AGE OF CHRIST, 1229.

The Age of Christ, one thousand two hundred twenty-nine.

The monastery of St. Francis, at Cork, was founded by Mac Carthy More (Dermot).

Murray O'Gormally[g], Prior of Inis-macnerin[h], and the most renowned in Connaught for piety and wisdom, died.

Dermot O'Fiach, Abbot of the church of Gilla-Molaisse O'Gillarain, of Tuaim, died, and was interred at Ardcarne.

of Kilronan he is called O Ᵹopmḟúilıġ ppıoıp peġléſſa ınnſı mac neıpın."

[h] *Inis-macnerin*, Inıſ mac nEpın, now generally called Church Island. It is situated in Lough Key, near Boyle, in the county of Roscommon. Archdall thought that this was the same as Eas-mac-neirc; but it appears, from the meaning of the words and from these Annals, that they were two distinct places. The *island* [ınıſ] of the sons of Erin could not be the same as the *cataract* [eaſ] of the son of Erc. The Cistercian Abbey of Boyle was that called by the Irish maınıſteıp aṫa ꝺa laapc. Eaſ mıc neıpc is the present Assylyn; and Inıſ mac n-eıpın, or more properly ınıſ mac nEıpnín, is the present Church-Island in Lough Key. Ware, Colgan, Archdall, and Weld, have confounded these names, because they had no accurate knowledge of the localities.—See notes under the years 1209 and 1222. That the correct name of this place is Inıſ mac nEıpnín appears from the Irish Calendar of the O'Clerys; and, that it received this name from St. Barrfionn Mac Ernin, and his brothers, who were the patrons of the place, and venerated there on the 22nd of September.

> "Sept. 22. Barrfhionn Mac Ernin.
> ——— The sons of Ernin of Inis-mac n-Eirnin in Lough Key, in Connaught."

The family of O'Gormaly are still numerous in this neighbourhood; but they are to be distinguished from the uí Ᵹaıpmleaꝺaıġ, or O'Gormlys of Tyrone, who are of a different lineage. This island, which now goes by the name of Church Island, contains the ruins of a small church of great antiquity.

Diarmait mac giollaċarraiġ, airċinneaċ tiġe baoiṫin, ⁊ uasal ṡacart décc. A adhlacadh i mainistir na trinoide iar ná ḃuain amaċ ó ċeart do na canančaiḃ, do ṁanċaiḃ mainistre na buille, ⁊ boí side trí hoiḋċe gan adlacadh ar badar na manaiġ agá ḟosdadh ina mainistir feisin.

Giraird ua caṫáin cananaċ dob eccnaiḋe ro ḃaoi don ord ċananaċ décc.

Duiḃeasa ingean Ruaiḋri bean caṫail mic diarmata do écc ina cailliġ duiḃ.

Diarmaid mag carṫaiġ tiġearna dSesmuṁan décc.

Dionis ua mórḋa espcop Shíl Muireḋhaiġ do treccedh a espuccóide ar dia.

Loċlainn ua mannċáin do ṁarḃadh lá dearbraṫair a aṫar.

AOIS CRIOSD, 1230.

Aois Criost, mile, dá ċéd, trioċa.

Florent ua cSerḃalláin espcop tíre heoġain, uasal ṡSenoir toccaide decc iar sé bliadhnaiḃ ochtmogat a aoisi.

Giollaiosa ua cléiriġ espcop Luiġne, iosep mac teċedain espcop conmaicne, Mac Raiṫ Mag Serraiġ espcop conmaicne, Rool petit espcop na miḋe Riaglóir toccaide, ⁊ milidh Criost, Giolla coimdeadh ua duilennáin comarba feiċin, ⁊ ab reicclésa cananaċ easrуadara, Muirsḋaċ ua gorm-ġaile priόir innsi mic nerin, Maolmuire ua maoleóin comarba ciaráin cluana mic nóis, giollacartaiġ ua heilgiusáin canánaċ ⁊ angcoire, donn-sleḃe ua hionmainen manaċ naoṁṫa ⁊ ardmaiġistir saoir mainistre na buille décc.

[i] *Died.*—His death is entered in the Annals of Ulster, but they make no mention of the contention about his body. The entry is thus given in the old translation: "A. D. 1229. Dermot Mac Gillcarrick, Erhenagh of Tybohin, and gentle priest, and best man for Almes & liberality in those parts of Connaught, *in Christo quieuit.*"

[k] *Had attempted to retain it,* badar na manaiġ ag a fosdadh, literally, "the monks were keeping it in their own monastery;" that is, they wished to have the honour of having so holy a man interred in their sanctuary.

[l] *Duvesa.*—In the Annals of Kilronan she is called the daughter of Roderic O'Conor: Duibessa ingen Ruaiḋri hí Conċuḃair, bean caṫuil meic Diarmada do eg ina cailliġ duiḃ.

[m] *Dionysius O'More.*—In the Annals of Clonmacnoise, as translated by Mageoghegan, he is called, "Denis O'More, Bushopp of Oilfynn." He resigned the duties of his bishopric to apply himself more sedulously to devotion.

[n] *Rool Petit.*—He is called Ralph Petit in Harris's edition of Ware's Bishops, p. 142. In

Dermot Mac Gillacarry, Erenagh of Tibohine, and a noble priest, died[i]. He was buried in the monastery of the Holy Trinity, his body having been by right obtained by the canons, from the monks of the monastery of Boyle, after it had remained three nights unburied, because the monks had attempted to retain it[k] in their own monastery.

Gerard O'Kane, the wisest of the order of canons, died.

Duvesa[l], daughter of Roderic [O'Conor], and wife of Cathal Mac Dermot, died a nun.

Dermot Mac Carthy, Lord of Desmond, died.

Dionysius O'More[m], Bishop of Sil-Murray [Elphin], resigned his bishopric for the sake of God.

Loughlin O'Monahan was killed by his father's brother.

THE AGE OF CHRIST, 1230.

The Age of Christ, one thousand two hundred thirty.

Florence O'Carolan, Bishop of Tyrone, a noble and select senior, died in the eighty-sixth year of his age.

Gilla-Isa O'Clery, Bishop of Leyny [Achonry]; Joseph Mac Techedan, Bishop of Conmaicne [Ardagh]; Magrath Mac Sherry, Bishop of Conmaicne; Rool Petit[n] (Rodolphus Petit), Bishop of Meath, a select ruler and soldier of Christ; Gilla-Coimdeadh O'Duileannain, Coarb of St. Feichin, and Abbot of the church of the Canons at Easdara [Ballysadare]; Murray O'Gormally, Prior of Inis-mac-nerin; Mulmurry O'Malone, Coarb of St. Kieran, of Clonmacnoise; Gilla-Carthy O'Helgiusain, a canon and anchorite; and Donslevy O'Hinmainen[o], a holy monk and the chief master of the carpenters of the monastery of Boyle, died.

the Annals of Kilronan his death is thus entered under the year 1229: "Rool Peıcıc epp̄. na mıḋe, *uir religiosus et caritatissimus, et Dei famulus in Christo quieuit.*"

[o] This passage is thus correctly translated in Archdall's Monasticon: "Died Donn Sleibhe O'Hionmaine, a reverend and holy monk, and now principal master of the carpenters of this Abbey."

In the Dublin copy of the Annals of Ulster his death is entered thus: A. D. 1230. Ꝺonnꞅleıbe hua ınmuınen naem ⁊ maıᵹıꞅceꞃ ꞅaeꞃ quıeuıc ın Chꞃıꞅco; and thus rendered in the old translation: "A. D. 1230. Dunleve O'Inmanen, a sacred monk and free master, died." In the Annals of Kilronan, he is styled Manaċ

Maolseċlainn mac firedind uasal saccart ⁊ maiġistir leiġinn décc ina noirst manaiġ i mainistir na buille.

Sloicceaḋ la hua ndomnaill (domnall mor) hi ccuicceaḋ Connaċt ind aghaiḋ Aoḋa mic Ruaiḋrí í Choncobair baoi hi ffriṫḃert fris co ro ṁill maġ naoí, ⁊ morán don tír, act ara aoí ní ro ġiallsat clann Ruaiḋri don dul sin.

Sloiccheaḋ la mac uilliam búrc i cconnaċtaiḃ gur milleaḋ morán do Connaċtaiḃ lais, ⁊ ro marbaḋ donn óg mag oireċtaiġ, ⁊ eiċtiġearn mac an

naoṁ ⁊ ardṁaiġisdir saor mainisdreċ na buille. "Monachus sanctus, et archimagister fabrorum Monasterii Buellensis." The word saor means cheap, free, noble, as an adjective, and an artificer, as a noun. It is very probable that it is a noun in this sentence, and in the genitive case plural, governed by maiġisdir. But if we take saor to be an adjective, and prefix it to mainisdreċ, thus: ardṁáiġistir saor-ṁainisdreċ na ḃúille, then it will mean "chief master of the free (or noble) monastery of Boyle; and if we make it an adjective belonging to ardṁaiġistir, the translation will be "noble or free head master (or teacher) of the monastery of Boyle."

p A. D. 1230. The Annals of Kilronan give a much longer account of the death of Donn Oge Mageraghty, and of the contentions between the son of William Burke and the Connacians, but under the year 1229. It is as follows:

"A. D. 1229. Hugh, the son of Roderic, and the Connacians in general, turned against the son of William Burke and the English, through the solicitations of Donn Oge, son of Donncahy Mageraghty, and of Cormac, the son of Tomaltagh Mac Dermot of the Rock, and his retainers, for they had pledged their word that they would not belong to any king who would bring them into the house of the English. Hugh, the son of Roderic, and the people of West Connaught, plundered the young son of William and Adam Duff; and Donn Oge and the sons of Manus [O'Conor], and the young soldiers of the Sil-Murray, plundered Mac Costello and Hy-Many. The son of William, however, mustered the greater part of the English of Ireland, and many of the Irish, and marched into Connaught, accompanied by Felim, the son of Cathal Crovderg, to give him the kingdom of Connaught, and to expel Hugh, the son of Roderic, and every Connacian who had joined him and opposed himself [the son of William]. They first advanced to the castle of Bun-Galvy" [i. e. the castle at the mouth of the River Gaillimh, which flows through the town of Galway], "to attack Hugh O'Flaherty. Then Hugh, the son of Roderic, went to the relief of Hugh O'Flaherty, and was joined by the Connacians under the conduct of the sons of Murtough [Muimhneach] O'Conor; and the Connacians were on the west side of the River Galliv, and the English on the east side, and great conflicts were daily carried on between them. The English, having remained here for some time, without having obtained either peace, hostages, or pledges from the Connacians, consulted together, and resolved upon going in pursuit of the cows and the people who had fled into the mountains and fastnesses of the country and upon the islands, and they went that night from the castle of Bungalvy to Droichead Inghine Goillin [i. e. the bridge of the daughter of Goillin] where the morning rose upon them.

Melaghlin Mac Firedinn, a noble priest and a professor of literature, died in his monastic noviciate in the monastery of Boyle.

An army was led by O'Donnell (Donnell More) into Connaught, against Hugh, the son of Roderic O'Conor, who was opposed to him, and destroyed Moynai and a great part of the country [province]. The sons of Roderic, however, did not give him hostages on this occasion.

An army was led by the son of William Burke into Connaught, and desolated a large portion of that country, and Donn Oge Mageraghty[p] and Egh-

Then the son of William inquired, 'Is there a pass between us and the lake, by which a party of the Connacians could come down?' The Guides answered and said, 'There is.' He then arrayed a party of horse to proceed to Cong and Kilmaine (or Inishmaine). At this time it happened that great numbers of the Connacians were coming early in the morning from Cong, having unwisely and unwarily passed the night before in parties of two and three, and a few of the better sort among them were slain under the conduct of the officers of Murtough, the son of Manus O'Conor, namely, Dermot O'Henaghan, Loughlin Mac Classan, and Teige Mac Gilchreest O'Mulrenin. With respect to the English, they proceeded after this fortunate occurrence to Mayo of the Saxons, and on the day following they went to Toberpatrick [the Abbey of Ballintober], where the canons and victuallers of the town came to the son of William and begged of him, for the love of God, not to stay with them that night. This request of their's was complied with, and the English moved onwards to Muine Maicin; and they would not have marched from Mayo so far, were it not that they had not obtained hostages or pledges from Manus, the son of Murtough Muimhneach. On the next day they proceeded to Achadh Fabhuir [Aghagower], and encamped in the town, on the east side of the church, that is, at Margenana, on the margin of Lough Crichan. Hither Manus, the son of Murtough, came into their house, and gave them hostages. On the day following the English returned to Muine Maicin, and remained there for a night, and on the next day they went to Magh Sine, and thence they passed through Leyny, and Ceis Corann; thence they set out for Coirshliabh [the Curlieu mountains], where though the guides missed the common pass, they crossed the whole mountain without meeting any accident. With respect to Hugh, the son of Roderic, and Cormac, the son of Tomaltagh of the Rock, who was the son of Conor Mac Dermot, and Donn Oge Mageraghty, and the Sil-Murray, they were at this time in a wood, and the resolution they proposed was this, as they had sent their cows and people into the fastnesses of Muintir-Eolais, and of Sliabh an Iarainn, not to come in collision with the English on this occasion; but Donn Oge said that he would not agree to this resolution; but that he would proceed to the west side of the English; and he set out forthwith for Fincarn, accompanied by his own brother, the youths of Sil-Murray, his English allies, the son of Donnell Bregach O'Melaghlin with his English, and Brian, the son of Turlough O'Conor. On his arrival at Fincarn, Donn sent forth to battle a body of his troops, who fought well with the English, while he himself remained on the top of the carn, earnestly looking on at the conflict. Then the English sent a countless number of

ḃreiṫeaṁain í ṁionaċain ⁊ sochaiḋe oile náċ áirimṫer, ⁊ ro hionnarbadh (tria anfforlann) Aoḋ mac Ruaiḋri Rí Connaċt lá mac uilliam, ⁊ lá gallaiḃ don ċur sin go haoḋ ua néill tre iompúḋ ḋó ar ġallaiḃ, ⁊ ro ríoġaḋ feiḋlim mac caṫail croiḃdeirg lá mac uilliam.

Aoḋ ó néill tiġearna tire heogain ríoġdaṁna Ereann uile, cosnaṁṫaċ leṫe cuinn ré gallaiḃ Ereann, ⁊ ré leṫ moġa nuaḋat. Fer ná tucc geill, eitirsḋa, ná cíos do ġall na do ġaoiḋeal, fer do rad maḋmanna, ⁊ ára móra mence for ġallaiḃ. Aircṫeoir gall ⁊ gaoiḋeal. Fer ro triall ionnsoiġiḋ Ereann uile décc gen gur saoileaḋ bás naile dfaġḃáil ḋó act a ṫuitim lá gallaiḃ.

Art mac airt uí ruairc do marḃaḋ lá raġnall ua ffinḋ i meaḃail.

Maolseaċlainn ua mannaċáin do ṁarḃaḋ la a ḃraiṫriḃ.

archers and horsemen towards the carn, and they were not perceived until they had the carn surrounded, and Donn Oge was thus left almost alone, being accompanied only by Brian, the son of Turlough O'Conor, and a few of his own relatives; and these were but a short time left thus together. Donn Oge, being left thus unprotected, was soon recognized, and many archers pressed upon him, and five arrows entered him; he was at length overtaken by one horseman, and though he had no weapon but a battle axe, he prevented the horseman from closing upon him, but the horseman drove his spear though him at each push. At last the archers surrounded him on every side, and he fell attempting to defend himself against an overwhelming number."

"With respect to Hugh, the son of Roderic, he was stationed at the east side of the English, and he did not wish to come to an engagement, and indeed it was against his will that Donn had done so, nor did he know that Donn had been killed. The routed forces were driven towards him, but Hugh escaped by the strength of his hand without discredit. One man pressed upon him, but he turned upon that man, and gave him a shot of the javelin which he held in his hand, and sent its shaft through him, after which he made his escape.

"The English, being fortunate in thus cutting off Donn Oge, carried away great spoils on their way to Sliabh an Iarainn, and they killed women and children, and stripped those they had not killed. They carried great booties to the English camp. In consequence of this spoliation many of the natives perished of cold and famine. On the next day the English departed, leaving the kingdom of Connaught to Felim, the son of Cathal Crovderg, and banished Hugh, the son of Roderic, to Hugh O'Neill."

In the Annals of Clonmacnoise, as translated by Mageoghegan, it is stated, under the year 1230, that Donn Og Mac Aireaghtie was killed by Ffelym O'Connor, and by Mac William Burke, at the mount called Slieve Seysie [the Curlieus].

[q] *Hugh O'Neill.*—The notice of the death and character of this O'Neill is thus given in the Annals of Clonmacnoise, as translated by Mageoghegan: "A. D. 1230. Hugh O Neale, King of Aileagh, the greatest spoyler of the Churchmen and Churches of Connaught, and the only banisher and extyrper of the English, and destroyer of the Irish, died." And thus in the

tighern, the son of the Brehon O'Minaghan, and many others not enumerated, were slain. Hugh, the son of Roderic, King of Connaught, was expelled by the son of William [Burke] and the English (by overwhelming numbers), on this occasion, to Hugh O'Neill, because he had risen up against the English; and Felim, the son of Cathal Crovderg, was proclaimed King [of Connaught] by the son of William [Burke].

Hugh O'Neill[q], Lord of Tyrone[r] and Roydamna [heir presumptive to the throne] of all Ireland,—the defender of Leth-Chuinn against the English of Ireland and [the people of] Leth-Mhogha Nuadhat; who had never rendered hostages, pledges, or tribute, to English or Irish; who had gained victories over the English, and cut them off with great and frequent slaughter; the plunderer of the English and Irish; a man who had attempted the subjugation of all Ireland,—died[s] [a natural death], although it was never supposed that he would die in any other way than to fall by [the hands of] the English.

Art, the son of Art O'Rourke, was treacherously[t] slain by Randal O'Finn.

Melaghlin O'Monahan was slain by his relatives[u].

old translation of the Annals of Ulster: "A. D. 1230. Hugh O Neile, King of the north of Ireland, and King of all Leithquin, and that shou'd bee King of all Ireland; a man that most killed and prayed" [preyed] "Galls, and broke most Castles of the Irish, died, and a man thought less to dye by the Galls." A much more patriotic character of him is given in the Annals of Kilronan under the year 1229, thus: "A. D. 1229. Hugh O'Neill died in this year. He was King of the Kinel-Owen, and inferior to none in renown and goodness; a king who had not given hostages or pledges to any man English or Irish; a king who had gained many victories over the English, and had slain many of them; a king who was the support of all the Irish; who had never been expelled or exiled; a king the most hospitable and defensive that had come of the Irish for a long period."

[r] *Tyrone*, τιρ Εoġαιn, comprised the present counties of Tyrone and Londonderry, and the baronies of Inishowen and Raphoe, in the county of Donegal. The inhabitants bore the generic name of Kinel-Owen, and had at this period branched off into various families, who were all tributary to one archchief, commonly called ριġ ċιnειl εoġαιn; and who was sometimes of the family of Mac Loughlin, sometimes of that of O'Neill, and, in one or two instances, of that of O'Flaherty, now Laverty, descended from Aedh Allan, who was one of the sixteen monarchs of the Kinel-Owen race. These once great family names are still numerous in this region; but none bearing them at present are above the rank of farmers, except those who have entered into holy orders.

[s] *Died*, δécc.—The phrase used in the Dublin copy of the Annals of Ulster, is "*quievit in Christo*."

[t] *Treacherously*, ι mεαḃαιl.—In the old translation of the Annals of Ulster, this sentence is rendered: "Art mac Art ORoirke killed by Ranall O Fin *mutherously*."

[u] *Relatives*, bραιṫριḃ.—The word bράṫαιρ in

AOIS CRIOSD, 1231.

Aois Criosd, mile, da ċéd triocha, a háon.

Dionis ua morḋa epscop ailfinn do crioċnuccaḋ a bethaḋ in oilen na trinóide ar loċ cé an .15. do december ⁊ donnchaḋ ua conċobair doirdneaḋ na ionaḋ.

Flann ua connaċtaiġ epscop ua mbriuin breifne décc.

Stefán ua braoin airċinneċ Maiġe eó [decc].

Céleċair ua dobailén airċinnech camċa fear derċaċ, craibdeaċ, eccnaiḋe, ernaiġteċ [decc].

Feṫḟoilge inġen ċonċobair mic diarmata bean muirceartaiġ muiṁniġ mic toirrḋealbaiġ móir [decc] maṫairriḋe Maġnusa mic Muircertaiġ, ċonċobair ruaiḋ, ṫuaṫail, ⁊ ṫoirrḋealbaiġ ṡaccairt, ⁊ priórir recclesa peadair ⁊ póil.

Dubcoblaiġ inġen conċobair mic diarmata décc i mainistir na búille.

Flaiṫbertaċ ua flannaccáin taoiseaċ cloinne caṫail meic muireḋaiġ muillṫain décc ina oiliṫre i mainistir na búille. Dubṫemraċ inġean uí ċuinn bean an Flaiṫbeartaiġ hisin décc.

Ualgarcc ua Ruairc tiġearna breifne décc ina ailiṫre ar sliġiḋ an tsroṫa.

Giollaiosa mac samraḋáin tiġearna teallaiġ eċdaċ, ⁊ duindín ua Maolconaire ollaṁ síl muireḋhaiġ muillṫain décc.

ancient manuscripts signifies a brother; but in the modern Irish language bráṫair means a kinsman, and dearbraṫair is the word used to denote a brother.

[w] *Bishop of Hy-Briuin Breifney.*—This is the Bishop of Kilmore, called Florence O'Conacty in Harris's Ware, vol. i. p. 226. In the Annals of Ulster he is called Bishop of Breifney, and in those of Kilronan, Bishop of Hy-Briuin.

[x] *Of Camma*, camċa.—A parish church in the barony of Athlone, and county of Roscommon, dedicated to St. Bridget. The small village of Tober Brighde, generally called in English Brideswell, is in it. We learn from a tract preserved in the Book of Lecan, fol. 92, treating of O'Kelly, and his people of Hy-Many, that all the Hy-Many were baptized here. "St. Bridget has the baptism of the race of Mainé, and although the children may not (always) be brought to her church to be baptized, her Coarb has the power to collect the baptismal penny from these tribes. This money is divided into three parts, of which she herself (*rectius* her Coarb) has one part, Druim Dreastan (now Drum parish) the second, and Cluain Eamhain (now Cloonoun) the other third part."—See *Tribes and Customs of Hy-Many*, printed for the Irish Archæological Society, p. 78, note [d], and map to the same work.

[y] *Fethfoilge.*—In the Annals of Kilronan she

THE AGE OF CHRIST, 1231.

The Age of Christ, one thousand two hundred thirty-one.

Dionysius O'More, Bishop of Elphin, closed his days on the Island of the Blessed Trinity on Lough Key, on the 15th of December, and Donough O'Conor was appointed in his place.

Flann O'Connaghty, Bishop of Hy-Briuin Breifney[w] [Kilmore], died.

Stephen O'Breen, Erenagh of Mayo [died].

Keleher O'Devlin, Erenagh of Camma[x], a charitable, pious, wise, and prayerful man [died].

Fethfoilge[y], daughter of Conor Mac Dermot, and wife of Murtough Muimhneach, the son of Turlough More [died]. She was the mother of Manus, Conor Roe, Tuathal, and Turlough the Priest, Prior of the Church of SS. Peter and Paul.

Duvcovlagh, daughter of Conor Mac Dermot, died in the monastery of Boyle.

Flaherty O'Flanagan, Chief of the race of Cathal, the son of Muireadhach Muilleathan[z], died on his pilgrimage in the monastery of Boyle. Duvtawragh, daughter of O'Quin, and wife of this Flaherty, died.

Ualgarg O'Rourke, Lord of Breifney, died on his way to the River [Jordan].

Gilla-Isa Magauran, Lord of Tealach Eachdhach[a], and Duinnin O'Mulconry, Ollave [chief poet] of the race of Muireadhach Muilleathan [the Sil-Murray], died.

is called Fethfailghe (Fefalia), and her death is thus noticed: "A. D. 1231. Fethfailghe, the daughter of Conor Mac Dermot, and the wife of Murtough Muimhneach, the son of Turlough More O'Conor, died this year. She was the largest, the most beautiful, the most hospitable, the most chaste, and the most famous woman of Leith Chuinn. She was the mother of Manus, Conor Roe, Tuathal, and Turlough the priest, i. e. the Prior of the Regles of SS. Peter and Paul."

[z] *The race of Cathal, son of Muireadhach Muilleathan.*—This was the tribe name of the O'Flanagans, the O'Morans, and their correlatives. The extent of their territory is still remembered in the neighbourhood of Elphin, Belanagare, and Mantua, between which it principally lies.—See note [h], under the year 1193, pp. 97, 98.

[a] *Tealach Eachdhach*, now sometimes called Tullaghagh, but generally Tullyhaw, a barony in the north-west of the county of Cavan, the ancient inheritance of the family of Magauran, or Magovern. The level part of this barony, containing the village of Ballymagovern, or Ballymagauran, i. e. Magauran's town, was anciently called Magh Sleacht.

Conċoḃar gott ua hEaġra tiġearna Luiġne décc.

Slóiccedh lá Domhnall ua nDomhnaill tiġearna tíre Conaill, ⁊ lá hAonġus mac Gillefinnéin co soċraide fear Manaċ do saiġidh i Raiġilliġ Caṫail. Ruccsat loinccsi leó for Loċ Uaċtair, ⁊ ro airccsit Eó inis. Tucsat ariar lá taoḃ seód maoíne ⁊ ionnmus an baile uile leó

Feidhlimidh mac Caṫail Croiḃdeirg do ġaḃail la mac Uilliam Búrc i míliucc tar slánaiḃ maiṫe Gall Éreann.

AOIS CRIOSD, 1232.

Aois Criost, míle, dá ċéd, tríoċa, a dó.

Faċtna ua hAllgaiṫ comorba Droma Mucadha, ⁊ oificel ua fFiaċraċ fer tiġe aoidhedh, leiġinn, ⁊ luḃra, ⁊ lersaiġṫe truaġ do écc.

Tempall Cille móire i ttír Briúin na Sionna do coisreccadh lá Donnchadh

[b] *Conor God*, Conċoḃar Gott.—In the Annals of Ulster and of Kilronan the name is written Concobor God. The adjective god is used in medical Irish MSS., to translate the Latin *balbus*, or *balbutiens*.

[c] *An army was led.*—This event is given somewhat more satisfactorily in the Annals of Kilronan, as follows:

"A. D. 1231. A great army was led by Donnell O'Donnell, King of Tirconnell, and by Aengus Mac Gilla-Finnen, against Cathal O'Reilly, and they brought a fleet [of boats and cots] with them upon Lough Oughter, and plundered Eo-inis, and killed the best white steed that was in Ireland, and carried away Cacht, the daughter of Mac Fiachrach, the wife of O'Reilly, and the jewels and goods of the whole town."

[d] *Mac Gilla-Finnen*, now made Mac Gillinnion.—The name is still very common in the west of the county of Fermanagh; but many have changed it to Leonard. This family is of the Kinel-Connell race, and descend from Flaherty Mac Loingsigh, who was Monarch of Ireland from the year 727 to 734. For the pedigree of this family see *Battle of Magh Rath*, printed for the Irish Archæological Society in 1842, p. 335.

[e] *Eo-inis.*—Archdall states that Eo-inis, or Inis-eo, was an island in Lough Erne; and even Colgan, in *Acta SS.*, p. 222, places Inis-eo, not Eo-inis, in Lough Erne; but this passage affords evidence to shew that Eo-inis was in Lough Oughter. It is at present the name of an island in Lough Oughter, Anglicised Eanish (Eá-inis, in accordance with the Ultonian pronunciation), but no remains of antiquity are to be seen on it, except an earthen fort.

[f] Under this year the Annals of Kilronan record, that Cormac, the son of Tomaltagh [Mac Dermot], commenced the erection of a market-town at Port na Cairrge. This is the place now called Rockingham, the well known and magnificent seat of Lord Lorton.

[g] *Faghtna.*—This entry is given somewhat differently and better in the Annals of Kilronan, as follows:

A. D. 1232. Faċtna O hAllgaiṫ comarba

Conor God[b] O'Hara, Lord of Leyny, died.

An army was led[c] by Donnell O'Donnell, Lord of Tirconnell, and Aengus Mac Gilla-Finnen[d], with the forces of Fermanagh, against O'Reilly (Cathal): they brought boats with them upon Lough Oughter, and plundered Eo-inis[e], and, after obtaining their own award, they carried away with them all the jewels, treasures, and wealth of the whole town.

Felim, the son of Cathal Crovderg (O'Conor), was taken prisoner by the son of William Burke, at Meelick, in violation of the guarantee given by all the English chieftains in Ireland[f].

THE AGE OF CHRIST, 1232.

The Age of Christ, one thousand two hundred thirty-two.

Faghtna[g] O'Hallgaith, Coarb of Drumacoo[h], and official of Hy-Fiachrach [Aidhne], who had kept an open house for strangers, the sick, and the indigent, and also for the instruction of the people, died.

The church of Kilmore[i], in Hy-Briuin na-Sinna, was consecrated by

dromma mucadha, 7 Oirpirdel ua Fiachrach, fear tighe aidheadh, 7 lubhra 7 leighinn 7 lessuighthi tíre 7 talman in oc anno quieuit.

"A. D. 1232. Faghtna O'Hallgaith, Coarb of Druim Mucadha, and official of Hy-Fiachrach, a man who had kept a house for the entertainment of strangers and of the sick, and also for the instruction and improvement of the country and the land, *in hoc anno quieuit.*"

[h] *Of Drumacoo*, Dromma mucadha.—A parish belonging to the diocese of Kilmacduagh, in the barony of Dunkellin, and county of Galway.—See Ordnance Map of the County of Galway, sheet 103; and also *Tribes and Customs of Hy-Many*, printed for the Irish Archæological Society in the year 1843, p. 71, note [b], where it is shewn that the territory of Hy-Fiachrach Aidhne was co-extensive with the present diocese of Kilmacduagh. See also the map prefixed to the same work, on which this church is shewn, under the name of druim mocua, as in the district of COILL UA BH-FIACHRACH, a short distance to the south-west of Kilcolgan, and not far from the margin of the Bay of Galway.

[i] *Kilmore*, in Hy-Briuin-na-Sinna,—now Kilmore, a parish church in the district now called Tirarune, but anciently Tir-Briuin, situated in the east of the county of Roscommon, stretching along the western bank of the River Shannon, and about six miles east of Elphin. Archdall has confounded this place with Coill-mor, near St. John's, at Lough Ree.

There is a curious stone inserted in the wall of the church-yard of Kilmore, exhibiting a fragment of an inscription in Saxon characters, which runs thus:

"A. D. M: CCC.L: VII. EATHEAN INGEAN MIC BRANAN ME FECIT."

"A. D. 1357. EATHEAN DAUGHTER OF MAC BRANAN, MADE ME."

ua Concoḃáir epscop ailfinn, ⁊ canánaiġ do ḋénaṁ isin mbaile ceona lá Conn ua Flannaccain baoí na prioir ann.

Tiobraitte ua braoin comorba commáin saoí cléirceċta, sḟncusa, ⁊ brḟitḟṁnasa décc in inis Cloṫrann ina ailiṫre.

Aoḋ mac amlaoiḃ mic domnaill uí fearġail toiseaċ muintire hangaile do loscaḋ ar inis loċa cúile lá cloinn aoḋa ciabaiġ mic murchaḋa uí ferġail iar ccaiṫḟṁ naoí mbliaḋan i ttoisiġeċt na hangaile dḟis murchaiḋ carraiġ í ferġail.

Maġnus mac aṁlaiḃ mic taiḋg mic maolruanaiḋ caindel einiġ, eangnaṁa, ⁊ craḃaiḋ décc.

Donnchaḋ mac tomaltaiġ meic diarmada saoí ar eineaċ, ⁊ ar ḟngnam, lettroman Connaċt do ecc is in aicideċt.

Concoḃar mac Aoḋa mic Ruaiḋri do éluḋ ó gallaiḃ, ⁊ clanna toíseaċ Connaċt do ṫionól ina ṫimċeall. ⁊ a ndol is na tuaṫaiḃ ar ionnsaiġiḋ. Ro marḃaḋ tra eirioṁ las na Tuathaiḃ, ⁊ giollaceallaiġ ua hḟiḋin, giolla-criost mac donnchaḋa mic diarmada, ⁊ sochaiḋe amaille friú. Asé an lá sin ro ġealsat na tuaṫa na saṁṫaċa uile, an tan atruḃrad fear saṁ-ṫaiġe gile do ṁarḃaḋ meic aodha.

Riġe do ṫaḃairt daoḋ mac Ruaiḋri lá mac uilliam búrc do ridire, ⁊ siṫ do dénaṁ dó ris iar ngaḃáil fḟiḋlim mic caṫail croiḃdeirg dó.

[k] *There.*—This passage is rendered as follows in the old translation of the Annals of Ulster: "A. D. 1232. The church of Kilmore sanctified, and canons made in the same by Con O'Flanagan."

[l] *Coarb of St. Coman*, i. e. the Abbot of Roscommon. Inisclothrann is an island, containing the ruins of seven churches, in Lough Ree, an expansion of the Shannon between the counties of Longford and Roscommon.—See note under the year 1193.

[m] *Auliffe*, aṁlaoiḃ.—He was the son of Teige, who was the son of Mulrony, the ancestor after whom the Mac Dermots of Moylurg were called Clann-Mulrony.

[n] *Aicideacht.*—Under the year 1206 Mac Dermot is called Lord of Moylurg, Airteach, and Aicidheacht; and at the year 1273, O'Quin is styled leṫṫoiseaċ na haicideaċta, from which it would appear that this was another name for the territory of the Clann Cuain, in which Mac Dermot had a house on an island in the lake called Claenloch, (see entry under the year 1187, p. 79, note[k]), and which O'Quin had placed under the protection of Mac Dermot about the year 1150. The word aiciḋeaċta is used in the Annals of Kilronan in such a manner as will shew that it was used to denote chiefry, as in the following passage: "A. D. 1225. Coimeirge coċta deirge is in mbliaḋain si la Toirrdealbaċ mac Ruaiḋri mic Toirrḋealbaiġ, 7 le h Aeḋ mac Ruaiḋri 7 le hAoḋ O Neill do cosnum cuicid Connaċt re hAeḋ mac Caṫail Croiḃdeirg tre forcongraḋ Duinn Oig meg oireaċtaiġ, riġ-

Donough O'Conor, Bishop of Elphin; and canons were appointed in the same town by Conn O'Flanagan, who was Prior there[k].

Tipraide O'Breen, Coarb of St. Coman[l], who was learned in theology, history, and law, died on the island of Inis-Clothran, on his pilgrimage.

Hugh, the son of Auliffe, who was son of Donnell O'Farrell, Chief of Annaly, was burned on the island of Inis Locha Cuile by the sons of Hugh Ciabach, the son of Morogh O'Ferrall, having been nine years Chief of Annaly, from the death of his predecessor, Morrogh Carrach O'Ferrall.

Manus, son of Auliffe[m], the son of Teige Mac Mulrony, lamp of hospitality, feats of arms, and piety, died.

Donough, son of Tomaltagh Mac Dermot, eminent for his hospitality and feats of arms, died in Aicideacht[n],—a great loss to Connaught.

Conor, son of Hugh, the son of Roderic, made his escape from the English, and the sons of the chiefs of Connaught assembled around him, and they made an incursion into the Tuathas; but Conor, with Gilla-Kelly O'Heyne, and Gilchreest, the son of Donough Mac Dermot, and many others along with them, were slain by the people of the Tuathas. This was the day on which [the people of] the Tuathas whitened[o] all the handles of their battle-axes, because it was rumoured that it was by a man who carried a white handled battle-axe that the son of Hugh had been slain.

The kingdom [of Connaught] was again given to Hugh, the son of Roderic, by the son of William Burke[p], who made peace with him after he had taken Felim, son of Cathal Crovderg, prisoner.

ṫaoiriġ ṡil Muireaḋaiġ a ndiġuil a ḟearainn 7 a aicideaċta do ḃuain de. i. e. A war was kindled in this year by Turlough, the son of Roderic, who was the son of Turlough, and Hugh, the son of Roderic, and by Hugh O'Neill, in contesting the province of Connaught with Hugh, the son of Cathal Crovderg, at the solicitation of Donn Oge Mageraghty, royal chieftain of Sil-Murray, in revenge of the loss of his lands and *Aicidheacht*."

[o] *Whitened*, ro ġealsat, i. e. a rumour having spread abroad, that the person who slew him carried a white-handled battle axe, each of those who had opposed him whitened the handle of his battle-axe, in order that his slayer might not be identified, from fear of the vengeance of his father, who was then very powerful, and became King of Connaught immediately after.

[p] *The son of William Burke.*—This was the celebrated Richard de Burgo, who was called the Great Lord of Connaught. He was the son of William Fitz-Adelm de Burgo, by Isabel, natural daughter of Richard I., and widow of Llewellyn, Prince of Wales. He is said to have struck off the arm of King Roderic O'Conor, in the Battle of Leithridh, near Dublin. He was

Caiplén bona gaillme do denam lá Riocapd de bupcc, ⁊ caiplén dúin iomgáin do ṫindpcſccal lá hadam Sdondún.

Giolla na naom ua dálaig paoí pé dán, ⁊ lé tíg aidead coitcſnn do congbáil do ṫpuaċcaib ⁊ do ṫpénaib décc.

Maeleóin bodap ua Maolconaipe do gabail cluana bolcáin.

Fſidlimid mac caṫail cpoibdeipg do léccad amaċ lá gallaib.

Concubap mac neill uí gaipmlſdhaig toipeaċ cenel Moain décc.

Sloigead lá domnall ua laċlainn tigeapna típe heogain co ngallaib, ⁊ co ngaoidealaib i ttíp conaill dia po mill móp hi ppánait, ⁊ tuc bpaigde domnaill uí baoigill, ⁊ uí taipceipt lſip.

Slóiccead lá hua ndomnaill i ttíp eogain co piaċt tulaċ nócc dia po ṁapb bú iomda dia po loipc apbanna, ⁊ dia po milleadh mopan, ⁊ tainic ap cúla co copccpach.

Midbeċ ⁊ ſaghimip do opccain lá cinél eogain uaip do poċtattap a

Lord Deputy of Ireland in 1227, and died on his passage to France in January, 1243, in proceeding to meet the King of England at Bourdeaux, attended by his barons and knights. He married Hodierna, daughter of Robert de Gernon, and grand-daughter, maternally, of Cathal Crovderg O'Conor, King of Connaught, and had by her two sons, Walter and William, the former of whom marrying Maud, daughter and heiress of Hugh de Lacy, Junior, became, in her right, Earl of Ulster on the death of his father-in-law, and had by her one son, Richard, commonly called the Red Earl, who was considered the most powerful subject in Ireland.—See Pedigree of the Earl of Clanrickard by Duald Mac Firbis, O'Clery, Lodge, and Burke; and the manuscript entitled *Historia Familiæ De Burgo*, preserved in the MS. Library of Trinity College, Dublin, F. 4, 13.

[q] *Of Bungalvy*, bona gaillme, i. e. of the mouth of the River of Galway, from which river the town takes its name. In Mageoghegan's translation of the Annals of Clonmacnoise, this name is Anglicised Bonagalvie, thus: "A. D. 1222. The Castle of Bonagalvie was made by the son of William Burk;" and in the old translation of the Annals of Ulster it is made Bun-Gallaway. Thus:

"A. D. 1232. An army by William Burke [*recte*, the son of William Burke] to the castle of Bun-Gallaway, and there made another castle." This castle was erected near the mouth of the River Galway, on the east side.

There had been an earlier castle erected here in the year 1124 by the Irish. See the earlier part of these Annals at the years 1124, 1132, 1149; see also O'Flaherty's Account of West Connaught, printed for the Irish Archæological Society in 1845, p. 31; and Hardiman's History of Galway, p. 47, note [u]; and the old map of Galway in the same work, at p. 30.

[r] *Dunamon*, Dun Iomguin.—A place on the River Suck, on the borders of the counties of Roscommon and Galway. Tradition says that Dunamon was originally the residence of O'Finaghty, whose territory, consisting of forty-eight ballys, or townlands, lay on both sides of the River Suck, and this tradition is curiously corroborated by a notice given of this family in

The castle of Bungalvy[q] was erected by Rickard de Burgo, and the erection of the castle of Dunamon[r] was commenced by Adam Staunton.

Gilla-na-naev O'Daly, a learned poet, who had kept a house of hospitality for the indigent and the mighty, died.

Malone Bodhar [the Deaf] O'Mulconry took Cluain Bolcain[s].

Felim, the son of Cathal Crovderg, was set at liberty by the English.

Conor, the son of Niall O'Gormly, Chief of Kinel-Moen, died.

Donnell O'Loughlin, Lord of Tyrone, at the head of an army composed of the English and Irish, made an incursion into Tirconnell, and did much injury in Fanat[t], and carried away the hostages of Donnell O'Boyle and O'Tairchirt.

An army was led by O'Donnell into Tyrone, and arrived at Tullaghoge, on which occasion he killed many cows, burned the corn crops, and did much injury, and *then* returned home in triumph.

Mevagh[u] and Aughnish[w] were plundered by the Kinel-Owen, for their ships

Mac Firbis's Book of Pedigrees, the original of which is in the possession of Lord Roden, and a faithful copy of it in the Library of the Royal Irish Academy. The literal translation of it is as follows:

"Conmhach was the son of Muireadhach, and he was his eldest son, and in consequence of this seniority, the descendants of Conmhach (though inferior in power) are entitled to great privileges from the descendants of the other sons of Muireadhach, viz., to drink the first cup at every feast and banquet of a king: and all the descendants of the other sons of Muireadhach must rise up before the representative of Conmhach, or Chief of Clann Conway. O'Finaghty was the royal chieftain of Clann Conway, and had forty-eight ballys about the Suck before the English Invasion; but the Burkes drove him from his patrimonial inheritance, so that there liveth not of the family of O'Finaghty, at the time of writing this Book (1650), any one more illustrious than the blessed and miraculous priest, James, whose brothers are William and Redmond, sons of Cathal, son of Donough, son of Hugh, son of Rory, son of Cathal, son of Teige Oge, son of Teige, son of Cathal."

Dunamon, ดun ıomǥuın, means the dun or fort of Iomghuin, a man's name: the dun is yet in existence.—See Ordnance Map of the County of Roscommon, sheet 38; and of Galway, sheets 8 and 20.

[s] *Fanat.*—A district in the north-east of the barony of Kilmacrenan, in the county of Donegal.—See note [s], under the year 1186, p. 70.

[t] *Cluain Bolcain.*—The O'Mulconrys were, and are still, seated at Clonahee, near Strokestown, in the county of Roscommon; but there is no place in that neighbourhood now called Cluain Bolcain.

[u] *Mevagh,* mıoḃeaċ.—A parish in the barony of Kilmacrenan, and county of Donegal, a part of which forms a well-known promontory called Ros Guill, extending into Sheephaven and the Atlantic Ocean.—See Ordnance Map of the County of Donegal, sheets 7 and 16.

[w] *Aughnish,* Eaǥınır, *recte* eaċ-ınır, i. e. *horse-island.*—An island in Lough Swilly, near Rathmelton, in the east of the barony of Kilmacrenan,

loingsiḃ an dú sin, ⁊ do rala drem do cenél conuill im mac neill uí doṁnaill ċuca, ro laḋ ár na loingsi lais, ⁊ ro marḃaḋ som ṗeisin hi ffrioṫguin.

Giolla na naem ó dálaiġ saoi i ndan décc.

AOIS CRIOST, 1233.

Aois Criost, mile, dá ċéd, tricha, atrí.

Gofraiġ ua daiġre airċinneċ doire colaim cille [decc].

Maoliosa ua Maonaiġ uasal ṡaccart nó ġabaḋ a ṡsaltair gaċ laoi aċt dia doṁnaiġ namá [do écc].

Donncathaiġ airċinneċ achaiḋ foḃair fer rsidiġṫe gaċa cúisi, ⁊ gaċa caingne, fer co nairmidin, ⁊ co nonóir decc an .15. do ḋecember.

Slóiġead lá feiḋlimiḋ mac caṫail croiḃdeirg i cconnaċtaiḃ, ⁊ do ḋeaċaiḋ corbmac mac tomaltaiġ (tiġearna maiġe luirg) ina ḋail, ⁊ tuc les i maiġ luirc é. Do rónaḋ longport leó occ druim gregraiġe. Ḃaoi corbmac, conċoḃar a ṁac, ⁊ na trí tuaṫa, dá ṁac muirċeartaiġ meic diarmada, .i. donnċaḋ, ⁊ Muirċeartaċ ina ṡarraiḋ annsin. Arí comairle do rónsat dol i ndiaiḋ aoḋa (ríġ Connaċt), ⁊ cloinne Ruaiḋri ar ċena. Iar ndol dóiḃ ina ndóċum, ro sraoíneaḋ for aoḋ mac Ruaiḋri ro marḃaḋ é féin, ⁊ aoḋ muiṁneċ

in the county of Donegal. The ruins of the original church of the parish of Aughnish are still to be seen on this island.—See Ordnance Map of the County of Donegal, sheets 37 and 46.

[x] *Gilla-na-naev.*—This is a repetition.

[y] *Excepting Sunday.*—In the old translation of the Annals of Ulster this passage is rendered as follows: "A. D. 1233. Moylisa O Moynig, a gentle priest that would repeat his psalter every day, Sunday excepted, died."

[z] *The Three Tuathas.*—These were three districts on the west side of the Shannon, in the east of the county of Roscommon.—See note [d], under the year 1189, p. 86.

[a] *Defeated Hugh, the son of Roderic.*—It is stated in the Annals of Kilronan, that this Hugh was King of Connaught for five years, and that he was the last of the descendants of Roderic that was King of Connaught; that the Pope offered Roderic, and his issue, for ever, the title to the sovereignty, and six married wives, if he would thenceforward abstain from the sin of the women;—that Roderic did not accept of this offer on such conditions; and, as he did not, that God deprived him and his race for ever of reign and sovereignty, in revenge of the sin of concupiscence. Deoḋḟlaiṫ ċloinni Ruaiḋri hí Concuḃair ri Erenn innsin. Uair tarcaiḋ an Papa ceart ar Erinn do féin ⁊ da ṡíol na ḋiaiḋ go braṫ, ⁊ seisear do mnáiḃ posda, ⁊ sgur do peccaḋ no mban ó sin amaċ; ⁊ nír ġaḃ Ruaiḋri sin, ⁊ ó nár ġaḃ do ḃean dia riġe ⁊ flaiteaṁnus da ṡíol co braṫ i ndioġoltas

touched at these places; but a party of the Kinel-Connell, with the son of Niall O'Donnell, came upon them, and slaughtered the crews, but the son of Niall himself was slain in the heat of the conflict.

Gilla-na-naev[x] O'Daly, an adept in poetry, died.

THE AGE OF CHRIST, 1233.

The Age of Christ, one thousand two hundred thirty-three.

Geoffry O'Deery, Erenagh of Derry-Columbkille [died].

Maelisa O'Maeny, a noble priest, who was wont to sing his psalter every day, excepting Sunday[y] only [died].

Donncahy, Erenagh of Aghagower, settler of every dispute and covenant, a man of esteem and honour, died on the 15th of December.

An army was led by Felim, the son of Cathal Crovderg, into Connaught, and Cormac, the son of Tomaltagh (Lord of Moylurg), went to meet him and brought him with him into Moylurg. A camp was formed by them at Druim Gregraighe, and Cormac, his son Conor, the people of the Three Tuathas[z], the two sons of Murtough Mac Dermot, namely, Donough and Murtough, joined him there. The resolution they adopted was to go in pursuit of Hugh, King of Connaught, and the other sons of Roderic. On overtaking them they attacked and defeated Hugh, the son of Roderic[a], slew himself and his brother,

peccaiḋ na mban. Dr. Hanmer, in the speech which he has manufactured and put into the mouth of Dermot Mac Murrough, King of Leinster, makes him say to the men of Leinster and the British knights: "The tyrant Roderic hath murdered his own naturall brother, he hath three wives alive, he hath eleven bastards by severall women. O villaine! to behold a mote in our eye, and cannot see a beam in his owne." *Hanmer's Chronicle*, Dublin Edition of 1809, p. 235. Whether Dr. Hanmer found materials for this speech in any old historical collection among the families of the English Pale in Ireland, or whether it is a pure fabrication of his own, the Editor has not been able to determine; but it is certain that Giraldus Cambrensis does not make Dermot charge King Roderic with any such crimes, in the speech which he puts into his mouth. In this speech no allusion whatever is made to Roderic's lasciviousness, but he is called a tyrant, and an artful, ambitious man: "Malleus ille malarum artium & ambitionum omnium magister & author, violento dominatu cunctos opprimere cupiens: ad nos iterum à patria pellendos, vel etiam in ipsa (quod absit) delendos, ecce super, capita nobis iam imminet. De multitudine superbus & elatus ambitionem suam brachio metitur. Sed inermi multitudini & inerti plerunq; gravis esse solet animosa paucitas et armata. Sed (si) Lageniam

a dearḃraṫair, ⁊ a ṁac, ⁊ donnchaḋ mór mac diarmada mic Ruaiḋri, ⁊ ile oile cenmoṫát. Ro marḃaḋ ann dana Raġallaċ ua flannagáin, ⁊ tomás bisis constapla na hEreann, eoan a braṫair, eoan guer, ⁊ gaill iomḋa ele ḃeós iar mbuain clog ⁊ baċall, iar ndénaṁ earsccaoine ⁊ baṫhaḋ coindell do cleirċiḃ Connaċt orra uair ro ṡáraiġ ⁊ ro slatt aoḋ muiṁneaċ teaġ baoiṫin, ⁊ cealla iomda ar cena gur ro ṫuitset féin in eneċ na naoṁ isa cealla ro ṡáraiġset. Ro benaḋ ríġe, ⁊ cennus Condaċt do cloinn Ruaiḋri mic toirrḋealḃaiġ is in ló sin. Gabaiḋ feḋlimiḋ mac caṫail croibdeirg riġe Connaċt iarttain, ⁊ na caislein do rónaḋ lá neart cloinne Ruaiḋri uí conċoḃair, ⁊ mic uilliam búrc do sgaoileaḋ lais iad, .i. caislén bona gaillṁe, caislen na circe, caislén na cailliġe, ⁊ caislén dúin iomgain.

Slóiċċeaḋ lá huilliam mac hugo de laċi (ingen Ruaiḋri uí conċoḃair a maṫair side), ⁊ lá gallaiḃ miḋe amaille fris is in mbreifne in dócum caṫail uí Raġallaiġ co ndearnsat creaċa móra. Ruccsat imorro drong do muintir ui Raġallaiġ for uilliam de laci, ⁊ for ṁaiṫiḃ an tslóiġ i ndeóiḋ na ccreaċ tuccsat caċar dia roile, marḃṫar ann uilliam brit, ⁊ drong do maiṫiḃ gall ar aon ris. Ro gonaḋ uilliam de laci co soċaiḋiḃ oile. Soaitt as an tír gan giall gan eittere. Do cear uilliam de laci ⁊ Serlus mac caṫail gaill uí concoḃair, feórus fionn mac na gaill riogna, ⁊ diarmaid bearnaċ ua maoilseclainn do na gonaiḃ do radaḋ forra in iomairecc Móna

quærit: quoniam alicui Connactensium aliquando subiecta fuit: Ea ratione & nos Connactiam petimus, quia nostris aliquoties cum totius Hiberniæ subdita fuerat monarchia. Nec ille more monarchæ dominari quærit: sed damnare, sed à patria propellere, & in omnium iura solus succedere: & omnia solus obtinere."—*Hibernia Expugnata*, lib. i. c. 8.

[b] *Castle-Kirk*, now called the Hen's Castle. Its ruins are still to be seen on a rocky island, in the north-west part of Lough Corrib, in that arm of the lake which receives the river of Bealanabrack, and belongs to the parish of Cong.

[c] *Caislen-na-Cailllighe*, now called the Hag's Castle, which is a translation of its Irish name. It stands on an artificial island in the east side of Lough Mask, said to have been formed by dropping stones into the lake.—See this castle referred to at the year 1195, p. 102, note [r].

[d] *William*.—He was the ancestor of the celebrated Pierce Lacy, of the county of Limerick; and also of the Lynches of Galway.—See note under the year 1186. In Mageoghegan's translation of the Annals of Clonmacnoise, this event is noticed as follows: "A. D. 1233. William Delacie, chiefest Champion in these parts of Europe, and the hardiest and strongest hand of any Englishman, from the Nicen seas to this place, or Irishman, was hurt in a skirmish in the Brenie, came to his house, and there died of the wound. Charles O'Connor was also wounded the same day, and died thereof. Neale Ffox, King of Teaffa-land, was likewise hurt in the said skirmishe, came to his house in like man-

Hugh Muimhneach, his son, Donough More, the son of Dermot, who was son of Roderic [O'Conor], and many others besides them. There were also slain on this occasion Raghallagh O'Flanagan, Thomas Biris, Constable of Ireland, John, his relative, John Guer, and many other Englishmen; after they had been cursed and excommunicated by the clergy of Connaught, by the ringing of bells with croziers, and the extinguishing of candles; for Hugh Muimhneach had violated and plundered Tibohine, and many other churches, so that he [*and his party*] fell in revenge of the saints whose churches they had violated. The kingdom and government of Connaught was on that day taken from the sons of Roderic, the son of Turlough. After this Felim, the son of Cathal Crovderg, assumed the government of Connaught, and demolished the castles which had been erected by the power of the sons of Roderic O'Conor, and the son of William Burke, namely, the castle of Bungalvy, Castle-Kirk[b], and Castle-na-Cally[c], and the castle of Dunamon.

An army was led by William[d], the son of Hugo de Lacy (whose mother was the daughter of Roderic O'Conor), accompanied by the English of Meath, into Breifny against Cathal O'Reilly, and committed great depredations; but a party of O'Reilly's people overtook William de Lacy, and the chiefs of his army, who were behind the preys, and they gave battle to each other, in which William Britt, and a number of the chiefs of the English along with him, were slain. William de Lacy, with many others, was wounded. They returned from the territory without hostage or pledge. And William de Lacy, Charles, the son of Cathal Gall[e] O'Conor, Feorus Finn[f], the son of the English Queen, and Dermot Bearnagh[g] O'Melaghlin, died of the wounds they received in that battle of Moin-crann-chaoin[h]. Niall Sinnagh O'Catharny, Lord of Teffia, was

ner, and, after receiving the sacraments of the altar and Extream Unction, died penitently."

[e] *Cathal Gall*, Caṫal gall, i. e. Cathal the Englishman; he was so called by way of reproach, for speaking the English language.

[f] *Feorus Finn*, i. e. *Pierce the Fair*.—He must have been half brother to Henry III., whose mother, Queen Isabella, who was the daughter and heir of Amerie, Earl of Angolesm, after the death of King John, married the Count de la Marche in France.—See Hanmer's Chronicle, Dublin edition of 1809, p. 353.

[g] *Bearnach*. — This word, which signifies gapped, is often applied to a person who had lost his front teeth.

[h] *Maoin-crann-caoin*, i. e. the bog or morass of the beautiful trees. There is no place at present bearing the name in the county of Cavan, which comprises the entire of the territory of Breifny O'Reilly.

crann ċaoin. Niall sionnaċ ua caṫarnaiġ tiġearna fear teaṫḃa do ġuin is in amus cedna, ⁊ a écc ina tigh iar ndénaṁ a ṫiomna, ⁊ iar na ongaḋ.

AOIS CRIOST, 1234.

Aois Criost, mile, dá céd, triocha, acſṫair.

Aongus ua maolfoġṁair epscop ua ffiaċraċ, Giolla na naomh mac airt uí braoin airċinneaċ Rosa commain, Maoliosa mac daniel uí gormġaile Prióir innsi mac nerin, Maolpeadair ua carmacáin maiġistir Rosa comáin, ⁊ giolla iosa ua gibellain manaċ ⁊ anċoire oiléin na trinoide décc.

Domnall mac aoḋa í néill tiġearna cenél eoġain, aḋḃar ríġ Ereann do ṁarḃaḋ la mag laclainn .i. doṁnall ⁊ lá cenél eoġain fodein, ⁊ doṁnall do gaḃáil tiġearnais.

Aonġus mac gillefindein tiġearna loċa hſirne do iompuḋ ar ua ndoṁnaill, ⁊ a ḋol ar creiċ i ttír conuill, ⁊ ó domnaill, .i. doṁnall mor, do brſiṫ air, ⁊ a ṁarḃaḋ a ndioġail eiccneaċáin.

Aoḋ ua hſġra tiġearna luiġne do ṁarḃaḋ lá donnchaḋ mac duarcáin í eagra (iar loscaḋ tiġe fair, ⁊ iar tteċt ass), a ndioġail a ḋearḃraṫar, ⁊ cóicc mac dearḃraṫar a aṫar do marḃsoṁ, ⁊ a dearḃraṫair ele do ḋallaḋ lais.

Diarmaid ua cuinn taoiseaċ muintire giollgain do marḃaḋ.

Riocard mac uilliam marascal do dol ind aġaiḋ Riġ saxan hi saxaiḃ,

[i] Under this year the Annals of Kilronan record the death of Donncatha, Erenagh of Aghagower, on the 18th of the Calends of January; a man respected in the Church and State for his wisdom and personal form; a man the most bountiful of his cotemporaries in bestowing cattle and food; protector of the poor and the mighty; the ornament of the country, and the guide and settler of every covenant among his own people, and all in general.

[j] *Mac Gillafinnen*, now Mac Gillinion.—Maguire was not as yet powerful in Fermanagh. The Mac Gillinions were afterwards chiefs of Muinter Pheodachain.

[k] *Muintir-Gillagan.*—This territory was distributed among the baronies of Ardagh, Moydow, and Shrule, in the county of Longford. The townlands of which it consisted are specified in an Inquisition taken at Ardagh, on the 4th of April, in the tenth year of the reign of James I., which found that thirty-five small cartrons of Montergalgan then belonged to O'Farrall Bane, and seventeen one-half cartrons of like measure to O'Farrall Boye's part of the county of Longford. The territory of Caladh na h-Anghaile, called in this Inquisition "the

also wounded in this battle, and died at his own house, after making his will and being anointed[i].

THE AGE OF CHRIST, 1234.

The Age of Christ, one thousand two hundred thirty-four.

Aengus O'Mulfover, Bishop of Hy-Fiachrach [Killala]; Gilla-na-naev, the son of Art O'Breen, Erenagh of Roscommon; Maelisa, the son of Daniel O'Gormally, Prior of Inismacnerin; Mulpeter O'Carmacan, Master at Roscommon; and Gilla-Isa (Gelasius) O'Gibellan, a monk and anchorite on Trinity Island, died.

Donnell, the son of Hugh O'Neill, Lord of the Kinel-Owen, and heir presumptive to the sovereignty of Ireland, was slain by Mac Loughlin (Donnell), and the Kinel-Owen themselves, and Donnell [i. e. Mac Loughlin], assumed the lordship.

Aengus Mac Gillafinnen[j], Lord of Lough Erne, turned against O'Donnell, and went into Tirconnell upon a predatory incursion; but O'Donnell (Donnell More), overtook him, and killed him in revenge of [the death of] Egneghan.

Hugh O'Hara, Lord of Leyny, was killed by Donough, the son of Duarcan O'Hara (after he had burned the house over him, and after Hugh had escaped out of it), in revenge of his brother, and the five sons of his father's brother, whom he [Hugh] had slain, and of another brother who had been plundered by him.

Dermot O'Quin, Chief of Muintir-Gillagan[k], was slain.

Richard, the son of William Mareschal[l], having rebelled against the King

Callow,"—a name still locally remembered as that of a low district in the barony of Rathcline,—lies between Muintir Gillagan and the Shannon. —See note on Magh Treagha, under the year 1255.

[l] *Richard, the son of William Mareschal.*—He was the second son of William Mareschal, or Marshall, or, as Hanmer will have it, Maxfield. He was Earl Marshall of England, Earl of Pembroke, in Wales, and of Ogie, in Normandy, and Prince of Leinster, in Ireland.—See Hanmer's Chronicle, Dublin Edition of 1809, pp. 346, 347. The Four Masters have given this account very imperfectly. They should have written it thus: "A. D. 1254. Richard, the son of William Mareschal, having rebelled against the King of England, came over to Ireland, and took possession of Leinster. The English of Leinster assembled to oppose him on behalf of the King, namely, Maurice Fitzgerald, the Justiciary,

⁊ toċt dó tairis anoir co ro gaḃ illaiġniḃ. Tionoilit goill Ereann na aġaiḋ ro ḋáiġ ríġ saxan, .i. mac Muiris iustis na hEreann, hugo de laci iarla ulaḋ, ⁊ ualtra de laci tiġearna na miḋe. Tangattar go cuirreċ life hillaiġniḃ gur ċuirriot caṫ fris an marasgal, ⁊ marbṫar an marascal, ⁊ ro gaḃaḋ Seffraiġ marascal, ⁊ ní raiḃe ag cur an ċaṫa acṫ esioṁ a aonar iar na ṫréigeḋ dia ṁuintir buḋéin.

AOIS CRIOST, 1235.

Aois Criost, mile, da ċéd trioċat, acúicc.

Isaac ua maoilḟoġṁair aircindeċ cille halaiḋ décc.

Matheus prioir oiléin na trinoide [décc].

Madadán ua madadáin tiġearna síl nanmchada décc.

Loċlainn mac eiċtiġern uí ċeallaiġ do ṁarḃaḋ la macaiḃ an ġiolla Riaḃaiġ uí ḃaoiġill.

Hugo de Lacy, Earl of Ulster, and Walter de Lacy, Lord of Meath. They came to Curragh-Liffey, in Leinster, where they had appointed to hold a conference with the Earl. But they quarrelled with him at the conference, and took him prisoner, after having first wounded him mortally, for, being deserted by his false friend, Geoffry de Marisco, he was left almost alone on the field, and his stubborn valour would not allow him to submit tamely to his betrayers."

[m] *Mac Maurice.*—This is a mistake, for the person who opposed Richard Mareschal was Maurice, the son of Gerald Fitzgerald. He might have been called Mac Maurice, patronimically, from his grandfather, but it does not appear that he ever was.

[n] *Currech-Liffey*, Cuirreċ life, i. e. *Curragh of the Liffey*—The Curragh of Kildare is so called throughout these Annals, from which it may be safely concluded, that the Curragh anciently extended eastwards as far as the River Liffey, for the enclosures which from time intruded on the plain have gradually narrowed it. The word cuirreċ, or, as it is now written, curraċ, has two significations, namely, a shrubby moor, and a level plain, or race course; and it appears from the derivations given of the word in Cormac's Glossary, that it has this two-fold application from a very early period.

[o] *Geoffry Mareschal.*—This is an error of name and fact, for there was none of the great family of the Mareschals called Geoffry, and the person evidently referred to was Geoffry de Marisco, who did not stand alone fighting in the field of battle, but, according to Mathew Paris, marched away with four score of the Earl's company, who had been bribed to this desertion.

The fact seems to be that the Irish annalists knew nothing of the insidious plot laid by the Anglo-Irish barons against Richard Mareschal, and therefore described it as a regular battle. The best account of the plot against Mareschal is given by Matthew Paris, who bestows fourteen folio pages on the story of the last days and death of this young nobleman. See Leland's

of England, in England, he came over to Ireland, and landed in Leinster. The English of Leinster assembled to oppose him, on behalf of the King: Mac Maurice[m], Lord Justice of Ireland; Hugo de Lacy, Earl of Ulster; and Walter de Lacy, Lord of Meath. They came to Cuirreach-Life[n], in Leinster, where they engaged with Mareschal, and killed him; and they made a prisoner of Geoffry Mareschal[o], who had stood alone fighting on the field of battle, after all his people had fled from him[p].

THE AGE OF CHRIST, 1235.

The Age of Christ, one thousand two hundred thirty-five.

Isaac O'Mulfover, Erenagh of Killala, died.

Matheus, Prior of Trinity Island [died].

Madden O'Madden, Lord of Sil-Anmchadha, died.

Loughlin, the son of Echtighern O'Kelly, was slain by the sons of Gilla-Reagh O'Boyle.

History of Ireland, book ii. c. 1, vol. i. pp. 213–219; and Moore's, vol. iii. pp. 16–19. Dr. Hanmer, who had read Matthew Paris, is guilty of an intentional forgery in his Chronicle, *ad ann.* 1233, where he says, that "Richard Marshall was mortally wounded in a battle near Kildare, uppon the great Heath called the Curragh, fighting against the O'Connors!"—Dublin Edition, p. 346.

In Mageoghegan's translation of the Annals of Clonmacnoise, the account of this rencounter at the Curragh of Kildare, is thus briefly and incorrectly entered: "A. D. 1234. William Marshall gave battle to the rest of the Englishmen of Ireland, where William himself was slain and Geoffry March was taken."

The compiler of the Annals of Kilronan also, who appears to have known nothing of the plot against the Earl, described the encounter on the Curragh as a regular battle, and adds, that the death of Richard was one of the most lamentable occurrences of these times.

[p] Under this year the Annals of Clonmacnoise record, that Felim O'Conor, King of Connaught, marched with his forces to Meath, and burned Ballyloughloe, Ardnurcher, and many other towns. Under this year also the Dublin copy of the Annals of Innisfallen record the death of Walter de Lacy, Lord of Meath, leaving no issue, except two daughters. They also record the erection of the great church of St. Canice, at Aghaboe, by the successor of St. Kieran of Saigher. The Annals of Ulster and of Kilronan record a great snow and frost in this year, as follows: "A. D. 1234. Sneċta mor ieir da nodluic, 7 sic iar sin co nimgidis daoini 7 eiċ fo neredaib prim loċa 7 aiḃne Ereann. It is thus rendered in the old translation of the Annals of Ulster: "A. D. 1234. Extreame snow betweene both Christmas's this yeare. Great frost after that. Men and horses, with their loads, went uppon" [the] "rivers and lakes of Ireland."

Taicleach mac aoḋa uí ḋuḃda tiġearna ua namalgaḋa ⁊ ua ffiaċraċ do ṁarḃaḋ daon urċar soiġde i nDoirrġaire i longport feiḋlimiḋ mic caṫail croiḃdeirg.

Sluaicceaḋ la gallaiḃ Ereann ar na ttionol lá Riocard mac uilliam búrc. Ariad roḃdar oirdearca ḃádar for an sluaiġeaḋ sin lais Mac muiris iustís na hEreann, hucco de laci iarla ulaḋ, ualtra Rittabard ard ḃarún laiġen co ngallaiḃ laiġen, ⁊ eoan gogan co ngallaiḃ muṁan, ⁊ Rúta ḋa Ereann araon riú. Tangattar tar aṫluain go roscomáin. Ro loiscset an baile. Assén co hoilfinn. Ro loiscset tempall mor ailfinn. Assén co mainistir aṫa dalaarcc for buill oiḋċe doṁnaiġ na trinóide do ṡonnraḋ. Do ċottar dronga dia ffianlaċ fon mainistir, brisit an scrista, tuccsat cailiġ aifrinn, eidiġe, ⁊ ionnmusa ass. Bá graín mór la maiṫiḃ gall in ní sin, ⁊ do ċuirsiot for ccúla gaċ ní fríṫ dioḃ sin, ⁊ ro íocsat dar cenn an nfiṫ ná fríṫ. Ro cuirset araḃárac sirṫe uaḋaiḃ co creit, co cairṫe muilcén, co tor glinne

[q] *The most illustrious.*—Ar iad roḃdar oirḋearca bádar for an sluaiġead sin is a very old and obsolete form of construction, which would stand in the Irish of the present day thus: is iad ba oirḋeirce ḃí ar an sluaiġeaḋ sin. Charles O'Conor, of Belanagare, in the preface to his Dissertations on the History of Ireland, says that the Four Masters had in their writings preserved the language of the sixth century; and though we cannot fully acquiesce in this opinion, it must be acknowledged that they used very ancient forms of expression, and had no scruple in borrowing phrases from the oldest specimens of composition in the language; but they generally abstracted the words of the older annalists, without much regard to strength or neatness of expression, or purity of style.

[r] *Mac Maurice.*—This name should be Maurice Fitzgerald.

[s] *Walter Rittabard.*—He is called Gualterus de Ridenesfordia by his cotemporary, Giraldus Cambrensis, in his *Hibernia Expugnata*, lib. ii. c. xxi; and Walter de Riddlesford by most modern writers. He had his chief castle at Tristerdermot, now Castledermot, in the territory of Omurethi, in the south of the now county of Kildare, whence he and his followers had expelled the O'Tooles, shortly after the English invasion.—See note under the year 1180, pp. 53, 54; and *Genealogies, Tribes, and Customs of Hy-Fiachrach*, pp. 400, 401, note [a].

[t] *John Goggan.*—O'Flaherty, in his Hiar-Connaught, quoting this passage, calls him, "the Lord John Cogan." The name is still numerous in Munster, but now generally Anglicised Goggan.

[u] *Routes.*—The word ruta, which is derived from the Norman-French word *route*, is Englished *Rowte* by Mageoghegan, in his translation of the Annals of Clonmacnoise, at the year 1237. It means a *band* or *company* in a military sense, but in a legal sense it signifies an assembly of persons going forcibly to commit an unlawful act. In Dr. Cowel's Law Dictionary this word is correctly explained *routa, turma, cohors*, and Jacob, in his Law Dictionary, derives it from the French *route*, and explains it, "a company or number." In the Annals of Kilronan, at the year 1225,

Taichleach, the son of Hugh O'Dowda, Lord of Tirawley and Tireragh, was killed by one shot of an arrow during his interference [to quell a quarrel] in the camp of Felim, the son of Cathal Crovderg.

An expedition was made by the English of Ireland [this year], being assembled by Richard, the son of William Burke. The most illustrious[q] of those who were with him on this expedition were Mac Maurice[r], Lord Justice of Ireland; Hugo de Lacy, Earl of Ulster; Walter Rittabard[s], the chief Baron of Leinster, who commanded the English of Leinster; and John Goggan[t], with the English of Munster, together with all the routes[u] *of soldiers* in Ireland. Crossing [the bridge] at Athlone, they proceeded to Roscommon, and burned the town; thence, going to Elphin, they burned the great church there, and proceeded from thence to the monastery of the Ath Dalaarg, on the [river] Boyle, on the night of Trinity Sunday precisely. Parties of their soldiers assailed the monastery, broke into the sacristy, and carried away chalices, vestments, and other valuable things[w]. The English chiefs, however, were highly disgusted at this, and sent back every thing they could find, and paid for what they could not find. Next day they sent marauding parties[x] to Creit, to Cairthe-muilchenn[y],

O'Neill's band, or company of soldiers, is called Rúṫ Eoġanaċ; and, at the same year, rúṫaḋa ceiṫeirne is used to denote bands, or companies, of kernes, or light-armed infantry.

[w] *Chalices, vestments, &c.*—The passage relating to the robbing of the abbey of Boyle is given as follows, in Mageoghegan's translation of the Annals of Clonmacnoise: "A. D. 1235. The English of Ireland went with their forces to Connoght, untill they came to the abbey of Boylle, where they encamped within the walls of the said abbey, tooke all the goods they cou'd finger, as well as holy vestments, Challices, as also the habitts of the Monks, and striped the fryers and Monks very irreverently of their habbitts in the middest of their Cloister. Took also a great prey from Cormack Mac Dermott, which was then generally called the prey of preys."

[x] *Marauding parties*, ṡirte.—In the Annals of Kilronan the reading is as follows: Do ċuireadar a ṡirṫe 7 a ſerſénaiġ ar abaraċ 7 aruṫaḋa ceiṫeirne go creit 7 co cairṫi muilċe, 7 as sin co tor ġlinne fearna. "They sent on the next day their scouts, their archers, and their routes [*cohortes*] of kerne to Creit, to Cairthi Muilche, and thence to Tor-Glinne-fearna." There is no place in the county of Leitrim now called Creit, unless it be Creagh, in Kiltogher parish.

[y] *Cairthe Muilchenn*, now called in Irish Gleann a Chairthe, and in English, Glencar. It is a valley, in the county of Leitrim, and adjoining the barony of Carbury, in the county of Sligo.—See its position marked on the map prefixed to *Genealogies, Tribes, and Customs of Hy-Fiachrach*, published by the Archæological Society in 1844. See also Ordnance Map of the County of Leitrim, sheet 6, and of the County of Sligo, sheet 9.

fearna, ⁊ tugsat creaċa móra leó co hard carna i ccoinde an iustis. Do ronsat goill comairle incleiṫe annsin tria arlaċ eoġain uí edin do ḋioġail a ċneaḋ ar muiṁneaċaiḃ, ⁊ ar ḋonnchaḋ cairpreċ ua mbriain, .i. roḋ ina ffriṫḟing is in conair ċéona hi ttír ṁaine, immaonmaiġ, ⁊ asside go tuaḋmuṁain gan rabad gan raṫugaḋ do muiṁneachaiḃ. Do rónaḋ creaċa dírime leo.

Od connairc feiḋlimid mac caṫail croiḃdeirg na goill do ḋul uaḋa ar comairle ro ċind dol cona soċraide i mbáiḋ muiṁneaċ, ⁊ iar roċtain dó dia soiġiḋ nó cuirdís deabṫa crodha gaċ laoi. An lá déiḋeanaċ tra do ċodar Connaċtaiġ, ⁊ muiṁniġ is in caṫlaṫair, ⁊ ro caṫaiġset co fíorḋa. Acht ċeana ro fortaṁlaiġ forlion na ngall neḋiġṫe, ⁊ an marcṡluaiġ forra fó ḋeóiḋ, ⁊ ro muḋuiġit sochaiḋe eatorra díḃlinib acht as mó ro dioláiṫriġeaḋ muiṁniġ tria toġaoís ḋonnchaḋa cairpriġ. Tangadar Connaċtaiġ iaroṁ dia ttiġiḃ. Do róine ua briain araḃárac síṫ re gallaiḃ, ⁊ do beart braiġde dóiḃ. Tangadar tra na goill tar anais go Connaċtaiḃ. Areaḋ lodar ceddus go haoḋ ua flaiṫḃeartaiġ, ⁊ do riġne side síṫ friú dar ceann a bó, ⁊ a ṁuinntire. Feḋlimiḋ immorro mac caṫail croibdeirg, así comairle ro sgrúd soṁ a mbaoi do buaiḃ a cconmaicne mara, ⁊ a cconmaicne cúile doneoċ ro gaḃ a ċomairle, ⁊ mac magnusa, ⁊ conċoḃar ruad mac muirceartaiġ muiṁniġ do breiṫ lais do ṡoiġiḋ í ḋomnaill, .i. domnall mór, ⁊ an tír uile dfásuccaḋ for cind gall. Iar sin tra tangadar goill go dún mugdord. Ro cuirriod teċta go magnus mac muirceartaiġ muiṁniġ diarraiḋ giall fair, ⁊ ní tard magnus síṫ na eitiredha doiḃ. Ro cuirset din goill ó ḋun mugdord slóġ diairmiḋe sa macaiḃ ruaiḋri gur ro airccset eccuill, ⁊ do beartsat creaċa iomḋa

[a] *Tor-Glinne-fearna*, i. e. the tower of Glenfarne, or the alder glen, a remarkable valley, in the parish of Clooneclare, near Manor-Hamilton, in the barony of Rossclogher, and county of Leitrim. Glenfarn Hall is in this valley.—See Ordnance Map of the County of Leitrim, sheet 13. The tower here referred to would not appear to have been a castle or steeple, but either a Cyclopean fort, or a natural rock resembling a tower, like the rocks called *tors* on the coast of Antrim and Donegal. There is no place now bearing the name in Glenfarn.

[b] *Moinmoy*, Maonṁaġ.—A level territory in the county of Galway, comprising Moyode, Finure, and all the champaign lands around the town of Loughrea, in the county of Galway. It was bounded on the east by the territory of Sil-Anmchadha; on the south by the mountain of Slieve Aughty; and on the west by the diocese of Kilmacduagh. This was the original inheritance of the O'Mullallys and O'Naghtans, who, shortly after the English Invasion, were driven from it by the

to Tor-Glinne-fearna[z], and they carried off great spoils from those places to the Lord Justice at Ardcarne. Here the English held a private consultation, at the request of Owen O'Heyne, who wished to be revenged on the Momonians, and on Donough Cairbreach O'Brien, and they determined on going back the same way through Hy-Many and Moinmoy[a], and thence to Thomond, without giving the Momonians any notice or forewarning of their intentions. [This they accordingly did], and committed great depredations.

Now when Felim, the son of Cathal Crovderg, saw that the English had departed, the resolution he came to was to proceed with his forces, to succour the Momonians. [This he did], and, on their joining them, spirited skirmishes took place every day. At last the Connacians and Momonians came to a pitched battle [with the English], and fought manfully. But the English cavalry and infantry, who were clad in armour, finally overcame them. Many were slain on both sides, but the Momonians suffered most loss, through the imprudence of Donough Cairbreach. The Connacians then returned home[b], and on the next day O'Brien made peace with the English, and gave them hostages. The English returned into Connaught, and went first to Hugh O'Flaherty, who made peace with them in behalf of his people and cattle. As to Felim, the son of Cathal Crovderg, the resolution which he adopted was to take with him to O'Donnell, i. e. Donnell More, all the cows belonging to such of the inhabitants of Conmaicne-mara and Conmaicne-Cuile who should take his advice, together with the son of Manus, and Conor Roe, the son of Murtough Muimhneach, and leaving the whole country desolate for the English. The English soon afterwards came to Dun-Mughdord[c], and sent messengers to Manus, the son of Murtough Muimhneach, to demand hostages from him; but Manus would not give them either peace or hostages. The English then sent from Dun-Mughdord a numerous force against the sons of Roderic, who plun-

Burkes, when the former settled in the barony of Dunmore, near Tuam, and the latter in the woody district of the Faes, in the barony of Athlone, in the county of Roscommon.—See *Tribes and Teiritories of Hy-Many*, printed for the Irish Archæological Society, p. 70, note [z], and the map prefixed to the same work.

[b] *Home.*—In the Annals of Kilronan it is stated that the Connacians returned from this battle, having gained great credit for their valour and skill, without having lost any man of distinction: Cancocap Connaċcaiġ aiṗde ṗo ṗceim engnuṁa 7 ṗoṁaiṗi gan duine ṗuaċenca do maṗbaḋ d'ib.

[c] *Dun-Mughdord*, now Doon, a castle in the parish of Aghagower, about three miles east of

leó go ꝺꞃuımm ní ı ccoımne gall. Ꞇanaıc ꝺana aoꝺ ua ꝼlaıṫbeaꞃꞇaıġ, ⁊ eoġan ua heꝺın ꞅluaġ móꞃ ele ꞇımċeall, ⁊ aꞃṫꞃaıġe leó aꞃ ná ꞇꞇaꞃꞃaıng co líonán ċınꝺ maꞃa. Ꞃanġaꞇꞇaꞃ na haꞃṫꞃaıġe ꞅın cona ꞅoċꞃaıꝺe, ⁊ an ıuꞅꞇíꞅ ına ccoınꝺe co ꝺꞃuımní co calaꝺ ınꞅı aonaıġ.

Ꝧaġnuꞅ, ımoꞃꞃo, baí ꞅıꝺe ⁊ a longa aꞃ ꞅꞅuṫ na hınnꞅı, ⁊ ꝺeabṫa meınce uaꝺa ꝼoꞃ ġallaıḃ, ⁊ ımaꞃeaċ ó ġallaıḃ ꝼaıꞃꞃıoṁ. Ꞃo ꞅcıṫıġıꞇ ꞇꞃa gaıll ꝼꞃıꞅ ꞅın, ⁊ aꞃeaꝺ ꝺo ꞃónꞅaꞇ a longꝼoꞃꞇ ꝺo bꞃeıṫ leó, ⁊ a naꞃṫꞃaıġe ꝺo ṫaꞃꞃaıng ċuca ı ccúıl ꞇꞃáġa móꞃ boí ıꞅ ın maıġın ꞅın. Ꝺꞃo ꞃaṫaıġ maġnuꞅ ınꝺꞅın ꝺo ċuaıꝺ ın ınıꞅ ꞃaıṫnı, ⁊ ꞃo cuıꞃ ꝺꞃong ꝺıa ṁuınꞇıꞃ ınꝺ ınıꞅ aonaıġ. Ꝺo connca-ꝺaꞃ gaıll maġnuꞅ cona ṁuınꞇıꞃ ꝺo ꝺol ꝼoꞃ na hoıléınaıḃ hıꞅın, ꞃo ṫóġḃaꝺaꞃ a naꞃṫꞃaıġe leó aꞃ ꝼuꝺ na ꞇꞃaġa, ⁊ ꞃo ċuıꞃꞅíꞇ ꝼoꞃ muıꞃ ıaꞇ, ⁊ ꞃo líonaıꞇ co hobann ꝺo ꞅluaġ, ⁊ ꝺo ꞅıꞃꞇhıḃ aꞃmṫa eꝺıġṫe, ⁊ loꞇuꞃ ꝼoꞃꞅ na hoıléınaıḃ ı mbaꝺaꞃ muınꞇıꞃ maġnuꞅa (cenmoṫá ınıꞅ ꞃaıṫın ı mbaoı maġnuꞅ ꝼeꞅın), ⁊ ꞃo ṁaꞃḃꞅaꞇ a ꝼꞅuaꞃaꝺaꞃ ꝺo ꝺaoınıḃ ınnꞇıḃ. Ꝺo ꝺeochaıꝺ maġnuꞅ ⁊ ı mbaoí ꝺıa ṁuınꞇıꞃ ın ınıꞅ ꞃaıṫne ına longaıḃ, ⁊ ꞃo ꝼaġaıḃꞅíꞇ an ınꞅı, ⁊ ꝺıambaꝺ ꞇaıꞃıꞅı lá maġnuꞅ muınꞇıꞃ ṁaılle ꞃo ċuıꞃꞃeaꝺ a longa hı ccínn loıngıꞅ na ngall.

Westport.—See Ordnance Map of the county of Mayo, sheet 88.

[d] *Achill*, Ecuıll, a well-known island in the barony of Burrishoole, and county of Mayo.—See its most remarkable features and antiquities shewn on the map prefixed to *Genealogies, Tribes, and Customs of Hy-Fiachrach*, published by the Irish Archæological Society in 1844.

[e] *Druimni*.—There is no place at present bearing this name in the barony of Burrishoole or of Murresk, in the county of Mayo.—See Ordnance Map of that county, sheet 87, &c.

[f] *Which they carried*.—Roderic O'Flaherty, in his Account of Hiar-Connaught, says that the boats of Lough Orbsen were drawn from Bonbonan for five miles [*recte* six miles and a-half] on this occasion.

[g] *Linan Cinn-mara*, is now called Leenaun, a well known place near the Killary Harbour, in Connamara, in the north-west of the county of Galway. It is described by O'Flaherty, in his Account of Hiar-Connaught, printed for the Archæological Society in 1845, as "Imair-an-Linain, antiently Linan Kinmara, a long green spot of land by the sea of Coelshaly Ro" [Killary].

[h] *The sound near the island*, ꞅꞅuṫ na hınꞅı.—In this part of Ireland ꞅꞅuṫ means a sound or inlet of the sea, into which the tide flows with the rapidity of a stream. Of this application of the word we have a striking illustration in the name ꞅꞅuṫ ċınn Eacla, at Achill head; baıle an ꞇꞅꞃoṫa, or streamstown, near Clifden, in Connamara; and ꞅꞅuṫ na maoıle, in the north of Ireland, near Ballyshannon.

[i] *Large strand*.—This strand lies to the north of Murresk Lodge, and extends from Bartraw point to Annagh Island, near the foot of Croaghpatrick.

[k] *Inis-raithni*, i. e. the Ferny Island, now corruptly Anglicised Inishraher. It is an island in the Bay of Westport.—See Ordnance Map of

dered Achill[d], and carried off great spoils to Druimni[e]. Hugh O'Flaherty and Owen O'Heyne also came round with a great army, having vessels with them, which they carried[f] [by land] as far as Linan Cinn-mara[g]. These vessels, with their forces, being met by the Lord Justice at Druimni, were brought to the Callow of Inis-Aenaigh.

Manus at this time was with his ships on the Sound near the island[h], and he made frequent attacks upon the English, and they upon him in return. The English, however, desisted for a time; they removed their camp, and drew their vessels into the angle of a large strand[i] at that place. When Manus observed this, he landed on Inis-raithni[k], and sent a party of his people on the Island of Inis-Aonaigh[l]. As soon, however, as the English perceived that Manus and his people had landed on these islands, they drew their boats along the strand, and having them on the sea, they quickly filled them with a numerous army and troops of well-armed and mail-clad soldiers; and these landed on the islands on which the people of Manus were (except Inis-Raithin[m], where Manus himself was), and killed all the people they found on them. Upon this Manus, and those who were with him on Inis-Raithin, took to their ships, and fled from the island. Had Manus, however, been on friendly terms with the O'Malleys, they would have sent their ships against the English fleet.

the county of Mayo, sheet 87. See also *Genealogies, Tribes, and Customs of Hy-Fiachrach*, p. 303, note [h], and the map prefixed to the same work.

[l] *Inis-Aonaigh*, i. e. the island of the fair or market, now correctly anglicised Inisheany. It is an island in the same bay, lying immediately to the east of Bartraw point, and nearly due-south of Inis-Raithin. It is nearer to the large strand alluded to in the text than Inis-Raithin.

[m] *Except Inis-Raithin*, cenmoṫa Inir Raiṫin. In these Annals cenmoṫa, like the Latin *præter*, has two opposite meanings, namely, *except* and *besides*, and it is sometimes not easy to determine which of these meanings is intended. At the year 1020 it is translated *præter* by Colgan in *Trias Thaum.*, p. 298; but at the year 1391 it means clearly *besides*. According to the Annals of Connaught and of Kilronan, from which the Four Masters seem to have abstracted their account of this transaction, the English landed on the two islands. These Annals state, that "when Manus O'Conor had perceived that the English had drawn their boats ashore, and that they could not be attacked, he sailed eastwards [*recte* north-eastwards], and landed on Inis-Rathain, and some of his people landed on Inis-Aonaigh, and took some sheep there to kill and eat them. When the English observed this they rose up actively and drew their boats along the strand with rapidity, and launching them on the sea, filled them with well-armed and mailed soldiers and archers, and, landing on the two islands [7 do ċuadar ar ar da oilen], they killed all the people they found on them. Manus

Ní baoí bó ar oilén in insiḃ Modh nár ċuirsiot goill ar calaḋ in aon ló, ⁊ nó tiocfadaís muinteara na mbó cona mbuar do na hoilénaiḃ hisin lá haiḋble a níotaiḋ ⁊ a nocarais mena beiṫ gaḃáil forra.

Ro marḃaid foḋaoine iomḋa lá gallaiḃ an oiḋċe sin. An aoine imorro ar ná ṁárac do cuas leó ar oilénaiḃ ṫuaiscirt uṁaill. Ro forcongraḋ lá toiseachaiḃ an tslóiġ gan daoine do ṁarḃaḋ ind onóir césta criost.

O ṫairnic tra lá gallaiḃ slad ⁊ creachaḋ huṁaill eitir ṁuir ⁊ tír tangadar riompu, ⁊ a mbú, ⁊ a ccreaċa leó go luġburdan. Do ċuadar as siḋe ina nuiḋedhaiḃ inṫeaċta co hEsdara co ndearnadar creiċ ar ua nDoṁnaill ar daiġin ionnarḃta feḋlimiḋ cuicce. Tangattar as siḋe i ccoirrsliaḃ na segsa, ⁊ go calaḋ puirt na cairrcce ar loċ cé dá ġaḃáil ar drung do ṁuintir feḋlimiḋ uí ċonċoḃair ⁊ ċorbmaic mic tomaltaiġ baoí occa ċoiṁéd. Tuccsat imorro gaill Ereann, ⁊ an lustis comairce ⁊ tearmann do ċlarus mac Mailin dairċideoċain oilefind, ⁊ do ċanánaċaiḃ oiléin na trinoide in onóir na naoṁ trinóide, ⁊ do ċóiḋ an iústis féin, ⁊ maiṫe na ngall do ḋéċain an ionaid sin, ⁊ do ḋénaṁ sléċtana ⁊ ernaiġṫe an dú sin.

Do rónsat gaill iaroṁ aiḋme iongnaiṫe daṁainsi ealaḋan ⁊ innleċta trias ro ġaḃsat Carrag loċa cé for ṁuintir feḋlimiḋ ⁊ corbmaic, ⁊ iar ná gaḃáil ro ḟágaiḃ an iustis luċt coiṁeda fuirre, ⁊ an ro ba lór leó do ḃiuḋ, ⁊ lionn, ⁊ ro fagaiḃsiot gaill connaċtaiġ don ċur sin gan biaḋ gan éḋaċ

and such of his people as were on Inis-Rathain, then went into their ships," &c.

[n] *Insi Modh.*—This is a general name for a group of islands in Clew Bay, said to be 365 in number.—See Ordnance Map of the County of Mayo, sheets 67, 76, and 87, and the Map to *Genealogies, Tribes, and Territories of Hy-Fiachrach*, already referred to; and also the paper on Inis Mochaoi, published by the Down and Connor and Dromore Architecture Society, in which the author, the Rev. William Reeves, corrects an error of Dr. O'Conor, who had stated that the Insi Modh were the Copeland Islands.

[o] *Luffertane*, luġburdán, a townland in the parish of Ballintober, in the county of Mayo, containing the ruins of a castle said to have been erected by the family of Burke.—See *Genealogies, Tribes, and Customs of Hy-Fiachrach*, printed for the Irish Archæological Society in 1844, p. 153, note [s], and p. 402. There is another place of the name in the parish of Boyle, in the county of Roscommon; it is a hill in Lord Lorton's demesne, and now pronounced luġḃardán in Irish, and Lurton in English.

[p] *Port-na-Carrick.*—This name is now anglicised Rockingham. It is situated in the county of Roscommon, near the shore of Lough Key, and is well known to tourists as the princely seat of Lord Lorton. The natives of the town of Boyle and its vicinity, when speaking Irish, always call Rockingham Port na cairge.

[q] *And pray there.*—This passage is given in the Annals of Boyle, as follows: Do cued imorro in iustís 7 maiti ngall Erenn du

There was not a single cow upon any of the Insi Modh[n] islands which the English did not carry off to the shore in one day; and those to whom these cows had belonged would have been obliged to come off their islands, in consequence of thirst and hunger, if they had not been [killed or] taken prisoners.

Many of the inferior sort were slain that night by the English. On the next day, which was Friday, the English went upon the islands north of Umallia; and the chiefs of the army ordered that no people should be slain on that day, in honour of the crucifixion of Christ.

After the English had plundered and devastated Umallia, both by sea and land, they marched on with their cows and spoils to Luffertane[o]; thence they proceeded, by regular marches, to Easdara [Ballysadare], where they took a prey from O'Donnell, because he had granted an asylum to Felim after his expulsion; and from thence to the Curlieu Mountains, and to Caladh-Puirt na Cairrge[p], on Lough Key, to take it from a party of the people of Felim O'Conor and Cormac, the son of Tomaltagh [Mac Dermot], who were guarding it. On this occasion the English of Ireland and the Lord Justice spared and protected Clarus, the son of Mailin, Archdeacon of Elphin, and the Canons of Trinity Island, in honour of the Blessed Trinity; and the Lord Justice himself, and the chiefs of the English, went to see that place, and to kneel and pray there[q].

The English afterwards, with great art and ingenuity, constructed wonderful engines[r], by means of which they took [the fortress of] the Rock of Lough Key from the people of Felim and Cormac; and the Lord Justice, after taking it, left warders in it, with as much provisions and beer as they deemed sufficient. By this expedition the English left the Connacians without food, rai-

déċſuin in inuit ſen ⁊ d'aiṗniċte ann do ṫabaiṗt caóiṗ do ġun ná llámad duni eaſonóiṗ in ninuit ſen. Which is thus most incorrectly translated by Dr. O'Conor: "Profecti sunt vero Justitiarius, et Magnates Alienigenarum Hiberniæ, ad expugnandam istam gentem istam, et transegerunt noctes ibi, dantes impetus in eam absque vulneratione Arcis durante eo tempore." The conduct of the English was, however, the very reverse, as will appear from the true translation, which is as follows: "The Justiciary and the chiefs of the English of Ireland went to see that place, and to pray and to pay veneration to it, so that none should offer dishonour to the place."

[r] *Wonderful engines.*—The Annals of Boyle contain a very curious account of the *pirrels*, or engines, constructed by the English for taking the Rock of Lough Key on this occasion; but Dr. O'Conor has mistranslated almost every sentence of it.

gan eallaċ, ⁊ ní ro ḟágaibsead síṫ ná sáiṁe innte, aċt maḋ gaoiḋil féin ag slat ⁊ ag marḃaḋ a ċéle. Ar a aoi ní ruccsat goill giall na eitere don ċur sin.

Do róine feḋlimiḋ síṫ sir in iursir, ⁊ tuccait cúig triucha an righ dórumh gan croḋ gan cíos orra.

Carrac loċa cé do ġabail lá corbmac mac diarmata i ccínn ṗiċít aiḋċe iarom iar ndol don consdapla imaċ co ndruing móir dá ṁuintir imme, ro iaḋ fear díoḃ féin, .i. ó hoistin an baile tar a néis, ⁊ do rad do corbmac iarttain. Ro hiodlaiceaḋ na gaill ar comairce co hoilén na trinóide, ⁊ ro cuireaḋ slán ar an tír iad. Trasgartar ⁊ múrtar an ċarracc lá corbmac iarom conaċ gaḃdaís gaill doriḋiri.

Doṁnall ⁊ muirceartaċ dá mac muireadaiġ uí ṁaille do ṁarḃaḋ lá doṁnall mac maġnusa mic muirceartaiġ uí concoḃair, ⁊ lá niall ruaḋ mac caṫail mic conċoḃair i cliara, ⁊ a naḋnacal innte ḃeós.

Tuaṫal mac muirceartaiġ uí ċonċoḃair do ṁarḃaḋ lá concoḃar mbuiḋe mac toirrḋealḃaiġ ui corcoḃair, ⁊ lá concoḃar mac aoḋa muiṁniġ.

Caislen Milic do ḃriseaḋ la feḋlimiḋ ua conċoḃair.

[s] *Free of tribute.*—According to the Annals of Kilronan, Felim was to receive rent and custom out of these five cantreds. Dr. O'Conor, in his suppressed work, Memoirs of the Life and Writings of Charles O'Conor of Belanagare, p. 41, states that Felim obtained a royal charter in the year 1257, "granting to him, and to his heirs for ever, free and peaceable dominion over five baronies, in as ample a manner as ever they were enjoyed by his ancestors." These five cantreds would seem to have constituted the mensal lands of the Kings of Connaught from time immemorial. According to the Annals of Clonmacnoise, Felim O'Conor was deprived of "the King's five cantreds" in the year 1236, when they were given to Brian, the son of Terlagh O'Connor." Thus, after describing the treacherous but unsuccessful attempt of the Justiciary to take Felim O'Conor prisoner, the following observation is made on the character of Brian O'Conor: "A. D. 1236. Bryen Mac Terlagh O'Connor was then established in the possession of the five cantredes belonging to the King of Connaught, who preyed the provence and destroyed it, without respect to either spirituall or temporall land."

[t] *Taken.*—The Annals of Kilronan state that O'Hoist remained inside the gate and closed it against the constable; and that thereupon the English fled to Clarus Mac Mailin, who afforded them protection. The same account is also given in the Annals of Boyle, but totally falsified by Dr. O'Conor.

[u] *Cliara*, so called at the present day in Irish, but anglicised Clare Island. It is a celebrated island in Clew Bay, still belonging to the O'Malleys, and containing the ruins of a castle and monastery erected by that family.—See Map prefixed to *Genealogies, Tribes, and Customs of Hy-Fiachrach*, and Ordnance Map of the County

ment, or cattle, and the country without peace or tranquillity, the Gaels [Irish] themselves plundering and destroying one another. The English, however, did not obtain hostages or pledges of submission on this expedition.

Felim made peace with the Lord Justice; and they [the English] gave him the King's five cantreds, free of tribute[s] or rent.

The Rock of Lough Key was taken[t], twenty nights afterwards, by Cormac Mac Dermot. As the constable and a great number of his people had gone out, O'Hostin, one of his own people, closed the gate of the fortress, and afterwards gave it up to Cormac. The English were conveyed [*recte* fled] to Trinity Island, and afterwards conducted out of the country in security. [The fortress of] the Rock was afterwards razed and demolished by Cormac, in order that the English might not take it again.

Donnell and Murtough, two sons of Murray O'Malley, were slain by Donnell, son of Manus, who was son of Murtough O'Conor; and by Niall Roe, son of Cathal, son of Conor [*recte* O'Conor], in Cliara[u], and were interred there.

Tuathal, the son of Murtough O'Conor, was slain by Conor Boy, the son of Turlough O'Conor, and by Conor, the son of Hugh Muimhneach [O'Conor].

The Castle of Meelick[w] was demolished by Felim O'Conor.

of Mayo, sheets 84, 85.

[w] *The Castle of Meelick* is near the Shannon, in the barony of Longford, and county of Galway.

Under this year (1235) the Dublin copy of the Annals of Innisfallen contain the following notices of the transactions of Munster, which have been omitted by the Four Masters.

"A. D. 1235. Teige Duvdedagh, the son of Dermot of Dundronan, who was the son of Donnell More na Curadh Mac Carthy, was slain by Cormac Finn and Donnell God, the two sons of Donnell More na Curadh Mac Carthy.

"The Irish were defeated by the English at Tralee, in a conflict, in which Cormac, the son of Cormac Finn, who was the son of Donnell More na Curadh Mac Carthy, Gasginach O'Driscoll, and Murtough, his brother, were slain."

Under this year the Annals of Kilronan record the death of Matheus, Prior of Trinity Island, and they enter the deaths of Gilla-an-Choimdedh O'Cuilin, *Prepositus* of Insula mac Nerin, and of the father of Clarus Mac Mailin, Archdeacon of Elphin, in the following words: "Gilla Coimdedh O'Cuilin, *Prepositus de Insula mac Nerin et Pater Clari Elfenensis, Archidiaconi, feliciter in Christo quieuit; et in insola Sancte Trinitatis est sepultus die Sancti Finniani, cujus anima requiescat in pace.*" The Editor has not been able to determine satisfactorily of what family this celebrated ecclesiastic, Clarus Mac Mailin, was; but inclines to think that he was a branch of the O'Mulconrys; for, in Mageoghegan's Annals of Clonmacnoise, under the year 1260, he is called, "Clarus Mac Moylyn O Moylchonrie."—See note under that year, respecting the removal of the canons of Trinity Island, in Lough Key, to Trinity Island, in Lough Oughter, in Breifny.

AOIS CRIOST, 1236.

Aois Criost, míle, dá céd, triocha, asé.

Macraiṫ mac maoilín Sagart cille Mic treana [decc].

Aoḋ ua giḃelláin Sagart cille Rodain. Bá cananaċ é ro deóiḋ in oilén na trinóide décc oiḋċe nodlac.

An iustis, .i. mac muiris do ṫionol gall Ereann na ċoinne co haṫ feorainne. Tainic fedlim mac caṫail croiḃdeirg Rí Connaċt is in coinne hisin. Isead bá meanmarc leó uile feall for feidlim ge ro ḃaoi na cairdeas críost ag an iustis, ⁊ bá he sin foċann a ttionoil co haon ṁaigin. Iar bfios sgéil ⁊ iar ffagḃáil raḃaḋ dfeiḋlimiḋ ro siacht ar in ccoinne uathaḋ marcsluaiġ co rosscomáin. Ro leanaḋ ar sen co droicht sliccige, ⁊ do ċuaiḋ in ucht uí ḋoṁnaill, ⁊ ó naċ ruccsat fair do rónsat creaċa móra ar ṫadg ua cconcoḃair, ⁊ rucsat deaġ ṁná imda i mbroid ⁊ i ndaoíre. Co rangattar gus na gaḃalaiḃ sin leó go druim ngreccraiġe i maiġ luirg, uair as ann baoi an iustis fén occa nurnaide. Bá iar ndol mic uilliam hi saxaiḃ do rónaḋ an coinne hísin.

Soḋais an iustis ⁊ na goill iar sin dia ttiġiḃ, ⁊ ro ḟagaiḃ forlaṁus an tíre ag brian mac toirrḋealḃaiġ.

Creaċa mora do ḋénaṁ lá brian ⁊ la haṁsaiḃ an iustís ar macaiḃ aoḋa mic caṫail croiḃḋeirg, ⁊ ar socaiḋiḃ oile do muintir ḟeiḋlimiḋ. Creaċa eile do ḋénaṁ lá macaiḃ aoḋa ar ġallaiḃ ⁊ ar a neascairdiḃ gaoiḋealda co ro loitsioḋ an tír eatorra imáreaċ amne.

Conċoḃar mac aoḋa muiṁniġ do ṁarḃaoh lá magnas mac muirċeartaigh uí ċonċobhair.

Maolmuire ua laċtnáin do ṫoga in esscopóide tuama, ⁊ a ḋul i saxaiḃ,

[x] *Kilmactranny*, Cill mic Treana.—Charles O'Conor adds: i ttir Oiliolla; but the Editor does not think it proper to give it in the text. Kilmactranny is a vicarage in the diocese of Elphin, situated in the barony of Tirerrill, in the county of Sligo.

[y] *Kilrodan*, Cill Rodain, an old church in the parish of Tibohine, or Airteach, in the north-west of the county of Roscommon.

[z] *Ath-feorainne*, now Afeoran, a townland on the east side of the River Suck, in the parish of Taghboy, barony of Athlone, and county of Roscommon.—See *Tribes and Customs of Hy-Many*, printed for the Irish Archæological Society in 1842, p. 115, where the situation of this place is distinctly pointed out in a quota-

THE AGE OF CHRIST, 1236.

The Age of Christ, one thousand two hundred thirty-six.

Magrath Mac Mailin, Priest of Kilmactranny[x], died.

Hugh O'Gibellan, Priest of Kilrodan[y], and finally canon on Trinity Island, died on the Christmas night.

The Lord Justice of Ireland, Mac Maurice, summoned the English of Ireland to meet him at Ath-feorainne[z], at which meeting Felim, the son of Cathal Crovderg O'Conor, was present. They all yearned to act treacherously towards Felim, although he was the gossip[a] of the Lord Justice; and this was the reason that the meeting had been called. Felim having received intelligence and forewarning of their design, departed from the assembly; and, attended by a few horsemen, proceeded to Roscommon. He was pursued [thither and] as far as the bridge of Sligo; he fled to O'Donnell for protection. As they did not overtake him they committed great acts of plunder upon Teige O'Conor, and carried away many respectable women into captivity and bondage; they then proceeded to Druim Gregruighe in Moylurg, where the Lord Justice awaited their return. The meeting above mentioned was called immediately after the departure of [Richard], the son of William Burke, for England.

After this the Lord Justice and the English returned home, leaving the government of the country to Brian, the son of Turlough [O'Conor].

Great depredations were committed by [this] Brian and the soldiers of the Lord Justice on the sons of Hugh, son of Cathal Crovderg, and others of the people of Felim. The sons of Hugh committed other depredations among the English and their own Irish enemies; so that the country was destroyed between both parties.

Conor, the son of Hugh Muimhneach, was slain by Manus, the son of Murtough O'Conor.

Mulmurry O'Laghtnan was appointed to the bishopric of Tuam, and went

tion from a grant, in 1612, to Captain Colla O'Kelly.

[a] *Gossip*, Ꞡe ꞃo baoı na ċaıꞃᵭeaꞅ cꞃíoꞅꞇ.—He was sponsor or godfather to one of his children. Cáıꞃᵭeaꞅ cꞃíoꞅꞇ is still the common term used in Ireland to denote gossip or sponsor.

⁊ grada do ṫabairt fair tria scribhennaiḃ comarba Petair, ⁊ tria coṁaonta ríġ Saxan.

Mac uilliam do ṫuiḋecht a saxaiḃ, ⁊ ní fer cecip tucht i tudchaiḋ fa fo síṫ nó fo eisíṫ.

Feḋlimiḋ mac caṫail croiḃḋeirg do ṫocht i cconnachtaiḃ doriḋisi iar ná ṫochuireaḋ do druing do connachtaiḃ .i. ua ceallaiġ ua flaind mec aoḋa mic caṫail croibdeirg, ⁊ mac airt uí ṁaoilṡeachlainn go rabatar uile cethre caṫa coṁṁóra ⁊ ro ionnsaiġset iaroṁ co rind dúin airm i mbádar bú an tíre uile ag brian mac toirrḋealbaiġ, ⁊ ag eoġan ua ḟiḋin, ⁊ ag concoḃar buiḋe mac toirrḋealḃaiġ, ⁊ ag mac goisdelb. Rangadar tra muintir feḋlimiḋ tar dúnclaḋ ⁊ tar daingean ċlasaiġ an oilen, ⁊ ro ċuir gaċ cenn slóiġ, ⁊ gaċ taoisioċ buiḋne dib a ffolartnaiḃ do na buaiḃ reampa aṁail só ġebttís ar a cconair iad ar a ccind. Ro sgaoilset muintir ḟeḋlimiḋ ar na hédalaiḃ co ná ro airis ina ḟocair dona ceiṫriḃ caṫaiḃ achtmaḋ aon cethrar marcaċ namá.

Od connairc brian mac toirrḋealbaiġ ⁊ eoġan ua heiḋin cona soċraiḋe muintir feḋlimiḋ go hesraoite lá a néḋalaiḃ, do eirġsedar go haṫlaṁ ésgaiḋ uathaḋ marcsluaiġ ⁊ amsaḋ ioṁḋa do ṡaiġiḋ uí concoḃair cona uaṫaḋ muintire, ní ro airis concoḃar buiḋe mac toirrḋealbaiġ ní conus tapla i ccenn mac naoḋa mic caṫail croiḃḋeirg i riocht a ṁuintire fein, ⁊ ro ṫuitsioṁ lá ruaiḋri mac aoda mic caṫail croibdeirg.

Ro ṁeabaiḋ for guṫ feḋlimiḋ (an airdriġ) occ fostaḋ ⁊ occ ioṁḟuireach a muintire ó a néḋalaiḃ fri hiombualaḋ a naġaiḋ a mbioḋḃaḋ. Ro marḃaḋ sochaiḋe ioṁḋa don tsluaiġ lá feḋlimiḋ cona ṁuintir is in maiḋm sin is in oilen ⁊ alla muiġ don oilén do macaiḃ mallacht, ⁊ do luċt déntma uilc acht

[b] *Mac William.*—In the Annals of Kilronan it is stated that he did not do much good for Ireland by his journey to England.

[c] *Rindown*, rinn dúin.—See note [x], under the year 1199, p. 120.

[d] *Dispersed with their spoils.*—The Annals of Kilronan, which describe this attack on Rindown more fully, have the following remark on the conduct of Felim's people on this occasion: "Lamentable was their conduct on this occasion; they abandoned their lord, their guarantee, and their valour, for the spoils which they met. They left their lord and king, attended only by four horsemen out of the four battalions which he brought with him, so that the king strained his voice calling them back."

[e] *Foot-soldiers*, amsaiḃ.—The Annals of Kilronan call them serrenaiġ, i. e. archers.

[f] *He fell by him.*—This is very lamely expressed by the Four Masters, who appear to

to England, where he was consecrated, after having received the Pope's letters, by consent of the King of England.

Mac William[b] returned from England, but whether with peace or with war was unknown.

Felim, the son of Cathal Crovderg, returned to Connaught, having been invited thither by some of the Connacians, namely, by O'Kelly, O'Flynn, the son of Hugh, who was son of Cathal Crovderg O'Conor, and the son of Art O'Melaghlin; all forming four equally strong battalions. They marched to Rindown[c], where Brian, the son of Turlough, Owen O'Heyne, Conor Boy, son of Turlough, and Mac Costello, had all the cows of the country. Felim's people passed over the ramparts and ditches of the island [*recte* peninsula], and every chief of a band and head of a troop among them drove off a proportionate number of the cows, as they found them on the way before them; after which they dispersed, carrying off their booty, in different directions, and of the four battalions, leaving only four horsemen with Felim.

When Brian, the son of Turlough, Owen O'Heyne, and their forces, observed that Felim's people were dispersed with their spoils[d], they set off actively and quickly with a small party of horse and many foot-soldiers[e] to attack Felim and his few men. Conor Boy, son of Turlough, did not perceive his situation until he came up with Rory, son of Hugh, son of Cathal Crovderg, and, mistaking him for one of his own people, he fell by him[f].

Felim (the King) strained his voice calling after his army, and commanding them to abandon the spoils and rally to fight their enemies. Many of the [enemy's] forces were killed in this rencounter by Felim and his people, upon the island and outside the island; all excommunicated persons[g] and doers of

have left the sentence unfinished. It is better told in the Annals of Kilronan, but it would swell this work to too great a size to notice differences of this kind.

[g] *Excommunicated persons*, macaiḃ mallaċt, literally, *sons of curses*.—In the Annals of Kilronan, the reading is: "Ro marḃaḋ soċaiḋe don tsluaġ is in oilén ⁊ allamoiġ don oilen do daoiniḃ mallaiġṫe coinniol-ḃáitte is in maiḋm sin, aċt maḋ Tuóc mac Cormaic mic Tomaltaiġ Mic Diarmada namá."

The Annals of Clonmacnoise, as translated by Mageoghegan, describe Felim's attack on Rindown as follows: "A. D. 1236. Felym O'Connor with an army came to Connoght again, and marched on untill he came to John's house, took all the spoiles of the town and islands thereof, and left nothing that they cou'd take or see from the door of the Castle foorth: Felym's camp lay at the markett cross of the town;

maḋ taḋg mac corbmaic mic tomaltaiġ mic diarmata namá. Do ċualaiḋ tra mac uilliam an maiḋm sin do ṫabairt ar gaċ aon dár iompoid fair, ro eiriġ lá hua conċobair dia ccſnnsucchaḋ. Do chuaiḋ dana diarmaid mac maġnusa iar ná cluinsin sin dionnsoiġiḋ maġnusa mic muirceartaiġ uí concobair.

Tanig iaraṁ mac uilliam gan raḃaḋ gan raṫuccaḋ go tuaim dá ġualann, ar sine go maiġ eó na saxan, ⁊ ní ro ḟágbaiḋ cruaċ na cliaḃ arḃa i relic ṁóir maiġe eó ná hi relic tſmpaill míchil árċaingil, ⁊ tucsat cſiṫri ficit cliaḃ ar na teamplaiḃ fſirin. Tangadar na ḋeadhaiḋ co turlaċ, ⁊ tucsat an diaċ ceona fair. Do ċuirſit dana sluaġ do ċreachaḋ ṁuintire diarmada mic maġnusa, ⁊ do rala muintir concoḃair ruaiḋ, ⁊ turloċa dóiḃ, ⁊ ro airgſit na sluaiġ sin iad uile hi ttrécomursc a ċele. Ro béigſin din do ṁaġnus muintir diarmada do ḋíochur ⁊ dionnarbaḋ uaḋa. Do chuaiḋ conċoḃar ruaḋ araḃarac hi tech mic uilliam, ⁊ do róine síṫ fris, ⁊ fuair aiseac a ċreċe dona buaiḃ trias ro hairgeaḋ, ⁊ an ro aṫinsſit luċt na cille dia ccruḋ do raḋaḋ doiḃ dorídise. Do ḋeachaiḋ ḃeos diarmaid mac maġnusa hi tteach gall tar cſnn a ḃó, ⁊ a ṁuintire doneoċ ro fágbaḋ occa. Luiḋ mac uilliam co balla, ⁊ ro boí oiḋċe ann, do chuaiḋ ais síde co tuaim dá ġualann, ⁊ ro faġaiḃ coicceaḋ connaċt gan riṫ ná saiṁe gan biaḋ i ccill ná hi ttuaiṫ innte.

Aeḋ ua flaiṫbeartaiġ tiġearna iarṫair Connaċt décc.

Diarmaid mac neill uí Ruairc do dallaḋ lá coinċonnaċt ua Raġallaiġ.

Caṫal riabaċ mac giolla bruide uí Ruairc tiġearna ua mbriuin do ecc.

many of the meaner sort of Felym's people were drownded in the puddle of that town; he left [behind] much of the small cattle of the said prey."

[h] *Went over to*, ċuaiḋ dionnsoiġiḋ.—This phrase simply means to go to, or towards. In the Annals of Kilronan the phrase used is, tánic a nuċt; which means that Dermot repaired to Manus for protection.

[i] *Turlagh*, now Turlagh, situated in the barony of Carra, and county of Mayo. It is a fair-town and a rectory, in the diocese of Tuam, where there is a round tower of considerable height, in good preservation.

[k] *Balla*, situated near the boundary between the baronies of Carra and Clanmorris, in the county Mayo; it is a fair-town and a vicarage in the diocese of Tuam. It contains the ruins of an ancient church and round tower.

[l] *Within it.*—This account of the desolation of the province of Connaught is given much better in the Annals of Kilronan. They state that on this occasion the people of Brian, the son of Turlough O'Conor, burned the church of Imlagh Brocadha over the head of O'Flynn's

evil, excepting only Teige, son of Cormac, who was son of Tomaltagh Mac Dermot. As soon as Mac William learned how O'Conor had defeated all who had turned against him, he joined him to reduce them. Dermot, the son of Manus, upon hearing this, went over to[h] Manus, the son of Murtough O'Conor.

After this Mac William proceeded to Tuam da ghualann, without notice or forewarning, and thence to Mayo of the Saxons, and left neither rick nor basket of corn in the large churchyard of Mayo, or in the yard of the church of St. Michael the Archangel, and carried away eighty baskets out of the churches themselves. They afterwards went to Turlagh[i], on which they inflicted a similar calamity. They then sent a body of men to plunder the people of Dermot, the son of Manus, and these falling in with the people of Conor Roe, and the inhabitants of Turlagh, they plundered them all indiscriminately; and Manus was compelled to expel and banish Dermot's people from him. On the following day Conor Roe went into Mac William's house, made peace with him, and received a restoration of the prey of cows which had been taken from him; and such part of their cattle as the people of the church [of Turlagh] were able to recognize as their own was restored to them. Dermot, the son of Manus, also went into the house of [i. e. submitted to] the English, that they might spare such of his people and cattle as were then remaining with him. Mac William proceeded to Balla[k], where he stopped for one night, and went thence to Tuam da ghualann. He left the province of Connaught without peace or tranquillity, and without food in any church or territory within it[l].

Hugh O'Flaherty, Lord of West Connaught, died.

Dermot, the son of Niall O'Rourke, was deprived of sight by Cuconnaught[m] O'Reilly.

Cathal Reagh, son of Gilla-Brude O'Rourke, Lord of Hy-Briuin, died.

people, while it was full of women, children, and nuns, and had also three priests within it; and that Tearmann Caoluinne was also burned by the Lord Justice.

[m] *Cuconnaught.*—Charles O'Conor, of Belanagare, anglicises this name Constantine. Cú connáct signifies the hero, or literally, dog of Connaught. There are several names of men similarly compounded, as Cú Ulaḋ, the hero of Ulster, a name translated *canis Ultoniæ*, by the compiler of the Annals of Ulster; Cu miḋe, the hero of Meath; Cu luaċra, the hero of Luachair; cu muṁan, the hero of Munster; Cú blaḋma, the hero of Slieve Bloom; Cú ċaisil, the hero of Cashel.

Fleochaḋ mór, doineann, ⁊ coccaḋ dearṁair is in mbliaḋainsi.

Maiḋm cluana caṫa do ṫabairt lá feḋlimiḋ ua cconcobair ar cloinn Ruaiḋri, ⁊ ar ċoncobar mac corbmaic meic diarmada.

Giolla Patraic mac giollaroid tiġearna ċenél aongusa décc.

Tearmann caelainne do losccaḋ las an lustis.

Sloiccheaḋ la hUa ndoṁnaill (doṁnall mor) in Ulltoiḃ co hiubar chinn choiche dar ṁill gaċ tír gus a rainicc, ⁊ dá ffuair geill ⁊ uṁla o urṁor ulaḋ.

AOIS CRIOSD, 1237.

Aois Criost, míle, dá ċéd, triocat, a seaċt.

Tomas ua ruaḋain epscop luiġne [decc].

Giollaísu mac an scélaiġi uí tormaiġ epscop Conmaicne [decc].

Giolla na nécc ua mannaċáin décc i mainistir na búille.

Sluaiġead lá feḋlimiḋ mac caṫail croibdeirg cona ḃraiṫriḃ hi cconnachtaiḃ. Cúconnaċt ua Raġallaiġ con uiḃ ḃriúin uile, ⁊ caṫal mag Raġnaill go cconṁaicniḃ immaille fris dionnsoiġiḋ ṡleaċta Ruaiḋri .i. brian mac toirrdealḃaiġ, Muirceartaċ ⁊ doṁnall meic diarmada mic Ruaiḋri, ⁊ conċobar mac corbmaic meic diarmada. Do deaċadar tar coirrṡliaḃ na seaghsa buḋ ṫuaiṫ indeadhaiḋ sleaċta ruaiḋri co rangadar druim raitte, ⁊ do ċuirriot sliocht Ruaiḋr aṁsa an iustis (battar ina bfarraḋ) do ṫabairt

[n] *Heavy rains.*—The Annals of Kilronan give a horrible account of the weather, wars, distresses, and crimes of this year.

[o] *Cluain Catha*, now Battlefield, a townland and gentleman's seat in the barony of Corran, and county of Sligo, about four miles southwards of Ballymote.

[p] *Tearmonn Caollainne.*—The Annals of Kilronan state that this act was committed by the Lord Justice, when he went to Connaught to assist the son of William Burke.—For the situation of Termonn Caelainne see note [b], under the year 1225, p. 238.

[q] *Iubhar Chinn Choiche.*—This is the more ancient name of the town of Newry, in the county of Down, which is now called in Irish *Iubhar Chinn Tragha.*—See *Battle of Magh Rath*, printed for the Irish Archæological Society in 1842, p. 276, note [c]. Under this year (1236) the Annals of Clonmacnoise, as translated by Mageoghegan, record the death of Hugh O'Malone, Bishop of Clonmacnoise, in the abbey of Kilbeggan. They also record the erection of the castle of Loughreagh by Mac William Burk, and of the castle of Ardrahan by the Lord Deputy Mac Maurice; also of the castle of Ullin Wonagh, but without mentioning by whom. Acording to the Annals of Kilronan, the castle of Muille Uanach was erected by the Justiciary Mac Maurice [Fitzgerald] after Felim O'Conor

Heavy rains[a], harsh weather, and much war prevailed in this year.

The victory of Cluain Catha[c] was gained by Felim O'Conor, over the sons of Roderic, and Conor, the son of Cormac Mac Dermot.

Gillapatrick Mac Gillaroid, Lord of Kinel-Aengusa, died.

Tearmonn Caollainne[p] was burned by the Lord Justice.

O'Donnell (Donnell More) marched with an army to Iubhar Chinn Choiche[q] in Ulidia, and destroyed every territory through which he passed: he also obtained hostages and submission from most of the Ulidians.

THE AGE OF CHRIST, 1237.

The Age of Christ, one thousand two hundred thirty-seven.

Thomas O'Rowan, Bishop of Leyny[r], [died].

Gilla-Isa Mac-an-Skealy O'Tormy, Bishop of Conmaicne [Ardagh], died.

Gilla-na-necc[s] O'Monahan died in the monastery of Boyle.

An army was led by Felim, the son of Cathal Crovderg [O'Conor], and his brothers, into Connaught, being joined by Cuconnaught O'Reilly, with all the Hy-Briuin, and by Cathal Mac Randal, with the Conmaicni[t], against the descendants of Roderic, namely, Brian, son of Turlough, Murtough, and Donnell, sons of Dermot, who was son of Roderic, and Conor, son of Cormac, who was son of Dermot. They went northwards across Coirrshliabh-na-Seaghsa[u], until they arrived at Drumraitte[w], in pursuit of the race of Roderic. The descendants of Roderic sent the soldiers of the Lord Justice, who were

had fled to O'Donnell, and while the son of William Burke was in England. The Annals of Kilronan record, under this year, the killing of Melaghlin O'Malley by Donnell, son of Manus who was the son of Murtough Muimhneach O'Conor, on the island of Oilen da Chruinde, which is a small island near Rinvile, in the barony of Ballinahinch, in the north-west of the county of Galway.

[r] *Bishop of Leyny*, i. e. of Achonry.

[s] *Gilla-na-necc.*—In the Annals of Kilronan the name is written more correctly, Gılla na neach, i. e. the *youth of the horses.*

[t] *Conmaicni*, i. e. the Conmaicni of Moy-Rein, who possessed the southern part of the county of Leitrim.—See note [r], under the year 1215, p. 186.

[u] *Coirrshliabh-na-Seaghsa.*—This is the Irish name of the Curlieu mountains, situated to the north of Boyle, in the county of Roscommon.

[w] *Drumraitte*, now Drumrat, a parish in the barony of Corran, and county of Sligo, situated to the north of the Curlieu mountains.

deabṫa dfeḋlimiḋ cona ṡocraide. Ro forcongair feḋlimiḋ fora ṡlóġaiḃ gan a ndiuḃracaḋ itir acht tocht dia niombualaḋ gan fuireaċ. Do rónad fairrioṁ sin, ni ro ḟulngsettar na hamsa go cian an iomtuarġain an tan ro sraoíneaḋ forra i ccénn a muintire. Ro marḃaḋ drong mór dioḃ im Mac mibricc don cur sin.

Od ċonncattar sliċt Ruaiḋri an sgaoileaḋ ⁊ an scainnreaḋ tugaḋ for a soċraide, ro iomġabsat an tionaḋ a mbattar gan aoínneaċ do ṁarḃaḋ díḃ. Do sgaoilsit a haiṫle an ṁaḋma sin cona baoí aittreabh hi síol muireaḋaiġ leo. Ro hairccead a muintir uile lá feḋlimiḋ, ⁊ do rónaḋ creaċa iomḋa ar concoḃar mac corbmaic hi ttir nailealla. Ruccusdar iaroṁ a loingsi for loċ cé, ⁊ ro ḋioċuir de corbmac mac diarmada tiġearna maiġe luirg, ⁊ ro airgc maġ luirgc uile. Faccbaid dana, tiġearnus an tíre ⁊ an loċa ag donnchaḋ mac muirċéṙtaiġ luaṫṙuiliġ.

Siṫ do ḋénaṁ don iustis ré feḋlimiḋ, ⁊ tuccaḋ cúig triuċa an rígh ḋóroṁ gan croḋ gan ċíos orra.—(*Vide supra*, 1230).

Maġnus mac diarmada mic maġnusa do ṁarḃaḋ lá doṁnall mac diarmada mic Ruaiḋri uí concoḃair.

Muirceartaċ mac diarmada mic Ruaiḋri uí concoḃair do ṁarḃaḋ lá mac maġnusa mic muirceartaiġ muiṁniġ.

Creaċ do denaṁ lá Concobair mac corbmaic for Ruaidri ua ngaḋra, ⁊ braṫair Ruaiḋri do ṁarḃaḋ.

Ḃraiġde Concoḃair mic corbmaic do ṁarḃaḋ lá feḋlimiḋ mac caṫail croiḃdeirg.

Mainistir canánaċ do tionnscnaḋ lá clarus mac mailín in oilen na trinóide ar loċ uaċtair iar na ċoṁairleaccaḋ dó ó caṫal ua Raġallaiġ.

[x] *Mac Mibric.*—This name is still extant in the county of Mayo, but always anglicised Merrick. This family, which is of Welsh extraction, was seated in the valley of Glenhest, to the west of Glen-Nephin, in the county of Mayo.—See *Genealogies, Tribes, and Customs of Hy-Fiachrach*, published by the Irish Archæological Society in 1844, pp. 331, 332, 401.

[y] *Lough Key.*—The Annals of Clonmacnoise state that Felim O'Conor took possession of Lough Key and Lough Arvagh [Lough Arrow], on this occasion.

[z] *Free of cattle-tribute or rent.*—This is scarcely true; for it appears, from an entry on a great roll of the Pipe, of the forty-sixth year of Henry III., A. D. 1262, that Ffethelmus O'Konechor owed 5000 marks and 2000 cows, for having three cantreds of land in Connaught in fee-farm, viz., the cantreds of Machney [maġ naoi], Tyrtotha [trí tuaṫa], and Moylurg.—See

along with them, to give battle to Felim and his forces. Felim, however, ordered his troops not to shoot at them at all, but to come to a close fight without delay. This was done according to his order; and the soldiers did not long sustain the charge, when they were routed towards their people. A great number of them were slain, and, among the rest, Mac Mibric[x].

When the descendants of Roderic saw the flight and confusion into which their forces were thrown, they retreated from their position without the loss of a man. After this defeat, however, they were dispersed in such a manner that they had no residence in [the territory of] Sil-Murray. All their people were plundered by Felim, and many preys were taken from Conor, son of Cormac, in Tirerrill. They [Felim's party] afterwards brought their fleet on Lough Key[y], and drove from thence Cormac Mac Dermot, Lord of Moylurg, and plundered all Moylurg; and the lordship of the territory and lake they gave to Donough, the son of Murtough Luath-Shuileach.

The Lord Justice made peace with Felim; and the five cantreds of the King were given him [Felim], free of cattle-tribute, or rent[z].—(*Vide supra*, 1230.)

Manus, son of Dermot, who was son of Manus, was slain by Donnell, son of Dermott, who was son of Roderic O'Conor.

Murtough, son of Dermott, who was son of Roderic, was slain by the son of Manus, son of Murtough Muimhneach [O'Conor].

A prey was taken by Conor, son of Cormac, from Rory O'Gara, and Rory's brother was slain.

The hostages of Conor, the son of Cormac, were put to death by Felim, son of Cathal Crovderg.

A monastery for canons was commenced by Clarus Mac Mailin, on Trinity Island[a] in Lough Oughter, under the patronage of Cathal O'Reilly.

Hardiman's History of Galway, p. 48, note [x].

[a] *Trinity Island in Lough Oughter.*—This island is in the upper or southern part of Lough Oughter, and belongs to the parish of Kilmore, in the barony of Upper Loughtee, and county of Cavan.—See Ordnance Map of this county, sheet 20, on which Trinity Abbey and grave-yard are shewn. The island contains 122 acres, 2 roods, and 11 perches, English measure. According to Ware this monastery was founded in the year 1249.—See Harris's edition of his Antiquities, p. 272.

Under this year (1237) the Annals of Kilronan and of Clonmacnoise record the death of Donat O'Fidhubhra, called in the latter O'Furie, Archbishop of Armagh.

ḃarúin na heireann do ṫoċt i cconnaċtaiḃ, ⁊ caislén do ṫinnscsctal dóiḃ do dénam innte.

AOIS CRIOST, 1238.

Aois Criost, mile, da cheḋ, triocat, a hocht.

Felix ua Ruanaḋa airdeps cop tuama iar ccor a epscoboide de ar ḋia riar an tan sin, ⁊ iar ngabáil habite manċsra ime hi ccill muire in aṫcliaṫ déġ.

Donnchaḋ uaiṫneaċ mac aoḋa mic Ruaiḋri uí concoḃair do ṁarḃaḋ lá taḋg mac aoḋa mic caṫail croiḃḋeirg.

Donnchaḋ mac duarcáin uí sġra tiġearna luiġne do gabáil lá taḋg mac aoḋa mic caṫail croiḃḋeirg, ⁊ an tan rugaḋ dia ċoiméd é ro marḃsat a ḃraiṫre buḋḋéin, .i. meic aoḋa uí sġra ar an sliġiḋ a ttír briúin na sionna.

Flaiṫbeartaċ mac Caṫṁaoil ardtaoíseaċ cenél fsraḋaiġ, ⁊ toiseaċ cloinne Congail, ⁊ ó ccsnnḟoda i ttír manaċ, feiġe gaisccid ⁊ einiġ tíre heoġain do ṁarḃaḋ lá donnchaḋ mac caṫṁaoil lá a ḃraṫair fsin tria ṫangnaċt.

Donnchaḋ mac muirceartaiġ do ḋol ir in mbreifne go hua Raġallaiġ, ⁊ ruġ sluaġ mór lais i cconnaċtaiḃ, ⁊ ro aircceist muintir cluana coirpṫi, ⁊ ro marḃaḋ sochaiḋe do ṁaiṫiḃ muintire heolais hi ttóraiġeaċt na creċe sin, ⁊ drong mór dona tuathaiḃ.

Maolruanaiḋ mac donnchaḋa ui ḋuḃda do ṁarḃaḋ lá maolseaċlainn

[b] Under this year the Annals of Kilronan state, that Donough, the son of Murtough O'Conor, granted the lands of Drumann iarthar, and the tract extending from Lathach Cille Braoin to the lake [Lough Key], both wood, bog, and plain, to the congregation of the Holy Trinity of Lough Key, and to Clarus Mac Mailin, and that he reigned but one month after making this grant.

[c] *Felix O'Rooney.*—In Harris's edition of Ware's Bishops, p. 605, in which he is called Felix O'Ruadan, it is stated that he was the uncle of King Roderic O'Conor, and that having resigned in the year 1235, he spent the remainder of his life in St. Mary's Abbey, near Dublin, where he died in the year 1238. It is stated in the annals of this abbey, that he covered the church and belfry of the Blessed Virgin, near Dublin, with lead; and that he was magnificently interred in the chancel of the church, at the steps of the altar, on the left hand side.

[d] *Cluain-Coirpthi.*—In the *Feilire Aenguis*, at the 15th of February, this place is described as i noiṫriḃ cenel doḃṫa i connaċtaiḃ, i. e. "in the desert or wilderness of Kinel-Dofa, in Connaught." For some account of this place, see

The barons of Ireland went to Connaught, and commenced erecting castles there[b].

THE AGE OF CHRIST, 1238.

The Age of Christ, one thousand two hundred thirty-eight.

Felix O'Rooney[c], Archbishop of Tuam, after having some time before resigned his bishopric for the sake of God, and after having assumed the monastic habit in Kilmurry [Mary's Abbey], in Dublin, died.

Donough Uaithneach, son of Hugh, who was son of Roderic O'Conor, was slain by Teige, son of Hugh, who was son of Cathal Crovderg.

Donough, son of Duarcan O'Hara, Lord of Leyny, was taken prisoner by Teige, the son of Hugh, who was son of Cathal Crovderg; and, while on his way to the place of confinement, he was killed in Hy-Briuin-na-Sinna, by his own kinsmen, namely, the sons of Hugh O'Hara.

Flaherty Mac Cawell, Chief of Kinel-Farry, and Clann-Congail, and of Hy-Kennoda in Fermanagh, the most illustrious in Tyrone for feats of arms and hospitality, was treacherously slain by Donough Mac Cawell, his own kinsman.

Donough, son of Murtough [Mac Dermot], went into Breifny to O'Reilly, and brought a great force with him into Connaught, and plundered the people of Cluain-Coirpthi[d]; and many of the chiefs of Muintir-Eolais[e] were slain in pursuit of the prey which had been taken in the country, as were also a great number of [inhabitants of] the Tuathas.

Mulrony, the son of Donough O'Dowda, was slain by Melaghlin, the son of

Colgan's *Acta Sanctorum*, at the 15th February, and the Irish Calendar of the O'Clerys, at the same day. St. Berach, or Barry, the original founder of this church, flourished about the year 580. The situation of Cluain Coirpthe, which has been mistaken by Archdall, and even by the accurate Dr. Lanigan (see his Ecclesiastical History, vol. ii. p. 325), is still well known to the natives of Kinel-Dofa, in the county of Roscommon. It is now called Kilbarry, and is situated in the parish of Termonbarry, in O'Hanly's country, near the Shannon. The ruins of several churches are still to be seen there, and there was a round tower standing near one of them in the memory of some old persons, with whom the Editor conversed in the year 1837, when he visited this celebrated locality.

[e] *Muintir-Eolais.*—The O'Ferralls were called Muintir Anghaile; the Mac Ranals Muintir Eolais.

mac concobair ruaiḋ mic muirceartaiġ muiṁniġ, ⁊ la mac tiġearnáin mic caṫail miccarain uí concobair.

Caislena do ḋénaṁ hi muintir murchaḋa hi cconmaicne cuile, ⁊ a ccſra lár na barúnaiḃ réṁráite.

Sluaiġeaḋ lá mac muiris iustís na herenn, ⁊ lá hugo de laci iarla ulaḋ hi ccenél eoġain ⁊ hi ccenél conaill. Ro aiṫriġſſt mag laċlainn (.i. doṁnall) ⁊ tucsat tiġearnus cenél eoġain do mac uí neill, ⁊ ro gaḃsat fſin braiġde an tuaisceirt.

Cloicṫeaċ eanaiġ dúin do denaṁ.

Caṫal mag riaḃaiġ taoiseaċ fear sceine décc.

AOIS CRIOSD, 1239.

Aois Criost, mile, da ċéd, triocat, anaoí.

Muircſrtaċ mac Doṁnaill uí briain do écc.

Caṫ cairn triaḋail do ṫabairt lá Doṁnall mag laċlainn dú in ro marbaḋ doṁnall taṁnaiġe ua néill, mag maṫġaṁna, Somairle ua gairmleaḋaiġ, caoċ bſrnais ua gairmleaḋaiġ, ⁊ maiṫe cenel moain go sochaiḋiḃ iomḋa

[f] *Muintir Murchadha.*—This was the tribe name of the O'Flahertys, and it became also that of the territory which they possessed, and which, before the English invasion, was nearly co-extensive with the barony of Clare, in the county of Galway. In an Inquisition taken at Galway, on the 20th of March, 1608, before Geffry Osbaldston, Esq., this territory is called Muinter-murroghoe, and described as forming the northern part of the barony of Clare, then a part of Clanrickard. The O'Flahertys seem to have been driven from this territory in the year 1238, or very soon afterwards, when they settled in that part of the county of Galway lying west of Lough Orbsen, where they became as powerful as ever they had been in their more original territory of Muintir Murchadha.

[g] *The son of O'Neill.*—Charles O'Conor writes *inter lineas*, .i. do Ḃhrian, i. e. to Brian.

[h] *Cloictheach* is the Irish name by which the round towers of Ireland are still known in their respective localities, as cloiġṫeaċ ċille riġ, in the county Kilkenny; cloicṫeaċ cluana Uaṁa, Cloyne steeple.—See O'Brien's Dictionary, *in voce* cloiġṫeac and cuilceaċ. In some parts of Ireland the word is made cuilcṫeaċ by metathesis, and in others clógas is the form used to express steeple or round tower. O'Brien gives *cloigtheach* and *cuilceach* as denoting a steeple or belfry; and clogas as a belfry or steeple. O'Reilly also gives both forms of the term.—See Petrie's Inquiry into the Origin and Uses of the Round Towers of Ireland, p. 390.

[i] *Annadown*, Eanaċ dúin.—A townland, containing the ruins of a monastery and several churches, near the margin of Lough Corrib, in the barony of Clare and county of Galway.

[k] *Mac Reevy*, mag riaḃaiġ, now generally an-

Conor Roe, who was son of Murtough Muimhneach, and by the son of Tiernan, who was son of Cathal Miccarain O'Conor.

Castles were erected in Muintir-Murchadha[f], in Conmaicne-Cuile, and in Carra, by the barons aforesaid.

An army was led by Mac Maurice, Lord Justice of Ireland, and Hugo de Lacy, Earl of Ulster, into Tyrone and Tirconnell. They deposed Mac Loughlin (Donnell), and gave the government of Tyrone to the son of O'Neill[g], and they themselves obtained the hostages of the north.

The Cloictheach[h] of Annadown[i] was erected.

Cathal Mac Reevy[k], Lord of Feara-Scedne[l], died[m].

THE AGE OF CHRIST, 1239.

The Age of Christ, one thousand two hundred thirty-nine.

Murtough, the son of Donnell O'Brien, died.

The battle of Carnteel[n] was fought by Donnell Mac Loughlin, where Donnell Tamnaighe O'Neill, Mac Mahon, Sorley O'Gormly, and Caech-

glicised Mac Creevy, or M'Greevy.

[l] *Feara-Scedne.*—The situation of this tribe, to whom there is no other reference in the Irish annals, has not been determined. Duald Mac Firbis, in his Genealogical Book (Lord Roden's copy, p. 783), gives a list of the families of the Feara Sgenne, consisting of Mac Riabhaigh, as chief, and thirty-one other families; but he does not inform us where they were located. O'Duggan, in his Topographical Poem, makes Mac Riabhaigh the ancient Chief of Moylurg, in the now county of Roscommon; but we cannot believe that he and his thirty-one families had any power in Moylurg at this period, unless as followers of the Mac Dermots, who were then its chief lords.

[m] Under this year (1238) the Annals of Clonmacnoise, as translated by Mageoghegan, contain the following passage, relating to the affairs of Ulster, of which the Four Masters have collected no notice: "A. D. 1238. Mac Gille Morie, a good chieftaine of Ulster, was killed by some of the people of Hugh Delacie, Earle of Ulster, as he was going to the Earle's house; whereupon Mac Donnsleyve, the King of Ulster's" [*recte* Uladh's, or Ulidia's] "son, Melaghlyn, Prince of Kynell Owen, and all the Chieftains of Ulster, took armes and banished the said Earle of Ulster out of the whole provence. The Earle of Ulster assembled together all the English of Ireland, and went the second time to Ulster where he possessed himself of all the lands again, in the three months of harvest, and banished Melaghlyn from thence into Connought. O'Neale the Read took the superioritie and principalitie of Tyre Owen afterwards."

[n] *Carnteel*, carn tSiaḋail, i. e. the Carn of Siadhail, Sheil, or Sedulius; a small village in a parish of the same name, in the barony of Dungannon, and county of Tyrone, a short dis-

immaille friú, ⁊ ro ġabh arís an tiġearnus, ⁊ ro benadh ḋe gan ḟuireach déis an ṁaḋma sin.

Toirrḋealbhach mac Ruaiḋri uí Conċobhair (Rí Connacht) décc.

Ferġal mac Conconnacht uí Raġallaiġ tiġearna Dartraiġe ⁊ cloinne Fermaiġe, ⁊ tiġearna Breifne ó ṡliabh sair, maḋ iar leabhar oile, do ṁarbhaḋ lá Maolruanaiḋ mac Fearġail ⁊ lá Conċobhar mac Corbmaic ar ndula ḋó ar creċ go mac Neill mic Conġalaiġ dia ro airecc iad, ⁊ diar ġabh teaġ orra, ⁊ tainic Muirċertaċ mac Néill ar bfiṫir as an tiġ amach. Ro ġabhaḋ é, ⁊ ro marbhaḋ fó ceḋóir déis mic uí Raġallaiġ do ṁarbhaḋ.

Creaċ do dénaṁ lá Gallaiḃ Ereann ar ua nDoṁnaill gur ró airgset Cairpri, ⁊ ro baoí an lustís fein occ Esrodara occa Rurnaiḋe, ⁊ do ḋeaċadar a ṡirṫi go Druim cliabh.

Lasairḟina ingen Caṫail Ċroibhḋerg bean huí Domnaill do ṫabhairt leiṫbhaile da fearonn ḟorsta .i. Ros ḃirn, do Clarus mac Maoilín, ⁊ do coiṁṫionól canánaċ oilén na Trinóide ar Loċ Cé in onoir na Trinóide ⁊ Muire.

Corbmac mac Airt huí Ṁaoileaċlainn déġ.

AOIS CRIOST, 1240.

Aois Criost, míle, da céd, ceṫrachat.

Maineistir do thóġbhail i bPurtlairge lá Sir Hugo Purpel do ḃraiṫriḃ .S. Fraincis.

Giolla na naoṁ ua Dreáin airċinneach Arda carna do écc.

tance to the north-east of Aughnacloy, on the road to Dungannon.

[o] *Caech-Bearnais*, i. e. the blind man of Barnis.

[p] *Mountain.*—The mountain of Breifny means Slieve-in-ierin.

[q] *Congallagh.*—See an entry under the year 1228, where this Niall, the son of Congalagh, is called O'Rourke, and said to have been Lord of Dartry and Clann-Fearmaighe.

[r] *The son of O'Reilly.*—This story, which is so briefly and imperfectly told, has been copied by the Four Masters from the Annals of Connaught.—See entry under the year 1240, from which it appears that the Mulrony and Conor here mentioned were sons of Cormac Mac Dermot, Chief of Moylurg.

[s] *Rosbirn.*—The Down Survey shews a denomination of land called Rossborne, near the mouth of the Ballysadare River, in the parish of Kilmacowen, barony of Carbury, and county of Sligo. This barony belonged, at this period, to O'Donnell, who must have given this, and other lands in its vicinity, as a *tinscra*, or dowry, to his wife, according to the old Irish custom.

[t] *Cormac.*—His death is noticed as follows in Mageoghegan's translation of the Annals of

Bearnais[o] O'Gormly, and the chiefs of Kinel Moen, with many others, were slain. Mac Loughlin reassumed the lordship after this battle, but was deprived of it without delay.

Turlough, the son of Roderic O'Conor (King of Connaught), died.

Farrell, the son of Cuconnaught O'Reilly, Lord of Dartry and Clann-Fermaighe, and, according to another book, Lord of Breifny, from the mountain[p] eastwards, was slain by Mulrony, son of Farrell, and Conor, son of Cormac [Mac Dermot], after he had gone on a predatory excursion to the son of Niall, the son of Congallagh[q] [O'Rourke], on which occasion he plundered them and took their house. Murtough, son of Niall, came out on parole, but was seized and killed, immediately after the son of O'Reilly[r] had been slain.

A prey was taken by the English of Ireland from O'Donnell, and they plundered Carbury; and the Lord Justice himself was awaiting them at Ballysadare, and his scouts went as far as Drumcliff.

Lasarina, daughter of Cathal Crovderg O'Conor, and the wife of O'Donnell, gave a half townland of her marriage dowry, viz., Rosbirn[s], to Clarus Mac Mailin, and the Canons of Trinity Island, in Lough Key, in honour of the Trinity and the Virgin Mary.

Cormac[t], the son of Art O'Melaghlin, died.

THE AGE OF CHRIST, 1240.

The Age of Christ, one thousand two hundred forty.

A monastery was founded at Waterford for Franciscan Friars by Sir Hugo Purcell.

Gilla-na-naev O'Dreain, Erenagh of Ardcarne, died.

Clonmacnoise: "A. D. 1238. Cormac mac Art O'Melaghlyn, the prince that most annoyed and hinder'd the English in his own time, and next successor of the Kingdome of Meath, if he had lived and were suffered by the English, died quietly in his bed, without fight or dissention, in Inis Dowgyn, upon the river of Sack."

The same Annals contain the following passages, under this year, which have been omitted by the Four Masters:

"A. D. 1238. Geffrye O'Dalie, an excellent poett, died in pilgrimage in Sruhir.

"Walter Delacie repaired to the King of England.

"The Earle of Ulster's sonn was killed by the Ulster men, and twenty-eight men in shirts of mail with him."

Sluaiġeaḋ mór lá Coinċonnaċt ua Raġallaiġ for Ċorbmac mac nDiarmata co ro airgg an tír uile co hArd Carna, ⁊ ro marḃ daoíne iomḋa i ndioġail a meic, ⁊ Corbmac mac Tomaltaiġ do aiṫríġaḋ, ⁊ Donnchaḋ mac Muirċſrtaiġ do gabáil tiġearnusa Muiġe Luirg.

Feḋlimiḋ ua Concoḃair do dol do laṫair riġ Saxan do ċosaoid Gall ⁊ Gaoiḋeal fris, ⁊ fuair onóir ṁór on riġ don ċur sin, ⁊ tainig slan dia ṫiġ.

Aoḋ mac Giolla na naoṁ Cruimm uí Seaċnusaiġ do ṁarḃaḋ lá Concoḃar mac Aoḋa mic Caṫail Croiḃdeirg, ⁊ lá Fiaċra ua Floinn.

Saḋḃ ingean uí Ċeinneidiġ bſn Donnchaiḋ Ċairbriġ uí Ḃriain décc.

Mainestir Tighe Molaga hi cCairpre isin Mumain in Escopoideċt Ruis do ṡonnraḋ do ṫógḃail do ḃraiṫriḃ .S. Franseis lá Mag Carṫaiġ riaḃaċ tiġearna Cairpreach ⁊ a tumba fein do denoṁ hi cCoraiḋ na mbraṫar. As innte ros aḋnaicṫſr an Barrach mor, ⁊ ó Maṫġamna Cairpreaċ, ⁊ Barún Cúrsach.

[u] *Felim O'Conor.*—In the Annals of Clonmacnoise, as translated by Connell Mageoghegan, the notice of Felim O'Conor's appearance before the King of England is given as follows: "A. D. 1240. Felym O'Connor went into England, because the English of Ireland refused to yeald him any justice; the King graunted him the five cantreds, which himself had, and [he] returned in safety."

Matthew Paris gives a curious account of the reception of Felim O'Conor at the English court, but he errs in giving John as the name of the De Burgo, against whom he lodged his complaints; for it does not appear from any trustworthy document, nor any authority whatever, except Matthew Paris himself, and Dr. Hanmer, a very careless chronicler, who merely copies him, that there was any powerful man named John de Burgo in Ireland at this time. So effectually did Felim plead his cause on this occasion, that King Henry III. ordered Maurice Fitzgerald, then Lord Justice of Ireland, "to pluck up by the root that fruitless sycamore, De Burgo, which the Earl of Kent, in the insolence of his power, had planted in those parts, nor suffer it to bud forth any longer." "Ut ipsius iniquæ plantationis, quam Comes Cantiæ Hubertus in illis partibus, dum suâ potentiâ debaccharet, plantavit, infructuosam sicomorum radicitus evulsam, non sinerat pullulare."—See Matthew Paris at this year. Dr. O'Conor states, in his suppressed work, *Memoirs of the Life and Writings of Charles O'Conor*, p. 42, that Felim O'Conor obtained a royal charter for five baronies in the year 1257, and that he shortly after built the abbeys of Roscommon and Tuamona. In the last edition of Rymer, vol. i. p. 240, there is a letter from Felim O'Conohur, King of Connaught, to Henry III., thanking him for the many favours which he had conferred upon him, and especially for his having written in his behalf against Walter de Burgo to his Justiciary, William Dene; but this letter, though placed under the year 1240 by Rymer, refers to a later period, as Dene was not Justiciary before 1260.

[v] *Sabia*, Saḋḃ.—This was very common as the proper name of a woman, till a recent period, in Ireland, but it is now nearly obsolete. The

A great army was led by Cuconnaught O'Reilly against Cormac Mac Dermot, and plundered the entire country as far as Ardcarne, and slew many people, in revenge of his son. Cormac, the son of Tomaltagh, was deposed, and Donough, the son of Murtough [Mac Dermot], assumed the lordship of Moylurg.

Felim O'Conor[u] went before the King of England to complain to him of the English and Irish, on which occasion he received great honour from the King; he then returned safe home.

Hugh, the son of Gilla-na-naev Crom O'Shaughnessy, was slain by Conor, son of Hugh, who was the son of Cathal Crovderg, and by Fiachra O'Flynn.

Sabia[v], daughter of O'Kennedy, and wife of Donough Cairbreach O'Brien, died.

The Monastery of Timoleague[w], in Carbery, in Munster, in the diocese of Ross, was founded for Franciscan Friars, by Mac Carthy Reagh, Lord of Carbery, and his own tomb was erected in the choir of the Friars. In this monastery also Barry More, O'Mahony of Carbery, and the Baron Courcy, are interred[x].

word signifies *goodness*.

[w] *Timoleague*, a monastery, now in ruins, in the barony of Barryroe, in the county of Cork. Ceać molaga signifies the house of St. Molaga, who probably erected a primitive Irish monastery at this place, but of this we have no record. This saint was a native of Fermoy, and his principal monastery was at a place in that territory called Tulach min Molaga.—See his Life given by Colgan, in his *Acta Sanctorum*, at 20th January, p. 148. The year of his death is not recorded, but it must have been after the year 665, as we learn from his life that he survived the great pestilence which raged in that year. Dr. Smith, in his description of this abbey, gives the following account of its tombs: "Here are several tombs of the Irish families, viz., Mac Carthy Reaghs, in the midst of the choir; west of it is an old broken monument of the O'Cullanes; and on the right a ruined tomb of the lords Courcy. The O'Donovans, O'Heas, &c., were also buried here."—*Natural and Civil History of Cork*, vol. i. p. 251. In the will of Daniell O'Donovane, made at Rahin, in August, 1629, and now preserved in the Registry of the Court of Prerogative in Ireland, he orders his "bodie to be buried in the Abby of Tymolege," but his descendants soon after placed their tomb in the churchyard of Myross. Most, if not all the other families have also discontinued to bury in this abbey.

[x] Under this year the Annals of Clonmacnoise, as translated by Mageoghegan, contain the following passages, which have been omitted by the Four Masters:

"A. D. 1240. William Delacie, Lord of Meath, the only son of Walter Delacie, and his wife, died in one week. Some say they were poysoned.

"There arose great dissentions in Ulster against the Earle of Ulster this year. Richard Tuite, with a company of 3000 soldiers, went to assist him."

AOIS CRIOST, 1241.

Aois Criost míle, dá céd, ceathrachatt a haon.

An tepscop ua Flaiṫbeartaiġ (.i. Muirċeartaċ), .i. epscop eanaiġ dúin [do ecc].

Coisearccaḋ teampaill na mbraṫar minúr in Áṫluain lá comarba Patraic.

Domhnall mór mac Éccneaċáin huí Doṁnaill tiġearna tíre Conaill, Fearmanaċ, ⁊ íoċtair Connaċt co Coirrsliaḃ, ⁊ Oirġiall ó clár anuas décc in aibítt manaiġ iar mbreiṫ buaḋa ó ḋoṁan, ⁊ o ḋeaṁan, ⁊ a aḋnacal co nonóir ⁊ go nairmitin i mainistir Easa Ruaiḋ is in foġṁar do ṡonnraḋ.

Maoilseaċlainn ua Doṁnaill do oirdneḋ i ttiġearnus tíre Conaill ind ionaḋ a aṫar. Ua Neill, .i. Brian do ṫeaċt ċuiġe iar ná ionnarbaḋ la Doṁnall Maġ Laċlainn, ⁊ ua Doṁnaill do ḋula cona ṡoċraiḋe lá Brian ua Néill hi cenél Eoġain, ⁊ tuccsat cath do Mag Laċlainn, .i. caṫ Caimeirge, ⁊ ro ṁarḃsat Doṁnall ua Laċlainn tiġearna Cenel Eoġain, ⁊ deicneaḃar da ḋerḃfine, ⁊ taoisiċh cenél Eoġain uile immaille fris, ⁊ ro hoirdneaḋ Brian don chur sin i ttiġearnus Cenel Eoġain.

Diarmaid mac Magnusa mic Toirrḋealḃaiġ ṁóir uí Ċonċoḃair saoí einiġ ⁊ eangnaṁa do ecc.

Sitriucc Ṁág Oireaċtaiġ taoíseaċ Cloinne Tomaltaiġ decc.

Ualtra de Laci tiġearna Miḋe ó Gallaiḃ, ⁊ ceann coṁairle Gall Ereann déġ hi Saxaiḃ.

Taḋg mac Ruaiḋri uí Gaḋra décc.

Taḋg ua Conċoḃair do argain Dartraiġe ⁊ Cloinne Fearmaiġe.

[y] *The plain*, clár.—The plain here referred to is Machaire Oirghiall, or the level part of the county of Louth, which was then in the possession of the English.

[z] *Caimeirge*.—There is no place of this name now in the ancient territory of Kinel-Owen. But tradition points out the site of a great battle between the rival families of O'Neill and Mac Loughlin, near Maghera, in the county of Londonderry, which the Editor inclines to believe to be that of the battle here referred to.

[a] *Walter de Lacy*.—His obituary is given as follows in Mageoghegan's translation of the Annals of Clonmacnoise:

"A. D. 1241. Walter Delacie, the bountifullest Englishman for horses, cloaths, money, and goold, that ever came before his time into this kingdom, died in England of a Wound."

His only son, William, died in 1240.—See

THE AGE OF CHRIST, 1241.

The Age of Christ, one thousand two hundred forty-one.

Bishop O'Flaherty (i. e. Murtough), i. e. the Bishop of Annadown, died.

The church of the Friars Minor in Athlone was consecrated by the successor of St. Patrick.

Donnell More, the son of Egnaghan O'Donnell, Lord of Tirconnell, Fermanagh, and Lower Connaught, as far as the Curlieu Mountains, and of Oriel, from the plain[y] northwards, died in the monastic habit, victorious over the world and the devil, and was interred with honour and respect in the monastery of Assaroe, in the harvest time.

Melaghlin O'Donnell was installed in the lordship of Tirconnell, in the place of his father. O'Neill (i. e. Brian), after having been expelled by Mac Loughlin, came to O'Donnell, and O'Donnell, with his forces, went with Brian O'Neill into Tyrone, and they gave battle to Mac Loughlin, i. e. the battle of Caimeirge[z], in which they slew Donnell O'Loughlin, Lord of the Kinel-Owen, and ten of his family, together with all the chieftains of the Kinel-Owen. And Brian [O'Neill] was then installed in the lordship of the Kinel-Owen.

Dermot, the son of Manus, son of Turlough More O'Conor, celebrated for hospitality and prowess, died.

Sitric Mageraghty, Chief of Clann-Tomalty, died.

Walter de Lacy[a], Lord of the English of Meath, and head of the council[b] of the English of Ireland, died in England.

Teige, the son of Rory O'Gara, died.

Teige O'Conor plundered Dartry and Clann-Fearmaighe [in the county of Leitrim].

note[x] under that year. This Walter left two daughters, co-heiresses, Margaret and Mabel, the elder of whom married Lord Theobald de Verdon, and the second, Geoffry de Geneville. The palatinate of Meath was divided between these two ladies, Lough Seudy, now Ballymore-Lough Seudy, in Westmeath, being the head of Verdon's moiety, and Trim that of Geneville's. In 1330, after Verdon's forfeiture, the palatinate was re-united in favour of Roger Mortimer, who married Geneville's grand-daughter and heiress.—Rot. Pat. 2 Hen. V. 137. See Grace's *Annals of Ireland*, edited by the Rev. Richard Butler, for the Irish Archæological Society, p. 30, note [t].

[b] *Head of the Council*, ceann aċcomairc, means nothing more than that he was so politic and prudent as to be always consulted by the Eng-

Sluaġ mór do dénaṁ lás an iustis, .i. muiris mac gearailt i maiġ naé go ro airccsít fiacra ua flainn, ⁊ donnchaḋ mac diarmada, ⁊ ruccsat uaṫaḋ do ṁuintir ui conċoḃair forra, ⁊ ro marḃaḋ leó nár mac giolla ċeallaiġ ⁊ sochaiḋe ele.

Doṁnall mag ḟlannchaḋa taoiseaċ dartraiġe do écc.

AOIS CRIOST, 1242.

Aois Criost, míle, da ċéd, cetraċad, adó.

Doṁnall mac airten do écc ina ċanánaċ hi ccill ṁóir.

Caibitil ṁór lá Príṁaiḋ arda maċa, ⁊ la habbadaiḃ cananach ereann i luġṁaḋ dia ro toġbaḋ moran do ṫaisiḃ do ṫionoil moċta on Róiṁ.

Donnchaḋ Cairpreaċ ua briain (tiġerna dail ccais) tuir ordain ⁊ oireaċais deisceirt Ereann, ⁊ a mac toirrdealbaċ mac donnchaḋa cairbriġ décc.

Conċoḃar ua briain do ġaḃail riġe tuadṁuṁan.

Aeḋ ua concoḃair (.i. an taiṫcleireaċ) mac aoḋa mic Ruaiḋri uí Chonċoḃair do ṁarḃaḋ la toirrdealbaċ mac aoḋa mic caṫail croibdeirg.

Brian mac donnchaiḋ uí dubda tiġearna ua ffiaċrach, ⁊ ua naṁalgaḋa ⁊ iorrais do ṁarḃaḋ ar slicchiḋ acc dol dá oiliṫre co mainistir na búille.

Sluaiġeaḋ mór las an lustis ⁊ lá gallaiḃ ereann archena, ⁊ lá feidlimiḋ mac caṫail croibdeirg hi cenel cconaill in diaiḋ taiḋg uí ċonċoḃair do ċóiḋ dionnsoiġiḋ cenél cconaill. Ro gaḃsad na slóiġ sin Longport i nDruim ṫuama, ⁊ ro ṁillsít a lán don ċuairt sin gén gur treigeaḋ taḋg dóiḃ. Taḋg ua Conċoḃair do ġaḃail iarttáin lá coinconnaċt ua Raġallaiġ tria forċongra ḟeiḋlimiḋ mic caṫail ċroiḃdeirg.

lish whenever they engaged in a war, or came on terms of peace with the Irish.

c *Nar.*—The Mac Gillakellys had this name from Nar, the eldest son of Guaire Aidhne, King of Connaught, from whose son Artghal they descend.—See *Genealogies, Tribes, and Customs of Hy-Fiachrach*, p. 69.

d *Primate.*—His name was Albert of Cologn.—See Harris's edition of Ware's Bishops, p. 65. In Mageoghegan's translation of the Annals of Clonmacnoise, he is called a *Scotchman*, the translator having mistaken Almaineaċ, a German, for Albanaċ, a Scotchman.

e *Mochta.*—In an epistle attributed to him, he styles himself, "*Mauchteus peccator presbyter, Sancti Patricii discipulus.*" He was by nation a Briton, and is generally supposed to have been the first Bishop of Louth. He died on the 19th

The Lord Justice, namely, Maurice Fitzgerald, mustered a great army with which he marched into Moynai [in the county of Roscommon], and plundered Fiachra O'Flynn and Donough Mac Dermot; a small party of O'Conor's people overtook them, and slew Nar[c] Mac Gillakelly, and many others.

Donnell Mac Clancy, Chief of Dartry, died.

THE AGE OF CHRIST, 1242.

The Age of Christ, one thousand two hundred forty-two.

Donnell Mac Airten died a Canon at Kilmore.

A great chapter was held by the Primate[d] of Armagh, and the abbots of the Canons Regular of Ireland, at Louth, on which occasion many of the relics which Mochta[e] had collected, and brought from Rome, were taken up.

Donough Cairbreach O'Brien, Lord of the Dalcassians, tower of the splendour and greatness of the south of Ireland, and his son Turlough, died.

Connor O'Brien assumed the lordship of Thomond.

Hugh O'Conor (i. e. the Aithchleireach[f]), son of Hugh, who was son of Roderic O'Conor, was slain by Turlough, son of Hugh, who was son of Cathal Crovderg.

Brian[g], son of Donough O'Dowda, Lord of Tireragh, Tirawley, and Erris, was killed on the way as he was going on a pilgrimage to the Abbey of Boyle.

A great army was led by the Lord Justice and all the English of Ireland, with Felim, the son of Cathal Crovderg O'Conor, into Tirconnell, in pursuit of Teige O'Conor, who had fled to Kinel-Connell. The army encamped at Drumhome, and they destroyed much on this expedition, but Teige was not abandoned to them. Teige O'Conor was afterwards taken by Cuconnaught O'Reilly, at the request of Felim, son of Cathal Crovderg.

of August, in the year 535.—See Colgan, *Acta Sanctorum*, p. 737; Irish Calendar of the O'Clerys, at 19th of August; and Lanigan's Ecclesiastical History of Ireland, vol. i. pp. 308–310.

[f] *Aithchleireach*, i. e. the denounced or superannuated clergyman.

[g] *Brian.*—Charles O'Conor writes, *inter lineas*, .ı. ḃριαn ʋeαρᵹ, i. e. "Brian the Red." It does not appear from the pedigree of the O'Dowdas, compiled by Duald Mac Firbis, that he left any descendants.—See *Genealogies, Tribes, and Customs of Hy-Fiachrach*, p. 115.

AOIS CRIOST, 1243.

Aois Criost, míle, da ċéd, ceaṫraċat atrí.

Petrus macraiṫ iar ccinneḋ a beṫhaḋ i ccanánchaiḃ oilén na trinóide ar loċ cé décc, ⁊ a adnacal lá féle martain.

Findaċta ua luġaḋa comarba beneoin [do ecc].

Maoleóin ua creċáin airċideochain tuama ar tteċt ṫairis (.i. tar muir) ina ṁaiġistir decc in áṫ cliaṫ.

Caṫasaċ ua sneḋiusa deaganaċ muintire maolruanaiḋ décc in ard ċarna an 10. august.

Taḋg mac aoḋa mic caṫail ċroiḃḋeirg do léccaḋ dua Raġallaiġ, ⁊ a ṫeaċt co mainistir na Buille cona ṡoċraide, dul dó iaromh co teaċ mic diarmada, Corbmac mac Tomaltaiġ, ⁊ é féin, ⁊ a bean inġen ṁéġ carṫaiġ (.i. etaoín inġen ḟinġin, ⁊ bá hiside mathair taiḋg buḋdein) do ġaḃáil, ⁊ a taḃairt do ċoinċonnaċt ua raġallaiġ mar ṁnaoí ar a ḟuasglaḋ féin.

Taḋg do ḋul doriḋisi fá ḟéil martain in uathaḋ sochaiḋe hi coinde go hua Raġallaiġ, ⁊ taḋg do ġabail dó hi fill, ⁊ a ṁuintir do ṁarbaḋ, ⁊ a beiṫ fein i láiṁ co féil bearaiġ ar ccind.

Sluaiġeaḋ mor do ṫionol lá Riġ Saxan do saiġiḋ riġ Franc, ⁊ teċta do ṫoċt ón ríġ diarraiḋ gall ereann cuige. Riocard mac uilliam búrc do ḋul ann i ccuma ċáich, ⁊ a écc ṫoir ar an sluaiċċeaḋ sin.

Caṫal mac aoḋa uí Concoḃair dalta muintire Raġallaiġ do iompuḋ orra, ⁊ creaċ do ḋenaṁ ḋó ar muirċeartaċ mac ġiollaṡúiliġ i muiġ nisse, ⁊

[h] *Coarb of St. Benen*, i. e. successor of St. Benignus, who was a disciple of St. Patrick and his immediate successor in the see of Armagh. The most celebrated of his monasteries were Druim lias, in the county of Leitrim, and Kilbannon, near Tuam, in the county of Galway. It is not easy to determine of which of these the Finaghty in the text was coarb.

[i] *Archdeacon*, airċideochain.—This term is to be distinguished from airċinneach, the former meaning the archdeacon, and the latter, the hereditary warden, prepositus, or chief farmer, or manager, of the church lands.

[k] *Festival of St. Bearach*, that is, of St. Bearach, or Barry, of Cluain Coirpthe, now Kilbarry, in Kinel-Dofa, or O'Hanly's country, in the east of the county of Roscommon. The memory of this saint was celebrated annually, on the 15th of February.—See the *Feilire Aenguis;* the Irish Calendar of the O'Clerys; and Colgan's *Acta Sanctorum*, at this day.

[l] *Moy-Nissi*, maġ nissi.—This is called maġ nesi in O'Dugan's topographical poem, and maġ neisi in the Book of Fenagh, in which it is

THE AGE OF CHRIST, 1243.

The Age of Christ, one thousand two hundred forty-three.

Petrus Magrath, after having retired to spend his life among the canons of Trinity Island, on Lough Key, died, and was interred on St. Martin's festival day.

Finaghty O'Lughadha, Coarb of St. Benen[h], died.

Malone O'Creghan [Crean], Archdeacon[i] of Tuam, after having returned across the sea as a professor, died in Dublin.

Cahasagh O'Snedhuisa, Deacon of Muintir-Mulrony [i. e. the Mac Dermots of Moylurg], died at Ardcarne on the 10th of August.

Teige, the son of Hugh, son of Cathal Crovderg, was set at liberty by O'Reilly, and he came with his forces to the Abbey of Boyle, and afterwards to the house of Mac Dermot (Cormac, son of Tomaltagh), whom he took prisoner, together with his wife, the daughter of Mac Carthy (viz., Edwina, daughter of Fineen), who was Teige's own mother, and gave her as wife to Cuconnaught O'Reilly, for his own ransom.

Teige went again on the festival of St. Martin following, with a small party, to a meeting appointed by O'Reilly. Teige was taken by treachery, and his people were slain, and he himself was kept in confinement until the festival of St. Bearach[k] ensuing.

A great army was mustered by the King of England, to oppose the King of France, and he sent ambassadors to [summon] the English of Ireland to his aid. Among the rest went Richard, the son of William Burke, and died on that expedition.

Cathal, son of Hugh O'Conor, the fosterson of the O'Reillys, turned against them, and committed depredations on Murtough Mac Gilhooly in Moy-Nissi[l], and made a prisoner of Murtough himself, whom he afterwards put to death

stated that it was granted to St. Caillin, the first abbot of Fenagh, who was of the same race as the Mac Rannalls, the head chieftains of Conmaicne of Moy-Rein. According to O'Dugan it was the patrimonial inheritance of the O'Mulveys, of whom the Mac Gilhoolys were an offshoot. Moy-Nissi was the name of a level tract of country on the east side of the Shannon, in the barony and county of Leitrim. The family name Mac Gilhooly is still common in this district, but the prefix Mac is usually rejected.—See note [t], p. 309, *infra*.

Muirceartaċ féin do ġabáil dó, ⁊ a ṁarbaḋ hi cill Sessin. Creaċ oile do dénoṁ dó fó ċeddóir ar cloinn Fearmaiġe ⁊ ar Dartraiġiḃ.

Creaċ Maiġe Rein lá Caṫal, ⁊ ro éiriġ coġaḋ eitir Ua cConcoḃair ⁊ Ua Raġallaiġ.

AOIS CRIOST, 1244.

Aois Criost, míle, dá céd, cetrachat a ceaṫair.

Donnċaḋ mac Finġin mic Maoilreaċlainn mic Aoḋa mic Toirrḋealbaiġ uí Concoḃair espcop Oile Finn décc an 23. April i nInis Cloċrann, ⁊ a aḋnacal i Mainistir na Buille.

Airċideochain Tuama do ḃáḋaḋ ar Glaislinn Cluana.

Donnchaḋ Mór Ua Dálaiġ saoí nár sáraiġeaḋ, ⁊ náċ sáireoċar lé dán do écc, ⁊ aḋnacal hi Mainistir na Búille.

Taḋg mac Aoḋa mic Caṫail Croiḃḋeirg do ḋallaḋ ⁊ do chrochadh la Coinconnaċt Ua Raġallaiġ i féil Ḃearaiġ occ Inis na Conaire for Loch Aillinne iar na ḃeiṫ illáiṁ aige ó ḟéil Martain gus an ionḃaiḋ sin. Ruaiḋri

[m] *Kill-Sessin*, now pronounced in Irish as if written cill tséisin, and Anglicised Kilteashin. It is the name of a townland in the west of the parish of Ardcarne, where, according to tradition, the Bishop of Elphin had formerly his palace.—See note under the year 1258.

[n] *Clann Fearmaighe*, was a territory in the county of Leitrim, adjoining Dartry, which is now called the barony of Rossclogher, and Tir Tuathail, in the county of Roscommon.

[o] *Moy-Rein*, maġ réin.—This comprised the southern or level part of the county of Leitrim. The inhabitants were called Conmaicne Maighe Rein, and also Muintir Eoluis, of whom, since the establishment of surnames in the tenth century, the Mac Rannalls were by far the most celebrated family. In the Book of Fenagh the name maġ réin is explained *plain of the track*, and the name is said to have been derived from the flight of the Fomorians, from the battle of Moy-Turey, who passed through it as far as Fenagh, where they were overtaken, slain, and interred, and where their graves are still pointed out.

[p] *Inishcloghran*.—An island in Lough Ree in the Shannon.—See note [l], under the year 1193, p. 98.

[q] *Glaislinn* signifies *green pool*, or pond.—There is no place at present bearing this name in the neighbourhood of Tuam, and there are so many places near it called Cluain that it is impossible to determine to which of them this pool or pond belonged.—See *Tribes and Customs of Hy-Many*, p. 130, where Glaislinn is referred to as at the head of Magh Finn, which was a territory in the barony of Athlone, in the county Roscommon.

[r] *Donough More O'Daly*.—In Mageoghegan's translation of the Annals of Clonmacnoise he is called "chief of Ireland for poetry." It is gene-

at Kill-Sessin[m]. Immediately after this he committed another predatory outrage in the territories of Clann-Fearmaighe[n] and Dartry [in the county of Leitrim].

In the same year Moy-Rein[o] was plundered by Cathal, and a war broke out between O'Conor and O'Reilly.

THE AGE OF CHRIST, 1244.

The Age of Christ, one thousand two hundred forty-four.

Donough (son of Fineen, the son of Melaghlin, son of Hugh, who was son of Turlough) O'Conor, Bishop of Elphin, died on the 23rd of April on Inish-cloghran[p], and was interred in the abbey of Boyle.

The Archdeacon of Tuam was drowned in the Glaislinn[q] of Cluain.

Donogh More O'Daly[r], a poet who never was and never will be surpassed, died, and was interred in the abbey of Boyle.

Teige, the son of Hugh, son of Cathal Crovderg, was blinded and hanged[s] by Cuconnaught O'Reilly, on the festival of St. Bearach, on Inis-na-Canaire[t] [an island], in Lough Allen, having been kept in confinement by him from the feast of St. Martin to that time. Rory, the son of Hugh, his brother, was

rally supposed that this Donough was Abbot of Boyle, but it does not appear from the Irish Annals, or any written authority, that he was an ecclesiastic. According to the tradition preserved in the north of the county of Clare, he was the head of the O'Dalys of Finnyvara, in the north of Burrin, where they still point out the site of his house and his monument. He is the ancestor of the O'Dalys of Dunsandle, whose ancestor came from Finnyvara with Ranailt Ny-Brien, the wife of Teige Roe O'Kelly, of Callow, in the latter part of the fifteenth century.—See *Tribes and Customs of Hy-Many*, p. 125.

O'Reilly says that he was called the Ovid of Ireland, and such, indeed, he may be regarded, though it must be acknowledged that he could bear no comparison with the Roman Ovid, in the soft luxuriance of his poetical imagery, or daring flights of his genius. His poems are principally of a religious or moral character, and possess considerable merit, though not so much as to entitle him to the unqualified praise bestowed upon his powers by the Four Masters.—See O'Reilly's Irish Writers, pp. 88–92, for a list of his poems.

[s] *Was blinded and hanged*, do ḃallaḋ 7 do ċrochaḋ.—Charles O'Conor writes *inter lineas* "do ṗroċaḋ *potius; vide infra*." In the Dublin copy of the Annals of Ulster the reading is, Do ḃallaḋ 7 do ṗbochuḋ, i. e. "was blinded and emasculated." The old translator of the Ulster Annals renders it, "Teige O'Conner blinded and maymed by Coconaght O'Rely."

[t] *Inis-na-Canaire* is now called variously Big

mac Aoḋa a dſrḃraṫair do ḃaḋaḋ ar an cuirrín connaċtach ag áṫliacc na sionna an 9. lá do ṁarta, ⁊ a aḋnacal i mainistir cluana tuaiscirt co hairṁiḋneaċ onóraċ.

Conċoḃar mac Aoḋa mic Caṫail croibḋeirg do écc hi ccind ṁíosa dear-rach.

Sluaiġeaḋ lá Feḋlimiḋ mac Caṫail croibḋeirg is in mBréifne sair go hUa Raġallaiġ do ḋioġail a ḋalta ⁊ a ḃraṫar fair, .i. Taḋg ua Conċoḃair. Ro ḃádar aḋaiġ longpuirt hi Fiodnaċ maiġe Rein, ní raiḃe an coṁarba is in baile an aiḋċe sin, ⁊ ní raiḃe cind for ṫeampall Fiodnaċa, ⁊ o naċ raiḃe ro loiscſtar drong don tslóiġ boṫa ⁊ bélscálána batar is in tempall hi seiġ gan cſt dá ndaġḋaoínib. Ro múchaḋ dalta de an comarba ant. Tainic an comarba feisin araḃaraċ co bfeircc ⁊ lonnus mór fo ḃás a ḋalta. Ro iarr a eraic ar ua cConċoḃair. Adbert ua Concoḃair co ttiobraḋ a ḃrſṫ fſin dó. Así mo ḃrſṫra ar an coṁarba an taon duine as fearr agaiḃ in eraic mo ḋalta dé do loscaḋ liḃ. Maġnus mac Muirceartaiġ Ṁuiṁniġ sin ar ua Concoḃair. Ní me itir ar Maġnus acht an tí as cſnn ar an sluaġ. Ní scérabsa riḃ ar an coṁarba co fFaġar éraic mo ḋalta. Loṫar an sluaġ iar sin as an baile amaċ, ⁊ do lean an coṁarba iad. Do ċóiḋsſt co haṫ na cirre forsin ngeirctiġ, ⁊ ro ḃaoí an tuile tar bruachaiḃ di, ⁊ ní ċaoṁnacatar toċt tairse gur ro scaoilsſt teaċ Sepel eóin baiste do

Island, Gilhooly's Island, Mary Fitzgerald's Island, and lastly, O'Reilly's Island, from the present head landlord. It lies near the southern extremity of Lough Allen, not far from Drumshambo.

[u] *Cuirreen-Connaughtagh*, Cuirrín Connaċtach, now locally called Curreen. It is the name of the southern extremity of the townland of Ballyclare, in the parish of Cloontuskert, near Lanesborough. It is often overflooded by Lough Ree.

[w] *Ath-liag-na-Sinna*, now béal aṫa liag, Anglicè Ballyleague, that part of Lanesborough lying on the Connaught side of the Shannon. The Aṫ liag mentioned in these Annals, under the years 1140, 1220, 1227, and 1244, is Ballyleague, or Lanesborough. The little town of Athleague, on the River Suck, to the south-west of the town of Roscommon, is the Ath liag mentioned by the Four Masters, at the year 1266.

[x] *Cluain-tuaiscirt*, now Cloontuskert, a parish containing the ruins of a small abbey, near Lanesborough, in the barony of South Ballintober, and county of Roscommon.—See Ordnance Map of that county, sheet 37. There is a larger abbey of the same name in the barony of Clonmacnowen, in the county of Galway.—See it marked on the Ordnance Map of that county, sheet 88.

[y] *Fenagh-Moy-Rein*, Fiodnaċ maiġe Réin, now Fenagh, in the barony and county of Leitrim. A monastery was erected here by St. Caillin, in the sixth century. It is now a parish church in the diocese of Ardagh. There is

drowned in Cuirreen Connaughtagh[u], at Ath-liag-na-Sinna[w], on the 9th day of March, and was interred in the monastery of Cluain-tuaiscirt[x], with great veneration and honour.

Conor, son of Hugh, who was son of Cathal Crovderg, died at the end of the first month of Spring.

An army was led by Felim, the son of Cathal Crovderg, eastwards, into Breifny, against O'Reilly, to take revenge of him for his [Felim's] fosterson and kinsman, Teige O'Conor. They encamped for a night at Fenagh-Moy-Rein[y]. The Coarb was not home[z] on that night, and there was no roof on the church of Fenagh, and as there was not, a party of the troops, without the permission of their chiefs, burned some tents and huts which were within the church, and the Coarb's ward was there suffocated. The Coarb himself, on coming home next day, was greatly angered and incensed at the death of his ward, and he demanded his *eric*[a] from O'Conor, who answered that he would give him his own award. "My award is," said the Coarb, "that you deliver up to me the very best man among you as *eric*, for your having burned my ward." "That is Manus, the son of Murtough Muimhneach," said O'Conor. "I am not at all," said Manus; "it is he who is head of the army." "I will not depart from you," said the Coarb, "until I obtain *eric* for my ward." The army then marched out of the town, and the Coarb followed them. They proceeded to Ath-na-Cuirre, on the River Geirctheach[b], but the flood had then over-

still extant a curious manuscript which belonged to Fenagh, and which enumerates the lands, privileges, and dues of the monastery. The original is preserved in the British Museum, and a copy made in 1517, by Maurice, son of Paidin O'Mulconry, was lately in the possession of a Rev. Mr. Rody, who lived near Fenagh, of which the Editor made a copy in the year 1829, which is now in the Library of the Royal Irish Academy. Clog-na-riogh still exists and is preserved in the chapel at Foxfield, near Fenagh, where it is regarded as a sacred relic, and held in great veneration. According to the Book of Fenagh, it was called *Clog-na-riogh*, i. e. Bell of the Kings, because it was used to contain the water in which nineteen Irish kings were baptized.

[z] *The Coarb was not at home.*—In the Annals of Connaught the language of this passage is better arranged, thus: "There was no roof on the church of Fenagh, and the Coarb was not at home that night; and as he was not, a party of Felim's troops, &c."

[a] *Eric.*—An amercement or fine for bloodshed; a mulct or reparation. It was exactly similar to the *were* or *wergild* of the Saxons.—See Harris's Ware, vol. ii. p. 71.

[b] *Geirctheach.*—This is the river now called the *Yellow River*, which is formed by a junction of several streams rising in Sliabh an Iarainn, and is subject to great floods; it passes through the

ḃaoí ind imeal ind áṫa dia ċur tarrsan aḃainn do ḋol táirrsi don tsluaġ. Do ḋeaċaiḋ Maġnus mac muirceartaiġ muiṁniġ is in tiġ, ⁊ concoḃar mac corbmaic mic diarmada. Ro raiḋ maġnus sis in bfsir baoí ar mullaċ an tiġe occa sccaoilead ag síneaḋ a cloideaṁ uaḋa suas, ag sin ar sé an tairrnge congḃus an maide gan tuitim. Aġá ráḋ sin dó ro ṫuit fécce an tíġe hi ccſnn maġnusa co ndearna bruiriġ dia ċind gur ḃo marḃ fó céddóir ar an laṫair sin, ⁊ ro haḋnaiceaḋ é hi ndorus teampaill fiodnaċa alla amuiġ, ⁊ tuccad trí lán cluig na ríġ dorrail ar a anmain, ⁊ deċ neċ ficſt. Gonaḋ amlaiḋ sin fuair coṁarba Caillín esraic a dalta. Do rónaḋ leċt do clochaiḃ snaitte, ⁊ cros caoindénṁaċ uas a ciṅd, ⁊ ro briseaḋ lá muintir ruairc iatt cioḋ iar ttsriol.

Corbmac mac tomaltaiġ mic conċoḃair mic diarmada tiġearna cloinne maoilruanaiḋ uile decc in aibit manaiġ léiṫ hi mainistir na búille is in fFoġṁar iar mbrſiṫ ḃuaḋa ó ḋoṁan ⁊ ó ḋeaṁan, iar ccaiṫſm sé mbliadan fiċeat a ttiġſrnus.

Fearġal mac taccadain do ṁarḃaḋ lá conċoḃar mac tiġearnáin i fill in inis fraoiċ for loċ gile.

AOIS CRIOST, 1245.

Aois Criost, míle, da ċéd, ceaṫraċatt acúicc.

Doṁnall ua flandaġáin abb cunga décc.

Conċoḃar ruaḋ mac muirceartaiġ ṁuiṁniġ mic toirrdealḃaiġ uí conco-ḃair do lot dua ṫimmaiṫ dá ṁaor buḋḋéin lá scín tria iomaccaillaim feirsci do ṫeċt ſtorra hi purt na leicci, ⁊ giollacriost mac ioṁar uí birn do

little town of Ballinamore, which it sometimes almost inundates.

[c] *Fractured it.*—This passage is given more briefly and somewhat differently in the Annals of Clonmacnoise, as translated by Mageoghegan, as follows: "A. D. 1244. Felym O'Connor with great forces went to be revenged for their sinister dailings on the O'Reillys and the Breniemen, and made havock of all they could meet withall in that country, without respect to either sex or age whatsoever. They killed both men and beasts without any remorse. At last they came to the Corre, where there was a tymber house of couples into which Magnus mac Mortagh and Connor mac Cormack entered, and immediately there arose a great blast of Winde which fell downe the house, whereof one couple fell on the said Magnus, and did put the topp of his head thro his brains to his very neck, and caused his neck to sinck into his breast; was strocken

flowed its banks, and they were not able to cross the ford; so they pulled down the chapel-house of St. John the Baptist, which was on the margin of the ford, that they might place its materials across the river, that the army might pass over it. Manus, the son of Murtough Muimhneach, and Conor, son of Cormac Mac Dermot, went into the house; and Manus called to the man who was on the top of the house throwing it down. "There," said he, pointing up his sword, "is the nail which prevents the stick from falling;" and while he was thus speaking, the rafter of the house fell down on his own head and fractured it[c], so that he died immediately on the spot. He was buried outside the door of the church of Fenagh; and three times the full of Clog-na-Riogh, together with thirty horses, were given as an offering for his soul; and thus it was that the Coarb of St. Caillin obtained *eric* for [the death of] his ward. A monument of hewn stone and a beautiful cross were raised over his head, but they were broken down not long afterwards by the O'Rourkes.

Cormac, son of Tomaltagh, the son of Conor Mac Dermot, Lord of all the Clann-Mulrony, died in Autumn, in the habit of a Grey Friar, in the abbey of Boyle, victorious over the world and the Devil, after having been in the lordship twenty-six years.

Farrell Mac Tagadain was treacherously slain by Conor Mac Tiernan on Inishfree[d], an island in Lough Gill.

THE AGE OF CHRIST, 1245.

The Age of Christ, one thousand two hundred forty-five.

Donnell O'Flanagan, Abbot of Cong, died.

Conor Roe, the son of Murtough Muimhneach, [who was] son of Turlough O'Conor, was wounded with a knife by O'Timmaith, his own steward, in consequence of an angry conversation that occurred between them at Port-na-leicce[e].

dead. This is the end of this man that escaped narrowly from many dangers before, lost his life in this manner by a blast of Wynde miserably."

[d] *Inishfree*, Inip ϝpaoich, i. e. *the Island of the heath*.—This island retains its name to this day. It lies near that extremity of Lough Gill, where it receives the River Buanaid (Bonet) from the county Leitrim.—See map prefixed to *Genealogies, Tribes, and Customs of Hy-Fiachrach*, on which the position of this island is shewn.

[e] *Port-na-leicce*.—This was the name of a

ṁarḃaḋ an ṁaoír sin, ⁊ concoḃar Ruaḋ do ḃreiṫ co mainistir na búille, ⁊ a écc don loc sin, ⁊ a aḋlacaḋ is in mainistir hísin iar mbuaidh ongṫa ⁊ aiṫriġe.

Caislén slicciġ do ḋénoṁ lá mac muiris mic gearailt, iustís na hereann, ⁊ re siol muiredaiġ uair ro forconġraḋ for feḋlim a ḋenaṁ ar a ṗinginġ féin, ⁊ cloċa, ⁊ aél, ⁊ tiġe spitel na trinóide do ṫarraing ċuicce iar ttaḃairt an ionaiḋ céona lar an iustis do ċlarus mac mailin in onóir na naoṁ trinóide.

Slóiġeaḋ mór la riġ saxan i mbreatnaiḃ, ⁊ ro ġaḃ longport oc caislén gannoc, ⁊ ro ṫoċuir ina ḋoċum an iustís co nGallaiḃ ereann, ⁊ feḋlimiḋ mac caṫail croibdeirg cona ṡocraide. O do ċuatar tra ro milleaḋ breatain leó, ⁊ ara aoí ní ro ġaḃsat ġéill na eiteirḃa don ċur sin. Bá honorach feḋlimiḋ ó conċoḃair ag an ríġ ar an slóicceaḋ sin.

Caislén áṫa an ċip ar brú maiġe nisse do ḋénaṁ lá miliḋ mac goisdelḃ.

Fiaċra mac dauid uí flainn taoíseach sil maoilepuain, décc.

Cearḃall buiḋe mac taiḋg mic aongusa finnabrach uí ḋálaiġ décc.

Caislén suicín do ḋénoṁ.

place on the Shannon, near Jamestown, in the county of Roscommon; but it is now obsolete.

[f] *Gannoc* is a castle in Caernarvonshire, near the shore of the Conwy, called Diganwy by the Welsh.—See Gough's Camden, p. 560, col. 2, where it is related that Henry III. was reduced to great straits under its walls in the year 1245.

[g] *He invited to his aid*, do ṫóċuir ina ḋoċum, literally, "he invited to him." The Irish annalists speak as if the King had no right to summon them. It appears that at this time the Irish barons, among other peculiar rights, claimed that they were not bound to attend the King beyond the realm, differing in this from the nobles of England, who were bound by law to assist the King in his expeditions, without as well as within the kingdom. That King Henry was aware of the exemption claimed by them is evident from the writs issued by him on this occasion, having been accompanied by an express declaration that their attendance now should not be brought forward as a precedent.—See Close Roll, 28 Henry III. Matthew Paris gives, in his Chronicle at this year, a letter, said to have been written at the time by a nobleman in Henry's camp, which conveys a vivid idea of the distressed condition of the English army before the Irish had joined them. Its substance is as follows: "The King with his army lyeth at Gannocke fortifying that strong castle, and we live in our tents, thereby watching, fasting, praying, and freezing with cold. We watch for fear of the Welshmen, who are wont to invade and come upon us in the night-time; we fast for want of meat, for the halfpenny loaf is worth five-pence; we pray to God to send us home speedily; we starve with cold, wanting our winter garments, having no more but a thin linen cloth between us and the wind. There is an arm of the sea under the castle where we lie, whereto the tide cometh, and many ships come up to the haven, which bring victuals to the camp from

The steward was killed by Ivor O'Beirne; and Conor Roe was conveyed to the abbey of Boyle, where he died of the wound, after Extreme Unction and Penance, and he was interred in that monastery.

The castle of Sligo was erected by Maurice Fitzgerald, Lord Justice of Ireland, and by the Sil-Murray; for Felim [O'Conor] was ordered to erect it at his own expense, and to convey the stones, lime, and houses of Trinity Hospital thither, after the Lord Justice had granted that place to Clarus Mac Mailin, in honour of the Holy Trinity.

A great army was led by the King of England into Wales, he pitched his camp at the castle of Gannoc[f]; and he invited to his aid[g] the Lord Justice, the English of Ireland, and Felim, son of Cathal Crovderg O'Conor, and his forces, to come to him. As soon as they had come they desolated all Wales, but obtained neither hostages nor pledges on this occasion. The King treated Felim O'Conor with great honour on this expedition.

The castle of Ath-an-chip [on the River Shannon], on the borders of Moy-Nissi [in the county of Leitrim], was erected by Myles Costello.

Fiachra, the son of David O'Flynn, Chief of Sil-Maelruain, died.

Carroll Boy, son of Teige, the son of Aengus Finnabhrach O'Daly, died.

The Castle of Suicin[h] was erected.

Ireland and Chester."—See Matthew Paris, *ad an.* 1245; Hanmer's Chronicle, Dublin edition of 1809, p. 393; and Moore's History of Ireland, vol. iii. p. 20. "All this time," says Matthew Paris, "the King was looking impatiently for the Irish forces, mused with himself, fretted with himself, the wind serving, and yet said nothing. At length their sails were descried, and Maurice Fitzgerald and the Prince of Connaught presented themselves in battle array before the King." Hanmer adds: "When all the forces joyned together, the Welshmen were overthrowne; the King manned and victualled his Castles, returned into England, gave the Irishmen leave to returne, winking awhile in policie at the tarriance and slow coming of Maurice Fitzgerald." Hanmer also remarks that, on the return of Maurice Fitzgerald, the Lord Justice, to Ireland, he performed a successful expedition against the Irish of Ulster, but that this was of no avail, for that the King, whose displeasure was inexorable, dismissed him from his office, and appointed Sir John, the son of Geoffry de Marisco, in his place. Maurice Fitzgerald, after some contests with the Irish, and the new Lord Justice, took upon him the habit of St. Francis, in the monastery of Youghal, where he died, in 1256.

[h] *The Castle of Suicin* was probably near the head of the Suck, in the county of Mayo. In the townland of Cashel and parish of Kiltullagh, and county of Roscommon, near the head of the Suck, which is called Bun Suicin, there is an ancient Irish cashel, or Cyclopean tower; but no ruins of a modern castle are now visible near Bun Suicin, excepting the site of O'Flynn's

Raġnall ua maoilmiadaiġ do ṁarbaḋ lá connaċtaiḃ.

Muirċertaċ mac muirġiusa mic caṫail mic diarmada do marbaḋ lá fearaiḃ breifne.

Sluaiġeaḋ lá hUa ndoṁnaill (Maoilechlainn) for gallaiḃ, ⁊ gaoidelaiḃ ioċtair ċonnacht co ttuccsat bú ⁊ edala iomda leo don turus sin.

AOIS CRIOSD, 1246.

Aois Criosd, míle, dá ċéd, cethracha, a sé.

Eóin ua hugróin mac coṁorba mochua, easpcop oilefinn an teóin sin do écc i Raiṫ aeda mec bric.

Ioain mac iagfri do ṫocht ina iustís in Erinn ⁊ Muiris mac gerailt do aiṫrigaḋ.

Druim lethain do loscaḋ an bliadainsi.

Maoilseaċlainn mac Concobair ruaiḋ mic muirchertaiġ muiṁniġ uí Concobair do ṁarbaḋ la hua ndubda, .i. muirchertaċ. Muirċertaċ do ionnarbaḋ tar muir dar an marbṫa sin.

Sluaiġeḋ do denaṁ do Muiris mac gerailt i ttir Conaill ⁊ é do ṫabairt

castle, near Ballinlough.—See note under Sil Maelruain, at the year 1200.

[i] *Rath-Aedha-mic Bric*, now Rahugh, a parish in the barony of Moycashel, about three miles south-east of Kilbeggan, in the county of Westmeath. The name signifies the fort of Hugh the son of Brec, a saint who founded a monastery there, within a rath or fort, in the sixth century.

"Hæc ecclesia est hodie Parochialis Dioecesis Midensis in regione de Kinel-fiacha et denominatione a viro sancto sumpta, vocatur *Rath-aodha*."

"Colitur in diversis ecclesiis, ut patronus, ut in Enach-Briuin, in regione Muscragiæ in Momonia; Sliebh-lieg in Tirconalliâ, ubi capella ipsi sacra, et solemnis perigrinatio; Rath-aodha in Kinel-Fiacha, et Killaria quæ vicus est in regione Midiæ quæ Magh-assuil appellatur. Obiit autem S. Aidus, anno 588 juxta Chronicon Cluanense aliosque nostros annales."—Colgan's *Acta SS.* p. 423, col. 2, notes 30, 31.

This St. Aedh is still vividly remembered at the foot of Slieve League, in the barony of Banagh, and county of Donegal, on which mountain his little chapel is yet to be seen in ruins. The Saint himself is called in English Hughy Breaky! He is also remembered at Killare, in the county of Westmeath, but not here at Rahugh.

[k] *John Fitz-Geoffry*, i. e. Sir John, the son of Geoffry de Marisco, who had been Lord Justice. Florilegus writes on the depriving of Fitzgerald as follows:

"Mauritium Hiberniæ Justiciarium eo quod ficte & tarde auxilium ab Hibernia domino Regi duxerat periclitanti a Justitiariâ deposuit."—See Hanmer's Chronicle, Dublin edition of 1809, p. 395.

John Fitz-Geoffry de Marisco was appointed

Randal O'Mulvey was slain by the Connacians.

Murtough, son of Maurice, who was son of Cathal Mac Dermot, was slain by the men of Breifny.

An army was led by O'Donnell (Melaghlin) against the English and Irish of Lower Connaught, and he carried away many cows and other property on that expedition.

THE AGE OF CHRIST, 1246.

The Age of Christ, one thousand two hundred forty-six.

John O'Hughroin, son of the Coarb of Mochua, Bishop of Elphin, died in Rath-Aedha-mic-Bric[i].

John Fitz-Geoffry[k] came to Ireland as Lord Justice, and Maurice Fitzgerald was deprived[l].

Drumlahan[m] was burned in this year.

Melaghlin, son of Conor Roe, the son of Murtough Muimhneach O'Conor, was slain by O'Dowda (Murtough), who was banished over sea after the commission of that deed.

Maurice Fitzgerald marched with an army into Tirconnell: he gave the

Lord Justice of Ireland on the 4th of November, 1245; and, it is quite clear that Maurice Fitzgerald performed the expedition into Ulster against O'Donnell after he was deprived of his office, notwithstanding Hanmer's assertion to the contrary. See the year 1247. Mr. Moore seems to think that Maurice Fitzgerald retired from the world immediately after being removed from office.—See his History of Ireland, vol. iii. p. 21; but it is evident from the older Irish annals that he continued his struggles with the native Irish, and even with the new Justiciary, for some years before he retired into the monastery of Youghal. After his removal the Geraldines for some time kept the state of an independent sept, supporting themselves by their own power, and making war and peace by their own authority They made mighty efforts to annihilate or reduce to a state of abject slavery the Irish of Desmond; but they received a great check from the fierce and warlike clan of the Mac Carthys in the year 1261.

[l] *Deprived*, aiṫrioġaḋ, literally *dethroned*, or *unkinged*, that being the term used by the annalists to express the deposing of their own petty kings or chieftains.

[m] *Drumlahan*, ḋruim lẏṫain, but more correctly ḋruim lẏṫan, i. e. the broad ridge or hill, now generally anglicised Drumlane, a townland and parish, remarkable for the ruins of a church and round tower, in the barony of Loughtee and county of Cavan, and about three miles from the town of Belturbet. St. Mogue, or Maidoc, of Ferns, is the reputed patron saint and founder of this church, which was monastic; but Dr. Lanigan thinks that a monastery had existed here

leithe thire Conaill do corbmac mac diarmada mic Ruaidri uí Concoḃair, ⁊ braiġde uí doṁnaill do ġabail ar an leiṫ oile. Na braiġde do ḟaccbail i ccaislén slicciġe.

Ua doṁnaill, .i. Maoilseaċlainn ⁊ maiṫe cenél cconaill do ṫeaċt la Saṁna go Slicceaċ. Baḋún an baile do loscaḋ doiḃ. Ni ro ḟéḋsat dol for an ccaislén, ⁊ ro chrochsat luċt an ċaislén a mbraiġdi ina ffiaḋnaisi iar na leccaḋ síos do ṁullaċ an chaislén, .i. ó Mianáin oide uí doṁnaill ⁊ a chomalta.

Murchaḋ ua hanluain ticcherna na nairther do marḃaḋ ar forcongra briain uí nell.

Aeḋ mac Aeḋa uí Concoḃair do ġabail ⁊ a argain.

Toirrdealḃaċ mac Aeḋa uí Concoḃair do éluḋ a crannóig locha leisi is in foġṁar. An luċt coiṁeda boí air do ḃáḋaḋ do, .i. corbmac ua muireaḋaiġ ⁊ dá ua ainmireaċ. Toirrḋealḃaċ do ġabail do riḋiri ar comairce espcoip ċluana ⁊ iar ná ṫabairt illaiṁ ġall a chur i ccaislén atha luain.

Albert almaineach airdespuc Arddamacha daṫruccaḋ doċum na hungari.

AOIS CRIOSD, 1247.

Aois Criosd, mile, da ċéd, ceathracha aseaċt.

Concoḃor ua Muireaḋaiġ espcop ua ffiachrach aiḋne do écc ⁊ mbristuma.

Aeḋ mac concailleaḋ abb ċluana heoaiss do écc.

Maoilseachlainn ó doṁnaill ticcherna thire Conaill, cenél Moáin, insi heoġain ⁊ fearmanaċ do ṁarḃaḋ la Muiris mac gearailt. Ba haṁlaiḋ so for caoṁnaccair riḋe. Sluaiġeaḋ mor do tionól la Muiris mac gearailt ⁊

before St. Maidoc was born.—See his Ecclesiastical History of Ireland, vol. ii. p. 336, note 122.

[n] *Lord of the Oriors*, tiġheaṙna na naiṙṫeaṙ, i. e. *dominus Orientalium*, i. e. of the two baronies of Orior, in the east of the county of Armagh. The inhabitants of these baronies were so called from their situation in the east of the territory of Oriel.

[o] *Command*, forċongra.—This word signifies order or command, and sometimes request or suggestion. In the old translation of the Annals of Ulster this passage is rendered thus: "A. D. 1246. O'Hanlon, King of Oirthir, killed, through the *persuasion* of Brien O'Neal."

[p] *Lough Leisi*.—This name is now obsolete.—See note under the year 1452, where it is shewn that Lough Leisi was the ancient name of Muckenagh Lough, near the old church of Kilglass, in O'Hanly's country, in the east of the county of Roscommon.

half of Tirconnell to Cormac, son of Dermot, who was son of Roderic O'Conor, and obtained hostages from O'Donnell for the other half. These hostages he left in the castle of Sligo.

O'Donnell (Melaghlin), and the chiefs of the Kinel-Connell, came on All-Saints' day to Sligo, and burned the bawn, but were not able to make their way into the castle; upon which the people of the castle hanged the hostages in their presence, having suspended them from the top of the castle, i. e. O'Mianain, the tutor of O'Donnell, and [another who was] his foster-brother.

Murrough O'Hanlon, Lord of the Oriors[n], was put to death by command[o] of Brian O'Neill.

Hugh, son of Hugh O'Conor, was taken prisoner and plundered.

Turlough, the son of Hugh O'Conor, made his escape from the Crannog [wooden house] of Lough Leisi[p] in Autumn, having drowned his keepers, namely, Cormac O'Murray, and the two O'Ainmireachs. He was again taken while under the protection of the Bishop of Cluain [Clonfert], and, being given up into the hands of the English, was confined in the castle of Athlone.

Albert, the German[q], Archbishop of Armagh, was translated to Hungary[r].

THE AGE OF CHRIST, 1247.

The Age of Christ, one thousand two hundred forty-seven.

Conor O'Murray, Bishop of Hy-Fiachrach Aidhne [Kilmacduagh], died at Bristol.

Hugh Mac Conchaille[s], Abbot of Clones, died.

Melaghlin O'Donnell, Lord of Tirconnell, Kinel-Moen, Inishowen, and Fermanagh, was slain by Maurice Fitzgerald. He was enabled to accomplish this in the following manner: A great army was led by Maurice Fitzgerald,

[q] *Albert, the German*, albeɼt almaıneach.—See note under the year 1242, and also Harris's edition of Ware's Bishops, p. 66, where it is stated that Albert of Cologne resigned his see in 1247, and died beyond seas.

[r] Under this year (1246) the Dublin copy of the Annals of Ulster record, that the Bishop of Rath Luraigh [Maghera], was elected to the archbishopric of Armagh.

[s] *Mac Conchaille*.—This name is still extant in the neighbourhood of Clones, in the county of Monaghan, and in the county of Fermanagh, but anglicised by some to Woods, and by others to Cox, because it is assumed that Caille, or

la gallaiḃ arċſna go riachtadar Sligeaċ ar tus, airriḋe co hEſſ aeḋa ruaiḋ mic badairn. Do ḋeachaiḋ corbmac mac diarmada mic Ruaiḋri uí Concoḃair ina thionól. Ba isin cſtaoine iar ffél pſttair ⁊ poil insin. Ro thionoil ua domnaill cenel Conaill ⁊ eoġain ar a ccind conar leccſſt gall na gaoiḋeal tar ath Sſnaiġ anunn re hſḋ seachtmaine ón trath go aroile Coniḋ e aireacc arrainicc leo corbmac ua concoḃair go sochraiḋe moir marcsluaiġ draoiḋſḋ triaran maġ siar ⁊ iompuḋ ar fud an ṁaiġe suas fri bord an mointiġ soir gan airiuġaḋ do neaċ co rainic bel aṫa ċuluain for Sirne. Ní ro airgſſt cenél cconaill ní conus facatar an marcsluaiġ do lſiṫ a ccúil ċuca don taoḃ dia raḃatar don aḃainn. Soait iaraṁ friú. Od conncatar goill aire cenél Conaill for an marcsluaiġ tangadar do lſiṫ a nordumann chuca, uair do baḋ dſrbh leó ná caoṁsatais i ffrſſdal diḃlinib, Ro ling-

Coille, the latter part of the name, may signify *of a wood*, or *of a cock*.

[t] *The cataract of Aedh Ruadh, the son of Badharn.*—This was the ancient name of the cataract called the Salmon Leap, at Ballyshannon, in the county of Donegal. The name is now pronounced as if written easa ruaḋ, and in English Assaroe, —See note [n], under the year 1194, p. 99.

[u] *Bethought them.*—Aireacc means a sudden thought or impulse of the mind. This passage, the language of which is so rudely constructed by the Four Masters, is much more clearly, though more briefly, given in the Annals of Ulster, and thus rudely Englished in the old translation of these annals:

" A. D. 1247. Melaghlin O'Donnell, King of Tirconnell, and Gilla Munelagh O'Boyl, and Mac Sowerly" [were] "killed by Mac Morris in Belascna. Kindred Conell defended the ford for a whole weeke, that there could not pass neither English nor Irish, untill Cormac O'Conner used craft at last; for he carried with him a number of horse along the fields westwards, and turned again upwards nere the bogs by Easterly, until he came to the ford of Cuil uone upon the Erne. And Kindred Conell wot nothing" [ni ro airiġset Cenel Conuill ni] "untill they saw the great troop of horse on the side of the river where they were. And as they noted the Horse on their backs, the Galls came over the Ford, so that Mac Maurice had their killing as aforesaid." The meaning of this passage, the language of which is so lamely constructed by the Four Masters, is evidently as follows. "When it was perceived by Fitzgerald's party, that they had no chance of being able to cross the ford at Ballyshannon, while the forces of O'Donnell were defending it, they had recourse to the following stratagem, which was suggested by Cormac, the grandson of King Roderic O'Conor, who had been appointed as chief of half the territory of Tir-Connell, a short time before, by Maurice Fitzgerald. Cormac proceeded at the head of a strong body of horse first westwards, along the plain of Moy-Ketne so as to make the Kinel-Connell believe that he was retreating into Connaught. He then turned upwards, that is, southwards, and proceeded in the direction of Connaught, till he was so far from those who were defending the ford, that they could no longer see him, when, wheeling round, he directed his course eastwards along the margin of the bog, until he arrived, unperceived by the enemy, at the ford of Belacooloon, on the River Erne, a

and the other English chiefs, first to Sligo, and thence to the Cataract of Aedh Roe, the son of Badharn[t]. Cormac, the son of Dermot, who was son of Roderic O'Conor, joined his muster. This was on the Wednesday after the festival of SS. Peter and Paul. O'Donnell assembled the Kinel-Connell and Kinel-Owen against them, so that they did not allow a single man, either English or Irish, to cross the ford of Ath-Seanaigh for a whole week. The English then bethought them[u] of sending Cormac O'Conor with a large body of cavalry westwards along the plain, who was to turn southwards through the plain, and then eastwards along the borders of the bog, unperceived by any one, until he should arrive at Bel-atha-Culuain [a ford] on the Erne. [This was accordingly done], and the Kinel-Connell knew nothing of the movement until they saw the body of cavalry advancing on their rear[w], on their side of the river; they then turned round to them. When the English saw that the attention[x] of the Kinel-Connell was directed towards the cavalry who had advanced on their rear[y], they rushed across the ford against them, being confident that they [the

short distance to the west of Belleek, which ford he crossed, and being then on the north side of the river, he proceeded towards Ballyshannon, and advanced on the rear of O'Donnell's forces, who were still defending the ford. The latter, who had expected no such manœuvre, being alarmed at the approach of a large body of fierce cavalry, suddenly turned their faces towards them to sustain their onset, leaving the ford unprotected. When Maurice Fitzgerald perceived that the defenders of the ford had turned their faces towards O'Conor's cavalry, he immediately ordered his troops to cross the ford, and to attack the rear of the enemy, thinking that the forces of O'Donnell would not be able to sustain the attack on both sides. In this he was not mistaken; for, although the Kinel-Connell, on observing his intention, had sent a party to prevent him from crossing, still he succeeded, and joined O'Conor's cavalry, and both united routed the Kinel-Connell, &c. &c."

[w] *On their rear*, do leiṫ a ccúil cuca.—In Grace's Annals of Ireland this sentence is thus given in Latin: "Occurrit O'Donell cum suis ex tota Kineoil Conaill ad vadum Athshani, eos cum preterire minime andirent ibidem 7 dies definuit, missus igitur Cormacus cum equitum parte clam ad vadum Cuiluaniæ, Erne fluminis, terga hostium aggreditur, qui statim in fugam conversi sunt, &c."

Grace places these events under the year 1242, and Dr. Hanmer under 1245, but both are evidently wrong.

[x] *That the attention, &c.*—When the Kinel-Connell had wheeled round to sustain the onset of the cavalry, their backs were turned towards Fitzgerald's forces, who were on the south side of the ford.

[y] *Who had advanced upon their rear*, an marcṡluaġ tanġadar do leiṫ a ndrumann chuca, i. e. *equitatus qui venerunt a tergo in eos.*—Here the nominative case to the verb tanġadar is the relative a, understood, for in ancient Irish compositions, which the Four Masters affected to imitate, the verb has a plural termina-

sſct an taċ furro go mbadar cenél cconaill in edirmſdón a mbioḋbaḋ iar niaḋaḋ ḋoiḃ iompo da gaċ lſiṫ. Aċt ċſna ro marḃaḋ ua doṁnaill ar an laṫair sin, an cammuinélaċ ua baoiġill priomṫaoiseaċ na ttrí ttuaṫ, Mac soṁairle ticchſrna airſrġaoiḋeal ⁊ maiṫi cenél Conaill arċſna. Ro baiḋit ⁊ ro marḃaid drong ṁór do ṡloġaiḃ mic gſrailt annsin. Ro baiḋid dana araill diḃ ar an ffinn buḋ ṫhuaiṫ ⁊ sochaiḋi oile don tsloiġ cſtna i ttſrmonn dabeócc i ttoraiġeaċt na ccreaċ ro teċsſt rſmpu im uilliam brit Sirriam Connaċt ⁊ im Ridire ócc oile ba dearḃraṫair dosiḋe. Ro hinnreaḋ ⁊ ro hairccſḋ an tír leó iarsin. Ro ḟaccaibsſd cſnnus cenél cconaill ag Ruaiḋri ua canannáin don cur sin.

Eaċmarcaċ ó caṫain ticchſrna cianaċta ⁊ ḟſr na craoiḃe do ṁarḃaḋ la maġnus ua ccaṫain ar ndol dó ar creċ ina ṫír go hairthſr ṁaiġe i ndáilriada.

Toirrḋealḃaċ mac aoḋa uí Conċoḃair do éluḋ a háṫ luain.

Miliḋ mac goisdelḃ do gaḃail ḟſḋa Conmaicne ⁊ caṫal mág Raġnaill do diochur esdiḃ ⁊ crannócc claſnlocha do gaḃail dó, ⁊ luċt a gaḃála do ḟágḃail do innte uaḋa ſen. Caṫal ⁊ toirrḋealḃaċ da ṁac aſḋa uí Conċoḃair do ċoiṁſirġe la mag Raġnaill do diochur meic goisdelḃ a ḟiḋ Conmaicne. Ro gaḃsad an ċrannócc ⁊ an loch, Ro Scaoilsſt caislén lecce deirge i saṫarn doṁnaiġ ċincidisi, uair do chuaiḋ toirrḋealḃaċ co hoilén na trinóide ar cſnn ċlarusa mic moilín an airċinniġ ar ní ro ḟaſṁsat na goill toċt as an caisslen amaċ muna ttíosdaoís ar comairce an airċinniġ dia niodhlacaḋ tar Sionainn anair co tuam mná. Tangadar le clarus iaroṁ, ⁊ ro diochuireaḋ clann goisdelḃ as in tír amaċ uile.

tion to agree with the relative when its antecedent is a noun of multitude, or of the plural number.—See the Editor's Irish Grammar, part iii. c. i. pp. 359, 360.

[z] *Chieftain of the Three Tuathas*, Toiseaċ na ttrí ttuaṫ.—These were three territories in the north-west of the county of Donegal. They passed afterwards into the possession of a branch of the Mac Sweenys, who received from them the appellation of Mac Suibhne na dtuath.

[a] *Argyle*, airer gaoiḋeal, i. e. *the district of the Gaels*.—This is the name by which Argyle in Scotland is always called by the Irish writers, and not Ard-na-Ngaodhal, as O'Flaherty very erroneously states in *Ogygia Vindicated*, Dedication, p. li.—See Colgan's *Trias Thaum.*, p. 115.

[b] *O'Canannan*.—There is not one of this name at present in Tirconnell, though they were the ancient chiefs of it preceding the O'Donnells.

[c] *Armoy*, airṫear maiġe.—An ancient ecclesiastical town in the barony of Carey, in the north of the county of Antrim.—See note [n], un-

Kinel-Connell] would not be able to attend to the attacks of both. The Kinel-Connell were now in the very centre of their enemies, who had surrounded them on every side. O'Donnell was slain on the spot, as well as the Cammhuinealach [Wry-necked] O'Boyle, the head Chieftain of the Three Tuathas[z], Mac Sorley, Lord of Argyle[a], and other chiefs of the Kinel-Connell. A great number of Fitzgerald's forces were slain and drowned here; others of them were drowned northwards in the River Finn, and many others at Termon Daveog, in pursuit of preys that fled before them; and among the rest William Britt, sheriff of Connaught, and his brother, a young knight. The country was then plundered and desolated by them [the English], and they left the chieftainship of the Kinel-Connell to Rory O'Canannan[b] on this occasion.

Eachmarcach O'Kane, Lord of Kienaghta and Firnacreeva, was slain by Manus O'Kane, after having gone on a predatory excursion into his country as far as Armoy[c] in Dal-Riada[d].

Turlough, the son of Hugh O'Conor, made his escape from Athlone.

Miles Mac Costello took possession of Feadha Conmaicne[e], and expelled Cathal Mac Rannall from thence: the Crannóg of Claenlough[f] was also taken for him, and he left those who had taken it to guard it for him. Hereupon Cathal and Turlough, two sons of Hugh O'Conor, rose up to assist Mac Rannall in expelling Mac Costello from Feadha-Conmaicne. They retook the Crannóg and the Lake, and demolished the castle of Leckderg on the Saturday before Whit-Sunday; and Turlough went to Trinity Island, to Clarus Mac Mailin, the Erenagh, for the English were not willing to come out of the castle, except on the condition that the Erenagh would protect and escort them westwards across the Shannon to Tuaim-mna[g]. Soon afterwards they went away with Clarus, and the Clann-Costello were all expelled from that country.

der the year 1177, p. 33.

[d] *Dal-Riada.*—A territory which comprehended that part of the county of Antrim north of Slemmish.—See Ussher's *Primordia*, p. 1029.

[e] *Feadha Conmaicne*, i. e. the woods of Conmaicne.—A district, near the River Shannon, in Mac Rannall's country, in the south of the county of Leitrim.

[f] *Claenlough.*—There is no lough at present bearing this name in the county of Leitrim, but the Down Survey shews "Clean logh" in the parish of Killarga, in the barony of Dromahaire, having the Duff, now Diffagher River, running from it to Lough Allen. This Lough is now called Belhavel Lough, and is shewn under this name on the Ordnance Survey of the county of Leitrim, sheet 15.

[g] *Tuaim-mna*, now Tumna, a parish in the

Coccaḋ mor la toirrḋealḃac mac aſḋa uí Concoḃair ⁊ lá donnchaḋ mac anmchaḋa mic donnchaḋa uí giollapatraicc do orrgaiḃ for ġallaiḃ Connaċt. Ro ṫionoil toirrḋealḃaċ clanna ticcſrnaḋ Connaċt go riachtadar fiḋ ua ndiarmada ⁊ muintir fachaiḋ. Ro marḃsat daoíne iomḋa. Rangadar arriḋe go cairlén ḃona gaillṁe. Ro loiscc̄ſtt an baile ⁊ an cairlén. Ro muḋaiġit daoine leó im mac Elget Senescal Connaċt ro marḃaḋ la donnchaḋ mac anmċaḋa. Leanaid goill iad iarttain Tuccsatt deaḃaiḋ ḋoiḃ, du in ro marḃaḋ drong do ġallaiḃ, Lodar uaṫa daiṁḋeóin co rangador cſra. Ro thionóil trá Siurtán dexſtra, Clann ádaim, ⁊ goill cſra go toirrḋealḃaċ Forráccaiḃ toirrḋealḃaċ an tír ḋoiḃ ó ná boí coiṁlíon friú.

Ḃuirgés ċinntrachta do loscaḋ la taḋg mac concoḃair ruaiḋ, ⁊ la taḋg mac tuaṫail mic muirċſrtaiġ muiṁniġ, aċt ċſna ní fuaradar goill Connaċt fri ré imċén roiṁe sin samail coccaḋ na rioġḋaṁnaḋ sorra don ċur sin. Cona boí tuaṫ no triocha ċſtt do ċrich ġall i Connaċtaiḃ gan crech gan arccain uaḋaiḃ.

Ross commáin ⁊ ard carna do loscaḋ la gallaiḃ.

Fionnġuala ingſn Ruaiḋri ui Conċoḃair do écc i ccunga ḟechín.

Loingſs do ṫeaċt do ua ḋuḃda ⁊ dua ḃaoiġill do arccain cairpri, ⁊ luċt luinge dib do ḃaḋaḋ occ insi ṫuaṫ sarr fa ṁaġnus ua mbaoiġill.

barony of Boyle, and county of Roscommon, adjoining the River Shannon. Archdall does not mention this monastery. In the Irish Calendar of the O'Clerys, the patron saint of this church is called Etaoin, at the 5th of July. Thus: "Etaoin o Tuaimná a maġ luirg le taoḃ aḃann Ḃuille, i. e. Etaoin of Tumna, in Moylurg, at the bank of the River Boyle." This virgin is still vividly remembered at this church, and her grave is shewn in the churchyard.—See note under the year 1249.

[h] *O'Gillapatrick.*—In Mageoghegan's translation of the Annals of Clonmacnoise he is more correctly called Donnogh mac Anmchie mac Donnogh Mac Gillepatrick.

[i] *Fiodh-Ua-n-Diarmada*, i. e. the wood of the territory of Hy-Diarmada, or O'Concannon's country, in the county of Galway.

[k] *The castle of Bungalvy*, Caislen bona Gaillṁe, i. e. the castle at the mouth of the River Galway. O'Flaherty, in combating the assertions of Ptolemy as to the tribes enumerated by him, thus speaks of this river: "Fluvius in occidentali Connactæ e lacu Orbsen (Lacus Curb) dilabens nunquam Ausoba aut Ausona, nomine innotuit, sed Gaillimh, a quo urbs celebris, Connactæ decus, in ostio nomen Galviam mutuavit."—*Ogygia*, pp. 16, 17.

[l] *Mac Elget.*—Mageoghegan calls him Mac Eligott. A family of this name, and probably the descendants of this seneschal, settled at Bally-Mac-Elligott, near Tralee, in the county of Kerry, where they were highly respectable till the close of the seventeenth century.

[m] *Buirges Chinntrachta*, i. e. the borough at the head of the strand.—That this place was in

A great war [was kindled] by Turlough, the son of Hugh O'Conor, and Donough, the son of Anmchadh O'Gillapatrick[h] of Ossory, against the English of Connaught. Turlough assembled the sons of the lords of Connaught, with whom he proceeded to Fiodh-Ua-n-Diarmada[i] and Muintir-Fahy, where they slew many persons. From thence they marched to the castle of Bungalvy[k] [Galway], and burned the town and the castle. Many persons were destroyed by them, with Mac Elget[l], Seneschal of Connaught, who was killed by [the aforesaid] Donough, the son of Anmchadh. The English afterwards pursued them, and gave them battle, in which a number of the English were slain; and the Irish retreated in despite of them into Carra, where Jordan de Exeter, the Clann-Adam, and the English of Carra, assembled against Turlough. Turlough left the country to them, as he had not forces equal to their's.

Buirges Chinntrachta[m] was burned by Teige, son of Connor Roe, and Teige, son of Tuathal, who was son of Murtough Muimhneach. The English of Connaught had not for a long time before experienced such a war as was waged with them by the Roydamnas [the royal heirs presumptive] on this occasion; for there was not a district or cantred of the possessions of the English in Connaught which they did not plunder[n] and devastate.

Roscommon and Ardcarne were burned by the English.

Finola[o], daughter of Roderic O'Conor, died at Conga-Fechin [Cong].

O'Dowda and O'Boyle brought a fleet to plunder Carbury; and the crew of one ship, under the command of Manus O'Boyle, were drowned at Inis-Tuathrass[p].

Connaught, and not Iubhar Chinntrachta, now Newry, in Ulster, no doubt can be entertained. It was in all probability the ancient name of Burriscarra, which is situated at the north-east extremity of Lough Carra, in the barony of Carra, and county of Mayo, and where the English fortified themselves in the year 1238.—See *Genealogies, Tribes, and Customs of Hy-Fiachrach*, pp. 202, 203.

[n] *Which they did not plunder*, literally, there was not a tuagh or cantred of the territory of the English in Connaught, without being preyed and plundered by them."

[o] *Finola*, pionnguala, signifying of the fair shoulders, was common as the name of a woman in Ireland, till the latter end of the seventeenth century; but it is now entirely obsolete.

[p] *Inis-Tuathrass*, i. e. the island of the district of the Roses. There is no island off the coast of Sligo, or Donegal, now bearing this name. It was probably the ancient name of Cruit Island, off the coast of Tuathrass, now the district of the Rosses, in the northwest of the barony of Boylagh, in the county of Donegal. The ship of Manus O'Boyle would seem to have been lost before she had cleared the coast of Tirconnell.

Tadhg mac Concobair ruaidh do loscadh insi moire claenlocha ⁊ ochtar ar ḟichit do ġallaiḃ do loscadh innte.

Mainestir do dſnoṁ i nGaillıṁ in airdeppscoitecht tuama lá huilliam burc tiġearna cloinne Riocaird do braiṫriḃ .S. ffrainseis. Do rónadh tuambada iomda la druing moir do maiṫiḃ an ḃaile is in mainestir sin.

Mainistir Inse i ttuadhṁuṁain in esscoitecht cille da Lua do denaṁ la hua mbriain conadh innte ḃios adhnacal ṡil mbriain.

Sloiġeadh mór la Mac Muiris mec gearailt ⁊ la gallaib ar tarraing gorrada uí doṁnaill go hess Ruaidh. Do thaot Ruaidhri ó canannain go ccenel cconaill ina naġaidh, ⁊ ni ró chumaingsſt ní ḋo iná dul seacha sin don chur sin.

AOIS CRIOSD, 1248.

Aois Criosd, mile, da ċéd, cſthraċa, a hocht.

Diarmaid ua cuana Saccart mor oile finn do écc ⁊ a adhnacal i ccill ṁóir.

Maiġisdir gillbert ua cſrḃaill do écc.

Orichin guer do ṁarḃadh do giollamoċoinne ua caṫail.

Coiṁſirġe do ḋſnaṁ do ṁac maġnusa ⁊ do mac Concoḃair ruaidh ⁊ iompudh ḋoiḃ for ġallaiḃ. Caislén meic enrg, .i. riasur rusſr do loscadh ḋoiḃ ⁊ a ċonstapla do ġaḃail, Creaċa ṫuaisceirt uṁaill do ḃrſiṫ leó ar insiḃ modh, Ro thionóil Siurtan dexetra, Seón buitilér, Robbſn laiglés ⁊ daoine imda immaille friú Tangadar go baile ṫobair patraicc aissiḋe go hachadh faḃair. Ro airccriod uṁall ar naḃarach thuaiṫ ⁊ tear. Tainicc

[q] *Claenlough*—This cannot be the Lough Cleane in the parish of Killarga, in the county of Leitrim above mentioned in note [f], because that lough contains no island. There is another lake which anciently bore this name near Castlebar, in the county of Mayo.

[r] *Race of Brian*, siol mbriain, i. e. of the race of Brian Borumha, Monarch of Ireland. These are the O'Briens of Thomond, and all the branches that shot off from them.

[s] *Were unable*, ni ro cumaingsſt ni do, literally, they were not able to do aught to him.

[t] *Or to proceed further*, dul seaċa sin, literally, "to go beyond that," i. e. beyond Assaroe, at Ballyshannon.

[u] *O'Cuana*.—This name is now Anglicised Cooney.

[w] *Kilmore*, i. e. the church of Kilmore na Sinna, to the north-east of the town of Elphin.

[x] *Inse Modha*,—named from Modha, one of the Clann Hua Mor, a tribe of the Firbolgs,—a cluster of islands in Clew Bay, between the baronies

Teige, the son of Conor Roe, burned Inishmore in Claenlough[q], on which occasion twenty-eight of the English were also burned.

A monastery was founded in Galway, in the archdiocese of Tuam, by William Burke, Lord of Clanrickard, for Franciscan friars. Many tombs were erected in this monastery by the chief families of the town.

The monastery of Ennis, in Thomond, in the diocese of Killaloe, was founded by O'Brien, and in this monastery is the burial-place of the race of Brian[r].

A great army was led by the son of Maurice Fitzgerald and the English to Assaroe [at Ballyshannon], at the desire of Godfrey O'Donnell. Rory O'Cannan, with the Kinel-Connell, came against them, and the English were unable[s] to do him any injury, or to proceed furthur[t] on that occasion.

THE AGE OF CHRIST, 1248.

The Age of Christ, one thousand two hundred forty-eight.

Dermot O'Cuana[u], the great priest of Elphin, died, and was buried at Kilmore[w].

Master Gilbert O'Carroll died.

Opichin Guer was slain by Gilla-Mochoinne O'Cahill.

The son of Manus and the son of Conor Roe rose up together against the English. The castle of Mac Henry, i. e. of Piers Poer, was burned by them, and its constable was taken prisoner. They carried the spoils of the north of Umallia along with them to [the islands called] Inse Modha[x]. Jordan de Exeter, John Butler, Robin Lawless, and many others, assembled, and marched to Ballytoberpatrick[y], and from thence to Aghagower[z]; and, on the next day,

of Murrisk and Erris, in the county of Mayo.

[y] *Ballytoberpatrick*, baile Copair Paccraicc, now called Ballintober. A village in the barony of Carra, in the county of Mayo, where the ruins of an abbey founded in the year 1189 or 1190, by Cathal Crovderg, King of Connaught, are still to be seen in good preservation.

[z] *Aghagower*, Achadh fabair, a parish church in the barony of Murrisk, county Mayo, east of the famous mountain called Cruach Phadraig, or St. Patrick's rick or stack. The author of the Tripartite Life of St. Patrick thus speaks of this place: "Progressus Patricius pervenit usque in Umalliam quæ est regio maritima occidentalis Connaciæ. Ibi extructæ Ecclesiæ de Achadh fobhair præfecit, et in Episcopum consecravit S. Senachum virum vitæ innocentiâ & animi submissione longè celebrem."—Lib. ii. c. 62. And again: "His peractis descendit de monte (Cruach Patraic) Patricius, ac in ecclesiâ

Enrí dana mor ṡluaiġeadh in uṁall (dia ṫír buḋéin) uair ar innte boí a aittreabhadh. Do roiġne din piarus Puer mac Enrí Siṫ re domhnall mac maġnusa. Ro ġeall dana domhnall go ttiobhradh sochraide ⁊ arṫraiġi dó do ċum dula ar a bhraiṫribh.

Dala mac uí Concobhair imorro do badur ar insibh moḋ, do foillsicchedh dóibh sochraide do ḋul o mac Enri a ccoinne arṫraiġedh do ċum domhnaill. Iar na ḟios sin da cloinn uí Concobhair lodar Rompo gur marbhadh leó o huain mac na Gaillsicche ⁊ Seón mac an gall ṡacairt. Ro marbhadh beos la diarmaid mac maġnusa ar an ccoimhsiġi sin Sneoitt guer ⁊ drong dia muinntir amaille fris. Rob e sin an taiṫsir gan aithsir uair ro marbhadh an cuingidh calma ⁊ an tairridh iorgaile .i. diarmaid mac maġnusa is in maiġin sin.

Taḋcc macc Concobhair ruaidh do marbhadh la gallaibh. Ba mór tra aḋuaṫ ⁊ imeacclu an taidhg sin for gallaibh ⁊ gaoidhealaibh doneoċ do bioḋ na aghaidh díobh go ffuair a aidheadh.

Sluaiġeadh la Muiris mac gearoilt i ttir conaill. Creaċa aiḋble, urtha, ⁊ aircene do ḋénamh lais. Ruaidhri ua canannáin do ionnarbadh ḋó i ccenél Eoġain ⁊ ticcheṙnus cenél cconaill do ḟaccbail ag gofraidh mac domhnaill uí domhnaill.

Sluaicchedh do ḋénamh la cenél neoġain ⁊ la hua ccanannáin i ttir Conaill doridhisi go ttugsad caṫ do goffraidh ⁊ do cenel cconaill gur marbhadh ua canannáin .i. Ruaidhri ⁊ iomad ina ḟochair don toirc sin.

Sluaicchedh oile la iustís na hEreann i ccenél neoġain go hua nell. Assi comhairli do rónsad cenél eoġain annsin braiġde do ṫabhairt uaṫa o do buí neart gall for gaoidhealaibh Ereann, ⁊ sith do ḋénamh riú tar cenn a ttíre. Ar don cur sin do ronsat goill droichet na banna ⁊ caislen droma tairsicch.

de Achadh-fobhair reliquam paschæ celebravit solemnitatem." Colgan has the following note on its situation, in *Trias Thaum.*, p. 178, col. *b*, note 118: "Ecclesia de Achadhfobhair est Diocesis Tuamensis et Comitatus Mageonensis in Connacia. Et licet hodie sit tantum parrochialis, & caput ruralis Decanatus, fuit olim sedes Episcopalis."—See *Genealogies, Tribes, and Customs of Hy-Fiachrach*, printed for the Irish Archæological Society, p. 150, note [b].

[a] *Umallia, north and south.*—North Umallia is the present barony of Burrishoole, and south Umallia is the barony of Murrisk. The former is called Umhall iochtrach, or lower Umhall, and the latter, Umhall Uachtrach, or upper Umhall, by the Irish, and both "the Owles" by English writers.

[b] *Lord Justice.*—According to the Dublin copy of the Annals of Innisfallen, this expedition against O'Neill was performed by Theobald

they plundered Umallia north and south[a]. Henry came with a numerous army into Umallia (his own country), for his residence was there. Pierce Poer, the son of Henry, made peace with Donnell, son of Manus, and Donnell promised that he would give him men and vessels to attack his kinsmen.

As to the sons of O'Conor, who were on the [islands of] Inse Modh, they received information that a body of men had gone from the son of Henry [Poer] to Donnell, for the purpose of bringing his ships; and O'Conor's sons, on learning this, went forth and killed O'Huain, son of the Englishwoman, and John, the son of the English priest. In the affray, Sinnott Guer, and a number of his people, were also slain by Dermot, the son of Manus; but this was a victory without triumph, for Dermot himself, the son of Manus, that valiant hero and stay in battle, was killed on the spot.

Teige, son of Conor Roe, was killed by the English. This Teige had been the dread and terror of such of the English and Irish as were opposed to him up to his death.

An army was led by Maurice Fitzgerald into Tirconnell, where he engaged in conflicts and committed great depredations and plunders. He banished Rory O'Canannan into Tyrone, and left the lordship of Kinel-Connell to Godfrey, the son of Donnell O'Donnell.

The Kinel-Owen and O'Canannan mustered a body of forces and marched into Tirconnell, and gave battle to Godfrey and the Kinel-Connell, on which expedition Rory O'Canannan and many others were slain.

Another army was led by the Lord Justice[b] of Ireland into Tyrone, against O'Neill. The Kinel-Owen held a council, in which they agreed that, as the English of Ireland had, at this time, the ascendancy over the Irish, it would be advisable to give them hostages, and to make peace with them for the sake of their country. It was on this expedition that the English erected the bridge of the Bann[c], and the castle of Druim Tairsigh[d].

Butler, who was then the Lord Justice.

[c] *The bridge of the Bann*, ᴅɲoıċſc nα bαnnα.—This is not the bridge now called Banbridge, in the county of Down, but a bridge on the Lower Bann at Coleraine. In the old translation of the Annals of Ulster this passage is given as follows:

"A. D. 1248. An army by the Galls of Ireland to Culraghan, and [they erected] the bridge of the Banna, and the castle of Dromtarsy, and a dwelling at Drom."

[d] *Druim Tairsigh.*—In the Dublin copy of the Annals of Ulster, the passage is given thus:

A. D. 1248. Iuſtıſ nα hEſeınn ᴅo ᴅul ſluαġ

Aṫṫraiġi do ṫabairt la brian ua neill ticchearna ṫire heoġain ó loch feaḃail i maġ níṫe tar tErmann da ḃeócc go rainicc loċ neirne go nderna creaċa dioairṁe ⁊ gur briss caislén ann.

Conmaicne mara uile dairccain do ġallaiḃ. Gaill do ḋul for sluaiġeaḋ do com ui flaithbertaiġ. Maiḋm do ṫabairt dó forra ⁊ sochaiḋe do marḃaḋ ḋiob.

Muirceartaċ ua duḃda .i. an taiṫcleireaċ (.i. tiġearna ó ċill darbile co traiġ) do marḃaḋ la mac feḋlimiḋ uí concoḃair.

Uilliam burc do écc i saxaiḃ. A ċorp do ṫabairt co heirinn ⁊ a aḋnacal in aṫ iseal.

Ri frank do ḋul co hierusalem do ċosnaṁ na criosdaiḋeachda.

Ioan trial do marḃaḋ la giollu na naeṁ ua bfergail.

Feḋlimiḋ mac caṫail croiḃḋeirg do ṫabairt raṫa na romanaċ do ċanánchaiḃ cille moire tre forcongra taiḋg ui mannaċáin an onóir naeṁ muire ⁊ .s. augustín.

Aṁlaoiḃ mac caṫail riaḃaiġ uí ruairc do ṁarḃaḋ la concoḃor carraċ mac donnchaiḋ tre ṫangnacht.

Facchartaċ ua doḃailén ticchearna an corainn do écc.

Raighned airdepscop arda macha do teċt on roiṁ iar ttabairt pallium lais, ⁊ aifrionn do raḋa dó leis a bfeil peḋair, ⁊ poil in ardmacha.

go cul raṫain, ⁊ caislen ⁊ droiċead do ḋenum ḋóiḃ ag druim ṫairsiċ, i. e. "The Justiciary of Ireland went to Coleraine with an army, and a bridge and a castle were built by them at Druim thairsich."

There is no place on the River Bann now called Druim Tairsigh, or Drumtarsy; but there can be no doubt that it was on the western side of that river, opposite Coleraine. According to Pope Nicholas's Taxation (in 1291), there was a parish of Drumtarsi, in the diocese of Derry, which must be somewhere about Killowen, as it is mentioned between Camus and Dunbo. In the year 1347, Donald O'Kenalar was parson of Drumtarsny, in the diocese of Derry; and, in 1382, the castle of Druntarcy was ordered to be repaired.

[e] *Vessels.*—These were cots, or small boats, which were carried by land on the shoulders of men, to be launched on lakes for plundering islands. This passage is not in the Dublin copy of the Annals of Ulster, but it is thus given in the old translation: "A. D. 1348. Shipping brought by Brian O'Nell, Archking of all the North of Ireland, from Lochfevail to Moynitha, over Termon Daveog to Logh Derge, till he came to Lough Erne, until he made a great prey and broke a castle there." Termon-Daveog is now called Termon Magrath, and its church was situated on an island in Lough Derg, near Pettigoe, in the county of Donegal.

Brien O'Neill, Lord of Tyrone, brought vessels[e] [small boats], from Lough Foyle into Magh-Ithe[f], and across Termon Daveog, until he reached Lough Erne, where he committed great depredations, and demolished a castle.

The entire of Conmaicne-mara [Conamara] was plundered by the English. The English went upon an expedition against O'Flaherty, who defeated them, and killed numbers of them.

Murtough O'Dowda, that is, the Aithchleireach, Lord of the tract of country extending from Kildarvilla[g] to the Strand, was killed by the son of Felim O'Conor.

William Burke died in England. His body was brought over to Ireland, and buried at Athassel[h].

The King of France went to Jerusalem in defence of Christianity.

John Tyrrell was slain by Gilla-na-naev O'Farrell.

Felim, son of Cathal Crovderg, gave, by order of Teige O'Monahan, Rath-na-Romhánach[i] to the canons of Kilmore, in the honour of the Blessed Virgin Mary and St. Augustine.

Auliffe, son of Cathal Reagh O'Rourke, was treacherously slain by Cathal Carrach Mac Donough.

Faghartach O'Devlin, Lord of Corran [in the county of Sligo], died.

Raighned[k], Archbishop of Armagh, came from Rome, bringing with him a pallium, in which he said Mass at Armagh on the festival of SS. Peter and Paul.

[f] *Lough Foyle into Moy-Ithe.*—The ancient Irish gave the name of Lough Foyle to the whole extent of water from the mouth of the lake to Lifford. They had no River Foyle. Magh Ithe lies to the west of what is now called the River Foyle.

[g] *Kildarvilla*, cill ꝺaiꞃḃile, i. e. *the church of St. Dervilla.*—This is a very ancient church in the south of the parish of Kilmore, in the barony of Erris, and county of Mayo. The strand here alluded to is Traigh Eothaile, near Tanrego, in the county of Sligo, which formed the eastern boundary of O'Dowda's country at this period. This O'Dowda was chief of the entire of the baronies of Erris, Tirawley, and Tireragh, in the counties of Mayo and Sligo.

[h] *Athassel*, aṫ ıꞅeal, i. e. *the low ford.*—A village situated in the barony of Clanwilliam, in the county of Tipperary, on the west side of the River Suir, where William Fitz-Adelm de Burgo founded a priory for canons regular of the order of St. Augustine.—See Ware and Archdall.

[i] *Rath-na-Romhánach* is the name of a townland in the parish of Kilmore in the territory of Tir-Briuin na Sinna, of which O'Monahañ was chief at this period. It is now called in English Rathnarovanagh.—See Ordnance Survey of the county of Roscommon, sheet 17.

[k] *Raighned.*—His real name was Reiner. For

AOIS CRIOSD, 1249.

Aois Criosd, mile, dá céd, ceathrachat a naoí.

Maolmuire ua lachtnáin airdepscop tuama, ⁊ maighistir a ccanóin do écc is in ngeimhreadh gar beacc ria nodlaicc.

Andrias mac gilla gér comorba fecin décc.

Maolciarain ua lenacháin uasal ṡaccart tuama mna, fear tighe aoidheadh choitcinn idir eacclais ⁊ tuaith do écc ar slicchidh ag dul go hardcarna deirdeacht senmora is in aoine re lucchnasadh ⁊ a adhnacal go huasal onorach in oilén na trinoide for loch ce.

Conn ua flannacain prióir cille móire na sionna do écc.

Mór ingen donncaidh uí dubhda ben an giollu muinelaigh ui baoighill do écc.

Tadhg ua mannacháin ticchearna ua mbriuin na sionna do écc an sesedh la do mí iúin ⁊ a adhnacal i ccill moir na sionna.

Coccadh mór ⁊ uilc iomdha do denamh do ḟinghin mag carthaigh ar gallaibh Dearmumhan.

Piarus puér mac Enri, dabith triú, ⁊ socaidhe do gallaibh ócca amaille riú do toidheacht le mac ḟeorais i cconnachtaibh co caislén sliccigh. Adcuas do mac feidlimidh ui concobhair innsin go ttucc airrcéis orra. Feachair deabaidh aithgér storra go ttorcair piarus puér ⁊ dabith triu amaille le druing dona gallaibh occa remraite ⁊ ruccadh a ccuirp co hEss dara da nadhnacal.

Imthusa mac feidlimidh iarsin tainic roimhe go tir fiachrach ⁊ ar sud chriche mic ḟeorais gur lomairec í ó mhuaidh co traicch neothuile an traoir.

some account of this archbishop, whose surname or country has not yet been determined, see Harris's edition of Ware's Bishops, p. 66. He returned from Rome in the year 1247.

[l] *A proficient in the canon law*, maighistir a ccanoin.—By this is meant that he was an eminent canonist.

[m] *Coarb of Fechin*, i. e. abbot of Cong, in the county of Mayo.

[n] *Tuam-mna.*—See note [s], *ad an.* 1248, p. 323. There is a tradition in the neighbourhood of Carrick-on-Shannon, that the chapel of Toomna was built by the family of Lenaghan. The name is still extant in the parish.

[o] *Gilla-Muinelach O'Boyle*, i. e. the wife of Gilla Cammhuinelach, or the wry-necked, O'Boyle, who was slain at Ballyshannon, in the year 1247.

[p] *Made a great war.*—This passage could not be literally rendered into English. The reader may form an idea of the construction by the following Latin version: "Bellum magnum et mala multa facta sunt per Florentium Mac Carthy in Anglos Desmoniæ."

THE AGE OF CHRIST, 1249.

The Age of Christ, one thousand two hundred forty-nine.

Mulmurry O'Laghtnan, Archbishop of Tuam, a proficient in the canon law[l], died in winter, a short time before Christmas.

Andreas Mac Gillager, Coarb of Fechin[m], died.

Mulkieran O'Lenaghan, a noble priest of Tuam-mna[n], who kept a house of hospitality for the clergy and the laity, died on the way as he was going to Ardcarne, to hear a sermon, on the Friday before Lammas, and was interred with pomp and honour on Trinity Island, in Lough Key.

Conn O'Flanagan, Prior of Kilmore of the Shannon, died.

More, daughter of Donough O'Dowda, and wife of Gilla-Muinelach O'Boyle[o], died.

Teige O'Monahan, Lord of Hy-Briuin-na-Sinna, died on the 6th day of June, and was buried at Kilmore-na-Sinna.

Fineen Mac Carthy made a great war[p] on the English of Desmond, and inflicted many evils upon them.

Pierce Poer, the son of Henry, David Trew, and a number of young men, went, along with Mac Feorais[q], into Connaught, to the castle of Sligo. The son of Felim O'Conor marched to meet them, and a fierce battle was fought, in which Pierce Poer, David Trew[r], and many of the youths aforesaid, were slain; and their bodies were carried to Ballysadare for interment.

As to the son of Felim, he proceeded after this to Tireragh, and through Mac Feorais's country, which he entirely plundered from the Moy[s] to Traigh Eothuile-

[q] *Mac Feorais*, now pronounced Mac Keorish, the initial ꝼ being aspirated. This was the Irish surname assumed by the Berminghams from Feorus, or Piarus, the son of Myler Bermingham, their ancestor.—See Harris's Ware, vol. ii. p. 59.

[r] *David Trew.*—Mageoghegan writes the name David Drew, in his translation of the Annals of Clonmacnoise.

[s] *The Moy.*—This river is the Moda of Adamnan, which Dr. Prichard takes to be Wexford Harbour.—See his Ethnography of the Celtic Race, sect. xii. par. 2. O'Flaherty thus speaks of this river, *Ogygia*, p. 165: "Muadus Adamnano Moda, Moadus Giraldo Cambrensi, Calgano Muadius, Moy Anglis, unde Moyus Waræo e Lugniâ districtus Sligoensis in Galengam Mayonensem dimanat, & oceanum ingrediens utrumque comitatum disterminat, Tirficria Sligoensi, & Tiramalgad Mayoensi ultra citraque positis."

Thus Colgan, *Trias Thaum.*, p. 374, col. *a*,

Leanaiss gereoitin mac ḟeorais iad co rug ar donnċaḋ mac maġnusa gur crochtnaiġeaḋ é lais. Gaḃṫar beos iar ná ġuin ⁊ berṫear e go dún contreaṫain. Leanaiss mac fedlimiḋ iad iaroṁ go ttucc mac maġnusa leis iar marḃaḋ gereoittin. Mac maġnusa do écc iaroṁ do biṫin an luit sin ⁊ ba moirearḃaiḋ eriḋe.

Mac muiris do tionol soċraide go ttainicc i cconnaċtaiḃ gur ben an méd ar a rucc dona creachaiḃ do mac fedlimiḋ. Od cuala fedlimiḋ mac caṫail croiḃdeirg tionól na ngall do beiṫ ina coṁfoccus tar és na mor olc do roiġne a mac orra ass i coṁairle do rinne a imirceacha do ċor tar sionainn soir is in mbreifni, ⁊ i ttuaisceart eireann. Tionoilis din an iustís goill miḋe ⁊ laiġfn go ttainicc sluaġ mor roiṁe tar athluain, airsiḋe i siol muireaḋaiġ ⁊ mac muiris don leiṫ araill, goill connaċt ⁊ muṁan maraon ris. Tangadar na sluaiġsi do gach taoiḃ go hoilfinn iar milleaḋ sil muireaḋaiġ rompo go sin, ⁊ tuccsat ċuca toirrḋealḃaċ mac aoḋa mic

note 35: "Moda fluvius est Connaciæ celebris, vulgo Muaidh & nobis Latine Moadus sive Muadus appellatus."

[t] Tráiġ Eoṫuile an traoir, i. e. *the strand of Eothuile the artifex*, anciently called tráiġ an ċáirn and tráiġ Ruis airgiḋ. A very large strand in the county of Sligo, near Ballysadare. It is thus described by O'Flaherty, *Ogygia*, p. 174, note 3: "Traigh an chairn, hodie Traighe eothuile in Sligoensi agro, littus marinum, ubi congeries lapidum (unde *Traigh-an-chairn* dictum videtur) etiamnum conspicitur in medio littore semper fluctibus mirabiliter eminens." This carn is now called Cairgin mor, and it is believed that it is never covered by the tide.

[u] *Gereoitin Mac Feorais*, i. e. little Garrett Bermingham. Mageoghegan calls him Gerdin Bremyngham, in his translation of the Annals of Clonmacnoise, under this year.

[w] *Them*, iad.—The most remarkable imperfection in the style of these Annals is in the management of the personal pronouns. The leading nominative in this sentence is *the son of Felim*, and yet the writer suddenly introduces iad, *them*, though there is no plural noun in the previous part of the sentence to which it could refer. This is to be attributed to the carelessness or want of skill in the writers, perhaps to both, not to any imperfection in the language, for nothing could be easier than to set the sentence right by introducing soċraide instead of iad.

[x] *Dun Contreathain*, now Donaghintraine, a townland in the parish of Templeboy, in the barony of Tireragh, and county of Sligo.—See Ordnance Map of that county, sheet 12; and *Genealogies, Tribes, and Customs of Hy-Fiachrach*, p. 283.

[y] *As much of the preys*, that is, as much as he could catch of those preys which the son of Felim had driven away from Tireragh, then in the possession of the Berminghams.

[z] *The Lord Justice*.—This passage is well translated as follows in Mageoghegan's Annals of Clonmacnoise under this year.

"The Deputie of Ireland assembled together all the English of Meath" [and] "Lynster, and with them came to Athlone, from thence to Silemoreye. Mac Morishe was of the other side, with

an-tsaoir[t]. Gereoitin Mac Feorais[u] pursued them[w] [i. e. the son of Felim and his forces], overtook Donough, the son of Manus, and wounded him; he was also taken, after being wounded, and led captive to Dun Contreathain[x]. The son of Felim afterwards followed them, killed Gereoitin, and rescued and carried with him the son of Manus, who afterwards died of his wounds. He was a great loss.

Mac Maurice [Fitzgerald] mustered an army, and, proceeding into Connaught, took from the son of Felim as much of the preys[y] as he could overtake. When Felim, the son of Cathal Crovderg, heard that an English muster was in his neighbourhood, and reflected on the great injuries which his son had done to the English, he adopted the resolution of sending his moveable property eastwards across the Shannon into Breifny, and into the north of Ireland. The Lord Justice[z] then assembled the English of Meath and Leinster, who marched a great army across [the bridge of] Athlone, and thence into Sil-Murray; and Mac Maurice [Fitzgerald], on the other side, had with him the English of Connaught and Munster. Both these armies, having first plundered

all the forces of the English of Connought and Munster. Both armies mett at Alfyn, destroying and spoyleing all Silmorey to that place, from whence they came to Terlagh Mac Hugh Mac Cahall Crovederg, who being come, was by them made King of Connought instead of Felym Mac Cahall Crovederg. They afterwards preyed and spoyled the lands of Brenie, and also made many great hurts in that contrey, and conveighed their preys along with them; remained twenty nights at Silemorey, ruining and destroying that Contrey, they took with them the spoyles of Loghke, Carrick, and their Islands. The Deputy returned to Meath, Mac Morish to Sligoe, and Terlagh O'Connor was left then in Connought, to ward and defend Silemorey.

"The Nobility of Connought went to Athenrie, to prey and spoyle that towne, on the day of our Lady the Blessed Virgin Mary, in the middest of harvest. There were there a great army, with Terlagh mac Hugh, the Sheriff of Connoght, with many Englishmen, were in the said towne before them, the Sheriff and Englishmen desired them, in honour of the Blessed Virgin Mary, whose day then was, to forbear with them that day, which the said Irish Nobility refused to give any respect, either in honour of the Blessed Virgin or holie roode; they assaulted the towne against the will of the said Terlagh, which Jordan de Exetra, the Sheriff, and Englishmen seeing, they rushed forthe to meet with the said Irishmen, where the Virgin Mary wrought miraculouslie against the said Nobility. When the Irish Nobility saw the Englishmen, well apoynted with harness, armes, and shirts of mail, make towards them, they were daunted and affirigted at their sight and presently discomfitted. Hugh mac Hugh O'Connor was killed in that pressence, Dermott roe Mac Cormac O'Melaghlyn, the two sons of O'Kellie, Bryen-an-Dery Mac Manus, Carrick an Tivall mac Neal O'Connor, Boythgalagh mac Keigan, the son of Dermott Bacagh O'Connor, the two sonns of Loghlyn O'Connor, Donell mac Cormack mac Dermodda, Finnanagh mac Brannan,

caṫail croiḃdeirg gur ríoghsad é an ionadh fedlimiḋ mic caṫail. Ro aircc-sscct crioċ brefni iaraṁ. Do ronsat uilc iomḋa innte da gaċ aird. Tucc-sad creaċa diriṁi eisdi. Badar fiche oiḋche gona laiḃ i siol muireaḋaiġ ga milleaḋ gur airccriod loċ ce gona oilénaiḃ ⁊ an ċarrac immaille friú. Do cuaiḋ tra an iustis isin miḋi iarsin ⁊ mac muiris go sliccea ċ. Faccbaid toirrḋealḃaċ ag coiṁéd sil muireaḋaiġ.

Sluaiccheaḋ la rioġḋaṁnaiḃ connaċt, .i. toirrḋealḃaċ ⁊ aeḋ da ṁac aeḋa mic caṫail croiḃdeirg go haṫ na riog da lorccaḋ ⁊ da lomarccain im fel muire imeḋón foġṁair. Baoi sirriam connaċt is in ḃaile ar a ccionn, ⁊ goill iomḋa ina ḟoċair. Iarraid na goill cairdi an laoi sin ar cloinn riġ connaċt an onóir naeṁ muire sa fel boí ann. Noċan fuairsit sin uacha. Giḋeaḋ boí toirrḋealḃaċ ga ttoirmeasc im an mbaile dionnsaiġiḋ, ⁊ noċar daṁsat uaisle an tsluaiġ gan a ṡaiġiḋ da aiṁdeóin. Od connairc siurtán go ngallaiḃ sin tangadar as is mbaile amaċ i ccoinne an tsloiġ, ⁊ iad arṁṫa éidiġte. Gaḃais tra eacclu ⁊ uirṁeatacht occbaiḋ an tsluaiġ araill ga bfaicsin saṁlaiḋ ina ccoirriġtiḃ caṫa ionnus gur meaḃsad rompo tre mior-ḃailiḃ mor muire sa fél inar diultsad an ċairde do hiarraḋ orra. Ro marḃaḋ da maiṫiḃ isuiḋe aeḋ mac aeḋa uí concoḃair, diarmaid ruaḋ mac corbmaic uí maoilṡeaċlainn, da mac uí ċeallaiġ, brian an doire mac maġnusa, carraċ in ṡiuḃail mac nell uí conċoḃair, baoṫġalaċ mac aeḋac-cain, da mac lochlainn uí concoḃair. Doṁnall mac corbmaic meic diar-mada, an fionnánaċ mac branáin, cumuṁan mac cassarlaiġ, ⁊ araill immaille riu.

Donnċaḋ ua giollapattraicc .i. mac anmċaḋa mic donncaiḋ dossraiġiḃ do ṁarḃaḋ lá gallaiḃ. Ro ḋlighsiod goill innsin, uair ba mór ro marḃ, ro

Cowmowan mac Cassurley, with many more, were killed in that place."

[a] *Twenty nights and days*, fiche oiḋche go na láiḃ, literally, "twenty nights with their days."

[b] *The rock.*—Mac Dermot's castle in Lough Key, in the barony of Boyle, and county of Roscommon.

[c] *Truce*, cáirde, literally, *respite*.

[d] *Donough O'Gillpatrick.*—This passage is given as follows in Mageoghegan's Annals of Clonmacnoise.

"Donnogh mac Anmchy mac Donnogh mac Gillepatrick, the best head of a companie that ever descended of Osserie, of the race of Colman mac Brickne high" [*recte* ḃicne ċaoiċ], "or Scanlan mac Kynfoyle down, for manhood, vallour, and bounty, was killed by the Englishmen of Forgi[illegible], as he deserved of the English divers times before, for he killed, preyed, and burnt many an Englishman before that day. Donnogh was the third Irish-

Sil-Murray on their route, proceeded to Elphin, and, having sent for Torlough, son of Hugh, who was son of Cathal Crovderg, they elected him King in the place of Felim, the son of Cathal. They afterwards plundered Breifny, and committed many injuries there in every direction, and carried away from thence innumerable spoils. They were twenty nights[a] and days in Sil-Murray ravaging it, so that they plundered Lough Key, with its islands, and also the Rock[b]. The Lord Justice then went to Meath, and the son of Maurice to Sligo, leaving Torlough in charge of Sil-Murray.

An army was led by the Roydamnas [heirs presumptive] of Connaught, namely, Turlough and Hugh, two sons of Hugh, the son of Cathal Crovderg, to Athenry, on Lady Day in mid-autumn, to burn and plunder it. The sheriff of Connaught was in the town before them, with a great number of the English. The English demanded a truce[c] for that day from the sons of the King of Connaught, in honour of the Blessed Virgin Mary, it being her festival day; but this they did not obtain from them; and although Turlough forbade his troops to assault the town, the chiefs of the army would not consent, but determined to make the attack, in spite of him. When Jordan and the English saw this, they marched out of the town, armed and clad in mail, against the Irish army. The youths of the latter army, on seeing them drawn up in battle array, were seized with fear and dismay, so that they were routed; and this was through the miracles of the Blessed Virgin Mary, on whose festival they had refused to grant the truce demanded from them. Of their chiefs were here killed Hugh, son of Hugh O'Conor; Dermot Roe, son of Cormac O'Melaghlin, the two sons of O'Kelly; Brian an Doire, the son of Manus; Carragh Inshiubhail, son of Niall O'Conor; Boethius Mac Egan; the two sons of Loughlin O'Conor; Donnell, son of Cormac Mac Dermot; Finnanach Mac Branan; Cumumhan Mac Cassarly, and others besides.

Donough O'Gillapatrick[d], i. e. the son of Anmchadh, son of Donough, one of the Ossorians, was killed by the English. This was a retaliation due to the English; for, up to that time, he had killed, burned, and destroyed many

man that [most] war'd against the Englishmen, after the first footing in this land, viz., Connor O'Melaghlyn, Connor of the Castles Mac Coghlan, and this Donnogh mac Anmchy; for the son of Anmchy in his own person, did use to goe to take view of the Englishmen's towns and forts, in the habbitt of a poor man, carpenter, turner, or other tradesman."

loırcc ⁊ ro lérıonnaır ᴅıob ᵹo rın. Ƅahé an ᴅonnċaᴅ ra an ᴛrearr ᵹaoıᴅeal buᴅ mó ᴅroᵹlaᴅ orra, .ı. Concobar ua maoılreaċlaınn, Conċobar na ccaırlén mac cochláın ⁊ Mac anmchaᴅha .ı. an ᴅonncaᴅ ra. Oır ar e ᴛeᵹeaᴅ ᴅo braᴛ na mbaılᴛeaᴅ marccaᴅ ı ccruᴛ ᴅuıne boıċᴛ, nó ṡaoír no ᴛornóra, no ealaᴅna, no ᴅo ᴅſnaṁ ceirᴅe cſnnaıᵹı, aṁaıl ro raıᴅſᴅ.

Ƅıᴅ na Shaer, bıᴅ na ᴛornóır,
Ƅıᴅ mo laoᵹ na leabróır
Ƅıᴅ aᵹ rec ṗíona ır ċroıcıonn,
mar a bṗaıcſnn re rſrmóın.

Ꝺún mór ᴅo lorccaᴅ ᴅo cloınn rıᵹ Connaċᴛ.

Sluaıccheaᴅ la hua nᴅoṁnaıll, .ı. ᵹorraıᴅ ın ıoċᴛar Connaċᴛ ᵹur mılleaᴅ ⁊ ᵹur lomaırcceaᴅ laır ó ċoırrrlıab co muaıᴅ co ᴛᴛaınıcc rlan ıar mor corccar ᴅon cur rın co néᴅalaıb ⁊ co mbraıᵹᴅıbh ıomᴅaıb.

AOIS CRIOSD, 1250.

Aoır Crıorᴅ, míle, ᴅá ċéᴅ, caocca.

Ꞇomár ua meallaıᵹ erpucc Eanaıᵹ ᴅúın ᴅo écc.

Eprcop ımlıᵹ ıubaır ᴅo écc.

Conᵹalaċ mac cıᴅneoıl eprcop na brſıpne ᴅo écc.

Ꞇoırrᴅealbaċ mac muırcſrᴛaıᵹ muımnıᵹ uí Concobaır prıoır réccleṛa pſᴛᴛaır ⁊ poıl ᴅo écc.

Ꝼeᴅlımıᴅ ua concobaır ᴅo ċoıᴅeachᴛ ar an ᴛuaırccearᴛ ᵹo roċraıᴅe móır laır a cenél neoᵹaın ᴅo ṡaıᵹıᴅ na brſıpne. Aırrıᴅe ır na ᴛuaċaıb ⁊ Concobar mac ᴛıccſrnáın maraon rırr. Aırrıᴅe ı ᴛᴛír maıne ᵹur ᴅıochuırrſᴅ ᴛoırrᴅealbaċ a Connaċᴛaıb amaċ ᵹo nᴅeachaıᴅ ın uchᴛ ġall ᴅorıᴅırı. Ꞇıonoılıᴅ ṗeᴅlım ımırceaċa Connaċᴛ laır ᴛar rlıab reᵹra ríor ᵹur cuırrıoᴅ

[e] *He is*, bıᴅ.—This translation is strictly literal, word for word, except that bıᴅ is in the consuetudinal present tense in Irish, which has no corresponding tense in English.

[f] *Dun mor*, i. e. the great fort, now the little town of Dunmore, about eight miles to the north of Tuam, in the county of Galway. A short distance to the west of the town are the ruins of a castle in tolerable preservation, which was originally erected by Hosty Mac Mebric, or Merrick, but which afterwards fell into the possession of the Berminghams.

of them. This Donough was, of the Irish, the third greatest plunderer of the English: the three plunderers were Conor O'Melaghlin, Conor Mac Coghlan, [surnamed] of the Castles, and the son of Anmchadh, viz., this Donough [Fitzpatrick]. He was in the habit of going about to reconnoitre their market towns, in the guise of a pauper, or a carpenter, or a turner, or poet, or of one carrying on the trade of a merchant, as was said [in the following quatrain]:

He is a carpenter, he is[e] a turner,
My nursling is a bookman,
He is selling wine and hides,
Where he sees a gathering.

Dunmore[f] was burned by the sons of the King of Connaught.

An army was led by O'Donnell (Godfrey), into Lower Connaught, and he destroyed and ravaged [that tract of country reaching] from the Curlieu Mountains to the Moy, and returned safe and in triumph, carrying with him great spoils and many hostages.

THE AGE OF CHRIST, 1250.

The Age of Christ, one thousand two hundred fifty.

Thomas O'Meallaigh, Bishop of Annadown, died.

The Bishop of Imleach Iubhair [Emly] died.

Congalagh Mac Kidnel[g], Bishop of Breifny [Kilmore], died.

Turlough, son of Mortough Muimhneach O'Conor, Prior of the church of SS. Peter and Paul, died.

Felim O'Conor came from the north, with a numerous force, out of Tyrone; he marched into Breifny, and thence into the Tuathas, accompanied by Conor, son of Tiernan [O'Conor]; thence into Hy-Many, and they expelled Turlough out of Connaught, who again went over to the English. He [Felim] then collected all the moveable property of Connaught, and proceeded with it down across Sliabh Seaghsa [the Curlieu Mountains], but the English sent messen-

[g] *Mac Kidnel.*—He is called Congalach Mac-Eneol in Harris's edition of Ware's Bishops, p. 226, where he is given as Bishop of Kilmore.

goill teachta na deoidh go nderrnadh sith fria, ⁊ a righ daireacc dó fén doridhisi.

Brighde Connacht do dallad in áth luain do gallaibh.

Creach mór do dénamh la feidlimidh for cathal ua Concobair ⁊ a atcor a connachtaibh.

Cairbre ua maoilseachlainn do marbhadh i ffell la dauit Roitsi.

Diarmaid ua hEgra tighearna luighne do écc i bpriosún ag mag geraild.

Sluaicchedh mor la muirir mac gearailt, cathal ua raghallaigh, cuconnacht ua raghallaigh, ⁊ maithe ua mbriúin uile immaille friú i ccenel eoghain go rabhadar teora hoidhce i tteulaigh ócc. Fuairriod mor dulc ⁊ dimneadh ainnsidhe. Nochar gabsat gell na eidireadha ó uibh nell don cur sin. Iar tteacht doibh tar a naiss i ccenél Conaill muirir mac gerailt do gabail uí canannain ticchearna cenel cconaill ar comairce an easpuicc uí cerbhalláin. A marbhadh doibh iarsin ⁊ é ag triall ar eccin uatha.

Finghin mág carthaigh do marbhadh la gallaibh deasmuman.

AOIS CRIOSD, 1251.

Aois Criosd, mile, da céd, caoccat a haen.

Raighnéd airdepscop ardamacha do dul do Róimh dia oilithre.

Flosint mac floinn doirdneadh la nodlac in airdeprcopoideacht tuama ar méd a eccna ⁊ a eolaisr.

Mainestir hi ccill na mullach in espscopóitteecht corcaighe do chumdach lásan mbarrach ⁊ togha adhnaicthe na mbarrach sin innte.

Giollumocoinne mac giollamocoinne uí cathail do marbhadh la Concobor mac aedha mic cathail croibhdeirg.

[h] *Were blinded*, do dallad.—This would appear to have been done, not by putting out the eyes, but by thrusting needles into them.—See *Genealogies, &c., of Hy-Fiachrach*, p. 337.

[i] *Bishop O'Carolan.*—He was German, or Gilla-Coimdedh O'Carolan, who was Bishop of Derry from the year 1230 till his death in 1279.—See Harris's edition of Ware's Bishops, p. 288.

[k] *Fineen Mac Carthy.*—According to the Dublin copy of the Annals of Innisfallen, he was slain by his own uncle, Donnell God Mac Carthy, who was assisted by the head of the Goggans, or De Cogans, though they were at peace with him. This Fineen was the son of Dermot of Dundronan, who was the son of Donnell More na Curra Mac Carthy.

[l] *Raighned.*—His real name was Reiner, as appears from the public records. He obtained

gers after him, and, a peace being concluded between them, his kingdom was again restored to him.

The hostages of Connaught were blinded[h] by the English at Athlone.

A great depredation was committed by Felim on Cathal O'Conor, and the latter was driven out of Connaught.

Carbry O'Melaghlin was treacherously slain by David Roche.

Dermot O'Hara, Lord of Leyny, died in prison, where he had been confined by Fitzgerald.

A great army was led by Maurice Fitzgerald, Cathal O'Reilly, Cuconnaught O'Reilly, and all the other chiefs of Hy-Briuin, into Tyrone, and remained three nights at Tullaghoge, where they sustained much injury and hardship, but obtained no pledges or hostages from the O'Neills on this expedition. On their return into Tirconnell Maurice Fitzgerald took O'Canannan, Lord of the Kinel-Connell, prisoner, under protection of Bishop O'Carolan[i]. He was afterwards killed as he was trying to make his escape from them.

Fineen [Florence] Mac Carthy[k] was slain by the English of Desmond.

THE AGE OF CHRIST, 1251.

The Age of Christ, one thousand two hundred fifty-one.

Raighned[l], Archbishop of Armagh, went on a pilgrimage to Rome.

Florentius Mac Flynn was, on Christmas Day, consecrated Archbishop of Tuam, for his wisdom and learning.

A monastery was founded at Kilnamullagh[m], in the diocese of Cork, by Barry, who chose a burial place for his family in it.

Gilla Mochoinne, son of Gilla Mochoinne O'Cahill, was slain by Conor, son of Hugh, the son of Cathal Crovderg.

the King's license for five months on the 11th of June, 1253, to repair to Rome, in order to settle some affairs relating to his church. He never returned, but died at Rome in 1256.—See Harris's edition of Ware's Bishops, p. 66.

[m] *Kilnamullagh*, cill na mullach, *church of the hills or summits.*—It is now called Buttevant, and is situated in the barony of Orrery, in the county of Cork.—See O'Sullivan Beare's History of the Irish Catholics, p. 159, where he translates this name "*Ecclesia tumulorum.*"

Tadhg mac tuathail mic muirchertaigh muimnigh uí Conchobair do marbhadh do gallaibh.

Da mac Ruaidhri uí nell do marbhadh i ccill moir ua niallain.

Ardgal ua laithbhertaigh coinnel gaiscidh ⁊ enigh tuaisceirt Ereann do écc.

Giollucriosd ua breislén toiseach fanad ⁊ a brathair do marbhadh la ceallach mbalbh ua mbuighill.

Donnchadh mac cathmaoil toiseach cenel fferadhaigh do marbhadh dairgiallaibh.

Iomhar mac madadháin toiseach cloinne ruadhrach do mharbhadh.

Concobor mac corbmaic mic tomaltaigh meic diarmada, Saí enigh ⁊ engnamha do écc.

Flaithbhertach ua cerbaill toiseach calraighe do marbhadh la hart mac airt uí Ruairc.

Muireadhach ua taidhg do ecc.

Cioth mor dfearthain la feli poil ⁊ pedair in uibh briúin go snamhadh eathor adhbal timcheal baile cille moire na Sionna, ⁊ go melfeadh muilenn ar an srut boí on srouaigh go hath na faithche i bfiodhnach fri ré ceileabharta earrparta.

Flann ó lachtnáin taeiseach an dá bhac do écc.

---

[n] *Kilmore-Oneilland*, cill mór ua niallain, i. e. *the great church of the territory of Hy-Niallain*, now the church of Kilmore, in the barony of Oneilland, and county of Armagh, and about three miles to the east of the city of Armagh.

[o] *Fanad.*—A territory in the north-east of the barony of Kilmacrenan, in the county of Donegal.—See note [s], under the year 1186, p. 76.

[p] *Kinel-Farry*, cinel fferadhaigh.—A territory in the barony of Clogher, in the county of Tyrone.

[q] *Calry*, calraighe, and Latinized Calrigia.—A territory in the north-east of Connaught, the name of which is still preserved in the parish of Calry, in the barony of Carbury, and county of Sligo; but it is quite clear from a passage in the Tripartite Life of St. Patrick, lib. ii. c. 103, that this territory originally comprised some part of the county of Leitrim, for *Druim da eithiar*, now Dromahaire, in the county of Leitrim, is mentioned as in the territory of Calrigia.

[r] *Hy-Briuin-na-Sinna* comprehends the parishes of Aughrim, Kilmore, and Clooncraff, in the east of the county of Roscommon. It was divided from Kinel-Dofa, or O'Hanly's country, by a chain of lakes now called Muckinagh, and separating the parish of Kilglass from those of Kilmore and Clooncraff; and from the territory of Corcachlann, by the River Uar, or Owenoor. Coradh na dtuath, the weir or dam of the Tuathas, now a bridge on an arm of the Shannon, and on the road from Rooskey to Drumsna, divided Tir Briuin from Kinel Dofa, and the ford of Bellanagrange, now spanned by a bridge on the road from Strokestown to Drumsna, is the point at which the three Tuathas met.—

Teige, son of Tuathal, who was son of Murtough Muimhneach O'Conor, was slain by the English.

The two sons of Rory O'Neill were slain in Kilmore-O'Neilland[n].

Ardgal O'Laverty, the lamp of the valour and hospitality of the north of Ireland, died.

Gilchreest O'Breslen, Chief of Fanad[o], and his brother, were slain by Kellagh Balbh [the Stammering] O'Boyle.

Donough Mac Cawell, Chief of Kinel-Farry[p], was slain by the men of Oriel.

Ivor Mac Madden, Chief of Clann-Ruadhrach, was slain.

Conor, son of Cormac, who was son of Tomaltagh Mac Dermot, illustrious for hospitality and prowess, died.

Flaherty O'Carroll, Chief of Calry[q], was slain by Art, son of Art O'Rourke.

Murray O'Teige died.

On the festival of SS. Peter and Paul, a great shower of rain fell in Hy-Briuin-na-Sinna[r], so that a large boat might have sailed round the town of Kilmore-na-Sinna; and a mill might grind on the stream which ran from the hill down to the ford of Ath-na-faithche, at Fenagh, during the time that vespers were being chaunted.

Flann O'Laghtnan, Chief of the Two Bacs, died[s].

See entries at the years 1398 and 1451, where the churches of Aughrim and Clooncraff are mentioned as in this territory.

[s] *Two Bacs*, an ꝺa ḃac.—This territory retains its ancient name to the present day, and is applied to a Roman Catholic parish, which comprises the ancient parishes of Ballynahaglish and Kilbelfad, in the barony of Tirawley and county of Mayo. But it appears from the Book of Hy-Fiachrach, as transcribed by Duald Mac Firbis, that Ardagh, Kilmore-Moy, and Rosserk, were originally comprised in this territory. It was bounded on the east by the River Moy, and on the west, to a considerable extent, by Lough Cullin and Lough Conn. See *Genealogies, Tribes, and Customs of Hy-Fiachrach*, p. 232, note [k], and note [r] under the year 1180, p. 56, *supra*. Under this year the Annals of Clonmacnoise and of Connaught contain the following notice of the death of Clarus Mac Mailin, Archdeacon of Elphin:

"Clarus Archidiaconus Olfyn, vir providus & discretus, qui Carnem suam jeiuniis et orationibus macerabat, qui patientiam et Coronam observabat, qui persecutionem a multis propter justitiam patiebatur, venerabilis fundator Locorum fraternitatis Sanctæ Trinitatis, per totam Hiberniam specialiter fundator Monasterij Sanctæ Trinitatis apud Loghke, vir Locum Sepulture ibidem elegit, et in Christo quievit Sabatho Penthecostes dominicæ, cuius animæ propitietur Deus omnipotens in Cœlo, cui ipse servivit in seculo, in cuius honore ecclesiam de Ryndoyne, et monasterium Sanctæ Trinitatis apud Athmoye, Ecclesiam Sanctæ Trinitatis apud Killruisse ædificavit."

AOIS CRIOSD, 1252.

Aois Criosd, mile, dá chéd, caocca, adó.

Maolmaedócc ua beolláin comharba cholaim cille in druim cliabh, fear ba mór cadhus ⁊ conach, ba hoirdheirc oineach, ba huille onóir ⁊ airmhidin ó ghallaibh ⁊ ó ghaoidhealaibh re a linn do écc.

Caislen chaoiluisce do dhénamh la mac muiris meic gearailt ⁊ caislén mhuighi cobha.

Concobhar ua dochartaigh toiseach ardha miodhair, tuir oinigh ⁊ eangnamha an tuaisceirt deg.

Concobhar mac cathmaoil toiseach cenel ffeardhaigh ⁊ ioltuath archena. Sloighedh Conaille, Eoghain, ⁊ oirghiall do marbhadh la muintir briain uí nell ag cosnamh a comairci friú, iar mbeith dho for slanaibh uí gairmleadhaigh ⁊ uí chathain.

Cuconnacht mac Consnamha toiseach muintire cinaith do écc.

Giolla isu ua cearbaill toiseach calraighi droma cliabh do écc.

Maghnus mac giolla duibh toiseach teallaigh gairbheth do écc.

Iustís na hEreann do theacht co hardmacha immaille re sluagh lánmhór, eirghidhe co huibh eachdhach, airisidhe tar a naiss co cluain fiachna. Brian ó nell dá noighréir annsin, ⁊ a dearbhrathair, Ruaidhri ó nell do thabhairt do

[t] *Cael-uisce*, i. e. Narrow-water.—This place retains its ancient name to the present day among those who speak Irish, but is always called in English Narrow-water. It is situated between Warren's Point and Newry, in the barony of Upper Iveagh, and county of Down. The name was originally applied to the narrow part of the river, near the head of Carlingford Lough.—See the Irish Calendar of the O'Clerys, at the 2nd of April, where the church of Cluain Dallain, now Clonallon, is described as near Snamh Each, i. e. the harbour which is near the Cael in Iveagh, in Ulidia. "Conall mac Aodha ó chluain dalláin a bfail snámha each .i. an cuan laimh fris in chaol i nUibh Eachach Uladh."—See also Dubourdieu's Statistical Survey of the County of Down, p. 294.

[u] *Moy-Cova*, magh cobha, i. e. the plain of Eochy-Cova, the ancestor of the tribe called Ui Eathach Cobha, located in the present baronies of Upper and Lower Iveagh, in the county of Down.—See O'Flaherty's *Ogygia*, part iii. c. 78. The Four Masters, and from them Colgan and others, have erred in placing this plain in Tyrone; and, Dr. Lanigan has been set astray by them, where he conjectures (Ecclesiastical History of Ireland, vol. iv. p. 11, note 26), that Magh Cobha was probably where the village now called Coagh is situated: but the situation of the plain of Magh Cobha is fixed by the older writers who place it in Uibh Eathach, now Iveagh, and who place in it the church of

THE AGE OF CHRIST, 1252.

The Age of Christ, one thousand two hundred fifty-two.

Maelmaedhóg O'Beóllain, Coarb of Columbkille, at Drumcliff, a man of great esteem and wealth, the most illustrious for hospitality, and the most honoured and venerated by the English and Irish in his time, died.

The castle of Caol-Uisce[t] was erected by Maurice Fitzgerald, as was also the castle of Moy-Cova[u].

Conor O'Doherty, Chief of Ardmire [in the county of Donegal], tower of the hospitality and feats of arms of the north, died.

Conor Mac Cawell, Chief of Kinel-Farry [in Tyrone], and many other territories, and peace-maker of Tirconnell, Tyrone, and Oriel, was slain by the people of Brian O'Neill, while defending his protegees against them, he himself being under the protection[w] of O'Gormly and O'Kane.

Cuconnaught Mac Consnava, Chief of Muintir-Kenny[x], died.

Gilla-Isa O'Carroll, Chief of Calry of Drumcliffe, died.

Manus Mac Gilduff, Chief of Tullygarvey[y], died.

The Lord Justice of Ireland came to Armagh with a very numerous army, and proceeded thence to Iveagh, from which he marched back to Cluain-Fiachna[z]. Brian O'Neill and his brother made submission to him, and Rory

Domhnach more Muighe Cobha, which is unquestionably the present Donaghmore, in the barony of Upper Iveagh, nearly midway between Newry and Loughbrickland.—See *Feilire Aenguis*, at 16th November; and Haliday's edition of Keating's History of Ireland, p. 318, where the plain of Magh Cobha, which is said to have been cleared of wood in the reign of Irial Faidh, is said to be situated in Aoibh Eachach, anglice Iveagh.—See note [q], under the year 1188, p. 81, *supra*.

[w] *Under the protection.*—This passage is not in the Dublin copy of the Annals of Ulster, but it is given in English as follows, in the old translation preserved in the British Museum: "A. D. 1252. Conner Mac Cathmoyl, kingly chief of Kindred Feragh and many other places, also the upholder of liberality and fortitude of the North of Ireland; the peace-maker of Connells and Owens, and Airgialls also, killed by the Rutes" [*cohortes*] "of Brien O'Neal, defending his *comrick* from them, being upon O'Garmely & O'Cahan's word himself."

[x] *Muintir-Kenny*, muintir cinaith.—The name of a tribe and territory in the barony of Dromahaire, in the county of Leitrim. The name is still locally known and applied to the district lying between Lough Allen and the River Arigna.

[y] *Teallach Gairbheth*, now the barony of Tullygarvey, in the north-east of the county of Cavan.

[z] *Cluain Fiachna*, i. e. St. Fiachna's lawn,

ḃraġaid doibh. Ar ar an sluaigheaḋ so tarlu imresain longpuirt etir ḟearaiḃ miḋe ⁊ ṁuiṁneaċaiḃ i ndun dealgan co ttorcradar sochaiḋe do ḟearaiḃ muṁan.

Tearbaċ mór ⁊ tiormaċ is in samraḋ go ttegtí tosaiḃ tiormaiḃ tar priomaibhniḃ Ereann. Arḃanna Ereann ḃeós gá mbuain fiche laiṫe ria luġnasaḋ. Na croinn gá ccoṁlosccaḋ le teas ngréne.

Monaḋ nua dordugaḋ do riġ Saxan do ḋenaṁ in eirinn ⁊ an tairccead boí innte ria sin do trecceaḋ.

Murċaḋ ua fallaṁain ardċonstapla Connaċt do marḃaḋ dfearaiḃ breifne i maigh rén.

Creachsluaiġeaḋ la goffraidh ua ndoṁnaill hi tir neoghain dia ttarraiḋ bú ⁊ braighde ile. Rucc brian ua néill fair ag fágbáil an tíre. Ro ficcheaḋ iomaireag aṁnus etorra adiú ⁊ anall go raíṁiḋ for cenél neoghain co ffargaibset ar cenn im druing ṁoir dia ndaghdaoiniḃ.

AOIS CRIOSD, 1253.

Aois Criosd, mile, da ċéd, caocca, a trí.

Alinn ua Suilleaḃáin espucc leasa móir do écc.

Dauit mac ceallaiġ uí giollupattraicc epscop cluana mic nois do écc, ⁊ tomas ua cuinn braṫair mionúr doirdneaḋ is in Roiṁ na ionaḋ.

Giollaceallaiġ ua Ruaiḋín espuc ua ffiachraċ do écc. Seón ua laidig braṫair dord .S. dominic doirdneaḋ ina ionaḋ i ccill alad ua ffiachraċ, ⁊ graḋa espuic do ṫabairt fair i ttuaim an dara doṁnaċ don geaṁcorgus.

Mainisdir do ḋenaṁ do ḃraiṫriḃ .S. Dominic i Slicceach.

meadow, or bog-island. It is mentioned at the years 1003 and 1069 as a monastery; but its exact situation, or modern name, has not been determined.

[a] *Discontinued*, do treicceaḋ, literally, *was abandoned*. In modern times this entry would be thus expressed: New coin was issued in Ireland by order of the King of England, and the old coin was called in.

[b] *Thomas O'Quin*.—He was a Franciscan friar, and was confirmed by King Henry III., on the 20th of February, 1252, English style.—See Harris's edition of Ware's Bishops, p. 171.

[c] *Gilla-Kelly O'Ruaidhin*.—See Harris's edition of Ware's Bishops, p. 650, where the Editor writes, under John O'Mailfagamair, who died in 1234: "I do not find who was his next successor. But it is certain the see was vacant

O'Neill was given up to him as a hostage. It was on this expedition a riot took place between the men of Meath and the men of Munster, in the [English] camp at Dundalk, and many of the men of Munster were killed.

Great heat and drought prevailed in this Summer, so that people crossed the [beds of the] principal rivers of Ireland with dry feet. The reaping of the corn crops of Ireland was going on twenty days before Lammas [the 1st of August], and the trees were scorched by the heat of the sun.

New money was ordered by the King of England to be made [coined] in Ireland, and the money previously in use was discontinued[a].

Murrough O'Fallon, High Constable of Connaught, was slain in Moy-Rein by the men of Breifny.

Godfrey O'Donnell made a predatory incursion into Tyrone, and took many cows and prisoners, but was overtaken as he was leaving the country by Brian O'Neill, and a fierce battle was fought between them, in which the Kinel-Owen were defeated, and left behind many heads, with a great number of their chieftains [i. e. as prisoners].

THE AGE OF CHRIST, 1253.

The Age of Christ, one thousand two hundred fifty-three.

Alinn O'Sullivan, Bishop of Lismore, died.

David, the son of Kellagh O'Gillapatrick, Bishop of Clonmacnoise, died and Thomas O'Quin[b], a friar minor, was consecrated at Rome as his successor.

Gilla-Kelly O'Ruaidhin[c], Bishop of Hy-Fiachrach [Killala], died, and John O'Laidig, a friar of the order of St. Dominic, was elected to succeed him at Killala in Hy-Fiachrach, and the degree of Bishop conferred on him at Tuam, on the second Sunday in Lent.

A monastery for Dominican Friars was founded at Sligo.

on the 22nd of June, 1253, on which day King Henry III. granted a licence to proceed to the election of a Bishop of Killala, as appears in the Records of the Tower of London." He then remarks, under O'Laidig: "I do not know whether he immediately succeeded *O'Mailfagamair*, or who intervened; but there is mention made in the Records, of a Bishop of *Killala* (whose name is not told) who went to England with *Florence Mac Flin*, Archbishop of Tuam, A. D. 1255, to complain of grievances."

Mainistir do ṫorainn dona braiṫribh cena ag aṫ lethan illuighnibh.

Cuirt do ḋenaṁ la tomaltaċ ua cconcobhair epscop oilifinn i ccill tésin.

Eoġan ua heḋin tigcherna ua ffiachraċ do écc.

Ingen an iarla ultoiġ ben miliḋ mic goirdealbhaiġ do écc ⁊ a haḋnacal i mainistir na búille.

Sluaiccheaḋ mor la gallaibh ereann im Mac Muiris go ndeachaiḋ i ttír neoghain do ṡaiġiḋ uí nell ⁊ nochar gabhsat gell na edireaḋa innte, uair tuccaḋ ár aḋbhal mór don dul sin orra.

Coccaḋ mór do denaṁ la brian ua nell flaiṫ cenel neoġain for gallaibh, ⁊ dul dó go moiġ coba gur trascraḋ a ċaislén leiss immaille le mor do caislénaibh oile. Loiscctea an Sradbaile leiss ⁊ folmaiġis maċaire ulaḋ.

Sluaiccheaḋ do ḋenaṁ do doṁnall ua Raġallaiġ ⁊ don caeċ ua Raġallaiġ do ċaṫal ua concobhair ⁊ do giollu na naeṁ ó ḟeargail i muintir eolaiss dionnsaighiḋ ċaṫail mecc Raġnaill gur aircceset an tir uile. Badar da oiḋċe longpuirt ag tulaiġ álainn, ⁊ an tres oiḋċe ag eanaċ ḋuibh. Deilġis giollu na naeṁ ua fergail friu annsin. Teaccaid muintir Raġallaiġ ⁊ caṫol ó concobhair go cluain conmaicne co mbadar aḋaiġ longpuirt innte. Od

[d] *Ath Leathan*, i. e. *the broad ford*, now Ballylahan, in the north of the parish of Templemore, in the barony of Gallen, and county of Mayo — See Ordnance Map of the county of Mayo, sheet 61. The Four Masters are wrong in placing this in the territory of Leyny, for it is certainly in the ancient territory of Gailenga, O'Gara's original country.

[e] *Killtesin*, now Kilteashin, the name of a townland in the west of the parish of Ardcarne, in the barony of Boyle, and county of Roscommon. There are at present no ruins of this palace to be seen here, but there is a mound called Suidhe an Easbuig, i. e. the Bishop's seat, near which, tradition says, the Bishop of Elphin had formerly a palace.—See entries under the years 1243 and 1258. It is sometimes called Cill Seisin by the annalists, but now always cill tSéisin, or Kilteashin, by the natives.

[f] *But far from obtaining*.—The language of this passage is rather carelessly constructed by the Four Masters. The literal translation is as follows: "A great hosting by the Galls of Ireland about Mac Maurice, so that they went into Tyrone against O'Neill, and they did not take hostages or pledges, for a prodigious great slaughter was, on that occasion, brought on them." It is thus Englished in the old translation of the Annals of Ulster: "A. D. 1253. A great army by Mac Morris, &c., went to Tyrone, and tooke" [i. e. obtained] "neither force nor might there. And the Galls lost a great navy" [*recte* army] "by that journey."

[g] *Chief of Kinel-Owen*.—In the Dublin copy of the Annals of Ulster he is called riġ ṫíre heoġain, i. e. King of Tyrone, and in the old translation of these Annals he is styled Archking of the North of Ireland. Thus:

"A. D. 1253. An army by Brien O'Neal, Archking of the North of Ireland, to Moycova,

Another monastery for the same order of friars was founded at Ath-Leathan[d] in Leyny.

A palace was erected by Tomaltagh O'Conor, Bishop of Elphin, at Killtesin[e].

Owen O'Heyne, Lord of Hy-Fiachrach [Aidhne], died.

The daughter of the Earl of Ulster, wife of Miles Mac Costello, died, and was interred in the Abbey of Boyle.

A great hosting by the English of Ireland, under the command of Mac Maurice (Fitzgerald), and they marched into Tyrone against O'Neill; but, far from obtaining[f] either hostages or pledges from him, they were cut off with very great slaughter on that occasion.

A great war was waged with the English by Brian O'Neill, Chief of Kinel-Owen[g]. He marched to Moy-Cova, the castle of which, with a great number of other castles, he demolished. He also burned Sradbhaile[h], and desolated Machaire-Uladh[i].

An incursion was made by Donnell O'Reilly and the Caech [Monoculus] O'Reilly, Cathal O'Conor, and Gilla-na-naev O'Farrell, into Muintir-Eolais, against Cathal Mac Rannall, and they plundered the entire country. They remained two nights encamped at Tulach-alainn[k], and stopped the third night at Annaghduff[l], where Gilla-na-naev separated from the others. The O'Reillys and Cathal O'Conor then marched to Cluain-Conmaicne[m], where they remained

broke down the castle, and many castles more in Ulster, &c." [killed] "many men in that journey."

[h] *Sradbhaile*, i. e. Street-town.—This is still the local name for the town of Dundalk, in the county of Louth; but sometimes the natives of its immediate vicinity call it simply an sráiḋ, i. e. "*the street*," without adding baile; in like manner as they call Drogheda [*Pontana civitas*] simply an ḋroiċeaḋ, i. e. "the bridge," without adding aṫa, i. e. of the ford. The strand near Dundalk was anciently called Traigh Bháile mhic Buain, i. e. the strand of Bailé, the son of Buan, but this has no connexion whatever with its more modern appellation of Sraḋḃaile, which simply means "*street-town.*"

[i] *Machaire Uladh*, i. e. the plain of Ulidia.—This was an ancient name for the level part of the county of Down, which was at this period called Uladh by the Irish.

[k] *Tulach-aluinn*.—The ancient name of a hill at the village of Carrigallen, in the county of Leitrim.

[l] *Annaghduff*, eanaċ ḋuiḃ.—A parish near Drumsna, in the county of Leitrim.

[m] *Cluain Conmaicne*.—Now the village of Cloone, in the barony of Mohill, and county of Leitrim. There was a monastery erected here in the sixth century by St. Cruimther Fraech, but there is not a vestige of it at present.—See

cuala aeḋ mac feḋlimiḋ sin tionoilis co tinnearnaċ a muinter. Lenaiss iadsom go cluain Tuccsat tresss aggarḃ dia roile gur moiḋiḋ for muintir Raġallaiġ, marḃtar ann donnchadh mac giollu iosu mic donncaiḋ uí Raġallaiġ, mac giollu toedócc ua bioḃraiġ, ⁊ sochaiḋe oile imaille friu.

Mainestir .S. Franseis in ardfearta do ḋénoṁ la Mac Muiris ciarraiġe.

AOIS CRIOSD, 1254.

Aois Criosd, míle, da ċéd, caocca, a ceaṫair.

Maolfinnén ua beolláin coṁorba droma cliaḃ do écc.

Murċaḋ ua maoilseaċlainn do ṁarḃaḋ la mac an trionnaiġ uí caṫarnaiġ.

Ainoilss ua hinnsrġi tuir engnaṁa thuaisccirt ereann do écc.

Piarus pramister ticchspna conmaicne duin móir do écc.

Mainistir braṫar .S. Dominic in aṫ leathan do loscaḋ uile.

Piarus Ristubartt ticchspna sil maoilruain, barún essiḋe, a marḃaḋ ar loch riḃ la murċaḋ ua maoilseaċlainn.

Sitreacc máġ ḟeanlaoiġ do gaḃail dḟeḋlimiḋ mac caṫail ċroiḃdeirg, ⁊ an seanḟuileaċ mac seanlaoich do dallaḋ laiss a loss aiṁlsa, óir do raiḋeaḋ sis co mbadar ag feallaḋ fair.

Donnchaḋ mac donnchaiḋ mic tomaltaiġ, ⁊ aṁlaoiḃ ua bioḃraiġ do marḃaḋ lá Connachtaiḃ i ccluain Conmaicne.

Maġnus ua gaḋra do marḃaḋ tre anḟochain do muintir mic feḋlimiḋ uí concoḃair.

Colgan's *Acta Sanctorum*, p. 346, and Lanigan's Ecclesiastical History of Ireland, vol. ii. p. 324. The name of this saint is now locally pronounced Cruffer Ree.

[n] *Ardfert* is a village in the barony of Clanmaurice, and county of Kerry, about four miles to the north-west of Tralee. The extensive ruins of this monastery are still to be seen a short distance to the east of the village.

[o] *O'Henery*.—The O'Henerys were seated in the valley of Glenconkeine, in the county of Londonderry. This passage is not in the Dublin copy of the Annals of Ulster; but it is found thus Englished in the old translation: "A. D. 1254. Anyles Hinerge, the threshold of manhood [eangnaṁa], in the North of Ireland, died."

[p] *Conmaicne of Dunmore*.—This territory is comprised in the barony of Dunmore, in the north of the county of Galway, which at this period belonged to the family of Bermingham, or Bramingham, of which name Pramister, in

encamped for a night. When Hugh, the son of Felim, heard this, he quickly assembled his forces, and followed them to Cluain. They gave each a fierce battle, in which the Muintir-Reilly were defeated, and Donough, son of Gilla-Isa, the son of Donough O'Reilly, the son of Gilla-Toedog O'Biobhsaigh, and many others, were slain.

The Franciscan monastery of Ardfert[n] was founded by Fitzmaurice of Kerry.

THE AGE OF CHRIST, 1254.

The Age of Christ, one thousand two hundred fifty-four.

Maelfinnen O'Beollain, Coarb of Drumcliff, died.

Murrough O'Melaghlin was slain by the son of the Sinnagh (the Fox) O'Caharny.

Aindiles O'Henery[o], tower of the valour of the north of Ireland, died.

Pierce Pramister, Lord of Conmaicne, of Dunmore[p], died.

The Dominican monastery of Ath-leathan [Ballylahan, in the county of Mayo] was totally destroyed by fire.

Pierce Ristubart[q], Lord of Sil-Mailruain[r], and a baron, was slain on Lough Ree, by Murrough O'Melaghlin.

Sitric Mac Shanly was taken prisoner by Felim, the son of Cathal Crovderg, who also caused Sean-Shuileach Mac Shanly to be blinded, for he had been told that they were forming treacherous plots against him.

Donough, son of Donough, who was son of Tomaltagh [Mac Dermot], and Auliffe O'Biobhsaigh, were slain by the Connacians, at Cluain-Conmaicne.

Manus O'Gara was unjustly[s] slain by the people of the son of Felim O'Conor.

the text, is obviously a corruption.

[q] *Pierce Ristubard.*—At the year 1235 the Four Masters call the Baron Walter de Riddlesford by the strange name of ḃalτaıṗ Rıτταbaṗṫ, and the probability is, that Ristubard is here an attempt at writing the same surname. If not, the name intended may be Rochfort. This sentence is rather carelessly constructed by the Four Masters. The literal translation is as follows: "Piarus Ristubardus, dominus de Sil-Mailruain,—Baro ille,—occisus est super Lacum Righe per Murchadum O'Melaghlin."

[r] *Sil-Maelruain.*—This was the tribe name of the O'Flynns of Ballinlough, in the west of the county of Roscommon, who appear to have been for a time subdued by this baron; but they recovered their possessions soon after his death.

[s] *Unjustly.*—Tre anḟoċain means *per nefas*; ḟoċain means cause; an-ḟoċain, wrong cause.

Ri franc do toiḋeacht o Ierusalem iar ndenaṁ sioḋa teora mbliaḋan edir na criosdaiġiḃ ⁊ na siorraisdiniḃ.

Mainestir glas cille dara do dénaṁ la hiarla cille dara, ⁊ atá tumba onorach aca i ssépél muire is in ṁainestir ċéttna.

AOIS CRIOSD, 1255.

Aois Criosd, míle, da ċéd, caocca, a cúig.

Donnsléḃe ó floinn abb recclésa Pedair ⁊ Poil in Ardmaċa do ecc, ⁊ Pattraicc ua muireaḋaiġ prioir an tiġe céдna do ṫoġa do ċum na habdaine.

Tomas mac Diarmada aircinneaċ oilefinn do écc. Pearsún maighi luirg airtiġ, ⁊ cloinne cuain eisiḋe.

Ua laidig aircinneaċ eanaiġ dúin do écc.

Aeḋ mac feḋlimiḋ ui concoḃair do dul i ttír eoġain ⁊ siṫ do ḋenamh ḋó edir a aṫair féin ⁊ tuaisccert Ereann ⁊ a raiḃe do connaċtaiḃ ar essiṫ isin tuaisccert do taḃairt less atuaiṫ tre lár a ḋergnaṁad cona nimersgiḃ, .i. mec Ruaiḋri ui concoḃair ⁊ goill, ⁊ nocha laṁdaois urċoid do ḋenaṁ doiḃ an naṁaid sin, .i. mec Ruaiḋri ⁊ na goill remraite.

Mac cerbaill do gaḃail airdespucoideaċta caisil muṁan.

Florens mac floinn airdespucc tuama do dul tar muir dagallaiṁ riġ

[t] Under this year the Dublin copy of the Annals of Innisfallen, and a fragment of a Munster copy of the same, contain the following notice of a local feud in Munster:

"A. D. 1254. Fingin Reanna róin, mac Domnaill Guid, 7 O Donnaḃáin do ṁarḃaḋ Diarmada ui Maṫġaṁna, a n-éiric an Chruim hui Dhonnaḃáin do marbaḋ ar Innse an Ḃéil, timċeall troda buaċaillide bó, le muintir hUi Mhaṫġaṁna.

"A. D. 1254. Fineen Reanna Róin [of Ringrone], the son of Donnell God [Mac Carthy], and O'Donovan, killed Dermot O'Mahony, in revenge of Crom O'Donovan, who had been slain at Inis an bheil [Phale, near Inishkeen, in the county Cork], about the fight of Cowboys, by the people of O'Mahony."

The Crom here mentioned is the ancestor of all the septs of the O'Donovan family in the baronies of Carbery, in the county of Cork, and of several others in Leinster. He gave name to Gleann a Chruim, i. e. Crom's Glen, a district in the county of Cork, comprising that portion of the parish of Fanlobus lying southwards of the River Bandon. According to the pedigree of O'Donovan, given by Duald Mac Firbis, this Crom had three sons, namely, Cathal, Aneslis, and Loughlin, who were the founders of three distinct septs, called Clann-Cahill, Sliocht-Aneslis, and Clann-Loughlin, which became the names

The King of France returned from Jerusalem, after having concluded a three years' peace between the Christians and the Saracens.

The Green Monastery at Kildare was founded by the Earl of Kildare; and they [his family] have a superb tomb in the chapel of the Blessed Virgin Mary in this monastery[t].

THE AGE OF CHRIST, 1255.

The Age of Christ, one thousand two hundred fifty-five.

Donslevy O'Flynn, Abbot of the Church of SS. Peter and Paul at Armagh, died, and Patrick O'Murray, Prior of the same house, was elected to the abbacy.

Thomas Mac Dermot, Erenagh[u] of Elphin, died; he was parson of Moylurg, Airteach, and Clann-Cuain.

O'Laidig, Erenagh of Annadown, died.

Hugh, son of Felim O'Conor, went to Tyrone, and made peace between his own father and the people of the North of Ireland; and he brought with him from the north all the Connacians who were there in a state of disturbance; he brought them, with their moveables, through the midst of his bitterest enemies, viz. the sons of Roderic O'Conor and the English, who did not dare to molest them.

Mac Carroll assumed the archbishopric of Cashel, in Munster.

Florence Mac Flynn, Archbishop of Tuam, crossed the sea to converse with

of three districts in the county of Cork, which are well defined in the public records. Cathal, the eldest son of Crom, had two sons, namely, Teige, the ancestor of the subsequent chiefs of Clann-Cahill, and Ivor, otherwise called Gilla-reagh, who is said to have built Castle-Ivor, in the parish of Myross, in the year 1251 [1351?], which remained in the possession of his descendants till the middle of the sixteenth century. This Ivor is still remembered in the wild traditions of the district as a celebrated navigator and necromancer, and it is firmly believed that he is enchanted in a lake called Lough Cluhir, near his castle, in the townland of Listarkin, in the parish of Myross, and that his magical ship is seen once every seventh year, with all her courses set and colours flying, majestically floating on the surface of that lake. John Collins, of Myross, who was intimately acquainted with the traditions and legends of these districts, writes, in his pedigree of the O'Donovans: "I have seen one person in particular *testify by oath* that he had seen this extraordinary phenomenon in the year 1778."

[u] *Erenagh*, aiрcinneaċ.—Mageoghegan calls him Archdean, but we have shewn elsewhere that this is a mistake.—See note [o], under the year 1179, p. 47.

ꞅaꞅan ⁊ gaċ ní ꝺaꞃ ꞅiꞃeaꞃꝺaiꞃ thoiꞃ ꝺꞅacchail ꝺó o onóiꞃ an ꞃioġ ⁊ a ċoiꝺeacht anoiꞃ ꝺo ꞃiꝺiꞃi.

Maṫġaṁain ó mannaċáin ꝺo ṁaꞃbaꝺ ag Ꝺuimlinn.

Ꝺiaꞃmaiꝺ ó cuinn aṁlaoiḃ a ṁac ⁊ maiṫi muintiꞃe giollccain immaille ꞃiú ꝺo ṁaꞃbaꝺ ag ꝼaꞃaꝺán moiġe tꞃeaġa la giollu na naꞅṁ ua ꝼꝼꞅꞃgail ⁊ a naꞃccain iaꞃaṁ.

Coinne moꞃ eꝺiꞃ ó cconċoḃaiꞃ, .i. ꝼeꝺlimiꝺ, ⁊ mac uilliam buꞃc ag toċoꞃ mona coinneaꝺa. Siṫ ꝺo ꝺꞅnaṁ ꝺoiḃ annꞅin ⁊ gaċ ꝺál ina ꞃaiḃe ꝼeꝺlimiꝺ ꝺo leccaꝺ leꞅꞅ.

Iuliana ingꞅn coṁoꞃba caillin ⁊ giollu na naꞅṁ a ꝺꞅꞃbꞃathaiꞃ ꝺo ecc.

Ragnailt ingꞅn uí ꝼꞅꞃgail ꝺo écc i nꝺaḃaiġ ꝼoṫꞃaicṫe.

AOIS CRIOST, 1256.

Aoiꞅ Cꞃioꞅt míle, ꝺa ċéꝺ, caocca aꞅé.

Ꝼlann mac ꝼloinn aiꞃꝺeꞃꞅcoꞃ tuama ꝺo écc i mbꞃiꞅtuma.

Aiꞃꝺeꞅꞅoc atha cliath ꝺo écc.

Giollu an coimꝺeaꝺ ua cinnꝼaelaiꝺ abb Eanaiġ ꝺuin ꝺo écc.

Ua giollaꞃáin abb eaccailꞅi na tꞃinoiꝺe i ttuaim ꝺo écc.

Ꝺꞃong ꝺo muintiꞃ Raġallaiġ ꝺo ṁaꞃbaꝺ la haꞅꝺ mac ꝼeꝺlimiꝺ, .i. caṫal ua ꞃaġallaiġ tiċhꞅꞃna muintiꞃe maoilṁoꞃꝺa ⁊ ċaṫa aꞅꝺa ꝼinn, a ꝺa mac imaille ꞃiꞅ .i. ꝺoṁnall ꞃuaꝺ ⁊ Niall, a ꝺꞅꞃḃꞃaṫaiꞃ cuconnaċt, tꞃi meic caṫail ꝺuiḃ uí ꞃaġallaigh i. goꝼꞃaiꝺ, ꝼꞅꞃgal, ⁊ ꝺoṁnall, ⁊ annaꝺ mac ꝺoṁnaill uí ꞃaġallaiġ ꝺo maꞃbaꝺ la Concobaꞃ mac tiċhꞅꞃnáin. Niall .i. an

ᵛ *Buimlinn*, now Bumlin, a vicarage near Strokestown, in the diocese of Elphin, in the barony and county of Roscommon. St. Midabaria, the sister of St. Berach, is the patron of this parish.—See Colgan's *Acta Sanctorum*, p. 344.

ʷ *Faradhan Moighe Treagha*, i. e. the meeting place of Magh Treagha, which is a territory in the barony and county of Longford, containing the parish of Clongesh. The townlands of this territory, which is called Moytra in Anglo-Irish documents, are enumerated in an Inquisition taken at Ardagh on the 10th of April, in the tenth year of the reign of James I., from which its exact extent may still be determined.

ˣ *Tochar Mona Coinneadha*, i. e. the togher or causeway of the bog of Coinneadh. The situation of this causeway is still well known. It is in the parish of Templetogher, between Ballimoe and Dunmore, in the north-east of the county of Galway, and the ruins of a church and castle are to be seen near it.—See note ⁿ, under the year 1225.

the King of England; and all that he requested was obtained by him from the king's honour; and he returned home again.

Mahon O'Monahan was slain at Buimlinn[v].

Dermot O'Quin, Auliffe, his son, together with the chiefs of Muintir Gillagan, were slain at Faradhan Moighe Treagha[w], by Gilla-na-naev O'Farrell, who afterwards pillaged their territory.

A great meeting took place at Tochar Mona Coinneadha[x] between O'Conor (Felim) and Mac William Burke. A peace was concluded between them, and all his conditions were conceded to Felim.

Juliana, daughter of the Coarb of St. Caillin[y], and Gilla-na-naev, his brother, died.

Ranailt, daughter of O'Farrell, died in a bath.

THE AGE OF CHRIST, 1256.

The Age of Christ, one thousand two hundred fifty-six.

Flann Mac Flynn died in Bristol.

The Archbishop of Dublin[z] died.

Gilla-an-Choimhdheadh O'Kinnfaela, Abbot of Annadown, died.

O'Gillaran, Abbot of Trinity Church at Tuam, died.

A party of the O'Reilly family were slain by Hugh, the son of Felim [O'Conor], namely, Cathal O'Reilly, Lord of Muintir-Maelmora[a], and of *all* the race of Hugh Finn[b]; his two sons, namely, Donnell Roe and Niall; his brother, Cuconnaught; the three sons of Cathal Duff O'Reilly, namely, Godfrey, Farrell, and Donnell; Annadh, son of Donnell O'Reilly, who was slain by Conor Mac

[y] *Coarb of St. Caillin.*—He was O'Rody, the hereditary warden and chief farmer of the lands of the church of Fenagh, in the county of Leitrim.

[z] *The Archbishop of Dublin.*—We learn from the Annals of Mary's Abbey that his name was Luke, but his surname no where appears. He had been Dean of St. Martin's, London, and Treasurer of the King's Wardrobe.—See Harris's edition of Ware's Bishops, pp. 320, 321.

[a] *Muintir-Maelmora* was the tribe name of the O'Reillys, which they derived from their ancestor Maelmordha, the fifteenth in descent from Duach Galach, King of Connaught.

[b] *Hugh Finn* was the fifth in descent from Duach Galach, King of Connaught, and the ancestor of the O'Rourkes, O'Reillys, and of all the tribes called Hy-Briuin Breifne. From this passage it would appear that O'Reilly was chief of the two Breifnys at this period.

caeċ ua raġallaiġ tiġearnan máġ brattaiġ, giollu michil mac taichliġ, donnċaḋ ua bioḃraiġ, Maġnus mac giollu ḋuiḃ ⁊ tuilleaḋ ar tri fichit do maiṫiḃ a muintire immaille riú. Caṫ ṁoiġe sleċt ar bru aṫa dearg ag alt na hellte uas bealaċ na beithiġe ainm an caṫasa. Ciḋ iad muintear Raġallaiġ tra torcradar drong do ṁaiṫiḃ an tsluaiġ boí na naġaiḋ leó, .i. diarmaid ó flannaġáin, flann macc oireachtaiġ, Murċaḋ fionn ó fearġail ⁊ Sochaiḋe gen mó thaittriḃe, ⁊ ro briseadar fo thrí an glasslaiṫ for ṫosaċ an tsluaiġ arailL no go rucc anfforlann orra fo ḋeoiḋ. Ag Sailtean na ngarán rug tossaċ an tsluaiġsi for muintir Raġallaiġ ceus ⁊ ro leanrad iad co háit ticche mec cuirrín airriḋe co laṫair an mor caṫa.

Iustis do thoċt in Erinn o riġ Saxan. Coinne do ḋénaṁ do fén ⁊ dafeḋ ua Concoḃair ag rinn duin. Siṫ do ceangal doiḃ reasoile annsin ar ċonnraḋ gan laġduġaḋ criche na fearainn Connaċt ar ua cconċoḃair an ccén buḋ iustís esioṁ.

Ruaiḋri ó gaḋra tiġearna Slebe luġa do ṁarḃaḋ la dabid mac Riocaird cúisin. Aeḋ mac feḋlimiḋ uí Concoḃair do arccain ḟearainn mic Ricaird cúisin a ndioġail ui gaḋra do ṁarḃaḋ dosom. Leaccais a caislen, Marḃaiḋ a mboí do ḋaoiniḃ ann ⁊ gaḃais oiléin locha techeatt uile.

[c] *Mac Tiernan.*—In the Dublin copy of the Annals of Ulster he is called conchubar mac tigernain hui Ruairc, "Conor, the son of Tiernan O'Rourke." There are two distinct families of Mac Tiernans; one located in the district of Tir Tuathail, in the north-east of the county of Roscommon, and also at Lanesborough; and the other in the barony of Tealach Dunchadha, now Tullyhunco, in the county of Cavan, who are of the same race as the O'Rourkes, and who Anglicise their name Mac Kiernan, and sometimes incorrectly Kiernan, without the prefix Mac.

[d] *Moy-Slecht.*—It appears from a manuscript Life of St. Maidoc, that Magh Sleacht, so celebrated in the lives of St. Patrick, as the plain on which stood the idol Crom Cruach, was the level part of the barony of Tullyhaw, in the north-west of the county of Cavan. The village of Ballymagauran is in it. It is bounded on the west by Magh Rein, the plain in which Fenagh, in the county of Leitrim, is situated.

[e] *Alt-na-heillte*, i. e. the precipice of the doe.—It is stated in the Dublin copy of the Annals of Ulster, under the year 1257, that it is situated at the extremity of Slieve an-Ierin. "Allt na heillti os bealach na beiṫiġe i cinn sleiḃe in iarainn." Magh Slecht, as already stated, was the level part of the barony of Tullyhaw, in which the village of Ballymagauran is situated.

[f] *Bealach-na-beithe*, i. e. road of the birch trees.—There is a townland of this name, now Anglicised Ballaghnabehy, in the parish of Cloonclare, barony of Dromahaire, and county of Leitrim; but it cannot be the same as that referred to in the text, which was in the plain of Magh Slecht, at the extremity of Slieve an-Ierin. By extremity of Slieve an-Ierin must be here under-

Tiernan[c]; Niall, i. e. the Caech [Monoculus] O'Reilly; Tiernan Mac Brady; Gilla-Michael Mac Taichligh; Donough O'Biobhsaigh; Manus, son of Mac Gilduff; and upwards of sixty others of the chiefs of their people were slain along with them. This engagement is called the Battle of Moy Slecht[d], and was fought on the margin of Athderg, at Alt-na-heillte[e], over Bealach-na-beithe[f].

The O'Reillys, however, slew a number of the chiefs of the opposite forces, namely, Dermot O'Flanagan, Flann Mageraghty, Murrough Finn, O'Farrell, and many others besides: their glaslaiths [recruits] even forced the van of the adverse army to give way three times, but they were at length overpowered by the main body. It was at Sailtean-na-nGasan[g] that the van of that army first came up with the O'Reillys, from which place they pursued them to Ait-Tighe-Mec-Cuirrin, and from thence to the field of the great battle.

A Justiciary[h] arrived in Ireland from the King of England. He and Hugh O'Conor held a conference at Rinn Duin, where a peace was ratified between them, on condition that so long as he should be Justiciary, the territory or lands of O'Conor in Connaught should not be circumscribed.

Rory O'Gara, Lord of Sliabh Lugha [in the County Mayo], was slain by David, son of Richard Cuisin[i]. Hugh, the son of Felim O'Conor, plundered the territory of the son of Richard Cuisin, in revenge of O'Gara; he demolished his castle, and killed all the people that were in it, and seized on all the islands of Lough Techet[k].

stood that portion of the mountain now called Bartonny, near the village of Ballinamore, in the county of Leitrim, which borders on the plain of Magh Slecht. The whole range of these mountains was originally called Sliaḃ an Iaṗainn, i. e. the mountain of the iron.

[g] *Sailtean-na-nGasan.* — There are several places in the county of Leitrim called Sailtean, Anglice Seltan; but the Sailtean alluded to in the text is evidently the townland now called Seltannahunshin, in the parish of Oughteragh, in the barony of Carrigallen, which townland is very near the plain of Magh Slecht, on which the parties came to the general engagement.

[h] *Justiciary.*—According to the list of the Chief Governors, &c., of Ireland, given in Harris's Ware, Alan de la Zouch, formerly Chief Justice of the King's Bench in England, was Lord Justice of Ireland from the year 1255 to 1259, so that he is the Justiciary above referred to in the text.

[i] *Cuisin.*—This name is now written Cushen.

[k] *Lough Techet*, now Lough Gara, in which the River Boyle, in the county of Roscommon, has its source. The following story in the Tripartite Life of St. Patrick, will at once shew the identity of Loch Techet with Lough Gara: "St. Patrick (when in the regions of Connaught) having resolved to visit Moylurg, passed through Bearnas Hua Noililla [the gap at Coloony], and moved onwards towards the River Buill [Boyle], which takes its rise in

Raġnall mac branáin tighearna corcachlann do écc.

Creaċsluaiġeaḋ la mac uilliam burc for Ruaiḋri ua flaiṫbeartaiġ goro aircceartair gnó mór ⁊ gnó beacc ⁊ ro gaḃardair loch oirbrion uile.

Donncachaḋ mac finnlaiċ do écc i mainistir na buille.

Coccaḋ mor deirge eidir aoḋ ó cconcoḃair ⁊ conn o Ruairc (.i. mac tigearnain) ger ḃaḋ gradach im aroile go sin. Ua Ruairc do dul i cceann gall iaraṁ. Siṫ do snaḋmaḋ riú do fen cona muintir gan ceo dfedlimiḋ ná da mac. Aeḋ ua conċoḃair do creachaḋ uí Ruairc iarsin an cedaoín ria nodlaic. Do gniad Siṫ frisoile ar a haiṫle.

Aṫ luain ⁊ dún doiġre do loscaḋ in en ló.

Sloiccheaḋ la hua ndoṁnaill, .i. Goffraiḋ hi ffearaiḃ manach da ffuair comṫa, ⁊ braiġde. Tainic arriḋe i mbreifne ui ruairc. Do radsat siḋe a oiġreir ḋó.

AOIS CRIOSD, 1257.

Aois Criosd, míle, da ċéd, caocca a seaċt.

Mac Robias abb cluana heoais do écc.

Muireaḋaċ mac maoilbriġde ui fairċeallaiġ coṁorba maedocc do écc.

Maolpattraicc mac cele airċinneaċ cille halaḋ do ṁarḃaḋ.

Loch Techet; but on crossing this river his chariot was upset in a certain ford on it, and himself thrown into the waters, which ford is for that reason called Ath Carbuid, or the ford of the chariot, and lies near the waterfall of Eas mac n-Eirc." The name of this ford is now forgotten in the country, but Eas mic n-Eirc is well known, being that now called Assylin.

[l] *Corcachlann*, a territory in the east of the county of Roscommon, comprising the parishes of Bumlin, Kiltrustan, Cloonfinlough, and the western half of the parish of Lissonuffy, which half was anciently called Templereagh. An Inquisition taken on the 1st of June, 34 Eliz., finds that "the rectory of Corcaghlan extended into all the townlands of the parishes of Bumlin, Kiltrustan, Cloonfenloughe, and Tamplereoghe."—See references to Cluain Seancha, under the year 1410; also Colgan's *Trias Thaum.*, p. 134, and the note to Kinel-Dofa, under the year 1210, p. 169, *supra*.

Mac Brannan, the chief of this territory, was descended from the noble Druid Ona, who presented Imleach-Ona, now Elphin, to St. Patrick. The present representative of the family is Hubert Brannan, of Bellmount, near Strokestown, who still enjoys a small property of about fifty-six acres in Corcachlann, one of the most ancient hereditary estates in the world.

[m] *Mac William.*—This was Walter de Burgo, the son of Richard More, and grandson of William Fitz-Adelm. He became Earl of Ulster in the year 1264, in right of his wife Maud, daughter of Hugo de Lacy the younger.

Randal Mac Brannan, Lord of Corcachlann[l], died.

Mac William[m] Burke set out on a predatory expedition against Rory O'Flaherty. He plundered Gno-More and Gno-Beg[n], and took possession of all Lough Oirbsion [Lough Corrib].

Donncahy Mac Shanly died in the Abbey of Boyle.

A great war broke out between Hugh O'Conor and Con O'Rourke [i. e. the son of Tiernan], though they had been till then upon amicable terms with each other. O'Rourke afterwards went to the English, and formed a league of peace with them for himself and his people, without the permission so to do by Felim or his son. Hugh O'Conor [the son of Felim] afterwards, to wit, on the Wednesday before Christmas Day, plundered O'Rourke. They afterwards made peace with each other.

Athlone and Dun-doighre[o] were burned on the one day.

O'Donnell, i. e. Godfrey, marched with an army into Fermanagh, by which he obtained property and hostages. From thence he procceded to Breifny-O'Rourke, where they gave him his own demand.

THE AGE OF CHRIST, 1257.

The Age of Christ, one thousand two hundred fifty-seven.

Mac Robias, Abbot of Clones, died.

Murray, son of Maelbrighde O'Faircheallaigh[p], Coarb of Maidoc, died.

Maelpatrick Mac Kele[q], Erenagh of Killala, was slain.

[n] *Gno-More and Gno-Beg.*—These two territories are comprised in the present barony of Moycullen, in the county of Galway. "Gnobegg was meared and bounded from Srawan Icarwan, or Srwan Igravan north, to Galway south, saving the liberties, and so along the River of Alley, or Donkelly west, to Galway east."—See History of Galway, p. 40.

[o] *Dun-doighre*, now Duniry, a townland and parish in the barony of Leitrim, and county of Galway, where the family of Mac Egan had a celebrated school.—See *Tribes and Customs of Hy-Many*, printed in 1843 for the Irish Archæological Society, p. 169, and the map prefixed to the same; and also the Ordnance Map of the County of Galway, sheet 116.

[p] *O'Faircheallaigh.*—This name is now anglicised Farrelly, and is very common in the neighbourhood of the church of Drumlahan, or Drumlane, in the county of Cavan, of which they were hereditary Erenaghs.—See note [b], under the year 1172.

[q] *Mac Kele*, mac céle.—This is probably the name now anglicised Mac Hale.

Tomás ua Maoilciaráin Saoí Erenn in eaccna do écc.

Mainistir muire i rosscommain do coisreacaḋ las an espucc tomaltaċ ua concoḃair do ḃraithriḃ .S. dominic.

Conn mac ticchernain ui Ruairc (.i. tiġearna bresne) do dul i tteaġ uí Concoḃair ⁊ a mec do daingniucchaḋa síoḋa riú ⁊ a mbrisit fein dersonn na bresne do taḃairt doibh immaille le cloich insi na ttorc ar loċ fionnmoiġe. Luċt coiṁeda do ċor innte doeḋ mac feḋlimiḋ.

Caṫal cairceaċ mac aeḋa mic caṫail croiḃdeirg ⁊ aeḋ mac concoḃair mic aeḋa mec caṫail croiḃdeirg do ḋallaḋ daeḋ mac feḋlimiḋ mic caṫail croiḃdeirg tré ṫnúth ⁊ ḟormad tar saruġaḋ laoċ, ċleireaċ, ⁊ mionn cconnaċt.

Cond mac caṫail uí raiġilliġ taoiseaċ muintire maoilmorḋa decc.

Cloch innsi na ttorc for loch fionnmaiġe do loscaḋ dua Ruairc, ⁊ luċt a coimhetta do léccaḋ este.

Sitreacc mac ualġairce ui ruairc do ċor i ttiċcernus dAoḋ ua ċoncoḃair hi ccend ċonċoḃair meic ticcernain uí ruairc, ⁊ doṁnall mac concoḃair do marbadh Sitrecca ar a los.

Coinne do ḋénaṁ dfeiḋlimiḋ ua ċoncoḃair in áth luain re lustis na hEreann ⁊ re Mac uilliam burc, ⁊ re maithibh gall arċena go ndearnsat sith re roile.

Creach mór do ḋenamh dAoḋ ua conċoḃair im ċáirce ar ua ruairc.

Cath cróḋa do taḃairt la goffraiḋ ua ndoṁnaill tiġerna tíre conaill for lustis na hEreann Muiris mac gerailt, ⁊ for ġallaiḃ Connaċt arċena ag Credrán cille hi ros cede hi ccrich coirpre fri Slicceach a tuaiḋ ag cosnaṁ a tire friú. Ro fiġedh iorġal aimarḋa aindrennda etorra. Ro ciorrbait cuirp, Ro leónait laoich, Ro buaiḋrit ceoraḋa ceċtarnae diḃ.

[r] *Cloch-inse-na-dtorc*, i. e. the stone fortress of Hog Island.—The ruins of this fortress are still to be seen. Garadice Lough, lying to the east of Ballinamore, in the barony of Carrigallen, and county of Leitrim, is called "L. Fenvoy" on the engraved map from the Down Survey; and this island, which is in the east side of the lake, is shewn, by a mistake of the engraver, under the name of "madark" [for I. nadork]. This island, which has received the new name of Cherry Island, contains the ruins of an old castle, in which the United Irishmen took shelter in the year 1798.

[s] *Cathal Cairceach*.—He is called Cathal Caech, i. e. the blind or purblind, in the Annals of Connaught. The word cairce, from which the adjective cairceaċ is derived, is glossed in a MS. in Trinity College, Dublin, H. 3. 18. p. 210,

Thomas O'Mulkieran, the most eminent man in Ireland for wisdom, died.

The monastery of the Virgin Mary, at Roscommon, was consecrated by Bishop Tomaltagh O'Conor, for Dominican friars.

Con, son of Tiernan O'Rourke, went into the house of O'Conor and his son, and ratified a treaty of peace with them, and gave them as much of the land of Breifny as they desired to have, together with the fortress of Cloch-inse-na-dtorc[r], in Lough Finvoy, in which Hugh, son of Felim, placed guards.

Cathal Cairceach[s], son of Hugh, who was son of Cathal Crovderg, and Hugh, son of Conor, son of Hugh, who was son of Cathal Crovderg, were blinded by Hugh, son of Felim, the son of Cathal Crovderg; and this was done through envy and rancour, and in violation of the guarantees of the laity, clergy, and relics of Connaught.

Con, son of Cathal O'Reilly, Chief of Muintir-Maelmora, died.

Cloch-inse-na-dtorc, in Lough Finvoy, was burned by O'Rourke, those who guarded it[t] being first permitted to come out of it.

Sitric, son of Ualgarg O'Rourke, was elected chief of his tribe, by Hugh O'Conor, in preference to Conor, son of Tiernan O'Rourke, in consequence of which Donnell, son of Conor, killed Sitric.

A conference was held by Felim O'Conor at Athlone, with the Lord Justice of Ireland, with Mac William Burke and the other English chiefs, and they made peace with one another.

A great depredation was committed by Hugh O'Conor on O'Rourke about Easter.

A brave battle was fought by Godfrey O'Donnell, Lord of Tirconnell, in defence of his country, with the Lord Justice of Ireland, Maurice Fitzgerald, and the other English nobles of Connaught, at Creadran-Cille in Ros-cede[u], in the territory of Carbury, to the north of Sligo. A desperate and furious battle was fought between them: bodies were mangled, heroes were disabled, and the senses were stunned on both sides. The field was vigorously maintained

by the modern word finna, i. e. a film on the eye.

[t] *Those who guarded it*, i. e. O'Conor's warders, who were in the castle.

[u] *Ros-cede*, now the Rosses.—Two townlands in the parish of Drumcliff, in the barony of Carbury, and county of Sligo. An arm of the sea runs up to Drumcliff, which divides the Rosses from the plain of Machaire Eabha.

Ro coṫaiġeaḋ an caṫlaṫair co coṁnart la cenél cconaill, ⁊ do bertsat brſisim dúr danarda for ġallaibh is in ngleo go ro sraoíneaḋ forra fo ḋſóiḋ go ro ladh a nár. Ar a aoi tra do tromġonaḋ goffraiḋ fſissin is in caiṫgleó sin, ar tarla síde enech in ionċaiḃ fris Muiris mac gearailt is in ngliaidh ísin go ro gonsatar aroile gan diċell. Ba tria ágh an chaṫa sin do díoċuireaḋ goill ⁊ gſaltaiġ a hioċtar Connaċt.

Gabtar bſos Mac grifin .i. Ridere erderc la muintir í doṁnaill is in ló céona. Loiscctear ⁊ lomairccṫſr Slicceaċ leó ara haithle. Ro marbaḋ dana mac corbmaic huí doṁnaill hi ffrithġuin is in cath sin creadrain. Soaid iaroṁ dia ttiġiḃ ar aba gona uí doṁnaill, ar muna gaḃdaois a ġona greim ḋe, do biaḋ maiḋm forra go muaidh. Ag filleaḋ ina ffriṫing do ġoffraiḋ ro traiċċeaḋ ⁊ ro díoscaoileaḋ lais caislén ċaoil uiscce do rónaḋ lá gallaiḃ feċt riaṁ dforbairi for ċenél cconaill.

Muiris mac Gſailt Iustis Ereann re hſdh díoscaoilteach gaoidheal décc.

Cairt do ṫabairt ó Righ Saxan dfelim ua conċoḃair ar ċuicc triuċa an riġ.

Coccaḋ mor etir Concoḃar ó mbriain ⁊ goill muṁan go ttuccaḋ ár na ngall lais. Creacha aidble do denaṁ do taḋg ua briain orra bſós.

Concoḃar mac ticcſrnáin uí ruairc do ṁarbaḋ ag ath na failme do Giolla bſraiġ ua laṁduiḃ dia ṁuintir fſin ⁊ do ṁuintir Maṫa uí Raiġilliġ tre ṫangnacht.

Caṫal ua mannacháin décc an seseḋ do december.

[r] *Felim O'Conor.*—Dr. O'Conor has the following notice of this fact:

"In 1240 Felim went to the court of England to complain of those English adventurers, who, headed by De Burgo, usurped part of his province; he appealed to the treaty of Windsor, strongly insisted, in the Latin language, on the justice of his cause, and returned home so well pleased with the reception he had met, that in 1245 he marched with a body of forces to join Henry in an expedition against the Welsh. But all this could not prevent the invaders of his province, who were secretly instigated by Henry himself to encroach on his dominions; hostilities were continued without interruption until 1255, when Felim sent the Archbishop of Tuam with ambassadors to England, and obtained, in 1257, a Royal Charter, granting to him and his heirs for ever, free and peaceable dominion over five baronies, in as ample a manner as ever they were enjoyed by his ancestors.

"After obtaining this grant he built the magnificent abbeys of Roscommon and Tumona, and died in 1264. Leland remarks, that in his remonstrance to Henry III. against the damages which he had sustained by Walter de Burgo, he

by the Kinel-Connell, who made such obstinate and vigorous onsets upon the English that, in the end, they routed them with great slaughter. Godfrey himself, however, was severely wounded; for he met Maurice Fitzgerald face to face in single combat, in which they wounded each other severely. In consequence of the success of this battle, the English and the Geraldines were driven out of Lower Connaught.

On the same day Mac Griffin, an illustrious knight, was taken prisoner by O'Donnell's people; and Sligo was afterwards burned and totally plundered by them. Donough, the son of Cormac O'Donnell, was killed in the heat of this battle of Creadran. They (O'Donnell's people) then returned home in consequence of O'Donnell's wounds; but, were it not that his wounds had oppressed him, he would have routed his enemies to the River Moy. Godfrey, on his return, prostrated and demolished the castle which had been erected by the English a short time before, at Cael-uisce, to carry on the war against the Kinel-Connell.

Maurice Fitzgerald, for some time Lord Justice of Ireland, [and] the destroyer of the Irish, died.

The King of England granted Felim O'Conor[v] a charter to hold the five cantreds of the King.

A great war between Conor O'Brien[w] and the English of Munster; and the English were slaughtered by him. Teige O'Brien[x] also committed great depredations upon them.

Conor, son of Tiernan O'Rourke, was treacherously slain at Ath-na-failme by Gillabarry O'Lamhduibh, one of his own people, and by the people of Matthew O'Reilly.

Cathal O'Monahan died on the 6th of December[y].

charges the burning of churches and the massacre of his clergy at a thousand marks."—*Memoirs of the Life and Writings of Charles O'Conor of Belanagare*, p. 41.

[w] *Conor O'Brien.*—He is the Conor O'Brien usually called Conchobhair na Siudaine in the pedigrees of the O'Briens.

[x] *Teige O'Brien.*—He is called Teige Cael-Uisce in the Dublin copy of the Annals of Innisfallen, in which his death is entered under the year 1256, which is certainly incorrect. He was the son of Concobhar na Siudaine.—See note [i], under the year 1258, p. 368.

[y] Under this year, 1257, the Annals of Clonmacnoise, as translated by Mageoghegan, record the founding and erecting of a house for friars of the Order of St. Dominic at Roscommon, by Felim O'Conor.

AOIS CRIOST, 1258.

Aois Criost, míle, da ċéd, caoccat a hocht.

Abraham ó conalláin, Airdepscop Ardamacha dfaġail ṗallium o cuirt na Roṁa, ⁊ aiffrionn do raḋa dó leir in ardmaċa an dara la do ṁí lún.

Uater de salerna airdepscop tuama ⁊ deccanaċ mor Londan do ecc hi Saxaiḃ iar na toġa is na ceimionnaiḃ remraite la riġ Saxan an bliaḋain roiṁe sin. Tomaltach ó concoḃair epscop oilefinn do ṫoġa docum airdepscopoidechta tuama.

Giollacrist o carmacain deccanach oilifinn décc.

An manach ua cuirnin saoi craḃaiḋ décc.

Matha mac giolla ruaidh uí roduibh, .i. an maiġistir decc.

Cuirt an epscoip in oilfinn, ⁊ cuirt cille Sesin do sgaoileaḋ dAoḋ ó concoḃair.

O Domhnaill gorraiḋ do beith in oṫairlighe a ecca re hed mbliaḋna ar loch beathach iar ccor ċaṫa credrain. Iar na fios sin dua neill (.i. brian) tionoiliḋ a ṡlogha in en ionad do tocht hi ttir Conuill, ⁊ faoiḋis techta uaḋa hi ccend uí doṁnaill do chuingiḋ giall, eidiredh ⁊ uṁla for ċonallcoibh, o ro batar gan tiġearna infedma aca deis Gorraḋa. Iar ttabairt aiṫisc dua doṁnaill do na teċtaiḃ lottur for ccúla, ⁊ aṁail as deini luiḋsiot.

Ro ḟorcongair ó domhnaill for ċonallċoiḃ tionol as gach aird ċuicce, ⁊ iar ttarcclamaḋ doiḃ fo ṫoġairm a ttiaccerna ro forail forra ona baí ionaisttir leó an tárach ina mbertaoi a ċorp fo ḋeoiḋ do ḋenaṁ ḋó, ⁊ a ċor ann, ⁊ a iomċar in eidirmedon a ṁuintire. Ro raidh riú calma do denaṁ ord baí fein etorra, ⁊ gan tren a nesccaracc do leicen forra.

[z] *Great Dean.*—He was Dean of St. Paul's, London. Harris states that he died in London, on his return from Rome, without ever seeing his bishopric, about the middle of April, 1258. See his edition of Ware's Bishops, p. 606.

[a] *The monk.*—In the old translation of the Annals of Ulster, this entry is rendered: "A.D. 1258. The munck O'Cuirnyn died in Christ."

[b] *Kilsesin.*—See note under the year 1253. The place is now called Cill tSéisin in Irish, and anglicised Kilteashin. The Irish word cúirt, which seems to have been borrowed from the English *court*, is now used to denote any large square house with many windows, without any regard to the dignity or title of the occupier.

[c] *Loch-Beathach*, i. e. Birch Lake.—This lake

THE AGE OF CHRIST, 1258.

The Age of Christ, one thousand two hundred fifty-eight.

Abraham O'Conallan, Archbishop of Armagh, received a Pallium from the Court of Rome, in which he said Mass, at Armagh, on the 2nd day of the month of June.

Walter de Salerna, Archbishop of Tuam, and Great Dean[a] of London, died in England, having been elected to those dignities in the preceding year by the King of England.

Tomaltagh O'Conor, Bishop of Elphin, was elected Archbishop of Tuam.

Gilchreest O'Carmacan, Deacon of Elphin, died.

The monk[a] O'Curnin, a pious sage, died.

Matthew, son of Gillaroe O'Rodiv, i. e. the Master [Professor], died.

The Bishop's palace at Elphin, and the palace of Kilsesin[b], were demolished by Hugh O'Conor.

O'Donnell (Godfrey) had now, for the space of a year, after having fought the battle of Creadran, been lying on his death-bed [in an island] in Loch-Beathach[c]. When O'Neill [i. e. Brian] obtained intelligence of this, he collected his forces together for the purpose of marching into Tirconnell, and sent messengers to O'Donnell to demand hostages, pledges, and submission, from the Kinel-Connell, as they had no capable chieftain since [the disabling of] Godfrey. When the messengers delivered their message to O'Donnell, they returned back with all the speed they could exert.

O'Donnell ordered the Kinel-Connell to assemble from all quarters and come to him; and after they had assembled at the summons of their lord, he ordered them, as he was not able to march with them, to make for him the bier[d] wherein his body would finally be borne, and to place him in it, and carry him in the midst of his people. He told them to exert their bravery, as he himself was among them, and not to suffer the might of their enemies to pre-

still retains this name, which is anglicised Lough Beagh and Lough Veagh. It is situated near the village of Church-Hill, in the parish of Gartan, barony of Kilmacrenan, and county of Donegal.

[d] *Bier*, ápaċ.—The word used in the modern language to denote bier is cpóċap. The word apaċ is thus explained by O'Clery, in his Glossary of ancient Irish words: "Apaċ .ı. cpóchap. Im ápach .ı. pa ċpóchap."

Rangattur rompa an tuċt sin ina rſimim la forcongra a ttiġſrna hi ccoinne sloigh í neill co ttarla an dá ṡluaiġ aghaidh in aghaidh imon aḃainn dianid ainm Suileach. Ro ionnsaighsiot a ċele gan coiccill do cairdſs no do coiṁḟiallus gur meaḃaidh for an sluaġ nſoġanach tar anair, gur ḟaccbattar daoine iomda, eiċ, ⁊ edála aidble. Acc tiontudh don tsluaġ conallach on maidhm ro lſicceadh an tárach i mboí ó domnaill ar sraidsliġe na congbála gonadh ann do ḋeachaidh a ainim ar do ġaſḃ cró na ngon, ⁊ na ccrecht do radadh fair hi ccath crſorain, ⁊ nír bó bás ar mioḋlaċus an bás hisin acht iar mbrſith buadha gach tan for a ḃioḋḃadaibh.

O ro clos tra la hua néill écc í domnaill ro ċuir teċta doridisi hi ccſnd ċonallach do ċuingidh giall ⁊ uṁla forra. Báttar cenél cconuill a ccoṁairle aga sccrúdadh cidh do ġendais fris sin, no cia toísreaċ dibh fſin da ttiubrattais uṁla, no aidide uair na bai tiġſrna erdalta oca oro écc gorraidh. Dia mbattar for na hiomraitiḃ sin at conncattar Domnall occ mac domnaill móir í domnaill cuca a halbain ina macaſṁ ócc aidſdach in aſis a oċt mbliadan ndécc, ⁊ do radsat cenel cconaill a ccſndus dó fo cedóir. Dſithbir ón ar dob eiride a fflaiṫ dílſs diongmala budhdſin, ⁊ o ro airnſidsiot cenél cconaill an taiṫſscc sin do bſrtsat teċta í neill ċuca (dosomh) ba forail laissiumh, ⁊ ba fairbrigh innsin. Conadh ann do raidh an trſinbriaṫar airdirc tria san ngaoidilcc nalbanaigh boí occa acc agallaiṁ na tteċtadh .i. go mbiadh a doṁan fſin ag gach fſr. Ba samail do ṫurus tuaṫail tſctmair tar muir anall a halbain iar noilgenn traoṡclann Ereann la haithechṫuaṫaibh an turus sin ḋomnaill oicc a halbain a lſiṫ

[e] *Suileach*, now the River Swilly, which discharges itself into Lough Swilly, near the town of Letterkenny, in the county of Donegal.

[f] *Street of Congbhail*, now Conwal, near Letterkenny, where there was anciently a monastery and village; but there are no ruins now to be seen at the place, except the walls of an old church of small dimensions. There is a tradition that the village was destroyed by an accidental fire first kindled by a cat, after which it was never rebuilt; but that the town of Letterkenny soon after supplied its place.

[g] *Donnell Oge*.—According to a marginal note in the handwriting of Charles O'Conor, of Belanagare, this Donnell Oge was the son of Donnell More O'Donnell, by a daughter of Cathal Crovderg O'Conor, King of Connaught. Though the Annals of Ulster and Clonmacnoise state that all the northern chiefs submitted to O'Neill at Cael-Uisce, it is more probable that this youthful chief did not; for though he was inaugurated about the same time, by the consent of O'Neill, it does not appear that any individual of the Kinel-Connell race assisted O'Neill in the unfortunate battle of Down, in 1260. This jealousy and emulation between the two great

vail over them. They then, by order of their lord, proceeded on their march against O'Neill's army; and the two armies met face to face, at the river called Suileach[e]. They attacked each other, without regard to friendship or kindred, until the Tyronian army was discomfited and driven back, leaving behind them many men, horses, and a great quantity of valuable property. On the return of the Tirconnelian army from this victory, the bier on which O'Donnell was carried was laid down in the street of Congbhail[f], and here his soul departed, from the venom of the scars and wounds which he had received in the battle of Creadran. This was not death in cowardice, but the death of a hero, who had at all times triumphed over his enemies.

When O'Neill heard of the death of O'Donnell, he again sent messengers to the Kinel-Connell, to demand hostages and submission from them. Hereupon the Kinel-Connell held a council, to deliberate on what they should do, and as to which of their own (petty) chiefs they would yield submission and obedience, as they had no certain lord since Godfrey died. Whilst they were engaged in such speeches, they saw approaching Donnell Oge[g], the son of Donnell More O'Donnell, a valiant youth, then eighteen years of age, who had arrived from Scotland, and the Kinel-Conell immediately conferred the chieftainship upon him. This they lawfully did, as he was their own legitimate and worthy lord. When the Kinel-Connell told him of the message which the emissaries of O'Neill had brought them, he deemed it extravagant and exorbitant[h]. It was on this occasion he repeated the celebrated proverb, in the Albanian Gælic, in which he conferred with the emissaries, namely, "That every man should have his own world." Similar to the coming of Tuathal Teachtmhar over the sea from Scotland, after the extirpation of the royal race of Ireland by the Attacots[i], was this coming of Donnell Oge, to consolidate the

races of Owen and Connell finally wrought the destruction of the chieftains of Ulster, as is quite evident from various passages in these Annals.

[h] *Extravagant and exorbitant*, ba forail lais-umh 7 ba fairbrigh innsin. The Irish word foráil is explained "iomarcaidh," i. e. excess, too much, by O'Clery, in his Glossary of ancient Irish words, and the word fairbrigh is nearly synonymous with it, and is explained "excess" in O'Reilly's Dictionary, and used in that sense by the Four Masters at ths year 1573. What the annalists mean is, that the young chieftain, who had been fostered and educated in Scotland, thought the demands of O'Neill exorbitant and extravagant.

[i] *Attacots*, aithechthuathaibh, i. e. the plebeian tribes.—These are said to have been tribes of the Firbolgs, who murdered the monarch Fiacha

le hiomuaim nairdrighe, le táṫucchaḋ tuaṫ, ⁊ le cosnaṁ a criche fein ar ċoiccriocaibh on ló in ro hoirdneaḋ é i tticcfernus gus an laithe fo deoidh a ffuair a oiḋeaḋ.

Mainistir clasna i Laiġnib in epscobóideċt cille dara do tógbáil do braiṫrib .S. fransis.

Sloiccéaḋ mór la haoḋ mac feidlimiḋ, ⁊ la taḋg ua mbriain hi ccoinne briain uí neill go caoluisce go ttuccsat na maiṫe sin leṫ ar leth cennus do brian ua neill for gaoiḋelaib iar ndénaṁ sioḋa dóib re roile. Braiġde Aoḋa uí ċoncobair dósom re comall, ⁊ braiġhde muintire raiġillig ⁊ ua mbriúin ó cenandus go druim cliab dAoḋ mac Feidlimiḋ mar an cceḋna.

Mac Somairle do teċt hi loingeas timcell Connaċt a hinsibh gall go

Finola, and all the kings and nobles of the royal Milesian blood in the second century. The Queen of Ireland, who was then pregnant, fled from the general massacre into Scotland, where she brought forth a son, named Tuathal, who afterwards returned to Ireland, conquered the plebeians, and restored the Milesian chieftains to their territories; after which he was elected monarch, and his subjects swore by the sun and moon, and all the elements, visible and invisible, that they and their posterity would be obedient to him and his royal issue for ever.

[j] *Claena*, now Clane, a fair-town in the county of Kildare, about fifteen miles from Dublin.

[k] *Cael Uisge.*—In the Dublin copy of the Annals of Ulster it is remarked, *inter lineas*, that this place was at Lec Ui Mhaildoraighe, which is unquestionably the place now called Bel lice, or Belleck, on the Erne, to the east of Ballyshannon.—See note [l], under the year 1200, p. 125.

[l] *Brian O'Neill.*—The account of this meeting of the Irish chieftains at Cael-Uisce is also given in the Annals of Ulster and of Clonmacnoise, at the year 1258; but it is entered in the *Caithreim Thoirdhealbhaigh*, and in the Dublin copy of the Annals of Innisfallen, under the year 1252, in which a different account of the meeting is given. In these authorities (if, indeed, they can be so called), it is stated, that a meeting of the Irish chieftains took place at Cael-Uisce, at the extremity of Lough Erne, for the purpose of electing a king over the Irish, to suppress the usurpation of the English; that Teige, the son of Conor na Siudaine O'Brien, sent one hundred horses over the river to be presented to O'Neill as wages of subsidy, but that O'Neill rejected the offer, and sent them back, with two hundred others, with their harnesses and with golden bits, to be presented to O'Brien as an earnest of the subordination and obedience due by him to O'Neill; that O'Brien sent them back again, and the result was, that the meeting broke up without electing a king or chief prince. Dr. O'Brien receives all this as authentic in his History of the House of O'Brien, published in Vallancey's *Collectanea de Rebus Hibernicis*, and states that Teige Cael Uisce O'Brien died in the year 1255. But it is quite evident, from the concurrence of the older annals, that this meeting took place in the year 1258, and that Teige O'Brien lived till the year 1259, under which year his death is entered in the Dublin copy of the Annals of Ulster. It will, however, be readily believed from the older annals, that the chiefs of Connaught and Ulster

monarchy, to cement territories, and to defend his own country against foreigners, from the day on which he was installed in the lordship until the day of his death.

The monastery of Claena[j], in Leinster, in the diocese of Kildare, was founded for Franciscan Friars.

A great host was led by Hugh, son of Felim, and Teige O'Brien, to meet Brian O'Neill, at Cael-Uisce[k]. The aforesaid chieftains, with one accord, conferred the sovereignty over the Irish on Brian O'Neill[l], after having made peace with each other; for the observance of which agreement the hostages of Hugh O'Conor were delivered up to him, and the hostages of Muintir-Reilly, and of all the Hy-Briuin[m], from Kells to Drumcliff.

Mac Sorley[n] sailed with a fleet from the Insi Gall [Hebrides] around

submitted to Brian O'Neill on this occasion, and rendered him hostages. The passage is thus given in Mageoghegan's translation of the Annals of Clonmacnoise, with which the more accurate Annals of Ulster agree: "A. D. 1258. Hugh mac Felym [O'Connor] and Teige O'Bryen had a meeting with Bryen O'Neale, at the Castle of Koyleuske, where peace was concluded between them, and" [they] "agreed that Bryan O'Neal shou'd be King of the Irish of Ireland" [tucadur na maiti sin uile ardceannus do ḃrian O Neill, *Ann. Ult.*], "whereupon Hugh mac Ffelym yealded Hostages to Bryan; also the chiefest of the Bryans [Hy-Briuin] and Montyr-Kellys, from Kelles to Dromkliew, yealded hostages to Hugh O'Connor." The Annals of Ulster add, that Donnell O'Donnell was inaugurated chief of Tirconnell on this occasion, and that all the Kinel-Connell rendered him hostages. This being the older account of this meeting at Cael-Uisce, it may be fairly asked whether the story about Teige Cael-Uisce O'Brien having attended a meeting here six years earlier, and the account of his refusing to acknowledge the superiority of O'Neill, may not have had its origin in the wild and creative fancy of John, the son of Rory Magrath, chief historiographer of Thomond, who wrote the *Caithreim Thoirdhealbhaigh*, or Triumphs of Turlough O'Brien, in the year 1459. It is a very strange fact that neither Leland nor Moore, the ablest writers of the history of Ireland, should have noticed this attempt of the Irish chieftains to unite against the English. O'Neill fought soon after, at the head of the chiefs of the north and west of Ireland, with all the valour and desperation of his royal ancestors; but, being inferior to his enemies in military accoutrements and discipline, he and his people were cut off with dreadful slaughter, and none of the O'Neills ever after acquired any thing like the monarchy of Ireland.

[m] *Hy-Briuin*, i. e. the Hy-Briuin Breifne.—These were the O'Reillys, O'Rourkes, and their correlatives.

[n] *Mac Sorley*.—This passage is thus given in Mageoghegan's translation of the Annals of Clonmacnoise:

"A. D. 1258. Mac Sowarle brought a great fleet with him from the Islands of Scotland, went about Ireland of the West, where they robbed a Marchant's shipp of all the goods therein, as wine, cloath, brass, and Irons. Jordan de Exetra, then Sheriff of Connought, pursued him at seas with a great Fleet of English-

rainicc Conmaicne mara gur ġabustair long ċſndaiġe annsin go ndſrna a hſoail eidir ḟíon, édach, uma, ⁊ iarn. Siurtán dexter Sirriam connacht do lſnmain mic Somairle gur an ailén in ro airis, ⁊ a longa for a nangcairibh ina ccomḟoccus. Feaċar iomairecc ſttorra, marbṫar Siurtan fo ċédoir, ⁊ Piarus accabard Ridere dia ṁuinntir, ⁊ soċaiḋe cenmoṫátsom. Mac Somairle gona muintir do tilleaḋ doridisi go haiṫeasach edalach go rainicc a ṫir búdéin.

Doṁnall mac Concoḃair mic tiġearnain uí ruairc baoí i mbraiġdſnus tar cſnn a aṫar ag fſiḋlimiḋ ó ċoncoḃair, ⁊ ga ṁac (.i. Aoḋ) do léccean amach doibh, ⁊ tiġſrnus na breifne do tabairt dó a nionaḋ a aṫar.

Macraith macc tigearnain toiseaċ tellaiġ dunchaḋa ḋo ṁarḃaḋ la doṁnall mac concoḃair ui ruairc. Ḃſnaid connaċtaiġ, ⁊ fir breifne go coitċionn a ṫiġſrnus do ḋoṁnall annsin, ⁊ marḃaitt teallach dunchaḋa a ḋſrḃraṫair, caṫal mac Concoḃair. Tuccaḋ ṫiġearnus ua mbriuin iarsin do Art mac caṫail riaḃaiġ uí ruairc, .i. o Sliaḃ roir.

Ḃrian macc rampaḋáin tiġearna ṫeallaiġ eachdaċ do ṁarḃaḋ la connaċtoiḃ.

Aṁlaoiḃ mac Airt uí ruairc tiġearna Ḃreifne o sliaḃ siar décc.

Tomas ó birn décc.

Ardġal ó concoḃair mac coṁarba comain decc.

Coccaḋ mor etir ġallaiḃ ⁊ concoḃar ua briain dár loisccead ardraṫain, cill colgan, arḃanna, ⁊ Sraḋḃailte ioṁḋa oile.

Coinne etir gallaiḃ, ⁊ gaoiḋealaiḃ Ereann in eccmais feḋlimiḋ uí Concoḃair, ⁊ sith do denamh eattorra.

men. Mac Sowarle did land upon an Island in the Seas, and did putt his Shipps at Anchor, and seeing the Sheriff with his people make towards them, Mac Sowarle gyrte himself with his armour and harness of steel, and so did all the companie that were with him out of hand; whereupon the Sheriff landed on the Island, where he was well served by Mac Sowarle. The Sheriff himself was instantly killed, with Sir Pyers Caward, a worthy knight, with many others. The English, after receiving this great loss, returned, and Mac Sowarle also returned, with the happy success of a ritch booty, to his own Contrey."

[o] *Conmaicne-mara*, i. e. the maritime Conmaicne, now the barony of Ballynahinch, in the north-west of the county of Galway. The name of this ancient territory is yet preserved, but shortened to Connamara.

[p] *Mac Tiernan*, now generally anglicised Kernan. This family of Tealach Dunċhadha, or Tullyhunco, in Breifny, are to be distinguished from the Mac Tiernans of the county of Roscommon, who are a branch of the O'Conors, and de-

Connaught, and at length put in at Conmaicne-mara[o], where he took a merchant ship, and plundered it of its wine, cloth, copper, and iron. Jordan de Exeter, Sheriff of Connaught, pursued Mac Sorley to the island on which he was stopping, with his ships at anchor near it. An engagement took place between them, in which Jordan was at once killed, as was also Pierce Agabard, a knight of his people. Mac Sorley and his people returned exultingly and enriched, and reached their own country [in safety].

Donnell, son of Conor, the son of Tiernan O'Rourke, who was until now detained in prison for his father, by Felim O'Conor and his son Hugh, was set at liberty by them; and the lordship of Breifny was given to him, in the place of his father.

Magrath Mac Tiernan[p], Chief of Teallach-Dunchadha, was slain by Donnell, son of Conor O'Rourke. The Connacians, and the men of Breifny in general, upon this took the lordship from Donnell, and the inhabitants of Tealach-Dunchadha slew his brother, Cathal, son of Conor. After this the lordship of Hy-Briuin, from the mountain eastwards[q], was conferred upon Art, son of Cathal Reagh O'Rourke.

O'Brian Magauran, Chief of Tealach Eachdhach[r], was slain by the Connacians.

Auliffe, son of Art O'Rourke, Lord of Breifny, from the mountain westwards, died.

Thomas O'Beirne died.

Ardgal O'Conor, son of the Coarb of Coman, died.

A great war [broke out] between the English and Conor O'Brien, during which were burned Ardrahen[s], Kilcolgan[t], and many street-towns, and much corn.

A conference took place between the English of Ireland and the Irish, in the absence of Felim O'Conor, and a peace was concluded between them.

scend from Tiernan, the son of Cathal Miogharan, son of Turlough More O'Conor, Monarch of Ireland.

[q] *Mountain eastwards.*—By "the mountain" is here meant the range of Slieve-an-ierin. Breifny from the mountain eastwards, means the county of Cavan; and Briefny from the mountain westwards, means the county of Leitrim.

[r] *Teallach Eachdhach*, now the barony of Tullaghagh, or Tullyhaw, in the north-west of the county of Cavan, in which the Magaurans, or Magoverns, are still very numerous.

[s] *Ardrahen*, a fair-town in the barony of Dunkellin, and county of Galway.

[t] *Kilcolgan*, a well-known place on the bay of Galway, in the same barony and county.

AOIS CRIOST, 1259.

Aois Criost, mile, dá céd, caocca anaoí.

Corbmac ua luimluinn epscop cluana fferta brenainn ⁊ aird eaccnaidhe na herenn décc ina naoimhsenoir cianaosda.

Tomaltach mac toirrdhealbhaigh mic maoileachlainn uí Conchobhair do thoidheacht on roimh iar na oirdneadh na airdepscop tuama i ccuirt an Papa, Pallium do thabhairt lais ⁊ Sochair mora don eacclais archena.

An giolla cam mac giolla chiaráin Saoí i lecchionn ⁊ i ndáimh décc.

Aedh ua Concobhair do thabhairt ionaidh amhlaoibh mic airt, do art beacc mac airt uí Ruairc ⁊ art mac cathail riabhaigh uí Ruairc do gabhail lais iar ccur Amhlaoibh is in ionat raibhe sin dó.

Aodh ua Concobhair do dul go doire cholaim chille do thabhairt ingene dubhgoill mic Somhairle.

Cathal mac Consnamha toiseach muintire cionaith do dallad la haodh ua Concobhair. braighde domhnaill uí Ruairc do dalladh dó beos, .i. niall mac donnchaidh ⁊ brian mac nell, ⁊ braighde ua mbriúin archena.

Coinne eitir aodh ua cconcobhair ⁊ brian ó nell ag daiminis locha herne.

Sith do denamh daodh ua cconcobhair le domhnall ua Ruairc ⁊ é do thabhairt tigherdnais na breifne do domhnall ar a haithle.

Taichleach mac diarmada do écc.

Milidh mac goirdelbhaigh do écc.

Gillbert mac goirdealbhaigh do gabhail la haodh ua cconcobhair ⁊ sliabh lugha do lomarcain dó uile. Gillbert do thabhairt a triar mac i mbraighdenus tar a cenn budhén, ⁊ aodh ua concobhair dá léccen fén amach ar a haithle.

Tadhg ua briain Riogdhamhna mumhan do écc.

Siudhraidh ua baoighill do mharbhadh da dearbhfine fesin.

[u] *Great benefits.*—This passage is given as follows in Mageoghegan's Annals of Clonmacnoise: "A. D. 1259. Thomas mac Terlagh mac Melaghlyn O'Conor came from Rome this year, where he received the orders of Bishopp, and brought his Pallium, with many other profitts, to the Church."

[w] *Devenish*, daimhinis, i. e. the Ox Island, or *bovis insula*, as it is translated in the Life of St. Maidoc. It is situated in Lough Erne, near Enniskillen, in the county of Fermanagh. Laisrean, or Molaisse, the patron saint of this island, flourished in the sixth century, having died, according to the Annals of the Four Masters, in

THE AGE OF CHRIST, 1259.

The Age of Christ, one thousand two hundred fifty-nine.

Cormac O'Luimlin, Bishop of Clonfert-Brendan, and the most illustrious man in Ireland for wisdom, died, a holy senior, of great age.

Tomaltagh, son of Turlough, who was son of Melaghlin O'Conor, returned from Rome, after having been consecrated Archbishop of Tuam at the Pope's court, bringing with him a pallium and great benefits[u] for the Church.

Gillacam Mac Gillakieran, a man eminent in literature and poetry, died.

Hugh O'Conor gave the place [seat] of Auliffe, son of Art, to Art Beg, son of Art O'Rourke, and made a prisoner of Art, son of Cathal Reagh, after he had removed Auliffe from his residence.

Hugh O'Conor went to Derry-Columbkille, to espouse the daughter of Dugald Mac Sorley [Mac Donnell].

Cathal Mac Consnamha, Chief of Muintir-Kenny [in the county of Leitrim], was blinded by Hugh O'Conor; the hostages of Donnell O'Rourke, namely, Niall, son of Donough, and Brian, son of Niall [O'Rourke], and all the other hostages of the Hy-Briuin, were also blinded by him.

Hugh O'Conor and Brian O'Neill held a conference at Devenish[w], in Lough Erne.

Hugh O'Conor made peace with Donnell O'Rourke, and afterwards gave him the lordship of Breifny.

Taichleach Mac Dermot died.

Miles Mac Costello died.

Hugh O'Conor made a prisoner of Gilbert Mac Costello, and ravaged all Sliabh-Lugha[x]. Gilbert delivered up his own three sons prisoners in the place of himself, upon which Hugh O'Conor liberated him.

Teige O'Brien, Roydamna [heir presumptive] of Munster, died.

Siry O'Boyle[y] was slain by his own tribe.

the year 563, but, according to the Annals of Ulster, in the year 570. The ruins of an ancient church and of an abbey of the fifteenth century, and a beautiful round tower in good preservation, are still to be seen on this island.

[x] *Sliabh-Lugha*, a mountain district in the barony of Costello, and county of Mayo.—See note ', under the year 1206, p. 150.

[y] *Siry O'Boyle.*—In the old translation of the Annals of Ulster this entry is rendered

O domhnaill (domhnall occ) do tionol sloicch lanmhoir in aoin ionad, ⁊ a dhol i ttír Eoghain. Aodh buidhe ó neill do theacht slocch ele ina choinne. An tir uile do milleadh leo, ⁊ a ndol assidhe in oirghiallaibh go ro ghiallad doibh gach ionadh inar ghabsatt go roadh doibh ina ffrithing.

Feidhlimidh ua tuathail tighearna Sil Muireadhaigh dó écc.

AOIS CRIOSD, 1260.

Aois Criosd, míle, da céd, Seasccatt.

Cionaoth ua birn prióir cille moire do écc.

Maolfinnén ua mithighen do écc.

Grada espuicc do thabhairt do comharba Pattraicc ar maoilseachlainn ua Concobhair ag dun dealgan.

Cath droma dheirg ag dún da lethghlass do thabhairt la brian ua nell ⁊ la hAodh ua cconchobhair do ghallaibh tuaisceirt Ereann, du i ttorchradar sochaide

thus: "Syry O'Boyle killed by his own brothers."

[a] *Hugh Boy O'Neill*, i. e. Hugh the Yellow.—This is the ancestor of the O'Neills of Clannaboy, or race of Hugh Boy, who shortly after this period acquired a new territory for themselves, in the counties of Down and Antrim. Davies and Leland seem to think that these territories were not wrested from the English settlers till after the murder of the Earl of Ulster, in the year 1333.—See Leland's History of Ireland, vol. i. p. 296, b. 2, ch. 4.

[a] *Sil-Muireadhaigh*.—Charles O'Conor writes, or ui, *inter lineas*. The prefix Sil is here a mistake for Ui, or Hy, as the O'Tuathails, or O'Tooles, were always called Ui Muireadhaigh, to be distinguished from the Sil-Muireadhaigh, which was the tribe name of the O'Conors of Connaught and their correlatives. The Hy-Muireadhaigh were originally located along the River Barrow, in the present county of Kildare, and the Sil-Muireadhaigh in the present county of Roscommon.—See note [e], under the year 1180, pp. 51–54, and note [m], under the year 1174, p. 12.

[b] Under this year (1259) the Dublin copy of the Annals of Innisfallen record, that the castles of Dunnamark, Dunnagall, Dundeady, Rathbarry, Innisonan, and Caislen an Uabhair, were burned upon the English of Desmond, by Fineen Reanna Roin, the son of Donnell God Mac Carthy.

[c] *Kilmore*.—From the name O'Beirne it is quite evident that this was the church of Kilmore near the Shannon, for O'Beirne's country was the district lying between Elphin and Jamestown, in the county of Roscommon.

[d] *O'Meehin*.—He was evidently O'Meehin of Ballaghmeehin, in the parish of Rossinver, in the north of the county of Leitrim.

[e] *Melaghlin O'Conor*.—He was Bishop of Elphin. See Ware's Bishops, by Harris, p. 629, where he is called "Milo, or Melaghlin, Mac-Thady O'Connor, Archdeacon of Clonmacnoise."

O'Donnell (Donnell Oge) assembled a very numerous army, and marched into Tyrone. Hugh Boy O'Neill[a] came with another army to meet him, and all the country was burned by them. They went from thence into Oriel, and hostages were given up to them in every place through which they passed, until their return.

Felim O'Tuathail, Lord of Sil-Muireadhaigh[a] [Omurethi], died[b].

THE AGE OF CHRIST, 1260.

The Age of Christ, one thousand two hundred sixty.

Kenny O'Beirne, Prior of Kilmore, died[c].

Mael-Finnen O'Meehin[d] died.

The dignity of bishop was conferred, by the Coarb of St. Patrick, upon Melaghlin O'Conor[e], at Dundalk.

The battle of Druim-dearg[f], near Dun-da-leath-ghlas [Downpatrick] was fought by Brien O'Neill and Hugh O'Conor, against the English of the North of Ireland. In this battle many of the Irish chieftains were slain, viz. Brian

He was consecrated by Abraham O'Conallan.

[f] *The battle of Druim dearg*, i. e. of the Red Hill or Ridge.—Sir Richard Cox, in his *Hibernia Anglicana*, p. 69, states that this battle was fought in the streets of Down. His words are: "*Stephen de long Espee*, Lord Justice (some call him Earl of Salisbury, and *Burlace* styles him Earl of *Ulster*; but I think there is no ground for either of the Titles), he encountered *O'Neale*, and slew him and three hundred and fifty-two Irishmen in the streets of Down; but not long after the Lord Justice was betrayed and murdered by his own people." Dr. Hanmer notices this battle under the year 1258, and Cox, Grace, and others, under 1259; but the Annals of Ulster, and those of Kilronan, Connaught, and Clonmacnoise, notice it under the year 1260. In the Dublin copy of the Annals of Innisfallen it is entered under the year 1258, and it is stated that it was fought on Sunday, and that O'Neill's head was sent to England. There is yet extant a poem composed by Gilla Brighde Mac Con Midhe (Mac Namee), in lamentation of Brian O'Neill and the other chieftains who were killed in this battle. In this poem Mac Namee, the bard of O'Neill, states, that the head of O'Neill, King of Tara, was sent to London to the King of England, and that the Irish fought at a great disadvantage, being dressed in satin shirts only, while their English antagonists were protected with shirts of mail.

Na goill ó Lunduin a le,
Na pubaill ó Portlairge,
Taguid na mbróin gealġluis guirm,
Na neanġlais óir is iaruinn.

Leattrom do ċuadar sa ċaṫ,
Gaill agus gaoidil teampaċ;
Léinte caoimṡroill ar ċloinn Ċuinn,
Goill ionna naonḃroin iaruinn.

do maiṫiḃ gaoiḋel, .i. Ḃrian ó nell uachtarán Erſnn, doṁnall ó cairre, diarmaid mácc lachloinn, Maġnus ua caṫain, Cian ua hinnerġe, donnsleḃe máġ cana, concoḃor ó duiḃdiorma ⁊ a ṁac, .i. aoḋ, aoḋ ua caṫáin, Muircſrtaċ ua caṫáin, aṁlaoiḃ ua gairmleadhaiġ, cuulaḋ ó hanluain, ⁊ niall ó hanluain. Acht chſna do marḃaḋ cuicc fir décc do maiṫiḃ muinntire caṫáin ar an laṫhair sin. Torcradar drong do maiṫiḃ Connaċt ann ḃeós, .i. giollu crioſd mac concoḃair mic corbmaic mic tomaltaiġ ticchſrna maiġe luirg, Caṫal mac ticchſrnáin ui Concoḃair, Maolruanaiḋ mac donnċaiḋ, Caṫal mac donnchaiḋ, mic muircſrtaiġ, aoḋ mac muircſrtaiġ finn, Taḋg mac caṫail mic briain ui maoilruanaiḋ, diarmaid mac taiḋg mic muireaḋaiġ mic tomaltaigh ui maoilruanaiḋ, Concoḃor mac giollu arraiṫ, Taḋg mac cén uí gaḋra, giollu bſraiġ ua cuinn, Carrolus mac an esruicc uí muireaḋaiġ ⁊ Sochaiḋe ṁor duaislib ⁊ danuaislib gaoiḋeal immaille riú.

Sloicchſḋ la mac uilliam búrc do com feḋlimiḋ ui Concoḃair do saiġiḋ goro inder an tír roiṁe go riacht Ros commáin. Nochar laṁarstair dulseaċa sin síos uair boí feḋlimiḋ ⁊ a ṁac, .i. aoḋ na ngall re a nuċt is na tuaṫaiḃ, ⁊ ba Connaċt ar a ccul is in dithreiḃ conaḋ í coṁairle do ronsat da gaċ taoiḃ Síṫ do ḋſnaṁ riſroile. Do gníad samlaiḋ. Iompaidis mac uilliam ina frithing ar a haithle.

"The Galls from London thither,
The hosts from Waterford,
Came in a bright green body,
In gold and iron armour.

"Unequal they entered the battle,
The Galls and the Irish of Tara;
Fair satin shirts on the race of Con,
The Galls in one mass of iron."

He lauds the hospitality, and laments the loss of Brian, King of Tara, in bardic eloquence; bewails the misfortunes of the Irish in losing him; enumerates the chiefs of the Kinel-Owen who fell along with him, among whom he mentions Manus O'Kane as the greatest loss next after the King himself. He preserves the date in the following quatrain, from which it is probable the Four Masters, and some of the older annalists, draw their date of 1260; but they must have had more authorities than this poem, as they have enumerated several chieftains who fell in this battle, not noticed in the poem.

Trí fiċid deug bliaḋain ḃán,
Mile o ġein ċriosd go coṁṡlán,
Gur ṫuit san fiaḋ gorm úrglas
Brian a long dun-da-leaṫġlais.

"Thirteen times twenty years exact,
And one thousand from the birth of Christ,
Until fell Brian on the rich green land
At the fortress of Dun-da-leath-glas."

Mac Namee observes, in a tone of grief and despondency, that all the former victories of the Kinel-Owen were more than counterbalanced by their defeat on this occasion.

O'Neill, the Chief of Ireland[g]; Donnell O'Cairre; Dermot Mac Loughlin; Manus O'Kane; Kian O'Henery; Donslevy Mac Cann; Conor O'Duvdirma, and his son Hugh; Hugh O'Kane; Murtough O'Kane; Auliffe O'Gormly; Cu-Uladh O'Hanlon; and Niall O'Hanlon. In a word, fifteen of the chiefs[h] of the family of O'Kane were slain on the field. Some of the chiefs of Connaught also fell there, namely, Gilchreest, son of Conor, son of Cormac, son of Tomaltagh [Mac Dermot], Lord of Moylurg; Cathal, son of Tiernan O'Conor; Mulrony Mac Donough; Cathal, son of Donough, the son of Murtough; Hugh, son of Murtough Finn; Teige, son of Cathal, son of Brian O'Mulrony; Dermot, son of Teige, son of Murray, son of Tomaltagh O'Mulrony; Conor Mac Gilla-Arraith; Teige, son of Kian O'Gara; Gillabarry O'Quin; Carolus, son of the Bishop[i] O'Murray; and many others, both of the Irish nobility and the plebeians.

An army was led by Mac William Burke against Felim O'Conor, and he plundered the country before him, until he reached Roscommon. He dared not, however, pass down beyond this, because Felim and his son Hugh na nGall were near him in the Tuathas, and the cows of Connaught were behind them[k] in the wilderness[l]; so that they came to a resolution, on both sides, to make peace with each other. Accordingly they did so, and then Mac William returned home.

In Mageoghegan's translation of the Annals of Clonmacnoise this battle is called the battle of Downe Daleglass, and it is stated that "Brian O'Neill is since called Bryan Catha in Duin, which is as much as to say in English, Bryan of the Battle of Downe." Manus O'Kane and other chiefs who fell in this battle are also called "Catha an Duin," i. e. "of the Battle of Down," in the pedigree of their descendants in all the Irish genealogical books.

[g] *Chief of Ireland*, uaċtaṗán Ereann.—In Mageoghegan's translation of the Annals of Clonmacnoise this is interpreted, "Bryan O'Neale, named the King of the Irish of Ireland." He is evidently so called by the annalists, because at the meeting held at Cael Uisce in 1258, the greater part of the Irish chiefs consented to submit to him as their chief leader.

[h] *Fifteen of the chiefs*.—This is rendered, "fifteen of the best of the O'Cahans were slayn at that present," in the old translation of the Annals of Ulster; and "fifteen of the chiefest of the Family of the O'Kaghans" in Mageoghegan's Annals of Clonmacnoise.

[i] *Son of the bishop*, mac an epscoig, &c.—In Mageoghegan's Annals of Clonmacnoise this is rendered: "Charles, the Bushopp O'Mory's son, with many others of the Noble and Ignoble sort."

[k] *Behind them*, ar ccúl.—This phrase generally means under their protection.

[l] *In the wilderness*, i. e. in the wilderness of Kinel-Dofa, or O'Hanly's country, in the east of the county of Roscommon. The church of Kilbarry, anciently called Cluain Coirpthe, was in this wilderness.

Sluaiccheḋ la mac muiris i ttuaḋmuṁain do saiġiḋ Concoḃair uí ḃriain, go ttarla ua briain i ccoill berráin ⁊ tionol ina timceal do maiṫiḃ a muintire ara cionnsoṁ. Maiḋter for gallaiḃ riú ro ceḋóir ⁊ marḃṫar dauit Prindercas Ridire roinnsermar essiḋe, an failgeaċ, Pearrún airdraṫain, Tomas baroit, ⁊ Sochaiḋe nach airimter ḋioḃ.

Maġnus mac aoḋa mecc oireachtaiġ do ṁarḃaḋ la doṁnall ua fflaichiṁ.

Lochlainn mac aṁlaoiḃ mic airt ui Ruairc ⁊ ticchernán a derḃraṫair do marḃaḋ daoḋ ua Concoḃair iar na ttoirbert dó la doṁnall mac nell mic Congalaiġ ui Ruairc.

Doṁnall mac Conċoḃair mic ticchernáin uí Ruairc do marḃaḋ la teallach ndúnċaḋa i meaḃail ⁊ Muirceartaċ a dearbraṫair do ṁarḃaḋ daoḋ ua Conċoḃair iar sin. Art beacc mac airt ui Ruairc do marḃaḋ daoḋ ua Concoḃair beos.

Taḋg duḃ mac nell mic Congalaiġ do marḃaḋ la maoilseaċlainn mac aṁlaoiḃ mic airt.

Creaċ mór la haoḋ ua cconcoḃair for tuaiṫ raṫa dár marḃaḋ Concoḃar mac branáin toiseaċ corc achlann, Muircertaċ ó maonaiġ, mac briain uí allaṁain ⁊ Sochaiḋe archena.

Creaċ do ḋenaṁ do mac muiris ar ua ndoṁnaill. Drong do muintir uí doṁnaill do breith orra i mbeannan brechmoiġe. Drem do losccaḋ ⁊ do marḃaḋ leó ḋioḃ.

Creaċ aḋḃal do ḋenaṁ dua doṁnaill ar mac muiris gur airccertar cairpre uile.

Longport Concoḃair uí ceallaiġ do losccaḋ la muintir aoḋa uí Concoḃair.

[m] *Mac Maurice.*—This was the celebrated Sir Gerald Sugagh Fitzgerald, who died soon after.

[n] *Coill-Bearain*, now Kilbarran, in the parish of Feakle, barony of Upper Tulla, county of Clare.

[o] *The Failgeach.*—He was the head of a Welsh sept called Clann an Fhailghe then in Ireland, but the Editor has not been able to determine their location.—See *Genealogies, Tribes, and Customs of Hy-Fiachrach*, p. 325, note [f], where it is shewn, that Clann an Fhailghe were a Welsh tribe. Under the year 1316, the Annals of Clonmacnoise, as translated by Mageoghegan, contain the following notice of this sept:

"A. D. 1316. Felym O'Connor took a prey from the sonns of Failge, killed Richard himself" [i. e. their chieftain], "and made a great slaughter of his people."

An army was led by Mac Maurice[m] into Thomond, to attack Conor O'Brien. O'Brien, attended by the chiefs of his people, met him at Coill-Bearain[n]; and the English were defeated at once, with the loss of David Prendergast, a most puissant knight; the Failgeach[o]; the parson of Ardrahin, Thomas Barrott; and others not mentioned.

Manus, the son of Hugh Mageraghty, was slain by Donnell O'Flahiff[p].

Loughlin, son of Auliffe, the son of Art O'Rourke, and Tiernan his brother, were slain by Hugh O'Conor, after they had been delivered up to him by Donnell, son of Niall, the son of Congalagh O'Rourke.

Donnell, son of Conor, son of Tiernan O'Rourke, was treacherously slain by the inhabitants of Tealach-Dunchadha [Tullyhunco]; and Murtough, his brother, was afterwards slain by Hugh O'Conor. Art Beg, son of Art O'Rourke, was also slain by Hugh O'Conor.

Teige Duff, son of Niall, the son of Congalagh, was slain by Melaghlin, son of Auliffe, who was son of Art (O'Rourke).

A great depredation was committed by Hugh O'Conor in Tuath-ratha[q]; on which occasion Conor Mac Branan, Chief of Corc-Achlann, Murtough O'Maeny, the son of Brian O'Fallon, and many others, were slain.

A depredation was committed by Mac Maurice on O'Donnell. A party of O'Donnell's men overtook them (i.e. the plunderers) at Beannan Breacmhoighe[r], and burned and killed some of them.

A great depredation was committed on Fitzmaurice by O'Donnell, who plundered the whole of Carbury.

The garrison of Conor O'Kelly was burned by the people of Hugh O'Conor.

[p] *O'Flahiff*, ua ḟlaıṫıṁ.—This name is now pronounced as if written O'ḟlaıṫıṁ, and anglicised Lahiff. This family is now respectable in the neighbourhood of Gort, in the south of the county of Galway.

[q] *Tuath-ratha*, now anglicised Tooraah, in the north-west of the county of Fermanagh. Hugh O'Conor went on this occasion to plunder O'Flanagan, Chief of Tooraan. All the persons mentioned as having been slain were of his own followers.

[r] *Beannan Breacmhoighe*, i. e. the hill of Breachmhagh. There are several places in the county of Donegal called Breachmhagh; the place here referred to is probably the townland of Breachmhagh, Anglice Breaghwy, in the parish of Conwal, in the barony of Raphoe.—See Ordnance Map of this county, sheet 45. There is a remarkable hill called Binnion in the parish of Taughboyne, in the same barony; but it is the place called beınnın in these Annals at the year 1557, and not the beannán here referred to.

Sitreacc mac fernlaich do marbhadh in áthluain do donncathaigh mag oireachtaigh ⁊ do tomaltach mag oireachtaigh.

Creachsluaicchеadh la hua ndomhnaill for ċenél neocchain tar eis caṫa dúin gur hairccеadh, ⁊ gur loisccеadh urmhor ċenel neocchain leis don cur sin.

Abraham ua conallain comorba Patraicc décc.

AOIS CRIOSD, 1261.

Aois Criosd, mile, da ċéd, Seascca, a haon.

Maolpatraicc ó Sccandail espoc Raṫa boṫ do toġa ina airdespoc in ardmaċa.

Se cleiriġ décc do maiṫib cleireaċ cenél cconaill do marbhadh la Concobar ua nell ⁊ la cenél neoġain i ndoire ċolaim ċille im Concobar ua ffirġil. Concobor ua nell do marbhadh fo cedoir tre miorbailib de ⁊ ċolaim ċille le donn ua mbreslén toiseaċ fanad.

Aedh mac maoilseachlainn ui Concobair do ṁarbhadh do maolḟabaill ua Edin.

Caṫal ó heaġra do marbhadh do gallaib ar tarraing mic ḟeorais ⁊ coicc fir oile do luiġnib do marbhadh imaille ris i ttempall mor fechin in eassdara.

Coccadh mor ⁊ uilc iomda do dénamh dfinġin mac domhnaill mecc carṫaiġ ⁊ dá braiṫrib ar ġallaib.

Sluaicchеadh mor la cloinn ġerailt i ndesmumain do saiġidh mecc carṫaiġ, .i. finġin. Macc carṫaiġ da ionnsaiġidh go ttucc maidm forra dar marbhadh ocht mbarúin ⁊ cuicc fir ridire im dreim ele duaislib gall is

[a] Under this year (1260) the Annals of Clonmacnoise contain the two passages following, which have been altogether omitted by the Four Masters:

"A. D. 1260. Carbrey O'Melaghlyn, a worthy prince for manhood, bounty, and many other good parts, was treacherously killed by David Roche in Athboye" [Ballyboy] "in the territory of Ffearkeall."

"Clarus Mac Moylyn O'Moylechonrie brought the White Cannons of the Order of Premonstra, neer Christmas, from Trinity Island, on Loghke, to Trinity Island on Logh Oghter, in the Brenie, and were there appointed by the Lycense of Cahall O'Reyllie, who granted the place after this manner: *In puram et perpetuam Elimozinam in*

Sitric Mac Shanly was slain at Athlone by Donncahy Mageraghty and Tomaltagh Mageraghty.

A predatory incursion was made by O'Donnell, against the Kinel-Owen, after the battle of Down; and the greater part of Kinel-Owen was plundered and burned by him on that occasion.

Abraham O'Conallan, Coarb of St. Patrick (Archbishop of Armagh), died[s].

THE AGE OF CHRIST, 1261.

The Age of Christ, one thousand two hundred sixty-one.

Maelpatrick O'Scannal, Bishop of Raphoe, was elected to the Archbishopric of Armagh.

Sixteen of the most distinguished of the clergy of Kinel-Connell were killed at Derry by Conor O'Neill and the Kinel-Owen, together with Conor O'Firgil[t]. Conor O'Neill was slain immediately afterwards by Donn O'Breslen, Chief of Fanad, through the miracles of God and St. Columbkille.

Hugh, son of Melaghlin O'Conor, was slain by Mulfaville O'Heyne.

Cathal O'Hara was slain by the English, by the procurement of Mac Feorais [Bermingham]; and five of the people of Leyny were also killed in the Great Church of Easdara [Ballysadare].

A great war was waged, and many injuries were inflicted, by Fineen Mac Carthy, son of Donnell Mac Carthy, and his brothers, on the English.

A great army was marched by the Clann-Gerald [Geraldines] into Desmond, to attack Mac Carthy, i. e. Fineen. Mac Carthy attacked and defeated them; and in this contest were slain eight barons and five knights, besides others of

Sancte Trinitatis, et idcirco Clarus hoc fecit in Domino qui Monstratenses" [*Permonstratenses*] "*gaudent consimili privilegio cum monachio ita quod ad ullam aliam ordinem transire possent.*"

This passage must have been misplaced by the transcriber, because the death of Clarus is entered under the year 1251.

"John de Verdon came over into Ireland this year."

"Robyn Lawless died on Easterday."

[t] *O'Firgil.*—This name, which was that of the hereditary coarbs of Kilmacrenan, is now Anglicised Freel. This passage is given as follows in the old translation of the Annals of Ulster: "A. D. 1261. The best of the clergy of Tirconnell was killed by Conor O'Nell and Kindred Oen, in Derry-Columbkill, about Conor O'Fergill. Conor O'Nell was killed soon after, through the miracles of Columbkill, by Don O'Brislen, Chief of Fanaght."

in ccliaṫaiġ sin imaille re Seon mac tomáis ⁊ sis an mbarraċ mór. Dioairmiḋi a ttorċair do daorsccorsluaġ gall is in ccaṫiorġail remraite.

Fingin mag carṫaiġ do marḃaḋ la gallaiḃ iar sin, ⁊ ticchſnus dſsmuṁan do gaḃail da dſrḃraṫair don aitċlſireaċ mág carṫaiġ.

Art mac caṫail riaḃaiġ ui Ruairc delúḋ o aoḋ ua conċoḃair, ⁊ toisiġ na breifne, ⁊ ċonmaicne do ṫaḃairt ċſnnais na breifne ḋó.

Doṁnall ua heaġra do ḋſnaṁ creċe for cloinn ḟeórais in dioġail marḃṫa caṫail ui eaġra doiḃ ⁊ ṡaraiġṫi ṫeampaill fechin gur marḃ Sefín mac ḟeorais, ⁊ an tattluicc tuccurtair a teampall earadara ar e baoí ima cſnn ag a marḃaḋ.

Brian ruaḋ ua briain do losccaḋ ⁊ do scaoileaḋ caislen uí ċonaing ⁊ ro marḃ a mboí do ḋaoiniḃ ann.

Longport aoḋa uí Concoḃair (ag snaṁ inredaiġ) do losccaḋ dfearaiḃ bſifni.

[u] *Battle.*—This battle is noticed in the Annals of Ulster and Multifernan, under the year 1261. It was fought at Callainn Gleanna O'Ruachtain, about five miles eastward of Kenmare, in the parish of Kilgarvan, in the barony of Glenarough, and county of Kerry. There is a much more satisfactory account of this battle given in the Annals of Innisfallen, under the year 1260. Dr. Hanmer has the following notice of it under the same year: "Anno 1260. William Denne was made Lord Justice, in whose time Green Castle, *Arx-Viridis*, was destroyed, and the Carties plaied the Divells in Desmond, where they burned, spoiled, preyed, and slue many an innocent; they became so strong, and prevailed so mightily, that for the space (so it is reported) of twelve yeeres the Desmond durst not put plow in ground in his owne country; at length, through the operation of Satan, a bane of discord was thrown betweene the Carties and the Odriscoles, Odonovaines, Mac Donoch, Mac Mahonna, Mac Swines, and the inhabittants of Muscrie, in so much that by their cruell dissention, they weakened themselves of all sides, that the Desmond in the end overcame and overtopped them all; but in the beginning of these Garboils, I find that the Carties slue of the Desmonds, John Fitz-Thomas, founder of the Momastery and Convent of Trally, together with Maurice his sonne, eight Barons, fifteen Knights, besides infinite others, at a place called Callan, where they were buried. Mine Authors are Iohn Clinne onely, and the Booke of Houth."—*Hanmer's Chronicle*, Dublin edition of 1809, p. 400. The same account of the battle is given in Coxe's *Hibernia Anglicana*, p. 69, except that the author adds, out of his own head, that the victory was gained "by ambuscade." But Dr. Leland, who had the English and Irish accounts of this battle before him, and who was too high-minded to distort facts or give any details without authority, has come to the conclusion that it was a fair battle; but he should have stated, on the authority of the Annals of Innisfallen, and other documents, that William Denn, the Justiciary, Walter de Burgo, Earl of Ulster, Walter de Riddlesford, the great Baron of Leinster, and Donnell Roe, the son of Cormac Finn

the English nobles, as also John Fitz Thomas and Barry More. Countless numbers of the English common soldiers were also killed in the aforesaid battle[u].

Fineen Mac Carthy was afterwards killed by the English[w], and the lordship of Desmond was assumed by his brother, the Aithcleireach Mac Carthy.

Art, son of Cathal Reagh O'Rourke, made his escape from [the custody of] Hugh O'Conor; and the nobles of Breifny and Conmaicne gave him the lordship of Breifny.

Donnell O'Hara committed a depredation upon the Clann-Feoracs [Berminghams], in revenge for their having slain Cathal O'Hara, and desecrated the church of St. Feichinn: he also killed Sefin Mac Feorais, who while being killed had upon his head the bell[x] which he had taken from the church of Ballysadare.

Brian Roe O'Brien burned and demolished Caislein ui Chonaing [Castle Connell], and killed all that were in it.

The Fortress of Hugh O'Conor (at Snamh-in-redaigh[y]) was burned by the men of Breifny.

Mac Carthy, with all his Irish followers, assisted the Geraldines against Mac Carthy Reagh and such of the Irish of the Eugenian race as espoused his cause.

After this signal defeat of the English, Fineen Reanna Roin, and the Irish chieftains of South Munster, burned and levelled the castles of Dun Mic-Toman, Duninsi, Dunnagall, Cuan Dore, Dundeady, Dunnalong, Macroom, Muirgioll, Dunnamark, Dunloe, Killorglin, and the greater part of the castles of Hy-Conaill-Gaura, and killed their English warders.

[w] *Killed by the English.*—According to the Dublin copy of the Annals of Innisfallen, Fineen Reanna Roin Mac Carthy, who was the greatest hero of the Eugenian line of Desmond that appeared since the English Invasion, was killed by Miles Cogan and the De Courcys, at the castle of Rinn Roin, or Ringrone, from which was derived his historical cognomen, which he never bore till after his death.

[x] *The bell,* that is, Sefin had on his head a blessed bell, which he had taken away from the church of Ballysadare, thinking that O'Hara would not attempt to strike him while he had so sacred a helmet on his head, even though he had obtained it by robbery.

[y] *Snamh-in-redaigh.*—This is probably the place now called Druim Snamha, Anglice Drumsna, on the Shannon, on the boundary between the counties of Leitrim and Roscommon. Dr. Lanigan supposes (in his Ecclesiastical History of Ireland, vol. i. p. 24), that Drumsnave in Leitrim might be the place anciently called Snamh da-en; but we have direct authority to prove that Snamh da-en was the ancient name of that part of the Shannon between Clonmacnoise, in the King's County, and Clonburren, in the county of Roscommon.—See *Tribes and Customs of Hy-Many*, p. 5, note [f]; also MS. in Trinity College, Dublin, H. 2, 16, p. 871.

Loscaḋ cluana suilionn, .i. longport feḋlim ui Concoḃair.

Toirrḋealḃaċ ócc mac aoḋa ui Concoḃair do taḃairt for altram dart ó ruairc.

Creaċ mór la haoḋ ua Concoḃair isin mbreifne co rainic druim lethain. Brisiḋ do ṫaḃairt annsin for blaiḋ da sluaġ gur marḃaḋ sochaiḋe nar boirrdeirc ḋioḃ.

Aoḋ buiḋe ua nell dionnarbaḋ, ⁊ Niall culánaċ ó nell doirdneaḋ ina ionaḋ.

Niall ua gairmleadhaiġ toiseaċ cenél moáin do écc.

Maiḋm mór la hua ndoṁnaill for niall ċulánach ó néill dú in ro marḃaḋ ⁊ in ro gaḃaḋ soċaiḋe do ṁaiṫiḃ ċenel eoġain fa ṁac caṫmaoil toiseaċ ċenel feradhaiġ co ndruing do ṁaiṫibh ele nach airiṁter sonn.

AOIS CRIOST, 1262.

Aois Criost, mile, dá céd, seascca, adó.

Maolpattraicc ó Sccannail Airdepscop ardamaċa do radha oiffrind le pallium (in octau Eoin baiste) in Ardmacha.

Maoilseacloinn mac taidcc ui concoḃair epscop oilesinn do écc.

Sluaiġeaḋ adbal mór la gallaiḃ ereann do saiġiḋ feḋlimiḋ mic caṫail croiḃdeirg ⁊ a mic aoḋ na ngall, gur cuir ua concoḃair urṁór bó Connaċt i ttir Conaill ar teċeaḋ na ngall, ⁊ buí fén in inis Saimera ar cúl a bó ⁊ a muinter. Tainic mac uilliam burc tar toċar móna coinneaḋa iniar, ⁊ slóġ mor immailli ris go ráinic oilfinn. Iustís na hereann ⁊ Eoan de uerdun

[z] *Cluain Suilionn*, now Cloonsellan, a townland in the parish of Kilteevan, barony of Ballintober south, and county of Roscommon.—See Ordnance Map of this county, sheets 40 and 42.

[a] *Drumlahan.*—This place is now more usually called Drumlane. It is situated near Belturbet, in the county of Cavan, and is remarkable for its round tower. Colgan states that it is situated on the boundary between the two Breifnys.

[b] Under this year the Dublin copy of the Annals of Innisfallen contain several notices of the affairs of Munster, which have been omitted or but slightly noticed by the Four Masters, under the year 1262; such as the landing of Richard de Rupella at Portnalong, in Ivahagh; a great battle between Cormac na Mangarton, the son of Donnell God Mac Carthy, and the English of Ireland, at Tuairin Chormaic, on the side of the Mangarton mountain, where Cormac was slain and his people slaughtered; and also a victory gained by Donnell Mael, the son of Donnell God Mac Carthy, over the English, on

Cluain Suilionn[z], i. e. the Fortress of Felim O'Conor, was burned.

Turlough Oge, son of Hugh O'Conor, was given in fosterage to Art O'Rourke.

A great depredation was committed by Hugh O'Conor in Breifny; and he advanced to Drumlahan[a], where a part of his army was defeated, and many of the less distinguished of them were slain.

Hugh Boy O'Neill was banished, and Niall Culanagh was elected in his place.

Niall O'Gormly, Chief of Kinel-Moen, died.

A great victory was gained by O'Donnell over Niall Culanagh O'Neill [in a battle], in which many of the chiefs of Kinel-Owen, under the conduct of Mac Cawell, Chief of Kinel-Farry, and many other chiefs not mentioned here, were killed or taken prisoners[b].

THE AGE OF CHRIST, 1262.

The Age of Christ, one thousand two hundred sixty-two.

Maelpatrick O'Scannail, Archbishop of Armagh, said Mass in a pallium (in the Octave of John the Baptist), at Armagh.

Melaghlin, son of Teige O'Conor, Bishop of Elphin, died.

A very great army was led by the English of Ireland against Felim, son of Cathal Crovderg O'Conor, and his son Hugh na ngall; upon which O'Conor sent off the greater number of the cows of Connaught into Tirconnell, away from the English, and remained himself on Inis Saimer[c] to protect his cows and people. Mac William Burke marched across Tochar Mona Coinneadha[d] from the west, with a great army, as far as Elphin; and the

which occasion he slew twelve of their knights, and the greater part of their muster.

These three brothers, the sons of Donnell God, were the most heroic of the Mac Carthy family since the English Invasion.

[c] *Inis Saimer.*—See O'Flaherty's *Ogygia*, c. ii. p. 163, where he describes Inis Samer as "*Erneo fluvio.*" It is now called Fish Island, and is situated in the River Erne, very close to the cataract of Assaroe at Ballyshannon.

[d] *Tochar Mona Coinneadha.*—A celebrated causeway in the parish of Templetogher, and barony of Ballymoe, in the north-east of the county of Galway.—See other references to it at the year 1177, pp. 34–36; also note [n], under the year 1225, p. 232; and note under the year 1255.

do ṫocht tar Aṫluain anoir go Roscommáin. Leccid siorṫa uaṫa i ccenél dobṫa mic aongusa gur airccsiod an méd ro an tar ér uí Concobair i cconnachtaibh don toisc sin, ⁊ do tórainnsiod áit caisléin i Roscommáin. Dala aodha uí concobair tra ro tionoilsiḋe a ṡochraiḋe, ⁊ luiḋ in iarṫar Connacht gur airgiostair ó Moiġ eó na Saxan, ⁊ o Ḃhalla iniar. Loisccit a mbailte ⁊ a narbanna go sliab luġa, ⁊ ro marbsatair daoine iomda eatorra sin. Cuiris a toiriġ ⁊ a ógṡlaṫa uaiḋ in uachtor Connacht gur loiscsiod, ⁊ gur airccsiod ó Tuaim da gualann go haṫluain, ⁊ ro marbsat a ttarla do daoinibh inḟeaḋma eatorra. Cuirid goill iaram teċta uaṫa doċum ui Concobair ⁊ a mic do tairccsin síoḋa dóibh. Ticc aoḋ iarsin ina ccoinne go hath doire ċuirc. Do gníaḋ siṫ ann re roile gan braighde gan etireaḋa ó cechtar na dá céle. Baoi aod ua concobair ⁊ mac uilliam burc in én leabaid an oiḋċe dér na síoḋa go subaċ soiṁeanmnaċ, ⁊ imtiġid goill arabaraḋ iar cceliobraḋ dua Concobair.

Aodh buiḋe ua Néll doirdneaḋ doriḋise, ⁊ Niall culánaċ daiṫríoġaḋ.

Crſċ mór do dénaṁ la gallaib na miḋe ar giolla na naoṁ ua fearġail tiġearna na hAngaile, ⁊ a oireachta fſin do ḋul uaiḋ i cclſiṫ gall. A aiṫríoġaḋ doiḃ, ⁊ a tiġearnus do tabairt do mac murchaiḋ carraiġ uí fſrġail. Uilc iomḋa, creaċa, gnearra, urṫa, ⁊ aircene, ⁊ marbṫa do ḋénaṁ do ġiolla na naoṁ for gallaib iarsin. Tiġearnus na hangoile do cosnaṁ dó ar éccin, ⁊ mac murchaiḋ carraiġ dionnarbaḋ dó ar an tír amaċ.

Donnslebe mac caṫmaoil taoiseaċ cenél fearadhaiġ do marbaḋ daoḋ buiḋe ua néll.

Sluaiġeaḋ la mac uilliam búrc ⁊ lá gallaib Ereann i nDeasmumain

[e] *The Lord Justice.*—He was Sir Richard de Rupella, or Capella.—See Harris's Ware, vol. ii. p. 103.

[f] *John de Verdun.*—According to the Annals of Clonmacnoise, as translated by Mageoghegan, he came to Ireland in 1260. He married Margaret, daughter of Walter de Lacy, in whose right he became Lord of Westmeath, and had his chief residence at Ballymore, Lough Seudy.—See Grace's Annals, edited by the Rev. Richard Butler, note [t], p. 30.

[g] *Kinel-Dofa-mic-Aengusa*, i. e. O'Hanly's country, to the east of Slieve Baune, in the county of Roscommon.—See note [e], under the year 1210, p. 169; and pedigree of O'Hanly, p. 171.

[h] *Sliabh Lugha.*—This was originally O'Gara's country, but it now belonged to the family of Mac Costello. It forms the northern part of the barony of Costello, in the county of Mayo.—See note [l], under the year 1206, p. 150; and also note [n], under the year 1224, pp. 215, 216.

Lord Justice[e] of Ireland and John de Verdun[f] came across [the bridge of] Athlone to Roscommon. They sent out marauding parties into Kinel-Dofa-mic-Aengusa[g], who plundered all that remained after O'Conor in Connaught; and they marked out a place for a castle at Roscommon. As to Hugh O'Conor, he assembled his troops, and marched into the West of Connaught, and plundered the country from Mayo of the Saxons, and from Balla, westwards; and he also burned their towns and corn as far as Sliabh Lugha[h], and slew many persons between them [these places]. He sent his chiefs and young nobles into Upper [i. e. South] Connaught, who burned and plundered [the country] from Tuam da ghualann to Athlone, and killed all they met who were fit to bear arms. The English afterwards dispatched messengers to O'Conor and his son, to offer them peace; and Hugh came to a conference with them at the ford of Doire-Chuirc[i], where they made peace with each other, without giving hostages or pledges on either side. After they had concluded this peace, Hugh O'Conor and Mac William Burke slept together in the one bed, cheerfully and happily[k]; and the English left the country on the next day, after bidding farewell to O'Conor.

Hugh Boy O'Neill was again elected, and Niall Culanagh deposed.

A great depredation was committed by the English of Meath on Gilla-na-naev O'Farrell, Lord of Annaly; and his own tribe forsook him, and went over to the English. He was deposed by them, and his lordship was bestowed on the son of Murrough Carragh O'Farrell. After this many evils, depredations, aggressions, spoliations, and slaughters, were committed by Gilla-na-naev on the English; and he asserted, by main force, the lordship of Annaly, and banished the son of Murrough Carragh from the country.

Donslevy Mac Cawell, Chief of Kinel-Farry, was slain by Hugh Boy O'Neill.

An army was led by Mac William Burke and the English of Ireland into

[i] *Derryquirk*, ooıpe cuıpc, a townland in the parish of Killuckin, in the barony and county of Roscommon.

[k] *Cheerfully and happily.*—This sentence is very rudely constructed by the Four Masters. They should have written it thus: "After the conclusion of this peace Hugh O'Conor and Mac William Burke (Walter, son of Richard, who was son of William Fitz-Adelm), passed the night together merrily and amicably, and even slept together in one bed. Hugh O'Conor and this Mac William were near relations, the former being the grandson, and the latter the great grandson of Cathal Crovderg O'Conor."

dionnsaiġiḋ Még carṫaiġ go rangadar mangartaċ loċa lén. Marbṫar gearalt roitsi annsin lá Mag carṫaiġ, ⁊ a dſirṫi gur béside an tsear barún do bfearr in erinn ina aimsir fſin. Ba háiṫſr go nanáiṫſr do dſsmumain sin uair do marḃaḋ corbmac mac domnaill guid még carṫaiġ don taċar so. Acht ċſna ba hſsbadaċ goill ⁊ gaoidil mun mangartaiġ an la remráitte.

Domnall ua mannaċáin do marḃaḋ do cloinn Ruaidri ⁊ taidcc uí Conċoḃair.

Sluaicċeaḋ la hua ndomnaill (domnall ócc) hi ffſraiḃ manach cetus, ⁊ assiḋe i ngairbtrian Connacht ⁊ go granard tſthba go ro iarrsat, ⁊ go ro ġiallsatt gach tir gus a rainicc dó, ⁊ tainicc dia tigh iar mbuaiḋ ccoscair.

AOIS CRIOSD, 1263.

Aois Criosd, mile, dá ċéd, sescat, atrí.

Tomás ua ceallaiġ espuc cluana fearta, ⁊ Maolciarain ua maoileoin (.i. ab cluana mic nois) déġ.

Dauith ua find ab mainistre na buille, ⁊ Giollapatraicc mac giolla na nguirén prioir Doirſin, Saoí craḃaiḋ ⁊ eniġ déġ.

Donn ua bresleń do marḃaḋ la domnall ua ndomnaill i ccuirt an espuicc i ráiṫ both.

Sluaiġheaḋ la mac uilliam dionnsaiġhiḋ feidlimiḋ ui concoḃair ⁊ a mſic go rangadar Roscomáin, ⁊ ro teiċsiod siol muireadaiġ rompa i ttuaisceart Connaċt, ⁊ nochan fuairsiod goill creaċa re a ndénaṁ don

[l] Mangartaċ loċa lein, now anglicised Mangarton, a lofty mountain over Lough Leane, in the barony of Magunihy, and county of Kerry.

[m] *Cormac, son of Donnell God.*—The Dublin copy of the Annals of Innisfallen notices this battle under the year 1261, and states that it was fought on Tuarain Chormaic, on the side of the Mangarton mountain.

[n] *On that day*, an la remráitte, literally, on the day aforesaid. This is incorrect writing, because no particular day is mentioned in the previous part of the sentence. Their usual phrase, don ċur sin, i. e. on that occasion, would be much more correct.

[o] *Granard in Teffia.*—Now Granard, a small market town in the county of Longford, four miles north of Edgeworthstown. The most remarkable feature of antiquity now to be seen at Granard is a large moat with a considerable part of two circumvallations around it. It is said that this moat was opened about fifty years ago, and that the arched vaults of a castle were found within it, built of beautiful square stones, which are well cemented with lime and

Desmond, against Mac Carthy, and arrived at Mangartagh[l], of Lough Leane. Here Gerald Roche, who was said to be the third best knight of his time in Ireland, was slain by Mac Carthy. This was a triumph without joy to Desmond, for Cormac, son of Donnell God[m] [the Stammering] Mac Carthy, was slain in this battle. Indeed, both the English and the Irish suffered great losses about the Mangartagh mountain on that day[n].

Donnell O'Monahan was slain by the sons of Rory and of Teige O'Conor.

An army was led by O'Donnell (Donnell Oge), first into Fermanagh, and thence into the Rough Third of Connaught, and to Granard in Teffia[o]; and every territory through which he passed granted him his demands and gave him hostages; and he returned home in triumph.

THE AGE OF CHRIST, 1263.

The Age of Christ, one thousand two hundred sixty-three.

Thomas O'Kelly, Bishop of Clonfert, and Mulkierian O'Malone, Abbot of Clonmacnoise, died.

David O'Finn, Abbot of the Monastery of Boyle, and Gillapatrick, son of Gilla-na-nguisen, Prior of Doirean[p], a man eminent for piety and hospitality, died.

Donn O'Breslen was slain by Donnell O'Donnell, in the bishop's court [palace] at Raphoe.

An army was led by Mac William Burke[q] against Felim O'Conor and his son. He reached Roscommon, and the Sil-Murray fled before him into the north of Connaught; and the English had no preys to seize upon on that occa-

sand mortar. Dr. O'Conor writes this name grian-ard, which he translates *collis solis*, i. e. as *hill of the sun*; but there is no authority for writing the first syllable grian. In Leabhar-na-h-Uidhre the name is written granaret. The town of Granard has been removed from its ancient site, which see marked on the Ordnance Map of the parish.

[p] *Doirean.*—This place is now so called in Irish at the present day, and anglicised Derrane, Durrane, &c. It is situated in the district of Fiodh Monach, a short distance to the north of the town of Roscommon.—See Ordnance Map of the county of Roscommon, sheet 35. According to the tradition in the country, this was a house of great importance; but the Irish Annals contain very few notices of it.

[q] *Mac William Burke.*—He was Walter, the son of Richard More, who was the son of William Fitz-Adelm de Burgo. He became Earl of

dul sin. Ro innsaiġ donnchadh ua floint ⁊ tadg a ṁac an sluaġ, ⁊ do marbsat céd diob edir maiṫ ⁊ saiṫ, im Aitin ruitsél ⁊ imma mac, ⁊ im cúic ṁacaib conconnaċt uí concobair imaille re sochaide oile. Soait an sluaġ fo mela dia ttiġib iar sin.

Maolfabaill ua hedin do marbad lá gallaib.

Diarmait clereaċ mac corbmaic meic diarmata do écc.

Aindiles mág ḟionnbarr taoiseaċ muintire gearadáin do écc.

Caislén do denaṁ la mac uilliam búrc ag ath angail isin ccorann.

Machair ua ruadáin do marbad la gallaib i ndorus tempaill cilli Sescnén.

Etaoin ingean uí ḟlannaccáin do écc.

Sluaiccéad la hua ndoṁnaill (doṁnall occ) hi cconnachtoib go ccompanaicc fri haodh ua cconcobair acc coirrsliab. Lottar assiḋe go cruaċain assiḋe tar Suca, assiḋe hi ccloinn riocaird gur milleadh ⁊ gur ler lomairccsḋ leo go heċtge ⁊ go gaillim, ⁊ iar niompud dAod ua ċoncobair ó ua ndoṁnaill, ro ascena ó doṁnaill tar Sruṫair, tar Rodba, ar fud tire haṁalgaid, ⁊ iaroṁ tar muaid, ⁊ do bsit a ógriar uadaib uile.

Creach mór do ḋenaṁ la haeḋ mac feḋlimiḋ ar gallaib slebe luġa, ⁊ i

Ulster very soon after this period.—See note [f], under 1264.

[r] *Muintir-Gearadhain.*—This territory, the name of which is anglicised Montergeran in old law documents, stretched along Lough Gowna, on the west side, in the north of the present county of Longford. According to an Inquisition taken at Ardagh, on the 4th of April, in the tenth year of the reign of James I., Montergeran, in the county of Longford, was divided from Clanmahon, in the county of Cavan, by that part of Lough Gowna called Snabeneracke. The townlands of Aghnekilly and Aghacannon, near Lough Gowna, belonging to Edmond Kearnan, who died in 1634, were a part of this territory.

[s] *Ath Anghail, in Corran.*—Corran is the name of a barony, in the county of Sligo; but there is no place in this barony now bearing the name of Ath Anghaile, i. e. Annaly's, or Hennely's, ford.

[t] *Kilsescnen*, Cill Sescnén, now anglicised Kilshesnan. It is an old church in ruins, in a townland of the same name, in the parish of Killosser, barony of Gallen, and county of Mayo.—See its situation shewn on the map to *Genealogies, Tribes, and Customs of Hy-Fiachrach*, printed in 1844, for the Irish Archæological Society. The family of Rowan are still in the neighbourhood of this church.

[u] *River Suck.*—The Suck rises from the hill of Eiscir ui Mhaonacain, in the townland of Culfearna, parish of Annagh, barony of Costello, and county of Mayo. In a tract on the ancient state of Hy-Many, preserved in the Book of Lecan, fol. 92, it is stated that the River Suck flows from a well in Sliabh Formaili, now Sliaḃ ui ḟloinn. "Dealbna, ó áṫ liag co Suca mar

sion. Donough O'Flynn and Teige, his son, attacked their army, and killed one hundred of them, noble and plebeian, with Aitin Russell and his son, the five sons of Cuconnaught O'Conor, and others. The army then returned to their homes in sorrow.

Mulfavill O'Heyne was slain by the English.

Dermot Cleireach, son of Cormac Mac Dermott, died.

Aindiles Mag-Fhionnbharr [Maginver], Chief of Muintir-Gearadhain[r], died.

A castle was erected by Mac William Burke at Ath-angail, in Corran[s].

Machair O'Ruadhain [Rowan] was slain by the English in the doorway of the church of Kilsescnen[t].

Edwina, daughter of O'Flanagan, died.

An army was led by O'Donnell (Donnell Oge) into Connaught, and joined Hugh O'Conor at the Curlieu mountains. They proceeded from thence to Croghan, thence across the River Suck[u], and thence into Clanrickard; and they totally ravaged the country as far as Echtge and Galway. O'Conor then separated from O'Donnell; and O'Donnell proceeded across the Rivers Sruthair[w] and Rodhba[x], through Tirawley, and afterwards across the Moy, and obtained his full demands from all.

A great depredation was committed by Hugh, son of Felim, on the English

a mbpúċtan ar a tobar ag Sliab formaili." But the River Suck does not, properly speaking, issue from a mountain, nor from a well. Its source, which is called Bun Suicin, is a small pool of dirty mountain waters, lying at the west side of a low Esker or ridge. It oozes through the Esker, and appears at the east side of it, not as a well, but in scattered tricklings of bog water. From the east side of the Esker onwards, a small mountain stream, called the Suck, runs eastwards into Lough Ui Fhloinn, at Ballinlough; hence it winds its way in an eastern direction, and passes under the bridge of Castlereagh, where it turns southwards, and, passing through Ballymoe, Dunamon, Athleague, Mount Talbot, Belafeorin, and Ballinasloe, pays its tribute to the Shannon, near the village of Shannon Bridge. It flows through a very level country, and is remarkable for its sinuosity and inundations.

[w] *Sruthair.*—This is the ancient name of the Blackriver, which flows through the village of Shrule (to which it gives name), and forms, for some miles, the boundary between the counties of Mayo and Galway.

[x] *Rodhba*, now the River Robe, which flows by a circuitous course through the south of the county of Mayo, passing through the demesne of Castlemagarret, and through the town of Ballinrobe, to which it gives name, and discharges itself into Lough Mask, opposite the island of Inis Rodhba, which also derives its name from it.

cciarraiġe, ⁊ ro marbaḋ ſochaiḋe ṁor do ġallaiḃ laiſ, ⁊ do rat buar iomḃa uaiḋiḃ.

AOIS CRIOST, 1264.

Aoiſ Criоſt, mile, da ċéd, ſeſcat, a cſtaiр.

Aonġuſ ua clumain eſpuc luiġne do écc imairiſtir na búille iar ccur a eſpaccóide de ré chian roime ſin.

Coccaḋ eidir Art ua maoilſeaċluinn, ⁊ goill na miḋe. Ar do taḃairt laiſ orra iman mbroſnaiġ eidir marḃaḋ ⁊ baḋhaḋ.

Muirceartaċ mac domnaill uí airt do marḃaḋ, ⁊ a muintir do loſcaḋ lá donn máġ uiḋir.

Creaċ mór do dénaṁ do dealḃnaiḃ ar Shiol nanmċaḋa, ⁊ cuic meic uí maḋaḋain do marḃaḋ don toiſc ſin.

Coinni eidir iuſdiſ na hEreann (gona gallaiḃ im iarla ulaḋ, ⁊ im muiriſ mac geraiłt gona ccoimtionól lſt ar leṫ) ⁊ ſeḋlimiḋ ua Concoḃair gon a

y *Sliabh Lugha, and in Ciarraighe.*—These two territories are included in the present barony of Costello, in the south-east of the county of Mayo.—See them completely defined at pp. 150, 215, 216, *supra*.

z Under this year the Annals of Clonmacnoise, as translated by Mageoghegan, contain the following curious entry: "Ebdon, King of Denmark, died in the islands of the Orcades, as he was on his journey to come to Ireland."

a *O'Cluman*.—This name, which is still common in the counties of Sligo and Mayo, is now generally anglicised Coleman. Cluman would sound nearly as well; but Irish families in anglicising their names are not influenced by sound, but by the respectability of those families with whose names they assimilate their own.

b *Brosna*.—A river which flows through the county of Westmeath and the King's County, and pays its tribute to the Shannon, near Banagher.—See Colgan's *Trias Thaum.*, p. 159. In Mageoghegan's translation of the Annals of Clonmacnoise, this passage is rendered as follows: "A. D. 1264. Art mac Cormac mac Art O'Melaghlyn made great warrs upon the English of Meath, and made great slaughter upon them at the river of Brosnagh, where he that was not killed of them was drowned in that river."

c *Donn Maguire*.—According to the tradition in the country, this is the first of the Maguire family who became Chief of Fermanagh. His spirit is believed to haunt the mountain of Binn Eachlabhra, near Swadlinbar, where he forbodes the approaching death of the head of the Maguires, by throwing down a huge mass of the rocky face of the mountain.

d *Delvin [Eathra]*, i. e. the barony of Garrycastle, in the King's County.—See note [b], under the year 1178, p. 44.

e *Sil-Anmchadha*, i. e. the O'Maddens, in the barony of Longford, in the county of Galway.—See note [k], under the year 1178, p. 44.

of Sliabh Lugha, and in Ciarraighe[y]: great numbers of the English were killed by him, and he carried off many cows from them[z].

THE AGE OF CHRIST, 1264.

The Age of Christ, one thousand two hundred sixty-four.

Aengus O'Cluman[a], Bishop of Leyny, died in the Abbey of Boyle, having resigned his bishopric long before.

A war broke out between Art O'Melaghlin and the English of Meath; and he destroyed great numbers of them near the River Brosna[b], both by killing and drowning.

Murtough, son of Donnell O'Hart, was killed; and his people were burned by Donn Maguire[c].

A great depredation was committed by the inhabitants of Delvin [Eathra[d]] on the Sil-Anmchadha[e]; and the five sons of O'Madden were slain on the occasion.

A conference was held this year at Athlone between the Lord Justice of Ireland (attended by the English, the Earl of Ulster[f], and Maurice Fitzgerald,

[f] *The Earl of Ulster.*—This was Walter Burke, or De Burgo, the grandson of William Fitz-Adelm. According to the Dublin copy of the Annals of Innisfallen, he obtained this title in the year 1264, after his marriage with [Maud] the daughter of Hugh de Lacy the younger. Dr. Hanmer has the same statement under the same year. His words are as follows: "*Anno* 1264. *Walter Bourke*, commonly called *Walterus de Burgo*, was made Earle of Vlster, hee had married the daughter and heire of Sir *Hugh Delacy*, the younger, and in her right enjoyed the Earledome.

"The Booke of *Houth* layeth down the descent, that this *Walter*, by the said heire of Vlster Vlster had issue, *Walter* [*recte* Richard], and he had issue five daughters; 1. *Ellen*, that married *Robert le Bruse*, King of Scotland; 2. *Elizabeth*, that married the Earle of Gloster; 3. *Johan*, that married *Thomas*, Earle of Kildare; 4. *Katherine*, that married the Earle of Louth; 5. *Margaret*, that married the Earle of Desmond; 6. *Ellinor*, that married with the Lord *Multon*. Notwithstanding these honourble matches and amity concluded in the outward sight of the world, there rose deadly warres between the *Geraldines* and *Burks*, which wrought blood sheds, troubles, by partaking throughout the Realme of Ireland; at the same time the fury of the *Giraldins* was so outrageous, in so much that *Morice Fitz Maurice*, the second Earle of Desmond, opposed himselfe against the sword, and took at Tristledermote, now called Castle Dermocke, *Richard de Capella*, the Lord Iustice, *Theobald le Butler*, and *Iohn*, or *Millis de Cogan*, and committed them to the prisons in Leix and Donamus; but the

mac in Aṫ luain. Eaccla, ⁊ anḃáṫaḋ intinne do gabail na ngall od conncadar Rí Connaċt ⁊ a ṁac go lionmar lſirṫionoilte ag toċt ina ccoṁdáil. Gonaḋ í comairli ar ar cinnsead síṫ diarraiḋ orra. Aontaiġis Fedlimiḋ ⁊ maiṫe a muintire an tsíṫ do dénaṁ, ⁊ ro scarsat re roile go sioṫċanta iaroṁ.

Coccaḋ dergi edir mac uilliam burc (.i. iarla ulaḋ), ⁊ muiris mac gearailt, gur milleaḋ urmór Ereann ſtorra, gur gaḃ an tiarla araibi do caislénaiḃ i cconnaċtaib ag mac gearailt, gur loisc a mainer, ⁊ gur airgſstair a muintir.

Art ua maoilseaċloinn do loscaḋ araiḃe do ċaislenaiḃ ⁊ do sráitt-ḃailtiḃ i ndealḃna, a ccalroiġi, ⁊ a mbrſghmaine gur díoċuirſstair a ngoill estiḃ uili. Gabhais braighde a ttoiseaċ ar a haiṫle.

Iusdis na hEreann, Seoan gogan, ⁊ teboid buitelér do gabáil do muiris mac gerailt i ttempal coisreccṫa.

Caislen loċa measca ⁊ caislén Aird raṫain do gabail do mac uilliam.

Airdepscop Ardamacha Maolpattraicc ó Sccannaill do ṫabairt na mbraṫar minur go hArdmacha, ⁊ asé mac domnaill gallócclaċ (do reir gnattcuimne) do ṫionnsgain in mainestir sin do ṫógḃail ó ṫosaċ.

yeere following, *Henry* the third not pleased with these commotions and hurly burlies, by mature advice taken of his Councell, pacified the variance between them; discharged *Denny* [Denn] of his Iusticeship, and appointed *David Barry* Lord Iustice in his place."—*Hanmer's Chronicle*, Dublin edition of 1809, pp. 401, 402.

The Book of Howth is, however, wrong in this genealogy; for we know from more authentic Irish and English authorities, that Walter, the first of the De Burgo family, who became Earl of Ulster, was the father, and not the grandfather, of the ladies above enumerated; and, that his eldest son was named Richard, not Walter.

[g] *Burned his manors.*—This and the preceding entry are given as follows in Mageoghegan's translation of the Annals of Clonmacnoise: "A. D. 1264. The Lord Deputy of Ireland, the Earle of Ulster, Mac Gerald, and the English nobility of Ireland, had a meeting with Ffelym O'Connor, and with Hugh, his son, in Athlone. The English nobility, seeing the great multitutes of people follow Ffelym and his sonn, were strocken with great fear; whereupon they advised with themselves that it were better for them to be in peace with Ffelym and his son, than in continual dissention, which [peace] was accepted of by Ffelym and concluded by them.

"Also there arose dissention between Mac William Burk, the Earl of Ulster, and Mac Gerald this year, [so] that the most part of the kingdome was brought to utter ruin by reason of all their warrs against one another, in so much that the said Earle took all the castles of Mac Gerald in Connought into his own hands, and burnt and destroyed all his manours."

[h] *Street-towns*, i. e. villages consisting of one street, without being defended by a castle.

with their respective forces), on the one side, and Felim O'Conor and his son on the other. The English were seized with fear and perplexity of mind when they saw the King of Connaught and his son approaching them with a numerous and complete muster of their forces, and came to the resolution of suing for peace. Felim and the chiefs of his people consented to make the peace, and they afterwards separated on amicable terms.

A war broke out between Mac William Burke (Earl of Ulster) and Maurice Fitzgerald, so that the greater part of Ireland was destroyed between them. The Earl took all the castles that Fitzgerald possessed in Connaught, burned his manors[g], and plundered his people.

Art O'Melaghlin burned all the castles and street-towns[h] in Delvin, Calry, and Brawney, and drove the English out of all of them; he then took hostages from their chieftains[i].

The Lord Justice of Ireland[j], John Goggan[k], and Theobald Butler, were taken prisoners by Maurice Fitzgerald in a consecrated church[l].

The castle of Lough Mask and the castle of Ardrahin were taken by Mac William Burke.

The Archbishop of Armagh, Maelpatrick O'Scannal, brought the Friars Minor to Armagh; and (according to tradition), it was Mac Donnell Galloglagh[m] that commenced the erection of the monastery.

[i] *From their chieftains*, that is, from the Irish chieftains whom he placed over these territories after the expulsion of the English. These were Mac Coghlan, Magawley, and O'Breen. The Delvin here mentioned is the present barony of Garrycastle, Mac Coghlans' country, in the King's County. Calry comprised all the parish of Ballyloughloe, in Westmeath, and Brawney is still the name of a barony adjoining Athlone and the Shannon in the same county, in which the O'Breens are still numerous, but have changed the name to O'Brien.

[j] *The Lord Justice.*—He was Richard de Rupella, or Capella.

[k] *John Goggan.*—In Mageoghegan's translation of the Annals of Clonmacnoise he is called John Cowgan, which seems more correct. The name is now usually written Goggan, and is very common all over the south of Ireland, particularly in the county of Cork.

[l] *In a consecrated church.*—This was the church of Castledermot, in the county of Kildare.—See Annals of Ireland by Camden and Grace. In the Dublin copy of the Annals of Innisfallen this passage is incorrectly given under the year 1266. According to Camden and Hanmer the prisoners were confined in the castles of Dunamase and Ley, then in the possession of the Geraldines.

[m] *Mac Donnell Galloglagh* of the Gallowglasses, or heavy-armed Irish soldiers, was chief of Clann Kelly, in Fermanagh.

AOIS CRIOST, 1265.

Aois Criost, míle, dá ċéd, sescat, acúicc.

Tomas mac Fearġail meic Diarmada espuc Oilfinn, Tomas ua Maicin espuc Luigne, ⁊ Maolbriġde uá Gruccáin airċinneaċ Oilefinn do écc.

Muiris mac Nell uí Concoḃair do toġa do cum espucóide Oilefinn.

Caislén Sliccigh do sgaoileaḋ la hAoḋ ua cConcoḃair, ⁊ la hua nDoṁnaill. Caislen an ḃFinnatta, ⁊ caislen Ráṫa aird craoiḃe do loscaḋ ⁊ do scaoil-eaḋ leó beós.

Mainistir Topair Patraicc do losccaḋ.

Tadg mag Fionnḃarr do marḃaḋ do Concoḃar mag Raġnaill ⁊ do mac Doṁnaill uí Fearġail.

Feḋlimiḋ mac Caṫail croiḃdeirg uí Concoḃair Ri Connaċt, fear cosanta ⁊ coṫaiġṫi a cuicciḋ féin, ⁊ a ċarad for gaċ taoiḃ, fear ionnarbṫa ⁊ airgṫe a easscarat, fear lan deineċ, deangnaṁ, ⁊ doirdercus, fear méa-daighṫe ord eccailseaċ, ⁊ ealadan, dosġadḃar ríġ Ereann ar uaisli, ar cruṫ, ar cróḋacht, ar ċéill, ar iocht, ar ḟírinne do écc iar mbuaiḋ nongṫa ⁊ naiṫrighi i mainistir braṫar .S. domenic i Roscomáin tucc féin roiṁe sin do Dia ⁊ don urd. Aoḋ ua Concoḃair a mac féin do ríogaḋ uas Connachtaiḃ dá és, ⁊ a creaċ ríġi do dénaṁ do ar uiḃ Failġe, ⁊ iar niompúḋ

[n] *Beannada*, now Banada, a small village near which are the ruins of an abbey, in the barony of Leyny, and county of Sligo.

[o] *Rath-ard-Creeva*.—This name is now obsolete.

[p] *Toberpatrick*, i. e. the great abbey of Ballintober, in the county of Mayo.

[q] *Mag-Finnvar*.—He was Chief of Muintir-Geran, a territory on the west side of Lough Gowna, in the north of the county of Longford

[r] *Felim*.—This passage is rendered as follows in Mageoghegan's translation of the Annals of Clonmacnoise:

"Felym mac Cahall Crovedearg O'Connor, king of Connoght, defender of his own province and Friends every where, and destroyer and banisher of his Enemies, where he could find them: one full of bounty, prowess" [eangnaṁ], "and magnanimity, both in England and Ireland, died penitently, and was buried in the Fryers Preachers' (monastery) of Roscommon, which he himself before granted to the said order, in honor of God and St Dominick. After whose death his own son, Hugh O'Connor (a vallarous and sturdy man), tooke upon him the name of King of Connought, and immediately made his first regal prey upon the countrey of Affailie, made great burnings and outrages in that countrey, and from thence returned to Athlone, where he put out the eyes of Cahall Mac Teige O'Connor, who, soone after the losing his eyes, died."

THE AGE OF CHRIST, 1265.

The Age of Christ, one thousand two hundred sixty-five.

Thomas, the son of Farrell Mac Dermot, Bishop of Elphin; Thomas O'Maicin, Bishop of Leyny; and Maelbrighde O'Grugan, Erenagh of Elphin, died.

Maurice, the son of Niall O'Conor, was elected to the bishopric of Elphin.

The castle of Sligo was demolished by Hugh O'Conor and O'Donnell. The castle of Beannada[n] and the castle of Rath-ard-Creeva[o] were also burned and destroyed by them.

The monastery of Toberpatrick[p] was burned.

Teige Mag-Finnvar[q] was slain by Conor Mac Rannal and the son of Donnel O'Farrell.

Felim[r], son of Cathal Crovderg O'Conor, the defender and supporter of his own province, and of his friends on every side; the expeller and plunderer of his foes,—a man full of hospitality, prowess[s], and renown; the exalter of the clerical orders and men of science; a worthy materies of a King of Ireland for his nobility, personal shape, heroism, wisdom, clemency, and truth, died, after the victory of [Extreme] Unction and penance, in the monastery of the Dominican Friars, at Roscommon[t], which he himself had granted to God and that order. Hugh O'Conor, his own son, was inaugurated king over the Connacians, as his successor. Hugh committed his regal depredation[u] in Offaly[w], and on his

[s] *Prowess*, eangnam, is used throughout these Annals in the sense of prowess or dexterity at arms.—See extract from the Annals of Kilronan, at the year 1235, where the phrase ro sgeimh eangnamha is used to express "with credit for prowess."

[t] *Roscommon*. — Dr. O'Conor, in his suppressed work, *Memoirs of the Life and Writings of Charles O'Conor of Belanagare*, writes, p. 43: "Felim was interred in his own abbey of Roscommon, and his monument, of which Mr. Walker has given a drawing in his Dress of the ancient Irish, is an object of melancholy curiosity to this day." And he adds in a note:— "Mr. Grose has given a faithful view of this abbey. The steeple of the abbey, of late undermined by a gentleman who wished to procure materials for building a house, fell about two years ago" [he was writing in 1796], "and the monument of Felim is covered with rubbish and with ruins." The Editor examined this monument in 1837, when it was very much injured, but could discover no fragment of an inscription upon it.

[u] *Regal depredation*, a chreach righi.—It appears that every king after his inauguration was expected to achieve some grand act of depredation.

[w] *Offaly*, a territory of considerable extent in

do go háṫ luain Caṫal mac taiḋcc uí concoḃair do dallaḋ lais, ⁊ a écc da ḃíthin.

Muirceartaċ mac caṫail mic diarmata mic taidg uí maoilruanaiḋ tiġearna muiġe luirg dég.

Giolla na naoṁ ua cuinn taoiseaċ muintire giollccáin, Caṫal mag raġnaill taoiseaċ muintire heolais, ⁊ Muireaḋaċ ua cearbaill taoiseaċ calroiġi do ecc ḃeós.

Coinne do denaṁ do Tomaltach ua Concoḃair (.i. airdespuc tuama) re dauiṫ prinndergás ⁊ re macaiḃ murchaḋa. Mórán do muintir an airdes-puic do marbaḋ an lá sin dóiḃ a ccill meaḋoin.

Dearbforgaill ingḟn ui dubda (maṫair an airdespuic thomaltaiġ uí Concoḃair) décc iar mbuaiḋ, ⁊c.

AOIS CRIOST, 1266.

Aois Criosd, mile, dá ċéd, sescat, asé.

Graḋa espuicc do tabairt ar braṫair dord .S. domenic (.i. ua Scopa) in ard Maċa do cum beiṫ i Raiṫ boṫ dó.

Tomas ua maolconaire aircideochain Tuama, ⁊ Maoilisu ua hanainn prioir Rosa commain, ⁊ Aṫa liacc, do écc.

Tomas ua miadaċain do gabail espocóide luigne.

Toġa espuicc do toċt on Róiṁ go cluain ferta brenainn, ⁊ graḋa espuicc do tabairt do fḟin ⁊ do tomas ó miadaċáin in Aṫ na ríoġ an dom-naċ ria Nodlaic.

Doṁnall ua hEġra tiġearna luigne do marbaḋ do gallaiḃ, ⁊ é ag loscaḋ Aird na riaġ.

Leinster.—See note [g], under the year 1178, p. 44; and note [e], under the year 1193, p. 96.

[x] *David Prendergast.*—The seal of this chief still exists, as would appear from an impression of it in the museum of Mr. Petrie. It bears his arms on a shield, and the legend is, "S. DAVID DE PRENDERGAST."

[y] *Kilmaine*, cill meaḋoin, i. e. the middle church, a parish and village in a barony of the same name, in the south of the county of Mayo. Harris, in his edition of Ware's Bishops, p. 607, says that this quarrel took place "at Kilmethan, a manor belonging to the archbishoprick."

[a] *Athleague*, aṫ liag.—This is aṫ liag maenacain, a village and parish on the River Suck, in the north-west of the barony of Athlone, in the county of Roscommon. It is to be distinguished from Athliag na Sinna, now Ballyleague, at

return to Athlone put out the eyes of Cathal, son of Teige O'Conor, who died in consequence.

Murtough, son of Cathal, the son of Dermot, son of Teige O'Mulrony, Lord of Moylurg, died.

Gilla-na-naev O'Quin, Chief of Muintir-Gillagan, Cathal Mac Rannall, Chief of Muintir-Eolais, and Murray O'Carroll, Chief of Calry, died.

A conference was held by Tomaltagh O'Conor (Archbishop of Tuam) with David Prendergast[x] and the Mac Murroughs; and many of the Archbishop's people were slain on that day by them at Kilmaine[y].

Dervorgilla, daughter of O'Dowda (the mother of the Archbishop Tomaltagh O'Conor), died, after the victory, &c.

THE AGE OF CHRIST, 1266.

The Age of Christ, one thousand two hundred sixty-six.

The dignity of bishop was conferred at Armagh on a friar of the order of St. Dominic (i. e. O'Scopa), and he was appointed to Raphoe.

Thomas O'Mulconry, Archdeacon of Tuam, and Maelisa O'Hanainn, Prior of Roscommon and Athleague[z], died.

Thomas O'Meehan[a] became Bishop of Leyny.

A bishop-elect[b] came from Rome to Clonfert-Brendan, and the dignity of bishop was conferred on him, and on Thomas O'Meehan, at Athenry, on the Sunday before Christmas.

Donnell O'Hara was killed by the English while he was in the act of burning Ardnarea[c].

Lanesborough, in the same county.

[a] *Thomas O'Meehan.*—In Harris's edition of Ware's Bishops, p. 659, he is called Dennis O'Miachan. His predecessor was Thomas.

[b] *Bishop-elect.*—Ware calls him John, an Italian, the Pope's nuncio; and says that he sat for many years, and was at last, in 1296, translated to the archbishopric of Benevento, in Italy. Ware thought that "the fair frontispiece at the west end of the church, adorned with a variety of statues of excellent workmanship," was built by him; but there can be little doubt that this frontispiece, or ornamented doorway, is at least two centuries older than his time.—See Harris's edition of Ware's Bishops, p. 639.

[c] *Ardnarea,* i. e. the height or hill of executions, now Anglicised Ardnaree. It may be now said to form the eastern part of the town of Ballina. On an old map of the coasts of Mayo, Sligo, and Donegal, preserved in the State Pa-

Mathgamain mac cSitriucc ui cSitriucc tigearna ciarraige do marbad la gallaib.

Mathgamain ua cuilSin tigearna claonglaisi do marbadh dá mnaoi féin den buille do Sccin tré éd.

Caislén tighi da choinne do bhriseadh, ⁊ Conmaicne uile dfásughadh.

Toirrdhealbhach mac Aodha mic cathail croibhdeirg décc i mainistir chnuic Muaide.

Diarmait ruadh mac Concobair mic corbmaic meic diarmata, ⁊ donnchathaigh mac duinn óicc még oirechtaigh do dallad daodh ua Concobair.

Buirgér beoil an tachair do loscadh do Flann ruadh ua Floinn, ⁊ morán do gallaibh an baile do marbadh dó.

Aodh ua Concobair Rí Connacht do dul isin mbreifne daithríoghadh Airt mic cathail riabhaigh, ⁊ tighearnus breifne do tabairt dó do concobar buidhe mac amhlaoibh mic airt uí ruairc, ⁊ braighde taoiseach na breifni uili do gabháil.

Sluaigheadh la huilliam búrc do soighidh uí maoilseachlainn. Morán do báthadh díbh in ath crochda, ⁊ a niompudh gan nSirt gan braighde do gabháil.

Ar mór do thabairt do droing do muintir ui concobair, .i. do Lochlainn mac diarmata mic muirchSirtaigh, do mac cSitriucc, ⁊ do mac domhnaill duibh ui Eaghra, ar bhSitnachaibh, ⁊ ar luighnibh in iarthar Connacht, ⁊ én ceann dég ar fichit do tiodhlacadh go hua cconcobair dóibh.

Corbmac mac giolla criost meic diarmada do lot, ⁊ a ecc trSimhid.

Sadb ingean cathail croibhdeirg, ⁊ Maoileoin bodhar ua maoilconaire ollamh Sil muireadhaigh i Seanchus do écc.

Maolpatraic ó Scandail Priomhaidh Aird macha do tabairt bráthar mionur go hard macha, ⁊ lSithaindíog lándomhain do dénamh lais im an eacclais iaramh.

pers Office, it is called "Monasturie, and Castle of Ardnaree."

[d] *O'Cuileain.*—This name is now Anglicised Collins all over the south of Ireland.

[e] *Claenghlais*, now Clonlish, a wild district in the barony of Upper Connello, in the southwest of the county of Limerick, adjoining the counties of Kerry and Cork. O'Cuilcain was originally Chief of Hy-Conaill-Gaura; but his territory was at this period narrowed by the encroachments of the English settlers.

[f] *Tigh da Choinne*, now Tiaquin in the county of Galway. The Conmaicne here mentioned must be Conmaicne Kinel-Dubhain, now the barony of Dunmore, in the county of Galway, and not the Conmaicne on the east side of the Shannon.

[g] *Bel-an-tachair*, now Ballintogher, a small

Mahon, son of Kehernagh O'Kerrin, Lord of Ciarraighe [in the County of Mayo], was slain by the English.

Mahon O'Cuilein[d], Lord of Claenghlaisi[e], was killed by his own wife with one stab of a knife, given through jealousy.

The castle of Tigh-da-Choinne[f] was demolished, and all Conmaicne was laid waste.

Turlough, son of Hugh, the son of Cathal Crovderg, died in the monastery of Knockmoy [in the county of Galway].

Dermot Roe, son of Conor, the son of Cormac Mac Dermot, and Donncahy, son of Donn Oge Mageraghty, were blinded by Hugh O'Conor.

The borough of Bel-an-tachair[g] was burned by Flann Roe O'Flynn, and many of the English of the town were slain by him.

Hugh O'Conor, King of Connaught, went into Breifny to depose Art, son of Cathal Reagh; and he gave the lordship of Breifny to Conor Boy, son of Auliffe, the son of Art O'Rourke, and took hostages from all the chiefs of Breifny.

An army was led by William Burke against O'Melaghlin; but many of his troops were drowned in Ath-Crochda[h], and he returned without conquest or hostages.

A party of O'Conor's people, namely, Loughlin, son of Dermot, who was son of Murtough [O'Conor], Mac Keherny, and the son of Donnell Duv O'Hara, made a great slaughter of the Welshmen[i] and the people of Leyny in West Connaught; and thirty-one of their heads were brought to O'Conor.

Cormac, son of Gilchreest Mac Dermot, received a wound, of which he died.

Sabia, daughter of Cathal Crovderg, and Malone Bodhar [the Deaf] O'Mulconry, Ollav of Sil-Murray in history, died.

Maelpatrick O'Scannal, Primate of Armagh, brought the Friars Minor to Armagh, and afterwards cut a broad and deep trench around their church.

village, near the boundary of the county of Leitrim, in the barony of Tirerill, and county of Sligo.

[h] *Ath-Crochda.*—More usually written Ath-Crocha. It was the name of a ford on the Shannon, at the place now called Shannon Harbour.—See *Tribes and Customs of Hy-Many*, note [g], p. 5, and map to the same work. See also note under the year 1547.

[i] *Welshmen.*—These were the Joyces, Bar-

AOIS CRIOST, 1267.

Aois Criost, mile, da ċéd, seasccat. a seaċt.

Epscop cluana ferta, .i. Rómanaċ do dul do soiġidh an ṗapa.

Murċadh mac Suiḃne do gabail in umall do domnall mac maġnusa uí Concoḃair, a tabairt ar laiṁ an iarla, ⁊ a écc i bpriosún aicce.

Brian mac toirrdhealḃaiġ mic Ruaidhri ui concoḃair do écc i mainistir ċnuic muaidhe.

Creaċ do denaṁ do mac uilliam ar ua cconcoḃair gur airgsiodair tir maine ⁊ clann uadaċ.

Creaċ do denaṁ do gallaiḃ iarṫair Connaċt i ccairpre droma cliaḃ, ⁊ Eas dara darccain dóiḃ.

Donnchadh mac Ruaidhri mic aoḋa ui concoḃair do marḃadh la gallaiḃ.

Galar treablaideaċ do gabail Ríġ Connaċt go ndeachaidh a ṫásc fo Erinn.

Alis ingean meic carrgamna do écc.

Aodh ua muirsidhaiġ taoiseaċ an lagáin do ṁarḃadh i ccill Alaidh la hua Maoilḟoġmair comarba na cille dia doṁnaiġ iar neisteaċt oiffrind.

AOIS CRIOST, 1268.

Aois Criost, míle, dá ċéd, seasccat, a hoċt.

Aodh mac Concoḃair uí flaiṫḃeartaiġ oiffícel Eanaiġ dúin do écc.

Tempall mór Arda maċa do tionnscnadh las an bpriomaidh, giollapatraicc ó Scandail.

Concobar ruadh ua briain tiġearna tuadhmuṁan, Seoinin a mac, a ingen,

retts, Merricks, Hostys, and others.—See *Genealogies, Tribes, and Customs of Hy-Fiachrach*, pp. 324–339.

[j] *Mac Sweeny.*—This is the first notice of the family of Mac Sweeny occurring in these Annals.

[k] *The Earl*, i. e. Walter Burke, or De Burgo, who was made Earl of Ulster in 1264.

[l] *Tir-Many*, i. e. Hy-Many, O'Kelly's country, in the counties of Roscommon and Galway.

[m] *Clann-Uadagh.*—O'Fallon's country, in the barony of Athlone, and county of Roscommon.—See note [r], under the year 1225, p. 236.

[n] *Mac Carroon.*—According to O'Flaherty, Mac Carrghamhna was seated in the barony of Cuircnia, or Kilkenny West, in the county of Westmeath.

THE AGE OF CHRIST, 1267.

The Age of Christ, one thousand two hundred sixty-seven.

The Bishop of Clonfert, who was a Roman, went over to the Pope.

Murrough Mac Sweeny[j] was taken prisoner in Umallia by Donnell, son of Manus O'Conor, who delivered him up to the Earl[k], in whose prison he died.

Brian, son of Turlough, who was son of Roderic O'Conor, died in the monastery of Knockmoy.

A depredation was committed by Mac William on O'Conor; and he plundered Tir-Many[l] and Clann-Uadagh[m].

A depredation was committed by the English of West Connaught in Carbury of Drumcliff, and they plundered Easdara [Ballysadare].

Donough, son of Rory, the son of Hugh O'Conor, was slain by the English.

A dangerous disease attacked the King of Connaught; and the report of it spread all over Ireland.

Alice, daughter of Mac Carroon[n], died.

Hugh O'Murray, Chief of Lagan[o], was slain at Killala by O'Mulfover, coarb of the church, on a Sunday, after hearing mass.

THE AGE OF CHRIST, 1268.

The Age of Christ, one thousand two hundred sixty-eight.

Hugh, son of Conor O'Flaherty, Official of Annadown, died.

The Great Church of Armagh was begun by the Primate, Gillapatrick O'Scannal.

Conor Roe O'Brien, Lord of Thomond, Seoinin, his son, his daughter, his

[o] *Lagan.*—The name and extent of this territory are still remembered. It is situated in the north of the barony of Tirawley, in the county of Mayo. It originally comprised the parishes of Kilbride and Doonfeeny, and extended eastwards to the strand of Lacken, where it adjoined the territory of Caeille Conaill. The O'Murrays were soon after dispossessed by the Barretts and Lynotts.—See *Genealogies, Tribes, and Customs of Hy-Fiachrach*, pp. 222, 223, notes [x] and [y].

Under the year 1267, the Dublin copy of the Annals of Innisfallen contain an account of the revolt of the tribes of Thomond against Conor na Siudaine O'Brien, of which the Four Masters have collected no account.

mac a inġine, .i. mac Ruaiḋri uí grada, dubloċlainn ua loċlainn, tomas ua beollain, ⁊ Soċaiḋe oile do marḃaḋ la diarmait mac muirċertaiġ ui briain ⁊ é féin do marḃaḋ inn iaraṁ. Ḃrian mac concoḃair uí briain do gaḃail tigearnais tuaḋmuman ar a haiṫle.

Toirrḋealḃaċ óg mac aoḋa mic feḋlimiḋ mic caṫail croiḃdeirg, dalta ua mbriúin eriḋe, do écc.

Aṁlaoiḃ ua fearġail tuir cosanta conmaicneaċ do marḃaḋ la gallaiḃ i ḃfell.

Concoḃar ua ceallaiġ tiġearna ua maine, Aongus ua dalaiġ Saoi ḟir dána ⁊ tiġe aoidheaḋ, Maġnus mag oirechtaiġ taoiseaċ cloinne tomaltaiġ, Doṁnall ua gradda taoiseaċ cenel dunġaile, ⁊ Duḃġall mac Ruaiḋri, tiġearna innsi gall, ⁊ airir gaoiḋeal do écc.

Muiris ruaḋ mac gearailt do ḃáthaḋ for muir go luċt luingi imaille ris ag toiḋecht ó Shaxaiḃ.

Ionnsaiġiḋ do taḃairt daoḋ ua concoḃair for gallaiḃ go haṫ luain. Na goill do toċt ina coinne gus na feadhaiḃ, tachor do cur eatorra, ḃriseaḋ for gallaib, ⁊ Sochaiḋe diḃ do marḃaḋ.

Donn mac taiḋg uí mannaċáin, ⁊ deiċneaḃar dá muintir do marbaḋ do taḋg ua ḟlannaccáin ⁊ do giolla criost ua birn.

Fearġal ua maoilmuaiḋ taoiseaċ fear cceall, ⁊ Maoilseaċlainn mag coċlain do marḃaḋ la gallaiḃ.

Aenġus ua maoilfoġmair do ṁarḃaḋ la huiḃ Muireaḋaiġ i ndioġail a ccinn ḟine.

[p] *Airer-Gaedheal*, i. e. the district or territory of the Gaels. This is the name by which Argyle, now Argyleshire in Scotland, is always called by correct Irish and Erse writers.

[q] *Maurice Roe Fitzgerald.*—This passage is given as follows in the Annals of Clonmacnoise as translated by Mageoghegan: "A. D. 1268. Morish Roe Mac Gerald was drownded in the sea coming from English to this kingdome, and a shipp full of passengers, being his own people, were drownded too." Sir Richard Cox says, in his *Hibernia Anglicana*, p. 70, that this Maurice Fitzgerald was not of Desmond, as the Annals say, but the son of Maurice, who was Lord Justice in 1272.

[r] *Faes*, na feaḋa, i. e. the woods. This was the name of O'Naghtan's country, in the barony of Athlone, and county of Roscommon. In an inquisition taken at Roscommon on the 26th of October, 1587, this territory is called "Les Ffaes, alias O'Naghten's Cuntry;" and it appears from another inquisition taken at the same place, on the 23rd of October, 1604, that "the territory of the Ffaes, or O'Naghten's Cuntry, contained thirty quarters of land."

[s] *With the loss of many.*—This passage is very

daughter's son, i. e. the son of Rory O'Grady, Duvloughlin O'Loughlin, Thomas O'Beollan, and a number of others, were slain by Dermot, the son of Murtough O'Brien, for which he himself was afterwards killed; and Brian, the son of Conor O'Brien, then assumed the lordship of Thomond.

Turlough Oge, the son of Hugh, son of Felim, son of Cathal Crovderg, the foster-son of the Hy-Briuin, died.

Auliffe O'Farrell, Tower of Protection to the Conmaicni, was treacherously slain by the English.

Conor O'Kelly, Lord of Hy-Many; Aengus O'Daly, a man eminent for poetry, and keeper of a house of hospitality; Manus Mageraghty, Chief of Clann-Tomalty; Donnell O'Grady, Chief of Kinel-Dongaly; and Dugald Mac Rory, Lord of Insi-Gall, and of Airer-Gaedheal[p] [Argyle], died.

Maurice Roe Fitzgerald[q] was drowned in the sea, together with a ship's crew, while on his return from England.

Hugh O'Conor set out for Athlone against the English, who came to the Faes[r] to oppose him; and a battle was fought between them, in which the English were defeated, with the loss of many[s].

Donn, son of Teige O'Monahan[ss], was slain, together with ten of his people, by Teige O'Flanagan and Gilchreest O'Beirne.

Farrell O'Molloy, Chief of Fircall, and Melaghlin Mac Coghlan, were slain by the English.

Aengus O'Mulfover was slain by the O'Murrays, in revenge of their Kennfinè[t].

abruptly constructed in the original. The literal translation of it is as follows: "An incursion was made by Hugh O'Conor upon the English to Athlone. The English came against him to the Faes. A battle was fought between them. A breach upon the English, and many of them were killed. The correct grammatical construction would read as follows: tuc aoḋ ua Conċoḃuir ionnsaiġiḋ go hAṫluain for Ġallaiḃ; do ċuaiḋ na goill ina ċoinne gus na Feaḋaiḃ, agus do cuireaḋ caṫ eatorra, i n-ar brisead for ġallaiḃ, agus i n-ar marḃaḋ socaiḋe ḋioḃ.

[ss] *O'Monahan.*—The head of this family was chief of the beautiful district of Tir-Briuin, lying between Elphin and Jamestown, in the east of the county of Roscommon, and had his residence at Lissadorn, near Elphin, till shortly after this period, when they were dispossessed by the O'Beirnes, who are still numerous and respectable in the territory.

[t] *Kenfinne*, ceann fine, i. e. head of a sept or tribe. This term is generally applied to the heads of minor families. There is a very curious dispute concerning the exact meaning of it in a report of a pleading between Teige O'Doyne, chief of Oregan, and his brother, Doctor Charles Dunne, preserved in Marsh's Library, Dublin, Class No. 3. Tab. 2. No. 26. pp. 221, 331.

AOIS CRIOST, 1269.

Aois Criost, míle, da ċéd, Sescat, anaoí.

Dauith ua bragain espucc cloċair do écc, ⁊ a aḋnacul i mainistir melifoint uair ba manaċ da manchaiḃ é.

Taḋg mac nell mic muireadhaiġ ui concoḃair do marḃaḋ in oilfinn dócc-láċ do muintir a ḃraṫar féin, ⁊ an tí do rinne an gníoṁ sin do tuitim inn.

Iomur ua birn ócclaċ ⁊ lainḟear grada aoḋa uí Concoḃair do ċor an tsaoġail de ar lár a cloinne ⁊ a ċonáiċ, ⁊ dul go mainistir Rosa comáin dó, gur caiṫ an seal baoí roime da saoġal eidir ḃraiṫriḃ .S. Domenic.

Brian mac doṁnaill duiḃ ui Eaġra do marḃaḋ do gallaiḃ i Sliccaċ.

Benmiḋe inġean toirrḋealḃaiġ meic Ruaiḋri, bḟn maolmuire meic Suiḃne, Seaffraiġ mac doṁnaill clannaiġ meic giollapatraicc tiġearna sleḃe blaḋma, ⁊ Aoḋ ua fionnaċta Saoí tiompánoiġ do écc.

Echmiliḋ macairtén do marḃaḋ dua anluain.

Domnall ua fearġoil, ⁊ aoḋ a mac, cáraid deġeiniġ dḟrlaiġṫeaċ do ṁarḃaḋ do giolla na naoṁ ua fḟrġail ⁊ do ġallaiḃ.

Cristina inġean uí neachtain bḟn diarmada miḋiġ meic diarmata, bḟn do bḟḟrr eneaċ ⁊ ionnracus don cineaḋ dá mbaoí, ⁊ as mó do ċuir dá comaoin ar an ord liaṫ do écc iar mbuaiḋ naiṫriġe.

Caislén Sliccíġ do denaṁ la mac muiris meic gearailt iar na ḃriseaḋ daoḋ ua Concoḃair ⁊ dua doṁnaill roime sin.

[u] *David O'Bragan.*—In Harris's edition of Ware's Bishops, he is called David O'Brogan.—See p. 182. In the Dublin copy of the Annals of Ulster, his death is entered under the year 1267, thus: "David ua Bragan Eps. Clochair, qui uirtuose et fideliter pro defensione iusticie ecclesie Clochorensis per tempus uite eius laborauit obiit hoc anno, &c."

[v] *Monks,* i. e. he had retired into the monastery some time before his death.

[w] *Duv,* duḃ, i. e. Black.

[x] *Of Slieve Bloom,* sleḃe blaḋma, a mountain on the confines of the King's and Queen's counties. Ussher calls it *Mons Bladina* by a mistake, in *Primordia*, p. 962, which O'Flaherty corrects in *Ogygia*, p. 3, c. 3. It was originally called Sliabh Smoil. See *Ogygia*, p. iii. c. 81, and *Vita Sancti Moluæ*, given by Colgan in his *Acta Sanctorum*, at 26th March.

[y] *Mac Artan* was Chief of Kinelarty, in the county of Down.

[z] *O'Hanlon* was Chief of Oriel, in the county of Armagh.

[a] *Two.*—Cáraid means a brace, pair, or couple.

[b] *Christina.*—The character of O'Naghtan's daughter is thus given in Mageoghegan's trans-

THE AGE OF CHRIST, 1269.

The Age of Christ, one thousand two hundred sixty-nine.

David O'Bragan[u], Bishop of Clogher, died, and was interred in the monastery of Mellifont, for he had been one of its monks[v].

Teige, son of Niall, the son of Murray O'Conor, was slain at Elphin, by a youth of his own brother's people; and the person by whom the deed was perpetrated was killed for it.

Ivor O'Beirne, chief servant and confidant of Hugh O'Conor, withdrew from the world, from the midst of his children and affluence, and entered the monastery of Roscommon, where he passed the rest of his life among the Dominican friars.

Brian, son of Donnell Duv[w] O'Hara, was slain by the English of Sligo.

Benmee, daughter of Turlough (son of Roderic O'Conor), and wife of Mulmurry Mac Sweeny; Jeffrey, son of Donnell Clannagh Mac Gillapatrick, Lord of Slieve Bloom[x]; and Hugh O'Finaghty, a learned minstrel, died.

Eghmily Mac Artan[y] was slain by O'Hanlon[z].

Donnell O'Farrell and Hugh, his son, two[a] truly hospitable and munificent men, were slain by Gilla-na-naev O'Farrell and the English.

Christina[b], daughter of O'Naghtan, and wife of Dermot Midheach Mac Dermot, the most hospitable and chaste[c] woman of her tribe, and the most bountiful to the order of Grey Friars, died, after the victory of penance[d].

The castle of Sligo was rebuilt by the son of Maurice Fitzgerald, after it had been demolished by Hugh O'Conor and O'Donnell.

lation of the Annals of Clonmacnoise: "Christin, O'Neaghtean's daughter, the wife of Dermod Myegh Mac Dermoda, a right exceeding beautiful woman, well lymmed, bountiful in bestowing, chaste of her body, and ingenious and witty delivery of her mind, devout in her prayers, and, finally, she was inferior to none other of her time for any good parts requisite in a noble gentlewoman, and charitable towards the order of Graye moncks, died with good penance."

[c] *The most hospitable and chaste.*—Literally, of the best hospitality and purity. Her character is stated in more correct language in the Annals of Ulster, and thus rendered in the old translation: *Anno* 1268 (rectius 1270). "Christina Ny-Neghtain, Dermot Myegh Mac Dermot's wife, a woman of best name and quality that was in her time, and that gave most to the White Order, *quievit.*"

[d] *Penance*, αιτριγe.—This word is generally used by the Four Masters, where the Annals of Ulster have *penitentia.*

Caislén Rosa comáin do denaṁ la Roibert deford iusdís na herionn, ⁊ aresaḋ fo dísa a denam, Aoḋ ua Concoḃair Rí Connaċt do beṫ easslan, ionnus nar tualaing taċar no teaccḃail do taḃairt do gallaiḃ, na toirmíscc do ċor ar an ccaislén do denaṁ. Connaċtaiġ do beiṫ ina cceḋiḃ creaċ (go herġi doraṁ doriḋise.) fo coraiḃ gall.

Flaithbertaċ ua Maoilḟiona taoiseaċ leithe Calraiġe Mhaighe héleóg do marḃaḋ dó gaiḃteacháin dó lethtaoiseach oile.

AOIS CRIOST, 1270.

Aois Criost, míle, da ċéd, seachtmogat.

Maolpattraicc ua Scandail airdespucc Aird maċa do dul do láṫair Riġ Saxan. An Rí da glacaḋ go honórac, ⁊ toiḋecht tar a ais dó imaille re mor ċumaċtaiḃ.

Coccaḋ mor eidir ua cconcoḃair ⁊ iarla ulaḋ uater a búrc, gur ṫionóil an tiarla maiṫe gall ereann im an ngiusdis, ⁊ a rann gaoideal

[e] *Robert de Ufford,* Roibert deford.—In the Annals of Ulster he is called Roibert dufford. According to the list of the Chief Governors of Ireland, given in Harris's edition of Ware's Antiquities, Robert de Ufford was Lord Justice of Ireland in 1268; and Richard de Oxonia, or D'Exeter, was Lord Justice in 1269. In Mageoghegan's translation of the Annals of Clonmacnoise, he is incorrectly called Hobert, or Robert Sufford, or Stafford. The entry is worded as follows: "A. D. 1269. Hobert or Robert Sufford, or Stafford, came over from England as Deputie of this kingdome, apointed by the King of England for the reformation of the lawes, customes, and statutes of this land, and made his first voyage" [expedition] "with his forces to Connaught, and, by the help of the English forces of Ireland, he built a castle at Roscommon. The opportunity and occasion of building of the said castle was, because Hugh O'Connor, King of Connaught, fell sick of a grievous disease, supposed to be irrecoverable."

[f] *O'Maelfina*, pronounced O'Molina, or O'Mulleena, but now generally Anglicised Mullany. The little town of Crossmolina, called in Irish, cros ui Mhaoilḟína, i. e. O'Molina's Cross, received its name from this family. The territory of Calry of Moy-heleog was nearly co-extensive with the parish of Crossmolina, in the barony of Tirawley.—See *Genealogies, Tribes, and Customs of Hy-Fiachrach*, pp. 13, 165, and the map prefixed to the same work. The family name Gaughan is still common all over the county of Mayo.—*Id.*, pp. 13, 238.

[g] *A great war.*—This is related more clearly in Mageoghegan's translation of the Annals of Clonmacnoise, as follows: "There arose great dissention and warrs between the King of Connaught and Walter Burke, Earl of Ulster, in so much that all the English and Irish of the kingdome could not separate them, or keep them from annoying each other. The Earle procured the Lord Deputy, with all the English forces of Ireland, to come to Connaught. They came to

The castle of Roscommon was erected by Robert de Ufford[e], Lord Justice of Ireland. He was induced to erect it because Hugh O'Conor, King of Connaught, was ill, and was therefore unable to give the English battle or opposition, or prevent the erection of the castle. The Connacians, until his recovery, were plundered and trodden under foot by the English.

Flaherty O'Maelfina[f], Chief of half the territory of Calry of Moy-heleog, was slain by Gaughan, Chief of the other half.

THE AGE OF CHRIST, 1270.

The Age of Christ, one thousand two hundred seventy.

Maelpatrick O'Scannal, Archbishop of Armagh, went over to the King of England: the King received him honourably; and he returned home with great privileges.

A great war[g] broke out between O'Conor and the Earl of Ulster, Walter Burke. The Earl assembled the chiefs of the English of Ireland, together

Roscommon the first night, thence to Portlike, where they encamped. The next day they advised that the Earl of Ulster, with the most part of the forces, should go eastwards of the River Synan, to the place on the river called the Foord of Connell's weir.

"As for Hugh O'Connor, King of Connaught, he was ready prepared with the five companies he had before the English at Moynishe. The Lord Deputy remained of [on] the west of the River Synen, at the Furney [ααα ꝼuꞃnαιδ]. After the Earle had passed to Ath-Cora-Connell as aforesaid, he was assaulted by a few of O'Connor's people in the woods of Convackne, where a few of the English armie were killed. The Englishmen never made any residence or stay until they came to Moynishe, which was the place where O'Connor encamped, where the English did likewise encampe that night. The Englishmen advised the Earle to make peace with Hugh O'Connor, and to yeald his brother, William Oge mac William More mac William, the Conqueror, in hostage to O'Connor, dureing the time he shou'd remain in the Earl's house concluding the said peace, which was accordingly condescended and done, as soone as William came to O'Connor's house he was taken, and also John Dolphin and his son were killed.

"When tyding came to the ears of the Earle how his brother was thus taken, he took his journey to Athenkip, where O'Connor beheaved himself as a fierce and froward lyon about his prey, without sleeping or taking any rest, that he did not suffer his enemies to take refection or rest all this time, and the next day soon in the morning, gott upp and betook him to his arms: the Englishmen, the same morning, came to the same foorde, called Athenkip, where they were overtaken by Terlogh O'Bryen. The Earle returned upon him and killed the said Terlogh, without the help of any other in that pressence. The Connoughtmen pursued the Englishmen,

arċéna go Connaċtaib go riaċtadar Ros comáin an ced adhaig, Oilfinn an dara hadaiġ, Airriḋ go port lecce. Gaḃaid forad ⁊ Saorlongport ann an oiḋċe sin. Tiaġaid daon ċomairle araḃaraċ in áṫ caraḋ conaill tar Sionainn soir.

Baoí Rí Connaċt mun am sin uathaḋ do maiṫiḃ a muintire i moiġ nire ar cionn na ngall, ⁊ do an an giusdis ⁊ bécán don tsluaġ ġall allaniar do Sionainn ga nurnaiḋe. Iar ndul don iarla tar aṫ caraḋ Conaill ro erġiodar uathaḋ do muintir uí concoḃair do na gallaiḃ i ccoillṫiḃ Conmaicne go ndearnsad marḃaḋ orra. Lodar iaram go maġ nire gur gabsad forlong-port ann in oiḋċi sin. Do gniad do comairle reroile ainnsíḋe Síṫ do denaṁ lé Ríġ connaċt, ⁊ dearḃraṫoir an iarla (uilliam óg mac Riocaird mic uilliam concuir) do ċor ar láiṁ muintire uí concoḃair an ccéin do beṫ sé fén i ttiġ an iarla ag snaḋmaḋ na sioḋa. Do gniṫeṡ samlaiḋ. Aċt céna do gabsad muintir ui concoḃair dearbraṫoir an iarla focedóir, ⁊ ro ṁarḃ-sad Seaan dolifín go na mac. Feargaigṫear an tiarla iar na clos sin dó. Rucc ar an adaiġ sin go himsníomaċ achtuirreach. Erccis i muiċdeaḋoil na maidne araḃárac gona gallaiḃ ⁊ gaoiḋealaiḃ ceangailte coirighṫe ina timċeal, ⁊ gluaisid do saiġiḋ ui concoḃair go rangadar aṫ an ċip. Do geḃid toirrḋealḃaċ ua briain ċuca aghaidh in aghaidh annsin, ⁊ é ag toċht i ccommbáiḋ uí concoḃair. Do ḃéir an tiarla fén a aġaiḋ ar toirrḋealḃaċ, ⁊ ro cuiṁniġ a eccraiḋes dó go ttorċair toirrḋealḃaċ lais focedoir. Dala Connaċt tra rucsad orra do ċom an aṫa don dul sin ionnus gur ḃrúcht-ḋoirtriod ina cceann do ċois ⁊ deaċ gur ḃriseadar for a ttosaċ, ⁊ gur ċuirsiod a ndeireaḋ ar a nionat dá naiṁdeóin. Marḃtar naonḃar do maiṫiḃ a Ridireaḋ don iarraiḋ si a ttimceal an áṫa imaille re Riocard

and made their hindermost part runn and break upon their outguard or foremost in such manner and foul discomfiture, that in that instant nine of their chiefest men were killed upon the bogge, aboute Richard ne Koylle and John Butler, who were killed over and above the said knights. It is unknown how many were slain in that conflict, save only that a hundred horses, with their saddles and other furniture, with a hundred shirts of mail, were left. After these things were thus done, O'Connor killed William Oge, the Earl's brother, that was given him before in hostage, because the Earle killed Terlagh O'Bryen that came to assist O'Connor against the Earle.

"O'Connor immediately tooke and brake down the castles of Athengalie, the castle of Sliew Louth, and the castle of Killcalman: also, he burnt Roscomon, Rynndwyne, alias Teagh Owen, and Ullenonach."

with the Lord Justice[h] and all his Irish faction, and marched into Connaught; the first night they arrived at Roscommon, and the second at Elphin; from thence they proceeded to Port-lecce, where they rested and encamped for that night; and on the next morning they marched, by common consent, eastwards, across the ford of Ath-Caradh-Conaill, on the Shannon.

The King of Connaught, attended by a small number of the chiefs of his people, was at this time in Moy-Nise, ready to meet the English; and the Lord Justice and a small part of the English army remained on the west side of the Shannon, awaiting the Connacians. After the Earl had crossed [the ford of] Ath-Caradh Conaill[i], a small party of O'Conor's people attacked the English at Coillte Conmaicne, and slew some of them. After this they went to Moy-Nise[j], where they encamped for that night; and they consulted together, and agreed to make peace with the King of Connaught, and to deliver up to his people the Earl's brother (William Oge, son of Richard, the son of William the Conqueror[k]), while he himself (i. e. O'Conor) should be in the Earl's house concluding the peace. This was accordingly done; but O'Conor's people took the Earl's brother prisoner at once, and slew John Dolifin and his son. When the Earl heard of this, he became enraged, and passed the night in sadness and sorrow; and he rose next morning at daybreak, with his English and Irish arranged and arrayed about him, and marched against O'Conor to Ath-an-chip[l], where they met face to face Turlough O'Brien, who had come to assist O'Conor. The Earl himself faced Turlough, mindful of the old enmity between them, and slew him at once; but the Connacians came up with the Earl's troops at the ford, where they poured down upon them, horse and foot, broke through their van, and forcibly dislodged their rear. In this onslaught at the ford, nine of the chief English knights were slain around the ford, together with Richard

[h] *Lord Justice.*—According to the list of Chief Governors of Ireland, given in Harris's edition of Ware's Antiquities, Sir James Audley, or de Aldithel, was Lord Justice of Ireland in the year 1270.

[i] *Ath-Caradh Conaill*, i. e. the ford of Connell's weir. This was the name of a ford on the Shannon, near Carrick-on-Shannon, but the name has been long obsolete.

[j] *Moy-Nise*, a level district in the county of Leitrim, on the east side of the Shannon.—See note under the year 1263.

[k] *William the Conqueror*, that is, William Fitz Adelm de Burgo, who is usually styled by Irish writers, the Conqueror, because it was believed that he conquered the province of Connaught.

[l] *Ath-an-chip*, i. e. the ford of the stock or trunk; a ford on the Shannon, near Carrick-

na coilleaḋ, ⁊ re Seaan buitelér, gan áirḟṁ ar a ttorcradar díoḃ edir maiṫ ⁊ saiṫ uaṫa so amaċ. Dírim ḃeós na hédála do ḃḟnaḋ diḃ darm, dédeaḋ, ⁊ deachaiḃ, ⁊c. Marbtar dearbraṫair an iarla (.i. uilliám ócc) iarsin lá hua cconcobair a nerait mic uí briain do marḃaḋ don iarla.

Caislén atha anguili, caislén slebi luġa ⁊ caislen cille calman do leaccaḋ dua concoḃair. Ros comain, Rinn dúin ⁊ Uillinn uanaċ do loscaḋ lais beós.

Brian ruaḋ ua briain diompúḋ for gallaiḃ. Airgti aidble do dénaṁ dó orra, ⁊ caislén cláir áṫa dá caraḋ do gabáil dó.

Creaċa móra do dénaṁ don iarla, ⁊ do gallaiḃ Connaċt i ttír noilealla ar muintir Aodha uí concoḃair, ⁊ dauiṫ cuisin do marḃaḋ don dul sin.

Mac murchaiḋ carraiġ ui fḟrgail, bḟiṫir ar ḃeoḋacht, oinċú ar ḟngnaṁ do marḃaḋ la gallaiḃ.

Tanaiḋe mór mac duinnín mic néḋe mic conaing ḃuiḋe uí maoilconaire doirdneaḋ in ardollaṁnacht connaċt, ⁊ foirċionn do ḋul for ollaṁnacht an duḃḟúiliġ ui maoilconaire ⁊ dunlaing uí maoilconaire.

Slicceach do loscaḋ la hua ndoṁnaill, ⁊ lá cenel Conaill ⁊ mac breal-laiġ an chairn uí maoilḃrénainn do ṁarḃaḋ don turus sin.

Cristina inġḟn uí Neachtain bḟn diarmada Midiġ meic diarmada do

on-Shannon, but the name has been long obsolete.

[m] *Richard na Coille*, i. e. Richard of the Wood. According to the Dublin copy, and the old translation of the Annals of Ulster, this Richard was the Earl's brother [brá̇ṫair]: "And this was one of the soarest battayles that the Irish ever gave to the Galls in Ireland, for Richard ne kill, the Earl's brother, and John Butler, and many more knights, and many English and Irish besides, and at least 100 horse, with their saddles, were left."—*Old Trans.*

[n] *John Butler.*—Hanmer, referring to Clinne, and the interpolated copy of the Annals of Innisfallen, state that the Lords Richard and John Verdon were slain on this occasion; but this is obviously an error. It has been, however, perpetuated by Cox and Moore.

[o] *Ath-Angaile.*—The castle of Ath-Angaile was in the territory of Corran, as appears from an entry under the year 1263. The name has been long obsolete. The castle of Sliabh Lugha is the one now called Castlemore-Costello, situated a short distance to the south-west of Kilcolman, in the same barony. Kilcolman castle stood near the old church of Kilcolman, in the parish of the same name, barony of Costello, and county of Mayo.—See Map to *Genealogies, Tribes, and Customs of Hy-Fiachrach*, on which its true position is shewn, though in the explanatory index to this map, p. 484, it is inadvertently placed in the barony of Clanmorris.

[p] *Uillin Uanagh.*—The name of this place has been variously corrupted by the transcribers of the original Irish Annals. The Four Masters

na Coille[m] and John Butler[n], exclusive of others, both noble and plebeian. Immense spoils were also taken from them, consisting of arms, armour, horses, &c. The Earl's brother (William Oge) was put to death after this battle by O'Conor, as an *eric* for the son of O'Brien, who had been slain by the Earl.

The castle of Ath-Angaile[o], the castle of Sliabh Lugha, and the castle of Cill Calman, were demolished by O'Conor. Rindown and Uillin Uanagh[p] were also burned by him.

Brian Roe O'Brien turned against the English, and committed great depredations upon them; and the castle of Clar-Atha-da-charadh[q] was taken by him.

Great depredations were committed by the Earl and the English of Connaught in Tirerrill on the people of Hugh O'Conor; and David Cuisin [Cushen] was killed on that occasion.

The son of Murrough Carragh O'Farrell, a bear in liveliness, and a leopard[r] in prowess[s], was slain by the English.

Tany More, son of Duinnin, son of Nedhe, son of Conaing Boy O'Mulconry, was elected to the chief ollavship[t] of Connaught; and the ollavships of Dubhshuileach O'Mulconry and Dunlang O'Mulconry were abolished.

Sligo was burned by O'Donnell and the Kinel-Connell; and the son of Breallagh-an-Chairn O'Mulrenin was killed on that occasion.

Christina[u], daughter of O'Naghtan, and wife of Dermot Midheach Mac

write it *Muilleann Guanach*, at the year 1225, but the Annals of Ulster and Kilronan make it *Muillibh Uanach*, while those of Connaught make it *Muillibh Uainidhe*. At the year 1236, it is written Muillibh Uanach in the Annals of Kilronan, and Ullum Wonaghe in Mageoghegan's translation of the Annals of Clonmacnoise. From the notice of it at the year 1225, it is quite obvious that it was in the barony of Athlone, and that it was the name of a hill or mill in the townland of Onagh, in the barony of Athlone, and county of Roscommon. The castle afterwards became the seat of that branch of the O'Kellys called Makeogh.—See *Tribes and Customs of Hy-Many*, p. 19, note [k].

[q] *Clar Atha-da-charadh*, i. e. plain of the ford of the two weirs. This is probably the original name of the town of Clare, near Ennis, in the county of Clare.

[r] *Leopard*, onċu.—The word onnċu is explained leopard by O'Reilly. It was borne on the standard of the King of Connaught, and his standard bearer was called feaṗ ıomċaıṗ na honċon.—See note under the year 1316.

[s] *Prowess*, eangnaṁ, prowess, dexterity at arms.

[t] *Chief Ollavship*, aṗdollamnaċt, i. e. the office of chief poet.

[u] *Christina*.—This is a repetition. See her death already entered under the last year. Her death is entered in the old translation of the Annals of Ulster as follows: "A. D. 1268 (*rectius* 1270). Christina ny Neghtain Dermot Myegh Mac Dermot's wife, a woman of best

écc, bfn ro buḋ maiṫ deirc ⁊ oineaċ, ⁊ do rad almrana iomda don ord liaṫ.

AOIS CRIOST, 1271.

Aoir Criort mîle, da ċéd, reachtmogat a haon.

Siomon maccraiṫ deccanach Arda carna do écc.

Uater a búrc iarla ulaḋ, ⁊ tiġearna gall Connaċt do écc i ccairlén na gaillṁe iar mbuaiḋ naiṫriġe do galar aithgearr.

Tomar mac muirir do écc i mbaile loċa mearcca.

Iomar ua birn laimḟear graḋa aoḋa ui concobair do écc i Ror comáin iar mbuaiḋ naiṫriġe, ⁊ a aḋnacul innte.

Aoḋ ua concoḃair mac comorba comáin do marbaḋ do tomár buitelér ag muine inġine crechain.

Doṁnall ua floinn do marḃaḋ do mac Robín laiglef ir in ló ceona i ccionn uachtaraċ rruṫra.

Maṫgaṁain ua Concoḃair do marḃaḋ do gallaiḃ dúin móir.

Niocol mac Seaain uerdún tiġearna óirġiall do marḃaḋ lá Seafrraiḋ ua ḃfearġail.

Concoḃar mac tiġearnáin ui concoḃair do marḃaḋ la maoilreaċluinn mac Airt uí ruairc, ⁊ la cloinn fearmuiġe.

Cairlén tiġe templa, cairlén Sliccig, ⁊ cairlen aṫa liacc do briread daoḋ ua concobair.

Aodh mac néill uí ḋuḃda do écc.

name and quality that was in her times, and that gave most to the white [grey ?] order, *quievit*."

[w] *Earl of Ulster*.—His death is thus entered in the Annals of Clonmacnoise, as translated by Mageoghegan: "A. D. 1271. Walter Burke, Earle of Ulster, and Lord of the English of Connaught, died in the castle of Gallway of one week's sickness, after good penance, and was entred [interred] in Rathcahall."

[x] *Thomas Mac Maurice*.—In Mageoghegan's translation of the Annals of Clonmacnoise he is called "Thomas Mac Morish Fitzgerald." Ballyloughmask is now called Lough Mask Castle, and is situated on the east side of Lough Mask, in the parish of Ballinchala, barony of Kilmaine, and county of Mayo. This castle was re-edified by Sir Thomas Burke, shortly after the battle of Kinsale.—See *Genealogies, Tribes, and Customs of Hy-Fiachrach*, pp. 202, 478.

[y] *Muine-inghine-Chrechain*, i. e. the hill or shrubbery of the daughter of Creaghan. The name is now obsolete.

[z] *Of Sruthair*, rruṫra.—This was the original

Dermot, died. She was a good, charitable, and hospitable woman, and had given much alms to the order of Grey Friars.

THE AGE OF CHRIST, 1271.

The Age of Christ, one thousand two hundred seventy-one.

Simon Magrath, Deacon of Ardcarne, died.

Walter Burke, Earl of Ulster[w], and Lord of the English of Connaught, died of a short sickness in the castle of Galway, after the victory of penance.

Thomas Mac Maurice[x] died at Ballyloughmask.

Ivor O'Beirne, the head and confidential servant of Hugh O'Conor, died at Roscommon, after penance, and was buried there.

Hugh O'Conor, son of the coarb of St. Coman, was killed at Muine-inghine-Chrechain[y], by Thomas Butler.

Donnell O'Flynn was slain on the same day, by the son of Robin Lawless, at the upper end of Sruthair[z].

Mahon O'Conor was slain by the English of Dunmore[a].

Nicholas, the son of John Verdun, Lord of Oriel, was slain by Geoffry O'Farrell.

Conor, son of Tiernan O'Conor, was slain by Melaghlin, son of Art O'Rourke, and by the Clann-Fearmaighe [in the County Leitrim].

The castle of Teagh Templa[b], the castle of Sligo, and the castle of Athliag [Ballyleague], were demolished by Hugh O'Conor.

Hugh, son of Niall O'Dowda, died.

name of the Black River, which flows through the village of Shrule, and forms for several miles the boundary between the counties of Mayo and Galway. The name was afterwards applied to a castle built by the Burkes on the north side of this river, and also to the village which grew up around it, and also to the parish.

[a] *Dunmore*, a village in a barony of the same name, about eight miles to the north of Tuam, in the county of Galway.

[b] *Teagh Templa*.—According to Ware, this castle belonged to the Knights Templars, and was erected by the English in the thirteenth century.—See Harris's edition, vol. ii. p. 271. According to an Irish manuscript in the possession of Major O'Hara, a castle was built here by the O'Haras, but the date of its erection is not added. The name is now anglicised Templehouse, and is that of the residence of Colonel Perceval, situated in the east of the barony of Leyny, in the county of Sligo.—See the position of this castle marked on the map prefixed to

AOIS CRIOST, 1272.

Aois Criost, míle, da chéd, sechtmoghat, adó.

Henri buitelér tighearna umhaill, ⁊ hoitse medbric do marbhadh do cathal mac Concobhair ruaidh, ⁊ do cloinn muirchertaigh ui concobhair.

Caislén Rosa comáin do bhriseadh do righ connacht, aodh ua concobhair.

Tadhg dall mac aodha mic cathail croibhdeirg do écc, ⁊ ba hésidhe adhbhar righ do bferr da cineadh no gur dallsad muintir Raighilligh é.

Iamas dodalaigh iusdis na hÉreann do marbhadh dua broin, ⁊ do Connachtaibh.

Muirgios mac donnchaidh mic tomaltaigh uí maoilruanaidh, Saoi enigh, ⁊ engnamha a chineadh do écc illongport uí domhnaill i murbhach, ⁊ a tabhairt go mainistir na buille dá adhnacul.

Donnchadh mac giolla na naomh még samhradháin do mharbhadh dá derbhrathair tomas.

Riocard diuid an barún do buaisle do gallaibh décc.

An midhe do loscadh go Granard daodh ua concobair.

Ath luain do loscadh lais beós, ⁊ a droichead do bhriseadh.

O domhnaill (domhnall ócc) do tionol sethar ⁊ bhád for loch eirne, ⁊ airsidhe for loch uachtair. Maithsa, ⁊ edala na tíre ina timchell (battar for innsib an locha sin) do bhein eisdibh, ⁊ a norccain lais co mbattar ar a

Genealogies, Tribes, and Customs of Hy-Fiachrach, printed for the Archæological Society in 1844, and Explanatory Index to the same map, p. 497. Sir Richard Cox states, under the year 1270, that the castles of "Aldleek, Roscomon, and Scheligah (perhaps Sligo), were destroyed." These incorrect names he took from Hanmer, who had taken them from some incorrect copy of Irish Annals. In the old translation of the Annals of Ulster the entry is thus given: "A. D. 1269 (*al.* 1271). The castle of Roscomon, the castle of Sligo" [Sligigh] "and the castle of Athleag, were broken by Hugh Mac Felim and Conaght."

[c] *Hosty Merrick*, hoistí medbric.—In the Annals of Clonmacnoise, as translated by Mageoghegan, he is called Hodge Mebric, and in the Dublin copy of the Annals of Ulster, hoidsi mac Meric. According to the tradition in the county of Mayo, this Hosty gave name to Glenhest in that county, and is the ancestor of the families of Hosty and Merrick.

[d] *Clann-Murtough O'Conor*, clann muircheartaigh ui chonchobhair.—These were the descendants of the celebrated Murtough Muimhneach, the son of Turlough More O'Conor, Monarch of Ireland.

[e] *James Dodaly*.—Hanmer, *ad ann.* 1270, calls him the Lord *James Audley*, and says he died "with the fall of a horse." Cox says that

THE AGE OF CHRIST, 1272.

The Age of Christ, one thousand two hundred seventy-two.

Henry Butler, Lord of Umallia, and Hosty Merrick[e], were slain by Cathal, son of Conor Roe, and by the Clann-Murtough[d] O'Conor.

The castle of Roscommon was demolished by Hugh O'Conor, King of Connaught.

Teige Dall (the Blind), son of Hugh, the son of Cathal Crovderg, died. He had been the best materies of a king of all his tribe, until he was blinded by the O'Reillys.

James Dodaly[e], Lord Justice of Ireland, was slain by O'Broin[f] and the Connacians.

Maurice, son of Donough, son of Tomaltagh O'Mulrony, the most hospitable and valiant[g] of his tribe, died in O'Donnell's garrison at Murvagh[h], and was conveyed to the abbey of Boyle, to be interred there.

Donough, son of Gilla-na-naev Magauran, was slain by his brother Thomas.

Richard Tuite[i], the noblest of the English barons, died.

Meath was burned, as far as Granard[k], by Hugh O'Conor. Athlone was also burned by him, and its bridge was broken down.

O'Donnell (Donnell Oge) collected the vessels and boats upon Lough Erne, and [proceeded] thence to Lough Oughter. The goods and valuables of the surrounding country (which were upon the islands of that lake) were seized

he was killed in Thomond, by a fall from his horse, on the 23rd of June, 1272.

[f] *O'Broin*, ua bpoın.—This is a mistake for O bpıaın. In Mageoghegan's translation of the Annals of Clonmacnoise this entry is thus given: "A. D. 1272. James Dowdall, Deputie of Ireland, was killed by O'Brien, and some Connoughtmen."

[g] *Valiant*, ꞅaoı eınıġ ⁊ eanġnaṁ.—The Irish word eanġnaṁ is used by the Irish annalists to denote *prowess*, *valour*, and *dexterity at arms*. See note [b], p. 277, where ꞅo ꞅceıṁ enġnuṁa is used to denote laudability, or credit of prowess, and note under the year 1270, where onċu aꞃ eanġnaṁ is used to express a leopard in prowess, or warlike activity.

[h] *Murvagh*, muꞃḃaċ, i. e. a sea plain, or salt marsh, now Murvagh, Ordnance Map, sheet 99 and 107, in the barony of Tirhugh, and county of Donegal, about one mile to the west of Ballyshannon. There is another place of the name about three miles south-west of the town of Donegal.

[i] *Richard Tuite.*—In Mageoghegan's translation of the Annals of Clonmacnoise he is called the "worthiest baron in all Ireland."

[k] *Granard*, a small town in the county of Longford.—See note under the year 1262.

ċumus, Tren ⁊ treisi do ġabáil dó in gach maiġin ina ccomfochraibh don ċur sin.

An céd éduard do ríoġadh os Saxaiḃ. 16. Nouember.

AOIS CRIOST, 1273.

Aois Criost, mile, da ċéd, seachtmoġat, atrí.

Flann ó tiġernaiġ tiġerna ciarra do marbaḋ dó Muiréadaiġ im thiġernus ciarra tria neart aodha mic feidlimiḋ uí conċobair.

Concoḃar buide mac Amlaoiḃ mic airt uí ruairc tiġearna breifne do marbaḋ do cloinn concoḃair mic tiġearnáin uí concoḃair, ⁊ do marbsom an mac do b fearr dibsiom tiġearnán.

Eochaiḋ mag maṫġaṁna tiġearna oirġiall, ⁊ Sochaiḋe imaille ris do marbaḋ dua anluain, ⁊ do cenél neoġain.

Creaċ do denaṁ do Siurtán dexetra isin ccorann. Uaṫaḋ do ríoġdaṁnaiḃ connaċt do breiṫ orra, aiṁgliocus coṁairle do dénaṁ dóiḃ ar furáileaṁ coda da ndaorsccorsluaġ, gur marbaḋ doṁnall mac donnchaiḋ mic maġnusa, Magnus mac airt, aireachtaċ mac aoḋaccáin, Aoḋ ua birn, ⁊ Sochaiḋe oile.

Morsluaġ la mac muiris meic geraiłt i ttuaḋṁuṁain gur gaḃ braiġdi ⁊ neart ar ua mbriain.

Corbmac mac diarmada mic Ruaiḋri décc.

[l] *Made king.*—Do ríoġadh literally signified to be *kinged*, or made king. This was the day of his father's death. He was then absent in the Holy Land, and was not crowned till the 15th day of August, 1274. Among the Irish themselves do ríoġaḋ means to be inaugurated king; but it appears from the dates given by them for the ríoġaḋ of the kings of England, that they merely meant their succession, which takes place the very instant their predecessors dies.—See Blackstone's Commentaries, vol. i. p. 249; see also the years 1199 and 1216, where the ríoġaḋ has been inadvertently rendered "was crowned." Hanmer has the following remark under this year (1272): "The most renowned King Henry the Third, having lived 65 yeeres, and reigned 56, and 28 dayes, ended his dayes, and was buried at Westminster. Edward, the first of that name, sonne of King Henry III., surnamed *Long Shankes*, of the age of 35 yeers, began his reigne, *anno* 1272."

[m] *O'Tierney.*—This name is now locally made Tiernan, and is still common in the barony of Carra, in the county of Mayo.

[n] *O'Murrays*, now Murrays, without the prefixed O.—See *Genealogies, Tribes, and Cus-*

on and carried off by him; and he acquired control and sway in every place in the neighbourhood on this expedition.

The first Edward was made king[l] over the English on the 16th of November.

THE AGE OF CHRIST, 1273.

The Age of Christ, one thousand two hundred seventy-three.

Flann O'Tierney[m], Lord of Carra, was slain by the O'Murrays[n] in a dispute concerning the lordship of Carra, and through the power of Hugh, son of Felim O'Conor.

Conor Boy, son of Auliffe, son of Art O'Rourke, Lord of Breifny, was slain by the sons of Conor, son of Tiernan O'Conor; and he killed the best of them, namely, Tiernan.

Eochy Mac Mahon, Lord of Oriel, and many others along with him, were slain by O'Hanlon and the Kinel-Owen.

A depredation was committed by Jordan d'Exeter in Corran[o]. A few of the young princes of Connaught overtook him; but these having adopted an imprudent plan, suggested by some of the common people[p], it fell out that Donnell, son of Donough, Manus, son of Art [O'Conor], Aireaghtagh Mac Egan, Hugh O'Beirne, and many others, were slain.

A great army was led by Mac Maurice Fitzgerald into Thomond, where he took hostages, and obtained sway[q] over O'Brien.

Cormac, son of Dermot, son of Roderic [O'Conor], died.

toms of Hy-Fiachrach, printed for the Irish Archæological Society in 1844, pp. 187, 189.

[o] *Corran*, coρann, now the barony of Corran, in the county of Sligo.

[p] *Common people*, ᴅαογccαρρluαġ.—In the Dublin copy of the Annals of Ulster, the term used is ᴅρoċᴅαίne, i. e. bad people. The whole passage is thus rendered in the old translation: "A. D. 1270 (*al.* 1272, *vel* 1273). A pray made by Jordan de Exeter in Coran, and a few of the nobles of Conaght came upon them, and used bad direction, through the persuasion of idle men, whereby Donell Mac Donogh Mac Manus, and Manus Mac Art, and Oreghtagh Mac Egan, and Hugh O'Birn, and many more" [were killed].

[q] *Obtained sway*, neαρτ ᴅo ġαβαil.—Mageoghegan has this passage as follows in his translation of the Annals of Clonmacnoise: "A. D. 1273. Morish Mac Gerald, with great forces, went to Thomond, and tooke hostages from the O'Bryens, and subdued the whole country."

Domnall iorrair mac magnusa mic muirchertaigh muimnigh dionnarbadh a humall ⁊ a hiorrus.

Ruaidhri ua flaithbhertaigh dionnarbadh a hiartar Connacht.

O domnaill (domnall ócc) do thocht slóigh lanmoir in aoin ionad do maithiph Conallach, ⁊ do maithibh Connacht, ⁊ dol dó i ttír neocchain, ⁊ an tír do milleadh lais.

Domnall ó cuinn lfth toiseach na haicidechta do marbadh la hua ndubhthaigh.

AOIS CRIOST, 1274.

Aois Criost, míle, dá céd, seachtmogat, a ceathair.

Aodh mac feidhlimidh mic cathail croibhdeirg Rí connacht, Rí ro folmaigh, ⁊ ro fasaigh Connachta ar gallaibh ⁊ gaoidhealaibh bidís na aghaidh, Rí do radh madhmanna mionca for hSaxanchaibh, ro thrasccair a ccúirti ⁊ a ccaislén, ro mudhaigh a ccuradha ⁊ a ccaithmilidh, Rí ro gabh braighdi ua mbriúin ⁊ catha aidhbha find, Rí bá mó gráin ⁊ coscear, eneach ⁊ oirdhercus, fear millte ⁊ leasoighthi Ereann eside, a écc iar mbuaidh naithrighi dia dardaoin ar aoí laithe, ⁊ an tres la do Samhradh eside. Eoghan mac Ruaidhri mic aodha mic cathail croibhdeirg do rioghadh ina ionad, ⁊ nocha raibe acht én ráithi is in ríghe an tan ro marbsat a derbhfine fesin e, .i. Ruaidhri mac toirrdhealbaigh mic aodha ui concobair i ttempall bráthar Rosa comáin, ⁊ Aodh mac cathail doill

[r] *Donnell Irrais.*—The Annals of Ulster record the death of this Donnell at the year 1271 or 1274. It is thus entered in the old translation: "A. D. 1271 (*rectius* 1274). Donell Mac Manus Mac Murtagh Muvnagh O'Coner, a tryed golden chief and perfect overseer to all, *quievit in pace.*"

[s] *O'Quin.*—This was O'Quin of Clann-Cuain, who was at this time tributary to Mac Dermot of Moylurg, who had a house on an island in Claenloch in Clann-Cuain.—See note [n], under the year 1232; see also the entry under the year 1206, where Mac Dermot is styled Lord of Moylurg, Airteach, and Aicideacht, p. 151.

[t] *A king the most successful, &c.*, Ri bá mo gráin 7 coscear.—In the old translation of the Annals of Ulster, this is rendered, "he that terrified and put down most of any." In Mageoghegan's translation of the Annals of Clonmacnoise the whole passage is given in English as follows: "A. D. 1274. Hugh Mac Felym O'Conor, King of Connaught for nine years, died the fifth of the noones of May, on Thursday, that is to say, upon the feast day of the Invention of the Cross. This is the king that wasted and destroyed Connaught upon the English; this is he that razed and broke down their houses and castles, made them even with the earth, and gave themselves many great overthrows and conflicts; this is he that took the

Donnell Irrais[r] [of Erris], son of Manus, son of Murtough Muimhneach, was banished from Umallia and Erris.

Roderic O'Flaherty was banished from West Connaught.

O'Donnell (Donnell Oge) assembled a considerable army, composed of the nobles of Tirconnell and Connaught, with whom he marched into Tyrone, and ravaged the country.

Donnell O'Quin[s], Semi-Chief of Aicideacht, was slain by O'Duffy.

THE AGE OF CHRIST, 1274.

The Age of Christ, one thousand two hundred seventy-four.

Hugh, son of Felim, the son of Cathal Crovderg, King of Connaught, a king who had desolated and devastated that part of Connaught possessed by his English or Irish enemies; a king who had given the English frequent overthrows, prostrated their manor-houses and castles, and cut off their heroes and warriors; a king who had obtained the hostages of the Hy-Briuin, and all the race of Aedh Finn; a king the most successful[t] and triumphant, the most hospitable and renowned; the destroyer and improver of Ireland, died, after gaining the victory of penance, on Thursday, the third day of the Summer. Hugh, son of Rory, son of Hugh, who was son of Cathal Crovderg, was made king in his place; but he was only one quarter of a year in the government, when he was slain, in the church of the Friars at Roscommon, by his kinsman, namely, Rory, son of Turlough, the son of Hugh O'Conor; upon which, Hugh, son of Cathal

hostages of Ombryan" [Hy-Briuin], "and Tyreconnell; this is he that spoyled and defended from others the spoiles of the provence of Connaught; and finally this is he that most was feared of [i. e. by] the English, of all the kings of Connaught that were before his time; and was with great reverence buried with the moncks in the abbey of Boyle. After whose death Owen mac Rowrie mac Hugh mac Cahall Crovederge was ordained King of Connaught, who reigned not long (butt one quarter of a year), when he was killed treacherously by his own kinsman or brother, Rowrie Mac Turlagh O'Connor, in the church of the Fryers Preachers at Roscommon.

"After him succeed Hugh mac Cahall Dall O'Connor, as king of that province, who did not reigne as long as his predecessors was short. Hugh Mac Cahall reigned but a fortnight, when he was killed by one Thomas Mac Oreaghty and O'Beyrne. After him succeeded, as King of Connaught, Teige Mac Terlagh Mac Cahall, the same year.

mic aodha mic caṫail croiḃdeirg do rioġaḋ do Connaċtaiḃ, ⁊ noċar ffaide a riġi sidhé uair ní raibe aċt én coicdís inte an tan do marbaḋ é la Mag oirechtaiġ, tomaltaċ, ⁊ la hua mbirn, ⁊ tadg mac toirrdealbaiġ mic aodha mic caṫail croiḃdeirg do rioġaḋ uas Connaċtaiḃ iaram.

Tiġearnan mac aodha uí ruairc tiġearna breifne, ⁊ Domhnall mac magnusa mic muircertaiġ muimniġ, Saoi eniġ, ⁊ engnamha Ereann uili déġ.

Giolla na naomh mac aodha mic amlaoiḃ uí fḟerġail tiġearna na hanġaile, comhrur ċoimhéda eniġ, ⁊ engnamha cloinne Rudhraide, fear lan duairli, ⁊ dinntleċt go nguairbertaiḃ for naimdiḃ go ccaoinsr lé cairdiḃ, do écc iar mbuaidh naiṫriġe.

Maoileaċlainn mac amhlaoiḃ mic Airt uí Ruairc tiġearna dartraiġi ⁊ cloinne fearmuiġe do marbaḋ la Concobar mac domhnaill mic neill uí ruairc.

Tadg mac cearbaill buidhe uí dalaiġ ollamh aodha uí concobair lé dán déġ.

Domhnall ócc mac domhnaill mic airt uí Ruairc, ⁊ Caṫal mag ḟlannċaidh taoiseaċ dartraiġi do écc.

Fferghal ó caithniadh tiġearna iorrais do écc i nua mic caecháin.

AOIS CRIOST, 1275.

Aois Criost, míle, da ċéd, sechtmogat, a cúicc.

Ua laidiġ esbucc cille halaidh, ⁊ Cairbre ua Scuapa esbucc Ráṫa boṫ i ttír Conaill do écc.

Ruaidhri mac toirrdhealbaiġ uí Concobair do gabáil dua Concobair (tadg mac toirrdhealbaiġ a braṫair). Ruaidhri delúdh iaram, ⁊ Concobar ua háinliġi da brsiṫ leis, Toraiġecht do breiṫ forra, ⁊ concobar ua háinliġi do marbaḋ dóiḃ.

Tadg mac caṫail meic diarmata darccain dua conċobair.

Concobar mac feargail mic donnċaidh mic muircertaiġ do marbaḋ da braiṫriḃ fḟein.

[u] *Prowess.*—eangnamh.

[w] *Hy-Mac-Caechain.*—This was the name of a district in the northern extremity of the barony of Erris, in the county of Mayo. The fort called Doonkeeghan, and the sand banks called Dumha Caechain, still point out the position of this territory.—See *Genealogies, Tribes, and Customs of Hy-Fiachrach*, pp. 173, 280.

[x] *O'Scuapa.*—According to the Annals of Clonmacnoise, as translated by Mageoghegan, he was

Dall, the son of Hugh, son of Cathal Crovderg, was made king by the Connacians; and his reign was not longer, for he had been but one fortnight in the government, when he was slain by Mageraghty (Tomaltagh) and O'Beirne; and Teige, son of Turlough, son of Hugh, son of Cathal Crovderg, was elected king over the Connacians.

Tiernan, son of Hugh O'Rourke, Lord of Breifny, and Donnell, son of Manus, who was son of Murtough Muimhneach, most illustrious throughout all Ireland for hospitality and prowess[u], died.

Gilla-na-naev, son of Hugh, the son of Auliffe O'Farrell, Lord of Annaly, supporter of the hospitality and prowess of the Clanna-Rury, a man full of nobleness and intellect, dangerous to his foes, and kind to his friends, died, after the victory of penance.

Melaghlin, son of Auliffe, the son of Art O'Rourke, Lord of Dartry and Clann-Fearmaighe, was slain by Conor, son of Donnell, the son of Niall O'Rourke.

Teige, son of Carroll Boy O'Daly, chief poet of Hugh O'Conor, died.

Donnell Oge, son of Donnell, son of Art O'Rourke, and Cathal Mac Clancy, Chief of Dartry, died.

Fergal O'Caithniadh, Lord of Erris, died in Hy-Mac-Caechain[w].

THE AGE OF CHRIST, 1275.

The Age of Christ, one thousand two hundred seventy-five.

O'Laidigh, Bishop of Killala, and Carbry O'Scuapa[x], Bishop of Raphoe, in Tirconnell, died.

Rory, son of Turlough O'Conor, was taken prisoner by the O'Conor (Teige, son of Turlough, his brother). Rory afterwards made his escape, and Conor O'Hanley took him with him; but they were pursued, and overtaken, and Conor O'Hanley was killed.

Teige, son of Cathal Mac Dermot, was plundered by O'Conor.

Conor, son of Farrell, son of Donough, son of Murtough [O'Conor], was slain by his own kinsmen.

first a friar of the order of Preachers.—See also Harris's edition of Ware's Bishops, p. 271, where it is stated, on the authority of the Annals of Lough-Kee, that he died at Rome in 1275.

Art mac caṫail riaḃaiġ uí ruairc tiġearna breifne do marḃaḋ la Mag ḟionnḃarr, ⁊ la gallaiḃ i ngranard, ⁊ ár a muintire do cur.

Maiḋm mor for gallaiḃ i nultaiḃ go ráinicc da céd eaċ, ⁊ dá céd ceann in áiriṁ diḃ an éccmais ar muḋaiġeaḋ da ndaorsccorsluaġ.

Tomas mag samraḋain do marḃaḋ la cenél luacáin.

Cenél Eocchain do ṫecht hi ttír Conaill co ro ṁillsiot bloḋ mór don tír, ⁊ ó domnáill (domnall ócc) do ṫionol a ṁuintire ina ḋocom, ⁊ a lenmain go huchṫ sleḃe truim go raoiniḋ forra go ffarccaibhriot ár daoine, eiċ iomḋa, faiḋb, airm ⁊ edeaḋa ag cenél cconaill don ċur sin.

AOIS CRIOST, 1276.

Aois Criost, míle, da céd, seaċtmogat asé.

Giolla an coimḋe ua cerḃalláin epscop tíre heoccain decc.

Aoḋ muiṁneaċ mac feḋlimiḋ mic caṫail croiḃdeirg do toiḋeċt as in mumhain i cconnaċtaiḃ. A dul iarsin i ccenn ui domnaill. O domnaill do toċt lais go líon a tionóil go heċnaċ, ua domnaill diompúḋ uaiḋ annsin, ⁊ aoḋ do ḟuireaċ i cconnaċtaiḃ.

Creaċ do denaṁ do cloinn toirrḋealḃaiġ ar mac feḋlimiḋ, ⁊ ar cloinn meic diarmata, ⁊ giolla criost ua maoilbrenainn do marḃaḋ dóiḃ.

[y] *Mac Finnbhar.*—He was chief of the territory of Muintir-Geran, situated on the west side of Lough Gowna, in the county of Longford.

[z] *Kinel-Luachain.*—This territory comprised the entire of the parish of Oughteragh, in the north of the barony of Carrigallen, in the county of Leitrim, adjoining the barony of Tullyhaw, Magauran's country.—See Irish Calendar of the O'Clerys at 7th July.

[a] *Slieve Truim.*—This name is now obsolete, but it is given on a map of Ulster, dated 1590, by Francis Jobson, under the anglicised form of Slevetrym. This name has been since changed by the proprietor to the unmeaning appellation of Bessy Bell. It is situated a short distance to the south of the village of Newtown-Stewart, in the barony of Strabane, and county of Tyrone.

[b] Under this year the Annals of Clonmacnoise, as translated by Mageoghegan, contain the two following entries, omitted by the Four Masters: "A. D. 1275. Art Mac Cormack O'Melaghlyn was hurt by O'Moylloy, and by those of Kynaleaghe, and the two sons of Mahon Magawlye were also killed by them. John de Verdon and thirteen knights were poysoned together in England.

[c] *Hugh Muimhneach*, i. e. Hugh the Momonian. He was an illegitimate son of King Felim O'Conor, and was called Muimhneach, or the Momonian, from his having been fostered in

Art, son of Cathal Reagh O'Rourke, Lord of Breifny, was slain by Mac Finnvar[y] and the English at Granard, and his people were slaughtered.

A great victory was gained over the English in Ulidia, so that there were counted two hundred horses and two hundred heads, besides all who fell of their plebeians.

Thomas Magauran was slain by the Kinel-Luachain[z].

The Kinel-Owen came into Tirconnell, and desolated a great part of the country. O'Donnell (Donnell Oge) assembled his people to oppose them, and pursued them to the breast of Slieve Truim[a], where they were defeated; and they left slaughtered men, many horses, accoutrements, arms, and armours behind them to the Kinel-Connell on this expedition[b].

THE AGE OF CHRIST, 1276.

The Age of Christ, one thousand two hundred seventy-six.

Gilla-an-Choimhdhe O'Carolan, Bishop of Tyrone (Derry), died.

Hugh Muimhneach[c], son of Felim, who was son of Cathal Crovderg, came from Munster into Connaught, and went thence to O'Donnell. O'Donnell and all his forces went with him to Echenach[d], and there parted from him, Hugh remaining in Connaught.

A depredation was committed by the sons of Turlough on the son of Felim and the sons of Mac Dermot; and Gilchreest O'Mulrenin was slain by them.

Munster, as we learn from the Annals of Clonmacnoise, as translated by Mageoghegan, in which this entry is given as follows: "A. D. 1276. A base son was presented to Felym Mac Cahall Crovederg O'Connor, after the death of the said Ffelym a long space, who was called Hugh Moyneagh, because he was nurished and brought up in Munster, and came to Connoght from thence, and as soon as he came and was known to be the son of Felym, Silemoreye and Clann-Moyleronie accepted of him, and had him in great accoumpt and reverence." This Aedh Muimhneach is also mentioned in the pedigree of the O'Conors, given in the Book of Lecan, fol. 72, *et sequen.* Thus: Feiblimiġ mac caṫail croibḋeirg, aen mac aici .i. aeḋ mac feiblimiġ, 7 mac aili ar na chur chuici .i. aeḋ muiṁneċ, 7 ro gob in taeḋ sin rigi Connaċt: "Felim, the son of Cathal Crovderg, had one son, namely, Hugh Mac Felim, and another son was fathered upon him, namely, Hugh Muimhneach, and this [latter] Hugh assumed the government of Connaught."

[d] *Echenach*, now Aughanagh; an ancient church said to have been built by St. Patrick,

Creaċ do denaṁ do mac feḋlimiḋ ar cloinn muircheartaiġ, ⁊ giolla na naingeal ua conroí do marḃaḋ do cloinn muircheartaiġ a ttóraiġecht a ccreiċi.

Creaċ do denaṁ do Ruaiḋri mac toirrḋealbaiġ ar muintir nechtain, ⁊ iadsaṁ do tabairt maḋma fair, ⁊ do ḃuain na creiċe ḋe. Doṁnall mac nell mic congalaiġ ui Ruairc (.i. giolla an ime), ⁊ sochaiḋe oile do muintir Ruairc do marḃaḋ doiḃ. Giollacriost ua neaċtain, do marḃaḋ do Ruaiḋri mac toirrḋelbaiġ iarsin.

Diarmaitt mag giolla muire tiġearna leithe cathail do écc.

AOIS CRIOST, 1277.

Aois Criost, mile, dá céd, seċtmogat aseacht.

Braon ua maoilmoiċéirġi ab cSnannois do écc.

Brian ruaḋ ua briain tiġearna tuaḋmuman do gabail i meaḃail do mac iarla claire. A ṫarraing eidir eachaiḃ ar a haiṫli iar ndenaṁ cairdis criost re roile doiḃ roiṁe sin, ⁊ do tabairt clocc ⁊ mionn da cele imma ccaradrad do comall.

Giollacriost ua birn fear gráḋa aoḋa ui concoḃair do marḃaḋ don giolla ruaḋ mac loċlainn ui concoḃair. Giolla na naoṁ ua birn do écc iar naiṫriġe.

Caislen rosa comain do leaccaḋ daoḋ mac feḋlimiḋ (.i. aoḋ muiṁneaċ) go cconnaċtaiḃ imme, ⁊ do doṁnall ua doṁnaill.

and which gives name to a parish in the barony of Tirerrill, and county of Sligo.—See *Genealogies, Tribes, and Customs of Hy-Fiachrach*, printed for the Irish Archæological Society in 1844, p. 490; and the map prefixed to the same work, on which this church is shewn, on the west side of Lough Arrow.

[e] *Clann-Murtough.*—These were the descendants of Murtough Muimhneach O'Conor, the son of Turlough More, Monarch of Ireland.

[f] *Lecale.*—Leaṫ Caṫail, i. e. Cathal's half, now the barony of Lecale, in the county of Down.

[g] Under this year, the Dublin copy of the Annals of Innisfallen gives an account of the expulsion of Brian Roe O'Brien out of Thomond, and the election of Turlough, the son of Teige Caeluisce O'Brien, in his place.

[h] *Brian Roe O'Brien.*—This passage is given in Mageoghegan's translation of the Annals of Clonmacnoise as follows: "A. D. 1277. The Earle of Clare his son, took Bryen Roe O'Bryen prisoner, very deceitfully, after they had sworn to each other all the oaths in Munster, as bells, relics of saints, and bachalls" [croziers], "to be true to each other for ever, and not endamage

A depredation was committed by the son of Felim on the Clann-Murtough[e]; and Gilla-na-n-Aingel O'Conroy was slain by Clann-Murtough, while pursuing the prey.

A depredation was committed by Rory, son of Turlough, on the O'Naghtans, but they defeated him, and deprived him of the booty. Donnell, son of Niall, son of Congalagh O'Rourke (i. e. Gilla-an-ime), and many others of the O'Rourkes, were slain by them. Gilchreest O'Naghtan and William O'Naghtan were afterwards slain by Rory, son of Turlough.

Dermot Mac Gillamurry, Lord of Lecale[f], died[g].

THE AGE OF CHRIST, 1277.

The Age of Christ, one thousand two hundred seventy-seven.

Braen O'Mulmoghery, Abbot of Kells, died.

Brian Roe O'Brien[h], Lord of Thomond, was treacherously taken by the son of the Earl of Clare, and afterwards drawn between horses, and this after both had entered into gossipred[i] with each other, and taken vows by bells and relics to retain mutual friendship.

Gilchreest O'Beirne, servant of trust to Hugh O'Conor, was slain by Gillaroe, son of Loughlin O'Conor.

Gilla-na-naev O'Beirne died, after penance.

The castle of Roscommon was pulled down by Hugh, son of Felim O'Conor [i. e. Hugh Muimhneach], aided by the Connacians and Donnell O'Donnell.

each other; also after they became sworne gossips, and for confirmation of this their indissoluble bond of perpetuall friendship, they drew part of the blood of each of them, which they putt in a vessall, and mingled it together: after all which protestations, the said Bryen was taken as aforesaid and bound to sterne steedes, and so was tortured to death by the said Earle's son." This passage is quoted by Mr. Moore, in a note in his History of Ireland, vol. iii. p. 33; but he does not mention what annals he quotes from. The Irish work called *Caithreim Thoirdhealbhaigh*, or Wars of Turlough O'Brien, contains a much more detailed account of the circumstances attending the murder of Brian Roe O'Brien. This murder is alluded to by the Irish chieftains in their remonstrance to Pope John XXII., as a striking instance of the treachery of the English and Anglo-Irish then in Ireland. They call the murderer of Brian Roe, the Duke of Gloucester's brother.—See *Memoirs of the Life and Writings of Charles O'Conor of Belanagare*, p. 74.

[i] *Gossipred.*—Iar ndenamh cairdis criost re aroile, i. e. after one of them had been sponsor to the other's child at baptism.

Creac mór do denaṁ do teallac ecdac for cenel luacáin a nglionn da duile dar marḃsat concoḃar mag dorchaiḋe ⁊ sochaiḋ immaille fris.

AOIS CRIOSD, 1278.

Aois Criosd, míle, dá céd, seachtmoġad, a hocht.

Tomás ua cuinn espucc cluana mic nóis do écc.

Flaiṫḃertac ua daiṁin tiġerna fermanac décc.

Tadcc mac toirrdhealḃaiġ mic aoḋa mic caṫail croiḃdeirg Rí connacht do ṁarḃadh la cloinn caṫail meic diarmada.

Ruaiḋri mac toirrdhealḃaiġ ui Concoḃair do marḃaḋ la giollu crisd máġ ḟlannchaiḋ, ⁊ la dartraiġiḃ ar bord droma cliaḃ, ⁊ an pearrún riaḃac mac tiġernáin uí Concoḃair, ⁊ sochaiḋe oile nác airiṁter sonn.

Donnchaḋ, fergal, ⁊ giollucriosd trí meic muirgesa meic donncaid mic tomaltaiġ do marḃaḋ la taḋcc mac doṁnaill iorrais.

Maiḋm cuince do ṫaḃairt do donnchaḋ mac briain ruaiḋ ⁊ do cloinn oile uí briain ar mac iarla claire gur loisccseḋ teampal cuince for a muintir ⁊ go ttuccsat ar diairṁe forra etir loscaḋ ⁊ marḃaḋ.

Tomaltac macc oireachtaiġ Rioġṫaoiseac síl muireaḋaiġ do marbhadh lar na tuathaiḃ.

[x] *Gleann-da-duile*, a valley in the parish of Oughteragh, barony of Carrigallen, and county of Leitrim. Kinel-Luachain, the territory of the Mac Dorcys, comprised the parish of Oughteragh, which adjoins Teallach Eachdhach, or the barony of Tullyhaw, in the northwest of the county of Cavan.

[l] Under this year the Dublin copy of the Annals of Innisfallen contains an interesting account, evidently abstracted from Magrath's *Caithreim Thoirdhealbhaigh*, of the coming of Thomas De Clare into Thomond to assist Brian Roe O'Brien, against Turlogh, the son of Teige Caeluisce. They also record the erection of the castle of Bunratty by Thomas de Clare, who dispossessed the old inhabitants of Tradry, and planted it with his own followers; and also the treacherous execution of Brian Roe O'Brien by the said Thomas de Clare, at the instigation of his (de Clare's) wife and father-in-law. These events are very unsatisfactorily treated of by the Four Masters. Under this year also, the Annals of Clonmacnoise, as translated by Mageoghegan, contain the following notice of the death of Conor O'Melaghlin, which has been omitted by the Four Masters: "A. D. 1277. Connor Mac Donnell Breagagh O'Melaghlyn, he that most warred with Englishmen in his owne time, a second Gwarie for bounty, a lyon for strength, and tyger for fierceness in time of enterprises and onsetts, and one hop'd to be king of Ireland, if he were suffered by the English,

A great depredation was committed by [the people of] Eachdhach upon the Kinel-Luachain, in Gleann-da-duile[k], during which they slew Conor Mac Dorcy, and a host of others[l].

THE AGE OF CHRIST, 1278.

The Age of Christ, one thousand two hundred seventy-eight.

Thomas O'Quin, Bishop of Clonmacnoise, died.

Flaherty O'Davine[m], Lord of Fermanagh, died.

Teige, son of Turlough, son of Hugh, son of Cathal Crovderg, King of Connaught, was slain by the sons of Cathal Mac Dermot.

Rory, son of Turlough O'Conor, was slain by Gilchreest Mac Clancy and the inhabitants of Dartry, on the borders of Drumcliff; and the Swarthy Parson, son of Tiernan O'Conor, and many others not numbered here.

Donough, Farrell, and Gilchreest, the three sons of Murrough, son of Donough, son of Tomaltagh, were slain by Teige, son of Donnell [O'Conor], of Erris.

The victory of Cuinche[n] was gained by Donough, son of Brian Roe, and the other sons of O'Brien, over the Earl of Clare; they burned the church of Cuinche over the heads of his people, and caused an indescribable destruction of them, both by burning and killing[o].

Tomaltagh Mageraghty, Royal Chieftain of Sil-Murray, was slain by the [people of the] Tuathas.

died penitently at Kilbeggann."

[m] *O'Davine*, ua daimhin.—This name is very common in the counties of Londonderry and Tyrone, where it is anglicised Devine. The family are of the same race as the Maguires and Mac Mahons of Oriel. The family of Maguire had not as yet obtained the chief sway in Fermanagh, though Donn Maguire had made great exertions to put down all rivals a few years before.

[n] *Cuinche*, now Quin, in the barony of Bunratty, about five miles to the east of Ennis. The church here referred to was an ancient Irish one, dedicated to St. Finghin. The great abbey of this place was not erected till the year 1402, or, according to Ware, till 1433.—See Harris's edition of Ware's Antiquities, p. 280.

[o] *Burning and killing.*—This passage is thus stated by Mageoghegan, in his translation of the Annals of Clonmacnoise: "Donnough Mac Bryen Roe O'Bryen gave the overthrow of Coynche to Thomas de Clare (the Earle), and burnt the church of Coynche over the heads of the said Earle and his people, where infinite numbers of people were both slain and killed therein, and

Aodh muimhneach mac feidhlimidh do ghabhail Righe Connacht.

Iomaireagh do thabhairt do bhrian ua ndubhda, ⁊ do Art na ccapall ua nEghra tighearna luighne, do cloinn Fheórais, gur ro sraoineadh for cloinn Fheorais, ⁊ ro marbhadh diar mac Mhaoilir móir, ⁊ Conchobhar ruadh mac Feórais, ⁊ aroile cén móthát.

AOIS CRIOSD, 1279.

Aois Criost, mile, dá céd, seachdmoghad, a naoi.

Tomaltach mac toirrdhelbhaigh mic maoilseachlainn ui Conchobhair airdepsucc tuama Saoi eirenn uile, i neaccna, i neólus ⁊ i ndeserc do écc iar mbuaidh naithrighe.

Giolla an choimdedh ó cerbhalláin epscop thíre heoghain do écc.

Concobhor mac diarmada mic maghnusa uí Concobhair do marbhadh.

Murchadh ó neachtain do mharbhadh do domhnall ó neachtain ⁊ comrac dfhoccra do Roibérd ua neachtain dearbhrathair murchaidh ar domhnall ⁊ Roibérd do marbhadh leis iarsin.

Domhnall mac giollucriost uí neachtain do marbhadh la haodh ó ccoincénainn.

Maolseachlainn mac toirrdhelbhaigh do mharbhadh.

Giolla íosa mór mac firbhisigh ollamh ua Fiachrach i seanchus do écc.

escaped narrowly himself, which escape myne author sayeth that himself was sorry for."

p *Hugh Muimhneach.*—Dr. O'Conor does not take any notice of this King of Connaught in his historical account of the family of O'Conor, prefixed to the Memoirs of the Life and Writings of Charles O'Oonor of Belanagare. In Mageoghegan's translation of the Annals of Clonmacnoise, this entry is in English as follows: "A. D. 1278. Hugh Moyneagh Mac Felym was ordained and made King of Connought." This is an instance of the inauguration of a bastard as King of Connaught, and of one who does not appear to have been ever acknowledged by his father.—See note under the year 1276. It appears from several authentic records that bastards, particularly muliers, were sometimes elected, at least, to minor chieftainries. Dr. Charles Dunne, in his arguments against his brother, Teige O'Doyne, Chief of Hy-Regan, in the reign of James I., asserts that for many hundred years "no bastard attained to the chiefrie of Iregaine in the Queen's County;" but this amounts to an acknowledgment that bastards had attained to the chiefry in more ancient times. In a Chancery record of a law-suit between Donell O'Donovan, Chief of Clancahill, in the county of Cork, and his brother, Teige, the latter states, "that by the usage and custome of the contrie of Carberie, an illegitimate, or base son, was to be secluded and put besides the chieftanrie, signorie, and inheritance, so that he that was lawfullie borne was ever interested by custome in them and no bastard."

Hugh Muimhneach[p], son of Felim, assumed the sovereignty of Connaught.

Brian O'Dowda and Art na g-Capall [of the Horses] O'Hara, Lord of Leyny, gave battle to the Clann-Feorais [Birminghams], in which the Clann-Feorais were defeated, and the two sons of Meyler More, Conor Roe Mac Feorais, and others besides, were slain.

THE AGE OF CHRIST, 1279.

The Age of Christ, one thousand two hundred seventy-nine.

Tomaltagh, son of Turlough, son of Melaghlin O'Conor, Archbishop of Tuam, the most illustrious man in all Ireland for wisdom, knowledge, and charity, died, after the victory of penance.

Gilla-an-Choimhdheadh O'Carolan[q], Bishop of Tyrone (Derry), died.

Conor, son of Dermot, son of Manus O'Conor, was killed.

Murrough O'Naghtan was slain by Donnell O'Naghtan; upon which a challenge was given to Donnell by Robert O'Naghtan, brother of Murrough; and Robert also fell by (the hand of) Donnell.

Donnell, son of Gilchreest O'Naghtan, was slain by Hugh O'Concannon.

Melaghlin, son of Turlough [O'Conor], was slain.

Gillo-Isa More Mac Firbis, Ollav of Tireragh in history, died.

But Donell, in his rejoinder, asserts, and his witnesses prove, that "the custome of the countrie waranteth that bastards, especiallie muliers, by the civill law, might be O'Donovans." The fact seems to be that bastards who were of a warlike character were preferred, in those lawless times, to legitimate children of less combative disposition, especially when they were of a higher or more powerful family by the mother's side than by the father's. The marriage ceremony does not appear to have stamped as much dignity on the character of the offspring, as the respectability and power of the mother's family, and their own bravery, which always commanded the admiration of the subalterns. We have a striking instance of this fact in the account given by the genealogists of the children of Turlough More O'Conor, King of Ireland, who were twenty-four in number, and of whom, according to the Book of Lecan, only three were by his married wife, and even these were thrown into the shade by the superior valour of their illegitimate brothers.

[q] *O'Carolan.*—His death has been already entered under the year 1276, which is the date assigned to it in the Dublin copy of the Annals of Ulster. In the old translation of the Ulster Annals, both dates are given thus: "A.D. 1276 (*al.* 1279). Gilcomy O'Cerballan, Bishop of Tiroen, *quievit.*" In Harris's edition of Ware's Bishops, p. 289, his death is assigned to the year 1279, on the authority of the Annals of Lough Kee.

AOIS CRIOSD, 1280.

Aois Criosd, mile, dá céd, ochtmoġat.

Seaan ua laidiġ easpocc cille halaḋ,[r] ⁊ Matha mac maġnusa uí Concoḃair abb na buille do écc.

Imreasain do ṡirge etir aoḋ ṁuiṁneaċ[s] mac feḋlimiḋ mic cathail croiḃḋeirg Ri Connaċt ⁊ clann muircheartaiġ muiṁniġ ui Concoḃair. Aoḋ muiṁneaċ do ṁarḃaḋ ḋoiḃ i ccoill in daingin[t] ⁊ maoilseaċlainn mac maġnusa do ġaḃail an la cédna ris. Ua domnaill da ḟuaslacaḋ uaṫa. Ceiṫri céd bó ⁊ fiche eaċ asséḋ fuairsiod ass.

Caṫal mac Conċoḃair ruaiḋ mic muircheartaiġ muiṁniġ mic toirrdealḃaiġ móir uí Concoḃair do ríoġaḋ do Connachtaiḃ iarsin.

Maoilseaċlainn ó gairmleadhaiġ toiseaċ cenél moáin, ⁊ Concoḃor ua gairmleadhaiġ do ṫuitim le teallaċ moḋaráin.[u]

AOIS CRIOSD, 1281.

Aois Criosd, mile, da céd, ochtmoġat a hoén.

Taḋg mac caṫail meic diarmada tighearna moiġe luirc, Saoí in eineaċ i nengnaṁ[w] ⁊ i nuairle do écc.

Caṫ dirint da ċrioch etir cenel cconaill ⁊ cenel eoġain. Aoḋ buiḋi mac domnaill óicc mic aoḋa méṫ mic aoda sir a raitti an macaomh toinleasc ⁊ goill ulaḋ imaille fris don dara leṫ. Domnall óg ua domnaill tighearna cenel cconaill, ḟer manaċ, airgiall, urmoir gaoiḋeal ulaḋ uile ⁊ Connaċt

[r] *O'Laidhigh.*—In the old translation of the Annals of Ulster he is called "John O'Loyn," and in Harris's edition of Ware's Bishops, p. 650, "Friar John O'Laidig, or O'Loyn."

[s] *Murtough Muimhneach.*—The descendants of this Mortogh are henceforward called Clann-Muircheartaigh in these Annals. They became very contentious, and are often mentioned.

[t] *Dangan.*—Daingean, a fastness, or fortress. There are several places of this name in Connaught. The Dangan here referred to is probably the townland of Dangan, now divided into the several portions of Danganbeg, Dangan Eighter, and Dangan Oughter, in the parish of Killererin, in the barony of Tiaquin, and county of Galway.—See Ordnance map of that county, sheet 44.

[u] *Teallach Modharain.*—There was a tribe of this name located near Corcaree in Westmeath. See note [n], p. 66, *supra.* But this tribe were in Ulster, and seated near Strabane, in Tyrone.

[w] *Prowess,* engnaṁ.—This word is translated

THE AGE OF CHRIST, 1280.

The Age of Christ, one thousand two hundred eighty.

John O'Laidhigh[r], Bishop of Killala, and Matthew, son of Manus O'Conor, Abbot of Boyle, died.

A contention arose between Hugh Muimhneach, son of Felim, son of Cathal Crovderg, King of Connaught, and the descendants of Murtough Muimhneach[s] O'Conor. Hugh Muimhneach was slain by these at the wood of Dangan[t]; and Melaghlin, son of Manus, was taken prisoner on the same day by them; but he was ransomed by O'Donnell, and they received four hundred cows and twenty horses for him.

Cathal, son of Conor Roe, son of Murtough Muimhneach, son of Turlough More O'Conor, was inaugurated king by the Connacians after this.

Melaghlin O'Gormly, Chief of Kinel-Moen, and Conor O'Gormly, fell by the tribe of Teallach-Modharain[u].

THE AGE OF CHRIST, 1281.

The Age of Christ, one thousand two hundred eighty-one.

Teige, son of Cathal Mac Dermot, Lord of Moylurg, illustrious for hospitality, prowess[w], and nobility, died.

The battle of Disert-da-chrioch[x] was fought by the Kinel-Connell and the Kinel-Owen, [that is], beween Hugh Boy, son of Donnell Oge, son of Hugh Meth, son of Hugh, who was usually called an Macaemh Toinleasc[y], assisted by the English of Ulster, on the one side; and Donnell Oge O'Donnell, Lord of Tirconnell, Fermanagh, Oriel, and the greater part of the Irish of Ulster, of

prowess by Mageoghegan, and *feats* by the old translator of the Annals of Ulster, by whom this passage is thus rendered: "A.D. 1278 (*al.* 1281). Teg Mac Cathall Mac Diermod, King of Moilurg, an excellent man in liberality and feats, *quievit.*" The original Irish is given as follows in the Dublin copy of the Annals of Ulster: "A. D. 1278. Taḋg mac caṫail mic Ḋiarmada ri muiġi luirg sai neiniġ 7 nengnoṁa quieuit in christo."

[x] *Disert-da-chrioch*, now Desertcreaght, a townland and parish in the north of the barony of Dungannon, in the county of Tyrone.

[y] *Macaemh Toinleasc.*—Mageoghegan Englishes this "Hugh Boye mac Donnel Oge mac Hugh, surnamed the Fatt, mac Hugh, who was called the leasy-arsed youth."

achd maḋ beacc ⁊ na breifne uile don leṫ araill. Ro ṁeabaiḋ tra an caṫ-so for cenel cconaill. Ro marbaḋ domnall ua domnaill ann .i. an taſn gaoiḋeal do bfſrr eneaċ, ſngnaṁ, aireachus ⁊ uaisle do ġaoiḋealaiḃ Ereann is in aimsir sin. Fechſṁ coitcionn iarṫair Eorpo uile eiriḋe ⁊ a aḋnacul i mainistir na mbraṫor i nDoire colaim cille iar mbreith buaḋa gacha maithſsa dó gó sin. Atiatt annso an luchd ro bfſrr dar marbaḋ ina ḟoċair Maolruanaiḋ ua baoiġill taoiseaċ na ttri ttuaṫ, Eoġan mac maoilseaċlainn mic domnaill móir ui ḋomnaill, Ceallaċ mac giollubriġde uí baoiġill an taſn taoiseaċ do bfſrr ſngnaṁ ⁊ eneaċ dexiḃ ⁊ dollaṁnaiḃ boí in ſnaimsir sirr, aindilſrr ó baoiġill, dubġall a ṁac som, giollu criosd mag ḟlannċaidh taoiseaċ dartraicche, domnall mac gille ḟinnén taoiseaċ muinntiri feodaċáin, Enna ó gairmleadhaiġ ardtaoiseaċ cenel moáin, Corbmac mac an ḟirleġinn uí domnaill taoiseaċ fanad, giollu an comḋeaḋ ua maolduin taoiseaċ luircc, Carmac mac carmaic ui domnaill, giollu na nócc mac dail le docair, Maoilseaċloinn mac nell ui ḃaoiġill, aindilſr mac muirceſrtaiġ ui domnaill, Maġnus mac cuinn, giollu na naſṁ ua heoċaccáin, muirċeſrtaċ ua flaithbſrtaiġ, muirceſrtach mac anultoiġ, flaithbſrtaċ macc buiḋeaċain ⁊ Sochaiḋe oile do macaibh tigchſrnaḋ ⁊ taoiseaċ nach airiṁtſr sonn.

Aoḋ mac domnaill oicc ui domnaill doirdneaḋ i nionaḋ a aṫar.

Caṫ edir na bairéḋċaiḃ ⁊ an ciomsóccaċ gur meabaiḋ for bairéḋċaibh. Ro marbaḋ ann uilliam bairéd, adam Plemend, ⁊ Sochaiḋe imaille friú. Ḃadar tra dias do gaoiḋealaiḃ ag congnaṁ las an cciomsoccaċ is in ccaṫh sa ro dſrrccnaiḋ ar goil ⁊ ġaisccead luṫ ⁊ laṁaċ da mbaoi ann, Taiċleaċ ó baoiġill, ⁊ taichleaċ ó dúbda iadside.

Aodh Muiṁneach mac toirrḋealbaiġ uí briain do écc.

[z] *O'Donnell.*—Charles O'Conor wrote *inter lineas*, "san 41 bliaḋain dia aois, i. e. in the forty-first year of his age."

[a] *Hospitality, prowess, &c.*, eneaċ, engnaṁ, &c.—The translation of this passage given by Mageoghegan in his Annals of Clonmacnoise, has a close agreement with the text of the Four Masters. Thus: "Donnell O'Donnell was slain; the best Irishman for bounty, prowess, worthiness, and many other perfections that lived in his time, and was buried in the church of Derie, after he had all things fallen out with him fortunately untill that day of his death."

[b] *The greatest commander*, fechem coitċionn iarṫair eorpa.—The old translator of the Annals of Ulster renders this, "the overseer of the west of Europe."

[c] *Dowell*, dubġall.—This name, which signifies black Gaul, or foreigner, is generally anglicised Dowell by the Irish, and Dugald by

Connaught, excepting a small portion, and of the entire of Breifny, on the other. In this battle the Kinel-Connell were defeated; and Donnell Oge O'Donnell[z], the most illustrious man of the Irish of his time for hospitality[a], prowess, splendour, and nobility, and the greatest commander[b] in the west of Europe, was slain; and he was interred in the monastery of Derry, having obtained the palm in every goodness up to that time. The most distinguished of those who fell along with him were the following, namely, Mulrony O'Boyle, Chief of the Three Tuathas; Owen, son of Melaghlin, son of Donnell More O'Donnell; Kellagh, son of Giolla-Brighde O'Boyle, one of the most illustrious chieftains of his time for prowess, and for munificence to learned men and ollavs; Andiles O'Boyle, and Dowell[c], his son; Gilchreest Mac Clancy, Chief of Dartry; Donnell Mac Gillafinnen, Chief of Muintir-Feodachain[d]; Enna O'Gormly, Chief of Kinel-Moen; Cormac, son of the Ferleighin [Lector] O'Donnell, Chief of Fanad; Gilla-an-Choimhdheadh O'Muldoon, Chief of Lurg[e]; Cormac, son of Cormac O'Donnell; Gilla-na-n-óg Mac Dail-re-docair; Melaghlin, son of Niall O'Boyle; Andiles, son of Murtough O'Donnell; Manus Mac Quin; Gilla-na-naev O'Heoghagan; Murtough O'Flaherty; Murtough Macan-Ulty; Flaherty Mac Buidheachain; and many others of the sons of lords and chieftains not enumerated here.

Hugh, son of Donnell Oge O'Donnell, was inaugurated in the place of his father.

A battle [was fought] between the Barretts and the Cusack, in which the Barretts were defeated, and William Barrett, Adam Fleming, and many others, were slain. There were assisting the Cusack in this battle two of the Irish, namely, Taichleach O'Boyle and Taichleach O'Dowda, who surpossed all that were there in bravery and valour, and in agility and dexterity at shooting[f].

Hugh Muimhneach, son of Turlough O'Brien, died[g].

the Scotch.

[d] *Muintir Feodachain.*—The territory of the Mac Gillinnions extended from the Arney River to western extremity of Belmore mountain, in the barony of Magheraboy, and county of Fermanagh.

[e] *Lurg*, is now the name of a barony in the north of the county of Fermanagh, in which the Muldoons are still numerous.

[f] *Dexterity at shooting*, lámac.—This passage is thus given in English in the old translation of the Annals of Ulster: "A. D. 1278 (*al.* 1281). A battell between the Barets and the Cusacks, where the Barets were put to flight, and William Baret was killed," [and also] "Adam Flemin, and many more men; and there were

AOIS CRIOSD, 1282.

Aoiꝼ Cꞃioꞅꝺ, mꞇle, ꝺá ċéꝺ, ochꞇmoᵹaꞇ, aꝺó.

Muiꞃċꞇꞃꞇaċ mac muꞃċaꝺa Rí laiᵹꞇn, ⁊ aꞃꞇ mac muꞃċaꝺa a ꝺꞇꞃḃꞃaṫaiꞃ ꝺo ṁaꞃḃaḋ la ᵹallaiḃ.

Taichleaċ mac maolꞃuanaiḋ uí ḋúḃꝺa ꞇicchꞇꞃna ua ffiaċꞃaċ, aon ꝺo bꞇꞃꞃ eneaċ ⁊ ionnꞅaicchiḋ ꝺa ċineaḋ ina aimꞅiꞃ ꝺo ṁaꞃḃaḋ la haꝺam cioṁꞅócc aꞃ ꞇꞃaicch Eoꞇhaile.

Laꞅꞅaiꞃꝼiona inᵹꞇn caṫail cꞃoiḃꝺeiꞃᵹ uí Concoḃaiꞃ bꞇn ꝺoṁnaill móiꞃ ui ꝺoṁnaill ⁊ maṫaiꞃ ꝺoṁnaill óicc, bainꞇꞇnn ban lꞇiṫe cuinn iꞅiꝺe ꝺo écc.

Maṫa ua Raᵹallaiᵹ ꞇicchꞇꞃna muinnꞇiꞃi maoilmoꞃḋa, ⁊ Ᵹiollu ioꞅu macc ꞇicchꞇꞃnáin ꝺo nᵹoiꞃṫi ᵹiollu ioꞅu móꞃ ꞇaoiꞅeaċ ꞇellaiᵹ ꝺunċaꝺa ꝺéᵹ.

Caṫal mac ᵹiollu na naꞇṁ ui ḟꞇꞃᵹail ꞇicchꞇꞃna na hanᵹaile ꝺo écc, i

two Irish on Cusack's side, that excelled all in courage and shooting, viz., Taichlegh O'Duvda, and Taichlegh O'Boyl."

It is thus given by Mageoghegan, in his translation of the Annals of Clonmacnoise: "A. D. 1281. There was a feild fought between the Barretts of the one side, and the Cusaks of the other, where the Barretts were vanquished. William Barrett and Adam Ffiemyng, with many others, were slain. There were two Irishmen of Cusack's side that surpassed the companys of both sides for prowes, manhood, dexteritie of handling of arms, hardiness, and all other parts of activitie, named Taihleagh O'Dowdie, and Taihleagh O'Boylle." According to the *Historia Familiæ De Burgo*, a manuscript in the Library of Trinity College, already referred to, this battle was fought at Moyne, in the barony of Tirawley, near the ancient church of Kilroe: "Bellum apud Mayn de Kilro per Adam Cymsog ex unâ parte, et William Bareth ex altera parte, ubi vulneratus et captus est idem William. Et postea de hiis vulneribus mortuus fuit. Adam Fleming et multi alii [occisi sunt]." The place here called Kilro retains that name to this day, and is remarkable for the remains of a very ancient church erected in the time of St. Patrick. Moyne abbey is a short distance to the south-east of it.—See *Genealogies, Tribes, and Customs of Hy-Fiachrach*, p. 328.

[g] Under this year the Dublin copy of the Annals of Inisfallen contain very curious notices of the feuds of Thomond, which was at this period the theatre of war and bloodshed, in consequence of the intrigues of Thomas de Clare, who set up Donough, the son of Brian Roe O'Brien, against Turlough, the son of Teige Caeluisce O'Brien.

[h] *Mac Murrough*.—According to Grace's Annals, these were slain at Arklow in 1282. Dr. Hanmer notices their death as follows, at 1281: "Murtough Mac Muroch, with Art, his brother, lost their heads at Wickloe: another saith at Artchloe, so Clyn and Dowling doe report."

[i] *O'Dowda*.—The notice of Taichleach O'Dowda's death is given as follows in Mageoghegan's translation of the Annals of Clonmacnoise:

THE AGE OF CHRIST, 1282.

The Age of Christ, one thousand two hundred eighty-two.

Murtough Mac Murrough[h], King of Leinster, and Art, his brother, were slain by the English.

Taichleach, son of Mulrony O'Dowda[i], Lord of Tireragh, the most hospitable and warlike of his tribe in his time, was slain by Adam Cusack on [the strand of] Traigh Eothaile.

Lasarina, daughter of Cathal Crovderg O'Conor, the wife of Donnell More O'Donnell, and the mother of Donnell Oge, head of the women of Leth-Chuinn[k], died.

Mathew O'Reilly, Lord of Muintir Maelmora, and Gilla-Isa Mac Tiernan[l], usually called Gilla-Isa More, Chief of Teallach-Dunchadha, died.

Cathal, son of Gilla-na-naev O'Farrell, Lord of Annaly, died on Inis-Cuan[m]

"A. D. 1282. Taithleaghe Mac Moyleronie O'Dowdie, prince of the country of Offiaghragh Moye, one of great prowes and bountie, and of great and of continuall dissention with the English and all foreigners, in defence of his contrey, was killed by Adam Cusack at Beerhaven." Here he renders Traigh Eothaile by Beerhaven, but this is a great error. Haliday, in his translation of Keating's History of Ireland, p. 193, falls into a similar error in supposing it to be Youghal. The Traigh Eothaile, mentioned by Keating at the page above referred to, is described by Duald Mac Firbis, a native of Tireragh, as in Tir Fiachrach: Tráiġ Ruiſ airgiḋ ré ráiḋtear Traiġ Eoṫuile iſ in Tír Ḟiaċraċ ſo a ṫáim, i. e. "the strand of Ros Airgid, which is called Traigh Eothuile, in this Tir Fiachrach in which we are."—*Lib. Geneal.* (Marquis of Drogheda's copy), p. 8. Traigh Eothuile is now generally called Trawohelly, and is a large and beautiful strand at the mouth of the Ballysadare River, in the barony of Tireragh, and county of Sligo. It extends from the Strand road to Beltraw, near Tanrego.—See *Genealogies, Tribes, and Customs of Hy-Fiachrach*, p. 117, and the map prefixed to the same work.

[k] *Leth-Chuinn*, i. e. Conn's half, means the northern half of Ireland. In the old translation of the Annals of Ulster, Lasarina is called "the gentlest woman in Ireland."

[l] *Mac Tiernan.*—In the old translation of the Annals of Ulster, this name is anglicised Mac Kiernan, which is the present anglicised form. This family of Teallach Dunchadha, now the barony of Tullyhunco, in the county of Cavan, is to be distinguished from Mac Tiernan, of the county of Roscommon, descended from Tiernan, the son of Cathal Migarain O'Conor.

[m] *Inis-Cuain, in the river of Cluain-lis-Becemic-Conla.*—These names are now obsolete. The nearest name to Cluain-lis, now remaining in the county of Longford, is the parish of Cloongish; but they cannot be considered identical, as Cloongish is called in Irish Cluain geiṙe.—See Irish Calendar of the O'Clerys, at 25th April.

ninisſ cuan for aḃainn cluain lis béce mic connla. Seaffraiḋ mac giollu na naſṁ ui fḟergail do ġaḃail ticcheſrnais na hangaile da ér.

AOIS CRIOSD, 1283.

Aois Criosd, míle, da ċéd, ochdṁogad, atrí.

Aoḋ buiḋe o nell ticcheſrna cenel eoġain, fecce eniġ ⁊ ġaiscciḋ gaoiḋeal, aon Roġa an tuaisccirt ar ṫioḋnacal ſéct ⁊ maoine, fer ba moa gráin ⁊ coscar da cenél ina aimsir. Ba rioġḋaṁna diongḃala dEirinn eisiḋe, do ṁarḃaḋ la mag maṫġaṁna, brian, ⁊ la hairġiallaiḃ ⁊ la giollu iosu ruaḋ mac doṁnaill ui Raġallaiġ.

Taḋg mac doṁnaill iorrais uí ċonċoḃair do loṫ la luiġhniḃ ⁊ a thairbirt do chathal ó ċoncoḃair ⁊ a écc iarsin do biṫhin a luit.

Ath cliaṫ ⁊ teampall criosd do loscaḋ.

AOIS CRIOST, 1284.

Aois Criosd, mile, dá ċéd, ochtmocchatt, a ceathair.

Muirir ua concoḃair epscop oile finn décc, ⁊ Aṁlaoiḃ ua tomaltaiġ do oirdneaḋ ina ionaḋ ⁊ a écc iarttain. Giolla iosa mac an liaṫanaiġ ui ċoncoḃair Abb oilen na trinóiḋe ar loch cé (dord pemonstra) do togha in epscoṗóiḋeċt oile finn iarsin.

[n] Under this year (1282), the Dublin copy of the Annals of Innisfallen contain some notices of the affairs of Thomond, which have been omitted by the Four Masters. They would appear to have been abstracted by the compiler of this Chronicle from the Irish work entitled *Caithreim Thoirdhealbhaigh*, or Wars of Turlough O'Brien.

[o] *O'Neill.*—In Mageoghegan's translation of the Annals of Clonmacnoise, he is called King of Aileagh.

[p] *Oriels.*—Oirġiallaiḃ, Mac Mahon's followers were so called.

[q] *Burned.*—In Grace's Annals of Ireland this event is recorded with equal brevity, but more correctly, thus: "A. D. 1283. Arsit Dubliniæ pars et Campanile Trinitatis." For a fuller account of this event, see Clynn's Annals, and Hanmer's Chronicle, *ad ann.* Under this year the Annals of Clonmacnoise, as translated by Mageoghegan, record the death of Art O'Melaghlin, surnamed "of the castles," in the following words: "A. D. 1283. Art Mac Cormack O'Melaghlyn, surnamed Art na Gaislean, the greatest warrior in Ireland in his time against the Englishmen, and he that killed most of the English and Irish; also he that broke down

[an island] in the river of Cluain-lis-Becc-mic-Conla; and Geoffrey, son of Gilla-na-naev O'Farrell, assumed the lordship of Annaly after him[n].

THE AGE OF CHRIST, 1283.

The Age of Christ, one thousand two hundred eighty-three.

Hugh Boy O'Neill[o], Lord of Kinel-Owen; head of the liberality and valour of the Irish; the most distinguished in the North for bestowing jewels and riches, the most formidable and victorious of his tribe in his time, and the worthy heir to the throne of Ireland; was slain by Mac Mahon (Brian) and the Oriels[p], and Gilla-Isa Roe, son of Donnell O'Reilly.

Teige, son of Donnell of Erris O'Conor, was wounded by the people of Leyny, and delivered up to Cathal O'Conor, and [soon] after this died of the effect of his wound.

Dublin and Christ's church were burned[q].

THE AGE OF CHRIST, 1284.

The Age of Christ, one thousand two hundred eighty-four.

Maurice O'Conor, Bishop of Elphin, died, and Auliffe O'Tomalty was consecrated his successor; but he died soon after. Gilla-Isa, son of Liathanagh O'Conor, Abbot of Trinity Island in Lough Ree (of the Premonstratentian[r] Order), was then elected to the bishopric of Elphin.

seven-and-twenty castles, both great and small, in the course of his warrs, and he that gave many great overthrows to the English and Irish, died with good penance; after whose death his son, Carbry, succeeded him in his place, and was constituted King of Meath."

Under this year the Dublin copy of the Annals of Inisfallen contains an account (abstracted from the *Caithreim Thoirdhealbhaigh*) of the battles between De Clare and Turlough O'Brien, and of the death of Donough, the son of Brian Roe O'Brien, who assisted De Clare. This latter event is briefly noticed by the Four Masters under the year 1284.

[r] *Premostratentian.*—The Premostratentian, or White Canons, were originally a branch of the Canons Regular, and lived according to the rule of St. Augustine. They were reformed by St. Norbert of Lorrain about the year 1120, at Premonstre, in the diocese of Laon in Picardy. Pope Calixtus the Second, confirmed this order, and gave them the title of Canons Regular. The habit of their order is a white cassock, with a rochet over it, a long white cloak, and a cap of the same colour.

Donnchaḋ ua briain tiġearna ṫuaḋṁuṁan do ṁarḃaḋ la toirrḋealḃaċ ua mbriain.

Duḃġall mac maġnusa ui ḃaoiġill taoiseach cloiche chinnḟaolaḋ do ṁarḃaḋ do ṁuintir ui ṁaoilġaoithe.

Mac na hoiḋche maġ dorchaiḋe taoiseach ċeinel luachain (no duachain) do écc.

Siomand dexetra do ṁarḃaḋ la brian ua ffloinn, ⁊ la da mac ui ḟlannaġáin, diarmaitt, ⁊ maoileaċloinn. Coccaḋ ⁊ easaonta déirġe hi cconnachtaiḃ tres an marḃaḋ sin. Creacha móra do dénoṁ do ġallaiḃ ara haiṫle ⁊ a nairsġ co hiomlán do ṁuintir oilén na trinóide, ⁊ do ṁanchaiḃ mainistre na buille.

Caislén cille colmáin do leaccaḋ la cathal mac concoḃair ruaiḋ (Ri connaċt).

Dún mór do loscaḋ la fiaċra ua ffloinn.

AOIS CRIOST, 1285.

Aois Criost, mile, da chéd, ochtṁocchat, a cúicc.

Siomón ó Ruairc epscop na breifne décc.

Ruaiḋri ua gaḋra tiġearna Slebe luġa do ṁarḃaḋ la Mac feorais for loch uí ġaḋra.

Muiris maol Mac Gerailt do écc.

[s] *Donough O'Brien.*—The Irish work called *Caithreim Thoirdhealbhaigh*, gives a detailed account of the death of this Donough, which has been abstracted by the compiler of the Dublin copy of the Annals of Innisfallen.

[t] *Cloch Chinnfaelaidh*, i. e. Kinfaela's stone. The name is now anglicised Cloghineely, and is that of a district in the north-west of the barony of Kilmacrenan, in the county of Donegal. This is one of the three Tuathas, or districts, which originally belonged to O'Boyle, and, more recently, to Mac Sweeny na-d-Tuath. The stone from which this district takes its name, and of which strange legends are told in the country, is to be seen near the small village of Crossroads, which is the present capital of the territory of Cloghineely.

[u] *Mac-na-h-Oidhche Mac Dorcy.*—Mac-na-h-Oidche signifies *son of the night*, and was rather a soubriquet, or nickname, than the baptismal name of a man. It is now obsolete. The territory of Kinel-Luachain, in which the Mac Dorcys are still extant, comprised the parish of Oughteragh, or Ballinamore, in the east of the county of Leitrim.

[w] *To the family, &c.*, that is, they gave up the spoils to the heads of these monasteries, to be disposed of as they should think proper.

Donough O'Brien[s], Lord of Thomond, was slain by Turlough O'Brien.

Dowell, son of Manus O'Boyle, Chief of Cloch Chinnfaeladh[t], was slain by the people of O'Mulgeeha.

Mac-na-h-Oidhche Mac Dorcy[u], Chief of Kinel-Luachain, died.

Simon de Exeter was slain by Brien O'Flynn and the two sons of O'Flanagan, Dermot and Melaghlin; in consequence of which war and dissensions arose in Connaught. After this the English committed great depredations; but they restored the whole of the spoils to the family[w] of Trinity Island[x], and the monks of the abbey of Boyle.

The castle of Kilcolman[y] was thrown down by Cathal, son of Conor Roe, King of Connaught.

Dunmore[z] was burned by Fiachra O'Flynn.

THE AGE OF CHRIST, 1285.

The Age of Christ, one thousand two hundred eighty-five.

Simon O'Rourke, Bishop of Breifny, died.

Rory O'Gara, Lord of Sliabh-Lugha[a], was slain by Mac Feorais [Bermingham] on Lough O'Gara[b].

Maurice Mael [the Bald] Fitzgerald died.

[x] *Trinity Island.*—See other notices of this island at the years 1231, 1234, 1235, 1236, 1237, 1239, 1243, 1247, and 1249; and see its situation in Lough Key, and the ruins of the abbey shewn on the Ordnance map of the county of Roscommon, sheet 6.

[y] *Kilcolman*, a townland in a parish of the same name in the barony of Costello, and county of Mayo.—See note under the year 1270.

[z] *Dunmore.*—This is the Dunmore in the county of Galway, eight miles to the north of Tuam, where are still to be seen the ruins of a strong castle erected by the family of Mac Feorais, or Bermingham.

Under this year (1284), the Dublin copy of the Annals of Innisfallen record the erection of the castle of Ennis, in Thomond, by Turlough, the son of Teige Caeluisce O'Brien.

[a] *Sliabh-Lugha.*—This name is sometimes Anglicised Slewlowe in old Anglo-Irish documents. See note [l] under the year 1206, p. 150.

[b] *Lough O'Gara.*—Loċ uı ġaḋpa, i.e. O'Gara's lake. This lake is now more usually called Lough Gara. It was anciently called Loch Techet, and received its present name from the family of O'Gara, who, after they had been driven from their original territories of Galenga and Sliabh Lugha, in the now county of Mayo, by the Jordans and Costelloes, settled in the present barony of Coolavin, in the county of Sligo, and erected a castle at Moygara, or Moy O'Gara, near the north-east extremity of this lake.

Enri mac giolla ḟinnéin do écc.

Maiḋm do thabairt do Maġnus ua cConcoḃair ar Adam Cioṁsócc ⁊ ar ġallaiḃ iarthair Connacht ag Earr dara dú inar marḃaitt daoíne ioṁḋa ⁊ inar gaḃaḋ coilin Cioṁsócc derbrathair Adaim.

Maidhm do thabairt do Pilib mac Goisdelḃaiġ ar ṁuintir Maġnusa uí ċoncoḃair ar Sliaḃ gaṁ dú in ro marḃaḋ sochaiḋe do muintir Maġnusa.

AOIS CRIOST, 1286.

Aois Criost, míle, dá cheḋ, ochtṁocchatt, a sé.

Sloiġeaḋ mór la hiarla Ulaḋ i cConnachtaiḃ gur ro milleaḋ moran do ṁainistribh ⁊ do cheallaiḃ seachnón Connacht lais. Ro ġaḃ neart in gaċ

[c] *Mac Gillafinnen*.—This name is now anglicised Mac Gillinnion, and sometimes changed to Leonard. The family were seated in the district of Muintir Feodachain, extending from the Arney River to the western extremity of Belmore mountain, in the barony of Magheraboy, and county of Fermanagh.

[d] *Sliabh Gamh*, a chain of mountains in the baronies of Leyny and Tireragh, in the county of Sligo. The name is now incorrectly translated Ox Mountains, because the natives believe that the true Irish form of the name is Sliaḃ ḋaṁ, i. e. mountains of the oxen; but this is a local error, for the name is spelled Sliaḃ gaṁ in all the ancient and modern Irish annals.

[e] Under this year the Annals of Clonmacnoise, as translated by Mageoghegan, contain the following passages, which have been altogether omitted by the Four Masters: "A. D. 1285. Hugh mac Hugh O'Conor and Flann O'Melaghlyn, with other noble youth in their companys, took a great prey from William Crocke, where" [*recte* but] "they were pursued and quite discomfitted, in so much that above twenty of them were slain and drownded, together with Bryan mac Donnell Breagagh O'Melaghlyn, a youth then of the age of fifteen years.

"Theobald Buttler, with his forces, accompanied with the forces of O'Kelly, of Elie O'Karroll, of Ormond, of Arye, of Ohne" [Owney] "O'Mulryan, of Sileanmchye, and Clann William of the Burks, came to Delvin Mac Coghlan to take the spoyles of that Contrey, and to destroy and subvert itself by their Power. Carbrey O'Melaghlyn, King of the Irish of Meath, hearing thereof, with such few forces as he on a sudden could make up, came to defend the Contrey from them, and gave them the onset at Lomclone O'Doynne, now called Lomclone Offlathrie" [now Lumcloon, or Lumploon, near the village of Cloghan, in the barony of Garrycastle, and King's County], "where there were killed on the sudden Sir William de la Rochelle, Knight, with many others, with Morrogh mac Cormack O'Connor, and divers of the chiefest of the said Theobald's army slain, besides many Captives that were taken, as Sir Hobert Dunn mac William Burke, Knight, with four other principall Englishmen with him.

"Theobald Buttler died at Beerehaven.

"Mac Gerald Genville and Bremyngham made up a great army with the forces of Meath,

Henry Mac Gillafinnen[c] died.

Manus O'Conor defeated Adam Cusack and the English of West Connaught at Easdara [Ballysadare], where many persons were killed, and Colin Cusack, the brother of Adam, was taken prisoner.

Philip Mac Costello defeated the people of Manus O'Conor on Slieve Gamh[d], where many of Manus's people were slain[e].

THE AGE OF CHRIST, 1286.

The Age of Christ, one thousand two hundred eighty-six.

A great army was led by the Earl of Ulster into Connaught; and many monasteries and churches throughout the province were destroyed by him. He obtained sway[f] in every place through which he passed, and took the hos-

and marched to the contrey of Affailie" [Offaly], "where they seized upon a great prey of Cowes, whereupon the inhabitants of the said contrey assembled together their forces, and went on the strengths and passages of the contrey to offend" [resist] "them, and said to Carbrey O'Melaghlyn, King of Meath, Clyncolman, and Irishrie of Meath, to come to aid them against the said armie, their adversaries, who came with a well appointed army of Soldiers, and mett the Englishmen in the field; the Irishrie of Meath and Inhabitants of Affalie striking stiffly to their head, and chief man Carbrey O'Melaughlin made fiercely and courageously towards the battle of the English, and gave a great overthrow to them, took Mac Gerald prisoner, and Sir Adam Pettitt Knight, and above three score knights and freehoulders, with a great slaughter of the inferiour sort.

"There was great snow this year, which from Christmas to Saint Bridgett's day continued.

"Gille Issa Mac Tiernan, Chief of Teallagh Donnogha, died."

[f] *Obtained sway*, po ᵹaḃ neapt.—The word neapt, when thus applied, signifies power, strength, or sway. In the old translation of the Annals of Ulster this passage is rendered as follows: "A. D. 1282 (*rectius* 1286). A great army by the Earle of Ulster into Connaght, and" [he] "spoyled many churches and abbyes and was strong" [po ᵹaḃ neapt] "in all places, as hee went and took the pledges of Connells and Owens, and deposed Donnell O'Nell, and made Nell Culanagh O'Nell King." It is given in Mageoghegan's translation of the Annals of Clonmacnoise as follows: "A. D. 1286. The Earle of Ulster repaired with great forces to Connought, committed great outrages in that Provence, and especially in the abbeys and church lands, and, notwithstanding their unruliness, the Earle had the victory of his enemies every where in that journey, and took hostages of O'Neale and O'Donnell, deposed Donnell mac Bryen O'Neale of his principallity, and gave the rule, government, and chief name of Ulster to Neale Culanagh O'Neale." The latter Annals contain the following passages under this year (1286), which have been omitted by the Four Masters:

conair dar ġaḃ, ⁊ ro ġaḃ braighde Connaċt uile. Rug iaram Connachtaiġ lais gur ro ġaḃ braiġde Conaill ⁊ Eoġain. Ro aiṫríġ domnall mac briain uí néill, ⁊ tug tiġearnus do niall ċúlánaċ.

Pilib mac goisdealbaiġ do écc.

AOIS CRIOST, 1287.

Aois Criost, mile, da chéd, ochtmoccat, a seacht.

Floirenc ó gibelláin airċideochain oilefinn feallsaṁ toġaiḋe do écc.

Giolla na nócc ó mannachain tiġerna na ttrí ttuaṫ do écc.

Diarmaitt miḋeach mac diarmada mic Muirgiusa mic cathail meic diarmada, tiġearna ṡil ṁaoílruain, fer ba ferr, ba sine, ⁊ ba huaisle da chineaḋ do écc.

Maolseachnaill mac tomaltaiġ meg oireċtaiġ do ṁarbaḋ la toirrḋealbaċ mac eoġain ui ċoncobair i ndioġal a athar do treġeaḋ don Tomoltaċ remráite.

Adam cioṁsócc, bean ṁuṁan ingen uí chatáin, ⁊ Domnall ó háinliġe taoíseaċ cenel dobtha do écc.

AOIS CRIOST, 1288.

Aois Criost, mile, da chéd, ochtmoccat a hochtt.

Stephan airdeaspob tuama do gualann décc.

Michael mac an tSaoir espcop clochair do écc.

Maghnus mac Concobair ruaiḋ uí Concobair (imaille re na bfuair do Chonnaċtaiḃ, do uiḃ briuin, ⁊ do Conṁaicniḃ) do ṫocht co háṫ Slisean du

"Finola Ny-Melaghlyn, archabbesse of Meath, died.

"Cahall O'Madden, Prince of Silanmchie, died.

"There was such scarsitie of victualls and corn in the Spring time and Summer of this year, that a Hoope or Cronnocke was sold for four shillings, and there was also a great morren of Cowes the said Spring."

[s] *Sil-Mailruain.*—This is a mistake for Clann-Mailruanaidh, or Clann-Mulrony, which was the tribe name of the Mac Dermots of Moylurg, in the county of Roscommon. Sil-Mailruain was the tribe name of the O'Flynns of Ballinlough, in the same county. In Mageoghegan's translation of the Annals of Clonmacnoise, this Donnell Midheach Mac Dermot is called "Chief of the O'Mulronies, the eldest and worthyest man of his own name," which is more

tages of all Connaught. He then brought the Connacians with him, and took the hostages of the Kinel-Connell and Kinel-Owen. He deposed Donnell, the son of Brian O'Neill, and gave the lordship to Niall Culanagh.

Philip Mac Costello died.

THE AGE OF CHRIST, 1287.

The Age of Christ, one thousand two hundred eighty-seven.

Florence O'Gibellan, Archdeacon of Elphin, a distinguished philosopher, died.

Gilla-na-nóg O'Monahan, Lord of the Three Tuathas [in the county of Roscommon], died.

Dermot Midheach [i. e. the Meathian], son of Dermot, who was son of Maurice Mac Dermot, Lord of Sil-Mailruain[g], the best, oldest, and noblest man of his tribe, died.

Melaghlin, son of Tomaltagh Mageraghty, was slain by Turlough, the son of Owen O'Conor, to avenge the desertion of his [Turlough's] father by the aforementioned Tomaltagh.

Adam Cusack, Benmumhan, daughter of O'Kane, and Donnell O'Hanly, Chief of Kenel-Dofa [in the county of Roscommon], died.

THE AGE OF CHRIST, 1288.

The Age of Christ, one thousand two hundred eighty-eight.

Stephen, Archbishop of Tuam[h], died.

Michael Mac-an-t-Sair[i], Bishop of Clogher, died.

Manus, the son of Conor Roe O'Conor, with as many as he was able to muster of the Connacians and of the Hy-Briuin and Conmaicne[k], proceeded to

correct than the text of the Four Masters.

[h] *Stephen, Archbishop of Tuam.*—His name was Stephen de Fulburn, or of Fulburn. He succeeded in 1286.—See Harris's edition of Ware's Bishops, p. 607.

[i] *Michael Mac-an-t-Sair.*—See Harris's edition of Ware's Bishops, p. 182, where it is stated that he succeeded in 1268, and died in 1285. The family name Mac an tsaoir, meaning son of the carpenter, is now sometimes anglicised Mac Intire, and sometimes translated Carpenter.

[k] *The Hy-Briuin and Conmaicne.*—These were

iraibe a dearbṫaṫair (Ri Connaċt) cona soċraide. Tachur do cur ſtorra lſth ar lſṫ. Cathal do ġabail lais iar maiḋm for a ṁuintir, ⁊ riġe Connaċt do ġabail ar eiccin do ṁaġnus ann sin ⁊ a dſrbḃrathair do aiṫriogaḋ. Teaċ do ġabail ar an Maġnus reimraitte do toirrḋealḃaċ mac Eoġain ui ċoncoḃair isin Ross mór, ⁊ Magnus do lot ann, ⁊ Niall gealbuiḋe ó concoḃair do lot beos. Raghnall mag Raġnaill taoiseaċ Mhuintire heolais do marḃaḋ an tan sin dosn urċur soiġde. Slóiġeaḋ la Maġnus ó cconcoḃair ar a haiṫle iar na leiġius i Siol Muirſdaiġ gur ġaḃ a neart, ⁊ a mbraighde.

Sloiġeaḋ las an Iarla ruaḋ, Risderd mac uater Iarla ulaḋ mic Riocaird mic uilliam conquerer dionnsaiġiḋ connaċt go riacht go Ross comáin mar i mbaoi maġnus mac Concoḃair ruaiḋ Ri Connaċt, Mac gſrailt ⁊ muintſr an riġ gur tionoilsſd uile ara chſnn, ⁊ grſnnaiġid ad tiarla sa ṫeacht seacha sin. Gonaḋ í comairle do ronaḋ las an iarla an tír dfaccḃáil, ⁊ a sluacch do scaoileaḋ iaraṁ.

AOIS CRIOSD, 1289.

Aois Criosd, mile, da ċéd, ochtṁoġad, a naoí.

Miles espocc Conmaicne, .i. an Gailleaspucc ⁊ Siomon ua finnaċta aircinneaċ oilefinn do écc.

the inhabitants of the present counties of Cavan and Leitrim.

[l] *Ath-Sliesan*, or Beal-atha-Sliesan, now Bellaslishen Bridge, on the road between Elphin and Strokestown, in the county of Roscommon, and within one mile of Elphin. It is on the River Uair, a silent, sluggish stream, which flows with such lenity that one could scarcely discern which way it glides. This river rises in Lough Mey, in the parish of Shankill, and meanders its way in a most extraordinary manner, passing under the bridges of Bellaslishen, Bellavahane, and Bellagrange, enters Cloonahee Lough near the seat of O'Mulconry, and then expands into a large lake now called Muickenagh, dividing Tir-Briun-na-Sinna from Kinel-Dofa, and finally glides into the embrace of the Shannon at the celebrated weir or dam called Caradh-na-dtuath, where there is now a good bridge in place of the old Irish caradh.—See references to this place at the years 1309, 1342, and 1595.

[m] *Rossmore*.—In Mageoghegan's translation of the Annals of Clonmacnoise it is stated that this house belonged to Flann O'Donollan, archpoet of Connaught. Thus: "A. D. 1288. Terlagh mac Owen mac Rowrie tooke a house upon Manus mac Connor Roe, burnt the house over his head, and afterwards Manus escaped against the said Terlagh. The house belonged to Flann O'Donollan, archpoet (for Irish poetry) of Connoght." It is the present townland of Rossmore, in the parish of Ballynakill, barony of Leitrim, and county of Galway.—See Ordnance map of

Ath-Slisean[l], where his brother [Cathal], the King of Connaught, was stationed with his troops. A battle was fought between them, in which Cathal was taken prisoner, and his people were defeated. Manus then took forcible possession of the sovereignty of Connaught, and deposed his brother. A house was [forcibly] taken from the same Manus by Turlough, the son of Owen O'Conor, at Rossmore[m], where Manus and Niall Gealbhuidhe O'Conor were wounded. Ranall Mac Ranall, Chief of Muintir-Eolais, was slain on this occasion by one shot of an arrow[n]. An army was led by Manus O'Conor, after his wounds were healed, against the Sil-Murray; and he obtained sway over them, and took their hostages.

An army was led by the Red Earl[o], Richard, son of Walter Earl of Ulster, son of Richard, son of William the Conqueror[p], against Connaught; and he arrived at Roscommon, where Manus, the son of Conor Roe, King of Connaught, Fitzgerald, and the people of the king, then were, all of whom assembled together, and openly defied the Earl to pass beyond that place; so that the Earl adopted the resolution of quitting that country, and he then dispersed his forces.

THE AGE OF CHRIST, 1289.

The Age of Christ, one thousand two hundred eighty-nine.

Miles, Bishop of Conmaicne[q], that is, the English bishop, and Simon O'Finnaghty, Erenagh of Elphin, died.

that county, sheet 132.

[n] *One shot of an arrow*, ᴅoen upċup ꞅoiᵹᴅe.—In the old translation of the Annals of Ulster, this is rendered "by one shot of an arrow."

[o] *The Red Earl.*—He was the second Earl of Ulster, and from his great possessions was esteemed the most powerful subject in Ireland. He died in the year 1326, and was succeeded by his grandson, William, the third and last Earl of Ulster of this family, who was murdered in the year 1333.—See Lodge's Peerage, and also the pedigree of De Burgo, as given by Duald Mac Firbis, and in the *Historia Familiæ De Burgo* already referred to.

[p] *William the Conqueror.*—This was William Fitz Adelm de Burgo, who was called the Conqueror, because he was said to have conquered the province of Connaught.

[q] *Miles, Bishop of Conmaicne*, i. e. of Conmaicne Moy-Rein and Annaly. The Conmaicne were the O'Farrells and Mac Rannalls, whose territories are comprised in the diocese of Ardagh. This bishop is called Milo de Dunstable by Ware, who states that he took that name from a town in Bedfordshire, where he seems to have been born.—See Harris's edition of Ware's Bishops, p. 251.

Maṫa ó Sccingín airḋ Sheanċaiḋ Ereann do écc.

Taḋcc ó flannagáin taoiseaċ cloinne caṫail do écc.

Sloicchеḋ la Riocard diuid, la gallaiḃ na miḋe ⁊ la magnus ua cconcoḃair Ri Connaċt do ṡaighiḋ uí maoilseaċloinn. O maoilseaċlainn do ṫionol ina naghaiḋ co rainicc crois Shliaḃ cona muinntir i ccoṁfoċraiḃ doiḃsioṁ. Ferṫar iomaireacc eatorra. Ro marḃaḋ riocard diuid ann .i. an barún mor cona braiṫriḃ ⁊ Siecus ó ceallaiġ.

Fiaċra ó floinn taoiseaċ ṡil maoilruain, fer ba ferr eineaċ ⁊ engnaṁ do ṫoiseachaiḃ Connaċt do dul do ḋenaṁ cleamnusa le gallaiḃ ⁊ a marḃaḋ i meaḃail la mac riocaird finn búrc, la mac uilliam ⁊ la mac feorais.

Sloiccheaḋ mor la mac feorais ⁊ la gallaiḃ illaiġniḃ docum an ċalḃaiġ uí Concoḃair. Ro feachaḋ caṫ eatorra. Maittear for Ġallaiḃ. Maoilir dexetra do marḃaḋ don dul sin ⁊ Sochaiḋe oile do ġallaiḃ imaille le hiomat eaċ ⁊ eḋala do ḃuain dioḃ.

[r] *Matthew O'Sgingin.*—The family of O'Sgingin were originally seated at Ardcarne, in the barony of Boyle, and county of Roscommon. A branch of them afterwards passed into Tirconnell, where they became chroniclers to the O'Donnells. This branch became extinct about the year 1382, and were succeeded by the O'Clerys.—See *Genealogies, Tribes, and Customs of Hy-Fiachrach*, pp. 76, 77, 78.

[s] *Clann-Chathail.*—According to the tradition in the county of Roscommon, this territory, of which O'Flanagan was the chief, extended from Belanagare to Elphin ; and the O'Flanagan resided at Mointeach, now refined to Mantua. This tradition agrees with the position of O'Flanagan on "Ortelius Improved," and is corroborated by a passage in these Annals under the year 1601, in which Elphin is mentioned as on the confines of Moylurg, Tir-Briuin, Clann Cathail, and Moy-Nai. The Abbe Mageoghegan makes this territory extend all the way from Elphin to Lough Arrow, which is a silly blunder, for Moylurg, Mac Dermot's country, lay between them. From various evidences derived from tradition and ancient documents it appears that Clann-Chathail, O'Flanagan's country, comprised the parishes of Kilmacumshy, Kilcorkey, and Shankill, and the greater part of the parishes of Creeve and Elphin. The following places were in it : 1st, Scor-mor, in the parish of Kilmacumshy, and in the very centre of the district, now called the Lathach riabhach, the present traditional name for O'Flanagan's country ; 2nd, Loch-na-ngasan, which cannot be identified ; 3rd, Kilnegoone, in O'Flanagan's country "did belong unto the Dominican abbey of Elphin," Inquis. 27, Eliz. ; 4th, Caldragh, in the parish of Shankhill,—Inquisition *tempore* Iac. I, finds "that Cormac O'Flenegan of Caldragh is seised of fee of the Cartrons of Caldragh and Cloneboyoge ;" 5th, Ballroddy, said by tradition to have been one of the seats of O'Flanagan, the *maer* or steward of the King of Connaught. In the fourteenth century O'Conor Roe crippled the power and circumscribed the territory of O'Flanagan, so that his territory was found to be very insignificant in the reign of Queen Elizabeth.

Matthew O'Sgingin[r], chief historian of Ireland, died.

Teige O'Flanagan, Chief of Clann-Chathail[s], died.

An army was led by Richard Tuite, the English of Meath, and Manus O'Conor, King of Connaught, against O'Melaghlin, who assembled his people to oppose them, and marched to Crois-Shliabh[t], in their vicinity. A battle was fought between them, in which Richard Tuite, i. e. the Great Baron, with his kinsmen, and Siecus [Jacques] O'Kelly were slain.

Fiachra O'Flynn, Chief of Sil-Maelruain, the most hospitable and expert at arms of all the chiefs of Connaught, went to form an alliance with the English by marriage, but was treacherously slain by the son of Richard Finn [the Fair] Burke, Mac William, and Mac Feorais [Bermingham].

An army was led by Mac Feorais [Bermingham] and the English, into Leinster, against Calvagh O'Conor[u]; and a battle was fought between them, in which the English were defeated, and Meyler de Exeter and many others of the English were slain; they were also deprived of many horses and other spoils[w].

Under this year the Annals of Clonmacnoise, as translated by Mageoghegan, contain the two following passages, which have been omitted by the Four Masters:

"A. D. 1288. There were fifteen ecclesiasticall men, both Abbotts and Priours, drownded this year coming from Rome, upon the coasts of Ireland.

"Donnell Breagagh O'Melaghlyn was killed, with the privitie of Carbrey O'Melaghlyn, by Melaghlyn O'Melaughlyn."

[t] *Crois-Shliabh.*—This name, which signifies cross-mountain, is now obsolete in Westmeath, and it is useless to conjecture what mountain it was the name of until some distinct evidence of its situation be discovered. The Annals of Clonmacnoise, which would probably give us the exact situation and modern name of this place, are defective at this period, the manuscript having lost ten years, i. e. from 1289 to 1299, before Connell Mageoghegan had translated it in 1627.

[u] *Calvagh O'Conor.*—He was O'Conor Faly, Chief of Offaly in Leinster. The name Calvagh is now anglicised Charles.

[w] The entries placed under this year in the Annals of the Four Masters are given under the year 1285, in the Dublin copy of the Annals of Ulster, which is decidedly incorrect; but the two dates are given in the old translation, in which they are rendered as follows:

"A. D. 1285, *al.* 1289. Teig O'Flanegan, Chief of Clancathal, died.

"Mathew O'Skingin, Arch-chronicler of all Ireland, died.

"Miles, Bishop of Conmaicne, i. e. the English Bishop, died.

"Symon O'Fynaghta, Airchinech of Olfin, *quievit.*

"An army by Richard Tuit, and Galls of Meath, and Manus O'Conner, King of Conaght, with him, to O'Melaghlin, who gave them a great overthrow, and Richard Tuit, the great Baron, was killed there, and his brothers, and Jaques [Secuṙ] Kelly, the Bishop's son.

"Fieghra O'Flin, chief of the Mulronies"

AOIS CRIOSD, 1290.

Aois Criosd, mile, da ċétt, nóchatt.

O Sédaċáin espucc cille mic duach do écc.

Cairpri ó maoileaċloinn Ri miḋe an macaoṁ bo moirġníoṁaiġe in Erinn ina aimsir do ṁarḃaḋ la maġ cochláin.

Sloiccéḋ la domnall mac briain uí nell i ccenel neoġain gur chuir niall culánaċ ó nell ar eccin esde ⁊ ticchṡrnus ċenél neoġain do ġaḃáil dó fen a los a laṁ.

Aoḋ mac domnaill óicc uí ḋomnaill daiṫriogaḋ da dḟrḃraṫair fén Toirrḋealḃaċ ua domnaill tre ċumaċtaiḃ ċiniḋ a maṫar, .i. cloinni domnaill ⁊ ghallócclaċ iomḋa ele ⁊ ticchṡrnus do gabáil do fén ar éccin.

AOIS CRIOSD, 1291.

Aois Criosd, mile, dá ċéd, nochatt, a haon.

Edru maccraṫ abb mainistreaċ na trinoide for loċ cé do écc.

Toirrḋealḃaċ mac Eoġain ui Concoḃair aoinḟsr ba mó eneaċ, ſngnaṁ ⁊ coscar re a linn in Erinn do marḃaḋ la niall ngealbuiḋe ó cconcoḃair.

[Sil mailruanaiġ], "the only man" [*recte* the most distinguished man] "in liberality and feats, and Comrick that was in Connaght" [in taen duine ro bfepp einec ⁊ engnom ⁊ comairce do ḃí i connaċtaiḃ], "went to marry one of the Galls, that he [was] killed by Makrickard Fin Bourk, Mac William, and Makoruis, by murther.

"A great army by Makoruis to Cellagh O'Conner, and the nobility of Leinster, but they were much discomfited, and Meiler de Setra, and many other Galls, and many horses, lost by him."

[x] *Mac Coghlan.*—This entry is given in the Annals of Clonmacnoise, as translated by Mageoghegan, under the year 1289: "A. D. 1289. Carbrey mac Art O'Melaghlyn, King of the Irishrie of Meath, was slain by David Mac Coghlan, prince of Delvin Mac Coghlan. David himself was the first that strocke him; his brother Gille-Koewgin mac Coghlan, with sixteen others of the Familie of the Mac Coghlans, did, in like manner, strike him, the said David being a Gossipp of the said Carbrey before; for which cause the Earle of Ulster spoyled and destroyed the said Mac Coghlan and his Contrey, tho' O'Melaghlyn was in the wrong at first.

"Morrogh O'Melaghlyn, son of the said Carbrey, succeeded him in his place."

On this David Mac Coghlan Mageoghegan has the following note:

"This David Mac Coghlan (as I take him to be) was the ancestor of Sleight Donnell, who was son of Donnell himself, and father of Ffy-

THE AGE OF CHRIST, 1290.

The Age of Christ, one thousand two hundred ninety.

O'Sedaghan, Bishop of Kilmacduagh, died.

Carbry O'Melaghlin, King of Meath, the most noble-deeded youth in Ireland in his time, was slain by Mac Coghlan[x].

An army was led by Donnell, the son of Brian O'Neill, into Kinel-Owen, whence he expelled Niall Culanagh O'Neill, and he himself then assumed the lordship of Kinel-Owen by force of arms.

Hugh, son of Donnell Oge O'Donnell, was deposed by his own brother, Turlough O'Donnell, aided by his mother's tribe, i. e. the Clann-Donnell [Mac Donnells of Scotland], and many other gallowglasses; and he himself assumed the lordship by force[y].

THE AGE OF CHRIST, 1291.

The Age of Christ, one thousand two hundred ninety-one.

Edru Magrath, Abbot of the monastery of the Blessed Trinity in Lough Key, died.

Turlough, the son of Owen O'Conor, the most hospitable, most expert at arms, and most victorious man of his time in Ireland, was slain by Niall Gealbhuidhe O'Conor.

nine and Donnough, of whom the two septs of Slight Ffynine and Slight Donnough descended. His brother, Gillecowgin, is the ancestor of the sept of Leackagh. His other brother, Rosse, was the ancestor of the sept of Clondownie, and his nephew, Mac Rosse, of the sept of Boynean."

[y] The transactions of this year are incorrectly given under the year 1286, in the Dublin copy of the Annals of Ulster. The old translation gives both dates as follows:

"A. D. 1286, *al.* 1290. William Brimingham made Archbishop." He was Archbishop of Tuam, to which dignity he succeeded in 1289, and died 1311. See Harris's edition of Ware's *Bishops*, pp. 608, 609.

"The Bishop O'Shedagan, Bishop of Kilmac-Duagh, died.

"Carbre O'Melaghlin, King of Meath, the Roiallest actor that was in Ireland in his tyme, killed.

"An army by Donnell mac Brian O'Neale to kindred Owen, and put Nel O'Nele out of the contry by force, and made himself king by strength of armes.

"Hugh O'Donel deposed by his brother, Tirlagh, by the force of his mother's kindred, viz., Clan Donell, and many other Gallow-glasses."

Conċobor ó dubda (.i. concobar conallach) ticchérna ua ffiaċraċ do baṫadh ar an sionainn.

Conġalaċ macc eochaccain taoiseċ ċenél ffiaċaċ do écc.

Sloicchéḋ la Riocard burc iarla uladh da ngoirthi an tiarla Ruadh i ttír neoġain dár aithrigh sé domhnall mac briain uí nell, ⁊ niall culánaċ ó nell doirdneadh dó iar ffaccbáil na tíre iarsin don iarla Marbtoir niall culanáċ la domhnall ua nell. Giḋeadh nir ḟoirbheaċ do ḋomhnall an gníomh sin, uair do hoirdneadh brian mac aoḋa buiḋe ui nell a hucht an iarla ċédna le mac mairtin ⁊ le mac Eóin, ⁊ ro dioċuireadh eisiomh a tír eoġain.

Sluaiccéḋ las an Iarla i ttír conaill do chum ṫoirrḋealbaiġ mic domhnaill óig, gur airgc an tír edir cill ⁊ tuaiṫ. Rainicc iarsin go hoil finn i cconnachdaib ⁊ tuccsat Connachdaiġ i mbraiġde do.

Comṫoccbail do ḋénaṁ do caṫal ó Concobair, do niall gelbuiḋe ⁊ do luċt a ccommbaḋa edir ġallaib ⁊ gaoiḋealaib daiṫríoġadh maġnusa. Iomaireacc do ṫabairt doib dia roile i ccúil maile[a]. Caṫal do loṫ, murċadh mac taiḋg do ṁarbadh ⁊ Sochaiḋi naċ airimthér. Maiḋm for maġnus dana ⁊ é fén do dul [as] fo laiṁ iar mbén moráin dia eachaib ḋe. Creaċa móra do ḋénaṁ i ccairpri do muinntir caṫail uí ċonċobair ⁊ nell ġealbuiḋe iar nguin caṫail. Dala maġnusa ui Chonċobair tra iar ttocht do Shiol muireadhaiġ dia aos gráḋa budén ⁊ do ġallaib Rosa commáin ina ḟoirithin arabarać iarsan maiḋm do cuaiḋ inaircis na ccreaċ go ttarla na ccénn é ar sraith an ḟeráin ⁊ ar an aonaċ. Na creaċa do buain díob ann sin ⁊ niall do dul ass a niort a ġaisccidh ⁊ a esiomail. Tomás mac goirdealbaiġ do ṁarbadh, a braṫair dauit mac goirdealbaiġ do gabail ⁊ a marbadh ina braiġdénus. Morán oile don tsluacch béos edir gallaib ⁊ ġaoiḋealaib do marbadh ⁊ do muḋuġadh. Tocht do niall is in tir iarsin ar siṫ ⁊ a ḟérann fén do ṫabairt dó. Do ronadh ſdarċoraoid mor ⁊ ionnlach adbal ſtorra[a] do ridisi go ro ḟóbair niall an tir dfaccbáil.

Brian ó floinn ticchérna ua ttuirtre do écc.

[a] *Cuil-Maile.*—In O'Flaherty's account of West Connaught, printed for the Irish Archæological Society in 1845, it is stated that this is Killoony, in the county of Sligo, by which he meant the present village of Coloony, in the barony of Tirerril, not far to the south of Ballysadare; and it appears from several passages in these Annals that he is right.—See note at the year 1598.

[a] *Between them*, ſtorra, i. e. between the parties of Cathal and Manus O'Conor.

Conor O'Dowda (i. e. Conor Conallagh), Lord of Hy-Fiachrach, was drowned in the Shannon.

Congalagh Mageoghegan, Chief of Kinel-Fiachach, died.

An army was led by Richard Burke, Earl of Ulster, usually called the Red Earl, into Kinel-Owen, where he deposed Donnell, son of Brian O'Neill, and installed Niall Culanagh O'Neill in his place; but after the Earl had left the country, Niall Culanagh was slain. This deed, however, was not a fortunate one for Donnell; for Brian, son of Hugh Boy O'Neill, was inaugurated, by the influence of the said Earl, by Mac Martin and Mac Eoin, and the other [Donnell] was banished from Tyrone.

An army was led by the Earl into Tirconnell against Turlough, son of Donnell Oge, and plundered the country, as well ecclesiastical as lay property. He then proceeded to Elphin in Connaught, and the Connacians rendered him their hostages.

An insurrection [was raised] by Cathal O'Conor, Niall Gealbhuidhe O'Conor, and their English and Irish adherents, to dethrone Manus [O'Conor]. They gave battle to each other at Cuil-Maile[a], where Cathal was wounded, and Murrough, son of Teige [O'Conor], and many others not enumerated here, were killed. Manus was defeated, and secretly effected his escape, after having been deprived of many of his horses. After Cathal had been wounded, his people, and those of Niall Gealbhuidhe, committed great depredations in Carbury. As to Manus O'Conor, being aided by the Sil-Murray, his own servants of trust, and the English of Roscommon, who came to his assistance on the day after his defeat, he went in pursuit of the preys, and came up with them at Srath-an-fherain, and at Aenach, where he deprived them of the prey; but Niall made his escape by dint of valour and prowess. Thomas Mac Costello was slain, and his brother, David Mac Costello, taken prisoner, and [afterwards] killed while in captivity. Many others of the army, both English and Irish, were slain or disabled. Niall afterwards returned to the country on terms of peace, and his own lands were restored to him; but great complaints and dissensions occurring between them[a], Niall thought fit to leave the country.

Brian O'Flynn [O'Lyn], Lord of Hy-Tuirtre[b] died.

[b] *Hy-Tuirtre.*—This was the ancient name of a territory in the present county of Antrim, lying to the east of Lough Neagh. See note [a] under the year 1176, p. 25, where the parish of Kil-

Creach mór do ḋenaṁ do magnus ó concobair ar niall gealbuiḋe.
Aodh ó follamhain do marḃadh no do ecc.

AOIS CRIOSD, 1292.

Aois Criosd, mile, da ċéd, nochatt, adó.

Aindiles ó dochartaiġ taoiseaċ arda miodair, fear einiġ coitcinn ⁊ donnċaḋ mac Eoġain ui Chonċoḃair do écc.

Soṁairle ua gairmleadhaiġ do ṁarḃaḋ la hua nell.

Niall gealbuiḋe ó Concoḃair do marḃaḋ do taḋg mac aindriasa ui Concoḃair ⁊ do tuaṫal mac muircertaiġ.

Mag cochláin tiġhearna dealḃna moire do ṁarḃaḋ do Shifin mac ḟeorais tre ḟursailem an iarla.

Congalach ó ceallaigh tiġerna breġh [do écc].

lead is inadvertently said to be a part of this territory. It should be the church of Kill-gad, which stood on the townland now corruptly called Gilgad, and situated in the parish of Connor.

[b] The events recorded under this year by the Four Masters are given in the Dublin copy of the Annals of Ulster under 1287, but both dates appear in the old translation, the words of which are here inserted, that the reader may be enabled to compare the translations:

"*Anno* 1287, *al.* 1291. Tirlagh mac Owen O'Conner, the" [largest] "most beautifull and best of liberality and otherwise in Ireland of his tyme, killed by Nell Galvoi O'Conner.

"An army by Richard Bourk, Earle of Ulster, into Tyrone, and deposed Donnell mac Brian O'Neale, and made Nell Culanagh king; and when the Earle left the country, Nell Culanagh was killed by Donel O'Neale, and Brian, son of Hugh Boy O'Neale, was made king after by consent of the Earle aforesaid, by Mac Martin and Mac Eoin mac Hugh Boy O'Neale; and Donell left the contrey.

"An army by the Earle into Tirconell, upon Tirlagh" [O'Donnell], "and preyed the contry spirituall and temporall, and came into Conaght to Olfin, and Conaght made him the feast of St. Briget" [tucadur connacta ḟelbraiġde do, i. e. the Connacians gave him treacherous hostages].

"Conor O'Duvda, King of Offieghragh, drowned upon the Shannon.

"A rising-out gathered by Cathal O'Coner and Nel Gelvoy, and all that they could procure of Galls and Irish, to depose Magnus, and were interrupted at Cara Culin" [*alias* Cul Maile], "where Cathal was wounded, and Morough mac Teige O'Conor killed, and other men, and many horses taken from Manus his men and" [Manus himself] "was put to flight, and escaped under hand; and great preys were made by Cathal O'Conor and Nell Gelvoy" [after] "Cathal being wounded at Carbry; and Manus O'Coner,—when Syl-Mureah, i. e. (Sept-Mureah) came to him and his own loving frends" [a aesa graḋa ḟein], "with the Galls of Roscomon to assist him on the morrow after the breach,—came to meete the prayes, and

A great depredation was committed by Manus O'Conor upon Niall Gealbhuidhe.

Hugh O'Fallon was killed (or died[b]).

THE AGE OF CHRIST, 1292.

The Age of Christ, one thousand two hundred ninety-two.

Aindiles O'Doherty, Chief of Ardmire, a man of universal hospitality, and Donough, son of Owen O'Conor, died.

Sorley O'Gormly was slain by O'Neill.

Niall Gealbhuidhe O'Conor was slain by Teige, son of Andreas O'Conor, and Tuathal[c], son of Murtough.

Mac Coghlan, Lord of Delvin More[d], was slain, by order of the Earl, by Sifin Mac Feorais [Birmingham].

Congalagh O'Kelly[e], Lord of Bregia, died.

overtooke them at Srath in Ferain and Inagh, tooke all the prayes from them, and Nell himself escaped hardly" [i. e. with difficulty]; "Thomas O'Gosteloy" [was] "killed there, and his brother David taken and killed in the same captivity, and many more of that army, both English and Irish. And Neale made peace, came into the country, and had his own land given him.

"Hugh O'Fallon *quievit in Christo.*

"Congalach Mageoghegan, chief of Kindred Fiegh, *mortuus est.*"

[c] *Tuathal.*—This name, which is now generally anglicised Toole, is rendered Tully in the old translation of the Annals of Ulster. Thus: "*Anno* 1288, *al.* 1292. Nell Galvoy O'Coner killed by Teig mac Anrias O'Coner, and by Tully mac Murtagh."

[d] *Delvin More.*—This is a mistake, it should be Delvin-Eathra, or Delvin simply. The entry is thus given in the Annals of Ulster: "A. D. 1288. Mag coċlan ri delḃna do marḃaḋ da ṡifin mac ḟeorais tre forgoll an iarla." And thus rendered in the old translation: "*Anno* 1288, *al.* 1292. Mac Coghlan, King of Delvin, killed by Seffin Brimingham, at the Earle's request."

[e] *Congalagh O'Kelly.*—Though he is here styled Lord of Bregia, it is highly probable that he retained but a small portion of his principality, as the English were at this period firmly established in Dublin and Meath. This once great family, who descended from Hugh Slainé, son of Dermot Mac Kervell, monarch of Ireland, have been since so dispersed that they cannot now be distinguished from the O'Kellys of other races and districts. Connell Mageoghegan, who translated the Annals of Clonmacnoise in the year 1627, has the following curious remarks upon this family and their territory of Bregia or Moybrea, under the year 778: "To the end that the reader may not be ignorant of Moybrea and the inhabitants thereof, I will, in a few words, shew the bounds thereof, and to whom it was allotted. Dermott mac Kervell, King of Ireland, of whom mention was made in this History, had

Sloiccheadh lar an Iarla Ruadh for Maghnus ua cConcobhair go raimicc go Ross comáin, ⁊ ro imthigh gan braighde gan neart don turus sin, go ro lean Maghnus an tiarla go Mílliuc go ttard a oighréir nodh.

AOIS CRIOST, 1293.

Aois Criost, mile, da ced, nochat, a trí.

Florint o cearbhallain espocc doire décc.

Taisi Patraig, Coluim cille, ⁊ Brighde do foillsiuccadh do Niocol mac

issue Hugh Slane, Colman More, and Colman Begg. To the race of Hugh was allotted this Moyvrey, extending from Dublinn to Bealaghbrick, westerlie of Kells, and from the hill of Houthe to the mount of Sliew Fwayde [Sliabh Fuaid] in Ulster. There reigned of King Hugh his race as monarchs of this kingdom nine kings, as shall be shewed when I come to the place where remembrance ought to be made of them.

"There were many other princes of Moyvrey besides the said kings, and behaved themselves as becomed them, and because they were neerer the invasions of the land than other Septs, they were sooner banished and brought low than others. The O'Kelly of Brey was the chief name of that race, though it hath many other names of by-septs, which, for brevity's sake, I omit to particulate. They are brought so low now-a-days that the best Chronicles in the kingdom are ignorant of their Discents, though the O'Kelly's are so common every where that it is unknown whether the dispersed parties in Ireland of them be of the Family of O'Kellys of Connaught or Brey, that scarcely one of the same Family knoweth not [*sic*] the name of his own great grandfather, and are turned to be meer churles, and poore labouring men, so as scarse there is a few parishes in the kingdom but hath some one or other of those Kellys; I mean of Brey."

[f] *The relics of Patrick, Columbkille, and Bridget.*—This passage is given in the Dublin copy of the Annals of Ulster under the year 1289, but in the old translation both dates are given, thus: "*Anno* 1289 *al.* 1293. The bones of Patrick, Columbkill, and Bridget, [were] revealed to Nichol Mac Moilisa, coarb of Patrick, to be in Patrick's Saval, and [he] digged them up, and after they were digged many miracles were sayd to be made [*sic*] and he did save them up in a saving Shryne honourably." The original Irish runs as follows in the Dublin copy of the Annals of Ulster:

"A. D. 1289.—Taissi Padraic ⁊ Colum cille ⁊ Brigde do foillsiughadh do nicol mac Mailissu, do comarba Padraic, do beith i Sabull Patraic, ⁊ a togbail do, ⁊ iar na togbail ferta mora ⁊ mirbuileadha do denum, ⁊ a cur dosun a scrin cumdaigh co honórach." It is very strange that no reference has been made to this passage in any of the discussions about the real place of St. Patrick's sepulture. According to Giraldus Cambrensis, in his *Topographia Hiberniæ*, Dist. iii. c. 18, the relics of these saints were found in the year in which the Earl John (John Earl of Morton, afterwards King John) first came to Ireland, which was 1185. In the Office of the Translation of the Relics of SS. Patrick, Columba, and Brigida, printed at Paris in 1620, and reprinted by Colgan, Messingham, and Ussher, a minute account of their discovery

An army was led by the Red Earl against Manus O'Conor; and he arrived at Roscommon, but departed without obtaining hostages or acquiring any power by this expedition. Manus, however, followed the Earl to Meelick, and gave him his full demands.

THE AGE OF CHRIST, 1293.

The Age of Christ, one thousand two hundred ninety-three.

Florence O'Carolan, Bishop of Derry, died.

It was revealed to Nicholas Mac Maelisa (Coarb of St. Patrick) that the relics[f]

in 1185 is given, and which has been abstracted by Dr. Lanigan in his Ecclesiastical History of Ireland, vol. iv. p. 274, *et sequen.* The substance of it is as follows: It being generally believed that the bodies of the three great patron saints of Ireland were in Down, Malachy its bishop used to pray fervently to God that he would vouchsafe to point out to him the particular place in which they were buried. On a certain night, while fervently praying in the cathedral church of Down, he saw a light like a sunbeam traversing the church: on seeing this he prayed more intensely that it might move to and stop at the spot where the bodies were interred. [De visione prædictâ Episcopus multum exultans intensius orabat ne radius ille discederet, quousque reliquias absconditas inveniret]. The light soon moved to the spot. Immediately procuring the necessary implements, Malachy dug that irradiated spot and found the bones of the three bodies, which he deposited in distinct boxes or coffins, and placed again under the ground. Having communicated his discovery to John de Courcy, then Lord of Down, they determined on sending messengers to Pope Urban III. for the purpose of procuring the translation of these relics to a more dignified part of the church. The Pope, agreeing with their request, sent as his legate on this occasion Vivian, cardinal priest of St. Stephen in Monte Caelio, who had been at Down about nine years before, and who had been acquainted with Sir John de Courcy and the Bishop Malachy. On his arrival the relics were removed to a more respectable part of the church, and deposited in the one monument, on the 9th of June, the festival of St. Columba.

It is a very strange fact that the body of St. Patrick, the apostle of Ireland, was said to have been pointed out by an angel at Glastonbury the year before. See Ussher's *Primordia*, p. 892. But the most extraordinary circumstance connected with the history of the relics of the Trias Thaumaturgæ is, that the Irish annalists, that is, such as wrote in the Irish language, do not appear to have ever heard of the discovery of them by Malachy in 1185, and hence it is but fair to conclude that Malachy's dream at Down was got up by the English party in order to add dignity to Down, then in the possession of Sir John de Courcy. It is quite evident that the mere Irish never heard, or at least never believed this story of their discovery at Down, in 1185; for, if they had been deposited in a costly shrine at Down in 1185, as stated by Giraldus, it is hard to believe that they would have been lost in the course of the next century, so as to make another revelation necessary for their discovery in 1293, when it would appear they were under the earth at Saul, in a spot unknown to all except Nicholas Mac Maelisa, the Archbishop of Armagh,

maoilísu (comarba Patraicc) do bhith i Saball, a ttóccbáil lais, Ferta móra ⁊ mìorbhaile do denamh dóibh iaramh ⁊ a ccur i Sccrín iar na cumdach go honorach ar a haithle.

Murchadh o Maoileachlainn Rí midhe decc.

Maghnas ó conchobhair Rí connacht, fer cogthach congalach bá moa gráin gaisccedh, ⁊ rún oinigh do ghaoidhelaibh Ereann ina aimsir décc, iar mbeith ráithe i ngalar dó, ⁊ Aodh mac eoghain do righadh ina ionadh tria neart an lustis, ⁊ an deachmadh lá iar na oirdneadh, ro gabhadh eisidhe la Mac gearailt, ⁊ ro marbhadh .l. dia muintir, ⁊ ro creachadh aroile díobh.

Cathal ó conchobhair do marbhadh do Ruaidhri mac donnchaidh riabhaigh.

Cathal ruadh ó Concobhair do ghabhail righe Connacht iar ngabhail Aodha mic Eoghain. A marbhadh a ccionn raithe iarsin la Ruaidhri mac donnchaidh riabhaigh uí concobhair. Aodh mac Eoghain do léccead as a braighdenas iaramh, ⁊ rígi Connacht do gabhail dó tre nert an lustis ⁊ muintire an righ. A ghabhail do mhac Gerailt i meabhail an dechmadh lá iar na rioghadh. Creacha móra do dhénamh air, ⁊ caocca da muintir do mharbhadh.

Ferghal ua Raighilligh tiicherna muintire maoilmórdha decc.

Mor ingen feidhlimidh ui concobhair décc.

to whom it was pointed out in a vision. It seems therefore quite clear that the discovery of them at Down in 1185 was, like the prophecy of Merlin, already alluded to under the year 1177, a scheme of Sir John De Courcy and his writers, and that their discovery at Saul in 1293 was a counter-scheme of Nicholas Mac Maelisa, who was one of the greatest opposers of the English that ever governed the see of Armagh. It may, however, have happened that both bishops had dreamed of bones, and that bones were found at both places.

[g] *Sabhall*, now Saul, a small village situated about two miles to the east of Downpatrick, in the county of Down. The name of this place is usually written in Irish Sábhall Phádruig, which the monastic Latin writers rendered *Zabulum vel Horreum Patricii*, i. e., Patrick's barn. See Ussher's *Primodia*, p. 847. The reason assigned by these writers for the church erected here by St. Patrick having received the appellation of sabhall or barn is, that it was built after the form and position of the barn of Dichu, St. Patrick's first convert; but Dr. Lanigan thinks that it was originally nothing else than a real barn belonging to Dichu, in which St. Patrick celebrated divine worship, "in the same manner," he adds, "as even in our own time barns have been used in Ireland for the same purpose."—*Ecclesiastical History of Ireland*, vol. i. pp. 212, 213.

[h] *Manus O'Conor, King of Connaught.*—The language of this and the subsequent entries is nearly the same in the Dublin copy of the Annals of Ulster, as in the text of the Four Masters, and are thus rendered in the old translation: "*Anno* 1289, *al.* 1293. Manus O'Conor, king of Conaght for the time of five years and a half, the best maker of peace and war, most

of Patrick, Columbkille, and Bridget were at Sabhall[g]; they were taken up by him, and great virtues and miracles were afterwards wrought by [means of] them, and, after having been honourably covered, they were deposited in a shrine.

Murrough O'Melaghlin, King of Meath, died.

Manus O'Conor[h], King of Connaught, a warlike and valiant man, the most victorious, puissant, and hospitable of the Irish of his time, died, having been ill a quarter of a year; and Hugh, son of Owen, was inaugurated his successor, through the influence of the Lord Justice; but on the tenth day after his election he was taken prisoner by Fitzgerald, and some of his people were slain, and others plundered.

Cathal O'Conor was slain by Rory, son of Donough Reagh.

Cathal Roe O'Conor, having made a prisoner of Hugh, son of Owen, assumed the kingdom of Connaught, but was killed a quarter of a year afterwards by Rory, son of Donough Reagh O'Conor. Hugh, son of Owen, afterwards received his liberty, and, aided by the power of the Lord Justice[i] and the people of the king [of England] took possession of the kingdom of Connaught; but on the tenth day after his election, he was taken prisoner by Fitzgerald[k], when great spoils were taken from him, and fifty of his people slain.

Farrell O'Reilly, Lord of Muintir-Maelmora, died.

More, daughter of Felim O'Conor, died.

frend[ly] and warlike, most liberall and venturous in his time of the Irish, sick a whole quarter of a year, died.

"Cathal O'Conor [was] killed by Rory mac Donogh Rievagh.

"Cathal Roe O'Connor taking the kingdome of Connaght, having taken Hugh mac Owen, and the same Cathal [was] killed after one quarter by Roary mac Donogh Rievagh O'Conor, and Hugh mac Owen set at liberty and tooke the kingdome of Conaght by the power of the Deputy.

"The castle of Sligo, made by John Fitz Thomas, and [he] went over to the King of England's house [Caiſlen Sliġiġ do denum do Seon Fitztomaſ, ⁊ a dul tairiſ co teċ riġ Saxan].

"Hugh mac Owen O'Conner tooke the kingdome of Conaght through the power of the Justice, and the King's army, and the tenth day of his raigne was treacherously made captive by Mac Geralt, and 50 of his men killed, and great prayes made uppon him.

"Ferall O'Rely, King of Muinter Mulmora, died.

"More, daughter to Felim O'Conor, *quievit*.

"Murtagh O'Flanagan, Chief of Clann Cathal, *quievit*.

"Tully mac Murtagh [O'Coner] killed by Munter Egra."

[i] *Lord Justice*.—He was William de Vescy, who is celebrated in English-Irish history for his dissensions with John Fitz Thomas Fitz Gerald, Baron of Offaley.

[k] *Taken prisoner by Fitzgerald*.—This is another version of the second last entry.

Muirchertach o flannaccain tighearna, no taoiseaċ, cloinne caṫail décc. Tuaṫal mac Muirchertaiġ ui Concoḃair do marḃaḋ la muintir Eghra.

Caislen Sliccigh do ṫaḃairt do Seon fitzthomas, ⁊ Seon buḋḋein do ḋol go Saxoibh.

AOIS CRIOST, 1294.

Aois Criost, mile, ḋa céḋ, nochat a cethair.

Creacha móra do ḋenoṁ la haeḋ ṁac eoġain ar cloinn Muirċertaiġ.

Muirchertach mac maġnasa uí ċoncoḃair adḃar coicceḋaiġ do ḃfearr da ċineḋ do marḃaḋ do tadg (.i. taḋg ua concoḃair) ⁊ do ḋoṁnall mac taidg.

Maoileaċlainn ó flannaccain taoiseaċ cloinne caṫail do marḃaḋ la caṫal mac taiḋcc meic diarmada ar Sráid sliccigh. Caṫal mac taidg meic diarmada tiġearna moiġe luircc decc iar sin, ⁊ Maolruanaiḋ mac giolla-crist meic diarmada do ġabhail a ionaiḋ.

Donnchaḋ mac Conṡnaṁa taoiseaċ muintire cionaoiṫ, Duarcán mac tiġearnáin tighearna, no taoiseaċ ṫeallaiġ dúnchaḋa, ⁊ Dearḃfail inġen taidg mic caṫail meic diarmata décc.

Caislén Sliccig do leccaḋ la hAoḋ mac Eoġain uí concoḃair.

Riocard a burc .i. an tiarla ruaḋ do gabail do ṁac gearailt. Buaiḋreaḋ Ereann do ṫeacht trésimitriḋe.

[1] *Went to England.*—It is said that he was summoned to England on this occasion, to answer to certain charges tendered against him by William de Vescy, Lord of Kildare. See Grace's Annals at the year 1294. The feud between these noblemen would appear to have originated in a dispute about their estates, as Vescy, in right of his mother Agnes, one of the daughters of Sibilla, Countess of Ferrers (to whom, as one of the sisters of the Earl Marshal, the county of Kildare was assigned), became entitled to a seventh part of Kildare. Being both admitted to plead their cause before the King, in council, they there showered upon each other speeches full of vulgar abuse and recrimination, of which a report professing to be faithful is preserved by Holingshed; but it is to be suspected that the speeches put into their mouths by that rude chronicler, were pure inventions of his own, or founded on very slender materials. For example, the following replication of De Vescy: "'A gentleman!' quoth the Lord Justice, 'thou bald Baron, I tell thee, the Vescies were gentlemen before the Giraldins were Barons of Ophaly; yea, and before that Welsh bankrupt thine ancestor feathered his nest in Leinster!'" The pleadings ended in a combat which was offered by the Baron of Offaley, and which his antagonist accepted; but when the day approached for the battle, De Vescy, "turning his great boast to small roast,

Murtough O'Flanagan, Lord, or Chieftain of Clann-Cathail, died.

Tuathal, son of Murtough O'Conor, was slain by the O'Haras.

The castle of Sligo was given to John Fitz-Thomas, and John himself went to England[l].

THE AGE OF CHRIST, 1294.

The Age of Christ, one thousand two hundred ninety-four.

Great depredations were committed by Hugh, son of Owen (O'Conor), upon the Clann-Murtough.

Murtough, the son of Manus O'Conor, the best materies of a provincial king of all his tribe, was slain by Teige (i. e. Teige O'Conor) and Donnell, the son of Teige.

Melaghlin O'Flanagan, Chief of Clann-Cathail, was slain by Cathal, son of Teige Mac Dermot, in the street of Sligo. Cathal, son of Teige Mac Dermot, Lord of Moylurg, died [shortly] afterwards; and Mulrony, the son of Gilchreest Mac Dermot, assumed his place.

Donogh Mac Consnava[m], Chief of Muintir-Kenny; Duarcan Mac-Tiernan, Lord, or Chieftain, of Teallach Dunchadha; and Dervilia, daughter of Teige, the son of Cathal Mac Dermot, died.

The castle of Sligo was razed by Hugh, son of Owen O'Conor.

Richard Burke, i. e. the Red Earl, was taken prisoner by Fitzgerald, in consequence of which all Ireland was thrown into a state of disturbance.

began to cry creak" [craven] "and secretly sailed into France." It is added that "King Edward being advertised thereof, bestowed De Vescy's lordships of Kildare and Rathangan on the Baron of Offaley; saying, that albeit De Vescy conveyed his person to France, yet he left his lands behind him in Ireland." See Cox's *Hibernia Anglicana*, p. 84, and Moore's History of Ireland, vol. iii. p. 39. These stories of Holingshed should not, however, be regarded as true history without being supported by contemporaneous writers, for he is by no means a trustworthy authority. In 1297, William De Vescy surrendered to King Edward the castle, manor, and county of Kildare, to wit, every thing he had or could have in Ireland, and the King directed his Justiciary, John Wogan, to take possession of them. *Rot. Canc. Antiq.* 45, 46. Kildare remained in the King's hands until the 14th of May, 1316, when Edward II., by Letters Patent, declared that he had granted to John Fitz-Thomas "castrum et villam de Kildare, cum terris, redditibus, et aliis pertinentiis, sub honore et nomine Comitis de Kildare, ipsumque præfecisse in comitem ejusdem loci."—See Lodge's Peerage, by Archdall—KILDARE.

[m] *Mac Consnava.*—Now anglicised Mac Kinaw, and often incorrectly Forde.

Moirerḟch meabla do denaṁ do mac gearailt ⁊ do ṁac pḟorais ar ċonnaċtaib. Aoḋ mac Eoġain do ḟaṁluċċaḋ daiṫrioghaḋ doiḃ. An tír do ṁillḟoh, ⁊ giḋḟḋ noċar ċuirrḟt do nḟrt uirre aċt a coṁbuaiḋreaḋ aṁlaiḋ.

Dauit mac giolla arraiṫ do ṁarbaḋ do ṁacaiḃ domnaill duiḃ uí Eaġra.

Domnall ua hḟġra tiġḟrna luiġne do écc.

An tiarla do ġabáil la mac gearailt, ⁊ buaiḋreaḋ Ereann uile do teċt trer an ngabáil sin.

Diarmaitt ó caḟṁáin do écc.

AOIS CRIOST, 1295.

Aois Criost, mile, da céd, nochat, a cúig.

An tiarla ruaḋ do lḟiccḟn as a ḃraiġdḟnus do ṁac Gearailt tre nḟrt Riġ Saxan, ⁊ braiġde maiṫe da ċinḟḋ pḟin do gabail ass.

Brian mac Aoḋa buiḋe uí neill tiġḟrna ċinel eoġain do ṁarbaḋ do domnall mac briain uí neill, ⁊ ár mór do ċor ar ġallaiḃ ⁊ ar ġaoiḋealaiḃ amaille fris.

Coiṁeirġe ċoccaiḋ i ttír ċonaill eidir Aoḋ mac domnaill óicc, ⁊ toirrdealbaċ a dḟrbraṫair imon tiġḟrnus gur milleaḋ mórán don tír ḟcorra etir ecclais ⁊ thuaiṫ. Toirrdealbaċ daiṫrioġaḋ iarsin, ⁊ a aṫcor a tír ċonaill, i ccḟnn cenél eoġain ⁊ cloinne domnaill.

Domnall ua ceallaiġ tiġḟrna ua maine, aon ba gliocca comairle ina aimsir déċc in aibíd manaiġ, ⁊ a aḋnacal i mainistir ċnuic muaiḋe.

Mac Branáin (.i. conn) taoisech corc achlann déċc. Tomaltaċ mac Branáin an taoíseaċ do ronaḋ ina ionad do marbaḋ la muintir conalláin a ndíoġail a aṫar do marbaḋ laissium peaċtriamh.

[n] *A state of disturbance.*—This general disturbance, "propter capcionem Ricardi de Burgo Comitis Ultonie per Johannem filium Thome," is mentioned in an entry in Rot. Pat. 13 Ed. II. 80.—See Grace's Annals of Ireland, edited by the Rev. Richard Butler, for the Irish Archæological Society in 1842, p. 43, note [m].

[o] *O'Caomhain.*—See note [1] under the year 1208, p. 160.

[p] *The Red Earl.*—According to Pembridge's Annals, Richard Earl of Ulster was taken prisoner "*cito post festum S. Nicolai*" (Dec. 6) and detained in the castle of Lea, "*ad festum S. Gregorii Papæ*" (March 12). It is stated in Grace's Annals of Ireland that the Earl of Ulster was set at liberty on this occasion by the King's Parliament at Kilkenny, and that John Fitz-Thomas, as a penalty, lost the castle of Sligo and all his possessions in the province of Connaught, and also the castle of Kildare.

A great depredation was treacherously committed upon the Connacians by Fitzgerald and Mac Feorais [Birmingham]. Hugh, son of Owen, was attempted to be deposed by them. The country was desolated; yet, though they thus disturbed the province, they acquired no power over it.

David Mac Giolla-Arraith was slain by the sons of Donnell Duv O'Hara.

Donnell O'Hara, Lord of Leyny, died.

The Earl was taken prisoner by Fitzgerald, in consequence of which capture Ireland was thrown into a state of disturbance[n].

Dermot O'Caomhain[o] died.

THE AGE OF CHRIST, 1295.

The Age of Christ, one thousand two hundred ninety-five.

The Red Earl[p] was let out of prison by Fitzgerald, through the power of the King of England; and good hostages of his own tribe were received in his stead.

Brian, the son of Hugh Boy O'Neill, Lord of Kinel-Owen, was slain by Donnell, the son of Brian O'Neill, and a great slaughter made of the English and Irish [who were] along with him.

Hostilities broke out in Tirconnell between Hugh, son of Donnell Oge, and Turlough, his brother, concerning the lordship, so that a great part of the country was destroyed between them, both lay and ecclesiastical property. Turlough was afterwards deposed, and banished from Tirconnell to the Kinel-Owen and the Clann-Donnell.

Donnell O'Kelly, Lord of Hy-Many, one of the most judicious men in counsel of his time, died in the habit of a monk, and was interred in the monastery of Knockmoy.

Mac Branan (i. e. Con), Chief of Corcachlann, died; and Tomaltagh Mac Branan, who was elected his successor, was slain by the Muintir-Conallan[q], in revenge of their father, who had been killed by him some time before.

[q] *Muintir-Conallan*, i. e., the family of the O'Conallan's, who were located in the Plain of Connaught, to the west of the territory of Corcachlann. This family are to be distinguished from the O'Quinlans of Iveleary near Trim, in Meath, and from the O'Coinghiollains, or Connellans, who are now numerous in the county of Sligo.

Caislén an baile nuí[p], ⁊ Caislén moighe brecroiġe[q] do leccadh la Seaff-raiḋ o bFſrġail, ⁊ caislen ṁuiġe duṁa[r] do lſgaḋ lais mar an ccſtna.

AOIS CRIOST, 1296.

Aois Criost, míle, da ċéd, nochat, asé.

Giolla iosa mac an liaṫánaiġ easpucc oilifinn ⁊ Maolpſdair ó duibġſn-nain airdideochain na breifne o ḋruimcliaḃ go cſnannus decc.

Aoḋ mac Eoġain uí Concoḃair daiṫriogaḋ lá a oireċt fſin. Clann Mhuir-cſrtaiġ[s] do ṫabairt ina ionaḋ. A ccſannus do tabairt doiḃ do ċoncobar ruaḋ[t] mac caṫail, ⁊ a mbraiġde. An tír uile eitir cill ⁊ tuaiṫ do milleaḋ tres an aithrioghaḋ sin. Morsluaicceaḋ do ṫionol im Aoḋ ó cconcobair do ġallaiḃ ⁊ gaoiḋelaiḃ im Uilliam búrc, ⁊ im teróid a búrc go ttucc don tír iatt go mbátar cſiṫre laiṫe cona noiḋċiḃ ga milleaḋ ⁊ ga mór arccain etir croḋ ⁊ arḃar. Teccait taoisiġ na tíre ina ċſnn iar sin, ⁊ rucc lſis iad do laṫair an iarla do denaṁ síṫe riú. Dala cloinne Muircſrtaiġ tra ro loisccsiott ⁊ ro millsiott críoċ Cairpre uile, ⁊ do ċuaiḋsiott fó a tſm-plaiḃ. Giḋſḋ ro ḋioġail dia, Muire, ⁊ colum cille sa tſmpail ro ṡáraigh-siott sin orra go haṫġoiritt ar a haiṫle.

Imṫúsa na ttaoiseaċ remráite iar ngeallaḋ doiḃ oiġrſir Aoḋa do ḋenaṁ ro ṫillsiott dia ttiġiḃ, ⁊ nír ansat a mbun a rioċṫána dAoḋ uair do

[p] *Baile-nui*, i. e. Newtown.—According to Grace's Annals of Ireland, which contain more copious and more authentic information respecting Leinster than the Annals of the Four Masters, this castle is in the county of Wicklow, and that called Newcastle M'Kynegan.

[q] *Magh-Breacruighe*.—There is no place in the county of Longford now called by this name, unless Barry be a corruption of it. Barry is a village in the parish of Taghshinny, near Ballymahon, where the ruins of a castle are now to be seen.

[r] *Magh-Dumha*.—Now Moydoe, or Moydow, the name of a parish and barony in the county of Longford. The castle of Moydoe, now in ruins, lies in the townland of Bawn and parish of Moydoe; it is surrounded by a fosse. There are two ruins of castles in the parish of Moydoe in this county, one called Bawn and the other Castlereagh, each giving its name to a townland; but it is not easy now to decide which of them is the one here referred to as demolished in the year 1295. A great part of Castlereagh is yet standing in tolerable preservation.

[s] *The Clann-Murtough*.—These were the descendants of Murtough or Muircheartach Muimhneach, son of Turlough More O'Conor, Monarch of Ireland.

[t] *Conor Roe*.—He was Conor Roe, the son of Cathal, who was son of Hugh Breifneach, who

The castle of Baile-nui[p] and the castle of Magh-Breacruighe[q] were razed to the ground by Jeffrey O'Ferrall; and the castle of Magh-Dumha[r] was also demolished by him.

THE AGE OF CHRIST, 1296.

The Age of Christ, one thousand two hundred ninety-six.

Gilla-Isa Mac-an-Liathanaigh, Bishop of Elphin, and Maelpeter O'Duigennan, Archdeacon of Breifny, from Drumcliff to Kells, died.

Hugh, the son of Owen O'Conor, was deposed by his own tribe, and the Clann-Murtough[s] were brought in his place. The chieftainship was conferred by them on Conor Roe[t], the son of Cathal, and their hostages were given up to him. In consequence of this dethronement, all the country, as well ecclesiastical as lay property, was spoiled. A great force was mustered to aid Hugh O'Conor, consisting of the English and Irish, among whom were William Burke and Theobald Burke; these he brought into the country, and for four days and four nights they continued destroying it and plundering it of its corn and cattle. The chieftains of the country then came to him [Hugh O'Conor], and he led them to the Earl, in order to conclude a peace with them. As to the Clann-Murtough, they burned and destroyed the whole territory of Carbury, and attacked its churches; but God, [the Virgin] Mary, and Columbkille, whose churches they had profaned, took revenge of them for this shortly afterwards.

As for the aforementioned chieftains, after they had promised submission to Hugh, they returned to their [respective] homes; but they did not remain long

was son of Cathal Roe, King of Connaught in 1279, who was son of Conor Roe, who was son of Murtough Muimhneach, who was son of Turlough More O'Conor, Monarch of Ireland. This passage is given in the old translation of the Annals of Ulster as follows: "*Anno* 1292, *al.* 1296. Hugh mac Owen O'Conner deposed by his own subjects, and Clan Murtagh brought into the contery in his place. Pledges given to Conner Roe mac Cathall, and all the country, both spirituall and temporall, spoyled through that deposing. All Crich Carbre burnt and spoyled by Clan Murtagh, and [they] rifled the churches of the contry; and God and Columb-Kill, and our Lady Mary, whose churches they rob'd, were revenged on them. Conor Roe mac Cathall killed by Mac Dermott prosecuting a pray, and Loughlin mac Conner taken. Manus mac Tomalti taken, and other men killed. This was done at the end of Keda" [now Keadew in the barony of Boyle], "in Tyrtohall. Hugh O'Conher, Mac Dermot, O'Farrall, and these men made

gabsat le cloinn Muirċeartaiġ doridisi. Aodh mac Eoġain do ṫeaċt isna tuaṫaib annsin, ó Feargail ⁊ macc Raġnaill cona ninnircib do ṫabairt leis dó, teaċta do ċor uaidh do ṡaiġidh meic Diarmata ⁊ uí Ḟlannagáin, iarsoṁ diompódh ar cloind Muirċeartaiġ tar na hoireaċtoib oile annsin, ⁊ gabáil doib le hAodh. Iar na clos sin do Ċoncobar ruadh tucc ionnsaiġidh ar ṁac nDiarmata go ndearna féin ⁊ a combraiṫre creach fair. Mac Diarmata do ḋol do ṫóraiġeaċt a creiche, fechair iomairecc eatorra, go ttorcair Concobar ruadh, ⁊ gur gabadh Lochlainn mac Conċobair, ⁊ Maġnus mac Tomaltaiġ iar marbadh Socraitte uaṫa leaṫ for leath, ⁊ a ttabairt do Mac Diarmata lais go hAodh. Aodh (.i. ó Concobair), ó Feargail, Mac Diarmata, Mag Raġnaill, ⁊ na hoireaċta reṁraite do denaṁ creiċe diogla ar muintir cloinne Muirċeartaiġ an la cedna. Loclainn mac Concobair do dalladh iarsin ⁊ a écc ina othar.

Sluaiccheadh la Riġ Saxan i nAlbain go ro gabh neart mór ar an ccrich sin. Do battar maithe Gall Ereann aran sluaiġeadh sin, .i. Riocard a Burc iarla Uladh, ⁊ Gearailt mac Gearailt, ⁊ Seon Fitzthomas, ⁊ ro gabsat for milleadh Alban eitir ṫuaiṫ ⁊ eacclais. Ro milleadh leo dana Mainestir braṫar baoí is in ccrich, ⁊ ro trasgairsead go talṁain conar fagaibsead cloċ for cloiċ for a háit iar marbadh druinge dia haos gradh, do ṁnaib, ⁊ do ḋaoinib nar bo hinechta itir.

AOIS CRIOST, 1297.

Aois Criost, míle, da céd, noċat, a seacht.

Maoilseachlainn mac Briain abb na Buille do ṫoġa do ċum espuccoide Ailefinn, ⁊ Marian ó Donnabair dord .S. Dominic do ṫoġa ria Maoileachlainn ⁊ a ndol araon don Roiṁ, ⁊ Maoilechlainn décc.

great prayes upon Clann Murtagh the same day."

[u] *An army.*—This passage is given in the old translation of the Annals of Uster as follows: "*Anno* 1292, *al.* 1296. "A forcible army by the King of England into Scotland, that he bare sway of all the country, and spoyled countries, and destroyed subjects and churches, especially an Abby of Friers, that he left no stone upon a stone of it, and killed many *savenrits* [*sic*] and women. And the best men of Ireland were at that army, viz., Richard Bourke, Earle of Ulster, [and] Mac Gerald, viz., John Fitz-Thomas."

[v] *Ecclesiastics*, aos gráidh.—This term, when applied to laymen, denotes servants of trust, or officers; but when applied to ecclesiastics it means friars, priests, &c.

[w] *Not able to bear arms.*—Daoine nar bo

at peace with him, for they [soon afterwards] again sided with the Clann-Murtough. Hugh, the son of Owen, then came into the Tuathas, bringing O'Farrell and Mac Rannall, with their troops, along with him, and sent messengers to Mac Dermot and O'Flanagan, upon which these turned out against the Clann-Murtough, in opposition to the other tribes, and sided with Hugh. When Conor Roe had heard of this, he made an attack upon Mac Dermot, and, in conjunction with his kinsmen, committed a depredation upon him. Mac Dermot went in pursuit of the prey; and a battle was fought between them, in which Conor Roe was slain, and Loughlin, his son, and Manus, son of Tomaltagh, were taken prisoners, after the loss of many on both sides. Mac Dermot brought the prisoners to Hugh. On the same day Hugh (i. e. the O'Conor), O'Farrell, Mac Dermot, Mac Rannall, and the abovementioned tribes, committed a retaliatory depredation on the people [followers] of the Clann-Murtough. Loughlin, the son of Conor, was afterwards blinded, in consequence of which he died.

An army[u] was led by the king of England into Scotland, and he acquired great power in that country. The chiefs of the English of Ireland, i. e. Richard Burke, Earl of Ulster, Gerald Fitzgerald, and John Fitzthomas, were on this expedition. They commenced ravaging Scotland, both territories and churches. A monastery of friars in that country was plundered by them, and they prostrated it to the ground, so that they left not one stone of it above another on its site, and this after they had killed many of its ecclesiastics[v], besides women and persons not able to bear arms[w].

THE AGE OF CHRIST, 1297.

The Age of Christ, one thousand two hundred ninety-seven.

Melaghlin Mac Brian, Abbot of Boyle, was elected to the bishopric of Elphin; and Marian O'Donnaver, a friar of the order of St. Dominic, who had been elected [to the same see] before Melaghlin[x], repaired both to Rome, where Melaghlin died.

h-ıneaċta, i. e. persons not fitted for action; ıneaċta, fitted for action; ın, in compound words, signifies meet, fit, or proper, as ınḋéanta, fit to be done; ınḟeaḋma, capable of doing a manly action; ınaıṗm, fitted to bear arms, &c.

[x] *Before Melaghlin.*—This entry is better

Enri macc oirechtaigh easpucc Condere décc, ⁊ a adhnacal i mainistir drochait átha. Manach eiside.

Uilliam ó dubhtoigh epscop cluana fearta do thuitim dia eách, ⁊ a ecc dia bithin.

Concobhar mac taichligh meic diarmata tighearna moighe luirg ⁊ airtigh, fer roba ferr trold, ⁊ tachar, goil, ⁊ gaisccedh, ionnsaighidh, ⁊ anadh, díon, ⁊ tearmonn, firinne ⁊ flaithemhnus ina comaimsir décc, ⁊ a adhnacal i mainistir na búille.

Maghnus ó hainlighi toiseach chenel dobhta décc.

Cuuladh ó hanluain tighearna oirthir, Aongus mág mathgamhna, ⁊ morán oile do maithibh a muintire do marbhadh la gallaibh dúin dealccan acc iompudh dia ttighibh doibh (.i. do na gallaibh) on iarla.

given in the Dublin copy of the Annals of Ulster, thus: "A. D. 1293 [1297]. Maelechlainn mac Briain, ab na búille, do thogha cum espocoide Oilfinn, 7 Marian O Dondobur, brathair preciur do thogha reimhe 7 a ndul don Roim in imcosnam na hespucoide cedna 7 [Maelechlainn] a eg don turus sin."

"A. D. 1293 [1297]. Melaghlin Mac Brian, abbot of Boyle, was elected to the bishopric of Elphin, and Marian O'Donnover, a Friar Preacher, who had been elected before him, went to Rome in contention for the same bishopric, and [Melaghlin] died on that journey."

This entry is not in the old translation of the Annals of Ulster, preserved in the British Museum.

[r] *Henry Mageraghty.*—In the Dublin copy of the Annals of Ulster, his death is thus entered under the year 1293: "*Anno Domini* 1293. Henri Magoirechtaigh espuc Connire, manach liath, quieuit in Christo, 7 a adlucudh i mainistir drochaid atha."

"*Anno Domini* 1293. Henry Mageraghty, Bishop of Connor, a grey monk, *quievit in Christo*, and was buried in the monastery of Drogheda." But in the old translation of the Ulster Annals it is entered as follows:

"*Anno* 1293 (*al.* 1297). Henry Mac Oreght, Bishop of Aghaconair, a grey monk, *quievit.*"

In Harris's edition of Ware's Bishops, p. 659, Henry Mac Oreghty, a Cistertian monk, is mentioned as Bishop of Achonry, and his death placed in the year 1297. In the same work, p. 288, mention is made of a Henry Mac Oreghty, Bishop of Derry, commonly called Henry of Ardagh, whose death is also placed in 1297. The fact would appear to be that he was Bishop of Derry (Doire) only, and that achaidh Conaire and Condere are mere mistakes of transcribers. We know from the public records that he was really Bishop of Derry, for he received the royal assent on the 3rd of March, 1294; but there seems to be no authority for making him Bishop of Achonry, except the old translation of the Annals of Ulster, which Ware and Harris seem to have used.—See note [l], *infra*.

[s] *Airtech.*—The text of the Annals of Ulster is very nearly the same as that of the Four Masters, but the old translator does not attempt a close version of it. He shortens it thus: "*Anno* 1293 (*al.* 1297). Conor mac Tachly mac Dermot, king of Moilurg and Arty, the elder, and lord of all Munter-Mulrony, a man [the most] praysable in all respects of all his own time,

Henry Mageraghty[y], Bishop of Conor, died, and was interred in the monastery of Drogheda. He was a monk.

William O'Duffy, Bishop of Clonfert, fell from his horse, and died in consequence.

Conor, the son of Taichleach Mac Dermot, Lord of Moylurg and Airteach[z], the best man of his time for combat and contest, valour and prowess, incursion and wealth, protection and refuge, veracity and governing authority, died, and was interred in the monastery of Boyle.

Manus O'Hanly, Chief of Kinel-Dofa, died.

Cu-Uladh[a] O'Hanlon, Lord of Orior, Aengus[b] Mac Mahon, and many others of the chiefs of his people, were slain by the English of Dundalk, on their return home from the Earl [of Ulster].

quievit." The original text is a remarkable example of the alliteration and tautology of the inflated prose style of the Irish writers of the fifteenth and sixteenth centuries.

The territory of Airteach extends from the western extremity of the parish of Tibohine, in the county of Roscommon, where it joins the county of Mayo, to the bog of Belanagare, which divides it from Machaire-Chonnacht, and from the northern boundary of Clann-Cheithearnaigh to Lough O'Gara. It comprised the parishes of Tibohine and Kilnamanagh in the west of the county of Roscommon, and was in ancient times the country of Mac Dermot Gall.—See notices of this territory at the years 1381, 1416, and 1415.

A stream called *Abhainn na Foraoise*, rising in the bog of Belanagare, and falling into the Breedoge River, divides Airteach from Machaire Chonnacht; and the River Breedoge which rises in Lough Bealaigh, in the parish of Kilcolagh, and falls into Lough O'Gara, is the boundary between it and Moylurg. Airteach lies between the Rivers Lung and Breedoge, and is bounded on the south by the parish of Kilkeevin, and on the east by the parish of Kilcorkey.

There were three Mac Dermots in the county of Roscommon, two of whom sprang up about the middle of the fourteenth century: 1st, the Mac Dermot himself, who was Chief of Moylurg, Airteach, and Tir-Tuathail; 2nd, Mac Dermot Gall, or the Anglicised, who possessed Airteach, but was tributary to the chief Mac Dermot; and, 3rd, Mac Dermot Roe, who was Chief of Tir-Tuathail, and tributary generally to the Mac Dermot of Moylurg, but sometimes to Mac Donough of Tirerrill, in the county of Sligo, who was another offshoot from the same family.

The family of Mac Dermot Gall, are interred in the church-yard of Cloonard, in the parish of Tibohine, where they have a separate square enclosure to themselves, in which they would allow no one to be buried but a Mac Dermot Gall, not even their wives when of a different family.

[a] *Cu-Uladh.*—This name, which is very common in the families of O'Hanlon, Mac Mahon, and others, is translated *Canis Ultoniæ*, by the compiler of the Annals of Ulster, and anglicised Cooley by Fynes Morrison, and other writers of the reign of Elizabeth; and Cowley by Connell Mageoghegan, in his translation of the Annals of Clonmacnoise.

[b] *Aengus.*—This name is still in use, but lati-

AOIS CRIOST, 1298.

Aoiꝼ Cꞃioꞅꞇ, míle, ꝺá ċéꝺ, nochaꞇ, a hochꞇꞇ.

Tomáꞅ ó haiꞃecꞇaigh abb eaꞅꞅa ꞃuaiꝺ ꝺécc.

Saꝺb inġín Aoꝺa buiꝺe uí neill bín ꞇaiꝺg mic ainꝺꞃiaꞅa uí ċoncobaiꞃ ꝺécc.

Bꞃian bꞃeaġach mac Samꞃaꝺáin ꞇaoiꞅeaċ ꞇeallaiġ echꝺach ꝺo ṁaꞃbaꝺ la hAoꝺ mbꞃeiꞅneaċ ó cconcobaiꞃ, ⁊ lá cloinn muiꞃcꞅꞃꞇaiġ aꞃċína.

Donnchaꝺ mac ꝺoṁnaill uí eaġꞃa an ꞇaonmac ꞇaoiꞅiġ ba ꝼeaꞃꞃ oineċ, ⁊ laṁ acc coꞅnamh a ꞇíꞃe ꝺo ṁaꞃbaꝺ ꝺá bꞃaꞇaiꞃ, bꞃian caꞃꞃaċ ó hÍġhꞃa.

Tomaꞅ Fizmuiꞃiꞅ baꞃun ꝺo ġꞅꞃalꞇaċaiḃ ꝼꞃiꞅ a nabaꞃꞇai on ꞇoiꝺꞃe cam ꝺo écc.

AOIS CRIOST, 1299.

Aoiꞅ Cꞃioꞅꝺ, mile, ꝺa céꝺ, noċaꞇ, a naoí.

Niocol mac maoilioꞅa Aiꞃꝺeꞅꞅcop Aꞃꝺamacha an ꞇaín cleꞃeċ ꞃo ba ꝺiaꝺha cꞃaibꝺiġe bai in Eꞃinn ina aimꞅiꞃ ꝺécc.

Feaꞃġal ua ꝼiꞃġil eꞅꞃucc Raꞇha boꞇh ꝺo écc. Ba heꞅiꝺe peaꞃꞃa ecclaiꞃi ꞃo ba mo ainm ꝺíꞃce, ⁊ ꝺaonnaċꞇa, cꞃaḃaꝺ, ⁊ caoínġnioṁ baoí ina aimꞅiꞃ.

Alxanꝺaiꞃ macc ꝺoṁnaill, aoin ḟeaꞃ ba ꝼíꞃꞃ eneċ, ⁊ enġnaṁ ꝺa ꞃaiḃe ꝺia ċinẏoh in Eꞃinn, ⁊ in albain ꝺo maꞃbaꝺ la halexanꝺaiꞃ mac ꝺuḃġaill, ⁊ áꞃ ꝺíꞃíṁe ꝺia muinꞇiꞃ amaille ꞃiꞅ.

nised to Æneas. It is made Enos by Mageoghegan, which is not far from its Irish pronunciation, which is Ennees in Connaught, Ennais in Munster, and Ennoos in Ulster.

[e] *O'Heraghty.*—This name is to be distinguished from Mageraghty, or Geraghty, which is that of a family of royal extraction in Connaught. The O'Heraghtys, who were never a family of any distinction, were located in the present county of Donegal, where they are still numerous; some of them are also on the island of Inishmurray, off the coast of Sligo, where they are beginning to change the name to Geraghty, while others of the same race and name, who have migrated to Leinster, have changed it to Harrington! The Mageraghtys, who are of the same race as the O'Conors, Kings of Connaught, were originally located in the district of Muintir-Rodiv, in the plain of Connaught, and are now very numerous in the counties of Roscommon, Galway, and Mayo, and even in Leinster, where they generally reject the Mac and shorten the name to Geraghty, and even to Gearty and Gerty, which latter forms are not to be approved of. O'Heraghty is as different from Mageraghty as O'Donnell is from Mac Don-

THE AGE OF CHRIST, 1298.

The Age of Christ, one thousand two hundred ninety-eight.

Thomas O'Heraghty[c], Abbot of Assaroe, died.

Sabia, daughter of Hugh Boy O'Neill, and wife of Teige, son of Andreas O'Conor, died.

Brian Breaghach [the Bregian] Magauran, Chief of Teallach-Eachdhach [Tullyhaw], was slain by Hugh Breifneach O'Conor, and the Clann-Murtough.

Donough, the son of Donnell O'Hara, a chieftain's son, of best hospitality and hand in defence of his country, was slain by his own kinsman, Brian Carragh O'Hara.

Thomas Fitzmaurice, a Baron of the Geraldines, usually called the Crooked Heir[d], died.

THE AGE OF CHRIST, 1299.

The Age of Christ, one thousand two hundred ninety-nine.

Nicholas Mac Maelisa, Archbishop of Armagh, the most godly and devout ecclesiastic of his time in Ireland, died.

Farrell O'Firghil, Bishop of Raphoe, died. He was the most celebrated man of his time for charity, humanity, piety, and benevolent actions.

Alexander Mac Donnell, the best man of his tribe in Ireland and Scotland for hospitality and prowess, was slain by Alexander Mac Dowell[e], together with a countless number of his people who were slaughtered.

nell, or O'Neill from Mac Neill. They differ in name, in descent, and in locality; the pedigree and history of the former is unknown, those of the latter are recorded with considerable minuteness till about the middle of the sixteenth century, when they sunk into comparative poverty and obscurity, though in 1585 there was a recognized chief of the name, and the Editor is informed that his lineal descendant is still living near Moylough, in the county of Galway.

[d] *Crooked heir.*—This passage is thus given in the Dublin copy of the Annals of Ulster: "Anno Domini 1294 [1298]. Tomas Fimuiris, barún mór do cloinn Gerailt risi na-bairṫea in teiġrin cam, quievit in Christo." And thus rendered in the old translation: "*Anno* 1294, *al.* 1298. Thomas Fitz Moris, Baron of the Fitzgeralds, that was called the Crooked heire, *quievit.*"

[e] *Mac Dowell.*—This surname is generally written Mac Dugald by the Scotch. This passage is thus given in the old translation of the Annals of Ulster: "*Anno* 1295, *al.* 1299. Alexander Mac Donell, one of the best of Ireland

AOIS CRIOST, 1300.

Aois Criost, míle, trí chétt.

Congalach ua lochlainn espucc corcmodruaḋ, saoí enigh ⁊ craḃaiḋ décc.

Ffiḋlimiḋ mág cárṫaig aḋbar tighfrna dfsmuman décc.

Caislén átha cliaṫ an ċorainn, .i. baile an móta do ṫionnsgnadh lár an iarla.

Seon Prinndrecas do marḃaḋ la mac piaċra uí floinn.

Teboitt buiteler ro baḋ barún oirdirc décc.

Adam Stondun barun mór ele eriḋe do écc.

Seoinin ócc mac muiris do marḃaḋ la Concoḃar ua fFloinn go ndaoiniḃ ele amaille fris.

AOIS CRIOST, 1301.

Aois Criost, míle, da ċéd, a haon.

Fionnġuala ingfn ṗḟiḋlimiḋ ui concoḃair banab cille craoḃnatt décc.

Cairbre mac corbmaic uí ṁaoilecḟlainn do ṁarḃaḋ tre aslaċ mic airt ui maoileachlainn a ḃrathar.

and Scotland, was killed by Alexander Mac Dubgall, with a great slaughter of his people."

The Annals of Clonmacnoise, as translated by Mageoghegan, record the death of Sir John Delamare this year in the following words:

"Sir John Delamare, knight, the best, worthiest, powerfullest, and bountifullest knight of all Meath, was killed by Geffrie O'Ferrall in pursuite and defence of his own preye."

"The families of Delamares, Ledwitches, Frenies, and Cabies, are of the remnant of the Danes that remaine in this kingdome."

[f] *Congalagh O'Loughlin.*—In Harris's edition of Ware's Bishops, p. 629, he is set down as Bishop of Kilfenora, which is perfectly correct, for the original country of the people, or tribe, called Corcomroe, was exactly coextensive with the diocese of Kilfenora. In after ages, however, this territory was divided into two parts between the rival chiefs O'Conor and O'Loughlin, and the eastern division, which was allotted to O'Loughlin, was called East Corcomroe, while the western, which fell to the share of O'Conor, was called West Corcomroe.—See the Irish work, called *Caithreim Thoirdheabbhaigh*, at the year 1311, where the present barony of Burren, in the north of the county of Clare, is called East Corcomroe. But in process of time East Corcomroe began to be more generally called Burren, i. e. the rocky district, and O'Loughlin, its chief, who previously to the fourteenth century, had been styled Chief of Corcomroe, was called O'Loughlin Burren. The extent of the western division of Corcomroe is now preserved in the barony of Corcomroe, while that of East Corcomroe is preserved in

THE AGE OF CHRIST, 1300.

The Age of Christ, one thousand three hundred.

Congalagh O'Loughlin[f], Bishop of Corcomroe, a man of learning, hospitality, and piety, died.

Felim Mac Carthy[g], heir-apparent to the lordship of Desmond, died.

The castle of Ath-Cliath-an-Chorainn (i. e. of Ballymote) was commenced by the Earl[h].

John Prendergast was slain by the son of Fiachra O'Flynn.

Theobald Butler, an illustrious baron, died.

Adam Staunton[i], another great baron, died.

Seoinin Oge Mac Maurice was slain by Conor O'Flynn, with many others along with him.

THE AGE OF CHRIST, 1301.

The Age of Christ, one thousand three hundred one.

Finola, daughter of Felim O'Conor, Abbess of Cill-Craebhnatt[j], died.

Carbry, son of Cormac O'Melaghlin[k], was slain at the instigation of the son of Art O'Melaghlin, his kinsman.

the barony of Burren. Thus we see the reason why the great abbey of Burren is, even to this day, called the abbey of Corcomroe. O'Loughlin retained all his division of Corcomroe (namely Burren) till the time of Cromwell, but the entire of O'Conor's portion of it was granted to Sir Donnell O'Brien, in the reign of Queen Elizabeth, except Ennistimon, which was left to O'Conor himself; but he lost it soon after.

[g] *Felim Mac Carthy.*—In Mageoghegan's translation of the Annals of Clonmacnoise he is called "Felym Mac Carrhie, young prince of Desmond."

[h] *The Earl.*—In Mageoghegan's translation of the Annals of Clonmacnoise, this passage is thus rendered: "A. D. 1300. The castle of Athkle-an-Corran, *alias* Ballenmote, was founded by the Reade Earle this year."

[i] *Adam Staunton.*—In Mageoghegan's translation of the Annals of Clonmacnoise he is called "Addam Stontan, Lord of Keera, died."

[j] *Cill Craebhnatt*, Cıll Cpuobnατε.—This nunnery, which is called Killcreunata by Ware and Archdall, is now called Kilcreevanty. It is situated in the county of Galway, about three miles to the north-west of Tuam. Extensive ruins of this nunnery still remain, but its architectural features are all destroyed, except one window which shews that the architecture was extremely beautiful. The situation of this nunnery was unknown to Archdall and even to Dr. Lanigan.

[k] *O'Melaghlin.*—Mageoghegan's translation of the Annals of Clonmacnoise contains the two

Uilliam mácc Flannchaidh toiseach Dartraighe do marbhadh la hualgarcc mac domhnaill mic airt uí ruairc.

Creach mór do dénamh dAodh mac cathail uí concobhair, ⁊ do cloinn muirchertaigh ar thadhg mac aindriasa i moigh ccedne.

Sluaiccheadh la Righ Saxan in Albain, ⁊ mac gerailt, ⁊ mac Feorais, ⁊ maithe barún Ereann uile cenmothá iarla uladh do dhol leis ar an sluaigheadh sin, ⁊ a bheith doibh o chaicthidhis ria lughnasadh go Samhain in Albain, ⁊ gan a lainnert do ghabháil doibh in airsett sin.

AOIS CRIOST, 1302.

Aois Criost, mile, trí chéd, adhó.

Stiamna ó braccáin airdeasppucc caisil [decc].

Milis esppucc luimnigh, mac meic eisiomh don Iarla laighnech, ⁊ esppucc corcaighe décc. Ba manach eisiumh réna oirdneadh ina esppuccóide.

passages following which have been omitted by the Four Masters: "Cormack Mac Cormack O'Melaghlyn was killed by the son of Art O'Melaghlyn, who was his own Cossen Germain, his father's brother's son."

"Gille Issie Mac Firvisse, chief chronicler of Tyrefiaghragh, wonderfull well skilled in histories, poetry, computation, and many other sciences, died.

[l] *Teige, the son of Andreas.*—This Andreas was the son of Brian Luighneach, the ancestor of O'Conor, Sligo.—See pedigree of the O'Conors of Connaught in the Book of Lecan, fol. 72, *et sequen.*

[m] *Moy-g-Cedne.*—Magh g-cedne, a plain situate between the rivers Drobhaois (Drowes) and Eirne (Erne), in the county of Donegal. The name and extent of this plain are still well known. In an Inquisition, 13 Jac. I. it is called Moygh, *alias* Moygene, and described as "inter flumina de Earne et Drohes [Drowes] in com' Donigall, Letrym, et Slygoe, vel eorum altero." For very early references to this plain, see O'Flaherty's *Ogygia*, Part iii. c. 14; and Duald Mac Firbis's genealogical work (Marquis of Drogheda's copy), p. 15.

[n] *Except the Earl of Ulster*, Cenmothá Iarla Uladh.—This would also bear to be translated "besides the Earl of Ulster," for the Irish cenmothá, like the Latin *præter*, sometimes means *besides*, and sometimes *except*. The phrase used in the Dublin copy of the Annals of Ulster is, a ningnais Iarla Uladh, i. e. "in the absence of the Earl of Ulster;" and yet in the old translation of these annals it is rendered "besides the Earle of Ulster." Thus: "*Anno* 1297, *al.* 1301. An army by the King of England into Scotland, and Mac Geralt and Mac Korus, and the best of the Barons of Ireland, *besides* the Earle of Ulster, with him in that journey, and were there from a fortnight before Lammas untill Allhallowtide, and made noe great hand there." It is rendered in Mageoghegan's translation of the Annals of Clonmacnoise as follows: "A. D. 1301. The King of England, with Mac Gerald, the Lord Bremyngham, with all the

William Mac Clancy, Chief of Dartry, was slain by Ualgarg, the son of Donnell, son of Art O'Rourke.

A great depredation was committed by Hugh, the son of Cathal O'Conor, and the Clann Murtough, upon Teige, the son of Andreas[l], in Magh g-Cedne[m].

An army was led by the King of England into Scotland. Fitzgerald, Mac Feorais [Bermingham], and all the other noble barons of Ireland, except the Earl of Ulster[n], accompanied him on this expedition. They remained in Scotland from a fortnight before Lammas[o] until Allhallowtide[p], but were not able to effect the total conquest of the country.

THE AGE OF CHRIST, 1302.

The Age of Christ, one thousand three hundred two.

Stephen O'Bragan, Archbishop of Cashel [died].

Miles, Bishop of Limerick[q], grandson of the Leinster Earl, and the Bishop of Cork[r], died. The latter had been a monk before he was consecrated Bishop.

forces of the English of Ireland, *save onely* the Earle of Ulster, went to Scotland to conquer the said kingdome, where they continued from a fortnight before Lammas untill Hollantide, and made no intire conquest thereof."

The probability is that the Earl of Ulster was not on this expedition, and that he did not go to assist King Edward into Scotland until the year 1303. The Editor, therefore, has translated cenmot by *except.*

[o] *Lammas.* — Lúġnaṡa, called in English Lammas, is the name by which the first of August is still known. The word is thus explained in Cormac's Glossary: luġnaṡṡaḋ .ı. naṡṡaḋ no auṗtaċ loġa mic Eıṫlıonꝺ .ı. oenaċ no ṗeṗta laıṡ ım ṫaıꝺe ṗoġaṁaıṗ ın ceċ blıaḋaın. Cluıċe no oenaċ no auṗtaċ ıṡ ꝺo ıṡ aınm naṡṡaḋ, i.e. "Lughnassadh, i.e. the games or festival of Lughaidh, the son of Eithliond. There was a fair held by him each year in the beginning of harvest. Nassadh signifies game, fair, or festival."

[p] *Allhallowtide.*—Saṁuın, is yet the name of the first of November: it is explained in O'Clery's glossary as follows: "Saṁuın q. d. ṡaṁṗuın .ı. ṗuın an tṡaṁṗaıḋ. ṗuın .ı. cṗíoċnuġaḋ." *Samhuin* q. d. *Samh-fhuin*, i. e. the end of summer; *fuin*, i. e. end."

[q] *Miles, Bishop of Limerick.*—The surname of this Miles, Bishop of Limerick, is not given in any of the Irish annals; but the Annals of Ulster and Clonmacnoise agree in calling him the grandchild [i. e. son of the son] of the Earl of Leinster. The person called the Earl of Leinster, by the Irish annalists, was evidently no other than the Earl William Marshall; and it is highly probable that this Miles was his (perhaps illegitimate) grandson. He would appear to be the Bishop of Limerick, called by Ware *Gerald le Marescall*, who died in 1301 (*English style*). The Fitzgeralds were not styled Earls of Leinster, or even of Kildare, till the year 1316.

[r] *The Bishop of Cork.*—His name was Robert

Doṁnall ruaḋ mag cartaiġ tiġḟrna dḟrṁuṁan, Donn carrach mág uidir céd tiġḟrna ṡil uiḋir i ffḟraiḃ manach, ⁊ Ruaiḋri mac domnaill uí eaġra adbar tiġearna luiġne décc.

Creach mór do ḋénamh dAoḋ mac caṫail ar ṫadg mac briain, ⁊ ar Shitriucc mac an ċairnigh még flannchaiḋ i moigh cceidne.

AOIS CRIOST, 1303.

Aois Criost, míle, trí ċéd, a trí.

Maoilechloinn mac briain espucc oile finn décc, ⁊ Donnchaḋ ó flannaccain abb na buille do gabáil na hespuccóide dia eis.

Toirrḋealḃaċ mac domnaill oicc uí doṁnaill da ngoirṫi toirrḋealḃaċ cnuic an maḋma tigearna tire conaill, tuir cocctach caṫach cosnaṁaċ, Cúculainn cloinne dálaiġ ar gaiscceaḋ, do marbaḋ la a dḟrbraṫair Aoḋ mac doṁnaill óicc iar ccoccaḋ imċian, ⁊ iar milleaḋ moráin dia ttír ḟttorra da gach taoiḃ, go nár adbal himaille ris do cenél eoġain, do ṁaiṫiḃ gall an tuaisceirt, ⁊ do Conallċaiḃ búḋén. Ba diḃriḋe Muirċḟrtaċ mág flannchaiḋ taoiseaċ dartraiġe. Donn ó caṫain tigearna fear na craoiḃe, ⁊ cianachta, donnchaḋ mac mḟnman, Aoḋ mac mḟanman, da ṁac mic an fir lḟiginn ui doṁnaill, niall mac neill uí baoiġill adbar taoisiġ na ttrí ttuath, mac hugossa, a ṁac ⁊ a dḟrbraṫair, Adam Sandál, goill, ⁊ gaoidil iomḋa ar ċḟna. Aoḋ mac doṁnaill oicc do bḟith i ttiġḟrnus tire conaill iarsin go roḋanaċ sóinmech an ccéin do ṁair.

Mac Donogh. He had been a Cistercian monk, and succeeded to this dignity in the year 1277.—See Harris's edition of Ware's Bishops, p. 559.

[s] *The Sil-Uidhir.*—The Sil-Uidhir are the Maguires, Mac Awleys, Mac Caffrys, Mac Manuses, and their correlatives in Fermanagh. In Mageoghegan's translation of the Annals of Clonmacnoise, the following notice occurs of this first of the Maguires who acquired the chieftainship of Fermanagh: "A. D. 1302. Donn Magwyre, prince of Fermanagh, the best of all Ireland for hospitality, liberality, and prowess, died. Great comparisons have been made between this Donn Magwyre and Donnell Roe Mac Carthy (before mentioned) for their bountys and hospitalities, which Donn Magwyre, by the judgment of a certain learned Irish poett (which remained for a long space in the houses of the said Donn and Donnell covertly, and in the habitt of a karrogh, or common gamester, to know which of them surpassed the other) was counted to excell Donnell in all good parts, as by this Irish verse, made by the said poet, you may know:

Donnell Roe Mac Carthy, Lord of Desmond; Donn Carragh Maguire, the first lord of the Sil-Uidhir[s] in Fermanagh; and Rory, the son of Donnell O'Hara, heir-presumptive to the lordship of Leyny, died.

A great depredation was committed by Hugh, son of Cathal, in Magh g-Ceidne, upon Teige, son of Brian, and Sitric, son of Cairneach Mac Clancy.

THE AGE OF CHRIST, 1303.

The Age of Christ, one thousand three hundred three.

Melaghlin Mac Brian[t], Bishop of Elphin, died; and Donough O'Flanagan took the bishopric after him.

Turlough, the son of Donnell Oge O'Donnell, usually called Turlough of Cnoc-an-Madhma[u], Lord of Tirconnell, a warlike tower of protection in battle, and the Cuchullin of the Clann-Daly in valour, was slain by his brother, Hugh, son of Donnell Oge, after a long war, during which much of their country was spoiled between them in every direction; and great numbers of the Kinel-Owen, of the chiefs of the English of the North, and of the Kinel-Connell themselves, were slaughtered along with him. Among these were Murtough Mac Clancy, Chief of Dartry; Donn O'Kane, Lord of Firnacreeva and Kienaghta; Donough Mac Menman, and Hugh Mac Menman; two grandsons of the Ferleighin [Lector] O'Donnell; Niall, son of Niall O'Boyle, heir presumptive to the Three Tuathas[v]; Mac Hugossa, his son, and brother; Adam Sandal; and many others, as well English as Irish. After this, Hugh, son of Donnell Oge, enjoyed the lordship of Tirconnell in happiness and prosperity as long as he lived.

"Donn Maguiḋir maḋ se sin,
Mó Deasṁúṁain 'ná ḋuṫaiḋ
Mó sa ḋó dolaiḋ Duinn
Aċt ciḋ mo doṁan Doṁnaill."

"which is as much to say in English, as notwithstanding Desmond, and the lands of Donnell Mac Carthie, be far greater than the lands of Donn Magwyre, yet Donn retaineth in his house twice as many as Donnell doth."

[t] *Melaghlin Mac Brian.*—See a notice of his going to Rome in 1297, to contest the bishopric of Elphin with Marian O'Donnaver. According to Ware he died at Rome about the close of the year 1302.

[u] *Cnoc-an-Madhma*, i. e. hill of the defeat. The Editor is not aware that any place retaining this name is now to be found in Tirconnell.

[v] *The Three Tuathas.*—These were three districts in the barony of Kilmacrenan, in the north-west of the county of Donegal, which afterwards belonged to a branch of the Mac

Doṁnall ócc maġ cártaigh ticcſrna dſrmuṁan décc.

Diarmait ó ḟlannaccáin taoiseaċ tuaiṫe rata, a ḋá mac, ⁊ sochaiḋe imaille friú do marḃaḋ lá druing do luċt tiġe doṁnaill mic taidg uí concoḃair i mbun duiḃe i ttóraiġeċt creiċe boí do brſiṫ lais a moiġ ccéidne.

Maġnas macc saṁradáin taoiseaċ teallaiġ echḋaċ, ⁊ Niall mac gille-ḟinnéin, décc.

Geroid Mac Gſrailt décc.

Creach mór do ḋenaṁ la cloinn Muirċſrtaiġ ar ṁuintir ċionaiṫ, ⁊ Muirceartaċ mac Consnaṁa adbar taoisiġ muintire cionaiṫ do marḃaḋ don ċur sin.

Sluaiġeaḋ mor la Riġ Saxan in Albain, ⁊ an tiarla, goill ⁊ gaoiḋil ioṁḋa do ḋol coblaċ mór a hErinn do congnaṁ lais. Caiṫreċa ioṁḋa do bſin amaċ doibh, ⁊ nſrt Alban do ġabail leó don ċur sin. Teroitt a burc dearbraṫair an iarla decc (.i. adhaiġ nodlac) hi ccarraic ḟſrġusa iar ttoiḋeċt dó don tsluaiġeaḋ sin.

Sweenys, called from them Mac Suiḃne na d-tuaṫ, i. e. Mac Sweeny of the *tuaths*, or districts.

[w] *Donnell Oge Mac Carthy.*—He was the son of Donnell Roe, Prince of Desmond, who died in 1302; who was the son of Cormac Finn, Prince of Desmond, who was the son of Donnell More na Curra, who was the fourth in descent from Carthach, the progenitor after whom the Mac Carthys have taken their surname. The silver seal of this Prince is in the possession of Mr. Petrie, and is in its style very similar to that of his cotemporary Felim O'Conor, which was found during the government of Lord Strafford, and given by that nobleman to King Charles I. Donnell is represented on horseback charging with sword in hand. The legend "S. Dovenaldi og fili D. Rogh Mac Arthy."

[x] *Bun Duibhe*, i. e. the mouth of the River Dubh, now Bunduff, a village in the barony of Carbery, in the county of Sligo. The names of many villages, townlands, &c. situated at the mouths of rivers, are compounded of bun, *foot, mouth*, and the name of the river, as bun Droḃaoíse, i. e. the mouth of the River Drowes, q. d. *Drowes-foot*, bun-na Mairge, now Bonamargy, in the county of Antrim; bun na Finne, the mouth of the River Fin.

[y] *Garrett Fitzgerald.*—He was the eldest son of John Fitz-Thomas, Baron of Offaly.—See Cox's *Hibernia Anglicana*, p. 87, A. D. 1304.

[z] *Mac Consnava*, Mac Consnaṁa.— This name is generally written Mac Conáṁa in the Dublin copy of the Annals of Ulster. It is now sometimes correctly anglicised Mac Kinnaw, and very incorrectly translated *Forde*. The territory of Muintir Cionaoith, which still retains its ancient name, lies in the county of Leitrim, to the west and north-west of Lough Allen, and is nearly co-extensive with the barony of Dromahaire.

[a] *Into Scotland.*—This passage is rendered as follows in the old translation of the Annals of Ulster: "*Anno* 1299, *al.* 1303. A great army by the King of England into Scotland; many cityes taken by them; and the Earle and Eng-

Donnell Oge Mac Carthy[w], Lord of Desmond, died.

Dermot O'Flanagan, Chief of Tuathratha, his two sons, and many others along with them, were slain at Bun Duibhe[x], by some of the household of Donnell, son of Teige O'Conor, who had pursued them, to deprive them of a prey which they were carrying off from Magh-g-Cedne.

Manus Magauran, Chief of Teallach Eachdhach [Tullyhaw, in the county of Cavan], and Niall Mac Gillafinnen, died.

Garrett Fitzgerald[y] died.

A great depredation was committed by the Clann-Murtough [O'Conor] in Muintir-Kenny, on which occasion Murtough Mac Consnava[z], Chief of Muintir-Kenny, was slain.

A great army was led by the King of England into Scotland[a]; and the [Red] Earl and many of the Irish and English went with a large fleet from Ireland to his assistance. On this occasion they took many cities, and gained sway[b] over Scotland. Theobald Burke[c], the Earl's brother, died after his return from this expedition, on Christmas night, at Carrickfergus[d].

lish and Irish went out of Ireland, a great navy, and conquered much there. Tibot Bourk, brother to the Earle, died after returning from that journey, at Carrigfergus, on Christmas eve."

Sir Richard Cox has the following remarks upon the Red Earl, in his *Hibernia Anglicana*, p. 87: "A. D. 1303. *Richard Burk*, Earl of Ulster, accompanied with *Eustace le Poer*, and a good Army, went to aid the King in *Scotland;* and the Earl made thirty-three knights in the castle of *Dublin* before he set out; and it is observable that in all commissions, and even in the Parliament Rolls, this Earl is always named before the Lord Justice."—See also Leland's History of Ireland, book ii. c. 2, vol. i. p. 258, where this historian has the following remark on the state of Ireland in the absence of these great lords:

"The absence of such powerful lords produced its natural effect in Ireland, in encouraging a licentious spirit of insurrection, and giving free course to the treachery and turbulence both of the English and Irish inhabitants. Several feuds broke out with new violence, and petty wars were carried on, to the utter desolation of the finest and most valuable of the English settlements. The disorder extended even to the seat of government; and the utmost efforts of the chief governour and the well-affected lords were scarcely sufficient to defend the province of Leinster."

[b] *Gained sway*, neaṗt alban do ġabail leó, i. e. the strength, power, or sway of Scotland was obtained by them. Neaṗt do ġabail signifies to obtain power, or to effect a conquest.

[c] *Christmas night*, aḋaiġ nodlac.—The Irish word aḋaiġ, *night*, is now always written oiḋċe, and the word seems to have lost an initial n, as it is evidently cognate with the Latin *nox*, *noctis*, and the English *night*.

[d] Under this year the Annals of Clonmacnoise, as translated by Mageoghegan, record the death of Morrishe mac William Gallda Mageoghegan, on the fourth of the Ides of June."

AOIS CRIOST, 1304.

Aois Criost, mile, trí céd, a cethair.

Concobhar mac Aodha uí concobhair do marbhadh la hoiberd ua fFlaithbheartaigh iar ndenamh mebhla dósomh ar dhonnchadh ua fFlaithbheartaigh, 7 hoiberd do tuitim inn focédóir.

An contaois bean Riocaird a burc iarla uladh, .i. an tiarla Ruadh, 7 Uater a burc oighre an iarla céona do écc.

AOIS CRIOST, 1305.

Aois Criost, mile, trí céd, a cúig.

O Concobhair failghe, .i. Muirchertach, Maolmordha, a bhrathair, 7 an calbhach ó concobhair amaille fri naonbhar ar ficit do mhaithibh a muintire do mharbhadh do Shir piarus mac fFeorais tre fheill 7 meabhail i ccaislen meic Feorais.

Caislen nua insi heoccáin do dhénamh las an iarla ruadh.

Maidhm la hAodh mac cathail uí concobhair, 7 la cloinn Mhuircheartaigh ar cenae ar mhuinntir Raighilligh da ttorchair pilip ó Raighilligh, 7 oighre cloinne suibhne, 7 mácc buirrche cenn na ngallócclach imaille fri cethrachat arcéd ina ffarradh.

[e] Under this year the Annals of Clonmacnoise, as translated by Mageoghegan, have the following entry, which is omitted by the Four Masters: "A. D. 1304. William Oge mac William Gallda Mageoghegan died, the prides of the Ides of October this year."

[f] *Mac Feorais's own castle.*—This is Castlecarbury in Birmingham's country, which comprised the present barony of Carbury, in the north-west of the county of Kildare. Extensive ruins of this castle are still to be seen.

[g] *Deceit.*—This entry is given in the Annals of Ulster and Clonmacnoise, as translated by Mageoghegan, in nearly the same words as in the text of the Four Masters, except that, by some unaccountable mistake, the latter annals represent the massacre as having taken place in the castle of Carrickfergus, instead of Carrick-Carbury. According to Grace's Annals of Ireland this massacre was perpetrated by Jordan Comin and his comrades, at the court of Peter Brimingham at Carrick in Carberia. It is referred to as an instance of the treachery of the English to their Irish neighbours in the Remonstrance sent by the Irish Chieftains to Pope John XXII. in 1315. It is stated in this document that Mauricius O'Conor and Peter Brumichehame were fellow-sponsors; that Peter, who was called the treacherous Baron, invited Mauritius and his brother, Calvacus, to an entertainment on the feast day of the Holy Trinity; and that the instant they stood up from the table, he cruelly

THE AGE OF CHRIST, 1304.

The Age of Christ, one thousand three hundred four.

Conor, son of Hugh O'Conor, was slain by Hubert O'Flaherty, after he had acted treacherously towards Donough O'Flaherty. Hubert was killed in retaliation immediately after this.

The Countess, wife of Richard Burke, Earl of Ulster, i. e. the Red Earl, and Walter de Burgo, heir of the same Earl, died[e].

THE AGE OF CHRIST, 1305.

The Age of Christ, one thousand three hundred five.

O'Conor Faly (Murtough), Maelmora, his kinsman, and Calvagh O'Conor, with twenty-nine of the chiefs of his people, were slain by Sir Pierce Mac Feorais [Bermingham] in Mac Feorais's own castle[f], by means of treachery and deceit[g].

The new castle of Inishowen[h] was erected by the Red Earl.

A victory was gained by Hugh, son of Cathal O'Conor, and the Clann-Murtough[i], over the O'Reillys, in a contest in which Philip O'Reilly, the heir of Clann-Sweeny, and Mac Buirche, head of the Gallowglasses, together with one hundred and forty others, were slain.

massacred them, with twenty-four of their followers, and sold their heads at a dear price to their enemies; and that, when he was arraigned before the King of England, no justice could be obtained against such a nefarious and treacherous offender."—See *Memoirs of the Life and Writings of Charles O'Conor of Belanagare*, p. 74, and also Grace's Annals of Ireland, edited for the Irish Archæological Society in 1842, by the Rev. Richard Butler, p. 58, note [e].

[h] *The new castle of Inishowen.*—Green Castle, near the western margin of Lough Foyle, in the parish of Moville, barony of Inishowen, and county of Donegal, is, even at the present day, called Caiſlean nua, i. e. *New Castle*, in Irish by the natives. The magnificent ruins of this castle sufficiently shew that it was a fortress of great strength and importance, and in every respect worthy of the princely Earl by whom it was erected in so important a situation, to subdue the O'Neills and O'Donnells, and check the incursions of the Scots.—See note under the year 1555. This castle is shewn on Mercator's Map of Ireland, under the name of Newcastle. According to Hanmer's Chronicle, and Grace's Annals of Ireland, Arx Viridis in Ultonia was thrown down in 1260; but the Annals of Ulster and Clonmacnoise agree in placing its first erection in the year 1305.

[i] *Clann-Murtough*, Clann Muiṗċeaṗtaiġ.—

Maṫa ócc ó raiġilliġ do marḃaḋ do ṫeallaċ ndunchaḋa.

Toirrḋealḃaċ mac néill ruaiḋ uí briain décc.

Aéḋh óg ó ferġail do écc.

AOIS CRIOST, 1306.

Aois Criost, mile, tri céd, a sé.

Donnchaḋ ó flaiṫbertaich espucc cille halaiḋ saoí cráḃaiḋ na ngaoiḋeal décc i ndún búinne ag dol go hath cliath dó, ⁊ a aḋnacal go honóraċ isin muilionn ċerr i ttigh muire.

Petrus ó tuaṫalain biocaire ċille espuicc broin, ⁊ Maiġistir Tomás ó náan aircideochain Ráṫa boṫ, ⁊ toġa easpuicc na hecclaisi cetna décc.

Toirrḋealḃaċ ua briain tigerna tuaḋmuman, fer ba hoirḋercda, ⁊ ba ferr craḃaiḋ, ⁊ caoiṁḋeirc, áġ, ⁊ engnaṁ boí in Erinn ina aimsir ddéc, ⁊ donnchaḋ a ṁac doirdneaḋ ina ionaḋ.

Doṁnall tuirtreċ ó néill do marḃaḋ in iomraiṫne la lucht tiġe uí neill.

Ferġal mag raġnaill taoiseaċ muintire heolais do ṁarḃaḋ la a derbraiṫriḃ ⁊ la druing dia oireacht féin.

Coccaḋ mór etir Aoḋ mac eoġain uí ċoncoḃair Rí Connaċt go maiṫiḃ ṡíl Muirḋaiġ imaille ris, ⁊ Aoḋ mac caṫail uí concobair go nderfim do macaiḃ taoiseaċ Connaċt, ⁊ go ttaoisechaiḃ ⁊ oireċtaiḃ na breifne ina farraḋ. Bádor da gach leṫ imi an Sionainn fri ré ceiṫeora mís. Do ġníaḋ drem do muintir Aoḋa meic caṫail forbais is na tuaṫaiḃ go ndernsat cre-

These were the descendants of Murtough Muimhneach, the son of Turlough More O'Conor, Monarch of Ireland.

[k] *Dunbuinne*, now Dunboyne, a small village in a barony of the same name, in the south of the county of Meath.

[l] *Mullingar.*—This is the first mention of Mullingar in these Annals. According to tradition the place took its name from a mill which stood on the River Brosna. It is said that Kilbixy was originally the head town of Westmeath.

[m] *O'Tuathalain.*—This name is now anglicised Toland, in the barony of Inishowen, in the county of Donegal, the original locality of the family; but in the Island of Achill, in the west of the county of Mayo, where some of the family settled with the O'Donnells, in the latter part of the seventeenth century, it is less correctly anglicised Thulis.

[n] *Killaspugbrone*, cill easpuicc Broin, i. e. the church of Bishop Bronus; a very ancient church, now in ruins and nearly covered with sands, in the south-west of the barony of Carbury, in the county of Sligo. For some account of the origin of this church the reader is re-

Matthew Oge O'Reilly was slain by the inhabitants of Teallach-Dunchadha.

Turlough, son of Niall Roe O'Brien, died.

Hugh Oge O'Farrell died.

THE AGE OF CHRIST, 1306.

The Age of Christ, one thousand three hundred six.

Donough O'Flaherty, Bishop of Killala, the most eminent of the Irish for piety, died at Dunbuinne[k], on his way to Dublin, and was interred with honour at Mullingar[l], in the house of the Blessed Virgin Mary.

Petrus O'Tuathalain[m], Vicar of Killaspugbrone[n], and Professor Thomas O'Naan, Archdeacon of Raphoe, and bishop-elect of the same church, died.

Turlough O'Brien, Lord of Thomond, a man the most illustrious, most pious, most humanely charitable, most prosperous, and most expert at arms, that was in Ireland in his time, died; and his son Donough was elected in his place.

Donnell Tuirtreach[o] O'Neill was slain through mistake by the household of O'Neill.

Farrell Mac Rannall, Chief of Muintir-Eolais [in the county of Leitrim], was slain by his brothers and a party of his own people.

A great war [broke out] between Hugh, son of Owen O'Conor, King of Connaught, assisted by the chiefs of the Sil-Murray and Hugh, son of Cathal O'Conor, joined by some of the sons of the chieftains of Connaught, and the chieftains and tribes of Breifny. They [the two armies] were for the space of four months encamped[p] at both sides of the Shannon. Some of Hugh's people encamped in the Tuathas, where they committed great depredations. Flann,

ferred to the Tripartite Life of St. Patrick as published by Colgan in his *Trias Thaum.*, and Lanigan's Ecclesiastical History of Ireland, vol. i. p. 346.

[o] *Tuirtreach*, i. e. of Hy-Tuirtre, a territory in the south of the county of Antrim, for the extent of which see note [a] under the year 1176, p. 25.

[p] *Encamped.*—The Irish word ꝼoꞃbaıꞅ, as appears from various examples of its use in ancient and modern manuscripts, signifies a siege, or encampment, as, Ꝼoꞃbaıꞅ Ꝺꞃoma Ꝺaṁ-ꝣaıꞃe, the encampment of Drom Damhghaire, now Knocklong, in the county of Limerick, which is made the subject of an ancient Irish story, by which the meaning of the word ꝼoꞃbaıꞅ is fully established.

acha, ⁊ airccne isuiḋe. Flann mac fiaċraċ uí floinn aḋbar taoísiġ ṡíl maoilruain, ⁊ brian mac donnchaiḋ riaḃaiġ uí ċoncoḃair go sochaiḋiḃ hi maille friu do marḃaḋ do muintir ainliġi báttar ag tóraigheaċt a ccreiche. Ar iad tra ba ḟír battar ar an fforbair sin Ruaiḋri mac caṫail uí concoḃair, donnchaḋ mac Concoḃair an ċopáin mic ḟírġail aḋbar tiġírna moiġe luircc ar aġ ⁊ einec gur an lá sin. Ciḋ tra acht ranccattar rompa na maiṫe sin gur an mío do ṁair da muintir cona ccreiċ leó go riaċtrat longport uí concobair. Loisccitt pailis riġ Connaċt annsin. Rucc Aoḋ mac Eoġain orra iar lorccaḋ an ríoġbaile doiḃ. Bíntar a ccreach díoḃ foċedóir, ⁊ marbṫar Donnchaḋ mac Concoḃair an ċopáin go ndruing dia muintir ina timċel.

Creaċ mór do ḋénaṁ do ċloinn muirċírtaiġ i ccríċ cairpre. Dauit ó ċaoṁáin (.i. taoiseaċ o tuaim da boḋar go glíoir) bruċċaiḋ toiċṫech tromconáiċ, donnchaiḋ mac buiḋeaċain, ⁊ soċaiḋe oile do marḃaḋ a ttimċel na críche isin.

O flannaccáin do marḃaḋ la Brian ccarrach ó neaghra.

AOIS CRIOST, 1307.

Aois Criost, míle, trí céd, a seachtt.

Luirint ó Laċtnáin (.i. manaċ liaṫ) epscop ċille meic ḋuaich, ⁊ Donnċaḋ ó Flannaccáin epscop oile finn décc.

[q] *Palace.*—Charles O'Conor writes, *inter lineas*, ".i. Pailis ċluain fraoiċ." The place is now called Cloonfree, and is a townland situated about one mile westwards of Strokestown, in the county of Roscommon. It is described as follows by the Rev. John Keogh of Strokestown, for Sir William Petty's intended Atlas in 1683: "Here is a kind of fort (like Rathcroghan) four-square, which anciently was the King of Connaught's palace, but so very long ago that the very ruins of the building, if there were any considerable, are defaced, and no remainder of it to be seen but the said fort, the wall whereof is only a green bank, together with some broad pavements annexed to it." The fort here described forms a square, the side of which measures fifty paces in length; but it does not bear any resemblance to Rathcroghan, as Keogh asserts in the above description.

[r] *Tuaim-da-Bhodar*, now Toomore, a parish near Foxford, in the barony of Gallen, and county of Mayo. Gleoir was the original name of the River Leafony, in the barony of Tireragh, in the county of Sligo.

[s] Under this year the Annals of Clonmacnoise, as translated by Mageoghegan, contain the following entries, which have been omitted by the

son of Fiachra O'Flynn, heir presumptive of Sil-Maelruain, and Brian, son of Donough Reagh O'Conor, together with many others, were slain by the O'Hanlys, who were in pursuit of them for their prey. The most distinguished of those who made this incursion were Rory, son of Cathal O'Conor; Donough, son of Conor of the Cup, the son of Farrell [Mac Dermot], heir presumptive to the lordship of Moylurg, by reason of his prosperity and hospitality up to that day. Howbeit, these chieftains marched on with their spoil, and as many of their people as had survived, until they arrived at O'Conor's fortress. They then burned the palace of the King of Connaught[q]. Hugh, the son of Owen, overtook them after they had burned the royal residence, and immediately deprived them of the prey, killed Donough, son of Conor of the Cup, and some of his people around him.

A great depredation was committed by the Clann-Murtough [O'Conor] in the territory of Carbury. David O'Caomhain, Chief of *that tract of country extending* from Tuaim-da-Bhodar[r] to Gleóir, a rich and affluent brughaidh [farmer], Donough Mac Buidheachain, and many others, were slain on this predatory incursion.

O'Flanagan was slain by Brian Carragh O'Hara[s].

THE AGE OF CHRIST, 1307.

The Age of Christ, one thousand three hundred seven.

Laurence O'Laghtnan[t] (i. e. a Grey Friar), Bishop of Kilmacduagh, and Donough O'Flanagan, Bishop of Elphin, died.

Four Masters, though they are in the Annals of Ulster: "A. D. 1306. Robert Bruise was crowned King of Scotland, against the King of England's will.

"Sir William Prendergrass, a noble and worthy knight, died.

"Nicholl O'Dorchie [*recte* O'Donchie], a priest and a virgin from his birth, was killed by the Black Horse [ᵹeaꞃꞃán ᴅuḃ] of the Barretts, without any occasion; and whosoever sayeth one *Pater Noster* and *Ave Maria* for his soule, he shall have plenary indulgence of his sinns as often as he sayeth it." It is thus given in the old translation of the Annals of Ulster: "*Anno* 1302 (*al.* 1306). Nichol O'Dunacha, a young priest that was in Drumkliew, killed by Gerran Duf of the Barretts, without any cause, but martirised him; and whosoever saieth a *Pater Noster* for his soule, he hath 26 dayes forgivnes of his sins as often as he sayth it."

[t] *Laurence O'Laghtnan and Donough O'Flanagan.*—O'Lachtnain is now generally anglicised Laughnan, and sometimes, incorrectly,

Doṁnall mac taidg mic briain mic aindriasa mic briain luighnigh mic toirrdhealḃaig moir tanairi Connacht, fſr lán dſngnaṁ, ⁊ denech, ⁊ Saoí coitċſnn coṁroġnaċ do marḃaḋ la hAoḋ mbreifnech mac caṫail ruaiḋ uí concobair.

Tadcc mac maoileċlainn mic donnchaiḋ mic doṁnaill mic maġnasa mic toirrdhealḃaiġ, saoí nſiniġ do marḃaḋ la caṫal mac doṁnaill mic taidcc.

Urṁór gall Rossa commain do marḃaḋ la donnchaḋ muiṁneaċ ó ccealllaiġ tiġſrna ó maine acc aṫ easccraċ cuan, dú i ttorċair pilip muinder, seaan muinder, ⁊ maiú driu imaille re soċaidhiḃ nach ainmniġtſr. Ro gaḃaḋ ann diarmaitt gall mac diarmata, corbmac mac cſiṫernaiġ, ⁊ Sirriam Rossa comáin, acht do lſigdſh iad iar ttrioll, ⁊ do ronsat siṫ ar son an ḃaile do loscaḋ le hemann buitiler. An donnchaḋ so ó ceallaiġ décc iarsna gniomaiḃ si, ⁊ nir bó bas iar miodhlachas sin acht ba hecc iar ngniomaiḃ gaile, ⁊ gaisccidh, iar ttiodhnacal séd ⁊ maíne.

Ailḃe ingſn taidcc uí concoḃair décc.

Maoileachlainn ó gairmlſdhaiġ taoiseaċ cenél moáin, ⁊ maġnus macc oireaċtaiġ décc.

Loftus. The notices of these ecclesiastics are more fully given in Mageoghegan's translation of the Annals of Clonmacnoise, and it would appear from these and various other entries that the Four Masters have not fully copied the original of these Annals. In Mageoghegan's translation these entries run as follows : "Laurence O'Laghtnan, abbott of Easroe, abbott of the Boyle for a time, afterwards abbott of Cnockmoy, and at last Bishop of Kilmacduagh, died.

"Donough O'Flanagan, abbott of Boylle for the space of five years, and Bushopp of Olfyn for three years and a half; a man famous for hospitalitie, devotion, and other good parts belonging to his function throughout all Europe. One that never refused any one whatsoever, neighter for meat or cloathes : one that maintained, protected, and made peace between the inhabitants of the province of Connaught : one full of wisedome and good delivery to maintain any thing he took in hand ; one charitable and free-hearted towards all men, died penitently, of 5 weeks sicknesse, the 10th of the Kallends of June."

The probability, however, is, that the manuscript from which Mageoghegan made his translation had lost some folios from Mageoghegan's time, 1627, till 1636, when the Four Masters compiled their Annals.

" *Donnell, son of Teige.*—This Donnell is the ancestor of O'Conor Sligo. According to the pedigree of the Conors, preserved in the Book of Lecan, fol. 72–74, he (Donnell) had seven sons, of whom Cathal, King of Connaught, was the most illustrious.

" *A man distinguished for hospitality*, saoi neiniġ.—The Irish word saoi means a gentleman, a worthy, generous man, and sometimes a learned man. It is the opposite of daoi, a clown.

[v] *Ath-easgrach-Cuan*, i. e., the ford of St. Cuan's *esker* or ridge, now Ahascragh, a small town

Donnell[t], son of Teige, son of Brian, son of Andreas, son of Brian Luighneach, who was son of Turlough More [O'Conor], Tanist of Connaught, a man of great prowess and hospitality, who was universally esteemed, was slain by Hugh Breifneach, the son of Cathal Roe O'Conor.

Teige, the son of Melaghlin, son of Donough, son of Donnell, son of Manus, son of Turlough [O'Conor], a man distinguished for his hospitality[u], was slain by Cathal, the son of Donnell, son of Teige [O'Conor].

The greater number of the English of Roscommon were slain by Donough Muimhneach O'Kelly, Lord of Hy-Many, at Ath-easgrach-Cuan[v], where Philip Muinder, John Muinder, and Main Drew, with many others whose names are not mentioned, were killed. Dermot Gall Mac Dermot, Cormac Mac Kaherny, and the sheriff of Roscommon, were taken prisoners; but they were afterwards set at liberty, and they made peace [*recte* restitution] for the burning of the town by Edmund Butler[w]. Donough O'Kelly, after he had performed these exploits, died; and his was not the death of one who had lived a life of cowardice, but the death of a man who had displayed prowess and bravery, and bestowed jewels and riches.

Alvy, daughter of Teige O'Conor, died.

Melaghlin O'Gormly, Chief of Kinel-Moen, and Manus Mageraghty, died.

on the Clonbrock river, in a parish of the same name, in the east of the county of Galway, where the memory of St. Cuan is still held in great veneration. See Ordnance Map of the county of Galway, sheet 61.

[w] *Edmond Butler.*—This passage, which is so very rudely given by the Four Masters, is thus rendered by Connell Mageoghegan, in his translation of the Annals of Clonmacnoise: "A. D. 1307. The Englishmen of Roscommon were all killed by Donnogh Moyneagh O'Kelly, before his death at Athaskragh, where Phillip Montyre, John Montyre, and Mathew Drew, with 70 other persons, were taken and killed. Also the sheriff of Roscommon, Dermott Gall Mac Dermott, and Cormack Mac Kehernie, were by him sett at libertie, and concluded peace with him for the burning of the town by Edmond Butler, then Deputie of Ireland."

It is thus less correctly rendered in the old translation of the Annals of Ulster: "*Anno* 1303 (*al.* 1307). The Galls of Roscomon all killed by Donogh O'Kelly, King of Omane, at Atheskragh, where Philip Munder, Magiu Drew, with many more, were killed and taken. Dermot Gall Mac Dermot, Cormac Mac Ketherny, and the sheriff of Roscomon, were taken, and were enlarged after a while, making peace for the towne."

It would appear that the town of Ahascragh had been burned by Edmond Butler (who became Lord Deputy of Ireland in 1312), and that O'Kelly had detained in captivity the sheriff of Roscommon, and his accomplices, Dermot Gall Mac Dermot and Cormac Mac Keherny, until they made restitution for the loss sustained

Concoḃar mac Fiaċraċ uí Floinn duine óg ba ferr oineaċ ⁊ gaisccedh baoí dia ċenél do écc.

An dara hEduard do ríoġadh os Saxaiḃ, ⁊ Iulij.

AOIS CRIOST, 1308.

Aois Criost, míle, trí céd, a hocht.

Saiġnen teinntiġe do ṫuitim i mainistir na mbraṫor i Ros comain go ros bris an ṁainistir.

Creaċ mór do denaṁ la Maolruanaiḋ mac Diarmata ar cloinn Doṁnaill uí Concoḃair i cCrich Coirpre, ⁊ crích oile beós do cloinn Muircheartaiġ orra iar ndenaṁ síoda riu roiṁe, ⁊ iar ttaḃairt braiġde doiḃ. Acht ro ḟellsatt orra iarttain. Gluaisit clainn Doṁnaill uí Concobair iarsin go Sliab da én, ⁊ noċa ruccsat leó acht a ních, a ndíoḋ, ⁊ a ngroiġe. Iar na clos do Gallaiḃ Ua Ffiaċraċ ⁊ Luiġne, tionoilitt ċuca, ⁊ lenaitt iad go mullach sleḃe da én. Iompaidid mic Doṁnaill riú. Feachair sccainnir sttorra, maidtear for Gallaiḃ, ⁊ baoí maiḋm orra go rangattar lec easa dara. Torċair Tomas mac Ualtair consapla Dúin ḟinne, a derbrathair, ⁊ soċaide imaille riú.

by O'Kelly in the burning of his town of Ahascragh. Mac Dermot Gall, i. e. the Englishman, was so called for speaking the English language, and joining the English against his own countrymen.

[x] *Was made king*, do ríoġadh, literally *was kinged.*—This term is applied by the Irish annalists to the inauguration of their own kings and chieftains, but not to the crowning of the kings of England, as is quite evident from the dates. Edward II., styled of Caernarvon, the place of his birth, began his reign on the 7th of July, 1307, and was crowned at Westminster on the 24th of February following. The Annals of Clonmacnoise, as translated by Mageoghegan, contain the following notice of the death of Edward I.: "A. D. 1307. Edward the Great, King of England, Wales, and Scotland, Duke of Gascoigne, and Lord of Ireland, died in the 35th year of his reign, and in the 66th year of his age. After whose death the crown of England, Wales, Ireland, and Scotland, was given to Edward, surnamed Edward of Carnarvan."

[y] Under this year the Annals of Clonmacnoise, as translated by Mageoghegan, contain the following passage, which has been omitted by the Four Masters: "A. D. 1307. Carolus Mac Anliahanye was elected to the Bishoprick of Alfyn, of the one part (and was abbott of Loghke, who received his orders at Ardmach, and enjoyed the profitts of the Bishoprick for the space of three years and a half); William Bremyngham did ellect Molassy Magooge [Mac Hugo, or Mac Aedha] of the other side, to be Bishopp of the said place, who resided in Rome for three years, and at last came" [home].—See

Conor, son of Fiachra O'Flynn, the most hospitable and valiant youth of his tribe, died.

Edward II. was made king[x] of England on the 7th of July[y].

THE AGE OF CHRIST, 1308.

The Age of Christ, one thousand three hundred eight.

Lightning[a] fell upon the monastery of the friars of Roscommon, and destroyed it.

A great depredation was committed by Mulrony Mac Dermot upon the sons of Donnell O'Conor, in the territory of Carbury; and another depredation was committed upon them by the Clann-Murtough, who had concluded a peace with them, and given them hostages, but afterwards acted treacherously towards them. The sons of Donnell O'Conor after this proceeded to Slieve-da-én, taking nothing with them but their steeds, horses, and accoutrements. As soon as the English of Tireragh and Leyny had heard of this, they assembled, and pursued them to the summit of Slieve-da-én[a]. Here the sons of Donnell turned on them, and a battle ensued, in which the English were routed and pursued as far as Leac-Easa-dara[b]. Thomas Mac Walter, Constable of Bunfinne[c], his brother, and many others, were slain[d].

also Harris's edition of Ware's Bishops, p. 631. This is the last year in the old translation of the Annals of Ulster, preserved in the British Museum. The Dublin Irish copy extends to the year 1504.

[a] *Lightning.*—Mageoghegan gives a strictly literal translation of this in his version of the Annals of Clonmacnoise: "A thunderbolt came from heaven and lighted upon the abbey of the Fryers of Roscommon, and broke down the said abbey on St. Stephen's night, in Christmas holy days."

[a] *Slieve-da-en.*—On an old map preserved in the State Papers' Office, London, this mountain is shewn as situated a few miles south of Sligo, between Lough Gill and Colloony.

[b] *Leac-Easa-dara*, i. e. the flat rock of Ballysadare. This was applied to a flat rock in the river.

[c] *Bunfinne* is now anglicised Buninna, which is the name of a townland in the parish of Drumard, barony of Tireragh, and county of Sligo. It is so called from its situation at the mouth of a small stream called the Finn.

[d] *Many others were slain.*—This passage is somewhat better given in the Annals of Clonmacnoise, as translated by Mageoghegan, as follows:-"A. D. 1308. Moyleronie Mac Dermoda tooke a great prey from the sonns of Donnell O'Connor in the land of Kriche Carbrey, in Connaught.

" Bryan O'Dowdie, and the English of

Creach dioġalta do dénoṁ dAoḋ mac caṫail ar a dearbraṫair ar Ruaiḋri mac caṫail, dia ro marḃaḋ Maġnus mac Maġnusa ndruing ele imaille fris.

AOIS CRIOST, 1309.

Aois Criost, mile, trí céd, anaoí.

Aoḋ mac eoġain mic Ruaiḋri mic aoḋa mic caṫail croiḃdírcc, Rí Connacht, ⁊ díġaḋbar airdríġ Erenn, aon gaoiḋel ba fírr eineċ ⁊ íngnaṁ ṫainic ina ríṁír do marḃaḋ la hAoḋ mbreifneaċ mac caṫail uí ċoncoḃair i ccoill in cloċain, ⁊ moran do maiṫiḃ a muintire imme. Ba diḃ riḋe concoḃar mac diarmata, diarmait ruaḋ mac taiḋg ui ċonċoḃair, diarmait mac caṫail carraiġ meic diarmata, Aoḋ mac muirċírtaiġ meic taiḋcc mic maolruanaiḋ,

Lwynie and Tyrefiaghragh, tooke another prey from the said parts.

"Clann-Mortagh also tooke another prey from the said sonns of Donnell O'Connor, after that they had agreed and delivered hostages for security of the peace before. After all which preys and spoyles taken the sons of Donnell aforesaid came to the Mount of Sleiw-da-ene, and took with them thither but their horses, armor and stood [stud]. The said Englishmen of the lands of Lwynie and Tyrefiaghragh, hearing of their being there, assembled their forces and followed them to the said Mounte. The sonns of Donnell and Mac Donnogh retrayted upon them, where they gave them an overthrow, and put them to flight, and pursued them to a place called Leack-eassa-dara, where they killed Thomas Mac Walter, Constable of the Castle of Bonnafinne, with his brother, and divers others."

[e] Under this year the Annals of Clonmacnoise, as translated by Mageoghegan, contain the two passages following, which have been omitted by the Four Masters: "A. D. 1308. Piers Gaveston, a great favourite of the King of England, came to this kingdome this year, and soone after his coming killed O'Dempsie. The Easter of this year was in the month of March, and there was a great morren of cattle therein." Under this year Grace's Annals of Ireland record the death of Peter Bermingham, the *noble tamer* of the Irish. He is the Piarus or Feorus who was commonly called the treacherous Baron by the Irish, and from whom the Berminghams seem to have taken the surname of Mac Feorais. See note under the year 1305.

[f] *Slain by Hugh Breifneach.*—It is stated in the Dublin copy of the Annals of Ulster, *manu recentiori inter lineas*, that he was slain with a hatchet by Dael O'Sochlachan, a clown of a tanner: "⁊ in Dael ua Sochlaċan do sín laṁ do da marḃaḋ le tuaiġ .i. bodaċ rudaire."

[g] *Coill an Clochain*, i. e. the wood of the clochan, or ford of the stepping stones. According to the Annals of Clonmacnoise, as translated by Mageoghegan, this place is situated in the territory of the Brenie (i. e. Breifny). It is probably the place now called Kilclogha, situated in the parish of Drumgoon, barony of Clankee, and county of Cavan. The whole passage is translated by Mageoghegan as follows: "A. D. 1309. Hugh mac Owen mac Rowrie mac Hugh mac

A retaliatory depredation was committed by Hugh, the son of Cathal [O'Conor], upon his brother Rory, son of Cathal, on which occasion Manus Mac Manus [O'Conor], and others, were killed[e].

THE AGE OF CHRIST, 1309.

The Age of Christ, one thousand three hundred nine.

Hugh, the son of Owen, son of Rory, son of Hugh, son of Cathal Crovderg, King of Connaught, and worthy heir to the monarchy of Ireland, the most hospitable and expert at arms of all the Irish born in his time, was slain by Hugh Breifneach[f], the son of Cathal O'Conor, at Coill-an-clochain[g], together with many of the chiefs of his people about him. Among these were Conor Mac Dermot; Dermot Roe, son of Teige O'Conor; Dermot, son of Cathal Car-

Cahall Crovederg O'Connor, King of Connaught, one for birth, prowes, liberality, and many other parts, worthy to be king of a [*recte* the] kingdom, was killed by Hugh Breffneagh mac Cahall Roe O'Connor, in Kilcloaghan, in the territory of the Brenie, with these ensuing persons that were killed at the said place with him, viz.: Connor Mac Dermoda, Dermot Roe mac Teig mac Andryas, Dermott mac Cahall Carragh mac Dermoda, Hugh mac Mortagh mac Teig mac Moyllronie, [and] Dermott Oge O'Helie, who was a modest, liberal, and great housekeeper; Moyledownie the Galloweglass, Gillernew, chief Brehon of Conaught, Fogartagh O'Dowailgie of the household men of Tomaltagh Mac Dermott, with many others, with the loss of a hundred more of them. After which deed Hugh Brenagh came to his house, where the three Thawthies, that is to say, the three thirds of the Provence [No, but the Three Tuathas in the east of the present county of Roscommon. Ed.] came to congratulate him.

"In the mean time Moyleronie Mac Dermoda, prince of Moylorge, with the assemblies and forces of his allies and friends of all parts, came to the middest of Sile Moriegh, to maintain the principalitie, and name of King of Connaught, for his own fosterson.

"Felym O'Connor sent his messengers to all his friends and allies of the English and Irish that they should come to him, to assist him in that enterprize; and William Burke, with his brothers and kinsmen came accordingly, and there encamped in the middest of the Provence, with their said many forces, fearing the inhabitants should join with Hugh Breffnagh (the aforesaid king-killer), to make him king of the Provence. The said Moyleronie took to himself the revenues and proffitts belonging to the King of Connaught, together with such Jewells and principalls as belonged to the place, and made the Inhabitants to take their oaths never to yeald to any other but to Felym, the said Mullronie's fosterson, whereupon William Burke returned to Olfyn.

"Hugh Brenagh went to Meath to meet with the Earle, and in his absence the Inhabitants of the Provence came upon the land of Oghter Tyrie, took a great prey which they consumed in their camp of Oghterhirie aforesaid."

⁊ diarmait ó helighi flaithbhruccaidh do bfshr ina aimsir. Torchair don leth araill, giolla na naomh mac aodhaccain ollamh Connacht i mbrethemhnas, ⁊ aoin fsr do dsrscnaidh do brethemhnaibh na haimsire i mbaoi. Fagartach ua dobailén, ⁊ daoíne oile nach airimhtsr. Siol muirfohaigh do tabhairt tighshrnais do Ruaidhri mac cathail uí concobhair. Ruaidhri ó concobhair iarsin, ⁊ ó floinn go mbuidhin marcsluaigh do thocht ar an machaire, ⁊ mac meic fsorais do marbhadh doibh.

Coinne do denamh duilliam burc ⁊ do connachtaibh (.i. don mfid boi ina rann diobh) re Ruaidhri mac cathail im ath slisfn. Brisfdh coinne doibh for aroile. Iomairsct do chur fstorra. Maidhfdh for Ruaidhri, ⁊ drsm da muintir do marbhadh. Uilliam búrc do dol go mainistir na builLe, ⁊ clann muirchsrtaigh do dol go tir noilella. Arbhanna iomdha do milleadh doibh, ⁊ loiscethe do denamh. Mac uilliam do thecht tar coirrsliabh anuas iarsin. Ruaidhri mac Cathail do chor as a longport dó, ⁊ donnchadh ua fionnachta do marbhadh do thosach sloigh meic uilliam, ⁊ daoine iomdha oile.

Creach do dhénomh do Mac uilliam i cloinn fsrmaighe, ⁊ creach oile go beinn ghulban.

Concobhar mac briain ruaidh uí bhriain do mharbhadh.

[h] *Brughaidh*, i. e., a farmer.

[i] *Chief Brehon.*—Ollamh Connacht i mbreithemhnas, i. e. chief ollav of Connaught in law; ollamh signifies a chief professor of any science. In Cormac's Glossary it is derived from oll, great, and dámh, a learned man.

[j] *Lordship*, tighshrnus.—This is not a very correct term used by the Four Masters; for although the territory of the O'Conors was at this time much circumscribed, the O'Conor was still inaugurated King of the Irish of Connaught, according to the ancient Irish ceremonies.

[k] *The Plain.*—An machaire, i. e. Machaire Connacht, i. e. the plain of Connaught. It is the level part of the county of Roscommon, and lies between Castlerea and Strokestown.

[l] *Ath Sliisean.*—This is still the name of a ford on the Abhainn Uar, a short distance to the south of the town of Elphin, in the county of Roscommon.—See note at the year 1288.

[m] *Clann-Murtough.*—These were the descendants of the celebrated Murtough Muimhneach O'Conor. They were at this time moving from territory to territory without any fixed possessions; but in the year 1342 they became so powerful that their chief leader, Hugh, the son of Hugh Breifneach, became King of Connaught in despite of the O'Conors of Sligo, or race of Brian Luighneach, and of the race of Cathal Crovderg: but in the succeeding century they sunk into obscurity, and disappeared from history. The pedigree of this tribe of the O'Conors is given as follows in the Book of Leccan, fol. 72, *et sequen.*: I. Murtough Muimhneach, the son of Turlough More O'Conor, monarch of Ireland, had four sons, namely, 1, Manus (the father of Donnell of Erris); 2, Conor Roe; 3, Donough

ragh Mac Dermot; Hugh, son of Murtough, son of Teige, son of Mulrony; and Dermot O'Healy, a princely brughaidh, the best of his time[h]. On the other side fell Gilla-na-naev Mac Egan, Chief Brehon[i] of Connaught, and the most illustrious of the Brehons of his time; Faghartach O'Devlin, and others not mentioned. The Sil-Murray then conferred the lordship[j] upon Rory, the son of Cathal O'Conor. Rory O'Conor and O'Flynn afterwards led a troop of cavalry to the Plain[k], and slew Mac Feorais [Bermingham].

A conference was held by William Burke and the Connacians (i. e. as many of them as were on his side) with Rory, son of Cathal, at Ath-Slisean[l]. They violated, however, the rules of a conference, and a battle was fought between them, in which Rory was defeated, and some of his people were slain. William Burke went to the abbey of Boyle, and the Clann-Murtough[m] went to Tirerrill, where they destroyed much corn, and made many conflagrations. Mac William then proceeded northwards, across the Curlieu Mountains, and drove Rory, the son of Cathal, from his fortress[n]. On this occasion Donough O'Finnaghty and many others were slain by the van of Mac William's army.

A depredation was committed by Mac William in Clan-Fearmaighe, and another at Binn-Gulban[o].

Conor, the son of Brian Roe O'Brien, was slain.

Reagh; and 4, Conor Gearr. II. Conor Roe, the second son of Murtough Muimhneach, had two sons, Cathal and Manus, who were both kings of Connaught. III. Cathal Roe, King of Connaught in 1279, had two sons, 1, Rory (the father of Teige, who was the father of Murtough Balbh); and 2, Hugh Breifneach, a warrior of great prowess and celebrity. IV. Hugh Breifneach had two sons, 1, Hugh, King of Connaught in 1342, and Cathal. V. Hugh, King of Connaught, the fifth in descent from the monarch Turlough More, had one son, Dermot, who is the last generation of this line given in the Book of Lecan; and his brother Cathal had seven sons, namely, 1, Owen; 2, Hugh; 3, Rory; 4, Manus; 5, Conor Roe; 6, Cathal Roe; 7, Murtough; of whose descendants no further account is given. They were afterwards thrown into the shade by the upspringing vigour and power of the descendants of Cathal Crovderg, and the O'Conors of Sligo.

[n] *His fortress*, longpopt, i. e., his fortified camp.

[o] *Binn-Gulban.*—This was the ancient name of a conspicuous mountain in the barony of Carbury, in the north of the county of Sligo. The name is now corrupted to Binbulbin. The language of this passage is very rudely constructed by the Four Masters. It is thus given in the Dublin copy of the Annals of Ulster: "A. D. 1305 [*recte* 1309]. Cpeċ do denam le Mac Uilliam i cloinn ḟepmuiġe; Cpeċ eile leir co beinn gulban 7 nír paide rír. A. D. 1305 [*recte* 1310]. A depredation was made by Mac William in Clann Fermuighe; another depredation by him as far as Benn Gulban, and further down" [i. e. northwards]. The meaning

AOIS CRIOST, 1310.

Aois Criost, mile, trí céd, adeich.

Concobar ua briain rioghdamhna do bfhrr ina aimsir do marbadh dona gallaibh dubha i meabail.

Moirchrecha dioghla do dénamh la hAodh mbreifneach ⁊ le cloinn muirchertaigh archena, ar maolruanaidh mac diarmatta. Donnchadh mac donnchaidh dargain dóibh. E fein ⁊ drong do maithibh a muintire do ghabail. Drem oile do marbadh, ⁊ do loscadh doibh, a bean ingen uí flannaccain do marbadh.

Ferghal mácc dorchaidh décc.

Fionnguala ingen Maghnusa uí concobair, ⁊ Una ingean Aodha mic Feidhlimidh décc.

Sloicceadh la Seffraidh ó bferghail go dún uabair, dú inar marbadh domhnall mac Aodha óicc uí ferghail, Aodh mac maoilíosa, ⁊ goffraidh mac muirchertaigh.

Caislen bona finne do loscadh ⁊ darccain do Ruaidhri mac cathail, daoh mac maghnusa, ⁊ do muintir Aodha breifnigh eitir cruachaibh ⁊ tighibh.

Aodh breifneach ó concobair adhbhar Righ Connacht do marbadh la Mac

intended to be conveyed is, that Mac William plundered the territory of Clann Fermaighe, in the county of Leitrim, and made another plundering excursion as far as the mountain of Binbulbin, and beyond it to the north.

[p] *Roydamna.*—Ríoghdamhna, signifies a king *in fieri*; a prince designed or fit to be a king. In the Dublin copy of the Annals of Ulster he is called the best son of a king in Leath Mogha, i. e. the southern half of Ireland. O'Flaherty thus explains this word: "Quisque e reliquis familiæ candidatus Ríoghdamhna dictus est; quod est regia materies; nimirum materies apta ad recipiendum regiam formam suæ familiæ. Si vero liberæ, aut Mechanicæ artis alumnus fuerit, adhbhar tantum, quod materiem etiam denotat vocatur; quippe materies disposita, ut tali professione informetur."—*Ogygia*, p. 58. Charles O'Conor, in his Dissertations on the History of Ireland, p. 61, objects to this definition, and says that Roydamhna was the king elect, or prince appointed to succeed the reigning monarch of the whole island, or of one of the provinces. But it is quite evident from the many examples of the use of the terms throughout these and the older annals that O'Flaherty's definition is correct. Adhbhar is indeed applied to kings and chieftains, as well as to professors of arts and sciences, but not so often.

[q] *By the black English.*—Do na gallaibh duba. The Editor does not know the meaning of duba in this passage. It is probably used to denote the English lately come over, who were black strangers in comparison with the Irish-English. The term is also used in the Dublin copy of the Annals of Ulster.

[r] *Retaliatory depredations*, moirchreacha dioghla, literally "great preys of revenge," i. e., preys

THE AGE OF CHRIST, 1310.

The Age of Christ, one thousand three hundred ten.

Conor O'Brien, the best roydamna[p] of his time, was treacherously slain by the black English[q].

Great retaliatory depredations[r] were committed by Hugh Breifneach and the Clann-Murtough upon Mulrony Mac Dermot. Donough Mac Donough was plundered by them, and many of the chiefs of his people were taken prisoners; others were killed and burned by them, and his [Mac Donough's] wife, the daughter of O'Flanagan, was killed.

Farrell Mac Dorcy died[s].

Finola, daughter of Manus O'Conor, and Una, daughter of Hugh, the son of Felim, died.

An army was led by Geoffrey O'Farrell to Dun-Uabhair,[t] where Donnell, son of Hugh Oge O'Farrell, Hugh, son of Maelisa, and Godfrey, son of Murtough, were slain.

The castle of Bunfinne[u], including both its houses and corn stacks, was burned and plundered by Rory, son of Cathal, Hugh, son of Manus, and the people of Hugh Breifneach.

Hugh Breifneach O'Conor, the worthy heir[v] to the kingdom of Connaught,

taken in reprisal for others, that had been taken by Mac Dermot from the Clann-Murtough.

[s] *Mac Dorcy.*—This family was located in the territory of Kinel Luachain, comprising the parish of Oughteragh, in the east of the county of Leitrim.

[t] *Dun Uabhair.*—This is described in other annals as in Mageoghegan's country of Kyneleagh, or Kinel-Fiachach, from which it is quite certain that it is the present Donore, near Ardnurcher, in the barony of Moycashel, and county of Westmeath. This passage is given as follows in Mageoghegan's translation of the Annals of Clonmacnoise: "Geffrey O'Ferall, with the forces of the Analie, came to Donover, in Kyneleagh, to take the spoyles and preys of that countrey, but the natives and inhabitants of the countrey so well behaved themselves against them in the defence of their countrey and goods, that they killed Donnell Mac Hugh Oge O'Ferrall, Hugh Mac Moylissa, and Geoffry Mac Mortagh."

[u] *The castle of Bunfinne*, near Tanrego, in the barony of Tireragh, and county of Sligo, in Connaught.

[v] *Worthy heir.*—Oιζαὁbαρ Rιġ Connαċτ, literally, "a good materies of a king of Connaught," that is, one who, from his descent and personal qualifications, might be elected King of Connaught, according to the ancient Irish custom. The ꝺeαġ αꝺbαρ, or worthy heir, was no always the eldest son of the last chief.

uidilin .i. Seonacc, baoí ar buannacht aicce fFin tre feill, ⁊ mebail, ⁊ ba tré loiġideacht do rinne innrin.

Fiche tonna fíona do cor i ttír i moiġ ccétne.

Cairlén Sliccigh do denam don iarla ruadh.

Feidlimidh mac Aodha mic eoġain uí concobair do ġabail ionaid a athar.

Corbmac ua flannaccáin taoiseach tuaithe ráta do marbadh la henri mac gillefinnéin taoíreach muintire peódacháin.

Macraith macc uidir tanairi fFir manach, ⁊ donn mac giollamichil taoiseach cloinne conġaile do lorccadh la roolb maġ matġamhna.

[w] *Mac Quillin*, Mac Uidilin.—The head of this family was chieftain of the Route, a territory in the north of the county of Antrim. This family was among the early Welsh settlers in this country about the year 1172. Duald Mac Firbis, in his account of the English and Irish families of Ireland (Lord Roden's copy, p. 832), states that the ancestor of the Mac Uidhilins, who was of Dalriedan descent, passed over into Wales, where his posterity remained until the reign of Henry II., when a branch of them returned and settled in the same part of Ireland from which their ancestor had emigrated many centuries before. This, however, is a mere legend, copied from a modern compilation by Mac Firbis, who remarks that he would not vouch for its authenticity: "ní ġabaim orm a n-iomláine acht feb fuarur róm."—*Id.*, p. 829.

[x] *For a bribe*.—It is stated in the Annals of Clonmacnoise, as translated by Mageoghegan, that Mac Quillin was bribed by Mac William Burke. As the account of this transaction is so imperfectly given by the Four Masters, the Editor deems it his duty to lay before the reader an account of it given in the Annals of Clonmacnoise, which is much fuller and more consecutive: "Hugh Breffneagh made a great prey called the prey of Toyten, or fire (Creach an toitean), upon Mulronie Mac Dermott in Clogher, where Donnogh Mac Dermott was taken prisoner, and his wife (O'Flannagan's daughter) was killed; women, children, and many others were also there killed; and encamped at Oghter heire, before Mac Dermott and the inhabitants of Sile Morie: which when Mac William Burke heard, he encamped at Kil Lomatt, in the sight of the said Hugh Breiffneagh. The latter sent privie message to his brother Rowrie mac Cahall, that he shou'd go then, in the absence of William Burke, to his castle of Bonnafynne, which he did accordingly, preyed and spoyled the castle of Bonnafynne aforesaid, and converted all they could there find to their own uses.

"Hugh Breffneagh staid there with his Bwannaghtmen, and their chief head, Johnock Mac Vuellen; and when this Johnock, with his heired Bwannaghtmen, saw Breffnagh all alone after the sending of the most part of all his forces with his brother to take the spoyles of Bonnafinne aforesaid, being provocked thereunto by William Burke, who promised him a certain stipend for killing the said Breffneagh, who accordingly getting the said opportunity killed the said Breffneagh according to his promise to William Burke before made.

"When tidings thereof came to William Burke, Mollronie Mac Dermoda, and Sile morie, to their camp at Killomatt, they immediately sent their forces to take the spoyles and preys of all the

was, by treachery and deceit, slain by Mac Quillin[w] (i. e. Johnock), who was on bonaght with him. It was for a bribe[x] that Mac Quillin did this.

Twenty tuns of wine were washed ashore in Magh-Cedne[y].

The castle of Sligo was erected[z] by the Red Earl.

Felim, the son of Hugh, son of Owen O'Conor, assumed the place of his father[a].

Cormac O'Flanagan, Chief of Tuathratha, was slain by Henry Mac Gilla-finnen, Chief of Muintir Feódacháin[b].

Magrath Maguire, Tanist of Fermanagh, and Donn Mac Gilla-Michil, Chief of Clann-Conghaile, were burned by Roolv[c] Mac Mahon[d].

followers and people that belonged to Hugh Brenagh. William Burk himself came to the middest of the country, and seized Mac Vuellen, with his rowte of 200 men upon them, so as there was not a towne in Silemorrey without a continual Bawnie, nor no parish without oppression, nor no good man without great wrong done him during the reign and government of William Burk, after the death of Hugh Brenagh.

"When Molronie Mac Dermott saw his fosterson Felym was sett naught by, and the revenews which of right belong'd to him taken by William Burk, and that the Englishmen exercised their captivities and imprisonments upon the Irishmen, to weaken and bring them lowe, who conjectured that if Molronie were cutt off, that there would be no resistance in Connaught, and that the whole provence shou'd be theirs without contradiction, he determined with himself to promote the said Felym to be King of Connaught, and thus he resolved to do, whether they would or no; whereupon he brought the said Felym with him to Carnefroeigh (where they then used to create their kings), and there made him King of Connaught after the manner used before in his predecessors' tymes; he was installed King with as great sollemnity, ceremonies, and other the customs theretofore practized, as any one of his ancestors since the time of his ancestor Bryan Mac Eaghy Moymeone, sometime King of Counaught: also the said Mollronie made a magnificent feast in honour thereof, with the assembly and presence of all the nobility of Connaught, such as none of his ancestors predecessors Kings of Connaught ever before him was heard or read in books to have made."

From this passage it is quite clear that the Four Masters did not fully copy the Annals of Clonmacnoise.

[y] *Magh-Cedne*, a plain in the south of the county of Donegal, lying between the rivers Drowes and Erne.

[z] *Was erected*, do dſnam.—In Mageoghegan's translation of the Annals of Clonmacnoise, this passage is thus rendered: "A. D. 1310. The Castle of Sleigeagh was repeared and made by the Earle this year."

[a] *Assumed the place of his father*, i. e. became King of the Irish of Connaught.

[b] *Muintir Feódacháin*.—A territory in the barony of Magheraboy, in the county of Fermanagh, extending from the Arney river to the western extremity of Belmore mountain.

[c] *Roolv.*—This is a Hibernicised form of Ralph, or Rodolph.

[d] Under this year the Annals of Clonmac-

AOIS CRIOST, 1311.

Aois Criost, mile, trí céd adeich, a háon.

Domhnall ó ruairc ticcſrna brſifne décc.

Creaċ adbal do dénaṁ la cloinn muirċſrtaiġ i cconnaċtaiḃ, ⁊ giolla-criost mac muirġſra meic donnchaidh mic diarmata, Aodh mac corbmaic, donnchadh mac tomaltaiġ, uilliam mac giolla arráiṫ, ⁊ soċaidhe cén motáo do marḃadh leo.

Sloicċeadh mór la huilliam búrc isin mumain in aghaidh an claraiġ, Cath do taḃairt doiḃ, maidhtear ror an cclaraċ. Baoi uilliam búrc ror dárachd ag leanmain an madhma. Iadhaid muintir an claraiġ uime ⁊ gaḃtar leó é, ara aoí aré ba coscċraċ is in ccath.

Tadhcc ó háinligi do marḃadh do Shiurtán dexetra.

Coccadh mór i ttuadhmumain. Caṫ do ṫaḃairt do donnchadh mac Conmara, ⁊ da oireaċt (.i. trioċat céd ó ccaisin) dua briain ⁊ drſraiḃ muṁan. Maidhtear ror mac Conmara, marḃtar éféin, ⁊ domhnall ó gráda ticcſrna cinel dungaile ar an laṫoir sin, ⁊ ár dírime don tsluaġ cſċtarda.

Donnchadh ua briain Ri muṁan, ⁊ adḃar riġ Ereann ar eineċ ⁊ gniom-arṫoiḃ do marḃadh la Murchadh mac maṫgaṁna uí briain i meaḃail iar sin, ⁊ Muirċſrtaċ ua briain do oirdneadh in ionadh.

Loċlainn riaḃaċ ó deaġadh do Marḃadh la Maṫgaṁain mac domhnaill ċonnachtaigh uí briain.

noise, as translated by Mageoghegan, have the following entries, which have been entirely omitted by the Four Masters:

"A. D. 1310. Tanaye More O'Mullconrie, chief Chronicler of Silemorrey, died in the Spring of this year.

"Joan, daughter of O'Connor of Affailie, and wife to Mortagh Mageoghegan, chieftain of Kyneleagh, died.

"Feral mac Mortagh More Mageoghegan was killed by these of the Analie."

[e] *A great army.*—Upon this dissension between Clarus and De Burgo, Mageoghegan writes the following remark, in his translation of the Annals of Clonmacnoise:

"But by the way this much I gather out of this Historian, whom I take to be an authentic and worthy prelate of the Church, that would tell nothing but truth, that there reigned more dissentions, strife, warrs, and debates between the Englishmen themselves in the beginning of the conquest of this kingdome, than between the Irishmen, as by perusing the warrs between the Lacies of Meath, John Coursey, Earle of Ulster, William Marshall, and the English of Meath and Munster, Mac Gerald, the Burks, Butler, and Cogan, may appear."

[f] *Hy-Caisin.*—This is the name of the origi-

THE AGE OF CHRIST, 1311.

The Age of Christ, one thousand three hundred eleven.

Donnell O'Rourke, Lord of Breifny, died.

A great depredation was committed in Connaught by the Clann-Murtough [O'Conor], on which occasion Gilchreest, son of Maurice, who was son of Donough Mac Dermot; Hugh, son of Cormac, son of Donough, son of Tomaltagh [Mac Dermot]; William Mac Giolla-Arraith; and many others besides, were slain by them.

A great army[e] was led by William Burke into Munster, against Clarus [De Clare], and a battle was fought, in which Clarus was defeated. William Burke pursued the routed enemy with great bravery, until the people of Clarus closed around him, and took him prisoner. He was, however, victorious in the battle.

Teige O'Hanly was slain by Jordan de Exeter.

A great war [broke out] in Thomond. Donough Mac Namara and his adherents (i. e. the inhabitants of the cantred of Hy-Caisin[f]) gave battle to O'Brien and the men of Munster; but Mac Namara was defeated, and he himself and Donnell O'Grady, Lord of Kinel-Dungaile[g], were slain on the battle field; and both armies suffered immense slaughter.

Donough O'Brien, King of Munster, and a materies for a monarch of Ireland for his hospitality and achievements, was treacherously slain by Murrough, son of Mahon O'Brien; and Murtough was elected in his place.

Loughlin Reagh O'Dea was slain by Mahon, the son of Donnell Connaghtagh O'Brien.

nal territory of the Mac Namaras, in the county of Clare, and is only their original tribe name transferred to their territory. The exact extent of it is preserved in the ecclesiastical division called the deanery of Ogashin, which contains the parishes of Quin, Tulla, Cloney, Dowry, Kilraghtis, Templemaley, Inchicronan, and Kilmurry-na-Gall; but after the year 1318, when the Hy-Bloid, who had inhabited the eastern part of the now county of Clare, were defeated by the descendants of Turlough O'Brien, aided by the Mac Namaras, the latter got possession of nearly the entire of that part of the county of Clare lying between the rivers Fergus and Shannon.

[g] *Kinel-Dungaile.*—This was the tribe name of the O'Gradys, and became, as usual, attached to their country. Since the year 1318, this district comprised the parishes of Tomgraney, Mayno, Inishcaltra, and Clonrush, of which the two latter parishes are now included in the county of Galway, though sixty years ago the

Seonacc mac uidilín do marbadh an gruidelaigh i mbaile topair brigde, ⁊ éfsin do marbadh inn foceddóir, ⁊ ba don ghsprramhtaigh ler marbsom Aodh breifnech roimhe sin do marbadh é buddsin.

Creach do dénamh la feilim ó cconcobair Rí Connacht ar cloinn muircsrtaigh ar bord moighe ccédne, ⁊ Maoileclainn mac Concobair sir a raitti cfnd an medil do marbadh ann, ⁊ socaide oile.

Diarmait cleirech ó briain décc.

Domhnall ó birn taoiseach tire briuin, ⁊ giolla íosu ó dálaigh ollamh le dán décc.

AOIS CRIOST, 1312.

Aois Criost, míle, tri chéd, a dech a dó.

Uilliam mac fsorais airdeasspucc tuama, ⁊ beneidicht ó braccáin esspucc luighne décc.

Maoileachloinn mácc aodha esspucc oilesinn do togha in airdespuccóideacht tuama iaramh.

parish of Inishcaltra was accounted a part of the county of Clare. Both, however, still belong to the diocese of Killaloe, and are a part of the deanery of O m-Bloid.

[h] *Ballytoberbride.*—Baile tobair brigde, now Ballintober, a small village which gives name to a barony in the county of Roscommon. The ruins of O'Conor Don's extensive castle are still to be seen here in tolerable preservation. It was a square bawne, defended at each of the four angles by a tower of considerable strength and size. The number of rooms in the four towers was about sixteen, and some of them were of good size. The north-west tower was rebuilt in 1627, as appears from a stone in the wall exhibiting that date and the name Rury. The other three towers were, according to tradition, built as early as the reign of King John. St. Bridget's well, from which the place took its name, is yet in existence here, but not regarded as a holy well. Charles O'Conor of Ballinagare, and his grandson, the late Dr. Charles O'Conor, the translator of the first part of the Annals of the Four Masters, are interred in the church of Ballintober, in the tomb of O'Conor Don, which is inscribed with the date 1636; but no epitaph appears for either.

[i] *Short axe,* gearrtuagh.—This passage is given as follows in Mageoghegan's translation of the Annals of Clonmacnoise: "A. D. 1311. Seonag or John Oge Mac Vuellin was killed in a fray at Ballentober-Bryde, by the same Galloweglasse" [axe] "wherewithall he" [had] "killed Hugh Brenagh before: Mine author prayeth God to reward him that killed him for murthering Hugh Brenagh, as before is recited."

[k] *Cean-an-Medhil.*—This passage is entered in the Dublin copy of the Annals of Ulster, under the year 1307, as follows:

"A. D. 1307. Crech do denumh le Feidlimid o concobuir ri connacht ar clainn muircer-

Johnock Mac Quillin slew Gruidelach at Ballytoberbride[h], where he himself was immediately after killed, in revenge of it; and it was with the same short axe[i] with which he had killed Hugh Breifneach [O'Conor] that he was killed himself.

A depredation was committed by Felim O'Conor, King of Connaught, upon the Clann-Murtough, on the border of Magh-Cedne, where Melaghlin, son of Conor, popularly called Ceann-an-Medhil[k], and many others, were slain.

Dermot Cleireach O'Brien died[l].

Donnell O'Beirne, Chief of Tir-Briuin[m], and Gilla-Isa O'Daly, an ollav in poetry, died.

THE AGE OF CHRIST, 1312.

The Age of Christ, one thousand three hundred twelve.

William Mac Feorais [Bermingham], Archbishop of Tuam, and Benedict O'Bragan, Bishop of Leyny [Achonry], died.

Melaghlin Mac Aedha[n], Bishop of Elphin, was afterwards elected to the bishopric of Tuam[o].

ταιġ αp bopb muιġι ceιτnι 7 mαelpeċlαιnn mαc concobuιp pυαιὁ pιpι pαιτeα ceαnn ιn meιġιl ϭo mαpbαϭ αnn 7 ϭαίne eιle."

"A. D. 1307. A depredation was committed by Felim O'Conor, King of Connaught, upon the Clann-Murtough, on the border of Magh Ceitni, and Melaghlin, the son of Conor Roe, usually called Ceann-an-Meighil, and other persons, were killed there.

[l] *Dermot Cleireach O'Brien.*—His death is recorded in the Dublin copy of the Annals of Ulster, under the year 1307: but in Mageoghegan's translation of the Annals of Clonmacnoise, Dermot Klereagh O'Bryen, King of Munster, is said to have been deposed in 1311, when Mortagh O'Bryen was constituted in his place, and the death of Dermott Klereagh is recorded under the year 1313.

[m] *Of Tir-Briuin*, i. e. of the territory of Tir-Briuin-na-Sinna, lying on the west side of the Shannon between Elphin and Jamestown, in the county of Roscommon.

[n] *Mac Aedha*, mαġ αoϭα.—This name is sometimes anglicised Magee and sometimes Mac Hugh.

[o] Under this year the Annals of Clonmacnoise, as translated by Mageoghegan, contain the following passages, which have been omitted by the Four Masters: "A. D. 1312. The Temples were destroyed thro' out all Christendum this year.

"Pyers Gaveston was killed, the King's mynione.

"Dervorgill, daughter of Manus O'Connor, King of Connaught, died.

"The feast of Easter this year was in the month of March. 26 *Martii Dominica Paschalis.*"

AOIS CRIOST, 1313.

Aois Criost, mile, trí chéd, a tri décc.

Tadcc mac aindriasa mic briain luighnigh, ⁊ Cathal mac Murchaidh carraigh uí ḟerghail decc.

Giolla iosa mag dorchaidh do marbhadh la Concobhar ccarrach mac diarmata.

AOIS CRIOST, 1314.

Aois Criost, mile, trí chéd, a dech, a cethair.

Matha macc uibne espucc na breifne décc.

Niall (.i. niall becc) mac maoileachlainn mic toirrdhelbhaigh cnuic an madhma uí domhnaill do marbhadh dAodh mac Aodha uí domhnaill.

Matha mág tigheernáin do marbhadh do cathal ó ruairc.

Roolbh mág mathghamhna do marbhadh dá bhráithribh fein.

Maidhm for muintir raighilligh ag druim lethan la Ruaidhri mac cathail uí choncobhair.

Niall mac briain uí néill, rioghdhamhna cenél neoghain fer rathmar ro conaigh eiridhe do écc.

Maghnas mac domhnaill í eaghra do marbhadh la Maghnas mac uilliam uí eaghra.

AOIS CRIOST, 1315.

Aois Criosd, mile, tri ched, a dech, a cúicc.

Loingeas mór do thecht a halbain go herinn la derbhrathair Righ alban la hedhuard go ro ghabsat i ccríochaibh uladh. Crecha mora do dhénamh doibh ar mhuintir an iarla ⁊ ar ghallaibh na midhe. Sluagh mór do thionól don iarla i nacchaidh na nalbanach. Feidhlimidh mac aodha uí concobhair co ndrúing móir

[p] *Maguibne.*—In Harris's edition of Ware's Bishops, p. 227, he is called Matthew Mac Duibne, and said to have been a man of great account in his country.

[q] *By his own kinsmen*, da bhraithribh féin.—Mageoghegan translates this: "Rohalve Mac Mahon was killed by his own brothers." The Irish word bráthair originally signified a bro-

THE AGE OF CHRIST, 1313.

The Age of Christ, one thousand three hundred thirteen.

Teige, son of Andreas, son of Brian Luighneach [O'Conor], and Cathal, son of Murrough Carragh O'Farrell, died.

Gilla-Isa Mac Dorcy was slain by Cathal Carragh Mac Dermot.

THE AGE OF CHRIST, 1314.

The Age of Christ, one thousand three hundred fourteen.

Mathew Maguibne[p], Bishop of Breifny [Kilmore], died.

Niall [i. e. Niall Beg], the son of Melaghlin, son of Turlough of Cnoc-an-madhma O'Donnell, was slain by Hugh, the son of Hugh O'Donnell.

Matthew Mac Tiernan was slain by Cathal O'Rourke.

Roolbh [Rodolph] Mac Mahon was slain by his own kinsmen[q].

The O'Reillys were defeated at Drumlahan by Rory, the son of Cathal O'Conor.

Niall, son of Brian O'Neill, heir presumptive of Kinel-Owen, a prosperous and very wealthy man, died.

Manus, son of Donnell O'Hara, was slain by Manus, son of William O'Hara.

THE AGE OF CHRIST, 1315.

The Age of Christ, one thousand three hundred fifteen.

A great fleet arrived in Ireland[r] from Scotland, commanded by Edward, the King of Scotland's brother, and landed in Ulster. They committed great depredations on the Earl's people and the English of Meath. The Earl mustered a great army to oppose the Scots, and was joined by Felim, son of Hugh

ther; but it is now generally used to denote a relative.

[r] *Arrived in Ireland.*—According to Grace's Annals of Ireland, Edward Bruce landed at Glondonne, i. e. the Glendun River, in the barony of Lower Glenarm, in the county of Antrim. Lodge (Peerage, Athenry) says that he landed at Olderfleet, which was the old name of Larne Lough, in the same county.

do ċonnaċtaiḃ do ḋul lar an iarla. Sluaġ mór ele do ṫionól la Ruaiḋri mac caṫail hi cconnaċtaiḃ co ro loisccead ⁊ go ro briseaḋ caislein ioṁḋa lais iar ffaccḃail na tíre dFeiḋlimiḋ.

Aoḋ (.i. aſ̃ḋ ballaċ) mac maġnnsa uí concoḃair do marḃaḋ la caṫal mac doṁnaill uí concoḃair.

Maġnas mac Maġnasa uí concoḃair an taoimḟſ̃r ba mó allaḋ ⁊ oirdearcus do rioġdaṁnaiḃ Connaċt mun am sin, ⁊ a dſ̃ḃraṫair Doṁnall do marḃaḋ beós lasan ccaṫal ccéḋna arnaḃárach.

Caṫ do ṫaḃairt don iarla ruaḋ ⁊ dedvard abriús cona sloġaibh dia roile, gor raimhiḋ ror an iarla. Gaḃtar ann uilliam búrc, ⁊ dá mac mſ̃ic an miliḋ.

Maṫġaṁain mag raġnaill taoiseaċ muintire heolais, ó maolmiaḋaiġ taoiseaċ muintire cſ̃rballain, ⁊ soċaiḋe dá muintir imaille riú do marḃaḋ la Maolruanaiḋ mac ndiarmata ticcſ̃rna moiġe luircc. Concobar ruaḋ mac Aoḋa breifniġ do marḃaḋ ro ḃaoí do lſ̃iṫ mſ̃ic diarmata an la sin.

O Doṁnaill, .i. Aoḋ mac doṁnaill óicc do ṫocht im ċaislén Slicciġ go morsluaġ imaille ris, An baile do gabáil dó, ⁊ mórán do millſ̃oh na ṫimceal.

Ruaiḋri mac doṁnaill uí ċonċoḃair do marḃaḋ la cſ̃iṫirn gallócclaċ ar furailſ̃m dſ̃rḃforgailli inġine maġnasa uí concoḃair tucc tuarfoċrait doibh aire.

Aṁlaoiḃ ó fſ̃rġail do écc.

Taḋhg ó huiginn saoi i ndán do écc.

[s] *Mac Anveely.*—This was the Irish name assumed by the Stauntons of Carra, in the now county of Mayo.

[t] *Muintir-Cearbhallain.*—This was the tribe-name of the O'Mulveys and their correlatives in the west of the county of Leitrim. Their country was otherwise called Magh Nisi.—See note at the year 1243 and 1270.

[u] As the events of this year are so very briefly and imperfectly treated of in the Annals of the Four Masters, the Editor deems it necessary to supply the deficiency by inserting here the account of the transactions of Edward Bruce, from Mageoghegan's translation of the Annals of Clonmacnoise, it being the most copious Irish account of his proceedings in Ireland yet discovered. It agrees very closely with the Irish of the Annals of Connaught:

"1315. Edward mac Robert Bruise, Earle of Carrick, and Brother of King Robert, King of Scotland, Landed with a fleet of 300 shipps in the north of Ulster, at whose coming all the Inhabitants of the Kingdom, both English and Irish, were stricken with great terrour, that it made the Lands and Inhabitants of Ireland to shake for fear; Immediately after his arrivall

O'Conor, and a great number of the Connacians. Rory, son of Cathal, mustered another great army in Connaught, and many castles were burned and broken down by him after Felim had left the country [province].

Hugh (i. e. Hugh Ballagh), the son of Manus O'Conor, was slain by Cathal, son of Donnell O'Conor.

Manus, the son of Manus O'Conor, the most famous and illustrious of the princes of Connaught at this time, and Donnell, his brother, were on the next day also slain by the same Cathal.

The Red Earl and Edward Bruce, with their armies, came to a battle with each other, in which the Earl was defeated, and William Burke and the two sons of Mac Anveely[o] were taken prisoners.

Mahon Mac Rannall, Chief of Muintir-Eolais, O'Mulvey, Chief of Muintir-Cearbhallain[p], and many of their people, were slain by Mulrony Mac Dermot, Lord of Moylurg. Conor Roe, son of Hugh Breifneach, who fought on Mac Dermot's side on that day, was [also] slain.

O'Donnell (Hugh, son of Donnell Oge) came with a great army to the castle of Sligo, took the town, and destroyed much around it.

Rory, son of Donnell O'Conor, was slain by a band of gallowglasses, at the instigation of Dervorgilla, daughter of Manus O'Conor, who gave them a reward for the deed.

Auliffe O'Farrell died

Teige O'Higgin, a learned poet, died[q].

he burnt the townes of Downedealgan, Athfirdia, and Rathmore" [i. e. Rathmore-Moylinny. —*Ann. Connaught*], "harried and spoyl'd all Ulster in generall, tooke their hostages, collected the revenews of that province to himself, and made the Ulstermen to consent and acknowledge him as their King, delivered him the Regalities belonging to the King, and gave him the name of King of Ireland.

"When Richard Burke, Earle of Ulster, heard that Edward Bruise was thus arrived, and that he usurped the name of King, and exercised the before recited tyranies, he out of all parts gathered a great army with him to Roscommon, from thence he marched on to Athlone, thro' the borders of Meath and Moyebrey, accompanied with ffelym O'Connor, King of Connought; their army consisted of twenty Cohortes.

"The English army never spared neighther spirituall nor Temporall Land, in every place where they came, without respect of Saint or Shrine, or sacred place, from the river of Synen of the South, to Cowlerayne of the North, and Innis Owen. As this great army was thus marching on, spoyleing and destroyeing all places in their way, they saw Edmond Butler, then Deputy of Ireland, likewise marching on to-

AOIS CRIOST, 1316.

Aois Criost, míle, trí ched, adech, aSé.

Morsloiccheaḋ do ṫionol la Feilim ó cconcobair, le Mac fforais, ⁊ le gallaiḃ iarṫair ċonnacht. Toċt doiḃ go tóċar mona coinneaḋa. Ruaiḋri

wards them with 30 Cohorts of well-appointed Soldiers, armed at all points, at whose sight the Earl was somewhat angry, alledging that himself was of sufficient power to expel Bruise and his Scottishmen out of all the Kingdome, and desired and advised the Deputie not to joyne with himself, and that he needed not his assistance.

"The Earle encamped that night at Athfirdia near the mounte called *Sleiwbrey* [re taoḃ sleiḃe breaġ.—*Ann. Connaught*], and Edward Bruise, with his Scottish and Ulstermen, at Innis-Koeyne; the Earle the next day followed him, and encamped at the towne of Louth. William Burke, to take some advantage of Bruise, skyrmished with him, where there were a few killed at either side.

"As for Edward Bruise, and his army, by the procurement of O'Neale and Ulstermen, he tooke his journey to Cowlerayne of the North and to the borders of Innisowen, and fell downe and broke the Bridge of Cowlerayne, to stopp the Earle's passage over the River of Bann, whom the Earle followed untill he came to the same river, and from thence thro' Ulster, where he marched holding on their course of spoyleing and destroying all places where they came, not spearing Church or Chappel [saḃall.—*Ann. Conn.*], in somuch that they did not leave neither field of Corne undestroyed, nor towne unransacked, nor unfrequented place (were it never so desert) unsearched and unburnt, and consumed to meere ashes, the very churches that lay in their way into the bear stones. The encounter of which armies of both sides of the river of Banne was so inconvenient, that neither party cou'd hender or offend the other, for they were severed from each other by the said deep, spatious, smooth running river; nevertheless they had daily some shooting of arrowes of both sides of the river.

"Edward Bruise hearing of the great fame of Felym O'Connor, King of Connaught, y[t] then was with the red Earle, he sent him privie message y[t] he would give him y[e] province of Connaught at his disposition, and to adhere to himself, and also to returne from the Earle to defend his own provence, to w[ch] offer the said Felym lystened and acknowledged to accept of him. In the mean time Rowrie m[c] Cahall roe O'Connor seeing himself to have his opportunity in the absence of Felym and his nobles that went with him in the journey of Ulster, he also made his repair towards Edward Bruise, with whom he had secrett communication, and promised the said Earle to banish all Englishmen from out of all Connaught, if Edward would be pleased to accept of his own service. Edward authorized him to warre against Englishmen, and not to meddle with the lands of Ffelym. But Rowrie having rec[d] that favour of Bruise he did not only war upon Englishmen, but also upon Ffelym and his partakers, and sought all means to gett the Kingdom of Connought into his own hands, and immediately assembled together Brenymen, and great companies of Gallowglasses and Connoughtmen, and made towards the middle parts of Silemorrey, where, first of all, he burnt the street town of Sligeagh, Athkle an Coran, the castle of Killcalman, the towne of Tobber-bride,

THE AGE OF CHRIST, 1316.

The Age of Christ, one thousand three hundred sixteen.

A great army was mustered by Felim O'Conor, by Mac Feorais [Birmingham], and the English of West Connaught. They marched to Tochar-mona-

Downeoman, with the Castles of Roscomon, Ryndoyne, als Teaoyn, and Athlone, together with all the houses that lay in his way between these places.

"After committing of wch great exploytes, he desired Mac Dermoda to give him the dutys due upon him belonging to the King of Connaught, and also to yeald him obedience, which Mac Dermott absolutely denied, and withall refused to give him hostages, but he rec^d hostages and pledges of the rest of the whole provence, incontinently went to Carne fraoigh, where he was invested King of Connought by the 12 chieftaines of Silemorie, 12 Coworbs, and other spiritualls that were accustomed to use the Ceremonies usuall at the time of the Investure of the King: remained for a time among Silemorrey, preying and destroying such of that countrey as he supposed to stick to Felym O'Connor, and that wou'd yeald him allegiance, and also the chiefest cause of his residence there, was tarying for the return of Felym and his forces from the North. In the mean time Felym O'Conor thought with himself that Rowrie wou'd usurp the rule of Connaught, in his absence he spoke to the Read Earle, and told him how Rowrie would warr against him in Connought, and seek to gett the whole government and rule of that Provence into his own hands, by this opportunity he had in their absence. Whereupon he intended to depart from the Earle, to defend his Lands in Connought, who in journeying thro' Ulster and Uriell had not one day of rest, but continuall assaults and skyrmishes untill he came to Granard, and to a place called Killnenawas [coill na namhar, *Ann. Conn.*] and to the people of his Uncle, his Mother's Brother, Shane Offerall, after great slaughters and losses of his people, and flight of some of them with their Goods. After his return he advised with his princes and Chieftains that were with him in that tumultuous journey, and in whose places Rory O'Connor did constitute others of his own side, that they and every of them shou'd returne to their places, and take and hold them of Rory dureing the time they should contend together for the preheminence, with condition that if he had overcome Rorye, they should hold of him as they did before; and as for his own ffoster ffather, Mc Dermott, of Moylorge, seeing it is thought that Rorye would not agree with him for any reasonable conditions of peace, he was content he should remaine with himself dureing his warres, untill he had seen the end and issue thereof.

"The read Earle and Englishmen seeing Ffelim and his Connoughtmen gave them no assistance against their enemyes, and saw them also departe in that manner, they returned backe again from Cowlerayne to the castle of Conyre, [condaire, *Ann. Conn.*], when the Scottish and Ulstermen followed them, and as they were att the point to meete and give battle, at the first onsett William Burke, with some of his knights, were taken, with the two sonnes of Mac an Miles, the read Earle himselfe took his flight, and was chased from thence to Connaght, after whose comeing into the province his allyes and friends, both of the English and Irish, flocked to his house, in hope to be relieved by him from the

Ua concobaip Rí Connacht do dul ina naghaidh líon a rochpaitte, lomaipecc do cop ſttoppa, bpireadh rop Ruaidhpi, E ρſin do mapbadh, ⁊ na maite ri ele

oppression of Rory O'Connor. These ensuing persons were the chiefest men of note that had recourse to him: Felym O'Connor, Kinge of Connaught; Mortagh O'Bryen, prince of Thomond; Mullronye Mac Dermott, prince of Moylorge; Gilbert O'Kelly, prince of Imanye; who all were banished out of their lands and possessions.

"When they were thus mett, and that Mullronye Mac Dermott saw so manie exiled Noblemen together in one house, he recounted with himselfe, was abashed, and said, that he would never after be reckoned amongst so many, or that number of deposed Chieftains, but would repayre to Teige O'Kelly, by whose intercession he thought to come in favour and credit of Rorye and get his own again, which accordingly was done, upon yielding of hostages by the said Mullronie to Rory O'Connor for keeping his allegiance and Fidelity with him.

"Hugh Ballagh O'Connor was treacherously killed by Cahall mac Donnell O'Connor; Hugh m[c] Art, and Dermot m[c] Symon ne Traye, were, in like manner, killed by him in revenge of his Father, that before was killed by the said Dermott.

"Donell the next day took a great preye from the sonnes of Mortaugh, where Magnus m[c] Magnus, and Donell his brother, were killed in pursuit thereof, and Tomaltagh m[c] Donnogh was taken captive, after committing of which exploite they took parte and partaked with the English for their own defence. When newes came to the eares of Felym O'Connor of these things, hee, with a few of his trustiest friends, went to the sonnes of Donnell O'Connor, vidz[t]. to Rorye, Magnus, Cahall, Mortagh, Donnogh, John, and Teige, and after someconference had, they, with the help of their kinsmen, and such others as joined with them, preyed Bryen O'Dowdye, took another prey from Arteagh of Dermott Gall, killed many of his people, and burnt his haggards and Corne, together with their houses, and alsoe took another prey from the sonnes of Cahall Offlanagan, which they tooke in their way to the weare, called Cara-Cowla-Cwirck, and they could not drive the prey by reason of the greate moisture of the bogge, because the feete of the Cattle waded so deep in the Moore, and also being pursued by a greate company, insomuch that all the forces of the sonnes of Cahall, and that partye did overtake them, with Mahon M[c] Granell, chieftain of Moyntireolis, with his kinsmen and followers. Mac Dermot, hearing the clamorous noise of the Drivers, and such as were about the said prey, coming to Cara [Cowla-Cwirc] aforesaid, he followed them to Kowlevaher, and seeyinge the preye stayed, and like to be kept, by the owners, he did not well like it, but had rather their prey should be taken by Felym and his adherents. Whereupon he imediately assisted Phelym, notwithstanding the greate multitudes that were against him, and, upon the suddaine, Connor Roe mac Hugh Breffnye O'Connor was killed, Mahon M[c] Granell, chieftaine of Moynterevolais O'Mullmyay, chief Moyinnter Kervallan, etc.; and discomfitted these that withheld their prey from Felym, took the preye himself, without restitution to the owners, came that night to the Abbey of Boyle, the next day over Segass North-easterlye from thence to Kowll Offynn, to the Korann, and to the Country of Lwynie, where Ffelym expected his coming. When Rorye O'Connor heard that Mullronye M[c] Dermott had done these private exploites, and that he joyned in Companye with his said ffoster-sonne Felym, he caused to be assembled

Coinneadha[v]. Rory, the son of Cathal O'Conor, King of Connaught, came against them with all his forces; and a battle was fought between them, in

from all parts his forces, and with them encamped that night at Ballymore O'fflyn; made little respect of the reverence due to the churches of Kill-Athrachta and Easse-da-chonna; and preyed the moncks of the abbey of Boyle.

"Tomaltagh m[c] Morgiessa M[c] Donnogh, with all his followers and dependants, went to assist Ffelym; Dermott Gall went to Crwachann, the King's Pallace, and Teig O'Kelly went to assist Rowrie, and there followed his promise of allegiance upon Mullronie Mac Dermott; and being so joined together they pursued Felym and Mullrony to Letter-Long [leitir luighne, *Ann. Conn.*], and to the borders of the mount of Sliewgawe, and also to the valley called Gleanfahrowe, where infinite numbers of Cowes, Gerans, and sheep were killed by them. They strip'd Gentlemen [mna uaisle, i. e. gentlewomen. *Ann. Conn.*] that could make no resistance of their cloaths to their naked skinns; destroyed and killed without remorse children, and little ones of that Journey. There was not seen so much hurt done in those parts before in any man's memory, without proffit to the doers of the harm. Mullronie Mac Dermott hearing that Dermott Gall sate in the privilege seat of his ancestors at Carrick of Loughke, and with honour conveighed to Cruachan [cruachan], to enjoye the principality belonging to himself as his right, and that he made havouck and killed all his Cowes at Gleanfahrowe (as before is specified), he, with his household, and such other as he had in readiness for the purpose, march'd towards Carrick, turned his back to Kara and Synen, and the three Kerryes, viz[t]. the Lower Kerrie, Kerrie Moy-Ie, and Kerrie Arthie, with their Cattle: it is thought that in these days there was not such an assault given, or such a prey taken, by any man whatsoever, for they made all the country to shake for their fear. The wife of Mac Dermott Gall was taken prisoner at once with the said prey, together with a few of her gentlewomen. Dermott Gall, after that day, never enjoyed any happy day; besaught restitution, and, upon refusall, preyed Moylorge; took all the cowes and horses they could meet, notwithstanding Dermott had warning before, which did nothing availe him, although he had a great assembly of people before them, and left Moylorg waste and voyde of cattle. There was no respect of either temporall or Church-land in that country; their cattle, corn, and other things were snatched even from the very altars, and delivered over to the Gallowglasses for their wages.

"The towne of Dunmore was burn't by Rowrie O'Connor.

"Eaghroym O'Manie (Aughrim), was burnt by the said Rowrie, and the Castles thereof fallen downe.

"The Cantred of Moynmoye was wasted and destroyed by Teig O'Kellie.

"Felym O'Connor, mac Dermod, Tomaltagh mac Donnogh, and the sons of Donnell O'Connor, partaked with the English of Ighter Connaught, and after they accorded peace with them they destroyed Tyrenna Tyrneaghten, Moyntyr Kreghan, and the demense of Dunmore, called Convacknie.

"Richard Burk, Earle of Ulster, called the red Earle, remained this year without force or power in any of the parts of Ireland.

"There reigned many diseases generally thro' out the whole Kingdom a great loss of the inhabitants, great scarcitie of Victualles and slaughter of people, and some ugly and fowle weather.

"Hugh O'Donnell, prince of Tyreconnell, came to the lands of Carbrey in Connaught, and destroyed all that Contrey, by the advice of his

don dul sin, .i. diarmait gall mac diarmata tiġſrna moiġe luircc, corbmac mac cſtearnaiġ taoiseaċ ciarraiġe, ⁊ soċaiḋe oile duaislib a ġallocclaċ, ⁊ a muintire sainrſoaiġi.

Riġe Connaċt do ġabáil dfelim arís. Slóġ mór do ṫecclamaḋ dó dionnsaiġiḋ áṫa lſtain, ⁊ an baile do loscaḋ lſs. Slemne dexetra tiċċſrna an baile do marbaḋ leó, ⁊ an goccánach beós, .i. an barún ba saoíre in Erinn ina aimsir, ⁊ iomat gall ele archeana ⁊ évala mora do denam doiḃ.

Sloiċċeaḋ lánṁór do ṫionól la felimiḋ ó cconcoḃair imaille re maiṫiḃ an ċúiccıḋ. Ba dia maitiḃ side Donnchaḋ ua briain go maithibh muṁan, O maoileachlainn Rí miḋe, Ualgarcc ua ruairc tiġſrna brefne, O fſrgail ticcſrna muintire hanġaile, tadg ua ceallaiġ tiġſrna ó maine, Maġnas mac doṁnaill uí concoḃair tanaisi Connaċt, Art ó hſġra tiġearna luiġne, ⁊ Brian ó dubda ticcſrna ua ffiaċraċ. Tiaġaitside uile go haṫ na rioġ. Ro

wife, the daughter of Magnus O'Connor, and came herself, with a greate route of Gallowglasses, and took all the spoyles of the churches of Drumkleiw, without respect to church or churchman of that place.

"The Castle of Sliegeagh was taken and fallen down by O'Donnell of that Journey."

[v] *Tochar mona Coinneadha.*—This is the name of a celebrated causeway in the parish of Templetogher, in the barony of Ballimoe (anciently called Clanconway), in the county of Galway. See it referred to at the years 1225, 1255, and 1262.

[w] *Ciarraighe.*—A territory in the county of Mayo, comprised in the present barony of Costello.

[x] *His own particular friends.*—This passage is repeated in the autograph by a mistake of the transcriber.

[y] *Ath leathan*, i. e., Broad ford, now Ballylahan in the barony of Gallen and county of Mayo, formerly the seat of Mac Jordan de Exeter.

[z] *A very great army.*—The account of the battle is more fully given in the Annals of Clonmacnoise, as translated by Mageoghegan, and is here inserted as proving the situation of Tochar mona Coinneadha.

"A. D. 1316. Felym O'Connor took a prey from the sonns of Failge, killed Richard himself" [Ricard Failgech fein.—*Ann. Conn.*]. "and made a great slaughter of his people.

"After which things Ffelym O'Connor gather'd together a huge armie both of Irish and Englishmen, among whom the Lord Bermyngham, Mullronie Mac Dermott, the sons of Donnell O'Connor, and other noblemen (which for brevity's sake I omitt), are not to be forgotten, to give battle to Rowrie mac Cahall Roe O'Connor, which [who] took the kingdom of Connaught before of the said Ffelym. Being so accompanied they marched on towards Silemorrey; which being told to Rowrie O'Connor, King of Connaught, as then sitting at the topp of Fie Ikie in Clyr convaye, watching the proceedings of Ffelym and his partakers, where he encamped, and being so sett, he saw Ffelym and his ffoster-father, Mullronie Mac Dermodda, with their squadrons well sett in battle arraye, fiercely make towards him, Ffelym himself and his foster-father, Mullronie, in the former" [foremost]

which Rory was defeated, and he himself slain, together with Dermot Gall Mac Dermot, Lord of Moylurg, Cormac Mac Keherny, Chief of Ciarraighe[w], and many others of the chiefs of his gallowglasses, and of his own particular friends[x].

Felim again assumed the government of Connaught; he mustered another army, and marched against Ath-leathan[y]; he burned the town, and slew Slevin de Exeter, Lord of the town, and also Goganagh [De Cogan], the noblest baron in his time in Ireland, and many others of the English, and acquired much booty.

A very great army[z] was mustered by Felim O'Conor and the chiefs of the province [of Connaught]. Among these chiefs were the following, viz. Donough O'Brien, with the chiefs of Munster; O'Melaghlin, King of Meath; Malgary O'Rourke, Lord of Breifny; O'Farrell, Lord of Annaly; Teige O'Kelly, Lord of Hy-Many; Manus, son of Donnell O'Conor, Tanist of Connaught; Art O'Hara, Lord of Leyny; and Brian O'Dowda, Lord of Hy-Fiachrach. They all marched to Athenry[a]. The English of West Connaught mustered their forces, to oppose

"rank, together with the most part of the English of Connaught, especially of that part of the Provence following them, and drawing to a place in his presence called Togher Mone Konneye. The Connoughtmen, with their King, Rowrie mac Cahall O'Connor, mett them in the same place, where King Rowrie and his army by the multiplicity of hands and arms against him, was quite overthrown and discomfitted; King Rowrie himself (a man of wonderful prowes; a destroyer of foreigners, and an expeller of them out of the Kingdom), was killed: also Dermott Gall Mac Dermott, prince of Moylorg; Cormack Kehearnie, prince of Kerrie; Gillechriste Mac Dermodda, Connegan Mac Cunneagan, Donnell Mac Coneagan, Donnogh Mac Rowrie, with a hundred Gallowglasses, and divers others, were killed: Dermott and Donnell O'Boyle, and also Robock Bremyngham of the other side were hurt. This battle was given the 7th of the Kalends of March in the year of our Lord 1316.

"Felym O'Connor afterwards took all the preyes and spoyles of all that belonged to Rowrie O'Connor, or that partaked with him before, and took himself the government and name of King of Connought, as before he had, which extends from Easroe in Ulster to Eaghtge; took hostages for the preservation of allegiance of the Breniemen; constituted Ualgarge O'Roirke as their King: also took the hostages of the O'Kellys, O'Maddens, O'Dermodaes, O'Haras, O'Dowdies, and, after setting himself, prepared an army with whome he went to banish the English of Connought; immediately burnt the town of Athlehan; killed Stephen Dexeter therein, Miles Cogan, William Prendergass, and John Stanton, Knights; and also William Lawless, with a great slaughter of their people. He burnt all the contrey from the place" [called] "Castlecorran to Roba; took all their preyes and spoyles; returned to his house with a ritch booty of his enemies, and a fortunate success in his affairs."

[a] *Athenry*, αṫ nα ρıġ. ı. *Athenria*, i. e. Regum Vadum.—*Ogygia*, p. 16. It was a borough or corporate town in a barony of the same name in the county of Galway, but now an obscure village

tionoilsiot tra goill iarṫair connaċt ina naghaiḋ, .i. uilliam búrc, an barún mac fſórais tiġſrna áṫa na rioġ, ⁊ urṁór gall lſiṫe cuinn uile. Ciḋ tra acht ro cuireaḋ caṫ croḋa curata ſttorra lſth for lſth. Sraointear for gaoiḋelaiḃ fo deóiḋ. Marḃṫar feḋlimiḋ ó concoḃair Ri Connaċt is in ccaiṫiorġail sin, ⁊ ba hesiḋe enġaoiḋel as móa re a raiḃe suil ag fearoiḃ Ereann. Ro marḃaḋ bſos taḋcc ó ceallaiġ ticċſrna ó maine ⁊ oċtar ar fiċit duaisliḃ ṡil cceallaiġ imaille fris, Maġnus mac doṁnaill uí Concoḃair tánaisi Connacht, Art ua heaġra tiġearna luiġne, Maoileachlainn carrach ó dubhda, Concoḃar ócc ó duḃda, Muircſrtach mac Concoḃair uí duḃda, diarmait mac diarmata adbar ticcſrna moiġe luircc, Muirceartaċ mac taichliġ meic diarmata, Muirceartaċ mac diarmata mic fſrgail, Maoilseċlainn ócc mac maġnusa, Seaan mac murchaiḋ uí madaḋáin, doṁnall mac Aoḋa uí conċſnainn ticcſrna ua ndiarmata, ⁊ Muircſrtaċ a ḋſrḃraṫair, Murchaḋ ó madadáin, doṁnall ó baoiġill, ⁊ donnchaḋ ua maolmuaiḋ cona muintir imaille fris, Murchaḋ mac Murchaiḋ még maṫġaṁna go ccéd da muintir ime, Niall sionnach tiġſrna fſr ttſṫba cona muintir, Fſrġal mac Seaain gallda uí fſrġail, uilliam mac Aoḋa óicc uí ḟſrġail, tomas mac aṁlaoiḃ uí fſrġail, coiccſr bſós do cloinn ndonnchaiḋ, .i. tomaltaċ mac giollacrist, Murchaḋ mac donnchaiḋ, concoḃar mac taidcc, muircſrtaċ mac donnchaiḋ, ⁊ Maelechlainn mac donnchaiḋ. Ro marḃaḋ tra is in caṫ céḋna Eoin mac aoḋaccáin brſiṫſṁ uí Concoḃair, Giolla na naoṁ mac dáil ré docair uí doḃailén fſr iomċarṫa ⁊ iomċoiṁéda brataiġe uí Concoḃair,

without a market. According to the Annals of Clonmacnoise, as translated by Mageoghegan, Felim O'Conor mustered this army to banish William Burke out of Connaught. Dr. O'Conor gives a curious account of the battle of Athenry in his suppressed work, *Memoirs of the Life and Writings of Charles O'Conor of Belanagare*, p. 79. He remarks that the English were well armed and drawn up in regular systematic array, commanded by Sir William de Burgo and Richard de Bermingham; and that the Irish fought without armour. He also gives the speech said to have been delivered to the Irish army by Felim O'Conor before the battle; but it is to be suspected that it is one drawn from his own imagination, as he does not tell us where it is preserved. However his remarks on it and the result of the battle are amusing, and shall be here laid before the reader:

"Such was the speech of Felim, and so great was the enthusiasm of his army that 10,000 of his men, and twenty-nine of the subaltern chiefs of Connaught were killed in this decisive engagement. Tradition says that, like the Fabian family, the O'Conors were so completely defeated, that throughout all Connaught not one man remained of the name, Felim's brother excepted, who could be found able to

them, namely, William Burke; the Baron Mac Feorais [Bermingham], Lord of Athenry; and the greater part of the English of Leath Chuinn. A fierce and spirited engagement took place between them, in which the Irish were at last defeated. Felim O'Conor, from whom the Irish had expected more than from any other Gael then living, was slain. There were also slain Teige O'Kelly, Lord of Hy-Many, and twenty-eight gentlemen of the O'Kellys; Manus, son of Donnell O'Conor, Tanist of Connaught; Art O'Hara, Lord of Leyny; Melaghlin Carragh O'Dowda; Conor Oge O'Dowda; Murtough, son of Conor O'Dowda; Dermot Mac Dermot, heir apparent to Moylurg; Murtough, son of Taichleach Mac Dermot; Murtough, son of Dermot O'Farrell; Melaghlin Oge Mac Manus; John, son of Murrough O'Madden; Donnell, son of Hugh O'Concannon, Lord of Hy-Diarmada, and his brother Murtough; Murrough O'Madden; Donnell O'Boyle; Donough O'Molloy, and his people along with him; Murrough, the son of Murrough Mac Mahon, and one hundred of his people; Niall Sinnagh [the Fox], Lord of the men of Teffia, and his people; Farrell, son of John Gallda O'Farrell; William, son of Hugh Oge O'Farrell; Thomas, son of Auliffe O'Farrell; and five of the Clann-Donough[b], namely, Tomaltagh, son of Gilchreest; Murrough, son of Donough; Conor, son of Teige; Murtough, son of Donough; and Melaghlin, son of Donough. In this battle were also slain John Mac Egan, O'Conor's Brehon; Gilla-na-naev, son of Dailredocair O'Devlin,

carry arms. The annals remark that they were defeated by the superiority of the English archers, who swept off everything that opposed them, and that Felim was killed on the field of battle in the twenty-third year of his age, and performed prodigies of valour, which shewed that he was as worthy as Bruce of the monarchy of all Ireland. Had he succeeded at the battle of Athunree it is probable that Ireland would be as independent as any other nation in Europe; nor can it be conjectured at this time how far that independence, with an alliance between the Scots of Ireland and the Scots of Albany, would have contributed to render the English, then at war with the Welch, and detested by all their neighbours, a tributary people, the inhabitants of a province remote from the seat of government, and the insulted sufferers of all the calamities which her mercantile monopoly has brought upon all three.

"Cox boasts that 'after this battle the Berminghams took a prey of 2000 cows from the O'Conors;' but certain it is that, considering the inferiority of the Irish arms, we find no cause of wonder that 8000 Irish, as Cox has it, or 11,000, as the Irish annals say, were slain at the battle of Athunree; and that the King of England, on receiving the news of this victory, granted to Richard de Birmingham the title of Baron of Athunree, which his descendants have enjoyed ever since.'"

[b] *Clann-Donough*, i. e. the Mac-Donoughs of Tirerrill, who are a branch of the Mac Dermots of Moylurg.

⁊ Tomás ó conallain. Acht cena ni heidir a faisneis, nó a innisin gacha ttorcrattar do maithibh Connacht, Mumhan, ⁊ Midhe is in ccath ccédna. Lá féle .S. Labhrás do shonnradh tuccadh an tromcath so. Teora bliadhna ar fichitt ba haois dFeidhlimidh an tan sin. Ruaidhri na bFedh mac donnchaidh mic Eoghain mic Ruaidhri uí Concobhair doirdneadh i ttighearnus Connacht iaramh.

Sloicceadh adbal re mac uilliam búrc i síol muiredhaigh. O concobhair ⁊ Síol muiredhaigh, ⁊ moran doireacht connacht, ⁊ dá nuaislibh do dénamh sithe ris. Acht cena nochar faomh mac diarmata antsíth do dénomh, Mac uilliam do shaighidh moighe luirc iarsin, Creacha aidble do dénamh dó im áth an chip ⁊ in uachtar tíre, An tír uile do losccadh ⁊ do milleadh dó. Acht cena ro imthighsiot gan cath gan comhadh ar a haithle. Ruaidhri mac donnchaidh daithrioghadh do mhac diarmata iar sin.

Dearbhforgaill ingean Maghnusa uí concobhair, bean Aodha uí domhnaill décc.

AOIS CRIOST, 1317.

Aois Criost, mile, trí chéd, a dech, aSeachtt.

Donnchadh ua briain, Rí mumhan do mharbhadh.

Toirrdelbhach mac Aodha mic Eoccain .i. mac Ruaidhri mic aedha mic cathail croibhdheirg do rioghadh do chonnachtoibh.

Roibert a briúis do thecht in Erinn a halbain imaille re morsluaigheadh dfortacht a bhrathar Edbhard a briuis, ⁊ do diochur gall a hEirinn.

Maoilir dexetra ticcearna átha letain do marbhadh la cathal mac domhnaill ui chonchobhair, ⁊ domhnall mac taidhg mic domhnaill iorrais uí chonchobhair

[c] *Thomas O'Conallan.*—In the Annals of Clonmacnoise, as translated by Mageoghegan, he is called "Thomas O'Connolan of the King's Guard." This family was located in the county of Galway, but the exact position of their territory has not been determined. They are to be distinguished from the O'Coindealbhains or Quinlans of Tullyard, near Trim, in Meath, as well as from the O'Caoindealbhains or Quinlivans of Munster, and from the O'Coinghiollains of Sligo.

[d] *Na-bhFeadh*, i. e. of the Faes, which was the name of O'Naghtan's country in the barony of Athlone, and county of Roscommon.

[e] *Ath-an-chip.*—The name of a ford on the Shannon, near the town of Carrick-on-Shannon.

[f] *Uachtar-tire*, i. e., the upper part of the country. The northern part of the barony of Boyle, containing the small village of Keadew, is still locally so called.

[g] *Donough O'Brien.*—There is a long account of the battle in which he was slain given in the

O'Conor's standard-bearer; and Thomas O'Conallan[c]. In short, it is impossible to enumerate or tell all the chiefs of Connaught, Munster, and Meath, who fell in this battle. This terrible battle was fought on the festival day of St. Lawrence [10th of August]. Felim O'Conor was twenty-three years of age at the time. Rory na-bhFeadh[d], the son of Donough, son of Owen, son of Rory O'Conor was then inaugurated King of Connaught.

A numerous army was led by William Burke into Sil-Murray; and O'Conor and the Sil-Murray, with many of the tribes and chiefs of Connaught, made peace with him. Mac Dermot, however, did not consent to make this peace; and Mac William [for that reason] afterwards made an incursion into Moylurg, committed great depredations about Ath-an-chip[e], and in Uachtar-tire[f], and burned and destroyed the whole country; but his men departed without fighting a battle, or obtaining pledges of submission. Rory, the son of Donough [O'Conor], was afterwards deposed by Mac Dermot.

Dervorgilla, the daughter of Manus O'Conor, and wife of Hugh O'Donnell, died.

THE AGE OF CHRIST, 1317.

The Age of Christ, one thousand three hundred seventeen.

Donough O'Brien[g], King of Munster, was slain.

Turlough, the son of Hugh, son of Owen, son of Rory, son of Hugh, son of Cathal Crovderg, was inaugurated by the Connacians as their king.

Robert Bruce came from Scotland to Ireland with a great army[h], to assist his brother, and expel the English from Ireland.

Meyler de Exeter, Lord of Athleathan [Ballylahan, in the county of Mayo], was slain by Cathal, son of Donnell O'Conor; and Donnell, the son of Teige, son of Donnell[i]-Erris O'Conor, was slain along with him, together with four-

Irish work called *Caithrem Toirdhealbhaigh*, from which it has been abstracted by the compiler of the Dublin copy of the Annals of Innisfallen.

[h] *Great army.*—In the Annals of Clonmacnoise, as translated by Mageoghegan, this passage is thus given: "A. D. 1317. Robert Bruise, King of Scotland, came this year to Ireland with a great army of Galloweglasses, to assist his brother, Edward Bruise, to conquer and bring in subjection this kingdome, and to banish all English here hence."

[i] *Donnell-Erris O'Conor.*—He was the son of Manus, who was the son of Murtough Muimneach, the son of King Turlough More O'Conor.

do ṁarbaḋ bfós amaille ris, ⁊ ceiṫre fir décc dia muintir imaraon friú. Ar bord methénaigi (.i. abann) droma cliaḃ do rónaḋ na gníoṁa sin.

Caislen aṫa cliaṫ an coraınn (.i. baile an móta) do briseaḋ.

Maoileċlainn carrach mac diarmata adbar tigerna moiġe luircc, Concobar ó concobair, .i. mac coṁorba comáin, ⁊ Maġnus ó ḟlannaccáin adbar taoisiġ cloinne caṫail do ṁarbaḋ la gillbert mac goirdealbaiġ co sochaidib oile.

Maiḋm cille móire for mac Ruaiḋri, ⁊ for fferaib breifne. Mac Aoḋa breifniġ uí ċoncobair do ġabail ann. Da mac neill uí ruairc, conċobar buiḋe mag tiġearnain taoiseaċ ṫeallaiġ dúnchaḋa, Maṫġaṁain macc tiġearnain, an giolla ruaḋ mac an airċinniġ mic tiġernáin, niocól mac an maiġistir, ⁊ secht bfichit gallócclaċ do ṁuintir ṁic Ruaiḋri do ṁarbaḋ ann, ⁊ soċaiḋe nach airnsioter.

Maeliosa ruaḋ mac aoḋaccáin saoi Ereann i bffeneaċus ⁊ i mbreiṫeṁnus décc.

Raġnall mag raġnaill taoiseaċ muintire heolais do ġabail i bfioll, ⁊ taoisech do ḋénaṁ do Sheffraiḋ mag raġnaill ina ionad.

AOIS CRIOST, 1318.

Aois Criost, mile, trí chéd, a dech, a hocht.

Maiḋm mór do ṫabairt i nélib ar ġalloib la hua ccerbaill dú i ttorċair Adam mares ⁊ Soċaiḋe do ġalloibh.

[j] *Ballymote* is in the barony of Corran, and county of Sligo.

[k] *Kilmore*, the seat of a bishopric in the county of Cavan.

[l] *Mac-an-Master.*—This name is still extant in the county of Cavan, but generally anglicised Masterson.

[m] *Mac Egan.*—Mageoghegan gives this entry in his version of the Annals of Clonmacnoise thus:

" Moyleissa Roe Mac Keigan, the best-learned in Ireland in the Brehon Lawe, in Irish called Fenechus, died." To this he adds the following note:

" This Fenechus or Brehon lawe, is none other but the civill Lawe, which the Brehons had in an obscure and unknown language, which none could understand except those that studied in the open schools they had. Some were judges and others were admitted to plead in the open air as barristers, and for their fees, costs, and all, received the eleventh part of the thing in demand of the party for whom it was ordered; the loser paid no costs.

" The Brehons of Ireland were divided into severall tribes and families, as the Mac Keigans, O'Deorans, O'Breasleans, and Mac Tholies.

teen of their people. It was on the brink of the Methenagh (i. e. a river) of Drumcliff, that these deeds were done.

The castle of Ath-cliath an Chorainn (i. e. of Ballymote[j]) was demolished.

Melaghlin Carragh Mac Dermot, heir to the lordship of Moylurg; Conor O'Conor (i. e. the son of the coarb of St. Coman); Manus O'Flanagan, heir to the chieftainship of Clann-Cathail, and many others, were slain by Gilbert Mac Costello.

The son of Rory and the men of Breifny were defeated at Kilmore[k], where the son of Hugh Breifneach O'Conor was taken prisoner, and the two sons of Niall O'Rourke, Conor Boy Mac Tiernan, Chief of Teallach Dunchadha, Mahon Mac Tiernan, Gillaroe, son of the Erenagh Mac Tiernan, Nicholas Mac-an-Master[l], one hundred and forty of the gallowglasses of the people of the son of Rory, and others not enumerated, were slain.

Maelisa Roe Mac Egan[m], the most learned man in Ireland in law and judicature, died.

Randal Mac Rannall[n], Chief of Muintir-Eolais [in the county of Leitrim], was treacherously taken prisoner, and Geoffrey Mac Rannall was made Chief in his place.

THE AGE OF CHRIST, 1318.

The Age of Christ, one thousand three hundred eighteen.

A great victory was gained[o] over the English in Ely[p], by O'Carroll; and Adam Mares and many other Englishmen were slain.

Every contrey had its peculiar Brehaive" [bpeıċeam] "dwelling within itself, that had power to decide the causes of that contrey, and to maintain their controversies against their neighbour contreys, by which they held their lands of the Lord of the Contrey where they dwelt. This was before the lawes of England were in full force in this Land, and before the kingdom was divided into Shyres."

[n] *Mac Rannall.*—This name is anglicised Magranell or Mac Granell, by Mageoghegan in his translation of the Annals of Clonmacnoise, in which this passage is given as follows: "A. D. 1317. Randalph Mac Granell was deposed of the chieftaineship by the people of his own contrey, and the captainrie given over by them to Geffrey Magranell as more worthy thereof."

[o] *A great victory was gained.*—maıḋm mop ᴅo ṫaḃaıpṫ, literally, "a great defeat was given."

[p] *Ely.*—The Ely of which O'Carroll was chief comprised the baronies of Ballybrit and Clonlisk, in the south of the present King's County; that is, that part of the King's County lying south of the boundary of the diocese of Meath.

Slóġ mór do ṫionól do Mhaolruanaiḋ mac diarmata tiġearna moiġi luirg do ṡaiġiḋ caṫail mic domhnaill uí concobair go Fassa coilleaḋ. Tainicc ar in sloiġeaḋ sin Toirrḋelḃaċ mac Aoḋa mic Eoġain uí concobair, Ualgarcc ua ruairc tiġearna breifne, concobar ó ceallaiġ tiġearna ua maine, ⁊ Tomaltaċ mac donnchaiḋ tiġearna tíre hoilella. Iar ndul go Fassa coilleaḋ do na maiṫiḃ sin ro tarccaiḋ Caṫal coṁṫa móra doiḃ, ⁊ giḋeaḋ noċar gabaḋ uaiḋ acht a ionnsaiġiḋ go lairmeaḋón a longpuirt. Ciḋ eisiḋhe ní ar ṫime ná ar tlás do ċúaiḋ sin dó uair do ḟreaccair iadsomh go ḟraochḋa foirniata, gur ḟearaḋ iomairecc áiṫ aṁnus eatorra, go ttorċair brian mac toirrḋealḃaiġ uí concobair ríoġḋaṁna Connacht, Concobar ó ceallaiġ, brian mac maġnusa, Caṫal mac giollacriost meic diarmata, ⁊ soċaiḋe oile duaislib ⁊ danradhaib an tsluaiġ archeana la caṫal co na muintir.

Caṫal mac domhnaill dionnsaiccidh uí ċoncobair ⁊ ṁeic diarmata iarsin, go ndearna creacha aiḋble i moiġ luirg, ⁊ gur haiṫriogaḋ toirrḋealḃaċ mac aoḋa lais. Gabhais féin ceannus Connacht iaraṁ, ⁊ teid toirrḋealḃaċ do ṡaiġiḋ uilliam burc ⁊ gall ar a haithle.

Seaan mac domhnaill uí neill do ṁarḃaḋ la hua ndomhnaill, .i. Aoḋ mac domhnaill óicc i ndoire choluim cille, ⁊ mac domhnaill, ⁊ soċaiḋe ele do ṁarḃaḋ ⁊ do báthaḋ.

[q] *Fassa-Coille.*—This was the name of a woody district in the barony of Carbury, in the north of the county of Sligo. See it mentioned again at the year 1397.

[r] *Cathal, son of Donnell O'Conor.*—From Murtough, the brother of this Cathal, O'Conor Sligo descended, thus: Murtough, father of Donnell, who was father of Owen, who was father of Donnell, who was father of Cathal Oge, who was father of Teige, who was father of Cathal Oge, who was father of Donnell O'Conor Sligo, who was father of Sir Calvagh or Sir Charles O'Conor Sligo. See Pedigree of O'Conor Sligo, given by Duald Mac Firbis in his Genealogical Work (Lord Roden's copy), p. 221.

[s] *Great presents.*—coṁṫa mora.—Mageoghegan renders this "great gifts and bribes," in his translation of the Annals of Clonmacnoise, in which the whole passage runs as follows:

"A. D. 1318. Molronie Mac Dermodda, prince of Moylorge, gathered together a great army consisting of the ensuing, viz., Terlagh O'Connor, King of Connought, Ularg O'Royrck, prince of the Brenie; Connor O'Kelly, prince of Imaine; and Tomaltagh Mac Donnogh, prince of Tyre-allella," [and] "marched towards Cahall mac Donnell O'Connor, who dwelt at Fasagh Koyllie. Cahall offered them great gifts and bribes, and not to come to" [annoy] "him; which they refused, and marched towards the middest of the place where he encamped; which he seeing, having none other remedy, he tooke hearte anew, and with a courageous stomack, without daunting, he issued from out his house, and made feircely towards the place he saw his enemies approache, and gave them a valourous onsett;

A great host was mustered by Mulrony Mac Dermot, Lord of Moylurg, with which he marched to Fassa-Coille[q], to attack Cathal, son of Donnell O'Conor[r]. In this army came Turlough, son of Hugh, son of Owen O'Conor; Ualgarg O'Rourke, Lord of Breifny; Conor O'Kelly, Lord of Hy-Many; and Tomaltagh Mac Donough, Lord of Tirerrill. On the arrival of these chieftains at Fassa-Coille, Cathal offered them great presents[s]; but these were not accepted from him, and they charged him in the very middle of his fortified camp. Cathal, however, was in nowise daunted[t] or disheartened at this, but resisted them with fierceness and bravery; and a furious and desperate battle was fought between them, in which Brian, the son of Turlough O'Conor, heir presumptive to the government of Connaught, Conor O'Kelly, Brian Mac Manus, Cathal, son of Gilchreest Mac Dermot, and many others of the nobles and plebeians of the army, were slain by Cathal and his people.

Cathal, son of Donnell, afterwards marched against the O'Conor and Mac Dermot, and committed great depredations in Moylurg, and deposed Turlough, the son of Hugh, and assumed the sovereignty of Connaught himself; upon which Turlough went to [seek refuge from] William Burke and the English.

John, son of Donnell O'Neill, was slain by O'Donnell (Hugh, the son of Donnell Oge) at Derry-Columbkille, and Mac Donnell[u] and many others were slain and drowned.

killed Connor O'Kelly, prince of Imaine at first; Bryan mac Terlagh O'Connor, Tanist or next successor of the Kingdom of Connought; Bryan mac Magnus, Cahall mac Gillechrist, and many others of the noble and ignoble sort were killed therein; and immediately afterwards" [he] "tooke a great prey from Dermodda; tooke the government and name of King of Connought to himself, and deposed Terlagh O'Connor thereof, and for his defence partaked with William Burke and the English of Connought."

[t] *In nowise daunted.*—This part of the passage is translated by Mageoghegan as follows, in his version of the Annals of Clonmacnoise: "Which he seeing, having none other remedy, he tooke heart anew, and with a couragious stomack, without daunting, he issued from out of his house, and made fiercely towards the place he saw his enemies approache, and gave them a valourous onsett: killed Connor O'Kelly, prince of Imaine, at first; Bryan Mac Terlagh, O'Connor, Tanist or next successor of the kingdome of Connaught; Bryan Mac Magnus; Cahall Mac Gillechrist, and many others of the noble and ignoble sort."

[u] *Mac Donnell.*—Mageoghegan, in his translation of the Annals of Clonmacnoise, gives this passage differently, as follows:

"A. D. 1318. John O'Neale's son, that is to say, the son of Donnell O'Neale, was killed by Hugh O'Neale in the town of Derry. The said Hugh and divers others were killed and drownded the same day."

Eduard a brius fſr millte Erenn go coitcenn etir gallaiḃ, ⁊ gaoidealaiḃ do marḃaḋ do ġallaiḃ tré nſrt caṫaiġte, ⁊ croḋaċta i nDún dealgan. Mac ruaiḋri tiġſrna innsi gall, Mac doṁnaill tigearna airir gaoidel, ⁊ iolar do maiṫiḃ alban imaille riú do ṁarḃaḋ ina ḟarraḋ, ⁊ noċa dearnaḋ re haimsir imċéin inErinn gníoṁ as mó as a ttáinic a lſs inás, uair táinic gorta coitċenn re linn an Eduaird si innte co mbidís daoine ag tomailt aroile fri ré na ttſóra mbliaḋan go lſiṫ baoísioṁ ſttorra.

Seaan ó Fſrġail do ṁarḃaḋ daon orċor soiġde dia ṁac fén.

Seaffraiḋ mac giolla na naoṁ uí ḟſrġail tiġſrna na hangaile décc.

Caṫal mac giolla crist meg raġnaill do marḃaḋ.

Giolla an choimdeaḋ mac cionaſoha uí ġormġaile ⁊ gormlaiṫ inġean meic branáin a bean do éġ.

AOIS CRIOST, 1319.

Aois Criost, mile, tri chéd, a dech, a Naoí.

Enri mac an crosain espucc ratha both do écc, ⁊ Tomás mac corbmaic uí doṁnaill abb easa ruaiḋ do ṫoġa in espuccoide Rátha both iaraṁ.

[y] *Edward Bruce.*—The Annals of Clonmacnoise, as translated by Mageoghegan, give the account of Bruce's death more fully, as follows:

"Edward Bruise, a destroyer of all Ireland, in generall, both English and Irish, was killed by the English in battle by their valour at Dundalk, the 14th of October, 1318, together with Mac Rowrie, King of the Islands, and Mac Donnel, prince of the Irish" [Gaels] "of Scotland, with many other Scottishmen. Edward Bruise seeing the Enemies encamped before his face, and fearing his brother, Robert Bruise, King of Scotland (that came to this kingdom for his assistance), would acquire and gett the glorie of that victorie, which he made himself believe he would gett, of the Anglo-Irish, which he was sure he was able to overthrow, without the assistance of his said brother, he rashly gave them the assault, and was therein slain himself, as is declared, to the great joye and comfort of the whole kingdome in generall, for there was not a better deed that redounded more to the good of the Kingdom since the creation of the World, and since the banishment of the Fine Fomores out of this land, done in Ireland than the killing of Edward Bruise, for there reigned scarcity of victuals, breach of promises, ill performances of covenants, and the loss of men and women thro' out the whole Kingdom for the space of three years and a half that he bore sway, insomuch that men did commonly eat one another for want of sustenance during his time."

The battle in which Edward Bruce was slain was fought near the hill of Faughard, within two miles of Dundalk, and the natives still point out the spot where he fell. It would appear from the Anglo-Irish accounts of this battle that the English owed the victory to the desperate bravery of John Maupas, an Anglo-Irish knight, who, under the persuasion that the death of Bruce

Edward Bruce[v], the destroyer of [the people of] Ireland in general, both English and Irish, was slain by the English, through dint of battle and bravery, at Dundalk, where also Mac Rory, Lord of the Inse-Gall [the Hebrides], Mac Donnell, Lord of Argyle, and many others of the chiefs of Scotland, were slain. And no achievement had been performed in Ireland for a long time before, from which greater benefit had accrued to the country than from this; for, during the three and a half years that this Edward spent in it, a universal famine prevailed to such a degree, that men were wont to devour one another[w].

John O'Farrell was slain by his son with one shot from an arrow[x].

Geoffrey, son of Gilla-na-naev O'Farrell, Lord of Annaly, died.

Cathal, son of Gilchreest Mag-Rannall, was slain.

Gilla an-Choimhdhe, son of Kenny O'Gormly, and Gormlaith, daughter of Mac Branan, his wife, died.

THE AGE OF CHRIST, 1319.

The Age of Christ, one thousand three hundred nineteen.

Henry Mac-an-Chrosain, Bishop of Raphoe, died; and Thomas, son of Cormac O'Donnell, Abbot of Ashroe, was then elected to the bishopric of Raphoe.

himself would ensure the victory to the English, rushed devotedly to the place where he saw him, and when, after the battle, the body of Bruce was discovered, that of John Maupas was found lying stretched across it. (See Campion's Historie of Ireland, A. D. 1318). Sir John Bermingham is said to have brought Bruce's head to the King, and received as a reward the earldom of Louth and the barony of Ardee. The hands and heart of Bruce are said to have been carried to Dublin, and his other limbs sent to different places; but tradition says that his body was buried in the churchyard of Faughard, where they still pretend to point out his grave. Barbour, however, says that Gib Harper wore Edward Bruce's armour, and that his body was consequently mistaken for that of Bruce, and his head salted in "a kest, and sent as a present to King Edward." See Grace's Annals of Ireland, edited by the Rev. Richard Butler, p. 95.

[w] *Were wont to devour one another.*—Grace and Pembridge state that some of the people were so pinched with famine that they dug up the graves in the church-yards, and, after they had boiled the flesh in the scull of the dead body, eat it up; but this is evidently an exaggerated account of this dearth, for, surely, if the famine had not consumed the pots as well as the food, they might have easily found better utensils for cooking human flesh than the sculls of men. Dr. Drummond thinks that this story owes its origin to the ambiguity of the word "scull," which is frequently used by old English writers to denote a covering for the head; but when it is considered that the chroniclers of the event wrote in the Latin language, this conjecture will be found to lose much of its ingenuity.

[x] *With one shot from an arrow*, daon orċor

Espucc doire, O bánáin Easpucc clochair, ⁊ Espucc cluana fſrta brenainn décc.

Aine inġean meic diarmata bſn ṁeic Consnáṁa décc.

Eachmarcach mac branáin taoiseaċ corcachlann do ṁarbaḋ Thomaltaiġ uí maoilbrénainn, giḋſḃ noċar marbaḋ in asccaiḋ sin uair fuairsiuṁ fſisin bás a ccionn an trſs laoí iar sin do biṫin na ngon tucc Tomaltaċ fair.

Doṁnall ó néill ticcſrna tíre heoccain daṫcor ar a flaithſs tre nſrt gall ⁊ cloinne Aoḋa buiḋe, ⁊ a ḋul co fſraiḃ manaċ ar comairci ḟlaiṫbſrtaiġ ṁég uiḋir, ⁊ fir manach do creaċaḋ a muinntire.

O neill, .i. doṁnall do gabail a ṫiġſrnais fſin do ridiri.

Brian mac doṁnaill ui neill tánaisi ċenel eoġain do marbaḋ la cloinn aoḋa buiḋe ⁊ la hannraoi mac daiull ag ráiṫ lúraiġ.

AOIS CRIOST, 1320.

Aois Criost, mile, trí chéd, afiche.

Mainestir bſndtraiġe i nduṫaiġ uí Suilleaḃáin in esscopóiteċt Ruis, do tógḃáil la hua Suilleáḃan do ḃraiṫriḃ .S. Franseis, ⁊ as is an mainestir sin baoi togha aḋnaicthe ui Shuilleaḃáin ⁊ moráin duaislib oile.

Coinne, ⁊ comḋáil eidir Caṫal ó ċoncoḃair ⁊ maolruanaiḋ mac diarmata, go ndſrnsat síṫ ċonnail cairdſṁail re roile, ⁊ mac diarmata do ṫoiḋeċt

soiġde.—Mageoghegan renders this passage thus: "A. D. 1318. John O'Farrell was killed by his own son with an arrow."

[y] *The Bishop of Derry.*—He was Odo or Hugh O'Neill, and succeeded in the year 1316. See Harris's Edition of Ware's Bishops, p. 289.

[z] *O'Banan.*—He is called Gelasius O'Banan by Ware. He succeeded in 1316.

[a] *The Bishop of Clonfert.*—The Bishop of Clonfert who died in this year was Gregory O'Brogy, who succeeded in 1308. See Harris's Edition of Ware's Bishops, p. 639.

[b] *He did not escape scathless.*—Giḋeadh noċar murbaḋ i nasraiḋ sin, literally signifies "he was not killed gratis, i. e., his death cost Mac Branain his own life.

[c] *The Clann-Hugh-Boy.*—These were the descendants of Hugh Boy O'Neill, who was slain in the year 1283, and were located in the territory of Clannaboy, in the counties of Down and Antrim.

[d] *Rath-lury,* Raṫ lúraiġ.—This place is now called Maghera, which is a small town in the county of Londonderry. St. Lurach's or Loury's well and grave are still pointed out. See note [l] under the year 1218, p. 193, *supra.*

[e] *Monastery of Bantry.*—Dr. Smith, in his *Natural and Civil History of Cork,* book ii. c. 5,

The Bishop of Derry[y], O'Banan[z], Bishop of Clogher, and the Bishop of Clonfert[a], died.

Aine, daughter of Mac Dermot, and wife of Mac Consnava, died.

Eachmarcach Mac Branan, Chief of Corcachlann, slew Tomaltagh O'Mulrenin; but he himself did not escape scathless[b], for, on the third day afterwards, he died of the wounds which Tomaltagh had inflicted upon him.

Donnell O'Neill, Lord of Tyrone, was expelled from his lordship through the power of the English and the Clann-Hugh-Boy[c], and went to Fermanagh under the protection of Flaherty Maguire; but the inhabitants of Fermanagh plundered his people.

O'Neill, i. e. Donnell, assumed his own lordship again.

Brian, son of Donnell O'Neill, Tanist of Tyrone, was slain by the Clann-Hugh-Boy and Henry Mac Davill at Rath-lury[d].

THE AGE OF CHRIST, 1320.

The Age of Christ, one thousand three hundred twenty.

The monastery of Bantry[e], in O'Sullivan's country, in the bishopric of Ross[f], was founded by O'Sullivan for Franciscan Friars. In this monastery O'Sullivan and many other nobles chose burial places for themselves.

A meeting and conference took place between Cathal O'Conor and Mulrony Mac Dermot: a kindly and amicable peace[g] was concluded between them,

states that this monastery was founded in 1460, by Dermot O'Sullivan; but he quotes no authority. No vestige of this building now remains.

[f] *Ross.*—This diocese comprised the western part of the county of Cork.—See Smith's Natural and Civil History of Cork, Book i. cc. 2 and 4; and Lanigan's Ecclesiastical History of Ireland, vol. ii. p. 194.

[g] *A kindly and amicable peace*, ṗíṫ ċonnail caiṗdeaṁail.—Mageoghegan, in his translation of the Annals of Clonmacnoise, renders this passage as follows: "Cahall O'Connor and Mullronie Mac Dermott had a meeting, where a friendly attonement was agreed and concluded between them; whereupon Mullronie upon some occasions of his left the countrey; [and] the said Cahall, contrary to his said agreement, tooke his advantage by the oportunity he had in his absence, and mett him at a place called Torawnagh, whom he instantly took prisoner, and also took Granie, daughter of Mac Magnus, wife of the said Mullronie, whom he found staying for a boat to pass over into the island of Carrick Logha Ke; he tooke the spoyles and preys of the contrey: also he tooke prisoner Mac Donnogh, Lord of the territorye called Tyreallealla in Connought."

dia tír féin iarrsin, michoingell do denaṁ don ċaṫal rémraitte ar mac nDiarmata ar a haiṫle ar mullach Doraṁnach, .i. a ġabail lais, ⁊ Grainne inġean meic Maġnusa bean meic Diarmata do ġabáil beós i bPurt na Cairrge. Maoilíosa donn mac Aoḋaccáin ⁊ a ṁac, ⁊ Tomaltach mac Donnchaiḋ tiġerna tíre hOilella do ġabail beós, ⁊ an tír do lomarccain iaraṁ.

Aoḋ mac Taiḋg uí Concobair deaġadbar righ Connacht ar deilb ar uaisle, ⁊ ar einech do marbaḋ do ṁac Mairtín, ⁊ éssein do marbaḋ ina dioġail.

Maṫġaṁain mac Doṁnaill Connachtaiġ uí Briain tanaisi Muṁan do marbaḋ do Cloinn Cuiléin.

Mór inġean uí Baoiġill bean uí Ferġail décc.

Mac Mairtín do ṁarbaḋ ina ṫiġ féin la hAodh mac Taidhg uí Concobair, Clann Mairtín, ⁊ clann Aeḋa Buiḋe do leanṁain Aoḋa go Clochar, ⁊ a ṁarbaḋ ann.

AOIS CRIOST, 1321.

Aois Criost, míle, trí chéd, fiche a haon.

Grainne inġen meic Maġnasa bean ṁaolruanaiḋ meic Diarmata décc.

Ruaiḋri na bfeḋ mac Donnchaiḋ mic Eoġain uí Concobair do marbaḋ do Ċaṫal mac Aoḋa mic Eoġain tre ṫangnocht.

Carracc Locha Cé do bríseaḋ la Caṫal mac Doṁnaill uí Concobair.

Maġnus ó hAnluain tiġerna Oirṫir do ḋallaḋ dá ḃraṫair féin Niall mac Conulaḋ uí Anluain cedaoín an ḃraith.

Niall ó hAnluain tiġerna Airṫir do ṁarbaḋ do Ġallaiḃ Dúin Dealgan i meabhail.

[h] *Mullagh Doramhnach.*—There is no place now bearing this name in Mac Dermot's country. It was probably the ancient name of the townland of Mullaghmore, in the parish of Killukin, barony of Boyle, and county of Roscommon.

[i] *Port-na-Cairrge.*—This was the name of the quay or bank opposite Mac Dermot's Castle, called Carraig Locha Ce, or the Rock of Lough Key. The spot is still so called by the natives when speaking Irish.

[k] *A good materies,* deaġadbar.—Mageoghegan renders this as follows, in his Annals of Clonmacnoise: "Hugh mac Teige O'Connor, a young man of great worth and expectation, and one sufficient for birth, composition of body, and liberalitye, to be a Kinge, was killed by Mac Martynn, who was killed in revenge thereof.

[l] *Clann-Cuilein.*—This was one of the tribe names of the Mac Namaras of Thomond.

[m] *Clann-Martin.*—This was a sept of the O'Neills of Tyrone. The Clann-Hugh Boy were

and Mac Dermot then returned to his own country. Cathal, however, afterwards violated the conditions of this peace, for he made a prisoner of Mac Dermot at Mullagh Doramhnach[h], and also of his wife, the daughter of Mac Manus, at Port-na-Cairrge[i]. Maelisa Don Mac Egan and his son, and Tomaltagh Mac Donough, Lord of Tirerrill, were also made prisoners, and the country was entirely plundered.

Hugh, son of Teige O'Conor, a good materies[k] of a King of Connaught, by reason of his personal shape, nobility, and hospitality, was slain by Mac Martin, who was himself slain in revenge of it.

Mahon, son of Donnell Connaghtagh O'Brien, Tanist of Munster, was slain by the Clann-Cuilein[l].

More, daughter of O'Boyle, and wife of O'Farrell, died.

Mac Martin was slain in his own house by Hugh, the son of Teige O'Conor; but the Clann-Martin[m] and the Clann-Hugh-Boy pursued Hugh to Clogher[n], where they killed him.

THE AGE OF CHRIST, 1321.

The Age of Christ, one thousand three hundred twenty-one.

Grainne, daughter of Mac Manus, and wife of Mulrony Mac Dermot, died.

Rory of the Faes[o], the son of Donough, son of Owen O'Conor, was treacherously slain by Cathal, the son of Hugh, son of Owen.

The Rock of Lough Key was destroyed by Cathal, son of Donnell O'Conor.

Manus O'Hanlon, Lord of Orior, was blinded on Spy-Wednesday by his own kinsman[p], Niall, son of Cu-Uladh O'Hanlon.

Niall O'Hanlon, Lord of Orior, was treacherously slain by the English of Dundalk.

also a sept of the same family, who, soon after this period, made themselves masters of an extensive territory in the counties of Down and Antrim, to which they gave their clan-name.

[n] *Clogher* is the head of a bishop's see, in a barony of the same name, in the county of Tyrone.

[o] *Of the Faes.*—He was so called from the territory of the Faes, or O'Naghtan's country, near Athlone, in the county of Roscommon, in which he was fostered.

[p] *Kinsman*, bꞃáċaıꞃ.—Mageoghegan renders it *brother* in his translation of the Annals of Clonmacnoise, thus: "A. D. 1321. Magnus O'Hanlon, prince of the Orhir was blinded by his own brother, and mightily oppressed by Neale mac Conuley O'Hanlon, upon Wednesday, the week before Easter."

Maidm adbal do ṫabairt do Aintriu mac fſorais ⁊ do ġallaiḃ na mide ar ṁacaibh riogh ua bfailġe.

Uilliam mac gille finnén, ⁊ Matha do ṁarbaḋ la henri mac giolla finnéin ina oirecht féin.

AOIS CRIOST, 1322.

Aois Criost, mile, trí chéd, fiche, adó.

Matha ua heothaiġ esrucc Conmaicne (no ardachaiḋ), ⁊ Aindrias macc maoilin ardṁaiġistir dliġiḋ nuiṗiadnairi ⁊ Shenreaċta i léx, ⁊ i ccanóin décc.

Lucás ua Muiredhaiġ airchideochain cluana do écc.

Murchaḋ mac giolla na naoṁ uí ḟſrġail tiġſrna na hanġaile do marbaḋ do ṁac a dſrbraṫar Seoinin ó fſrgail i ccluain lis bſicc tré meḃail. Muirċſrtaċ mac amlaoiḃ uí ḟſrġail do marbaḋ an lá céDna dia braiṫribh fſirsin (lochluinn, ⁊ Roibſrd) tre meḃail. Loċlainn mac aṁlaoiḃ uí ḟſrgail do marbaḋ la Seoinin iar sin.

Donnchaḋ mac donnchaiḋ meic diarmata décc.

Hannraoi mac gilleḟinnéin taoiseaċ muintire feodaċáin do ṁarbaḋ la cloinn Aṁlaoibh még uidir.

Gillibert ó ceallaiġ tiġſrna ó maine décc.

Maolruanaiḋ mac diarmatta do ġabail lé concoḃar mac taidg uí concoḃair, ⁊ do luċt tiġe caṫail uí concoḃair i ccluain cummuiscc, ⁊ an baile darccain doibh.

Riocard mac fſorais tiġſrna áṫa na riog décc.

Maidm mor do ṫabairt do ḃrian ó ḃriain for ġallaiḃ.

Giolla na naoṁ mac Serraiḋ mic giolla na naoṁ uí ḟſrġail do ġabail tiġearnais na hanġaile.

Uilliam liaṫ búrc mac uilliam moir décc.

Maolruanaiḋ mac giollacriost mic concoḃair mic corbmaic mic tomaltaiġ na cairrge tiġſrna moiġe luirce [décc].

[q] *Cluain-lis-Bec.*—This name, which was that of a seat of one of the O'Farrells, in the county of Longford, is now obsolete.

[r] *The sons of Auliffe Maguire.*—The descendants of this Auliffe took the tribe name of Clann-Auliffe, and gave name to a barony in the county of Fermanagh, now anglicised Clanawley, and sometimes incorrectly Glenawley.

[s] *Cluain-Cumuisc.*—This name would be anglicised Clooncummisk, but there is no place

A great defeat was given by Andrew Mac Feorais [Bermingham] and the English of Meath to the sons of the Chieftains of Offaly.

William and Matthew Mac Gillafinnen were slain by Henry Mac Gillafinnen, at a meeting of his own tribe.

THE AGE OF CHRIST, 1322.

The Age of Christ, one thousand three hundred twenty-two.

Mathew O'Hoey, Bishop of Conmaicne or Ardagh, and Andreas Mag-Mailin, Chief Professor of the Law of New Witness, of the Ancient Law, and of the Canon Law, died.

Lucas O'Murray, Archdeacon of Cluain, died.

Murrough, the son of Gilla-na-naev O'Farrell, Lord of Annaly, was treacherously slain at Cluain-lis-Bec[q] by his brother's son, Seoinin O'Farrell. Murtough, the son of Auliffe O'Farrell, was treacherously slain on the same day, by his own kinsmen (Loughlin and Robert). Loughlin, the son of Auliffe O'Farrell, was afterwards slain by Seoinin [O'Farrell].

Donough, the son of Donough Mac Dermot, died.

Henry Mac Gillafinnen, Chief of Muintir-Feodachain, was slain by the sons of Auliffe Maguire[r].

Gilbert O'Kelly, Lord of Hy-Many, died.

Mulrony Mac Dermot was taken prisoner by Conor, son of Teige O'Conor, and by the household of Cathal O'Conor, at Cluain-Cummuisc[s], which town they plundered.

Richard Mac Feorais [Bermingham], Lord of Athenry, died.

The English suffered a signal defeat[t] from Brian O'Brien.

Gilla-na-naev, the son of Geoffrey, son of Gilla-na-naev O'Farrell, assumed the lordship of Annaly.

William Liath[u] Burke, son of William More, died.

Mulrony [Mac Dermot], the son of Gilchreest, son of Conor, son of Cormac, son of Tomaltagh of the Rock, Lord of Moylurg [died].

known to the Editor now bearing the name in the county of Roscommon.

[t] *Suffered a signal defeat.*—Literally, "A great defeat was given by Brian O'Brian to the English."

[u] *Liath*, i. e. grey, hoary.

Muiris ṁac an ċomarba do éġ.

Osgar mac lochlainn ṁég uidir do ṁarbaḋ la caṫal ó Ruairc.

Petrus ó brſlén ollaṁ brſiṫſṁan fſrmanaċ do écc.

Fingin ó cairide ollaṁ fſrmanaċ i leiġius do écc.

Fearġal ruaḋ mac Saṁradain ⁊ Giolla iosa mac Saṁradáin do ṁarbaḋ la cloinn Amlaoiḃ ṁég uidir.

AOIS CRIOST, 1323.

Aois Criost, míle, trí chétt, fiche, a trí.

Giolla airnín ó cathusaiġ airchinneaċ cluana da Raṫ[a] do écc.

Cairpre an sccreccain (.i. Ri miḋe) mac corbmaic uí maoileċlainn ri miḋe do ṁarbaḋ la doṁnall ua maoilmuaiḋ tria ṫangnaċt.

Maolmorḋa mag eochaccáin décc.

Seoinin ua fſrġail do ṁarbaḋ do cloinn tSeaain ui ḟſrġail.

O heaġra (.i. fſrġal) do ṁarbaḋ dua ċonnmacháin[b] dá oirecht féin.

Ruaiḋri ṁag ṁaṫġamna mac tiġearna oirġiall, ⁊ Maolseaċlainn ó Sſgannáin, ⁊ mac Maeileḋúin do ṁarbaḋ la caṫal ó Ruairc i mbeol Atha Conaill.

Niall mac néill ċaim do ṁarbaḋ la lochlainn ó Raġallaiġ, ⁊ la Maelseaċlainn.

Sloiġeaḋ mór tainic Mac ḟeorais ⁊ goill do forḃairi ar ḋoṁnall mac Seaain uí fſrġail go coill na namus dia ro marbaḋ an cerac ⁊ an calbac, ⁊ goill iomḋa imaille friú.

Maolmſḋa ingſn ṁég tiġearnain bean briain ṁég Saṁradáin décc.

Giollapatraicc ó duibġſnnain ollaṁ Conmaicni i sſnċus, ⁊ lucas a mac do ṁarbaḋ la concoḃar mac gairḃiṫ még uidir.

Loċlainn mac eoġain uí dalaiġ do ṁarbaḋ la cloinn aſḋa buiḋe uí néill.

[a] *Cluain-da-rath.*—Cluain da raṫ, i. e. the pasturage of the two forts, now Clondara, a townland and village, containing the ruins of an abbey, in the parish of Killashee in the west of the county of Longford.—See Ordnance Map of that county, sheets 8 and 13. The Inquisition of the 27th January, 37 Queen Elizabeth, finds that there were here an hospital and Termon, Irenagh, or Corbeship, endowed with four cartrons of land.—See *Archdall's Monasticon*, p. 438, with MS. additions, in the library of the Royal Irish Academy.

[b] *O'Connmhachain.*—This name is still extant in the district of Ballycroy, in the county of

Maurice, son of the Coarb, died.

Henry Mac Gillafinnen, Chief of Muintir-Feodachain was slain by the sons of Auliffe Maguire.

Osgar, the son of Loughlin Maguire, was slain by Cathal O'Rourke.

Petrus O'Breslen, Chief Brehon of Fermanagh, died.

Fineen O'Cassidy, Chief Physician of Fermanagh, died.

Farrell Roe Magauran and Gilla-Isa Magauran were slain by the sons of Auliffe Maguire.

THE AGE OF CHRIST, 1323.

The Age of Christ, one thousand three hundred twenty-three.

Gilla-airnin O'Casey, Erenagh of Cluain-da-rath[v], died.

Carbry an Sgregain, son of Cormac O'Melaghlin, King of Meath, was treacherously slain by Donnell O'Molloy.

Maelmora Mageoghegan died.

Seoinin O'Farrell was slain by the sons of John O'Farrell.

O'Hara (Farrell) was slain by O'Connmachain[w], one of his own people.

Rory Mac Mahon, son of the Lord of Oriel, Melaghlin O'Seagannain, and Mac Muldoon, were slain by Cathal O'Rourke at Bel-atha-Chonaill[x].

Niall, son of Niall Cam, was slain by Loughlin and Melaghlin O'Reilly.

Mac Feorais (Bermingham) and the English marched with a great army against Donnell, son of John O'Farrell, to Coill-na-n-amhas[y], where Kepagh and Calvagh, and many of the English, were slain.

Maelmeadha, daughter of Mac Tiernan, and wife of Magauran, died.

Gillapatrick O'Duigennan, Chief Historian of Conmaicne, and Lucas, his son, were slain by Conor, the son of Garvey Maguire.

Loughlin, the son of Owen O'Daly, was slain by the tribe of Hugh Boy O'Neill.

Mayo, and is now generally anglicised Conway.

[x] *At Bel-atha-Chonaill.*—Im ḃeol Ꭿṫa Connaill, now Ballyconnell, a village in the barony of Tullaghagh, or Tullyhaw (ṫeallaċ eċḋach), in the county of Cavan, and about eleven miles to the north-east of the town of Cavan.

[y] *Coill-na-n-amhas*, i. e. wood of the hireling soldiers, now Kilnaneawse, near Edgeworthstown, in the county of Longford. It appears from an Inquisition taken at Longford, on the 1st of August, 1627, that this and ten other townlands in the same neighbourhood had been

Goffraiḋ mac giolla íosa uí ḋálaiġ do ṁarbaḋ la brian mac Ruaiḋri uí Concobair.

AOIS CRIOST, 1324.

Aois Criost, mile, trí ċéd, fiche acſthair.

Caṫal (.i. Rí connaċt) mac domnaill mic taidcc mic briain mic ainḋriasa mic briain luiġniġ mic toirrḋealbaiġ móir, aon duine ba bſoḋa, ba mó maiṫſs, ⁊ mór aiṫſs dá mbaoí in aon aimsir ris do marbaḋ la toirrḋealbaċ ó cconcobair i ttír briúin na Sionna, ⁊ Mac uí domnaill, .i. Maoileaċlainn mac toirrḋealbaiġ ċnuic an maḋma, mic domnaill oícc, tánaisi tíre conaill iar na ionnarbaḋ dua domnaill, .i. Aoḋ mac domnaill óicc ⁊ Giollacriost ócc mac donnchaiḋ, ⁊ soċaiḋe oile do marbaḋ annsin bſós im ċaṫal ó cconcobair, ⁊ Toirrḋealbaċ do gabail ċſnnais Connaċt ar a haiṫle.

Raġnall ócc máġ raġnaill taoiseaċ muintire heolais do marbaḋ.

Uilliam búrc mac uilliam ṁoir do écc.

Tadhg ua Ruairc ⁊ tiġearnán mag Ruairc do ġabail la cloinn Matha uí Raġallaiġ, ⁊ iadsoṁ dia ttairbert do Mhag ṁathġaṁna, ⁊ a marbaḋ lais a ndioġail a ṁeic Ruaiḋri ro marbaḋ riasan tan sin.

Donnchaḋ mac giollapatraicc tiġearna osraiġe do écc.

Brian ó Raġallaiġ ⁊ giollacriost do ṁarbaḋ lá muintir Ruairc.

AOIS CRIOST, 1325.

Aois Criost, mile, trí chéd, fiche a cúig.

Domnall mac briain uí néill tiġearna ċenél nſoġain do écc occ loch laoghoire.

Cuulaḋ mac domnaill mic briain uí neill dſġaḋbar ticcſrna tire heoġain do ṁarbaḋ la cloinn néill mic briain, clann dſrbraṫar a aṫor.

in the possession of Francis Edgeworth, then lately deceased.

[s] *Along with Cathal O'Conor.*—This passage, which is given in a very confused manner by the Four Masters, is somewhat better in the Annals of Clonmacnoise, as translated by Mageoghegan, thus:

"A. D. 1324. Cahall mac Donnell, King of Connaught, was killed by Terlagh mac Hugh mac Owen, who" [*recte* he] "was held to be the hardiest and substantiallest Irishman of his time. Melaghlyn mac Terlagh O'Donnell and Gille-

Godfrey, son of Gilla-Isa O'Daly, was slain by Brian, the son of Rory O'Conor.

THE AGE OF CHRIST, 1324.

The Age of Christ, one thousand three hundred twenty-four.

The King of Connaught, Cathal, the son of Donnell, son of Brian, son of Andreas, son of Brian Luighneach, son of Turlough More [O'Conor], the most energetic, the best, and the most successful man of his time, was slain by Turlough O'Conor, in Tir-Briuin-na-Sinna; and the son of O'Donnell, i. e. Melaghlin, the son of Turlough of Cnoc-an-madhma, son of Donnell Oge, Tanist of Tirconnell, who had been banished by O'Donnell, i. e. Hugh, the son of Donnell Oge, Gilchreest Oge Mac Donough, and many others, were slain along with Cathal O'Conor[z]. Turlough assumed the government of Connaught after him.

Rannall Oge Mac Rannall, Chief of Muintir Eolais, was slain.

William Burke, son of William More, died.

Teige O'Rourke and Tiernan Mac Rourke were made prisoners by the sons of Matthew O'Reilly, and delivered by them into the hands of Mac Mahon, by whom they were put to death in revenge of his son Rory, whom they had slain some time before.

Donough Mac Gillapatrick, Lord of Ossory, died.

Brian O'Reilly and Gilchreest [O'Reilly] were slain by the O'Rourkes.

THE AGE OF CHRIST, 1325.

The Age of Christ, one thousand three hundred twenty-five.

Donnell, the son of Brian O'Neill, Lord of Tyrone, died at Lough-Laeghaire[a].

Cu-Uladh, the son of Donnell, son of Brian O'Neill, a good materies of a Lord of Tyrone, was slain by the sons of Niall, the son of Brian, i. e. the sons of his father's brother.

christe Oge Mac Donnogh, with many others, were killed at once with him" [i. e. along with him], "in the Contrey of Tyrbryen, the seventh of the Kallends of September, after he had reigned King of Connaught six years and a half, against the wills of the Irish and English; after whose death Terlagh O'Connor succeeded in the kingdome of Connought."

[a] *Lough Laeghaire*, i. e. Leary's lake.—This lake is said to have taken its name from Leary

Giollacriost clereċ mac diarmatta ⁊ brian ó gaḋra décc.

Diarmait ó maoilbrenainn arḋtaoiseaċ cloinne Concoḃair do écc.

Maolseachlainn ó flannagáin taoiseaċ tuaithe Rátha do marbadh la macaiḃ diarmada uí flannagáin.

Diarmait ua Maoílḃrenainn (an taoiseċ dioġain), Manannán taoiseaċ Connaċt ina aimsir do écc.

Tomás ó coinderi oſganaċ na breifne deg.

Maidm do ṫabairt la cloinn toirrḋealbaiġ uí briain ar ċloinn briain ruaiḋ ⁊ brian mac Maṫġaṁna do ṁarbaḋ co ndruing oile imaille fris.

Raghnall ó huiginn ⁊ Niocol mac coṁarba Maoḋóg do écc.

Raġnailt ingín Anḋaiḋ uí Raġallaiġ bín donnchaḋa meg bradaiġ do écc.

Donnchaḋ mac cionaiṫ do ṁarḃaḋ in eacclais ṁég Mathġaṁna.

AOIS CRIOST, 1326.

Aois Criost, míle, trí chéd, fiche, aSé.

Luirint ó lactnain epsucc oilefinn décc, ⁊ Seón ó fíonnaċta do ṫoġa do ċum na hepsuccóide ceḋna iar sin.

Risdírd a burc, .i. an tiarla ruaḋ ticcírna ulaḋ ⁊ connaċt durmor, aon roġa gall Ereann uile do écc a ndírſḋ Saṁraiḋ.

the victorious, one of the heroes of the Red Branch in Ulster, in the first century. The name is now obsolete; but, as appears from several references to it, the lake was situated in the barony of Clogher, in the county of Tyrone.—See other references to it at the years 1431, 1436, 1500, and 1509.

[b] *Dermot O'Mulrenin.*—This is the same Dermot mentioned in the second last entry, and the transcriber writes dermad, "a mistake," before this entry.

[c] *Manannan.*—He was generally surnamed Mac Lir, i. e. the son of the sea, and said to have been a great navigator and merchant of the Tuatha De Danann colony, who made the Isle of Man his principal depot. In Cormac's Glossary (*voce* Manannan) he is described as a famous merchant of the Isle of Man, and the best navigator in the western world, and for that reason called the God of the sea by the Scots and Britons: "Inde Scoti Britonesque eum deum vocaverunt maris, eumque filium maris esse dixerunt, i. e. Mac Lir." It is added that the Isle of Man derived its name from him. There exists a tradition in the county of Londonderry, that the spirit of this celebrated navigator lives in an enchanted castle in the *tuns*, or waves of Magilligan, opposite Inishowen, and that his magical ship is seen there once every seventh year. O'Mulrenin is called the Manan-

Gilchreest Cleireach Mac Dermot and Brian O'Gara died.

Dermot O'Mulrenin, Head Chieftain of Clann-Conor, died.

Melaghlin O'Flanagan, Chief of Tuath-ratha [in Fermanagh], was slain by the sons of Dermot O'Flanagan.

Dermot O'Mulrenin[b] (the great chieftain), the Manannan[c] of the chiefs of Connaught in his time, died.

Thomas O'Connery, Deacon of Breifny, died.

A victory was gained by the sons of Turlough O'Brien, over the sons of Brian Roe O'Brien ; and Brian, the son of Mahon O'Brien, and many others, were slain.

Randal O'Higgin and Nicholas[d], son of the Coarb of St. Maidoc, died.

Raghnailt, daughter of Annadh O'Reilly, and wife of Donough Mac Brady, died.

Donough Mac Kenna[e] was slain in Mac Mahon's church.

THE AGE OF CHRIST, 1326.

The Age of Christ, one thousand three hundred twenty-six.

Laurence O'Laghtnan, Bishop of Elphin, died; and John O'Finnaghty[f] was elected his successor in the bishopric.

Richard Burke, i. e. the Red Earl, Lord of Ulster, and of the greater part of Connaught, the choicest[g] of all the English of Ireland, died at the close of Summer.

nan of the chieftains of Connaught, in consequence of his being an experienced sailor.

[d] *Nicholas*, i. e. Nicholas O'Farrelly, son of the coarb of St. Maidoc, or Mogue, of Drumlane, in the county of Cavan.

[e] *Mac Kenna.*—He was chief of the territory of Trough, anciently called Triocha ched an chladaigh, now the barony of Trough, in the north of the county of Monaghan, whence a branch of the same family removed to the parish of Maghera, in the county of Londonderry, in the middle of the seventeenth century, where the name is now very numerous.

[f] *John O'Finnaghty.*—In his Patent of restitution to the temporalities, dated 1st March, 1326, he is called John of Roscommon. He died in 1354, and was buried in the cathedral of Elphin. See Harris's Edition of Ware's Bishops, p. 631.

[g] *The choicest.*—This entry is rendered as follows by Mageoghegan in his translation of the Annals of Clonmacnoise:

"A. D. 1326. Richard Burke, Earle of Ulster and Lord of Connought, the choyce Englishman of all Ireland, this yeare died, a little before Lamas day."

Iomar mág ragnaill taoiseach muintire heólais do marbhadh la a braithribh.

Niocol ó hEdhin decc.

Toirrdhealbhach mac an chaoich do éc.

Toirrdhealbhach mag mathghamhna do écc.

An tres Eduard do rioghadh os Saxaibh. 25. Ianuarii.

Creach maighe hionais do denamh la hua Ruairc, ualgarg, airm in ro marbhadh gorraidh mág garraidh la cathal ua Ruairc.

Maidhm do thabhairt la Domhnall cairbreach mág carthaigh ar Mac tomais ⁊ ar ghallaibh mumhan du in ro marbait Ridereadha iomdha.

Amhlaoibh Mhag uidhir do écc.

AOIS CRIOST, 1327.

Aois Criost, míle, trí chéd, fiche, a Seacht.

Flaithbheartach mag uidhir tighearna fear manach, ⁊ Gormlaith ingean meic diarmata bean mághnasa mic domhnaill uí concobhair tánaisi connacht re head, bean choncobhair uí cheallaigh tighearna ó maine ara haithle, ⁊ bean fhearghail uí eaghra tighearna luighne iarsin, décc iar mbuaidh naithrighe enigh, ⁊ oirdearcais.

Maoilechloinn riabhach mac domhnaill mic taidhg uí choncobhair decc do galar breac.

Fearghal mac ualghairg uí Ruairc, Cuilén ua diomasaigh, ⁊ Sadb ingean meic aodhaccáin décc.

Cogadh mór eitir Righ Saxan ⁊ a bean, .i. ingean Righ frranc, ⁊ Rí Saxan do aithrioghadh las an mnaoi chétna, ⁊ a mac do ghabail righe is in mbliadhain

[h] *By his kinsmen*, la a braithribh.—"Was killed by his own brothers."—Mageoghegan, in *Ann. Clonmacnoise*.

[i] *Magh hionais*.—This was the name of a level district in the present barony of Clanawley, in the south of the county of Fermanagh. It is to be distinguished from Samh Inis Maighe (now ridiculously anglicised Inismacsaint), which is situated in the north-west of the same county.

[j] *Mac Thomas*.—It is stated in Harris's edition of Ware's Antiquities, p. 59, that a branch of the Desmond Fitzgeralds, seated in the county of Waterford, took the name of Mac Thomas.

[k] *After the victory of penance*, iar mbuaidh naithrighe.—This passage, the language of which is so oddly constructed by the Four Masters, is translated by Mageoghegan as follows, in his version of the Annals of Clonmacnoise:

"A. D. 1327. Gormphley, the daughter of Mac Dermodda, first married to Magnus mac Don-

Ivor Mac Rannall, Chief of Muintir-Eolais, was slain by his kinsmen[h].

Nicholas O'Heyne died.

Turlough Mac-an-Chaoich [O'Reilly] died.

Turlough Mac Mahon died.

Edward III. was made King of England on the 23rd of January.

O'Rourke, Ualgarg, plundered Magh-hionais[i], where Godfrey Mac Caffrey was slain by Cathal O'Rourke.

A victory was gained by Donnell Cairbreach Mac Carthy over Mac Thomas[j] and the English of Munster. Many knights were slain.

Auliffe Maguire died.

THE AGE OF CHRIST, 1327.

The Age of Christ, one thousand three hundred twenty-seven.

Flaherty Maguire, Lord of Fermanagh, and Gormlaith, the daughter of Mac Dermot, and wife of Manus, son of Donnell O'Conor, Tanist of Connaught, for some time afterwards wife of Conor O'Kelly, Lord of Hy-Many, and afterwards wife of Farrell O'Hara, Lord of Leyny, died, after the victory of penance[k], hospitality, and renown.

Melaghlin Reagh, son of Donnell, son of Teige O'Conor, died of *Galar breac.*

Farrell, son of Ualgarg O'Rourke, Cuilen O'Dempsey, and Sabia, daughter of Mac Egan, died.

A great war [broke out] between the King of England and his queen, the daughter of the King of France. The king had been dethroned by this woman, and her son had in the past year[l] assumed the government by her order, in

nell O'Connor, Tanist of Connought for a time, afterwards married to Connor O'Kelly, prince of Imaine, and lastly to Fferrall O'Hara, the best woman for liberality, manners, and hospitality of her sept, died, after good penance."

In the last year, is in mbliaḋain sſċmaṫa. The word sſċmaṫa is used by the best Irish writers to denote *past*, or *last past*. It is thus used by the Four Masters at the year 1582: "ó ṫús foġṁair na bliaḋna seaċmaṫa go mí meaḋoin foġṁair na bliaḋna sreaċnairce, i. e. from the beginning of the autumn of the past year to the month of mid-autumn of the present year."

In the Annals of Clonmacnoise, as translated by Mageoghegan, the dethroning of King Edward is entered under the year 1326, thus: "A. D. 1326. There arose great warrs between

seachmata inaghaiḋ a athar tria forcongra a maṫar, ⁊ a oirdneaḋ la comairle Shaxan.

Rí alban do tocht in erinn.

Cogaḋ eitir ṁuintir Ruairc ⁊ muintir Raġallaiġ, ⁊ cloch locha huachtair do lorcadh la cathal ua Ruairc.

Cairlén locha huachtair do ġabail la hua Ruairc, trisgair ar ḟiċit bó.

Giollacriost dall ṁag Raġnaill do ṁarbaḋ la Mac uí ṁaoil Mhiaḋaigh ina leabaiḋ féin.

Teiḋm galair bric ar ḟud ereann dia ro écsat ile.

AOIS CRIOST, 1328.

Aois Criost, míle, trí chéd, fiche a hocht.

Esscop na bréifne ó cridagan do éc.

Tomas ó mellaiġ espucc eanaiġ dúin décc isin Roiṁ.

Muirir ó gibelláin ardmaiġistir ereann i ndliġeaḋ nua ⁊ i sendlicċeaḋ, i ccanóin ⁊ i léx, fellsoṁ físeolaċ, saoí ḟirdána, cananaċ coraḋ i ttuaim dá gualann, i noilfinn, i nachaḋ conaire, i ccill alaiḋ, i neanaċ dúin, ⁊ i ccluain ferta, oiffiċél ⁊ breiṫeṁ coitċionn na hairdeasbuccoide, décc.

the King of England and his Queen, the French King's daughter, where at last the King was deposed of his Crown, and given [*recte* which was given] to his own son Edward, by the advice of the counsell of England."

Under the year 1327 the same chronicle notices his death in the following words:—"A. D. 1327. King Edward the Second was pressed to death by pressing a great Table on his belly, this year, with many other tortures, in the Castle of Berckley, and was entered in Glocester."

Edward III. was proclaimed King of England on the 25th of January, 1327, and crowned on the 1st of February following.

[m] *The King of Scotland*, i. e. Robert Bruce.—According to Grace's Annals of Ireland, Robert Bruce landed at Carrickfergus in the year 1328, and sent word to the Justiciary and the Council that he came to make peace between Ireland and Scotland, and that he would meet them at Green Castle, but that, the latter failing to come to the meeting, he returned to Scotland.

[n] *The castle of Lough Oughter.*—This is more usually called *Cloch Locha Uachtair*, i. e. the stone, or rock, of Lough Oughter. It is a round castle of great strength in the lake of Lough Oughter, not far from Kilmore, in the county of Cavan.—See other references to it at the years 1369 and 1370.

[o] *Galar Breac*, literally the speckled disease. This passage is thus rendered by Mageoghegan, in his translation of the Annals of Clonmacnoise:

opposition to his father. He was crowned by the council [i. e. the parliament] of England.

The King of Scotland[m] came to Ireland.

A war broke out between the O'Rourkes and O'Reillys ; and the castle of Lough Oughter[n] was taken by Cathal O'Rourke.

The castle of Lough Oughter was taken by O'Rourke by cunning, for twenty cows.

Gilchreest Dall Mac Rannall was slain in his own bed by the son of O'Mulvey.

The Galar Breac[o] raged throughout Ireland, of which many died.

THE AGE OF CHRIST, 1328.

The Age of Christ, one thousand three hundred twenty-eight.

The Bishop of Breifny [Kilmore], O'Cridagain, died.

Thomas O'Meallaigh, Bishop of Annadown, died at Rome.

Maurice O'Gibellan[p], Chief Professor of the New Law, the Old Law, and the Canon Law, a truly profound philosopher, a learned poet, and a canon chorister of Tuam, Elphin, and Achad-Chonaire[q], Killala, Annadown, and Clonfert, the official and the general Brehon [i. e. Judge] of the archbishopric, died.

"A. D. 1327. There reigned a disease called the pied pox, or little pox, in Ireland in general, and took away persons both great and small." Throughout the province of Connaught, ꞅalaꞃ bꞃeac means the small-pox ; but, in the south of Ireland, where bolꞅaċ is used to denote the small-pox, ꞅalaꞃ bꞃeac is used to denote the spotted fever. It is highly probable, however, that the Four Masters intended the term to denote the small-pox, as their cotemporary Mageoghegan translates it, "pied pox, or little pox."—See Dublin P. Journal, March 30, 1833, vol. i. p. 314.

[p] *Maurice O'Gibellan.*—This passage is thus rendered by Mageoghegan, in his translation of the Annals of Clonmacnoise :

"A. D. 1328. Morishe O'Gibelan, master of art, one exceeding well learned in the old and new laws, Civille and Canon, a cunning and skillful philosopher, an excellent poet in Irish, an elegant and exact speaker of the speech which in Irish is called Ogham, and, in some [sum], one that was well seen in many other good sciences. He was a Canon and Singer at Twayme, Olfyn, Aghaconary, Killalye, Enaghe Downe, and Clonfert."

[q] *Achad-Chonaire*, now anglicised Achonry, a small village in the barony of Leyny, county of Sligo, situated about sixteen miles to the south-west of Sligo. It was formerly an episcopal see, but is at present united to Killala.

Giolla na naingel ó taichligh airchinnech Daimhinnsi décc.

Maoilsechloinn ó faighilligh tigherna muintire maoilmordha do lot do ghallaibh na midhe, a ghabhail doibh iarsin go bfuairsiot braighde air, a écc dia ghonaibh ina tigh féin iar na haithle.

Giolla Adamhnain ó firghil comharba Adamhnain décc.

Toirneach ⁊ teintech adhbal is in samhradh go ro milleadh mes, ⁊ torrtha ereann go diomhór, ⁊ gur fásatar arbanna fionna fása.

Tedhom galair go coitcenn fechnóin ereann (da ngoirthi Slaotán), ⁊ a bheith tri laithe, no a ceathair ar gach aon da ngabhadh gur bo tanaisi báis doibh é.

Uilliam burc, .i. an tiarla donn mac Sir Seon (.i. iarla) mac an iarla ruaidh do thocht in erinn.

Donnchadh ruadh ó gadhra ⁊ cúiccer da chineadh imaille fris do marbhadh.

Concobhar mac branáin adhbar taoisigh corcachlainn do marbhadh la muintir na hangaile.

Sluaicceadh la Uater a búrc i cconnachtaibh gur hairceadh lais morán daor ghrádha toirrdhealbhaigh uí concobhair righ Connacht.

Sir Seon mac fheorais iarla Lughmhaigh, aon barún ba fhearr féile, bhioghmaire, ⁊ ba fherr oinech do ghallaibh Ereann, do marbhadh i feill da muintir féin .i. do gallaibh oirghiall, ⁊ sochaide imaille fris do ghallaibh ⁊ do gaoidhelaibh. Ba dibh-

[r] *Gilla-na-nangel O'Taichligh.*—The transactions of this year are incorrectly placed under 1325, in the Dublin copy of the Annals of Ulster. This entry reads as follows: Gilla na naingel o taichligh airchinnech Daimhinnsi mortuus est, i. e. Gilla-na-n-angel O'Taichligh, Erenagh of Devenish, *mortuus est.*

[s] *Great thunder and lightning.*—This passage is thus rendered by Mageoghegan, in his translation of the Annals of Clonmacnoise: "There was great thunder and lightning this year, that it destroyed great part of the corns of the kingdom, that they grew *whitish* by reason they lost their substance."

[t] *Slaedan*, a cough, or influenza. This passage is thus rendered by Mageoghegan in his translation of the Annals of Clonmacnoise: "There was a general disease throughout all Ireland called the Murre, which continued for the space of three or four days, and brought divers even to the point of death."

[u] *An-t-Iarla Donn*, i. e. the Brown Earl. He was so called from the colour of his hair. He is called "the Dun Earl" by Mageoghegan in his translation of the Annals of Clonmacnoise, in which the whole passage is rendered thus:

"A. D. 1328. The Earle of Ulster, called the Dunn Earle, grandchild to the Read Earle, called William Burke, Sir John Burke's sonn, came to Ireland."

[w] *Sir John Mac Feorais.*—This passage is thus given in the Annals of Clonmacnoise, as translated by Mageoghegan:

"Sir John Bermingham, Earl of Louth, the best Earl for worthiness, bounty, prowes, and vallour of his hands, was treacherously killed

Gilla-na-nangel O'Taichligh[r], Archdeacon of Innis [*recte* Devenish], died.

Melaghlin O'Reilly, Lord of Muintir-Maelmora, was wounded by the English of Meath, who afterwards took him prisoner, and received hostages for his ransom. He afterwards died of his wounds in his own house.

Gilla-Adamnan O'Firghil [O'Freel], Coarb of St. Adamnan [at Raphoe], died.

Great thunder and lightning[s] occurred in the summer [of this year], by which the fruits and crops of Ireland were very much injured, and the corn grew whitish and unprofitable.

A disease, called Slaedán[t], raged universally throughout Ireland, which afflicted, for three or four days successively, every person who took it. It was second [in pain] only to the agony of death.

William Burke, i. e. an-t-Iarla Donn[u], the son of Sir John (i. e. Earl), the son of the Red Earl, came to Ireland.

Donough Roe O'Gara and five of his tribe were killed.

Conor Mac Branan, heir to the chieftainship of Corcachlann, was slain by the people of Annaly.

An army was led by Walter Burke into Connaught. Many of the retainers of Turlough O'Conor, King of Connaught, were plundered by him,

Sir John Mac Feorais[w] [Birmingham], Earl of Louth[x], the most vigorous, puissant, and hospitable of the English of Ireland, was treacherously slain by his own people, namely, by the English of Oriel. With him were also slain

by his people, the English of Uriel, and" [*recte* who] "also killed at once with him, many good and worthy English and Irishmen: Mulronie Mac Kervel, chief Musician of the Kingdome, and his brother Gillekeigh, were killed in that company, of whom it's reported that no man in any age ever heard, or shall hereafter hear, a better Timpanist." The original Irish of the part of this passage relating to the minstrel is given as follows in the Dublin copy of the Annals of Ulster, in which it is entered under the year 1325: "In caeċ mac Cerḃaill .i. Maelruanaiġ, aen raġa timpánaċ Erenn 7 Alban, 7 in domain uile 7 ni derb-ṫar a leiṫeid do ṫeaċt riaṁ o ṫuis domain ris in eladain sin a marbaḋ fein 7 a derb-raṫair maiṫ eile doiḃ ar in laṫair cedna."

[x] *Earl of Louth.*—Pembridge and Grace state that this squabble took place between the Anglo-Irish families of Uriel at Balebragan, now Bragganstown, in the county of Louth. They give a far better account of the results of the conflict than the Irish annals; and it is curious to remark that, while the Irish annalists record no name except that of the Earl of Louth and Mac Carroll, "as great a minstrel as the world ever heard," the English chroniclers, who regarded the minstrel as a mere harper, or

sidhe an caoċ ó cerbaill, .i. Maolruanaiḋ, aon roġa tiompanaċ ereann, ⁊ alban eriḋe ina aimsir.

Brian mac Tomaltaigh meic donnchaiḋ do marḃaḋ do ḃrian mac taiḋg meic donnchaiḋ.

Morsluaiġeaḋ la hiarla ulaḋ, ⁊ la Toirrḋealḃaċ ua cconċoḃair (Ri Connaċt), ⁊ la Muircertaċ ua mbriain Ri muṁan, in aghaiḋ briain báin uí briain. Maiḋm do ṫaḃairt la brian mban ó mbriain forrasoṁ annsin. Concobar ua briain deġadbar ríġ ereann ar cruṫ, ar céill, ar einеċ, ⁊ oirdearcus do ṁarḃaḋ don dul sin amaille re ceiṫre ficit do deghdaoinibh ⁊ do daorsccarsluagh do ṫuitim ina ḟochair.

Tadcc mac toirrḋelḃaiġ uí concoḃair do ṁarḃaḋ la diarmait ua ngaḋra.

Comḋal ċoinne im áth ċinn locha teċet, etir Uáter mac uilliam burc. Gillbert mac goisdealḃaiġ don dara leiṫ, ⁊ maolruanaiḋ mac diarmata, ⁊ Tomaltaċ a ṁac, ⁊ Tomaltaċ mac donnchaiḋ go maiṫiḃ cloinne Maoilruanaiḋ. Maiḋm do ḃriseaḋ re mac ndiarmata for Uáter ⁊ for Gillbert cona muintir.

Donnchaḋ gallda mac doṁnaill uí ċoncoḃair do marḃaḋ la hAoḋ mac taidg mic maoilechlainn mic maghnasa.

Matha riaḃaċ mac gaffraiḋ do ṁarḃaḋ do ṁuintir gearadáin.

Ioṁar ṁág Raghnaill toísseaċ muintire heolais do marḃaḋ la cloind giollacriost ṁeg Raghnaill.

Duiḃessa ingen uí ḟergail ben meic Murchada an tslebe do écc.

An caoch mac cerḃaill diar ḃainm Maolruanaiḋ, aon rogha ṫiompanaċ ereann ina aimsir do marḃaḋ.

Edaoin ingen még Mathgamna ben Még uiḋir do écc.

Duiḃeasa ingen uí Eliġe ben Doṁnaill mic taiḋg uí ċoncoḃair do écc.

give only a long list of the distinguished Anglo-Irish gentlemen who fell in the conflict.

[y] *Minstrel.*—Tiompánaċ is explained by O'Brien, a harper or minstrel.

[z] *Conor O'Brien.*—This part of the passage is thus given in the Annals of Clonmacnoise, as translated by Mageoghegan:

"Connor O'Brien was killed, who was a young man of great expectation, bounty, comeliness of personage, and sufficient to govern a monarchy, and with him 80 persons were killed."

[a] *A meeting.*—This passage is thus rendered by Mageoghegan in his translation of the Annals of Clonmacnoise: "There was a general meeting at a place called Athkynlogha Techye between Walter Mac William Burke, Gilbert Mac Cossdelye, of the one side, and Mulronie Mac Dermodda, Tomaltagh, his son, Donnell

many others of the English and Irish, amongst whom was the Blind O'Carroll [*recte* Mac Carroll], i. e. Mulrony, Chief Minstrel[y] of Ireland and Scotland in his time.

Brian, the son of Tomaltagh Mac Donough, was slain by Brian, the son of Teige Mac Donough.

A great army [was led] by the Earl of Ulster, Turlough O'Conor, King of Connaught, and Murtough O'Brien, King of Munster, against Brian Bane O'Brien; but they were defeated by Brian Bane. Conor O'Brien[z], a good materies for a King of Ireland, by reason of his personal shape, wisdom, hospitality, and renown, was slain on this occasion, as were also eighty persons, including chieftains and plebeians.

Teige, son of Turlough O'Conor, was slain by Dermot O'Gara.

A meeting[a] for a conference took place at Ath-chinn-Locha Techet[b] between Walter, son of William Burke, and Gilbert Mac Costello, on the one side; and Mulrony Mac Dermot, Tomaltagh, his son, Tomaltagh Mac Donough, and the chiefs of Clann-Mulrony, on the other: and Walter, Gilbert, and their people, were defeated by Mac Dermot.

Donough Gallda, the son of Donnell O'Conor, was slain by Hugh, the son of Teige, son of Melaghlin, son of Manus [O'Conor].

Matthew Reagh Mac Caffrey was slain by Muintir Gearan[c].

Ivor Mac Rannall, Chief of Muintir-Eolais, was slain by the sons of Gilchreest Mac Rannall.

Duvesa, daughter of O'Farrell, and wife of Mac Murrough of the Mountain, died.

The Blind Mac Carroll[d], whose name was Mulrony, the chief of the minstrels of Ireland in his time, was slain.

Edwina, daughter of Mac Mahon, and wife of Maguire, died.

Duvesa, the daughter of O'Healy, and wife of Donnell, the son of Teige O'Conor, died.

Mac Donnough, and Clann Mulroney, or that family, of the other side: whereupon some distastful words that passed between them, from words they fell to blows of armes; in the end Mac William Burke was overthrown."

[b] *Ath-chinn-Locha Techet*, i. e. the ford at the head of Lough Techet. This lake is now called Lough Gara.

[c] *Muintir Gearan.*—A territory and tribe in the north-east of the county of Longford, lying along Lough Gowna, on the west side.

[d] *The Blind Mac Carroll.*—This is a repetition.

Sluaiġeaḋ oile la Muirċſrtaċ ó mbriain, ⁊ la cloinn cuiléin dionnsaiġiḋ ḃriain uí ḃriáin doridiri dia ro sraoineaḋ for muirċſrtaċ, ⁊ día ro marḃaḋ concoḃar ó briain, ⁊ doṁnall na ndoṁnall, ⁊ Maccon mac conmara go soch-aidiḃ oile.

Maiḋm mór do tabairt lá Mág eochagáin ar ġallaiḃ dú in ro marḃaḋ cúig céd décc ar fichit céd gall im ḋalatúnachaiḃ, ⁊ im ṁac an Ridere Uallaiġ.

Aṁlaoiḃ mag findbairr do marḃaḋ la Cathal ua Ruairc.

AOIS CRIOST, 1329.

Aois Criost, mile trí chéd fiche, aNaoí.

Augustin abb lſsa gaḃail for loch Eirne décc.

Caṫal mac doṁnaill uí ruairc dſgaḋḃar ticcſrna na breifne do marḃaḋ la cloinn tSeoin uí ḟſrgail, ⁊ do ġallaiḃ miḋe tre feill, ⁊ daoine oile imaille ris i tigh Riocaird diúid i Mainistir ḟoḃair.

Muirċſrtaċ mac doṁnaill uí Concoḃair ticcſrna cairpre, ⁊ dſghaḋḃar righ Connacht décc.

Caṫal mac Aoḋa mic Eoġain uí ċoncoḃair do ḋíochur ar eiccin as na sſḋaiḃ ⁊ a tir maine tre forcongra Uater a búrc ar Shíol cceallaiġ, ⁊ ar uiḃ maine ar ċſna.

Coccaḋ mór etir Toirrdealḃaċ ó cconcoḃair ⁊ clann maolruanaiḋ gur milleaḋ morán eattorra diḃlionaiḃ.

[a] *Three thousand five hundred.*—This number is decidedly an error of transcription, for it is incredible that the petty chief Mageoghegan, with his few followers, could have killed so great a number of their enemies,—a number greater than all the inhabitants of his territory of Kinel Fiachach. According to Pembridge and Grace, the number of the English common soldiers slain on this occasion was about 140, besides several distinguished knights; and nothing is more evident than that the number of common soldiers recorded by the original annalist was 135, i. e. cúig déc ar ḟicit ar ċed gall, and that the introduction of the word céd twice into the text is a modern falsification. This falsification, however, may not have been committed by the Four Masters; but it looks strange that the passage is not to be found in the Dublin copy of the Annals of Ulster, in the Annals of Clonmacnoise, as translated by Mageoghegan, in which there is no apparent chasm at this year, in the Annals of Kilronan, or in the Annals of Connaught. The Abbe Mageoghegan, in describing this battle, writes as if the 140 com-

Another army was led by Murtough O'Brien and the Clann-Cuilein [the Mac Namaras] against Brian; but Murtough was defeated, and Conor O'Brien, Donnell of the Donnells, the son of Cumara Mac Namara, with many others, were slain.

The English sustained a great defeat from Mageoghegan, three thousand five hundred[e] of them being slain in the contest, together with some of the Daltons, and the son of the Proud Knight.

Auliffe Mac Finnvar was slain by Cathal O'Rourke.

THE AGE OF CHRIST, 1329.

The Age of Christ, one thousand three hundred twenty-nine.

Augustine, Abbot of Lisgabhail[f] on Lough Erne, died.

Cathal, the son of Donnell O'Rourke, a good materies of an Earl of Breifny, and others, were treacherously slain by the sons of John O'Farrell, and the English of Meath, in the house of Richard Tuite, at the monastery of Fore[g].

Murtough, the son of Donnell O'Conor, Lord of Carbury, and a good materies of a King of Connaught, died.

Cathal, the son of Hugh, son of Owen O'Conor, was forcibly expelled from the Faes and from Tir-Many by order[h] of Walter Bourke, to the O'Kellys, and the other tribes of Hy-Many.

A great war [broke out] between Turlough O'Conor and the Clann-Mulrony, and much property was destroyed between them.

mon soldiers were knights or commanders (see his *Histoire D'Irlande*, tom. ii. p. 104), and quotes Pembridge, who gives the account very differently.—See Ware's Annals, *ad ann.* 1329; and Grace's Annals, edited for the Irish Archæological Society by the Rev. Richard Butler, p. 115.

[f] *Lisgabhail*, lιoꞅ ꞡaḃaιl, i. e. the fort of the fork, now anglicised Lisgole or Lisgool. The place is situated on the west bank of Lough Erne, a short distance southwards of Enniskillen, in the barony of Clanawley and county of Fermanagh. The monastery of this place existed to a late period.

[g] *Fore*, ꞅaḃaꞃ.—See note [s] under the year 1176, p. 22. The place now belongs to the Marquis of Westmeath, not to the Tuites.

[h] *By order*, i. e. Walter Burke issued an order to the O'Kellys to banish Cathal O'Conor from their territory, which order was executed. The passage is thus rendered by Mageoghegan in his translation of the Annals of Clonmacnoise: "A. D. 1329. Walter mac William Burck, called Mac William, procured the banishment of Cahall mac Hugh mac Owen O'Connor out of the Fewes and the Territory of Many of the O'Kellys."

Creaċ do denaṁ la tomaltaċ mac diarmata ar diarmait ó bflannaccáin taoiseaċ cloinne caṫail.

Aine inġean Fſrġail uí Raiġilliġ bſn Tomaltaiġ meic diarmata décc.

Taḋg mac toirrḋealbaiġ mic Maṫġaṁna uí ċoncobair do ṁarbaḋ la hua ngáḋra ⁊ la lucht Airtigh.

Sith do denoṁ do ṁac uilliam búrc ⁊ diarla ulaḋ re Mac tomáis.

Dabac dond mac uilliam Ridire uasal morconaiġ do écc.

Donnchaḋ mac giollapatraicc do marbaḋ la hiarla ulaḋ.

Maoilíosa donn mac Aodhagain ardollaṁ connacht do écc.

Guirt gan buain go hiar ffeil Michil ar ḟud ereann lar an ffleachaḋ.

AOIS CRIOST, 1330.

Aois Criost, míle trí chéd tríochatt.

Maoílíosa ó coinel comarba droma cliaḃ do écc.

Benidicht o flannaccáin Prióir cille moire na Sionna décc.

Maġnas mac Aoḋa breifniġ uí concoḃair do marḃaḋ la caṫal mac aoḋa mic Eoġain ui concoḃair i bfſronn na darach, ⁊ Siomann mac in ḟailgiġ do ṁarḃadh ina ḟarraiḋ.

Giollaíssu ruaḋ ó raiġilliġ ticcſrna muintire maoilmorḋa ⁊ na breifne uile re haimsir nimċéin décc ina Shſndattaiḋ iar mbreiṫ buaḋa ó ḋoṁan ⁊ ó ḋſṁan ⁊ a aḋnacal i mainistir in cabain i naibíd na mbráṫar mionúr, ⁊ ba hſiḋe céd fundúir na mainistre reṁraite.

Maoilechlainn mac carmaic bruġaiḋ céḋach conaich do écc.

Sluaiġeaḋ la hualġarcc ua ruairc go fiodh an atha. Goill an ḃaile déirġe dó iarsin. Maiḋm do ṫaḃairt for muintir uí ruairc, ⁊ Art ó ruairc adbar airdticcſrna breifne do marḃaḋ do ġallaiḃ, ⁊ soċaiḋe imaille fris im Ruaiḋri mac Saṁradhain.

Amas longpuirt do ṫaḃairt do Toirrdealḃaċ ó cconcoḃair Rí Connaċt

[i] *Fearonn-na-darach*, i. e. land of the oak. The name is now obsolete.

[k] *Mac-in-Fhailghe*, was the name of a Welsh tribe, but their location has not been determined. It is probably the name now anglicised Mac Nally, or Mac Anally.—See note under the year 1316.

[l] *Brughaidh Cedach*, a farmer who had one hundred of each kind of cattle.

[m] *Fiodh-an-atha*, i. e. the wood of the ford,

A depredation was committed by Tomaltagh Mac Dermot upon Dermot O'Flanagan, Chief of Clann-Cathail.

Aine, daughter of Farrell O'Reilly, and wife of Tomaltagh Mac Dermot, died.

Teige, the son of Turlough, son of Mahon O'Conor, was slain by O'Gara and the people of Airteach.

Mac William Burke and the Earl of Ulster made peace with Mac Thomas.

Daboc Donn Mac William [Burke], a noble and wealthy knight, died.

Donough Mac Gillapatrick was slain by the Earl of Ulster.

Maelisa Donn Mac Egan, Chief Ollav of Connaught, died.

The [corn] fields remained unreaped throughout Ireland until after Michaelmas, in consequence of wet weather.

THE AGE OF CHRIST, 1330.

The Age of Christ, one thousand three hundred thirty.

Maelisa O'Coinel, Coarb of Drumcliff, died.

Benedict O'Flanagan, Prior of Kilmore-na-Sinna, died.

Manus, the son of Hugh Breifneach O'Conor, was slain at Fearonn na-darach[i] by Cathal, the son of Hugh, son of Owen O'Conor; and Simon Mac-in-Fhailghe[k] was slain with him.

Gilla-Isa Roe O'Reilly, Lord of Muintir-Maelmora, and of the entire territory of Breifny for a long time previously, died at an advanced age, victorious over the world and the devil. He was interred in the Abbey of the Friars Minor in Cavan, of which he himself was the original founder.

Melaghlin Mac Carmaic, a wealthy Brughaidh Cedach[l], died.

An army was led by Ualgarg O'Rourke to Fiodh-an-atha[m], whereupon the English of that town rose up against him. O'Rourke's people were defeated; and Art O'Rourke, a materies of a chief lord of Breifny, Rory Magauran, and many others, were slain by the English.

An attack was made by Turlough O'Conor, King of Connaught, upon the

now anglicised Finae, a fair town in the barony of Half Fowre, and county of Westmeath. It is a small but neat village on a stream which unites the two lakes of Loċ Sileann and Loċ Eiṫne. Over this stream there is a bridge, which separates the counties of Westmeath and Cavan.

for uáter mac uilliam búrc i Leccmoiġ i moiġ luircc, ⁊ a ruaccaḋ dó airriḋe go cairṫe liacc fatta. Gillbert mac goisdelbaiġ (tigerna plebe luġa mun am sin) do ṫecht go líon a ṁuintire do ċuidiuccaḋ le mac uilliam. Tomaltaċ mac donnchaiḋ cona muintir do toċt do ċommoraḋ meic uilliam beór iar niompóḋ for ua cconcobair doiḃ. Na sluaiġ sin diblionaiḃ dionnsaiġiḋ uí ċoncobair. Ro cuirset iomairecc etorra let for leiṫ go rangatar áth disirt nuadan. Donnchaḋ mac domnaill mic maṫgaṁna, mac giolla comdáin, ⁊ uathaḋ do muintir uí concobair do ṁarbaḋ im an áth. Ua concobair go maiṫiḃ a muintire do dol da naiṁdeóin uaṫa go ráinicc gus na tuaṫaiḃ. Longport do ġabail do mac uilliam i ccill lomatt i ccoṁfoċraiḃ dua cconcobair. Sloiġeaḋ Connaċt eitir ġallaiḃ ⁊ ġaoiḋelaiḃ (don ṁéd ro gaḃ a pairt diob) do tecclamadh la mac uilliam do gabail riġe connaċt dó buḋéin iar sin, ⁊ a mbeiṫ ullaṁ aicce do ċum uí ċoncobair daithrioghadh. Iar na ḟios sin do Mhac diarmata iompóḋ for Mhac uilliam dó, ⁊ páirt uí concobair do ġabail ionnus gur cenglattar síṫ connail ċairdeṁail etorra dibhlionaiḃ.

Maiḋm mór do ṫabairt do ċoncobar mac Taidg mic briain mic aindriasa mic briain luiġniġ for ḋartraiġiḃ, ⁊ Soċaiḋe díoḃ do marbaḋ lais.

Toirrḋealbaċ ua concobair do dul uaṫaḋ deghdaoine do laṫair uilliam burc, .i. an tiarla donn diarraiḋ a chonganta in aghaiḋ ṁeic uilliam.

Brian mac giollacriost meg Raghnaill do ṁarbaḋ la tadhg mag Raġnaill.

[n] *Leagmhagh*, now Legvoy, a townland in the parish of Killukin, not far from Carrick-on-Shannon, in the barony of Boyle, and county of Roscommon.

[o] *Cairthe-liag-fada*, now probably the townland of Cnoc a ċarṫa, in the parish of Killukin, in the county of Roscommon. The place is so called from a large carṫa, or pillar stone, which stands on the top of the hill, and said to have been thrown by a giant from a distant locality.

[p] *Ath-Disirt-Nuadhan*, i. e. the ford of Disert Nuadhan.—This name is written aṫ disirt nuaḋat in the Dublin copy of the Annals of Ulster, and now corruptly called in Irish tirs Nuaḋáin, and strangely anglicised Eastersnow, which is the name of a parish in the barony of Boyle and county of Roscommon. This parish was dedicated to a Saint Nuadhan, of whom no account is found in the Irish Calendars, unless he be the Nuadha Anchorite set down in the Irish calendar of the O'Clerys at 3rd of October. His holy well, called tobar nuaḋain, is still in existence, but at present very seldom resorted to by pilgrims. There is a tradition in the country that there was a town here, but no trace of it now remains. The following extract from an Inquisition taken in the reign of Elizabeth seems to corroborate this tradition:

"Quod est quoddam forum sive mercatum in die Sabbatis qualibet septimana quondo non est guerra in patria, juxta templum Sancti Wogani vulgarite Temple-Issetnowne in baroniâ de Moylurg."

In another part of this Inquisition it is angli-

camp of Walter, the son of William Burke, at Leagmagh[n], in Moylurg, and forced him to retreat from thence to Cairthe-liag-fada[o]. Gilbert Mac Costello (at that time Lord of Slieve-Lugha) came with all his forces to aid Mac William; and Tomaltagh Mac Donough, with his people, having turned against O'Conor, came also to Mac William's assistance. These combined forces attacked O'Conor, and an engagement took place between both parties at Ath-Disirt-Nuadan[p], where Donough, son of Donnell Mac Mahon, Mac Gillacowan, and a few of O'Conor's people, were slain. Around the ford O'Conor and the chiefs of his people effected a retreat into the Tuathas by force; and Mac William (then) pitched his camp at Killomad[q], near O'Conor. The forces of Connaught, both English and Irish (i. e. all those who sided with him), were assembled by Mac William, in order to obtain the kingdom of Connaught for himself, and he had them in readiness to depose O'Conor. When Mac Dermot received intelligence of this, he turned against Mac William, and took part with O'Conor ; and a kindly and amicable peace was concluded[r] between both.

A great defeat was given by Conor, son of Teige, son of Brian, son of Andreas, son of Brian Luighneach [O'Conor], to the people of Dartry[s], and many of them were killed by him.

Turlough O'Conor, attended by a few distinguished persons, went to William Burke, i. e. the Dun Earl, to request his assistance against Mac William.

Brian, the son of Gilchreest Mac Rannall, was slain by Teige Mac Rannall.

cised Issertnowne. The Irish word Disert, which signifies a desert, wilderness, and sometimes a hermit's retreat, has been variously anglicised Ister, Ester, Easter, Tristle, Desert, and Dysart.

[q] *Killumod*, a parish in the barony of Boyle and county of Roscommon.

[r] *Peace was concluded.*—This passage is rendered by Mageoghegan as follows in his translation of the Annals of Clonmacnoise:

"A. D. 1330. Terlagh O'Connor, King of Connought, gave an assault to Walter Mac William Burke, at a place called Leakmoye, in Moylorg, and from thence chased him to Carhalyagefad. Gilbert Mac Cosdeally, with a great company, came to assist Mac William; and also Tomaltagh Mac Dermod came to relieve him too, and being mett and joined together, retrayted upon O'Connor to Athdisert Nwan, and there, about that forde, killed a few of his people, with Donnough mac Donnell mac Mahone, and the son of Gillecowgan with others that for prolixity's [*recte* brevity's] sake I omitt here to name, and so O'Connor escaped vallourously and came to the Twathies, whom Mac William followed, and encamped at Kill-lomatt in his presence; whereupon Mac William assembled all the forces of the English and Irish of Connought, with intent to take the kingdom and name of King of Connought to himself. Mac Dermott and O'Connor came to a friendly agreement, and peace was concluded between them."

[s] *Dartry*, i. e. Dartry Mac-Clancy, now the

Aedh ⁊ diarmait dá ṁac Murchaidh uí fferghail do ṁarbadh la haedh ó fferghail.

Pétrus mac comarba Maedóige do ṁarbadh la gallaib cenannsa.

AOIS CRIOST, 1331.

Aois Criost, míle, trí céd, triochat, a haon.

Coṁarba Caillín, .i. giolla na naoṁ mac cele do écc i mainistir Maothla.

Maolruanaidh mac diarmata ticcerna maiġe luircc dfaccbail a tiġernais, ⁊ aibíd ṁanaiġ do gabail dó i mainistir na búille, ⁊ tomaltach mac diarmata (a mac) do ġabáil ticcernais maiġe luircc an. 7. la Mai.

Ferghal mac maoileachlainn carraiġ meic diarmata do ṁarbadh la tadhg mac caṫail mic domhnaill uí concobair.

Sloicceadh la Uater mac uilliam burc i maigh luircc. An tír uile dionnradh dó acht cealla namá, uair tucc comairce ⁊ cadhas doibhside. Tomaltach mac diarmata cona ṁuintir dia nionnraighidh. Goill do ṫabairt amais fair ar a haithle gur marbsat foirenn dia ṁuintir. Ossadh do ḋenaṁ doi re roile ⁊ uáter dfagbail na tíre.

Maoilir ṁág eochagáin décc.

Murchadh mag Mathġaṁna do ṁarbadh la Seaan mag Mathġaṁna, ⁊ la gallaib machaire airġiall.

Tómás mac conċairrge uí ḟloinn do écc.

barony of Rossclogher, in the north of the county of Leitrim.

[t] *Caillin.*—He was the patron saint of Fenagh, in the county of Leitrim.

[u] *Maethail*, now *Mohill*, a village in a barony of the same name in the county of Leitrim. St. Manchan erected a monastery here in the year 652. See Colgan's *Acta Sanctorum*, p. 332, and Ussher's *Primordia*, p. 989. There are no remains of the monastery at present, and its site is occupied by the parish church of Mohill.

[v] *Mulrony Mac Dermot.*—This passage is given as follows by Mageoghegan in his version of the Annals of Clonmacnoise:

"A. D. 1331. Mulronie Mac Dermoda, prince of the territorie of Moylorg, forsook his government and principallity, and entered into religion, in the order of Gray Monks, in the abbey of Boylle, and within a short while after died, after whose death his sonn Tomaltagh, the 6th of May, succeeded him in his place."

[w] *An army was led.*—This passage is somewhat better given in Mageoghegan's translation of the Annals of Clonmacnoise, as follows:

"A. D. 1331. Walter Burke (called Mac William), with a great army repaired to Moylorge,

Hugh and Dermot, two sons of Murrough O'Farrell, were slain by Hugh O'Farrell.

Petrus, son of the Coarb of St. Maidoc, was slain by the English of Kells.

THE AGE OF CHRIST, 1331.

The Age of Christ, one thousand three hundred thirty-one.

The Coarb of [St.] Caillin[t], Gilla-na-naev Mac Cele, died in the monastery of Maethail[u].

Mulrony Mac Dermot[v], Lord of Moylurg, resigned his lordship, and assumed the habit of a monk in the abbey of Boyle; and Tomaltagh Mac Dermot, his son, assumed the lordship of Moylurg on the 7th of May.

Farrell, son of Melaghlin Carragh Mac Dermot, was slain by Teige, son of Cathal, son of Donnell O'Conor.

An army was led[w] by Walter Mac William Burke into Moylurg, and he plundered all the country, excepting only the churches, to which he gave protection and respect. Tomaltagh, with his people, opposed them, but the English attacked Tomaltagh, and killed some of his people. They [afterwards] made peace with each other, and Walter left the country.

Meyler Mageoghegan died.

Murrough Mac Mahon was slain by John Mac Mahon and the English of Machaire Oirghiall[x].

Thomas, the son of Cuchairrge O'Flynn, died.

where he burnt, preyed, and destroyed all places in that contrey, save only churches and church-lands, which he reverenced and had in great respect. But Tomaltagh Mac Dermot cou'd not well brook that Mac William should be suffered to enjoye any rest in that contrey, and therefore they suddainly betooke themselves to their arms, which they then held to be their best and readiest friends in time of greatest need, and gave them the onsett, but Mac William and his people, taking their hearts anew, gave a fresh encounter to Tomaltagh, chased him and his people, and killed divers of them, which Tomaltagh did not leave unrevenged, for he could not digestt that so many of his people were killed, and that they shou'd not escape without rendering him an accompt of so many heads of theirs, too, for entring so boldlie into his territory."

[x] *Machaire-Oriel*, Ṁaċaıpe Oıpġıall, i. e. the plain of Oriel. This was one of the ancient names of the level part of the county of Louth. It was also called maġ muıpṫéıṁne and Conaılle muıpṫeıṁne.

AOIS CRIOST, 1332.

Aois Criost, mile, trí céd, triocha, a dó.

Uater mac Sir uilliam búrc do gaḃail las an iarla ndonn, ⁊ a breiṫ lais iaram co caislén nua innsi heoġain, a écc do ġorta ar a haithle hi bprisún an ċaisléin reṁraite.

Maiḋm ḃfirne an ṁíl for ṫomaltach mac ndiarmata, ⁊ for ṁac uilliam re mac an iarla, ⁊ re tomaltaċ mac donnchaiḋ, ⁊ soċaiḋe dá ṁuintir do marbhadh.

Uilliam gallda mac Muirċertaiġ moir még eochagain, ticcerna ceneoil ḟiachach do écc.

AOIS CRIOST, 1333.

Aois Criost, mile, trí céd, trioċa, atrí.

Florent mac an oglaich airchideochain chille hoiriḋ do écc.

Uilliam búrc iarla ulaḋ do ṁarḃaḋ la gallaiḃ ulaḋ. Na goill do roiġne an gníoṁ sin do ḃasucchaḋ go heccsaṁail la muintir righ Saxan. Drong do crochaḋ, drong do crochaḋ, drong do ṁarḃaḋ, ⁊ drong do ṫarraing o ċéle dibh ina dioghail.

[y] *Walter.*—In Grace's Annals of Ireland he is incorrectly called Richard de Burgo. The starving of this Walter in the prison of Green Castle, was the chief cause of the murder of the Earl of Ulster in the following year.

[z] *The new castle.*—Green Castle, in the barony of Inishowen, near the mouth of Lough Foyle, in the north-east of the county of Donegal, is still called caislean nua in Irish by the natives.

[a] *Kinel-Fiachach*, now the barony of *Moycashel* in the south of the county of Westmeath.

[b] *Cill-Oiridh*, now *Killery*, an old church which gives name to a parish near Lough Gill, in the barony of Tirerrill and county of Sligo, and adjoining the county of Leitrim. See map prefixed to *Genealogies, Tribes, and Customs of Hy-Fiachrach;* on which the situation of this church is shewn. See another reference to Cill Oiridh under the year 1416.

[c] *Earl of Ulster.*—There is a much more circumstantial account of the death of this Earl of Ulster given by Pembridge and Grace under this year. Lodge gives the following particulars of it: "He was murdered on Sunday, June 6, 1333, by Robert Fitz-Richard Mandeville (who gave him his first wound), and others his servants, near to the Fords, in going towards Carrickfergus, in the 21st year of his age, at the instigation, as was said, of Gyle de Burgh, wife of Sir Richard Mandeville, in revenge for his having imprisoned her brother Walter and others."

This young earl left an only child, Elizabeth, who was married in the year 1352 to Lionel,

THE AGE OF CHRIST, 1332.

The Age of Christ, one thousand three hundred thirty-two.

Walter[y], son of Sir Walter Burke, was taken prisoner by the Dun Earl, and brought to the new castle[z] of Inishowen; and he afterwards died of hunger in the prison of this castle.

Tomaltagh Mac Dermot and Mac William were defeated, with the loss of numbers of their people, at Berna-an-mhil, by the son of the Earl, and by Tomaltagh Mac Donough.

William Gallda, son of Murtough More Mageoghegan, Lord of Kinel-Fiachach[a], died.

THE AGE OF CHRIST, 1333.

The Age of Christ, one thousand three hundred thirty-three.

Florence Mac-an-Oglaich, Archdeacon of Cill-Oiridh[b], died.

William Burke, Earl of Ulster[c], was killed by the English of Ulster. The Englishmen who committed this deed were put to death, in divers ways, by the people of the King of England; some were hanged, others killed, and others torn asunder[d], in revenge of his death.

third son of King Edward III., and this prince was then created, in her right, Earl of Ulster and Lord of Connaught, and these titles were enjoyed through marriage or descent by different princes of the royal blood, until at length, in the person of Edward IV., they became the special inheritance and revenue of the crown of England. Immediately on the Earl's death the chiefs of the junior branches of the family of Burke or De Burgo, then seated in Connaught, fearing the transfer of his possessions into strange hands by the marriage of the heiress, seized upon his estates in Connaught. The two most powerful of these were Sir William or Ulick, the ancestor of the Earls of Clanrickard, and Sir Edmund Albanagh, the progenitor of the Viscounts of Mayo. These, having confederated together and declared themselves independent, renounced the English dress and language, and adopted Irish names, Sir William taking the name of Mac William Oughter, or the Upper, and Sir Edmund that of Mac William Eighter, or the Lower. Under these names these two powerful chieftains tyranized over the entire province of Connaught, and though Lionel Duke of Clarence, in right of his wife, laid claim to their usurped possessions, the government appears to have been too weak to assert the authority of the English laws, so that the territories of the Burkes were allowed to descend in course of tanistry and gavelkind. See Hardiman's History of Galway, pp. 56, 57.

[d] *Torn asunder*, i. e. torn limb from limb. Mageoghegan renders it "hanged, drawn, and quartered."

Tomaltach mac donnchaiḋ meic diarmata tiġerna tire hoilella, fer ba ferr firinne, caḋus, ⁊ comairce da mbaí in en aimsir fris decc.

Feidhlimidh Ua doṁnaill an tanaisi tiġerna fa huaisle, fa hairegda ⁊ as mó ris a raibe súil dfirionnchaibh décc.

Gillibert mac goisdelbaiġ do ṁarbaḋ ar lar a tighe fein le caṫal mac diarmata gall tre mebail.

Aoḋ mac Consnaṁa taoiseaċ muintire cionaiṫ décc.

Mac na hoiḋce óg mág flannchaḋa do marbaḋ la connaċtaiḃ .i. la toirrdealbaċ ua cconcobair Rí connaċt ⁊ lá tiġernán mag Ruairc, ⁊ tiġernus na breifne do tabairt dua Raġallaiġ.

Donnchaḋ mac Aoḋa uí ċeallaiġ do ġabail do ṫoirrdealbaċ ó cconcobair Rí Connaċt.

Sith dfoccra do ċloinn uilliam burc o righ Saxan.

Concobar mac branáin taoiseaċ corc achlann décc.

Aodh mac domhnaill oicc í doṁnaill tiġerna ċenel cconaill, ċenel moáin innsi heoghain, ḟermanach, ioċtair ċonnacht, ⁊ na breifne, ⁊ adbar righ uladh uile bfós, aon roba mó grain ⁊ aḋuaṫ a eccratt roiṁe baoí do gaoidelaibh a aimsire, aon as mó les ċuit do ġallaiḃ ⁊ do gaoidelaibh battar ina aghaidh, aon ro bferr smaċt, reaċt, ⁊ riaghail bai ina comhfochraib, feichem coitcenn iarṫair eorpa ar eineach ⁊ derlaccadh décc iar mbreiṫ buaḋa o doman ⁊ deman in aibítt manaigh i nInis Saimer, ⁊ a aḋnacal co nonoir, ⁊ co nairmidin móir i mainistir easa ruaidh. Concobar ua doṁnaill (a ṁac) do ġabail a ionaid. Ro fás iaram ioṁcosnaṁ etir ċoncobar ⁊ Art (a ḋerbraṫair) imon fflaiṫeas go ro marbadh Art a ttraitte la concobar.

[e] *Mac Donough Mac Dermot.*—The Mac Donoughs of Tirerrill, in the county of Sligo, are a branch of the Mac Dermots of Moylurg in the county of Roscommon.

[f] *Mac Dermot Gall.*—He was located in the territory of Airteach, in the county of Roscommon, adjoining the barony of Costello in the county of Mayo. This passage is thus translated by Mageoghegan in his Annals of Clonmacnoise:

"Cahall Mac Dermodda Gall killed Gillebert Mac Cosdeally in the middest of his own house treacherously."

[g] *Inis Saimer.*—This is a small island in the river Erne, close to the cataract of Assaroe at Ballyshannon. It is to be distinguished from the monastery of Assaroe, which is situated on the north side of the river, about one mile to the west of the town of Ballyshannon.

[h] Mageoghegan translates it thus, in his version of the Annals of Clonmacnoise :

Tomaltagh Mac Donough Mac Dermot[e], Lord of Tirerrill, the most celebrated man of his time for veracity, honour, and protection, died.

Felim O'Donnell, a Tanist Lord, the noblest and most illustrious, and from whom the Irish people expected most, died.

Gilbert Mac Costello was treacherously slain in the middle of his own house by Cathal Mac Dermot Gall[f].

Hugh Mac Consnava, Chief of Muintir-Kenny, died.

Mac-na-h-Oidhche Oge Mac Clancy was slain by the Connacians (i. e. by Turlough O'Conor, King of Connaught, assisted by Tiernan Mag-Ruairc); and the lordship of Breifny was given to O'Reilly.

Donough, son of Hugh O'Kelly, was taken prisoner by Turlough O'Conor, King of Connaught.

A peace was proclaimed by the King of England to the Clann-William Burke.

Conor Mac Branan, Chief of Corcachlann, died.

Hugh, the son of Donnell Oge O'Donnell, Lord of Tirconnell, Kinel-Moen, Inishowen, Fermanagh, and Breifny, and a materies of a king of Ulster; of all the Irish the most successful, and the most dreaded by his enemies; he who had slain the largest number both of the English and Irish who were opposed to him; the most eminent man of his time for jurisdiction, laws, and regulations, and the chief patron of the hospitality and munificence of the West of Europe, died, victorious over the world and the devil, in the habit of a monk, on the island of Inis-Saimer[g], and was interred with great honour and solemnity in the monastery of Assaroe. Conor O'Donnell (his son) assumed his place. A dispute afterwards arose between this Conor and Art, his brother, concerning the lordship; and Art was soon killed by Conor in combat[h].

"Hugh O'Donnell, King of Tyreconnell and Fermanagh, one that took hostages of the territory of Carbry and Sligeagh, and Brenie; one deputed to be next successor of the Kingdom of Ulster, the best man in Ireland for bounty, prowess, magnanimity, rule, and good government, and in summer he that killed most of the English and Irish that were his enemies, died in this year, after he had overcome the world and the devill, and also after he had reigned fortunately in the principality of Tyrconnell fifty years, and after he had entred into religion in the habitt of a gray monck, receiving the sacraments of Penance and Extream Unction. After whose death his son, Connor O'Donnell, was constituted to succeed him," &c.

AOIS CRIOST, 1334.

Aois Criost, míle trí chéd, triochatt, a cethair.

Mórsloigheadh la connachtaibh uile etir ghallaibh ⁊ gaoidhealaibh is in mumhain do shaighidh mhic Conmara go ro ghabhsat a braighde ⁊ gur cuirset a nsmacht air. Teampall do loscadh do dhruing don tsluaigh sin ina mbattar ochtmoghat ar chéd do dhaoínibh, ⁊ diar Saccart imaille riú, ⁊ gan aon diobh do therna dh as gan oghlosgadh.

Dechneabhar do mhuintir donnchaidh mic Maoileachloinn carraigh meic diarmata do bhathadh ar loch techt.

Tadcc mac cathail mic domhnaill uí concobair décc.

Donnchadh mac Consnamha taoiseach muintire cionaith, ⁊ Seonacc mac Muirchertaigh móir meg eochaccáin tighearna chenel fiachach décc.

Uilliam mhág eochagán do écc.

Concobar mac branáin do écc.

Eóin mac giolla ultain do mharbhadh la domhnall mac aedha.

AOIS CRIOST, 1335.

Aois Criost, míle trí chéd, triochatt, a cúicc.

Fionnghuala ingen uí bhriain bean toirrdhealbhaigh uí concobhair decc.

Seaan mac airt uí eaghra do ghabhail le mac an iarla, ⁊ forgla a muintire do airccain.

Creach le cloinn domhnaill uí chonchobhair ar cloinn muiris Shuccaigh meic gearailt dar marbhadh mac meic muiris. Creach oile la cloinn mhuiris ina dioghail sin for cloinn domhnaill.

Iarthar chonnacht uile do milleadh la hemonn a búrc.

Uilc dirimhe eidir loscadh ⁊ marbhadh do denamh dó bheós ar mhac in iarla, ⁊ ar cloinn Riocaird a búrc, ⁊ Síth do denamh doibh re roile iarttain.

Giolla na naingeal ó cairide ollamh leighis fearmanach do écc.

[i] *Loch Techet.*—Now Lough Gara, near Boyle, in the county of Roscommon, on the borders of the county of Sligo.

[j] Under this year the Annals of Clonmacnoise as translated by Mageoghegan, have:

"There was such a great snow in the spring of

THE AGE OF CHRIST, 1334.

The Age of Christ, one thousand three hundred thirty-four.

A great army, both of English and Irish, was led by the Connacians into Munster against Mac Namara; and they took hostages from him, and obtained sway over him. A party of this army burned a church, in which were one hundred and eighty persons, and two priests along with them; and not one of them escaped the conflagration.

Ten of the people of Donough, the son of Melaghlin Carragh Mac Dermot, were drowned in Loch Techet[i].

Teige, the son of Cathal, son of Donnell O'Conor, died.

Donough Mac Consnava, Chief of Muintir-Kenny, and Johnock, son of Murtough More Mageoghegan, Lord of Kinel-Fiachach, died.

Conor Mac Branan died.

John Mac Gilla-Ultan was slain by Donnell Mac Hugh.

THE AGE OF CHRIST, 1335.

The Age of Christ, one thousand three hundred thirty-five.

Finola, the daughter of O'Brien, and wife of Turlough O'Conor, died.

John, son of Art O'Hara, was taken prisoner by the son of the Earl; and the greater part of his people were plundered.

A depredation was committed by the sons of Donnell O'Conor upon the descendants of Maurice Sugach Fitzgerald, on which occasion the son of Mac Maurice was killed. Another depredation was committed in retaliation by the Clann-Maurice upon the sons of Donnell.

The entire of the West of Connaught was desolated by Edmond Burke. Great evils were also wrought by him, both by burning and slaying, upon the son of the Earl and the race of Richard Burke. They afterwards made peace with one another.

Gilla-na-n-Angel O'Cassidy, Chief Physician of Fermanagh, died[j].

this year that the most part of the fowle of Ireland died."

It appears strange that this entry should have been omitted by the Four Masters, as they state

AOIS CRIOST, 1336.

Aois Criost, mile, trí chéd, triochatt, a sé.

Trinoit ó naan ardṁaigistir i nealadhnaibh iomda, i léx ⁊ i ccanóin décc.

Tomaltaċ gerr (na ccrech ttimcil) mac diarmata, tigearna muige luircc. Aon lá mó cosccur ar easccairdiḃ, ba ferr cádus, ⁊ comairce, engnaṁ, ⁊ eineaċ da mbaoí don ċineaḋ dia raiḃe décc oiḋċe ḋoṁnaiġ na trionóide ina tigh fein i ccalaḋ na cairrce, ⁊ a adhnacul i mainistir na buille go honorach. Concoḃar a ṁac do ġabail tiġernais tar a éis.

Teaboid a burc mac uilliam ⁊ Maoilir mac Siurtan dexetra décc.

Maiḋm do ṫabairt deoġan ó madaḋáin for cloinn Riocaird a búrc, ⁊ socaiḋe da muintir do marḃadh uatha .i. seiser ⁊ tri fichit.

Creach mor la cloinn diarmata gall, ⁊ la mac feidlimiḋ uí concoḃair for cloinn ġoisdelḃaiġ, ⁊ Maidiuc mac uaillorín do marḃaḋ ina tóraigheaċt.

Creach la hémann mac uilliam burc ar cloinn ċathail dar hairccead concoḃar ua flanngain ⁊ daoine iomḋa oile. Maoileachlainn ua flannagain do ṁarḃaḋ i toraiġeacht na ccreach don dul sin, ⁊ brathair do mac an mileaḋ do ġabail don toraiġ iarom, ⁊ braiġe do denam de.

Concoḃar mac diarmata tiġearna maiġe luircc, Aoḋ mac feidlimiḋ mic aedha uí Concoḃair go lucht tiġi uí Concoḃair imaille ris, ⁊ clann ndonnchaiḋ, ⁊ corbmac mac Ruaiḋri go nglaslaithiḃ criche coirpre do dul ar

that they had the original Annals of Clonmacnoise before them.

[k] Now a field close to Rockingham, the beautiful seat of Lord Lorton, in the county of Roscommon, near Boyle. It is still called Port-na-Cairge by the old natives of the district. The low, level part of the townland of Rockingham, verging on Lough Key, is the locality called Cala-na-Cairge, i. e., the callaw or strath of the rock (the castle on the opposite island in the lake so called). We learn from the Annals of Boyle that Cormac, the son of Tomaltach Mac Dermot, commenced the erection of a market-town here in 1231:

"1231. Cormac mac Tomaltaiġ incepit bailli margaiḋ do ḋenuḃ i port na Cairge."

The Rev. John Keogh, in his Account of the County of Roscommon, drawn up for Sir William Petty's intended Atlas in 1683, states that Carraig Mac Dermott was then named Rockingham:

"Carrig Mac Dermot, newly named Rockingham, is not now noted for many dwellers, of which, I doubt not, Sir Robert King will give a

THE AGE OF CHRIST, 1336.

The Age of Christ, one thousand three hundred thirty-six.

Trionoit O'Naan, Chief Professor of many Sciences, and of the Civil and Canon Laws, died.

Tomaltagh Gearr na-g-creach timchil Mac Dermot, Lord of Moylurg, the most victorious man of his tribe over his enemies, the most honourable man, the best protector, and the most expert at arms, and hospitable, died on the night of Trinity Sunday, at his own house at Cala-na-Cairrge[k], and was interred with honour in the abbey of Boyle. Conor, his son, assumed the lordship after him.

Theobald Burke Mac William and Meyler Mac Jordan de Exeter died.

Owen O'Madden defeated[l] the Clanrickard Burke, and killed sixty-six of them.

A great depredation was committed by the sons of Dermot Gall [Mac Dermot] and the son of Felim O'Conor, upon the Clann-Costello; and Maiduic Mac Waldrin was slain while in pursuit of the booty.

A depredation was committed by Edmond Mac William Burke upon the Clann-Cathail, on which occasion Conor O'Flanagan and many others were plundered. Melaghlin O'Flanagan was slain while in pursuit of the prey, and a brother of Mac Aveely[m] was taken and carried away as a prisoner.

Conor Mac Dermot, Lord of Moylurg, Hugh, the son of Felim, son of Hugh O'Conor, accompanied by O'Conor's household and the Clann-Donough, and Cormac, the son of Rory, with the young soldiers of the territory of Carbury, set out on a predatory excursion into Tireragh, and advanced as far as Mul-

true account." Keogh, however, here confounds Port-na-Cairge, the townland on which Rockingham House now stands, with the Carrig itself, which is an island in Lough Key, on which the castle still remains.

Longphort mic Diarmada is now called Longford Hill, and is situated in Lord Lorton's demesne, not far from Rockingham House.

[l] *Defeated.*—Literally, "a defeat was given by Owen O'Madden upon the clan Clanrickard Burke, and many of their [his] people were killed, viz., six and three score." It is rendered thus by Mageoghegan in his Annals of Clonmacnoise:

"A. D. 1236. Owen O'Madden gave an overthrow to the Burkes, when sixty-six of them were killed."

[m] *Mac Aveely*, mac an mileaḋ, i. e., son of the knight. This was the Irish name adopted by the family of Staunton, who were seated in the barony of Carra, in the county of Mayo, where they still retain it, and where there are many respectable persons of the name.

creiċ hi tír Fiaċrach go rangattar mullach Ratha. Ba na tíre do theichead rompo. Mairḃedala mora, iomad capall, beaccan deachaiḃ, ⁊ fochroḋ ilarḋa do ṫaḃairt leo, ⁊ daoine diairṁe do ṁarḃaḋ doiḃ, ⁊ iad féin diompud slán dia ttighiḃ.

Diarmaitt ó Flannagain tiġearna cloinne cathail décc.

Toirrdealbach ua Concoḃair Rí Connaċt do thionól imirceaḋ na ttuaṫ cloinne caṫail, cloinne Conċoḃair, ⁊ moigh luirg co hairteach. Caislén mor meic goisdealḃaiġ do gabail dua Concoḃair don toisce sin, ⁊ a bhriseaḋ, ⁊ césthsin congṁala an ḃaile do tocht amach ar comairce meic diarmata.

Doṁnall mac Seaain mic doṁnaill uí Concoḃair décc.

Niall mac Concoḃair mic taiḋg do ṁarbadh.

Mainestir .S. Fransеis hi ccarraic na Siúire in esscocoitteċt leasa móir do thógḃail la hiarla Urṁuṁan Semas buitilér.

Machġaṁain ó Raighilliġ do ṁarḃaḋ la gallaiḃ.

O Michiḋéin comarba Molaisi do écc.

[n] *Mullagh-Ratha*, i.e. "the summit of the fort." It would appear from various references to this place in the writings of the Mac Firbises of Lecan, that it was the original name of the townland of Rathlee in the parish of Easkey, in the barony of Tireragh and county of Sligo. See *Genealogies, Tribes, and Customs of Hy-Fiachrach*, p. 251, note [b], and the Ordnance map of the county of Sligo, sheets 10 and 11.

[o] *Were driven off.*—Literally, fled before them. The whole passage is given as follows in Mageoghegan's translation of the Annals of Clonmacnoise: "A. D. 1336. Connor Mac Dermoda, prince of Moylorg, Hugh mac Ffelim mac Hugh O'Connor, and the household mene of O'Conor, together with the families of Clanndonnogh and the O'Connors of Carbrey (now called the Territory of Sligoe), with Cormock mac Rowry O'Connor, repaired to take the preys and spoyles of Tyrefiaghragh, came to Mullagh Rath, from whom all the cowes of the contrey fledd; notwithstanding they returned not empty-handed, for they had some moveables, gerans, and a few horses, and committed slaughter in that contrey, returned safe and sound without bloodshed or loss of any of themselves."

[p] *Inanimate spoils.*—Mairḃedála, signifies literally *inanimate spoils*, meaning corn, furniture, gold, or silver, in contradistinction to animate spoils, such as cows, horses, sheep, &c.

[q] *Horses* [*of burden*].—In some parts of Ireland the word capall denotes a mare; but the original signification seems to have been a draught horse. It is thus derived in Cormac's Glossary: "capul .i. cap, carr ⁊ peall, eaċ. Capull, i. e., *Cap*, a car, and *peall*, a horse, i. e., a car-horse; the Greek word Καββαλλης, signifies a work horse.

[r] *Steeds.*—Eaċ signifies a *steed*; Lat. *Equus*; Æolian Greek, Ικκος.

[s] *Small cattle.*—Foċroḋ, small cattle; Fo, in compound words, implies little, inferior, small, mean, &c.; fo-ċroḋ, small cattle; fo-ḋuine, a mean man; foḃard, a bardling; foġéag, a small branch.

[t] *Castlemore-Costello* is situated in the barony

lagh-Ratha[o]. The cows of the country were driven off[o] before them. They carried away many inanimate spoils[p], many horses [of burden[q]], a few steeds[r], and many flocks of small cattle[s]; and after they had killed countless persons they returned in safety to their houses.

Dermot O'Flanagan, Lord of Clann-Cathail, died.

Turlough O'Conor, King of Connaught, collected the flitting forces of the Tuathas, Clann-Chathail, Clann-Conor, and Moylurg, and conveyed them to Airteach. Castlemore-Costello[t] was taken and demolished by O'Conor on this occasion, and the kern[u] who guarded it came out under protection of Mac Dermot.

Donnell, the son of John, son of Donnell O'Conor, died.

Niall, the son of Conor Mac Teige, was killed.

The Franciscan Monastery at Carrick-on-Suir, in the diocese of Lismore, was founded by James Butler, Earl of Ormond.

Mahon O'Reilly[w] was slain by the English.

O'Meehin[x], Coarb of St. Molaisse, died.

of Costello and county of Mayo, not far from the district of Airteach in the county of Roscommon. See map to *Genealogies, Tribes, and Customs of Hy-Fiachrach.*

[u] *Kern.*—Mageoghegan renders this, in his translation of the Annals of Clonmacnoise, thus: "A. D. 1336. Terlagh O'Connor, King of Connought, with all the forces of Twahes and Clann Kahill, with Moylorg, went to Arteagh; took Castlemore of Mac Gosdeallie, and afterwards broke downe the same, the warde of which castle came foorth upon Mac Dermott's protection, whose lives he saved accordingly."

The word cethern is explained by O'Flaherty: "Militum Manipulus et a cohorte Latinâ non abludit." *Ogygia*, p. 208. The kerns were a light-armed infantry. Ware thus speaks of them in his *Antiquities of Ireland*, c. xxi. : "Alii levioris armaturæ Henrico Marleburgensi Turbiculi, quibusdam Turbarii vulgo Kernii dicti; jaculis amentatis, machaeris et cultris, sive sicis Skeynes vocatis demicabant. In Rotulo Clauso anno 5 Edward III. Membr. 25, inter articulos in Hibernia observandos sextus est contra sustentatores, et ductores Kernorum et gentis vocatæ Idlemen nisi in Marchiis suas proprias ad Custas."

The etymology of this word, *Cethern*, is thus given in Cormac's Glossary: "Ceċeрn .ı. coıрe aımbe, unde dicitur ceıċıрnae : ceċeрn bın. cıċ, caċ ocoр орn, орꝺaın."

"Cethern, i. e. a band of soldiers; unde dicitur Cethirnach, i. e. manipularius seu unus e *cohorte*; cethern, then, i. e. cıċ, a battle, and upn, a slaughter; q. d. a slaughter in battle."

[w] *Mahon O'Reilly.*—He is the ancestor of that sept of the O'Reillys called Clann-Mahon, who gave name to the barony of Clannmahon in the west of the county of Cavan.

[x] *O'Meehin.*—He was the coarb of the church of Ballaghmeehin, in the parish of Rossinver, in the north of the county of Leitrim, where his lineal descendant and representative still farms the termon lands.

AOIS CRIOST, 1337.

Aoir Crioſt, mile, trí chéd, triochatt, a Seachtt.

Lughaidh ó dálaigh epscop cluana mic noir décc iar ndeighbeathaidh.

Tómár mac cormaic uí domhnaill epscop Ratha both saoi in eccna, ⁊ i ccrabhadh décc.

An maighistir ó Rothlain décc.

Sith do dénamh duilliam mac iarla uladh, ⁊ do brian ó briain (.i. brian bán) re aroile, ⁊ na fearoinn do folmaigh re ó mac an iarla do leigſin dó ara a ccíos fein do tabhairt arda.

Forlongport do dénomh do righ Connacht ag áth liag inaghaidh Emainn a búrc.

Seaan ua follamhain tighſrna cloinne huadach décc.

Tadhcc mac flannchadha tigearna dartraighe do marbhadh la corbmac mac Ruaidhri mic domhnaill uí Concobhair re rochraide oile, ⁊ i ndioghail Seaain mic Domhnaill. Creacha móra do dſnomh ar dartraighi dó ar a haithle ⁊ mac Muirir mecc flannchaidh do marbhadh ina ttoraigheacht.

Tadhg, ⁊ Maoileachloinn, da mhac Iomair megh Rághnaill do ghabail la Cathal mágh Raghnaill. Cathal do marbhadh iar sin i ttoraigheacht cloinne hIomhair da combraithribh iar ttionol lán rochraide, dóibh im uilliam mag mathghamhna, ⁊ im da mac oile Iomhair még ragnaill, Concobhar ⁊ Tomaltach. Magnus ó fearghail do mharbhadh dóibh an lá cedna. Taoiseach do dénomh do Tadhg mac Iomhair megh Raghnaill iarsin.

Domhnall Ruadh ó maille ⁊ corbmac a mac do marbhadh la cloinn Mebric, ⁊ do ghallaibh oile immaille friu oidhche fele Stephain.

Macha ua huiginn saoi re dan, ⁊ re daonnacht décc.

Enrí mac Mairtin do mharbhadh.

[r] *O'Rothlain.*—This name is now usually anglicised Rowley in the county of Mayo, where there are several respectable persons of the name.

[s] *Bryan Bane.*—This passage is given as follows by Mageoghegan in his translation of the Annals of Clonmacnoise: "That as much lands as Bryan Bane wasted of the demesne of William Burke, should be held by Bryan Bane for the valuable rent thereof."

[t] *Clann Uadagh.*—A territory in the barony of Athlone, south of the county of Roscommon. Laurence Fallon, Esq., of Mount Prospect, and Malachy Fallon of Ballynahan, Esq., are the pre-

THE AGE OF CHRIST, 1337.

The Age of Christ, one thousand three hundred thirty-seven

Lughaidh O'Daly, Bishop of Clonmacnoise, died after a well-spent life.

Thomas, the son of Cormac O'Donnell, Bishop of Raphoe, a man eminent for wisdom and piety, died.

The Master [Professor] O'Rothlain[y] died.

A peace was concluded between William, son of the Earl of Ulster, and Brian *Bán*[z] (the Fair) O'Brien ; and the lands which O'Brien had taken from the son of the Earl were given back to him at their former rent.

A camp was pitched at Athleague by the King of Connaught, to oppose Edmond Burke

John O'Fallon, Lord of Clann-Uadagh[a], died.

Teige Mac Clancy, Lord of Dartry, was slain by Cormac, the son of Rory, son of Donnell O'Conor, as were also numbers of others, in revenge of John, the son of Donnell.

Great depredations were afterwards committed in Dartry by O'Conor; and the son of Maurice Mac Clancy was killed while in pursuit of the preys.

Teige and Melaghlin, two sons of Ivor Mac Rannall, were taken prisoners by Cathal Mac Rannall. Cathal was afterwards slain by their kinsmen, who, having collected a considerable force, being joined by William Mac Mahon, and by Conor and Tomaltagh, the two other sons of Ivor Mac Rannall, went to rescue the sons of Ivor. Manus O'Farrell was slain by them on the same day. Teige, the son of Ivor Mac Rannall, was then made chieftain.

Donnell Roe O'Malley and Cormac, his son, were slain on St. Martin's night by Clann-Merrick[b], and other Englishmen who were along with them.

Matthew O'Higgin, a man eminent for poetry and humanity, died.

Henry Mac Martin[c] was slain.

sent representatives of the O'Fallons of Clann Uadagh.

[b] *The Clann-Merrick.*—This family, which is of Welsh descent, is still numerous in the county of Mayo, where they have received the inglorious sobriquet of bunoún meıobpıc, which does not admit of translation. See *Genealogies, Tribes, and Customs of Hy-Fiachrach*, pp. 331, 332.

[c] *Mac Martin.*—This became the surname of a collateral branch of the O'Neills of Clannaboy. See note [b], under the year 1291, p. 454.

Donnchaḋ mac Muirchertaiġ moir Ṁéġ Eochagáin tiġerna Cenél Ḟiachach do ṁarḃaḋ la hUiḃ Failġe.

Síth do dénuṁ dAoḋ reaṁar ó Néill re hOirġiallaiḃ, ⁊ re Feraiḃ Manach.

Donnchaḋ mór ó Dubda tanaisi Ua bFiaċrach do écc.

AOIS CRIOST, 1338.

Aois Criost, míle, trí chéd, triochatt a hochtt.

Ruaiḋri an Einigh Mag Uiḋir tiġerna Fermanach aoinḟer as mó do ṫoirḃir dairgett ⁊ dédach deachaiḃ, ⁊ dinniliḃ uaiḋ déigriḃ, ⁊ dollaṁnaiḃ Erionn ina aimsir féin do Ṡíol Uidhir décc.

Donnchadh mac Ruaiḋri uí Concoḃair do ṁarḃaḋ.

Mac Iarla Ulad, .i. Emand do ġaḃail Demann a Búrc, Cloch do cor fo a braġaitt, ⁊ a badhaḋ i loch Measca lais. Milleaḋ Gall Connaċt, ⁊ a chineaḋ féin do ṫeċt trias an ngníoṁ sin. Toirdealḃaċ ó Concoḃair Rí Connaċt dionnarḃaḋ Émainn mec Uilliam Burc iar sin a Connachtaiḃ amach iar milleaḋ na ttuaṫ ⁊ na cceall go haḋbal eatorra in Iarṫar Connaċt, ⁊ nert na tíre co coitċenn do ghaḃail dUa Conċoḃair ar a haithle.

Coblach mor do longaiḃ ⁊ barcaiḃ do thionol la hEmann a Burc iarsin ⁊ a beith for oilénaib mara athaḋ imchian da éis.

Luiġni ⁊ an Corann dfolṁuġaḋ ⁊ dfasuġaḋ imma nGallaiḃ, ⁊ a ttiġearnus do ġabail da nGaoiḋelaiḃ duthchassa buḋdéin ar ndíochur a nGall estoibh.

Tadhg mac Ruaiḋri mic Cathail uí Chonċoḃair (fir a ráiti bratach righin) do ġaḃail do Thómás mac Sampadhain, ⁊ moran da muintir do ṁarḃadh. Mac Shampaḋain (.i. Tómas) do dul go tech uí Concoḃair iarsin, ⁊ ag teacht tara ais dó, clann Muirchertaiġ ⁊ Muinter-Eolais do chomchruinniuġaḋ ara chionn, ⁊ a ġaḃail iar marḃaḋ morain dia ṁuintir.

[d] *The people of Offaly*, i. e. the O'Conors Faly.

[e] *Hugh Reamhar*, i. e. Hugh the gross or fat.

[f] *Rory an einigh*, i. e. Roger or Roderick of the hospitality, or the hospitable.

[g] *Sil-Uidhir*, i. e. the progeny of Odhar, who was the progenitor of the Maguires of Fermanagh. This tribe name is now locally pronounced *Sheel-Ivvir*.

[h] *The son of the Earl of Ulster*.—This passage is given as follows in the Annals of Clonmacnoise, as translated by Mageoghegan: "A. D. 1338.

Donough, son of Murtough More Mageoghegan, Lord of Kinel-Fiachach, was slain by the people of Offaly[d].

Hugh Reamhar[e] O'Neill made peace with the people of Oriel and Fermanagh.

Donough More O'Dowda, Tanist of Hy-Fiachrach, died.

THE AGE OF CHRIST, 1338.

The Age of Christ, one thousand three hundred thirty-eight.

Rory-an-einigh[f] Maguire. Lord of Fermanagh, a man who had bestowed more silver, apparel, steeds, and cattle, on the learned men and chief professors of Ireland, than any other of the Sil-Uidhir[g], in his time, died.

Donough, son of Rory O'Conor, was killed.

The son of the Earl of Ulster[h], i. e. Edmond, was taken prisoner by Edmond Burke, who fastened a stone to his neck and drowned him in Lough Mask. The destruction of the English of Connaught, and of his own [in particular], resulted from this deed. Turlough O'Conor afterwards banished Edmond Mac William Burke out of Connaught, after the territories and churches of the west of Connaught had been greatly destroyed between them; and O'Conor then assumed the sway of the whole province.

A large fleet of ships and barks was, after this, collected by Edmond Burke; and he remained for a long time on the islands of the sea.

Leyny and Corran were laid waste and wrested from the English, and the chieftainship of them assumed by the hereditary Irish chieftains, after the expulsion of the English.

Teige, son of Rory, son of Cathal O'Conor (who was usually called Bratach Righin[i]), was taken prisoner by Thomas Magauran, and many of his people were killed. Magauran (i. e. Thomas) afterwards went to the house of O'Conor; but, on his return, the Clann-Murtough[ii], and the Muintir-Eolais, assembled to meet him, and took him prisoner, after having slain many of his people.

Edmond, the Earle of Ulster's son, was taken by the other Edmond Burke, and [he] died.

[i] *Bratach Righin*, i. e. the tough or stiff standard.

[ii] *Clann Murtough*, i. e. the descendants of Murtough Muimhneach O'Conor, the son of Turlough More and brother of Brian Luighneach,

Aeḋh an ċleitiġ mac Ruaiḋri uí ċonċobair do lot ar deireaḋ a sluaiġ féin, ⁊ a écc da biṫin.

Derḃail inġen Cathail meic Murchaḋa ben donnchaiḋ meic Aedha óig décc.

AOIS CRIOST, 1339.

Aois Criost, míle, trí ched, triochatt, anaé.

Ruaiḋri ua ceallaiġ tiġerna ó maine do ṁarbaḋ la cathal mac aoḋa mic eoġain uí Conċobair ag dol o thig uí Conċobair ag dol o thiġ uí concobair dochum a thiġhe féin.

Tomás Mag Shaṁraḋain do leġean amach do cloinn Muircertaiġ.

Sloiġeaḋ mór la haeḋ reamhar ó néill go tír conaill. Mac Seaain uí néill do ṁarbaḋ ⁊ goffraiḋh ua doṁnaill don tsluaiġeaḋ sin la muintir uí dochartaiġ.

Emann mac uilliam burc gona loingeas dionnarbaḋ doiléanaiḃ na fairrge for a mboí do ḟoighiḋ ulaḋ la toirrdealbaċ ua cconcoḃair ri Connacht.

Ingen toirrdealḃaiġ uí briain ben meic iarla ulaḋ do tabairt do toirrdealbaċ ua cconcoḃair, ⁊ derḃail ingean aoḋa uí doṁnaill do leiccen dó.

Coccaḋ mór ar ḟud na miḋe eittir gallaiḃ ⁊ ġaoiḋealaiḃ.

Teampall cille Ronain do ḋénam la ferġal muiṁneaċ ua nduiḃgennáin.

the ancestor of O'Conor Sligo. See pedigree of the O'Conors of Connaught, in the Book of Lecan, fol. 72, *et sequen.*

[j] *Hugh an chletigh*, i. e. Hugh of the quill, a soubriquet applied to him because his mother could weave. It is so explained by Mageoghegan in his version of the Annals of Clonmacnoise.

[k] *Dearbhail.*—This entry is copied word for word from the Annals of Ulster.

[l] *The Clann-Murtough.*—These were a sept of the O'Conors, who descended from the celebrated Muircheartach or Murtough Muimhneach, the son of King Turlough.

[m] *Hugh Reamhar*, i. e. Hugh the fat or gross. He was the son of Donnell O'Neill, who was the son of Brian of the battle of Down, who was slain in 1260. He is the ancestor of all the succeeding chiefs of the O'Neills of Tyrone.

[n] *Taken to wife*, do ṫabairt, i. e. *ducta est in matrimonium.* Pósaḋ, the modern Irish word for marriage, a word evidently derived from the French, is very seldom used by the Irish Annalists.

[o] *Kilronan*, Cill Ronain, i. e. the church of St. Ronan.—An old church which gives name to a parish in the north of the barony of Boyle, in the county of Roscommon, verging on Lough Allen. See a notice of this church at the year 1586, where it is stated that it is on the confines of Breifny, Moylurg, and Tirerrill. It has not been yet determined which of the many saints

Hugh an Chletigh[j], son of Rory O'Conor, was wounded in the rear of his own army, and died in consequence.

Dearbhail[k], daughter of Cathal Mac Murrough, and wife of Donough, son of Hugh Oge, died.

THE AGE OF CHRIST, 1339.

The Age of Christ, one thousand three hundred thirty-nine.

Rory O'Kelly, Lord of Hy-Many, was slain by Cathal, son of Hugh O'Conor, while he was returning from O'Conor's residence to his own.

Thomas Magauran was liberated by the Clann-Murtough[l].

A great army was led by Hugh Reamhar[m] O'Neill into Tirconnell; and the son of John O'Neill and Godfrey O'Donnell were slain in the course of this expedition by the people of O'Doherty.

Edmond Mac William Burke was driven, with all his fleet, from the islands of the sea into Ulster, by Turlough O'Conor, King of Connaught.

The daughter of Turlough O'Brien, wife of the son of the Earl of Ulster, was taken to wife[n] by Turlough O'Conor, who put away Dearbhail, daughter of Hugh O'Donnell.

A great war [broke out] in Meath between the English and Irish.

The church of Kilronan[o] was erected by Farrell Muimhneach[p] O'Duigenan[q].

of this name in the Irish calendar was the patron of this church.

The ruins of this church still remain in tolerable preservation, and the character of the architecture perfectly corresponds with that of all the Irish churches of this period. The O'Duigenans were the Erenaghs of this church, as well as the chroniclers of the Clanmulrony.

[p] *Muimhneach*, i. e. the Momonian or Munsterson: O'Duigenan was certainly so called from his having been fostered in the province of Munster.

[q] The Annals of Clonmacnoise, as translated by Mageoghegan, give the entries under this year as follows:

"A. D. 1339. Edmond Burke with his shipps were banished into Ulster.

"The daughter of Terlagh O'Bryen, late wife of the Earle of Ulster's son, was taken to wife by Terlagh O'Connor, and he put away his own wife, the Lady Dervaile, Hugh O'Donnell's daughter.

"There arose great dissention, warrs, and debate between the English and Irish of Meath this year.

"All the corn of Ireland were destroyed, whereupon ensued a generall famine in this kingdome."

This entry, it will be observed, has been entirely omitted by the Four Masters.

"Ferall Moyneagh O'Dowgennan founded the church of Killronan."

AOIS CRIOST, 1340.

Aois Criost, mile, trí chéd, cethrachatt.

Mainistir oirḃealaigh hi ccarraic an chiúil ag an ccenn ṫoir do loch léin in esspoccoittecht arda ferta is in muṁain do ṫógḃail durd .S. ffranseis la Még cártaiġ mór prionnsa deasṁuṁan, doṁnall mac taiḋg, ⁊ do ṫoghsat iomatt do ṁaithiḃ an tire a naḋnacal is in mainistir sin. As diḃsiḋe ó Suilleaḃan mór ⁊ an dá ua donnchaḋa.

Coiṁṫógbail cogaiḋ eitir Maineachaiḃ, .i. eittir taḋg mac taiḋg uí ċeallaiġ da ttucc Toirrḋealḃach ua concobair (Ri Connacht) urláṁus ua maine, ⁊ uilliam mac donnchaḋa muiṁnig uí ċeallaiġ go ro cuireaḋ uilliam a tír maine amach ⁊ gé do ḟagaiḃ an tír, tug taḋg ua ceallaiġ gona braiṫriḃ ⁊ cona muintir toraiġeacht dó co ndeachsat i náit iombuailte chuige. Iompaiḋis uilliam ⁊ a muintir friú fochetóir go ro ferad caithghleó etorra. Act chena ro marbaḋ donnchaḋ mac aodha uí cheallaiġ, ⁊ ro ġabaḋ taḋg ó ceallaiġ iar na lot co ndeachaiḋ décc de iaroṁ.

Maoilseachlainn ua gairmleaḋaiġ taoiseach cenél Moain décc.

[r] *Oirbhealach.*—This name is anglicised Irrelagh by Ware, who states that the monastery was founded in the year 1440.

[s] *Carraig-an-chiuil*, i. e. the rock of the music. According to the tradition in the country, and a MS. description of Kerry, written about the year 1750, and now preserved in the Library of the Royal Irish Academy, the site on which this abbey was to be built, was pointed out to Mac Carthy More in a vision, which warned him not to erect his monastery in any situation except at a place called Carraig-an-chiuil; and there being no locality of that name known to him, he sent out a number of his faithful followers to discover where, within his principality, this place was situated. The story goes on to state that, after searching various places, they were returning home in despair; but passing by Oirbhealach, i. e. the eastern road or pass, they heard the most enchanting music issuing from a rock, from which they concluded that it must be the locality of Carraig-an-chiuil, or rock of the music, shewn to their chief in the vision; and they returned home stating what had occurred. Mac Carthy, on hearing their story, felt satisfied that they had found the true locality intended by Heaven for his monastery, and he accordingly commenced the erection of it there without delay.

[t] *Loch Lein.*—This is the ancient and present name of the lower lake of Killarney in the county of Kerry. The abbey of Irrelagh, or, as it is now usually called, Muckruss, is situated near the rocky shore of a small bay at the eastern end of the lower lake of Killarney, and within the demesne of Muckruss, from which it has taken its modern appellation.

[u] *Donnell, son of Teige.*—Here is a most glaring

THE AGE OF CHRIST, 1340.

The Age of Christ, one thousand three hundred forty.

The monastery of Oirbhealach[r] at Carraig-an-chiuil[s], at the eastern end of Loch Lein[t], in the diocese of Ardfert, in Munster, was founded for Franciscan Friars by Mac Carthy More, Prince of Desmond (Donnell, the son of Teige[u]); and the chiefs of the country selected burial places for themselves in this monastery. Among these were O'Sullivan More and the two O'Donohoes.

A war arose between the Hy-Manians, namely, between Teige, the son of Teige O'Kelly (to whom Turlough O'Conor, King of Connaught, had given the chieftainship of Hy-Many), and William, the son of Donough Muimhneach O'Kelly: and William was banished from Hy-Many, and, though he had left the country, Teige O'Kelly, with his kinsmen and people, went in pursuit of him; and when they had reached a spot upon which to fight a battle, William and his people turned round on them [their pursuers]; and a fierce battle was fought between them, in which Donough, the son of Hugh O'Kelly, was killed; and Teige O'Kelly was captured, after having received wounds, of which he died [soon] afterwards.

Melaghlin O'Gormly, Chief of Kinel-Moen, died.

anachronism; but it is probable that it is a mere error of transcription for Donnell, son of Cormac, for he was really the prince of Desmond in 1340. The Editor has not been able to find the record of the erection of this monastery in any of the older Annals, and has never been able to discover where the Four Masters found it. Nothing can be more certain than that both Ware and the Four Masters are wrong in ascribing the foundation of this monastery to Donnell, son of Teige Mac Carthy, for he lived a century later, having died in the year 1468. Teige, the father of this Donnell, was, according to tradition, the original founder of this monastery, and this is corroborated by the fact that he is called *Tadhg Mainistreach*, i. e. Teige of the Monastery, in the authentic pedigrees of the Mac Carthys. But the Four Masters have lost sight of all chronology in placing the erection of this monastery under the year 1340, after ascribing it to Donnell the son of Teige, prince of Desmond, inasmuch as Teige his father did not, according to themselves, become king or prince of Desmond till the death of his father in 1391, that is, fifty-one years after its supposed erection by his son Donnell! The fact seems to be, that the foundation of the monastery was laid some years previously to 1440, by Teige Mainistreach (not by Donnell, as Ware has it), and that the work was completed by his son Donnell in 1440. For some curious notices of the modern state of the ruins and tombs of this abbey, see an interesting article by Mr. Petrie in the Dublin P. Journal, vol. i. pp. 409–11.

Clann ualgairg uí Ruairc, domhnall, aedh, giollacriost ⁊ Ruaidhri do dol for creich dionnsoighidh cathail mic aedha breifnigh co ndernsat creach air. Concobhar mac donnchadha riabhaigh meic Maghnusa mic Muirchertaigh muimhnigh do marbhadh leo an la cedna ⁊ sochaidhe immaille friss. Conadh í sin cédfhola muintire Ruairc ⁊ cloinne Muirchertaigh muimhnigh fria aroile. Cathal mac aedha brefnigh do thoraigheacht a chreche iarsin go rug ar cloinn ualghairce uí Ruairc. Ro feradh iorghal amnus etorra. Domhnall ua Ruairc (aon rogha na breifne dadhbhar tighearna) do mharbhadh don chur soin go sochaidhi moir immaille ris. Giollacriost ua Ruairc ⁊ mac Consnamha do ghabhail iar maidhm for a muintir. Tadhg mac Ruaidhri mic cathail ui Concobhair do baoí illaimh ag ua Ruairce do leigen amach ar comhfhuaslaccadh giollacriost uí Ruairc.

Aodh mac fedhlimidh uí choncobhair do ghabhail do righ Connacht, ⁊ a cor i ccaislén Rossa commain da choimhéd. Coccadh mór ⁊ combuaidhreadh deirghe eittir ua cconcobhair ⁊ mac diarmada trés an ngabháil sin gur ro milleadh morán eatorra da gach taobh. Gluasacht ⁊ gergabhad dfaghail dua Concobhair iarsin dionnsoighidh tucc mac diarmatta chuicce don corann gor cuireadh go haimhdheonach é i mbaile an motaigh isteach, ⁊ síth do cengal dóibh re aroile ara haithle.

Siúrtan Ruadh mac goirdealbhaigh do mharbhadh do cathal mac diarmata gall.

Cathal mac diarmata gall, aon rogha a chinidh ina aoís fein ar ghoil ar ghaisccedh ar treisi ar talchaire do mharbhadh la donnchadh riabhach mac Maoileachloinn charraigh Mec Diarmada tre cheilg i lios Sealbhaigh i cloinn Conchobair.

[v] *The sons of Ualgarg O'Rorke.*—The descendants of this Ualgarg took the surname of Mac Ualghairg, and are still numerous in the county of Leitrim, where they anglicise the name Magolrick or Magoalrick.

[w] *Cathal, son of Hugh Breifneach.*—He seems to have been the principal leader of the turbulent Clann-Murtough O'Conor at this period. His line of descent is given as follows in the pedigree of the O'Conors preserved in the Book of Lecan, fol. 72: "Cathal, son of Hugh Breifneach, son of Cathal Roe, King of Connaught [A.D. 1279], son of Conor Roe, son of Murtough Muimhneach, son of Turlough More O'Conor, monarch of Ireland." This Cathal had seven sons, Owen, Hugh, Rory, Manus, Conor Roe, Cathal Roe, and Murtough, who are the last generation of the pedigree of the Clann-Murtough given in the Book of Lecan, from which it looks highly probable that the tribe disappeared from history soon after.

[x] *Took a prey from him.*—This passage is given more clearly in the Dublin copy of the Annals of Ulster, in which, however, it is incorrectly entered under the year 1337.

The sons of Ualgarg O'Rourke[v], Donnell, Hugh, Gilchreest, and Rory, went upon a predatory excursion against Cathal, the son of Hugh Breifneach[w], and took a prey from him[x]. Conor, the son of Donough Reagh, son of Manus, son of Murtough Muimhneach, and many others, were slain by them on the same day. This was the first rupture between the O'Rourkes and the race of Murtough Muimhneach. Cathal, son of Hugh Breifneach, afterwards went in pursuit of the prey, and overtook the sons of Ualgarg O'Rourke. A fierce battle was fought between them, in which Donnell O'Rourke (only choice of Breifny for a materies of a lord), and many others with him, were slain. Gilchreest O'Rourke and Mac Consnava were taken prisoners, after the defeat of their people. Teige, the son of Rory, son of Cathal O'Conor, who had been imprisoned by O'Rourke, was liberated as the condition of the ransom of Gilchreest O'Rourke.

Hugh, the son of Felim O'Conor, was taken prisoner by the King of Connaught, and sent to be confined in the Castle of Roscommon. A great war and disturbance arose between O'Conor and Mac Dermot, in consequence of this capture, and much destruction was caused by them on both sides. O'Conor was in jeopardy and extreme peril on the occasion of an incursion which Mac Dermot made against him into Corran, when he was forcibly driven into [the Castle of] Ballymote[y], where they afterwards concluded a peace with each other.

Jordan Roe Mac Costello was slain by Cathal Mac Dermot Gall.

Cathal Mac Dermot Gall[z], the only choice of his tribe for his prowess, valour, might, and puissance, was treacherously slain by Donough Reagh, the son of Melaghlin Carragh Mac Dermot, at Lis-sealbhaigh[a] in Clann-Conor.

[y] *Into [the castle] of Ballymote.*—This passage is rendered as follows in Mageoghegan's translation of the Annals of Clonmacnoise:

"A. D. 1340. Hugh Mac Felym O'Conor was taken by Terlagh O'Conor, King of Connaught, and committed to the Castle of Roscommon to be safely kept; for which cause there grew great debate between the King of Connought and Mac Dermott. Mac Dermott, in a skirmish between him and the said King, chased him into the castle of Ballenmotte, which saved the King's life; and afterwards they grew to a composition of peace."

[z] *Cathal Mac Dermot Gall.*—He was chief of Airteach, in the north-west of the county of Roscommon; and it is stated in the Annals of Ulster that he extended his sway over the adjoining territory of Sliabh Lugha, ar euraḋ a laṁ láidire, i. e. by the power of his strong hand.

[a] *Lis-sealbhaigh*, now Lissalway, in the parish

Magnas mac cathail mic doṁnaill uí choncoḃair do ṁarḃaḋ la cathal mac aedha breifniġ uí Concoḃair.

Brian occ macc Shamradháin do ṁarḃaḋ le teallach ndúnchadha.

Eoghan ua heóin tiġearna ua ffiaċrach aiḋne do ṁarḃaḋ la a braithrib féin.

Eoghan mac Seffraiḋ mecc Raġnaill, ⁊ aſdh ua maoílmiaḋaiġ do ṁarḃaḋ aroile.

Pilib ó duibgſndáin ollaṁ Conṁaicne décc.

Uilliam mac gillibert mic goisdealbaiġ do ṁarḃaḋ ar ġrſss is in mbreifne do tellach eaċdaċ.

Ruaiḋri mac maġnusa uí ſgra décc.

Mathġaṁain mac andaiḋ uí Raghallaiġ do marbaḋ la hAindrear mac briain uí Raiġilliġ ⁊ creacha móra do ḋénoṁ ḋó isin mbolgán ara haithle.

Teampall ċille Rónain do loscadh.

Niall ua huiginn saoi firḋána do ḃáthaḋ.

Conċoḃar ua domnaill tiġearna tire conaill cona ṫionol do ḋul i connaċtaiḃ.

AOIS CRIOST, 1341.

Aois Criost, mile, tri chéd, cethrachatt, a hoén.

Muirchſrtach mac an goḃann abb clochair décc.

Maiḋm mór do ṫaḃairt do ṁac uilliam burc ar cloinn Muiris dú inar marḃaḋ tomás mac Muiris, Muiris Mac Seonaic ruaiḋ ⁊ seachtmoghat fſr maraon riú.

Domnall mac donchaiḋ taoiseach cenel duacháin décc.

Donnchaḋ mac meic na hoiḋchi ṁéġ ḟlannchaḋa do marḃaḋ lá haeḋ mac Taḋg még ḟlannchaḋa.

O gairmilſdaiġ taoiseaċ cenél Moáin déġ.

Cathal mac cſitſrnaiġ do marḃaḋ do ſccor.

of Baslick, barony of Ballintober, and county of Roscommon. This fixes the position of the O'Mulrenins, who bore the tribe-name of Clann-Conor.—See note [b], under the year 1193, p. 97, *supra*.

[b] *Bolgan*.—A district near Belturbet, in the north of the county of Cavan, coextensive with the parish of Drumlane. In the year 1454, Donnell Bane O'Reilly had the territory of Bolgan, *alias* Drumlahan, in the neighbourhood

Manus, the son of Cathal, son of Donnell O'Conor, was slain by Cathal, son of Hugh Brefneach O'Conor.

Brian Oge Magauran was slain by the people of Teallach Dunchadha.

Owen O'Heyne, Lord of Hy-Fiachrach-Aidhne, was slain by his own kinsmen.

Owen, son of Geoffrey Mac Rannall, and Hugh O'Mulvey, slew each other.

Philip O'Duigenan, Ollav [i. e. Chief Poet] of Conmaicne, died.

William, the son of Gilbert Mac Costello, was slain in a conflict in Breifny by the people of Teallach-Eachdhach.

Rory, the son of Manus O'Hara, died.

Mahon, the son of Annadh O'Reilly, was slain by Andreas, the son of Brian O'Reilly, who afterwards committed great depredations in the [district of] Bolgan[b].

The church of Kilronan was burned.

Niall O'Higgin, a learned poet, was drowned.

Conor O'Donnell, Lord of Tirconnell, proceeded with his troops into Connaught.

THE AGE OF CHRIST, 1341.

The Age of Christ, one thousand three hundred forty-one.

Murtough Mac-an-Gowan[c], Abbot of Clogher, died.

The Clann-Maurice sustained a severe defeat from Mac William Burke. Thomas Mac Maurice, Maurice, son of Johnock Roe, and seventy men along with him, were slain in the battle.

Donnell Mac Dorcy, Chief of Kinel-Duachain[d], died.

Donogh, grandson of Mac-na-h-Oidhche Mac Clancy, was slain by Hugh, son of Teige Mac Cany.

O'Gormly, Chief of Kinel-Moen, died.

Cathal Mac Keheeny was killed by a fall.

of Belturbet, for his appenage. This name is still well known in the country; and Bolgan is given in Carlisle's Topographical Dictionary as an *alias* name for the parish of Drumlane.

[c] *Mac-an-Gowan*, mac an ᵹoƀann, i. e. son of the smith. This name is generally anglicised Mac Gowan in the north of Ireland, but in Meath and Leinster it is often translated Smith.

[d] *Kinel Duachain.*—More usually called Kinel Luachain, the name of a tribe and territory

Caislén Rossa commain do ghabháil la toirrdhealbhach ua cconchobhair, 7 aedh mac felim boí i mbraighdhenus ann do leigen amach, 7 fuasgladh do thabhairt ass.

Seaan mág mathghamhna do chur a hairghiallaibh.

Brian ua floinn tigearna tellaigh cuirnain décc.

Cuconnacht ua cuinn taoiseach muintire giollgain décc.

Diarmait ruadh mac corbmaic óig meic diarmata dég i naibitt manaigh i mainistir na buille.

AOIS CRIOST, 1342.

Aois Criost, míle, trí chéd, cethrachatt, a dó.

Coimhérghe coccaidh eidir toirrdhealbhach ua cconchobhair 7 conchobhar mac diarmada tighearna moighe luirg. Emann a burc déirghe a ccommbaidh meic diarmata in aghaidh uí chonchobhair.

Aodh mac feidlimidh uí chonchobhair 7 donnchadh ua birn taoiseach tíre briúin na Sionna do chor toirrdhealbhaigh uí Choncobhair i tteampall oile finn iar ndol dó do ghabháil gill creche do rorsat muintir birn ar hoiberd a burc, 7 cuid do galloglachaibh uí chonchobhair do mharbhadh doibh immaille re na consabal, .i. mac Ruaidhri.

Coccadh coitchenn déirghe hi cconnachtaibh iar sin. Clann muirchertaigh do dhol i rann uí conchobhair ar túr in aghaidh meic diarmata, lompúdh doibh iaromh la mac diarmada 7 le mac uilliam. Feall gráineamhail do dénomh do cloinn Muiris iar sin ina noirechtar fein ar cloinn uilliam burc, 7 tomas

nearly co-extensive with the parish of Oughteragh or Ballinamore, in the county of Leitrim.

[e] *A ransom was given*, &c.—This entry is differently worded in the Dublin copy of the Annals of Ulster. In the Annals of Clonmacnoise, as translated by Mageoghegan, it is given thus: "A. D. 1341. The castle of Roscommon was taken by Terlagh O'Connor, King of Connought; [it] was betrayed and yealded over to the said Terlagh by Hugh mac Ffelym O'Conor, before mentioned, that was prisoner therein."

[f] *Muintir-Gilligan.*—A territory in the county of Longford. See note [k], under the year 1234, p. 270.

[g] *To obtain reprisals.*—Mageoghegan renders this passage as follows in his Annals of Clonmacnoise: "O'Byrne chased King O'Connor into the church of Olfin, where some of his gallowglasses were killed, together with their constable and head, Mac Rory. This was done upon an occasion of King Terlagh coming to O'Byrne's contrey to distrain for a prey that O'Byrne took before from Robert Burke, whereof ensued great

The Castle of Roscommon was taken by Turlough O'Conor; and Hugh, the son of Felim, who was a prisoner therein, was liberated, and a ransom was given for him[e].

John Mac Mahon was banished from Oriel.

Brian O'Flynn, Lord of Teallach-Curnain, died.

Cuconnaught O'Quin, Chief of Muintir-Gillagan[f], died.

Dermot Roe, son of Cormac Oge Mac Dermot, died in the habit of a monk, in the Abbey of Boyle.

THE AGE OF CHRIST, 1342.

The Age of Christ, one thousand three hundred forty-two.

A war broke out between Turlough O'Conor and Conor Mac Dermot, Lord of Moylurg; and Edmond Burke rose to assist Mac Dermot against O'Conor.

Hugh, son of Felim O'Conor, and Donough O'Beirne, Chief of Tir-Briuin-na-Sinna, drove Turlough O'Conor into the church of Elphin, after he had gone to obtain reprisals[g] for a prey which O'Beirne's people had carried off from Hubert Burke. On this occasion some of O'Conor's gallowglasses, and his constable, Mac Rory[h], were slain by them.

After this a general war broke out in Connaught. The Clann-Murtough [O'Conor], at first took part with O'Conor against Mac Dermot; but afterwards turned over to the side of Mac Dermot and Mac William [Burke]. An abominable act of treachery was committed by the Clann-Maurice at a meeting[i]

and uncommon calamities thro' out the whole provence," &c. &c.

[h] *Mac Rory.*—He was the leader of a Scottish band of Gallowglasses from the western islands of Scotland, who were at this period in the pay of the King of Connaught. The Mac Rorys descend from Rory the brother of Donnell, the ancestor of the Mac Donnells of Scotland and Ireland. The Mac Rorys, Mac Donnells, and Mac Dowells, were called the Clann-Samhairle, or Clann-Sorley.

[i] *A meeting,* oıpeaċtaṗ, is translated "Assembly" by Mageoghegan. The word is still understood in the north of Ireland. Ꝺaṗoᵹ an oıpeaċtaıṗ was the name of a large oak tree which stood at Blackhill, in the parish of Desertmartin, county of Derry, and the people understand that it means "the tree of the meeting or assembly." This word is used to denote the meetings which the Irish held on hills in the open air, to which reference is often made in the old English statutes, in which it is anglicised *Iraghtes.* For a good example of the use of the word the reader is referred to an extract from the Privy Council Book (of 25 Eliz.), quoted in Hardiman's Irish Min-

burc do ṁarḃaḋ doiḃ, ⁊ Seoinin a burc do ṁarḃaḋ la cloinn Riocaird ar an ccor ccſona tria ḟoraileaṁ cloinne Muiris ⁊ ui ċoncoḃair. Cathal mac giollacriost meic diarmada do ṁarḃaḋ dfſrġal ua thaiḋg ar an ccogaḋ cedna, ⁊ Fearghal mac giollacriost finn mic Corbmaic do ṁarḃaḋ air ḃeós.

Commarcc crodha do thabairt do mac diarmatta gus na huaislib batar ina ḟarraḋ dua cconcoḃair i mbél Atha Slisſn dar lingead an táċ fair ⁊ diarmaitt mac briain uí fſrgail, fſr a aoisi do bḟſrr do conmaicnib, mac hoiberd a burc, ⁊ concobar mac Donnchaḋa duiḃ uí éiliġe do ṁarḃaḋ don chur sin.

Seaan ṁag mathġaṁna tiġſrna oirġiall do dul ar creich go haedh mac Rooilḃ ṁég ṁathġaṁna, ⁊ a ṁarḃaḋ ar dersſḋ na creche, ⁊ a ġallocclaċaiḃ immaille ris do ṁarḃadh ⁊ do badhaḋ.

Corbmac mac Ruaiḋri mic doṁnaill uí ċoncoḃair do ġaḃail la conċoḃar mac taiḋg, ⁊ le Ruaiḋri mac cathail uí Concoḃair. Concobar mac taiḋg do ġaḃail le brian mac Ruaiḋri iarsin, ⁊ a tabairt ḋó i laiṁ concobair meic diarmada, ⁊ a cor da coiṁéd i ccarraic locha cé.

Doṁnall ua dochartaiġ toiseach arda Miodhair ⁊ triocha ched tíre hénda, fear lán deineaċ, ⁊ dſngnaṁ décc, ⁊ Seaan ó doċartaiġ do gabail a ionaid.

Siol Muireadhaiġ uile do iompuḋ ar toirrdealbaċ mac aſdha mic Eoghain immaille ris na maithiḃ oile batar ga toirneaḋ. As iad as oirſghda do eiriġ ḋó an ionbaiḋ sin, Emann mac uilliam burc, Concoḃar mac diarmada tighſrna maigi luirg cona braiṫriḃ, ⁊ cona oireċt uile, aoḋ mac aſḋa breifniġ mic cathal ruaidh uí Concoḃair, Tadhg mac Ruaidhrí uí chóncobhair, Cathal mac aſdha breifniġ mic cathail ruaiḋ go sochraidi na breifne ⁊ ċonmaicne arċſna, ⁊ aſdh mac felim mic aodha mic Eoghain uí ċonċoḃair. Tionól dóiḃsioṁ uile ind agaiḋ ui ċoncoḃair, ⁊ a athċor go haiṁdeonaċ as a ṫír ⁊ as a thaloṁ feisin conaḋ í coṁairle tuccsat a charaid ḋó iarsin dol do ṡaiġiḋ meic diarmada co hincleithe gan raṫugaḋ do ṁorán dfios a ndiongnaḋ siṫ ris. Giḋſḋ fuarattar clann Muirċſrtaiġ sgéla na

strelsy, vol. ii. p. 159: "Item, he shall not assemble the Queen's people upon hills, or use any *Iraghtes.* or *parles upon hills.*"

j *Seoinin*, i. e. little John.

k *Beal-atha-slissen*, i. e. mouth of the ford of the beetles. This ford still retains this name, and is on the Abhainn Uar near Elphin, as already stated. See note under the year 1288.

of their own people against the Clann-William Burke: Thomas Burke was killed by them; and, with similar treachery, Seoinin[j] Burke was slain by the Clann-Rickard, at the instigation of the Clann-Maurice and O'Conor. In the same war Cathal, son of Gilchreest Mac Dermot, was slain by Farrell O'Teige; and Farrell, the son of Gilchreest Finn Mac Cormac, was slain also.

Mac Dermot, and the chieftains who assisted him, gave O'Conor a fierce battle at Beal-atha-Slisen[k], where they crossed the ford in despite of him. Dermot, the son of Brian O'Farrell, the best man of the Conmaicni in his time, the son of Hubert Burke, and Conor, the son of Donough Duv[l] O'Healy, were slain on this occasion.

John Mac Mahon, Lord of Oriel, set out upon a predatory excursion against Hugh, son of Roolv [Rodolph] Mac Mahon; and was slain in the rere of the prey, and his gallowglasses were destroyed by killing and drowning.

Cormac, the son of Rory, son of Donnell O'Conor, was taken prisoner by Conor, the son of Teige, and Rory, the son of Cathal O'Conor; and Conor, the son of Teige, was afterwards taken prisoner by Brian, the son of Rory, and delivered up by him to Conor Mac Dermot, who sent him to be imprisoned in the Rock of Lough Key.

Donnell O'Doherty, Chief of Ardmire, and of the cantred of Tir-Enda, a man full of hospitality and prowess, died, and John O'Doherty assumed his place.

All the Sil-Murray turned against Turlough, the son of Hugh, son of Owen [O'Conor], and joined the other chieftains who were for deposing him. Of those who rose up against him at that time, the following were the most distinguished, namely, Edmond Mac William Burke; Conor Mac Dermot, Lord of Moylurg, with his brothers, and all their adherents; Hugh, son of Hugh Breifneach, son of Cathal Roe O'Conor; Teige, the son of Rory O'Conor; Cathal, son of Hugh Breifneach, son of Cathal Roe, with all the forces of Breifny, and Conmaicne; and Hugh, son of Felim, who was son of Hugh, son of Owen O'Conor. All these assembled against O'Conor, and banished him by force from his country and lands; whereupon his friends advised him to go secretly, and without acquainting any with his intention, to Mac Dermot, to ascertain if he would make peace with him. But the Clann-Murtough[m] had

[l] *Duv*, ‍ꝺub, black.—This epithet is sometimes anglicised *duff*, and sometimes *doo*.

[m] *Clann-Murtough*, i. e. the descendants of Murtough Muimhneach O'Conor, of whom Hugh,

coṁairle sin, ⁊ fios na haidche dáiriḋe ina ttiocfaḋ ua concobair do ṡoiġid meic diarmada, ionnus gur inleadar iatt féin roiṁe ar bḟērnaḋaiḃ baoġail na conaire i ngebaḋ co longport meic diarmata. Aċt ċēna do chuaiḋ toirrḋealḃaċ en triar marcaċ tarra no gur heirġēḋ ḋó ar tócar an longpuirt. Loittēr cathal mac aedha breifniġ lais fo cēttóir, ⁊ ger ḃuathaḋ i naghaiḋ iolair eiriom gona ṫriar oile i mēg na sochaiḋe batar ina aghaiḋ, do chuaiḋ uatha da naiṁḋeóin gan fuiliuġaḋ gan forḋērgaḋ air fein ina ar aon dia ṁuintir. Cioḋ tra acht nochar bfear do mac diarmada toirrḋealḃaċ do beiṫ is in móirécēn sin no go ccuala an tēġim, an mairgneaċ ⁊ an mallachaḋ mór ga ḋénaṁ seachnon an longpuirt, ⁊ iar ffaġḃáil sgél ḋó cuiris daoine tairisi ós iseal i coinne uí ċoncoḃair dia breiṫ gus an ccarraic da caoṁna go ffēsaḋ fēin an ffréḋsaḋ a ṡíḋ do ḋénaṁ. Baoí ó concoḃair iar sin seċtmain, ⁊ maithe na tíre ag tocht ar cuairt chuige, ⁊ uadha ar furaileaṁ mec diarmada. Giḋeaḋ ó naċ bfuair mac diarmada cēḋ na síthe do ḋénaṁ téiḋ fein buiḋēn marcsloiġ les gur ro faġḃatar é i Ros commain.

Conċoḃar (.i. concoḃar ruaḋ) mag Eochagáin tiġērna cenél ḟiachach do ṁarḃaḋ la gallaiḃ.

Tomás ua cinga, Muiris mag Eochagain, Siommon mac concobair mic Siommoin meic giolla arraith taoiseaċ do ṫaoiseaċaiḃ luiġne décc.

Murchaḋ mac tomoltaiġ uí flannagain an trēs fēr do bfērr da chinēḋh do ṁarbad do gallócclachaiḃ meic cathail.

Aodh ṁac aēḋha breifniġ mic cathail ruaiḋ uí ċoncoḃair do riġaḋ do connachtaiḃ ⁊ do ṁac uilliam burc an céd luan do geimreaḋ iar naithriġeaḋ

the son of Hugh Breifneach was now the chief leader.

[n] *Intention*, coṁairle.—The literal meaning of coṁairle is counsel or advice; but it is often used in the same sense as the Latin *consilium*.

[o] *They posted themselves*.—This part of the passage is better expressed in the Annals of Ulster and of Connaught. It is also somewhat better given in the Annals of Clonmacnoise, as translated by Mageoghegan, as follows: "Whereupon he advised with his best friends to come to Mac Dermod's house, whereof Clanmortagh having had intelligence lay privily in ambush in his way, as he was passing with four or five horsemen in his companie in the dark of the night to Mac Dermott's house [but he] escaped narrowly by the force of his vallourous and hardy hand" [tainic uaiṫiḃ artaraḋ a laṁa laidire.—*Ann. Ult.*] "grievously wounded Cathall mac Hugh, Breffneagh (one of these that lay in the ambush), whereof Mac Dermott had no notice until, O'Connor was ferried over into Mac Dermott's

intelligence of this intention[n], and of the particular night on which O'Conor would come to Mac Dermot; and they posted themselves[o] at the several dangerous passes of the road by which he was to pass to Mac Dermot's fortress. Turlough, nevertheless, accompanied by only three horsemen, passed them all, and was not attacked until he had reached the causeway of the fortress. Cathal, the son of Hugh Breifneach, was at once wounded by him; and although he and his three attendants were but the few against the many, compared with the great body of men who opposed them, he made his escape without receiving himself, or any of his attendants, the slightest wound or injury. Mac Dermot, in the mean while, did not know the exceeding danger that Turlough was in, until he heard the cries, groans, and imprecations that were uttered through the garrison; but as soon as he had obtained information, he privately dispatched trusty persons to conduct O'Conor to the [castle of the] Rock, to protect him until he should determine whether he could make peace for him. Here O'Conor remained for a week, during which time, by order of Mac Dermot, the chieftains of the country visited him; but Mac Dermot, not having obtained permission [from the other chieftains] to conclude peace with him, he escorted him with a troop of cavalry, and left him at Roscommon.

Conor (i. e. Conor Roe) Mageoghegan, Lord of the Kinel-Fiachach, was slain by the English.

Thomas O'Kinga, Maurice Mageoghegan [and] Simon, son of Conor, son of Simon Mac Gillaarraith, one of the chieftains of Leyny, died.

Murrough, son of Tomaltagh O'Flanagan, the third best man of his tribe, was slain by the Gallowglasses of the son of Cathal [O'Conor].

Hugh, the son of Hugh Breifneach, son of Cathal Roe O'Conor, was inaugurated by the Connacians and Mac William Burke, on the first Monday of winter, after the deposing of Turlough; and the Tanistship of Connaught was

house of Carrick, where being come Mac Dermott heard the Crys and Lamentations made for the hurting of Cahall; nevertheless he kept O'Conor with him for the space of a sevenight, useing him in his house with such reverence as befitted him, giving liberty to such of his friends and allies to have access to him to converse with him. At last when Mac Dermott could not be licensed to come to an agreement of peace with him, he sent him with safe conduct to the castle of Roscommon, where he left him. Hugh mac Hugh Breafneagh O'Connor was constituted King of

toirrḋealbaiġ dóiḃ, ⁊ tanaiseċt connacht do thabairt dAeḋ mac Feidlimiḋ ui Concobair. Tir noilella do thaḃairt dFſrgal mac Diarmatta.

Tadg mac Tomaltaiġ mic Muirġiusa meic Donnchaiḋ dionnarbaḋ as a ḋuṫaiġ fſin lá Concoḃar mac Diarmata ⁊ la a ḃraiṫribh, ⁊ é do beiṫ i ffarraḋ toirrdealbaiġ uí Concoḃair, ⁊ Fſrġal mac Tomaltaiġ do ġaḃail ṫire hoilella dia ér.

An giolla duḃ Ṁag Uiḋir do bathaḋ for loch éirne.

Matha mac Magnusa bruġaiḋ coitcinn conaiġ na ro diúlt fri dreich nduine do truaġ nó do trén déġ.

Conċoḃar mac Aodha mic Domnaill oíg uí Ḋomnaill tiġſrna ċenel cconuill, íochtair ċonnacht, Ḟſrmanach cenel Moáin ⁊ insi heóġain, Soiḋeach diongṁala dairdriġe Erenn ar chruṫ, ar chéill, ar oineaċ, ar oirrḋſrcus, ar ghaois, ar ġliocus, ar mſnmnaiġe, ar móirċſtraiḋ, ar croḋaċt, ar calmatas, ar craḃaiḋ, ⁊ ċoinderce, do ṁarḃaḋ la a dearḃrathair Niall ó Domnaill iar ttaḃairt ammaiss oiḋċe fair ina longport fſin i Murḃach, ⁊ Niall feisin do ġaḃáil a ionaiḋ.

Flann óg ó Domnalláin ollaṁ connacht i nDán do écc.

Domnall ó Coinleisg saoí ḟſnchaiḋ do ṁarḃaḋ la huiḃ Diarmada gan ria ccairg.

Tomas mac Giollacoisgliġ saoi ar eineaċ ⁊ ar ſngnaṁ do écc.

Piarus Albanaċ do ṁarḃaḋ la cloinn Maoilir meic Feórais.

Connought by Mac William Burke and Connoughtmen, the first Monday of Winter, and also Hugh mac Ffelym was made Tanist of Connought. The territory of Tyreallella was granted to Fferall Mac Dermott, Teig mac Tomulty mac Dermott [being] deposed thereof, and banished by Connor Mac Dermoda, whereupon Teig joyned with Terlagh O'Connor."

[p] *He went over to.*—Literally, "he was along with Turlough O'Conor." Mageoghegan renders it: "Whereupon Teig joyned with Terlagh O'Connor."

[q] *Gilladuv*, an giolla duḃ, i. e. *juvenis niger*. This name is variously anglicised Gillduff, Gillyduff, Kilduff; and, in the surname of Mac Gilla duibh, often shortened to Illduff.

[r] *Matthew Mac Manus.*—According to the Dublin copy of the Annals of Ulster he dwelt on Lough Erne. The head of the family of Mac Manus of Fermanagh had his residence at Belle Isle, in Upper Lough Erne, which is still called Ballymacmanus by the natives. This family is a branch of the Maguires, and is to be distinguished from Mac Manus of Tir-Tuathail, who descended from Manus, the son of Turlough More O'Conor, monarch of Ireland.

[s] *Murbhach.*—There is a place of this name about three miles to the south-west of the town of Donegal. See note [h] under the year 1272, p. 417.—See also *Genealogies, Tribes, and Cus-*

given to Hugh, the son of Felim O'Conor. Tirerrill was given to Farrell Mac Dermot.

Teige, son of Tomaltagh, son of Maurice Mac Donough, was banished from his own patrimony by Conor Mac Dermot and his kinsmen; whereupon he went over[p] to Turlough O'Conor; and Farrell, the son of Tomaltagh [Mac Dermot] took possession of Tirerrill after him.

Gilladuv[q] Maguire was drowned in Lough Erne.

Matthew Mac Manus[r] a general and wealthy Brughaidh [farmer], who never rejected the countenance of man, whether mean or mighty, died.

Conor, the son of Hugh, son of Donnell Oge O'Donnell, Lord of Kinel-Connell, Lower Connaught, Fermanagh, Kinel-Moen, and Inishowen, and worthy heir to the monarchy of Ireland by reason of his personal form, wisdom, hospitality, renown, discretion, and ingenuity, magnanimity, intellectuality, valour, prowess, and his piety and charity, was slain by his brother, Niall O'Donnell, who attacked him by night in his own fortress at Murbhach[s]: and Niall himself assumed his place.

Flann Oge O'Donnellan[t], Ollav of Connaught in poetry, died.

Donnell O'Coinleisg, a learned historian, was slain, a short time before Easter, by the Hy-Diarmada[u].

Thomas Mac Gilla Coisgligh[v], celebrated for his hospitality and prowess, died.

Pierce Albanagh was slain by the sons of Meyler Mac Feorais [Bermingham].

toms of Hy-Fiachrach, p. 297, where the daughter of O'Donnell is called "the woman of Murbhach."

In the margin of the copy of the Annals of the Four Masters, preserved in the library of Trinity College, Dublin, H. 2. 11, the following words are added to the above passage in the hand-writing of Roderic O'Flaherty, author of the *Ogygia*: "In ostio domus suæ apud Findrois a Niello, filio Patris sui combustæ corruit.—*O'Mulconry*."

[t] *O'Donnellan.*—This family had a small district in Hy-Many, called Clann-Breasail; but our annalists have preserved no account of them as chieftains of that district. The only notices of the name to be found in the Annals relate to poets. For a short account of the celebrated persons of the family of O'Donnellan of Ballydonnellan in modern times, the reader is referred to *Tribes and Customs of Hy-Many*, p. 167.

[u] *Hy-Diarmada.*—This was the tribe-name of the O'Concannons of Killtullagh in Hy-Many in the county of Galway.—See note [s], under the year 1201, p. 131, *supra*.

[v] *Mac Gilla choisgle.*—This name is still common in the county of Fermanagh, and in the neighbourhood of Clones in the county of Monaghan, where it is anglicised Cuskly, and, sometimes, Cosgrove.

AOIS CRIOST, 1343.

Aois Criost, mile, trí chéd, ceathrachatt, a trí.

Seaan Mac Eoaigh epscop conmaicne décc.

Iohannes ó Laithimh epscop cille haladh, ⁊ cathal mac an liathanaigh abb na trinoitte décc.

Donnchadh clerech ó Maoilbhrénainn canánach coraidh oile finn do marbhadh durchur soighde le muintir hoiberd mic dabid duinn meic uilliam.

Slaine ingen uí bhriain ben toirrdhealbhaigh uí chonchobhair righ Connacht décc.

Cathal ó Madadháin saoí einigh ⁊ oirrdearcuis a chenél féin do marbhadh la cloinn Ricairtt.

Derbháil ingen aodha uí domhnaill do thoidheacht ar cuairt co hinis doighre drechain meic diarmada, ⁊ galar a hécca do gabháil annsin co bfuair bás ⁊ ro hadhnaicedh go huasal onórach i mainistir na buille, ⁊ nocha ttainicc roimpe dia cineadh aoinbhen rug barr a maithesa.

Dubhchabhlaigh ingen meic diarmada bean uí birn décc.

Muirchertach ua briain tigearna tuadhmuman decc, ⁊ diarmaitt ua briain do gabháil an tighearnais, ⁊ a athchor ar a flaithes la brian ua mbriain, ⁊ maithe tuadhmhuman do umhlughadh do brian iarsin

Tomas macc Shamhradhain taoiseach teallaigh eachdhach décc.

Uilleac mac Riocaird mic uilliam léith, macaomh gall ereann in eneach ⁊ in engnomh décc.

Maidhm mór ria ccloinn feórais ⁊ ria ccloinn riocaird for uíbh maine dú in ro marbhadh aoinfer décc duaislibh maineach im Concobhar cerrbhach ó cheallaigh.

w *Mac Eoaigh.*—In Harris's edition of Ware's Bishops, p. 252, he is set down under the name of John Mageoi, as Bishop of Ardagh, from the year 1331 to 1343.

x *O'Laithimh.*—This name is now usually anglicised Lahiff, but some have rendered it Guthrie, from an erroneous notion that it is derived from lathaigh, i. e. of the slough or puddle. In Harris's edition of Ware's Bishops, p. 650, this bishop is incorrectly called John O'Laitin. In the Dublin copy of the Annals of Ulster, his name is written iohannes ollaitaim (the t and m left unaspirated), and his death placed under the year 1340.

y *Inis Doighre.*—This is probably the island in the river Boyle now called Inishterry. See the Ordnance Map of the County of Roscommon, sheet 7.

z *Nobly and honourably interred,* go huasal onorach.—This is the Irish mode of expressing "She

THE AGE OF CHRIST, 1343.

The Age of Christ, one thousand three hundred forty-three.

John Mac-Eoaigh[w], Bishop of Conmaicne [Ardagh], died.

Johannes O'Laithimh[x], Bishop of Killala, and Cathal Mac-an-Liathanaigh, Abbot of the Monastery of the Blessed Trinity, died.

Donough Cleireach O'Mulrenin, a Canon chorister of Elphin, was slain with one shot of an arrow by the people of Hubert, son of David Donn Mac William [Burke].

Slaine, daughter of O'Brien, and wife of Turlough O'Conor, King of Connaught, died.

Cathal O'Madden, the most distinguished of his own tribe for hospitality and renown, was slain by the Clann Rickard.

Dearbhail, daughter of Hugh O'Donnell, came on a visit to Mac Dermot to Inis-Doighre[y], where she was seized with a fatal sickness and died, and was nobly and honourably interred[z] in the monastery of Boyle. There never was born[a] a woman of her tribe who surpassed her in goodness.

Duvcowlagh, daughter of Mac Dermot, and wife of O'Beirne, died.

Murtough O'Brien, Lord of Thomond, died; and Dermot O'Brien assumed the lordship, but he was banished from his chieftainship by Brian O'Brien; and the chieftains of Thomond then submitted to Brian.

Thomas Magauran, chief of Teallach Eachdhach [Tullyhaw], died.

Ulick, the son of Richard[b], son of William Liath [Burke], the most illustrious of the English youths of Ireland for hospitality and expertness at arms, died.

The Hy-Many suffered a great defeat from the Clann-Feorais [Berminghams], and the Clann-Rickard, on which occasion eleven of the chieftains[c] of Hy-Many, together with Conor Cearbhach[d] O'Kelly were slain.

was buried with great pomp and solemnity."

[a] *There never was born.*—The literal translation is: "There came not before her of her tribe any woman who surpassed her in goodness."

[b] *Ulick, son of Richard.*—This agrees with the text of the Dublin copy of the Annals of Ulster; but in Mageoghegan's translation of the Annals of Clonmacnoise it is given as follows:

"A. D. 1243. Ulick mac Ulick mac Richard mac Ulick, surnamed Ulick Leigh, chief of all the English of Ireland for bounty and prowes, died."

[c] *Chieftains.*—Mageoghegan renders it: "where Connor Karavagh O'Kelly, with eleven princes' sons of that family were slain.

[d] *Cearbhach*, i. e. the gamester or gambler.

Niall ó doṁnaill do cor ar a flaiṫes la haengus ua ndoṁnaill ⁊ le doṁnall (.i. doṁnall dubh) ua mbaoighill, le hua ndochartaigh le nert aodha reaṁair uí néill, ⁊ le cloinn suibne, ⁊ aengus mac concobair mic aedha mic doṁnaill óig do chor hi ttighernus tíre conaill.

Clann Muirċeartaigh do diochur ar an mbreifne la hualgarg ua Ruairc le toirrdealbaċ ua Concobair, ⁊ la Tadg mág Ragnaill co ndeaċsat go tír aedha dionnsoighiḋ uí doṁnaill, ⁊ tug aengus (.i. ó doṁnaill) tír aodha doibh. Tachar do ṫeccṁail iarsin eidir aongus ⁊ Niall (.i. in achaḋ mona) ⁊ clann muircertaigh deirge la haongus in agaiḋ Néill, maiḋm do thabairt leo for niall gona ṁuintir. Aindilis ua baoighill taoíseaċ thíre ainmireaċ cona mac, Eogan mac Airt uí ḋoṁnaill ⁊ sochaiḋe oile do ṁarbaḋ an tan sin, ⁊ aengus do ḃreiṫ buaḋa.

Dauit mág oirechtaigh coṁorba Patraicc décc.

Eóin mag ḋuibne airchideochain droma leathain do écc.

Conċobar mac diarmata tighearna muighe luirg tuile ordain, ⁊ oireachais cloinne maolruanaiḋ moir mic taidg mic caṫail mic concobair do ecc ina tigh féin seċtṁain ria samain dia saṫairn ar aoi laiṫe seaċtmuine iar mbreiṫ buadha o doṁan ⁊ o ḋeṁan, ⁊ a aḋnacal i mainistir na búille, ⁊ Feargal mac diarmata a ḋearbraṫhair féin do oirdneaḋ ina ionad.

Ruaiḋri mag craith ollaṁ leithe moga le dan do ecc.

[e] *Achadh mona*, i. e. bog-field, now Aghawoney, a townland in the parish and barony of Kilmacrenan, and county of Donegal.—See the Ordnance Map of the County of Donegal, sheets 36 and 45.

[f] *Tir-Ainmirech*, i. e. the territory of Ainmire, son of Sedna. This was not O'Boyle's original territory, for, previously to the arrival of the Mac Sweenys from Scotland, he was chief of the Tri-Tuatha, in the north-west of the barony of Kilmacrenan. Tir-Ainmirech was the ancient name of the present barony of Boylagh, in the west of the county of Donegal.

[g] *David Mageraghty.*—This name agrees with that in the Dublin copy of the Annals of Ulster at the year 1342; but he is called O'Hiraghty by Grace and Pembridge, who state that he died in the year 1337. See Harris's edition of Ware's Bishops, p. 81, and Grace's Annals, edited by the Rev. Richard Butler, p. 131. According to a note in O'Flaherty's hand-writing, in the College copy of the Annals of the Four Masters, this David died in the year 1346.

[h] *Mulrony More.*—He was the brother, and, according to some genealogists, the eldest brother of Aedh an gha bhearnaigh, or Hugh of the broken Spear, O'Conor, King of Connaught, who was slain in the year 1067. From this Mulrony the Mac Dermots and Mac Donoughs derived their tribe name of Clann-Mulrony.

[i] *Teige*, i. e. Tadhg *an eich ghil*, or Teige of the White Steed, King of Connaught, who was slain in the year 1030.

[j] *Cathal.*—He was King of Connaught, and

Niall O'Donnell was driven from his principality by Aengus O'Donnell, Donnell Duv O'Boyle and O'Doherty, by the power of Hugh Reamhar O'Neill and the Mac Sweenys ; and Aengus, the son of Conor, son of Hugh Oge, son of Donnell Oge [O'Donnell], was installed in the lordship of Tirconnell.

The Clann-Murtough [O'Conor], were driven out of Breifny by Ualgarg O'Rourke, Turlough O'Conor, and Teige Mac Rannall. They passed into Tirhugh to O'Donnell ; and Aengus (i. e. the O'Donnell), made them a grant of the territory of Tirhugh. Some time afterwards a battle was fought at Achadh-mona[e] between Aengus and Niall; and the Clann-Murtough rose up with Aengus against Niall, and they defeated Niall and his people. In this battle Aindiles O'Boyle, chief of Tir-Ainmirech[f], with his son, Owen, son of Art O'Donnell, and many others, were slain, and Aengus gained the victory.

David Mageraghty[g], coarb of St. Patrick, died.

John Mac Duibhne, Archdeacon of Drumlahan, died.

Conor Mac Dermot, Lord of Moylurg, fountain of the splendour and pre-eminence of the race of Mulrony More[h] the son of Teige[i], son of Cathal[j], son of Conor[k], died at his own house a week before Allhallowtide, on a Saturday, after having overcome the world and the devil, and was buried in the abbey of Boyle. Farrell Mac Dermott, his own brother, was installed his successor[l].

Rory Magrath[m], Ollav of Leth-Mogha in poetry, died[n].

died in the year 1009.

[k] *Conor*, Concoбup.—He was King of Connaught, and the progenitor after whom the O'Conors of Connaught have taken their surname. He died in the year 972. From this it appears that the Mac Dermots of Moylurg are virtually O'Conors, and that their real name is Mac Dermot O'Conor. See *Genealogies, Tribes, and Customs of Hy-Fiachrach*, p. 213, note [k].

[l] *His successor.*—Mageoghegan translates this passage as follows in his version of the Annals of Clonmacnoise:

"Connor Mac Dermodda, prince of Moylurg, the fountain and well-spring of all goodnesss of the family of Clanmolronie, and the son of Teig mac Cahall mac Connor, died in his house on Saturday, seven days before Alhallontide, and was buried in the abbey of Boylle ; in whose place succeeded his own son as prince of Moylorge, namel Fferall mac Connor."

The Dublin copy of the Annals of Ulster contains a quotation from a contemporaneous poet, who asserted that this Conor Mac Dermot excelled all the chieftains of the Irish race of his time in wisdom, valour, hospitality, and bounty. It also states that the Farrell or Ferall was his brother, not his son, as Mageoghegan makes him.

[m] *Rory Magrath.*—He was chief poet and historian to O'Brien in Thomond.

[n] Under this year the Annals of Clonmacnoise, as translated by Mageoghegan, record that Turlough O'Conor, King of Connaught, was restored to his kingdom, and that peace was concluded between him and Mac Dermot.

AOIS CRIOST, 1344.

Aois Criost, mile, tri chéd, ceathrachatt, a ceathair.

Epscob luighne décc.

Murchaḋ mac ṁaoilṁuáiḋ uí ſghra abb na buille ⁊ aḋḃar epscoip luiġne do écc.

Niocól maccraiṫ coṁorba tſrmainn dabeoucc decc.

Art mór mac corbmaic uí ṁaoileaclainn ri miḋe do ṁarḃaḋ la corbmac mballaċ ua maoíleachlainn, ⁊ é fſin do ġabail a ionaid.

Aodh mac Rooilḃ meg Mathġamna tiġearna oirġiall décc, ⁊ Murchaḋ óg ṁág maṫgaṁna do ġabáil an tiġearnais na ḋeoiḋ, ⁊ a écc hi cinn seachtṁaine. Maġnus mac Eocha mic Rooilḃ még ṁathgaṁna do ġabáil an tiġearnais iarsin.

Uilliam mac maṫgamna ṁég Raġnaill do ṁarḃaḋ la macaiḃ cathail ṁeg raġnaill.

Mathġamain mac giollacriost clerig meic diarmata do ṁarḃaḋ la muintir neliġe ar an ccoirrsliaḃ.

Brian mac Ruaiḋri ṁég uiḋir décc.

AOIS CRIOST, 1345.

Aois Criost, mile, trí chéd, ceathrachatt, a cúig.

Giolla na naoṁ ó cianáin abb leasa gabail do écc.

Toirrḋealbach mac aodha mic eoghain uí ċoncobair Rí Connacht do marḃadh durċar do ṡoighitt (.i. is in foġmar) i ffioḋ doradha hi muintiri eolais iar ndol do ċongnaṁ ḋó lá tadhg mag Raġnaill i naġaiḋ ċloinne Muircſrtaiġ muiṁniġ uí ċoncoḃair co loċ airinn. Clann Muircſr-

[o] *Intended bishop*, aḋḃar easpoig, i. e. Materies Episcopi, i. e. Episcopus in fieri. In Mageoghegan's translation of the Annals of Clonmacnoise he is called "Murrogh mac Bryen of the Chalices of the mass."

[p] *Termon-Daveog* is now called Termon Magrath, and is situated in the south of the county of Donegal, near Pettigoe. See note [x], under the year 1196, p. 104.

[q] *Ballagh*, ballaċ, i. e. freckled.

[r] *Muintir-Healy*, i. e. the family of O'Healy. This passage is entered in the Dublin copy of the Annals of Ulster as follows, under the year 1341:

THE AGE OF CHRIST, 1344.

The Age of Christ, one thousand three hundred forty-four.

The Bishop of Leyny [Achonry] died.

Murrough, son of Molloy O'Hara, Abbot of Boyle, and intended Bishop[o] of Leyny, died.

Nicholas Magrath, coarb of Termon-Daveog[p], died.

Art More, son of Cormac O'Melaghlin, King of Meath, was slain by Cormac Ballagh[q] O'Melaghlin, who installed himself in his place.

Hugh, son of Roolbh [Rodolph] Mac Mahon, Lord of Oriel, died, and Murrough Oge Mac Mahon next assumed the lordship, but died in a week afterwards; and the lordship was then assumed by Manus, son of Cochy, son of Rodolph Mac Mahon.

William, the son of Mahon Mac Rannall, was slain by the sons of Cathal Mac Rannall.

Mahon, the son of Gilchreest Cleireach Mac Dermot, was slain on the Coirsliabh [the Curlieu Mountain], by Muintir-Healy[r].

Brian, son of Rory Maguire, died.

THE AGE OF CHRIST, 1345.

The Age of Christ, one thousand three hundred forty-five.

Gilla-na-naev O'Keenan, Abbot of Lisgabhail[s], died.

Turlough, the son of Hugh, son of Owen O'Conor, King of Connaught, was killed in Autumn by one shot of an arrow, at Fidh doradha[t], in [the territory of] Muintir-Eolais, after he had gone to Loch-Airinn[u] to aid Teige Mac Rannall

"*Anno Domini* 1341. Maṫa mac ġillicrist cleriġ mic diarmada do marbaḋ le muintir n-Eilide ar in coirrsliaḃ." Here it is to be noted that cleiriġ, which is a cognomen of ġillicrist, is in the genitive case singular to agree with it.

[s] *Lisgabhail*, now Lisgool, on the margin of Lough Erne, near Enniskillen, in the county of Fermanagh.

[t] *Fidh doradha*, now Fedaro, a townland in the parish of Annaduff, barony of Mohill, and county of Leitrim.—See Ordnance map of that county, sheet 32. The territory of Muintir-Eolais comprised the barony of Mohill, and all that level portion of the county of Leitrim, south of the range of Slieve-an-ierin.

[u] *Loch Airinn.*—This name is still in use, but

taig, ⁊ an chuid oile do muintir eolais dia leanmain go fioḋ doradha, ⁊ a marbaḋ ar guirtín na spideóige, ⁊ nocha ttorchair do ġaoiḋealaiḃ re hathaiḋ roiṁe imċéin sgel buḋ mó inas, ⁊ Aoḋ mac toirrḋealbaiġ do ríoġaḋ ina ionatt.

Brian ua fſrġail dſghaḋbar tiġearna na hanġaile decc. Fear na ro ṫuill imdeargaḋ im ní da bfuair is in mbiṫ, co rug buaiḋ o ḋoṁan, ⁊ o deman.

Aoḋ ó Néill do dul coblaċ ar loch eachach, ⁊ clann aeḋa buiḋe co na ttionól do breiṫ fair, ⁊ daoine iomḋa do lot ⁊ do ṁarbaḋ ſtarra. Aċt ċſna tearna aeḋ ina longaiḃ uaidhiḃ dia naimḋeoin.

Magnus ó floinn line do marbaḋ la doṁnall donn, ⁊ la brian o néill.

Corbmac mac Ruaiḋri uí ċonċobair do écc.

Corrmac mac Muirċſrtaiġ meic lochlainn do ṁarbaḋ la macaiḃ ualġairg meic fſrġail.

AOIS CRIOST, 1346.

Aois Criost, míle, trí chéd, cſṫrachat, a sé.

Coccaḋ do ḟás eitir ua Ruairc, .i. ualgarg, ⁊ Ruaiḋri mac cathail uí ċonċobair. Tachar do ṫſgṁail ſtorra i ccalraiġe locha gile, ⁊ Sraineaḋ

it is generally anglicised Rinn Lough, or Lough a Rinn, which is that of a lake situated a short distance to the south of the town of Mohill, in the barony of Mohill and county of Leitrim. The ruins of a small castle of the Mac Ranalls are still to be seen on the margin of this lake.

[w] *The rest.*—In the Dublin copy of the Annals of Ulster the reading is bloḋ do muinntir Eoluis, i. e. "Some of the Muinter Eolais," which is better.

[x] *Gurtin na Spideoige*, i. e. the little garden or field of the robin redbreast. This name is now forgotten. The place so called was in the immediate vicinity of Fedaro townland. In an inquisition taken in the year 1631, Federree and Cornespedoge are mentioned as in the barony of Mohill and county of Leitrim.

[y] *There had not fallen.*—This passage is translated by Mageoghegan in his version of the Annals of Clonmacnoise, as follows:

"A. D. 1345. Terlagh O'Connor, King of Connaught, after he had reigned twenty-one years, was killed by the shoote of an arrow in Ffyedorowe in Moynter-Eolas, being [having] purposely gone thither to assist Teige Mac Ranell against Clann Mortagh, at Logh Aryn, whom the said Clann Mortagh and the rest of the inhabitants of Moyntir Eolas pursued to Fydorowe, and there, at a place called Gortyn Spideoge, was killed by an arrow, as aforesaid. There was not a greater exploit done by an arrow since Neale of the Nine Hostages was killed by Eochie mac Enna Kynseallagh at the Tyrhian seas; in whose [i e. Terlagh's] place Hugh Mac Terlagh was

against the descendants of Murtough Muimhneach O'Conor. The Clann-Murtough and the rest[w] of the Muinter-Eolais pursued him as far as Fidh Doradha, and killed him at Gurtin-na-spideoige[x]. For a long time before there had not fallen[y] of the Gaels, any one more to be lamented than he. Hugh, son of Turlough, was inaugurated King in his place.

Brian O'Farrell, worthy materies of a lord of Annaly, died. He was a man who never earned censure[z] on account of anything he ever acquired, even up to the hour when he overcame the world and the devil.

Hugh O'Neill went with a fleet on Lough Neagh, and the Clann-Hugh-Boy[a], with their muster, overtook him, and many persons were wounded and killed [in the contest] between them ; but Hugh made his escape, in despite of them, in his ships.

Manus O'Flynn[b] Line [i. e. of Moylinny], was slain by Donnell Donn and Brian O'Neill.

Cormac, the son of Rory O'Conor, died.

Cormac, son of Murtough Mac Loughlin, was slain by the sons of Ualgarg, son of Farrell [O'Rourke][c].

THE AGE OF CHRIST, 1346.

The Age of Christ, one thousand three hundred forty-six.

A war broke out between O'Rourke, i. e. Ualgarg, and Rory, the son of Cathal O'Conor; and an engagement took place between them in Calry-Lough-

constituted King of Connaught."

[z] *Earned censure.*—In the Dublin copy of the Annals of Ulster the reading is, "ꞃαınıc ᵹαn αen ᵹuꞇ αċmoꞃαın ó éᵹꞃıƀ ⁊ ó ollαmnαıƀ Єꞃenn," i. e. "he passed through life without any reproach from the literati or chief poets of Ireland." The meaning is, that he had been so generous to the poets that none of them attempted to lampoon him.

[a] *Clann-Hugh-Boy*, i. e. the race of Hugh Boy O'Neill, who was slain in the year 1283. They possessed, at this period, an extensive territory to the east of Lough Neagh in the present counties of Down and Antrim, and which was called Clann Aodha Buidhe,—*Anglice*, Clannaboy,—from their tribe-name.

[b] *O'Flynn.*—This name is now usually anglicised O'Lyn, by aspirating the initial ḟ, which seems to have been also the mode of pronouncing the name at a very early period. See note [s] under the year 1176, pp. 24, 25.

[c] Under this year O'Flaherty adds, in the College copy, the following passages from the Annals of Lecan :

for ua Ruairc ⁊ a gallocclaċa uile do ṁarḃaḋ, .i. máġ buirrce [⁊] mac neill caimm co na muintir. O Ruairc do leanṁain do Ruaiḋri ua cconcoḃair ⁊ do cloinn nDonnchaiḋ ara haithle, ⁊ a ṁarḃaḋ la maolruanaiḋ mac donnchaiḋ, ⁊ ro buḋ móirécht eriḋe.

Ceithre meic cathail mic an ċaoich még Raġnaill do ġabail ar loċ an sguir do chonchoḃar mag Raġnaill, Tomaltaċ mág Raġnaill da mbreith lais co Cairiol coirccraigh, ⁊ a marḃaḋ dó ann sin.

Cuulaḋ mac cathmaoil toísreaċ cenél fſradhaiġ do marḃaḋ la doṁnall mac caṫmaoil.

Maiḋm la brian mág maṫġamna for ġallaiḃ go ráinicc trí ċétt cſnn in airſmh ḋiḃ.

Niall ó doṁnaill, clann Muirchſrtaiġ, mac feḋlimiḋ uí concoḃair, ⁊ Muirġſr mac diarmata do lſnṁain Ruaiḋri mic cathail go cúil maoile go ttugsat maiḋm fair, ⁊ for cloinn nDonnchaiḋ annsin gur cuireaḋ ár orra, ⁊ a ccreachaḋ ara haithle ḋóiḃ go mbaoí a lor ḋaochain creach lais.

Mac diarmada gall do ṁarḃaḋ tre feill ina tiġ féin la cloinn Uailrin meic goirdealḃaiġ ⁊ corrmac caoch mac fínġin do ṁarḃaḋ ḋóiḃ imaille fris.

Concoḃar ua birn do ṁarḃaḋ

Iomar mac Murchaḋa uí fſrġail do ṁarḃaḋ la brian mac tiġearnain, ⁊ la cloinn meic Muircſrtaiġ.

Art mac tomáir uí Ruairc do ṁarḃaḋ la doṁnall mag tiġearnain.

"Odo O'Roirk Rodericum filius Cathaldi O'Conor apud fara coilleaḋ deprædatus, in templum cille hoiriġ confugit, et templo incenso occiditur.—MS. L."

"Amlaus (Donaldus rector) O'Flaherty occidentalis Connaciæ dominus obiit.—MS. L."

"Jacobus O'Corcrain, Archidiaconus Brefiniæ, et Florentius O'Corcrain insignis Cytharædus obierunt."—MS. L.

[d] *Calry-Lough-Gill*, calraiġe loċa gile, was a territory in the county of Sligo, bordering upon Lough Gill. The name is still preserved in Calry or Colry, a parish bordering upon this lake.

[e] *Galloweglasses.*—The Irish of the middle ages trained two kinds of infantry; one, called gallowglasses, were armed with an iron helmet, a coat of mail and a cuirass, and carried in one hand a fine-edged battle-axe, like that used by the ancient Gauls, of whom Marcellinus speaks in his 19th Book; the other were light-armed, and are called by Henry of Marleburgh Turbiculi, by others Turbarii, and popularly kerns: they fought with javelins tied with strings, darts, and knives called *skeynes*. In an Act passed in the fifth year of Edward III., c. 25, among the articles to be observed in Ireland the sixth was "against the leaders and supporters of kerns and the people called idlemen, unless on the confines

Gill[d], in which O'Rourke was routed, and all his gallowglasses[e] slain, i. e. Mac Buirrce, and Mac Neill Cam[f] with their people. O'Rourke was afterwards pursued by Rory O'Conor and the Clann-Donough, and was killed by Mulrony Mac Donough. This was a lamentable deed[g].

The four sons of Cathal, the son of the Caech [Monoculus] Mac Rannall, were taken prisoners on Loch-an-Sguir[h] by Conor Mac Rannall. Tomaltagh Mac Rannall afterwards brought them to Caisiol Cosgraigh, where they were put to death by him.

Cu-Uladh Mac Cawell, chief of Kinel-Farry, was slain by Donnell Mac Cawell.

A victory was gained by Brian Mac Mahon over the English, and three hundred of their heads[i] were counted [after the battle].

Niall O'Donnell, the Clann-Murtough [O'Conor], the son of Felim O'Conor and Maurice Mac Dermot, pursued Rory, the son of Cathal [O'Conor] to Cul-Maoile [Coloony], where they defeated him and the Clann-Donough with great slaughter. They afterwards plundered them, and carried off abundance of booty.

Mac Dermot Gall was treacherously killed in his own house by the sons of Waldrin Mac Costello; and Cormac Caech Mac Fineen was slain along with him.

Ivor, the son of Murrough O'Farrell, was slain by Brian Mac Tiernan and the Clann Murtough.

Art, son of Thomas O'Rourke, was slain by Donnell Mac Tiernan.

of the enemy's territory, and at their own expense."—*Ware's Antiquit.* c. xxi.

"The gallowglass succeeded the horseman, and he is commonly armed with a skull, a shirt of mail, and a Gallowglass axe," &c. &c.—*Barnabie Riches' New Irish Prognostication*, p. 37.

[f] *Mac Buirrce, &c.*—The Four Masters have omitted the 7, αγυγ, which renders this passage obscure, but the Editor has restored it from the Dublin copy of the Annals of Ulster. Mac Buirrce and Mac Neill Cam were Scots, and captains of gallowglasses employed in O'Rourke's service.

[g] *Lamentable deed.*—This entry is more briefly but far more correctly given in the Dublin copy of the Annals of Ulster, in which it is stated that the killing of O'Rourke is the most lamentable event that had occurred in Ireland since the killing of Cormac Mac Cullennan.

[h] *Loch-an-Sguir*, now Lough Scur. It is situated in the parish of Kiltubbrid, in the barony and county of Leitrim, near the village of Keshcarrigan. There is an island in this lake called Castle Island, on which stand the ruins of a castle called Caiplean Seóin, or John's castle, and another island called Prison Island on which, according to tradition, Mac Rannall was wont to confine his prisoners.

[i] *Three hundred heads.*—This is very rudely

AOIS CRIOST, 1347.

Aois Criost, míle, trí chéd, ceaṫrachatt, a Seacht.

Maolmaoḋóg ó táiċliġ oifficél locha herne do écc.

Giolla na naoṁ mac Seaffraiḋ mic giolla na naoṁ uí ḟerghail tiġearna na hangaile cenn coranta conṁaicneaċ ar ġoil ar gaisccidh, ar eneach, ⁊ ar oirrdearcus do écc i ccluain lis béic iar mbeiṫ athaiḋ imchian in airdċennus na hanġoile ḋó ⁊ é do breiṫ buaḋa ó ḋoman ⁊ ó ḋeman. Cathal mac murchaḋa mic giolla na naoṁ uí ḟerġail do ġabail tiġearnais na hangaile iaroṁ.

Muirġius mac diarmata do ṁarḃaḋ la Seaan ruaḋ mac dauid a burc.

Taḋg máġ Raġnaill taoiseach ṁuintire heólais do ġabail do cloinn Muirceartaiġ.

Uilliam Mac dauid do ṁarḃaḋ do ṫaḋg ruaḋ mac diarmata gall i mbaile an tobair.

Tomas mac artain tiġearna ua neachḋaċ ulaḋ do chrochaḋ la gallaiḃ.

Eoghan ua madaḋain taoiseach Sil nanmchadha décc ⁊ Murchaḋ a ṁac do ġabail cennais Sil nanmchaḋa.

Aengus mac gaḋra uí Madaḋain do écc.

Teampall chille Rónáin do chor suas dfearġal ua duiḃgionnáin.

Finnguala inġen meic fingin bean ḟerġail uí duiḃgionnain décc.

Enrí mac aedha buiḋe uí neill, fionnġuala inġean Maoilseaċlainn uí Raiġilliġ, ⁊ an giolla duḃ mac gille Mochua decc.

Donnchaḋ mac aedha óig uí ferġhail décc.

Síoraḋ ó cuirnín saoí ḟileaḋ ⁊ ollaṁ na breifne eriḋe do ecc.

stated by the Four Masters. In the Dublin copy of the Annals of Ulster the reading is: "Maḋm la brian mag maṫġaṁna ar gallaiḃ da ruinic tri c. ceann co laṫair," i.e. "a defeat was given by Brian Mac Mahon to the English, of whose heads three hundred were brought in his presence."

[j] *Cluain-lis-Bec.*—See other references to this place at the years 1282 and 1322.

[k] *Mac David Burke.*—He was chief of the territory of Clanconow or Clanconway, on the west side of the river Suck in the barony of Ballimoe and county of Galway. See note [s], under the year 1225.

[l] *Ballintober*, baile an tobair, i.e. the town of the well. This is the Ballintober in the county of Roscommon, which is usually called by the annalists baile tobair Ḃriġde, i.e. the town of St. Bridget's well, to distinguish it from baile tobair Páḋraig, now Ballintober, in the county of Mayo. Mac Dermot Gall was Chief of Airteach, in the county of Roscommon.

THE AGE OF CHRIST, 1347.

The Age of Christ, one thousand three hundred forty-seven.

Maelmaedhog O'Taichligh, Official of Lough Erne, died.

Gilla-na-naev, the son of Geoffrey, son of Gilla-na-naev O'Farrell, Lord of Annaly, chief protector of the Conmaicni, for his prowess, valour, hospitality, and renown, died at Cluain-lis-bec[j], after having been for a long time Chief of Annaly, and after having gained the victory over the world and the devil. Cathal, the son of Murrough, son of Gilla-na-naev O'Farrell, assumed the lordship of Annaly after him.

Maurice Mac Dermot was slain by John Roe Mac David Burke[k].

Teige Mac Rannall, Chief of Muintir-Eolais, was taken prisoner by the Clann-Murtough [O'Conor].

William Mac David [Burke] was slain at Ballintober[l] by Teige Roe Mac Dermot Gall.

Thomas Mac Artan, Lord of Iveagh[m], in Ulidia, was hanged by the English.

Owen O'Madden, Chief of Sil-Anmchadha, died; and Murrough, his son, assumed the chieftainship of Sil-Anmchadha[n].

Aengus, the son of Gara O'Madden, died.

The church of Kilronan was re-erected by Farrell O'Duigenan[o].

Finola, daughter of Mac Fineen, and wife of Farrell O'Duigenan, died.

Henry, son of Hugh Boy O'Neill; Finola, daughter of Melaghlin[p] O'Reilly; and Gilladuv Mac Gillamochua, died.

Donough, the son of Hugh Oge O'Farrell, died.

Siry O'Curnin[q], a learned poet and Ollav of Breifny, died.

[m] *Lord of Iveagh.*—The Mac Artans did not retain this dignity long, for the Magennises appear henceforward as lords of this territory.

[n] *Sil-Anmchadha.*—This is pronounced Sheel-Anmchy: for its situation and extent see note [k] under the year 1178, p. 44, *supra*.

[o] *O'Duigenan.*—This passage is better given from O'Mulconry's Annals, by O'Flaherty, in the College copy, H. 2. 11, thus:

"Finola, daughter of Owen Mac Fineen, and wife of Farrell Muimhneach O'Duigenan, Erenagh of Kilronan, died."

[p] *Melaghlin*, Maolpeaclainn.—This name, which is sometimes written Maoilpeacnaill, and Maoileaclainn is usually anglicised *Malachy*, but with what degree of propriety may be questioned, as it signifies the servant or devotee of St. Seachlainn or Secundinus, disciple of St. Patrick.

[q] *O'Curnin.*—The Annals of Lecan, as quoted

AOIS CRIOST, 1348.

Aois Criost, míle, trí chéd, cſthrachatt a hocht.

Giolla na naomh ua cianain abb lſsa gabail do écc.

Niall garbh ua domhnaill tighſrna tíre conaill, iar bfaghbail mór nimrſsna dó hi ttighſrnus ⁊ ria ttighſrnus, do marbhadh la Maghnuss meabhlach ua ndomhnaill tria cheilg ⁊ fiongail (.i. i port insi Saimer). Ba cur crodha comnart cosnamhach an ti niall go sin, ⁊ ba liach a aoidead amhlaidh sin. Aonghus mac conchobhair uí dhomhnaill baoi in imresain fri niall do ghabhail an tighearnais.

Cathal ó fſrgail tighearna na hangaile décc.

Maoileachlainn mág oireachtaigh taoiseac muintire roduibh, ⁊ Donnchadh mag bradaigh taoiseach cuile brighde décc.

Coimheirghe choccadh eidir fſrgal mac diarmada ⁊ Ruaidhri mac cathail mic domhnaill uí chonchobhair. Longport meic diarmada do loscadh la Ruaidhri. Mac diarmata do thionol a charad ara haithle co ndeachsatt i ndiaidh Ruaidhri go a longport go baile an mhotaigh gur ro loisceadh an baile leó eittir cloich ⁊ crann, ⁊ ni ro cuiread na naghaidh gur tillſett dia ttighibh doridhisi. Tugsat mac uí Ruairc baoí i mbraighdeanus is in mbaile ass immaille re gach braghaid oile da ffuairſett ann.

Clann feorais do ionnarbhadh la hémann a búrc gur bo heigſn do Mac feorais tocht dia chothughadh go teagh uí concobhair.

by O'Flaherty in the College copy of these Annals, call him "a learned poet and musician;" and add, that he died "in religione et peregrinatione."

[r] *O'Keenan.*—His death has been already entered under the year 1345.

[s] *Murderously*, i fiongail.—Properly means the murder of a kinsman.

[t] *Meabhlach*, i. e. the deceitful.

[u] *Inis-Saimer.*—At Ballyshannon. See note [b] under the year 1197, p. 111.

[w] *Melaghlin Mageraghty.*—In the Annals of Ulster he is called "impir in einigh, feithmeoir na feile ⁊ didneoir na daennachta, i. e. the emperor of hospitality, the servant of generosity, and the shelterer of benevolence." And it is added, that the professors of poetry and the sciences were grieved and broken-hearted on hearing of the death of this kind chieftain.

[x] *Cuil-Brighde.*—This, which is more generally written Cuil Brighdein, was the name of Mac Brady's territory, comprising the district round Stradone, in the county of Cavan. See other notices of it at the years 1378 and 1412. The name Mac Brady is now always made Brady, without the prefix Mac.

[y] *Mac Dermot's fortress*, longport meic diar-

THE AGE OF CHRIST, 1348.

The Age of Christ, one thousand three hundred forty-eight.

Gilla-na-naev O'Keenan[r], Abbot of Lisgabhail, died.

Niall Garve O'Donnell, Lord of Tirconnell, after having experienced much contention, before and during the term of his lordship, was treacherously and murderously[s] slain by Manus Meabhlach[t] O'Donnell, his kinsman, at the port of Inis-Saimer[u]. Niall was a brave, puissant, and defensive hero till then, and it was a sorrowful thing that he should have died in such a way. Aengus, the son of Conor O'Donnell, who had been in contention with Niall, assumed the lordship.

Cathal O'Farrell, Lord of Annaly, died.

Melaghlin Mageraghty[w], Chief of Muinter Rodiv, and Donough Mac Brady, Chief of Cuil Brighde[x], died.

A war broke out between Farrell Mac Dermot, and Rory, the son of Cathal, son of Donnell O'Connor. Mac Dermot's fortress[y] was burned by Rory. Mac Dermot afterwards assembled his friends, and they pursued Rory to his fortress at Ballymote, and burned the town, both stone and wooden edifices, and they did not meet any opposition until they reached home[z]. They took away the son of O'Rourke, that was in captivity in the town, together with every other captive they found there.

The Clann-Feorais [the Berminghams], were banished by Edmond Burke, and Mac Feorais[a] was compelled to go to the house of O'Conor for his support[b].

maoa.—This was not the castle in Lough Key commonly called Carraig Locha Cé, or the rock of Lough Key; but a fortification situated on Longford hill, now enclosed in Lord Lorton's demesne.

[z] *Until they reached home.*—This is the literal translation; but the idea intended to be conveyed is, that they returned home without having met any opposition. The words, as constructed in the original Irish, might imply that they did receive opposition on their return home; but although this is obviously not the meaning intended, the Editor has thought proper to preserve the order of the original construction, to give the reader an exact idea of the style of the original.

[a] *Mac Feorais*, i. e. the head of the Berminghams.

[b] *Support.*—O'Flaherty adds from the Annals of Lecan, in H. 2. 11 (Trinity College, Dublin):

"Gelasius Mac Tigernan obiit.—MS. L."

"An cluiche multos e vita sustulit.—MS. L."

AOIS CRIOST, 1349.

Aois Criost, míle, trí chéd, cſthrachatt, anaoí.

Maiḋm do ṫabairt la haoḋ ua Ruairc ar ḟlaiṫbſrtach ua Ruairc ar donnchaḋ ua nDoṁnaill, ⁊ ar Dartraiġiḃ. Aoḋ macc flannchaiḋ taoiseaċ Dartraiġe giollacriost mag ḟlannchaḋa, lochlainn mac aindilis uí ḃaoíghill ⁊ sochaiḋe immaille friú do ṁarḃaḋ don commarc hisin.

Eoin duḃ mac doṁnaill do ṁarḃaḋ la Maġnus mac eochaḋa ṁéġ maṫġaṁna.

Giolla na naoṁ ó huiginn Saoí le dán décc.

Coimeirġe do denoṁ eidir mac nDiarmada do Riḋiri ⁊ Ruaiḋri ua concoḃair gur ro ṫionóil Mac diarmada an méd fuair do ġallaiḃ, ⁊ gaoiḋealaiḃ im cloinn Muirċſrtaiġ ⁊ im cenél cconaill ḋo ṡoiġiḋ mic caṫail. Ruaiḋri do ġluasaċt rompa, ⁊ a ċur go cloinn fſrmaiġe ḋóiḃ. Giḋeaḋ nochar ḟédsatt uile eittir ġallaiḃ ⁊ gaoiḋealaiḃ greim do gabail air. Iompaíd ara haiṫle gan nſrt gan eidirſḋha. Ruaiḋri do ṫhionol soċraide iarsin gur loisg, gur mill, ⁊ gur airccſttair urṁór maighe luirg uile.

Plaiġ mór in erind, ⁊ go hairiḋe i muiġ luirg co ttugaḋ ár diarṁiḋe ar ḋaoíniḃ da bíṫin. Matha mac cathail uí Ruairc décc don plaiġ hisin.

Donnchaḋ riaḃach mac Maoileachloinn carraiġ meic diarmada do ġaḃail la corbmac boḋar mac diarmata, ⁊ é da breiṫ lais i nairteach, ⁊ a marḃaḋ i nduinetháiḋe do ṁuintir airtiġ, do mac giollacriost mic taiċliġ, ⁊ dua cearnaiġ.

Risderd ua Raġallaiġ tiġearna na breifne thoir, ⁊ mac an iarla do écc.

Gillebert ua flandagáin taoiseach tuaithe Ratha do marḃaḋ do ṁacaiḃ briain uí flannagáin.

[c] *Mac Clancy.*—This name is now anglicised Clancy, without the prefix Mac. It is locally pronounced in Irish as if written mag lannaċaiḋe.

[d] *Dartry.*—This territory comprised the present barony of Rossclogher, in the north of the county of Leitrim, where the Clancys, or Maglanchys, are still numerous.

[e] *The son of Cathal*, i. e. Rory O'Conor, who was at this time the chief leader of the race of Brian Luighneach, the ancestor of O'Conor Sligo. The Clann-Murtough were the descendants of Murtough-Muimhneach, the brother of Brian Luighneach.

[f] *Plague.*—This plague is noticed in Mageoghegan's version of the Annals of Clonmacnoise, under the year 1348, as follows:

"A. D. 1348. There was a generall plague in

THE AGE OF CHRIST, 1349.

The Age of Christ, one thousand three hundred forty-nine.

Hugh O'Rourke defeated Flaherty O'Rourke, Donough O'Donnell, and the people of Dartry; and Hugh Mac Clancy[e], Chief of Dartry[d], Gilchreest Mac Clancy, Loughlin, son of Aindiles O'Boyle, and many others, were slain in the engagement.

John Duv Mac Donnell was slain by Manus, son of Eochy Mac Mahon.

Gilla-na-naev O'Higgin, a learned poet, died.

Another contest arose between Mac Dermot and Rory O'Conor. Mac Dermot assembled all the English and Irish whom he found to aid him, together with the Clann-Murtough and the Kinel-Connell, against the son of Cathal[e]. Rory moved before these, and they drove him to Clann-Fermaighe, but the entire body of them, both English and Irish, were unable to take him. They afterwards returned without acquiring power or obtaining hostages; and Rory then mustered a force and burned, wasted, and plundered the greater part of Moylurg.

A great plague [raged] in Ireland, and more especially in Moylurg, by which great numbers were carried off. Matthew, the son of Cathal O'Rourke, died of this plague[f].

Donough Reagh, the son of Melaghlin Carragh Mac Dermot, was taken prisoner by Cormac Bodhar[g] Mac Dermot, who led him to Airteach; and he was killed in secret murder[h] by the people of Airteach, i. e. by the son of Gilchreest Mac Taichligh and O'Kearney.

Richard O'Reilly, Lord of East Breifny, and the son of the Earl, died.

Gilbert O'Flanagan, Chief of Tuath-Ratha[i], was slain by the sons of Brian O'Flanagan.

Moylurg and all Ireland in general, whereof the Earle of Ulster's grandchild died: also Mathew mac Cahall O'Royrck died of it."

[g] *Bodhar* (pronounced *bower*), i. e. the deaf. From this the Hiberno-English word *bother* is supposed to have been formed.

[h] *Secret murder.*—This is written ḋunaṫaiḋe in the Dublin copy of the Annals of Ulster, in which this passage is entered under the year 1346. In a manuscript in the Library of the Royal Irish Academy, No. 315, p. 288, this term is thus defined: "Duinaṫaiḋe, .i. marḃaḋ duine i ffell, ꞅa ċorp do ḟolċaḋ iar ꞅin, i. e. *Duinathaide*, to kill a man in treachery, and to conceal his body afterwards."

[i] *Tuath-ratha.*—Now anglicised Tooraah. It

Muirċ̄ṡrtach riaccánach ṁág aonghusa do ṁarbaḋ lá a ḃráiṫriḃ buḋḋéin.

Ruaiḋri ua cathain tighḟrna na craoiḃe, ⁊ airdi cianaċta do écc.

Aoḋ ua Raghallaigh do écc.

An giolla caéch ṁág dorchaiḋ do écc.

Muirghḟs mac donnchaiḋ taoíseaċ an ċorainn fear lán daiṫne, ⁊ deneaċ do écc.

Maiḋm mór do ṫaḃairt lar an lustis ⁊ la gallaiḃ na Miḋe ar ua Maoileachloinn ⁊ ar ġaoiḋealaiḃ na Miḋe dú i ndorcratar sochaiḋe dia maiṫiḃ.

AOIS CRIOST, 1350.

Aois Criost, míle, trí chéd, caoccatt.

Uilliam ó dubhda Epscop chille hAladh, fḟr tógbala ceall ⁊ neimhḟdh, Saoí diadha, deircach, daonnachtaċ do écc.

Aodh (.i. rí connaċt) mac aḟdha bréifnicch uí ċoncobair ris a ráití ua concobair do ṁarbaḋ la haeḋ ua ruairc i moigh angaidhe.

Fḟrgal ua ruairc mac ualgaircc do ṁarbaḋ do mac cathail cleirig meic donnchaḋa.

Brian mac diarmada aḋbar tigearna ṁaighe luircc do ṁarbaḋ i Ros commain la muintir an epscoip uí finaċta daon urchar soighde co tḟgṁaiseaċ, ⁊ an fear ar ar cuireaḋ an troigead do chaiṫḟiṁ (Ruaiḋri an creompa ó donnchaḋa) do ċiorrbaḋ fo ċéttóir ina éraic.

is still the local name of a district in the county of Fermanagh, lying between Lough Melvin and Lough Erne, and comprising the parishes of Inismacsaint and Boho. See note [q] under the year 1260, p. 379.

[k] *Kinsmen*, ḃráiṫriḃ. — In Mageoghegan's translation of the Annals of Clonmacnoise this is rendered "brothers," thus:

"A. D. 1348. Mortagh Riaganach Magenos was killed by his own brothers."

[l] *Ard-Keanaghta.*—The prefix *ard* here is evidently a mistake.

[m] *A defeat was given.*—This is the literal translation. It would be better expressed in English as follows:

"A great victory was gained by the Justiciary and the English of Meath over O'Melaghlin and the Irish of Meath, and many of the Irish chieftains were slain."

[n] *Man*, saoi.—The word saoi, which is rendered doctor by Colgan, has the same meaning in the ancient Irish as duine uasal has in the modern. It might be translated "gentleman" throughout, but the Editor has translated it by "learned man," "eminent man," or "distinguished man" throughout.

[o] *Magh-Angaidhe.*—This is probably the place in Breifny, now called Moy, *alias* Newtown-

Murtough Riaganagh Magennis was slain by his own kinsmen[k].

Rory O'Kane, Lord of Creeve and Ard-Keanaghta[l], died.

Hugh O'Reilly died.

Gilla-Caech Mac Dorcy died.

Maurice Mac Donough, Chief of Corran, a man full of intelligence and hospitality, died.

A great defeat was given[m] by the Lord Justice and the English of Meath to O'Melaghlin and the Irish of Meath, in which many of their chieftains were slain.

THE AGE OF CHRIST, 1350.

The Age of Christ, one thousand three hundred fifty.

William O'Dowda, Bishop of Killala, founder of many churches and sanctuaries, and a godly, charitable, and humane man[n], died.

Hugh (i. e the King of Connaught), the son of Hugh Breifneach O'Conor, and who was called the O'Conor, was slain in Magh-Angaidhe[o] by Hugh O'Rourke.

Farrell O'Rourke, the son of Ualgarg, was slain by the son of Cathal Cleirach Mac Donough.

Brian Mac Dermot, materies of a lord of Moylurg, was accidentally slain at Roscommon with one shot of a javelin[p] by the people of Bishop O'Finaghty[q]; and the man who was charged with having cast the dart (Rory-an-t-Seomra O'Donohoe[r]), was immediately mangled[s] as an *eric* [retaliation] for him [Brian].

Gore.—See Ordnance map of the county of Leitrim, sheet 26.

[p] *Of a javelin*, ꞅoıġꝺe.—The Irish word ꞅoıġeaꝺ or ꞅaıġeaꝺ, which is cognate with the Latin *sagitta*, generally signifies a shaft or arrow; but it sometimes also denotes a javelin not discharged from a bow, but thrown by the hand.

[q] *Bishop O'Finaghty.*—He was John O'Finaghty, Bishop of Elphin, called John of Roscommon, in his Patent of restitution to the temporalities, 1st March, 1326. In Harris's edition of Ware's Bishops he is erroneously called *John O'Findsa*, an error which arose from mistaking the contracted writing of the name, o ꝼınꝺꞅa, in the Annals of Ulster or of Lough Kee.

[r] *O'Donohoe.*—He was evidently one of the sept of O'Donnchadha of Hy-Cormaic in Moinmoy. See *Tribes and Customs of Hy-Many*, p. 76, note [w].

[s] *Was mangled*, ꝺo cıoꞃꞃbaḋ.—In the Dublin copy of the Annals of Ulster the reading is "ꝺo cıꞃꞃbaḋ 7 ꝺo maꞃbuḋ ann, was mangled and killed for it."

briain mac domnaill mic briain ruaiḋ uí briain do ṁarḃaḋ tre ḟeill la macaiḃ lorcáin meic ceoach. Ar dó ro raiḋeaḋ

> Truagh aon ṁac domnaill dala,
> Truaġ oighir briain boraṁa,
> Truaġ a ḋul mar na faoileaḋ
> Truaġ clann ċeoch da chomṁaoiḋſm.

Toirḋealḃaċ ócc ó briain do ṁarḃaḋ ré bfear ndécc do ċloinn ceoach i ndioġail a miġnioṁa, a bfſronn ⁊ a ccroḋ do ḃein díoḃ ḃeós.

Ruaiḋri mac caṫail mic domnaill uí ċonċoḃair do ṁarḃaḋ i fell i ngarrḋa na fiongaile ar brecsliaḃ la cloinn fſrġail meic donnchaiḋ ar forcongra aſḋha mic toirrḋealḃaiġ.

Aoḋ mac toirrḋealḃaiġ daiṫríoġaḋ do mac uilliam burc ⁊ do ṫuaṫaiḃ connacht, ⁊ aeḋ mac feiḋlimiḋ do ríoġaḋ dóiḃ ina aghaiḋ.

Cúċoiccriche mór máġ eochaġáin tiġſrna cenél fiachach, aoḋ mac aṁlaoiḃ meguiḋir, ⁊ Muirġſs mac donnchaḋa décc.

Aonghus ruaḋ ua dalaiġ saoí ereann i ndán, ⁊ aonghoss ua heoḋosa dſghfſar dana décc.

AOIS CRIOST, 1351.

Aois Criost, míle, trí chéd, caoccatt, a haon.

Mainestir Ruis oirbealaiġ in esscoiboidecht tuama do ḋénoṁ do braiṫriḃ .S. ffransois.

Eoghan na lathaiġi mac Suiḃne do marḃaḋ lá Maġnus ua ndoṁnaill.

Pilib máġ uiḋir taoiseaċ muintire phcodaċáin, ⁊ Enna ó flannaġáin taoiseach tuaithe ratha décc.

[t] *Pity his going, &c.*—i. e. Pity he perished by a death unlooked for.

[u] *The Clann-Keogh.*—These were evidently the family that gave name to Ballymakeogh, in the territory of Owney, in the county of Tipperary, which afterwards belonged to the head of the Ryans of that neighbourhood.

[w] *Garrdha-na-fiongaile*, would be now anglicised Garrynafinely, but the name is obsolete.

[x] *Brecshliabh.*—Now anglicised Bricklieve,—a mountain in the baronies of Tirerrill and Corran in the county of Sligo, lying between Lough-naleiby and Kesh-corran.—See *Genealogies, Tribes, and Customs of Hy-Fiachrach*, p. 481, and map prefixed to the same. See this mountain again referred to at the year 1512. Bricklieve townland and castle are shewn on the Ordnance map of the county of Sligo, sheet 34.

[y] *The inhabitants of the Tuathas*,—i. e. the O'Hanlys, Mac Brannans, O'Monahans, and their

Brian, the son of Donnell, son of Brian Roe O'Brien, was treacherously slain by the sons of Lorcan Mac Lorcan. Of him was said:

Pity the only son of Donnell of the meeting;
Pity the heir of Brian Borumha;
Pity his going[t] as was not expected;
Pity the Clann-Keogh should triumph over him.

Turlough Oge O'Brien killed sixteen of the Clann-Keogh[u] in revenge of this evil deed, and despoiled them, besides, of their lands and cattle.

Rory, the son of Cathal, son of Donnell O'Conor, was treacherously slain at Garrdha-na-Fiongaile[w] on Brecshliabh[x], by the sons of Farrell Mac Donough, at the instigation of Hugh, the son of Turlough.

Hugh, the son of Turlough, was deposed by Mac William Burke and by the people of the Tuathas[y] of Connaught; and Hugh, the son of Felim, was inaugurated by them in opposition to him.

Cucogry More Mageoghegan, Lord of Kinel-Fiachach, Hugh, the son of Auliffe Maguire, and Maurice Mac Donough, died.

Aengus Roe O'Daly, the most learned of the poets of Ireland, and Aengus O'Hosey, a good poet, died.

THE AGE OF CHRIST, 1351.

The Age of Christ, one thousand three hundred fifty-one.

The monastery of Ros-Oirbhealagh[z], in the diocese of Tuam, was erected for Franciscan friars.

Owen-na-Cathaighe Mac Sweeny was slain by Manus O'Donnell.

Philip Maguire, Chief of Muinter-Pheodachain[a], and Enna O'Flanagan, Chief of Tuath-ratha[b], died.

correlatives, who dwelt round Slieve Bann in the east of the county of Roscommon. See note [d] under the year 1189, p. 86.

[z] *Ros-Oirbheallaigh.*—Roſ Oıpḃeallaıġ, now Rosserelly, on the river of Ross, near Headford, in the barony of Clare, and county of Galway, where the extensive ruins of a monastery still remain in good preservation.

[a] *Muinter-Pheodachain.*—A well-known district in the barony of Maheraboy in the county of Fermanagh. It had belonged to the family of Mac Gillafinnen before this Philip Maguire wrested it from them, and they recovered it soon after. See note [d] under the year 1281, p. 435.

[b] *Tuath-ratha.*—See note [e] under the year 1349.

Aodh mac toirrdealbaiġ do ġabail neirt doridisi, braighdi connaċt do ṫabairt dó ⁊ aċt Feidlimid dionnarbaḋ ar an tír.

Aoḋ ua Ruairc do ġabail do mac Pilbín mic uilliam burc ag teċt ó cruaiċ Patraicc dó, ⁊ Mac diarmata deirge i naġaiḋ cloinne pilbin tríd sin. Creaċa ⁊ comairccne móra do ḋénoṁ ettorra deriḋe.

Mathġaṁain mac consnáṁa do ṁarbaḋ la cloinn donnchaiḋ meic consnaṁa.

Gairm ċoṁċoitcenn sniġ do ṫabairt duilliam mac donnchaḋa muiṁniġ uí ceallaiġ im Notlaicc do daṁscolaib ereann da lucht siubail da bochtaib, ⁊ da haiḋilgneaḋaib, ⁊ fuairsit uile a noighreir eidir maiṫ ⁊ saiṫ, iseal ⁊ uasal gursat buiḋiġ uile desiuṁ ⁊ dia ṁac, .i. do Maeleachloinn.

AOIS CRIOST, 1352.

Aois Criost, mile trí chéd, caoccatt, adó.

Aoḋ mac toirrḋealbaiġ uí ċonċobair do ghabail na righe doridisi daimh-ḋeóin a mbaoi ina aghaiḋ do ġallaib ⁊ do ġaoiḋealaib.

Aodh ó ruairc tiġerna breifne do ṁarbaḋ la cathal mac aeḋa bréifniġ uí concobair, ⁊ la cloinn muircertaiġ, ⁊ ár do ċur ar ġallócclachaib cloinne suibni an tan sin.

Aoḋ ua maoilbrénainn, ⁊ a ḋá mac do ṁarbaḋ la haeḋ mac feḋlimid uí ċoncobair.

[c] *Croaghpatrick.*—A celebrated mountain about five miles to the west of the town of Westport, in the barony of Murresk, in the county of Mayo. O'Rourke had gone thither on a pilgrimage, and on his return to Breifny he had to pass by Mac Philbin's castle of Doon. This passage is given in the Annals of Clonmacnoise, as translated by Mageoghegan, as follows:

"Hugh O'Royrck was taken by Mac Phillipin Mac William Burke, as he was returning from the pilgrimage of Crwagh Patrick."

This mountain is still visited by pilgrims, particularly on the last Sunday in summer, which is called Doṁnaċ Chruim Duiḃ in this neighbourhood.

[d] *Mac Philbin.*—This name was assumed by a branch of the Burkes who resided at the Castle of Doon, about three miles to the east of Westport, in the county of Mayo.

[e] *O'Kelly.*—This passage is given in Mageoghegan's translation of the Annals of Clonmacnoise, as follows:

"William Mac Donnough Moyneagh O'Kelly invited all the Irish Poets, Brehons, Bards, Harpers, Gamesters, or Common Kearroghs, Jesters, and others of their kind in Ireland to his house upon Christmas upon this year, where every one of them was well used during Christ-

Hugh, son of Turlough, having again acquired power, the hostages of Connaught were delivered up to him; and Hugh, son of Felim, was banished from the country.

Hugh O'Rourke, on his return from Croagh-Patrick[c], was taken prisoner by Mac Philbin[d] Mac William Burke; in consequence of which act Mac Dermot rose up against the Clann-Philbin. Great ravages and depredations were mutually committed by them on account of it.

Mahon Mac Consnava was slain by the sons of Donough Mac Consnava.

A general invitation was given at Christmas by William, the son of Donough Muimhneach O'Kelly[e], to the learned of Ireland, travellers, the poor and the indigent, and they were all served to their satisfaction, both good and bad, noble and ignoble, so that they were all thankful to him and his son, Melaghlin.

THE AGE OF CHRIST, 1352.

The Age of Christ, one thousand three hundred fifty-two.

Hugh, the son of Turlough O'Conor, assumed the government [of Connaught] again[f], in despite of all the English and Irish who were opposed to him.

Hugh O'Rourke, Lord of Breifny, was slain by Cathal, the son of Hugh the Breifneach O'Conor and the Clann-Murtough, and a great slaughter was made of the gallowglasses of the Mac Sweenys on the occasion[g].

Hugh O'Mulrenin and his two sons were slain by Hugh, the son of Felim O'Conor.

mas holydays, and gave contentment to each of them at the time of their departure, so as every one of them was well pleased, and extolled William for his bounty, one of which assembly composed certain Irish verses in commendation of William and his house, which begin thus:

"Filiḋ Ereann go haointeaċ.

[The poets of Erin to one house.]"

For an account of the descendants of this William, see *Tribes and Customs of Hy-Many*, pp. 104, 105, 106.

[f] *Assumed the government of Connaught again.*—This, and the passage next following it, are rendered by Mageoghegan as follows, in his version of the Annals of Clonmacnoise:

"A. D. 1352. Hugh mac Terlagh O'Connor tooke upon him the name of King of Connought, in spight of such of the English and Irish race as opposed him.

"Hugh O'Royrck, prince of the Brenie, was killed by Cahall mac Hugh Breaffneagh O'Connor and Clann Mortagh, and a great slaughter of the Gallowglasses belonging to the families of the Mac Swynes was also made."

[g] *On the occasion*, an tan sin.—Literally, at that time.

Aongur mac concobaiꞃ mic aꞅ́dha mic domhnaill óig uí domhnaill tigeaꞃna tíꞃe Conaill ꝼꞅ́ꞃ beóda boꞃꞃꝼadac, ⁊ aon ba ꝼꞅ́ꞃꞃ ꞅ́ngnomh ⁊ uairle i nultaib immón amm ꞅoin do marbad la Maghnur ua ndomhnaill. Felim ua domhnaill. do gabáil a ionaid ⁊ Seaan mac Concobaiꞃ uí domhnaill do beith acc cogad ꝼꞃiꞅ im an ttigeaꞃnaꞅ.

Combac baile an dúin la haꞅ́d mac toiꞃꞃdealbaig uí concobaiꞃ.

Concobaꞃ mac Muiꞃgꞅ́ꞃa meic donnchaidh peicꞅ́m coitcinn daoꞃ gaca cꞅ́iꞃde, Dabucc diolmain mac uillic umaill cꞅ́nn cꞅ́ithꞃne ⁊ diolmainec connacht, tomáꞃ mag Raghnaill, ⁊ tadhg mac Siacaꞅa uí ceallaig décc.

AOIS CRIOST, 1353.

Aoiꞃ Cꞃioꞅt, mile, tꞃí chéd, caoccatt, a tꞃí.

Eóin ua caiꞃbꞃe comaꞃba tigꞅ́ꞃnaig cluana heóaiꞃ décc.

Goꞃmlaith ingꞅ́n uí domhnaill bꞅ́n uí neill décc, ⁊ nocha ꞃaibe in én aimꞃiꞃ ꝼꞃia bꞅ́n ꞃo budh mó clú, ⁊ oiꞃꞃdeaꞃcuꞃ iná iꞅi.

Aodh mac Ruaidꞃi uí neill décc.

Mathgamhain mac giolla na naomh uí ꝼꞅ́ꞃgail tigꞅ́ꞃna na hangaile décc.

Tadg mág Raghnaill taoiꞅeac muinntiꞃe heólaiꞃ do marbad la cloinn tSeꝼꝼꞃaidh meg ꞃaghnaill.

Aodh mac toiꞃꞃdealbaig do aithꞃiogad ⁊ mac bꞃanáin do [dá] congmail iꞅ in tíꞃ.

Maineꞅtiꞃ cille conaill in eꞅꞅcopóittecht cluana ꝼꞅ́ꞃta hi connachtaib do thógbáil do bꞃaithꞃib .S. ꝼꞃanꞅeiꞅ la huilliam ua cceallaig tigeaꞃna ua Maine.

[h] *Baile-an-duin*, i. e. town of the *dun* or earthen fort, now Ballindoon, a village remarkable for the ruins of a monastery, situated near Lough Arrow, in the barony of Tirerrill and county of Sligo.

[i] *Was demolished*, combac.—In the Dublin copy of the Annals of Ulster the reading is, "commac baile in duin la haed mac toiꞃꞃdelbaig hui concobuiꞃ, 7 dith bo 7 caeꞃac ann. The demolition of Ballindoon by Hugh, son of Turlough O'Conor, and cows and sheep were destroyed there." The word comac is explained bꞃiꞅead, i. e. breaking, by O'Clery, in his Glossary of ancient Irish words.

[k] Under this year O'Flaherty adds the following entries from the Annals of Lecan and of O'Mulconry, in H. 2. 11 (Trinity College, Dublin):

"Odo O'Roirk, aodóꞃ aiꞃdꞃig ó mbꞃiuin, filios Murcherti apud Gleann gaible spoliat, et Majo proximo a Cathaldo, filio Odonis Brefinii et Tadæo filio Roderici O'Conor, et aliis necatur.—MS. L."

Aengus, the son of Conor, son of Hugh, son of Donnell Oge O'Donnell, Lord of Tirconnell, a vigorous and high-spirited man, the most distinguished in Ulster at this time for prowess and nobleness, was slain by Manus O'Donnell. Felim O'Donnell assumed his place; but John, the son of Conor O'Donnell, warred [contended] with him for the lordship.

Baile an Duin[h] was demolished[i] by Hugh, son of Turlough O'Conor.

Conor, the son of Maurice Mac Donough, general patron of men of all arts; Dabuck Dillon, the son of Ulick of Umallia, Chief of the kerns and of the Dillons of Connaught; Thomas Mac Rannall, and Teige, the son of Siacus O'Kelly, died[k].

THE AGE OF CHRIST, 1353.

The Age of Christ, one thousand three hundred fifty-three.

John O'Carbry[l], Coarb of Tighernach of Cluain-eois[m], died.

Gormlaith, daughter of O'Donnell, and wife of Hugh O'Neill, died; and there was not in her time a woman of greater name and renown.

Hugh, the son of Rory O'Neill, died.

Mahon, son of Gilla-na-naev O'Farrell, Lord of Annaly, died.

Teige Mac Rannall, Chief of Muintir-Eolais, was slain by the sons of Geoffrey Mac Rannall.

Hugh, the son of Turlough, was deposed; and Mac Branan detained him in the country.

The monastery of Kilconnell, in the diocese of Clonfert, in Connaught, was founded for Franciscan friars by William O'Kelly[n], Lord of Hy-Many.

"Flathbertus O'Roirk dominus Brefiniæ obiit.—*O'Mulconry*, 1353."

"Matthæus Magdorchaidh cæsus per filios Murcherti.—MS. L." "Dermitium mac Ceeeapnaıġ.—MS. L."

"Finola filia Domini Mac Dermott obiit.—MS. L. *et O'Mulconry.*"

"Tadæus filius Siacusi O'Kelly obiit.—MS. L. and *O'Mulconry.*"

[l] *John O'Carbry.*—The name of this John O'Carbry is inscribed on the *cumhdach*, or case of St. Patrick's copy of the Gospels given to St. Mac Carthenn of Clogher.—See the account of the ancient Irish Reliquary, called the *Domnach-Airgid*, printed in the eighteenth volume of the Transactions of the Royal Irish Academy, Antiquities, p. 16, and plate at p. 24.

[m] *Cluain eois.*—Now Clones, a small town in the barony of Dartry in the county of Monaghan, where a monastery was founded by St. Tighernach in the sixth century.

[n] *William O'Kelly.*—On this date, ascribed to

aois criost, 1354.

Aoís Críost, míle, trí chéd, caoccat, a ceathair.

An tepscob ó lachtnáin, .i. easpcop connacht, ⁊ Seaan ua fínachta easpcop oile finn décc.

Mac Murchadha do bárugadh la gallaibh, ⁊ coccadh mór do fás deiside eitir gallaibh ⁊ gaoidhelaibh.

Rudhraidhe ó mórdha tighearna laoighisi do marbhadh la a bhraithribh féin ⁊ la a lucht tighe.

Brian ó dubhda flaithchfnn tíre fiachrach décc, ⁊ a mac domhnall do ghabháil a ionaidh.

Brian mac aodha móir uí neill, Cathal mac néill uí Ruairc Seffraidh mág raghnaill, Seffraidh ua raghallaigh, Siteiucc macc Sampadain, ⁊ Fearghall macc eochagain taoiseach ceneóil fiachach do écc.

Ruaidhri mac Seaan mecc mathghamhna do marbhadh i longport még mathghamhna.

Maidhm mór do thabhairt la cloinn aodha buidhe uí néill, ⁊ la gallaibh dúine dealgan ar aodh ua néill i drong mor do marbhadh is in maidhm hisin.

Derbhforgaill ingean uí concobhair, Feidhlimidh mac cathail uí concobhair ⁊ hoiberd a burc do écc.

Flaithbheartach mac giolla finnein ⁊ a bhrathair do marbhadh la a muintir féin.

Murchadh mac cathail uí fearghail ⁊ Tadhg mac Seanlaich do écc.

Saerbhrethach mac Maoilíosa dhuinn meic aodhagáin ollamh conmhaicne do écc i ninis clothrann.

Maoilseachlainn mac Ritbeartaigh ollamh fearmanach i ndán décc.

the erection of the abbey of Kilconnell, O'Flaherty writes the following remark in the College copy of the Annals of the Four Masters (H. 2. 11):

"Quare perperam 1414 Waræus in Ant. Hib. habet, cum fundator ipse in summa senectute A°. 1381, decesserit, 74 annis post mortem patris A°. 1307 mortui."

It is quite evident, however, that the William O'Kelly intended by Ware is William, the grandson of this William Boy, who died in 1420, and who was the ancestor of the O'Kellys of Aughrim.

[o] *O'Laghtnan.*—In Mageoghegan's translation of the Annals of Clonmacnoise, he is called "O'Laghtna, Bishop of Twayme [Tuam] and Connought." Ware does not mention him in his list of the Archbishops of Tuam.

[p] *Of Leix,* laoighise.—This territory comprised

THE AGE OF CHRIST, 1354.

The Age of Christ, one thousand three hundred fifty-four.

O'Laghtnan[o], Bishop of Connaught, and John O'Finaghty, Bishop of Elphin, died.

Mac Murrough was put to death by the English ; in consequence of which a great war broke out between the English and Irish.

Rory O'More, Lord of Leix[p] was slain by his own kinsmen and household.

Brian O'Dowda, Chief of Tireragh, died, and his son, Donnell, assumed his place.

Brian, the son of Hugh More O'Neill ; Cathal, the son of Niall O'Rourke ; Geoffrey Mac Rannall ; Geoffrey O'Reilly ; Sitric Magauran ; and Farrell Mageoghegan, Chief of Kinel-Fiachach, died.

Rory, the son of John Mac Mahon, was slain in Mac Mahon's fortress.

Hugh O'Neill received a great defeat[q] from the race of Hugh Boy O'Neill[r], and the English, in which many were slain.

Dervorgilla, the daughter of O'Conor ; Felim, the son of Cathal O'Conor, and Hubert Burke, died.

Flaherty Mac Gillafinnen and his kinsman, were killed by their own people.

Murrough, the son of Cathal O'Farrell, and Teige Mac Shanly, died.

Saerbhreathach[s], son of Maelisa Donn Mac Egan, Ollave of Conmaicne, died on Inis Cloghrann[t].

Melaghlin Mac Rithbheartaigh[u], Ollav of Fermanagh, in poetry, died[w].

the greater part of the Queen's county. See note [f] under the year 1196, pp. 105, 106, *supra*.

[q] *Received a great defeat.*—Literally, " A great defeat was given by the Clann-Hugh-Boy O'Neill and the English of Dundalk to Hugh O'Neill, and a great number was slain in that defeat." It is translated by Mageoghegan, in his version of the Annals of Clonmacnoise, as follows:

"A. D. 1354. The O'Neals of Clannaboye, with the help of the English of Dundalk, gave a great overthrow to Hugh O'Neale [and the people of Tyrone], and made a great slaughter of them."

[r] *Race of Hugh Boy.*—This tribe as well as their country, in the counties of Down and Antrim, is called the Clannaboy by English writers.

[s] *Saerbhreathach.*—This name is usually latinised Justinus, and anglicised Justin. It signifies " the noble judge."

[t] *Inis Clothrann.*—An island in Lough Ree, belonging to the county of Longford. See note [i] under the year 1193, p. 98, *supra*.

[u] *Mac Rithbheartaigh.*—This name is still extant in Fermanagh, and usually anglicised Mac-Crifferty. It is to be distinguished from O'Rafferty and Magroarty.

[w] Under this year O'Flaherty adds, in H. 2.

AOIS CRIOST, 1355.

Aoiſ Cſioſt, míle, trí chéd, caoccatt, a cúicc.

Concobar mac consnáṁa epſcop na bréifne ó druim ċlíaḃ go cſnannuſ mac gallġaoidil prioir na trinoide, ⁊ mac cathail abb Sruthra décc.

Donnchaḋ mac felim mic aſdha mic domnaill óig uí domnaill do ṁarḃad ag tabairt ġormlaṫa inġine aſdha ruaiḋ ṁég uidir (.i. mág uidir) ar éccin lais, ⁊ donn mac murchaḋa as é ro ṁarḃ eiſioṁ i longport ṁég uidir.

Domnall mac Seaain uí ḟſrġail tiġearna na hAngaile décc.

Diarmait ua maoílṁiaḋaiġ taoíseach ṁuintire cſrḃallain do ṁarḃaḋ la muintir birn ⁊ sochaiḋe do muintir eolais imaille fris.

Cathal ó cuinn taoiseaċ muintire giollgáin do ṁarḃaḋ do cloinn tSeaain, ⁊ do ċloind aſdha ⁊ coigſar da braithriḃ immaille fris.

Corbmac ṁág Raġnaill taoiseaċ muintire heólais do ṁarḃaḋ la cloinn ioṁair ṁég raġnaill.

Fſrġal mac fearġail mic muircſrtaiġ ṁóir mic conġalaiġ ṁég ſochagáin toiseaċ cenel fiachach déġ.

Murchaḋ mac cathail uí ḟſrġail, Derbforgaill inġſn uí ḟſrġail, ⁊ tadhg mac aſdhagain saoí i feineachas décc.

Maiḋm do ṫabairt do ġallaiḃ iarthair connacht for mac uilliam, ⁊ mórán do ṁarḃaḋ dia ṁuintir.

11, the following entries from the Annals of Lecan, and of O'Mulconry, which he has translated into Latin:

"Amlaus filius Dermitii O'Ffarell a Mac Oirebeard Cæsus.—MS. L."

"Lasaria (dearḃforgaill,—C. Ecin), filia Domini O'Conor Odonis obiit.—MS. L."

"Odo filius Cormaci buiḋir occisus a filiis Donchadi riaḃaiġ.—*O'Mulconry*."

"Odo Magshamhradhain (Magauran) ab O'Foelan cæsus.—*O'Mulconry, et* MS. L. ad 1355."

"Giolla iosa mac aoḋa do écc.—MS. L." [Gilla-Isa Mac Aedha, died.]

"Diermitius O'Curnin, aḋḃar ollaṁan na breifne, et Magister Lucas O'Curnin obierunt."

[x] *Sruthair*, now corruptly called in Irish mainistir Sruille, and anglicised Abbeyshrule, a well-known place in the barony of Shrule, in the south of the county of Longford.

[y] *Donn.*—In the Dublin copy of the Annals of Ulster the slayer of O'Donnell is called domnall mac murchaiḋ.

[a] *Muinter-Birn*, i. e. the O'Beirnes of Tir-Briuin, a territory lying between Elphin and Jamestown in the county of Roscommon. The Muinter-Eolais were the Mac Rannalls and their correlatives, who were seated in the southern or level portion of the county of Leitrim, on the opposite side of the Shannon.

THE AGE OF CHRIST, 1355.

The Age of Christ, one thousand three hundred fifty-five.

Conor Mac Consnava, Bishop of Breifny [Kilmore], from Drumcliff to Kells, died.

Mac Gallgael, Prior of the [monastery of the] Blessed Trinity, died.

Mac Cathail, Abbot of Sruthair[x], died.

Donough, the son of Felim, son of Hugh, son of Donnell Oge O'Donnell, was slain as he was carrying off Gormaith, daughter of Hugh Roe Maguire (i. e. the Maguire), by force. It was Donn[y] Mac Murrough who slew him in Maguire's fortress.

Donnell, son of John O'Farrell, Lord of Annaly, died.

Dermot O'Mulvey, Chief of Muintir-Carolan, and many of the Muintir-Eolais, were slain by the Muintir-Birn[z].

Cathal O'Quin, Chief of Muintir-Gillagan[a], and five others, were slain by the Clann-Shane and the Clann-Hugh[b].

Cormac Rannall, Chief of Muintir-Eolais, was slain by the sons of Ivor Mac Rannall.

Farrell, the son of Farrell, son of Murtough More, son of Congalagh Mageoghegan, Chief of Kinel-Fiachach, died.

Murrough, the son of Cathal O'Farrell; Dervorgilla, the daughter of O'Farrell; and Teige Mac Egan, a man learned in the Fenechas[c], died.

The English of West Connaught defeated[d] Mac William [Burke], and killed many of his people.

[a] *Muinter-Gillagan.*—A district in the county of Longford, for the extent of which see note [k] under the year 1234, p. 270, *supra*.

[b] *Clann-Shane and Clann-Hugh.*—These were septs of the O'Farrells. The Clann-Hugh were located in the barony of Longford, adjoining the district of Magh Treagh, and the townlands of which they were possessed are specified in an inquisition taken at Ardagh, on the 4th of April, in the tenth year of the reign of James I.

[c] *The Fenechas*, i. e. the old laws of Ireland, commonly called the Brehon Laws by English writers.

[d] *Defeated.*—Literally "a defeat was given by the English of West Connaught to William Burke, and many of his people were killed." Mageoghegan renders it as follows in his version of the Annals of Clonmacnoise:

"A.D. 1355. The English of West Connought gave an overthrow to Mac William, and killed divers of his people."

Emann mac uilliam mic Riocaird do marbadh la siol nanmchadha.

Maidhm mór do thabairt la Riocard óg ar lucht tighe meic uilliam, .i. Emann ⁊ ar siol nanmchadha dar marbadh Stiamna mac Siurtáin enrí mac Pilbin ⁊ sé fir décc duaislibh sil nanmchadha.

Niall mág mathghamhna do marbadh la cloinn treaain még mathghamna.

Adhuc mac uidilín do marbadh la hoirtfsaibh.

Deich nuain do breith in aoínfecht daon chaoiridh.

AOIS CRIOST, 1356.

Aois Criost, míle, trí chéd, caoccatt, a Sé.

Ffrghal mac ferrfaidh még Raghnaill Priomhaidh Ardamacha, ⁊ fir ionaid Patraicc décc.

Nicol mac catharaigh epscop oirghiall décc.

Solamh ó meallán maor cluig an fdachta dég. Pecfm coitcfnn do cliaraibh ereann eridhe.

Aodh mac toirrdealbaigh uí concobair, Ri connacht do marbadh i mbaile locha deacair la donnchadh carrach ua ceallaigh, ⁊ la cloinn meic an baird ar forailfm maineach i ccionaidh inghfne Seóinin a burc bfn uí cheallaigh do brfith leis ar aitheadh, ⁊ ar elódh roimhe sin.

[e] *The Sil-Anmchadha*, i. e. O'Maddens in the barony of Longford, in the county of Galway.

[f] *Were brought forth*, do breith.—This verb is applied in Irish to the parturition of all animals. Mageoghegan renders the passage as follows in his version of the Annals of Clonmacnoise:

"A. D. 1355. One sheep had ten lambs this year."

[g] Under this year O'Flaherty has the following note on the chronology of the Irish annalists about this period, in the College copy of the Annals of the Four Masters, H. 2. 11:

"Quæ habentur in MS. L. ab anno 1355, ad 1373, inclusive, per annos 19, uno anno posteriora sunt, quam ut in his et O'Mulconry Annalibus præter pauca, quæ suis locis notabo."

He also adds the following entries from the Annals of Lecan, of O'Mulconry, and of Clonmacnoise:

"Hiberni Lageniæ retulerunt victoriam de Anglis Dublinii.—*O'Mulconry*."

"Tuamia .i. tuaim da ghualann, cremata a Cathaldo óg O'Conor et a Mac William (i. e. Edmundo de Burgo).—*O'Mulconry*, et War: in Tuam præsul. 1356, et Cod. Cluain. 1355."

"Rex Galliæ cum filio in Angliam captivi ducti 5. Febr. 1355–6, Cod. Cl."

"Una ovis decem agnos hoc anno peperit."—C. Ecin.

[h] *Mac Rannall*.—This is evidently a mistake of the Four Masters, as we know from the public records that the Primate of Armagh was Richard

Edmond, the son of William, son of Richard [Burke], was slain by the Sil-Anmchadha[e].

A great defeat was given by Richard Oge [Burke], to the household of Mac William (i. e. Edmond), and to the Sil-Anmchadha, in which Stephen Mac Jordan, Henry Mac Philbin, and sixteen of the chiefs of Sil-Anmchadha, were slain.

Niall Mac Mahon was slain by the sons of John Mac Mahon.

Aduc (Mac Quillin) was slain by the people of Oirthear.

Ten lambs were brought forth[f] at once by one sheep[g].

THE AGE OF CHRIST, 1356.

The Age of Christ, one thousand three hundred fifty-six.

Farrell, the son of Jeffrey Mac Rannall[h], Primate of Armagh, and representative of St. Patrick, died.

Nicholas Mac Cahasy[i], Bishop of Oriel [Clogher], died.

Solomon O'Mellan, the keeper of the Clog-an-Eadhachta[k], died. He was the general patron of the clergy of Ireland.

Hugh, the son of Turlough O'Connor, King of Connaught, was slain at Baile-Locha-Deacair[l] by Donough Carragh O'Kelly and the sons of Mac-an-Ward, at the instigation of the Hy-Many. This was in revenge of his having some time before carried off privately and clandestinely the daughter of Seoinin Burke, the wife of O'Kelly.

Fitz-Ralph, who was certainly not one of the Mac Rannalls. See Prince's ***Danmonii orientales illustres***, p. 294, and Harris's edition of Ware's Bishops, p. 81. The Editor has not been able to discover this entry in any of the older Irish Annals, and believes it to be a blunder.

[i] *Mac Cahasy*, mac catasaiġ.—This name is now made Mac Casey and Casey simply.

Ware writes the name *Mac Catasaid*, without aspirating the *t* or *d*. See Harris's edition of Ware's Bishops, p. 184, where it is stated that this bishop succeeded in 1320, and died in Autumn, 1356.

[k] *Clog an Eadhachta*, i. e. the bell of the testament. It is called cloᵹ an úbaċta in the Dublin copy of the Annals of Ulster, and by the Four Masters at the year 1425, q. v. It was evidently so called because it was mentioned in an ancient document called the ubaċt, or Testament of St. Patrick. This bell still exists in excellent preservation, and is now in the Cabinet of George Petrie, Esq., Author of the Essay on the ancient ecclesiastical Architecture of Ireland. It had belonged to the church of Donaghmore, near Dungannon in Tyrone.

[l] *Baile Locha Deacair*, i. e. the town or townland of Loch-Deacair. This is now anglicised Balloughdacker, and is the name of a townland

Aoḋ mac feḋlimiḋ uí ċoncobair do ġabáil lain ríġe connacht iaroṁ.

Conċobar mac taiḋg uí cheallaiġ do ṁarbaḋ la taḋg mac diarmada uí cheallaiġ.

Toirrḋealbach mac aeḋha bréifniġ uí concobair do ṁarbaḋ la cloinn ndonnchaiḋ.

Diarmaid mac diarmada ṁécc carṫaiġ ⁊ donnchaḋ a ṁac do ṁarbaḋ la mac uí Suilleabáin.

Mór ingḟn uí concobair décc, bḟn uí ḟḟrġail iriḋe.

Muirċḟrtach mac Seaain uí neill do ṁarbaḋ la Pilib máġ uiḋir.

Dubġhall mac Suibne do ṁarbaḋ do ḋoṁnall ua concobair.

Ruaiḋri mac aeḋha uí Choncobair, ⁊ doṁnall mac aeḋha breifniġ uí Chonċobair décc.

Donnchaḋ mac Conmara mac toiriġ do bḟḟr illeth moḋha ina aimsir fén do ṁarbaḋ la síol mbriain.

Donnchaḋ ppóirtceach do ṁarbaḋ la dir dia ṁuintir fḟin tria cheilg.

Gearoittin triel do bárugaḋ la muintir Riġ Saxan ar faitche áṫa cliaṫ.

Murchaḋ mac briain uí néill do écc.

Felim mac aeḋha mic doṁnaill óicc tiġḟrna ṫíre conaill do ṁarbaḋ la mac a dearḃbrathar fḟin Seaan mac concobair uí ḋoṁnaill, ⁊ Seaan do ġabáil tiġearnais tire conaill gan imrearain.

AOIS CRIOST, 1357.

Aois Criost, míle, trí chétt, caoccatt, a Seacht.

Clement ó duibġḟnnáin biocaire cille Ronáin décc. Saccart na sionnaċ atberṫí fris.

Maġnus máġ mathġaṁna tighḟrna oirġiall, Lochlainn mac Muirchḟrtaiġ

containing a lough, in the parish of Athleague, barony of Killian, and county of Galway.—See the Ordnance map of that county, sheets 20 and 33.

[m] *Clann-Donough*, i. e. the Mac Donoughs of Tirerrill, in the county of Sligo, who are a branch of the Mac Dermots of Moylurg.

[n] O'Flaherty adds, in H. 2. 11: "25 Januarii, 1355–6, Sir Mauricius Filius Thomæ Comes Desmoniæ, et Hiberniæ Justiciarius, obiit.—*Cambd. annal. O'Mulconry*, 1355, MS. L. 1356."

"Fercarius O'Fallon dynasta de Clann-uadach, obiit.—*O'Mulconry*."

"Gearoitín trial do ċarraing (no do bārucáḋ do ṁuintir riġ Saxan ar faiċċe aṫa cliaṫ, a regiis quibus a Daltonis traditus.—

Hugh, son of Felim O'Conor, then assumed the entire government of Connaught.

Conor, the son of Teige O'Kelly, was slain by Teige, the son of Dermot O'Kelly.

Turlough, the son of Hugh Breifneach O'Conor, was slain by the Clann-Donough[m].

Dermot, the son of Dermot Mac Carthy, and Donough, his son, were slain by the son of O'Sullivan.

More, daughter of O'Conor, died. She was the wife of O'Farrell

Murtough, son of John O'Neill, was slain by Philip Maguire.

Dowell Mac Sweeny was slain by Donnell O'Conor.

Rory, son of Hugh O'Conor, and Donnell, son of Hugh Breifneach O'Conor, died

Donough Mac Namara, the best son of a chieftain in Leth-Mogha in his time, was slain by the O'Briens.

Donough Proisteach was treacherously slain by two of his own people.

Gearoidin Tyrrell was put to death on the green of Dublin by the people of the King of England.

Murrough, the son of Brian O'Neill, died.

Felim, the son of Hugh, son of Donnell Oge [O'Donnell], Lord of Tirconnell, was slain by the son of his own brother, viz. John, son of Conor O'Donnell, and John then assumed the lordship of Tirconnell without opposition[n].

THE AGE OF CHRIST, 1357.

The Age of Christ, one thousand three hundred fifty-seven.

Clement O'Duigenan, Vicar of Kilronan, died. He was called Sagart-na-Sinnach[o].

Manus Mac Mahon, Lord of Oriel; Loughlin, son of Murtough; and Farrell

MS. L. 1356, *et Cod. Cl.*"

"Justitiarius Dublinii, obiit.—(Sc. Sir Thomas Rokesby, Cambd. 1356, 1357). MS. L."

"Dominus Bermingham ab Anglis cæsus.—*O'Mulconry*, 1357, & MS. L."

[o] *Sagart-na-Sinnach*, i. e. priest of the Foxes. It is not easy to determine why he was so called, as he does not appear to have had any connexion with the Sinnachs, or Foxes, chiefs of Teffia, in Westmeath.

uí Choncobaiṗ, ⁊ Fḟeṗgal muiṁneaċ ua duibgſennán ollaṁ conṁaicne ⁊ cloinne maoilruanaiḋ ṫíṗ ⁊ tuaṗ déġ.

Seaan mac briain uí Raġallaiġ do ṁarbaḋ la gallaiḃ.

Brian mac giollacriost uí Ruairc ⁊ Maghnus buiḋe mag Shampadain do ṁarbaḋ i rúta meic uidilin la haoḋ ó néill.

Donnsléḃe mac cſerbaill saorṁaiġistir ſenma ⁊ airphiteach do buḋ ſeṗṗ ina aimsir fén décc.

Sith coitchenn eitir an dá chathal, cathal mac aodha bréifnigh ⁊ cathal ócc mac caṫail mic doṁnaill.

AOIS CRIOST, 1358.

Aois Criost, míle, trí cheḋ, caoccatt, a hocht.

Brian mac cathmaoil epscop uirġiall decc.

Maġnus ṁácc uidir do ṁarbaḋ la cloinn cathṁaoil.

Doṁnall ua heġra tighſerna luiġne décc lá cárg.

Concobar ó hainliġe taoiseach ċenél dobtha mic aenġusa décc, iar mbreith ḃuaḋa ó domhan ⁊ ó ḋeaṁan dó.

Maiḋm do thabairt daodh ua néill for airgiallaiḃ, ⁊ for feraiḃ manaċ dú in ro marbaḋ aeḋ mac caba, ⁊ mac an epscoip uí ḋuḃda (.i. maoileaċlainn) co sochaiḋiḃ imaille friú.

Maiḋm mór do thabairt dua morḋa for gallaiḃ átha cliaṫ, ⁊ dá ḟichitt décc do marbaḋ ar én lathair lais díoḃ.

[p] *Clann-Mulrony, Lower and Upper.*—The Lower Clann-Mulrony were the Mac Donoughs, who were seated in the barony of Tirerrill, in the county of Sligo; and the Upper Clann-Mulrony were the Mac Dermots of Moylurg.

[q] *The Route.*—This is still the name of a territory forming the northern portion of the county of Antrim. The name is supposed to be a corruption of Dal Riada.—See Ussher's *Primordia*, p. 1029, and O'Flaherty's *Ogygia*, Part iii. c. 63.

[r] *Cathal, the son of Hugh Breifneach.*—He was the chief leader of that sept of the O'Conors called the Clann-Murtough. His pedigree is thus given in the Book of Lecan: "Cathal, son of Hugh Breifneach, son of Cathal Roe, King of Connaught in 1279, son of Conor Roe, son of Murtough Muimhneach (the ancestor of the Clann-Murtough), who was the son of Turlough More O'Conor, monarch of Ireland.

[s] *Cathal Oge, the son of Cathal.*—He was at this time the chief leader of the O'Conors of Sligo, and the most heroic that hitherto appeared of that sept of the O'Conors. He was the son of Cathal, King of Connaught, who was the son of Donnell, Tanist of Connaught, who was son of Teige, son of Brian, son of Andreas,

Muimhneach O'Duigennan, Ollav of Conmaicne and Clann-Mulrony, Lower and Upper[p], died.

John, son of Brian O'Reilly, was slain by the English.

Brian, son of Gilchreest O'Rourke, and Manus Boy Magauran, were slain in the Route[q], Mac Quillin's territory, by Hugh O'Neill.

Donslevy Mac Caroll, a noble master of music and melody, the best of his time, died.

A general peace was ratified between the two Cathals, namely, between Cathal, the son of Hugh Breifneach[r], and Cathal Oge, the son of Cathal[s], son of Donnell[t].

THE AGE OF CHRIST, 1358.

The Age of Christ, one thousand three hundred fifty-eight.

Brian Mac Cawell, Bishop of Oriel [Clogher], died.

Manus Maguire was slain by the Clann-Cawell[u].

Donnell O'Hara, Lord of Leyny, died on Easter day.

Conor O'Hanly, Chief of the Race of Dofa, son of Aengus, died, after gaining victory over the world and the Devil.

A victory was gained by Hugh O'Neill over the people of Oriel and Fermanagh [in a battle], in which Hugh Mac Cabe, Melaghlin, the son of the Bishop O'Dowda[w], and many others were slain.

A great defeat was given[x] to the English of Dublin by O'More; and two hundred and forty of them were killed by him on the field of battle.

son of Brian Luighneach, the ancestor of the O'Conors of Sligo, who was the son of Turlough More O'Conor, monarch of Ireland.

[t] O'Flaherty adds to this year in H. 2. 11:

"Comes Desmonia transfretando submersus. *O'Mulconry, et Cod. Cl.*"

"Fedlimius O'Donell et filius ejus Ragnallus capti.—*Cod. Cl.*"

"A Joanne O'Donell cæsi.—*O'Mulconry*, 1356, *supra.*"

"Mathgamanius Ꞡallba Maguir obiit.—MS. L."

"Padinus mop O'Mælchonary Archiantiquarius Connaciæ obiit æstate post mortem Odonis O'Conor domini sui.—MS. L."

[u] *The Clann-Cawell*, i. e. the family of Mac Cawell, who were located in the present barony of Clogher, in the county of Tyrone.

[w] *The Bishop O'Dowda.*—He was William O'Dowda, Bishop of Killala, who died in 1350.—See *Genealogies, Tribes, and Customs of Hy-Fiachrach*, p. 117.

[x] *A great defeat was given.*—Mageoghegan translates this passage as follows, in his version

Toirrḋealḃach mac aoḋa na fioḋḃaiḋe uí neill ⁊ mac aintriu meic feoruis décc.

Cioth mór dfrsheáin i crich coirpre is in Samhradh co nar mó fiaḋuball ina gach cloch de.

Senicin mac uidilin ardconstabla cuigid ulaḋ do écc.

Mac giolla íosa uí ḟlannagáin do ṁarbaḋ la Magnus mac caṫail mic aoḋha bréifniġ.

AOIS CRIOST, 1359.

Aois Criost, míle, trí cheḋ, caoccatt, a naoí.

Corbmac mac cárṫaiġ tiġerna dearṁuṁan, ⁊ Domnall mac taiḋg uí maṫġaṁna décc.

Maiḋm mór do thabairt do ċaṫal óg mac caṫail uí concoḃair occ áth Seanaiġ ar Sheaan mac conċoḃair uí ḋoṁnaill, ⁊ ar ċonallchaiḃ. Seaan ó dochartaiġ taoiseaċ arda miodhair, Eoghan connachtach, Toirrḋealḃaċ mac Suiḃne do ġaḃáil do ṁac uí Concoḃair don chur soin, ⁊ daoíne iomda do marbaḋ lais.

Matha macc Shamradhain adbar toisiġ ṫeallaiġ eachdhaċ do lot an lá so ⁊ a écc da bithin iar rochtain a thighe fein dó. Cathal bodar mac cathail uí ruairc, ⁊ maolseachlainn ó gairmleadhaiġ do coṁthuitim re aroile ar an ccoccaḋ ccédna so iar mbreiṫ sloiġ do ridiri do chathal ó

of the Annals of Clonmacnoise: "A. D. 1358. O'More, of the Contrey of Lease, gave a great discomfiture to the English of Dublin, where were killed of them 240 persons."

[r] *Hugh na Fidhbhaighe*, i. e. Hugh of the wood.

[s] *Wild apple.*—Mageoghegan translates this passage as follows, in his version of the Annals of Clonmacnoise:

"A. D. 1358. There was a great shower of hail in the Summer-time of this year in the territory of Carbrey; every stone thereof was no less than a crabb."

To this entry O'Flaherty adds, in H 2. 11:

"Et sementes clientum Cathaldi Og O'Conor multum corrupit.—MS. L."

[a] *Manus.*—According to the pedigree of the O'Conors, given in the Book of Lecan, he was the fourth son of Cathal.

[b] To this year O'Flaherty adds the following entries, H. 2. 11:

"Matthæus filius Thomæ O'Roirk obiit.—MS. L. 1357, *O'Mulconry, et Cod. Cl. et* C. Ecin."

"Murchertus filius Tigernani O'Roirk obiit. MS. L."

"Caċt inġean ui cheallaiġ bean muirġesa mic Donnchaḋa déġ [i. e. Cacht, daughter of

Turlough, the son of Hugh na Fidhbhaighe[y] O'Neill, and the son of Andrew Mac Feorais [Bermingham], died.

A heavy shower [of hail] fell in Carbury in the summer, each stone of which was not smaller than a wild apple[z].

Senicin [Jenkin] Mac Quillin, High Constable of the province of Ulster, died.

The son of Gilla-Isa O'Flanagan was slain by Manus[a], the son of Cathal, son of Hugh Breifneach O'Conor[b].

THE AGE OF CHRIST, 1359.

The Age of Christ, one thousand three hundred fifty-nine.

Cormac Mac Carthy, Lord of Desmond, and Donnell, the son of Teige O'Mahony, died.

A great victory was gained at Ballyshannon by Cathal Oge[c], the son of Cathal O'Conor, over John, the son of Conor O'Donnell, and the Kinel-Connell. John O'Doherty, Chief of Ardmire, Owen Connaghtagh, and Turlough Mac Sweeny, were taken prisoners on this occasion by the son of O'Conor, and many persons were slain by him. Matthew Magauran, materies[d] of a lord of Teallach Eachdhach was wounded on that day, and died of his wounds after his return to his own house. During the same war Cathal Bodhar, the son of Cathal O'Rourke, and Melaghlin O'Gormly, fell by each other's hand in the same war[e]. This occurred when Cathal O'Conor marched with a second army

O'Kelly, and wife of Maurice Mac Donough, died.]—MS. L."

[c] *Cathal Oge.*—He was the son of O'Conor Sligo, and the most heroic of the O'Conors at this period.

[d] *Materies of a lord*, aḋbar tiġerna.—Mageoghegan translates this, "next successor of Teallaghaagh," in his version of the Annals of Clonmacnoise. Thus:

"A. D. 1359. Cahall Oge O'Connor gave an overthrow to the Inhabitants of Tyreconnell at Belaseanie, where John O'Dochortie, Cheiftain of Ardmire, and Terlagh Mac Swynie were taken, and a great many others slain besides. Mathew Magawran, next successor of Teallaghaagh, was hurt in the same place, from thence was conveighed to his house, and died of the wound. The said Cahall went to the lands of O'Gormley, where Cahall (surnamed the deaf) O'Ruwyrck was killed by Melaughlyn O'Gormley."

[e] *During the same war.*—Cathal Oge, the son of O'Conor Sligo, made great efforts to conquer Tirconnell at this period; and it is stated in the Dublin copy of the Annals of Ulster, under the year 1356 [*recte* 1359], that he became prince

concoḃair go tír ċonaill go rangatar drong da ṁuintir duteaiḋ uí gairmleḋaiġ im ċathal boḋar ua Ruairc.

Muirċertach mac tomais uí ḟloinn line aḋḃar tiġearna ua tuirtre do ṁarḃaḋ daoḋ mac briain mic aodha buiḋe uí néill.

Brian mac donnchaiḋ adbar tiġſrna ua nailella do marbaḋ do mac rſnċa doireachT uí ġaḋra.

Enrí mac uilliccc mic Riocaird a búrc décc.

Murchaḋ ócc mac mathġaṁna adbar tiġearna corco baiscind do marḃaḋ la síol mbriain.

Maghnas ua dubda mac tiġearna ua fiaċrach ⁊ Aoḋ mac Conċoḃair meic aſḋaccáin décc aſn roga brſtheaman ereann.

Doṁnall mac taiḋg uí ṁathġaṁna do ṁarḃaḋ.

Art mac Amlaoiḃ uí Ruairc do ṁarḃaḋ la Mág aſnġusa.

AOIS CRIOST, 1360.

Aois Criost, mile, trí chéd, a seasccatt.

Maolruanaiḋ mac an chammuinélaiġ uí baoiġill toiseaċ na trí tuaṫ, saoi oirrderc ar eineach, ar uaisle, ar chéill ar cosccur, ⁊ ar comairge décc.

Aṁlaoiḃ mac Seaffraiḋ ṁéġ Raghnaill do ṁarḃaḋ.

Sir Roibſrd Saḃaoís ⁊ diarmaitt ó hainliġe décc.

Ros commain, daiṁinis, Slicceċ, Mainistir lſsa gaḃail, fiodhnach ⁊ druim lias do loscaḋ.

Seaan mac giollacriost uí Ruairc do marḃaḋ daeḋ mág ḋorchaiḋ.

Diarmait ua briain daiṫriogaḋ do ṁac a brathar buḋḋein.

of Tirconnell: "Riġi tire conaill do gabail do mac i Concobuir." The Four Masters, however, who had the Annals of Ulster before them, have suppressed this passage, thinking that it would derogate from the glory of the O'Donnells!

This passage is given from the Annals of Lecan by O'Flaherty, in the margin of H. 2. 11, as follows. It should be observed, however, that it was in Irish in the original, and that the Latin is O'Flaherty's translation:

"Cathaldus Og filius Cathaldi O'Conor et Odo mór O'Neill diem statuunt ad ſruaiḋ verum Odo bellis implicitus ad statum diem non pervenit: quo comperto Johannis O'Donell Tirconalliæ dominus cum copiis inter ſruaiḋ et Doriam conflatis Cathaldum Domini O'Conor

into Tirconnell, and a party of his people arrived in O'Gormly's territory under the command of Cathal Bodhar O'Rourke.

Murtough, the son of Thomas O'Flynn Line[f], heir-apparent to Hy-Tuirtre, was slain by Hugh, the son of Brian, son of Hugh Boy O'Neill.

Brian Mac Donnell, heir to the lordship of Tirerrill, was slain by Mac Seancha, one of the adherents of O'Gara.

Henry, the son of Ulick, son of Richard Burke, died.

Murrough Oge Mac Mahon, heir apparent to the lordship of Corco-Vaskin, was slain by the O'Briens.

Manus O'Dowda, son of the Lord of Hy-Fiachrach, and Hugh, the son of Conor Mac Egan, the choicest of the Brehons of Ireland, died.

Donnell, son of Teige O'Mahony, was slain.

Art, the son of Auliffe O'Rourke, was slain by Magennis[g].

THE AGE OF CHRIST, 1360.

The Age of Christ, one thousand three hundred sixty.

Mulrony, son of the Cammhuinelach [the Wry-necked] O'Boyle, Chief of the three Tuathas, a man illustrious for his hospitality, nobleness, wisdom, conquests, and protection, died.

Auliffe, son of Geoffrey Mac Rannall, died.

Sir Robert Savadge[h] and Dermot O'Hanly died.

Roscommon, Devenish, Sligo, the monastery of Lisgool, Fenagh, and Druimlias[i], were burned.

John, son of Gilchreest O'Rourke, was slain by Hugh Mac Dorcy.

Dermot O'Brien was deposed by the son of his own brother.

filium paucis ad fœdus feriendum comitatum aggreditur: verum Cathaldus victor (ut supra) Tirconalliæ dominium ea vice adeptus est. Eugenius Wardeus, ollam tıpe conaıll, in hac pugna occubuit.—MS. L."

[f] *O'Flynn Line*, i. e. O'Lyn of Moylinny, Chief of Hy-Tuirtre. This family was soon after dispossessed by that sept of the O'Neills called the Clannaboy, who took possession of all Hy-Tuirtre.—See note [z] under the year 1176, pp. 24, 25, *supra*.

[g] *Magennis*.—He was Chief of Iveagh, in the county of Down.

[h] *Savadge*.—This family was seated in Aṗo Ulaḋ, now the Ardes, in the east of the county of Down.

[i] *Druimlias*, now Drumlease, an old church in ruins, near the east extremity of Lough Gill,

Diarmait mac donnchaḋa riabaiġ meic diarmata do ṁarḃaḋ la caṫal óg mac cathail uí ċoncobair.

Ingen toirrdealbaiġ uí concobair bean ferġail uí Raiġilliġ do ṁarbaḋ dearsgar.

Droichet clochaelta do ḋenaṁ la caṫal óg ó cconcobair ar abainn esra dara.

Ferġal mac Seaffraiḋ ṁeg Raġnaill ⁊ tuathal ua fionaċta décc.

Naomhacc ó duibgennan décc.

Cathal mac an caoich meg Raġnaill do marbaḋ.

Giolla na naoṁ ó connmaiġ ollaṁ túaḋmuṁan le seinm décc.

Mac riġ Saxan do tocht in Erind.

Art mac giolla riabaiġ ṁég aengusa do marḃaḋ la cloinn an tsráḃaoisiġ ⁊ la mac Muircertaiġ Riaġánaiġ ṁég aonġusa i meabail.

Sluaiġeḋ la cathal i tír naṁalgaḋa gur ro mill tighe ⁊ templa iomḋa.

AOIS CRIOST, 1361.

Aois Criost, mile, trí chéd, Seascat a háon.

Benidecht ua mocháin airchinneach cille hatracht décc.

Art mac Murchaḋa Rí laiġen ⁊ doṁnall riabach rioghḋaṁna laiġean

in the barony of Dromahaire, and county of Leitrim.

[j] *Eas-dara*, i. e. Ballysadare, in the county of Sligo.

[k] *O'Connmhaigh*.—This name is now locally pronounced in Irish as if written O'Connúġa, and anglicised Conway, without the prefix O.

[l] *The son of the King of England*.—He was Lionel, Duke of Clarence, third son of Edward III. He landed in Dublin with a body of 1500 men on the 15th of September, and held the office of Lord Lieutenant of Ireland for nearly three years, when he returned to England; and, though during that period he achieved nothing worthy of notice in Ireland, he was in the course of the three years following twice intrusted with the same office. It was during his administration, in the year 1367, that the memorable Parliament was held at Kilkenny, which passed the celebrated Statute known generally by the name of the Statute of Kilkenny; an ordinance which contains some enactments full of that penal spirit which kept the aborigines of this island in a state of warfare with the English Pale for centuries after. This Statute was edited for the first time, with a translation and notes, for the Irish Archæological Society, by James Hardiman, Esq., Author of the History of Galway, and requires no comment here. For some curious particulars respecting Lionel and his officers, the reader is referred to Davis's Discovery, pp. 23, 24; and to Grace's Annals of Ireland, edited by the Rev. Richard Butler, p. 153.

Dermot, son of Donough Reagh Mac Dermot, was slain by Cathal Oge, son of Cathal O'Conor.

The daughter of Turlough O'Conor, and wife of Farrell O'Reilly, was killed by a fall.

A bridge of lime and stone was built by Cathal O'Conor across the river of Eas-dara[j].

Farrell, the son of Geoffrey Mac Rannall, and Tuathal O'Finnaghty, died.

Naevag O'Duigennan died.

Cathal, son of the Caoch Mac Rannall, was slain.

Gilla-na-naev O'Conmhaigh[k], Chief Professor of Music in Thomond, died.

The son of the King of England[l] came to Ireland.

Art, son of Gillareagh Magennis, was treacherously slain by the sons of Savadge and the son of Murtough Riaganagh Magennis.

Cathal (O'Conor) marched with an army into Tirawley, and destroyed many of its houses and churches[m].

THE AGE OF CHRIST, 1361.

The Age of Christ, one thousand three hundred sixty-one.

Benedict O'Mochain, Erenagh of Killaraght[n], died.

Art Mac Murrough, King of Leinster, and Donnell Reagh, heir apparent

[m] To this year O'Flaherty adds the following entries in H. 2. 11:

"Giolla anndriar mac Maoilpóil en daoi Ereann re timpánacht, ar dobaréain 7 ar droċfeinm, do éġ: [i. e. Gilla Andreas Mac Maelpoil, the only clown of Ireland for tympanship, penury, and bad music, died.]—MS. L."

"Filia O'Gairmleodha uxor Magni Eoganaiġ O'Donell, et ejusdem mulieris mater filia O'Cahan obierunt.—MS. L."

"Joannes filius Sinicin Mac Uidhilin occisus. —*O'Mulconry.*" "A filio Savagii in dolo.—MS. L."

"Mac Riġ Saxan do ṫoċt i nErind.—MS. L., 8 Sept. 1361, *Dublinii appulit;—Cambd. Annal.;* 1360, *Cod. Cl.*"

"Sluaiġeaḋ les (.i. le Caṫal óg ó Concobair) do ċum Sir Emann a burc, 7 dar airg crić ṁic Uilliam co caislen na leṫinse:" [i. e. an army was led by him (i. e. by Cathal Oge O'Conor) to Sir Edmond Burke, by which he plundered Mac William's country as far as the castle of Lehinch.]—MS. L."

[n] *Killaraght.*—Cill aṫraċt, i. e. church of Athracht, a virgin, who took the veil from St. Patrick; it is the name of a parish in the barony of Coolavin, in the south of the county of Sligo, where the memory of this virgin is still held in great veneration.

do ġaḃail la Mac ríġ Saxan ina tiġ fein tre cheilg, ⁊ a nécc ar a haiṫle ina mbraighdeanas.

Corbmac ballaċ ó maoileachlainn Ri miḋe, Donnchaḋ ua lochlainn tiġearna corcomdruadh, cathal ⁊ muirchſrtach da ṁac aſdha mic eoġain, Dubócc ingſn aſdha még uidir bſn ċonċonnact mic pilip ṁég maṫgamna, Tomas mag tiġſrnain taoiseaċ teallaiġ dunchaḋa, Niocol ó fionaċta Tuathal ó Máille, iadsiḋe dég uile.

Sir émann a búrc, Remann mac burcaiġ an muine, Uater Stondún ⁊ Gillebert mac maoilir décc.

Cluithe an ríġ i nérinn uile co comcoitchionn ⁊ Risderd Sauaois décc da bithin.

Mac Raiṫ ua find ollaṁ fil Muireḋaiġ i rſinm ⁊ i tiompánaċt décc.

Creacha mora do denaṁ la Mac uilliam burc, ⁊ la Mac feorais, ⁊ la gallaiḃ connaċt uile ar ċaṫal óg mac caṫail uí concoḃair go ro creachsat, ⁊ go ro airgſt luiġne ⁊ tír fiachraċ. Sluaiġeaḋ la caṫal iſrttain do ḋioġail i ndearnsat go ro airgc oireċt meic feorais, ⁊ crioch emainn meic hoiberd gur ro mill ⁊ gur ro loit an tír go léir.

AOIS CRIOST, 1362.

Aoís Criost, mile, tri chéd, Seascat, a dó.

O beollam coṁarba droma cliaḃ, giolla an coimdeaḋ mac Muġroin oircindeċ cille an iomaire Oireachtach mac branain oircindeach oile find

° *Sir Edmond Burke.*—O'Flaherty adds, in H. 2. 11: "Hospitalitate, fortitudine, prudentia, peritia et justitia clarissimus hic Edmundus [vocatur] in Libro Mic Firbisiġ."

What O'Flaherty here calls *Liber* Mic Firbisiġ, is evidently the copy of the *Chronicon Scotorum* in the handwriting of Duald Mac Firbis, now preserved in the Library of Trinity College, Dublin.

ᵖ *Burke of Muine.*—In Mageoghegan's translation of the Annals of Clonmacnoise, he is called "Redmond Burke of the Moniemore."

ᑫ *Cluithe an righ.*—This passage is given as follows in the Dublin copy of the Annals of Ulster, but entered under the year 1158:

"A. D. 1158. Cluiċe in ríġ do beiṫ co tiuġ is in mbliaḋain si i nErinn. Risderd Saḃais dec de."

"A. D. 1158. The game of the King was *thick* [i. e. rife] this year in Ireland. Richard Savadge died of it."

It is thus given by Mageoghegan, in his Annals of Clonmacnoise, under the correct date:

"A. D. 1361. The King's Game was used generally throughout Ireland. Richard Savadge thereof died."

to the throne of Leinster, were treacherously made prisoners by the son of the King of England. They afterwards died in prison.

Cormac Ballach O'Melaghlin, King of Meath; Donough O'Loughlin, Lord of Corcomroe; Cathal and Murtough, two sons of Hugh, son of Owen [O'Conor]; Dubliόg, daughter of Hugh Maguire, and wife of Cuconnaught, son of Philip Mac Mahon; Thomas Mac Tiernan, Chief of Teallach-Dunchadha [Tullyhunco, in the county of Cavan]; Nicholas O'Finnaghty, and Tuathal O'Malley, all died.

Sir Edmond Burke[o], Redmond, son of Burke of Muine[p], Walter Staunton, and Gilbert Mac Meyler, died.

Cluithe an righ[q] [was rife] throughout all Ireland in general, and Richard Savadge died of it.

Magrath O'Finnaghty, Chief Musician and Tympanist to the Sil-Murray, died.

Great depredations were committed by Mac William Burke and Mac Feorais [Bermingham], and by the English of all Connaught, upon Cathal Oge, son of Cathal O'Conor; and they ravaged and wasted Leyny and Tireragh. An army was led by Cathal afterwards, to take revenge for what they had done; and he plundered Mac Feorais's people and the territory of Edmund Mac Hubert [Burke], and spoiled and destroyed the whole country.

THE AGE OF CHRIST, 1362.

The Age of Christ, one thousand three hundred sixty-two.

O'Beollan, Coarb of Drumcliff; Gilla-an-choimhdhe Mac Mughroin, Erenagh of Cill-an-iomaire[r]; Oireachtach Mac Branan, Erenagh of Elphin; Aengus

O'Flaherty, in H. 2. 11, glosses "cluiċe an riġ," by ".i. an plaiġ," i. e. the plague.

This must have been a name for some epidemic disease; but the Editor has not discovered anything to prove what was the exact nature of it, or why it was called Cluithe an righ, or "the King's Game." The scrofulous disease called the King's evil, is so called for no other reason than because it was commonly believed to be cured by the royal touch; and it may be safely conjectured that the name *cluithe an righ* for this plague had its origin in some similar notion.

[r] *Cill-an-iomaire.*—Cill an iomaire, i. e. the church of the ridge, now Killanummery, a parish in the barony of Dromahaire, and county of Leitrim.

Aongur mac an ócclaoich airchinnceaċ chille hairiḋ, o ṗṡrghara biocaire iomtha, ⁊ Murchaḋ manach mac taiḋg ḋécc.

Eoghan fionn ua concoḃair mac riġ Connacht Maolruanaiḋ ó ḋuḃḋa, ⁊ a ḃſn ingean meic ḋonnchaiḋ, Niall macc Shamraḋain taoiseaċ teallaiġ eachḋach Diarmaitt mac Seaain uí ḟſrġail tiġearna na hangaile, Cairpre ó cuinn taoíseaċ muintire giollgain, Domnall mac Ruaiḋri uí ceallaiġ, Tomaltach ua birn, Muircheartach ḋonn macc oireachtaiġ, eóghan ua máille, ḋiarmaitt a ṁac tiġearnaḋa umaill iaḋsoṁ ḋo écc.

Cúcoigcriche mag eochagain, mac ḋiarmaḋa meg eochagain, ⁊ Muirir mac muirchſrtaiġ meg eochagain ḋécc.

Cathal óg ⁊ mac feḋlimiḋ uí ċoncobair ḋo gabail cairlen baile an topair.

Sluaigeaḋ aḋbal mor la riġ connaċt aoḋ mac feḋlimiḋ, ⁊ la caṫal óg ua cconcoḃair ir in miḋe gur ro loirgrſt co haṫair miḋe. Cill cainḋiġ ḋo loscaḋ leo go cceiṫriḃ tſmplaiḃ ḋécc ina mbatar forlongrort ag gallaiḃ, ⁊ uilc iomḋa ḋo ḋſnoṁ forra ḋon chur rin, a niomroḋ slán ḋia ttighiḃ iaraṁ.

Taḋg mac conċoḃair mic toirrḋealḃaiġ uí briain ḋo ṁarḃaḋ la cloinn ċoiléin.

Cathal óg ó concoḃair an tén rioghḋaṁna ba mó allaḋ, ⁊ oirrḋearcur neart, ⁊ niaḋachur, eneach, ⁊ ſngnoṁ in aon aimrir rir ḋo écc, i Sligeach ḋo ṗláigh.

[s] *Cill-airidh.*—This is called cill oiriḋ in the Dublin copy of the Annals of Ulster, and the same spelling is used by the Four Masters at the years 1333 and 1416. The name is now anglicised Killerry, and is that of a parish near Lough Gill, in the barony of Tirerrill, and county of Sligo.—See *Genealogies, Tribes, and Customs of Hy-Fiachrach*, p. 486, and map to the same.

[t] *Of Imaidh*, ioṁta.—This name is latinised Imagia by Colgan, and anglicised Imay by Roderic O'Flaherty. The name is now usually written Omey, and is that of an island on the coast of Connamara, in the north-west of the county of Galway. Guaire, the hospitable King of Connaught, bestowed it on St. Fechin, who founded an abbey on it in the seventh century. Imagia was a parish church in the time of Colgan (1645).—See his *Acta Sanctorum*, pp. 140, 141; see also O'Flaherty's *Iar-Connaught*, printed for the Irish Archæological Society, p. 113, where he says, "St. Fechin erected an abbey therein, but now the parish church is only extant, whereof St. Fechin is patron, the 20th of January worshipped." Colgan had a manuscript Irish life of St. Fechin, which belonged to this church.

[u] *Ballintober.*—This is the first notice of this castle occurring in these Annals. For some account of the present state of the ruins of it see note [h] under the year 1311, p. 500.

[v] *Kilkenny*, i. e. Kilkenny west, in a barony of the same name in the county of Westmeath.

Mac an Oglaoich, Erenagh of Cillairedh[s]; O'Fergusa, Vicar of Imaidh[t]; and Murrough, the monk, Mac Teige, died.

Owen Finn O'Conor, son of the King of Connaught; Mulrony O'Dowda and his wife, daughter of Mac Donough; Niall Magauran, Chief of Teallach Eachdhach [Tullyhaw]; Dermot, son of John O'Farrell, Lord of Annaly; Carbry O'Quin, Chief of Muintir-Gillagan; Donnell, son of Rory O'Kelly; Tomaltagh O'Beirne, Murtough Donn Mageraghty, Owen O'Malley, and Dermot, his son, Lords of Umallia, died.

Cucogry Mageoghegan, the son of Dermot Mageoghegan, and Maurice, the son of Murtough Mageoghegan, died.

The castle of Ballintober[u] was taken by Cathal Oge and the son of Felim O'Conor.

A very great army was led by the King of Connaught, Hugh, son of Felim, and Cathal O'Conor, into Meath, which they triumphantly desolated by fire. They burned the church of Kilkenny[v] and fourteen other churches, in which the English had garrison. Many other injuries they also did them [the English], after which they returned in safety to their homes.

Teige, son of Conor, son of Turlough O'Brien, was slain by the Clann-Coilen[w].

Cathal Oge O'Conor, a Roydamna[x] of more fame, renown, strength, heroism, hospitality, and prowess, than any in his time, died of the plague at Sligo.

This passage is given somewhat better in Mageoghegan's translation of the Annals of Clonmacnoise, as follows:

"A. D. 1362. Hugh mac Felym O'Connor, King of Connought, and Cahall Oge O'Connor, marched with their forces to Meath, burnt and destroyed all places where they came, to [as far as] the hill of Cnock-Aysde in Kynaleaghe. Of that journey they burnt 14 Churches, and the church of Kilkenny, in Machairie Kwyrcknie [Macaıpe Cuıpcne]; committ'd many outrages upon the English of Meath, and were so many that it were hard to recoumpt them; returned at last to their houses in safety."

[w] *The Clann-Coilen*, i. e. the Mac Namaras, who were otherwise called Hy-Caisin. They were seated in the county of Clare, between the River Fergus and the Shannon.—See note [f] under the year 1311, pp. 498, 499, *supra*.

[x] *Roydamna*, i. e. *materies regis*, or one who, from his descent, personal form, and valour, might be elected a king. This passage is translated by Mageoghegan in his version of the Annals of Clonmacnoise, as follows:

"A. D. 1362. Cahall Oge O'Connor, the hardiest and man of greatest valour of any nobleman of his time, died of the plague at Sligeagh, the 3rd of November."

This Cathal Oge was the son of Cathal, King of Connaught, who was the son of Donnell, Ta-

Muirchertach mac Tomáis mic Cathail riabhaigh uí Ruairc do écc.

Domhnall mac uí Cheallaigh do écc.

Cúconnacht ó Duibhgennain biocaire cille Rónain dég.

Amhlaoibh mac Firbhisigh adhbhar ollamhan ó ffiachrach, Fearghal mac Taidhg meic Aedhagáin saoi breithemhan, Seaan mac Donnchaidh meic Firbhisigh adhbhar ollamhan ó ffiachrach, Diarmaid mac Meg Carthaigh, Concobhar mac Maoileachlainn carraigh uí Dubhda, ⁊ Muircheartach a mhac iaidsidhe uile do égh.

AOIS CRIOST, 1363.

Aois Criost, míle, trí chéd, Seascatt, a trí.

Maghnas eóghanach mac Concobhair mic Aedha mic Domhnaill óig uí Domhnaill, ⁊ Aodh ruadh mág uidhir tighearna Fermanach décc.

Maghnus (meblach) mac Aedha uí Domhnaill adbhar tighearna tíre conaill fer as mó do righne duaisle ⁊ do ghuaisbhertaibh ina aimsir do marbhadh la Maghnus mac Cathail riabhaigh uí Chonchobhair.

Tadhg mac Consnamha taoiseach muintire Cionaith do lot do Chathal mac Aedha breifnigh, ⁊ a ghabhail do iarsin go bfuair bás ina braighdeanus.

Lasairfhiona ingen uí Fherghail ben uí Raghailligh décc.

Muircheartach ruadh mac Domhnaill Iorrais uí Choncobhair do marbhadh do mac Maghnusa (.i. Tadhg).

Bebinn ingen Még Eochagain ben an Trionnaigh décc.

Cathal mac Donnchaidh do marbhadh do mhuintir Muighe luirg.

Gaoth adhbhal mhór do bhriseadh iomad teampall ⁊ cumhtaighthi is in mbliadhain si, ⁊ iolar long, ⁊ laoidheang do bhathadh di beós.

Concobhar ua Dubhda do marbhadh la Donnchadh ua nDubhda ⁊ la Muircheartach mac Donnchaidh uí Dhubhda.

nist of Connaught, and ancestor of the O'Conors of Sligo.

Intended Ollav, adhbhar ollamhan, literally, *materies* of an ollav, or chief professor of poetry or history.

[z] To this year O'Flaherty adds the two following notices in II. 2. 11:

"Item Gillapatricius mac Oireachtaigh taoiseach muintire Roduibh peste obiit.—MS. L."

"Cormacus Ballagh O'Maelseachlainn, Rex Midiæ obiit.—*Cod. Cl. et* C. E."

[a] *Eoghanach*, i. e. of Tyrone. He was so called from his having been fostered in Tyrone.

[b] *Meabhlach*, i. e. the guileful, treacherous, or crafty.

[c] *Perilous*, do ghuaisbheartaibh.—Literally, of

Murtough, the son of Thomas, son of Cathal Reagh O'Rourke, died.

Donnell, the son of O'Kelly, died.

Cuconnaught O'Duigennan, Vicar of Kilronan, died.

Auliffe Mac Firbis, intended Ollav[y] of Tireragh; Farrell, the son of Teige Mac Egan, a learned Brehon; John, son of Donough Mac Firbis, intended Ollav of Tireragh; Dermot, son of Mac Carthy; Conor, son of Melaghlin Carragh O'Dowda, and Murtough, his son, all died[z].

THE AGE OF CHRIST, 1363.

The Age of Christ, one thousand three hundred sixty-three.

Manus Eoghanach[a], the son of Conor, son of Hugh, son of Donnell Oge O'Donnell, and Hugh Roe Maguire, Lord of Fermanagh, died.

Manus Meabhlach[b], son of Hugh O'Donnell, heir to the lordship of Tirconnell, a man who had performed a greater number of noble and perilous[c] actions than any other man of his time, was slain by Manus, son of Cathal Sramach[d] O'Conor.

Teige Mac Consnava, Chief of Muintir-Kenny, was wounded, and afterwards taken prisoner, by Cathal, son of Hugh Breifneach O'Conor. He died in his confinement.

Lasarina[e], daughter of O'Farrell, and wife of O'Reilly, died.

Murtough Roe, the son of Donnell-Erris O'Conor, was slain by Teige Mac Manus.

Bevin, the daughter of Mageoghegan, and wife of the Sinnach [the Fox], died.

Cathal Mac Donough was slain by the people of Moylurg.

A very great storm in this year threw down several churches and houses, and also sank many ships and boats.

Conor O'Dowda was slain by Donough O'Dowda, and Murtough, son of Donough O'Dowda.

dangerous deeds, i. e. deeds the achievement of which was attended with peril.

[d] *Sramach*, i. e. the blear-eyed.

[e] *Lasarina.*—Charles O'Conor writes, *inter lineas*, "no caċaıpıona." To this year O'Flaherty adds the following passages in H. 2. 11:

"Grania filia Donaldi O'Conor; filia Donaldi puaḋ O'Mally uxor Donaldi O'Dowd; Mael-

AOIS CRIOST, 1364.

Aois Criost, míle, trí chéd, Seasccat, a ceathair.

Aodh ua néill Rí ċinél neoġain an taon ġaoiḋeal do bfſrr ina aimsir décc iar mbuaiḋ niochta, ⁊ nenig áiġ ⁊ oirrdearcais.

Diarmaid ua briain tiġearna tuaḋmuṁan, Maoileachloinn mac murchaiḋ mic giolla na naoṁ mic aoḋa mic aṁlaoiḃ tiġſrna na hanġaile, Derbail ingean uí ḋoṁnaill bſn ṁéġ uidir, Mairgreg ingſn uatér a burc bſn aoḋa mic feiḋlimiḋ uí concoḃair, Doṁnall ṁág uiḋir taoíseach cloinne fſrġaile, Giolla na naoṁ ua duiḃdaḃoireann ollaṁ corcomdruaḋ le ḃrſṫſmnas, Aiffric ingean briain uí Raġallaiġ bſn briain meic tiġearnáin déġ.

Doṁnall mac Ruaiḋri uí ċeallaiġ aḋbar tiġearna ó Maine do éġ.

Giolla na naoṁ mac gobann na scél saoí ṡſnchaḋa, Diarmaid ó sgingin ollam ċenel conaill re sſnchas, ⁊ Mairġreg ingſn uátéir a búrc bean aſḋa mic feidlimiḋ uí concobair ri Connacht déġ.

AOIS CRIOST, 1365.

Aois Criost, mile, trí chéd, Seasccat, a cúig.

Paidín ó congaile pſrsún ⁊ airchinneach Rossa airṫir décc.

Ruaiḋri mac doṁnaill ui néill do ṁarḃaḋ daon urċar soiġde la Maoileachlainn mac an ghirr meic caṫmaoíl.

sechlunnius filius Murgesi Mac Donogh; Fergallus Mac Consnaṁa; et Odo Mac Maġnusa, obierunt.—MS. L."

"Diermitius mac laiṁe .i. mac mic Diarmada meg Carṫaiġ, cæsus.—MS. L." [Dermot Mac Laimhe, i. e. son of the son of Dermot Mac Carthy, was slain.]

[f] *After gaining the palm.*—This passage is given somewhat differently as follows in Mageoghegan's translation of the Annals of Clonmacnoise:

"A. D. 1364. Hugh O'Neale, King of Ulster, the best King of any province in his time, died, after good pennance, as a good Christian."

[g] *O'Duvdavoran.*—This name is now shortened to Davoran. The head of this family was originally seated at Lisdoonvarna, in the southwest of the barony of Burren, in the county of Clare. There are still many respectable persons of the name in the county.

[h] *Na Sgel,* i. e. of the tales or stories.

[i] To this year O'Flaherty adds the two following obits in H. 2. 11:

"Niellus Mag Cagadan occisus a Mac Diarmada Gall.—MS. L."

"Brannus O'Broin insignis Cytharædus obiit.

THE AGE OF CHRIST, 1364.

The Age of Christ, one thousand three hundred sixty-four.

Hugh O'Neill, King of Kinel-Owen, the best man of the Irish of his time, died, after having gained the palm[f] for humanity, hospitality, valour, and renown.

Dermot O'Brien, Lord of Thomond; Melaghlin, the son of Murrough, son of Gilla-na-naev, son of Hugh, son of Auliffe [O'Farrell], Lord of Annaly; Derbhail, daughter of O'Donnell, and wife of Maguire; Margaret, daughter of Walter Burke, and wife of Hugh, son of Felim O'Conor; Donnell Maguire, Chief of Clann-Fergaile; Gilla-na-naev O'Duvdavoran[g], Chief Brehon of Corcomroe; and Affrica, daughter of Brian O'Reilly, and wife of Brian Mac Tiarnan, died.

Donnell, son of Rory O'Kelly, heir to the lordship of Hy-Many, died.

Gilla-na-naev Mac Gowan, [surnamed] na Sgel[h], a learned historian; Dermot O'Sgingin, Ollav of Tirconnell in History; and Margaret, daughter of Walter Burke, and wife of Felim O'Conor, King of Connaught, died[i].

THE AGE OF CHRIST, 1365

The Age of Christ, one thousand three hundred sixty-five.

Paidin O'Congaile[j], Parson and Erenagh of Ross-Airthir[k], died.

Rory, the son of Donnell O'Neill, was killed with one shot of an arrow[l] by Melaghlin Mac-an-Girr Mac Cawell.

—*O'Mulconry*, 1365, MS. L. 1364, C. C. Ɛ." [i. e. Bran O'Byrne, a celebrated harper, died.]

[j] *Paidin O'Conghaile.*—In modern times this name would be anglicised Paddy Conneely. The name O'Conghaile, which is pronounced as if written O'Conaoile, is to be distinguished from O'Congalaiġ, which is pronounced O'Connálaiġ, and now always anglicised Connolly, without the prefix O.

[k] *Ross-Airthir.*—This name is more usually written Ros oirṫir, and is now anglicised Rossorry. It is situated on the west side of the narrow part of Lough Erne, a short distance to the south of Enniskillen, in the county of Fermanagh.

[l] *One shot of an arrow.*—This might be also rendered "one cast of a javelin." The passage is translated by Mageoghegan as follows, in his version of the Annals of Clonmacnoise:

"A. D. 1365. Rowrie mac Donnell O'Neale was killed by Melaughlyn mac Engyrr Mac Cathmoyle by the shott of an arrow."

Feidhlimidh an einigh mac domhnaill uí concobhair tighearna corcomodhruadh saoí gan aithbe neimigh, ⁊ nirghnomha décc.

Tomar mac Murchadha uí ferghail dég.

Ionnsoighidh do thabhairt do cloinn goirdealbhaigh ar luighnibh dia ro marbhadh corbmac ua hegra ⁊ seisear do maithibh a chineadh imaille frir.

Aodh mac diarmada do dul i muintir eolair, Creacha móra do dénomh orra, ⁊ nochar creacha gan dioghail iaidridhe, uair do marbhadh corbmac mac diarmada ruaidh biatach coitchionn connacht, dá mac tomaltaigh uí birn, .i. Maoileachlainn dall ⁊ giollacriort (imaille re rochaidibh oile) la heolarachaibh i ttoraigheacht a ccreach. Ro gabsat beór diarmait mac diarmatta, ⁊ maolruanaidh mac donnchaidh riabhaigh iar maidhm a muintire.

Brian mac matha meic tighearnáin taoiseach teallaigh dunchadha, aon ba mó ágh oirrdearcur clu ⁊ ceannar do taoiseachaibh breifne do écc. Ar do ro raidheadh

Brian mac tighearnáin na ttreas,
Re a eineach nir chóir coimmear,
Ro lean gan fíoch an fele
Budh neimh crioch a caithreime.

Brian mac aedha meg mathgamhna do gabail tighearnais oirgiall. Cleamnar dforailsemh do ar Somairle mac Eoin duibh meic domhnaill (adbar tighearna insi gall, ⁊ ardconrubal cuigidh uladh). Go ttuc air ingean uí Raghallaigh do leigean, ⁊ a ingen fein do thabairt. Nir bo cian iar sin go ttuc Mag math-

[m] *Felim-an-einigh*.—This passage is thus rendered by Mageoghegan in his version of the Annals of Clonmacnoise:

"A. D. 1365. Felym Aneny, in English called Felym the bountifull, son of Donnell O'Connor of Corcomroe, died."

[n] *Unebbing*.—The word aithbe is explained by Michael O'Clery, in his Glossary of ancient Irish words, as follows: "Aithbe .i. traghadh, no laghdughadh na mara. Aithbhe, i. e. the ebbing or lessing of the sea."

[o] *Muintir-Eolais*, i. e. the Mac Ranalls and their followers in the southern or level portion of the county of Leitrim.

[p] *Not with impunity*.—Literally, "but these were not depredations unrevenged."

[q] *Mac Tiernan*.—This name is now always anglicised Kiernan, in the barony of Tullyhunco, in the west of the county of Cavan, where it is very common.

[r] *Brian, the son of Hugh Mac Mahon*.—This story is very differently told in the Annals of Clonmacnoise, as translated by Mageoghegan, as follows:

"A. D. 1365. Bryan mac Hugh Magmahon tooke upon him the principallitye of the contreys of Uriel, tooke to wife the daughter of Sowarle mac Eon Duffe Mac Donnell, archcon-

Felim an-einigh[m], son of Donnell O'Conor, Lord of Corcomroe, a man of unebbing[n] hospitality and prowess, died.

Thomas, son of Murrough O'Farrell, died.

An attack was made by the Clann-Costello upon the people of Leyny, on which occasion Cormac O'Hara, and six of the chiefs of his tribe along with him, were slain.

Hugh Mac Dermot made an incursion into [the country of] the Muintir Eolais[o], and committed great depredations upon them, but not with impunity[p]; for Cormac Mac Dermot Roe, General Biatach of Connaught; the two sons of Cormac O'Beirne, Melaghlin Dall and Gilchreest, and many others, were slain by the Muintir Eolais, who went in pursuit of the prey. After the defeat of their people, Dermot Mac Dermot and Mulrony, son of Donough Reagh, were taken prisoners.

Brian, the son of Matthew Mac Tiernan[q], Chief of Teallach Dunchadha [Tullyhunco], the most distinguished for valour, renown, fame, and power, of the sub-chieftains of Breifny, died. Of him was said:

Brian Mac Tiernan of the battles,
Whose hospitality was incomparable;
He followed generosity without hatred,
And heaven was the goal of his career.

Brian, the son of Hugh Mac Mahon[r], assumed the lordship of Oriel. He sued for an alliance by marriage with Sorley, son of Owen Duv Mac Donnell, heir to the lordship of the Insi-Gall, and High Constable of the province of Ulster; and he induced him to put away O'Reilly's daughter, and espouse his

stable and head of the galloglasses of Ulster; was procured to put away the daughter of O'Rellye that was formerly married to him. Not long after Sowarle invited his said sonne-in-law to his house, and being conveyed to an inner roome therein, as though to pass the time in conversation and drinking of wine, was filthily taken by his said Father-in-law, and committed him to a strong place on a lough to bee kept, for which cause Sawarle was banished from out of the whole country."

In the Dublin copy of the Annals of Ulster, however, Brian Mac Mahon is made the perpetrator of this horrid deed, and it is added that Somairle was the son of Eoin Dubh, who was the son of Alexander, heir to the kingdom of Insi Gall. Alexander, the father of Eoin Dubh, was the son of Aengus More, who was the son of Donnell, the progenitor of the Mac Donnells of Scotland, who was the son of Randal, who was the son of Somhairle, the progenitor of all the Clann-Sorley, namely, the Mac Donnells,

ġaṁna esioṁ ar cuireaḋ chuige, ⁊ iar mbeith ḋóiḃ athaiḋ ag ól tarla imresain etorra. Iaḋais brian a laṁa ina thimcioll-soṁ, ⁊ tucc fodeara a cengal go daingen dosgaoilte, ⁊ a chur is in loch baoi ina comḟogus gur ro baitheaḋ é fochetóir. Doṁnall mac aodha uí néill cona braiṫriḃ, brian mac enrí uí néill go maiṫiḃ cloinne aoḋa buiḋe, ⁊ toirrḋealḃaċ mor mac doṁnaill cona raiḃe da chineaḋ i nultaiḃ do thionól hi cenn aroile iarsin. Dul dóiḃ dén láiṁ ⁊ dén aonta go hairġiallaiḃ co rangattar hi comḟocraiḃ Ráṫa tulach longport meg maṫġaṁna. Raḃaḋ do rochtain rompa co brian gur teichestair, ⁊ go ro fágbaḋ an baile fás folaṁ ara ccionn. Iadsoṁ do leanṁain még maṫġaṁna, ⁊ éfein ⁊ maithe an tíre do beiṫ hi ttimċeall a ccruiḋ, ⁊ a ccethra da ccur fo daingean an tíre. Maiḋm do ṫaḃairt for airġiallaiḃ annsin, a néde, ⁊ a ninnile do ḃuain díoḃ. Mag maṫġaṁna daṫchur ar a ḋuṫaiḋ feisin i nucht muintire maoilṁórḋa iarsin, ⁊ a ḃean ⁊ a ingen do ġabail.

Cúċonnacht ó Raiġilliġ tiġerna breifne do dul is na braiṫriḃ, ⁊ a thiġearnas do ḟagḃail aga derḃrathair Pilib.

Aoḋ mac Neill uí doṁnaill (.i. adbar tiġearna ṫíre conuill) do ṁarḃaḋ la doṁnall mac Muirchertaiġ uí concoḃair. Taḋg mac maġnusa uí concoḃair do breiṫ ar ḋoṁnall an la cedna, ⁊ briseaḋ do ṫaḃairt air, ⁊ drong da ṁuintir do ṁarḃaḋ im aoḋ mac concoḃair mic taiḋg.

Roiberd mac uatin baired do écc.

Mac ríġ Saxan do ḟágbáil erenn.

Mac Dowells, Mac Rorys, O'Gnimhas (now Agnews), and Mac Eoins of Ardnamurchon.

[a] *This being accordingly done.*—This sentence is very rudely constructed by the Four Masters. It is far better given in the Annals of Ulster as follows:

"Gerr ar a aiṫle sin co tuc cuigi ina teċ féin é dol fina, ⁊ mar do ṡail in sin d'faġḃail is e cuireḋ fuair gur iad brian fein a da laim tairis ⁊ a ġabail co doċrac domiaḋaċ ⁊ a togbail amaċ ⁊ uathaḋ da muinntir ina ḟoċair, gur crapled ⁊ gur cenglaḋ a ċosa ⁊ a laṁa dá ċeile, ⁊ gur cuireḋ a loċ é, ⁊ ni fes a sgela o sin amaċ. Do ligeḋ fon tir, ⁊ gaċ inaḋ a friṫ a muinntir do marḃaḋ ⁊ do hairgeḋ iat. Mairg doṁan ⁊ talam ⁊ uisci inar folchaḋ in traerċlann soceneoil .i. adbar riġ innsi gall, mac eoin duiḃ mic alaxandair."

"Shortly after this he invited him to his own house to drink wine; and when he expected to get the wine, the treatment he received was this: Brian himself folded his arms about him, and seized him roughly and disrespectfully, and carried him out, with a few of his people along with him; and his hands and legs were crippled and tied to each other, and he was thus cast into a lake, and no further tidings of him were

own. Not long after this Mac Mahon invited him [Mac Donnell] to a feast, and they continued drinking for some time. Anon a dispute arose between them; whereupon Brian threw his arms about him [Sorley], and ordered that he should be fast and strongly fettered, and cast into a neighbouring lake: [and this being accordingly done[s]] he was at once drowned. Upon this Donnell, son of Hugh O'Neill, and his brother, Brian, son of Henry O'Neill, with the chief of Clannaboy[t], and Turlough More Mac Donnell, with all of his tribe in Ulster, assembled together, and, with one accord, marched into Oriel as far as the confines of Rath-Tulach[u], the mansion-seat of Mac Mahon. Intelligence of this having reached Brian, he fled, leaving the town empty and desolate to them. They, however, pursued Mac Mahon, who, with the chiefs of his territory, was engaged placing their herds and flocks in the fastnesses of the country. The men of Oriel were defeated, and deprived of their arms and cattle[w]. After this Mac Mahon was banished from his own country to Muintir-Maelmora[x], and his wife and his daughter were made prisoners.

Cuconnaught O'Reilly, Lord of Breifny, retired among the friars, and resigned his lordship to his brother Philip.

Hugh, the son of Niall O'Donnell, heir to the lordship of Tirconnell, was slain by Donnell, the son of Murtough O'Conor. On the same day Teige, the son of Manus O'Conor, encountered Donnell, and defeated him, with the loss of a great number of his people, among whom was Hugh, the son of Conor, son of Teige.

Robert Mac Wattin[y] Barrett, died.

The son of the King of England left Ireland.

heard. Parties were dispatched throughout the country, and wherever his people were found they were killed and plundered. Wo to the world, the land, and the water where this noble offspring was submersed, i. e. the materies of a king of the Innsi Gall, the son of Eoin Dubh, son of Alexander."

[t] *Clannaboy*, in the original Clann Aodha-buidhe, i. e. the descendants of Hugh Boy O'Neill.

[u] *Rath-Tulach.*—This was a place in the barony and county of Monaghan, but the name is now obsolete.

[w] *Cattle.*—It is stated in the Dublin copy of the Annals of Ulster, that they were pursued as far as Lough Erne, where they were deprived of their flocks and herds by the men of Fermanagh, as well as by the forces who pursued them.

[x] *Muintir-Maelmora.*—This was the tribe name of the O'Reillys of the county of Cavan, then called East Breifny.

[y] *Robert Mac Wattin.*—O'Flaherty remarks in H. 2. 11, that he is called Robug mac uaein, in the Annals of Lecan, in which his death is entered under the year 1366, and that he is

AOIS CRIOST, 1366.

Aois Críost, míle, trí chéd, Seascat a Sé.

Epscop rátha both, .i. mac Maengail do écc.

Cathal mac aodha breifniġ mic caṫail ruaiḋ, Maġnus ócc a mac, ⁊ Muircṡrtaċ mac dáil re docair, Muirġius ó maoltuile, diarmaid mac Siomóin, ⁊ diarmaid mac giolla bṡraiġ do ṁarḃaḋ i fell la fearaiḃ manaċ ar sraṫ fear luirg, ⁊ creacha aiḋble do denaṁ ḋóiḃ ar cloinn Muircṡrtaiġ, ⁊ iad do denoṁ sioḋa re muintir Ruairc, ⁊ do maiṫṁ a ffoltanais ḋóiḃ ar ulc re cloinn Muircṡrtaiġ, ⁊ muintir Ruairc do denaṁ an cedna frisoṁ. Mac Ruaiḋri uí ċoncoḃair do gaḃail ionaid cathail iaroṁ. Muintir Ruairc do dul for imirce a ccoṁḋail fṡr manach. Greiss timchill do denoṁ dóġbaiḃ cloinne muircheartaiġ gur ro marḃsat cathal máġ flannchaiḋ taoiseaċ dartraiġe.

Muircṡrtaċ mac Raġnaill mic Raġnall móir meg raġnaill aḋḃár toísiġ gan ffresabra do marḃaḋ i fell lá Maoileacloinn máġ raġnaill taoiseaċ muintire heolais, ⁊ maoileaċloinn fein décc i ccionn dá mís da éis sin.

Corbmac donn mag carṫaiġ tiġearna ó ccairbre, ⁊ ó neachḋach muṁan do marḃaḋ i fell da brathair mac domnaill na ndomnall.

Conċoḃar ua concobair tiġearna ciarraiġe luaċra do ṁarḃaḋ do branachaiḃ.

Ruaiḋri mac muirceartaiġ uí ċoncoḃair do ḃathaḋ for sionainn.

Maiḋm do thabairt la taḋg mac maġnusa uí concoḃair ar seaan ua

called tiġearna bairéḋac [i. e. Lord of the Barretts] in O'Mulconry's Annals.

[a] *Mac Maengail.*—His name was Patrick.—See Harris's edition of Ware's Bishops, p. 272. The name is still extant in the county of Donegal, where it is anglicised Mac Monigal.

[a] *Srath-Fear-Luirg*, i. e. the strath or holm of the men of Lurg, an ancient territory, now a barony in the north of the county of Fermanagh. It is probably the place called Stranahone, in this barony.—See Ordnance map of Fermanagh, sheets 2 and 6.

[b] *Excursion.*—According to the Dublin copy of the Annals of Ulster, this excursion was made by the O'Rourkes into Breifny, by which is meant that part of Breifny in which the Clann-Murtough O'Conor had established themselves, and from whence they had driven out the original proprietors.

[c] *Melaghlin.*—O'Flaherty adds to this entry in H. 2. 11: "Qui Mælsechlunnius Conmacniorum fulcrum et columen erat.—MS. L."

[d] *Carbery.*—A large district in the south-west of the county of Cork.

THE AGE OF CHRIST, 1366.

The Age of Christ, one thousand three hundred sixty-six.

The Bishop of Raphoe, i. e. Mac Maengail[z], died.

Cathal, the son of Hugh Breifneach, son of Cathal Roe, and Manus, his son, and also Murtough Mac Dail-re-docair, Maurice O'Maeltuile, Dermot Mac Simon, and Dermot Mac Gilla-Bearaigh, were treacherously slain at Srath-Fear-Luirg[a] by the people of Fermanagh, who, to annoy the Clann-Murtough, made peace with the O'Rourkes, and forgave them all their past hostilities; and the O'Rourkes agreed to their proposals. The son of Rory O'Conor after this assumed the place of Cathal. The O'Rourkes went on a migratory excursion[b], accompanied by the people of Fermanagh; but the youths of the Clann-Murtough attacked and surrounded them, and killed Cathal Mac Clancy, Chief of Dartry.

Murtough Mac Rannall, the son of Randal More Mac Rannall, [who was] a materies of a chieftain without dispute, was treacherously slain by Melaghlin Mac Rannall, Chief of Muintir-Eolais. Melaghlin[c] himself died in two months afterwards.

Cormac Don Mac Carthy, Lord of Carbery[d], and of Ivahagh of Munster[e], was treacherously slain by his relative, the son of Donnell na-n-Domhnall[f].

Conor O'Conor, Lord of Ciarraighe-Luachra[g], was slain by the Branaghs[h].

Rory, son of Murtough O'Conor, was drowned in the Shannon.

A victory was gained by Teige, the son of Manus O'Conor, over John

[e] *Ivahagh of Munster.*—This was the ancient name of the country of O'Mahony Finn, otherwise called O'Mahony the Western. In the manuscript entitled *Carbriæ Notitia*, its extent is described thus: "The whole peninsula from Ballydehab to Dunmanus bay is called Ivagh, and did formerly belong to O'Mahone Fune, the best man of that name. The whole of this territory paid tribute to Mac Carthy Reagh for several centuries; but before the English Invasion, both it and the whole of Carbery had belonged to O'Driscoll.

[f] *Na-n-Domhnall.*—Mageoghegan renders this "Donnell of the Donnells." He was probably so called from having many men of the name Donnell among his household.

[g] *Ciarraighe-Luachra.*—This was the original name of a territory comprising about the northern half of the present county of Kerry.

[h] *Branaghs.*—This was the name of an English family seated in the neighbourhood of O'Kerry. O'Flaherty in H. 2. 11, makes the a in bpánaċaiḃ long, and adds "familia scilicet Anglica ei vicinâ.—*O'Mulconry.*"

nDomhnaill gona ġallócclachaiḃ du in ro marḃaḋ sochaiḋe. Mac Suiḃne ⁊ drong do ṁaitiḃ ṫíre conaill do ġabail ⁊ braighde do dſnoṁ ḋíoḃ.

Tionol do dſnaṁ do ḋomhnall ua Neill ⁊ do cloinn nDomhnaill, .i. do ṫoirrḋealbaċ mac domhnaill ⁊ do Alaxanduir a ṁac, dionnsoiġiḋ neill uí néill. Mac cathṁaoil do ċor ar an tír doiḃ co nDeachaiḋ i rann neill uí néill gona éḋiḃ ⁊ inDiliḃ. Iarttroṁ do breiṫ ar dſireaḋ muintire meic cathṁaoil cona ccſthraiḃ, ⁊ laṁ do ṫabairt tarra gur bſnratt a ccroḋ ḋíoḃ. Raġnall mac alaxandair oiġre cloinne Alaxandair do ṫeċt a hinnsib gall mun ammsoin i ccommbáiḋ Néill uí néill. An cſthſrn do gach taoiḃ do tſġṁail i ccomġar dia roile, .i. airecta cloinne domhnaill. Raġnall do ċor teachtaḋ mar araiḃe toirrḋealbaċ ⁊ a mac alaxandair co na muintir diarraiḋ an tsliġe do leiġſn dó i nonóir a sinnsirecta ⁊ do ṫaoḃ a mbrachairsi re aroile. Do ronaḋ dimbriġ leósoṁ don aithſsg hisin uair do ionnsaiġſít gus an áṫ a bfacadar eisioṁ ag triall tairis. Tucsat tachar trén tinnſsnach da chéile hisuiḋe gur marḃaḋ ⁊ gur loitſḋ drong dirím dioḃ da gach leiṫ. Marḃṫar mac do raġnall, i ccommarcc caich la toirrḋealbach, ⁊ gaḃṫar mac toirrḋealbaiġ (alaxandair) la muintir Raġnaill gur ḃreaṫnaiġſít a ṁarḃaḋ fo ċéttóir. Aċt cſna nir comairlécc Raġnall dóib uair ro ráiḋ naċ biaḋ a mac ⁊ a brathair in aoinḟeaċt an la sin da earbaiḋ.

Coccaḋ mór eitir ġallaib connacht. Mac muiris dionnarbad as an tír do ṁac uilliam co nDeachaiḋ do soiġiḋ cloinne Riocaird. Sloiġeaḋ do ḋſnoṁ do mac uilliam, daoḋ ua cconcobair, rí connaċt, ⁊ duilliam ó ceallaiġ tigearna ó maine in uachtar connacht go cloinn Riocaird, ⁊ a mbeiṫ forgla Raiṫe i bforbairi for aroile. Nſrt do ġaḃáil do mac uilliam fa ḋeoiḋ, ⁊ braiġde

[1] *His son and his kinsman.*—This entry is given in Mageoghegan's translation of the Annals of Clonmacnoise, as follows:

"A. D. 1366. Donell O'Neale made great preparations and assemblies to warre against Neale O'Neale, banished Mac Cathmoyle out of his country. Randolph mac Alexander, chief of the Mac Donells, came out of the Isles to assist Neale O'Neale in that warre, where the two forces of the Mac Donells met, that is to saye, Randolph, of the one side, and his kinsmen, the other Mac Donells, of the other side, Terlagh, and his son Alexander. Randolph sent Alexander, his son and heire, and Terlagh Mac Donell, to his kinsmen, desireing them, in regard they were his kinsmen, and he cheife of the house they were of, that they would be pleased to desist from contending against him. They, little regarding the entreaties, made fiercely towards the foorde where they saw Randolph stand, which was answered by the like courage and fierceness by Randolph and

O'Donnell and his gallowglasses. Many were slain in the conflict; and Mac Sweeny and many of the chiefs of Tirconnell were taken and led away prisoners.

An army was mustered by Donnell O'Neill and the Clann-Donnell, i. e. Turlough, the son of Donnell, and Alexander, his son; and they marched against Niall O'Neill. They expelled Mac Cawell from the country, upon which he went over to the side of Niall O'Neill. They came up with the rear body of Mac Cawell's people and their cattle; and, having worsted them, they took their cattle from them.

Randal, son of Alexander, the heir to Clann-Alexander, arrived at this time from the Inis-Gall [the Hebrides], to assist Niall O'Neil. The kerns of both parties met close together, i. e. the troops of the Clann-Donnell. And Randal sent messengers to Turlough and his son Alexander, with their people, to request of them to permit him to pass in honour of his seniority, and for sake of their mutual relationship; but this request was made light of by the others, for they advanced to the ford, which they saw him [Randal] crossing. Here they gave each other a fierce and stubborn battle, in which countless numbers were killed and wounded on both sides. One of Randal's sons was killed by Turlough in the heat of the conflict; and Turlough's son, Alexander, was taken prisoner by Randal's people, who meditated putting him to death at once; but Randal did not consent to this, for he said that he would not be deprived of his son and his kinsman[l] on the one day.

A great war broke out between the English of Connaught. Mac Maurice was banished from his territory by Mac William; and Mac Maurice fled for protection to the Clann-Rickard. Mac William, Hugh O'Conor, King of Connaught, and William O'Kelly, Lord of Hy-Many, marched with an army to Upper Connaught against the Clann-Rickard, and remained there nearly three months engaged in mutual hostilities, until at last Mac William subdued the

his companye. At last the son of Randolph was killed, and Alexander Mac Donell was taken by Randolph's Company, whome the company would kill in revenge of Randolph's son, but they were not suffered by Randolph himself, who worthilie said to them that were so intended to kill Alexander, that he wou'd not loose his son and kinsman together, and that he thought the killing of his son a sufficient loss, and not to suffer his own men to kill his kinsman too. Also there was great slaughter of Donell O'Neale's people in that pressence."

cloinne Riocaird do ṫabairt ar a laiṁ, ⁊ a ṫoideċt ro buaid ccorgair dia tir iarom.

Seaan mac goirdealbaiġ tigearna plebe lugha décc.

Huigin trial tiġearna fir ttulach do marbad la cloinn feorais.

AOIS CRIOST, 1367.

Aois Criost, mile, tri cheud, Seascat aSeacht.

An tepscop (.i. maolseaclainn) ó fferġail, .i. epscop Ardachaid, Saoí gan earbaid i ccrabad, i ndéirc, i ndeénnacht, ⁊ i neagna, ⁊ Malachias mag uidir airchideochain oirgiall do éc.

Cúconnacht ua Raghallaiġ tiġerna breifne no gur treicc í ar dia do dul i clerċeċt, ⁊ pilib do gabail a ionaid.

Clann muirċertaiġ do teċt ar imerce go maġ nisse. Ionnsoiġid do thabairt doib i muiġ luirg. Ba hiad ba hoirsġda ar an siobal sin, Tadg mac Ruaidri uí concobair. Fearġal mac tiġernain tiġearna ṫeallaiġ dúnchada, ⁊ diarmait mag Raġnaill tiġearna ṁuintire heólais, ⁊ galloclaċa ioṁda ina bfarrad. Longport aodha meic diarmada do losgad leó. Ferġal mac diarmata tiġearna maiġe luirg do breiṫ orra, ⁊ Aod mac diarmada immaille fris. Tachar do tabairt doib, ⁊ daoine ioṁda do marbad eatturra leaṫ ar leṫ. Iompód do ṫadg ó Concoḃair ⁊ do Mhág Raghnaill iarsin gan creich gan ċoṁaidh.

Maidm do ṫabairt la doṁnall mac Muirċertaiġ uí Concoḃair, la muintir Ruairc ⁊ la cloinn ndonnchaid cona ccéithirn congbala ar ṫadg mac maġnusa uí Conċoḃair for traiġ neóṫuile an traoís. Galloglaiġ mic maġnusa

[k] *Fer-Tulach*.—Now the barony of Fertullagh, in the south-east of the county of Westmeath. This was Tyrrell's country, from the period of the Anglo-Norman invasion till their forfeiture in 1641; but previously to their arrival it was the patrimonial inheritance of the O'Dooleys, as we learn from these Annals at the years 978, 1021, 1144, and from O'Dugan's topographical poem, in which O'Dooley is thus mentioned:

"O'Duḃlaiġe ra diogainn rath
Ri b-fear d-triaċ-uasal d-tulach."

For some account of the migration of the O'Dooleys to Ely O'Carroll, where they are yet numerous, see Duald Mac Firbis's pedigree of O'Melaghlin.

[l] Under this year O'Flaherty adds the following entries in H. 2. 11:

"Magister Florentius mac an oglaoiċ obiit. *O'Mulconry*."

Clann-Rickard; whereupon the hostages of these latter were delivered up to him, and he returned to his country in triumph.

John Mac Costello, Lord of Sliabh Lugha, died.

Huggin Tyrrell, Lord of Fer-Tulach[k], was slain by the Clann-Feorais [Berminghams[l]].

THE AGE OF CHRIST, 1367.

The Age of Christ, one thousand three hundred sixty-seven.

The Bishops O'Farrell (i. e. Melaghlin), Bishop of Ardagh, a sage not wanting in piety, charity, humanity, or wisdom; and Malachias Maguire, Archdeacon of Oriel [Clogher], died.

Cuconnaught O'Reilly, Lord of Breifny until he resigned the lordship for the sake of God, took holy orders; and Philip assumed his place.

The Clann-Murtough came upon a migratory excursion to Magh-nisse[m], and made an incursion into Moylurg. The most illustrious of those who set out on this incursion were Teige, son of Rory O'Conor; Farrell Mac Tiernan, Lordof Teallach Dunchadha; and Dermot Mac Rannall, Lord of Muintir-Eolais: these were accompanied by many gallowglasses. They burned the fortified residence of Hugh Mac Dermot; but Farrell Mac Dermot and Hugh Mac Dermot, Lord of Moylurg, opposed them; and a battle ensued, in which many were slain on both sides. Teige O'Conor and Mac Rannall then returned, without having gained either booty or consideration.

A victory was gained by Donnell, the son of Murtough O'Conor, the O'Rourkes, and the Clann-Donough, with their retained kerns, over Teige, the son of Manus, on Traigh Eothuile an t-Saoir[n]. The gallowglasses of the son of

"Joannes Mac Costellow Dominus Sleıbı luġa obiit."

"Dermitius Ua heılıġe dominus Mac Oglaich obiit.—*Mac Firb.* (1397. MS. L.)"

"Wilielmus mac an ṗeaրրuın (.i. filius Rickardi de Burgo Rectoris de Loghreagh. *Annal: domini Mac William*) filii Wilielmi de Burgo, occisus per Clannrickardios in monasterio Conga. *Mac Firb.* (1367. MS. L.)"

"Conchavarus (filius Cathaldi. MS. L.) domini O'Farell filius obiit.—*Mac Firb.*"

"Jordanus Dexeter, Albia filia O'Flannagan uxor Cathaldi filii Donaldi, et Mac Conmara, dynasta de Cloinn Colen decesserunt.—*Mac Firb.* (1367. MS. L.)"

[m] *Magh Nisse*, now the name of a level district lying in the county of Leitrim, immediately to the east of Jamestown and Carrick-on-Shannon.

[n] *Traigh Eothuile an t-Saoir* is the name of a

do marbaḋ ann dechneabar ⁊ seacht ffiċit ro ríṁeaḋ dibsiḋe do muḋuġaḋ im ḋoṁnall mac Soṁairle im ḋoṁnall óg a mac im an dá Mac Suibne im ṁac an epscoip uí ḋubda ⁊ fa uilliam mac Sithiġ.

Dearḃáil inġean Maolruanaiḋ móir meic diarmada ben ualgaircc uí Ruairc do ṁarbaḋ la cloinn Muirchertaiġ.

Maoilseaċlainn mac Seaffraiḋ meic giollapatraicc, ⁊ drong dia ṁuintir do ṁarbaḋ i fell la gallaiḃ.

Tadg mág Shaṁradain, ⁊ Aenġuss mac an degánaiġ még Saṁradáin décc.

Tadg ⁊ lochlainn da ṁac aongusa Ruaiḋ uí ḋalaiġ, ⁊ Maolmaire óg mag craiṫ dég.

Mag Muiris na mbriġ, Eoghan mac Ruaiḋrí uí cheallaiġ, Muirchertach mac Muirchertaiġ uí concoḃair, ⁊ Beḃinn inġen ualgairg uí Ruairc ben tomaltaiġ meic donnchaḋa décc.

Iondsoiġiḋ do ṫabairt la cloinn Muirchertaiġ for ḟeraiḃ manach dar airccsit inis móir, loch mberraid, ⁊ Seanadh mac Maġnusa, ⁊ édála ioṁḋa do thabairt leo, ⁊ tilleaḋ slán dóiḃ do Riḋiri.

AOIS CRIOST, 1368.

Aois Criost, míle, trí chéd, Seascat, a hocht.

Comarba Maoḋócc ⁊ airċideochain na breifne fear lan do raṫ an Spioratu naoiṁ décc iar mbreiṫ ḃuaḋa ó ḋoṁan ⁊ ó ḋeaṁon.

great and well-known strand, near Ballysadare, in the county of Sligo.

[o] *The son of the Bishop O'Dowda.*—O'Flaherty adds in H. 2. 11, that his name was "Cosnamhach," and quotes "MS. L."—See also *Genealogies, Tribes, &c. of Hy-Fiachrach*, p. 117, note [c].

[p] *Na-m-Brigh*, i. e. of Bryze, or Brees, a well-known castle in the parish of Mayo, barony of Clanmorris, in the bounty of Mayo.—See *Genealogies, Tribes, and Customs of Hy-Fiachrach*, p. 482.

[q] *Inis-mor, Loch m-Bearraid.*—These names are now obsolete. Inis-mor was the name of an island in Upper Lough Erne, near Belle-isle; and Loch m-Bearraid was the name of a branch of Lough Erne.

[r] *Senad-Mac-Manus.*—This place is now called Ballymacmanus by the natives, but it is more generally known by the name of Belle-Isle. It is a very beautiful island in the Upper Lough Erne, and is now the property of the Rev. Gray Porter of Kilskeery.

[s] O'Flaherty adds the following passages to this year in H. 2. 11:

"Donaldus, filius Murcherti O'Conor cum

Manus, one hundred and fifty in number, were slain; as were also Donnell, son of Sorley, Donnell Oge, his son, the two Mac Sweenys, the son of the Bishop O'Dowda[o], and William Mac Sheehy.

Derbhail, daughter of Mulrony More Mac Dermot, and wife of Ualgarg O'Rourke, was killed by the Clann-Murtough.

Melaghlin, the son of Geoffry Mac Gillapatrick, and a party of his people, were treacherously slain by the English.

Teige Magauran and Aengus, son of the Deacon Magauran, died.

Teige and Loughlin, two sons of Aengus Roe O'Daly, and Mulmurry Oge Magrath, died.

Mac Maurice na-m-Brigh[p]; Owen, son of Rory O'Kelly; Murtough, son of Murtough O'Conor; and Bebinn, daughter of Ualgarg O'Rourke and wife of Tomaltagh Mac Donough, died

The Clann-Murtough made an incursion into Fermanagh, and plundered Inis-mór, Loch m-Berraid[q], and Senad Mac Manus[r]; and, after carrying off a great quantity of booty, returned home in safety[s].

THE AGE OF CHRIST, 1368.

The Age of Christ, one thousand three hundred sixty-eight.

The Coarb of St. Maidoc and Archdeacon of Breifny, a man filled with the grace of the Holy Ghost, died, after overcoming the world and the devil.

Mac Dermott, Hoberto filio Walteri, et Theobaldo filio Wilielmi óg .i. uilleag (de Burgo.—*O'Mulc.*) sub quo Clann-Swiny, duce Tordelvaco Mac Swiny merebantur, Ruarkis et Clanndonoghis, duce Tadæo Mac Donogh in Tirfiachriam Mullach Ruadh usque irruit, prædasque egit. Tadæus filius Magni O'Conor ad Traigheothuile cum illis congressus evertitur.—*Mac Firb.*"

"Mac William spoliat Tirolillam: captis O'Hara, Joanne O'Hara et Wilielmo O'Mally.—*Mac. Firb.*"

"Pax inter Anglos et Hibernos.—*Ibid.*"

"Ibir Eirionnchaib 7 albancaib.—*O'Mulconry.*"

"Tadæus filius Magni O'Conor (paulo ante cladem de traig eothuile et eadem æstate.—MS. L.) victor contra incolas Montis Lughy: cæsis Milone Mac Jordan dubh, Davide Mac Philip, Seonaco filio Joannis Mac Jordan dubh, et Wilielmo Mac Jordan Ruaidh cum multis de Clann-Gosdelvais; et ex parte victoris Murcherto filio Matthæi O'Durnin. Idem Tadæus violavit fœdus cum O'Roirk Clanndonnochis fidejussoribus ictum: quapropter Cormacus Mac Donogh ab eo ad Donaldum filium Murcherti

Aoḋ mac Feiḋlimiḋ uí concoḃair Rí connacht cenn gaile ⁊ gaisccidh gaoiḋeal, Luġ lamḟada leithe cuinn i naġaiḋ gall ⁊ earccaradh do écc iar mbuaiḋ naithriġe i Ros ċommain. Ruaiḋri mac toirrḋealḃaiġ do ġabáil cennais connachtt.

Crioch coirpre do roinn ar ḋó eittir mac Maġnusa ⁊ domhnall mac Muirceartaiġ.

Ferġal mac diarmada tiġearna ṁaiġe luirg, leoṁan uaisle ⁊ engnaṁa a ċiniḋ, Tomaltaċ mac fearġail meic diarmada tanaisi maiġi luirg, ⁊ Corbmac mac diarmada do écc.

Aodh mac Conċoḃair meic diarmada do ġaḃail tiġearnais maiġe luirg.

Ruaiḋri mac Seonuicc ṁég eochagáin Seaḃac uaisle ⁊ engnaṁa a chiniḋ, aon ba fele ó áth cliath go háṫ luain, ⁊ Tiġearnán mac cathail uí Ruairc décc.

Diarmaid mac corbmaic duinn még cárṫaiġ do ġaḃail do ṁág carṫaiġ cairpreaċ. A tioḋnacal do ġallaiḃ ⁊ a básuġaḋ doiḃ iarsin.

Dauiṫ ua tuaṫail do ṁarḃaḋ la gallaiḃ átha cliaṫ.

Uilliam Saxanaċ mac Sir Emainn a burc oiġre na nuilliamaċ do écc don ġalar breac i ninis cua.

Fiaċra ó floinn aḋbar taoisiġ sil maoilruain, aon do bferr da chineaḋ fein ina aimsir décc cona ṁnaoi.

O'Conor descivit. Itaque Donaldus, Cormacus, et Tigernanus O'Roirk eum apud cṡrḃ mic taiḋg in ċoillin mic an ḟirleiġinn spoliant. Ille prædam apud Dromcliabh assecutus equum a Cormaco, et Tadæo oᵹ O'Durnin equum a Donaldo cæsos amisit. Donaldus partem prædæ in Brefiniam, et filius Magni fil. Cathaldi O'Dowd, et O'Hara aliam ad Mucolt in Lugnia retulerunt.—*Mac Firb.* Eundem Tadæum Dominus O'Donell, Clanndonnoghi, et O'Roirk apud Nemus spissum deprædantur.—*Ibid.*"

"Murchadus riaḃaċ filius mic Murchaḋa f. Lucæ ab agnatis cæsus.—*Ibid.*"

"Jonacus Mac Philbin obiit.—*Ibid.*"

"Cathaldus filius Imari Mac Tigernan obiit. —*Mac Firb.*"

"Fergallus O'Reylly fortuito cæsus.—*Ibid.*"

"Fedlim O'Reylly obiit.—*Ibid.*"

"Lasairḟiona ingean tomais Meg ṡaṁraḋain bean ṁaoileaċlainn uí Ruairc do écc.—*Ibid.*" [i. e. Lasarina, the daughter of Thomas Magauran, and wife of Melaghlin O'Rourke, died.]

[t] *Lughaidh Long-handed.*—He was a King of the Tuatha de Danann, and is much celebrated in Irish stories for his valour, and particularly for his having been the first that instituted the Games of Tailtenn in Meath, which continued to be celebrated down to the reign of Roderic O'Conor, the last monarch of the Irish.—See O'Flaherty's *Ogygia*, Part iii. c. 13. This passage is translated by Mageoghegan thus, in his version of the Annals of Clonmacnoise:

"Hugh Mac Felym O'Connor, King of Con-

Hugh, son of Felim O'Conor, King of Connaught, the foremost among the Irish for valour and prowess, and the Lughaidh Long-handed[t] of Leth-Chuinn, against the English and his other enemies, died, after penance, at Roscommon; and Rory, the son of Turlough, assumed the government of Connaught.

The territory of Carbury was partitioned equally between the son of Manus and Donnell, the son of Murtough [O'Conor].

Farrell Mac Dermot, Lord of Moylurg, the lion of the nobility and valour of his tribe; Tomaltagh, son of Farrell Mac Dermot, Tanist of Moylurg; and Cormac Mac Dermot, died.

Hugh, son of Cormac Mac Dermot, assumed the lordship of Moylurg.

Rory[u], the son of Johnock Mageoghegan, the hawk of the nobility and prowess of his tribe, and the most hospitable man from Dublin to Drogheda; and Tiernan, the son of Cathal O'Rourke, died.

Dermot, the son of Cormac Donn Mac Carthy, was taken prisoner by Mac Carthy, of Carbery, and by him delivered up to the English, who afterwards put him to death.

David O'Toole was slain by the English of Dublin.

William Saxonagh, the son of Sir Edmond Burke, the heir of the Mac Williams, died of the small-pox on Inis-Cua[w].

Fiachra O'Flynn, heir to Sil-Maelruain, the best man of his tribe in his time, died; and his wife died also.

naught, a prince both hardy and venturous, worthy to be compared to Lowaie Lawady for prowess and manhood in all his attempts, as well against the English as Irish that were against him, after 12 years reign as King of Connaught, died, with good penance at Roscommon. The territory called Crich Carbry was, after his death, divided into two parts, whereof one part was allotted to Donnell mac Mortagh, and the other part to the son of Manus O'Connor."

[u] *Rory.*—Mageoghegan has the following remark upon this man: "Tho' mine Author maketh this greate account of this Rowrie, that he extolleth him beyond reason, yett his Issue now, and for a long time past, are of the meanest of their own name."

[w] *Inis-Cua*, now Inishcoe, a townland extending into Lough Conn, in the south-east of the parish of Crossmolina, in the barony of Tirawley, and county of Mayo.—See *Genealogies, Tribes, and Customs of Hy-Fiachrach*, p. 114, n. [p], and p. 124, n. [s]. This passage is given as follows in Mageoghegan's translation of the Annals of Clonmacnoise:

"William Saxanagh, son of Sir Redmond Burke, Heyre of the Mac Williams, died of the *little pox* at Innis-Kwa."

O'Flaherty adds, in H. 2. 11: "i. e. in domo Wilielmi Barett.—*O'Mulconry.*"

Sloiġeaḋ mór la Niall ua Néill Rí ċineil nEoġain i noirġiallaiḃ, ⁊ maiṫe an coiġiḋ uile deirġe lais dforbaisi ar briain ṁag machġaṁna. Longport do ġabail doiḃ i meḋón an tíre. Coṁtha móra do thairgsin do ṁág maṫġaṁna dó, .i. leaṫ airġiall do ṫabairt do niall mac Murchaiḋ mic briain na ccoileaċ noiffrenn, .i. an tiġearna baoi roiṁe ar an tír, ⁊ comtha aiḋble oile dua néill buḋdéin in íoc meic doṁnaill. Ua néill do aontuġaḋ síoṫchána dó ar na coṁṫaiḃ sin. Mac murchaiḋ méġ maṫġaṁna ⁊ Alaxandair óg mac doṁnaill tiġearna na ngallocclaċ do gluasacht dén comairle, trí coiriġṫe cḟitḟirne dionnsoiġiḋ méġ machġaṁna gan ceaduġaḋ dua néill, ⁊ ammus longpuirt do chabairt dóiḃ air. Maġ ṁaṫġaṁna go líon a ṫṡlaiġ do beiṫ ar a ccoiṁéd, ⁊ iad armtha innilte im a longport ionnus gur eirġedar doiḃsiom gan chairde. Fearthar gliaiḋ naṁnais naichgeir eatorra. Brisstear ria mág maṫġaṁna orrasoṁ Ro marḃaḋ mac Murchaiḋ méġ maṫġaṁna tanaisi oirġiall, Alaxandair mac toirrḋealḃaiġ méc doṁnaill consabal na ngalloglaċ, ⁊ Eoghan mac toirrḋealḃaiġ mic maoileachloinn uí doṁnaill don ċur sin immailli re soċaiḋiḃ ele.

Tomas ua floinn tiġearna ttuirtre fír lan deineaċ ⁊ doirrdearcus deġ.

Taḋġ mac Maġnusa mic caṫail mic doṁnaill uí ċoncobair do gabáil tre cheilg do Ruaiḋri mac toirrḋealḃaiġ (dua ċonċobair) ina longport fein i nArd an ċoillín iar na breṫ leis do ċorbmac mac donnchaiḋ go tígh uí ċoncoḃair, ⁊ a ṫairbert do doṁnall mac Muircheartaigh uí ċoncoḃair ar a haiṫle, ⁊ a marḃaḋ ra ḋeoiḋ la doṁnall i ccaislén Sligicch. Acht ċena ar fhis na gníoṁaiḃsi do roiġneaḋ ar mac Maġnusa uí concoḃair do saṁailtí gach olc, gur bo seanfocal suaiṫniḋ lá cach nár mísa gabáil no marḃaḋ

[x] *In the very centre*, i ccéirtmeḋón.—The word used in the Annals of Ulster is, "i ṁbolgán in tire," i. e. *umbilico territorii.*

[y] *Na g-Coileach n-Oifrinn*, i. e. of the chalices of the Mass.

[z] *Without O'Neill's permission.*—The meaning evidently is, that they made this attack upon Mac Mahon without asking O'Neill's permission.

[a] *O'Flynn*, now O'Lyn. This Thomas could not have been lord of all the district of Hy-Tuirtre, for the O'Neills of the race of Hugh Boy were certainly possessed of the territory of Hy-Tuirtre at this period.

[b] *Teige, son of Manus.*—He was the near relative and rival of Donnell Mac Murtough O'Conor of Sligo. He was of an older branch of the descendants of Brian Luighneach than his slayer, being the son of Manus, who was son of Cathal, King of Connaught in 1324, whose brother, Murtough, was the father of Donnell, the slayer of Teige, and the founder of the family of the O'Conors of Sligo.

[c] *Ard-an-choillin*, i. e. height, or hill of the

A great army was led by Niall O'Neill, King of the Kinel-Owen, who was joined by the chieftains of the entire province [of Ulster], into Oriel, to attack Brian Mac Mahon; and they pitched a camp in the very centre[x] of the territory. Mac Mahon offered him great terms, namely, to cede one-half of the territory of Oriel to Niall, the son of Murrough, son of Brian na g-Coileach n-Oifrinn[y], i. e. he who had been lord over the territory before himself; and other great gifts to O'Neill himself, as eric for [the death of] Mac Donnell. O'Neill consented to make peace with him on these conditions; but the son of Murrough Mac Mahon and Alexander Oge Mac Donnell, Lord of the Gallowglasses, without O'Neill's permission[z], marched, with one accord, with three battalions of kerns against Mac Mahon, and made an assault upon his fortress; but Mac Mahon and his household, being upon their guard, armed and accoutred within their fortress, they responded without delay to the attack; and a fierce and furious conflict ensued, in which they [the assailants] were defeated by Mac Mahon. The son of Murrough Mac Mahon, Tanist of Oriel; Alexander, the son of Turlough Mac Donnell, Constable of the Gallowglasses; and Owen, the son of Turlough, son of Melaghlin O'Donnell, together with a great number of others, were slain on that occasion.

Thomas O'Flynn[a], Lord of Hy-Tuirtre, a man full of hospitality and renown, died.

Teige, the son of Manus[b], son of Cathal, son of Donnell O'Conor, was treacherously taken prisoner by Rory, the son of Turlough (i. e. the O'Conor), in his [Rory's] own fortress at Ard-an-choillin[c], after he had been brought thither by Cormac Mac Donough to O'Conor's house. He was afterwards given up to Donnell, son of Murtough O'Conor, by whom he was at last killed in the castle of Sligo. It was afterwards common to compare any evil deed with those acts committed against the son of Manus O'Conor; so that it became a proverb familiar with every one, that "the taking and killing[d] of the son of

little wood, now Ardakillin, a townland in the parish of Killukin, in the barony and county of Roscommon. No ruins are now to be seen here except three earthen forts.—See the year 1388.

[d] *Taking and killing.*—This passage is given more clearly as follows by Mageoghegan, in his version of the Annals of Clonmacnoise:

"A. D. 1368. Teig mac Magnus mac Cahall was deceitfully taken by the King of Connought, in his house of Ard-an-Killin, being brought tither to the King's house by Cormack Mac Donnogh upon his security, of which villainous dealing that old Irish proverb grew by comparing thereof to any wicked art: 'The

mec maġnusa, ina ġibe feilġníoṁ do ċluinti do dénoṁ. Cogaḋ mór do ḟás hi cconnaċtaiḃ eittir ua cconcoḃair, Mac uilliam, ⁊ mac diarmata tré an ngaḃáil sin ⁊ tres an marḃaḋ.

Cúulaḋ mac an ġirr mic caṫmaíl cinn a chiniḋ féin, ⁊ an mac baoi aige ina maighistir foirccṫe dfírscaiġṫe i nealaḋnaiḃ décc i Saxaiḃ.

Uilliam mac donnchaiḋ muiṁniġ uí ċeallaiġ tiġearna ua maine do ġaḃáil la hua Madaḋáin ⁊ la cloinn mic neoġain. Doṁnall mac concoḃair uí ċeallaiġ, ⁊ arḋgal óg ó concenainn do ṁarḃaḋ la ua Madaḋáin an lá sin.

Doṁnall mac conmara do écc.

Slemni mac uiḋlin consabal coiġiḋ ulaḋ do écc.

Muireaḋaċ ó fairċeallaiġ coṁarba Maedóg, ⁊ airċideochain na breifne do écc.

Diarmait laiṁdearg mac Murchaḋa rí laiġen do ġaḃáil la gallaiḃ. Ba heiriḋe cóiġedaċ ro ba cróḋa baoi ina aimsir.

AOIS CRIOST, 1369.

Aois Criost, míle trí chéd, Seascca, anaoi.

Aoḋh ua néill epscop clochair, Saoi craiḃdeach coindercleach, ⁊ Riocard ó Raiġilliġ epscop cille móir décc.

An deaccanach ó bardain décc.

taking of mac Manus is no worse.' He was within a little while after worse used, for he was given over to Donnell mac Mortagh O'Connor, who vilely did put him to death in the castle of Sligeagh; whereof ensued great contentions and generall discords throughout all Connought, especially between O'Connor, Mac William, and Mac Dermoda."

[e] *Professor of sciences.*—This passage is in the Dublin copy of the Annals of Ulster; but the Editor has not been able to discover any account as to what part of England he taught in. There were several bishops and other very distinguished ecclesiastics of this family, but no literary man of the name appears in Ware's Irish Writers, except the celebrated archbishop, Hugh Mac Caghwell, who wrote the Commentaries upon the works of *Duns Scotus*, and other works, in the beginning of the seventeenth century.

[f] *Clann-mic-n-Eoghain*, i. e. the race of the son of Eoghan. These were a branch of the O'Kellys descended from Eoghan, the third son of Donnell More O'Kelly, Chief of Hy-Many, who died in the year 1224. This sept gave name to the barony of Clanmacnowen, in the east of the county of Galway, in which they were seated.—See *Tribes and Customs of Hy-Many*, pp. 102, 165.

[g] To this year O'Flaherty adds the following passages in H. 2. 11:

Manus was not worse than whatever treacherous deed they used to hear of being perpetrated." In consequence of this taking and killing, a great war broke out in Connaught between O'Conor, Mac William, and Mac Dermot.

Cu-Uladh Mac-an-Ghirr Mac Cawell, chief of his own tribe, and a son of his, who was a learned and illustrious Professor of Sciences[e], died in England.

William, son of Donough Muimhneach O'Kelly, Lord of Hy-Many, was taken prisoner by O'Madden and the Clann-mic-n-Eoghain[f]. On the same day Donnell, son of Conor O'Kelly, and Ardgal Oge O'Concannon, were slain by O'Madden.

Donnell Mac Namara died.

Slevny Mac Quillin, Constable of the Province of Ulster, died.

Murray O'Farrelly, Coarb of St. Maidoc, and Archdeacon of Breifny [Kilmore], died.

Dermot, the Redhanded, Mac Murrough, King of Leinster, was taken prisoner by the English. He was the most valiant of the [Irish] provincial kings in his time[g].

THE AGE OF CHRIST, 1369.

The Age of Christ, one thousand three hundred sixty-nine.

Hugh O'Neill, Bishop of Clogher, a pious and humane man, and Richard O'Reilly[h], Bishop of Kilmore, died.

The Deacon O'Bardon died.

"Mora filia O'Roirk Odonis uxor Mac Donogh obiit.—MS. L. (1367. *O'Mulconry*)."

"Mathgamanius O'Tuathail ab Anglis cæsus. —MS. L." (*Mac Firb.* 1367.)

"Mac Magnusa de Tirtuathail obiit.—MS. L." (1367. *Mac Firb.*)

"Imarus filius Tomalti O'Birn obiit.—*Mac Firb.*"

"Laighsechus filius Davidis O'Morra suo cultro cæsus.—*Ibid.*"

"Donaldus filius Mac Conmara obiit.—*Ibid.*" (MS. L. 1369.)

"Anna filia O'Durnin uxor Tadæi O'Huigin obiit.—*Mac Firb.*"

"Crıċ Caıpbpe ꝺo ġaḃaıl ꝺo Ḋoṁnall mac Muıpċeapṫaıġ.—1369. MS. L." [i. e. the country of Carbury was taken by Donnell, the son of Murtough.]

"Ard an choillin, Roderici domus in Machaire Connaght infra ad ann. 1388."

[h] *Richard O'Reilly.*—His death is set down in the Dublin copy of the Annals of Ulster, under the year 1366, which should be 1369. Immediately after the notice of the death of Richard O'Reilly, those Annals enter the death of William, Archdeacon of Breifny; of Brian, the son of Murtough O'Conor; of John, son of Edmond Mac Hubert [Burke]; of Randal O'Hanly, and

Cúconnaċt ó Raġallaiġ tiġearna bréifne do écc.

Pilib ua Raiġilliġ do ġabáil la a braiṫriḃ fein, ⁊ a cur doiḃ i cloiċ locha huachtair go ndochar ceangail ⁊ cuibriġṫe fair. Maġnus ua Raġallaiġ do ġabáil tiġearnais annsin. Coccaḋ ⁊ comḃuaiḋreaḋ deirġe isin mbreifne triar an ġabail sin. Sluaġ mór do ṫionol dAnnaḋ mac Risderd uí Raġallaiġ. Mág Ṁathġaṁna ⁊ maithe oirġiall do ṫocht ina comḋáiḋ do chabaċ pilib uí Raiġilliġ ar Ṁaġnus. Maġnus cona braithriḃ ⁊ go lion a ttionoil do dul dentaoiḃ do ċosnaṁ na tire doiḃ buḋḋén. Caithgleo do chur eatorra. Maiḋm do ṫabairt for Mhaġnus i mblén ċupa. Trí meic corbmaic uí Fearġail, Seoinín, Maoileaċloinn, ⁊ Fearġus, Feidlimiḋ mac aodha an cleitiġ uí concobair, da mac flaithim móir mec conruḃa .i. donn, ⁊ brian, Sitreacc na Spóna mac an ṁaiġhistir ⁊ sochaiḋi oile do marḃaḋ don taċur sin.

Gearalt caoṁanach ríoghḋaṁna laiġen do marḃaḋ don Ridire duḃ.

Tiġearnán ua Ruairc do dul for creich i lurg. Creach mór do ṫabairt lais dó, ⁊ Aoḋ óg mac aoḋa uí Ruairc do ṁarḃaḋ la hua maolḋúin luirg in iarmóraċt na creċe.

Diarmaitt laiṁdearg mac murchaḋa Rí laiġen do ḃarúġaḋ la gallaiḃ aṫa cliaṫ iar na beiṫ aimsir imchian i mbraiġdenus aca.

Mathġaṁain maonṁaiġe ua briain, tiġearna tuaḋmuṁan, gaoiḋeal do ḃearr ⁊ do bairfasḋa i lech moḋha décc ina longport fein iar mbuaiḋ naiṫriġe. Brian ó briain do ġabáil tiġearnais tuaḋmuman tar es Maṫġaṁna.

O Maolḋúin (.i. domnall) taoíseaċ tuaithe luirg do ṁarḃaḋ la cloinn

Cormac O'Hanly, both of whom were carried off by the plague called cluiċe in ríġ; of Hugh O'Beirne, who perished of the same plague (don plaiḋ cedna); of John Mac Egan, and Gilbert O'Bardan, two professional youths of Conmaicne; and of Melaghlin Mac Mahon, heir to the lordship of Oriel. The Anglo-Irish annalists do not call this plague by any name. Under the year 1370, Grace has: "Incepit tertia pestis que nobiles permultos, aliosque innumeros sustulit."

[i] *Castle of Lough Oughter.*—The ruins of this fortress still exist. It is of the same architectural character with Reginald's Tower at Waterford, and with the keep of the castle of Dundrum, in the county of Down. The island in which it stands is said to have been formed by dropping stones into the lake. The Editor examined this castle in May, 1836, when it was in a tolerable state of preservation.

[k] *Blen-Cupa* is now anglicised Blencup, and is a townland in the parish of Kilmore, about four miles to the west of the town of Cavan. Blean means the groin, and, topographically, a little creek.

[l] *Sitric na Srona*, i. e. Sitric of the nose.

Cuconnaught O'Reilly, [some time] Lord of Breifny, died.

Philip O'Reilly was taken prisoner by his kinsmen, and was placed by them in [the castle of] Clough-Lough Oughter[i], severely bound and fettered. Manus O'Reilly then assumed the lordship. In consequence of this capture, war and disturbance broke out in Breifny. A great army was mustered by Annadh, the son of Richard O'Reilly, who was joined by Mac Mahon and all the other chiefs of Oriel, to rescue Philip O'Reilly from Manus by force. Manus and his kinsmen, however, came, together with their entire forces, to contest the [chieftainship of the] country for themselves. A battle was fought between them at Blen-cupa[k], where Manus was defeated. In this conflict were slain the three sons of Cormac O'Farrell, viz. Johnin, Melaghlin, and Fergus; Felim, son of Hugh an Chleitigh O'Conor; the two sons of Flaithim More Mac Conruva, namely, Donn and Brian; Sitric na Srona[l] Mac Master, and a number of others.

Gerald Kavanagh, heir to the kingdom of Leinster, was slain by the Black Knight[m].

Tiernan O'Rourke went upon a predatory excursion into Lurg, and carried off a great prey; but Hugh Oge, son of Hugh O'Rourke, was slain by O'Muldoon, Chief of Lurg[n], who had followed in pursuit of it.

Dermot Lavderg[o] Mac Murrough, after having been confined for a long time by the English of Dublin, was put to death[p] by them.

Mahon Moinmoy O'Brien, Lord of Thomond, the best and most illustrious of the Irish, died in his own fortress, after the victory of penance. Brian O'Brien assumed the lordship of Thomond after Mahon.

O'Muldoon (Donnell), Lord of the territory of Lurg, was slain by the sons

[m] *Black Knight*.—O'Flaherty adds, in H. 2. 11, that this "ριδιρe δub" was "δo ġallaiḃ áṫa cliaṫ," i. e. one of the English of Dublin.

[n] *Lurg*, now the barony of Lurg, in the north of the county of Fermanagh.

[o] *Dermot Lavderg*, i. e. of the Red Hand. He was the son of Gerald, who was the son of Murtough Roe, who was son of Maurice, who was the son of Murtough, who was the son of Donnell, who was the son of Donnell Kavanagh, who was, according to Giraldus Cambrensis, the bastard son of Dermot Mac Murrough, King of Leinster, in whose time the English first invaded Ireland. From this Dermot Lavderg descended a celebrated sept of the Kavanaghs, called Sliocht Diarmada Laimhdheirg; but they are now reduced to obscurity and poverty. O'Flaherty adds in the margin of H. 2. 11: "ab Equite nigro dolose captus.—*O'Mulconry*."

[p] *Was put to death*.—O'Flaherty adds in H. 2. 11: "facinus illis temporibus tristissimum.—*O'Mulconry*."

nell uí domnaill, ⁊ a ċreach do breiṫ leo fór oilén doilenaiḃ locha herne dianad ainm badḃa ⁊ Pilib maġ uidir tiġearna seacht tuaṫ do dul loingsi lanṁór do ḋioġail a óglaoiċ ar cloinn uí ḋomnaill ⁊ niall óg mac neill gairḃ mic aedha mec domnaill óig do ṁarḃaḋ lais i ttroid loingsi ar fionnloċ la taoḃ an oiléin.

Brian mac aedha buiḋe uí néill deaghadhḃar riġ ereann duaisle, deineaċ, ⁊ deaghghnaṁ do éġ.

Maiḋm mór adḃal do thabairt la brian ua briain tiġearna tuaḋṁuman for ġallaiḃ muṁan. Geroid iarla dearmuṁan, ⁊ morán do maiṫib gall do ġabail lais ⁊ ar diaisnéisi do chur for an ccuid oile ḋíoḃ. Luimneaċ do loscaḋ don turus sin la tuaḋṁuiṁneachaiḃ, ⁊ la cloinn cuilén. Lucht an baile do giallaḋ dua briain ⁊ Síoda cam mac ingine uí ḋuiḃidir do ġabail ḃardachta an baile cuige, ⁊ feallaḋ dona gallaiḃ batar is in mbaile fair gur ro ṁarḃsat é. Ba mór an techt hisin i leṫ re mac taoísiġ.

Pilib maġ uidir tiġearna fear manach do ḃreiṫ loingis go loch uachtair, ⁊ caislén cloiche uachtair do gabail dó. Pilib ua raiġilliġ (.i. tiġearna breifne) do léccen amach do máġ uidir, ⁊ a ṫiġearnus fein do ġabail dó doridisi.

Maolseachlainn maġ mathġamna adbar tighsirna oirġiall, Brian mac muirċeartaiġ uí Choncobair, Seaan mac Einainn mic hoiberd, Donnchaḋ ó birn taoiseaċ tíre briúin, Raghnall ó háinliġe, corbmac ó háinliġe, Eoin mac aedhagain, ⁊ Gillebert ó bardain da saor macaom cruitealadnach Conmaicne déġ.

Uilliam ó sairċeallaiġ comarba Maedóġ, ⁊ airchideochain na breifne do écc

[q] *Badhbha.*—This island still retains this name, but it is generally anglicised Boa Island. It is usually called by the natives of Tuath Ratha dwelling on the south side of Lough Erne, opposite this island, who speak Irish well, Inis badḃann, or Oileán badḃann. It is the largest island in Lower Lough Erne, and is situated not far from its northern shore, a short distance to the south of the village of Pettigoe.

[r] *The seven Tuathas*, i. e. the seven Tuathas, or districts, comprised in the principality of Fermanagh, of which Maguire was, at this period, the chief lord.

[s] *Oglach.*—This word literally means, a young hero or soldier; but it is often used in the sense of vassal, such as O'Muldoon was to Maguire. From ógláċ, in this sense, is derived ógláċas, vassallage, servitude.

[t] *Finn-loch*, i. e. the white lake. This was evidently the name of the Lower Lough Erne, which might have been locally so called to distinguish it from the Upper Lough Erne, as being a brighter sheet of water, and less studded with islands.

[u] *Clann Culein*, i. e. the Mac Namaras.

[w] *Brought vessels*, i. e. he carried boats by

of Niall O'Donnell, who carried the spoils of his territory with them to one of the islands of Lough Erne which is called Badhbha[q]. Philip Maguire, Lord of the Seven Tuathas[r], set out with a large fleet to take revenge upon the sons of O'Donnell for the death of his Oglach[s]; and a naval engagement took place, in which Niall Oge, son of Niall Garv, the son of Hugh, son of Donnell Oge [O'Donnell], was slain on Finn-loch[t], close to the island.

Brian, son of Hugh Boy O'Neill, a good materies of a king of Ireland, for his nobleness, hospitality, and prowess, died.

A great defeat was given by Brian O'Brien, Lord of Thomond, to the English of Munster. Garrett, Earl of Desmond, and many of the chiefs of the English, were taken prisoners by him, and the remainder cut off with indescribable slaughter. Limerick was burned on this occasion by the Thomonians and the Clann-Culein[u], upon which the inhabitants of the town capitulated with O'Brien. Sheeda Cam [Mac Namara], son of the daughter of O'Dwyre, assumed the wardenship of the town; but the English who were in the town acted treacherously towards him, and killed him. This was a lamentable treatment of the son of a chieftain.

Philip Maguire, Lord of Fermanagh, brought vessels[w] to Lough Oughter, took [the castle of] Clough-Lough-Oughter[x], and liberated Philip O'Reilly, who was confined therein, and who thereupon re-assumed the lordship.

Melaghlin Mac Mahon, heir to the lordship of Oriel; Brian, the son of Murtough O'Conor; John, the son of Edward Mac Hubert; Donough O'Beirne, Chief of Tir-Briuin; Randal O'Hanly; Cormac O'Hanly; [also] John Mac Egan, and Gilbert O'Bardan, two accomplished young harpers of Conmaicne, died[y].

William O'Farrelly, Coarb of St. Maidoc[z], and Archdeacon of Breifny, died[a].

land from Lough Erne, in the county of Fermanagh, to Lough Oughter, in the county of Cavan. The boats thus carried were mere curraghs or cots, such as they have on those lakes at the present day.

[x] *Clogh-Lough-Oughter*, i. e. the stone, or stone fortress of Lough Oughter.

[y] *Died.*—All these died of the plague called cluiċe an ṗiġ, or the King's game.—See note[b], pp. 645, 646, *supra.*

[z] *Coarb of St. Maidoc.*—O'Farrelly was coarb of St. Maidoc, or Mogue, at Drumlahan, or Drumlane, near Belturbet, in the county of Cavan. Archdeacon of Breifny means Archdeacon of the diocese of Kilmore.

[a] O'Flaherty adds the following entries to this year in H. 2. 11:

"Joannes O'Donellan Connaciæ Poeta obiit.—MS. L. (*Mac Firb.* 1368)."

"Rodericus filius Joannis O'Hara Tirfiach-

AOIS CRIOST, 1370.

Aois Criost, míle, trí chéd, seachtmoġatt.

Síth daingſn deaghtairisi do ḋénoṁ do ċenél eoghain ſtoppa féin. Braighde do ṫabairt ó doṁnall do niall ré gan cur a naġaiḋ imón tiġearnus. Roinn forba 7 ſſroinn ó Niall do doṁnall iarsin.

Giollapatraicc mac cathṁaoil taoiseaċ chenél fſradaiġ, cúulaḋ a ṁac 7 inġean maġnusa ṁéġ ṁathġaṁna a bſn, do ṁarbaḋ la cloinn aſda meic caṫṁaoil tre ḟeill. Murchaḋ a dſrbrathair do ġabáil a ionaid is in taoisiġeċt iarsin.

Cathaoir ua concobair adbor tiġearna ó bfailge, 7 muirceartaċ ua morḋa do ṫuitim ar creiċ la gallaiḃ laiġſn.

Dubcoblaiġ inġſn uí Raghallaiġ bſn pilip meg uiḋir do écc.

Maġnus ó Raġallaiġ do ġabail la cloinn tomais mic Maṫġamna uí Raiġilliġ, 7 a chur i cloich locha huachtair.

Cathal mac dabug uí ċoncſnainn tiġearna ua ndiarmada, Siobán ċam inġſn meg cartaiġ bſn mec conmara, Síoda chille cainniġ mac Seaain meic conmara, Seaan ó hſġra adbar tiġearna luigne, 7 Diarmaitt mac caṫail óig uí concobair do écc.

Brſisim maḋma do ṫabairt la Niall ua néill tiġearna ċeneil eóġain ar brian mag maṫġaṁna tiġearna oirġiall, 7 dronga dearṁara do muintir Méġ ṁaṫġaṁna do ṁarbaḋ 7 do baṫaḋ.

Doṁnall mac Maeileaċloinn, 7 taḋg mac lochlainn uí ċeallaiġ cona ḋiar mac do écc.

riam Muaiḋe diripiens ab incolis et Scotis occisus.—MS. L. (*Mac Firb.* 1368)."

" Cormacus boḋar Mac Dermott obiit.—MS. L. (*Mac Firb.* 1368)."

" Dermitius filius Thomæ Finn Mic Murchaḋa, obiit.—MS. L. (*Mac Firb.* 1368)."

" Finnuala filia Briani O'Dowd obiit.—*Mac Firb.*"

" Brianus filius Henrici. fil. Odonis flavi Ultoniæ hæres obiit.—*Mac Firb.*"

" Brianus Og O'Flaherty (.i. brian na noirreaċ) occidentalis Connaciæ hæres a Rickardo Og de Burgo captus.—MS. L. (*Mac Firb.* 1368)."

" Brianus Mac Mahon Anglos Orgielliæ spoliat: ubi Mælsechlunnius Mac Mahon per Sefin Fait prædam insequentem cæsus.—*Mac Firb.* (MS. L. 1370)."

" Wilielmus Mac Uidhilin Ultoniæ Constabularius obiit.—*Mac Firb.*"

" Adamus Alamar filius Mac Hoirebert obiit.—*Mac Firb.*"

" Multi Anglorum Midiæ mortui.—*Mac Firb.* (*peste reor de quo Cambd.* 1370)."

" Sequentia, MS. L. ad annum 1370.—*Mac*

THE AGE OF CHRIST, 1370.

The Age of Christ, one thousand three hundred seventy.

A firm and sincere peace was made by the Kinel-Owen with each other. Donnell [O'Neill] gave hostages to Niall [as pledges], that he would not contest the lordship with him; and Niall then gave Donnell a share of territory and lands.

Gillapatrick Mac Cawell, Chief of Kinel-Farry; Cu-uladh, his son, and his wife, the daughter of Manus Mac Mahon, were treacherously slain by the sons of Hugh Mac Cawell. Murrough, his [Gillapatrick's] brother then became Chieftain of Kinel-Farry.

Cahir[b] O'Conor, heir of Offaly, and Murtough O'More, were killed on a predatory excursion by the English of Leinster.

Duvcovla, the daughter of O'Reilly, and wife of Philip Maguire, died.

Manus O'Reilly was taken prisoner by the sons of Thomas, the son of Mahon O'Reilly, and confined in [the castle of] Clough-Lough-Oughter.

Cathal, son of Davock O'Concannon, Lord of Hy-Diarmada; Joanna Cam, daughter of Mac Carthy, and wife of Mac Namara; Sheeda, of Kilkenny, son of John Mac Namara; John O'Hara, heir to the lordship of Leyny; and Dermot[c], son of Cathal Oge O'Conor, died.

Niall O'Neill, Lord of Kinel-Owen, routed Brian Mac Mahon, Lord of Oriel; and very great numbers of Mac Mahon's people were cut off by slaying and drowning.

Donnell, son of Melaghlin, and Teige, son of Loughlin O'Kelly, with his two sons, died.

Firb. 1369, habent."

"Honoria filia Mac William de Burgo (ingꝼn uilleg.—MSS. L.) uxor Roderici O'Conor Regis Connaciæ obiit."

"Mælsechlunnius O'Hanluain Orientalium dominus obiit."

"Cahir O'Conor Hyfalgiæ hæres ab Anglis cæsus."

"O'Roirk, O'Farell Maguir et O'Conor expulerunt posteros Murcherti Muimnig O'Conor ad Muintir eolais: unde ipsi, et Mac Tigernan ad dominum Mac William confugerunt (*O'Mulconry* ad ann. 1370, et infra prope finem) e quibus Conchovarus ruaḋ filius Cathaldi fil. Odonis Brefinii obiit, A. D. 1371.—MS. L."

"Murchertus Sinnach Teffiorum dominus obiit 19 Febr. 1370.—*O'Mulconry*."

[b] *Cahir*, Caṫaoir.—This name is now, and has been for the last two centuries, anglicised Charles.

[c] *Dermot.*—He was the eighth son of the hero, Cathal Oge O'Conor, who was the son of

Maelseaċlainn connaċtaċ ó fferġail, ⁊ Caṫal óg ó fferġail do écc.

Taḋg ó Ruairc do ġabáil tiġearnais na breifne. Clann Muirceartaiġ ⁊ Mág tiġernain da indarbaḋ, ⁊ concobar ruaḋ mac caṫail mic aeḋa breifniġ, ⁊ a ċur i criċ mic uilliam.

Uilliam dono mac uillec do écc.

AOIS CRIOST, 1371.

Aois Criost, míle, trí chéd, seachtmoghat, a haon.

Airdepscop tuama .i. Seaan ó grada cenn eaccna ⁊ eniġ a aimsire do écc.

Fearġal mag coċlain do écc i láiṁ ag ua ccinnéidiġ.

Fearġal mag eoċaccáin do écc.

Murchaḋ ó madaḋáin (.i. mac eoġain) fercheaṁ coitċionn cliar, aiḋelgneaċ, ⁊ fíorḃocht Erenn do marḃaḋ daon orcor soiġde ar deireaḋ crece i nurmuṁain.

Brian ua cinneidiġ tiġerna urmuṁan do marḃaḋ i bfell lá gallaiḃ.

Emann ó cinneidiġ adḃar tiġearna urṁuṁan do écc.

Taḋg óg mac maġnusa uí concobair do marḃaḋ i bfell do domnall mac muirċertaiġ uí concoḃair i ccaislén slicciġ iar na cur do Riġ connacht (Ruaiḋri mac toirrdealḃaiġ) cuicce, do rér mar do raiḋeaḋ roṁainn.

Eachmarcaċ mac maġnusa mic Ruaiḋri mic maġnusa mic duinn móir meg uiḋir, bruġaiḋ coitcionn do baoi ar loċ éirne do écc.

Cathal, King of Connaught in 1324, who was the son of Donnell, Tanist of Connaught, and the ancestor of O'Conor Sligo.

[d] *Conor Roe.*—He was at this time the chief leader of that sept of the O'Conors called Clann-Murtough. This sentence is very rudely constructed by the Four Masters. It should stand thus:

"Teige O'Rourke assumed the lordship of Breifny, but was soon after banished from Breifny, and forced to take shelter in the country of Mac William Burke, by the Clann-Murtough, headed by Conor Roe (the son of Cathal, who was the son of Hugh Breifneach O'Conor), who was joined by Mac Tiernan O'Conor."

[e] To this year O'Flaherty adds the following entries in H. 2. 11:

"1370. David Bruis Rex Scotiæ obiit.—*Mac Firb.* (MS. L. 1371)."

"Supremus Christianorum Papa obiit.—*Mac Firb.* (1371, MS. L. *et Bellarm*)."

"Verum 19 Dec. 1370. Onuphrius ponit mortem Urbani 5."

"Midia .i. bean miḋe, filia Cathaldi O'Conor obiit.—*Mac Firb.*"

Melaghlin Connaughtagh O'Farrell, and Cathal Oge O'Farrell, died.

Teige O'Rourke assumed the lordship of Breifny; but the Clann-Murtough, Mac Tiernan, and Conor Roe[d], the son of Cathal, son of Hugh Breifneach, banished him to the territory of Mac William.

William Donn, the son of Ulick [Burke], died[e].

THE AGE OF CHRIST, 1371.

The Age of Christ, one thousand three hundred seventy-one.

John O'Grady[f], Archbishop of Tuam, the leading man[g] for wisdom and hospitality in his time, died.

Farrell Mac Coghlan died while detained in prison by O'Kennedy.

Farrell Mageoghegan died.

Murrough O'Madden (i. e. the son of Owen), general patron of the literati, the poor, and the destitute of Ireland, was killed by one shot of an arrow[h], in the rear of a predatory party in Ormond.

Brian O'Kennedy, Lord of Ormond, was treacherously slain by the English.

Edmond O'Kennedy, heir to the lordship of Ormond, died.

Teige Oge, the son of Manus O'Conor, was treacherously killed[i] in the castle of Sligo by Donnell, the son of Murtough O'Conor, after he had been sent to him, as already mentioned[k], by the King of Connaught (Rory, the son of Turlough).

Eachmarcach, the son of Manus, son of Rory, son of Manus, son of Donn More Maguire, a general brughaidh [farmer], who dwelt on Lough Erne, died.

[f] *John O'Grady.*—O'Flaherty adds, in H. 2. 11, "that he is called Sir John O'Grady, Archbp. of Connaught, in MS. L. and *O'Mulconry.*"

[g] *The leading man.*—Literally, "the head of the wisdom and hospitality of his time."

[h] *By one shot of an arrow*, daon orcor soiġde, i. e. *uno jactu sagittæ*. This may also mean "with one cast or shot of a javelin."

[i] *Killed*, do marḃaḋ, or "put to death."

[k] *As already mentioned.*—Literally, "accordingly as was said before us."—See note [b], under the year 1368. It is stated in the Dublin copy of the Annals of Ulster, that Donnell killed Teige with his own hand while in confinement, and that the act was the most repulsive and abominable deed ever committed in Ireland. To this passage O'Flaherty adds the following clause, in H. 2. 11, from *O'Mulconry*, MS. L. and *Mac Firb.*:

"Ipsius Donaldi manu confossus, postquam ab anno 1368 detentus ab eo in vinculis. Anno 1372, MS. L."

Maoilir mac hoibſrd do ṁarḃaḋ la hua cconcoḃair.

Creacha móra do ḋenaṁ la hua nduḃda (domnall) hi tír ḟiaċrach ṁuaiḋe go ro hairgeaḋ co leir an tír lais, ⁊ go ro ġaḃ a caislén .i. caislén áird na riaġ, ⁊ caislen mic conċoḃair, ⁊ i mbaoi innte do ġallaiḃ do ḋíochur eirtiḃ, ⁊ an tír do roinn ar a ḃraiṫriḃ, ⁊ ar a ṁuintir féin ar a haiṫle.

AOIS CRIOST, 1372.

Aois Criost, mile, trí ċéd, Seachtṁoġat, adó.

Brian mór máġ ṁathgamna tiġſrna oirġiall do triall i ccoinne gall do taḃairt taċair doiḃ, ⁊ gallocclaċ da muintir fén dá ṁarḃaḋ go hinċleiṫe i bfell, ⁊ é buḋen déluḋ ar an sluaġ iarsin.

Seaan mór ó duḃaccáin Saoi ḟeancaḋa ⁊ ollaṁ ó maine do écc iar mbuaiḋ nongṫa ⁊ naithriġe, i Rinn dúin ag muintir eoin baisde.

Muirċſrtaċ muimneaċ mac muirceartaiġ moir mécc eoċaccáin, taoiseaċ cenéil ḟiachach do écc iar mbuaiḋ naiṫriġe.

Mac feórais do ġaḃail dua ceallaiġ ⁊ da ċloinn, ⁊ Risderd mac feórais a oiḋre do marḃaḋ.

[l] *Tir-Fhiachrach Muaidhe*, i. e. Tir-Fhiachrach of the River Moy, now the barony of Tireragh, in the county of Sligo, which is bounded on the west by the River Moy.

[m] *Ard-na-riagh*, now Ardnarea, forming the eastern portion of the town of Ballina, in the barony of Tirawley, and county of Mayo.—See note [c], under the year 1266, p. 399, *supra*.

[n] *Castle-mic-Conor*, Caislen mic conċoḃair, i. e. the castle of the son of Conor. This was originally called Dún ṁic Conċoḃair, i. e. the Dun, or earthen fort, of the son of Conor. The name is now applied to a townland and parish, situated on the east side of the River Moy, in the barony of Tireragh and county of Sligo.—See the Ordnance map of that county, sheet 22. The townland contains the ruins of a castle standing on the site of the ancient dun, or earthen fort, on a hill called cnocán uí ḋuḃda, or O'Dowda's hillock, on a point of land extending into the River Moy.—See *Genealogies, &c. of Hy-Fiachrach*, pp. 175, 282. To this passage O'Flaherty adds the following clause in H. 2. 11:

"Divisitque [O'Dowd] regionem illam inter suos clientes pro modico vectigali; eam subjiciens suæ familiæ et posteris suis.—*Mac Firb.*"

[o] To this year O'Flaherty adds the following entries in H. 2. 11:

"Dermitius filius Cormaci fil. Dermitii Rufi a Clannrickardis cæsus.—MS. L. (*Mac Firb.* 1370)."

"Madiu mac an ridire, Hobertus et David filii Walteri Oġ, Fefalgia, filia Mac Donogh, mater filiorum Murcherti O'Conor (viz. Donaldi O'Conor.—MS. L.) et filiorum Walteri óġ filii Rickardi, matrona pia, ac eleemozinaria, decesserunt.—MS. L. 1371; *Mac Firb.* 1370."

"Comes Desmoniæ redemptus.—MS. L. 1371;

Meyler Mac Hubert was slain by O'Conor.

Great depredations were committed by O'Dowda (Donnell) in Tir-Fhiachrach[l] Muaidhe; the whole country was ravaged by him, and its castles were taken, namely, the castles of Ard-na-riagh[m] and Castle-mic-Conor[n], and all the English that were in them were driven out; and the country was after this parcelled out amongst his kinsmen and his own people[o].

THE AGE OF CHRIST, 1372.

The Age of Christ, one thousand three hundred seventy-two.

Brian More MacMahon, Lord of Oriel, marched to give battle to the English; but he was privily and treacherously slain by a gallowglass of his own people, who thereupon fled from the army.

John More O'Dugan[p], a learned historian and ollav of Hy-Many, died, after the victory of Extreme Unction and penance, at Rinn-duin, among the monks of John the Baptist.

Murtough Muimhneach, son of Murtough More Mageoghegan, Chief of Kinel-Fiachach, died, after the victory of penance.

Mac Feorais [Bermingham] was taken[q] prisoner by O'Kelly and his sons; and Richard Mac Feorais, his heir, was slain.

Mac Firb. 1370."

"Donnchadus O'Birn obiit.—*Mac Firb., et O'Mulc.*"

[p] *John More O'Dugan.*—It is stated in the Dublin copy of the Annals of Ulster, that this John More O'Dugan was the chief historian of all Ireland, and that he had been seven years in the monastery of Rinn-duin before his death, which this chronicle places incorrectly under the year 1370. He was the author of a curious topographical poem, in which he gives the names of the principal tribes and districts in Ulster, Connaught, and Meath, and the chiefs who presided over them before they were dispossessed by the English, or by other Irish tribes. He was also the author of several poems and poetical prose pieces addressed to the O'Kellys, his patrons, of which copies are preserved in a fragment of the Book of Hy-Many, in the Library of Trinity College, Dublin (H. 2. 7), and in the possession of Denis H. Kelly, of Castlekelly, Esq. For some account of this remarkable man and his works, the reader is referred to O'Reilly's Irish Writers, pp. 99, 100, 101.

[q] *Mac Feorais was taken.*—O'Flaherty adds to this passage in H. 2. 11, so as to make it read as follows:

"Mac Feorais do gabáil dua ceallaiġ ⁊ da ċloinn, ⁊ demund mac hoibeird, ⁊ Risderd mac Feorais a oiḋre do marḃaḋ.—MS. L. 1371, *Mac Firb. et Athenry Regest.*"

He also adds the two obits following:

Uilliam mac uillicc, ceann suarcusa ⁊ saoirḃér búrcać, ⁊ Uilliam occ ó ceallaiġ adḃor tiġearna ó maine do écc.

"Gillajesus filius Tigernani Magauran hæres Tellachachæ, obiit.—MS. L."

"Murchertus Mac Donogh obiit.—*Mac Firb.*"

' To this year O'Flaherty adds the following passages in H. 2. 11:

"Magister Nic. Mac Tegheden Officialis Cluan, obiit.—*Mac Firb.*"

"Mac William Burke aggressus est Donaldum filium Murcherti O'Conor optimatibus inferioris Connaciæ stipatum apud Turlach de . . .

William, the son of Ulick, the most distinguished man of the Burkes for gaiety and polite manners, and William Oge O'Kelly, heir to the lordship of Hy-Many, died[r].

[sic] sed Donaldus liberorum et satellitii sui viribus evasit et Mac Donogh captus est.—*Mac Firb.*"

" Ad ann. 1372. Tempestas in vigilia S. Brigidiæ domos et templa diruit.—*Mac Firb. et* MS. L."

CPSIA information can be obtained at www.ICGtesting.com
Printed in the USA
BVOW06*0650110716

454613BV00025B/199/P

9 781298 635259